T0345054

THE FAMA PORTFOLIO

THE FAMA PORTFOLIO

. . .

SELECTED PAPERS OF EUGENE F. FAMA

. . .

Edited by John H. Cochrane and Tobias J. Moskowitz

THE UNIVERSITY OF CHICAGO PRESS

Chicago and London

The University of Chicago Press, Chicago 60637

The University of Chicago Press, Ltd., London

© 2017 by The University of Chicago

Published 2017

Printed in the United States of America

26 25 24 23 22 21 20 19 18 17   3 4 5

ISBN-13: 978-0-226-42684-6 (cloth)

ISBN-13: 978-0-226-42698-3 (e-book)

DOI: 10.7208/chicago/9780226426983.001.0001

Library of Congress Cataloging-in-Publication Data

Names: Cochrane, John H. (John Howland), 1957– editor, author. | Moskowitz, Tobias J.
    (Tobias Jacob), 1971– editor, author. | Fama, Eugene F., 1939– Works. Selections.
Title: The Fama portfolio : selected papers of Eugene F. Fama / edited by John H. Cochrane
    and Tobias J. Moskowitz.
Description: Chicago : The University of Chicago Press, 2017.
Identifiers: LCCN 2016036174 | ISBN 9780226426846 (cloth : alk. paper) | ISBN 9780226426983
    (e-book)
Subjects: LCSH: Capital market. | Finance. | Efficient market theory. | Stocks—Rate of
    return.
Classification: LCC HG4523 .F36 2017 | DDC 332/.0415—dc23 LC record available at https://
    lccn.loc.gov/2016036174

♾ This paper meets the requirements of ANSI/NISO Z39.48-1992
(Permanence of Paper).

CONTENTS

. . .

PREFACE

. . .

John H. Cochrane and Tobias J. Moskowitz

In October 2014, colleagues, students, and friends joined to celebrate Gene Fama's 50 years at the University of Chicago and his record of scholarship, teaching, service, and leadership. In December 2013, Gene received the Nobel Prize in Economics. These events inspired us to create this volume.

This volume provides an introduction to Gene's work for a new generation of readers who did not study all of Fama's papers as they came along. It provides an entry point and a collection of some of his most influential work.

Putting together the list of papers to include was not an easy task. Which Fama papers should one read? Well, all of them! But one must select, and we did our best.

Of course we included the initial, most famous papers in each area. But for Gene Fama, as for the rest of us, ideas often get clearer and simpler over time. Also, early papers in any science have to spend a lot of time on robustness checks, exploring other ways of doing things, and so forth. Later papers can take that for granted, focus on the main point, and branch out to wider and more interesting applications. Therefore, in many cases, we have also included papers later in a series. Though these papers are not as famous or highly cited, they often are a better place for readers to start.

This volume intertwines essays written by ourselves and many of our colleagues. Gene's work is notable of course for its influence, how it changed ideas, and how others took Gene's ideas and used them in many other areas and investigations. Many of Gene's ideas seem commonplace and obvious in retrospect, but they were not so at the time. So we asked our essayists to explain some of the background of each series of papers, to tie together some of the larger literature in each area—both Gene's papers that we left out and contemporaneous work of others—and to explain a bit how we now understand issues after further rounds of digestion and simplification.

However, we have not tried, and we have not asked the other authors to try, to write a history of thought. Like all great ideas, modern financial economics has many parents. Gene is the first to acknowledge all the giants on whose shoulders he stood and the fundamentally collaborative and conversational process by which ideas develop. Many of Gene's papers are synthetic, bringing together a vast array of facts discovered by others and weaving them together in a big picture. Nor have we spent a lot of time tracing all the subsequent literature and how it was influenced by Gene's work, which would be an even larger task. Doing a bad job of attribution is worse than doing no job at all, so with apologies to all our hundreds of colleagues whose work deserves to be mentioned as antecedents, contemporaneous contributions, or important followers, we do not attempt to trace anyone else's contributions. Our essays have essentially no references, even to ourselves. This volume is about Gene.

Each of us has learned a tremendous amount from Gene, not only from reading his papers but from our decades of personal interactions. Gene is not just a profoundly influential researcher, he is also an outstanding teacher and colleague. He read our papers and offered essential comments and often trenchant criticism. He came to our workshops and pointed out important avenues for improvement and new ways of thinking, as well as fatal flaws. He has been generous toward us with the one commodity he guards most closely: his time. And he has shown by example how to be a great member of our academic community: how one should referee papers, evaluate candidates, run workshops, and contribute to a school and a profession. So, with our deep gratitude, we dedicate this volume to Gene, representing ourselves, our colleagues, and so many in our field who feel likewise.

INTRODUCTIONS

. . .

MY LIFE IN FINANCE

. . .

Eugene F. Fama

FOREWORD

I was invited by the editors to contribute a professional autobiography for the *Annual Review of Financial Economics*. I focus on what I think is my best stuff. Readers interested in the rest can download my vita from the website of the University of Chicago, Booth School of Business. I only briefly discuss ideas and their origins, to give the flavor of context and motivation. I do not attempt to review the contributions of others, which is likely to raise feathers. *Mea culpa* in advance.

Finance is the most successful branch of economics in terms of theory and empirical work, the interplay between the two, and the penetration of financial research into other areas of economics and real-world applications. I have been doing research in finance almost since its start, when Markowitz (1952, 1959) and Modigliani and Miller (1958) set the field on the path to become a serious scientific discipline. It has been fun to see it all, to contribute, and to be a friend and colleague to the giants who created the field.

ORIGINS

My grandparents emigrated to the U.S. from Sicily in the early 1900s, so I am a third generation Italian-American. I was the first in the lineage to go to university.

My passion in high school was sports. I played basketball (poorly), ran track (second in the state meet in the high jump—not bad for a 5'8" kid), played football (class B state champions), and baseball (state semi-finals two years).

Reprinted with permission from the *Annual Review of Financial Economics* 3, no. 1 (December 2011): 1–15. © 2011 by Annual Reviews.

The comments of Andy Lo and George Constantinides are gratefully acknowledged. Special thanks to John Cochrane, Kenneth French, and Tobias Moskowitz.

I claim to be the inventor of the split end position in football, an innovation prompted by the beatings I took trying to block much bigger defensive tackles. I am in my high school's (Malden Catholic) athletic hall of fame.

I went on to Tufts University in 1956, intending to become a high school teacher and sports coach. At the end of my second year, I married my high school sweetheart, Sallyann Dimeco, now my wife of more than 50 years. We have four adult children and ten delightful grandchildren. Sally's family contributions dwarf mine.

At Tufts I started in romance languages but after two years became bored with rehashing Voltaire and took an economics course. I was enthralled by the subject matter and by the prospect of escaping lifetime starvation on the wages of a high school teacher. In my last two years at Tufts, I went heavy on economics. The professors, as teachers, were as inspiring as the research stars I later profited from at the University of Chicago.

My professors at Tufts encouraged me to go to graduate school. I leaned toward a business school Ph.D. My Tufts professors (mostly Harvard economics Ph.D.s) pushed Chicago as the business school with a bent toward serious economics. I was accepted at other schools, but April 1960 came along and I didn't hear from Chicago. I called and the dean of students, Jeff Metcalf, answered. (The school was much smaller then.) They had no record of my application. But Jeff and I hit it off, and he asked about my grades. He said Chicago had a scholarship reserved for a qualified Tufts graduate. He asked if I wanted it. I accepted and, except for two great years teaching in Belgium, I have been at the University of Chicago since 1960. I wonder what path my professional life would have taken if Jeff didn't answer the phone that day. Serendipity!

During my last year at Tufts, I worked for Harry Ernst, an economics professor who also ran a stock market forecasting service. Part of my job was to invent schemes to forecast the market. The schemes always worked on the data used to design them. But Harry was a good statistician, and he insisted on out-of-sample tests. My schemes invariably failed those tests. I didn't fully appreciate the lesson in this at the time, but it came to me later.

During my second year at Chicago, with an end to course work and prelims in sight, I started to attend the Econometrics Workshop, at that time the hotbed for research in finance. Merton Miller had recently joined the Chicago faculty and was a regular participant, along with Harry Roberts and Lester Telser. Benoit Mandelbrot was an occasional visitor. Benoit presented in the workshop several times, and in leisurely strolls around campus, I learned lots from him about fat-tailed stable distributions and their apparent relevance in a wide range of economic and physical phenomena. Merton Miller became my mentor in finance and economics (and remained so throughout his lifetime). Harry Roberts, a statistician, instilled a philosophy for empirical work that has been my north star throughout my career.

EFFICIENT MARKETS

Miller, Roberts, Telser, and Mandelbrot were intensely involved in the burgeoning work on the behavior of stock prices (facilitated by the arrival of the first reasonably powerful computers). The other focal point was MIT, with Sydney Alexander, Paul Cootner, Franco Modigliani, and Paul Samuelson. Because his co-author, Merton Miller, was now at Chicago, Franco was a frequent visitor. Like Merton, Franco was unselfish and tireless in helping people think through research ideas. Franco and Mert provided an open conduit for cross-fertilization of market research at the two universities.

At the end of my second year at Chicago, it came time to write a thesis, and I went to Miller with five topics. Mert always had uncanny insight about research ideas likely to succeed. He gently stomped on four of my topics, but was excited by the fifth. From my work for Harry Ernst at Tufts, I had daily data on the 30 Dow-Jones Industrial Stocks. I proposed to produce detailed evidence on (1) Mandelbrot's hypothesis that stock returns conform to non-normal (fat-tailed) stable distributions and (2) the time-series properties of returns. There was existing work on both topics, but I promised a unifying perspective and a leap in the range of data brought to bear.

Vindicating Mandelbrot, my thesis (Fama 1965a) shows (in nauseating detail) that distributions of stock returns are fat-tailed: there are far more outliers than would be expected from normal distributions—a fact reconfirmed in subsequent market episodes, including the most recent. Given the accusations of ignorance on this score recently thrown our way in the popular media, it is worth emphasizing that academics in finance have been aware of the fat tails phenomenon in asset returns for about 50 years.

My thesis and the earlier work of others on the time-series properties of returns falls under what came to be called tests of market efficiency. I coined the terms "market efficiency" and "efficient markets," but they do not appear in my thesis. They first appear in "Random Walks in Stock Market Prices," paper number 16 in the series of *Selected Papers of the Graduate School of Business, University of Chicago,* reprinted in the *Financial Analysts Journal* (Fama 1965b).

From the inception of research on the time-series properties of stock returns, economists speculated about how prices and returns behave if markets work, that is, if prices fully reflect all available information. The initial theory was the random walk model. In two important papers, Samuelson (1965) and Mandelbrot (1966) show that the random walk prediction (price changes are iid) is too strong. The proposition that prices fully reflect available information implies only that prices are sub-martingales. Formally, the deviations of price changes or returns from the values required to compensate investors for time and risk-bearing have expected value equal to zero conditional on past information.

During the early years, in addition to my thesis, I wrote several papers on market efficiency (Fama 1963, 1965c, Fama and Blume 1966), now mostly forgotten. My main contribution to the theory of efficient markets is the 1970 review (Fama 1970). The paper emphasizes the joint hypothesis problem hidden in the sub-martingales of Mandelbrot (1966) and Samuelson (1965). Specifically, market efficiency can only be tested in the context of an asset pricing model that specifies equilibrium expected returns. In other words, to test whether prices fully reflect available information, we must specify how the market is trying to compensate investors when it sets prices. My cleanest statement of the theory of efficient markets is in chapter 5 of Fama (1976b), reiterated in my second review "Efficient Markets II" (Fama 1991a).

The joint hypothesis problem is obvious, but only on hindsight. For example, much of the early work on market efficiency focuses on the autocorrelations of stock returns. It was not recognized that market efficiency implies zero autocorrelation only if the expected returns that investors require to hold stocks are constant through time or at least serially uncorrelated, and both conditions are unlikely.

The joint hypothesis problem is generally acknowledged in work on market efficiency after Fama (1970), and it is understood that, as a result, market efficiency per se is not testable. The flip side of the joint hypothesis problem is less often acknowledged. Specifically, almost all asset pricing models assume asset markets are efficient, so tests of these models are joint tests of the models and market efficiency. Asset pricing and market efficiency are forever joined at the hip.

EVENT STUDIES

My Ph.D. thesis and other early work on market efficiency do not use the CRSP files, which were not yet available. When the files became available (thanks to years of painstaking work by Larry Fisher), Jim Lorie, the founder of CRSP, came to me worried that no one would use the data and CRSP would lose its funding. He suggested a paper on stock splits, to advertise the data. The result is Fama, Fisher, Jensen, and Roll (1969). This is the first study of the adjustment of stock prices to a specific kind of information event. Such "event studies" quickly became a research industry, vibrant to this day, and the main form of tests of market efficiency. Event studies have also found a practical application—calculating damages in legal cases.

The refereeing process for the split study was a unique experience. When more than a year passed without word from the journal, we assumed the paper would be rejected. Then a short letter arrived. The referee (Franco Modigliani) basically said: it's great, publish it. Never again would this happen!

There is a little appreciated fact about the split paper. It contains no formal tests (standard errors, t-statistics, etc.) The results were apparently so convincing as confirmation of market efficiency that formal tests seemed irrelevant. But this was before the joint hypothesis problem was recognized, and only much later did we come to appreciate that results in event studies can be sensitive to methodology, in particular, what is assumed about equilibrium expected returns—a point emphasized in Fama (1998).

Michael Jensen and Richard Roll are members of a once-in-a-lifetime cohort of Ph.D. students that came to Chicago soon after I joined the faculty in 1963. Also in this rough cohort are (among others) Ray Ball, Marshall Blume, James MacBeth, Myron Scholes, and Ross Watts. I think I was chairman of all their thesis committees, but Merton Miller and Harry Roberts were deeply involved. Any investment in these and about 100 other Ph.D. students I have supervised has been repaid many times by what I learn from them during their careers.

FORECASTING REGRESSIONS

In 1975 I published a little empirical paper, "Short-Term Interest Rates as Predictors of Inflation" (Fama 1975). The topic wasn't new, but my approach was novel. Earlier work uses regressions of the interest rate on the inflation rate for the period covered by the interest rate. The idea is that the expected inflation rate (along with the expected real return) determines the interest rate, so the interest rate should be the dependent variable and the expected inflation rate should be the independent variable. The observed inflation rate is, of course, a noisy proxy for its expected value, so there is a measurement error problem in the regression of the ex ante interest rate on the ex post inflation rate.

My simple insight is that a regression estimates the conditional expected value of the left-hand-side variable as a function of the right-hand-side variables. Thus, to extract the forecast of inflation in the interest rate (the expected value of inflation priced into the interest rate) one regresses the ex post inflation rate on the ex ante interest rate. In hindsight, this is the obvious way to run the forecasting regression, but again it wasn't obvious at the time.

There is a potential measurement error problem in the regression of the ex post inflation rate on the ex ante (T-bill) interest rate, caused by variation through time in the expected real return on the bill. The model of market equilibrium in "Short-Term Interest Rates as Predictors of Inflation" assumes that the expected real return is constant, and this seems to be a reasonable approximation for the 1953–1971 period of the tests. (It doesn't work for any later period.) This result raised a furor among Keynesian macroeconomists who postulated that the expected real return was a policy variable that played a central role in controlling investment and business cycles. There was a full day seminar on my paper at MIT, where my simple result was heatedly attacked. I argued that I didn't know what the fuss was about, since the risk premium component of the cost of capital is surely more important than the risk-free real rate, and it seems unlikely that monetary and fiscal actions can fine tune the risk premium. I don't know if I won the debate, but it was followed by a tennis tournament, and I think I did win that.

The simple idea about forecasting regressions in Fama (1975) has served me well, many times. (When I have an idea, I beat it to death.) I have many papers that use the technique to extract the forecasts of future spot rates, returns, default premiums, etc., in the term structure of interests rates, for example Fama (1976a,c, 1984b, 1986, 1990b, 2005), Fama and Schwert (1979), Fama and Bliss (1987). In a blatant example of intellectual arbitrage, I apply the technique to study forward foreign exchange rates as predictors of future spot rates, in a paper (Fama 1984a) highly cited in that literature. The same technique is used in my work with Kenneth R. French and G. William Schwert on the predictions of stock returns in dividend yields and other variables (Fama and Schwert 1977, Fama and French 1988, 1989). And regressions of ex post variables on ex ante variables are now standard in forecasting studies, academic and applied.

AGENCY PROBLEMS AND THE THEORY OF ORGANIZATIONS

In 1976 Michael Jensen and William Meckling published their groundbreaking paper on agency problems in investment and financing decisions (Jensen and Meckling 1976). According to Kim, Morse, and Zingales (2006), this is the second most highly cited theory paper in economics published in the 1970–2005 period. It fathered an enormous literature.

When Mike came to present the paper at Chicago, he began by claiming it would destroy the corporate finance material in what he called the "white bible" (Fama and Miller, *The Theory of Finance* 1972). Mert and I replied that his analysis is deeper and more insightful, but in fact there is a discussion of stockholder-bondholder agency problems in chapter 4 of our book. Another example that new ideas are almost never completely new!

Spurred by Jensen and Meckling (1976), my research took a turn into agency theory. The early papers on agency theory emphasized agency problems. I was interested in studying how competitive forces lead to the evolution of mechanisms to mitigate agency problems. The first paper, "Agency Problems and the Theory of the Firm" (Fama 1980a) argues that managerial labor markets, inside and outside of firms, act to control managers faced with the temptations created by diffuse residual claims that reduce the incentives of individual residual claimants to monitor managers.

I then collaborated with Mike on three papers (Fama and Jensen 1983a,b, 1985) that study more generally how different mechanisms arise to mitigate the agency problems associated with "separation of ownership and control" and how an organization's activities and the special agency problems they pose, affect the nature of its residual claims and control mechanisms. For example, we argue that the redeemable residual claims of a financial mutual (for example, an open end mutual fund) provide strong discipline for its managers, but redeemability is cost effective only when the assets of the organization can be sold quickly with low transactions costs. We also argue that the nonprofit format, in which no agents have explicit residual claims to net cash flows, is a response to the agency problem associated with activities in which there is a potential supply of donations that might be expropriated by residual claimants. Two additional papers (Fama 1990a, 1991b) spell out some of the implications of Fama (1980a) and Fama and Jensen (1983a,b) for financing decisions and the nature of labor contracts.

Kim, Morse, and Zingales (2006) list the 146 papers published during 1970–2005 that have more than 500 cites in the major journals of economics. I'm blatantly bragging, but Fama (1980a) and Fama and Jensen (1983a) are among my six papers on the list. (The others are Fama 1970, Fama and MacBeth 1973, Fama and French 1992, 1993. If the list extended back to ancient times, Fama 1965a and Fama, Fisher, Jensen, and Roll 1969 would also make it.) I think of myself as an empiricist (and a simple-minded one at that), so I like my work in agency theory since it suggests that occasionally theoretical ideas get sprinkled into the mix.

MACROECONOMICS

Toward the end of the 1970s, around the time of the agency theory research, my work took a second turn into macroeconomics and international finance. Fischer Black had similar interests, and I profited from many long discussions with him on this and other issues during the years he spent at Chicago in the office next to mine.

Since they typically assume away transactions costs, asset pricing models in finance do not have a natural role for money. Fama and Farber (1979) model a world in which financial markets are indeed frictionless, but there are transactions costs in consumption that are reduced by holding money. Money then becomes a portfolio asset, and we investigate how nominal bonds (borrowing and lending) allow consumer-investors to split decisions about how much money to hold for transactions purposes from decisions about how much of the purchasing power risk of their money holdings they will bear. We also investigate the pricing of the purchasing power risk of the money supply in the context of the CAPM.

Extending the analysis to an international setting, Fama and Farber (1979) show that exchange rate uncertainty is not an additional risk in international investing when purchasing power parity (PPP) holds, because PPP implies that the real return on any asset is the same to the residents of all countries. The point is obvious, on hindsight, but previous papers in the international asset pricing literature assume that exchange rate uncertainty is an additional risk, without saying anything about PPP, or saying something incorrect.

Three subsequent papers (Fama 1980b, 1983, 1985) examine what the theory of finance says about the role of banks. The first two (Fama 1980b, 1983) argue that in the absence of reserve requirements, banks are just financial intermediaries, much like mutual funds, that manage asset portfolios on behalf of depositors. And like mutual fund holdings, the quantity of deposits has no role in price level determination (inflation). Bank deposits also provide access to an accounting system of exchange (via checks and electronic transfers) that is just an efficient mechanism for moving claims on assets from some consumer-investors to others, without the intervention of a hand-to-hand medium of exchange like currency. Because it pays less than full interest, currency has an important role in price level determination. The role of deposits in price level determination is, however, artificial, induced by the requirement to hold "reserves" with the central bank that pay less than full interest and are exchangeable for currency on demand.

CORPORATE FINANCE

As finance matured, it became more specialized. The teaching and research of new people tends to focus entirely on asset pricing or corporate finance. It wasn't always so. Until several years ago, I taught both. More of my research is in asset-pricing-market-efficiency (66 papers and 1.5 books), but as a result of longtime exposure to Merton Miller, I have always been into corporate finance (15 papers and half a book).

The burning issue in corporate finance in the early 1960s was whether the propositions of Modigliani and Miller (MM 1958) and Miller and Modigliani (MM 1961) about the value irrelevance of financing decisions hold outside the confines of their highly restrictive risk classes (where a risk class includes firms with perfectly correlated net cash flows). With the perspective provided by asset pricing models, which were unavailable to MM, it became clear that their propositions do not require their risk classes. Fama (1978) tries to provide a capstone. The paper argues that the MM propositions hold in any asset pricing model that shares the basic MM assumptions (perfect capital market, including no taxes, no transactions costs, and no information asymmetries or agency problems), as long as either (i) investors and firms have equal access to the capital market (so investors can undo the financing decisions of firms), or (ii) there are perfect substitutes for the securities issued by any firm (with perfect substitute defined by whatever happens to be the right asset pricing model).

The CRSP files opened the gates for empirical asset pricing research (including work on efficient markets). Compustat similarly provides the raw material for empirical work in corporate finance. Fama and Babiak (1968) leap on the new Compustat files to test Lintner's (1956) hypothesis that firms have target dividend payouts but annual dividends only partially adjust to their targets. Lintner estimates his model on aggregate data. We examine how the model works for the individual firms whose dividend decisions it is meant to explain. It works well in our tests, and it continues to work in subsequent trials (e.g., Fama 1974). But the speed-of-adjustment of dividends to their targets has slowed considerably, that is, dividends have become more "sticky" (Fama and French 2002). The more interesting fact, however, is the gradual disappearance of dividends. In 1978 almost 80% of NYSE-Amex-Nasdaq listed firms paid dividends, falling to about 20% in 1999 (Fama and French 2001).

Post-MM corporate finance has two main theories, the pecking order model of Myers (1984) and Myers and Majluf (1984) and the tradeoff model (which has many authors). These theories make predictions about financing decisions when different pieces of the perfect capital markets assumption of MM do not hold. The pecking order model does reasonably well, until the early 1980s when new issues of common stock (which the model predicts are rare) become commonplace (Fama and French 2005). There is some empirical support for the leverage targets that are the centerpiece of the tradeoff model, but the speed-of-adjustment of leverage to its targets is so slow that the existence of targets becomes questionable. (This is the conclusion of Fama and French 2002 and other recent work.) In the end, it's not clear that the capital structure irrelevance propositions of Modigliani and Miller are less realistic as rough approximations than the popular alternatives. (This is the conclusion of Fama and French 2002.)

In my view, the big open challenge in corporate finance is to produce evidence on how taxes affect market values and thus optimal financing decisions. Modigliani and Miller (1963) suggest that debt has large tax benefits, and taxation disadvantages dividends. To this day, this is the position commonly advanced in corporate finance courses. Miller (1977), however, presents a scenario in which the tax benefits of debt due to the tax deductibility of interest payments at the corporate level are offset by taxation of interest receipts at the personal level, and leverage has no effect on a firm's market value. Miller and Scholes (1978) present a scenario in which dividend and debt choices have no effect on the market values of firms. Miller (1977) and Miller and Scholes (1978) recognize that that there are scenarios in which taxes do affect optimal dividend and debt decisions. In the end, the challenge is empirical measurement of tax effects (the marginal tax rates implicit) in the pricing of dividends and interest. So far the challenge goes unmet.

Fama and French (1998) take a crack at this first order issue, without success. The problem is that dividend and debt decisions are related to expected net cash flows—the main determinant of the market value of a firm's securities. Because proxies for expected net cash flows are far from perfect, the cross-section regressions of Fama and French (1998) do not produce clean estimates of how the taxation of dividends and interest affects the market values of a firm's stocks and bonds. There are also papers that just assume debt has tax benefits that can be measured from tax rate schedules. Without evidence on the tax effects in the pricing of interest, such exercises are empty.

THE CAPM

Without being there one can't imagine what finance was like before formal asset pricing models. For example, at Chicago and elsewhere, investments courses were about security analysis: how to pick undervalued stocks. In 1963 I taught the first course at Chicago devoted to Markowitz' (1959) portfolio model and its famous offspring, the asset pricing model (CAPM) of Sharpe (1964) and Lintner (1965).

The CAPM provides the first precise definition of risk and how it drives expected return, until then vague and sloppy concepts. The absence of formal models of risk and expected return placed serious limitations on research that even grazed the topic. For example, the path breaking paper of Modigliani and Miller (1958) uses arbitrage within risk classes to show that (given their assumptions) financing decisions do not affect a firm's market value. They define a risk class as firms with perfectly correlated net cash flows. This is restrictive and it led to years of bickering about the applicability of their analysis and conclusions. The problem was due to the absence of formal asset pricing models that define risk and how it relates to expected return.

The arrival of the CAPM was like the time after a thunderstorm, when the air suddenly clears. Extensions soon appeared, but the quantum leaps are the intertemporal model (ICAPM) of Merton (1973a), which generalizes the CAPM to a multiperiod world with possibly multiple dimensions of risk, and the consumption CAPM of Lucas (1978), Breeden (1979), and others.

Though not about risk and expected return, any history of the excitement in finance in the 1960s and 1970s must mention the options pricing work of Black and Scholes (1973) and Merton (1973b). These are the most successful papers in economics—ever—in terms of academic and applied impact. Every Ph.D. student in economics is exposed to this work, and the papers are the foundation of a massive industry in financial derivatives.

There are many early tests of the CAPM, but the main survivors are Black, Jensen, and Scholes (BJS 1972) and Fama and MacBeth (1973). Prior to these papers, the typical test of the CAPM was a cross-section regression of the average returns on a set of assets on estimates of their market βs and other variables. (The CAPM predicts, of course, that the β premium is positive, and β suffices to describe the cross-section of expected asset returns.) BJS were suspicious that the slopes in these cross-section regressions seemed too precise (the reported standard errors seemed too small). They guessed rightly that the problem was the OLS assumption that there is no cross-correlation in the regression residuals.

Fama and MacBeth (1973) provide a simple solution to the cross-correlation problem. Instead of a regression of average asset returns on their βs and other variables, one does the regression month-by-month. The slopes are then monthly portfolio returns whose average values can be used to test the CAPM predictions that the β premium is positive and other variables add nothing to the explanation of the cross-section of expected returns. (The point is explained best in chapter 8 of Fama 1976b.) The month-by-month variation in the regression slopes captures all effects of the cross-correlation of the regression residuals, and these effects are automatically embedded in the time-series standard errors of the average slopes. The approach thus captures residual covariances without requiring an estimate of the residual covariance matrix.

The Fama-MacBeth approach is standard in tests of asset pricing models that use cross-section regressions, but the benefits of the approach carry over to panels (time series of cross-sections) of all sorts. Kenneth French and I emphasize this point (advertise is more accurate) in our corporate finance empirical work (e.g., Fama and French 1998, 2002). Outside of finance, research in economics that uses panel regressions has only recently begun to acknowledge that residual covariance is a pervasive problem. Various new robust regression techniques are available, but the Fama-MacBeth approach remains a simple option.

Given the way my recent empirical work with Kenneth French dumps on the CAPM, it is only fair to acknowledge that the CAPM gets lots of credit for forcing money managers to take more seriously the challenges posed by the work on efficient markets. Before the CAPM, money management was entirely active, and performance reporting was shoddy. The CAPM gave us a clean story about risk and expected return (i.e., a model of market equilibrium) that allowed us to judge the performance of active managers. Using the CAPM, Jensen (1968) rang the bell on the mutual fund industry. Performance evaluation via the CAPM quickly became standard both among academics and practitioners, passive management got a foothold, and active managers became aware that their feet would forever be put to the fire.

THE THREE-FACTOR MODEL

The evidence in Black, Jensen, and Scholes (1972) and Fama and MacBeth (1973) is generally favorable to the CAPM, or at least to Black's (1972) version of the CAPM. Subsequently, violations of the model, labeled anomalies, begin to surface. Banz (1981) finds that β does not fully explain the higher average returns of small (low market capitalization) stocks. Basu (1983) finds that the positive relation between the earning-price ratio (E/P) and average return is left unexplained by market β. Rosenberg, Reid, and Lanstein (1985) find a positive relation between average stock return and the book-to-market ratio (B/M) that is missed by the CAPM. Bhandari (1988) documents a similar result for market leverage (the ratio of debt to the market value of equity, D/M). Ball (1978) and Keim (1988) argue that variables like size, E/P, B/M, and D/M are natural candidates to expose the failures of asset pricing models as explanations of expected returns since all these variables use the stock price, which, given expected dividends, is inversely related to the expected stock return.

The individual papers on CAPM anomalies did not seem to threaten the dominance of the model. My guess is that viewed one at a time, the anomalies seemed like curiosity items that show that the CAPM is just a model, an approximation that can't be expected to explain the entire cross-section of expected stock returns. I see no other way to explain the impact of Fama and French (1992), "The Cross-Section of Expected Stock Returns," which contains nothing new. The CAPM anomalies in the paper are those listed above, and the evidence that there is no reliable relation between average return and market β was available in Reinganum (1981) and Lakonishok and Shapiro (1986). Apparently, seeing all the negative evidence in one place led readers to accept our conclusion that the CAPM just doesn't work. The model is an elegantly simple and intuitively appealing *tour de force* that laid the foundations of asset pricing theory, but its major predictions seem to be violated systematically in the data.

An asset pricing model can only be dethroned by a model that provides a better description of average returns. The three-factor model (Fama and French 1993) is our shot. The model proposes that along with market β, sensitivities to returns on two additional portfolios, SMB and HML, explain the cross-section of expected stock returns. The size factor, SMB, is the difference between the returns on diversified portfolios of small and big stocks, and the value/growth factor, HML, is the difference between the returns on diversified portfolios of high and low B/M (i.e., value and growth) stocks. The SMB and HML returns are, of course, brute force constructs designed to capture the patterns in average returns related to size and value versus growth stocks that are left unexplained by the CAPM.

Ken French and I have many papers that address questions about the three-factor model and the size and value/growth patterns in average returns the model is meant to explain. For example, to examine whether the size and value/growth patterns in average returns observed by Fama and French (1992) for the post 1962 period are the chance result of data dredging, Davis, Fama, and French (2000) extend the tests back to 1927, and Fama and French (1998) examine international data. The results are similar to those in Fama and French (1992). Fama and French (1996, 2008) examine whether the three-factor model can explain the anomalies that cause problems for the CAPM. The three-factor model does well on the anomalies associated with variants of price ratios, but it is just a model and it fails to absorb some other anomalies. The most prominent is the momentum in short-term returns documented by Jegadeesh and Titman (1993), which is a problem for all asset pricing models that do not add exposure to momentum as an explanatory factor. After 1993, work, both academic and applied, directed at measuring the performance of managed portfolios routinely use the benchmarks provided by the three-factor model, often augmented with a momentum factor (for example, Carhart 1997, and more recently Kosowski et al. 2006 or Fama and French 2009).

From its beginnings there has been controversy about how to interpret the size and especially the value/growth premiums in average returns captured by the three-factor model. Fama and French (1993, 1996) propose a multifactor version of Merton's (1973a) ICAPM. The weakness of this position is the question it leaves open. What are the state variables that drive the size and value premiums, and why do they lead to variation in expected returns missed by market β? There is a literature that proposes answers to this question, but in my view the evidence so far is unconvincing.

The chief competitor to our ICAPM risk story for the value premium is the overreaction hypothesis of DeBondt and Thaler (1987) and Lakonishok, Shleifer, and Vishny (1994). They postulate that market prices overreact to the recent good times of growth stocks and the bad times of value stocks. Subsequent price corrections then produce the value premium (high average returns of value stocks relative to growth stocks). The weakness of this position is the presumption that investors never learn about their behavioral biases, which is necessary to explain the persistence of the value premium.

Asset pricing theory typically assumes that portfolio decisions depend only on the properties of the return distributions of assets and portfolios. Another possibility, suggested by Fama and French (2007) and related to the stories in Daniel and Titman (1997) and Barberis and Shleifer (2003), is that tastes for other characteristics of assets, unrelated to properties of returns, also play a role. ("Socially responsible investing" is an example.) Perhaps many investors simply get utility from holding growth stocks, which tend to be profitable fast-growing firms, and they are averse to value stocks, which tend to be relatively unprofitable with few growth opportunities. If such tastes persist, they can have persistent effects on asset prices and expected returns, as long as they don't lead to arbitrage opportunities.

To what extent is the value premium in expected stock returns due to ICAPM state variable risks, investor overreaction, or tastes for assets as consumption goods? We may never know. Moreover, given the blatant empirical motivation of the three-factor model (and the four-factor offspring of Carhart 1997), perhaps we should just view the model as an attempt to find a set of portfolios that span the mean-variance-efficient set and so can be used to describe expected returns on all assets and portfolios (Huberman and Kandel 1987).

The academic research on the size and value premiums in average stock returns has transformed the investment management industry, both on the supply side and on the demand side. Whatever their views about the origins of the premiums, institutional investors commonly frame their asset allocation decisions in two dimensions, size and value versus growth, and the portfolio menus offered by money managers are typically framed in the same way. And it is testimony to the credibility of research in finance that all this happened in a very short period of time.

CONCLUSIONS

The first 50 years of research in finance has been a great ride. I'm confident finance will continue to be a great ride into the indefinite future.

ADDENDUM—PROVIDED BY THE TENURED FINANCE FACULTY OF CHICAGO BOOTH

When my paper was posted on the Forum of the website of the Chicago Booth Initiative on Global Markets, the tenured finance faculty introduced it with the following comments. EFF

> This post makes available an autobiographical note by Gene Fama that was commissioned by the *Annual Review of Financial Economics*. Gene's remarkable career and vision, to say nothing of his engaging writing style, make this short piece a must read for anyone interested in finance. However, as his colleagues, we believe his modesty led him to omit three crucial aspects of his contributions.

First, Gene was (and still is) essential to shaping the nature of the finance group at Chicago. As he explains in a somewhat understated fashion, he and Merton Miller transformed the finance group, turning it into a research-oriented unit. For the last 47 years he has held court on Tuesday afternoons in the finance workshop, in a room that now bears his name. Through the workshop, generations of students, colleagues, and visitors have been and continue to be exposed to his research style of developing and rigorously testing theories with real world data that has become the hallmark of Chicago finance.

Second, and equally important, is his leadership. Rather than rest on his laurels or impose his own views on the group, Gene has always sought the truth, even when it appeared at odds with his own views. He has promoted a contest of ideas and outlooks, all subject to his exceptional standards of quality. The makeup of the group has shifted as the world and what we know about it has changed. The current finance group at Chicago includes a diverse set of people who specialize in all areas of modern finance, including behavioral economics, pure theory, and emerging, non-traditional areas such as entrepreneurship and development that were unheard of when Gene arrived at Chicago. Contrary to the caricatured descriptions, there is no single Chicago view of finance, except that the path to truth comes from the rigorous development and confrontation of theories with data.

Finally, each of us has our own personal examples of Gene's generosity, kindness and mentorship. He is an impeccable role model. He is in his office every day, and his door is always open. By personal example, he sets the standards for the values and ethics by which we do research and run our school. All of us have learned enormously from Gene's generous willingness to discuss his and our work, and gently and patiently to explain and debate that work with generations of faculty. Gene likely enjoys as high a ranking in the "thanks for comments" footnotes of published papers as he does in citations. He has made the finance group an exciting, collegial, and welcoming place to work. He has greatly enhanced all of our research careers and accomplishments. He is a great friend, and we can only begin to express our gratitude.

We hope you enjoy reading Gene's description of his career that might just as well be described as the story of how modern finance evolved at Chicago.

Gene's Tenured Finance Faculty Colleagues at Chicago Booth

John H. Cochrane, George M. Constantinides, Douglas W. Diamond,
Milton Harris, John C. Heaton, Steven Neil Kaplan, Anil K. Kashyap,
Richard Leftwich, Tobias J. Moskowitz, Lubos Pastor, Raghuram G. Rajan,
Richard Thaler, Pietro Veronesi, Robert W. Vishny, and Luigi Zingales

LITERATURE CITED

Ball R. 1978. Anomalies in relationships between securities' yields and yield-surrogates, *Journal of Financial Economics*. 6:103–126.

Banz RW. 1981. The relationship between return and market value of common stocks. *Journal of Financial Economics*. 9:3–18.

Barberis N, Shleifer A. 2003. Style investing. *Journal of Financial Economics*. 68:161–199.

Basu S. 1977. Investment performance of common stocks in relation to their price-earnings ratios: A test of the efficient market hypothesis. *Journal of Finance*. 12:129–56.

Basu S. 1983. The relationship between earnings yield, market value, and return for NYSE common stocks: Further evidence. *Journal of Financial Economics*. 12:129–56.

Bhandari LC. 1988. Debt/equity ratio and expected common stock returns: Empirical evidence. *Journal of Finance*. 43:507–28.

Black F. 1972. Capital market equilibrium with restricted borrowing. *Journal of Business*. 45:444–454.

Black, F, Jensen MC, Scholes M. 1972. The capital asset pricing model: Some empirical tests. In *Studies in the Theory of Capital Markets*. Jensen MC, ed. New York: Praeger. 79–121.

Black F, Scholes M. 1973. The pricing of options and corporate liabilities. *Journal of Political Economy*. 81: 638–654.

Breeden DT. 1979. An intertemporal asset pricing model with stochastic consumption and investment opportunities. *Journal of Financial Economics*. 7:265–296.

Carhart MM. 1997. On persistence in mutual fund performance. *Journal of Finance* 52:57–82.

Daniel K, Titman S. 1997. Evidence on the characteristics of cross sectional variation in stock returns. *Journal of Finance*. 52:1–33.

Davis JL, Fama EF, French KR. 2000. Characteristics, covariances, and average returns: 1929–1997. *Journal of Finance*. 55:389–406.

DeBondt WFM, Thaler RH. 1987. Further evidence on investor overreaction and stock market seasonality. *Journal of Finance*. 42:557–581.

Fama EF. 1963. Mandelbrot and the stable paretian hypothesis. *Journal of Business*. 36:420–429.

Fama EF. 1965a. The behavior of stock market prices. *Journal of Business*. 38:34–105.

Fama EF. 1965b. Random walks in stock market prices. *Financial Analysts Journal* September/October. 55–59.

Fama EF. 1965a. Tomorrow on the New York Stock Exchange. *Journal of Business*. 38:285–299.

Fama EF. 1970. Efficient capital markets: A review of theory and empirical work. *Journal_of Finance.* 25:383–417.

Fama EF. 1974. The Empirical relationships between the dividend and investment decisions of firms. *American Economic Review.* 64:304–318.

Fama EF. 1975. Short-term interest rates as predictors of inflation. *American Economic Review* 65:269–282.

Fama EF. 1976a. Forward rates as predictors of future spot rates. *Journal of Financial Economics.* 3:361–377.

Fama EF. 1976b. *Foundations of Finance.* New York: Basic Books.

Fama EF. 1976c. Inflation uncertainty and expected returns on Treasury bills. *Journal of Political Economy.* 84: 427–448.

Fama EF. 1978. The effects of a firm's investment and financing decisions on the welfare of its securityholders. *American Economic Review.* 68:272–284.

Fama EF. 1980a. Agency problems and the theory of the firm. *Journal of Political Economy.* 88:288–307.

Fama EF. 1980b. Banking in the theory of finance. *Journal of Monetary Economics.* 6:39–57.

Fama EF. 1983. Financial intermediation and price level control. *Journal of Monetary Economics.* 12:7–28.

Fama EF. 1984a. Forward and spot exchange rates. *Journal of Monetary Economics.* 14:319–338.

Fama EF. 1984b. The information in the term structure. *Journal of Financial Economics.* 13:509–528.

Fama EF. 1984c. Term premiums in bond returns. *Journal of Financial Economics.* 13:529–546.

Fama EF. 1985. What's different about banks? *Journal of Monetary Economics.* 15:29–39.

Fama EF. 1986. Term premiums and default premiums in money markets. *Journal of Financial Economics.* 17:175–196.

Fama EF. 1990a. Contract costs and financing decisions. *Journal of Business.* 63:S71–91.

Fama EF. 1990b. Term structure forecasts of interest rates, inflation, and real returns. *Journal of Monetary Economics.* 25:59–76.

Fama EF. 1991a. Efficient markets II. *Journal of Finance.* 46:1575–1617.

Fama EF. 1991b. Time, salary, and incentive payoffs in labor contracts. *Journal of Labor Economics.* 9:25–44.

Fama EF. 1998. Market efficiency, long-term returns, and behavioral finance. *Journal of Financial Economics.* 49:283–306.

Fama EF. 2005. The behavior of interest rates. *Review of Financial Studies.* 19:359–379.

Fama EF, Babiak H. 1968. Dividend policy of individual firms: An empirical analysis. *Journal of the American Statistical Association.* 63:1132–1161.

Fama EF, Bliss RR. 1987. The information in long-maturity forward rates. *American Economic Review.* 77:680–692.

Fama EF, Blume M. 1966. Filter rules and stock market trading. *Journal of Business.* 39:226–241.

Fama EF, Farber A. 1979. Money, bonds and foreign exchange. *American Economic Review.* 69:639–649.

Fama EF, Fisher L, Jensen M, Roll R. 1969. The adjustment of stock prices to new information. *International Economic Review.* 10: 1–21.

Fama EF, French KR. 1988. Dividend yields and expected stock returns. *Journal of Financial Economics.* 22: 3–25.

Fama EF, French KR. 1989. Business conditions and expected returns on stocks and bonds. *Journal of Financial Economics.* 25: 23–49.

Fama EF, French KR. 1992. The cross-section of expected stock returns. *Journal of Finance* 47:427–465.

Fama EF, French KR. 1993. Common risk factors in the returns on stocks and bonds. *Journal of Financial Economics.* 33:3–56.

Fama EF, French KR. 1995. Size and book-to-market factors in earnings and returns. *Journal of Finance.* 50:131–156.

Fama EF, French KR. 1996. Multifactor explanations of asset pricing anomalies. *Journal of Finance.* 51:55–84.

Fama EF, French KR. 1997. Industry costs of equity, *Journal of Financial Economics.* 43:153–193.

Fama EF, French KR. 1998. Value versus growth: The international evidence, *Journal of Finance.* 53: 1975–1999.

Fama EF, French KR. 1998. Taxes, financing decisions, and firm value. *Journal of Finance.* 53:819–843.

Fama EF, French KR. 2001, Disappearing dividends: Changing firm characteristics or lower propensity to pay? *Journal of Financial Economics.* 60:3–43.

Fama EF, French KR. 2002. Testing tradeoff and pecking order predictions about dividends and debt. *Review of Financial Studies.* 15:1–33.

Fama EF, French KR. 2005, Financing decisions: Who issues stock? *Journal of Financial Economics.* 76:549–582.

Fama EF, French KR. 2006, The value premium and the CAPM. *Journal of Finance.* 61:2163–2185.

Fama EF, French KR. 2007, Disagreement, tastes, and asset prices. *Journal of Financial Economics.* 83:667–689.

Fama EF, French KR. 2008, Dissecting Anomalies. *Journal of Finance.* 63:1653–1678.

Fama EF, French KR. 2009. Luck versus skill in the cross-section of mutual fund returns. manuscript, University of Chicago, December, forthcoming in the *Journal of Finance.*

Fama EF, Jensen MC. 1983a. Separation of Ownership and Control. *Journal of Law and Economics.* 26:301–25.

Fama EF, Jensen MC. 1983b. Agency problems and residual claims. *Journal of Law and Economics.* 26:327–49.

Fama EF, Jensen MC. 1985. Organizational forms and investment decisions. *Journal of Financial Economics.* 14:101–120.

Fama EF, MacBeth JD. 1973. Risk, return, and equilibrium: Empirical tests. *Journal of Political Economy.* 81:607–636.

Fama EF, Miller MH. 1972. *The Theory of Finance.* New York: Holt, Rinehart, and Winston.

Fama EF, Schwert GW. 1979. Inflation, interest and relative prices. *Journal of Business.* 52:183–209.

Fama EF, Schwert GW. 1977. Asset returns and inflation. *Journal of Financial Economics.* 5:115–146.

Huberman G, Kandel S. 1987. Mean-variance spanning. *Journal of Finance.* 42: 873–888.

Jegadeesh N, Titman S. 1993. Returns to buying winners and selling losers: Implications for stock market efficiency. *Journal of Finance.* 48:65–91.

Jensen MC. 1968. The performance of mutual funds in the period 1945–1964. *Journal of Finance.* 23:2033–2058.

Jensen MC, Meckling WH. 1976. Theory of the firm: Managerial behavior, agency costs and ownership structure. *Journal of Financial Economics.* 3:305–60.

Keim DB. 1988. Stock market regularities: A synthesis of the evidence and explanations, in *Stock Market Anomalies.* Dimson E (ed.). Cambridge: Cambridge University Press.

Kim EH, Morse A, Zingales L. 2006. What has mattered in economics since 1970. *Journal of Economic Perspectives,* 20:189–202.

Kosowski R, Timmermann A, Wermers R, White H. 2006. Can mutual fund "stars" really pick stocks? New evidence from a bootstrap analysis. *Journal of Finance.* 61:2551–2595.

Lakonishok J, Shapiro AC. 1986. Systematic risk, total risk, and size as determinants of stock market returns. *Journal of Banking and Finance.* 10:115–132.

Lakonishok J, Shleifer A, Vishny RW. 1994. Contrarian investment, extrapolation, and risk. *Journal of Finance.* 49:1541–1578.

Lintner J. 1956. Distribution of incomes of corporations among dividends, retained earnings and taxes. *American Economic Review.* 46:97–113.

Lintner J. 1965. The valuation of risk assets and the selection of risky investments in stock portfolios and capital budgets. *Review of Economics and Statistics.* 47:13–37.

Lucas RE Jr. 1978. Asset prices in an exchange economy. *Econometrica.* 46:1429–1446.

Mandelbrot B, 1966. Forecasts of future prices, unbiased markets, and martingale models. *Journal of Business* (Special Supplement, January). 39:242–255.

Markowitz H. 1952. Portfolio selection. *Journal of Finance.* 7:77–99.

Markowitz H. 1959. *Portfolio Selection: Efficient Diversification of Investments.* Cowles Foundation Monograph No. 16. New York: John Wiley & Sons, Inc.

Merton RC. 1973a. An intertemporal capital asset pricing model. *Econometrica.* 41:867–887.

Merton RC. 1973b. Theory of rational options pricing. *Bell Journal of Economics and Management Science.* 4:141–183.

Miller MH. 1977. Debt and taxes. *Journal of Finance.* 32:261–275.

Miller MH, Modigliani F. 1961. Dividend policy, growth, and the valuation of shares. *Journal of Business.* 34:422–433.

Miller MH, Scholes MS. 1978. Dividends and taxes. *Journal of Financial Economics.* 6:333–64.

Modigliani F, Miller MH. 1958. The cost of capital, corporation finance, and the theory of investment. *American Economic Review.* 48:261–97.

Modigliani F, Miller MH. 1963. Corporate income taxes and the cost of capital: A correction. *American Economic Review.* 53:433–443.

Myers SC. 1984. The capital structure puzzle. *Journal of Finance.* 39:575–592.

Myers SC, Majluf NS. 1984. Corporate financing and investment decisions when firms have information the investors do not have. *Journal of Financial Economics.* 13:187–221.

Reinganum MR. 1981. A New Empirical Perspective on the CAPM. *Journal of Financial and Quantitative Analysis.* 16:439–462.

Rosenberg B, Reid K, Lanstein R. 1985. Persuasive evidence of market inefficiency. *Journal of Portfolio Management.* 11:9–17.

Samuelson P. 1965. Proof that properly anticipated prices fluctuate randomly. *Industrial Management Review.* 6:41–49.

Sharpe WF. 1964. Capital asset prices: A theory of market equilibrium under conditions of risk. *Journal of Finance.* 19:425–442.

THINGS I'VE LEARNED FROM GENE FAMA

· · ·

Kenneth R. French

Gene Fama has taught us a lot over the last 50 years. The other papers in this volume focus on his contributions to asset pricing, corporate finance, and banking. I take a broader perspective and describe some of the things Gene has taught me about doing research, writing papers, and life in general.

Gene is a wonderful mentor who has extraordinary insights and shares them generously. Some of the lessons I describe are clearly things he meant to teach. Others, however, are inferences I have drawn from our interactions. Since these inferences may be wrong, I worry that Gene will deny or even vehemently disagree with what I say. I am usually surprised and often dismayed when I hear students summarize what they learned in my Investments class. I hope Gene does not have the same reaction to this essay.

USE YOUR TIME WISELY

Most of Gene's students and colleagues know his first recommendation about time management: if you are not willing to do something now, don't agree to do it later. The logic is straightforward. You will probably be as busy later as you are now, so unless the benefits will be substantially higher in the future, if you don't want to do something now you will probably regret having to do it later.

Gene's second recommendation is less well known: resist deadlines. Obviously, this advice is not intended for those who need deadlines to get anything done. But for the rest of us, there is no reason to let deadlines determine our priorities or make us work harder than we want.

Gene typically gives students and colleagues detailed comments on their papers a day or two after he is asked. He does referee reports almost as quickly. Together, Gene's first two time management recommendations explain this peculiar behavior. Assume you will actually do everything you plan to do and set your own priorities. Then the benefit of immediacy should determine what you do today. Start with the task whose payoff per hour of labor declines most quickly. In Gene's case, quick feedback enhances a colleague's productivity and sends a strong signal about the value Gene places on the colleague's research. Similarly, a quick referee report improves the author's productivity and the reputation of the journal. If the benefit of immediacy is highest for these tasks, they should be at the top of the stack—and that is where Gene puts them.

RANDOMNESS HAPPENS

Many years ago, while trying to convince Gene that a marginal candidate deserved tenure, I compared the candidate to one of our less productive tenured colleagues. His response destroyed my argument: "You make enough mistakes by mistake; don't make one on purpose."

This is one of my favorite Fama quotes. Gene was making a specific point— don't let a bad draw reduce your standard for future decisions—but I interpret his statement more broadly: even with unbiased forecasts, the effect of uncertainty can be asymmetric. This is obvious when we consider things like risk aversion and option pricing, but it may not be so obvious in other contexts.

While writing this essay, I finally figured out why my life always seems more frenetic than Gene's. I have been ignoring estimation error when deciding what I should agree to do. Whenever it looks like I'll have some slack in my schedule, I commit to do more and, if things turn out better than expected, I add even more. Unfortunately, this strategy leaves no room for tasks that take longer than expected. Even ignoring the optimism in my forecasts, my approach ensures that if anything goes wrong I am in trouble.

MAKE GOOD STATISTICAL INFERENCES

Gene has trained himself to make good statistical inferences, both professionally and in more general settings. When I was about 40, a younger friend passed away. While chatting with Gene about the tragedy, I said it bothered me not only because I had lost a friend, but also because his death at a young age caused me to reassess my own mortality. Without a pause, Gene replied, "Don't worry, I saw a 94-year-old yesterday."

Gene's ability to avoid statistical traps probably contributes to his skepticism about behavioral finance. Many of us read research about flawed decision making and say, "Sure, that seems like a plausible description of people's behavior." Gene looks at the same research and thinks, "Why would anyone do that?"

ALL INTERESTING MODELS ARE FALSE

Gene is arguably the best empiricist in finance. Although there are lots of reasons for his success, three of the most important are easy to describe. First, his empirical approach fully embraces the fact that models simplify the world. This insight implies that all interesting models are false and that most of the hypotheses people test in finance are also false. For example, no continuous random variable actually has an expected value of zero. With enough data we will always reject such a precise null.

Gene's goal when doing empirical work is to improve our understanding of important real world phenomena. He is not interested in testing models he knows are false. When presenting results, he emphasizes parameter estimates and the precision of the estimates, not formal tests. This emphasis explains why he says, for example, an estimate is *reliably* different from zero, not *significantly* different from zero. It also explains his aversion to papers that focus only on test statistics or, even worse, *p*-values.

SIMPLER IS BETTER

When asked to describe my research, a colleague who does theoretical work once said, "All Ken does is calculate averages . . . but he does it very well." I'm not sure whether that was meant as a compliment, but after working with Gene for 30 years, I view it as high praise. Simplicity is a hallmark of Gene's research. When writing papers, he works hard to make his logical arguments and statistical tests as simple as possible. He rarely uses a formal model to motivate his empirical work, and when he turns to the data he says, "If you can't see it in the averages, it's probably not there."

KNOW THE DATA

One of the most important reasons for Gene's success as an empiricist is his investment in the data. It is obvious that anyone who hopes to do good empirical work must pay attention to the data. But Gene's commitment goes far beyond that. When he begins working with new data, he spends days simply getting familiar with them. When he looks at empirical tests, he pores over the output, memorizing the central results and developing a thorough understanding of the rest. And when Gene considers someone else's work, he usually starts with the tables and then decides whether to read the text.

I try to replicate Gene's commitment, studying each new database and poring over test results. What I cannot replicate is his amazing memory. While

I struggle to remember the paper we just finished, he can describe the evidence from ancillary tests we did 25 years ago. After five decades of study, Gene knows more about financial data than Google. The value of this is apparent not only in his own research, but also in his advice to students, his suggestions in seminars, and his comments on colleagues' papers.

How can those of us without Gene's memory compete? They are not perfect substitutes, but I replace his facts with rules of thumb. The annual US equity premium for 1926 to 2013 is roughly 8% and the annual volatility is about 20%. The autocorrelations in equity returns are small and can often be ignored. The slopes in most regressions to explain US stock returns don't change a lot if we switch from nominal to real returns, but nominal or real does matter for bonds, especially short-term bonds. And so on. Obviously, these rules are not as good as Gene's detailed knowledge, but they usually provide the perspective I need.

CLARITY, BREVITY, PRECISION . . . AND NO FOOTNOTES

Mike Jensen, one of Gene's earliest students, once told me, "Our job is not to write papers, our job is to get people to read papers." That summarizes Gene's attitude toward writing. After hundreds, if not thousands, of arguments with Gene about the best word and the appropriate use of a comma, I can attest that he cares passionately about the quality of everything he writes. I can also attest that he works hard to deliver that quality. Because even the best colleagues rarely read anything more than once, Gene will not circulate a paper until it is as good as he can make it. As a result, most of his papers go through at least five and sometimes more than ten full revisions before he distributes them.

Gene tries to be clear, succinct, and precise. He can usually have all three, but when there is a conflict he sacrifices clarity and brevity for precision. His emphasis on communication affects even his research design. When choosing between two sensible empirical tests, the easier to explain has the inside track.

Finally, Gene rarely uses footnotes. Most are distractions that sidetrack the reader and expose a lazy writer. If the content is important, Gene includes it in the text. If the content is not worth space in the text, how can it justify a footnote that interrupts the reader's focus and train of thought?

COLLEGIALITY MATTERS

I am tempted to write that I have never seen Gene be rude or unkind, but I can anticipate his wife Sally's reaction: "Geesh French, I didn't realize you're blind."

So to be precise, in over 30 years of close observation, I recall Gene being discourteous only three times. Once a decade is a good record. He is blunt occasionally, but that is efficient, not rude.

Gene's behavior had a big impact on the level of collegiality at the Booth School when I was on the faculty and I assume it still does. Given his prominence in the field and the hundreds of former colleagues and students he has around the world, I think Gene's example has also had a big impact on the behavior of finance faculty more broadly. In other areas of economics, intellectual disagreements often lead to personal animosity. This rarely happens in finance. Gene's friendship with Dick Thaler illustrates the point. A sociologist could probably identify many contributing factors for the cultural norms in finance, but the example Gene sets must be important.

Gene's collegiality is not an accident. Soon after we started working together, we were talking about people the business school might hire. When I suggested one of the top researchers in finance, Gene said hiring him would be a mistake because he does not treat his colleagues with respect. Since that exchange, I have spent a lot of time trying to figure out what behavior contributes the most to a productive academic environment. I've concluded that, at least for business school faculty, Gene's behavior is a pretty good model.

NO AD HOMINEM ATTACKS

Gene once said a former colleague had won lots of arguments he should have lost. Nonacademics might be puzzled to discover that Gene meant this as strong criticism. His point was simple. Using sarcasm or a sharp wit to undermine those who disagree with you poisons the intellectual environment. Gene rejects all ad hominem attacks. He consistently focuses on the idea he is arguing about, not the person he is arguing with. For example, he says a reporter's question doesn't make sense, not that the reporter is a pompous, arrogant fool.

The first time I saw Gene insulted in an academic discussion—by a visiting accounting professor!—I was surprised by his response: he simply ignored the attack. Because of his prominence and outspoken views about market efficiency and monetary policy, Gene has been the victim of many personal attacks since then and, as far as I know, has ignored them all. He argues that his behavior is optimal, but doing is harder than knowing. Gene's ability to consistently remain on the intellectual high ground demonstrates remarkable emotional discipline.

GIVE REFEREES THE BENEFIT OF THE DOUBT

No one likes to hear that his or her child is not perfect. Most academics experience something like this every time we get a referee report. My solution is to skim the report when it arrives and then put it away. Twenty-four hours later I am ready to be constructive. Gene's response is more mature. He reads the report and immediately starts thinking about the most productive way to address the referee's concerns. I stopped complaining about referees' mistakes a long time ago because I know what Gene will say: "It's our fault if a smart, careful reader does not understand the paper." He does not always agree with the referee, and he will not make significant changes that reduce the quality of the paper, but he always assumes the referee is acting in good faith and he always starts with the presumption that the referee is right.

Gene also does not protest when a paper is rejected. He argues it is better to move on to another journal than to make the editor's difficult job even harder. As a result, he has not appealed an editorial decision in over 50 years of rejections.

CONCLUSION

Gene Fama has made remarkable contributions to our understanding of finance and economics for over 50 years. Gene's insights about research and the broader production function of academics—and his disciplined implementation of those insights—are equally remarkable. The goal of all his insights and discipline is to maximize his contribution to the intellectual environment of the University of Chicago. The big beneficiaries are the colleagues and students Gene has worked with over the years, especially me.

GENE FAMA'S IMPACT

A QUANTITATIVE ANALYSIS

. . .

G. William Schwert and René M. Stulz

Gene Fama has been the most prominent empiricist in finance for 50 years. He is the founder of empirical research in modern finance. For somebody who believes in numbers as he does, it is fitting to evaluate his impact using quantitative measures. We do so in this paper. As we collected data, we learned more about how exceptional Gene's impact is.

A scholar impacts the world because his research increases our knowledge. The most straightforward measure of how research increases our knowledge is a count of how often it is cited. We focus on a broad measure of citations, namely citations from Google Scholar, as our main measure. Per Google Scholar, Gene has more than 140,000 citations. To put this number in perspective, we compare Gene's citations to those of the Fellows of the American Finance Association. The median number of Google Scholar citations for the Fellows of the American Finance Association is 32,902. Only four Fellows have more than 100,000 citations.

We then explore in more detail which papers are most highly cited. Gene has three papers that have both more than 2,000 citations in the Social Sciences Citation Index and more than 11,000 Google citations. Strikingly, only one of these papers is an empirical paper. It is the paper with Ken French titled "Common Risk Factors in the Returns on Stocks and Bonds," published by the *Journal of Financial Economics*. The other two papers are "Efficient Capital Markets: A Review of Theory and Empirical Work" and the paper with Michael Jensen titled "Separation of Ownership and Control."

Our examination of Gene's citations shows how broad his range of interest was through his career. Of his top three papers, two are in asset pricing and one is in corporate finance.

Originally published as *Simon Business School Working Paper* No. FR 14–17 (September 2014). © 2014 by G. William Schwert and René M. Stulz.

"Efficient Capital Markets" is, in many ways, Gene's most influential paper. The citations do not show it partly because the contribution of the paper is to define the concept of efficient capital markets in a way that has lasted for more than 40 years. When authors talk about efficient capital markets, they refer to Gene's definition, but they rarely cite him. This is the ultimate mark of a paper's influence—its contribution becomes so embedded in a field's way of thinking and communicating that there is no need to cite the original paper when referring to its key concept.

Gene's influence has spread through students. Gene has advised a large number of Ph.D. students. We attempted to create a complete list of students advised either as chair or as a member of the student's committee and found 102 students. These students have gone on to conduct their own influential research. A simple way to see the success of Gene as an adviser is that 11 of his students have more than 10,000 Google citations. Six of his former students have been president of the American Finance Association and one received the Nobel Memorial Prize in Economic Sciences.

We conclude the paper with an attempt to explain why Gene has been so successful and for so long. Gene's professional life spans four complete decades. In each one of these decades, he published at least 15 papers. For the last complete decade, he was in his 60s. The decade in which he produced papers with the highest average number of citations is the 1990s, when he was in his 50s. His three most cited works are each published in a different decade. This lifecycle pattern of production is unusual among Nobel Prize winners. We speculate that it is the product of a person with a fierce intellect who loves what he is doing and has an unparalleled work ethic.

SECTION 1. GENE FAMA'S IMPACT ON FINANCE.

A scholar can impact the world at large as well as his academic discipline. There are no easy quantitative measures of this impact. But we know Gene's impact is enormous. "Efficient markets" is a household name throughout the world. The efficient markets view inspired countless laws, regulations, accounting practices, and policies, many of which you will read about in subsequent essays in this volume. It affects how investors make their investment decisions and evaluate their performance. It also has been (mistakenly, in our view, but a measure of influence nonetheless) blamed for a financial crisis.

The limitations of citation counts are well-known, but despite these limitations, citation counts provide the most straightforward and objective assessment of a scholar's impact. There are two distinct approaches to counting citations. The most traditional approach is to use the Social Sciences Citation Index (SSCI). The other approach is to use Google Scholar. Searching within Google Scholar is made easier with a program called "Publish or Perish" (Harzing 2007). Results with Google Scholar can be sensitive to how the search is conducted. To minimize the risk of errors, we conducted the search multiple times. Two research assistants conducted the search separately for each name. We then worked to reconcile their results when they were materially different. The number of citations in Google Scholar to SSCI is roughly 5 to 1.

With Google Scholar, Gene has 140,562 citations. Using SSCI instead, Gene has 30,154 citations. To put the number of citations in perspective, we collect the citations of all the Fellows of the American Finance Association (AFA). The list of the Fellows includes all past presidents of the AFA who were alive in 2000 when the Fellows list was created, as well as elected Fellows. Each year at least one Fellow has been elected. Gene is the first elected Fellow of the AFA. All winners of the Nobel Memorial Prize in Economics with work in finance who were alive in 2000 are Fellows. This list does not provide a perfect comparison group, as some highly cited financial economists are not Fellows. For instance, Tim Bollerslev is not a Fellow, but he would be among the top ten most highly cited Fellows as his citation count is 63,678. Table 1 shows the Google citations for all Fellows with more than 20,000 Google citations.

Thirteen fellows have less than 20,000 Google citations. Figure 1 plots the distribution of the number of citations for AFA Fellows.

Table 1 and Figure 1 show clearly how large Gene's impact is compared to the typical Fellow. The mean Google citations for all 47 AFA Fellows (excluding Gene) is 39,790. The distribution is skewed as the median is 32,902. Gene's cites are more than three times the mean and more than four times the median. The standard deviation of the number of Google citations for AFA Fellows is 32,240. Consequently, Gene's number of Google citations is more than three standard deviations above the mean. The top five AFA Fellows in Google citations are, in order: Andrei Shleifer, Gene Fama, Michael Jensen, Kenneth Arrow, and Robert Engle. Not surprisingly, three of the five have received the Nobel Memorial Prize in Economics.

With the introduction of the World Wide Web, the number of downloads has become a new measure of interest in a scholar's work. The Social Science Research Network (SSRN) publishes download statistics on the top authors. Gene's papers have been downloaded an astounding 386,573 times on SSRN. Gene has been involved with the SSRN since its inception. He is Chair of the Board of Trustees of SSRN.

TABLE 1. Google Scholar citations to Fellows of the American Finance Association Showing all Fellows with 20,000 or more citations. There are 47 Fellows as of 2014.

		Total Citations				Total Citations
1	Andrei Shleifer	168,336		19	Myron S. Scholes*	38,455
2	Eugene F. Fama*	140,562		20	Jeremy Stein	37,932
3	Michael C. Jensen	123,957		21	Sheridan Titman	37,389
4	Kenneth Arrow*	112,621		22	Sanford J. Grossman	35,902
5	Robert F. Engle*	84,429		23	Harry Markowitz*	33,261
6	Robert E. Lucas, Jr.*	69,926		24	William F. Sharpe*	33,012
7	Richard Thaler	68,839		25	Richard Roll	32,792
8	Paul Samuelson*	68,410		26	Darrell Duffie	30,917
9	Kenneth R. French	64,030		27	Douglas W. Diamond	27,553
10	Robert C. Merton*	59,972		28	Franklin Allen	26,670
11	John Y. Campbell	55,381		29	Lars Peter Hansen*	26,082
12	Stephen A. Ross	54,710		30	John C. Cox	25,311
13	Stewart C. Myers	48,867		31	Eduardo S. Schwartz	24,759
14	Franco Modigliani*	46,571		32	Burton G. Malkiel	24,550
15	Raghuram Rajan	45,559		33	Michael J. Brennan	21,219
16	René Stulz	45,397		34	John H. Cochrane	20,451
17	Robert Shiller*	43,261				
18	Bengt Holmström	41,357				

* Winners of the Sveriges Riksbank Prize in Economic Sciences in Memory of Alfred Nobel.

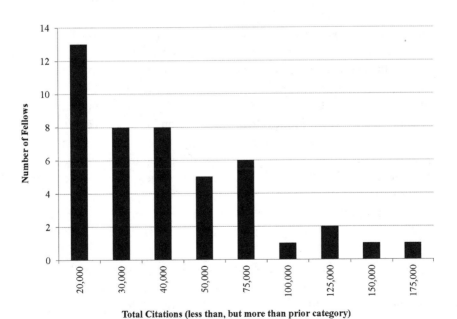

Figure 1. Distribution of citations to AFA Fellows

SECTION 2. WHERE DOES THE IMPACT COME FROM?

We now turn to a more detailed examination of the citation impact of Gene's work. Google Scholar reports citations to 107 papers and 2 books. In Table 2, we separate the papers into six groups: asset pricing, efficient markets, corporate control, banking, dividend policy and capital structure, and interest rates, exchange rates, and futures prices. (Though dividing papers across these groups is straightforward in most cases, some of our decisions are admittedly subjective.)

Gene's impact is strongest in the first three groups. In each of these groups, Gene has at least two papers with more than 1,000 cites in SSCI and at least one paper with 10,000 Google sites. The other three groups have distinctly less impact—by Gene's standards, but not by the standards of almost all members of the finance profession—as no paper has more than 500 SSCI citations or more than 2,000 Google citations.

Figure 2 shows the distribution of the number of papers across areas. The asset pricing group has the most papers—a total of 37. The interest rate and foreign exchange area—a close cousin of asset pricing—is the second most active group. The corporate control and banking groups are the least active.

Yet Figure 3 shows that the corporate control group has the most citations per paper. This success is due to two enormously successful papers. The first one, with Michael Jensen, is "Separation of Ownership and Control." The second one is by Gene alone, "Agency Problems and the Theory of the Firm." The first paper has 2,321 SSCI citations and the second has 1,743.

The efficient markets group is the second most successful group in terms of average citations per paper. This group includes "Efficient Capital Markets," which has 2,432 SSCI and 11,658 Google Scholar citations. Gene's dissertation, "The Behavior of Stock-Market Prices," is the second most cited article in that group with 1,373 SSCI citations and 6,598 Google Scholar citations. Finally, the asset pricing group is the third most successful group in citations per paper. That group includes three papers that have more than 1,000 SSCI citations. These three papers include two papers with Ken French published in the 1990s, "Common Risk Factors in the Returns on Stocks and Bonds" and "The Cross-Section of Expected Stock Returns." The third paper is the one with Jim Mac-Beth from the 1970s titled "Risk, Return, and Equilibrium: Empirical Tests."

Gene has both empirical papers and theoretical papers. His first theoretical paper was published in 1965, which is the first year that he appeared in scholarly journals. Some of the theory papers have a mathematical model. Others

TABLE 2. Google Scholar and Social Sciences Citation Index citations to papers and books by Eugene Fama

	Google Scholar	SSCI	Authors	Title	Year	Publication
Asset Pricing						
1	11,697	2,430	EF Fama, KR French	Common risk factors in the returns on stocks and bonds	1993	Journal of Financial Economics
2	10,515	1,801	EF Fama, KR French	The cross-section of expected stock returns	1992	Journal of Finance
3	7,584	1,620	EF Fama, JD MacBeth	Risk, return, and equilibrium: Empirical tests	1973	Journal of Political Economy
4	3,287	727	EF Fama, KR French	Industry costs of equity	1997	Journal of Financial Economics
5	2,571	627	EF Fama, KR French	Business conditions and expected returns on stocks and bonds	1989	Journal of Financial Economics
6	2,498	587	EF Fama, KR French	Permanent and temporary components of stock prices	1988	Journal of Political Economy
7	2,448	446	EF Fama, KR French	Size and book-to-market factors in earnings and returns	1995	Journal of Finance
8	2,375	553	EF Fama, KR French	Dividend yields and expected stock returns	1988	Journal of Financial Economics
9	1,940	435	EF Fama	Stock returns, real activity, inflation, and money	1981	American Economic Review
10	1,894	509	EF Fama, GW Schwert	Asset returns and inflation	1977	Journal of Financial Economics
11	1,558	252	EF Fama, KR French	Value versus growth: The international evidence	1998	Journal of Finance
12	1,064	215	EF Fama	Stock returns, expected returns, and real activity	1990	Journal of Finance
13	984	178	EF Fama, KR French	The equity premium	2002	Journal of Finance
14	784	152	JL Davis, EF Fama, KR French	Characteristics, covariances, and average returns: 1929 to 1997	2000	Journal of Finance
15	750	94	EF Fama, KR French	The capital asset pricing model: Theory and evidence	2004	Journal of Economic Perspectives
16	549	176	EF Fama	Multi-period consumption-investment decisions	1968	American Economic Review
17	512	66	EF Fama	Components of investment performance	1972	Journal of Finance
18	424	35	EF Fama, KR French	The CAPM is wanted, dead or alive	1996	Journal of Finance
19	404	129	EF Fama	Risk, return and equilibrium: Some clarifying comments	1968	Journal of Finance
20	389	133	EF Fama	Portfolio analysis in a stable Paretian market	1965	Management Science
21	321	49	EF Fama, KR French	The value premium and the CAPM	2006	Journal of Finance
22	267	44	EF Fama, KR French	Luck versus skill in the cross-section of mutual fund returns	2010	Journal of Finance
23	239	45	EF Fama	Multifactor portfolio efficiency and multifactor asset pricing	1996	Journal of Financial and Quantitative Analysis
24	210	56	EF Fama	Risk, return, and equilibrium	1971	Journal of Political Economy
25	189	49	EF Fama, GW Schwert	Human capital and capital market equilibrium	1977	Journal of Financial Economics
26	146	35	EF Fama, KR French	Disagreement, tastes, and asset prices	2007	Journal of Financial Economics

(Continued)

TABLE 2. (Continued)

	Google Scholar	SSCI	Authors	Title	Year	Publication
27	109	45	EF Fama, JD MacBeth	Tests of the multiperiod two-parameter model	1974	Journal of Financial Economics
28	90	6	EF Fama, KR French	Size, value, and momentum in international stock returns	2012	Journal of Financial Economics
29	71	14	EF Fama	A note on the market model and the two-parameter model	1973	Journal of Finance
30	56	9	DG Booth, EF Fama	Diversification returns and asset contributions	1992	Financial Analysts Journal
31	53	10	EF Fama, KR French, DG Booth, R Sinquefield	Differences in the risks and returns of NYSE and NASD stocks	1993	Financial Analysts Journal
32	51	11	EF Fama	Determining the number of priced state variables in the ICAPM	1998	Journal of Financial and Quantitative Analysis
33	49	14	EF Fama, KR French	Average returns, B/M, and share issues	2008	Journal of Finance
34	39	13	EF Fama, JD MacBeth	Long-term growth in a short-term market	1974	Journal of Finance
35	32		EF Fama, KR French	The economic fundamentals of size and book-to-market equity	1992	Unpublished working paper, University of Chicago
36	31	31	EF Fama, KR French	The CAPM: Theory and evidence	2003	Center for Research in Security Prices (CRSP)
37	26	11	EF Fama	Ordinal and measurable utility	1972	Studies in the Theory of Capital Markets
	56,206	11,576	Subtotal			
Efficient Markets						
1	11,658	2,432	EF Fama	Efficient capital markets: A review of theory and empirical work	1970	Journal of Finance
2	6,598	1,373	EF Fama	The behavior of stock-market prices	1965	Journal of Business
3	4,251	794	EF Fama, KR French	Multifactor explanations of asset pricing anomalies	1996	Journal of Finance
4	4,206	834	EF Fama	Efficient capital markets: II	1991	Journal of Finance
5	3,563	627	EF Fama	Market efficiency, long-term returns, and behavioral finance	1998	Journal of Financial Economics
6	3,265	815	EF Fama, L Fisher, M Jensen, R Roll	The adjustment of stock prices to new information	1969	International Economic Review
7	741	100	EF Fama	Random walks in stock market prices	1965	Financial Analysts Journal

#	Citations	Authors	Title	Year	Journal
8	732	EF Fama, ME Blume	Filter rules and stock-market trading	1966	Journal of Business
9	669	EF Fama	Mandelbrot and the stable Paretian hypothesis	1963	Journal of Business
10	495	EF Fama, KR French	Dissecting anomalies	2008	Journal of Finance
11	468	EF Fama, R Roll	Parameter estimates for symmetric stable distributions	1971	Journal of the American Statistical Association
12	438	EF Fama, R Roll	Some properties of symmetric stable distributions	1968	Journal of the American Statistical Association
13	166	EF Fama, AB Laffer	Information and capital markets	1971	Journal of Business
14	110	EF Fama	Efficient capital markets: Reply	1976	Journal of Finance
15	62	EF Fama	Tomorrow on the New York Stock Exchange	1965	Journal of Business
16	58	EF Fama, KR French	The anatomy of value and growth stock returns	2007	Financial Analysts Journal
17	57	EF Fama	Perfect competition and optimal production decisions under uncertainty	1972	Bell Journal of Economics and Management Science
18	45	EF Fama	Perspectives on October 1987, or, What did we learn from the crash?	1988	Journal of Finance
19	45	EF Fama, KR French	Luck versus skill in the cross section of mutual fund alpha estimates	2009	Journal of Finance
	37,627	7,871 Subtotal			
Corporate Control					
1	11,421	EF Fama, MC Jensen	Separation of ownership and control	1983	Journal of Law and Economics
2	8,716	EF Fama	Agency problems and the theory of the firm	1980	Journal of Political Economy
3	3,520	EF Fama, MC Jensen	Agency problems and residual claims	1983	Journal of Law and Economics
4	506	EF Fama, MC Jensen	Organizational forms and investment decisions	1985	Journal of Financial Economics
5	152	EF Fama	Contract costs and financing decisions	1990	Journal of Business
6	91	EF Fama	Time, salary, and incentive payoffs in labor contracts	1991	Journal of Labor Economics
7	88	EF Fama, AB Laffer	The number of firms and competition	1972	American Economic Review
	24,494	4,942 Subtotal			

(Continued)

TABLE 2. (Continued)

	Google Scholar	SSCI	Authors	Title	Year	Publication
Banking						
1	1,813	378	EF Fama	What's different about banks?	1985	Journal of Monetary Economics
2	889	192	EF Fama	Banking in the theory of finance	1980	Journal of Monetary Economics
	2,702	570	Subtotal			
Dividend Policy and Capital Structure						
1	1,730	279	EF Fama, KR French	Testing trade-off and pecking order predictions about dividends and debt	2002	Review of Financial Studies
2	1,704	295	EF Fama, KR French	Disappearing dividends: Changing firm characteristics or lower propensity to pay?	2001	Journal of Financial Economics
3	744	169	EF Fama, H Babiak	Dividend policy: An empirical analysis	1968	Journal of the American Statistical Association
4	551	87	EF Fama, KR French	Taxes, financing decisions, and firm value	1998	Journal of Finance
5	540	119	EF Fama, KR French	Forecasting profitability and earnings	2000	Journal of Business
6	501	87	EF Fama, KR French	Financing decisions: who issues stock?	2005	Journal of Financial Economics
7	391	82	EF Fama, KR French	New lists: Fundamentals and survival rates	2004	Journal of Financial Economics
8	352	84	EF Fama	Risk-adjusted discount rates and capital budgeting under uncertainty	1977	Journal of Financial Economics
9	307	63	EF Fama	The effects of a firm's investment and financing decisions on the welfare of its security holders	1978	American Economic Review
10	250	47	EF Fama, KR French	Profitability, investment and average returns	2006	Journal of Financial Economics
11	206	38	EF Fama	The empirical relationships between the dividend and investment decisions of firms	1974	American Economic Review
12	193	21	EF Fama, KR French	The corporate cost of capital and the return on corporate investment	1999	Journal of Finance
13	138	59	GD Eppen, EF Fama	Cash balance and simple dynamic portfolio problems with proportional costs	1969	International Economic Review
14	110	22	EF Fama	Discounting under uncertainty	1996	Journal of Business

#			Authors	Title	Year	Journal
15	73	30	GD Eppen, EF Fama	Solutions for cash-balance and simple dynamic-portfolio problems	1968	Journal of Business
16	63	26	GD Eppen, EF Fama	Three asset cash balance and dynamic portfolio problems	1971	Management Science
17	25		EF Fama, KR French	Dividends, debt, investment, and earnings	1997	Management Science
	7,878	1,508	Subtotal			

Interest Rates, Exchange Rates, and Futures Prices

#			Authors	Title	Year	Journal
1	1,458	385	EF Fama	Forward and spot exchange rates	1984	Journal of Monetary Economics
2	1,074	411	EF Fama	Short-term interest rates as predictors of inflation	1975	American Economic Review
3	1,033	252	EF Fama, RR Bliss	The information in long-maturity forward rates	1987	American Economic Review
4	669	208	EF Fama	The information in the term structure	1984	Journal of Financial Economics
5	626	203	EF Fama, KR French	Commodity futures prices: Some evidence on forecast power, premiums, and the theory of storage	1987	Journal of Business
6	483	147	EF Fama, MR Gibbons	Inflation, real returns and capital investment	1982	Journal of Monetary Economics
7	417	97	EF Fama	Term-structure forecasts of interest rates, inflation and real returns	1990	Journal of Monetary Economics
8	315	105	EF Fama, MR Gibbons	A comparison of inflation forecasts	1984	Journal of Monetary Economics
9	281	77	EF Fama, KR French	Business cycles and the behavior of metals prices	1988	Journal of Finance
10	221	93	EF Fama	Inflation uncertainty and expected returns on Treasury bills	1976	Journal of Political Economy
11	221	82	EF Fama	Forward rates as predictors of future spot rates	1976	Journal of Financial Economics
12	211	75	EF Fama, A Farber	Money, bonds, and foreign exchange	1979	American Economic Review
13	202	76	EF Fama	Term premiums in bond returns	1984	Journal of Financial Economics
14	159	39	EF Fama	Term premiums and default premiums in money markets	1986	Journal of Financial Economics
15	132	44	EF Fama	Financial intermediation and price level control	1983	Journal of Monetary Economics
16	122	42	EF Fama	Interest rates and inflation: The message in the entrails	1977	American Economic Review
17	119	35	EF Fama	Inflation, output, and money	1982	Journal of Business
18	60	22	EF Fama, GW Schwert	Inflation, interest, and relative prices	1979	Journal of Business
19	57	12	EF Fama	The behavior of interest rates	2006	Review of Financial Studies
20	47		EF Fama	A pricing model for the municipal bond market	1977	Manuscript, University of Chicago

(Continued)

TABLE 2. (Continued)

	Google Scholar	SSCI	Authors	Title	Year	Publication
21	38	11	EF Fama	Transitory variation in investment and output	1992	Journal of Monetary Economics
22	3		EF Fama	Annual inflation and money growth	1979	
23	2		EF Fama	Money and inflation	1979	
24	2		EF Fama	A price model for the municipal bond market	1977	Unpublished manuscript, University of Chicago
25	1		EF Fama	Short-term inflation and money growth	1979	
	7,953	2,416	Subtotal			
Books						
1	2,237	772	EF Fama	Foundations of finance: Portfolio decisions and securities prices	1976	
2	1,465	499	EF Fama, MH Miller	The theory of finance	1972	
	3,702	1,271	Subtotal			

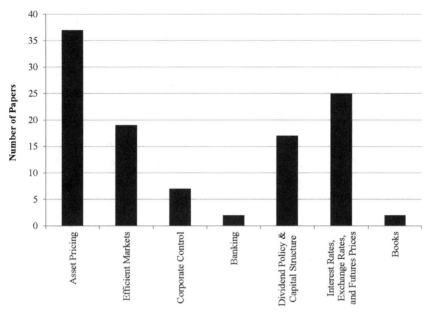

Figure 2. Distribution of Fama papers across research areas

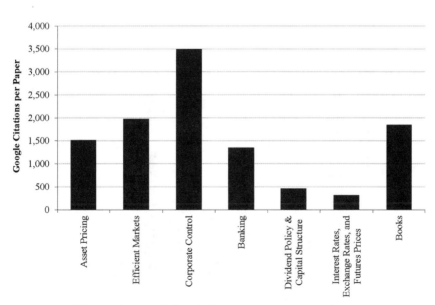

Figure 3. Average citations to Fama papers across research areas

are more conceptual. Two of the three most impactful papers are theoretical conceptual papers: "Efficient Capital Markets" and "Separation of Ownership and Control."

Gene has theoretical papers in each of the groups we identify. However, the impact of these papers differs according to the group. The top five papers in the corporate control group are all theoretical papers. They have a total of 24,315 Google citations. Fifteen out of 44 AFA Fellows have fewer Google citations for their whole career output. Both of Gene's banking papers are theoretical. In the efficient markets group, three of the top five papers are conceptual theoretical papers, with a total of 19,427 Google citations. In the asset pricing and interest rates and exchange rates group, no theoretical paper is among the top 10 papers. In the dividend policy and capital structure group, two theoretical papers are among the top 10 cited papers. However, neither paper has a large number of citations by Gene's standards. Specifically, "Risk-Adjusted Discount Rates and Capital Budgeting under Uncertainty" has 352 Google citations while "The Effects of a Firm's Investment and Financing Decisions on the Welfare of Its Security Holders" has 307 Google citations.

We collect data on where Gene published his papers. Figure 4 shows that he published 23 papers in the *Journal of Finance*, followed closely by the *Journal of Financial Economics* with 20 papers.

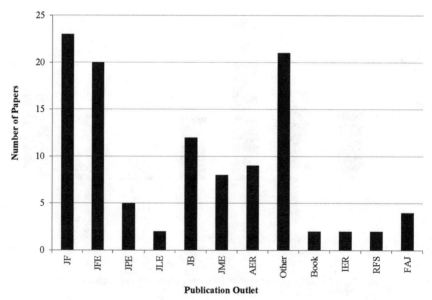

Figure 4. Distribution of Fama papers across journals

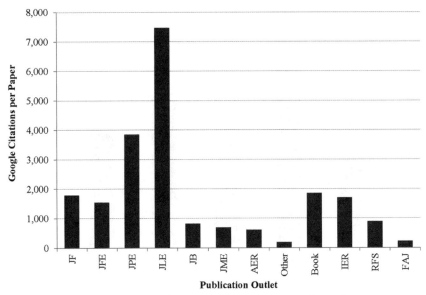

Figure 5. Average citations per Fama paper across journals

In contrast, he published only two papers in the *Review of Financial Studies*. He also published in the main economics journals with nine papers in the *American Economic Review* and five in the *Journal of Political Economy*. Figure 5 shows the average number of citations per paper across the journals in which Gene published.

His highest average number of citations per paper is in the *Journal of Law and Economics*. Only three of Gene's papers are published in that journal and they are all coauthored with Michael Jensen. These papers have a total of 23,657 citations.

Finally, it is amazing to see that Gene's work spans parts of six decades. Figure 6 shows the number of papers he published in each decade from the 1960s through the current decade.

Since the first and last decades only include about five years when Gene was publishing, it is not surprising that the number of papers is smaller, but the sustained quantity of output reflected in this graph is truly unique in our experience.

Figure 7 shows the average citations per paper across decades. The 1980s and 1990s, which include much of the Fama-French asset pricing research and the Fama-Jensen corporate control work, have the highest average levels of

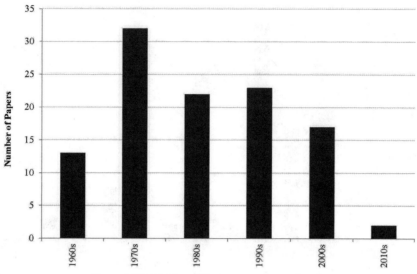

Figure 6. Distribution of Fama papers across decades

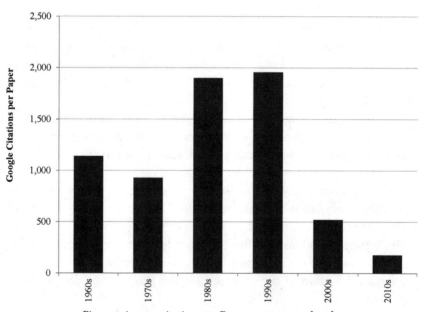

Figure 7. Average citations per Fama paper across decades

citations per paper. Nevertheless, papers from all of these decades have extremely high levels of average citations.

SECTION 3. GENE'S IMPACT THROUGH HIS STUDENTS.

Scholars have an impact on the field through the students they train who go on to themselves have an impact on the field. In that dimension, Gene's achievement is impressive, perhaps uniquely so. He advised 102 Ph.D. students either as chair or as a member of the committee. Collectively, these students have 585,645 Google citations. Of these 102 students, he was the chair for 48 students. These students have 438,353 Google citations. The average number of citations per Ph.D. student whose dissertation committee was chaired by Gene is 9,132.

Among the students for whom Gene was the adviser, Michael Jensen has the largest number of Google citations with 123,957. Without him, the average number of citations per Ph.D. student advised by Gene drops to 6,689. The students with more than 20,000 Google citations include Campbell Harvey, Richard Roll, Myron Scholes, and one of the authors of this article, G. William Schwert. The list includes two former editors of the *Journal of Finance*, the founding editor and the current editor of the *Journal of Financial Economics*, editors of the *Journal of Accounting and Economics* and the *Journal of Accounting Research*, and five former presidents of the American Finance Association.[1]

In keeping with the relevance of Gene's work for the world of investments, it is not surprising that several of his former students are investment managers. Clifford Asness and John Liew cofounded AQR Capital Management in 1998. As of March 2016, AQR has over $142 billion in assets under management. Dimensional Fund Advisors (DFA), which was started in 1981 by two of Gene's students, David Booth and Rex Sinquefield, has designed its menu of products and services around the Fama-French asset pricing research. As of March 2016, DFA had over $388 billion assets under management. Gene has been an active part of DFA's success as a director and consultant. The success of DFA has been very beneficial for the University of Chicago, as reflected in the naming of the Booth School of Business in 2008. Many of Gene's other PhD students now work at the top echelons of the investment world.

---

1. We include Campbell Harvey in the list of AFA presidents as he will hold the title in two years

SECTION 4. SOME COMMENTS ON GENE'S UNIQUENESS.

The numbers do not tell the whole story of Gene's remarkable impact on finance and economics.

In addition to Gene's impact through his own work and through his students, for over 50 years Gene has had a significant influence on his professional colleagues. This influence is most obvious through his interactions with the faculty at the University of Chicago. Scholars also benefit from comments from Gene on their papers even when they are not at the university. Both of us were visitors at Chicago and we know countless other visitors whose approach to finance was influenced by Gene and whose work, like ours, has benefitted and still benefits from interacting with him. His uniquely economical e-mails commenting on papers are always valuable. Many colleagues have benefited from his one-word, red-ink, hand-written comments on a paper draft.

One of Gene's biggest contributions has been his presence in the finance seminar at the University of Chicago. The ultimate test for a paper by an empiricist has long been whether Gene would find it credible and interesting. In that seminar, Gene has always had the ability to keep people honest with their work and with what the data were saying. There is always a possibility that Gene could ask for the code, as he is known to have done. As a result, he made the work presented at the seminar better, whether it was presented by faculty members or by individuals coming from the outside.

Gene has never hesitated to say what he thinks about papers he reads or papers that he listens to. As we know from experience, the fact that a paper is a lead article in a leading journal does not prevent Gene from concluding that the empirical results of the paper are not credible. To Gene, science can only progress with absolute honesty.

As journal editors, both of us have interacted with Gene as an author and as a referee for more than 35 years. He has been a role model. When one of us (René Stulz) created the "Tips for Authors" list on the *Journal of Finance* website (which migrated to the *Journal of Financial Economics* website when René finished his terms as *JF* editor), many of the examples of how authors should write papers and react to referees' reports are based directly on Gene's behavior.

We have both been privileged to observe Gene as a referee of others' papers. Gene is the longest continuously active editor at the *JFE*, having been a coeditor when it was first published in 1974. Many people who achieve much more modest success in our profession often find it too taxing to continue to serve as a referee or editor, reading, thinking about, and offering constructive criticism to authors who are hoping to get their papers published in an academic journal. Gene, in contrast, has always found time to contribute his time and thoughts to his professional colleagues, usually without any direct recognition for his efforts since referee reports are anonymous to the author. As shown in Figure 8, since 1994 Gene averages more than four referee reports per year for the *JFE*, which is higher than the average workload for the rest of the editorial board.

Figure 9 shows that his average turnaround time is a little more than 10 days, compared to about 32 days for the rest of the editorial board and over 40 days for ad hoc referees. His behavior as a referee for the *Journal of Finance* from 1988 to 2000 (Rene Stulz's tenure as editor) was similar.

It is rare for a scholar to maintain such an intense involvement with research at the forefront of the field for 50 years as Gene has done. Empirical research on the lifecycle of the impact of Nobel prizewinners in economics shows that authors of theoretical/conceptual contributions peak early in life (see Weinberg and Galenson 2005). More empirically oriented researchers appear to make their contributions later in life. Gene made highly impactful contributions in his 20s, but the Nobel Prize committee cites work form his 50s as well. He published seven asset pricing papers with more than 1,000 Google

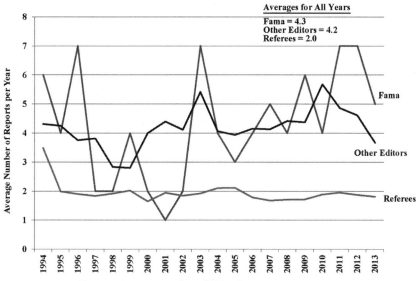

Figure 8. Average number of JFE *referee reports, 1994–2013*

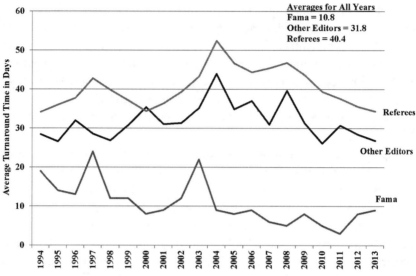

Figure 9. Average turnaround time for JFE referee reports, 1994–2013

citations in his 50s. In his 60s, he had two corporate finance papers with more than 1,000 cites. His three most highly cited papers were published in 1970, 1983, and 1993.

What is it that makes these papers special? None of the papers is a technical tour de force. None uses the most advanced econometric or theoretical techniques. Instead, each one of these papers opens up a new way for financial economists to think about their field. The 1970 paper does so by making sense of what market efficiency means and why it has to be taken seriously. The 1983 paper sets up a framework to understand corporate governance. The 1993 paper proposes an empirical asset pricing model that has been the benchmark model for finance research ever since. Though often using apparently simple econometric techniques, however, Gene is immensely influential as an empirical methodologist. Fama-MacBeth regressions, portfolio sorts, event studies, and assessing luck versus skill are just some of Gene's defining empirical methods that lasted decades.

Why have these papers been so successful? Why has Gene been so successful? Gene always works on his papers relentlessly. He has always understood that it is not enough to have insights or results. They have to be communicated so that they will impact the profession. Gene keeps rewriting his drafts. He has strong opinions on how papers should be written. As editors, both of us have imposed some of these opinions on countless authors. Gene also works intelligently and efficiently. Gene's discipline is unparalleled. He avoids distractions that make most of us less productive, but doing so allows him to be in his office with a regularity that would be close to impossible to replicate for most of his colleagues in finance. This discipline has not stood in the way of him being a kind and considerate person. One of us, René Stulz, remembers that one of the first phone calls he received after back surgery was from Gene. It is often said that for a paper to be highly cited, it is important to travel far and wide to present the paper and to work hard at selling it through personal interactions. This view may be correct, but if it is, Gene is a huge exception. Finally, and most importantly, Gene has always loved and respected research—and data. When the facts change, so does Gene's mind.

REFERENCES

Harzing, A. W. 2007. "Publish or Perish." Available at http://www.harzing.com/pop.htm.

Weinberg, B. A., and D. W. Galenson. 2005. "Creative Careers: The Life Cycles of Nobel Laureates in Economics." Working paper 11799, National Bureau of Economic Research, Cambridge, MA.

EFFICIENT MARKETS

· · ·

EFFICIENT MARKETS AND EMPIRICAL FINANCE

. . .

John H. Cochrane and Tobias J. Moskowitz

In 1970, Gene Fama defined a market to be "informationally efficient" if prices at each moment incorporate available information about future values.

> A market in which prices always "fully reflect" available information is called "efficient."—Fama (1970)

Informational efficiency is a natural consequence of competition, relatively free entry, and low information costs. If there is a signal that an asset's future value will be higher than its current value, competitive traders will try to buy the asset today. They bid prices up, until prices reflect the new information. We illustrate the process in the picture below.

As an immediate consequence, in a competitive asset market, price *changes* should not be predictable. This is a powerful result, which finance practitioners—whose job is to predict price changes—have great trouble digesting even as a matter of theory.

Like all good theories, it only seems simple in retrospect. It was a much harder and deeper intellectual achievement than our story suggests. It took

Figure 1

nearly a century to figure out the *basic predictions* of market efficiency, from Bachelier's random walk, Samuelson's proof that price changes should not be predictable, through Fama's efficient market essay, to the stochastic discount factor expression—price equals expected discounted payoff—that constitutes today's distillation of the theory.

EFFICIENCY AND EMPIRICAL FINANCE

The famous 1970 essay with which we start this volume is usually considered important as a statement of theory. The textbook treatment usually runs through Gene's catalog of "strong" to "weak" form predictions. But that is, in our view, not its key contribution. Rather, Gene showed how the simple idea of informational efficiency can organize and give purpose to a vast empirical project. Gene's contributions are more like Darwin's than Einstein's. Evolution by natural selection is a simple-sounding principle, with a lot of hard thinking needed to make it useful, that organized a vast empirical project in biology. Without evolution, natural history would have just been a collection of curious facts about plants and animals. Efficient markets is a simple-sounding principle, with a lot of hard thinking needed to make it useful, that organized a vast empirical project in financial economics. Without the efficient markets hypothesis, empirical finance would have just been a collection of Wall-Street anecdotes, how-I-got-rich stories, and technical-trading newssheets.

That empirical work consists, fundamentally, of applying scientific method to financial markets. Modern medicine doesn't ask old people for their health secrets. It does double-blind clinical trials. To this, we owe our ability to cure and prevent many diseases. Modern empirical finance doesn't ask Warren Buffet to share his pearls of investment wisdom, as the media does. We study a survivor-bias-free sample of funds sorted on some ex ante visible characteristic to separate skill from luck, and we correct for exposure to systematic risk. To this we owe our wisdom, and maybe, as a society, a lot of wealth as well.

Empirical work is not easy, either. The efficient markets hypothesis doesn't just hand you "predictions." The empirical implications of the efficient markets hypothesis are subtle and often deeply counterintuitive. Empirical work often tackles tough anomalies, each of which looks superficially like a glaring violation of efficiency, and each endorsed by a cheering crowd of rich (or perhaps lucky?) traders and hoping-to-be-rich current students. Like any nonexperimental science, distinguishing cause from effect is tough. There are always at least two stories for every correlation. It took hard work and great insight to account for risk premiums, selection biases, reverse causality, and endogenous variables, and to develop the associated statistical procedures. It took genius to sort through the mountains of charts and graphs that computers can spit out, to see the basic clear picture and a framework to organize it.

For example, efficiency implies that trading rules—"buy when the market went up yesterday"—should not work. The surprising result is that, when examined scientifically—and especially when accounting for the selection bias that only successful traders leave a paper trail—trading rules, technical systems, market newsletters, and so on have essentially no power beyond that of luck to forecast stock prices. That was true in 1970 and remains true today. This statement is not a theorem, an axiom, a philosophy, a tautology, or a religion: it is an empirical prediction that could easily have come out the other way.

If markets are efficient, then professional managers should do no better than monkeys with darts. This prediction too bore out remarkably well in the data in 1970 and still does to a large extent. It too could have come out the other way.

As Ray Ball points out, stock prices move on all sorts of information, which we as students of the market do not observe. How can you tell that prices are reacting correctly? It took genius to invert the question and to look instead at the average response to known pieces of information. And there, to see almost perfect stair-step reactions to information as predicted by the efficient markets view.

Already in 1970, Gene found that prices are not always efficient. For example, prices rise on the release of inside information, so that information, though known by someone, was not reflected in the original price. Perfect efficiency, like perfect competition, is always an ideal, toward which markets may be closer or further away.

This is *great* news. Only a theory that can be proved wrong has any content at all. Theories that can "explain" anything are as useless as "prices went down because the Gods are angry." Still, Gene found in 1970 that asset returns displayed patterns surprisingly close to efficient markets predictions, and surprisingly far from the assertions of most practitioners.

RISK, RETURN, AND MARKET EQUILIBRIUM

In a competitive market, investments that carry more risk must offer better returns on average. Therefore, if one finds a high expected return (i.e., an "underpriced" security), that fact does not necessarily imply inefficiency. It might represent a risk premium. The simple idea that price changes should not be predictable obviously needs amendment for allowable variation in risk premiums.

The joint hypothesis theorem in Gene's 1970 article is at least as important as the definition and characterization of efficiency. How much price or expected return variation can risk premiums account for?

> The theory only has empirical content, however, within the context of a more specific model of market equilibrium . . . (Fama 1970)

And, without specifying a model of market equilibrium, the theory (or its antitheses) therefore has *no* empirical content.

In more modern language, absent arbitrage opportunities we can write price as the expected discounted payoff,

$$\Lambda_t p_t = E_t\left[\Lambda_{t+1}(p_{t+1} + d_{t+1})\right] = \sum_s \pi(s)\Lambda_{t+1}(s)(p_{t+1}(s) + d_{t+1}(s))$$

where Λ_t is the stochastic discount factor, for example $\Lambda_t = \beta^t u'(c_t)$ in the canonical consumption based model, d_t are dividends, and s denotes states of nature. Really, *discounted* price changes, after correction for dividends, are unpredictable.

Informational efficiency says that the probabilities $\pi(s)$ forming the expectation E_t incorporate all available information. Risk aversion, risk premiums, and a "model of market equilibrium" are encoded in the discount factor Λ_t.

But, as the equation makes perfectly clear, $\pi(s)$ and $\Lambda_{t+1}(s)$ always enter together. You can't say anything about probabilities without saying something about discount factors, and vice versa. And, as seen most clearly in the utility formulation, the discount factor depends on the general equilibrium allocation of consumption c, as well as preferences and risk aversion encoded in u.

This theorem is a vital guiding light for empirical work. To this day, paper after paper looks at patterns in prices and declares them to be "irrational" or a "bubble" or otherwise "inefficient." But Fama proved in 1970 that such statements are simply empty, devoid of "empirical content." There is always some "model of market equilibrium" that will "explain" any price. At a minimum, one must state what kinds of models one finds plausible and verify that they do not generate risk premiums that, quantitatively, can explain a proposed anomaly.

In our view, the joint-hypothesis problem associated with efficient markets is as important as the theory itself. It has been key in organizing an ever-expanding set of pricing facts, and it is the more important organizing principle for today's active empirical work.

EFFICIENT MARKETS II

So, nearly a half-century later, how is the efficient markets hypothesis—and its organizing principle for empirical work—doing?

We included Gene's "Efficient Capital Markets II" in this volume as his progress report. It was written halfway through the second revolution in empirical finance—the understanding that risk premiums ("rational" or not) vary through time and across assets in large and unexpected ways. Also, "Efficient Capital Markets II" is one of those papers that, though less influential as measured by citations and influence on the profession, is perhaps a better summary and distillation for readers new to the field than was the original.

Between 1970 and 1990, evidence that returns are predictable mounted, and we cover several key Fama, and Fama and French, papers in that discovery later. As Gene emphasizes here, the evidence lies right where macroeconomic risk premiums lurk. Time-varying expected returns are most visible at long horizons, correlated across markets, and strongly correlated with business conditions where one might expect risk premiums to affect prices.

Event studies are perhaps the cleanest grounds to watch the incorporation of information into prices without joint-hypothesis problems, and here efficiency has stood up well. The surprising inability of professional managers to make money has continued in the vast literature Gene covers here.

BEHAVIORAL FINANCE

In 1970, there really wasn't a coherent alternative to efficient markets. "It takes a model to beat a model," Gene reminds us frequently. "People are dumb," while perhaps a trenchant observation on the human condition, or perhaps just an illusion of superiority, is not a theory. Or it's too good a theory—it can "explain" anything.

Starting in the late 1970s, a large literature that came to be known as "behavioral finance" worked to construct a coherent alternative model in which prices don't "efficiently" reflect information—people's probability assessments remain biased even though they may receive lots of information. These authors appealed to social psychology and the findings about how people misperceive probabilities in systematic ways in laboratory settings. By doing so, they hoped to avoid the charge of residual-naming. These insights from psychology were then applied to financial decision making and markets, providing both an alternative view of markets as well as some unique insights.

Gene always carefully read the empirical literature, even "behavioral," and here took on the evidence and its behavioral interpretation. A possible summary of his judgment is that the literature really didn't escape residual-naming and is not yet constrained by its theory. He finds that "under-reaction" is as frequent as "over-reaction."

Behavioral finance has, in our minds, had an important beneficial effect on the finance profession. In the 1970s, journals demanded that one have a "hypothesis" to "test." Facts for facts' sake didn't get published. This attitude was a valiant defense against fishing, but in the end was unproductive in that effort and stifled the production of facts that challenge theory. By adducing a behavioral "theory" that an empirical investigation was testing, the range of facts that empirical finance got to chew on grew dramatically. Yes, quite often one could transplant a "risk premium" introduction and a "behavioral" introduction on the same set of tables—the value effect comes to mind here—but the result is we all got to digest a vastly expanded set of facts. Hard sciences develop theories after uncomfortable facts, too. In the end, finding the truth must come from both sides—theory that the data hopes to verify, and facts in the data that theory needs to explain. Finance stands out in economics for the deep interplay between theory and often uncomfortable facts, a point Gene has made often.

STILL CONTENTIOUS

Forty-four years later, "efficiency" remains contentious.

Some of that contention reflects a simple misunderstanding of what social scientists do—and what they should do. What *about* Warren Buffet? What about Joe here, who predicted the market crash in his blog? Well, "data" is not the plural of "anecdote." These are no more useful questions to social science than "How did Grandpa get to be so old, even though he smokes?" is to medicine. Empirical finance looks at *all* the managers and all their predictions, tries to separate luck from ex ante measures of skill, and collects clean data.

Another part of that contention reflects simple ignorance of the definition of informational "efficiency." Every field of scholarly inquiry develops a technical terminology, often appropriating common words and giving them meanings quite different from the colloquial ones. "Efficient" estimators in statistics and "Pareto-Efficient" allocations in economics also have precise definitions, little related to the colloquial meaning of "efficiency." But people who don't know those definitions can say and write nonsense about the academic work.

"Efficiency" in finance means information, and only information. An *informationally* efficient market can suffer *economically inefficient* runs and crashes—so long as those crashes are not predictable. An informationally efficient market can have very badly regulated banks. An informationally efficient market need not process orders quickly or "efficiently."

People who say "the huge size of the 2008 (or 1987, or 1929) crash proves markets are inefficient" or "the fact that finance experts didn't foresee the crash proves that markets are inefficient" simply don't know what the word "efficiency" means. The main prediction of efficient markets is exactly that price movements should be unpredictable! And that returns must be balanced by risk. Steady profits without risk *would* be a clear rejection of efficient markets. The efficient markets hypothesis says nothing about how volatile or non-normal returns can be.

Cochrane once told a reporter that he thought markets were pretty "efficient." The reporter misquoted him as saying that markets are "self-regulating." Sadly, even famous academics say silly things like this all too frequently.

Part of the contention over efficiency reflects a misunderstanding of what financial economics, as a social science, tries to do. We're not here to "explain" the latest market gyration or provide market commentary. "The will of the gods" provided a perfectly good ex post story. The central idea of efficient markets, and markets as aggregators of information in the Hayekian tradition, is exactly that nobody can explain ex post why most prices move, nor predict movements ex ante.

Efficient markets taught us to evaluate theories by their rejectable predictions and by the numbers, and to do real, scientific, empirical work, not to read newspapers and tell stories. When someone asks, "Yes, but why *did* Warren Buffet get so rich?" the real answer is just "sir, that's a poorly posed question." Like "Why did uncle Joe not get cancer even though he smoked his whole life?" Medicine is useful, though it does not answer such questions. We recognize that this is unsatisfactory to journalists. Sadly, many academics still offer ex post stories for market movements on morning TV shows. Gene isn't one of them.

When Gene labeled the swift incorporation of information into prices as "efficiency," it was, perhaps, a bit of marketing genius. There is a fascinating story here, worth study by historians and philosophers of science and its rhetoric. What would have happened had Gene used another word? What if he had called it the "reflective" markets hypothesis, stating that prices "reflect" information? Would we still be arguing at all?

WHERE ARE WE TODAY?

With 40 years' hindsight, *are* markets efficient? Not always, and Gene said so in 1970. More recently, in our view, we have seen evidence that short-sales constraints and other frictions can lead to prices that are clearly information-ally inefficient. The empirical question has always been to what degree a given phenomenon approaches an unattainable ideal.

Still, the answer today is much closer to "yes" than to "no" in the vast majority of serious empirical investigations. It certainly is a lot closer to "yes" than anyone expected in the 1960s or than the vast majority of practitioners believe today. There are strange fish in the water, but most are surprisingly small fry. And having conquered 157 anomalies with patient hard work, many of us can be excused for suspecting that just a little more work will make sense of the 158th.

Admittedly, how one measures "close" is contentious. A small, persistent expected return anomaly can add up to a large difference in price. As we survey below, small prediction R^2 can add up to large 1–10 portfolio mean spreads. A tenth of a percent of arbitrage is worth billions if you can lever it up enough.

Today, empirical finance is less devoted to debating whether markets are efficient and more to assessing how efficient markets are. The vast majority of academic work agrees that market prices quickly reflect most visible pieces of information. Current efficiency debates include whether there is some slow diffusion of information on top of a large immediate reaction, or extended overreaction to an initial price reaction, or even to what extent prices move when there is no information and why. The current broad consensus that fully efficient markets are a theoretical ideal, real markets are always somewhat inefficient, the goal of research is to quantify how much, and the answer is "a lot better than you thought," pretty much sums up Gene's 1970 essay. In that sense, efficient markets won.

Moreover, most debates apparently about "efficiency" today are really about the nature of the "model of market equilibrium." Most current research really explores the amazing variety and subtle economics of risk premiums—focusing on the "joint hypothesis" rather than the "informational efficiency" part of Gene's 1970 essay. The discovery that risk premiums vary over time and across assets far more than anyone expected in 1970 counts as the major finding of the second revolution in empirical finance. Since the financial crisis of 2008, the major methodological debate has been between models that see macroeconomic sources of these risk premiums versus models that see risk premiums driven by "institutional finance" agency frictions. In this latter view, prices are "wrong" because markets are temporarily segmented and only leveraged intermediaries are "marginal." They require higher risk premiums than a fully integrated market would produce. Even much behavioral finance is not about mishandling of *information*, it's about misperceptions of *risk*. In all this work, slow diffusion of information into prices is just not an interesting mechanism for understanding the puzzles before us. But "models of market equilibrium" are much more important than we thought. The debate largely shifted from "do prices incorporate information efficiently?" to "what's the right pricing model?"

This is also great news. Healthy fields settle debates with evidence and move on to new discoveries. But don't conclude that efficient markets are passé. As evolution lies quietly behind the explosion in modern genetics, markets that are broadly efficient, in which prices quickly reflect information, quietly underlie all the interesting things we do today. This is the best fate any theory can aspire to.

Efficient markets are also important to the world at large, in ways that we can only begin to touch on here. The assurance that market prices are in some sense basically "right" lies behind many of the enormous changes we have seen in the financial and related worlds, from index funds, which have allowed for wide sharing of the risks and rewards of the stock market, to mark-to-market accounting, quantitative portfolio evaluation and benchmarking, modern risk management, and law and regulation.

The efficient markets hypothesis also is a close cousin, or perhaps uncle, to rational expectations and more deeply to the revolution that brought people and time into macroeconomics. This revolution became a hallmark of the University of Chicago economics department later in the 1970s.

Empirical financial economics, and the part that thinks about how information is incorporated into prices, is a live field, asking all sorts of interesting and important questions, with great discoveries left to be made. Is the finance industry too large or too small? Why do people continue to pay active managers so much? What accounts for the monstrous amount of trading? How is it, exactly, that information becomes reflected in prices through the trading process? Do millisecond traders help or hurt? How prevalent are runs? How many of the hundreds of return forecasting variables in the current literature are real? How many of the dozens of current risk factors do we really need? The ideas, facts, and empirical methods of informational efficiency continue to guide these important investigations.

The empirical focus of finance, inaugurated by Gene Fama in the 1970 essay, has been one of its greatest strengths, and largest influence. Economics has followed finance and become much more empirical in the last few decades.

Gene's bottom line is always: Look at the facts. Collect the data. Test the theory. Every time we look, the world surprises us totally. And it will again.

THE GREAT DIVIDE

· · ·

Clifford Asness and John Liew

Every December the Royal Swedish Academy of Sciences awards the Sveriges Riksbank Prize in Economic Sciences in Memory of Alfred Nobel. The Nobel committee recently recognized work on the efficient market hypothesis (EMH) with a dramatic splitting of the prestigious prize between EMH pioneer Eugene Fama and EMH critic Robert Shiller. (University of Chicago economist Lars Hansen also shares the $1.2 million prize, but his work is less central to our story.) This event, commemorated in this volume, makes now a great time to review EMH, its history, its controversies, and where things stand today.

Our contribution to the discussion, relative to other authors in this volume, emphasizes the lessons we have learned about EMH from our careers in the finance industry, and our observations on how EMH ideas and the EMH debate are perceived in and have impacted the finance industry.

We both received our PhDs at the University of Chicago under Gene Fama, and we consider him one of the great mentors of our lives and an extraordinary man. This fact might reasonably worry a reader that we are biased. But for the past 20 years, we've also pursued investment strategies whose success we think is at least partly explained by market inefficiencies. We pursued these strategies through the Asian crisis in 1997, the liquidity crisis of 1998, the tech bubble of 1999–2000, the quant crisis of August 2007, the real estate bubble and ensuing financial crisis culminating in 2008, and (for Cliff) the New York Rangers' not making the National Hockey League playoffs for seven years in a row, starting in 1997. Throughout this experience we have more than once come face-to-face with John Maynard Keynes's old adage that "markets can remain irrational longer than you and I can remain solvent," a decidedly folksier and earlier version of what has come to be known as the limits of arbitrage. We could arrogantly describe our investment strategies as a balanced

This essay is adapted from "The Great Divide," originally published as the cover story for the March 2014 Americas edition of *Institutional Investor*.

CLIFFORD ASNESS AND JOHN LIEW

and open-minded fusion of Fama and Shiller's views, but we admit they could also be described uncharitably as "risk versus behavioral schizophrenia."

All of this has put us somewhere between Fama and Shiller on EMH. We usually end up thinking the market is more efficient than do Shiller and most practitioners—especially active stock pickers, whose livelihoods depend on a strong belief in inefficiency. As novelist Upton Sinclair, presumably not a fan of efficient markets, said, "It is difficult to get a man to understand something, when his salary depends upon his not understanding it!" However, we also likely think the market is less efficient than Fama does. Our background and how we've come to our current view make us, we hope, qualified—but perhaps, at the least, interesting—chroniclers of this debate.

Last, we make a small contribution to the EMH conversation by offering what we think is a useful and modest refinement of Fama's thoughts on how to test whether markets are in fact efficient. We hope this refinement can help clarify and sharpen the debate around this important topic. Essentially, we strategically add the word "reasonable" and don't allow a market to be declared efficient if it's just efficiently reflecting totally irrational investor desires. If you thought that last line was confusing, good. Keep reading.

The concept of market efficiency has been confused with everything from the reason that you should hold stocks for the long run (and its mutated cousins, arguments like the tech bubble's "Dow 36,000") to predictions that stock returns should be normally distributed to even simply a belief in free enterprise. Though it may have implications for many of these things, market efficiency is not directly about any of these ideas.

So what does it mean for markets to be efficient? As Fama says, it's "the simple statement that security prices fully reflect all available information." But Fama also cautioned in 1970 that you cannot say anything about market efficiency by itself. You can only say something about the coupling of market efficiency and some security pricing model. What does it mean to reflect information? If the information is that a company just crushed its earnings target, should prices double? Triple? To be able to make any statement about market efficiency, you need to make some assertion of how the market *should* reflect information.

Suppose your joint hypothesis is that EMH holds and the capital asset pricing model (CAPM) is how prices are set. The CAPM says the expected return on any security is proportional to the risk of that security as measured by its market beta. Nothing else should matter. EMH says the market will get this right. Say you then turn to the data and find evidence against this pairing, as has been found. The problem is that you don't know which of the two (or both) ideas is wrong. EMH may be true, but CAPM may be a poor model of how investors set prices. Perhaps prices indeed reflect all information, but there are other risk factors that investors are getting compensated for bearing. Perhaps the CAPM describes risk premiums, but prices are wrong because investors wrongly assess the probability of a good outcome, due to behavioral biases or errors. Or maybe both EMH and CAPM are wrong. This seems like an impossible situation, but we'll show below how we believe that in practice one can still make useful judgments about market efficiency.

The CAPM + EMH framework held up well for many years, especially in event studies that showed information was rapidly incorporated into security prices. However, over time some serious challenges or "anomalies" have come up. These can be broadly grouped into two categories: microchallenges and macrochallenges.

The microchallenges center on what are called return anomalies. Researchers have identified characteristics that seem to explain differences in expected returns across securities, even controlling for market beta. Value and momentum are two of the most robust and important examples.

Starting in the mid-1980s, academic researchers began investigating simple value strategies. As is often the case, the value strategy was invented and popularized decades earlier, by Benjamin Graham and David Dodd. When they looked, the academics found that Graham and Dodd had been on to something. Stocks with lower price multiples tended to produce higher average returns than stocks with higher price multiples. As a result, the simplest diversified value strategies seemed to work. Importantly, the low-priced, high average return stocks did not have higher betas. The value strategy worked after accounting for the effects of the CAPM. Fama and French's papers in this volume represent the academic acceptance and digestion of the value phenomenon.

How do we interpret the value effect? Academics have split into two camps: risk versus behavior. The risk camp says that we learn from value that the CAPM is the wrong model of how prices are set. Market beta is not the only source of risk. Price multiples that forecast returns are related to another dimension of risk for which rational, informed investors must be compensated, and the low prices of value stocks fully reflect all that information.

Behaviorists say instead that markets aren't efficient. Behavioral biases exist, causing price multiples to represent mispricing, not risk. For instance, investors may overextrapolate either good or bad news and thus pay too much or too little for some stocks. Simple price multiples may capture these discrepancies. Value stocks are simply underpriced.

Similarly, in the late 1980s researchers including Narasimhan Jegadeesh, Sheridan Titman, and Cliff Asness (yes, the dissertation of one of the authors— bias alert) began empirical studies of diversified momentum strategies. The studies found that stocks with good momentum, as measured quite simply by returns over the previous six months to a year, tended to have higher average returns going forward than stocks with poor momentum, again fully adjusting for any return differences implied by CAPM or any other rational equilibrium model known at the time—more evidence against the joint hypothesis.

Momentum has been harder to deal with for efficient-market proponents. Cheap (value) stocks tend to stay cheap for a long time. They are usually crappy companies (we apologize for the technical term). Thus, it is not a stretch to believe there is something risky about value stocks for which the willing holder gets compensated. But price momentum changes radically from year to year. This year's positive momentum winner stock is likely to be next year's negative momentum loser stock. What kind of risk changes so quickly? Can a stock be risky one year and then safe the next? You can't dismiss such a thing. Extreme performance in either direction may inherently change risk characteristics. But most researchers, including EMH fans, still find it quite hard to devise a story, a vaguely plausible "model of market equilibrium" that reconciles the success (net of CAPM and value) of momentum with a risk factor story.

In addition, value and momentum are negatively correlated factors. This observation adds to the challenge. Negative correlation means that a portfolio of the two reduces risk because when one is hurting your portfolio, the other tends to be helping. So, a portfolio of value plus momentum presents an even greater challenge to the joint hypothesis of EMH and an equilibrium pricing model.

Furthermore, value and momentum are robust within stock markets around the world, as well as within a broad array of other asset classes, including bonds, currencies, and commodities. The larger the total risk-adjusted return generated by a market-neutral (no exposure to CAPM) strategy, the bigger the challenge.

The bottom line is that there are some factors, like momentum, that at this point seem to pose a considerable challenge to EMH. The verdict is more mixed for value, but most would agree that it still presents an additional challenge. Add to that the power of combining value and momentum, and at the very least it is fair to say there are important microchallenges to EMH.

On the macro side—meaning, dealing with the whole market, not relative value—Bob Shiller points out a puzzling observation in his now-famous 1981 paper, "Do Stock Prices Move Too Much to Be Justified by Subsequent Changes in Dividends?" Stock prices should be the present value of future dividends. Shiller determines what he calls an "ex post rational" price for the stock market as a whole by computing the present value of actual future dividends. This is obviously cheating, because in real life you don't know the value of future dividends. But the volatility of the *expected* present value of dividends should be less than the volatility of Shiller's ex post present value of dividends. Yet actual market prices swing more wildly than Shiller's "cheating" ex post rational price.

However, you can't escape Gene's joint hypothesis theorem. Proponents of efficient markets point out that Shiller uses a constant discount rate. Yet there can be times (recessions, financial crises) when people require a higher rate of return (or discount rate) to bear the risk of owning stocks, and there can be times (booms, low volatility, "reach-for-yield" events) when people require a lower rate. If discount rates vary over time, even without any change in expected future dividends, prices should change. Shiller and his fans retort, "Sure, but can reasonable equilibrium models produce the magnitude of time-varying required rates of return on the stock market?" And the debate ensues.

In later research, Shiller's volatility tests turn out to be exactly equivalent to long-horizon return forecasts, such as those covered in this volume. The fact is unified, but the interpretation is not. The expected returns needed to explain volatility tests are exactly those found by direct regressions. But those expected returns vary (one standard deviation) from roughly 1% to 9%, around a mean of 5%. Is it really true that sometimes the market rationally only delivers 1% risk premium, and at other times there are no buyers at 9%?

So where do we stand? Spoiler alert: after a lot of discussion and 20 years of implementing much of what we have discussed, and a lot more than just value and momentum, we're still confused. Our strategies seem to work. But really, just why? What is there about markets—efficiency or risk premiums—that makes our strategies work? This is why finance is such a live and interesting field.

We started our careers in the early 1990s, when as a young team in the asset management group at Goldman, Sachs & Co. we were asked to develop a set of quantitative trading models. Why Goldman let a small group of 20-somethings do these things we'll never know, but we're thankful that they did. Being newly minted University of Chicago PhDs and students of Gene Fama and Ken French, the natural thing for us to do was develop models in which one of the key inputs was value. We also used momentum from the get-go (as Cliff had written his dissertation on it), but here we'll focus on the simple value story, as it explains most of what happened in the early days.

(One of Cliff's favorite stories is asking Fama, no natural fan of momentum investing, if he could write his thesis on momentum, and Fama responding, "If it's in the data, write the paper" and then fully supporting it. That kind of intellectual honesty doesn't come along too often.)

Figure 1 displays the cumulative returns to Fama and French's "high minus low" (HML) trading strategy. The strategy buys a diversified portfolio of cheap US stocks (high book-to-market value ratios) and goes short a portfolio of expensive US stocks (measured by their low book-to-market ratios). Since it is a long-short strategy, it essentially has no market beta. As the graph shows, this strategy has produced strong positive returns over about 85 years.

The circled part is when we started our careers. Standing at that time, just before the big dip, we found both the intuition and the 65 years of data behind

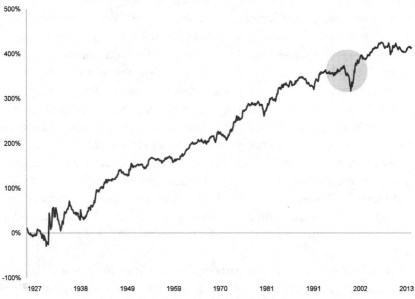

Figure 1. Cumulative returns to the HML value strategy

this strategy pretty convincing. Obviously, it wasn't perfect, but if you were a long-term investor, here was a simple strategy that produced positive average returns that weren't correlated to the stock market. Who wouldn't want some of this in their portfolio?

The first few years of our live experience with HML's performance were decent, and that helped us to establish a nice track record managing both Goldman's proprietary capital and the capital of some of our early outside investors. This start also laid the groundwork for us to team up with a fellow Goldman colleague, David Kabiller, and set up our firm, AQR Capital Management.

As fate would have it, we launched our first AQR fund in August 1998. You may remember that as an uneventful little month containing the Russian debt crisis, a huge stock market drop, and the beginning of the rapid end of hedge fund firm Long-Term Capital Management. It turned out that those really weren't problems for us. That month we did fine. We truly were fully hedged long-short, which saved our bacon. But when this scary episode was over, the tech bubble began to inflate.

We were long cheap stocks and short expensive stocks, right in front of the worst period for value strategies since the Great Depression. We were not long cheap stocks alone, which simply languished, but we were also short expensive growth stocks—just what boomed! We remember a lot of long-only value managers whining at the time that they weren't making money while all the crazy stocks soared. They didn't know how easy they had it. At the nadir of our performance, a typical comment from our clients after hearing our case was something along the lines of "I hear what you guys are saying, and I agree: these prices seem crazy. But you guys have to understand, I report to a board, and if this keeps going on, it doesn't matter what I think, I'm going to have to fire you." Fortunately for us, value strategies turned around, but few know the "limits of arbitrage" like we do.

With this experience in mind, let's go back to the debate over whether the value premium is the result of a value-related risk premium or behavioral biases. What does it feel like sitting in our seats as practitioners who have traded on value for the past 20 years? To us, it feels like some of both at work.

The risk story is actually quite compelling. One prerequisite for this story is that for risks to command a risk premium, they must not be diversifiable. What we saw in the tech bubble was an extreme version of exactly that. Cheap stocks would get cheaper across the board at the same time. It didn't matter if the stock was an automaker or an insurance company. When value was losing, it was losing everywhere. We saw the same phenomenon on the expensive side—all the growth stocks (which we were short) rose together. This comovement among stocks in an investment category holds within most asset classes we've looked at and sharply limits diversification, just as the arbitrage pricing theory (APT) says it should. This comovement doesn't prove that value is a risk factor—it could be occurring in a model based on correlated irrationality, and the joint hypothesis theorem says there is no proof without a model—but it is a very direct implication of a rational risk-based model.

However, there are reasons to believe some or even a lot of the efficacy of value strategies (at times) is behavioral. In addition to the long list of reasons that behaviorists put forth, we'll offer a couple of thoughts.

Throughout our experience managing money, we've seen that a lot of individuals and groups, and particularly committees, have a strong tendency to rely on three- to five-year performance evaluation horizons. Looking at the data, this is exactly the horizon over which securities most commonly become cheap and expensive. Put these two observations together and you get a large set of investors acting anticontrarian. We like to say that these investors act like momentum traders over a value-time horizon. To the extent that the real world is subject to price pressure—to the extent that there are limited numbers of people like us willing to do the opposite, and buy things that have gone down for three to five years and sell things that have gone up for three to five years, when these investors are doing the opposite—this behavior will lead to at least some mispricing (inefficiency) in the direction of value.

Now, many practitioners offer value-tilted products and long-short products that go long value stocks and short or at least avoid growth stocks. But if value works because of risk, there should be a market for people who want the opposite. If value works because of risk, for every investor who says, "Thank you, that's a great deal for me because I don't particularly care about value stocks, I'll buy," there should be an investor who says, "Thank you, but value stocks drop exactly at the most inconvenient time for me. I would like to short value despite the higher returns, just as I pay an insurance premium on my house." Real risk has to hurt. If some earn money by selling insurance, some must want to pay money to buy insurance. As Gene reminds us in his "equilibrium accounting," every portfolio allocation other than the market is a zero-sum game. For every buyer there must be a seller. In a rational market, we can't all just be smarter or less behavioral than average.

However, we know of nobody offering the systematic opposite product (long expensive, short cheap). When we have explained our strategy, its risks and its rewards, we have never met a customer who wants to short it. We would be curious to know if anyone has ever met such a customer. Although this is far from a proof, we find the complete lack of such products a bit vexing for the purely rational risk-based story.

In the real world, it seems likely to us that both rational (risk, "alternative beta") and irrational (mispricing because people get probabilities wrong) forces may be at work.

Furthermore, this mix is likely to vary over time. In our view, it's likely that at most times risk plays a significant role in value's effectiveness as a strategy. However, we believe that even the most ardent EMH supporters will admit, if only when they are alone at night, that in February 2000 (the peak of the dot-com bubble) they thought the world had gone at least somewhat mad. We are tempted to say there are no pure EMH believers in foxholes, or on trading desks.

The tech bubble wasn't just a cross-sectional "micro" phenomenon (value versus growth within the stock market), but the whole market itself was priced to extremely high levels, at least versus any measure of fundamentals, using any discount rate that we find vaguely plausible. This observation returns us to Shiller's macro critique of EMH, and Fama and French's return regressions. How is it possible that prices rationally vary so much given the relative stability of dividends? How is it possible that expected returns vary so much? Take a look at Figure 2, which we called "The Scariest Chart Ever!" in our first-quarter

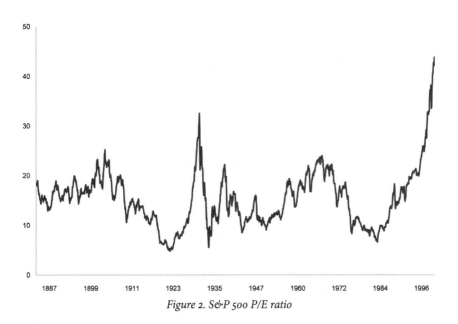

Figure 2. S&P 500 P/E ratio

2000 letter to investors (in which we also pleaded with them not to fire us). It's a graph of the Shiller P/E from 1881 to the end of March 2000.

Is it possible that a rational market could ever be priced so high without making absolutely incredible assumptions about future dividends? We think not. Is it possible that investors were really holding stocks, and growth stocks in particular, fully knowing that dividends would not rise by miraculous amounts, but willingly accepting the minuscule, even negative, discount rates that such prices require? We don't think so. We think the discount rate would have to be implausibly low to save EMH from Shiller this time. We think this one was a bubble.

Efficient marketers often point to the fact that it seems to be very difficult for active managers to consistently beat the market. But does this mean the market is efficient? Not necessarily. The market can be inefficient—prices not equal to rationally expected and correctly discounted present values—but still hard to beat, because arbitrage is limited and costly. And the biases of money managers, their clients, and whomever their clients report to add limits of arbitrage, especially the sort of patient long-term arbitrage, willing to bear losses for many years on the way to eventual gain.

For example, using the Gordon Growth formula $P/D = 1/(r - g)$, if the price/dividend ratio is $25 = 1/0.04$, an expected return that is 1% too low will irrationally boost the price/dividend ratio to $33 = 1/0.03$. One percent is about the annual cost of a short position. So this small average return error means a very large 32% price error!

When arbitrage is limited, only the coordinated rationality of every long-only investor drives price to its correct value.

Along these lines, as much deserved recognition as Shiller has gotten for calling the stock market bubble, remember that he was saying very similar things at least as far back as 1996. That was also when Federal Reserve chairman Alan Greenspan famously accused the market of "irrational exuberance." But the market kept climbing for four more years. Someone listening to Shiller or Greenspan starting in 1996 likely would have lost money without much recovery, as few if any investors could have stuck with this recommendation through four years of losses to reap the ultimate reward so far down the road. Thankfully for us, our value strategies, when combined with all else we did, only began hurting a year or so before the bubble burst. We doubt we could have survived losing for significantly longer than that.

Although failure to beat the market doesn't mean markets are efficient, the opposite would have clear implications. If we found the market was easy to beat with great regularity, it would be a blow to efficiency as well as to most equilibrium models. It's asymmetric. Nobody said this was fair. But that is an honor to Efficiency. Only hypotheses that can be rejected can start to call themselves scientific. Ex post explanations that can't be disproved aren't worth much.

Along these lines, some critics of EMH get a lot of joy pointing to the handful of long-term successful money managers, such as Warren Buffett, and, less well known outside the hedge fund world, the amazing returns of James Simons's Renaissance Technologies. Taking billions of dollars out of the market at low risk for a handful of people is a big deal to the manager in question (call that a mastery of the blindingly obvious).

But, as perhaps the exceptions that prove the rule, even these observations are not much of a blow against EMH in general. As rich as these few have become, they are still very small versus the size of markets and much easier to identify after the fact than before. As the academic research summarized in this volume emphasizes, such traders are awfully hard to identify ahead of time, and there are just about as many of them as one would expect due to chance. That one happy gambler leaves Las Vegas with a pocketful of coins does not mean the slots are loaded in your favor.

The joint hypothesis theorem says you can't say anything about efficiency without a model of market equilibrium. But the perfect model of market equilibrium is always just over the horizon. The behavioral-rational barroom fight has been going on for 60 years. Is there no way out?

We think there is. Without achieving the perfect model of market equilibrium, we can constrain market efficiency somewhat by requiring that the models of market equilibrium needed to reconcile a strategy as consistent with efficiency must be reasonable.

For instance, event studies usually use the CAPM or three-factor model for risk adjustment around the event. If they find short-term profits after the event, one could in principle "explain" that as unmeasured changing exposure to some new factor risk. But nobody ever does. Implicitly, researchers believe that no reasonable equilibrium model could explain consistent short-term profits if such are found.

As concrete examples, explaining things like the 1999–2000 bubble with tastes for specific securities really does not count. That's unverifiable, and indistinguishable from behavioral attachment to specific securities. Discount rates that vary beyond a plausible amount, or that are uncorrelated with real macroeconomic risks, are unreasonable.

CLIFFORD ASNESS AND JOHN LIEW

Do the above thoughts, distilled from our experience in the world of practical finance, make us behaviorists? We think most declared behaviorists go too far. Reading the behaviorist literature, you get the impression that anomalies are everywhere and easily profited from and that everyone but the author is just a moron. We've spent many years both studying and trading on these anomalies. Our experience, though certainly a net positive, is that many of these are out-of-sample failures. It's relatively easy to find something that looks like it predicts return on paper, and it's also relatively easy to come up with a seemingly plausible behavioral rationale for why markets might be missing something. But when you actually try to trade on the anomaly (the best kind of out-of-sample test if done for long enough in a consistent manner), in our experience most of these things don't work. Value, momentum, and a few other strategies have in fact stood the test of time and the test of implementation, but many others have not. Obviously, the flexibility of behavioral finance is both its strength and its weakness.

Are we therefore efficient marketers? Generally, yes, at least as the base case. We find that the concept of efficient markets is a healthier and more correct beginning point for thinking about markets and investing than a view that we are a whole lot smarter and less behavioral than the average investor. But, as Fama himself says, we don't believe markets are perfectly efficient all the time, and there's room for some factors (for example, part of the value return and probably much of the momentum return) to survive and thrive in the limited amount of inefficiency out there, and especially in occasional times of clearly crazy pricing.

So if markets are not perfectly efficient but not grossly inefficient either—though occasionally pretty darn wacky—what should investors do? We believe the vast majority would be better off acting like the market was perfectly efficient than acting like it was easily beatable. Active management is hard. Finding a good active manager, if you are an investor, is harder.

In our experience, actually running these strategies is much trickier than what you see in the academic literature. In addition to the tendency for returns to vanish shortly after publication, implementation details matter. With sloppy trading you can easily throw away any expected return premium—whatever its source—that might exist around these strategies. Academic papers often ignore transactions costs.

One of the worst misuses of "efficiency" is the common notion that the 2007–2008 credit and real estate bubble and ensuing financial crisis, and perhaps other bubbles, were caused by a belief in market efficiency, or "market fundamentalism," or even by efficient-markets academics, starting with Gene Fama. If there are bubbles, they are likely caused by people who think they are getting an extraordinarily impossibly good deal, not a fair deal in an efficient market. Efficient markets says just passively hold the market portfolio, so no efficient marketer was ever there bidding up a bubble. To say it's believers in efficient markets that cause bubbles is simply an ignorant (literally, because they don't know the definition of "efficiency") political slur—and a backward one at that.

The impact of the efficient market hypothesis has gone well beyond academia. It's hard to remember what finance was like before EMH. It was not a science; it was barely even abstract art. Before EMH, it was simply taken for granted that a smart corporate treasurer added lots of value by carefully choosing among debt and equity for his capital structure, or that any diligent, hardworking portfolio manager could beat the market. We may still argue over whether a few good managers add value above their fees—we certainly believe AQR does so—but the evidence is devastating because the vast majority of active management does not do so. Therefore, at a minimum, index funds and the general focus on cost and diversification are perhaps the most direct practical result of EMH thinking, and we'd argue the most investor-welfare-enhancing financial innovation of the past 50 years. Not bad.

So where does that leave us as students of Gene Fama, and practitioners for the past 20 years of much of what he taught us? Simply put, we'd have nothing without EMH. It is our North Star even if we often or always veer 15 degrees left or right of it. But despite this incredible importance, the idea that markets are literally perfect is extreme and silly, and thankfully (at least for us), there's plenty of room to prosper in the middle. Apparently, the Nobel committee agrees.

***

The views and opinions expressed herein are those of the authors and do not necessarily reflect the views of AQR Capital Management, its affiliates, or its employees.

EFFICIENT CAPITAL MARKETS

A REVIEW OF THEORY AND EMPIRICAL WORK

. . .

Eugene F. Fama

I. INTRODUCTION

The primary role of the capital market is allocation of ownership of the economy's capital stock. In general terms, the ideal is a market in which prices provide accurate signals for resource allocation: that is, a market in which firms can make production-investment decisions, and investors can choose among the securities that represent ownership of firms' activities under the assumption that security prices at any time "fully reflect" all available information. A market in which prices always "fully reflect" available information is called "efficient."

This paper reviews the theoretical and empirical literature on the efficient markets model. After a discussion of the theory, empirical work concerned with the adjustment of security prices to three relevant information subsets is considered. First, *weak form* tests, in which the information set is just historical prices, are discussed. Then *semi-strong form* tests, in which the concern is whether prices efficiently adjust to other information that is obviously publicly available (e.g., announcements of annual earnings, stock splits, etc.) are considered. Finally, *strong form* tests concerned with whether given investors or groups have monopolistic access to any information relevant for price formation are reviewed.[1] We shall conclude that, with but a few exceptions, the efficient markets model stands up well.

Though we proceed from theory to empirical work, to keep the proper historical perspective we should note to a large extent the empirical work in this

Reprinted with permission from the *Journal of Finance* 25, no. 2 (May 1970): 383–417. © 1970 by John Wiley and Sons.

Research on this project was supported by a grant from the National Science Foundation. I am indebted to Arthur Laffer, Robert Aliber, Ray Ball, Michael Jensen, James Lorie, Merton Miller. Charles Nelson. Richard Roll. William Tavlor. and Ross Watts for their helpful comments.

1. The distinction between weak and strong form tests was first suggested by Harry Roberts.

area preceded the development of the theory. The theory is presented first here in order to more easily judge which of the empirical results are most relevant from the viewpoint of the theory. The empirical work itself, however, will then be reviewed in more or less historical sequence.

Finally, the perceptive reader will surely recognize instances in this paper where relevant studies are not specifically discussed. In such cases my apologies should be taken for granted. The area is so bountiful that some such injustices are unavoidable. But the primary goal here will have been accomplished if a coherent picture of the main lines of the work on efficient markets is presented, along with an accurate picture of the current state of the arts.

II. THE THEORY OF EFFICIENT MARKETS

A. Expected Return or "Fair Game" Models

The definitional statement that in an efficient market prices "fully reflect" available information is so general that it has no empirically testable implications. To make the model testable, the process of price formation must be specified in more detail. In essence we must define somewhat more exactly what is meant by the term "fully reflect."

One possibility would be to posit that equilibrium prices (or expected returns) on securities are generated as in the "two parameter" Sharpe [40]-Lintner [24, 25] world. In general, however, the theoretical models and especially the empirical tests of capital market efficiency have not been this specific. Most of the available work is based only on the assumption that the conditions of market equilibrium can (somehow) be stated in terms of expected returns. In general terms, like the two parameter model such theories would posit that conditional on some relevant information set, the equilibrium expected return on a security is a function of its "risk." And different theories would differ primarily in how "risk" is defined.

All members of the class of such "expected return theories" can, however, be described notationally as follows:

$$E\left(\tilde{p}_{j,t+1} \mid \Phi_t\right) = \left[1 + E\left(\tilde{r}_{j,t+1} \mid \Phi_t\right)\right] p_{jt,} \qquad (1)$$

where E is the expected value operator; p_{jt} is the price of security j at time t; $p_{j,t+1}$ is its price at $t+1$ (with reinvestment of any intermediate cash income from the security); $r_{j,t+1}$ is the one-period percentage return $(p_{j,t+1} - p_{jt})/p_{jt}$; Φ_t is a general symbol for whatever set of information is assumed to be "fully reflected" in the price at t; and the tildes indicate that $p_{j,t+1}$ and $r_{j,t+1}$ are random variables at t.

The value of the equilibrium expected return $E\left(\tilde{r}_{j,t+1} \mid \Phi_t\right)$ projected on the basis of the information Φ_t would be determined from the particular expected return theory at hand. The conditional expectation notation of (1) is meant to imply, however, that whatever expected return model is assumed to apply, the information in Φ_t is fully utilized in determining equilibrium expected returns. And this is the sense in which Φ_t is "fully reflected" in the formation of the price p_{jt}.

But we should note right off that, simple as it is, the assumption that the conditions of market equilibrium can be stated in terms of expected returns elevates the purely mathematical concept of expected value to a status not necessarily implied by the general notion of market efficiency. The expected value is just one of many possible summary measures of a distribution of returns, and market efficiency per se (i.e., the general notion that prices "fully reflect" available information) does not imbue it with any special importance. Thus, the results of tests based on this assumption depend to some extent on its validity as well as on the efficiency of the market. But some such assumption is the unavoidable price one must pay to give the theory of efficient markets empirical content.

The assumptions that the conditions of market equilibrium can be stated in terms of expected returns and that equilibrium expected returns are formed on the basis of (and thus "fully reflect") the information set Φ_t have a major empirical implication—they rule out the possibility of trading systems based only on information in Φ_t that have expected profits or returns in excess of equilibrium expected profits or returns. Thus let

$$X_{j,t+1} = p_{j,t+1} - E\left(\tilde{p}_{j,t+1} \mid \Phi_t\right). \tag{2}$$

Then

$$E\left(\tilde{x}_{j,t+1} \mid \Phi_t\right) = 0 \tag{3}$$

which, by definition, says that the sequence $\{x_{jt}\}$ is a "fair game" with respect to the information sequence $\{\Phi_t\}$. Or, equivalently, let

$$z_{j,t+1} = r_{j,t+1} - E\left(\tilde{r}_{j,t+1} \mid \Phi_t\right), \tag{4}$$

then

$$E\left(\tilde{z}_{j,t+1}|\Phi_t\right) = 0, \tag{5}$$

so that the sequence $\{z_{jt}\}$ is also a "fair game" with respect to the information sequence $\{\Phi\}$.

In economic terms, $x_{j,t+1}$ is the excess market value of security j at time $t + 1$: it is the difference between the observed price and the expected value of the price that was projected at t on the basis of the information Φ_t. And similarly, $z_{j,t+1}$ is the return at $t + 1$ in excess of the equilibrium expected return projected at t. Let

$$\alpha(\Phi_t) = \left[\alpha_1(\Phi_t), \alpha_2(\Phi_t), \cdots, \alpha_n(\Phi_t)\right]$$

be any trading system based on Φ_t which tells the investor the amounts $\alpha_j(\Phi_t)$ of funds available at t that are to be invested in each of the n available securities. The total excess market value at $t + 1$ that will be generated by such a system is

$$V_{t+1} = \sum_{j=1}^{n} \alpha_j(\Phi_t)\left[r_{j,t+1} - E\left(\tilde{r}_{j,t+1}|\Phi_t\right)\right],$$

which, from the "fair game" property of (5) has expectation,

$$E\left(\tilde{V}_{t+1}|\Phi_t\right) = \sum_{j=1}^{n} \alpha_j(\Phi_t)E\left(\tilde{z}_{j,t+1}|\Phi_t\right) = 0.$$

The expected return or "fair game" efficient markets model[2] has other important testable implications, but these are better saved for the later discussion of the empirical work. Now we turn to two special cases of the model, the submartingale and the random walk, that (as we shall see later) play an important role in the empirical literature.

2. Though we shall sometimes refer to the model summarized by (1) as the "fair game" model, keep in mind that the "fair game" properties of the model are *implications* of the assumptions that (i) the conditions of market equilibrium can be stated in terms of expected returns, and (ii) the information Φ_t is fully utilized by the market in forming equilibrium expected returns and thus current prices.

The role of "fair game" models in the theory of efficient markets was first recognized and studied rigorously by Mandelbrot [27] and Samuelson [38]. Their work will be discussed in more detail later.

B. The Submartingale Model

Suppose we assume in (1) that for all t and Φ_t

$$E\left(\tilde{p}_{j,t+1} \mid \Phi_t\right) \geq p_{jt}, \text{ or equivalently, } E\left(\tilde{r}_{j,t+1} \mid \Phi_t\right) \geq 0. \tag{6}$$

This is a statement that the price sequence $\{p_{jt}\}$ for security j follows a submartingale with respect to the information sequence $\{\Phi_t\}$, which is to say nothing more than that the expected value of next period's price, as projected on the basis of the information Φ_t, is equal to or greater than the current price. If (6) holds as an equality (so that expected returns and price changes are zero), then the price sequence follows a martingale.

A submartingale in prices has one important empirical implication. Consider the set of "one security and cash" mechanical trading rules by which we mean systems that concentrate on individual securities and that define the conditions under which the investor would hold a given security, sell it short, or simply hold cash at any time t. Then the assumption of (6) that expected returns conditional on Φ_t are non-negative directly implies that such trading rules based only on the information in Φ_t cannot have greater expected profits than a policy of always buying-and-holding the security during the future period in question. Tests of such rules will be an important part of the empirical evidence on the efficient markets model.[3]

C. The Random Walk Model

In the early treatments of the efficient markets model, the statement that the current price of a security "fully reflects" available information was assumed

3. Note that the expected profitability of "one security and cash" trading systems vis-à-vis buy-and-hold is not ruled out by the general expected return or "fair game" efficient markets model. The latter rules out systems with expected profits in excess of equilibrium expected returns, but since in principle it allows equilibrium expected returns to be negative, holding cash (which always has zero actual and thus expected return) may have higher expected return than holding some security.

And negative equilibrium expected returns for some securities are quite possible. For example, in the Sharpe [40]-Lintner [24, 25] model (which is in turn a natural extension of the portfolio models of Markowitz [30] and Tobin [43]) the equilibrium expected return on a security depends on the extent to which the dispersion in the security's return distribution is related to dispersion in the returns on all other securities. A security whose returns on average move opposite to the general market is particularly valuable in reducing dispersion of portfolio returns, and so its equilibrium expected return may well be negative.

to imply that successive price changes (or more usually, successive one-period returns) are independent. In addition, it was usually assumed that successive changes (or returns) are identically distributed. Together the two hypotheses constitute the random walk model. Formally, the model says

$$f\left(r_{j,t+1} \mid \Phi_t\right) = f\left(r_{j,t+1}\right), \tag{7}$$

which is the usual statement that the conditional and marginal probability distributions of an independent random variable are identical. In addition, the density function f must be the same for all t.[4]

Expression (7) of course says much more than the general expected return model summarized by (1). For example, if we restrict (1) by assuming that the expected return on security j is constant over time, then we have

$$E\left(\tilde{r}_{j,t+1} \mid \Phi_t\right) = E\left(\tilde{r}_{j,t+1}\right). \tag{8}$$

This says that the mean of the distribution of $r_{j,t+1}$ is independent of the information available at t, Φ_t, whereas the random walk model of (7) in addition says that the entire distribution is independent of Φ_t.[5]

We argue later that it is best to regard the random walk model as an extension of the general expected return or "fair game" efficient markets model in the sense of making a more detailed statement about the economic environment. The "fair game" model just says that the conditions of market equilibrium can be stated in terms of expected returns, and thus it says little about

4. The terminology is loose. Prices will only follow a random walk if price changes are independent, identically distributed; and even then we should say "random walk with drift" since expected price changes can be non-zero. If one-period returns are independent, identically distributed, prices will not follow a random walk since the distribution of price changes will depend on the price level. But though rigorous terminology is usually desirable, our loose use of terms should not cause confusion; and our usage follows that of the efficient markets literature.

Note also that in the random walk literature, the information set Φ_t in (7) is usually assumed to include only the past return history, $r_{j,t}, r_{j,t-1}, \ldots$

5. The random walk model does not say, however, that past information is of no value in assessing distributions of future returns. Indeed since return distributions are assumed to be stationary through time, past returns are the best source of such information. The random walk model does say, however, that the *sequence* (or the order) of the past returns is of no consequence in assessing distributions of future returns.

the details of the stochastic process generating returns. A random walk arises within the context of such a model when the environment is (fortuitously) such that the evolution of investor tastes and the process generating new information combine to produce equilibria in which return distributions repeat themselves through time.

Thus it is not surprising that empirical tests of the "random walk" model that are in fact tests of "fair game" properties are more strongly in support of the model than tests of the additional (and, from the viewpoint of expected return market efficiency, superfluous) pure independence assumption. (But it is perhaps equally surprising that, as we shall soon see, the evidence against the independence of returns over time is as weak as it is.)

D. Market Conditions Consistent with Efficiency

Before turning to the empirical work, however, a few words about the market conditions that might help or hinder efficient adjustment of prices to information are in order. First, it is easy to determine *sufficient* conditions for capital market efficiency. For example, consider a market in which (i) there are no transactions costs in trading securities, (ii) all available information is costlessly available to all market participants, and (iii) all agree on the implications of current information for the current price and distributions of future prices of each security. In such a market, the current price of a security obviously "fully reflects" all available information.

But a frictionless market in which all information is freely available and investors agree on its implications is, of course, not descriptive of markets met in practice. Fortunately, these conditions are sufficient for market efficiency, but not necessary. For example, as long as transactors take account of all available information, even large transactions costs that inhibit the flow of transactions do not in themselves imply that when transactions do take place, prices will not "fully reflect" available information. Similarly (and speaking, as above, somewhat loosely), the market may be efficient if "sufficient numbers" of investors have ready access to available information. And disagreement among investors about the implications of given information does not in itself imply market inefficiency unless there are investors who can consistently make better evaluations of available information than are implicit in market prices.

But though transactions costs, information that is not freely available to all investors, and disagreement among investors about the implications of given information are not necessarily sources of market inefficiency, they are potential sources. And all three exist to some extent in real world markets. Measur-

[82]

ing their effects on the process of price formation is, of course, the major goal of empirical work in this area.

III. THE EVIDENCE

All the empirical research on the theory of efficient markets has been concerned with whether prices "fully reflect" particular subsets of available information. Historically, the empirical work evolved more or less as follows. The initial studies were concerned with what we call *weak form* tests in which the information subset of interest is just past price (or return) histories. Most of the results here come from the random walk literature. When extensive tests seemed to support the efficiency hypothesis at this level, attention was turned to *semi-strong form* tests in which the concern is the speed of price adjustment to other obviously publicly available information (e.g., announcements of stock splits, annual reports, new security issues, etc.). Finally, *strong form* tests in which the concern is whether any investor or groups (e.g., managements of mutual funds) have monopolistic access to any information relevant for the formation of prices have recently appeared. We review the empirical research in more or less this historical sequence.

First, however, we should note that what we have called *the* efficient markets model in the discussions of earlier sections is the hypothesis that security prices at any point in time "fully reflect" *all* available information. Though we shall argue that the model stands up rather well to the data, it is obviously an extreme null hypothesis. And, like any other extreme null hyposthesis, we do not expect it to be literally true. The categorization of the tests into weak, semi-strong, and strong form will serve the useful purpose of allowing us to pinpoint the level of information at which the hypothesis breaks down. And we shall contend that there is no important evidence against the hypothesis in the weak and semi-strong form tests (i.e., prices seem to efficiently adjust to obviously publicly available information), and only limited evidence against the hypothesis in the strong form tests (i.e., monopolistic access to information about prices does not seem to be a prevalent phenomenon in the investment community).

A. Weak Form Tests of the Efficient Markets Model
1. Random Walks and Fair Games: A Little Historical Background
As noted earlier, all of the empirical work on efficient markets can be considered within the context of the general expected return or "fair game" model, and much of the evidence bears directly on the special submartingale expected return model of (6). Indeed, in the early literature, discussions of the efficient

markets model were phrased in terms of the even more special random walk model, though we shall argue that most of the early authors were in fact concerned with more general versions of the "fair game" model.

Some of the confusion in the early random walk writings is understandable. Research on security prices did not begin with the development of a theory of price formation which was then subjected to empirical tests. Rather, the impetus for the development of a theory came from the accumulation of evidence in the middle 1950's and early 1960's that the behavior of common stock and other speculative prices could be well approximated by a random walk. Faced with the evidence, economists felt compelled to offer some rationalization. What resulted was a theory of efficient markets stated in terms of random walks, but usually implying some more general "fair game" model.

It was not until the work of Samuelson [38] and Mandelbrot [27] in 1965 and 1966 that the role of "fair game" expected return models in the theory of efficient markets and the relationships between these models and the theory of random walks were rigorously studied.[6] And these papers came somewhat after the major empirical work on random walks. In the earlier work, "theoretical" discussions, though usually intuitively appealing, were always lacking in rigor and often either vague or *ad hoc*. In short, until the Mandelbrot-Samuelson models appeared, there existed a large body of empirical results in search of a rigorous theory.

Thus, though his contributions were ignored for sixty years, the first statement and test of the random walk model was that of Bachelier [3] in 1900. But his "fundamental principle" for the behavior of prices was that speculation should be a "fair game"; in particular, the expected profits to the speculator should be zero. With the benefit of the modern theory of stochastic pro-

---

6. Basing their analyses on futures contracts in commodity markets, Mandelbrot and Samuelson show that if the price of such a contract at time t is the expected value at t (given information Φ_t) of the spot price at the termination of the contract, then the futures price will follow a martingale with respect to the information sequence $\{\Phi_t\}$; that is, the expected price change from period to period will be zero, and the price changes will be a "fair game." If the equilibrium expected return is not assumed to be zero, our more general "fair game" model, summarized by (1), is obtained.

But though the Mandelbrot-Samuelson approach certainly illuminates the process of price formation in commodity markets, we have seen that "fair game" expected return models can be derived in much simpler fashion. In particular, (1) is just a formalization of the assumptions that the conditions of market equilibrium can be stated in terms of expected returns and that the information Φ_t is used in forming market prices at t.

cesses, we know now that the process implied by this fundamental principle is a martingale.

After Bachelier, research on the behavior of security prices lagged until the coming of the computer. In 1953 Kendall [21] examined the behavior of weekly changes in nineteen indices of British industrial share prices and in spot prices for cotton (New York) and wheat (Chicago). After extensive analysis of serial correlations, he suggests, in quite graphic terms:

> The series looks like a wandering one, almost as if once a week the Demon of Chance drew a random number from a symetrical population of fixed dispersion and added it to the current price to determine the next week's price [21, p. 13].

Kendall's conclusion had in fact been suggested earlier by Working [47], though his suggestion lacked the force provided by Kendall's empirical results. And the implications of the conclusion for stock market research and financial analysis were later underlined by Roberts [36].

But the suggestion by Kendall, Working, and Roberts that series of speculative prices may be well described by random walks was based on observation. None of these authors attempted to provide much economic rationale for the hypothesis, and, indeed, Kendall felt that economists would generally reject it. Osborne [33] suggested market conditions, similar to those assumed by Bachelier, that would lead to a random walk. But in his model, independence of successive price changes derives from the assumption that the decisions of investors in an individual security are independent from transaction to transaction—which is little in the way of an economic model.

Whenever economists (prior to Mandelbrot and Samuelson) tried to provide economic justification for the random walk, their arguments usually implied a "fair game." For example, Alexander [8, p. 200] states:

> If one were to start out with the assumption that a stock or commodity speculation is a "fair game" with equal expectation of gain or loss or, more accurately, with an expectation of zero gain, one would be well on the way to picturing the behavior of speculative prices as a random walk.

There is an awareness here that the "fair game" assumption is not sufficient to lead to a random walk, but Alexander never expands on the comment. Similarly, Cootner [8, p. 232] states:

> If any substantial group of buyers thought prices were too low, their buying would force up the prices. The reverse would be true for sellers.

Except for appreciation due to earnings retention, the conditional expectation of tomorrow's price, given today's price, is today's price.

In such a world, the only price changes that would occur are those that result from new information. Since there is no reason to expect that information to be non-random in appearance, the period-to-period price changes of a stock should be random movements, statistically independent of one another.

Though somewhat imprecise, the last sentence of the first paragraph seems to point to a "fair game" model rather than a random walk.[7] In this light, the second paragraph can be viewed as an attempt to describe environmental conditions that would reduce a "fair game" to a random walk. But the specification imposed on the information generating process is insufficient for this purpose; one would, for example, also have to say something about investor tastes. Finally, lest I be accused of criticizing others too severely for ambiguity, lack of rigor and incorrect conclusions,

By contrast, the stock market trader has a much more practical criterion for judging what constitutes important dependence in successive price changes. For his purposes the random walk model is valid as long as knowledge of the past behavior of the series of price changes cannot be used to increase expected gains. More specifically, the independence assumption is an adequate description of reality as long as the actual degree of dependence in the series of price changes is not sufficient to allow the past history of the series to be used to predict the future in a way which makes expected profits greater than they would be under a naive buy-and hold model [10, p 35].

We know now, of course, that this last condition hardly requires a random walk. It will in fact be met by the submartingale model of (6).

But one should not be too hard on the theoretical efforts of the early empirical random walk literature. The arguments were usually appealing; where they fell short was in awareness of developments in the theory of stochastic processes. Moreover, we shall now see that most of the empirical evidence in the random walk literature can easily be interpreted as tests of more general expected return or "fair game" models.[8]

7. The appropriate conditioning statement would be "Given the sequence of historical prices."

8. Our brief historical review is meant only to provide perspective, and it is, of course, somewhat incomplete. For example, we have ignored the important contributions to the

2. Tests of Market Efficiency in the Random Walk Literature

As discussed earlier, "fair game" models imply the "impossibility" of various sorts of trading systems. Some of the random walk literature has been concerned with testing the profitability of such systems. More of the literature has, however, been concerned with tests of serial covariances of returns. We shall now show that, like a random walk, the serial covariances of a "fair game" are zero, so that these tests are also relevant for the expected return models.

If x_t is a "fair game," its unconditional expectation is zero and its serial covariance can be written in general form as:

$$E\left(\tilde{x}_{t+\tau}\tilde{x}_t\right) = \int_{x_t} x_t E\left(\tilde{x}_{t+\tau} \mid x_t\right) f(x_t) dx_t,$$

where f indicates a density function. But if x_t is a "fair game,"

$$E\left(\tilde{x}_{t+\tau} \mid \tilde{x}_t\right) = 0. [9]$$

From this it follows that for all lags, the serial covariances between lagged values of a "fair game" variable are zero. Thus, observations of a "fair game" variable are linearly independent.[10]

---

early random walk literature in studies of warrants and other options by Sprenkle, Kruizenga, Boness, and others. Much of this early work on options is summarized in [8].

9. More generally, if the sequence $\{x_t\}$ is a fair game with respect to the information sequence $\{\Phi_t\}$ (i.e., $E(\tilde{x}_{t+1} \mid \Phi_t) = 0$ for all Φ_t), then x_t is a fair game with respect to any Φ'_t that is a subset of Φ_t (i.e., $E(\tilde{x}_{t+1} \mid \Phi'_t) = 0$ for all Φ'_t). To show this, let $\Phi_t = (\Phi'_t, \Phi''_t)$. Then, using Stieltjes integrals and the symbol F to denote cumulative distinction functions, the conditional expectation

$$E(\tilde{x}_{t+1} \mid \Phi'_t) = \int_{\Phi''_t} \int_{x_{t+1}} x_{t+1} \, dF(x_{t+1}, \Phi''_t \mid \Phi'_t) = \int_{\Phi''_t} \left[\int_{x_{t+1}} x_{t+1} \, dF(x_{t+1} \mid \Phi'_t, \Phi''_t) \right] dF(\Phi'_t \mid \Phi'_t).$$

But the integral in brackets is just $E(\tilde{x}_{t+1} \mid \Phi_t)$ which by the "fair game" assumption is 0, so that

$$E(\tilde{x}_{t+1} \mid \Phi'_t) = 0 \quad \text{for all } \Phi'_t \subset \Phi_t.$$

10. But though zero serial covariances are consistent with a "fair game," they do not imply such a process. A "fair game" also rules out many types of non linear dependence. Thus using arguments similar to those above, it can be shown that if x is a "fair game," $E(\tilde{x}_t \tilde{x}_{t+1} \cdots \tilde{x}_{t+\tau}) = 0$ for all τ, which is not implied by $E(\tilde{x}_t \tilde{x}_{t+\tau}) = 0$ for all τ. For example, consider a three-period case where x must be either ± 1. Suppose the process is $x_{t+2} = \text{sign} (x_t x_{t+1})$, i.e.,

But the "fair game" model does not necessarily imply that the serial covariances of *one-period returns* are zero. In the weak form tests of this model the "fair game" variable is

$$z_{j,t} = r_{j,t} - E\left(\tilde{r}_{j,t} \mid r_{j,t-1}, r_{j,t-2}, \ldots\right). \quad \text{(Cf.fn. 9)} \tag{9}$$

But the covariance between, for example, r_{jt} and $r_{j,t+1}$ is

$$E\left(\left[\tilde{r}_{j,t+1} - E(\tilde{r}_{j,t+1})\right]\left[\tilde{r}_{jt} - E(\tilde{r}_{jt})\right]\right)$$
$$= \int_{r_{jt}} \left[r_{jt} - E(\tilde{r}_{jt})\right]\left[E\left(\tilde{r}_{j,t+1} \mid r_{jt}\right) - E\left(\tilde{r}_{j,t+1}\right)\right] f(r_{jt}) dr_{jt},$$

and (9) does not imply that $E\left(\tilde{r}_{j,t+1} \mid r_{jt}\right) = E\left(\tilde{r}_{j,t+1}\right)$: In the "fair game" efficient markets model, the deviation of the return for $t+1$ from its conditional expectation is a "fair game" variable, but the conditional expectation itself can depend on the return observed for t.[11]

In the random walk literature, this problem is not recognized, since it is assumed that the expected return (and indeed the entire distribution of returns) is stationary through time. In practice, this implies estimating serial covariances by taking cross products of deviations of observed returns from

x_t	x_{t+1}	$\rightarrow$	x_{t+2}
+	+	$\rightarrow$	+
+	−	$\rightarrow$	−
−	+	$\rightarrow$	−
−	−	$\rightarrow$	+ .

If probabilities are uniformly distributed across events,

$$E(\tilde{x}_{t+2} \mid x_{t+1}) = E(\tilde{x}_{t+2} \mid x_t) = E(\tilde{x}_{t+1} \mid x_t) = E(\tilde{x}_{t+2}) = E(\tilde{x}_{t+1}) = E(\tilde{x}_t) = 0,$$

so that all pairwise serial covariances are zero. But the process is not a "fair game," since $E(\tilde{x}_{t+2} \mid x_{t+1}, x_t) \neq 0$, and knowledge of (x_{t+1}, x_t) can be used as the basis of a simple "system" with positive expected profit.

11. For example, suppose the level of one-period returns follows a martingale so that

$$E(\tilde{r}_{j,t+1} \mid r_{jt}, r_{j,t-1} \ldots) = r_{jt}.$$

Then covariances between successive returns will be nonzero (though in this special case first differences of returns will be uncorrelated).

[88]

TABLE 1 (FROM [10]). First-order serial correlation coefficients for one-, four-, nine-, and sixteen-day changes in $\log_e$ price

| | | Differencing Interval (Days) | | |
Stock	One	Four	Nine	Sixteen
Allied Chemical	.017	.029	−.091	−.118
Alcoa	.118*	.095	−.112	−.044
American Can	−.087*	−.124*	−.060	.031
A. T. & T.	−.039	−.010	−.009	−.003
American Tobacco	.111*	−.175*	.033	.007
Anaconda	.067*	−.068	−.125	.202
Bethlehem Steel	.013	−.122	−.148	.112
Chrysler	.012	.060	−.026	.040
Du Pont	.013	.069	−.043	−.055
Eastman Kodak	.025	−.006	−.053	−.023
General Electric	.011	.020	−.004	.000
General Foods	.061*	−.005	−.140	−.098
General Motors	−.004	−.128*	.009	−.028
Goodyear	−.123*	.001	−.037	.033
International Harvester	−.017	−.068	−.244*	.116
International Nickel	.096*	.038	.124	.041
International Paper	.046	.060	−.004	−.010
Johns Manville	.006	−.068	−.002	.002
Owens Illinois	−.021	−.006	.003	−.022
Procter & Gamble	.099*	−.006	.098	.076
Sears	.097*	−.070	−.113	.041
Standard Oil (Calif.)	.025	−.143*	−.046	.040
Standard Oil (N.J.)	.008	−.109	−.082	−.121
Swift & Co.	−.004	−.072	.118	−.197
Texaco	.094*	−.053	−.047	−.178
Union Carbide	.107*	.049	−.101	.124
United Aircraft	.014	−.190*	−.192*	−.040
U.S. Steel	.040	−.006	−.056	.236*
Westinghouse	−.027	−.097	−.137	.067
Woolworth	.028	−.033	−.112	.040

*Coefficient is twice its computed standard error.

the overall sample mean return. It is somewhat fortuitous, then, that this procedure, which represents a rather gross approximation from the viewpoint of the general expected return efficient markets model, does not seem to greatly affect the results of the covariance tests, at least for common stocks.[12]

For example, Table 1 (taken from [10]) shows the serial correlations between successive changes in the natural log of price for each of the thirty stocks of the Dow Jones Industrial Average, for time periods that vary slightly from stock to stock, but usually run from about the end of 1957 to September 26, 1962. The serial correlations of successive changes in $\log_e$ price are shown for differencing intervals of one, four, nine, and sixteen days.[13]

The results in Table 1 are typical of those reported by others for tests based on serial covariances. (Cf. Kendall [21], Moore [31], Alexander [1], and the results of Granger and Morgenstern [17] and Godfrey, Granger and Morgenstern [16] obtained by means of spectral analysis.) Specifically, there is no evidence of substantial linear dependence between lagged price changes or returns. In absolute terms the measured serial correlations are always close to zero.

Looking hard, though, one can probably find evidence of statistically "significant" linear dependence in Table 1 (and again this is true of results reported by others). For the daily returns eleven of the serial correlations are more than twice their computed standard errors, and twenty-two out of thirty are positive. On the other hand, twenty-one and twenty-four of the coefficients for the four and nine day differences are negative. But with samples of the size underlying Table 1 (N = 1200–1700 observations per stock on a daily basis) statistically "significant" deviations from zero covariance are not necessarily a basis for rejecting the efficient markets model. For the results in Table 1, the standard errors of the serial correlations were approximated as $(1/(N-1))^{1/2}$, which for the daily data implies that a correlation as small as .06 is more than twice its standard error.

12. The reason is probably that for stocks, changes in equilibrium expected returns for the common differencing intervals of a day, a week, or a month, are trivial relative to other sources of variation in returns. Later, when we consider Roll's work [37], we shall see that this is not true for one week returns on U.S. Government Treasury Bills.

13. The use of changes in $\log_e$ price as the measure of return is common in the random walk literature. It can be justified in several ways. But for current purposes, it is sufficient to note that for price changes less than fifteen per cent, the change in $\log_e$ price is approximately the percentage price change or one-period return. And for differencing intervals shorter than one month, returns in excess of fifteen per cent are unusual. Thus [10] reports that for the data of Table 1, tests carried out on percentage or one-period returns yielded results essentially identical to the tests based on changes in $\log_e$ price.

But a coefficient this size implies that a linear relationship with the lagged price change can be used to explain about .36% of the variation in the current price change, which is probably insignificant from an economic viewpoint. In particular, it is unlikely that the small absolute levels of serial correlation that are always observed can be used as the basis of substantially profitable trading systems.[14]

It is, of course, difficult to judge what degree of serial correlation would imply the existence of trading rules with substantial expected profits. (And indeed we shall soon have to be a little more precise about what is implied by "substantial" profits.) Moreover, zero serial covariances are consistent with a "fair game" model, but as noted earlier (fn. 10), there are types of nonlinear dependence that imply the existence of profitable trading systems, and yet do not imply nonzero serial covariances. Thus, for many reasons it is desirable to directly test the profitability of various trading rules.

The first major evidence on trading rules was Alexander's [1, 2]. He tests a variety of systems, but the most thoroughly examined can be decribed as follows: If the price of a security moves up at least y%, buy and hold the security until its price moves down at least y% from a subsequent high, at which time simultaneously sell and go short. The short position is maintained until the price rises at least y% above a subsequent low, at which time one covers the short position and buys. Moves less than y% in either direction are ignored. Such a system is called a y% filter. It is obviously a "one security and cash" trading rule, so that the results it produces are relevant for the submartingale expected return model of (6).

After extensive tests using daily data on price indices from 1897 to 1959 and filters from one to fifty per cent, and after correcting some incorrect presumptions in the initial results of [1] (see fn. 25), in his final paper on the subject, Alexander concludes:

14. Given the evidence of Kendall [21], Mandelbrot [28], Fama [10] and others that large price changes occur much more frequently than would be expected if the generating process were Gaussian, the expression $(1/(N-1))^{1/2}$ understates the sampling dispersion of the serial correlation coefficient, and thus leads to an overstatement of significance levels. In addition, the fact that sample serial correlations are predominantly of one sign or the other is not in itself evidence of linear dependence. If, as the work of King [23] and Blume [7] indicates, there is a market factor whose behavior affects the returns on all securities, the sample behavior of this market factor may lead to a predominance of signs of one type in the serial correlations for individual securities, even though the population serial correlations for both the market factor and the returns on individual securities are zero. For a more extensive analysis of these issues see [10].

In fact, at this point I should advise any reader who is interested only in practical results, and who is not a floor trader and so must pay commissions, to turn to other sources on how to beat buy and hold. The rest of this article is devoted principally to a theoretical consideration of whether the observed results are consistent with a random walk hypothesis [8], p. 351).

Later in the paper Alexander concludes that there is some evidence in his results against the independence assumption of the random walk model. But market efficiency does not require a random walk, and from the viewpoint of the submartingale model of (6), the conclusion that the filters cannot beat buy-and-hold is support for the efficient markets hypothesis. Further support is provided by Fama and Blume [13] who compare the profitability of various filters to buy-and-hold for the individual stocks of the Dow-Jones Industrial Average. (The data are those underlying Table 1.)

But again, looking hard one can find evidence in the filter tests of both Alexander and Fama-Blume that is inconsistent with the submartingale efficient markets model, if that model is interpreted in a strict sense. In particular, the results for very small filters (1 per cent in Alexander's tests and .5, 1.0, and 1.5 per cent in the tests of Fama-Blume) indicate that it is possible to devise trading schemes based on very short-term (preferably intra-day but at most daily) price swings that will on average outperform buy-and-hold. The average profits on individual transactions from such schemes are miniscule, but they generate transactions so frequently that over longer periods and ignoring commissions they outperform buy-and-hold by a substantial margin. These results are evidence of persistence or positive dependence in very short-term price movements. And, interestingly, this is consistent with the evidence for slight positive linear dependence in successive daily price changes produced by the serial correlations.[15]

15. Though strictly speaking, such tests of pure independence are not directly relevant for expected return models, it is interesting that the conclusion that very short-term swings in prices persist slightly longer than would be expected under the martingale hypothesis is also supported by the results of non-parametric runs tests applied to the daily data of Table 1. (See [10], Tables 12–15.) For the daily price changes, the actual number of runs of price changes of the same sign is less than the expected number for 26 out of 30 stocks. Moreover, of the eight stocks for which the actual number of runs is more than two standard errors less than the expected number, five of the same stocks have positive daily, first order serial correlations in Table 1 that are more than twice their standard errors. But in both cases the statistical "significance" of the results is largely a

But when one takes account of even the minimum trading costs that would be generated by small filters, their advantage over buy-and-hold disappears. For example, even a floor trader (i.e., a person who owns a seat) on the New York Stock Exchange must pay clearinghouse fees on his trades that amount to about .1 per cent per turnaround transaction (i.e., sales plus purchase). Fama-Blume show that because small filters produce such frequent trades, these minimum trading costs are sufficient to wipe out their advantage over buy-and-hold.

Thus the filter tests, like the serial correlations, produce empirically noticeable departures from the strict implications of the efficient markets model. But, in spite of any statistical significance they might have, from an economic viewpoint the departures are so small that it seems hardly justified to use them to declare the market inefficient.

3. Other Tests of Independence in the Random Walk Literature

It is probably best to regard the random walk model as a special case of the more general expected return model in the sense of making a more detailed specification of the economic environment. That is, the basic model of market equilibrium is the "fair game" expected return model, with a random walk arising when additional environmental conditions are such that distributions of one-period returns repeat themselves through time. From this viewpoint violations of the pure independence assumption of the random walk model are to be expected. But when judged relative to the benchmark provided by the random walk model, these violations can provide insights into the nature of the market environment.

For example, one departure from the pure independence assumption of the random walk model has been noted by Osborne [34], Fama ([10], Table 17

---

reflection of the large sample sizes. Just as the serial correlations are small in absolute terms (the average is .026), the differences between the expected and actual number of runs on average are only three per cent of the total expected number.

On the other hand, it is also interesting that the runs tests do not support the suggestion of slight negative dependence in four and nine day changes that appeared in the serial correlations. In the runs tests such negative dependence would appear as a tendency for the actual number of runs to exceed the expected number. In fact, for the four and nine day price changes, for 17 and 18 of the 30 stocks in Table 1 the actual number of runs is less than the expected number. Indeed, runs tests in general show no consistent evidence of dependence for any differencing interval longer than a day, which seems especially pertinent in light of the comments in footnote 14.

and Figure 8), and others. In particular, large daily price changes tend to be followed by large daily changes. The signs of the successor changes are apparently random, however, which indicates that the phenomenon represents a denial of the random walk model but not of the market efficiency hypothesis. Nevertheless, it is interesting to speculate why the phenomenon might arise. It may be that when important new information comes into the market it cannot always be immediately evaluated precisely. Thus, sometimes the initial price will overadjust to the information, and other times it will under-adjust. But since the evidence indicates that the price changes on days following the initial large change are random in sign, the initial large change at least represents an unbiased adjustment to the ultimate price effects of the information, and this is sufficient for the expected return efficient markets model.

Niederhoffer and Osborne [32] document two departures from complete randomness in common stock price changes from transaction to transaction. First, their data indicate that reversals (pairs of consecutive price changes of opposite sign) are from two to three times as likely as continuations (pairs of consecutive price changes of the same sign). Second, a continuation is slightly more frequent after a preceding continuation than after a reversal. That is, let $(+\,|\,++)$ indicate the occurrence of a positive price change, given two preceding positive changes. Then the events $(+\,|\,++)$ and $(-\,|\,--)$ are slightly more frequent than $(+\,|\,+-)$ or $(-\,|\,-+)$.[16]

Niederhoffer and Osborne offer explanations for these phenomena based on the market structure of the New York Stock Exchange (N.Y.S.E.). In particular, there are three major types of orders that an investor might place in a given stock: (a) buy limit (buy at a specified price or lower), (b) sell limit (sell at a specified price or higher), and (c) buy or sell at market (at the lowest selling or highest buying price of another investor). A book of unexecuted limit orders in a given stock is kept by the specialist in that stock on the floor of the exchange. Unexecuted sell limit orders are, of course, at higher prices than unexecuted buy limit orders. On both exchanges, the smallest non-zero price change allowed is ⅛ point.

Suppose now that there is more than one unexecuted sell limit order at the lowest price of any such order. A transaction at this price (initiated by an order

---

16. On a transaction to transaction basis, positive and negative price changes are about equally likely. Thus, under the assumption that price changes are random, any pair of non-zero changes should be as likely as any other, and likewise for triplets of consecutive non-zero changes.

to buy at market[17]) can only be followed either by a transaction at the same price (if the next market order is to buy) or by a transaction at a lower price (if the next market order is to sell). Consecutive price increases can usually only occur when consecutive market orders to buy exhaust the sell limit orders at a given price.[18] In short, the excessive tendency toward reversal for consecutive non-zero price changes could result from bunching of unexecuted buy and sell limit orders.

The tendency for the events $(+\,|\,+\,+)$ and $(-\,|\,-\,-)$ to occur slightly more frequently than $(+\,|\,+\,-)$ and $(-\,|\,-\,+)$ requires a more involved explanation which we shall not attempt to reproduce in full here. In brief, Niederhoffer and Osborne contend that the higher frequency of $(+\,|\,+\,+)$ relative to $(+\,|\,+\,-)$ arises from a tendency for limit orders "to be concentrated at integers (26, 43), halves (26½, 43½), quarters and odd eighths in descending order of preference."[19] The frequency of the event $(+\,|\,+\,+)$, which usually requires that sell limit orders be exhausted at at least two consecutively higher prices (the last of which is relatively more frequently at an odd eighth), more heavily reflects the absence of sell limit orders at odd eighths than the event $(+\,|\,+\,-)$, which usually implies that sell limit orders at only one price have been exhausted and so more or less reflects the average bunching of limit orders at all eighths.

But though Niederhoffer and Osborne present convincing evidence of statistically significant departures from independence in price changes from transaction to transaction, and though their analysis of their findings presents interesting insights into the process of market making on the major exchanges, the types of dependence uncovered do not imply market inefficiency. The best documented source of dependence, the tendency toward excessive reversals in pairs of non-zero price changes, seems to be a direct result of the ability of investors to place limit orders as well as orders at market, and this negative dependence in itself does not imply the existence of profitable trading rules.

17. A buy limit order for a price equal to or greater than the lowest available sell limit price is effectively an order to buy at market, and is treated as such by the broker.

18. The exception is when there is a gap of more than ⅛ between the highest unexecuted buy limit and the lowest unexecuted sell limit order, so that market orders (and new limit orders) can be crossed at intermediate prices.

19. Their empirical documentation for this claim is a few samples of specialists' books for selected days, plus the observation [34] that actual trading prices, at least for volatile high priced stocks, seem to be concentrated at integers, halves, quarters and odd eighths in descending order.

Similarly, the apparent tendency for observed transactions (and, by implication, limit orders) to be concentrated at integers, halves, even eighths and odd eighths in descending order is an interesting fact about investor behavior, but in itself is not a basis on which to conclude that the market is inefficient.[20]

The Niederhoffer-Osborne analysis of market making does, however, point clearly to the existence of market inefficiency, but with respect to strong form tests of the efficient markets model. In particular, the list of unexecuted buy and sell limit orders in the specialist's book is important information about the likely future behavior of prices, and this information is only available to the specialist. When the specialist is asked for a quote, he gives the prices and can give the quantities of the highest buy limit and lowest sell limit orders on his book, but he is prevented by law from divulging the book's full contents. The interested reader can easily imagine situations where the structure of limit orders in the book could be used as the basis of a profitable trading rule.[21] But the record seems to speak for itself:

> It should not be assumed that these transactions undertaken by the specialist, and in which he is involved as buyer or seller in 24 per cent of all market volume, are necessarily a burden to him. Typically, the specialist sells above his last purchase on 83 per cent of all his sales, and buys below his last sale on 81 per cent of all his purchases ([32], p. 908).

20. Niederhoffer and Osborne offer little to refute this conclusion. For example ([32], p. 914): Although the specific properties reported in this study have a significance from a statistical point of view, the reader may well ask whether or not they are helpful in a practical sense. Certain trading rules emerge as a result of our analysis. One is that limit and stop orders should be placed at odd eights, preferably at ⅞ for sell orders and at ⅛ for buy orders. Another is to buy when a stock advances through a barrier and to sell when it sinks through a barrier.

The first "trading rule" tells the investor to resist his innate inclination to place orders at integers, but rather to place sell orders ⅛ below an integer and buy orders ⅛ above. Successful execution of the orders is then more likely, since the congestion of orders that occur at integers is avoided. But the cost of this success is apparent. The second "trading rule" seems no more promising, if indeed it can even be translated into a concrete prescription for action.

21. See, for example, ([32], p. 908). But it is unlikely that anyone but the specialist could earn substantial profits from knowledge of the structure of unexecuted limit orders on the book. The specialist makes trading profits by engaging in many transactions, each of which has a small average profit; but for any other trader, including those with seats on the exchange, these profits would be eaten up by commissions to the specialist.

Thus it seems that the specialist has monopoly power over an important block of information, and, not unexpectedly, uses his monopoly to turn a profit. And this, of course, is evidence of market inefficiency in the strong form sense. The important economic question, of course, is whether the market making function of the specialist could be fulfilled more economically by some non-monopolistic mechanism.[22]

4. Distributional Evidence

At this date the weight of the empirical evidence is such that economists would generally agree that whatever dependence exists in series of historical returns cannot be used to make profitable predictions of the future. Indeed, for returns that cover periods of a day or longer, there is little in the evidence that would cause rejection of the stronger random walk model, at least as a good first approximation.

Rather, the last burning issue of the random walk literature has centered on the nature of the distribution of price changes (which, we should note immediately, is an important issue for the efficient markets hypothesis since the nature of the distribution affects both the types of statistical tools relevant for testing the hypothesis and the interpretation of any results obtained). A model implying normally distributed price changes was first proposed by Bachelier [3], who assumed that price changes from transaction to transaction are independent, identically distributed random variables with finite variances. If transactions are fairly uniformly spread across time, and if the number of transactions per day, week, or month is very large, then the Central Limit Theorem leads us to expect that these price changes will have normal or Gaussian distributions.

Osborne [33], Moore [31], and Kendall [21] all thought their empirical evidence supported the normality hypothesis, but all observed high tails (i.e., higher proportions of large observations) in their data distributions vis-à-vis what would be expected if the distributions were normal. Drawing on these findings and some empirical work of his own, Mandelbrot [28] then suggested that these departures from normality could be explained by a more general

---

22. With modern computers, it is hard to believe that a more competitive and economical system would not be feasible. It does not seem technologically impossible to replace the entire floor of the N.Y.S.E. with a computer, fed by many remote consoles, that kept all the books now kept by the specialists, that could easily make the entire book on any stock available to anybody (so that interested individuals could then compete to "make a market" in a stock) and that carried out transactions automatically.

form of the Bachelier model. In particular, if one does not assume that distributions of price changes from transaction to transaction necessarily have finite variances, then the limiting distributions for price changes over longer differencing intervals could be any member of the stable class, which includes the normal as a special case. Non-normal stable distributions have higher tails than the normal, and so can account for this empirically observed feature of distributions of price changes. After extensive testing (involving the data from the stocks in Table 1), Fama [10] concludes that non-normal stable distributions are a better description of distributions of daily returns on common stocks than the normal. This conclusion is also supported by the empirical work of Blume [7] on common stocks, and it has been extended to U.S. Government Treasury Bills by Roll [37].

Economists have, however, been reluctant to accept these results,[23] primarily because of the wealth of statistical techniques available for dealing with normal variables and the relative paucity of such techniques for non-normal stable variables. But perhaps the biggest contribution of Mandelbrot's work has been to stimulate research on stable distributions and estimation procedures to be applied to stable variables. (See, for example, Wise [46], Fama and Roll [15], and Blattberg and Sargent [6], among others.) The advance of statistical sophistication (and the importance of examining distributional assumptions in testing the efficient markets model) is well illustrated in Roll [37], as compared, for example, with the early empirical work of Mandelbrot [28] and Fama [10].

23. Some have suggested that the long-tailed empirical distributions might result from processes that are mixtures of normal distributions with different variances. Press [35], for example, suggests a Poisson mixture of normals in which the resulting distributions of price changes have long tails but finite variances. On the other hand, Mandelbrot and Taylor [29] show that other mixtures of normals can still lead to non-normal stable distributions of price changes for finite differencing intervals.

If, as Press' model would imply, distributions of price changes are long-tailed but have finite variances, then distributions of price changes over longer and longer differencing intervals should be progressively closer to the normal. No such convergence to normality was observed in [101 (though admittedly the techniques used were somewhat rough). Rather, except for origin and scale, the distributions for longer differencing intervals seem to have the same "high-tailed" characteristics as distributins for shorter differencing intervals, which is as would be expected if the distributions are non-normal stable.

5. "Fair Game" Models in the Treasury Bill Market

Roll's work is novel in other respects as well. Coming after the efficient markets models of Mandelbrot [27] and Samuelson [38], it is the first weak form empirical work that is consciously in the "fair game" rather than the random walk tradition.

More important, as we saw earlier, the "fair game" properties of the general expected return models apply to

$$z_{jt} = r_{jt} - E\left(\tilde{r}_{jt} \mid \Phi_{t-1}\right).$$ (10)

For data on common stocks, tests of "fair game" (and random walk) properties seem to go well when the conditional expected return is estimated as the average return for the sample of data at hand. Apparently the variation in common stock returns about their expected values is so large relative to any changes in the expected values that the latter can safely be ignored. But, as Roll demonstrates, this result does not hold for Treasury Bills. Thus, to test the "fair game" model on Treasury Bills requires explicit economic theory for the evolution of expected returns through time.

Roll uses three existing theories of the term structure (the pure expectations hypothesis of Lutz [26] and two market segmentation hypotheses, one of which is the familiar "liquidity preference" hypothesis of Hicks [18] and Kessel [22]) for this purpose.[24] In his models r_{jt} is the rate observed from the term structure at period t for one week loans to commence at $t + j - 1$, and can be thought of as a "futures" rate. Thus $r_{j+1, t-1}$ is likewise the rate on one week loans to commence at $t + j - 1$, but observed in this case at $t - 1$. Similarly, L_{jt} is the so-called "liquidity premium" in r_{jt}; that is

$$r_{jt} = E\left(\tilde{r}_{0,t+j-1} \mid \Phi_t\right) + L_{jt}.$$

In words, the one-week "futures" rate for period $t + j - 1$ observed from the term structure at t is the expectation at t of the "spot" rate for $t + j - 1$ plus a "liquidity premium" (which could, however, be positive or negative).

---

24. As noted early in our discussions, all available tests of market efficiency are implicitly also tests of expected return models of market equilibrium. But Roll formulates explicitly the economic models underlying his estimates of expected returns, and emphasizes that he is simultaneously testing economic models of the term structure as well as market efficiency.

In all three theories of the term structure considered by Roll, the conditional expectation required in (10) is of the form

$$E\left(\tilde{r}_{j,t} \mid \Phi_{t-1}\right) = r_{j+1,t-1} + E\left(\tilde{L}_{jt} \mid \Phi_{t-1}\right) - L_{j+1,t-1}.$$

The three theories differ only in the values assigned to the "liquidity premiums." For example, in the "liquidity preference" hypothesis, investors must always be paid a positive premium for bearing interest rate uncertainty, so that the L_{jt} are always positive. By contrast, in the "pure expectations" hypothesis, all liquidity premiums are assumed to be zero, so that

$$E\left(\tilde{r}_{jt} \mid \Phi_{t-1}\right) = r_{j+1,t-1}.$$

After extensive testing, Roll concludes (i) that the two market segmentation hypotheses fit the data better than the pure expectations hypothesis, with perhaps a slight advantage for the "liquidity preference" hypothesis, and (ii) that as far as his tests are concerned, the market for Treasury Bills is efficient. Indeed, it is interesting that when the best fitting term structure model is used to estimate the conditional expected "futures" rate in (10), the resulting variable z_{jt} seems to be serially independent! It is also interesting that if he simply assumed that his data distributions were normal, Roll's results would not be so strongly in support of the efficient markets model. In this case taking account of the observed high tails of the data distributions substantially affected the interpretation of the results.[25]

6. Tests of a Multiple Security Expected Return Model

Though the weak form tests support the "fair game" efficient markets model, all of the evidence examined so far consists of what we might call "single se-

---

25. The importance of distributional assumptions is also illustrated in Alexander's work on trading rules. In his initial tests of filter systems [1], Alexander assumed that purchases could always be executed exactly (rather than at least) y% above lows and sales exactly y% below highs. Mandelbrot [28] pointed out, however, that though this assumption would do little harm with normally distributed price changes (since price series are then essentially continuous), with non-normal stable distributions it would introduce substantial positive bias into the filter profits (since with such distributions price series will show many discontinuities). In his later tests [2], Alexander does indeed find that taking account of the discontinuities (i.e., the presence of large price changes) in his data substantially lowers the profitability of the filters.

curity tests." That is, the price or return histories of individual securities are examined for evidence of dependence that might be used as the basis of a trading system for *that* security. We have not discussed tests of whether securities are "appropriately priced" vis-à-vis one another.

But to judge whether differences between average returns are "appropriate" an economic theory of equilibrium expected returns is required. At the moment, the only fully developed theory is that of Sharpe [40] and Lintner [24, 25] referred to earlier. In this model (which is a direct outgrowth of the mean-standard deviation portfolio models of investor equilibrium of Markowitz [30] and Tobin [43]), the expected return on security j from time t to t + 1 is

$$
E\left(\tilde{r}_{j,t+1} \mid \Phi_t\right) = r_{f,t+1} + \left[\frac{E\left(\tilde{r}_{m,t+1} \mid \Phi_t\right) - r_{f,t+1}}{\sigma\left(\tilde{r}_{m,t+1} \mid \Phi_t\right)} \right] \frac{\mathrm{cov}\left(\tilde{r}_{j,t+1}, \tilde{r}_{m,t+1} \mid \Phi_t\right)}{\sigma\left(\tilde{r}_{m,t+1} \mid \Phi_t\right)}, \tag{11}
$$

where $r_{f,t+1}$ is the return from t to t + 1 on an asset that is riskless in money terms; $r_{m,t+1}$ is the return on the "market portfolio" m (a portfolio of all investment assets with each weighted in proportion to the total market value of all its outstanding units); $\sigma^2(\tilde{r}_{m,t+1} \mid \Phi_t)$ is the variance of the return on m; $\mathrm{cov}(\tilde{r}_{j,t+1}, \tilde{r}_{m,t+1} \mid \Phi_t)$ is the covariance between the returns on j and m; and the appearance of Φ_t indicates that the various expected returns, variance and covariance, could in principle depend on Φ_t. Though Sharpe and Lintner derive (11) as a one-period model, the result is given a multiperiod justification and interpretation in [11]. The model has also been extended in [12] to the case where the one-period returns could have stable distributions with infinite variances.

In words, (11) says that the expected one-period return on a security is the one-period riskless rate of interest $r_{f,t+1}$ plus a "risk premium" that is proportional to $\mathrm{cov}(\tilde{r}_{j,t+1}, \tilde{r}_{m,t+1} \mid \Phi_t) / \sigma(\tilde{r}_{m,t+1} \mid \Phi_t)$. In the Sharpe-Lintner model each investor holds some combination of the riskless asset and the market portfolio, so that, given a mean-standard deviation framework, the risk of an individual asset can be measured by its contribution to the standard deviation of the return on the market portfolio. This contribution is in fact $\mathrm{cov}\,(\tilde{r}_{j,t+1}, \tilde{r}_{m,t+1} \mid \Phi_t) / \sigma(\tilde{r}_{m,t+1} \mid \Phi_t)$.[26] The factor

$$
\left[E\left(\tilde{r}_{m,t+1} \mid \Phi_t\right) - r_{f,t+1} \right] / \sigma\left(\tilde{r}_{m,t+1} \mid \Phi_t\right),
$$

26. That is,

$$
\sum_j \mathrm{cov}\left(\tilde{r}_{j,t+1}, \tilde{r}_{m,t+1} \mid \Phi_t\right) / \sigma\left(\tilde{r}_{m,t+1} \mid \Phi_t\right) = \sigma\left(\tilde{r}_{m,t+1} \mid \Phi_t\right).
$$

which is the same for all securities, is then regarded as the market price of risk.

Published empirical tests of the Sharpe-Lintner model are not yet available, though much work is in progress. There is some published work, however, which, though not directed at the Sharpe-Lintner model, is at least consistent with some of its implications. The stated goal of this work has been to determine the extent to which the returns on a given security are related to the returns on other securities. It started (again) with Kendall's [21] finding that though common stock price changes do not seem to be serially correlated, there is a high degree of cross-correlation between the *simultaneous* returns of different securities. This line of attack was continued by King [23] who (using factor analysis of a sample of monthly returns on sixty N.Y.S.E. stocks for the period 1926–60) found that on average about 50% of the variance of an individual stock's returns could be accounted for by a "market factor" which affects the returns on all stocks, with "industry factors" accounting for at most an additional 10% of the variance.

For our purposes, however, the work of Fama, Fisher, Jensen, and Roll [14] (henceforth FFJR) and the more extensive work of Blume [7] on monthly return data is more relevant. They test the following "market model," originally suggested by Markowitz [30]:

$$\tilde{r}_{j,t+1} = \alpha_j + \beta_j \tilde{r}_{M,t+1} + \tilde{u}_{j,t+1} \tag{12}$$

where $r_{j,t+1}$ is the rate of return on security j for month t, $r_{M,t+1}$ is the corresponding return on a market index M, α_j and β_j are parameters that can vary from security to security, and $u_{j,t+1}$ is a random disturbance. The tests of FFJR and subsequently those of Blume indicate that (12) is well specified as a linear regression model in that (i) the estimated parameters $\hat{\alpha}_j$ and $\hat{\beta}_j$ remain fairly constant over long periods of time (e.g., the entire post-World War II period in the case of Blume), (ii) $r_{M,t+1}$ and the estimated $\hat{u}_{j,t+1}$, are close to serially independent, and (iii) the $\hat{u}_{j,t+1}$ seem to be independent of $r_{M,t+1}$.

Thus the observed properties of the "market model" are consistent with the expected return efficient markets model, and, in addition, the "market model" tells us something about the process generating expected returns from security to security. In particular,

$$E\left(\tilde{r}_{j,t+1}\right) = \alpha_j + \beta_j E\left(\tilde{r}_{M,t+1}\right). \tag{13}$$

The question now is to what extent (13) is consistent with the Sharpe-Lintner expected return model summarized by (11). Rearranging (11) we obtain

$$E\left(\tilde{r}_{j,t+1} \mid \Phi_t\right) = \alpha_j(\Phi_t) + \beta_j(\Phi_t) E\left(\tilde{r}_{m,t+1} \mid \Phi_t\right), \tag{14}$$

where, noting that the riskless rate $r_{f,t+1}$ is itself part of the information set Φ_t, we have

$$\alpha_j(\Phi_t) = r_{f,t+1}\left[1 - \beta_j(\Phi_t)\right], \tag{15}$$

and

$$\beta_j(\Phi_t) = \frac{\operatorname{cov}\left(\tilde{r}_{j,t+1}, \tilde{r}_{m,t+1} \mid \Phi_t\right)}{\sigma^2\left(\tilde{r}_{m,t+1} \mid \Phi_t\right)}. \tag{16}$$

With some simplifying assumptions, (14) can be reduced to (13). In particular, if the covariance and variance that determine $\beta_j(\Phi_t)$ in (16) are the same for all t and Φ_t, then $\beta_j(\Phi_t)$ in (16) corresponds to β_j in (12) and (13), and the least squares *estimate* of β_j in (12) is in fact just the ratio of the sample values of the covariance and variance in (16). If we also assume that $r_{f,t+1}$ is the same for all t, and that the behavior of the returns on the market portfolio m are closely approximated by the returns on some representative index M, we will have come a long way toward equating (13) and (11). Indeed, the only missing link is whether in the estimated parameters of (12)

$$\hat{\alpha}_j \cong r_f(1 - \hat{\beta}_j). \tag{17}$$

Neither FFJR nor Blume attack this question directly, though some of Blume's evidence is at least promising. In particular, the magnitudes of the estimated $\hat{\alpha}_j$ are roughly consistent with (17) in the sense that the estimates are always close to zero (as they should be with monthly return data).[27]

In a sense, though, in establishing the apparent empirical validity of the "market model" of (12), both too much and too little have been shown *vis-à-*

27. With least squares applied to monthly return data, the estimate of α_j in (12) is

$$\hat{\alpha}_j = \bar{r}_{j,t} - \hat{\beta}_j \bar{r}_{M,t},$$

vis the Sharpe-Lintner expected return model of (11). We know that during the post-World War II period one-month interest rates on riskless assets (e.g., government bills with one month to maturity) have not been constant. Thus, if expected security returns were generated by a version of the "market model" that is fully consistent with the Sharpe-Lintner model, we would, according to (15), expect to observe some non-stationarity in the estimates of α_j. On a monthly basis, however, variation through time in one-period riskless interest rates is probably trivial relative to variation in other factors affecting monthly common stock returns, so that more powerful statistical methods would be necessary to study the effects of changes in the riskless rate.

In any case, since the work of FFJR and Blume on the "market model" was not concerned with relating this model to the Sharpe-Lintner model, we can only say that the results for the former are somewhat consistent with the implications of the latter. But the results for the "market model" are, after all, just a statistical description of the return generating process, and they are probably somewhat consistent with other models of equilibrium expected returns. Thus the only way to generate strong empirical conclusions about the Sharpe-Lintner model is to test it directly. On the other hand, any alternative model of equilibrium expected returns must be somewhat consistent with the "market model," given the evidence in its support.

B. Tests of Martingale Models of the Semi-Strong Form

In general, semi-strong form tests of efficient markets models are concerned with whether current prices "fully reflect" all obviously publicly available information. Each individual test, however, is concerned with the adjustment of security prices to one kind of information generating event (e.g., stock splits, announcements of financial reports by firms, new security issues, etc.). Thus each test only brings supporting evidence for the model, with the idea that by accumulating such evidence the validity of the model will be "established."

---

where the bars indicate sample mean returns. But, in fact, Blume applies the market model to the wealth relatives $R_{jt} = 1 + r_{jt}$ and $R_{Mt} = 1 + r_{Mt}$. This yields precisely the same estimate of β_j as least squares applied to (12), but the intercept is now

$$\hat{\alpha}'_j = \bar{R}_{jt} - \hat{\beta}_j \bar{R}_{Mt} = 1 + \bar{r}_{jt} - \hat{\beta}_j (1 + \bar{r}_{Mt}) = 1 - \hat{\beta}_j + \hat{\alpha}_j.$$

Thus what Blume in fact finds is that for almost all securities, $\hat{\alpha}'_j + \hat{\beta}_j \cong 1$, which implies that $\hat{\alpha}_j$ is close to 0.

In fact, however, though the available evidence is in support of the efficient markets model, it is limited to a few major types of information generating events. The initial major work is apparently the study of stock splits by Fama, Fisher, Jensen, and Roll (FFJR) [14], and all the subsequent studies summarized here are adaptations and extensions of the techniques developed in FFJR. Thus, this paper will first be reviewed in some detail, and then the other studies will be considered.

1. Splits and the Adjustment of Stock Prices to New Information

Since the only apparent result of a stock split is to multiply the number of shares per shareholder without increasing claims to real assets, splits in themselves are not necessarily sources of new information. The presumption of FFJR is that splits may often be associated with the appearance of more fundamentally important information. The idea is to examine security returns around split dates to see first if there is any "unusual" behavior, and, if so, to what extent it can be accounted for by relationships between splits and other more fundamental variables.

The approach of FFJR to the problem relies heavily on the "market model" of (12). In this model if a stock split is associated with abnormal behavior, this would be reflected in the estimated regression residuals for the months surrounding the split. For a given split, define month o as the month in which the effective date of a split occurs, month 1 as the month immediately following the split month, month -1 as the month preceding, etc. Now define the average residual over all split securities for month m (where for each security m is measured relative to the split month) as

$$u_m = \sum_{j=1}^{N} \frac{\hat{u}_{jm}}{N},$$

where $\hat{u}_{jm}$ is the sample regression residual for security j in month m and N is the number of splits. Next, define the cumulative average residual U_m as

$$U_m = \sum_{k=-29}^{m} u_k.$$

The average residual u_m can be interpreted as the average deviation (in month m relative to split months) of the returns of split stocks from their normal relationships with the market. Similarly, U_m can be interpreted as the cumulative deviation (from month -29 to month m). Finally, define u_m^+, u_m^-, U_m^+ and U_m^- as the average and cumulative average residuals for splits followed by "increased" ($+$) and "decreased" ($-$) dividends. An "increase" is a case where the percentage change in dividends on the split share in the year after the split is greater than the percentage change for the N.Y.S.E. as a whole, while a "decrease" is a case of relative dividend decline.

The essence of the results of FFJR are then summarized in Figure 1, which shows the cumulative average residuals U_m U_m^+, and U_m^- for $-29 \le m \le 30$. The sample includes all 940 stock splits on the N.Y.S.E. from 1927–59, where the exchange was at least five new shares for four old, and where the security was listed for at least twelve months before and after the split.

For all three dividend categories the cumulative average residuals rise in the 29 months prior to the split, and in fact the average residuals (not shown here) are uniformly positive. This cannot be attributed to the splitting process, since in only about ten per cent of the cases is the time between the announcement and effective dates of a split greater than four months. Rather, it seems that firms tend to split their shares during "abnormally" good times—that is, during periods when the prices of their shares have increased more than would be implied by their normal relationships with general market prices, which itself probably reflects a sharp improvement, relative to the market, in the earnings prospects of these firms sometime during the years immediately preceding a split.[28]

After the split month there is almost no further movement in U_m, the cumulative average residual for all splits. This is striking, since 71.5 per cent (672 out of 940) of all splits experienced greater percentage dividend increases in the year after the split than the average for all securities on the N.Y.S.E. In light of this, FFJR suggest that when a split is announced the market interprets this (and correctly so) as a signal that the company's directors are probably confident that future earnings will be sufficient to maintain dividend payments at a higher level. Thus the large price increases in the months immediately preceding a split may be due to an alteration in expectations concerning the

---

28. It is important to note, however, that as FFJR indicate, the persistent upward drift of the cumulative average residuals in the months preceding the split is not a phenomenon that could be used to increase expected trading profits. The reason is that the behavior of the average residuals is not representative of the behavior of the residuals for individual securities. In months prior to the split, successive sample residuals for individual securities seem to be independent. But in most cases, there are a few months in which the residuals are abnormally large and positive. The months of large residuals differ from security to security, however, and these differences in timing explain why the signs of the average residuals are uniformly positive for many months preceding the split.

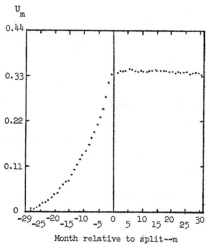

Figure 1a. Cumulative average
residuals—all splits

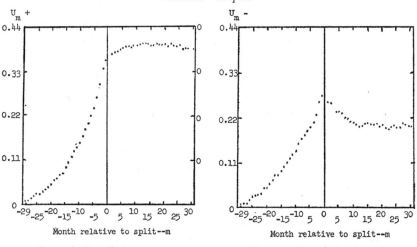

Figure 1b. Cumulative average
residuals for dividend "increases"

Figure 1c. Cumulative average
residuals for dividend "decreases"

future earning potential of the firm, rather than to any intrinsic effects of the split itself.

If this hypothesis is correct, return behavior subsequent to splits should be substantially different for the cases where the dividend increase materializes than for the cases where it does not. FFJR argue that in fact the differences are in the directions that would be predicted. The fact that the cumulative average residuals for the "increased" dividends (Figure 1b) drift upward but only slightly in the year *after* the split is consistent with the hypothesis that when the split is *declared,* there is a price adjustment in anticipation of future dividend increases. But the behavior of the residuals for stock splits associated with "decreased" dividends offers even stronger evidence for the split hypothesis. The cumulative average residuals for these stocks (Figure 1c) rise in the few months before the split, but then fall dramatically in the few months after the split when the anticipated dividend increase is not forthcoming. When a year has passed after the split, the cumulative average residual has fallen to about where it was five months prior to the split, which is about the earliest time reliable information about a split is likely to reach the market. Thus by the time it becomes clear that the anticipated dividend increase is not forthcoming, the apparent effects of the split seem to have been wiped away, and the stock's returns have reverted to their normal relationship with market returns.

Finally, and most important, although the behavior of post-split returns will be very different depending on whether or not dividend "increases" occur, and in spite of the fact that a large majority of split securities do experience dividend "increases," when all splits are examined together (Figure 1a), subsequent to the split there is no net movement up or down in the cumulative average residuals. Thus, apparently the market makes unbiased forecasts of the implications of a split for future dividends, and these forecasts are fully reflected in the prices of the security by the end of the split month. After considerably more data analysis than can be summarized here, FFJR conclude that their results lend considerable support to the conclusion that the stock market is efficient, at least with respect to its ability to adjust to the information implicit in a split.

2. Other Studies of Public Announcements

Variants of the method of residual analysis developed in [14] have been used by others to study the effects of different kinds of public announcements, and all of these also support the efficient markets hypothesis.

Thus using data on 261 major firms for the period 1946–66, Ball and Brown [4] apply the method to study the effects of annual earnings announcements. They use the residuals from a time series regression of the annual earnings of a firm on the average earnings of all their firms to classify the firm's earnings for a given year as having "increased" or "decreased" relative to the market. Residuals from regressions of monthly common stock returns on an index of returns (i.e., the market model of (12)) are then used to compute cumulative average return residuals separately for the earnings that "increased," and those that "decreased." The cumulative average return residuals rise throughout the year in advance of the announcement for the earnings "increased" category, and fall for the earnings "decreased" category.[29] Ball and Brown [4, p. 175] conclude that in fact no more than about ten to fifteen percent of the information in the annual earnings announcement has not been anticipated by the month of the announcement.

On the macro level, Waud [45] has used the method of residual analysis to examine the effects of announcements of discount rate changes by Federal Reserve Banks. In this case the residuals are essentially just the deviations of the daily returns on the Standard and Poor's 500 Index from the average daily return. He finds evidence of a statistically significant "announcement effect" on stock returns for the first trading day following an announcement, but the magnitude of the adjustment is small, never exceeding .5%. More interesting from the viewpoint of the efficient markets hypothesis is his conclusion that, if anything, the market anticipates the announcements (or information is somehow leaked in advance). This conclusion is based on the non-random patterns of the signs of average return residuals on the days immediately preceding the announcement.

Further evidence in support of the efficient markets hypothesis is provided in the work of Scholes [39] on large secondary offerings of common stock (ie., large underwritten sales of existing common stocks by individuals and institutions) and on new issues of stock. He finds that on average secondary issues are associated with a decline of between one and two per cent in the cumulative average residual returns for the corresponding common stocks. Since the magnitude of the price adjustment is unrelated to the size of the issue, Scholes concludes that the adjustment is not due to "selling pressure" (as is commonly believed), but rather results from negative information implicit in the fact that somebody is trying to sell a large block of a firm's stock. Moreover, he presents evidence that the value of the information in a secondary depends to some extent on the vendor; somewhat as would be expected, by far the largest negative cumulative average residuals occur where the vendor is the corporation itself or one of its officers, with investment companies a distant second. But the identity of the vendor is not generally known at the time of the secondary, and corporate insiders need only report their transactions in their own company's stock to the S.E.C. within six days after a sale. By this time the market

29. But the comment of footnote 28 is again relevant here.

on average has fully adjusted to the information in the secondary, as indicated by the fact that the average residuals behave randomly thereafter.

Note, however, that though this is evidence that prices adjust efficiently to public information, it is also evidence that corporate insiders at least sometimes have important information about their firm that is not yet publicly known. Thus Scholes' evidence for secondary distributions provides support for the efficient markets model in the semi-strong form sense, but also some strong-form evidence against the model.

Though his results here are only preliminary, Scholes also reports on an application of the method of residual analysis to a sample of 696 new issues of common stock during the period 1926–66. As in the FFJR study of splits, the cumulative average residuals rise in the months preceding the new security offering (suggesting that new issues tend to come after favorable recent events)[30] but behave randomly in the months following the offering (indicating that whatever information is contained in the new issue is on average fully reflected in the price of the month of the offering).

In short, the available semi-strong form evidence on the effect of various sorts of public announcements on common stock returns is all consistent with the efficient markets model. The strong point of the evidence, however, is its consistency rather than its quantity; in fact, few different types of public information have been examined, though those treated are among the obviously most important. Moreover, as we shall now see, the amount of semi-strong form evidence is voluminous compared to the strong form tests that are available.

C. Strong Form Tests of the Efficient Markets Models

The strong form tests of the efficient markets model are concerned with whether all available information is fully reflected in prices in the sense that no individual has higher expected trading profits than others because he has monopolistic access to some information. We would not, of course, expect this model to be an exact description of reality, and indeed, the preceding discussions have already indicated the existence of contradictory evidence. In particular, Niederhoffer and Osborne [32] have pointed out that specialists on the N.Y.S.E. apparently use their monopolistic access to information concerning unfilled limit orders to generate monopoly profits, and Scholes' evidence [39]

---

30. Footnote 28 is again relevant here.

indicates that officers of corporations sometimes have monopolistic access to information about their firms.

Since we already have enough evidence to determine that the model is not strictly valid, we can now turn to other interesting questions. Specifically, how far down through the investment community do deviations from the model permeate? Does it pay for the average investor (or the average economist) to expend resources searching out little known information? Are such activities even generally profitable for various groups of market "professionals"? More generally, who are the people in the investment community that have access to "special information"?

Though this is a fascinating problem, only one group has been studied in any depth—the managements of open end mutual funds. Several studies are available (e.g., Sharpe [41, 42] and Treynor [44]), but the most thorough are Jensen's [19, 20], and our comments will be limited to his work. We shall first present the theoretical model underlying his tests, and then go on to his empirical results.

1. Theoretical Framework

In studying the performance of mutual funds the major goals are to determine (a) whether in general fund managers seem to have access to special information which allows them to generate "abnormal" expected returns, and (b) whether some funds are better at uncovering such special information than others. Since the criterion will simply be the ability of funds to produce higher returns than some norm with no attempt to determine what is responsible for the high returns, the "special information" that leads to high performance could be either keener insight into the implications of publicly available information than is implicit in market prices or monopolistic access to specific information. Thus the tests of the performance of the mutual fund industry are not strictly strong form tests of the efficient markets model.

The major theoretical (and practical) problem in using the mutual fund industry to test the efficient markets model is developing a "norm" against which performance can be judged. The norm must represent the results of an investment policy based on the assumption that prices fully reflect all available information. And if one believes that investors are generally risk averse and so on average must be compensated for any risks undertaken, then one has the problem of finding appropriate definitions of risk and evaluating each fund relative to a norm with its chosen level of risk.

Jensen uses the Sharpe [40]-Lintner [24, 25] model of equilibrium expected returns discussed above to derive a norm consistent with these goals. From (14)-(16), in this model the expected return on an asset or portfolio j from t to t+1 is

$$E\left(\tilde{r}_{j,t+1}|\Phi_t\right)=r_{f,t+1}\left[1-\beta_j(\Phi_t)\right]+E\left(\tilde{r}_{m,t+1}|\Phi_t\right)\beta_j(\Phi_t), \qquad (18)$$

where the various symbols are as defined in Section III. A. 6. But (18) is an *ex ante* relationship, and to evaluate performance an *ex post* norm is needed. One way the latter can be obtained is to substitute the realized return on the market portfolio for the expected return in (18) with the result[31]

$$E\left(\tilde{r}_{j,t+1}|\Phi_t, r_{m,t+1}\right)=r_{f,t+1}\left[1-\beta_j(\Phi_t)\right]+r_{m,t+1}\beta_j(\Phi_t). \qquad (19)$$

Geometrically, (19) says that within the context of the Sharpe-Lintner model, the expected return on j (given information Φ_t and the return $r_{m,t+1}$ on the market portfolio) is a linear function of its risk

$$\beta_j(\Phi_t)=\mathrm{cov}\left(\tilde{r}_{j,t+1},\tilde{r}_{m,t+1}|\Phi_t\right)/\sigma^2\left(\tilde{r}_{m,t+1}|\Phi_t\right),$$

as indicated in Figure 2. Assuming that the value of $\beta_j(\Phi_t)$ is somehow known, or can be reliably estimated, if j is a mutual fund, its *ex post* performance from t to t + 1 might now be evaluated by plotting its combination of realized return $r_{j,t+1}$ and risk in Figure 2. If (as for the point a) the combination falls above the expected return line (or, as it is more commonly called, the "market line"), it has done better than would be expected given its level of risk, while if (as for the point b) it falls below the line it has done worse.

Alternatively, the market line shows the combinations of return and risk provided by portfolios that are simple mixtures of the riskless asset and the market portfolio m. The returns and risks for such portfolios (call them c) are

31. The assumption here is that the return $\tilde{r}_{j,t+1}$ is generated according to

$$\tilde{r}_{j,t+1}=r_{f,t+1}\left[1-\beta_j(\Phi_t)\right]+r_{m,t+1}\beta_j(\Phi_t)+\tilde{u}_{j,t+1},$$

and

$$E\left(\tilde{u}_{j,t+1}|r_{m,t+1}\right)=0 \quad \text{for all} \quad r_{m,t+1},$$

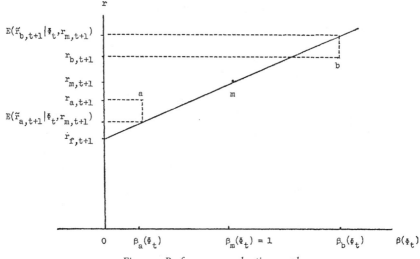

Figure 2. Performance evaluation graph

$$\tilde{r}_{c,t+1} = \alpha r_{f,t+1} + (1-\alpha)r_{m,t+1}$$

$$\beta_c(\Phi_t) = \frac{\text{cov}\left(\tilde{r}_{c,t+1}, \tilde{r}_{m,t+1} \mid \Phi_t\right)}{\sigma^2(\tilde{r}_{m,t+1} \mid \Phi_t)} = \frac{\text{cov}\left((1-\alpha)\tilde{r}_{m,t+1}, \tilde{r}_{m,t+1} \mid \Phi_t\right)}{\sigma^2(\tilde{r}_{m,t+1} \mid \Phi_t)} = 1-\alpha,$$

where α is the proportion of portfolio funds invested in the riskless asset. Thus, when $1 \geq \alpha \geq 0$ we obtain the combinations of return and risk along the market line from $r_{f,t+1}$ to m in Figure 2, while when $\alpha < 0$ (and under the assumption that investors can borrow at the same rate that they lend) we obtain the combinations of return and risk along the extension of the line through m. In this interpretation, the market line represents the results of a naive investment strategy, which the investor who thinks prices reflect all available information might follow. The performance of a mutual fund is then measured relative to this naive strategy.

2. Empirical Results

Jensen uses this risk-return framework to evaluate the performance of 115 mutual funds over the ten year period 1955–64. He argues at length for measuring return as the nominal ten year rate with continuous compounding (i.e., the natural log of the ratio of terminal wealth after ten years to initial wealth) and for using historical data on nominal one-year rates with continuous compounding to estimate risk. The Standard and Poor Index of 500 major common stocks is used as the proxy for the market portfolio.

The general question to be answered is whether mutual fund managements have any special insights or information which allows them to earn returns above the norm. But Jensen attacks the question on several levels. First, can the funds in general do well enough to compensate investors for loading charges, management fees, and other costs that might be avoided by simply choosing the combination of the riskless asset f and the market portfolio m with risk level comparable to that of the fund's actual portfolio? The answer seems to be an emphatic no. As far as net returns to investors are concerned, in 89 out of 115 cases, the fund's risk-return combination for the ten year period is below the market line for the period, and the average over all funds of the deviations of ten year returns from the market time is −14.6%. That is, on average the consumer's wealth after ten years of holding mutual funds is about fifteen per cent less than if he held the corresponding portfolios along the market line.

But the loading charge that an investor pays in buying into a fund is usually a pure salesman's commission that the fund itself never gets to invest. Thus one might ask whether, ignoring loading charges (i.e., assuming no such charges were paid by the investor), in general fund managements can earn returns sufficiently above the norm to cover all other expenses that are presumably more directly related to the management of the fund portfolios. Again, the answer seems to be no. Even when loading charges are ignored in computing returns, the risk-return combinations for 72 out of 115 funds are below the market line, and the average deviation of ten year returns from the market line is −8.9%.

Finally, as a somewhat stronger test of the efficient markets model, one would like to know if, ignoring all expenses, fund managements in general showed any ability to pick securities that outperformed the norm. Unfortunately, this question cannot be answered with precision for individual funds since, curiously, data on brokerage commissions are not published regularly. But Jensen suggests the available evidence indicates that the answer to the question is again probably negative. Specifically, adding back all other published expenses of funds to their returns, the risk-return combinations for 58 out of 115 funds were below the market line, and the average deviation of ten year return from the line was −2.5%. But part of this result is due to the absence of a correction for brokerage commissions. Estimating these commissions from average portfolio turnover rates for all funds for the period 1953–58, and adding them back to returns for all funds increases the average deviation from the market line from −2.5% to .09%, which still is not indicative of the existence of special information among mutual fund managers.

But though mutual fund managers in general do not seem to have access to information not already fully reflected in prices, perhaps there are individual funds that consistently do better than the norm, and so provide at least some strong form evidence against the efficient markets model. If there are such funds, however, they escape Jensen's search. For example, for individual funds, returns above the norm in one subperiod do not seem to be associated with performance above the norm in other subperiods. And regardless of how returns are measured (i.e., net or gross of loading charges and other expenses), the number of funds with large positive deviations of returns from the market line of Figure 2 is less than the number that would be expected by chance with 115 funds under the assumption that fund managements have no special talents in predicting returns.[32]

Jensen argues that though his results apply to only one segment of the investment community, they are nevertheless striking evidence in favor of the efficient markets model:

Although these results certainly do not imply that the strong form of the martingale hypothesis holds for all investors and for all time, they provide strong evidence in support of that hypothesis. One must realize that these analysts are extremely well endowed. Moreover, they operate in the securities markets every day and have wide-ranging contacts and associations in both the business and financial communities. Thus, the fact that they are apparently unable to forecast returns accurately enough to recover their research and transactions costs is a striking piece of evidence in favor of the strong form of the martingale hypothesis—at least as far as the extensive subset of information available to these analysts is concerned [20, p. 170].

32. On the other hand, there is some suggestion in Scholes' [39] work on secondary issues that mutual funds may occassionally have access to "special information." After corporate insiders, the next largest negative price changes occur when the secondary seller is an investment company (including mutual funds), though on average the price changes are much smaller (i.e., closer to 0) than when the seller is a corporate insider.

Moreover, Jensen's evidence itself, though not indicative of the existence of special information among mutual fund managers, is not sufficiently precise to conclude that such information never exists. This stronger conclusion would require exact data on unavoidable expenses (including brokerage commissions) of portfolio management incurred by funds.

IV. SUMMARY AND CONCLUSIONS

The preceding (rather lengthy) analysis can be summarized as follows. In general terms, the theory of efficient markets is concerned with whether prices at any point in time "fully reflect" available information. The theory only has empirical content, however, within the context of a more specific model of market equilibrium, that is, a model that specifies the nature of market equilibrium when prices "fully reflect" available information. We have seen that all of the available empirical literature is implicitly or explicitly based on the assumption that the conditions of market equilibrium can be stated in terms of expected returns. This assumption is the basis of the expected return or "fair game" efficient markets models.

The empirical work itself can be divided into three categories depending on the nature of the information subset of interest. *Strong-form* tests are concerned with whether individual investors or groups have monopolistic access to any information relevant for price formation. One would not expect such an extreme model to be an exact description of the world, and it is probably best viewed as a benchmark against which the importance of deviations from market efficiency can be judged. In the less restrictive *semi-strong-form* tests the information subset of interest includes all obviously publicly available information, while in the *weak form* tests the information subset is just historical price or return sequences.

Weak form tests of the efficient market model are the most voluminous, and it seems fair to say that the results are strongly in support. Though statistically significant evidence for dependence in successive price changes or returns has been found, some of this is consistent with the "fair game" model and the rest does not appear to be sufficient to declare the market inefficient. Indeed, at least for price changes or returns covering a day or longer, there isn't much evidence against the "fair game" model's more ambitious offspring, the random walk.

Thus, there is consistent evidence of positive dependence in day-to-day price changes and returns on common stocks, and the dependence is of a form that can be used as the basis of marginally profitable trading rules. In Fama's data [10] the dependence shows up as serial correlations that are consistently positive but also consistently close to zero, and as a slight tendency for observed numbers of runs of positive and negative price changes to be less than the numbers that would be expected from a purely random process. More important, the dependence also shows up in the filter tests of Alexander [1, 2] and those of Fama and Blume [13] as a tendency for very small filters to produce profits in excess of buy-and-hold. But any systems (like the filters) that attempt to turn short-term dependence into trading profits of necessity generate so many transactions that their expected profits would be absorbed by even the minimum commissions (security handling fees) that floor traders on major exchanges must pay. Thus, using a less than completely strict interpretation of market efficiency, this positive dependence does not seem of sufficient importance to warrant rejection of the efficient markets model.

Evidence in contradiction of the "fair game" efficient markets model for price changes or returns covering periods longer than a single day is more difficult to find. Cootner [9], and Moore [31] report preponderantly negative (but again small) serial correlations in weekly common stock returns, and this result appears also in the four day returns analyzed by Fama [10]. But it does not appear in runs tests of [10], where, if anything, there is some slight indication of positive dependence, but actually not much evidence of any dependence at all. In any case, there is no indication that whatever dependence exists in weekly returns can be used as the basis of profitable trading rules.

Other existing evidence of dependence in returns provides interesting insights into the process of price formation in the stock market, but it is not relevant for testing the efficient markets model. For example, Fama [10] shows that large daily price changes tend to be folowed by large changes, but of unpredictable sign. This suggests that important information cannot be completely evaluated immediately, but that the initial first day's adjustment of prices to the information is unbiased, which is sufficient for the martingale model. More interesting and important, however, is the Niederhoffer-Osborne [32] finding of a tendency toward excessive reversals in common stock price changes from transaction to transaction. They explain this as a logical result of the mechanism whereby orders to buy and sell at market are matched against existing limit orders on the books of the specialist. Given the way this tendency toward excessive reversals arises, however, there seems to be no way it can be used as the basis of a profitable trading rule. As they rightly claim, their results are a strong refutation of the theory of random walks, at least as applied to price changes from transaction to transaction, but they do not constitute refutation of the economically more relevant "fair game" efficient markets model.

Semi-strong form tests, in which prices are assumed to fully reflect all obviously publicly available information, have also supported the efficient markets hypothesis. Thus Fama, Fisher, Jensen, and Roll [14] find that the information in stock splits concerning the firm's future dividend payments is on average fully reflected in the price of a split share at the time of the split. Ball and Brown [4] and Scholes [39] come to similar conclusions with respect to the information contained in (i) annual earning announcements by firms and (ii) new issues and large block secondary issues of common stock. Though only a few different types of information generating events are represented here, they are among the more important, and the results are probably indicative of what can be expected in future studies.

As noted earlier, the strong-form efficient markets model, in which prices are assumed to fully reflect all available information, is probably best viewed as a benchmark against which deviations from market efficiency (interpreted in its strictest sense) can be judged. Two such deviations have in fact been observed. First, Niederhoffer and Osborne [32] point out that specialists on major security exchanges have monopolistic access to information on unexecuted limit orders and they use this information to generate trading profits. This raises the question of whether the "market making" function of the specialist (if indeed this is a meaningful economic function) could not as effectively be carried out by some other mechanism that did not imply monopolistic access to information. Second, Scholes [39] finds that, not unexpectedly, corporate insiders often have monopolistic access to information about their firms.

At the moment, however, corporate insiders and specialists are the only two groups whose monopolistic access to information has been documented. There is no evidence that deviations from the strong form of the efficient markets model permeate down any further through the investment community. For the purposes of most investors the efficient markets model seems a good first (and second) approximation to reality.

In short, the evidence in support of the efficient markets model is extensive, and (somewhat uniquely in economics) contradictory evidence is sparse. Nevertheless, we certainly do not want to leave the impression that all issues are closed. The old saw, "much remains to be done," is relevant here as elsewhere. Indeed, as is often the case in successful scientific research, now that we know we've been in the past, we are able to pose and (hopefully) to answer an even more interesting set of questions for the future. In this case the most pressing field of future endeavor is the development and testing of models of market equilibrium under uncertainty. When the process generating equilibrium expected returns is better understood (and assuming that some expected return model turns out to be relevant), we will have a more substantial framework for more sophisticated intersecurity tests of market efficiency.

REFERENCES

1. Sidney S. Alexander. "Price Movements in Speculative Markets: Trends or Random Walks." *Industrial Management Review,* 2 (May 1961), 7–26. Also reprinted in [8], 199–218.

2.———. "Price Movements in Speculative Markets: Trends or Random Walks. No. 2," in [8], 338–72.

3. Louis Bachelier. *Théorie de la Speculation* (Paris: Gauthier-Villars, 1900), and reprinted in English in [8], 17–78.

4. Ray Ball and Phillip Brown. "An Empirical Evaluation of Accounting Income Numbers." *Journal of Accounting Research,* 6 (Autumn, 1968), 159–78.

5. William Beaver. "The Information Content of Annual Earnings Announcements." *Empirical Research in Accounting: Selected Studies, 1968,* supplement to Vol. 7 of the *Journal of Accounting Research,* 67–92.

6. Robert Blattberg and Thomas Sargent. "Regression with Non-Gaussian Disturbances: Some Sampling Results," forthcoming in Econometrica.

7. Marshall Blume. "The Assessment of Portfolio Performance." Unpublished Ph.D. thesis, University of Chicago, 1968. A paper summarizing much of this work will appear in the April, 1970, Journal of Business.

8. Paul Cootner (ed.). *The Random Character of Stock Market Prices.* Cambridge: M.I.T., 1964.

9.———. "Stock Prices: Random vs. Systematic Changes." *Industrial Management Review,* 3 (Spring 1962), 24–45. Also reprinted in [8], 231–52.

10. Eugene F. Fama. "The Behavior of Stock Market Prices." *Journal of Business,* 38 (January, 1965), 34–105.

11.———. "Multiperiod Consumption-Investment Decisions." *American Economic Review,* (March, 1970).

12.———. "Risk, Return and Equilibrium." Report No. 6831, University of Chicago, Center for Math. Studies in Business and Economics, June, 1968.

13.——— and Marshall Blume. "Filter Rules and Stock Market Trading Profits." *Journal of Business,* 39 (Special Supplement, January, 1966), 226–41.

14.———, Lawrence Fisher, Michael Jensen and Richard Roll. "The Adjustment of Stock Prices to New Information." *International Economic Review,* X (February, 1969), 1–21.

15.——— and Richard Roll. "Some Properties of Symmetric Stable Distributions." *Journal of the American Statistical Association,* 63 (September, 1968), 817–36.

16. Michael D. Godfrey, C. W. J. Granger and O. Morgenstern. "The Random Walk Hypothesis of Stock Market Behavior." *Kyklos,* 17 (1964), 1–30.

17. C. W. J. Granger and O. Morgenstern. "Spectral Analysis of New York Stock Market Prices," *Kyklos,* 16 (1963), 1–27. Also reprinted in [8], 162–88.

18. John R. Hicks. *Value and Capital.* Oxford: The Clarendon Press, 1946.

19. Michael Jensen. "The Performance of Mutual Funds in the Period 1945–64," *Journal of Finance,* 23 (May, 1968), 389–416.

20.———. "Risk, the Pricing of Capital Assets, and the Evaluation of Investment Portfolios," *Journal of Business,* 42 (April, 1969), 167–247.

21. Maurice G. Kendall. "The Analysis of Economic Time-Series, Part I: Prices," *Journal of the Royal Statistical Society,* 96 (Part I, 1953), 11–25.

22. Ruben A. Kessel. "The Cyclical Behavior of the Term Structure of Interest Rates," National Bureau of Economic Research Occasional Paper No. 91. New York: Columbia University Press, 1965.

23. Benjamin F. King. "Market and Industry Factors in Stock Price Behavior," *Journal of Business,* 39 (Special Supplement January, 1966), 139–90.

24. John Lintner. "Security Prices, Risk, and Maximal Gains from Diversification," *Journal of Finance,* 20 (December, 1965), 587–615.

25.———. "The Valuation of Risk Assets and the Selection of Risky Investments in Stock Portfolios and Capital Budgets," *Review of Economics and Statistics,* 47 (February, 1965), 13–37.

26. Fredrich A. Lutz. "The Structure of Interest Rates," *Quarterly Journal of Economics,* 40 (1940–41).

27. Benoit Mandelbrot. "Forecasts of Future Prices, Unbiased Markets, and Martingale Models," *Journal of Business,* 39 (Special Supplement, January, 1966), 242–55.

28.———. "The Variation of Certain Speculative Prices." *Journal of Business,* 36 (October, 1963), 394–419.

29.——— and Howard M. Taylor. "On the Distribution of Stock Price Differences." *Operations Research,* 15 (November-December, 1967), 1057–62.

30. Harry Markowitz. *Portfolio Selection: Efficient Diversification of Investment.* New York: John Wiley & Sons, 1959.

31. Arnold Moore. "A Statistical Analysis of Common Stock Prices. Unpublished Ph.D. thesis, Graduate School of Business, University of Chicago, 1962.

32. Victor Niederhoffer and M. F. M. Osborne. "Market Making and Reversal on the Stock Exchange." *Journal of the American Statistical Association,* 61 (December, 1966), 897–916.

33. M. F. M. Osborne. "Brownian Motion in the Stock Market," *Operations Research,* 7 (March-April, 1959), 145–73. Also reprinted in [8], 100–28.

34.———. "Periodic Structure in the Brownian Motion of Stock Prices." *Operations Research,* 10 (May-June, 1962), 345–79. Also reprinted in [8], 262–96.

35. S. James Press. "A compound Events Model for Security Prices." *Journal of Business,* 40 (July, 1968), 317–35.

36. Harry V. Roberts. "Stock Market 'Patterns' and Financial Analysis: Methodological Suggestions." *Journal of Finance,* 14 (March, 1959), 1–10.

37. Richard Roll. "The Efficient Market Model Applied to U.S. Treasury Bill Rates." Unpublished Ph.D. thesis, Graduate School of Business, University of Chicago, 1968.

38. Paul A. Samuelson. "Proof That Properly Anticipated Prices Fluctuate Randomly." *Industrial Management Review,* 6 (Spring, 1965), 41–9.

39. Myron Scholes. "A Test of the Competitive Hypothesis: The Market for New Issues and Secondary Offerings." Unpublished PH.D. thesis, Graduate School of Business, University of Chicago, 1969.

40. William F. Sharpe. "Capital Asset Prices: A Theory of Market Equilibrium under Conditions of Risk." *Journal of Finance,* 19 (September, 1964), 425–42.

41.————. "Mutual Fund Performance." *Journal of Business,* 39 (Special Supplement, January, 1966), 119–38.

42.————. "Risk Aversion in the Stock Market." *Journal of Finance,* 20 (September, 1965), 416–22.

43. James Tobin. "Liquidity Preference as Behavior Towards Risk," *Review of Economic Studies,* 25 (February, 1958), 65–85.

44. Jack L. Treynor. "How to Rate Management of Investment Funds." *Harvard Business Review,* 43 (January-February, 1965), 63–75.

45. Roger N. Waud. "Public Interpretation of Discount Rate Changes: Evidence on the 'Announcement Effect.'" forthcoming in *Econometrica.*

46. John Wise. "Linear Estimators for Linear Regression Systems Having Infinite Variances." Unpublished paper presented at the Berkeley-Stanford Mathematical Economics Seminar, October, 1963.

47. Holbrook Working. "A Random Difference Series for Use in the Analysis of Time Series." *Journal of the American Statistical Association,* 29 (March, 1934), 11–24.

EFFICIENT CAPITAL MARKETS

II

· · ·

Eugene F. Fama

Sequels are rarely as good as the originals, so I approach this review of the market efficiency literature with trepidation. The task is thornier than it was 20 years ago, when work on efficiency was rather new. The literature is now so large that a full review is impossible, and is not attempted here. Instead, I discuss the work that I find most interesting, and I offer my views on what we have learned from the research on market efficiency.

I. THE THEME

I take the market efficiency hypothesis to be the simple statement that security prices fully reflect all available information. A precondition for this strong version of the hypothesis is that information and trading costs, the costs of getting prices to reflect information, are always 0 (Grossman and Stiglitz (1980)). A weaker and economically more sensible version of the efficiency hypothesis says that prices reflect information to the point where the marginal benefits of acting on information (the profits to be made) do not exceed the marginal costs (Jensen (1978)).

Since there are surely positive information and trading costs, the extreme version of the market efficiency hypothesis is surely false. Its advantage, how-

Reprinted with permission from the *Journal of Finance* 46, no. 5 (December 1991): 1575–1617. © 2012 by John Wiley and Sons.

The comments of Fischer Black, David Booth, Michael Bradley, Michael Brennan, Stephen Buser, John Campbell, Nai-fu Chen, John Cochrane, George Constantinides, Wayne Ferson, Kenneth French, Campbell Harvey, Richard Ippolito, Michael Jensen, Gautam Kaul, Josef Lakonishok, Bill McDonald, Robert Merton, Mark Mitchell, Sam Peltzman, Marc Reinganum, Jay Ritter, Harry Roberts, Richard Roll, G. William Schwert, H. Nejat Seyhun, Jay Shanken, Robert Shiller, Andrei Shleifer, Rex Sinquefield, René Stulz, Richard Thaler, Robert Vishny, and Jerold Warner are gratefully acknowledged. This research is supported by the National Science Foundation.

ever, is that it is a clean benchmark that allows me to sidestep the messy problem of deciding what are reasonable information and trading costs. I can focus instead on the more interesting task of laying out the evidence on the adjustment of prices to various kinds of information. Each reader is then free to judge the scenarios where market efficiency is a good approximation (that is, deviations from the extreme version of the efficiency hypothesis are within information and trading costs) and those where some other model is a better simplifying view of the world.

Ambiguity about information and trading costs is not, however, the main obstacle to inferences about market efficiency. The joint-hypothesis problem is more serious. Thus, market efficiency per se is not testable. It must be tested jointly with some model of equilibrium, an asset-pricing model. This point, the theme of the 1970 review (Fama (1970b)), says that we can only test whether information is properly reflected in prices in the context of a pricing model that defines the meaning of "properly." As a result, when we find anomalous evidence on the behavior of returns, the way it should be split between market inefficiency or a bad model of market equilibrium is ambiguous.

Does the fact that market efficiency must be tested jointly with an equilibrium-pricing model make empirical research on efficiency uninteresting? Does the joint-hypothesis problem make empirical work on asset-pricing models uninteresting? These are, after all, symmetric questions, with the same answer. My answer is an unequivocal no. The empirical literature on efficiency and asset-pricing models passes the acid test of scientific usefulness. It has changed our views about the behavior of returns, across securities and through time. Indeed, academics largely agree on the facts that emerge from the tests, even when they disagree about their implications for efficiency. The empirical work on market efficiency and asset-pricing models has also changed the views and practices of market professionals.

As these summary judgements imply, my view, and the theme of this paper, is that the market efficiency literature should be judged on how it improves our ability to describe the time-series and cross-section behavior of security returns. It is a disappointing fact that, because of the joint-hypothesis problem, precise inferences about the degree of market efficiency are likely to remain impossible. Nevertheless, judged on how it has improved our understanding of the behavior of security returns, the past research on market efficiency is among the most successful in empirical economics, with good prospects to remain so in the future.

II. THE MAIN AREAS OF RESEARCH

The 1970 review divides work on market efficiency into three categories: (1) weak-form tests (How well do past returns predict future returns?), (2) semi-strong-form tests (How quickly do security prices reflect public information announcements?), and (3) strong-form tests (Do any investors have private information that is not fully reflected in market prices?) At the risk of damning a good thing, I change the categories in this paper.

Instead of weak-form tests, which are only concerned with the forecast power of past returns, the first category now covers the more general area of *tests for return predictability,* which also includes the burgeoning work on forecasting returns with variables like dividend yields and interest rates. Since market efficiency and equilibrium-pricing issues are inseparable, the discussion of predictability also considers the cross-sectional predictability of returns, that is, tests of asset-pricing models and the anomalies (like the size effect) discovered in the tests. Finally, the evidence that there are seasonals in returns (like the January effect), and the claim that security prices are too volatile are also considered, but only briefly, under the rubric of return predictability.

For the second and third categories, I propose changes in title, not coverage. Instead of semi-strong-form tests of the adjustment of prices to public announcements, I use the now common title, *event studies.* Instead of strong-form tests of whether specific investors have information not in market prices, I suggest the more descriptive title, *tests for private information.*

Return predictability is considered first, and in the most detail. The detail reflects my interest and the fact that the implications of the evidence on the predictability of returns through time are the most controversial. In brief, the new work says that returns are predictable from past returns, dividend yields, and various term-structure variables. The new tests thus reject the old market efficiency-constant expected returns model that seemed to do well in the early work. This means, however, that the new results run head-on into the joint-hypothesis problem: Does return predictability reflect rational variation through time in expected returns, irrational deviations of price from fundamental value, or some combination of the two? We should also acknowledge that the apparent predictability of returns may be spurious, the result of data-dredging and chance sample-specific conditions.

The evidence discussed below, that the variation through time in expected returns is common to corporate bonds and stocks and is related in plausible ways to business conditions, leans me toward the conclusion that it is real and rational. Rationality is not established by the existing tests, however, and the joint-hypothesis problem likely means that it cannot be established. Still, even if we disagree on the market efficiency implications of the new results on return predictability, I think we can agree that the tests enrich our knowledge of the behavior of returns, across securities and through time.

Event studies are discussed next, but briefly. Detailed reviews of event studies are already available, and the implications of this research for market efficiency are less controversial. Event studies have, however, been a growth industry during the last 20 years. Moreover, I argue that, because they come closest to allowing a break between market efficiency and equilibrium-pricing issues, event studies give the most direct evidence on efficiency. And the evidence is mostly supportive.

Finally, tests for private information are reviewed. The new results clarify earlier evidence that corporate insiders have private information that is not fully reflected in prices. The new evidence on whether professional investment managers (mutual fund and pension fund) have private information is, however, murky, clouded by the joint-hypothesis problem.

III. RETURN PREDICTABILITY: TIME-VARYING EXPECTED RETURNS

There is a resurgence of research on the time-series predictability of stock returns, that is, the variation (rational or irrational) of expected returns through time. Unlike the pre-1970 work, which focused on forecasting returns from past returns, recent tests also consider the forecast power of variables like dividend yields (D/P), earnings/price ratios (E/P), and term-structure variables. Moreover, the early work concentrated on the predictability of daily, weekly, and monthly returns, but the recent tests also examine the predictability of returns for longer horizons.

Among the more striking new results are estimates that the predictable component of returns is a small part of the variance of daily, weekly, and monthly returns, but it grows to as much as 40% of the variance of 2- to 10-year returns. These results have spurred a continuing debate on whether the predictability of long-horizon returns is the result of irrational bubbles in prices or large rational swings in expected returns.

I first consider the research on predicting returns from past returns. Next comes the evidence that other variables (D/P, E/P, and term-structure variables) forecast returns. The final step is to discuss the implications of this work for market efficiency.

[125]

A. Past Returns
A. 1. Short-Horizon Returns

In the pre-1970 literature, the common equilibrium-pricing model in tests of stock market efficiency is the hypothesis that expected returns are constant through time. Market efficiency then implies that returns are unpredictable from past returns or other past variables, and the best forecast of a return is its historical mean.

The early tests often find suggestive evidence that daily, weekly, and monthly returns are predictable from past returns. For example, Fama (1965) finds that the first-order autocorrelations of daily returns are positive for 23 of the 30 Dow Jones Industrials and more than 2 standard errors from 0 for 11 of the 30. Fisher's (1966) results suggest that the autocorrelations of monthly returns on diversified portfolios are positive and larger than those for individual stocks. The evidence for predictability in the early work often lacks statistical power, however, and the portion of the variance of returns explained by variation in expected returns is so small (less than 1% for individual stocks) that the hypothesis of market efficiency and constant expected returns is typically accepted as a good working model.

In recent work, daily data on NYSE and AMEX stocks back to 1962 [from the Center for Research in Security Prices (CRSP)] makes it possible to estimate precisely the autocorrelation in daily and weekly returns. For example, Lo and MacKinlay (1988) find that weekly returns on portfolios of NYSE stocks grouped according to size (stock price times shares outstanding) show reliable positive autocorrelation. The autocorrelation is stronger for portfolios of small stocks. This suggests, however, that the results are due in part to the nonsynchronous trading effect (Fisher 1966). Fisher emphasizes that spurious positive autocorrelation in portfolio returns, induced by non-synchronous closing trades for securities in the portfolio, is likely to be more important for portfolios tilted toward small stocks.

To mitigate the nonsychronous trading problem, Conrad and Kaul (1988) examine the autocorrelation of Wednesday-to-Wednesday returns for size-grouped portfolios of stocks that trade on both Wednesdays. Like Lo and MacKinlay (1988), they find that weekly returns are positively autocorrelated, and more so for portfolios of small stocks. The first-order autocorrelation of weekly returns on the portfolio of the largest decile of NYSE stocks for 1962–1985 is only .09. For the portfolios that include the smallest 40% of NYSE stocks, however, first-order autocorrelations of weekly returns are around .3, and the autocorrelations of weekly returns are reliably positive out to 4 lags.

The results of Lo and MacKinlay (1988) and Conrad and Kaul (1988) show that, because of the variance reduction obtained from diversification, portfolios produce stronger indications of time variation in weekly expected returns than individual stocks. Their results also suggest that returns are more predictable for small-stock portfolios. The evidence is, however, clouded by the fact that the predictability of portfolio returns is in part due to nonsynchronous trading effects that, especially for small stocks, are not completely mitigated by using stocks that trade on successive Wednesdays.

An eye-opener among recent studies of short-horizon returns is French and Roll (1986). They establish an intriguing fact. Stock prices are more variable when the market is open. On an hourly basis, the variance of price changes is 72 times higher during trading hours than during weekend nontrading hours. Likewise, the hourly variance during trading hours is 13 times the overnight nontrading hourly variance during the trading week.

One of the explanations that French and Roll test is a market inefficiency hypothesis popular among academics; specifically, the higher variance of price changes during trading hours is partly transitory, the result of noise trading by uniformed investors (e.g., Black (1986)). Under this hypothesis, pricing errors due to noise trading are eventually reversed, and this induces negative autocorrelation in daily returns. French and Roll find that the first-order autocorrelations of daily returns on the individual stocks of larger (the top three quintiles of) NYSE firms are positive. Otherwise, the autocorrelations of daily returns on individual stocks are indeed negative, to 13 lags. Although reliably negative on a statistical basis, however, the autocorrelations are on average close to 0. Few are below $-.01$.

One possibility is that the transitory price variation induced by noise trading only dissipates over longer horizons. To test this hypothesis, French and Roll examine the ratios of variances of N-period returns on individual stocks to the variance of daily returns, for N from 2 days to 6 months. If there is no transitory price variation induced by noise trading (specifically, if price changes are i.i.d.), the N-period variance should grow like N, and the variance ratios (standardized by N) should be close to 1. On the other hand, with transitory price variation, the N-period variance should grow less than in proportion to N, and the variance ratios should be less than 1.

For horizons (N) beyond a week, the variance ratios are more than 2 standard errors below 1, except for the largest quintile of NYSE stocks. But the fractions of daily return variances due to transitory price variation are apparently small. French and Roll estimate that for the average NYSE stock, the upper bound on the transitory portion of the daily variance is 11.7%. Adjusted for the spurious negative autocorrelation of daily returns due to bid-ask effects (Roll (1984)), the estimate of the transitory portion drops to 4.1%. The smallest quintile of NYSE stocks produces the largest estimate of the transitory portion of price variation, an upper bound of 26.9%. After correction for bid-ask effects, however, the estimate drops to 4.7%—hardly a number on which to conclude that noise trading results in substantial market inefficiency. French and Roll (1986, p. 23) conclude, "pricing errors . . . have a trivial effect on the difference between trading and non-trading variances. We conclude that this difference is caused by differences in the flow of information during trading and non-trading hours."

In short, with the CRSP daily data back to 1962, recent research is able to show confidently that daily and weekly returns are predictable from past returns. The work thus rejects the old market efficiency-constant expected returns model on a statistical basis. The new results, however, tend to confirm the conclusion of the early work that, at least for individual stocks, variation in daily and weekly expected returns is a small part of the variance of returns. The more striking, but less powerful, recent evidence on the predictability of returns from past returns comes from long-horizon returns.

A. 2. Long-Horizon Returns

The early literature does not interpret the autocorrelation in daily and weekly returns as important evidence against the joint hypothesis of market efficiency and constant expected returns. The argument is that, even when the autocorrelations deviate reliably from 0 (as they do in the recent tests), they are close to 0 and thus economically insignificant.

The view that autocorrelations of short-horizon returns close to 0 imply economic insignificance is challenged by Shiller (1984) and Summers (1986). They present simple models in which stock prices take large slowly decaying swings away from fundamental values (fads, or irrational bubbles), but short-horizon returns have little autocorrelation. In the Shiller-Summers model, the market is highly inefficient, but in a way that is missed in tests on short-horizon returns.

To illustrate the point, suppose the fundamental value of a stock is constant and the unconditional mean of the stock price is its fundamental value. Suppose daily prices are a first-order autoregression (AR1) with slope less than but close to 1. All variation in the price then results from long mean-reverting swings away from the constant fundamental value. Over short horizons, however, an AR1 slope close to 1 means that the price looks like a random walk and returns have little autocorrelation. Thus in tests on short-horizon returns, all price changes seem to be permanent when fundamental value is in fact constant and all deviations of price from fundamental value are temporary.

In his comment on Summers (1986), Stambaugh (1986) points out that although the Shiller-Summers model can explain autocorrelations of short-horizon returns that are close to 0, the long swings away from fundamental value proposed in the model imply that long-horizon returns have strong negative autocorrelation. (In the example above, where the price is a stationary AR1, the autocorrelations of long-horizon returns approach −0.5.) Intuitively, since the swings away from fundamental value are temporary, over long horizons they tend to be reversed. Another implication of the negative autocorrelation induced by temporary price movements is that the variance of returns should grow less than in proportion to the return horizon.

The Shiller-Summers challenge spawned a series of papers on the predictability of long-horizon returns from past returns. The evidence at first seemed striking, but the tests turn out to be largely fruitless. Thus, Fama and French (1988a) find that the autocorrelations of returns on diversified portfolios of NYSE stocks for the 1926–1985 period have the pattern predicted by the Shiller-Summers model. The autocorrelations are close to 0 at short horizons, but they become strongly negative, around −0.25 to −0.4, for 3- to 5-year returns. Even with 60 years of data, however, the tests on long-horizon returns imply small sample sizes and low power. More telling, when Fama and French delete the 1926–1940 period from the tests, the evidence of strong negative autocorrelation in 3- to 5-year returns disappears.

Similarly, Poterba and Summers (1988) find that, for N from 2 to 8 years, the variance of N-year returns on diversified portfolios grows much less than in proportion to N. This is consistent with the hypothesis that there is negative autocorrelation in returns induced by temporary price swings. Even with 115 years (1871–1985) of data, however, the variance tests for long-horizon returns provide weak statistical evidence against the hypothesis that returns have no autocorrelation and prices are random walks.

Finally, Fama and French (1988a) emphasize that temporary swings in stock prices do not necessarily imply the irrational bubbles of the Shiller-Summers model. Suppose (1) rational pricing implies an expected return that is highly autocorrelated but mean-reverting, and (2) shocks to expected returns are uncorrelated with shocks to expected dividends. In this situation, expected-return shocks have no permanent effect on expected dividends, discount rates, or prices. A positive shock to expected returns generates a price decline (a discount rate effect) that is eventually erased by the temporarily higher expected returns. In short, a ubiquitous problem in time-series tests of market efficiency, with no clear solution, is that irrational bubbles in stock prices are indistinguishable from rational time-varying expected returns.

A. 3. The Contrarians

DeBondt and Thaler (1985, 1987) mount an aggressive empirical attack on market efficiency, directed at unmasking irrational bubbles. They find that the NYSE stocks identified as the most extreme losers over a 3- to 5-year period tend to have strong returns relative to the market during the following years, expecially in January of the following years. Conversely, the stocks identified as extreme winners tend to have weak returns relative to the market in subsequent years. They attribute these results to market overreaction to extreme bad or good news about firms.

Chan (1988) and Ball and Kothari (1989) argue that the winner-loser results are due to failure to risk-adjust returns. (DeBondt and Thaler (1987) disagree.) Zarowin (1989) finds no evidence for the DeBondt-Thaler hypothesis that the winner-loser results are due to overreaction to extreme changes in earnings. He argues that the winner-loser effect is related to the size effect of Banz (1981); that is, small stocks, often losers, have higher expected returns than large stocks. Another explanation, consistent with an efficient market, is that there is a risk factor associated with the relative economic performance of firms (a distressed-firm effect) that is compensated in a rational equilibrium-pricing model (Chan and Chen (1991)).

We may never be able to say which explanation of the return behavior of extreme winners and losers is correct, but the results of DeBondt and Thaler and their critics are nevertheless interesting. (See also Jagedeesh (1990), Lehmann (1990), and Lo and MacKinlay (1990), who find reversal behavior in the weekly and monthly returns of extreme winners and losers. Lehmann's weekly reversals seem to lack economic significance. When he accounts for spurious reversals due to bouncing between bid and ask prices, trading costs of 0.2% per turnaround transaction suffice to make the profits from his reversal trading rules close to 0. It is also worth noting that the short-term reversal evidence of Jegadeesh, Lehmann, and Lo and MacKinlay may to some extent be due to CRSP data errors, which would tend to show up as price reversals.)

B. *Other Forecasting Variables*

The univariate tests on long-horizon returns of Fama and French (1988a) and Poterba and Summers (1988) are a statistical power failure. Still, they provide suggestive material to spur the search for more powerful tests of the hypothesis that slowly decaying irrational bubbles, or rational time-varying expected returns, are important in the long-term variation of prices.

There is a simple way to see the power problem. An autocorrelation is the slope in a regression of the current return on a past return. Since variation through time in expected returns is only part of the variation in returns, tests based on autocorrelations lack power because past realized returns are noisy measures of expected returns. Power in tests for return predictability can be enhanced if one can identify forecasting variables that are less noisy proxies for expected returns that past returns.

B. 1. The Evidence

There is no lack of old evidence that short-horizon returns are predictable from other variables. A puzzle of the 1970's was to explain why monthly stock returns are negatively related to expected inflation (Bodie (1976), Nelson (1976), Jaffe and Mandelker (1976), Fama (1981)) and the level of short-term interest rates (Fama and Schwert (1977)). Like the autocorrelation tests, however, the early work on forecasts of short-horizon returns from expected inflation and interest rates suggests that the implied variation in expected returns is a small part of the variance of returns—less than 3% for monthly returns. The recent tests suggest, however, that for long-horizon returns, predictable variation is a larger part of return variances.

Thus, following evidence (Rozeff (1984), Shiller (1984)) that dividend yields (D/P) forecast short-horizon stock returns, Fama and French (1988b) use D/P to forecast returns on the value-weighted and equally weighted portfolios of NYSE stocks for horizons from 1 month to 5 years. As in earlier work, D/P explains small fractions of monthly and quarterly return variances. Fractions of variance explained grow with the return horizon, however, and are around 25% for 2- to 4-year returns. Campbell and Shiller (1988b) find that E/P ratios, especially when past earnings (E) are averaged over 10–30 years, have reliable forecast power that also increases with the return horizon. Unlike the long-horizon autocorrelations in Fama and French (1988a), the long-horizon forecast power of D/P and E/P is reliable for periods after 1940.

Fama and French (1988b) argue that dividend yields track highly autocorrelated variation in expected stock returns that becomes a larger fraction of return variation for longer return horizons. The increasing fraction of the variance of long-horizon returns explained by D/P is thus due in large part to the slow mean reversion of expected returns. Examining the forecast power of variables like D/P and E/P over a range of return horizons nevertheless gives striking perspective on the implications of slow-moving expected returns for the variation of returns.

B. 2. Market Efficiency

The predictability of stock returns from dividend yields (or E/P) is not in itself evidence for or against market efficiency. In an efficient market, the forecast power of D/P says that prices are high relative to dividends when discount rates and expected returns are low, and vice versa. On the other hand, in a world of irrational bubbles, low D/P signals irrationally high stock prices that will move predictably back toward fundamental values. To judge whether the forecast power of dividend yields is the result of rational variation in expected returns or irrational bubbles, other information must be used. As always, even with such information, the issue is ambiguous.

For example, Fama and French (1988b) show that low dividend yields imply low expected returns, but their regressions rarely forecast negative returns for the value- and equally weighted portfolios of NYSE stocks. In their data, return forecasts more than 2 standard errors below 0 are never observed, and more than 50% of the forecasts are more than 2 standard errors above 0. Thus there is no evidence that low D/P signals bursting bubbles, that is, negative expected stock returns. A bubbles fan can argue, however, that because the unconditional means of stock returns are high, a bursting bubble may well imply low but not negative expected returns. Conversely, if there were evidence of negative expected returns, an efficient-markets type could argue that asset-pricing models do not say that rational expected returns are always positive.

Fama and French (1989) suggest a different way to judge the implications of return predictability for market efficiency. They argue that if variation in expected returns is common to different securities, then it is probably a rational result of variation in tastes for current versus future consumption or in the investment opportunities of firms. They show that the dividend yield on the NYSE value-weighted portfolio indeed forecasts the returns on corporate bonds as well as common stocks. Moreover, two term-structure variables, (1) the default spread (the difference between the yields on lower-grade and Aaa long-term corporate bonds) and (2) the term spread (the difference between the long-term Aaa yield and the yield on 1-month Treasury bills), forecast returns on the value- and equally weighted portfolios of NYSE stocks as well as on portfolios of bonds in different (Moodys) rating groups.

Keim and Stambaugh (1986) and Campbell (1987) also find that stock and bond returns are predictable from a common set of stock market and term-structure variables. Harvey (1991) finds that the dividend yield on the S&P 500 portfolio and U.S. term-structure variables forecast the returns on portfolios of foreign common stocks, as well as the S&P return. Thus the variation in expected returns tracked by the U.S. dividend yield and term-structure variables is apparently international.

Ferson and Harvey (1991) formally test the common expected returns hypothesis. Using the asset-pricing models of Merton (1973) and Ross (1976), they try to link the time-series variation in expected returns, captured by dividend yields and term-structure variables, to the common factors in returns that determine the cross-section of expected returns. They estimate that the common variation in expected returns is about 80% of the predictable time-series variation in the returns on Government bonds, corporate bonds, and common-stock portfolios formed on industry and size. They can't reject the hypothesis that all the time-series variation in expected returns is common.

Fama and French (1989) push the common expected returns argument for market efficiency one step further. They argue that there are systematic patterns in the variation of expected returns through time that suggest that it is rational. They find that the variation in expected returns tracked by D/P and the default spread (the slopes in the regressions of returns on D/P or the default spread) increase from high-grade bonds to low-grade bonds, from bonds to stocks, and from large stocks to small stocks. This ordering corresponds to intuition about the risks of the securities. On the other hand, the variation in expected returns tracked by the term spread is similar for all long-term securities (bonds and stocks), which suggests that it reflects variation in a common premium for maturity risks.

Finally, Fama and French (1989) argue that the variation in the expected returns on bonds and stocks captured by their forecasting variables is consistent with modern intertemporal asset-pricing models (e.g., Lucas (1978), Breeden (1979)), as well as with the original consumption-smoothing stories of Friedman (1957) and Modigliani and Brumberg (1955). The general message of the Fama-French tests (confirmed in detail by Chen (1991)) is that D/P and the default spread are high (expected returns on stocks and bonds are high) when times have been poor (growth rates of output have been persistently low). On the other hand, the term spread and expected returns are high when economic conditions are weak but anticipated to improve (future growth rates of output are high). Persistent poor times may signal low wealth and higher risks in security returns, both of which can increase expected returns. In addition, if poor times (and low incomes) are anticipated to be partly temporary, expected returns can be high because consumers attempt to smooth consumption from the future to the present.

For the diehard bubbles fan, these arguments that return predictability is rational are not convincing. Common variation in expected returns may just mean that irrational bubbles are correlated across assets and markets (domestic and international). The correlation between the common variation in expected returns and business conditions may just mean that the common bubbles in different markets are related to business conditions. On the other hand, if there were evidence of security-specific variation in expected returns, an efficient-markets type could argue that it is consistent with uncorrelated variation through time in the risks of individual securities. All of which shows that deciding whether return predictability is the result of rational variation in expected returns or irrational bubbles is never clearcut.

My view is that we should deepen the search for links between time-varying expected returns and business conditions, as well as for tests of whether the links conform to common sense and the predictions of asset-pricing models. Ideally, we would like to know how variation in expected returns relates to productivity shocks that affect the demand for capital goods, and to shocks to tastes for current versus future consumption that affect the supply of savings. At a minimum, we can surely expand the work in Chen (1991) on the relations between the financial market variables that track expected returns (D/P and the term-structure variables) and the behavior of output, investment, and saving. We can also extend the preliminary attempts of Balvers, Cosimano and McDonald (1990), Cechetti, Lam, and Mark (1990) and Kandel and Stambaugh (1990) to explain the variation through time in expected returns in the confines of standard asset-pricing models.

B. 3. A Caveat

The fact that variation in expected returns is common across securities and markets, and is related in plausible ways to business conditions, leans me toward the conclusion that, if it is real it is rational. But how much of it is real? The standard errors of the slopes for the forecasting variables in the return regressions are typically large and so leave much uncertainty about forecast power (Hodrick (1990), Nelson and Kim (1990)). Inference is also clouded by an industry-level data-dredging problem. With many clever researchers, on both sides of the efficiency fence, rummaging for forecasting variables, we are sure to find instances of "reliable" return predictability that are in fact spurious.

Moreover, the evidence that measured variation in expected returns is common across securities, and related to business conditions, does not necessarily mean that it is real. Suppose there is common randomness in stock and bond returns due to randomness in business conditions. Then measured variation in expected returns that is the spurious result of sample-specific conditions is likely to be common across securities and related to business conditions. In short, variation in expected returns with business conditions is plausible and consistent with asset-pricing theory. But evidence of predictability should always be met with a healthy dose of skepticism, and a diligent search for out-of-sample confirmation.

C. Volatility Tests and Seasonals in Returns
C. 1. Volatility Tests

Volatility tests of market efficiency, pioneered by LeRoy and Porter (1981) and Shiller (1979, 1981), have mushroomed into a large literature. Excellent reviews (West (1988), LeRoy (1989), Cochrane (1991)) are available, so here I briefly comment on why I concur with Merton (1987), Kleidon (1988), and Cochrane (1991) that the tests are not informative about market efficiency.

A central assumption in the early volatility tests is that expected returns are constant and the variation in stock prices is driven entirely by shocks to expected dividends. By the end of the 1970's, however, evidence that expected stock and bond returns vary with expected inflation rates, interest rates, and other term-structure variables was becoming commonplace (Bodie (1976), Jaffe and Mandelker (1976), Nelson (1976), Fama (1976a, b), Fama and Schwert (1977)). With all the more recent evidence on return predictability, it now seems clear that volatility tests are another useful way to show that expected returns vary through time.

The volatility tests, however, give no help on the central issue of whether the variation in expected returns is rational. For example, is it related in sensible ways to business conditions? Grossman and Shiller (1981) and Campbell and Shiller (1988a) attempt to move the volatility tests in this direction. Predictably, however, they run head-on into the joint hypothesis problem. They test market efficiency jointly with the hypothesis that their versions of the consumption-based asset-pricing model capture all rational variation in expected returns.

C. 2. Return Seasonality

The recent literature includes a spate of "anomalies" papers that document "seasonals" in stock returns. Monday returns are on average lower than returns on other days (Cross (1973), French (1980), Gibbons and Hess (1981)). Returns are on average higher the day before a holiday (Ariel 1990), and the last day of the month (Ariel (1987)). There also seems to be a seasonal in intraday returns, with most of the average daily return coming at the beginning and end of the day (Harris (1986)). The most mystifying seasonal is the January effect. Stock returns, especially returns on small stocks, are on average higher in January than in other months. Moreover, much of the higher January return on small stocks comes on the last trading day in December and the first 5 trading days in January (Keim (1983), Roll (1983)).

Keim (1988) reviews this literature. He argues that seasonals in returns are anomalies in the sense that asset-pricing models do not predict them, but they are not necessarily embarassments for market efficiency. For example, Monday, holiday, and end-of-month returns deviate from normal average daily returns by less than the bid-ask spread of the average stock (Lakonishok and Smidt (1988)). Turn-of-the-year abnormal returns for small stocks are larger, but they are not large relative to the bid-ask spreads of small stocks (Roll (1983)). There is thus some hope that these seasonals can be explained in terms of market microstructure, that is, seasonals in investor trading patterns that imply innocuous seasonals in the probabilities that measured prices are at ask or bid. The evidence in Lakonishok and Maberly (1990) on Monday trading patterns, and in Reinganum (1983), Ritter (1988), and Keim (1989) on turn-of-the-year trading are steps in that direction.

We should also keep in mind that the CRSP data, the common source of evidence on stock returns, are mined on a regular basis by many researchers. Spurious regularities are a sure consequence. Apparent anomalies in returns thus warrant out-of-sample tests before being accepted as regularities that are likely to be present in future returns. Lakonishok and Smidt (1988) find that the January, Monday, holiday, and end-of-month seasonals stand up to replication on data preceding the periods used in the original tests. The intramonth seasonal (most of the average return of any month comes in the first half) of Ariel (1987), however, seems to be specific to his sample period. Connolly (1989) finds that the Monday seasonal in NYSE returns is weaker after 1974.

Recent data on the premier seasonal, the January effect, tell an interesting story. Table I shows that for the 1941–1981 period, the average monthly January return on a value-weighted portfolio of the smallest quintile of CRSP stocks is 8.06% (!), versus 1.34% for the S&P 500. During the 1941–1981 period, there is only 1 year (1952) when the S&P January return is above the CRSP bottom-quintile return. Moreover, for 1941–1981, all of the advantage of the CRSP small-stock portfolio over the S&P comes in January; the February-to-December average monthly returns on the two portfolios differ by only 4 basis points (0.88% for CRSP Small versus 0.92% for the S&P).

For 1982–1991, however, the average January return on the CRSP small-stock portfolio, 5.32%, is closer to the January S&P return, 3.20%. More striking, the average January return on the DFA U.S. Small Company Portfolio, a passive mutual fund meant to roughly mimic the CRSP bottom quintile, is

TABLE I. Comparison of returns on the S&P 500, the smallest quintile of CRSP stocks, and the DFA U.S. Small Company Portfolio: 1941–81 and 1982–91

The value-weighted CRSP small-stock portfolio (CRSP Small) contains the bottom quintile of NYSE stocks, and the AMEX and NASDAQ stocks that fall below the size (price times shares) breakpoint for the bottom quintile of NYSE stocks. The portfolio is formed at the end of each quarter and held for one quarter. Prior to June 1962, CRSP Small contains only the bottom quintile of NYSE stocks. AMEX stocks are added in July 1962 and NASDAQ stocks in January 1973. The DFA U.S. Small Company Portfolio (DFA Small) is a passive mutual fund meant to roughly mimic CRSP Small. DFA Small returns are only available for the 1982–1991 period.

Average Monthly Returns for January, February to December, and All Months

Portfolio	1941–1981			1982–1990 (91 for January)		
	Jan	Feb–Dec	All	Jan	Feb–Dec	All
S&P 500	1.34	0.92	0.96	3.20	1.23	1.39
CRSP Small	8.06	0.88	1.48	5.32	0.17	0.60
DFA Small				3.58	0.66	0.90

Year-by-Year Comparison of January Returns for 1982–1991

Year	S&P	CRSP Small	DFA Small	CRSP-S&P	DFA-S&P
1982	−1.63	−1.53	−1.96	0.10	−0.33
1983	3.48	10.01	6.28	6.53	2.80
1984	−0.65	0.26	−0.08	0.91	0.57
1985	7.68	13.41	10.59	5.73	2.91
1986	0.44	3.82	1.12	3.38	0.68
1987	13.43	10.91	9.43	−2.52	−4.00
1988	4.27	7.58	5.56	3.31	1.29
1989	7.23	4.79	4.04	−2.44	−3.19
1990	−6.71	−6.38	−7.64	0.33	−0.93
1991	4.42	10.28	8.41	5.86	3.99

3.58%, quite close to the January S&P return (3.20%) and much less than the January return for the CRSP small-stock portfolio (5.32%). The CRSP small-stock portfolio has a higher return than the DFA portfolio in every January of 1982–1991. But January is the exception; overall, the DFA portfolio earns about 3% per year more than the CRSP bottom quintile.

Why these differences between the returns on the CRSP small-stock portfolio and a mimicking passive mutual fund? DFA does not try to mimic exactly the CRSP bottom quintile. Concern with trading costs causes DFA to deviate from strict value weights and to avoid the very smallest stocks (that are, however, a small fraction of a value-weighted portfolio). Moreover, DFA does not sell stocks that do well until they hit the top of the third (smallest) decile. This means that their stocks are on average larger than the stocks in the CRSP bottom quintile (a strategy that paid off during the 1982–1991 period of an inverted size effect.)

The important point, however, is that small-stock returns, and the very existence of a January bias in favor of small stocks, are sensitive to small changes (imposed by rational trading) in the way small-stock portfolios are defined. This suggests that, until we know more about the pricing (and economic fundamentals) of small stocks, inferences should be cautious for the many anomalies where small stocks play a large role (e.g., the overreaction evidence of DeBondt and Thaler (1985, 1987) and Lehmann (1990), and (discussed below) the size effect of Banz (1981), the Value Line enigma of Stickel (1985), and the earnings-announcement anomaly of Bernard and Thomas (1989, 1990)).

Finally, given our fascination with anomalies that center on small stocks, it is well to put the relative importance of small stocks in perspective. At the end of 1990, there were 5135 NYSE, AMEX, and NASDAQ (NMS) stocks. Using NYSE stocks to define size breakpoints, the smallest quintile has 2631 stocks, 51.2% of the total. But the bottom quintile is only 1.5% of the combined value of NYSE, AMEX, and NASDAQ stocks. In contrast, the largest quintile has 389 stocks (7.6% of the total), but it is 77.2% of market wealth.

IV. CROSS-SECTIONAL RETURN PREDICTABILITY

At the time of the 1970 review, the asset-pricing model of Sharpe (1964), Lintner (1965), and Black (1972) was just starting to take hold. Ross's (1976) arbitrage-pricing model and the intertemporal asset-pricing models of Merton (1973), Rubinstein (1976), Lucas (1978), Breeden (1979), and Cox, Ingersoll, and Ross (1985) did not exist. In the pre-1970 efficient markets literature, the common "models" of market equilibrium were the informal constant expected returns model (random-walk and martingale tests) and the market model (event studies, like Fama, Fisher, Jensen, and Roll (1969)).

This section considers the post-1970 empirical research on asset-pricing models. This work does not place itself in the realm of tests of market efficiency, but this just means that efficiency is a maintained hypothesis. Depending on the emphasis desired, one can say that efficiency must be tested conditional on an asset-pricing model or that asset-pricing models are tested conditional on efficiency. The point is that such tests are always joint evidence on efficiency and an asset-pricing model.

Moreover, many of the front-line empirical anomalies in finance (like the size effect) come out of tests directed at asset-pricing models. Given the joint hypothesis problem, one can't tell whether such anomalies result from misspecified asset-pricing models or market inefficiency. This ambiguity is sufficient justification to review tests of asset-pricing models here.

We first consider tests of the one-factor Sharpe-Lintner-Black (SLB) model. I argue that the SLB model does the job expected of a good model. In rejecting it, repeatedly, our understanding of asset-pricing is enhanced. Some of the most striking empirical regularities discovered in the last 20 years are "anomalies" from tests of the SLB model. These anomalies are now stylized facts to be explained by other asset-pricing models.

The next step is to review the evidence on the multifactor asset-pricing models of Merton (1973) and Ross (1976). These models are rich and more flexible than their competitors. Based on existing evidence, they show some promise to fill the empirical void left by the rejections of the SLB model.

The final step is to discuss tests of the consumption-based intertemporal asset-pricing model of Rubinstein (1976), Lucas (1978), Breeden (1979), and others. The elegant simplicity of this model gives it strong appeal, and much effort has been devoted to testing it. The effort is bearing fruit. Recent tests add to our understanding of the behavior of asset returns in ways that go beyond tests of other models (e.g., the equity-premium puzzle of Mehra and Prescott (1985)). On the other hand, the tests have not yet taken up the challenges (like the size effect) raised by rejections of the SLB model.

A. The Sharpe-Lintner-Black (SLB) Model
A. 1. Early Success

The early 1970's produce the first extensive tests of the SLB model (Black, Jensen, and Scholes (1972), Blume and Friend (1973), Fama and MacBeth (1973)). These early studies suggest that the special prediction of the Sharpe-Lintner version of the model, that portfolios uncorrelated with the market have expected returns equal to the risk-free rate of interest, does not fare well. (The average returns on such "zero-β" portfolios are higher than the risk-free rate.) Other predictions of the model seem to do better.

The most general implication of the SLB model is that equilibrium pricing implies that the market portfolio of invested wealth is ex ante mean-variance efficient in the sense of Markowitz (1959). Consistent with this hypothesis, the early studies suggest that (1) expected returns are a positive linear function of market β (the covariance of a security's return with the return on the market portfolio divided by the variance of the market return), and (2) β is the only measure of risk needed to explain the cross-section of expected returns. With this early support for the SLB model, there was a brief euphoric period in the 1970's when market efficiency and the SLB model seemed to be a sufficient description of the behavior of security returns.

We should have known better. The SLB model is just a model and so surely false. The first head-on attack is Roll's (1977) criticism that the early tests aren't much evidence for the SLB model because the proxies used for the market portfolio (like the equally weighted NYSE portfolio) do not come close to the portfolio of invested wealth called for by the model. Stambaugh's (1982) evidence that tests of the SLB model are not sensitive to the proxy used for the market suggests that Roll's criticism is too strong, but this issue can never be entirely resolved.

A. 2. Anomalies

The telling empirical attacks on the SLB model begin in the late 1970's with studies that identify variables that contradict the model's prediction that market β's suffice to describe the cross-section of expected returns. Basu (1977, 1983) shows that earnings/price ratios (E/P) have marginal explanatory power; controlling for β, expected returns are positively related to E/P. Banz (1981) shows that a stock's size (price times shares) helps explain expected returns; given their market β's, expected returns on small stocks are too high, and expected returns on large stocks are too low. Bhandari (1988) shows that leverage is positively related to expected stock returns in tests that also include market β's. Finally, Chan, Hamao, and Lakonishok (1991) and Fama and French (1991) find that book-to-market equity (the ratio of the book value of a common stock to its market value) has strong explanatory power; controlling for β, higher book-to-market ratios are associated with higher expected returns.

[140]

One argument says that the anomalies arise because estimates of market β's are noisy, and the anomalies variables are correlated with true β's. For example, Chan and Chen (1988) find that when portfolios are formed on size, the estimated β's of the portfolios are almost perfectly correlated (-0.988) with the average size of stocks in the portfolios. Thus, distinguishing between the roles of size and β in the expected returns on size portfolios is likely to be difficult. Likewise, theory predicts that, given a firm's business activities, the β of its stock increases with leverage. Thus leverage might proxy for true β's when β estimates are noisy.

Another approach uses the multifactor asset-pricing models of Merton (1973) and Ross (1976) to explain the SLB anomalies. For example, Ball (1978) argues that E/P is a catch-all proxy for omitted factors in asset-pricing tests. Thus, if two stocks have the same current earnings but different risks, the riskier stock has a higher expected return, and it is likely to have a lower price and higher E/P. E/P is then a general proxy for risk and expected returns, and one can expect it to have explanatory power when asset-pricing follows a multifactor model and all relevant factors are not included in asset-pricing tests.

Chan and Chen (1991) argue that the size effect is due to a distressed-firm factor in returns and expected returns. When size is defined by the market value of equity, small stocks include many marginal or depressed firms whose performance (and survival) is sensitive to business conditions. Chan and Chen argue that relative distress is an added risk factor in returns, not captured by market β, that is priced in expected returns. Fama and French (1991) argue that since leverage and book-to-market equity are also largely driven by the market value of equity, they also may proxy for risk factors in returns that are related to relative distress or, more generally, to market judgments about the relative prospects of firms.

Other work shows that there is indeed spillover among the SLB anomalies. Reinganum (1981) and Basu (1983) find that size and E/P are related; small stocks tend to have high E/P. Bhandari (1988) finds that small stocks include many firms that are highly levered, probably as result of financial distress. Chan, Hamao, and Lakonishok (1991) and Fama and French (1991) find that size and book-to-market equity are related; hard times and lower stock prices cause many stocks to become small, in terms of market equity, and so to have high book-to-market ratios. Fama and French (1991) find that leverage and book-to-market equity are highly correlated. Again, these links among the anomalies are hardly surprising, given that the common driving variable in E/P, leverage, size, and book-to-market equity is a stock's price.

How many of the SLB anomalies have separately distinguishable roles in expected returns? In tests aimed at this question, Fama and French (1991) find that for U.S. stocks, E/P, leverage, and book-to-market equity weaken but do not fully absorb the relation between size and expected returns. On the other hand, when size and book-to-market equity are used together, they leave no measurable role for E/P or leverage in the cross-section of average returns on NYSE, AMEX, and NASDAQ stocks. Chan, Hamao, and Lakonishok (1991) get similar results for Japan. The strong common result of Chan, Hamao, and Lakonishok (1991) and Fama and French (1991) is that for Japanese and U.S. stocks, book-to-market equity is the most powerful explanatory variable in the cross-section of average returns, with a weaker role for size. Thus, book-to-market equity seems to have displaced size as the premier SLB anomaly.

In truth, the premier SLB anomaly is not size or book-to-market equity but the weak role of market β in the cross-section of average returns on U.S. stocks. For example, Fama and French (1991) find that the relation between β and average returns on NYSE, AMEX, and NASDAQ stocks for 1963–1990 is feeble, even when β is the only explanatory variable. Their estimated premium per unit of β is 12 basis points per month (1.44% per year), and less than 0.5 standard errors from 0. Stambaugh (1982) and Lakonishok and Shapiro (1986) get similar results for NYSE stocks for 1953–1976 and 1962–1981.

Chan and Chen (1988) find that when the assets used in tests of the SLB model are common-stock portfolios formed on size, there is a strong relation between average returns and β in the 1954–1983 period. Fama and French (1991) show, however, that this result is due to the strong correlation between the β's of size portfolios and the average size of the stocks in the portfolios (-0.988 in Chan and Chen). Fama and French find that when portfolios are formed on size and β (as in Banz 1981), there is strong variation in β that is unrelated to size (the range of the β's just about doubles), and it causes the relation between β and average returns to all but disappear after 1950. In short, the rather strong positive relation between β and the average returns on U.S. stocks observed in the early tests of Black, Jensen, and Scholes (1972) and Fama and MacBeth (1973) does not seem to extend to later periods.

Finally, Stambaugh (1982) shows that when the assets in the SLB tests are extended to include bonds as well as stocks, there is a reliable positive relation between average returns and β in the post-1953 period. His results, along with those of Lakonishok and Shapiro (1986) and Fama and French (1991), suggest two conclusions. (1) As predicted by the SLB model, there is a positive relation between expected returns and β across security types (bonds and stocks).

(2) On average, however, the relation between expected returns and β for common stocks is weak, even though stocks cover a wide range of β's.

A. 3. Market Efficiency

The relations between expected returns and book-to-market equity, size, E/P, and leverage are usually interpreted as embarrassments for the SLB model, or the way it is tested (faulty estimates of market β's), rather than as evidence of market inefficiency. The reason is that the expected-return effects persist. For example, small stocks have high expected returns long after they are classified as small. In truth, though, the existing tests can't tell whether the anomalies result from a deficient (SLB) asset-pricing model or persistent mispricing of securities.

One can imagine evidence that bears on the matter. If a past anomaly does not appear in future data, it might be a market inefficiency, erased with the knowledge of its existence. (Or, the historical evidence for the anomaly may be a result of the profession's dogged data-dredging.) On the other hand, if the anomaly is explained by other asset-pricing models, one is tempted to conclude that it is a rational asset-pricing phenomenon. (But one should be wary that the apparent explanation may be the result of model-dredging.) In any case, I judge the maturity of the tests of other asset-pricing models in part on how well they explain, or at least address, the anomalies discovered in tests of the SLB model.

A. 4. The Bottom Line

With the deck of existing anomalies in hand, we should not be surprised when new studies show that yet other variables contradict the central prediction of the SLB model, that market β's suffice to describe the cross-section of expected returns. It is important to note, however, that we discover the contradictions because we have the SLB model as a sharp benchmark against which to examine the cross-section of expected returns. Moreover, the SLB model does its job. It points to empirical regularities in expected returns (size, E/P, leverage, and book-to-market effects) that must be explained better by any challenger asset-pricing model.

The SLB model also passes the test of practical usefulness. Before it became a standard part of MBA investments courses, market professionals had only a vague understanding of risk and diversification. Markowitz' (1959) portfolio model did not have much impact on practice because its statistics are relatively complicated. The SLB model, however, gave a summary measure of risk, market β, interpreted as market sensitivity, that rang mental bells. Indeed, in spite of the evidence against the SLB model, market professionals (and academics) still think about risk in terms of market β. And, like academics, practitioners retain the market line (from the riskfree rate through the market portfolio) of the Sharpe-Lintner model as a representation of the tradeoff of expected return for risk available from passive portfolios.

B. Multifactor Models

In the SLB model, the cross-section of expected returns on securities and portfolios is described by their market β's, where β is the slope in the simple regression of a security's return on the market return. The multifactor asset-pricing models of Merton (1973) and Ross (1976) generalize this result. In these models, the return-generating process can involve multiple factors, and the cross-section of expected returns is constrained by the cross-sections of factor loadings (sensitivities). A security's factor loadings are the slopes in a multiple regression of its return on the factors.

The multifactor models are an empiricist's dream. They are off-the-shelf theories that can accommodate tests for cross-sectional relations between expected returns and the loadings of security returns on any set of factors that are correlated with returns. How have tests of the models fared?

One approach, suggested by Ross' (1976) arbitrage-pricing theory (APT), uses factor analysis to extract the common factors in returns and then tests whether expected returns are explained by the cross-sections of the loadings of security returns on the factors (Roll and Ross (1980), Chen (1983)). Lehmann and Modest (1988) test this approach in detail. Most interesting, using models with up to 15 factors, they test whether the multifactor model explains the size anomaly of the SLB model. They find that the multifactor model leaves an unexplained size effect much like the SLB model; that is, expected returns are too high, relative to the model, for small stocks and too low for large stocks.

The factor analysis approach to tests of the APT leads to unresolvable squabbles about the number of common factors in returns and expected returns (Dhrymes, Friend, and Gultekin (1984), Roll and Ross (1984), Dhrymes, Friend, Gultekin, and Gultekin (1984), Trzcinka (1986), Conway and Reinganum (1988)). The theory, of course, is no help. Shanken (1982) argues that the factor analysis approach to identifying the common factors in returns and expected returns is in any case doomed by fundamental inconsistencies.

I think the factor analysis approach is limited, but for a different reason. It can confirm that there is more than one common factor in returns and expected returns, which is useful. But it leaves one hungry for economic insights about how the factors relate to uncertainties about consumption and portfolio opportunities that are of concern to investors, that is, the hedging arguments for multifactor models of Fama (1970a) and Merton (1973).

Although more studies take the factor analysis approach, the most influential tests of the multifactor model are those of Chen, Roll, and Ross (1986). The alternative approach in Chen, Roll, and Ross is to look for economic variables that are correlated with stock returns and then to test whether the loadings of returns on these economic factors describe the cross-section of expected returns. This approach thus addresses the hunger for factors with an economic motivation, left unsatisfied in the factor analysis approach.

Chen, Roll, and Ross examine a range of business conditions variables that might be related to returns because they are related to shocks to expected future cash flows or discount rates. The most powerful variables are the growth rate of industrial production and the difference between the returns on long-term low-grade corporate bonds and long-term Government bonds. Of lesser significance are the unexpected inflation rate and the difference between the returns on long and short Government bonds. Chen, Roll, and Ross (1986) conclude that their business conditions variables are risk factors in returns, or they proxy for such factors, and the loadings on the variables are priced in the cross-section of expected returns.

Chen, Roll, and Ross confront the multifactor model with the SLB model. They find that including SLB market β's has little effect on the power of their economic factors to explain the cross-section of expected returns, but SLB market β's have no marginal explanatory power. They get similar results in tests of the multifactor model against the consumption-based model (see below). Moreover, Chan, Chen, and Hsieh (1985) argue that the business conditions variables in Chen, Roll, and Ross, especially the difference between low-grade corporate and Government bond returns, explain the size anomaly of the SLB model. These successes of the multifactor model are, however, tempered by Shanken and Weinstein (1990), who find that the power of the economic factors in Chen, Roll, and Ross is sensitive to the assets used in the tests and the way factor loadings are estimated.

The Chen, Roll, and Ross approach (identifying economic factors that are correlated with returns and testing whether the factor loadings explain the cross-section of expected returns) is probably the most fruitful way to use multifactor models to improve our understanding of asset-pricing. As in Ferson and Harvey (1991), the approach can be used to study the links between the common economic factors in the cross-section of returns and the financial (dividend-yield and term-structure) variables that track variation in expected returns through time. Since the approach looks for economic variables that are related to returns and expected returns, it can also be useful in the critical task of modelling the links between expected returns and the real economy (Chen (1991)). In the end, there is some hope with this approach that we can develop a unified story for the behavior of expected returns (cross-section and time-series) and the links between expected returns and the real economy.

There is an important caveat. The flexibility of the Chen, Roll, and Ross approach can be a trap. Since multifactor models offer at best vague predictions about the variables that are important in returns and expected returns, there is the danger that measured relations between returns and economic factors are spurious, the result of special features of a particular sample (factor dredging). Thus the Chen, Roll, and Ross tests, and future extensions, warrant extended robustness checks. For example, although the returns and economic factors used by Chen, Roll, and Ross are available for earlier and later periods, to my knowledge we have no evidence on how the factors perform outside their sample.

C. Consumption-Based Asset-Pricing Models

The consumption-based model of Rubinstein (1976), Lucas (1978), Breeden (1979), and others is the most elegant of the available intertemporal asset-pricing models. In Breeden's version, the interaction between optimal consumption and portfolio decisions leads to a positive linear relation between the expected returns on securities and their consumption β's. (A security's consumption β is the slope in the regression of its return on the growth rate of per capita consumption.) The model thus summarizes all the incentives to hedge shifts in consumption and portfolio opportunities that can appear in Merton's (1973) multifactor model with a one-factor relation between expected returns and consumption β's.

The simple elegance of the consumption model produces a sustained interest in empirical tests. The tests use versions of the model that make strong assumptions about tastes (time-additive utility for consumption and constant relative risk aversion (CRRA)) and often about the joint distribution of consumption growth and returns (multivariate normality). Because the model is then so highly specified, it produces a rich set of testable predictions about the time series and cross-section properties of returns.

[146]

The empirical work on the consumption model often jointly tests its time-series and cross-section predictions, using the pathbreaking approach in Hansen and Singleton (1982). Estimation is with Hansen's (1982) generalized method of moments. The test is based on a χ^2 statistic that summarizes, in one number, how the data conform to the model's many restrictions. The tests usually reject. This is not surprising since we know all models are false. The disappointment comes when the rejection is not pursued for additional descriptive information, obscure in the χ^2 test, about which restrictions of the model (time-series, cross-section, or both) are the problem. In short, tests of the consumption model sometimes fail the test of usefulness; they don't enhance our ability to describe the behavior of returns.

This is not a general criticism. Much interesting information comes out of the tests of the consumption model. For example, one result, from the so-called unconditional tests, that focus on the predictions of the model about the cross-section of expected returns, is the equity-premium puzzle (Mehra and Prescott (1985)). It says that the representative consumer, whose tastes characterize asset prices, must have high risk aversion to explain the large spread (about 6% per year) of the expected returns on stocks over low-risk securities like Treasury bills. In healthy scientific fashion, the puzzle leads to attempts to modify assumptions to accomodate a large equity premium. For example, Constantinides (1990) argues that a large premium is consistent with models in which utility depends on past consumption (habit formation).

The habit formation argument has a ring of truth, but I also think that a large equity premium is not necessarily a puzzle; high risk aversion (or low intertemporal elasticity of substitution for consumption) may be a fact. Roughly speaking, a large premium says that consumers are extremely averse to small negative consumption shocks. This is in line with the perception that consumers live in morbid fear of recessions (and economists devote enormous energy to studying them) even though, at least in the post-war period, recessions are associated with small changes in per capita consumption.

Moreover, the equity-premium puzzle is a special feature of unconditional tests that focus on the cross-section properties of expected returns. In these tests, estimates of the risk-aversion parameter are imprecise. Conditional tests, that also include the time-series predictions of the model, lead to reasonable estimates of the risk-aversion parameter of the representative consumer (Hansen and Singleton (1982, 1983)).

The central cross-section prediction of Breeden's (1979) version of the consumption model is that expected returns are a positive linear function of consumption β's. On this score, the model does fairly well. Breeden, Gibbons, and Litzenberger (1989) test for linearity on a set of assets that includes the NYSE value-weighted portfolio, 12 industry stock portfolios, and 4 bond portfolios. They argue that the expected returns on these assets are a positive linear function of their consumption β's. Wheatley (1988a) comes to a similar conclusion.

Wheatley (1988b) also cannot reject the hypothesis that the same linear relation between expected returns and consumption β's (with β's measured from U.S. consumption) holds for an opportunity set that includes portfolios of the common stocks of 17 international markets, as well as U.S. Government bonds, corporate bonds, and common stocks. Wheatley thus cannot reject the hypothesis that securities are priced as if the consumption-based model holds and capital markets are internationally integrated.

The plots in Breeden, Gibbons, and Litzenberger (1989) and Wheatley (1988a,b) suggest, however, that as in Stambaugh's (1982) tests of the SLB model, the evidence for a positive relation between expected returns and consumption β's comes largely from the spread between bonds (low β's and low average returns) and stocks (high β's and high average returns). The existence of a positive tradeoff among the stock portfolios is less evident in their plots, and they give no tests for stocks alone.

Breeden, Gibbons, and Litzenberger (1989) and Wheatley (1988a,b) bring the tests of the consumption model to about where tests of the SLB model were after the studies of Black, Jensen, and Scholes (1972), Blume and Friend (1973), and Fama and MacBeth (1973). In particular, a positive relation between expected returns and consumption β's is observed, but there is no confrontation between the consumption model and competing models.

Mankiw and Shapiro (1986) test the consumption model against the SLB model. They argue that in univariate tests, expected returns on NYSE stocks are positively related to their market β's and perhaps to their consumption β's. When the two β's are included in the same regression, the explanatory power of market β's remains, but consumption β's have no explanatory power. These results are, however, clouded by a survival bias. The sample of stocks used by Mankiw and Shapiro is limited to those continuously listed on the NYSE during the entire 1959–1982 period. Not allowing for delistings gives upward-biased average returns, and the bias is probably more severe for higher β (consumption or market) stocks.

Chen, Roll, and Ross (1986) include consumption β's with the β's for the economic variables used in their tests of multifactor models. Again, consumption β's have no marginal explanatory power. Thus Chen, Roll, and Ross reject the prediction of the consumption model that the explanatory power of other variables in the multifactor model is subsumed by consumption β's.

Finally, so far, the tests of the consumption model make no attempt to deal with the anomalies that have caused problems for the SLB model. It would be interesting to confront consumption β's with variables like size and book-to-market equity, that have caused problems for the market β's of the SLB model. Given that the consumption model does not seem to fare well in tests against the SLB model or the multifactor model, however, my guess is that the consumption model will do no better with the anomalies of the SLB model.

D. Where Do We Stand?
D. 1. The Bad News

Rejections of the SLB model are common. Variables like size, leverage, E/P, and book-to-market equity have explanatory power in tests that include market β's. Indeed, in recent tests, market β's have no explanatory power relative to the anomalies variables (Fama and French (1991)). The SLB model is also rejected in tests against multifactor models (Chen, Roll, and Ross (1986)).

If anything, the consumption-based model fares worse than the SLB model. It is rejected in combined (conditional) tests of its time-series and cross-section predictions (Hansen and Singleton (1982, 1983)). The equity-premium puzzle of Mehra and Prescott (1985) is ubiquitous in (unconditional) cross-section tests. And the model seems to fail miserably (consumption β's have no marginal explanatory power) in tests against the SLB model (Mankiw and Shapiro (1986)) and the multifactor model (Chen, Roll, and Ross (1986)).

The multifactor model seems to do better. It survives tests against the SLB and consumption-based models (Chen, Roll, and Ross (1986)). It helps explain the size anomaly of the SLB model (Chan, Chen, and Hsieh (1985), Chan and Chen (1991)). On the other hand, the evidence in Shanken and Weinstein (1990) that the results in Chen, Roll, and Ross and Chan, Chen, and Hsieh are sensitive to the assets used in the tests and the way the β's of economic factors are estimated is disturbing.

One can also argue that an open competition among the SLB, multifactor, and consumption models is biased in favor of the multifactor model. The expected-return variables of the SLB and consumption models (market and consumption β's) are clearly specified. In contast, the multifactor models are licenses to search the data for variables that, *ex post,* describe the cross-section of average returns. It is perhaps no surprise, then, that these variables do well in competitions on the data used to identify them.

D. 2. The Good News

Fortunately, rejections of the SLB model and the consumption model are never clean. For the SLB model, it is always possible that rejections are due to a bad proxy for the market portfolio and thus poor estimates of market β's. With bad β's, other variables that are correlated with true β's (like size) can have explanatory power relative to estimated β's when in fact asset pricing is according to the SLB model.

Estimating consumption β's poses even more serious problems. Consumption is measured with error, and consumption flows from durables are difficult to impute. The model calls for instantaneous consumption, but the data are monthly, quarterly, and annual aggregates. Finally, Cornell (1981) argues that the elegance of the consumption model (all incentives to hedge uncertainty about consumption and investment opportunities are summarized in consumption β's) likely means that consumption β's are difficult to estimate because they vary through time.

In this quagmire, it is possible that estimates of market β's are better proxies for consumption β's than estimates of consumption β's, and, as a result, the consumption model is mistakenly rejected in favor of the SLB model. It is even less surprising that the consumption model is rejected in favor of the multifactor model. Since the multifactor model is an expansion of the consumption model (Constantinides (1989)), the estimated β's of the multifactor model may well be better proxies for consumption β's than poorly estimated consumption β's.

These arguments against dismissal of the SLB and consumption models would be uninteresting if the predictions of the models about the cross-section of expected returns are strongly rejected. This is not the case. At least in univariate tests that include both bonds and stocks, expected returns are positively related to market β's and consumption β's, and the relations are approximately linear. Although other predictions of the SLB and consumption models are rejected, the rough validity of their univariate predictions about the cross-section of expected returns, along with their powerful intuitive appeal, keeps them alive and well.

Finally, it is important to emphasize that the SLB model, the consumption model, and the multifactor models are not mutually exclusive. Following Constantinides (1989), one can view the models as different ways to formalize the asset-pricing implications of common general assumptions about tastes (risk aversion) and portfolio opportunities (multivariate normality). Thus, as long as the major predictions of the models about the cross-section of expected returns have some empirical content, and as long as we keep the empirical shortcomings of the models in mind, we have some freedom to lean on one model or another, to suit the purpose at hand.

V. EVENT STUDIES

The original event study (of stock splits) by Fama, Fisher, Jensen and Roll (1969) is a good example of serendipity. The paper was suggested by James Lorie. The purpose was to have a piece of work that made extensive use of the newly developed CRSP monthly NYSE file, to illustrate the usefulness of the file, to justify continued funding. We had no clue that event studies would become a research industry. And we can't take much credit for starting the industry. Powerful computers and the CRSP data made it inevitable.

Event studies are now an important part of finance, especially corporate finance. In 1970 there was little evidence on the central issues of corporate finance. Now we are overwhelmed with results, mostly from event studies. Using simple tools, this research documents interesting regularities in the response of stock prices to investment decisions, financing decisions, and changes in corporate control. The results stand up to replication and the empirical regularities, some rather surprising, are the impetus for theoretical work to explain them. In short, on all counts, the event-study literature passes the test of scientific usefulness.

Here I just give a flavor of the results from event studies in corporate finance. The reader who wants a more extensive introduction is well served by the reviews of research on financing decisions by Smith (1986) and corporate-control events by Jensen and Ruback (1983) and Jensen and Warner (1988). Moreover, I mostly ignore the extensive event-study literatures in accounting, industrial organization, and macroeconomics. (See the selective reviews of Ball (1990), Binder (1985), and Santomero (1991).) I dwell a bit more on the implications of the event-study work for market efficiency.

A. Some of the Main Results

One interesting finding is that unexpected changes in dividends are on average associated with stock-price changes of the same sign (Charest (1978), Ahrony and Swary (1980), Asquith and Mullins (1983)). The result is a surprise, given that the Miller-Modigliani (1961) theorem, and its refinements (Miller and Scholes (1978)), predict either that dividend policy is irrelevant or that dividends are bad news because (during the periods of the tests) dividends are taxed at a higher rate than capital gains. The evidence on the response of stock prices to dividend changes leads to signalling models (Miller and Rock (1985)) and free-cash-flow stories (Easterbrook (1984), Jensen (1986)) that attempt to explain why dividend increases are good news for stock prices.

Another surprising result is that new issues of common stock are bad news for stock prices (Asquith and Mullins (1986), Masulis and Korwar (1986)), and redemptions, through tenders or open-market purchases, are good news (Dann (1981), Vermaelen (1981)). One might have predicted the opposite, that is, stock issues are good news because they signal that the firm's investment prospects are strong. Again, the evidence is the impetus for theoretical models that explain it in terms of (1) asymmetric information [managers issue stock when it is overvalued (Myers and Majluf (1984))], (2) the information in a stock issue that cash flows are low (Miller and Rock (1985)), or (3) lower agency costs when free cash flows are used to redeem stock (Jensen (1986)).

Like financing decisions, corporate-control transactions have been examined in detail, largely through event studies. One result is that mergers and tender offers on average produce large gains for the stockholders of the target firms (Mandelker (1974), Dodd and Ruback (1977), Bradley (1980), Dodd (1980), Asquith (1983)). Proxy fights (Dodd and Warner (1983)), management buyouts (Kaplan (1989)), and other control events are also wealth-enhancing for target stockholders. The political pressure to restrict the market for corporate control is strong, but my guess is that without the barrage of evidence that control transactions benefit stockholders, the pressure would be overwhelming.

An aside. The research on corporate control is a good example of a more general blurring of the lines between finance and other areas of economics. Many of the corporate-control studies appear in finance journals, but the work goes to the heart of issues in industrial organization, law and economics, and labor economics. The research is widely known and has contributors from all these areas. Likewise, research on time-varying expected returns and asset-pricing models (especially the consumption-based model) is now important in macroeconomics and international economics as well as in finance. At this point, it is not clear who are the locals and who are the invaders, but the cross-breeding between finance and other areas of economics has resulted in a healthy burst of scientific growth.

The cursory review above highlights just a smattering of the rich results produced by event studies in corporate finance. My focus is more on what this literature tells us about market efficiency.

B. Market Efficiency

The CRSP files of daily returns on NYSE, AMEX, and NASDAQ stocks are a major boost for the precision of event studies. When the announcement of an event can be dated to the day, daily data allow precise measurement of the speed of the stock-price response—the central issue for market efficiency. Another powerful advantage of daily data is that they can attenuate or eliminate the joint-hypothesis problem, that market efficiency must be tested jointly with an asset-pricing model.

Thus, when the stock-price response to an event is large and concentrated in a few days, the way one estimates daily expected returns (normal returns) in calculating abnormal returns has little effect on inferences (Brown and Warner (1985)). For example, in mergers and tender offers, the average increase in the stock price of target firms in the 3 days around the announcement is more than 15%. Since the average daily return on stocks is only about 0.04% (10% per year divided by 250 trading days), different ways of measuring daily expected returns have little effect on the inference that target shares have large abnormal returns in the days around merger and tender announcements.

The typical result in event studies on daily data is that, on average, stock prices seem to adjust within a day to event announcements. The result is so common that this work now devotes little space to market efficiency. The fact that quick adjustment is consistent with efficiency is noted, and then the studies move on to other issues. In short, in the only empirical work where the joint hypothesis problem is relatively unimportant, the evidence typically says that, with respect to firm-specific events, the adjustment of stock prices to new information is efficient.

To be fair, and to illustrate that efficiency issues are never entirely resolved, I play the devil's advocate. (Attacks on efficiency belong, of course, in the camp of the devil.) Although prices on average adjust quickly to firm-specific information, a common finding in event studies (including the original Fama-Fisher-Jensen-Roll split study) is that the dispersion of returns (measured across firms, in event time) increases around information events. Is this a rational result of uncertainty about new fundamental values? Or is it irrational but random over and underreaction to information that washes out in average returns? In short, since event studies focus on the average adjustment of prices to information, they don't tell us how much of the residual variance, generated by the deviations from average, is rational.

Moreover, when part of the response of prices to information seems to occur slowly, event studies become subject to the joint-hypothesis problem. For example, the early merger work finds that the stock prices of acquiring firms hardly react to merger announcements, but thereafter they drift slowly down (Asquith (1983)). One possibility is that acquiring firms on average pay too much for target firms, but the market only realizes this slowly; the market is inefficient (Roll (1986)). Another possibility is that the post-announcement drift is due to bias in measured abnormal returns (Franks, Harris, and Titman (1991)). Still another possiblity is that the drift in the stock prices of acquiring firms in the early merger studies is sample-specific. Mitchell and Lehn (1990) find no evidence of post-announcement drift during the 1982–1986 period for a sample of about 400 acquiring firms.

Post-announcement drift in abnormal returns is also a common result in studies of the response of stock prices to earnings announcements (e.g., Ball and Brown (1968)). Predictably, there is a raging debate on the extent to which the drift can be attributed to problems in measuring abnormal returns (Bernard and Thomas (1989), Ball, Kothari, and Watta (1990)).

Bernard and Thomas (1990) identify a more direct challenge to market efficiency in the way stock prices adjust to earnings announcements. They argue that the market does not understand the autocorrelation of quarterly earnings. As a result, part of the 3-day stock-price response to this quarter's earnings announcement is predictable from earnings 1 to 4 quarters back. This result is especially puzzling, given that earnings are studied so closely by analysts and market participants. The key (if there is one) may be in the fact that the delayed stock-price responses are strongest for small firms that have had extreme changes in earnings.

In short, some event studies suggest that stock prices do not respond quickly to specific information. Given the event-study boom of the last 20 years, however, some anomalies, spurious and real, are inevitable. Moreover, it is important to emphasize the main point. Event studies are the cleanest evidence we have on efficiency (the least encumbered by the joint-hypothesis problem). With few exceptions, the evidence is supportive.

VI. TESTS FOR PRIVATE INFORMATION

The 1970 review points to only two cases of market inefficiency due to the information advantages of individual agents. (1) Neiderhoffer and Osborne (1966) show that NYSE specialists use their monopolistic access to the book of limit orders to generate trading profits, and (2) Scholes (1972) and others show that corporate insiders have access to information not reflected in prices. That specialists and insiders have private information is not surprising. For efficiency buffs, it is comfortable evidence against (in the old terms) strong-form efficiency. Moreover, Jensen's (1968, 1969) early evidence suggests that private information is not common among professional (mutual-fund) investment managers.

What has happened since 1970 that warrants discussion here? (1) The profitability of insider trading is now established in detail. (2) There is evidence that some security analysts (e.g., Value Line) have information not reflected in stock prices. (3) There is also some evidence that professional investment managers have access to private information (Ippolito (1989)), but it is seems to be more than balanced by evidence that they do not (Brinson, Hood, and Beebower (1986), Elton, Gruber, Das, and Hklarka (1991)).

A. Insider Trading

In the 1970's, with the early evidence (Black, Jensen, and Scholes (1972), Fama and MacBeth (1973)) that the SLB model seemed to be a good approximation for expected returns on NYSE stocks, the thinking was that the model should be used routinely in tests of market efficiency, to replace informal models like the market model and the constant expected returns model. Jaffe's (1974) study of insider trading is one of the first in this mold.

Like earlier work, Jaffe finds, not surprisingly, that for insiders the stock market is not efficient; insiders have information that is not reflected in prices. His disturbing finding is that the market does not react quickly to public information about insider trading. Outsiders can profit from the knowledge that there has been heavy insider trading for up to 8 months after information about the trading becomes public—a startling contradiction of market efficiency.

Seyhun (1986) offers an explanation. He confirms that insiders profit from their trades, but he does not confirm Jaffe's finding that outsiders can profit from public information about insider trading. Seyhun argues that Jaffe's outsider profits arise because he uses the SLB model for expected returns. Seyhun shows that insider buying is relatively more important in small firms, whereas insider selling is more important in large firms. From Banz (1981) we know that relative to the SLB model, small stocks tend to have high average returns and large stocks tend to have low average returns. In short, the persistent strong outsider profits observed by Jaffe seem to be a result of the size effect.

There is a general message in Seyhun's results. Highly constrained asset-pricing models like the SLB model are surely false. They have systematic problems explaining the cross-section of expected returns that can look like market inefficiencies. In market-efficiency tests, one should avoid models that put strong restrictions on the cross-section of expected returns, if that is consistent with the purpose at hand. Concretely, one should use formal asset-pricing models when the phenomenon studied concerns the cross-section of expected returns (e.g., tests for size, leverage, and E/P effects). But when the phenomenon is firm-specific (most event studies), one can use firm-specific "models," like the market model or historical average returns, to abstract from normal expected returns without putting unnecessary constraints on the cross-section of expected returns.

B. Security Analysis

The *Value Line Investment Survey* publishes weekly rankings of 1700 common stocks into 5 groups. Group 1 has the best return prospects and group 5 the worst. There is evidence that, adjusted for risk and size, group 1 stocks have higher average returns than group 5 stocks for horizons out to 1 year (Black (1973), Copeland and Mayers (1982), and Huberman and Kandel (1987, 1990)).

Affleck-Graves and Mendenhall (1990) argue, however, that Value Line ranks firms largely on the basis of recent earnings surprises. As a result, the longer-term abnormal returns of the Value Line rankings are just another anomaly in disguise, the post-earnings-announcement drift identified by Ball and Brown (1968), Bernard and Thomas (1989), and others.

Stickel (1985) uses event-study methods to show that there is an announcement effect in rank changes that more clearly implies that Value Line has information not reflected in prices. He finds that the market takes up to 3 days to adjust to the information in changes in rankings, and the price changes are permanent. The strongest price changes, about 2.44% over 3 days, occur when stocks are upgraded from group 2 to group 1 (better to best). For most other ranking changes, the 3-day price changes are less than 1%.

The information in Value Line rank changes is also stronger for small stocks. For the smallest quintile of stocks, a change from group 2 to group 1 is associated with a 3-day return of 5.18%; for the largest quintile, it is 0.7%. Stickel argues that these results are consistent with models in which higher information costs for small stocks deter private information production. As a result, public information announcements (like Value Line rank changes) have larger effects on the prices of small stocks.

The announcement effects of Value Line rank changes are statistically reliable evidence against the hypothesis that information advantages do not exist. But except for small stocks upgraded from group 2 to 1 (or downgraded from

1 to 2), the price effects of rank changes (less than 1% over 3 days) are small. Moreover, Hulbert (1990) reports that the strong long-term performance of Value Line's group 1 stocks is weak after 1983. Over the 6.5 years from 1984 to mid-1990, group 1 stocks earned 16.9% per year compared with 15.2% for the Wilshire 5000 Index. During the same period, Value Line's Centurion Fund, which specializes in group 1 stocks, earned 12.7% per year—live testimony to the fact that there can be large gaps between simulated profits from private information and what is available in practice.

Finally, Lloyd-Davies and Canes (1978), and Liu, Smith, and Syed (1990) find that the touts of the security analysts surveyed in the *Wall Street Journal's* "Heard on the Street" column result in price changes that average about 1.7% on the announcement day, an information effect similar to that for Value Line rank changes.

The evidence of Stickel (1985), Lloyd-Davies and Canes (1978), and Liu, Smith, and Syed (1990) is that Value Line and some security analysts have private information that, when revealed, results in small but statistically reliable price adjustments. These results are consistent with the "noisy rational expectations" model of competitive equilibrium of Grossman and Stiglitz (1980). In brief, because generating information has costs, informed investors are compensated for the costs they incur to ensure that prices adjust to information. The market is then less than fully efficient (there can be private information not fully reflected in prices), but in a way that is consistent with rational behavior by all investors.

C. Professional Portfolio Management

Jensen's (1968, 1969) early results were bad news for the mutual-fund industry. He finds that for the 1945–1964 period, returns to investors in funds (before load fees, but after management fees, and other expenses) are on average about 1% per year below the market line (from the riskfree rate through the S&P 500 market portfolio) of the Sharpe-Lintner model, and average returns on more than half of his funds are below the line. Only when all published expenses of the funds are added back do the average returns on the funds scatter randomly about the market line. Jensen concludes that mutual-fund managers do not have private information.

Recent studies do not always agree. In tests on 116 mutual funds for the February 1968 to June 1980 period, Henriksson (1984) finds that average returns to fund investors, before load fees but after other expenses, are trivially different (0.02% per month) from the Sharpe-Lintner market line. Chang and

Lewellen (1984) get similar results for 1971–1979. This work suggests that on average, fund managers have access to enough private information to cover the expenses and management fees they charge investors.

Ippolito (1989) provides a more extensive analysis of the performance of mutual funds. He examines 143 funds for the 20-year post-Jensen period 1965–1984. He finds that fund returns, before load fees but after other expenses, are on average 0.83% per year above the Sharpe-Lintner market line (from the 1-year Treasury bill rate through the S&P 500 portfolio). He finds no evidence that the deviations of funds from the market line are related to management fees, other fund expenses, or turnover ratios. Ippolito concludes that his results are in the spirit of the "noisy rational expectations" model of Grossman and Stiglitz (1980), in which informed investors (mutual fund managers) are compensated for their information costs.

Ippolito's mutual-fund evidence is not confirmed by performance tests on pension plans and endowment funds. Brinson, Hood, and Beebower (1986) examine the returns on 91 large corporate pension plans for 1974–1983. The individual plans range in size from $100 million in 1974 to over $3 billion in 1983. Individual plans commonly have more than 10 outside managers, and large influential professional managers are likely to be well-represented in the sample. The plans on average earn 1.1% per year less than passive benchmark portfolios of bonds and stocks—a negative performance measure for recent data much like Jensen's early mutual fund results. Beebower and Bergstrom (1977), Munnell (1983), and Ippolito and Turner (1987) also come to negative conclusions about the investment performance of pension plans. Berkowitz, Finney, and Logue (1988) extend the negative evidence to endowment funds.

How can we reconcile the opposite recent results for mutual funds and pension funds? Performance evaluation is known to be sensitive to methodology (Grinblatt and Titman (1989)). Ippolito (1989) uses the Sharpe-Lintner model to estimate normal returns to mutual funds. Brinson, Hood, and Beebower (1986) use passive portfolios meant to match the bond and stock components of their pension funds. We know the Sharpe-Lintner model has systematic problems explaining expected returns (size, leverage, E/P, and book-to-market equity effects) that can affect estimates of abnormal returns.

Elton, Gruber, Das, and Hklarka (1991) test the importance of the SL methodology in Ippolito's results. They find that during Ippolito's 1965–1984 period, his benchmark combinations of Treasury bills with the S&P 500 portfolio produce strong positive estimates of "abnormal" returns for passive portfolios of non-S&P (smaller) stocks—strong confirmation that there is a problem with the Sharpe-Lintner benchmarks (also used by Jensen (1968, 1969), Henriksson (1984), and Chang and Lewellen (1984)).

Elton, Gruber, Das, and Hklarka then use a 3-factor model to evaluate the performance of mutual funds for 1965–1984. The 3 factors are the S&P 500, a portfolio tilted toward non-S&P stocks, and a proxy for the market portfolio of Government and corporate bonds. As in Brinson, Hood, and Beebower (1986), the goal of the Elton-Gruber-Das-Hklarka approach is to allow for the fact that mutual funds hold bonds and stocks that are not in the universe covered by the combinations of Treasury bills and the S&P 500 that Ippolito uses to evaluate performance. In simplest terms, the Elton-Gruber-Das-Hklarka benchmarks are the returns from passive combinations of Treasury bills with S&P stocks, non-S&P stocks, and bonds.

Elton-Gruber-Das-Hklarka find that for Ippolito's 1965–1984 period, their benchmarks produce an abnormal return on mutual funds of −1.1% per year, much like the negative performance measures for pension funds (Brinson, Hood, and Beebower (1986)) and endowments (Berkowitz, Finney, and Logue (1988)). Moreover, unlike Ippolito, but in line with earlier work (Sharpe (1966)), Elton, Gruber, Das, and Hklarka find that abnormal returns on mutual funds are negatively related to fund expenses (including management fees) and turnover. In short, if mutual, pension, and endowment fund managers are the informed investors of the Grossman-Stiglitz (1980) model, they are apparently negating their inframarginal rents by pushing research and trading beyond the point where marginal benefits equal marginal costs.

VII. CONCLUSIONS

The past 20 years have been a fruitful period for research on market efficiency and asset-pricing models. I conclude by reviewing briefly what we have learned from the work on efficiency, and where it might go in the future. (Section IV.D above provides a summary of tests of asset-pricing models.)

A. Event Studies

The cleanest evidence on market-efficiency comes from event studies, especially event studies on daily returns. When an information event can be dated precisely and the event has a large effect on prices, the way one abstracts from expected returns to measure abnormal daily returns is a second-order consideration. As a result, event studies can give a clear picture of the speed of adjustment of prices to information.

There is a large event-study literature on issues in corporate finance. The results indicate that on average stock prices adjust quickly to information about
investment decisions, dividend changes, changes in capital structure, and
corporate-control transactions. This evidence tilts me toward the conclusion
that prices adjust efficiently to firm-specific information. More important, the
research uncovers empirical regularities, many surprising, that enrich our understanding of investment, financing, and corporate-control events, and give
rise to interesting theoretical work.

It would be presumptuous to suggest where event studies should go in the
future. This is a mature industry, with skilled workers and time-tested methods. It continues to expand its base in accounting, macroeconomics, and industrial organization, with no sign of a letup in finance.

B. Private Information

There is less new research on whether individual agents have private information that is not in stock prices. We know that corporate insiders have private
information that leads to abnormal returns (Jaffe (1974)), but outsiders cannot profit from public information about insider trading (Seyhun (1986)). We
know that changes in Value Line's rankings of firms on average lead to permanent changes in stock prices. Except for small stocks, however, the average
price changes are small (Stickel (1985)). The stock-price reactions to the private
information of the analysts surveyed in the *Wall Street Journal's* "Heard on the
Street" column are likewise statistically reliable but small.

The investors studied in most detail for private information are pension
fund and mutual fund managers. Unlike event studies, however, evaluating
the access of investment managers to private information involves measuring abnormal returns over long periods. The tests thus run head-on into the
joint-hypothesis problem: measured abnormal returns can result from market
inefficiency, a bad model of market equilibrium, or problems in the way the
model is implemented. It is perhaps no surprise, then, that Ippolito (1989),
using the 1-factor benchmarks of the Sharpe-Lintner model, finds that mutual fund managers have private information that generates positive abnormal
returns. In contrast, using 2- and 3-portfolio benchmarks that are consistent
with multifactor asset-pricing models, Elton, Gruber, Das, and Hklarka (1991)
and Brinson, Hood, and Beebower (1986) find that mutual funds and pension
funds on average have negative abnormal returns.

The 1-factor Sharpe-Lintner model has many problems explaining the
cross-section of expected stock returns (e.g., the size and book-to-market eq-

uity anomalies, and, worst of all, the weak relation between average returns and β for stocks). Multifactor models seem to do a better job on expected returns (Chen, Roll, and Ross (1986), Chan and Chen (1991), Fama and French (1991)). These results lean me toward the conclusion that the multifactor performance evaluation methods of Elton, Gruber, Das, and Hklarka (1991) and Brinson, Hood, and Beebower (1986), and their negative conclusions about the access of investment managers to private information, are more reliable than the positive results of Ippolito (1989) and others that are based on the Sharpe-Lintner model. In truth, though, the most defensible conclusion is that, because of the joint-hypothesis problem and the rather weak state of the evidence for different asset-pricing models, strong inferences about market efficiency for performance evaluation tests are not warranted.

Since we are reviewing studies of performance evaluation, it is well to point out here that the efficient-markets literature is a premier case where academic research has affected real-world practice. Before the work on efficiency, the presumption was that private information is plentiful among investment managers. The efficiency research put forth the challenge that private information is rare. One result is the rise of passive investment strategies that simply buy and hold diversified portfolios (e.g., the many S&P 500 funds). Professional managers who follow passive strategies (and charge low fees) were unheard of in 1960; they are now an important part of the investment-management industry.

The market-efficiency literature also produced a demand for performance evaluation. In 1960, investment managers were free to rest on their claims about performance. Now, performance measurement relative to passive benchmarks is the rule, and there are firms that specialize in evaluating professional managers (e.g., SEI, the data source for Brinson, Hood, and Beebower (1986)). The data generated by these firms are a resource for tests for private information that academics have hardly tapped.

C. Return Predictability

There is a resurgence of interesting research on the predictability of stock returns from past returns and other variables. Controversy about market efficiency centers largely on this work.

The new research produces precise evidence on the predictability of daily and weekly returns from past returns, but the results are similar to those in the early work, and somewhat lacking in drama. The suggestive evidence in Fama (1965) that first-order autocorrelations of daily returns on the stocks of large firms are positive (but about 0.03) becomes more precise in the longer samples in French and Roll (1986). They also show that the higher-order autocorrelations of daily returns on individual stocks are reliably negative, but reliably small. The evidence in Fisher (1966) that autocorrelations of short-horizon returns on diversified portfolios are positive, larger than for individual stocks, and larger for portfolios tilted toward small firms is confirmed by the more precise results in Lo and MacKinlay (1988) and Conrad and Kaul (1988). This latter work, however, does not entirely allay Fisher's fear that the higher autocorrelation of portfolio returns is in part the spurious result of nonsynchronous trading.

In contrast to the work on short-horizon returns, the new research on the predictability of long-horizon stock returns from past returns is high on drama but short on precision. The new tests raise the intriguing suggestion that there is strong negative autocorrelation in 2- to 10-year returns due to large, slowly decaying, temporary (stationary) components of prices (Fama and French (1988a), Poterba and Summers (1988)). The suggestion is, however, clouded by low statistical power; the data do not yield many observations on long-horizon returns. More telling, the strong negative autocorrelation in long-horizon returns seems to be due largely to the Great Depression.

The recent evidence on the predictability of returns from other variables seems to give a more reliable picture of the variation through time of expected returns. Returns for short and long horizons are predictable from dividend yields, E/P ratios, and default spreads of low- over high-grade bond yields (Keim and Stambaugh (1986), Campbell and Shiller (1988b), Fama and French (1988b, 1989)). Term spreads (long-term minus short-term interest rates) and the level of short rates also forecast returns out to about a year (Campbell (1987), Fama and French (1989), Chen (1991)). In contrast to the autocorrelation tests on long-horizon returns, the forecast power of D/P, E/P, and the term-structure variables is reliable for periods after the Great Depression.

D/P, E/P, and the default spread track autocorrelated variation in expected returns that becomes a larger fraction of the variance of returns for longer return horizons. These variables typically account for less than 5% of the variance of monthly returns but around 25–30% of the variances of 2- to 5-year returns. In short, the recent work suggests that expected returns take large, slowly decaying swings away from their unconditional means.

Rational variation in expected returns is caused either by shocks to tastes for current versus future consumption or by technology shocks. We may never be able to develop and test a full model that isolates taste and technology shocks and their effects on saving, consumption, investment, and expected returns. We can, however, hope to know more about the links between expected returns and the macro-variables. The task has at least two parts.

1. If the variation in expected returns traces to shocks to tastes or technology, then the variation in expected returns should be common across different securities and markets. We can profit from more work, like that in Keim and Stambaugh (1986), Campbell (1987), and Fama and French (1989), on the common variation in expected returns across bonds and stocks. We can also profit from more work like that in Harvey (1991) on the extent to which the variation in expected returns is common across international markets. Most important, closure demands a coherent story that relates the variation through time in expected returns to models for the cross-section of expected returns. Thus we can profit from more work like that in Ferson and Harvey (1991) on how the variation through time in expected returns is related to the common factors in returns that determine the cross-section of expected returns.

2. The second interesting task is to dig deeper and establish (or show the absence of) links between expected returns and business conditions. If the variation through time in expected returns is rational, driven by shocks to tastes or technology, then the variation in expected returns should be related to variation in consumption, investment, and savings. Fama and French (1989) argue that the variation in expected returns on corporate bonds and common stocks tracked by their dividend yield, default spread, and term spread variables is related to business conditions. Chen (1991) shows more formally that these expected-return variables are related to growth rates of output in ways that are consistent with intertemporal asset-pricing models. Output is an important variable, and Chen's work is a good start, but we can reasonably hope for a more complete story about the relations between variation in expected returns and consumption, investment, and saving.

In the end, I think we can hope for a coherent story that (1) relates the cross-section properties of expected returns to the variation of expected returns through time, and (2) relates the behavior of expected returns to the real economy in a rather detailed way. Or we can hope to convince ourselves that no such story is possible.

[163]

REFERENCES

Affleck-Graves, John and Richard R. Mendenhall, 1990, The relation between the Value Line enigma and post-earnings-announcement drift, Unpublished manuscript, College of Business Administration, University of Notre Dame.

Ahrony, Joseph and Itzhak Swary, 1980, Quarterly dividend and earnings announcements and stockholders' returns: An empirical analysis, *Journal of Finance* 35, 1–12.

Ariel, Robert A., 1987, A monthly effect in stock returns, *Journal of Financial Economics* 18, 161–174.

———, 1990, High stock returns before holidays: Existence and evidence on possible causes, *Journal of Finance* 45, 1611–1626.

Asquith, Paul, 1983, Merger bids, uncertainty and stock holder returns, *Journal of Financial Economics* 11, 51–83.

——— and David W. Mullins, 1983, The impact of initiating dividend payments on shareholders' wealth, *Journal of Business* 56, 77–96.

——— and David W. Mullins, 1986, Equity issues and offering dilution, *Journal of Financial Economics* 15, 61–89.

Ball, Ray, 1978, Anomalies in relationships between securities' yields and yield-surrogates, *Journal of Financial Economics* 6, 103–126.

———, 1990, What do we know about market efficiency? Unpublished manuscript, William E. Simon Graduate School of Business Administration, University of Rochester.

——— and Philip Brown, 1968, An empirical evaluation of accounting income numbers, *Journal of Accounting Research* 6, 159–178.

———, S. P. Kothari, and Ross L. Watts, 1990, The economics of the relation between earnings changes and stock returns, Working paper, University of Rochester.

——— and S. P. Kothari, 1989, Nonstationary expected returns: Implications for tests of market efficiency and serial correlation in returns, *Journal of Financial Economics* 25, 51–74.

Balvers, Ronald J., Thomas F. Cosimano, and Bill McDonald, 1990, Predicting stock returns in an efficient market, *Journal of Finance* 45, 1109–1128.

Banz, Rolf W., 1981, The relationship between return and market value of common stocks, *Journal of Financial Economics* 9, 3–18.

Basu, Sanjoy, 1977, Investment performance of common stocks in relation to their price-earnings ratios: A test of the efficient market hypothesis, *Journal of Finance* 32, 663–682.

———, 1983, The relationship between earnings yield, market value, and return for NYSE common stocks: Further evidence, *Journal of Financial Economics* 12, 129–156.

Beebower, Gilbert L. and Gary L. Bergstrom, 1977, A performance analysis of pension and profit-sharing portfolios: 1966–75, *Financial Analysts Journal* 33, (May/June), 31–42.

Berkowitz, Stephen A., Louis D. Finney, and Dennis E. Logue, 1988, *The Investment Performance of Corporate Pension Plans* (Quorum Books, New York, NY).

Bernard, Victor L. and Jacob K. Thomas, 1989, Post-earnings-announcement drift: Delayed price response or risk premium?, *Journal of Accounting Research* 27 (Supplement), 1–36.

—— and Jacob K. Thomas, 1990, Evidence that stock prices do not fully reflect the implications of current earnings for future earnings, *Journal of Accounting and Economics* 13, 305–340.

Bhandari, Laxmi Chand, 1988, Debt/Equity ratio and expected common stock returns: Empirical evidence, *Journal of Finance* 43, 507–528.

Binder, John J., 1985, Measuring the effects of regulation with stock price data, *Rand Journal of Economics* 16, 167–182.

Black, Fischer, 1972, Capital market equilibrium with restricted borrowing, *Journal of Business* 45, 444–455.

——, 1973, Yes Virginia, there is hope: Tests of the Value Line ranking system, *Financial Analysts Journal*, 29, 10–14.

——, 1986, Noise, *Journal of Finance* 41, 529–543.

——, Michael C. Jensen, and Myron Scholes, 1972, The capital asset pricing model: Some empirical tests, in M. Jensen, ed., *Studies in the Theory of Capital Markets* (Praeger, New York, NY).

Blume, Marshall E. and Irwin Friend, 1973, A new look at the capital asset pricing model, *Journal of Finance* 28, 19–33.

Bodie, Zvi, 1976, Common stocks as a hedge against inflation, *Journal of Finance* 31, 459–470.

Bradley, Michael, 1980, Interfirm tender offers and the market for corporate control, *Journal of Business* 53, 345–376.

Breeden, Douglas T., 1979, An intertemporal asset pricing model with stochastic consumption and investment opportunities, *Journal of Financial Economics* 7, 265–296.

——, Michael R. Gibbons, and Robert H. Litzenberger, 1989, Empirical tests of the consumption-oriented CAPM, *Journal of Finance* 44, 231–262.

Brinson, Gary P., L. Randolph Hood and Gilbert L. Beebower, 1986, Determinants of portfolio performance, *Financial Analysts Journal* 43, (July/August), 39–44.

Brown, Stephen J., and Jerold B. Warner, 1985, Using daily stock returns: The case of event studies, *Journal of Financial Economics* 14, 3–32.

Campbell, John Y., 1987, Stock returns and the term structure, *Journal of Financial Economics* 18, 373–399.

—— and Robert Shiller, 1988a, The dividend-price ratio and expectations of future dividends and discount factors, *Review of Financial Studies* 1, 195–228.

—— and Robert Shiller, 1988b, Stock prices, earnings and expected dividends, *Journal of Finance* 43, 661–676.

Cechetti, Stephen G., Pok-Sang Lam, and Nelson C. Mark, 1990, Mean reversion in equilibrium asset prices, *American Economic Review* 80, 398–418.

Chan, K. C., 1988, On the contrarian investment strategy, *Journal of Business* 61, 147–163.

—— and Nai-fu Chen, 1988, An unconditional asset-pricing test and the role of firm size as an instrumental variable for risk, *Journal of Finance* 43, 309–325.

—— and Nai-fu Chen, 1991, Structural and return characteristics of small and large firms, *Journal of Finance* 46, 1467–1484.

——, Nai-fu Chen, and David A. Hsieh, 1985, An exploratory investigation of the firm size effect, *Journal of Financial Economics* 14, 451–471.

Chan, Louis K. C., Yasushi Hamao, and Josef Lakonishok, 1991, Fundamentals and stock returns in Japan, *Journal of Finance* 46, 1739–1764.

Chang, Eric C. and Wilbur G. Lewellen, 1984, Market timing and mutual fund investment performance, *Journal of Business* 57, 57–72.

Charest, Guy, 1978, Dividend information, stock returns, and market efficiency—II, *Journal of Financial Economics* 6, 297–330.

Chen, Nai-fu, 1983, Some empirical tests of the theory of arbitrage pricing, *Journal of Finance* 38, 1393–1414.

——, 1991, Financial investment opportunities and the macroeconomy, *Journal of Finance* 46, 529–554.

——, Richard Roll, and Stephen A. Ross, 1986, Economic forces and the stock market, *Journal of Business* 56, 383–403.

Cochrane, John H., 1991, Volatility tests and efficient markets: A review essay, *Journal of Monetary Economics* 27, 463–485.

Connolly, Robert A., 1989, An examination of the robustness of the weekend effect, *Journal of Financial and Quantitative Analysis* 24, 133–169.

Conrad, Jennifer, and Gautam Kaul, 1988, Time-variation in expected returns, *Journal of Business* 61, 409–425.

Constantinides, George M., 1989, Theory of valuation: Overview and recent developments, in S. Bhattacharya and G. Constantinides, eds., *Theory of Valuation* (Roman and Littlefield, City).

——, 1990, Habit formation: A resolution of the equity premium puzzle, *Journal of Political Economy* 98, 519–543.

Conway, Delores A. and Marc R. Reinganum, 1988, Stable factors in security returns: Identification using cross-validation, *Journal of Business and Economic Statistics* 6, 1–15.

Copeland, Thomas E. and David Mayers, 1982, The value line enigma: A case study of performance evaluation issues, *Journal of Financial Economics* 10, 289–321.

Cornell, Bradford, 1981, The consumption based asset pricing model: A note on potential tests and applications, *Journal of Financial Economics* 9, 103–108.

Cox, John C., Jonathan E. Ingersoll, and Stephen A. Ross, 1985, An intertemporal general equilibrium model of asset prices, *Econometrica* 53, 363–384.

Cross, Frank, 1973, The behavior of stock prices on Fridays and Mondays, *Financial Analysts Journal* 29 (November/December), 67–69.

Dann, Larry V., 1981, Common stock repurchases: An analysis of returns to bondholders and stockholders, *Journal of Financial Economics* 9, 113–38.

DeBondt, Werner F. M., and Thaler, Richard H., 1985, Does the stock market overreact, *Journal of Finance* 40, 793–805.

——— and Thaler, Richard H., 1987, Further evidence on investor overreaction and stock market seasonality, *Journal of Finance* 42, 557–581.

Dodd, Peter, 1980, Merger proposals, management discretion and stockholder wealth, Journal of Financial Economics 8, 105–137.

——— and Richard S. Ruback, 1977, Tender offers and stockholder returns: An empirical analysis, *Journal of Financial Economics* 5, 351–374.

——— and Jerold B. Warner, 1983, On corporate governance: A study of proxy contests, *Journal of Financial Economics* 11, 401–438.

Dhrymes, Phoebus J., Irwin Friend, Mustafa N. Gultekin, and N. Bulent Gultekin, 1984, New tests of the APT and their implications, *Journal of Finance* 40, 659–674.

———, Irwin Friend, and N. Bulent Gultekin, 1985, A critical reexamination of the empirical evidence on the arbitrage pricing theory, *Journal of Finance* 39, 323–346.

Easterbrook, Frank, H., 1984, Two agency-cost explanations of dividends, *American Economic Review* 74, 650–659.

Elton, Edwin J., Martin J. Gruber, Sanjiv Das, and Matt Hklarka, 1991, Efficiency with costly information: A reinterpretation of evidence from managed portfolios, Unpublished manuscript, New York University.

Fama, Eugene F., 1965, The Behavior of Stock Market Prices, *Journal of Business* 38, 34–105.

———, 1970a, Multiperiod consumption-investment decisions, *American Economic Review* 60, 163–174.

———, 1970b, Efficient capital markets: A review of theory and empirical work, *Journal of Finance* 25, 383–417.

———, 1976a, Forward rates as predictors of future spot rates, *Journal of Financial Economics* 3, 361–377.

———, 1976b, Inflation uncertainty and expected returns on Treasury bills, *Journal of Political Economy* 84, 427–448.

———, 1981, Stock returns, real activity, inflation, and money, *American Economic Review* 71, 545–565.

———, Lawrence Fisher, Michael C. Jensen, and Richard Roll, 1969, The adjustment of stock prices to new information, *International Economic Review* 10, 1–21.

——— and Kenneth R. French, 1988a, Permanent and temporary components of stock prices, *Journal of Political Economy* 96, 246–273.

——— and Kenneth R. French, 1988b, Dividend yields and expected stock returns, *Journal of Financial Economics* 22, 3–25.

——— and Kenneth R. French, 1989, Business conditions and expected returns on stocks and bonds, *Journal of Financial Economics* 25, 23–49.

———a nd Kenneth R. French, 1991, The cross section of expected stock returns, Unpublished manuscript, Graduate School of Business, University of Chicago.

——— and James MacBeth, 1973, Risk, return and equilibrium: Empirical tests, *Journal of Political Economy* 81, 607–636.

——— and G. William Schwert, 1977, Asset returns and inflation, *Journal of Financial Economics* 5, 115–146.

Ferson, Wayne E. and Campbell R. Harvey, 1991, The variation of economic risk premiums, *Journal of Political Economy* 99, 385–415.

Fisher, Lawrence, 1966, Some new stock-market indexes, *Journal of Business* 39, 191–225.

Franks, Julian, Robert S. Harris, and Sheridan Titman, 1991, The postmerger share price performance of acquiring firms, *Journal of Financial Economics,* 29, 81–96.

French, Kenneth R., 1980, Stock returns and the weekend effect, *Journal of Financial Economics* 8, 55–69.

——— and Richard Roll, 1986, Stock return variances: The arrival of information and the reaction of traders, *Journal of Financial Economics* 17, 5–26.

Friedman, Milton, 1957, *A Theory of the Consumption Function* (Princeton University Press, Princeton, NJ).

Gibbons, Michael R., and Patrick Hess, 1981, Day of the week effects and asset returns, *Journal of Business* 54, 3–27.

Grinblatt, Mark, and Sheridan Titman, 1989, Mutual fund performance: An analysis of quarterly portfolio holdings, *Journal of Business* 62, 393–416.

Grossman, Sanford J., and Robert J. Shiller, 1981, The determinants of the variability of stock market prices, *American Economic Review* 71, 222–227.

——— and Joseph E. Stiglitz, 1980, On the impossibility of informationally efficient markets, *American Economic Review* 70, 393–408.

Hansen, Lars P., 1982, Large sample properties of generalized method of moments estimators, *Econometrica* 50, 1029–1054.

——— and Kenneth J. Singleton, 1982, Generalized instrumental variables estimation in nonlinear rational expectations models, *Econometrica* 50, 1269–1286.

——— and Kenneth J. Singleton, 1983, Stochastic consumption, risk aversion, and the temporal behavior of asset returns, *Journal of Political Economy* 91, 249–265.

Harris, Lawrence, 1986, A transaction data study of weekly and intradaily patterns in stock returns, *Journal of Financial Economics* 16, 99–117.

Harvey, Campbell R., 1991, The world price of covariance risk, *Journal of Finance* 46, 111–157.

Henriksson, Roy T., 1984, Market timing and mutual fund performance: An empirical investigation, *Journal of Business* 57, 73–96.

Hodrick, Robert J., 1990, Dividend yields and expected stock returns: Alternative procedures for inference and measurement, Unpublished manuscript, Northwestern University, and National Bureau of Economic Research.

Huberman, Gur and Shmuel Kandel, 1987, Value Line rank and firm size, *Journal of Business* 60, 577–589.

—— and Shmuel Kandel, 1990, Market efficiency and Value Line's record, *Journal of Business* 63, 187–216.

Hulbert, Mark, 1990, Proof of pudding, *Forbes*, (December 10), 316.

Ippolito, Richard A., 1989, Efficiency with costly information: A study of mutual fund performance, 1965–84, *Quarterly Journal of Economics* 104, 1–23.

——a nd John A. Turner, 1987, Turnover, fees and pension plan performance, *Financial Analysts Journal* 43 (November/December), 16–26.

Jaffe, Jeffrey F., 1974, Special information and insider trading, *Journal of Business* 47, 410–428.

—— and Gershon Mandelker, 1976, The "Fisher effect" for risky assets: An empirical investigation, *Journal of Finance* 31, 447–458.

Jegadeesh, Narasimhan, 1990, Evidence of predictable behavior of security returns, *Journal of Finance* 45, 881–898.

Jensen, Michael C., 1968, The performance of mutual funds in the period 1945–64, *Journal of Finance* 23, 389–416.

——, 1969, Risk, the pricing of capital assets, and the evaluation of investment portfolios, *Journal of Business* 42, 167–247.

——, 1978, Some anomalous evidence regarding market efficiency, *Journal of Financial Economics* 6, 95–101.

——, 1986, The agency costs of free cash flows, corporate finance and takeovers, *American Economic Review* 76, 323–329.

—— Richard S. Ruback, 1983, The market for corporate control: The scientific evidence, *Journal of Financial Economics* 11, 5–50.

—— and Jerold B. Warner, 1988, The distribution of power among corporate managers, shareholders, and directors, *Journal of Financial Economics* 20, 3–24.

Kandel, Shmuel and Robert F. Stambaugh, 1990, Expectations and volatility of consumption and asset returns, *Review of Financial Studies* 3, 207–232.

Kaplan, Steven, 1989, The effect of management buyouts on operating performance and value, *Journal of Financial Economics* 24, 217–254.

Keim, Donald B., 1983, Size-related anomalies and stock return seasonality, *Journal of Financial Economics* 12, 13–32.

——, 1988, Stock market regularities: A synthesis of the evidence and explanations, in *Stock Market Anomalies,* Elroy Dimson, (Cambridge University Press, Cambridge, UK).

——, 1989, Trading patterns, bid-ask spreads, and estimated security returns: The case of common stocks at calendar turning points, *Journal of Financial Economics* 25, 75–97.

—— and Robert F. Stambaugh, 1986, Predicting returns in the stock and bond markets, *Journal of Financial Economics* 17, 357–390.

Kleidon, Allan W., 1988, Bubbles, fads and stock price volatility tests: A partial evaluation: Discussion, *Journal of Finance* 43, 656–659.

Lakonishok, Josef and Seymour Smidt, 1988, Are seasonal anomalies real?: A ninety year perspective, *Review of Financial Studies* 1, 435–455.

—— and Edwin Maberly, 1990, The weekend effect: Trading patterns of individual and institutional investors, *Journal of Finance* 45, 231–243.

—— and Alan C. Shapiro, 1986, Systematic risk, total risk and size as determinants of stock market returns, *Journal of Banking and Finance* 10, 115–132.

Lehmann, Bruce N., 1990, Fads, martingales, and market efficiency, *Quarterly Journal of Economics* 105, 1–28.

—— and David M. Modest, 1988, The empirical foundations of the arbitrage pricing theory, *Journal of Financial Economics* 21, 213–254.

LeRoy, Stephen F., 1989, Efficient capital markets and martingales, *Journal of Economic Literature* 27, 1583–1621.

—— and Richard D. Porter, 1981, The present-value relation: Tests based on implied variance bounds, *Econometrica* 49, 555–574.

Lintner, John, 1965, The valuation of risk assets and the selection of risky investments in stock portfolios and capital budgets, *Review of Economics and Statistics* 47, 13–37.

Liu, Pu, Stanley D. Smith, and Azmat A. Syed, 1990, Security price reaction to the Wall Street Journal's securities recommendations, *Journal of Financial and Quantitative Analysis* 25, 399–410.

Lloyd-Davies, Peter and Michael Canes, 1978, Stock prices and the publication of second-hand information, *Journal of Business* 51, 43–56.

Lo, Andrew W. and A. Craig MacKinlay, 1988, Stock market prices do not follow random walks: Evidence from a simple specification test, *Review of Financial Studies* 1, 41–66.

—— and A. Craig MacKinlay, 1990, When are contrarian profits due to stock market overreaction?, *Review of Financial Studies* 3, 175–205.

Lucas, Robert E., 1978, Asset prices in an exchange economy, *Econometrica* 46, 1429–1445.

Mandelker, Gershon, 1974, Risk and return: The case of merging firms, *Journal of Financial Economics* 1, 303–336.

Mankiw, N. Gregory and Matthew D. Shapiro, 1986, Risk and return: Consumption beta versus market beta, *Review and Economics and Statistics* 48, 452–459.

Markowitz, Harry, 1959, *Portfolio Selection: Efficient Diversification of Investments* (Wiley, New York, NY).

Masulis, Ronald W. and Ashok W. Korwar, 1986, Seasoned equity offerings: an empirical investigation, *Journal of Financial Economics* 15, 91–118.

Mehra, Rajnesh and Edward C. Prescott, 1985, The equity premium: A puzzle, *Journal of Monetary Economics* 15, 145–161.

Merton, Robert C., 1973, An intertemporal capital asset pricing model, *Econometrica* 41, 867–887.

Merton, Robert C., 1987, On the current state of the stock market rationality hypothesis, in *Macroeconomics and Finance: Essays in Honor of Franco Modigliani,* Rudiger

Dornbusch, Stanley Fischer, and John Bossons, eds. (MIT Press, Cambridge, MA), 93–124.

Miller, Merton H., and Franco Modigliani, 1961, Dividend policy, growth, and the valuation of shares, *Journal of Business* 34, 411–433.

—— and Myron Scholes, 1978, Dividends and taxes, *Journal of Financial Economics* 6, 333–364.

—— and Kevin Rock, 1985, Dividend policy under asymmetric information, *Journal of Finance* 40, 1031–1052.

Mitchell, Mark L. and Kenneth Lehn, 1990, Do bad bidders become good targets?, *Journal of Political Economy* 98, 372–398.

Modigliani, Franco and Richard Brumberg, 1955, Utility analysis and the consumption function, in K. Kurihara, ed., *Post Keynesian Economics,* (G. Allen, London).

Munnell, Alicia H., 1983, Who should manage the assets of collectively bargained pension plans?, *New England Economic Review* (July/August), 18–30.

Myers, Stewart C. and Nicholas S. Majluf, 1984, Corporate financing and investment decisions when firms have information that investors do not have, *Journal of Financial Economics* 13, 187–221.

Neiderhoffer, Victor and M. F. M. Osborne, 1966, Market making and reversal on the stock exchange, *Journal of the American Statistical Association* 61, 897–916.

Nelson, Charles R., 1976, Inflation and Rates of return on common stocks, *Journal of Finance* 31, 471–483.

—— and Myung J. Kim, 1990, Predictable stock returns: Reality or statistical illusion, Unpublished manuscript, Department of Economics, University of Washington.

Poterba, James and Lawrence Summers, 1988, Mean reversion in stock prices: Evidence and implications, *Journal of Financial Economics* 22, 27–59.

Reinganum, Marc R., 1981, Misspecification of capital asset pricing: Empirical anomalies based on earnings yields and market values, *Journal of Financial Economics* 12, 89–104.

——, 1983, The anomalous stock market behavior of small firms in January, *Journal of Financial Economics* 12, 89–104.

Ritter, Jay R., 1988, The buying and selling behavior of individual investors at the turn of the year, *Journal of Finance* 43, 701–717.

Roll, Richard, 1977, A critique of the asset pricing theory's tests' Part I: On past and potential testability of the theory, *Journal of Financial Economics* 4, 129–176.

——, 1983, Vas ist Das? The turn-of-the-year effect and the return premia of small firms, *Journal of Portfolio Management* 9, 18–28.

——, 1984, A simple implicit measure of the bid/ask spread in an efficient market, *Journal of Finance* 39, 1127–1139.

—— 1986, The hubris hypothesis of corporate takeovers, *Journal of Business* 59, 197–216.

—— and Stephen A. Ross, 1980, An empirical investigation of the arbitrage pricing theory, *Journal of Finance* 35, 1073–1103.

——— and Stephen A. Ross, 1984, A critical reexamination of the empirical evidence on the arbitrage pricing theory: A reply, *Journal of Finance* 39, 347–350.

Ross, Stephen A., 1976, The arbitrage theory of capital asset pricing, *Journal of Economic Theory* 13, 341–360.

Rozeff, Michael, 1984, Dividend yields are equity risk premiums, *Journal of Portfolio Management* 11, 68–75.

Rubinstein, Mark, 1976, The valuation of uncertain income streams and the pricing of options, *Bell Journal of Economics and Management Science* 7, 407–425.

Santomero, Anthony, 1991, Money supply announcements: A retrospective, *Journal of Economics and Business* 43, 1–23.

Scholes, Myron, 1972, The market for securities: Substitution versus price pressure and the effects of information on share prices, *Journal of Business* 45, 179–211.

Seyhun, H. Nejat, 1986, Insiders' profits, costs of trading, and market efficiency, *Journal of Financial Economics* 16, 189–212.

Shanken, Jay, 1982, The arbitrage pricing theory: Is it testable, *Journal of Finance* 37, 1129–1140.

——— and Mark I. Weinstein, 1990, Macroeconomic variables and asset pricing: Estimation and tests, Unpublished manuscript.

Sharpe, William F., 1964, Capital asset prices: A theory of market equilibrium under conditions of risk, *Journal of Finance* 19, 425–442.

———, 1966, Mutual fund performance, *Journal of Business* 39, 119–138.

Shiller, Robert J., 1979, The volatility of long-term interest rates and expectations models of the term structure, *Journal of Political Economy* 87, 1190–1219.

———, 1981, Do Stock prices move too much to be justified by subsequent changes in dividends? *American Economic Review* 71, 421–436.

———, 1984, Stock prices and social dynamics, *Brookings Papers on Economic Activity* 2, 457–510.

Smith, Clifford W. Jr., 1986, Investment banking and the capital acquisition process, *Journal of Financial Economics* 15, 3–29.

Stambaugh, Robert F., 1982, On the exclusion of assets from tests of the two-parameter model: A sensitivity analysis, *Journal of Financial Economics* 10, 237–268.

———, 1986, Discussion, *Journal of Finance* 41, 601–602.

Stickel, Scott E., 1985, The effect of value line investment survey rank changes on common stock prices, *Journal of Financial Economics* 14, 121–144.

Summers, Lawrence H., 1986, Does the stock market rationally reflect fundamental values?, *Journal of Finance* 41, 591–601.

Trzcinka, Charles, 1986, On the number of factors in the arbitrage pricing model, *Journal of Finance* 41, 347–368.

Vermaelen, Theo, 1981, Common stock repurchases and market signalling: An empirical study, *Journal of Financial Economics* 9, 139–183.

West, Kenneth D., 1988, Bubbles, fads, and stock price volatility tests: A partial evaluation, *Journal of Finance* 43, 639–655.

Wheatley, Simon, 1988a, Some tests of the consumption-based asset pricing model, *Journal of Monetary Economics* 22, 193–215.

———, 1988b, Some tests of international equity integration, *Journal of Financial Economics* 21, 177–212.

Zarowin, Paul, 1989, Does the stock market overreact to corporate earnings information?, *Journal of Finance* 44, 1385–1399.

MARKET EFFICIENCY, LONG-TERM RETURNS, AND BEHAVIORAL FINANCE

. . .

Eugene F. Fama

1. INTRODUCTION

Event studies, introduced by Fama et al. (1969), produce useful evidence on how stock prices respond to information. Many studies focus on returns in a short window (a few days) around a cleanly dated event. An advantage of this approach is that because daily expected returns are close to zero, the model for expected returns does not have a big effect on inferences about abnormal returns.

The assumption in studies that focus on short return windows is that any lag in the response of prices to an event is short-lived. There is a developing literature that challenges this assumption, arguing instead that stock prices adjust slowly to information, so one must examine returns over long horizons to get a full view of market inefficiency.

If one accepts their stated conclusions, many of the recent studies on long-term returns suggest market inefficiency, specifically, long-term underreaction or overreaction to information. It is time, however, to ask whether this literature, viewed as a whole, suggests that efficiency should be discarded. My answer is a solid no, for two reasons.

First, an efficient market generates categories of events that individually suggest that prices over-react to information. But in an efficient market, apparent underreaction will be about as frequent as overreaction. If anomalies split randomly between underreaction and overreaction, they are consistent with market efficiency. We shall see that a roughly even split between apparent

Reprinted with permission from the *Journal of Financial Economics* 49 (September 1998): 283–306. © 1998 by Elsevier limited.

The comments of Brad Barber, David Hirshleifer, S.P. Kothari, Owen Lamont, Mark Mitchell, Hersh Shefrin, Robert Shiller, Rex Sinquefield, Richard Thaler, Theo Vermaelen, Robert Vishny, Ivo Welch, and a referee have been helpful. Kenneth French and Jay Ritter get special thanks.

overreaction and underreaction is a good description of the menu of existing anomalies.

Second, and more important, if the long-term return anomalies are so large they cannot be attributed to chance, then an even split between over- and underreaction is a pyrrhic victory for market efficiency. We shall find, however, that the long-term return anomalies are sensitive to methodology. They tend to become marginal or disappear when exposed to different models for expected (normal) returns or when different statistical approaches are used to measure them. Thus, even viewed one-by-one, most long-term return anomalies can reasonably be attributed to chance.

A problem in developing an overall perspective on long-term return studies is that they rarely test a specific alternative to market efficiency. Instead, the alternative hypothesis is vague, market inefficiency. This is unacceptable. Like all models, market efficiency (the hypothesis that prices fully reflect available information) is a faulty description of price formation. Following the standard scientific rule, however, market efficiency can only be replaced by a better specific model of price formation, itself potentially rejectable by empirical tests.

Any alternative model has a daunting task. It must specify biases in information processing that cause the same investors to under-react to some types of events and over-react to others. The alternative must also explain the range of observed results better than the simple market efficiency story; that is, the expected value of abnormal returns is zero, but chance generates deviations from zero (anomalies) in both directions.

Since the anomalies literature has not settled on a specific alternative to market efficiency, to get the ball rolling, I assume reasonable alternatives must choose between overreaction or underreaction. Using this perspective, Section 2 reviews existing studies, without questioning their inferences. My conclusion is that, viewed as a whole, the long-term return literature does not identify overreaction or underreaction as the dominant phenomenon. The random split predicted by market efficiency holds up rather well.

Two recent papers, Barberis et al. (1998) and Daniel et al. (1997), present behavioral models that accommodate overreaction and underreaction. To their credit, these models present rejectable hypotheses. Section 3 argues that, not surprisingly, the two behavioral models work well on the anomalies they are designed to explain. Other anomalies are, however, embarrassing. The problem is that both models predict post-event return reversals in response to long-term pre-event abnormal returns. In fact, post-event return continuation is about as frequent as reversal—a result that is more consistent with market efficiency than with the two behavioral models.

Section 4 examines the problems in drawing inferences about long-term returns. Foremost is an unavoidable bad-model problem. Market efficiency must be tested jointly with a model for expected (normal) returns, and all models show problems describing average returns. The bad-model problem is ubiquitous, but it is more serious in long-term returns. The reason is that bad-model errors in expected returns grow faster with the return horizon than the volatility of returns. Section 4 also argues that theoretical and statistical considerations alike suggest that formal inferences about long-term returns should be based on averages or sums of short-term abnormal returns (AARs or CARs) rather than the currently popular buy-and-hold abnormal returns (BHARs).

In categorizing studies on long-term returns, Sections 2 and 3 do not question their inferences. Dissection of individual studies takes place in Section 5. The bottom line is that the evidence against market efficiency from the long-term return studies is fragile. Reasonable changes in the approach used to measure abnormal returns typically suggest that apparent anomalies are methodological illusions.

2. OVERREACTION AND UNDERREACTION: AN OVERVIEW

One of the first papers on long-term return anomalies is DeBondt and Thaler (1985). They find that when stocks are ranked on three- to five-year past returns, past winners tend to be future losers, and vice versa. They attribute these long-term return reversals to investor overreaction. In forming expectations, investors give too much weight to the past performance of firms and too little to the fact that performance tends to mean-revert. DeBondt and Thaler seem to argue that overreaction to past information is a general prediction of the behavioral decision theory of Kahneman and Tversky (1982). Thus, one could take overreaction to be the prediction of a behavioral finance alternative to market efficiency. For the most part, however, the anomalies literature has not accepted the discipline of an alternative hypothesis.

An exception is Lakonishok et al. (1994). They argue that ratios involving stock prices proxy for past performance. Firms with high ratios of earnings to price (*E/P*), cashflow to price (*C/P*), and book-to-market equity (*BE/ME*) tend to have poor past earnings growth, and firms with low *E/P, C/P,* and *BE/ME* tend to have strong past earnings growth. Because the market over-reacts to past growth, it is surprised when earnings growth mean reverts. As a result, high *E/P, C/P,* and *BE/ME* stocks (poor past performers) have high future returns, and low *E/P, C/P,* and *BE/ME* stocks (strong past performers) have low future returns.

I also classify the poor long-term post-event returns of initial public offerings (IPOs) (Ritter, 1991; Loughran and Ritter, 1995) and seasoned equity offerings (SEOs) (Loughran and Ritter, 1995; Spiess and Affleck-Graves, 1995) in the overreaction camp. Mitchell and Stafford (1997) show that SEOs have strong stock returns in the three years prior to the issue. It seems safe to presume that these strong returns reflect strong earnings. It also seems safe to presume that IPOs have strong past earnings to display when going public. If the market does not understand that earnings growth tends to mean revert, stock prices at the time of the equity issue (IPO or SEO) are too high. If the market only gradually recognizes its mistakes, the overreaction to past earnings growth is corrected slowly in the future. Finally, Dharan and Ikenberry (1995) argue that the long-term negative post-listing abnormal stock returns of firms that newly list on the NYSE or Amex are due to overreaction. Firms list their stocks to take advantage of the market's overreaction to their recent strong performance.

If apparent overreaction was the general result in studies of long-term returns, market efficiency would be dead, replaced by the behavioral alternative of DeBondt and Thaler (1985). In fact, apparent underreaction is about as frequent. The granddaddy of underreaction events is the evidence that stock prices seem to respond to earnings for about a year after they are announced (Ball and Brown, 1968; Bernard and Thomas, 1990). More recent is the momentum effect identified by Jegadeesh and Titman (1993); stocks with high returns over the past year tend to have high returns over the following three to six months.

Other recent event studies also produce long-term post-event abnormal returns that suggest underreaction. Cusatis et al. (1993) find positive post-event abnormal returns for divesting firms and the firms they divest. They attribute the result to market underreaction to an enhanced probability that, after a spinoff, both the parent and the spinoff are likely to become merger targets, and the recipients of premiums. Desai and Jain (1997) and Ikenberry et al. (1996) find that firms that split their stock experience long-term positive abnormal returns both before and after the split. They attribute the post-split returns to market underreaction to the positive information signaled by a split. Lakonishok and Vermaelen (1990) find positive long-term post-event abnormal returns when firms tender for their stock. Ikenberry et al. (1995) observe similar results for open-market share repurchases. The story in both cases is that the market under-reacts to the positive signal in share repurchases about future performance. Finally, Michaely et al. (1995) find that stock prices seem to under-react to the negative information in dividend omissions and the positive information in initiations.

Some long-term return anomalies are difficult to classify. For example, Asquith (1983) and Agrawal et al. (1992) find negative long-term abnormal returns to acquiring firms following mergers. This might be attributed to market underreaction to a poor investment decision (Roll, 1986) or overreaction to the typically strong performance of acquiring firms in advance of mergers, documented in Mitchell and Stafford (1997). Ikenberry and Lakonishok (1993) find negative post-event abnormal returns for firms involved in proxy contests. One story is that stock prices under-react to the poor performance of these firms before the proxy contest, but another is that prices over-react to the information in a proxy that something is likely to change.

Given the ambiguities in classifying some anomalies, and given that the review above is surely incomplete, I shall not do a count of underreaction versus overreaction studies. The important point is that the literature does not lean cleanly toward either as the behavioral alternative to market efficiency. This is not lost on behavioral finance researchers who acknowledge the issue:

> We hope future research will help us understand why the market appears to overreact in some circumstances and underreact in others. (Michaely et al., 1995, p. 606).

The market efficiency hypothesis offers a simple answer to this question—chance. Specifically, the expected value of abnormal returns is zero, but chance generates apparent anomalies that split randomly between overreaction and underreaction.

Is the weight of the evidence on long-term return anomalies so overwhelming that market efficiency is not a viable working model even in the absence of an alternative that explains both under- and overreaction? My answer to this question is no, for three reasons.

First, I doubt that the literature presents a random sample of events. Splashy results get more attention, and this creates an incentive to find them. That dredging for anomalies is a rewarding occupation is suggested by the fact that the anomalies literature shows so little sensitivity to the alternative hypothesis problem. The same authors, viewing different events, are often content with overreaction or underreaction, and are willing to infer that both warrant rejecting market efficiency.

Second, some apparent anomalies may be generated by rational asset pricing. Fama and French (1996) find that the long-term return reversals of DeBondt and Thaler (1985) and the contrarian returns of Lakonishok et al. (1994) are captured by a multifactor asset pricing model. In a nutshell, return covariation among long-term losers seems to be associated with a risk premium that can explain why they have higher future average returns than long-term winners. Fama and French (1996) discuss the quarrels with their multifactor model, but their results suffice to illustrate an important point: Inferences about market efficiency can be sensitive to the assumed model for expected returns.

Finally, but most important, a roughly even split between overreaction and underreaction would not be much support for market efficiency if the long-term return anomalies are so large they cannot possibly be attributed to chance. Section 5 argues, however, that even viewed individually, most anomalies are shaky. They tend to disappear when reasonable alternative approaches are used to measure them.

3. BEHAVIORAL MODELS OF UNDERREACTION AND OVERREACTION

Before examining individual long-term return studies, I first consider two behavioral models, recently proposed by Barberis, Shleifer, and Vishny (BSV 1998) and Daniel, Hirshleifer, and Subramanyam (DHS 1997), to explain how the judgment biases of investors can produce overreaction to some events and underreaction to others.

The BSV model is motivated by evidence from cognitive psychology of two judgment biases. (i) The representativeness bias of Kahneman and Tversky (1982): People give too much weight to recent patterns in the data and too little to the properties of the population that generates the data. (ii) Conservatism, attributed to Edwards (1968): The slow updating of models in the face of new evidence.

In the model of stock prices proposed by BSV to capture the two judgment biases, earnings are a random walk, but investors falsely perceive that there are two earnings regimes. In regime A, which investors assume is more likely, earnings are mean-reverting. When investors decide regime A holds, a stock's price under-reacts to a change in earnings because investors mistakenly think the change is likely to be temporary. When this expectation is not confirmed by later earnings, stock prices show a delayed response to earlier earnings. In regime B, which investors think is less likely, a run of earnings changes of the same sign leads investors to perceive that a firm's earnings are trending. Once investors are convinced that the trending regime B holds, they incorrectly extrapolate the trend and the stock price over-reacts. Because earnings are a random walk, the overreaction is exposed by future earnings, leading to reversal of long-term returns.

Regime A in the BSV model is motivated by the evidence of short-term momentum in stock returns (Jegadeesh and Titman, 1993) and the evidence of delayed short-term responses of stock prices to earnings announcements (Ball and Brown, 1968; Bernard and Thomas, 1990). Regime B is meant to explain the long-term return reversals of DeBondt and Thaler (1985) and the returns to the contrarian investment strategies of Lakonishok et al. (1994). How does the model do on other anomalies?

The prediction of regime B is reversal of long-term abnormal returns. Specifically, persistent long-term pre-event returns are evidence of market over-reaction which should eventually be corrected in post-event returns. In addition to DeBondt and Thaler (1985) and Lakonishok et al. (1994), other events consistent with this prediction are seasoned equity offerings (Loughran and Ritter, 1995; Mitchell and Stafford, 1997), new exchange listings (Dharan and Ikenberry, 1995), and returns to acquiring firms in mergers (Asquith, 1983). All these events are characterized by positive long-term abnormal returns before the event and negative abnormal returns thereafter.

But long-term return reversal is not the norm. Events characterized by long-term post-event abnormal returns of the same sign as long-term pre-event returns include dividend initiations and omissions (Michaely et al., 1995), stock splits (Ikenberry et al., 1996; Desai and Jain, 1997), proxy contests (Ikenberry and Lakonishok, 1993), and spinoffs (Miles and Rosenfeld, 1983; Cusatis et al., 1993).

In short, and not surprisingly, the BSV model does well on the anomalies it was designed to explain. But its prediction of long-term return reversal does not capture the range of long-term results observed in the literature. On the whole, the long-term return literature seems more consistent with the market efficiency prediction that long-term return continuation and long-term return reversal are equally likely chance results.

The DHS model has different behavioral foundations than the BSV model. In DHS there are informed and uninformed investors. The uninformed are not subject to judgment biases. But stock prices are determined by the informed investors, and they are subject to two biases, overconfidence and biased self-attribution. Overconfidence leads them to exaggerate the precision of their private signals about a stock's value. Biased self-attribution causes them to downweight public signals about value, especially when the public signals contradict their private signals. Overreaction to private information and underreaction to public information tend to produce short-term continuation of stock returns but long-term reversals as public information eventually overwhelms the behavioral biases. Thus, though based on different behavioral premises, the DHS predictions are close to those of BSV, and the DHS model shares the empirical successes and failures of the BSV model. This last comment also applies to Hong and Stein (1997).

DHS make a special prediction about what they call selective events. These are events that occur to take advantage of the mispricing of a firm's stock. For example, managers announce a new stock issue when a firm's stock price is too high, or they repurchase shares when the stock price is too low. This public signal produces an immediate price reaction that absorbs some of the mispricing. But in the DHS model, the announcement period price response is incomplete because informed investors overweight their prior beliefs about the stock's value. (The conservatism bias of the BSV model would produce a similar result.) Eventually, the mispricing is fully absorbed as further public information confirms the information implied by the event announcement. The general prediction for selective events is thus momentum; stock returns after an event announcement will tend to have the same sign as the announcement period return.

Does the DHS prediction about selective events stand up to the data? Table 1 summarizes the signs of short-term announcement returns and long-term post-announcement returns for the major long-term return studies. Except for earnings announcements, all these events seem selective. As predicted by DHS, announcement and post-announcement returns have the same sign for SEOs, dividend initiations and omissions, share repurchases, stock splits, and spinoffs. But announcement and post-announcement returns have opposite signs for new exchange listings and proxy fights, and the negative post-event returns to acquiring firms in mergers are not preceded by negative announcement returns. Most embarrassing for the DHS prediction, the long-term negative post-event returns of IPOs (the premier long-term return anomaly) are preceded by positive returns for a few months following the event (Ibbotson, 1975; Ritter, 1991).

TABLE 1. Signs of long-term pre-event, announcement, and long-term post-event returns for various long-term return studies

Event	Long-term pre-event return	Announcement return	Long-term post-event return
Initial public offerings (IPOs) (Ibbotson, 1975; Loughran and Ritter, 1995)	Not available	+	−
Seasoned equity offerings (Loughran and Ritter, 1995)	+	−	−
Mergers (acquiring firm) (Asquith, 1983; Agrawal et al., 1992)	+	0	−
Dividend initiations (Michaely et al., 1995)	+	+	+
Dividend omissions (Michaely et al., 1995)	−	−	−
Earnings announcements (Ball and Brown, 1968; Bernard and Thomas, 1990)	Not available	+	+
New exchange listings (Dharan and Ikenberry, 1995)	+	+	−
Share repurchases (open market) (Ikenberry et al., 1995; Mitchell and Stafford, 1997)	0	+	+
Share repurchases (tenders) (Lakonishok and Vermaelen, 1990; Mitchell and Stafford, 1997)	0	+	+
Proxy fights (Ikenberry and Lakonishok, 1993)	−	+	− (or 0)
Stock splits (Dharan and Ikenberry, 1995; Ikenberry et al., 1996)	+	+	+
Spinoffs (Miles and Rosenfeld, 1983; Cusatis et al., 1993)	+	+	+ (or 0)

Finally, given the demonstrated ingenuity of the theory branch of finance, and given the long litany of apparent judgment biases unearthed by cognitive psychologists (DeBondt and Thaler, 1995), it is safe to predict that we will soon see a menu of behavioral models that can be mixed and matched to explain specific anomalies. My view is that any new model should be judged (as above) on how it explains the big picture. The question should be: Does the new model produce rejectable predictions that capture the menu of anomalies better than market efficiency? For existing behavioral models, my answer to this question (perhaps predictably) is an emphatic no.

The main task that remains is to examine the long-term return anomalies one at a time to see if they deliver on their claims. We set the stage with a discussion of some of the general problems that arise in tests on long-term returns.

4. DRAWING INFERENCES FROM LONG-TERM RETURNS

Fama (1970) emphasizes that market efficiency must be tested jointly with a model for expected (normal) returns. The problem is that all models for expected returns are incomplete descriptions of the systematic patterns in average returns during any sample period. As a result, tests of efficiency are always contaminated by a bad-model problem.

The bad-model problem is less serious in event studies that focus on short return windows (a few days) since daily expected returns are close to zero and so have little effect on estimates of unexpected (abnormal) returns. But the problem grows with the return horizon. A bad-model problem that produces a spurious abnormal average return of x% per month eventually becomes statistically reliable in cumulative monthly abnormal returns (CARs). The reason is that the mean of the CAR increases like N, the number of months summed, but the standard error of the CAR increases like $N^{1/2}$. In AARs (averages of monthly abnormal returns), the pricing error is constant at x%, but the standard error of the AAR decreases like $N^{-1/2}$. Bad-model problems are most acute with long-term buy-and-hold abnormal returns (BHARs), which compound (multiply) an expected-return model's problems in explaining short-term returns.

This section discusses various approaches that attempt to limit bad-model problems. It also discusses a related issue, the relevant return metric in tests on long-term returns. I argue that theoretical and statistical considerations alike suggest that CARs (or AARs) should be used, rather than BHARs.

4.1. Bad-Model Problems

Bad-model problems are of two types. First, any asset pricing model is just a model and so does not completely describe expected returns. For example, the CAPM of Sharpe (1964) and Lintner (1965) does not seem to describe expected returns on small stocks (Banz, 1981). If an event sample is tilted toward small stocks, risk adjustment with the CAPM can produce spurious abnormal returns. Second, even if there were a true model, any sample period produces systematic deviations from the model's predictions, that is, sample-specific patterns in average returns that are due to chance. If an event sample is tilted toward sample-specific patterns in average returns, a spurious anomaly can arise even with risk adjustment using the true asset pricing model.

One approach to limiting bad-model problems bypasses formal asset pricing models by using firm-specific models for expected returns. For example, the stock split study of Fama et al. (1969) uses the market model to measure abnormal returns. The intercept and slope from the regression of a stock's return on the market return, estimated outside the event period, are used to estimate the stock's expected returns conditional on market returns during the event period. Masulis's (1980) comparison period approach uses a stock's average return outside the event period as the estimate of its expected return during the event period.

Unlike formal asset pricing models, the market model and the comparison period approach produce firm-specific expected return estimates; that is, a stock's expected return is estimated without constraining the cross-section of expected returns. Thus, these approaches can be used to study the reaction of stock prices to firm-specific events (splits, earnings, etc.). But they cannot identify anomalies in the cross-section of average returns, like the size effect of Banz (1981), since such anomalies must be measured relative to predictions about the cross-section of average returns.

The hypothesis in studies that focus on long-term returns is that the adjustment of stock prices to an event may be spread over a long post-event period. For many events, long periods of unusual pre-event returns are common. Thus, the choice of a normal period to estimate a stock's expected return or its market model parameters is problematic. Perhaps because of this problem, event studies often control for expected returns with approaches that constrain the cross-section of expected returns. An advantage of these approaches is that they do not require out-of-sample parameter estimates. A disadvantage is that constraints on the cross-section of expected returns always produce imperfect descriptions of average returns, and so can lead to bad-model problems.

For example, one approach estimates an abnormal return as the difference between an event firm's return and the return on a non-event firm or portfolio that is similar on characteristics known to be related to average returns. The hope in this matching approach is to control for cross-firm variation in average returns due both to differences in expected returns and to chance sample-specific patterns in average returns. For example, following Banz' (1981) evidence that small stocks have higher average returns than predicted by the CAPM, an event stock's abnormal return is often estimated as the difference between its return and the return on non-event stocks matched to the event stock on size. Following the evidence of Fama and French (1992) that average stock returns are also related to book-to-market equity (*BE/ME*), it is now common to estimate abnormal returns by matching event stocks with non-event stocks similar in terms of size and *BE/ME*.

When we analyze individual event studies, we shall see that matching on size can produce much different abnormal returns than matching on size and *BE/ME*. And size and *BE/ME* surely do not capture all relevant cross-firm variation in average returns due to expected returns or sample-specific patterns in average returns. In short, the matching approach is not a panacea for bad-model problems in studies of long-term abnormal returns.

Another method of estimating abnormal returns is to use an asset pricing model to estimate expected returns. Early studies of long-term abnormal returns (Jaffe, 1974; Mandelker, 1974; Asquith, 1983) use the CAPM. Some recent studies use the three-factor model of Fama and French (1993). Like all asset pricing models, however, the CAPM and the Fama–French model are incomplete descriptions of average returns. The shortcomings of the CAPM are well known (Fama and French, 1992). Fama and French (1993) show that their three-factor model does not even provide a full explanation of average returns on portfolios formed on size and *BE/ME,* the dimensions of average returns that the model's risk factors are designed to capture.

In short, bad-model problems are unavoidable, and they are more serious in tests on long-term returns. When we review individual studies in Section 5, the tracks of the bad-model problem will be clear. Different models for expected returns produce different estimates of long-term abnormal returns. And a reasonable change of models often causes an anomaly to disappear. I argue that when this happens, the anomaly is not much evidence against market efficiency.

4.2. *The Return Metric*

Studies of long-term returns are also sensitive to the way the tests are done. Average monthly abnormal returns (AARs or CARs) can produce different inferences than buy-and-hold abnormal returns (BHARs). Equal-weight returns produce different results than value-weight returns. And failure to account for the cross-correlation of event firm returns during long post-event periods can affect inferences. These implementation issues are discussed next.

4.2.1. The Return Metric: Theoretical Issues

In principle, the model of market equilibrium jointly tested with market efficiency specifies the unit of time for returns. For example, if the model defines equilibrium in terms of monthly expected returns, average monthly returns should be the metric used to test market efficiency. To examine how prices respond over periods longer than a month, one can average (AARs) or sum (CARs) the average monthly abnormal returns. Beginning with Fama et al. (1969), AARs and CARs are a common approach to examining long-term returns.

A criticism of this approach is that an average monthly return does not accurately measure the return to an investor who holds a security for a long post-event period. Long-term investor experience is better captured by compounding short-term returns to obtain long-term buy-and-hold returns. Much of the recent literature tests buy-and-hold abnormal returns for periods up to five years after an event.

Investor experience is interesting, and long-term BHARs are thus interesting. But formal tests for abnormal returns should use the return metric called for by the model invoked to estimate expected (normal) returns. The problem, of course, is that discrete-time asset pricing models are silent on the relevant interval for expected returns. Nevertheless, there are at least three theoretical reasons to lean toward shorter intervals:

(i) Asset pricing models, like the Sharpe (1964)–Lintner (1965) CAPM and the discrete-time version of Merton's (1973) ICAPM, commonly assume normally distributed returns. Normality is a better approximation for short horizons like a month than for longer horizons, where skewness becomes increasingly important (Fama, 1976, 1996).

(ii) The empirical tests of asset pricing models, invoked to justify applying the models in tests of market efficiency, typically use monthly returns. I know of no tests of asset pricing models on five-year returns.

(iii) Mitchell and Stafford (1997) point out that BHARs can give false impressions of the speed of price adjustment to an event. The reason is that BHARs can grow with the return horizon even when there is no abnormal return after the first period. For example, suppose returns for the first year after the event are 10% for event firms and zero for benchmark firms, so the first-year abnormal return is 10%. Suppose event and benchmark firms both have a 100% buy-and-hold return over the next four years. Although there is no abnormal return after the first year, the BHAR after five years grows to 20% [i.e., $(1.1 \times 2.0) - (1.0 \times 2.0)$].

4.2.2. The Return Metric: Statistical Issues

AARs and CARs also pose fewer statistical problems than long-term BHARs. Barber and Lyon (1997) provide the most complete discussion of the inference problems in tests on long-term returns. [See also Kothari and Warner (1997).] Barber and Lyon favor BHARs, but their tests show that inferences are less problematic for average monthly returns (AARs or CARs). In a follow-up paper, Lyon et al. (1997) develop elaborate techniques for correcting some of the inference problems of BHARs. But they acknowledge that their improved methods for BHARs produce inferences no more reliable than simpler methods applied to monthly AARs or CARs. The reason is that average monthly returns avoid the problems (e.g., extreme skewness) produced by compounding monthly returns to get long-term BHARs.

Brav (1997) emphasizes that all existing methods for drawing inferences from BHARs, including those in Lyon et al. (1997), fail to correct fully for the correlation of returns across events not absorbed by the model used to adjust for expected returns. The problem is more severe in long-term BHARs because more firms have events within, say, a given five-year window than within a three-day window. Brav (1997) presents an elaborate scheme to adjust for the cross-correlation of long-term BHARs in special cases (e.g., when it is due to industry effects). But a full solution is not typically available because the number of return covariances to be estimated is greater than the number of time-series observations.

In contrast, if average monthly returns are used, there has long been a full solution to the cross-correlation problem. Suppose the post-event period of interest is five years. For each calendar month, calculate the abnormal return on each stock that had an event in the last five years. (Abnormal returns can be estimated in any reasonable way, for example, with a matching firm or matching portfolio approach, or with an asset pricing model.) Then average the abnormal returns for the calendar month across stocks to get the abnormal return for the month on the portfolio of stocks with an event in the last five years. Re-form the portfolio every month. The time-series variation of the monthly abnormal return on this portfolio accurately captures the effects of the correlation of returns across event stocks missed by the model for expected returns. The mean and variance of the time series of abnormal portfolio returns can be used to test the average monthly response of the prices of event stocks for five years following the event. The approach can also be refined to allow for heteroskedasticity of the portfolio's abnormal return due to changes through time in the composition of the portfolio. This rolling portfolio approach (with refinements) was first used by Jaffe (1974) and Mandelker (1974).

A referee suggests that the portfolio approach described above can cause an anomaly to be understated if events bunch in time because firms exploit pricing errors during windows of opportunity. For example, Loughran and Ritter (1995) suggest that IPOs bunch because particular industries tend to be overvalued at specific times. This criticism of the portfolio approach is valid if monthly abnormal portfolio returns are weighted equally in calculating an overall average monthly abnormal return. One solution to the problem is to adjust for heteroskedasticity. Specifically, following Jaffe (1974) and Mandelker (1974), divide the abnormal portfolio return for each month by an estimate of its standard deviation. The overall abnormal return is then estimated by averaging the standardized monthly abnormal returns. This approach is attractive because it weights each month's abnormal return by its statistical precision, which seems like the right way to capture the increased information due to event bunching. More generally, however, one can weight the portfolio abnormal return for a month in any way that captures the economic hypothesis of interest.

4.2.3. The Return Metric: Value Weights versus Equal Weights

In the review of individual studies that follows, we find that apparent anomalies in long-term post-event returns typically shrink a lot and often disappear when event firms are value-weighted rather than equal-weighted. One can argue that value-weight returns give the right perspective on an anomaly because they more accurately capture the total wealth effects experienced by investors. But I am more concerned about bad-model problems. All the common asset pricing models, including the Fama–French (1993) three-factor model, have systematic problems explaining the average returns on categories of small stocks. Since equal-weight portfolio returns give more weight to small stocks, bad-model problems are more severe in inferences from equal-weight returns.

Many readers suggest that more serious mispricing of small stocks is a general prediction of behavioral finance. It is thus worth noting that the two behavioral pricing models reviewed in Section 3 do not produce this prediction. In Barberis et al. (1998), pricing is dominated by a representative investor, and there is no prediction that the judgment biases of this investor are more severe for small stocks. In Daniel et al. (1997), pricing is dominated by informed investors subject to judgment biases. Uninformed investors have no such biases. Thus, if large stocks attract more interest from informed investors (e.g., security analysts), mispricing problems might be more severe for large stocks.

Most important, the cognitive psychology literature does not seem to say that different classes of people are more subject to judgment biases. The same biases that plague college students (the subjects of most cognitive psychology experiments) also occur among experts (see the references in Barberis et al.). Thus, cognitive psychology, the basis of behavioral finance, does not seem to provide a basis for the common presumption that small stocks are more likely to be mispriced.

5. THE RELIABILITY OF INDIVIDUAL STUDIES

The summary of long-term return studies in Sections 2 and 3 accepts the conclusions of the papers at face value. Now the gloves come off. Examining long-term return anomalies one at a time, I argue that most are fragile. Abnormal returns often disappear with reasonable changes in the way they are measured.

5.1. IPOs and SEOs

Among the more striking of the long-term return anomalies is the study of initial public offerings (IPOs) and seasoned equity offerings (SEOs) by Loughran and Ritter (1995). They find that the total wealth generated at the end of five years if one invests $1 in each IPO or SEO immediately following the event is about 70% of that produced by the same buy-and-hold strategy applied to a sample of stocks matched to the IPOs and SEOs on size.

IPOs and SEOs clearly have poor long-term returns during the Loughran–Ritter sample period (1970–1990). The interesting question is whether the returns are really abnormal or whether they are shared with non-event firms similar on characteristics related to average returns. During the Loughran–Ritter period, variables known to be related to average stock return include size and book-to-market equity (Fama and French, 1992), and short-term past return (Jegadeesh and Titman, 1993). Since the long-term buy-and-hold returns in Loughran and Ritter only control for size, their results might be affected by other variables that are systematically related to average return.

Following up on this possibility, Brav and Gompers (1997) compare five-year buy-and-hold returns on IPOs with the returns on portfolios that match the IPOs on size and book-to-market equity (*BE/ME*) but exclude SEOs as well as IPOs. The five-year wealth relative (the ratio of five-year buy-and-hold wealth for IPOs to five-year buy-and-hold wealth for the benchmarks) rises from about 0.7 with the Loughran–Ritter size benchmarks to a bit more than 1.0 (that is, the anomaly disappears) when the benchmarks control for *BE/ME* as well as size. Similarly, Brav et al. (1995) find that the five-year buy-and-hold returns on SEOs are close to those of non-event portfolios matched on size and *BE/ME*.

Brav (1997) and Mitchell and Stafford (1997) show that IPOs and SEOs are typically small growth stocks. Fama and French (1993) show that such stocks have low returns during the post-1963 period. The results of Brav and Gompers (1997) and Brav et al. (1995) then suggest that explaining the IPO-SEO anomaly reduces to explaining why small growth stocks in general have poor returns during the IPO-SEO sample period. In other words, if there is a mispricing problem, it is not special to IPO-SEO stocks.

Brav and Gompers (1997) and Brav et al. (1995) also find that when IPOs and SEOs are value-weighted, five-year abnormal buy-and-hold returns shrink a lot, whatever the benchmark. For IPOs, value-weight five-year wealth relatives are 0.86 or greater for all benchmarks, and four of six benchmarks produce wealth relatives in excess of 0.9. For SEOs, value-weight five-year wealth relatives are 0.88 or greater for all benchmarks; three of six are in excess of 0.98. The message is that many IPO and SEO stocks are tiny, and they are influential in the returns observed when sample firms are equal-weighted. This result is general. We shall see that apparent anomalies typically shrink a lot when viewed in terms of value-weight returns.

Loughran and Ritter (1995), Brav and Gompers (1997), and Brav et al. (1995) do not engage in the treacherous game of drawing statistical inferences from long-term buy-and-hold returns. Their inferences are based on average monthly returns. Every month they calculate the return on a portfolio that contains all firms with an IPO or SEO in the last five years. The three-factor model of Fama and French (FF 1993) is then used to estimate the portfolio's abnormal returns. The average monthly abnormal return during the five-year post-event period is the intercept, a_p, of the time-series regression

$$R_{pt} - R_{ft} = a_p + b_p[R_{Mt} - R_{ft}] + s_p \text{SMB} + h_p \text{HML} + \varepsilon_{pt}, \tag{1}$$

where R_{pt} is the monthly return on the IPO or SEO portfolio, R_{ft} is the one-month Treasury bill rate, R_{Mt} is the monthly return on a value-weight market portfolio of NYSE, Amex, and Nasdaq stocks, SMB is the difference between the returns on portfolios of small and big stocks (below or above the NYSE median), and HML is the difference between the returns on portfolios of high- and low-*BE/ME* stocks (above and below the 0.7 and 0.3 fractiles of *BE/ME*).

Brav et al. (1995) estimate the intercepts in (1) for equal- and value-weight portfolios of the SEOs of their 1975–92 sample period. The intercept for the equal-weight portfolio is −0.42% per month ($t = −4.8$), but the intercept for the value-weight portfolio is −0.14% per month ($t = −1.18$). Similarly, Brav and Gompers (1997) find that the intercepts for equal- and value-weight portfolios of IPOs that are not backed by venture capitalists are −0.52% ($t = −2.80$) and −0.29% ($t = −1.84$). For IPOs backed by venture capitalists, the intercepts are slightly positive. Loughran and Ritter (1995) only show re-gressions that combine IPOs and SEOs, but their results are similar: Equal-weight portfolios produce reliably negative intercepts, but abnormal returns for value-weight portfolios are economically and statistically close to zero.

Since inferences about abnormal returns from estimates of (1) on rolling post-event portfolio returns are common in the recent anomalies literature, it is important to note three potential problems.

First, since the firms in the event portfolio change through time, the true slopes on the risk factors in (1) are time-varying. Mitchell and Stafford (1997) confirm that for three important events (mergers, share repurchases, and SEOs), changes in the composition of the event portfolio generate substan-tial variation in the slopes in (1). For SEOs, they find that the intercepts for their 1960–93 period for equal- and value-weight portfolios drop from −0.38 ($t = 4.47$) and −0.14 ($t = −1.51$) in the constant slope regressions, to −0.24 ($t = −3.64$) and −0.07 ($t = −0.81$) in the regressions that allow the slopes to vary through time.

Second, the number of firms in the event portfolio changes through time, creating residual heteroskedasticity that can affect inferences about the inter-cept. [Solutions to this problem like those in Jaffe (1974) and Mandelker (1974) are apparently a lost technology.]

Third, but most important, Fama and French (1993) show that the three-factor model is not a perfect story for average returns. This bad-model problem can produce spurious anomalies in event studies. For example, IPOs and SEOs tend to be small, low-*BE/ME* firms. Fama and French (1993) show that the three-factor model overestimates average returns on such firms during the IPO-SEO sample periods. This bad-model problem can explain why estimates of (1) on equal-weight IPO and SEO portfolios produce reliably negative intercepts, but estimates on value-weight portfolios produce intercepts close to zero. It can also explain why the intercepts in (1), which control for loadings on risk factors related to size and *BE/ME,* suggest abnormal post-event returns for equal-weight IPO and SEO portfolios. But with direct benchmark matching on size and *BE/ME,* the abnormal returns largely disappear.

I emphasize, however, that the results for IPOs and SEOs do not imply that benchmark matching on size and *BE/ME* is always superior to estimating abnormal returns as the intercepts from (1). All methods for estimating abnormal returns are subject to bad-model problems, and no method is likely to minimize bad-model problems for all classes of events. The important general message from the IPO-SEO results is one of caution: Two approaches that seem closely related (both attempt to control for variation in average returns related to size and *BE/ME*) can produce much different estimates of long-term abnormal returns.

In sum, I read Brav and Gompers (1997) and Brav et al. (1995) as showing that the poor long-term buy-and-hold returns following IPOs and SEOs are not a special anomaly. The low returns are shared with other firms similar on two dimensions, size and *BE/ME,* known to be related to average return. Moreover, when IPOs and SEOs are value-weighted, abnormal returns shrink for all benchmarks, and they are not reliably different from zero. Thus, if there is an IPO-SEO anomaly, it seems to be largely restricted to tiny firms.

5.2. Mergers

Asquith (1983) and Agrawal et al. (1992) find negative abnormal returns for acquiring firms for up to five years following merger announcements. Using a comprehensive sample of mergers for 1960–93, Mitchell and Stafford (1997) also find negative long-term abnormal returns for acquiring firms. Since these studies produce similar results, I focus on Mitchell and Stafford (MS 1997).

MS find that the three-year post-event buy-and-hold return for equal-weighted acquiring firms is on average 4% lower than for portfolios matched to acquiring firms on size and *BE/ME.* In economic terms, this is not a dramatic anomaly. For formal inferences, MS estimate the three-factor model (1) on the monthly returns on a rolling portfolio that includes firms with acquisitions during the preceding three years. When the acquirers are equal-weighted, the intercept in Eq. (1), that is, the average monthly abnormal return for the three years after a merger, is −0.25% per month (−25 basis points, $t = -3.49$), which is larger than but roughly consistent with the BH returns. When acquiring firms are value-weighted, the intercept in Eq. (1) drops to −0.11% per month ($t = -1.55$). Thus, if there is an anomaly, it is more important for smaller acquiring firms. Finally, MS and Loughran and Vijh (1997) show that abnormal post-announcement average returns to acquiring firms are limited to mergers financed with stock, that is, mergers that are also SEOs. When mergers are financed without issuing stock, the negative abnormal post-event returns disappear. This suggests that there is no distinct merger anomaly. Any merger anomaly may be the SEO anomaly in disguise.

5.3. Stock Splits

Desai and Jain (1997) and Ikenberry et al. (1996) find that for the 17-year 1975–91 period, stock splits are followed by positive abnormal returns of about 7% in the year after the split. Abnormal returns are calculated relative to benchmarks that control for size, BE/ME, and, in Desai and Jain, past one-year return.

One way to test whether such an anomaly is real or the sample-specific result of chance is to examine a different sample period. Fama et al. (1969) examine splits during the 33-year 1927–59 period. They find no drift in cumulative abnormal returns during the 30 months following splits. Since the split anomaly fails the out-of-sample test provided by FFJR, it seems reasonable to conclude that the 1975–91 anomaly is not real, unless the market has recently become inefficient.

Desai and Jain (1997) and Ikenberry et al. (1996) do provide neat evidence on one of the pitfalls in using buy-and-hold abnormal returns to judge the long-term return drift associated with an event. As noted earlier, Mitchell and Stafford (1997) point out that BHARs are likely to grow with the return horizon even when there is no abnormal return after the first period. For the 1975–91 period, the abnormal return is about 7% for the first year following stock splits, but it is close to zero in the following two years (slightly negative in the second and slightly positive in the third). BHARs, however, rise from 7% to about 12% after three years.

One way to avoid the distorted perspective on long-term drift produced by BHARs is to examine ratios rather than differences of the cumulative wealths generated by event and benchmark firms, as in Ritter (1991) and Loughran and Ritter (1995). Another is the time-worn CAR approach of FFJR, which sums returns rather than compounding them, or the rolling portfolio average monthly abnormal return (AAR) approach of Jaffe (1974) and Mandelker (1974).

5.4. Self-Tenders and Share Repurchases

Lakonishok and Vermaelen (1990) examine long-term returns following self-tender offers (tenders by firms for their own shares) during the 1962–86 period. Ikenberry et al. (1995) examine long-term returns following share repurchases during the 1980–90 period. Mitchell and Stafford (1997) study both self-tenders and repurchases for the 1960–93 period. Since the MS results are similar to but more comprehensive than those in the earlier papers, the discussion focuses on them.

MS find that three-year post-event BHARs, computed relative to matching portfolios that control for size and *BE/ME*, are 9% for self-tenders (475 events) and 19% for the much larger sample of 2,542 repurchases. When they estimate the three-factor regression (1) for the monthly returns on an equal-weight portfolio that contains all self-tenders and repurchases in the last three years, however, the average abnormal monthly return is puny, 0.11% per month ($t = 1.62$). Any hint of significance, economic or statistical, disappears entirely when the stocks in the rolling portfolio are value-weighted. The intercept for the value-weight portfolio of self-tenders and repurchases is −0.03% (−3 basis points per month, $t = -0.34$). In short, viewed from the perspective of the three-factor model of Eq. (1), there is no share repurchase anomaly.

Note, once again, that two apparently similar methods for estimating abnormal returns, (i) a matching portfolio control for size and *BE/ME* and (ii) an asset pricing regression that adjusts for sensitivity to risk factors related to size and *BE/ME*, produce somewhat different results. This again illustrates that estimates of long-term abnormal returns can be sensitive to apparently small changes in technique.

5.5. Exchange Listings

Dharan and Ikenberry (1995) find that during the 1962–90 period, stocks that newly list on the NYSE, or move from Nasdaq to Amex, have negative post-listing abnormal returns. When returns are risk-adjusted using matching portfolios formed on size and *BE/ME*, the three-year average abnormal return is −7.02%. The *t*-statistic for this CAR is −2.78, but this is without a full adjustment for the correlation of abnormal returns across firms. Moreover, Dharan and Ikenberry show that the negative post-listing abnormal returns are limited to firms below the NYSE-Amex median in size. Thus, once again, an apparent anomaly is limited to small stocks.

Mitchell and Stafford (1997) offer concrete perspective on how significance levels can be overstated because of the failure to adjust for the correlation across firms of post-event abnormal returns. Using the three-factor model (1), they calculate the standard deviations of abnormal returns for portfolios of firms with an event during the most recent 36 months. The proportions vary somewhat through time and across their three event classes (mergers, share repurchases, and SEOs), but on average the covariances of event-firm abnormal returns account for about half the standard deviation of the event portfolio's abnormal return. Thus, if the covariances are ignored, the standard error of the abnormal portfolio return is too small by about 50%! This estimate need not apply intact to the exchange listings of Dharan and Ikenberry (1995), but it suggests that a full adjustment for the cross-correlation of post-listing abnormal returns could cause the statistical reliability ($t = -2.78$) of their -7.02% post-event three-year CAR to disappear.

Dharan and Ikenberry's explanation of their negative post-listing abnormal returns is that firms are opportunistic, and they list their stocks to take advantage of the market's overreaction to their recent good times. This explanation seems shaky, however, given that any overreaction to past performance has already occurred and will soon be reversed. Moreover, standard signaling theory (e.g., Ross, 1977) does not predict that firms will incur costs to make a false signal whose price effects are soon obliterated. On the contrary, since listing involves costs, it should be a signal that the firm is under-valued.

5.6. Dividend Initiations and Omissions

Michaely et al. (1995) find that during the 1964–88 period, firms that initiate dividends have positive abnormal stock returns for three years after the event, and firms omitting dividends have negative abnormal returns. For the same sample, Brav (1997) finds that the three-year post-event abnormal return following initiations disappears with benchmarks that control for size and *BE/ME*. Michaely et al. (1995) show that the negative three-year abnormal returns following omissions, confirmed by Brav (1997), are largely concentrated in the second half of their 1964–88 sample period. All this suggests that inferences about long-term returns following changes in dividends should probably await an out-of-sample test.

The finding that stock prices under-react to dividend announcements is suspect on other grounds. It seems reasonable that underreaction would occur because the market underestimates the information in dividends about future earnings. However, from Watts (1973) to Benartzi et al. (1997), there is little evidence that changes in dividends predict changes in earnings.

5.7. Spinoffs

Cusatis et al. (1993) study the post-event returns of spinoffs and their parents for the 1965–88 period. The benchmarks are firms matched to the event firms on size and industry, and abnormal returns are BHARs. Both parents and spinoffs have positive abnormal returns in the three years after the event. The abnormal returns are, however, limited to event firms (parents and spinoffs) acquired in mergers. The conclusion is that the market does not properly assess the increased probability of takeover (and the attendant buyout premiums) following spinoffs.

The t-statistics for the three-year BHARs for spinoffs range from 0.58 to 2.55, hardly overwhelming. Moreover, in calculating the t-statistics, the BHARs of the event firms are assumed to be independent. It would not take a large adjustment for cross-correlation to produce t-statistics that suggest no real anomaly.

5.8. Proxy Contests

Ikenberry and Lakonishok (1993) examine stock returns following proxy contests during the 1968–87 period. They find negative post-event abnormal returns relative to benchmarks that control for market β and size. In the results for all proxy contests, the post-event abnormal returns are not statistically reliable. The negative post-event returns are only statistically reliable for the 50-odd proxy contests in which the dissidents win board representation. Since this result is not an ex ante prediction, the weak evidence for the overall sample seems more relevant, and it does not suggest a reliable anomaly. This is more or less the conclusion of the authors.

5.9. Summary

If a reasonable change in the method of estimating abnormal returns causes an anomaly to disappear, the anomaly is on shaky footing, and it is reasonable to suggest that it is an illusion. Included in this category are IPOs, SEOs, self-tenders, share repurchases, and dividend initiations. Moreover, the doubts about these anomalies are the result of replication and robustness checks that followed publication of the original studies. Other anomalies will likely fall prey to the same process.

Other long-term return anomalies are economically or statistically marginal. The negative post-event abnormal returns to acquiring firms in mergers are economically small. For exchange listings, spinoffs, and proxy contests, a full correction for the cross-correlation of long-term post-event abnormal returns could easily reduce them to former anomalies.

Some anomalies do not stand up to out-of-sample replication. Foremost (in my mind) is the stock split anomaly observed after 1975, which is contradicted by the earlier FFJR study. The long-term negative post-event returns of dividend-omitting firms also seem sensitive to sample period.

Whenever value-weight returns are examined, apparent anomalies shrink a lot and typically become statistically unreliable. At a minimum, this suggests that anomalies are largely limited to small stocks. But a reasonable alternative explanation is that small stocks are just a sure source of bad-model problems. Small stocks always pose problems in tests of asset pricing models, so they are prime candidates for bad-model problems in tests of market efficiency on long-term returns.

Which anomalies are above suspicion? The post-earnings-announcement drift first reported by Ball and Brown (1968) has survived robustness checks, including extension to more recent data (Bernard and Thomas, 1990; Chan et al., 1996). Again, though, the anomaly is stronger for small stocks. The short-term continuation of returns documented by Jegadeesh and Titman (1993) is also an open puzzle, but it is still rather new and further tests are in order.

6. CONCLUSIONS

The recent finance literature seems to produce many long-term return anomalies. Subjected to scrutiny, however, the evidence does not suggest that market efficiency should be abandoned. Consistent with the market efficiency hypothesis that the anomalies are chance results, apparent overreaction of stock prices to information is about as common as underreaction. And post-event continuation of pre-event abnormal returns is about as frequent as post-event reversal. Most important, the long-term return anomalies are fragile. They tend to disappear with reasonable changes in the way they are measured.

REFERENCES

Agrawal, A., Jaffe, Mandelker, G., 1992. The post-merger performance of acquiring firms: a re-examination of an anomaly. Journal of Finance 47, 1605–1621.

Asquith, P., 1983. Merger bids, uncertainty and stockholder returns. Journal of Financial Economics 11, 51–83.

Ball, R., Brown, P., 1968. An empirical evaluation of accounting income numbers. Journal of Accounting Research 6, 159–178.

Banz, R., 1981. The relationship between return and market value of common stocks. Journal of Financial Economics 9, 3–18.

Barber, B., Lyon, J., 1997. Detecting long-horizon abnormal stock returns: the empirical power and specification of test statistics. Journal of Financial Economics 43, 341.

Barberis, N., Shleifer, A., Vishny, R., 1998. A model of investor sentiment. Journal of Financial Economics 49, 307–343 (this issue).

Benartzi, S., Michaely, R., Thaler, R., 1997. Do dividend changes signal the future or the past. Journal of Finance 52, 1007–1034.

Bernard, V., Thomas, J., 1990. Evidence that stock prices do not fully reflect the implications of current earnings for future earnings. Journal of Accounting and Economics 13, 305.

Brav, A., 1997. Inference in long-horizon event studies: a re-evaluation of the evidence. Unpublished working paper. Graduate School of Business, University of Chicago.

Brav, A., Gompers, P., 1997. Myth or reality? The long-run underperformance of initial public offerings: evidence from venture and nonventure capital-backed companies. Journal of Finance 52, 1791–1821.

Brav, A., Geczy, C., Gompers, P., 1995. The long-run underperformance of seasoned equity offerings revisited. Unpublished working paper. Graduate School of Business, University of Chicago.

Chan, L., Jegadeesh, N., Lakonishok, J., 1996. Momentum strategies. Journal of Finance 51, 1681–1713.

Cusatis, P., Miles, J., Woolridge, J., 1993. Restructuring through spinoffs. Journal of Financial Economics 33, 293–311.

Daniel, K., Hirshleifer, D., Subrahmanyam, A., 1997. A theory of overconfidence, self-attribution, and security market under- and over-reactions. Unpublished working paper. University of Michigan.

DeBondt, W., Thaler, R., 1985. Does the stock market overreact? Journal of Finance 40, 793–805.

DeBondt, W., Thaler, R., 1995. Financial decision-making in markets and firms: a behavioral perspective. In: Jarrow, R. et al. (Eds.), Handbooks in OR and MS, vol. 9, Elsevier, Amsterdam, pp. 385–410.

Desai, H., Jain, P., 1997. Long-run common stock returns following splits and reverse splits. Journal of Business 70, 409–433.

Dharan, B., Ikenberry, D., 1995. The long-run negative drift of post-listing stock returns. Journal of Finance 50, 1547–1574.

Edwards, W., 1968. Conservatism in human information processing. In: Kleinmutz, B. (Ed.), Formal Representation of Human Judgement. Wiley, New York.

Fama, E., 1970. Efficient capital markets: a review of theory and empirical work. Journal of Finance 25, 383–417.

Fama, E., 1976. Foundations of Finance. Basic Books, New York.

Fama, E., 1996. Discounting under uncertainty. Journal of Business 69, 415–428.

Fama, E., Fisher, L., Jensen, M., Roll, R., 1969. The adjustment of stock prices to new information. International Economic Review 10, 1–21.

Fama, E., French, K., 1992. The cross-section of expected stock returns. Journal of Finance 47, 427–465.

Fama, E., French, K., 1993. Common risk factors in the returns on stocks and bonds. Journal of Financial Economics 33, 3–56.

Fama, E., French, K., 1996. Multifactor explanations of asset pricing anomalies. Journal of Finance 51, 55–84.

Hong, H., Stein, J., 1997. A unified theory of underreaction, momentum trading, and overreaction in asset markets. Unpublished working paper. Sloan School of Management, Massachusetts Institute of Technology.

Ibbotson, R., 1975. Price performance of common stock new issues. Journal of Financial Economics 2, 235–272.

Ikenberry, D., Lakonishok, J., 1993. Corporate governance through the proxy contest: evidence and implications. Journal of Business 66, 405–435.

Ikenberry, D., Lakonishok, J., Vermaelen, T., 1995. Market underreaction to open market share repurchases. Journal of Financial Economics 39, 181–208.

Ikenberry, D., Rankine, G., Stice, E., 1996. What do stock splits really signal? Journal of Financial and Quantitative Analysis 31, 357–377.

Jaffe, J., 1974. Special information and insider trading. Journal of Business 47, 410–428.

Jegadeesh, N., Titman, S., 1993. Returns to buying winners and selling losers: implications for stock market efficiency. Journal of Finance 48, 65–91.

Kahneman, D., Tversky, A., 1982. Intuitive predictions: biases and corrective procedures. Reprinted in Kahneman, Slovic, and Tversky, Judgement under Uncertainty: Heuristics and Biases. Cambridge University Press, Cambridge, England.

Kothari, S., Warner, J., 1997. Measuring long-horizon security price performance. Journal of Financial Economics 43, 301–339.

Lakonishok, J., Shleifer, A., Vishny, R., 1994. Contrarian investment, extrapolation, and risk. Journal of Finance 49, 1541–1578.

Lakonishok, J., Vermaelen, T., 1990. Anomalous price behavior around repurchase tender offers. Journal of Finance 45, 455–477.

Lintner, J., 1965. The valuation of risk assets and the selection of risky investments in stock portfolios and capital budgets. Review of Economics and Statistics 47, 13–37.

Loughran, T., Ritter, J., 1995. The new issues puzzle. Journal of Finance 50, 23–51.

Loughran, T., Vijh, A., 1997. Do long-term shareholders benefit from corporate acquisitions? Journal of Finance 52, 1765–1790.

Lyon, J., Barber, B., Tsai, C., 1997. Improved methods for tests of long-run abnormal returns. Unpublished working paper. Graduate School of Management, University of California, Davis.

Mandelker, G., 1974. Risk and return: the case of merging firms. Journal of Financial Economics 1, 303.

Masulis, R., 1980. The effects of capital structure changes on security prices: a study of exchange offers. Journal of Financial Economics 8, 139–177.

Merton, R., 1973. An intertemporal capital asset pricing model. Econometrica 41, 867–887.

Michaely, R., Thaler, R., Womack, K., 1995. Price reactions to dividend initiations and omissions. Journal of Finance 50, 573–608.

Miles, J., Rosenfeld, J., 1983. The effect of voluntary spinoff announcements on shareholder wealth. Journal of Finance 38, 1597–1606.

Mitchell, M., Stafford, E., 1997. Managerial decisions and long-term stock price performance. Unpublished working paper. Graduate School of Business, University of Chicago.

Ritter, J., 1991. The long-term performance of initial public offerings. Journal of Finance 46, 3–27.

Roll, R., 1986. The hubris hypothesis of corporate takeovers. Journal of Business 59, 197–216.

Ross, S., 1977. The determinants of financial structure: the incentive signaling approach. Bell Journal of Economics 8, 23–40.

Sharpe, W., 1964. Capital asset prices: a theory of market equilibrium under conditions of risk. Journal of Finance 19, 425.

Spiess, D., Affleck-Graves, J., 1995. Underperformance in long-run stock returns following seasoned equity offerings. Journal of Financial Economics 38, 243–267.

Watts, R., 1973. The information content of dividends. Journal of Business 46, 191–211.

EFFICIENCY APPLIED

EVENT STUDIES AND SKILL

. . .

FAMA, FISHER, JENSEN, AND ROLL (1969)

RETROSPECTIVE COMMENTS

. . .

Ray Ball

INTRODUCTION

Fama, Fisher, Jensen, and Roll (1969), or FFJR as it is commonly abbreviated, is a seminal Gene Fama paper, even if somewhat upstaged by his other works. To modern researchers in empirical asset pricing, the Fama-French papers are the gold standard, and his early 1980s papers on corporate control laid the foundation for a considerable literature. As Bill Schwert and René Stulz document in this volume, twelve of his other papers are more highly cited. FFJR garners but 2.3% of his 140,562 total cites. Even among the papers containing Gene's conception and consistent advocacy of market efficiency, FFJR is ranked only sixth in Google citations.

Nevertheless, a strong case can be made that FFJR had a much larger impact on the literature and on practice than citation counts indicate. Why? Because *at the time the research was conducted, it was instrumental in reframing how we think about asset prices.* Its impact on thought was so fundamental and so pervasive that we now take that way of thinking—and the paper's contribution—for granted.

The paper was like none before it. Its contributions, listed in what I regard as increasing order of importance, include

1. documenting share price behavior around the time of splits;
2. implementing the first control for the market factor, hence creating the precursor to the influential Fama-French models;
3. conducting the first event study;
4. providing the first direct test of market efficiency; and
5. demonstrating the wisdom and validity of Fama's (1965) framing of stock price behavior in terms of information economics.

These are discussed further below, ending with what in my view is the paper's most important (and perhaps the least appreciated in hindsight) contribution:

demonstrating empirically that stock price changes can be described in economic (as distinct from statistical) terms and, more specifically, showing that price changes can be usefully modelled in terms of information arrival, as first proposed in Fama's (1965) seminal paper. While this might seem obvious in retrospect, it was completely novel at the time, and in the following sections I will outline the case that it irreversably changed how we think about asset prices.

BACKGROUND TO THE STUDY

The FFJR publication date is 1969, but the *International Economic Review* first received the manuscript on May 31, 1966, and the revised version arrived on October 3, 1966. Among the authors, Gene Fama needs no further introduction, except to note that in mid-1966 he was about to be promoted to associate professor at Chicago, just three years after joining the faculty and two years after receiving his doctorate. His coauthors were:

- Larry Fisher, who had joined the finance faculty in 1957 after graduating from the Economics Department at Chicago. He was Associate Director of the Center for Research in Security Prices (CRSP) from its creation in 1960, and he put together the CRSP file, which was the first comprehensive machine-readable archive of price and return data. It would be fair to say that he knew more about the data than any other person.[1]
- Mike Jensen, who was a doctoral student in finance and graduated in 1968. He subsequently pursued a distinguished career in finance, corporate governance, and strategy, and is best known for his pioneering work on agency relations with William H. Meckling.
- Richard Roll, who also was a doctoral student in finance who graduated in 1968. He too has a distinguished career in finance. Like Mike Jensen, he is a past president of the American Finance Association.

The Chicago research climate at the time was electric. New ideas poured out of economists the likes of Coase, Fogel, Friedman, and Stigler, all of whom subse-

---

1. As students taking Larry's doctoral class in 1967, we joked that writing software to download data from the CRSP file was unnecessary; Larry could simply recite all the numbers for you. A sense of Larry's meticulous scrutiny of the data can be gleaned from a talk he gave while the file was being completed, which is reproduced at http://www.crsp.com/50/images/fisher.pdf. James Lorie conceived the file and orchestrated its development, but Larry Fisher constructed it.

quently were awarded Nobel Prizes. Merton Miller, another subsequent Nobel Prize winner, had brought economic reasoning to finance through the Miller-Modigliani debt and dividend irrelevance theorems. All ideas were open to question. Research workshops were intense. The most common question one heard was "What is the evidence for that?" It was no accident that the CRSP file emanated from this research cauldron and that Gene's natural home was at Chicago.

The idea behind FFJR originated with James Lorie.[2] Miller and Modigliani (1961) had demonstrated that correctly priced firm values are independent of their dividend distribution policies. (If a firm pays less dividends, then the retained earnings become assets of the firm, and the stock price is larger exactly by the amount that the dividend is smaller. The value of the firm, including the dividend paid, is unchanged.) Yet there was ample anecdotal evidence that dividend changes are associated with value changes. They had proposed (p. 430) a reconciliation along the lines that dividend changes convey information about firm value. Lorie suggested an empirical verification of this conjecture using the recently created CRSP price file. As they say, the rest is history.

DOCUMENTING SHARE PRICE BEHAVIOR AROUND THE TIME OF SPLITS

At its most concrete level, FFJR is the first systematic, large-sample documentation of how prices behave around the time of stock splits. (In a stock split, the company exchanges one old share for, say, two new shares. If markets are efficient, the price of the new shares should be exactly half the price of the old shares. The split should have no effect on returns to investors, unless the decision to split reveals information to the market.) FFJR documented substantial excess returns starting well before splits, and particularly in the months immediately prior to the splits. By partitioning the sample based on whether the split-adjusted dividend payout increased around the time of the splits, they were able to confirm the Miller-Modigliani conjecture that information about firm value was being released. They reported evidence that the price reaction to the split was essentially completed by the event date, consistent with market efficiency. By any standards, being the first to investigate splits this systematically would be a marvelous contribution in its own right. But that is just the beginning.

2. FFJR acknowledged this in their first footnote. Lorie was the director of (and the person who conceived of) CRSP.

IMPLEMENTING THE FIRST CONTROL
FOR THE MARKET FACTOR

I believe FFJR is the first research to control for the market factor when investigating asset pricing.[3] (FFJR wanted to check that the stock price movement around a split was not just due to the movement of the market as a whole.) In that sense, it was the precursor to the Fama-French multifactor models that are commonly used to this day. This is another dimension on which FFJR was like no other paper before it.

CONDUCTING THE FIRST EVENT STUDY

Many people would view conducting the first ever event study, as they later became known, as FFJR's greatest contribution. (An "event study" measures the economics of an event such as a share split or corporate action by measuring the path of stock prices around that event.) It spawned a substantial literature not only in finance but also spanning accounting, antitrust, compensation, economics, marketing, M&A, and many other areas. Event studies are also used routinely in securities litigation cases and in some antitrust litigation. The cottage industry conducting event studies is so robust that there is a German fee-based system that automates them for you.[4] Initiating the event study research design is yet another remarkable and continuing contribution of FFJR.

Some sense of how profoundly the event study impacted research at the time can be gleaned from how it affected an area with which I am closely familiar: the relation between asset prices and financial accounting information. A paper that Philip Brown and I coauthored, "An Empirical Evaluation of Accounting Income Numbers" (1968), studied price behavior as a function of firms' annual earnings announcements. That paper overturned prior theories on the usefulness of accounting information, is viewed as having founded the modern empirical literature in accounting, and produced the first anomalous evidence in the literature of predictable abnormal returns. The research could

3. Around the same time, the doctoral dissertations of Mike Jensen, Richard Roll, and Myron Scholes at Chicago implemented market factor controls. They were completed in 1967 and 1968, so the May 31, 1966, journal submission date of FFJR suggests it came first.

4. See http://eventstudymetrics.com/. Much of the demand appears to come from student projects.

not have been conducted without FFJR preceding it.[5] Nor could have the many event studies and derivative research designs that since have proliferated in accounting, economics, finance, and other areas.

PROVIDING THE FIRST DIRECT TEST OF
EFFICIENT PRICING OF INFORMATION

As FFJR noted in their introduction, all previous evidence on market efficiency had shown that "successive price changes in individual common stocks are very nearly independent" (p. 1) and that, while consistent with efficient pricing, that evidence provided an only indirect test because it did not study information flows directly. They noted that "there has been very little actual testing of the speed of adjustment of prices to specific kinds of new information." They then designed and implemented such a test.

Subsequently, what had previously been known in academic and practitioner circles as the Random Walk Hypothesis (based on statistical properties of returns, and more specifically whether returns can be predicted from past returns) became replaced by "the efficient markets hypothesis" (based on speed of adjustment to information, and whether returns can be predicted from past information). This was a major step in the development of our knowledge of asset price behavior, as should become clear from the following section.

DEMONSTRATING THE WISDOM AND VALIDITY
OF FAMA'S (1965) FRAMING OF STOCK PRICE
BEHAVIOR IN TERMS OF INFORMATION

FFJR demonstrated in a clear and simple fashion that prices are a systematic function of information flows. Obvious as that may seem in hindsight, I can attest that in the late 1960s and early 1970s many finance and accounting academics first looked upon FFJR's Figure 2b (p. 13) with near disbelief.

Why was the FFJR evidence such a revelation at the time? One must cast one's mind back to the time and note two things: economists did not make studying the stock market a high priority, and information was seldom viewed as important in general discourse, and in economics and finance in particular.

---

5. Ball and Brown (1968) was the first event study to be published, but the research was conducted after FFJR had been submitted for publication in May of 1966. That FFJR preceded us is clear from our acknowledgement of it in the reference list and at various points in the paper (footnotes 4, 11, 16, and 26).

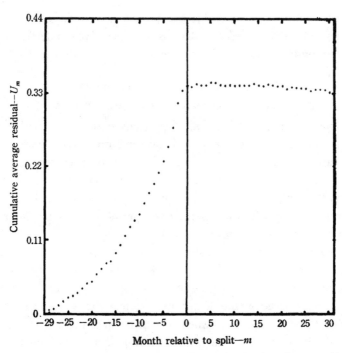

Figure 1. Cumulative average residuals—all splits (FFJR's Figure 2b)

That financial economists did not make studying the stock market a high priority is, if anything, an understatement. The term "financial economics" was unheard of. Some indication can be gleaned from Cootner's (1964) compilation of the important works of the day, in which only one of the 22 papers on the behaviour of prices had been published in the finance literature.[6] This is not surprising because economists had no empirically useful lens through which to view share price behavior. The general concept that price should be the expected present value of earnings was understood, though not with modern sophistication. But expectations could be anything, it seemed, so the proposition was not helpful. With no structure to add to a lay perspective, share price behavior appeared unfathomable to economists.

6. See Roberts (1959). Harry Roberts was a Chicago statistician whose influence on the research of his colleagues in finance was substantial (and was acknowledged in footnote 1 of FFJR).

Nor was information an important concept in economics generally. The Information Age generally is viewed as having commenced after the personal desktop computer became available in the late 1970s.[7] Some idea of the background against which FFJR arrived can be gleaned from the following:

- Computing was extraordinarily primitive and expensive by today's standards. The University of Chicago computer was an IBM 7094 with only 32 kilobytes of addressable memory, approximately one four-millionth of the memory of a current-generation 128 gigabyte Apple iPhone 6. It cost over $20 million at 2013 prices.[8] It operated in batch processing, so when you had a job running, you were the only person on campus who was computing.
- There were no word processors and no mass courier services. Letters were typed or written by hand and sent by mail.
- By today's standards, copying was time-consuming, low quality, and messy. The plain-paper, dry-process office photocopier had just been introduced by Haloid Xerox.
- There was no Internet and no e-mail. Interstate phone calls were very expensive and rare; international calls extremely so.

In economics, Hayek had published "The Use of Knowledge in Society" in 1945, arguing that the economy is too large and complicated for all the information about supply and demand to be gathered in a single place. While it later became viewed as a classic piece, the paper met with a poor reception among economists for decades, and even then was viewed as a critique of central planning and not as advocating greater attention to information by the economics profession.

In 1961 George Stigler had published another now-classic piece, "The Economics of Information," arguing that information can be considered an important economic good. The article commenced with the words, "One should hardly have to tell academicians that information is a valuable resource: knowledge is power. And yet it occupies a slum dwelling in the town of economics. Mostly it is ignored. . . ."

In financial practice, there was the tickertape, but no continuous coverage of financial markets on the web or on cable TV. Most investors learned about

7. See, for example, http://en.wikipedia.org/wiki/Information_Age.
8. See http://en.wikipedia.org/wiki/IBM_7090.

prices and information events from reading the local press, the *Wall Street Journal*, or *Barron's*. To finance academics, the CRSP file was the only electronically accessible and comprehensive historical account of asset prices, and it had only recently become available and was not widely used.

These facts give some appreciation of how novel it was at the time to view stock price behavior through the lens of response to information, something today's economists take as given.

Previous research on asset prices had modelled well-functioning asset markets in terms of the marketplace being a fair game and had tested the implication that successive price changes, like outcomes from the toss of unbiased dice, are independent. The early evidence was reasonably consistent with this prediction, and in the absence of an economic explanation the result was described (for approximately a decade) in statistical language as the "random walk hypothesis." (Alternatively, the term "Brownian motion" was adopted from physics.) Statistical dependence in security returns was interpreted as evidence of unexploited economic rents and as inconsistent with rational investor behavior in competitive markets—that is, as evidence of what later became known as "market inefficiency"—but the notion of information as an important economic good remained largely absent.[9]

Against this background, Fama (1965) made the conceptual breakthrough of framing stock prices as a function of information flows, and the efficient markets hypothesis was born. But the concept of market efficiency is only one implication of framing price behavior in terms of information. Notably, framing price behavior in this fashion paved the way for scholars such as Robert Shiller and Richard Thaler to apply theories of cognitive bias in information processing to asset markets, such as the prospect theory of Kahneman and Tversky (1979). Theories assuming both rational and irrational processing of information therefore possess a common heritage that emerged in the 1960s. Taken for granted now, framing price behavior in terms of responses to information was a crucial breakthrough in thinking that permeates modern financial economics.

To most people—in my experience, that included most academics in economics, finance, and accounting at the time FFJR was published—asset price behavior appears chaotic. That is because the lay perspective on the relation be-

---

9. In the introduction to his influential book of readings, *The Random Character of Stock Market Prices*, Cootner (1964, p. 2) presaged Fama's focus on prices and information but took it no further. The word "information" does not even appear in Samuelson's (1965) famous proof.

tween information and prices resides largely in calendar time. On a given calendar date, the lay person observes share prices changing in response to a large cross-section of heterogeneous information events, ranging from macro news of national and international political and economic events, to industry and competitor information, to firm-level news about products, prices, sales, technologies, factor costs, financing, governance, analyst forecasts, earnings announcements, and myriad other information events. From the lay perspective, it is difficult or impossible to see order in such complexity: on a given calendar date, prices are responding to a bewildering number of heterogeneous events, most of which no one person can ever observe, and therefore prices appear chaotic.

FFJR solved this problem neatly by inverting the lay perspective. Instead of observing the price response on a given calendar day to a cross-section of heterogeneous events, they observed the price response on a cross-section of calendar days to a given homogeneous event—in their case, the occurrence of a stock split.[10] And they observed order, not chaos.

This clever inversion is a key to many of Fama's insights in applying the idea of efficiency to the data. Rather than ask, "Why did Apple go up yesterday?" one asks, "How do stocks go up, on average, on days when companies announce a new product?" By averaging, we even out other pieces of information and focus on one. Rather than ask, "Why did Warren Buffet get so rich?" we ask, "How do all fund managers who follow a given strategy or use a given type of information do, averaging out the luck?" This idea is central to making "efficiency" a scientifically testable proposition, not an ex post story for price changes. That step is Gene's central contribution, and FFJR is one classic example.

However efficient or inefficient one believes asset markets to be, one cannot dispute that FFJR's Figure 2b (p. 13) irreversibly transformed our view of how asset prices behave. In the late 1960s and early 1970s many academics first looked upon FFJR's Figure 2b with near disbelief. Where they had previously seen unfathomable complexity, they now saw a seemingly orderly functional relation between prices and information.

POSTSCRIPT

By today's standards, the FFJR research design would not pass muster. They used monthly data, controlled only for a single market factor, collected event announcement dates for only a subsample of 52 of their 940 splits, and offered

---

10. This would not have been feasible without the CRSP file, which contained memory of the price response to past information events that no single person possessed.

no test statistics. A reader wishing to conduct an event study should emulate the refinements of more recent work. It would be churlish in the extreme to emphasize these issues, especially with the advantage of almost five decades of hindsight. That is how knowledge progresses: fresh insights, which are more obvious in retrospect than in prospect, are followed by researchers who add, modify, qualify, refine, and expand. FFJR shows us that the scarcest and most valuable insights are obtained from those who see them first, as Gene Fama has done so many times.

REFERENCES

Ball, Ray, and Philip Brown. 1968. "An Empirical Evaluation of Accounting Income Numbers." *Journal of Accounting Research* 6, 159–178.

Cootner, Paul H. 1964. *The Random Character of Stock Market Prices*. Cambridge: MIT Press.

Fama, Eugene F. 1965. "The Behavior of Stock-Market Prices." *Journal of Business* 38, 34–105.

Fama, Eugene F., Lawrence Fisher, Michael C. Jensen, and Richard Roll. 1969. "The Adjustment of Stock Prices to New Information." *International Economic Review* 10, 1–21.

Hayek, F.A. 1945. "The Use of Knowledge in Society." *American Economic Review* 35, 519–530.

Kahneman, D., and A. Tversky. 1979. "Prospect Theory: An Analysis of Decisions under Risk." *Econometrica* 47, 263–291.

Miller, Merton H., and Franco Modigliani. 1961. "Dividend Policy, Growth and the Valuation of Shares." *Journal of Business* 34, 411–433.

Roberts, Harry V. 1959. "Stock Market 'Patterns' and Financial Analysis: Methodological Suggestions." *Journal of Finance* 14, 1–10.

Samuelson, Paul A. 1965. "Proof that Properly Anticipated Prices Fluctuate Randomly." *Industrial Management Review* 6, 41–49.

Stigler, George J. 1961. "The Economics of Information." *Journal of Political Economy* 69, 213–225.

EUGENE FAMA AND INDUSTRIAL ORGANIZATION

· · ·

Dennis W. Carlton

It is a pleasure to write this short essay on Gene's contributions to the field of industrial organization because it is nice to honor a friend and brilliant scholar.

Readers may wonder what exactly is the link between Gene and industrial organization, since with the exception of his well-known work on the theory of the firm in the *Journal of Political Economy* (*JPE*) and *Journal of Law and Economics* (*JLE*), Gene is not mentioned as much as he should be in the industrial organization literature. The reason is that one of the techniques that Gene was instrumental in developing, the event study (Fama et al. 1969), is used so routinely without attribution in industrial organization that I suspect many industrial organization economists are unaware that Gene helped figure it out. If Gene were a young assistant professor awaiting a tenure decision or egotistical about number of cites, I am sure he would be greatly upset. However, that is not a description of Gene.

In this short essay, I cannot comprehensively review all the topics in industrial organization influenced by event studies, but let me hit just a few key ones, with apologies to the many authors whom I do not have space to mention. I end with a brief discussion of another area where Gene's work is likely to influence industrial organization: the risk characteristics of small value firms.

Merger policy is a fundamental topic in industrial organization. It is of practical as well as academic interest, as staffs of PhD economists at the FTC and Department of Justice routinely have to figure out which mergers to allow and which to challenge.

The recent Antitrust Modernization Commission was charged with analyzing whether merger policy in the United States should be changed. Event study literature about mergers was one of the key areas of academic research it examined.[1]

1. I was the sole economist on this 12 member congressional commission and was fortunate to convince Steven Kaplan to submit testimony in this area. His testimony (Kaplan 2006) provides an excellent summary that I draw upon here.

Starting with Eckbo (1983) and Stillman (1983), industrial organization economists have asked how the anticompetitive features of a merger could be analyzed by event studies. The logic goes as follows: Suppose Firm A announces that it will merge with Firm B, and the value of the sum of the two firms post-announcement exceeds the sum of the values of the two firms before the announcement. That increase could occur either because the merger is efficient or because the merger will reduce competition and lead to elevated pricing. If the merger is expected to lead to higher prices, then the rivals of the merged firm will benefit. However, if the merger will not increase market power but instead will create a more efficient firm, then the values of the rivals of the merged firm should fall. So, by examining the response of rival firms' stock prices to a merger announcement, regulators can tell whether the proposed merger represents increased efficiency, or increased monopoly. This procedure exploits the more general and deeper shift in understanding introduced by Gene's efficient markets concept, as emphasized in Ray Ball's essay, that stock prices collect, reflect, and convey information otherwise held by dispersed market participants.

There are of course many caveats to such an analysis. For example, an event study requires that one define when the information about the merger starts leaking out to the market, how expectations change along the lengthy antitrust review process, and whether one can look at only equity values and not debt. Moreover, because firms sell many different products, the value of the firm may consist of so many different industry segments that the effect of a merger in one segment will be hard to detect by examining the effect on the firm's value.

Despite all these caveats, the results of these studies have been remarkably consistent over time. Mergers don't seem to create market power but do seem to create efficiencies. There is an overall gain in value to the merged firm somewhere in the range of 0–10% (e.g., Andrade et al. [2001] report a 2% gain) above the value of the separate firms' values, and that gain seems unrelated to market power. This result, of course, does not mean that mergers never create market power—just that any attempt by merger authorities to become more stringent in merger enforcement must recognize that given our limited ability to identify such anticompetitive mergers ex ante, any significant toughening of standards runs the risk of deterring efficiency-enhancing mergers.

Event studies can also give guidance on whether government challenges to mergers have been perceived by the market as preventing antitrust harm. If the government challenges a merger that would lead to higher consumer prices because of the elimination of competition, that challenge should lead to a decline in the value of the merged firm's rivals, who would benefit from the general increased price level. Fee and Thomas (2004) investigate that possibility and do not find evidence to support it. There may be anticompetitive mergers going on, but government agencies don't seem to be able to identify them in their challenges.

More research is needed to reconcile these event studies with post-merger pricing and accounting information. If the merged firm is more efficient than the pre-merger firms, presumably measured profits should rise. That link has been hard to establish. Perhaps that is because of the difficulty of using accounting information, but I find that explanation unsatisfying. Some detailed studies of individual mergers have been more successful. There is evidence that CEOs that fail to deliver the anticipated value of a merger get replaced. But there is more work to be done to reconcile these results with the stock price behavior documented by event studies. Moreover, there have been relatively few merger retrospectives on pricing in the industrial organization literature, but that is changing. Linking up these post-merger studies on profits and individual pricing with event studies at the time of the merger would fill a missing gap in the literature. All of these advances are made possible by Gene's contribution from decades before.

The effect of regulation is another question of great interest to industrial organization economists. Schwert (1981) describes clearly how event studies can assist in the study of regulation. Since that article was published, a large number of studies have done what Schwert suggests. Event studies have proven enormously valuable here, though again there are many complicated issues related to identification of the right event windows and figuring out how the regulations have affected the riskiness of the firms. The obvious question is how proposed and implemented regulations have affected the value of firms in the industry. If regulation protects consumers by limiting the exercise of market power on prices, then regulations should reduce the profits of firms and lower their value. On the other hand, if producer groups use regulations to their advantage, for example by reducing competition, then greater regulation might increase stock market value.

There have now been numerous event study investigations of the effects of regulation and deregulation. Prager (1989) uses an event study to show that the creation of the Interstate Commerce Commission (ICC) in 1890 can be viewed as an attempt by the railroads to create a regulatory authority that would limit the amount of railroad competition to the detriment of consumers. The creation of that regulatory authority is associated with an increase in the value of railroads. Early court decisions that limited the power of the ICC to protect railroads from competition typically reduced the value of railroads. The ICC subsequently was captured by the customers of railroads and wound up harming the value of railroads.

There also have been numerous studies of the effect of deregulation of various industries using event studies. For example, Rose (1985) uses an event study to show that deregulation of trucking in the 1980s led to large declines in the value of certain trucking firms, suggesting that the earlier regulations were used to prevent competition in trucking. Dann and James (1982) show that the permission to issue variable rate money market certificates in the 1970s lowered the value of Savings and Loans. The 1980 deregulations which allowed banks to offer a greater variety of services helped large banks and hurt small ones (e.g., Millon-Cornett and Tehranian 1989). Czyrnik and Klein (2004) use event studies to show that repeal of the Glass-Steagall Act increased the value of commercial and investment banks.

Event studies have also proven useful in industrial organization to measure the value of reputation. Reputation is hard to evaluate but by looking at what happens to stock prices when an event hurts a firm's reputation, one can quantify the harm to reputation aside from the direct harm from the unfortunate event. See Jarrell and Peltzman (1985). For example, Mitchell and Maloney (1989) examine what happens to the value of an airline when it experiences a crash. They find that the crash has a negative effect on firm value only if the crash was due to pilot error. If it was not pilot error, then the interpretation is that the airline has insurance to cover the direct costs of the crash and there is no further reputational loss.

Event studies have also been useful in the current controversy regarding patent assertion entities, sometimes pejoratively referred to as patent trolls (Bessen et al. 2011). The concern is that some firms do nothing but amass a large portfolio of patents of questionable validity and then go around suing lots of other firms, who then settle the case rather than fight the case in court in order to avoid high litigation costs. Such suits could deter innovative activity and could be viewed as a tax on producing firms. Event studies have shown that such suits have decreased the value of defendants in lawsuits by about $500 billion over the last decade. There is much concern that the original inventors of these patents obtain little of this bonanza, so there are no positive incentive effects on invention.

I conclude with a topic not associated with event studies. The Fama and French (1993) article "Common Risk Factors in the Returns on Stocks and Bonds" focuses on small value firms. There is literature in industrial organization that looks at the birth and death of small firms. (As far as I know it does not identify value firms.) That literature recently (see, e.g., Fort et al. 2013) has shown that it is not small but young firms that have distinguishing growth prospects from other firms. Reconciling and further investigating the connection between this literature in industrial organization and the finance literature in this area should have big research payoffs in identifying the risks facing small firms, and potentially in understanding the source of the small stock and value stock premiums in asset markets, and resolving puzzles such as the surprisingly bad stock market performance of small growth firms, identified by Fama and French. Another great contribution from Gene, seemingly unrelated to industrial organization, may yet prove its importance to that area.

***

The author thanks Greg Pelnar and David Ross for assistance.

REFERENCES

Andrade, Gregor, Mark Mitchell, and Erik Stafford. 2001. "New Evidence and Perspectives on Mergers." *Journal of Economic Perspectives* 15, 103.

Bessen, James, Jennifer Ford, and Michael J. Meuer. 2011–2012. "The Private and Social Costs of Patent Trolls." *Regulation* (Winter), 26.

Czyrnik, Kathy, and Linda Schmid Klein. 2004. "Who Benefits from Deregulating the Separation of Banking Activities? Differential Effects on Commercial Bank, Investment Bank, and Thrift Stock Returns." *Financial Review* 39, 317.

Dann, Larry Y., and Christopher M. James. 1982. "An Analysis of the Impact of Deposit Rate Ceilings on the Market Values of Thrift Institutions." *Journal of Finance* 337, 1259.

Eckbo, B. Espen. 1983. "Horizontal Mergers, Collusion, and Stockholder Wealth." *Journal of Financial Economics* 11, 241.

Fama, Eugene F., Lawrence Fisher, Michael C. Jensen, and Richard Roll. 1969. "The Adjustment of Stock Prices to New Information." *International Economic Review* 10, 1.

Fama, Eugene F., and Kenneth R. French. 1993. "Common Risk Factors in the Returns on Stocks and Bonds." *Journal of Financial Economics* 33, 3.

Fee, C. Edward, and Shawn Thomas. 2004. "Sources of Gains in Horizontal Mergers: Evidence from Customer, Supplier, and Rival Firms," *Journal of Financial Economics* 74, 423.

Fort, Teresa, John Haltiwanger, Ron S. Jarmin, and Javier Miranda. 2013. "How Firms

Respond to Business Cycles: The Role of Firm Age and Firm Size." *IMF Economic Review* 61, 520.

Jarrell, Gregg A., and Sam Peltzman. 1985. "The Impact of Product Recalls on the Wealth of Sellers." *Journal of Political Economy* 93, 512.

Kaplan, Steven N. 2006. "Mergers and Acquisitions: A Financial Economics Perspective." Testimony before the Antitrust Modernization Commission. Available at http://govinfo.library.unt.edu/AMC/commission_hearings/PDF/kaplan_statement.pdf.

Millon-Cornett, Marcia H., and Hassan Tehranian. 1989. "Stock Market Reactions to the Depository Institutions Deregulation and Monetary Control Act of 1980." *Journal of Banking and Finance* 13, 81.

Mitchell, Mark L., and Michael T. Maloney. 1989. "Crisis in the Cockpit? The Role of Market Forces in Promoting Air Travel Safety." *Journal of Law and Economics* 32, 329.

Prager, Robin A. 1989. "Using Stock Price Data to Measure the Effects of Regulation: The Interstate Commerce Act and the Railroad Industry." *Rand Journal of Economics* 20, 280.

Rose, Nancy L. 1985. "The Incidence of Regulatory Rents in the Motor Carrier Industry." *Rand Journal of Economics* 16, 299.

Schwert, G. William. 1981. "Using Financial Data to Measure Effects of Regulation." *Journal of Law and Economics* 24, 121.

Stillman, Robert. 1983. "Examining Antitrust Policy towards Horizontal Mergers." *Journal of Financial Economics* 11, 225.

THE ADJUSTMENT OF STOCK
PRICES TO NEW INFORMATION

. . .

Eugene F. Fama, Lawrence Fisher, Michael C. Jensen,

and Richard Roll[1]

1. INTRODUCTION

There is an impressive body of empirical evidence which indicates that successive price changes in individual common stocks are very nearly independent.[2]
Recent papers by Mandelbrot (1966) and Samuelson (1965) show rigorously
that independence of successive price changes is *consistent* with an "efficient"
market, i.e., a market that adjusts rapidly to new information.

It is important to note, however, that in the empirical work to date the usual
procedure has been to *infer* market efficiency from the observed independence
of successive price changes. There has been very little actual testing of the
speed of adjustment of prices to *specific kinds* of new information. The prime
concern of this paper is to examine the process by which common stock prices
adjust to the information (if any) that is implicit in a stock split.

2. SPLITS, DIVIDENDS, AND NEW
INFORMATION: A HYPOTHESIS

More specifically, this study will attempt to examine evidence on two related
questions: (1) is there normally some "unusual" behavior in the rates of return
on a split security in the months surrounding the split?[3] and (2) if splits are

Reprinted from the *International Economic Review* 10, no. 9 (February 1969): 1–21.

1. This study way suggested to us by Professor James H. Lorie. We are grateful to
Professors Lorie, Merton H. Miller, and Harry V. Roberts for many helpful comments
and criticisms.

The research reported here was supported by the Center for Research in Security
Prices, Graduate School of Business, University of Chicago, and by funds made available
to the Center by the National Science Foundation.

2. Cf. Cootner (1964) and the studies reprinted therein, Fama (1965a), Godfrey,
Granger, and Morgenstern (1964) and other empirical studies of the theory of random
walks in speculative prices.

3. A precise definition of "unusual" behavior of security returns will be provided below.

associated with "unusual" behavior of security returns, to what extent can this be accounted for by relationships between splits and changes in other more fundamental variables?[4]

In answer to the first question we shall show that stock splits are usually preceded by a period during which the rates of return (including dividends and capital appreciation) on the securities to be split are unusually high. The period of high returns begins, however, long before any information (or even rumor) concerning a possible split is likely to reach the market. Thus we suggest that the high returns far in advance of the split arise from the fact that during the pre-split period these companies have experienced dramatic increases in expected earnings and dividends.

In the empirical work reported below, however, we shall see that the highest average monthly rates of return on split shares occur in the few months immediately preceding the split. This might appear to suggest that the split itself provides some impetus for increased returns. We shall present evidence, however, which suggests that such is not the case. The evidence supports the following reasoning: Although there has probably been a dramatic increase in earnings in the recent past, in the months immediately prior to the split (or its announcement) there may still be considerable uncertainty in the market concerning whether the earnings can be maintained at their new higher level. Investors will attempt to use any information available to reduce this uncertainty, and a proposed split may be one source of such information.

In the past a large fraction of stock splits have been followed closely by dividend increases—and increases greater than those experienced at the same

---

4. There is another question concerning stock splits, which this study does not consider. That is, given that splitting is not costless, and since the only apparent result is to multiply the number of shares per shareholder without increasing the shareholder's claims to assets, why do firms split their shares? This question has been the subject of considerable discussion in the professional financial literature. (Cf. Bellemore and Blucher (1956).) Suffice it to say that the arguments offered in favor of splitting usually turn out to be two-sided under closer examination—e.g., a split, by reducing the price of a round lot, will reduce transactions costs for some relatively small traders but increase costs for both large and very small traders (i.e., for traders who will trade, exclusively, either round lots or odd lots both before and after the split). Thus the conclusions are never clear-cut. In this study we shall be concerned with identifying the factors which the market regards as important in a stock split and with determining how market prices adjust to these factors rather than with explaining why firms split their shares.

time by other securities in the market. In fact it is not unusual for the dividend change to be announced at the same time as the split. Other studies (cf. Lintner (1956) and Michaelsen (1961)) have demonstrated that, once dividends have been increased, large firms show great reluctance to reduce them, except under the most extreme conditions. Directors have appeared to hedge against such dividend cuts by increasing dividends only when they are quite sure of their ability to maintain them in the future, i.e., only when they feel strongly that future earnings will be sufficient to maintain the dividends at their new higher rate. Thus dividend changes may be assumed to convey important information to the market concerning management's assessment of the firm's long-run earning and dividend paying potential.

We suggest, then, that unusually high returns on splitting shares in the months immediately preceding a split reflect the market's anticipation of substantial increases in dividends which, in fact, usually occur. Indeed evidence presented below leads us to conclude that when the information effects of dividend changes are taken into account, the apparent price effects of the split will vanish.[5]

3. SAMPLE AND METHODOLOGY

a. *The data.* We define a "stock split" as an exchange of shares in which at least five shares are distributed for every four formerly outstanding. Thus this definition of splits includes all stock dividends of 25 per cent or greater. We also decided, arbitrarily, that in order to get reliable estimates of the parameters that will be used in the analysis, it is necessary to have at least twenty-four successive months of price-dividend data around the split date. Since the data cover only common stocks listed on the New York Stock Exchange, our rules require that to qualify for inclusion in the tests a split security must be listed on the Exchange for at least twelve months before and twelve months after the split. From January 1927, through December 1959, 940 splits meeting these criteria occurred on the New York Stock Exchange.[6]

5. It is important to note that our hypothesis concerns the information content of dividend changes. There is nothing in our evidence which suggests that dividend *policy* per se affects the value of a firm. Indeed, the information hypothesis was first suggested by Miller and Modigliani (1961, p. 430), where they show that, aside from information effects, in a perfect capital market dividend policy will not affect the total market value of a firm.

6. The basic data were contained in the master file of monthly prices, dividends, and capital changes, collected and maintained by the Center for Research in Security Prices

b. *Adjusting security returns for general market conditions.* Of course, during this 33 year period, economic and hence general stock market conditions were far from static. Since we are interested in isolating whatever *extraordinary* effects a split and its associated dividend history may have on returns, it is necessary to abstract from general market conditions in examining the returns on securities during months surrounding split dates. We do this in the following way: Define

P_{jt} = price of the j-th stock at end of month t.

$P'_{jt} = P_{jt}$ adjusted for capital changes in month $t+1$. For the method of adjustment see Fisher (1965).

D_{jt} = cash dividends on the j-th security during month t (where the dividend is taken as of the ex-dividend data rather than the payment date).

$R_{jt} = (P_{jt} + D_{jt})/P'_{j,t-1}$ = price relative of the j-th security for month t.

L_t = the link relative of Fisher's "Combination Investment Performance Index" (Fisher (1966), table A1). It will suffice here to note that L_t is a complicated average of the R_{jt} for all securities that were on the N.Y.S.E. at the end of months t and $t-1$. L_t is the measure of "general market conditions" used in this study.[7]

One form or another of the following simple model has often been suggested as a way of expressing the relationship between the monthly rates of return provided by an individual security and general market conditions:[8]

(Graduate School of Business, University of Chicago). At the time this study was conducted, the file covered the period January, 1926 to December, 1960. For a description of the data see Fisher and Lorie (1964).

7. To check that our results do not arise from any special properties of the index L_t we have also performed all tests using Standard and Poor's Composite Price Index as the measure of market conditions; in all major respects the results agree completely with those reported below.

8. Cf. Markowitz (1959, pp. 96–101), Sharpe (1963; 1964) and Fama (1965b). The logarithmic form of the model is appealing for two reasons. First, over the period covered by our data the distribution of the monthly values of $\log_e L_t$ and $\log_e R_{jt}$ are fairly symmetric, whereas the distributions of the relatives themselves are skewed right. Symmetry is desirable since models involving symmetrically distributed variables present fewer estimation problems than models involving variables with skewed distributions. Second, we shall see below that when least squares is used to estimate α and β in (1), the sample residuals conform well to the assumptions of the simple linear regression model.

Thus, the logarithmic form of the model appears to be well specified from a statistical point of view and has a natural economic interpretation (i.e., in terms of monthly rates

$$\log_e R_{jt} = \alpha_j + \beta_j \log_e L_t + u_{jt} \tag{1}$$

where α_j and β_j are parameters that can vary from security to security and u_{jt} is a random disturbance term. It is assumed that u_{jt} satisfies the usual assumptions of the linear regression model. That is, (a) u_{jt} has zero expectation and variance independent of t; (b) the u_{jt} are serially independent; and (c) the distribution of u_j is independent of $\log_e L$.

The natural logarithm of the security price relative is the rate of return (with continuous compounding) for the month in question; similarly, the log of the market index relative is approximately the rate of return on a portfolio which includes equal dollar amounts of all securities in the market. Thus (1) represents the monthly rate of return on an individual security as a linear function of the corresponding return for the market.

c. *Tests of model specification.* Using the available time series on R_{jt} and L_t least squares has been used to estimate α_j and β_j in (1) for each of the 622 securities in the sample of 940 splits. We shall see later that there is strong evidence that the expected values of the residuals from (1) are non-zero in months close to the split. For these months the assumptions of the regression model concerning the disturbance term in (1) are not valid. Thus if these months were included in the sample, estimates of α and β would be subject to specification error, which could be very serious. We have attempted to avoid this source of specification error by excluding from the estimating samples those months for which the expected values of the residuals are apparently non-zero. The exclusion procedure was as follows: First, the parameters of (1) were estimated for each security using all available data. Then for each split the sample regression residuals were computed for a number of months preceding and following the split. When the number of positive residuals in any month differed substantially from the number of negative residuals, that month was excluded from subsequent calculations. This criterion caused exclusion of fifteen months before the split for all securities and fifteen months after the split for splits followed by dividend decreases.[9]

---

of return with continuous compounding). Nevertheless, to check that our results do not depend critically on using logs, all tests have also been carried out using the simple regression of R_{jt} on L_t. These results are in complete agreement with those presented in the text.

9. Admittedly the exclusion criterion is arbitrary. As a check, however, the analysis of regression residuals discussed later in the paper has been carried out using the regres-

TABLE 1. Summary of frequency distributions of estimated coefficients for the different split securities

Statistic	Mean	Median	Mean absolute deviation	Standard deviation	Extreme values	Skewness
$\hat{\alpha}$	0.000	0.001	0.004	0.007	−0.06, 0.04	Slightly left
$\hat{\beta}$	0.894	0.880	0.242	0.305	−0.10*, 1.95	Slightly right
$\hat{r}$	0.632	0.655	0.106	0.132	−0.04*, 0.91	Slightly left

*Only negative value in distribution.

Aside from these exclusions, however, the least squares estimates $\hat{\alpha}_j$ and $\hat{\beta}_j$ for security j are based on all months during the 1926–60 period for which price relatives are available for the security. For the 940 splits the smallest effective sample size is 14 monthly observations. In only 46 cases is the sample size less than 100 months, and for about 60 per cent of the splits more than 300 months of data are available. Thus in the vast majority of cases the samples used in estimating α and β in (1) are quite large.

Table 1 provides summary descriptions of the frequency distributions of the estimated values of α_j, β_j, and r_j, where r_j is the correlation between monthly rates of return on security j (i.e., $\log_e R_{jt}$) and the approximate monthly rates of return on the market portfolio (i.e., $\log_e L_t$). The table indicates that there are indeed fairly strong relationships between the market and monthly returns on individual securities; the mean value of the $\hat{r}_j$ is 0.632 with an average absolute deviation of 0.106 about the mean.[10]

Moreover, the estimates of equation (1) for the different securities conform fairly well to the assumptions of the linear regression model. For example, the first order autocorrelation coefficient of the estimated residuals from (1) has been computed for every twentieth split in the sample (ordered alphabetically by security). The mean (and median) value of the forty-seven coefficients is −0.10, which suggests that serial dependence in the residuals is not a seri-

---

sion estimates in which no data are excluded. The results were much the same as those reported in the text and certainly support the same conclusions.

10. The sample average or mean absolute deviation of the random variable x is defined as

$$\frac{\sum_{t=1}^{N} |x_t - \bar{x}|}{N}$$

where $\bar{x}$ is the sample mean of the x's and N is the sample size.

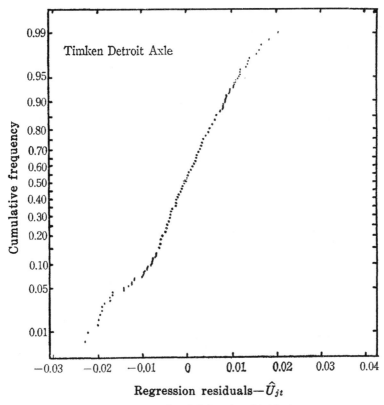

Figure 1. Normal probability plot of residuals

The lower left and upper right corners of the graph represent the most extreme sample points. For clarity, only every tenth point is plotted in the central portion of the figure.

ous problem. For these same forty-seven splits scatter diagrams of (a) monthly security return versus market return, and (b) estimated residual return in month $t + 1$ versus estimated residual return in month t have been prepared, along with (c) normal probability graphs of estimated residual returns. The scatter diagrams for the individual securities support very well the regression assumptions of linearity, homoscedasticity, and serial independence.

It is important to note, however, that the data do not conform well to the normal, or Gaussian linear regression model. In particular, the distributions of the estimated residuals have much longer tails than the Gaussian. The typical normal probability graph of residuals looks much like the one shown for Timken Detroit Axle in Figure 1. The departures from normality in the distributions of regression residuals are of the same sort as those noted by Fama (1965a) for the distributions of returns themselves. Fama (following Mandelbrot (1963)) argues that distributions of returns are well approximated by the non-Gaussian (i.e., infinite variance) members of the stable Paretian family. If the stable non-Gaussian distributions also provide a good description of the residuals in (1), then, at first glance, the least squares regression model would seem inappropriate.

Wise (1963) has shown, however, that although least square estimates are not "efficient," for most members of the stable Paretian family they provide estimates which are unbiased and consistent. Thus, given our large samples, least squares regression is not completely inappropriate. In deference to the stable Paretian model, however, in measuring variability we rely primarily on the mean absolute deviation rather than the variance or the standard deviation. The mean absolute deviation is used since, for long-tailed distributions, its sampling behavior is less erratic than that of the variance or the standard deviation.[11]

In sum we find that regressions of security returns on market returns over time are a satisfactory method for abstracting from the effects of general market conditions on the monthly rates of return on individual securities. We must point out, however, that although (1) stands up fairly well to the assumptions of the linear regression model, it is certainly a grossly over-simplified model of price formation; general market conditions alone do not determine the returns on an individual security. In (1) the effects of these "omitted variables" are impounded into the disturbance term u. In particular, if a stock split is associated with abnormal behavior in returns during months surrounding the split date, this behavior should be reflected in the estimated regression residuals of the security for these months. The remainder of our analysis will concentrate on examining the behavior of the estimated residuals of split securities in the months surrounding the splits.

4. "EFFECTS" OF SPLITS ON RETURNS: EMPIRICAL RESULTS

In this study we do not attempt to determine the effects of splits for individual companies. Rather we are concerned with whether the process of splitting is in

11. Essentially, this is due to the fact that in computing the variance of a sample, large deviations are weighted more heavily than in computing the mean absolute deviation. For empirical evidence concerning the reliability of the mean absolute deviation relative to the variance or standard deviation see Fama (1965a, pp. 94–8).

general associated with specific types of return behavior. To abstract from the eccentricities of specific cases we can rely on the simple process of averaging; we shall therefore concentrate attention on the behavior of cross-sectional averages of estimated regression residuals in the months surrounding split dates.

a. *Some additional definitions.* The procedure is as follows: For a given split, define month o as the month in which the effective date of a split occurs. (Thus month o is not the same chronological date for all securities, and indeed some securities have been split more than once and hence have more than one month o)."[12] Month 1 is then defined as the month immediately following the split month, while month −1 is the month preceding, etc. Now define the average residual for month m (where m is always measured relative to the split month) as

$$u_m = \frac{\sum_{j=1}^{Nm} \hat{u}_{jm}}{N_m}$$

where $\hat{u}_{jm}$ is the sample regression residual for security j in month m and n_m is the number of splits for which data are available in month m.[13] Our principal tests will involve examining the behavior of u_m for m in the interval $-29 \leqq m \leqq 30$, i.e., for the sixty months surrounding the split month.

We shall also be interested in examining the cumulative effects of abnormal return behavior in months surrounding the split month. Thus we define the cumulative average residual U_m as

$$U_m = \sum_{k=-29}^{m} u_k .$$

The average residual u_m can be interpreted as the average deviation (in month m relative to the split month) of the returns of split stocks from their normal relationships with the market. Similarly, the cumulative average residual U_m can be interpreted as the cumulative deviation (from month −29 to month m); it shows the cumulative effects of the wanderings of the returns of split stocks from their normal relationships to market movements.

12. About a third of the securities in the master file split. About a third of these split more than once.

13. Since we do not consider splits of companies that were not on the New York Stock Exchange for at least a year before and a year after a split, n_m will be 940 for $-11 \leqq m \leqq 12$. For other months, however, $n_m < 940$.

Since the hypothesis about the effects of splits on returns expounded in Section 2 centers on the dividend behavior of split shares, in some of the tests to follow we examine separately splits that are associated with increased dividends and splits that are associated with decreased dividends. In addition, in order to abstract from general changes in dividends across the market, "increased" and "decreased" dividends will be measured relative to the average dividends paid by all securities on the New York Stock Exchange during the relevant time periods. The dividends are classified as follows: Define the dividend change ratio as total dividends (per equivalent unsplit share) paid in the twelve months after the split, divided by total dividends paid during the twelve months before the split."[14] Dividend "increases" are then defined as cases where the dividend change ratio of the split stock is greater than the ratio for the Exchange as a whole, while dividend "decreases" include cases of relative dividend decline."[15] We then define u_m^+, u_m^- and U_m^+, U_m^- as the average and cumulative average residuals for splits followed by "increased" $(+)$ and "decreased" $(-)$ dividends.

These definitions of "increased" and "decreased" dividends provide a simple and convenient way of abstracting from general market dividend changes in classifying year-to-year dividend changes for individual securities. The definitions have the following drawback, however. For a company paying quarterly dividends an increase in its dividend rate at any time during the nine months before or twelve months after the split can place its stock in the dividend "increased" class. Thus the actual increase need not have occurred in the year after the split. The same fuzziness, of course, also arises in classifying dividend "decreases." We shall see later, however, that this fuzziness fortunately does not obscure the differences between the aggregate behavior patterns of the two groups.

b. *Empirical results.* The most important empirical results of this study are summarized in Tables 2 and 3 and Figures 2 and 3. Table 2 presents the aver-

14. A dividend is considered "paid" on the first day the security trades ex-dividend on the Exchange.

15. When dividend "increase" and "decrease" are defined relative to the market, it turns out that dividends were never "unchanged." That is, the dividend change ratios of split securities are never identical to the corresponding ratios for the Exchange as a whole.

In the remainder of the paper we shall always use "increase" and "decrease" as defined in the text. That is, signs of dividend changes for individual securities are measured relative to changes in the dividends for all N.Y.S.E. common stocks.

age residuals, cumulative average residuals, and the sample size for each of the two dividend classifications ("increased" and "decreased") and for the total of all splits for each of the sixty months surrounding the split. Figure 2 presents graphs of the average and cumulative average residuals for the total sample of splits and Figure 3 presents these graphs for each of the two dividend classifications. Table 3 shows the number of splits each year along with the end of June level of the stock price index.

Several of our earlier statements can now be substantiated. First, Figures 2a, 3a and 3b show that the average residuals (u_m) in the twenty-nine months prior to the split are uniformly positive for all splits and for both classes of dividend behavior. This can hardly be attributed entirely to the splitting process. In a random sample of fifty-two splits from our data the median time between the announcement date and the effective date of the split was 44.5 days. Similarly, in a random sample of one hundred splits that occurred between 1/1/1946 and 1/1/1957 Jaffe (1957) found that the median time between announcement date and effective date was sixty-nine days. For both samples in only about 10 per cent of the cases is the time between announcement date and effective date greater than four months. Thus it seems safe to say that the split cannot account for the behavior of the regression residuals as far as two and one-half years in advance of the split date. Rather we suggest the obvious—a sharp improvement, relative to the market, in the earnings prospects of the company sometime during the years immediately preceding a split.

Thus we conclude that companies tend to split their shares during "abnormally" good times—that is during periods of time when the prices of their shares have increased much more than would be implied by the normal relationships between their share prices and general market price behavior. This result is doubly interesting since, from Table 3, it is clear that for the exchange as a whole the number of splits increases dramatically following a general rise in stock prices. Thus splits tend to occur during general "boom" periods, and the particular stocks that are split will tend to be those that performed "unusually" well during the period of general price increase.

It is important to note (from Figure 2a and Table 2) that when all splits are examined together, the largest positive average residuals occur in the three or four months immediately preceding the split, but that after the split the average residuals are randomly distributed about 0. Or equivalently, in Figure 2b the *cumulative* average residuals rise dramatically up to the split

TABLE 2. Analysis of residuals in months surrounding the split

| (1) | Split followed by Dividend "increases" | | | Split followed by Dividend "decreases" | | | All Splits | | |
| | (2) | (3) | (4) | (5) | (6) | (7) | (8) | (9) | (10) |
Month m	Average u_m^+	Cumulative U_m^+	Sample size N_m^+	Average u_m^-	Cumulative U_m^-	Sample size N_m^-	Average u_m	Cumulative U_m	Sample size N_m
−29	0.0062	0.0062	614	0.0033	0.0033	252	0.0054	0.0054	866
−28	0.0013	0.0075	617	0.0030	0.0063	253	0.0018	0.0072	870
−27	0.0068	0.0143	618	0.0007	0.0070	253	0.0050	0.0122	871
−26	0.0054	0.0198	619	0.0085	0.0155	253	0.0063	0.0185	872
−25	0.0042	0.0240	621	0.0089	0.0244	254	0.0056	0.0241	875
−24	0.0020	0.0259	623	0.0026	0.0270	256	0.0021	0.0263	879
−23	0.0055	0.0315	624	0.0028	0.0298	256	0.0047	0.0310	880
−22	0.0073	0.0388	628	0.0028	0.0326	256	0.0060	0.0370	884
−21	0.0049	0.0438	633	0.0131	0.0457	257	0.0073	0.0443	890
−20	0.0044	0.0482	634	0.0005	0.0463	257	0.0033	0.0476	891
−19	0.0110	0.0592	636	0.0102	0.0565	258	0.0108	0.0584	894
−18	0.0076	0.0668	644	0.0089	0.0654	260	0.0080	0.0664	904
−17	0.0072	0.0739	650	0.0111	0.0765	260	0.0083	0.0746	910
−16	0.0035	0.0775	655	0.0009	0.0774	260	0.0028	0.0774	915
−15	0.0135	0.0909	659	0.0101	0.0875	260	0.0125	0.0900	919
−14	0.0135	0.1045	662	0.0100	0.0975	263	0.0125	0.1025	925
−13	0.0148	0.1193	665	0.0099	0.1074	264	0.0134	0.1159	929
−12	0.0138	0.1330	669	0.0107	0.1181	266	0.0129	0.1288	935
−11	0.0098	0.1428	672	0.0103	0.1285	268	0.0099	0.1387	940
−10	0.0103	0.1532	672	0.0082	0.1367	268	0.0097	0.1485	940
−9	0.0167	0.1698	672	0.0152	0.1520	268	0.0163	0.1647	940
−8	0.0163	0.1862	672	0.0140	0.1660	268	0.0157	0.1804	940
−7	0.0159	0.2021	672	0.0083	0.1743	268	0.0138	0.1942	940
−6	0.0194	0.2215	672	0.0106	0.1849	268	0.0169	0.2111	940
−5	0.0194	0.2409	672	0.0100	0.1949	268	0.0167	0.2278	940
−4	0.0260	0.2669	672	0.0104	0.2054	268	0.0216	0.2494	940
−3	0.0325	0.2993	672	0.0204	0.2258	268	0.0289	0.2783	940
−2	0.0390	0.3383	672	0.0296	0.2554	268	0.0363	0.3147	940
−1	0.0199	0.3582	672	0.0176	0.2730	268	0.0192	0.3339	940
0	0.0131	0.3713	672	−0.0090	0.2640	268	0.0068	0.3407	940
1	0.0016	0.3729	672	−0.0088	0.2552	268	−0.0014	0.3393	940
2	0.0052	0.3781	672	−0.0024	0.2528	268	0.0031	0.3424	940
3	0.0024	0.3805	672	−0.0089	0.2439	268	−0.0008	0.3416	940
4	0.0045	0.3951	672	−0.0114	0.2325	268	0.0000	0.3416	940
5	0.0048	0.3898	672	−0.0003	0.2322	268	0.0033	0.3449	940
6	0.0012	0.3911	672	−0.0038	0.2285	268	−0.0002	0.3447	940
7	0.0008	0.3919	672	−0.0106	0.2179	268	−0.0024	0.3423	940
8	−0.0007	0.3912	672	−0.0024	0.2155	268	−0.0012	0.3411	940
9	0.0039	0.3951	672	−0.0065	0.2089	268	0.0009	0.3420	940
10	−0.0001	0.3950	672	−0.0027	0.2062	268	−0.0008	0.3412	940
11	0.0027	0.3977	672	−0.0056	0.2006	268	0.0003	0.3415	940
12	0.0018	0.3996	672	−0.0043	0.1963	268	0.0001	0.3416	940
13	−0.0003	0.3993	666	0.0014	0.1977	264	0.0002	0.3418	930
14	0.0006	0.3999	653	0.0044	0.2021	258	0.0017	0.3435	911
15	−0.0037	0.3962	645	0.0026	0.2047	258	−0.0019	0.3416	903

TABLE 2. (Continued)

(1)	Split followed by Dividend "increases"			Split followed by Dividend "decreases"			All Splits		
	(2)	(3)	(4)	(5)	(6)	(7)	(8)	(9)	(10)
Month m	Average u_m^+	Cumulative U_m^+	Sample size N_m^+	Average u_m^-	Cumulative U_m^-	Sample size N_m^-	Average u_m	Cumulative U_m	Sample size N_m
16	0.0001	0.3963	635	−0.0040	0.2007	257	−0.0011	0.3405	892
17	0.0034	0.3997	633	−0.0011	0.1996	256	0.0021	0.3426	889
18	−0.0015	0.3982	629	0.0025	0.2021	255	−0.0003	0.3423	883
19	−0.0006	0.3976	620	−0.0057	0.1964	251	−0.0021	0.3402	871
20	−0.0002	0.3974	604	0.0027	0.1991	246	0.0006	0.3409	850
21	−0.0037	0.3937	595	−0.0073	0.1918	245	−0.0047	0.3361	840
22	0.0047	0.3984	593	−0.0018	0.1899	244	0.0028	0.3389	837
23	−0.0026	0.3958	593	0.0043	0.1943	242	−0.0006	0.3383	835
24	−0.0022	0.3936	587	0.0031	0.1974	238	−0.0007	0.3376	825
25	0.0012	0.3948	583	−0.0037	0.1936	237	−0.0002	0.3374	820
26	−0.0058	0.3890	582	0.0015	0.1952	236	−0.0037	0.3337	818
27	−0.0003	0.3887	582	0.0082	0.2033	235	0.0021	0.3359	817
28	0.0004	0.3891	580	−0.0023	0.2010	236	−0.0004	0.3355	816
29	0.0012	0.3903	580	−0.0039	0.1971	235	−0.0003	0.3352	815
30	−0.0033	0.3870	579	−0.0025	0.1946	235	−0.0031	0.3321	814

month, but there is almost no further systematic movement thereafter. Indeed during the first year after the split, the cumulative average residual changes by less than one-tenth of one percentage point, and the total change in the cumulative average residual during the two and one-half years following the split is less than one percentage point. This is especially striking since 71.5 per cent (672 out of 940) of all splits experienced greater percentage dividend increases in the year after the split than the average for all securities on the N.Y.S.E.

We suggest the following explanation for this behavior of the average residuals. When a split is announced or anticipated, the market interprets this (and correctly so) as greatly improving the probability that dividends will soon be substantially increased. (In fact, as noted earlier, in many cases the split and dividend increase will be announced at the same time.) If, as Lintner (1956) suggests, firms are reluctant to reduce dividends, then a split, which implies an increased expected dividend, is a signal to the market that the company's directors are confident that future earnings will be sufficient to maintain dividend payments at a higher level. If the market agrees with the judgments of the directors, then it is possible that the large price increases in the months immediately preceding a split are due to altering expectations concerning the

TABLE 3. Number of splits per year and level of the stock market index

Year	Number of splits	Market Index* (End of June)
1927	28	103.5
28	22	133.6
29	40	161.8
1930	15	98.9
31	2	65.5
32	0	20.4
33	1	82.9
34	7	78.5
35	4	73.3
36	11	124.7
37	19	147.4
38	6	100.3
39	3	90.3
1940	2	91.9
41	3	101.2
42	0	95.9
43	3	195.4
44	11	235.0
45	39	320.1
46	75	469.2
47	46	339.9
48	26	408.7
49	21	331.3
1950	49	441.6
51	55	576.1
52	37	672.2
53	25	691.9
54	43	818.6
55	89	1190.6
56	97	1314.1
57	44	1384.3
58	14	1407.3
59	103	1990.6

*Fisher's "Combination Investment Performance Index" shifted to a base January, 1926=100. See (1966) for a description of its calculation.

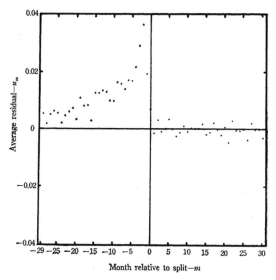

Figure 2a. Average residuals—all splits

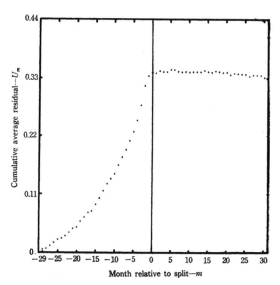

Figure 2b. Cumulative average residuals—all splits

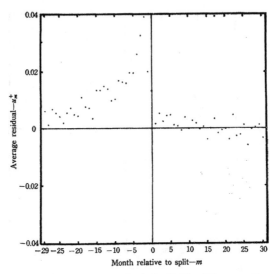

Figure 3a. Average residuals for dividend "increases"

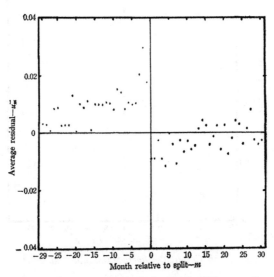

Figure 3b. Average residuals for dividend "decreases"

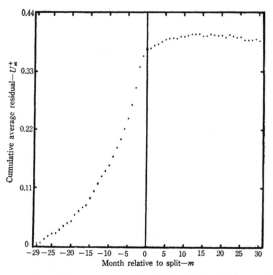

Figure 3c. Cumulative average residuals for dividend "increases"

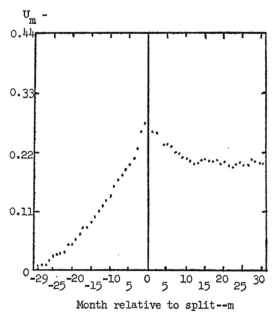

Figure 3d. Cumulative average residuals for dividend "decreases"

future earning potential of the firm (and thus of its shares) rather than to any intrinsic effects of the split itself.[16]

If the information effects of actual or anticipated dividend increases do indeed explain the behavior of common stock returns in the months immediately surrounding a split, then there should be substantial differences in return behavior subsequent to the split in cases where the dividend increase materializes and cases where it does not. In fact it is apparent from Figure 3 that the differences are substantial—and we shall argue that they are in the direction predicted by the hypothesis.

The fact that the cumulative average residuals for both dividend classes rise sharply in the few months before the split is *consistent* with the hypothesis that the market recognizes that splits are usually associated with higher dividend payments. In some cases, however, the dividend increase, if it occurs, will be declared sometime during the year after the split. Thus it is not surprising that the average residuals (Figure 3a) for stocks in the dividend "increased" class are in general slightly positive, in the year after the split, so that the cumulative average residuals (Figure 3c) drift upward. The fact that this upward drift is only very slight can be explained in two (complementary) ways. First, in many cases the dividend increase associated with a split will be declared (and the corresponding price adjustments will take place) before the end of the split month. Second, according to our hypothesis when the split is declared (even if no dividend announcement is made), there is some price adjustment in anticipation of future dividend increases. Thus only a slight *additional* adjustment is necessary when the dividend increase actually takes place. By one year after the split the returns on stocks which have experienced dividend "increases" have resumed their normal relationships to market returns since from this point onward the average residuals are small and randomly scattered about zero.

The behavior of the residuals for stock splits associated with "decreased" dividends, however, provides the strongest evidence in favor of our split hy-

16. If this stock split hypothesis is correct, the fact that the average residuals (where the averages are computed using all splits (Figure 2)) are randomly distributed about 0 in months subsequent to the split indicates that, on the average, the market has *correctly* evaluated the implications of a split for future dividend behavior and that these evaluations are fully incorporated in the price of the stock by the time the split occurs. That is, the market not only makes good forecasts of the dividend implications of a split, but these forecasts are fully impounded into the price of the security by the end of the split month. We shall return to this point at the end of this section.

pothesis. For stocks in the dividend "decreased" class the average and cumulative average residuals (Figures 3b and 3d) rise in the few months before the split but then plummet in the few months following the split, when the anticipated dividend increase is not forthcoming. These split stocks with poor dividend performance on the average perform poorly in each of the twelve months following the split, but their period of poorest performance is in the few months immediately after the split—when the improved dividend, if it were coming at all, would most likely be declared.[17] The hypothesis is further reinforced by the observation that when a year has passed after the split, the cumulative average residual has fallen to about where it was five months prior to the split which, we venture to say, is probably about the earliest time reliable information concerning a possible split is likely to reach the market.[18] Thus by the time it has become clear that the anticipated dividend increase is not forthcoming, the apparent effects of the split seem to have been completely wiped away, and the stock's returns have reverted to their normal relationship with market returns. In sum, our data suggest that once the information effects of associated dividend changes are properly considered, a split *per se* has no net effect on common stock returns."[19]

Finally, the data present important evidence on the speed of adjustment of market prices to new information. (a) Although the behavior of post-split returns will be very different depending on whether or not dividend "increases" occur, and (b) in spite of the fact that a substantial majority of split securities do experience dividend "increases," when all splits are examined together (Figure 2), the average residuals are randomly distributed about 0 during the year after the split. Thus there is no net movement either up or down in the

17. Though we do not wish to push the point too hard, it is interesting to note in Table 2 that after the split month, the largest negative average residuals for splits in the dividend "decreased" class occur in months 1, 4, and 7. This "pattern" in the residuals suggests, perhaps, that the market reacts most strongly during months when dividends are declared but not increased.

18. In a random sample of 52 splits from our data in only 2 cases is the time between the announcement date and effective date of the split greater than 162 days. Similarly, in the data of Jaffe (1957) in only 4 out of 100 randomly selected splits is the time between announcement and effective date greater than 130 days.

19. It is well to emphasize that our hypothesis centers around the information value of dividend changes. There is nothing in the empirical evidence which indicates that dividend policy per se affects the market value of the firm. For further discussion of this point see Miller and Modigliani (1961, p. 430).

cumulative average residuals. According to our hypothesis, this implies that on the average the market makes unbiased dividend forecasts for split securities and these forecasts are fully reflected in the price of the security by the end of the split month.

5. SPLITS AND TRADING PROFITS

Although stock prices adjust "rapidly" to the dividend information implicit in a split, an important question remains: Is the adjustment so rapid that splits can in no way be used to increase trading profits? Unfortunately our data do not allow full examination of this question. Nevertheless we shall proceed as best we can and leave the reader to judge the arguments for himself.

First of all, it is clear from Figure 2 that expected returns cannot be increased by purchasing split securities after the splits have become effective. After the split, on the average the returns on split securities immediately resume their normal relationships to market returns. In general, prices of split shares do not tend to rise more rapidly after a split takes place. Of course, if one is better at predicting which of the split securities are likely to experience "increased" dividends, one will have higher expected returns. But the higher returns arise from superior information or analytical talents and not from splits themselves.

Let us now consider the policy of buying splitting securities as soon as information concerning the possibility of a split becomes available. It is impossible to test this policy fully since information concerning a split often leaks into the market before the split is announced or even proposed to the shareholders. There are, however, several fragmentary but complementary pieces of evidence which suggest that the policy of buying splitting securities as soon as a split is *formally announced* does not lead to increased expected returns.

First, for a sample of 100 randomly selected splits during the period 1946–1956, Bellemore and Blucher (1956) found that in general, price movements associated with a split are over by the day after the split is announced. They found that from eight weeks before to the day after the announcement, 86 out of 100 stocks registered percentage price increases greater than those of the Standard and Poor's stock price index for the relevant industry group. From the day after to eight weeks after the announcement date, however, only 43 stocks registered percentage price increases greater than the relevant industry index, and on the average during this period split shares only increased 2 per cent more in price than nonsplit shares in the same industry. This suggests that even if one purchases as soon as the announcement is made, split shares will not in general provide higher returns than nonsplit shares.[20]

Second, announcement dates have been collected for a random sample of 52 splits from our data. For these 52 splits the analysis of average and cumulative average residuals discussed in Section 4 has been carried out first using the split month as month 0 and then using the announcement month as month 0. In this sample the behavior of the residuals after the announcement date is almost identical to the behavior of the residuals after the split date. Since the evidence presented earlier indicated that one could not systematically profit from buying split securities after the effective date of the split, this suggests that one also cannot profit by buying after the announcement date.

Although expected returns cannot in general be increased by buying split shares, this does not mean that a split should have no effect on an investor's decisions. Figure 4 shows the cross-sectional mean absolute deviations of the residuals for each of the sixty months surrounding the split. From the graph it is clear that the variability in returns on split shares increases substantially in the months closest to the split. The increased riskiness of the shares during this period is certainly a factor which the investor should consider in his decisions.

In light of some of the evidence presented earlier, the conclusion that splits cannot be used to increase expected trading profits may seem a bit anomalous. For example, in Table 2, column (8), the cross-sectional average residuals from the estimates of (1) are positive for at least thirty months prior to the split. It would seem that such a strong degree of "persistence" could surely be used to increase expected profits. Unfortunately, however, the behavior of the *average* residuals is not representative of the behavior of the residuals for *individual securities;* over time the residuals for individual securities are much more randomly distributed about 0. We can see this more clearly by comparing the average residuals for all splits (Figure 2a) with the month by month behavior of the cross-sectional mean absolute deviations of residuals for all splits (Figure 4). For each month before the split the mean absolute deviation

20. We should note that though the results are Bellemore and Blucher's, the interpretation is ours.

Since in the vast majority of cases prices rise substantially in the eight weeks prior to the announcement date, Bellemore and Bluener conclude that if one has advance knowledge concerning a contemplated split, it can probably be used to increase expected returns. The same is likely to be true of all inside information, however.

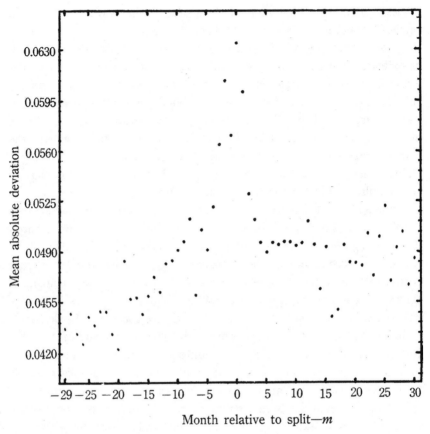

Figure 4. *Cross-sectional mean absolute deviation of residuals—all splits*

of residuals is well over twice as large as the corresponding average residual, which indicates that for each month the residuals for many *individual* securities are negative. In fact, in examining residuals for individual securities the following pattern was typical: Prior to the split, successive sample residuals from (1) are almost completely independent. In most cases, however, there are a few months for which the residuals are abnormally large and positive. These months of large residuals differ from security to security, however, and these differences in timing explain why the signs of the *average* residuals are uniformly positive for many months preceding the split.

Similarly, there is evidence which suggests that the extremely large positive average residuals in the three or four months prior to the split merely reflect the fact that, from split to split, there is a variable lag between the time split information reaches the market and the time when the split becomes effective. Jaffe (1957) has provided announcement and effective dates for the 100 randomly chosen splits used by herself and Bellemore (1956). The announcement dates occur as follows: 7 in the first month before the split, 67 in the second and third months, 14 in the fourth month, and 12 announcements more than four months before the split. Looking back at Table 2, column (8), and Figure 2a we see that the largest average residuals follow a similar pattern: The largest average residuals occur in the second and third months before the split; though smaller, the average residuals for one and four months before the split are larger than those of any other months.

This suggests that the pattern of the average residuals immediately prior to the split arises from the averaging process and thus cannot be assumed to hold for any particular security.

6. CONCLUSIONS

In sum, in the past stock splits have very often been associated with substantial dividend increases. The evidence indicates that the market realizes this and uses the announcement of a split to re-evaluate the stream of expected income from the shares. Moreover, the evidence indicates that on the average the market's judgments concerning the information implications of a split are fully reflected in the price of a share at least by the end of the split month but most probably almost immediately after the announcement date. Thus the results of the study lend considerable support to the conclusion that the stock market is "efficient" in the sense that stock prices adjust very rapidly to new information.

The evidence suggests that in reacting to a split the market reacts only to its dividend implications. That is, the split causes price adjustments only to the extent that it is associated with changes in the anticipated level of future dividends.

Finally, there seems to be no way to use a split to increase one's expected returns, unless, of course, inside information concerning the split or subsequent dividend behavior is available.

REFERENCES

Bellemore, Douglas H. and Lillian Blucher (Jaffee). 1956. "A Study of Stock Splits in the Postware Years." *Financial Analysts Journal* 15: November 1956, pp 19–26.

Cootner, Paul H., ed. 1964. *The Random Character of Stock Market Prices.* Cambridge, MA: MIT press.

Fama, Eugene F. 1965a. "The Behavior of Stock Market Prices." *Journal of Business* 37: January 1965, pp 34–105.

Fama, Eugene F. 1965b. "Portfolio Analysis in a Stable Paretian Market." *Management Science* 11: January 1965, pp 404–41.

Fisher, Lawrence. 1965. "Outcomes for 'Random' Investments in Common Stocks Listed on the New York Stock Exchange." *Journal of Business* 38: April 1965, pp 149–161.

Fisher, Lawrence. 1966. "Some New Stock Market Indexes." *Journal of Business* 39: January, 1966 Supplement, pp 191–225.

Fisher, Lawrence and James H. Lorie. 1964. "Rates of Return on Investments in Common Stocks." *Journal of Business* 37: January 1964, pp 1–21.

Godfrey, Michael D., Clive W. J. Granger, and Oscar Morgenstern. 1964. "The Random Walk Hypothesis of Stock Market Behavior." *Kyklos* 17: pp 1–30.

Jaffe (Blucher), Lillian H. 1957. A Study of Stock Splits, 1946–1956, New York University.

Lintner, John. 1956. "Distribution of Incomes of Corporations Among Dividends, Retainted Earnings and Taxes." *American Economic Review* XLVI: May 1956, pp 97–113.

Mandelbrot, Benoit. 1963. "The Variation of Certain Speculative Prices." *Journal of Business* 36: October, pp 394–419.

Mandelbrot, Benoit. 1966. "Forecasts of Future Prices, Unbiased Markets, and 'Martingale' Models." *Journal of Business* 39, no. Part 2: pp 242–255.

Markowitz, Harry. 1959. *Portfolio Selection: Efficient Diversification of Investments.* New York: Wiley.

Michaelson, Jacob B. 1961. The Determinants of Dividend Policies: A Theoretical and Empirical Study. Unpublished Doctoral Dissertation, University of Chicago.

Miller, Merton H. and Franco Modigliani. 1961. "Dividend Policy, Growth and the Valuation of Shares." *Journal of Business* 34: October, pp 411–433.

Samuelson, Paul A. 1965. "Proof That Property Anticipated Prices Fluctuate Randomly." *Industrial Management Review* Spring: pp 41–49.

Sharpe, William F. 1963. "A Simplified Model for Portfolio Analysis." *Management Science* 19: September, pp 425–442.

Sharpe, William F. 1964. "Capital Asset Prices: A Theory of Market Equilibrium under Conditions of Risk." *Journal of Finance* 19: September, pp 425–442.

Wise, John. 1963. "Linear Estimators for Linear Regression Systems Having Infinite Variances". Unpublished paper presented at the Berkeley-Stanford Mathematical Economics Seminar.

LUCK VERSUS SKILL

. . .

John H. Cochrane and Tobias J. Moskowitz

We include one paper on performance evaluation, "Luck versus Skill in the Cross-Section of Mutual Fund Returns," written with Ken French.

Gene's 1970 essay introduced fund performance evaluation as a test of "semi-strong form" efficiency. If prices already reflect publicly available information, then managers using such information won't be able to generate special or "abnormal" returns.

One must control for risk (that's the "normal" part). Funds can earn apparently better returns by leveraging, by investing in higher beta stocks, and so forth. But such strategies don't require any skill or special information—the investor can borrow and invest in a market index, without paying any fees.

The CAPM inaugurated the alpha-beta performance evaluation to control for risk. Betas measure a portfolio's exposure to risk and the return the investor can obtain by indexing; alphas measure the average return after correcting for risk and the return that requires skill or special information of the manager. Returns don't reveal skill or justify fees, alphas do. But measuring alphas and betas, especially in portfolios that are frequently changing, is not as easy as it seems, and this difficulty is especially strong as performance evaluation is extended to hedge funds and other less-stable investments, and to indices beyond the market portfolio.

The most fundamental issue is highlighted in the title of Gene and Ken's paper: Even if one controls for risk or benchmarks by looking at alphas, many funds will have large alphas just by chance. How do we tell skill from luck? The previous academic answer is straightforward: find a group of funds and then follow them—all of them, even the ones that go out of business—through time.

Overcoming the selection and survivor bias—we are much more likely to have data on ex post successful funds—is also not easy. Nonetheless, correcting for risk and selection bias, as Gene reviewed in 1970 and Gene and Ken remind us here, funds don't outperform indices on average.

We have gotten so used to this finding that we forget how remarkable it is. It should have come out the other way! In any other field of human endeavor, seasoned professionals systematically outperform amateurs. Tiger Woods will beat you at golf. You should hire a good plumber and a better tax lawyer. Why not hire a stock picker? But other fields are not as ruthlessly competitive, and free to enter, as financial markets.

Here the conversation between academics and practitioners has always run into a rough patch. The practitioner (or want-to-be practitioner) will ask, "Well, what about Warren Buffet? If markets are so efficient, how did he get so rich?" The academic answer "well, maybe he just got lucky" is not satisfying. How do we tell if a single investor, ex post, was skilled or lucky? But pointing out shared ignorance is not an effective rebuttal to the seemingly solid evidence of Mr. Buffet's vast wealth.

Furthermore, the practitioner may admit that the *average* fund doesn't outperform indexing. But surely the "good" funds have skill. But, as reviewed by Gene in 1970, there is a way to study this question: name an ex ante criterion for finding "good" funds, and look at the performance of that whole group, adjusting for risk, over time. There is a bit of fishing danger here too, as one out of twenty selection criteria will have a significant t-statistic. Selection criteria such as "invest with guys named Buffett" or "follow all funds in Nebraska" will lead to spurious results. But that's the same problem as all alpha-producing characteristics that we examine for stocks using historical data, as we must, rather than announcing skill indicators and waiting 20 years for the returns to roll in.

This procedure is an example of the clever inversion that Ray Ball describes, and shows quite how much genius had to go between the idea of informational efficiency and teasing out its predictions for markets. Rather than look for the information that made Buffet rich, look at the performance of all investors using a similar strategy, averaging out the luck.

The most natural indicator of skill or information advantage is past performance: look at groups of funds that did well in the past and see if they collectively do well in the future. Mark Carhart's (1997) study of one- and five-year performance persistence stands as a modern classic of this approach. The answer is, past performance tells you essentially nothing about performance going forward.

Still, the practitioner might note that the uncertainty in measuring average returns makes return histories very noisy signals of skill. The one-year return histories that Carhart found most powerful for predicting returns before risk adjustment are and should be nearly meaningless measures of long-term average performance. So the practitioner might retort, "I know the good funds, you're just using very noisy signals of who is good." So far, a large number of other indicators of skill have been tried in the academic literature, such as Morningstar Ratings, education of the manager, and so on, and few have found substantial skill or information advantage. (Inside information does work, but poses legal risks.) But the practitioner, or salesman, trying to convince you that his fund, with an eye-popping return history, really will violate the adage that past performance is no guide to the future, can still claim that the academic literature just isn't good enough at shopping for the "good" funds to notice them.

THE PAPER

Enter Fama and French. This paper is especially innovative for asking the question in a completely different way, but with the usual "now why didn't I think of that?" simplicity. Fama and French ask, if funds really have no alpha, what is the chance of seeing funds with good performance? How likely is it in a universe of 6,000 funds, that we see a fund with Buffet's performance?

They tabulate the distribution of fund alpha t-statistics—alpha / standard error of alpha—to put funds on the same basis despite varying lifespans and tracking errors. Then they ask how many funds should by luck alone produce large alpha t-statistics if the true alphas are all zero. The heart of the paper is a careful simulation approach to this question, which handles cross-correlation and non-normality. However, if you read the tables, the numbers are not far from standard t distributions. About 2.5% of funds should, if there is no skill at all, have alpha t-statistics above about 1.96.

The result: when adjusted with the Fama-French three- or four-factor model, there is a tiny amount of skill in gross returns, before fees. The upper tail of alphas is just a little bit bigger than it should be if there were no skill at all. After fees, there is essentially no positive skill in net returns to investors. And there is a puzzle, in our view: the average and median fund has negative alpha, both gross and net. And the *left* tail is much too big. There are far too many funds with *negative* alpha than pure chance would allow. In an efficient market, investors can't systematically lose money either, except by lack of diversification or by blowing money on trading costs and fees!

The immense novelty of this paper is that it does not rely on the researcher to come up with a signal of skill. So it answers the practitioner's challenge directly—no matter how clever you are at finding skill ex ante, the number of funds that have it is quite small. The weakness, from an investor's point of view, is that it does not tell you how to find the skilled funds, if there are any.

THE FUTURE

A half century after it started, performance evaluation remains a hot topic. A whole new class of funds has sprung up to study, including hedge funds, sovereign wealth funds, university endowments, private equity, and institutional proprietary trading. These are more active and spread across more markets. More importantly, the fundamental ideas behind performance evaluation are changing quickly.

Fama and French's paper reports a controversy with Berk and Green (2004), which will, we think, expand. For 50 years, academics have been deploring active management. But how does it survive? If efficient marketers would not allow "irrationality" as an "explanation" for a 50-year pricing puzzle, why do we allow it for a quantity puzzle? And though individuals are finally moving to indexing, supposedly sophisticated investors, including university endowments, are moving to more active and higher-fee management.

Berk and Green's article is, in our eyes, a watershed, because it writes down a simple, coherent supply-and-demand model in which the basic facts of performance evaluation and the larger academic study of active management make some sense. In their model, some managers do have skill, but only at limited scale. Investors move to the skilled managers until returns to investors are no more than investors can achieve by indexing. Managers capture all the skill in fees.

However, the Berk and Green model has not been quantitatively matched to the data. You can see this process beginning in Fama and French's comments. In Berk and Green's model, investors receive zero alpha after fees. In Fama and French's paper, the average fund delivers negative alpha after fees, which they cite as evidence against Berk and Green's model. Berk and van Binsbergen (2013) retort that Fama and French's factors don't include transactions costs, investors didn't know about value and momentum factors in the 1970s, investors could not trade those factors if they did know about them, and we should measure skill by alphas times assets under management not by raw alphas. Ten basis points on a billion dollars is a lot of skill. Using available tradeable factors, they climb back up to zero alpha. The argument has a long way to go.

Negative alphas and harmful fees are a deep puzzle. The fund literature (e.g., Carhart 1997) finds that fees and turnover cut returns to investors one-for-one. While we have repeated this mantra so often it seems natural, reflect a moment that this result is really puzzlingly bad. The fund manager says, "We charge fees and turnover to achieve our alpha. We then pass on the good returns to our investors." The most cynical Chicago economist would predict zero correlation between fees, turnover, and returns to investors: investors should get paid their outside opportunity, namely the market index, just as we each pay the same price to the electric company and the cleaners. Funds would chew up all the extra performance in fees, but no more. The fact that fees and turnover lower returns to investors is a huge puzzle even to that most cynical Chicago view. Why don't the investors just leave? The janitors don't take a pay cut at high-fee firms. Berk and Green assert the puzzle isn't there. Clearly, this discussion will continue.

More questions remain. Does the strength of fund flows following performance quantitatively match Berk and Green's Bayesian learning theory? We'll see. To our casual eyes, money flows faster than real information about skill in the latest returns. But nobody has checked this question yet.

A deeper intellectual shift is hiding in the transition from CAPM to multifactor models for performance evaluation. When the CAPM was the only model, well, you used the CAPM to risk adjust managers like everything else. Now that multifactor models, following Fama and French's size and book-to-market models, are the standard, which model should you use to adjust performance? Or should we be using deeper models, like the consumption-based model?

The answer in Fama and French is that the choice of factors for *performance evaluation* reflects much different criteria than, say, a model one would use to decide if booms and busts were "rational" or not. As the best example, Fama and French here use a momentum factor, as did Carhart (1997), despite their clear reservations whether the momentum premium is rational.

Why? Because the question here is, can a manager deliver something that I cannot get by mechanical trading strategies, for which I don't need to pay high fees? Any "factor" that the investor can trade mechanically or get in a passive, low-fee vehicle goes on the right-hand side in this thinking. If a manager offers a better, more efficient, lower cost of providing value or momentum, that is still valuable. However, net of fees, and benchmarked to a tradeable portfolio, that manager will still show alpha.

But is this logic correct? Adjusting with the market return makes abundant sense, whether or not the CAPM holds, because most investors have access to cheap market indices and have thought through their allocation to the market portfolio. They don't need to pay for beta through a manager.

But value is alpha to an investor who hasn't thought about value. How many investors have thought about momentum or short-volatility exposure? How many are in any position to trade those "factors," "mechanical" though they appear to us academics, without getting swamped by transactions costs?

As another example, should we benchmark with fixed or time-varying betas? Suppose a manager bought only the S&P 500 ETF, but changed his exposure based on some publicly observable signal, which he is not going to tell you about, and suppose his signal works. Suppose further we could measure his beta ex post with high-frequency data. Should we benchmark him to this time-varying beta and conclude he has no alpha? Should we at least worry about time-varying risk exposure? Or should we listen to his sputtering complaints that knowing when to increase beta *is* his alpha, and we should only benchmark to factors that we the investors already understand and trade?

The larger picture painted by the second generation of empirical work in the multifactor context is, in our evaluation, that "alpha," interpreted as pure information that is not incorporated in market prices, is hard to find. But the model of market equilibrium question, raised in Gene's 1970 essay, remains and has grown in importance. There are now many flavors of "beta." The function of most funds is simply to understand betas that investors don't understand or don't know how to trade efficiently. If that is our world, then just how one should benchmark, and the very definition of "skill," changes dramatically.

You can see hints of this fact in Fama and French's appendix tables, where they risk adjust only using the CAPM. Lo and behold, now there is a substantial tail of funds with positive "skill." Who are they? Well, they are value funds of course, perhaps even including Dimensional Fund Advisors (the fund specializing in small and value stocks based on Fama and French's research).

Finally, the "equilibrium accounting" that Fama and French emphasize is a deep puzzle of all active trading. Positive alphas are not really a puzzle. Negative alphas are a puzzle! It is natural to think that professional traders can, by paying attention, find information not incorporated into prices—somebody's got to do it—buy a little low, and sell a little high. In doing so, they take a little money from the "liquidity" trader, as all models of trading specify.

But the average investor must hold the market portfolio. The average alpha, relative to the market portfolio, must be zero. For every winner, there must be a loser. For every seller, there must be a buyer. Beating the market is a completely zero-sum game. (We repeat because practitioner analysis so routinely ignores this simple fact.)

There is a way for any of us to avoid being the liquidity trader with negative alpha: hold only the value-weighted market index, and refuse any offer to trade away from those weights. If we did, traders with information would simply bid prices up to efficient values, with no trading and no profit. Why does anyone agree to be the negative alpha? That remains the basic puzzle of information trading.

In sum, Fama and French give us a deeply innovative analysis and point the way to an ongoing, active area of research, not one that is just repeating 45-year-old arguments.

REFERENCES

Berk, Jonathan B., and Richard C. Green. 2004. "Mutual Fund Flows and Performance in Rational Markets." *Journal of Political Economy* 112, 1269–1295.

Berk, Jonathan, and Jules H. van Binsbergen. 2013. "Measuring Managerial Skill in the Mutual Fund Industry." Manuscript, Stanford University.

Carhart, Mark M. 1997. "On Persistence in Mutual Fund Performance." *Journal of Finance* 52, 57–82.

LUCK VERSUS SKILL AND FACTOR SELECTION

. . .

Campbell R. Harvey and Yan Liu

INTRODUCTION

In the universe of thousands of mutual funds, a substantial number will out-perform their benchmarks purely by luck. Fama and French (2010) develop an innovative approach that presents substantial progress on the economically important problem of distinguishing luck from skill in performance evaluation. Their methods can also be applied to distinguishing luck from performance in other important areas of finance. This article represents one such application to the reliability of return-predicting factors or characteristics.

LUCK

Fama and French address a classic problem in statistics called multiple testing. When many tests are conducted, some will appear "significant" by luck, using statistics designed to measure the chance of one, and only one, test coming out well.

Suppose every one of the 3,000 mutual funds has a true alpha of zero. Under this assumption, the t-statistics of the estimated alphas approximately follow standard normal distributions. Therefore, by pure chance, the maximum alpha t-statistic will be 3.6 on average, and 1% of the funds should show alpha t-statistics greater than 2.3. Though an individual fund only has a 1% chance of showing a 2.3 t-statistic, and therefore declaring its return "statistically significant," it is nearly certain that 30 funds with 2.3 t-statistics will exist just due to luck. It would clearly be a mistake to proclaim that finding such funds proves the presence of skill or market inefficiency.

In principle, multiple testing is easily handled. If the investigator is willing to write down the multiple testing procedure—choose the best of 100 mutual funds, say—then one can easily work out the probability distribution of the multiple test—the distribution of the greatest alpha t-statistic in 100 funds. The trouble is that the investigator is seldom so explicit about the multiple testing process. The profession as a whole—the tendency for only "significant" results to be published, for example—is even less explicit. Statistics which correct for multiple testing are therefore difficult to calculate. Thus, empirical work rarely corrects explicitly for multiple testing. The fact that published finance empirical work often fails out of sample is not surprising.

PRECURSORS

Kosowski, Timmermann, Wermers, and White (2006) use a bootstrap technique to study the distribution of alpha t-statistics under the null that funds have no true alpha. They deserve credit for advancing the "how many funds should we see outperforming" test rather than the more conventional tests for skill that look for persistence in performance or alphas in portfolios of funds sorted on the basis of some ex ante measure of skill. Their technique allows us to make statements about whether mutual funds exhibit skill in general, without the researcher needing to specify how to find the good funds. It therefore is less useful in evaluating the skill of a particular fund manager or helping investors in their quest to find the good funds.

They find that mutual fund "stars" are still stars after their adjustment: there are more successful funds than there should be, just due to chance.

The Kosowski et al. (2006) approach allows us to see if the best funds, with large individual t-statistics, do better than they should due to chance. Kosowski et al. thus generalize White (2000) in that White looks at the distribution of the maximum test statistics while Kosowski et al. calculate the whole distribution.

FAMA AND FRENCH

However, Kosowski et al. independently bootstrap each fund's returns. This method ignores potential correlation between the return residuals. If, beyond factor exposures, fund A and fund B both take the same "idiosyncratic" bets, then it is less likely that the better of the two has a large alpha t-statistic than would be the case if their residuals were uncorrelated. In the extreme case that all residuals are perfectly correlated, we essentially have only one fund and there is no need for multiple testing adjustment at all.

If the average correlation among the residuals is positive, then it seems that the multiple testing adjusted threshold should be lower than what Kosowski et al. suggest. However, funds often take opposite (idiosyncratic) bets against each other, and this tendency varies over time. In that case, there will be more high t-statistic funds due to chance than the Kosowski et al. approach calculates.

Fama and French solve this problem by bootstrapping the residuals across all funds, which is a key innovation. For example, suppose we have a $60 \times 3{,}000$ panel of fund returns in which rows are dates (months) and columns are funds. Fama and French resample an entire row. Resampling by row accommodates arbitrary cross-correlation of the residual risks. Fama's insight on this issue reaches back to the Fama-MacBeth procedure, which also allows arbitrary cross-sectional correlation. (One can block-bootstrap adjacent time periods as well, to maintain temporal correlations or include lags in the underlying regressions. However, time-series autocorrelations of fund returns are small, so this modification likely has little practical effect.)

Using this bootstrap and a four-factor performance attribution model, Fama and French find, among other things, that the top 1% fund's empirical alpha t-statistic of 2.5 is only very slightly above the first percentile of "luck" alphas (simulated p-value = 36.96%). Therefore, even for the top funds, there is little to no significant outperformance.

BUILDING ON THESE INSIGHTS

Fama and French and Kosowski et al. do not provide an overall test statistic. What is the probability of seeing the entire distribution of observed alphas, or one by some metric more extreme, if all the underlying alphas are zero? It's fun to look at the upper 1%, or upper 5%, but an arbitrariness lies in that choice. To produce an overall statistic, we would need to understand the joint properties of the values at each point of the distribution. What is the joint distribution of, say, the number of funds that exceed t-statistics of 2.0 and the number that exceed t-statistics of 3.0? (Such a test would likely reject the null that all alphas are zero, but because of the puzzlingly large number of funds with negative alphas, not positive alphas!)

Both Fama and French and Kosowski et al. also assume the joint null that none of the funds has skill. They do not tell us what would happen if a portion of these funds actually do have skill. Fama and French add a table of "injected alpha" predictions—they assume that true alphas are random draws from a normal distribution with a zero mean and find the variance estimate that best fits the realized alphas. But they do not reverse engineer the distribution of injected alpha that best matches the data, nor offer measures of uncertainty about this distribution. Reverse engineering the implied distribution of injected alpha is a straightforward calculation, and we encourage researchers to do it even though Fama and French did not.

As a result, Fama and French do not tell us just how many funds have skill, and how much they have, or whether a particular fund has significant skill or not. These concerns inspired a sequence of follow-up papers. To study the joint properties of the tests, recent work draws on the statistics literature that proposes the false discovery rate, which is defined as the expected number of false discoveries among all discoveries. In particular, Barras, Scaillet, and Wermers (2010) use the false discovery rate to correct for the bias in estimating the proportion of skilled funds. Harvey, Liu, and Zhu (2016) use false discovery rate as the multiple testing counterpart of the Type I error and provide multiple testing adjusted benchmark t-ratios. To evaluate the performance of tests under alternative hypotheses, Barras, Scaillet, and Wermers group the universe of mutual funds into three and use the distributional information in the t-statistics to estimate the proportion of false discoveries. Ferson and Chen (2014) refine their method by removing the perfect power assumption (i.e., the test will never confuse a good fund with a fund that has a zero or negative mean return) as well as incorporating the possibility that a bad fund (i.e., a fund that has a negative mean return) can be falsely identified as a good fund (i.e., a fund that has a positive mean return), and vice versa. Harvey, Liu, and Zhu parametrically model the distribution of mean returns for true discoveries in a multiple testing framework. By explicitly modeling the distribution of the test statistics under both the null and the alternative hypotheses, they are able to make inferences on the fraction of true discoveries.

APPLICATION TO OTHER AREAS OF FINANCE

Test multiplicity haunts finance research. For the fund evaluation literature, it is termed *luck versus skill*. For the return predictability and risk factor literature, it is called *data snooping* or *data mining*: some variables will appear to predict returns, and some factors (portfolios of stocks) will appear to have large average returns, based on one-at-a-time test statistics, if one looks at many candidates and chooses the best ones.

The fact that we do not observe the tests that are tried but failed is an important source of multiple-test bias. Harvey, Liu, and Zhu (2016) take this bias into account by explicitly modeling the missing data process. They assume that researchers drop all insignificant tests—tests that have t-statistics below a certain threshold. Following this assumption, observed t-statistics follow a truncated distribution, and they back out the underlying number of unreported tests. They estimate that more than four times the number of observed tests are missing (i.e., unpublished) for the academic literature on the cross-section of expected returns. That is, we observe only one in five tests.

Building on Fama and French's insight, however, we must also adjust test statistics for the fact that all variables share economy-wide shocks in fundamentals or liquidity conditions.

The return prediction literature faces an additional problem: the left-hand side variables are the same while researchers try multiple right-hand side variables. Time-series research tries to forecast the same, usually market return, with many right-hand side variables. In cross-sectional estimates, either in the form of Fama-MacBeth regressions, Gibbons-Ross-Shanken panel regressions, or portfolios formed on the basis of predictor variables, the cross-section of stock returns is the same left-hand side variable as one tries hundreds of forecasting variables.

FAMA-FRENCH APPLIED TO FACTOR SELECTION

Fama and French's technique can help us overcome these deep problems of empirical asset pricing. To illustrate, we apply Fama and French's technique to address multiple comparison problems in factor selection. Factor returns are long-short zero-cost investment strategies based on return predicting variables. Fama and French's "high minus low" (HML)—long (buy) value stocks with high book-to-market ratios, and short growth stocks with low book-to-market ratios—is the classic example. There is not much of a jump between evaluating the viability of a long-short investment strategy and evaluating the viability of a particular investment manager.

We study the Standard and Poor's (S&P) Capital IQ database of "alphas." S&P sells data on the historical performance of synthetic long-short strategies. We focus on 484 strategies for the US equity market from 1985 to 2014. These strategies are cataloged into eight groups based on the types of risks that they are exposed to (e.g., market risk) or the nature of the forecasting variables (e.g., characteristics). The database has a good coverage of well-known return signals, including CAPM beta (Capital Efficiency Group), size (Size Group), value (Valuation Group), and momentum (Momentum Group).

Following Fama and French, we first calculate the t-statistics for the average return (raw returns without factor adjustment) of each long-short strategy, and we rank these t-ratios. We then demean the long-short portfolio returns and bootstrap their return observations. In bootstrapping, we keep the entire cross-section intact for each resampled time period, again following Fama and French.

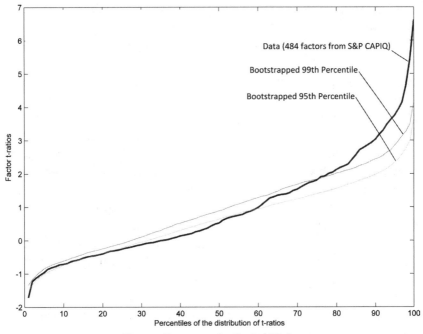

Figure 1. Factor tests for Capital IQ data

We obtain 484 (pre-transaction costs) long-short strategy returns from S&P Capital IQ. The curve labeled "Data" shows the *t*-statistic percentiles for these strategies. After demeaning each of the 484 strategies, the other two curves show the 99th and the 95th percentiles of the bootstrapped *t*-statistic percentiles, respectively.

Figure 1 presents the results. The line labeled "Data" shows the empirical *t*-ratio percentiles for the Capital IQ strategies. The x-axis presents the percentile of the 484 strategies in their rank by average return *t*-statistic. The y-axis shows the value of the alpha *t*-statistic for each fund. The dashed lines show the 99th and 95th percentiles in the bootstrapped percentiles of the no-mean-return distribution.

The top percentiles of the data are generally well above their 99th and 95th percentile bounds. In particular, the maximum *t*-ratio for the data is 6.62 and the 99th percentile for the simulated maximum *t*-ratios is 4.13; the 90th percentile for the data is 3.11 and the 99th percentile for the simulated 90th percentiles is 2.45. Based on the graph, we have confidence to reject the null hypothesis that none of the 484 factors has a positive expected return.

These results for the S&P Capital IQ factors contrast with Fama and French's mutual fund results. First, Fama and French find scant evidence that mutual funds outperform their four-factor benchmark. Figure 1 suggests that a number of the Capital IQ factors appear to outperform—that is, generate a mean return that is significantly positive. This is perhaps not surprising given that there is considerable evidence that some of these strategies (such as the equity premium and the return to value-oriented investing) generate positive returns. However, the bulk of the Capital IQ returns are less widely known long-short strategies. Second, Fama and French find significant underperformance (negative alphas) for the worst performing fund managers. There is no evidence of significant underperformance in the Capital IQ data.

However, our illustrative example makes no effort to overcome survivorship and selection bias. S&P may have culled significant underperformers and included in-sample successful strategies (backfill bias). Our point is to demonstrate the widespread usefulness of Fama and French's statistical method. Their research also includes meticulous data work to include all the dead funds and overcome survivor bias, selection bias, backfill bias, and so forth.

The Fama-French method does not tell us which of the factors have positive expected returns. For example, the 80th percentile of t-statistics seems to lie above the 99th percentile confidence band. We should not conclude that each strategy in the upper 20% is significant.

We also do not observe all the factors that have been tried. Although the IQ sample covers almost 500 factors, thousands more could have been tried but not reported. Harvey, Liu, and Zhu (2016) provide some tools to deal with this problem. They provide a truncated distributional framework to back out the number of missing predictor variables.

A CUTOFF

A simple tool for evaluating the effects of multiple testing, and that allows us to consider the significance of a given fund or strategy return, would be very useful. To that end, we now find a t-ratio cutoff that classifies a statistically significant factor, correcting for multiple testing.

Consider the mutual fund evaluation problem. In every bootstrap iteration, we calculate t-ratios for, say, 3,000 funds. We save the maximum t-ratio. We iterate 10,000 times and get the distribution of the maximum t-ratio. We then look at the max t-ratio among the fund managers. If the t-ratio of the best-performing fund manager is larger than the 95th percentile of the max of the bootstrapped distribution (under the null of no skill), we declare the manager "skilled."

The maximum may be sensitive to outliers. Tail percentiles may be better. However, there is a tradeoff. The max has more power to reject the null while percentiles are less affected by extreme observations. Here we use max as an illustration.

Next, for the manager declared skilled, we alter the null distribution to include that manager's alpha. Hence, 2,999 funds have a zero mean return and one fund will have a positive mean. We repeat the bootstrap. We compare the distribution of the second highest t-ratio to the t-ratio of the second best performing manager. If the manager is again better than the 95th percentile of the null, we declare that manager to be skilled, and insert her alpha into the null and continue. If the manager does not exceed the 95th percentile, we stop.

Essentially, at each step of our method, our null hypothesis is that some managers have skill, their levels of skill are set at the in-sample estimates, and the rest of the managers have a skill of zero. We use the t-statistic of the best performing manager among those that have not been identified as skillful to test this null. The first time the null is rejected, we record the t-statistic. This is the t-statistic threshold that our method identifies. Managers that have a t-statistic above this threshold are declared to have skill.

We can apply the same idea to factors. We find the fraction of statistically significant factors by sequentially injecting the in-sample means of the factors we declare as significant. In particular, we add back the means of the top p percent of factors. We then bootstrap to generate the distribution of the cross-section of t-ratios. In essence, this distribution is based on the hypothesis that the top p percent of factors are significant, their means equal their in-sample fit, and the remaining $1 - p$ percent of factors have a mean of zero. To test this hypothesis, we compare the $(1 - p)$th percentile of the bootstrapped distribution with the $(1 - p)$th percentile of t-ratios for the real data. We sequentially increase the level of p until the null hypothesis is not rejected. Our estimate of the fraction of significant factors will be p.

Figure 2 presents the results. When we inject the top 5% of factors into the null ($q = 5.0$, top panel), the 95th percentile of t-ratios of the real data is above the 95th percentile of the simulated 95th percentiles. Hence, inserting the means of the top 5% of factors into the null is not enough to explain the observed 95th percentile of t-ratios. Hence, we would declare the top 5% as "significant." We gradually increase q. When $q = 13.0$ (i.e., bottom panel), the 87th percentile of t-ratios of the real data meets the 95th percentile of the simulated 87th percentiles. The corresponding t-ratio cutoff is 2.71. We therefore conclude that 63 ($= 484 \times 13\%$) out of the 484 factors are "significant."

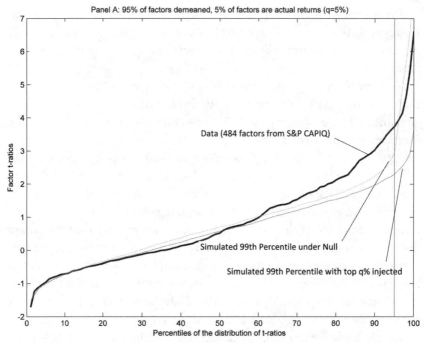

Figure 2. Estimating the fraction of significant factors

We obtain 484 (pre-transaction costs) long-short strategy returns from S&P Capital IQ. The curves labeled "Data" in both panels show the *t*-statistic percentiles for these strategies. After demeaning each of the 484 strategies, a curve in each panel shows the 99th percentiles of the bootstrapped *t*-statistic percentiles. In Panel A, we demean the bottom 95% of strategies (and keep the top 5% intact), and the third curve in the top panel shows the 99th percentiles of the bootstrapped *t*-statistic percentiles of this new sample, which we refer to as "simulated 99th percentile with top 5% injected." In panel B, we demean the bottom 87% of strategies (and keep the top 13% intact), and the third curve in the bottom panel shows the 99th percentiles of the bootstrapped *t*-statistic percentiles.

Again, this analysis is contingent on the integrity of the data provided by S&P Capital IQ. In addition, transactions costs are not included. Given the prominence of a few existing factors (e.g., market, size, value, and momentum), sometimes we are interested in the incremental alpha of a strategy after adjusting for prominent factors. But our method is easily extended to accommodate this.

Inspired by this example, Harvey and Liu (2015) propose a general method to estimate regression models in the presence of multiple testing. They first

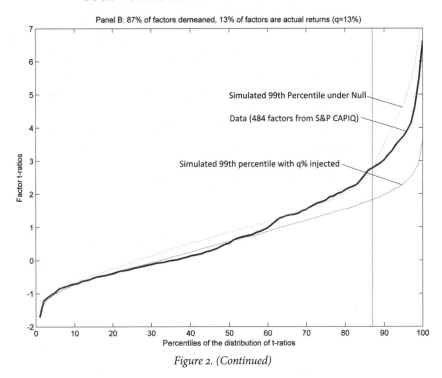

Figure 2. (Continued)

orthogonalize the right-hand variables so that they have no in-sample explanatory power. This is similar to Fama and French. They then bootstrap to test whether a "true" variable exists among a candidate set of right-hand side variables. To control for multiple testing, they use the max statistic, similar to White (2000). The final step of their method is to recursively identify the set of significant right-hand side variables, one variable at a time. Their framework is general enough to encompass most regressions models in asset pricing applications. In particular, they show how their method applies to predictive regressions, Gibbons-Ross-Shanken panel regressions, and Fama-MacBeth regressions. Harvey and Liu (2016) probe the multiple testing issue from a different angle. They propose a structural approach that allows us to pool information from the cross-section to adjust the inference on a particular entity within the cross-section.

CONCLUSION

Fama and French provide an innovative approach to distinguish between luck and skill in investment manager performance. We show that their insights touch a wide swath of financial research. In empirical research in finance, we often have many candidate variables or a large number of economic agents/ units that might provide an answer to an important economic question. Two issues hinder such investigations. First, inference is often incorrectly drawn from a statistic designed for independent rather than multiple testing. Second, financial variables are correlated in complicated ways. The large number of potential return-forecasting variables makes the accurate modeling of the correlation structure among these variables almost impossible. Fama and French deal with both of these hurdles. While they focus their application on investment manager evaluation, their insights apply to a broader spectrum of research in financial economics.

***

The authors appreciate the detailed comments of John Cochrane and Tobias Moskowitz.

REFERENCES

Barras, L., O. Scaillet, and R. Wermers. 2010. "False Discoveries in Mutual Fund Performance: Measuring Luck in Estimated Alphas." *Journal of Finance* 65, 179–216.

Fama, E. F., and J. D. MacBeth. 1973. "Risk, Return, and Equilibrium: Empirical Tests." *Journal of Political Economy* 81, 607–636.

Fama, E. F., and K. R. French. 2010. "Luck versus Skill in the Cross-Section of Mutual Fund Returns." *Journal of Finance* 65, 1915–1947.

Ferson, W. E., and Y. Chen. 2014. "How Many Good and Bad Fund Managers Are There, Really?" Working paper, University of Southern California.

Gibbons, M. R., S. A. Ross, and J. Shanken. 1989. "A Test of the Efficiency of a Given Portfolio." *Econometrica* 57, 1121–1152.

Harvey, C. R., Y. Liu, and H. Zhu. 2016. ". . . And the Cross-Section of Expected Returns." *Review of Financial Studies* 29, 5–68.

Harvey, C. R., and Y. Liu. 2015. "Lucky Factors." Working paper, Duke University.

Harvey, C. R., and Y. Liu. 2016. "Rethinking Performance Evaluation." Working paper, Duke University.

Kosowski, R., A. Timmermann, R. Wermers, and H. White. 2006. "Can Mutual Fund 'Stars' Really Pick Stocks? New Evidence from a Bootstrap Analysis." *Journal of Finance* 61, 2551–2595.

White, H. 2000. "A Reality Check for Data Snooping." *Econometrica* 68, 1097–1126.

LUCK VERSUS SKILL IN THE CROSS-SECTION OF MUTUAL FUND RETURNS

· · ·

Eugene F. Fama and Kenneth R. French

There is a constraint on the returns to active investing that we call equilibrium accounting. In short (details later), suppose that when returns are measured before costs (fees and other expenses), passive investors get passive returns, that is, they have zero α (abnormal expected return) relative to passive benchmarks. This means active investment must also be a zero sum game—aggregate α is zero before costs. Thus, if some active investors have positive α before costs, it is dollar for dollar at the expense of other active investors. After costs, that is, in terms of net returns to investors, active investment must be a negative sum game. (Sharpe (1991) calls this the arithmetic of active management.)

We examine mutual fund performance from the perspective of equilibrium accounting. For example, at the aggregate level, if the value-weight (VW) portfolio of active funds has a positive α before costs, we can infer that the VW portfolio of active investments outside mutual funds has a negative α. In other words, active mutual funds win at the expense of active investments outside mutual funds. We find that, in fact, the VW portfolio of active funds that invest primarily in U.S. equities is close to the market portfolio, and estimated before expenses, its α relative to common benchmarks is close to zero. Since the VW portfolio of active funds produces α close to zero in gross (pre-expense) returns, α estimated on the net (post-expense) returns realized by investors is negative by about the amount of fund expenses.

The aggregate results imply that if there are active mutual funds with positive true α, they are balanced by active funds with negative α. We test for the

Reprinted with permission from the *Journal of Finance* 65, no. 5 (October 2010): 1915–47. © 2010 by John Wiley and Sons.

We are grateful for the comments of Juhani Linnainmaa, Sunil Wahal, Jerry Zimmerman, and seminar participants at the University of Chicago, the California Institute of Technology, UCLA, and the Meckling Symposium at the University of Rochester. Special thanks to John Cochrane and the journal Editor, Associate Editor, and referees.

existence of such funds. The challenge is to distinguish skill from luck. Given the multitude of funds, many have extreme returns by chance. A common approach to this problem is to test for persistence in fund returns, that is, whether past winners continue to produce high returns and losers continue to underperform (see, e.g., Grinblatt and Titman (1992), Carhart (1997)). Persistence tests have an important weakness. Because they rank funds on short-term past performance, there may be little evidence of persistence because the allocation of funds to winner and loser portfolios is largely based on noise.

We take a different tack. We use long histories of individual fund returns and bootstrap simulations of return histories to infer the existence of superior and inferior funds. Specifically, we compare the actual cross-section of fund α estimates to the results from 10,000 bootstrap simulations of the cross-section. The returns of the funds in a simulation run have the properties of actual fund returns, except we set true α to zero in the return population from which simulation samples are drawn. The simulations thus describe the distribution of α estimates when there is no abnormal performance in fund returns. Comparing the distribution of α estimates from the simulations to the cross-section of α estimates for actual fund returns allows us to draw inferences about the existence of skilled managers.

For fund investors the simulation results are disheartening. When α is estimated on net returns to investors, the cross-section of precision-adjusted α estimates, $t(\alpha)$, suggests that few active funds produce benchmark-adjusted expected returns that cover their costs. Thus, if many managers have sufficient skill to cover costs, they are hidden by the mass of managers with insufficient skill. On a practical level, our results on long-term performance say that true α in net returns to investors is negative for most if not all active funds, including funds with strongly positive α estimates for their entire histories.

Mutual funds look better when returns are measured gross, that is, before the costs included in expense ratios. Comparing the cross-section of $t(\alpha)$ estimates from gross fund returns to the average cross-section from the simulations suggests that there are inferior managers whose actions reduce expected returns, and there are superior managers who enhance expected returns. If we assume that the cross-section of true α has a normal distribution with mean zero and standard deviation σ, then σ around 1.25% per year seems to capture the tails of the cross-section of α estimates for our full sample of actively managed funds.

The estimate of the standard deviation of true α, 1.25% per year, does not imply much skill. It suggests, for example, that fewer than 16% of funds have α greater than 1.25% per year (about 0.10% per month), and only about 2.3% have α greater than 2.50% per year (about 0.21% per month)—before expenses.

The simulation tests have power. If the cross-section of true α for gross fund returns is normal with mean zero, the simulations strongly suggest that the standard deviation of true α is between 0.75% and 1.75% per year. Thus, the simulations rule out values of σ rather close to our estimate, 1.25%. The power traces to the fact that a large cross-section of funds produces precise estimates of the percentiles of $t(\alpha)$ under different assumptions about σ, the standard deviation of true α. This precision allows us to put σ in a rather narrow range.

Readers suggest that our results are consistent with the predictions of Berk and Green (2004). We outline their model in Section II, after the tests on mutual fund aggregates (Section I) and before the bootstrap simulations (Sections III and IV). Our results reject most of their predictions about mutual fund returns. Given the prominence of their model, our contrary evidence seems an important contribution. The paper closest to ours is Kosowski et al. (2006). They run bootstrap simulations that appear to produce stronger evidence of manager skill. We contrast their tests and ours in Section V, after presenting our results. Section VI concludes.

I. THE PERFORMANCE OF AGGREGATE PORTFOLIOS OF U.S. EQUITY MUTUAL FUNDS

Our mutual fund sample is from the CRSP (Center for Research in Security Prices) database. We include only funds that invest primarily in U.S. common stocks, and we combine, with value weights, different classes of the same fund into a single fund (see French (2008)). To focus better on the performance of active managers, we exclude index funds from all our tests. The CRSP data start in 1962, but we concentrate on the period after 1983. During the period 1962 to 1983 about 15% of the funds on CRSP report only annual returns, and the average annual equal-weight (EW) return for these funds is 5.29% lower than for funds that report monthly returns. As a result, the EW average return on all funds is a nontrivial 0.65% per year lower than the EW return of funds that report monthly returns. Thus, during 1962 to 1983 there is selection bias in tests like ours that use only funds that report monthly returns. After 1983, almost all funds report monthly returns. (Elton, Gruber, and Blake (2001) discuss CRSP data problems for the period before 1984.)

A. The Regression Framework

Our main benchmark for evaluating fund performance is the three-factor model of Fama and French (1993), but we also show results for Carhart's (1997) four-factor model. To measure performance, these models use two variants of the time-series regression

$$R_{it} - R_{ft} = a_i + b_i(R_{Mt} - R_{ft}) + s_i SMB_t + h_i HML_t + m_i MOM_t + e_{it}. \qquad (1)$$

In this regression, R_{it} is the return on fund i for month t, R_{ft} is the risk-free rate (the 1-month U.S. Treasury bill rate), R_{Mt} is the market return (the return on a VW portfolio of NYSE, Amex, and NASDAQ stocks), SMB_t and HML_t are the size and value-growth returns of Fama and French (1993), MOM_t is our version of Carhart's (1997) momentum return, a_i is the average return left unexplained by the benchmark model (the estimate of α_i), and e_{it} is the regression residual. The full version of (1) is Carhart's four-factor model, and the regression without MOM_t is the Fama–French three-factor model. The construction of SMB_t and HML_t follows Fama and French (1993). The momentum return, MOM_t, is defined like HML_t, except that we sort on prior return rather than the book-to-market equity ratio. (See Table I below.)

Regression (1) allows a more precise statement of the constraints of equilibrium accounting. The VW aggregate of the U.S. equity portfolios of all investors is the market portfolio. It has a market slope equal to 1.0 in (1), zero slopes on the other explanatory returns, and a zero intercept—before investment costs. This means that if the VW aggregate portfolio of passive investors also has a zero intercept before costs, the VW aggregate portfolio of active investors must have a zero intercept. Thus, positive and negative intercepts among active investors must balance out—before costs.

There is controversy about whether the average SMB_t, HML_t, and MOM_t returns are rewards for risk or the result of mispricing. For our purposes, there is no need to take a stance on this issue. We can simply interpret SMB_t, HML_t, and MOM_t as diversified passive benchmark returns that capture patterns in average returns during our sample period, whatever the source of the average returns. Abstracting from the variation in returns associated with $R_{Mt} - R_{ft}$, SMB_t, HML_t, and MOM_t then allows us to focus better on the effects of active management (stock picking), which should show up in the three-factor and four-factor intercepts.

From an investment perspective, the slopes on the explanatory returns in (1) describe a diversified portfolio of passive benchmarks (including the risk-

TABLE I. Summary statistics for monthly explanatory returns for the three-factor and four-factor models

R_M is the return on a value-weight market portfolio of NYSE, Amex, and NASDAQ stocks, and R_f is the 1-month Treasury bill rate. The construction of SMB_t and HML_t follows Fama and French (1993). At the end of June of each year k, we sort stocks into two size groups. Small includes NYSE, Amex, and NASDAQ stocks with June market capitalization below the NYSE median and Big includes stocks with market cap above the NYSE median. We also sort stocks into three book-to-market equity (B/M) groups, Growth (NYSE, Amex, and NASDAQ stocks in the bottom 30% of NYSE B/M), Neutral (middle 40% of NYSE B/M), and Value (top 30% of NYSE B/M). Book equity is for the fiscal year ending in calendar year $k-1$, and the market cap in B/M is for the end of December of $k-1$. The intersection of the (independent) size and B/M sorts produces six value-weight portfolios, refreshed at the end of June each year. The size return, SMB_t, is the simple average of the month t returns on the three Small stock portfolios minus the average of the returns on the three Big stock portfolios. The value-growth return, HML_t, is the simple average of the returns on the two Value portfolios minus the average of the returns on the two Growth portfolios. The momentum return, MOM_t, is defined like HML_t, except that we sort on prior return rather than B/M and the momentum sort is refreshed monthly rather than annually. At the end of each month $t-1$ we sort NYSE stocks on the average of the 11 months of returns to the end of month $t-2$. (Dropping the return for month $t-1$ is common in the momentum literature.) We use the 30th and 70th NYSE percentiles to assign NYSE, Amex, and NASDAQ stocks to Low, Medium, and High momentum groups. The intersection of the size sort for the most recent June and the independent momentum sort produces six value-weight portfolios, refreshed monthly. The momentum return, MOM_t, is the simple average of the month t returns on the two High momentum portfolios minus the average of the returns on the two Low momentum portfolios. The table shows the average monthly return, the standard deviation of monthly returns, and the t-statistic for the average monthly return. The period is January 1984 through September 2006.

	Average Return				Standard Deviation				t-statistic			
	$R_M - R_f$	SMB	HML	MOM	$R_M - R_f$	SMB	HML	MOM	$R_M - R_f$	SMB	HML	MOM
1984–2006	0.64	0.03	0.40	0.79	4.36	3.38	3.17	4.35	2.42	0.13	2.10	3.01

free security) that replicates the exposures of the fund on the left to common factors in returns. The regression intercept then measures the average return provided by a fund in excess of the return on a comparable passive portfolio. We interpret a positive expected intercept (true α) as good performance, and a negative expected intercept signals bad performance.[1]

Table I shows summary statistics for the explanatory returns in (1) for January 1984 through September 2006 (henceforth 1984 to 2006), the period used in our tests. The momentum factor (MOM_t) has the highest average return, 0.79% per month ($t = 3.01$), but the average values of the monthly market premium ($R_{Mt} - R_{ft}$) and the value-growth return (HML_t) are also large, 0.64% ($t = 2.42$) and 0.40% ($t = 2.10$), respectively. The size return, SMB_t, has the smallest average value, 0.03% per month ($t = 0.13$).

B. Regression Results for EW and VW Portfolios of Active Funds

Table II shows estimates of regression (1) for the monthly returns of 1984 to 2006 on EW and VW portfolios of the funds in our sample. In the VW portfolio, funds are weighted by assets under management (AUM) at the beginning of each month. The EW portfolio weights funds equally each month. The intercepts in (1) for EW fund returns tell us whether funds on average produce returns different from those implied by their exposures to common factors in returns, whereas VW returns tell us about the fate of aggregate wealth invested in funds. Table II shows estimates of (1) for fund returns measured gross and net of fund expenses. Net returns are those received by investors. Monthly gross returns are net returns plus 1/12th of a fund's expense ratio for the year.

The market slopes in Table II are close to 1.0, which is not surprising since our sample is funds that invest primarily in U.S. stocks. The HML_t and MOM_t slopes are close to zero. Thus, in aggregate, active funds show little exposure to the value-growth and momentum factors. The EW portfolio of funds produces a larger SMB_t slope (0.18) than the VW portfolio (0.07). We infer that smaller funds are more likely to invest in small stocks, but total dollars invested in active funds (captured by VW returns) show little tilt toward small stocks.

---

1. Formal justification for this definition of good and bad performance is provided by Dybvig and Ross (1985). Given a risk-free security, their Theorem 5 implies that if the intercept in (1) is positive, there is a portfolio with positive weight on fund i and the portfolio of the explanatory portfolios on the right of (1) that has a higher Sharpe ratio than the portfolio of the explanatory portfolios. Similarly, if the intercept is negative, there is a portfolio with negative weight on fund i that has a higher Sharpe ratio than the portfolio of the explanatory portfolios.

TABLE II. Intercepts and slopes in variants of regression (1) for equal-weight (EW) and value-weight (VW) portfolios of actively managed mutual funds

The table shows the annualized intercepts (12 * α) and t-statistics for the intercepts ($t(Coef)$) for the CAPM, three-factor, and four-factor versions of regression (1) estimated on equal-weight (EW) and value-weight (VW) net and gross returns on the portfolios of actively managed mutual funds in our sample. The table also shows the regression slopes (b, s, h, and m, for $R_M - R_f$, SMB, HML, and MOM, respectively), t-statistics for the slopes, and the regression R^2, all of which are the same to two decimals for gross and net returns. For the market slope, $t(Coef)$ tests whether b is different from 1.0. Net returns are those received by investors. Gross returns are net returns plus 1/12th of a fund's expense ratio for the year. When a fund's expense ratio for a year is missing, we assume it is the same as other actively managed funds with similar assets under management (AUM). The period is January 1984 through September 2006. On average there are 1,308 funds and their average AUM is $648.0 million.

| | 12 * a | | | | | | |
	Net	Gross	b	s	h	m	R^2
EW Returns							
Coef	−1.11	0.18	1.01				0.96
t(Coef)	−1.80	0.31	1.12				
Coef	−0.93	0.36	0.98	0.18	−0.00		0.98
t(Coef)	−2.13	0.85	−1.78	16.09	−0.24		
Coef	−0.92	0.39	0.98	0.18	−0.00	−0.00	0.98
t(Coef)	−2.05	0.90	−1.78	16.01	−0.25	−0.14	
VW Returns							
Coef	−1.13	−0.18	0.99				0.99
t(Coef)	−3.03	−0.49	−2.10				
Coef	−0.81	0.13	0.96	0.07	−0.03		0.99
t(Coef)	−2.50	0.40	−5.42	7.96	−3.22		
Coef	−1.00	−0.05	0.97	0.07	−0.03	0.02	0.99
t(Coef)	−3.02	−0.15	−5.03	7.78	−3.03	2.60	

The intercepts in the estimates of (1) summarize the average performance of funds (EW returns) and the performance of aggregate wealth invested in funds (VW returns) relative to passive benchmarks. In terms of net returns to investors, performance is poor. The three-factor and four-factor (annualized) intercepts for EW and VW net returns are negative, ranging from −0.81% to −1.00% per year, with t-statistics from −2.05 to −3.02. These results are in line with previous work (e.g., Jensen (1968), Malkiel (1995), Gruber (1996)).

The intercepts in (1) for EW and VW net fund returns tell us whether on average active managers have sufficient skill to generate returns that cover the costs funds impose on investors. Gross returns come closer to testing whether managers have any skill. For EW gross fund returns, the three-factor and four-factor intercepts for 1984 to 2006 are positive, 0.36% and 0.39% per year, but they are only 0.85 and 0.90 standard errors from zero. The intercepts in (1) for VW gross returns are quite close to zero, 0.13% per year ($t = 0.40$) for the three-factor version of (1), and -0.05% per year ($t = -0.15$) for the four-factor model.

Table II also shows estimates of the CAPM version of (1), in which $R_{Mt} - R_{ft}$ is the only explanatory return. The annualized CAPM intercept for VW gross fund returns for 1984 to 2006, -0.18% per year ($t = -0.49$), is again close to zero and similar to the estimates for the three-factor and four-factor models. It is not surprising that the intercepts of the three models are so similar (-0.18%, 0.13%, and -0.05% per year) since VW fund returns produce slopes close to zero for the non-market explanatory returns in (1).

We can offer an equilibrium accounting perspective on the results in Table II. When we add back the costs in expense ratios, α estimates for VW gross fund returns are close to zero. Thus, before expenses, there is no evidence that total wealth invested in active funds gets any benefits or suffers any losses from active management. VW fund returns also show little exposure to the size, value, and momentum returns, and the market return alone explains 99% of the variance of the monthly VW fund return. Together these facts say that during 1984 to 2006, active mutual funds in aggregate hold a portfolio that, before expenses, mimics market portfolio returns. The return to investors, however, is reduced by the high expense ratios of active funds. These results echo equilibrium accounting, but for a subset of investment managers where the implications of equilibrium accounting for aggregate investor returns need not hold.

C. Measurement Issues in the Tests on Gross Returns

The benchmark explanatory returns in (1) are before all costs. This is appropriate in tests on net fund returns where the issue addressed is whether managers have sufficient skill to produce expected returns that cover their costs. Gross returns pose more difficult measurement issues.

The issue in the tests on gross fund returns is whether managers have skill that causes expected returns to differ from those of comparable passive benchmarks. For this purpose, one would like fund returns measured before all costs and non-return revenues. This would put funds on the same pure return basis as the benchmark explanatory returns, so the regressions could focus on manager skill. Our gross fund returns are before the costs in expense ratios (including management fees), but they are net of other costs, primarily trading costs, and they include the typically small revenues from securities lending.

We could attempt to add trading costs to our estimates of gross fund returns. Funds do not report trading costs, however, and estimates are subject to large errors. For example, trading costs are likely to vary across funds because of differences in style tilts, trading skill, and the extent to which a fund demands immediacy in trade execution. Trading costs also vary through time. Our view is that estimates of trading costs for individual funds, especially actively managed funds, are fraught with error and potential bias, and are likely to be misleading. We prefer to stay with our simple definition of gross returns (net returns plus the costs in expense ratios), with periodic qualifications to our inferences.

An alternative approach (suggested by a referee) is to put the passive benchmarks produced by combining the explanatory returns in (1) in the same units as the gross fund returns on the left of (1). This involves taking account of the costs not covered in expense ratios that would be borne by an efficiently managed passive benchmark with the same style tilts as the fund whose gross returns are to be explained. Appendix A discusses this approach in detail. The bottom line is that for efficiently managed passive funds, the costs missed in expense ratios are close to zero. Thus, adjusting the benchmarks produced by (1) for estimates of these costs is unnecessary.

This does not mean our tests on gross fund returns capture the pure effects of skill. Though it appears that all substantial costs incurred by efficiently managed passive funds are in their expense ratios, this is less likely to be true for actively managed funds. The typical active fund trades more than the typical passive fund, and active funds are likely to demand immediacy in trading that pushes up costs. Our tests on gross returns thus produce α estimates that capture skill, less whatever net costs (costs minus non-return revenues) are missed by expense ratios. Equivalently, the tests say that a fund's management has skill only if it is sufficient to cover the missing costs (primarily trading costs). This seems like a reasonable definition of skill since an efficiently managed passive fund can apparently avoid these costs. More important, this is the definition of skill we can accurately test, given the unavoidable absence of accurate trading cost estimates for active funds.

The fact that our gross fund returns are net of the costs missed in expense ratios, however, does affect the inferences about equilibrium accounting we can draw from the aggregate results in Table II. Since the α estimates for VW gross fund returns in Table II are close to zero, they suggest that in aggregate funds show sufficient skill to produce expected returns that cover some or all of the costs missed in expense ratios. If this is the correct inference (precision is an issue), equilibrium accounting then says that the costs recovered by funds are matched by equivalent losses on investments outside mutual funds.

II. BERK AND GREEN (2004)

Readers contend that our results (Table II and below) are consistent with Berk and Green (2004). Their model is attractive theory, but our results reject most of its predictions about mutual fund returns.

In their world, a fund is endowed with a permanent α, before costs, but it faces costs that are an increasing convex function of AUM. Investors use returns to update estimates of α. A fund with a positive expected α before costs attracts inflows until AUM reaches the point where expected α, net of costs, is zero. Outflows drive out funds with negative expected α. In equilibrium, all active funds (and thus funds in aggregate) have positive expected α before costs and zero expected α net of costs.

Our evidence that the aggregate portfolio of mutual funds has negative α net of costs contradicts the predictions of Berk and Green (2004). The results below on the net returns of individual funds also reject their prediction that all active managers have zero α net of costs. In fact, our results say that for most if not all funds, true α in net returns is negative.

Finally, equilibrium accounting poses a theoretical problem for Berk and Green (2004). Their model focuses on rational investors who optimally choose among passive and active alternatives. In aggregate, their investors have positive α before costs and zero α after costs. Equilibrium accounting, however, says that in aggregate investors have zero α before costs and negative α after costs.

III. BOOTSTRAP SIMULATIONS

Table II says that, on average, active mutual funds do not produce gross returns above (or below) those of passive benchmarks. This may just mean that managers with skill that allows them to outperform the benchmarks are balanced by inferior managers who underperform. We turn now to simulations that use individual fund returns to infer the existence of superior and inferior managers.

A. Setup

To lessen the effects of "incubation bias" (see below), we limit the tests to funds that reach 5 million 2006 dollars in AUM. Since the AUM minimum is in

2006 dollars, we include a fund in 1984, for example, if it has more than about $2.5 million in AUM in 1984. Once a fund passes the AUM minimum, it is included in all subsequent tests, so this requirement does not create selection bias. We also show results for funds after they pass $250 million and $1 billion. Since we estimate benchmark regressions for each fund, we limit the tests to funds that have at least 8 months of returns after they pass an AUM bound, so there is a bit of survival bias. To avoid having lots of new funds with short return histories, we only use funds that appear on CRSP at least 5 years before the end of our sample period.

Fund management companies commonly provide seed money to new funds to develop a return history. Incubation bias arises because funds typically open to the public—and their pre-release returns are included in mutual fund databases—only if the returns turn out to be attractive. The $5 million AUM bound for admission to the tests alleviates this bias since AUM is likely to be low during the pre-release period.

Evans (2010) suggests that incubation bias can be minimized by using returns only after funds receive a ticker symbol from NASDAQ, which typically means they are available to the public. Systematic data on ticker symbol start dates are available only after 1998. We have replicated our tests for 1999 to 2006 using CRSP start dates for new funds (as in our reported results) and then using NASDAQ ticker dates (from Evans). Switching to ticker dates has almost no effect on aggregate fund returns (as in Table II), and has only trivial effects on the cross-section of $t(\alpha)$ estimates for funds (as in Table III below). We conclude that incubation bias is probably unimportant in our results for 1984 to 2006.

Our goal is to draw inferences about the cross-section of true α for active funds, specifically, whether the cross-section of α estimates suggests a world where true α is zero for all funds or whether there is nonzero true α, especially in the tails of the cross-section of α estimates. We are interested in answering this question for 12 different cross-sections of α estimates—for gross and net returns, for the three-factor and four-factor benchmarks, and for the three AUM samples. Thus, we use regression (1) to estimate each fund's three-factor or four-factor α for gross or net returns for the part of 1984 to 2006 after the fund passes each AUM bound.

The tests for nonzero true α in actual fund returns use bootstrap simulations on returns that have the properties of fund returns, except that true α is set to zero for every fund. To set α to zero, we subtract a fund's α estimate from its monthly returns. For example, to compute three-factor benchmark-adjusted gross returns for a fund in the $5 million group, we subtract its three-factor α estimated from monthly gross returns for the part of 1984 to 2006 that the fund is in the $5 million group from the fund's monthly gross returns for that period. We calculate benchmark-adjusted returns for the three-factor and four-factor models, for gross and net returns, and for the three AUM bounds. The result is 12 populations of benchmark-adjusted (zero-α) returns. (CAPM simulation results are in Appendix B.)

A simulation run is a random sample (with replacement) of 273 months, drawn from the 273 calendar months of January 1984 to September 2006. For each of the 12 sets of benchmark-adjusted returns, we estimate, fund by fund, the relevant benchmark model on the simulation draw of months of adjusted returns, dropping funds that are in the simulation run for less than 8 months. Each run thus produces 12 cross-sections of α estimates using the same random sample of months from 12 populations of adjusted (zero-α) fund returns.

We do 10,000 simulation runs to produce 12 distributions of t-statistics, $t(\alpha)$, for a world in which true α is zero. We focus on $t(\alpha)$, rather than estimates of α, to control for differences in precision due to differences in residual variance and in the number of months funds are in a simulation run.

Note that setting true α equal to zero builds different assumptions about skill into the tests on gross and net fund returns. For net returns, setting true α to zero leads to a world where every manager has sufficient skill to generate expected returns that cover all costs. In contrast, setting true α to zero in gross returns implies a world where every fund manager has just enough skill to produce expected returns that cover the costs missed in expense ratios.

Our simulation approach has an important advantage. Because a simulation run is the same random sample of months for all funds, the simulations capture the cross-correlation of fund returns and its effects on the distribution of $t(\alpha)$ estimates. Since we jointly sample fund and explanatory returns, we also capture any correlated heteroskedasticity of the explanatory returns and disturbances of a benchmark model. We shall see that these details of our approach are important for inferences about true α in actual fund returns.

Defining a simulation run as the same random sample of months for all funds also has a cost. If a fund is not in the tests for the entire 1984 to 2006 period, it is likely to show up in a simulation run for more or less than the number of months it is in our sample. This is not serious. We focus on $t(\alpha)$, and the distribution of $t(\alpha)$ estimates depends on the number of months funds are in a simulation run through a degrees of freedom effect. The distributions of $t(\alpha)$ estimates for funds that are oversampled in a simulation run have more degrees of freedom (and thinner extreme tails) than the distributions of $t(\alpha)$ for the actual returns of the funds. Within a simulation run, however, over-sampling of some funds should roughly offset undersampling of others, so a simulation run should produce a representative sample of $t(\alpha)$ estimates for simulated returns that have the properties of actual fund returns, except that true α is zero for every fund. Oversampling and undersampling of fund re-turns in a simulation run should also about balance out in the 10,000 runs used in our inferences.

A qualification of this conclusion is in order. In a simulation run, as in the tests on actual returns, we discard funds that have less than 8 months of re-turns. This means we end up with a bit more oversampling of fund returns. As a result, the distributions of $t(\alpha)$ estimates in the simulations tend to have more degrees of freedom (and thinner tails) than the estimates for actual fund returns. This means our tests are a bit biased toward finding false evidence of performance in the tails of $t(\alpha)$ estimates for actual fund returns.

There are two additional caveats. (i) Random sampling of months in a sim-ulation run preserves the cross-correlation of fund returns, but we lose any ef-fects of autocorrelation. The literature on autocorrelation of stock returns (e.g., Fama (1965)) suggests that this is a minor problem. (ii) Because we randomly sample months, we also lose any effects of variation through time in the regres-sion slopes in (1). (The issues posed by time-varying slopes are discussed by Ferson and Schadt (1996).) Capturing time variation in the regression slopes poses thorny problems, and we leave this potentially important issue for future research.

To develop perspective on the simulations, we first compare, in qualita-tive terms, the percentiles of the cross-section of $t(\alpha)$ estimates from actual fund returns and the average values of the percentiles from the simulations. We then turn to likelihood statements about whether the cross-section of $t(\alpha)$ estimates for actual fund returns points to the existence of skill.

B. First Impressions

When we estimate a benchmark model on the returns of each fund in an AUM group, we get a cross-section of $t(\alpha)$ estimates that can be ordered into a cu-mulative distribution function (CDF) of $t(\alpha)$ estimates for actual fund returns. A simulation run for the same combination of benchmark model and AUM group also produces a cross-section of $t(\alpha)$ estimates and its CDF for a world in which true α is zero. In our initial examination of the simulations we compare (i) the values of $t(\alpha)$ at selected percentiles of the CDF of the $t(\alpha)$ estimates from actual fund returns and (ii) the averages across the 10,000 simulation runs of the $t(\alpha)$ estimates at the same percentiles. For example, the first percentile of three-factor $t(\alpha)$ estimates for the net returns of funds in the $5 million AUM group is -3.87, versus an average first percentile of -2.50 from the 10,000 three-factor simulation runs for the net returns of funds in this group (Table III).

For each combination of gross or net returns, AUM group, and benchmark model, Table III shows the CDF of $t(\alpha)$ estimates for actual returns and the average of the 10,000 simulation CDFs. The average simulation CDFs are similar for gross and net returns and for the two benchmark models. This is not surprising since true α is always zero in the simulations. The dispersion of the average simulation CDFs decreases from lower to higher AUM groups. This is at least in part a degrees of freedom effect; on average, funds in lower AUM groups have shorter sample periods.

B.1. Net Returns

The Berk and Green (2004) prediction that most fund managers have sufficient skill to cover their costs fares poorly in Table III. The left tail percentiles of the $t(\alpha)$ estimates from actual net fund returns are far below the corresponding average values from the simulations. For example, the 10th percentiles of the actual $t(\alpha)$ estimates, -2.34, -2.37, and -2.53 for the $5 million, $250 million, and $1 billion groups, are much more extreme than the average estimates from the simulation, -1.32, -1.31, and -1.30. The right tails of the $t(\alpha)$ estimates also do not suggest widespread skill sufficient to cover costs. In the tests that use the three-factor model, the $t(\alpha)$ estimates from the actual net returns of funds in the $5 million group are below the average values from the simulations for all percentiles below the 98th. For the $1 billion group, only the 99th percentile of three-factor $t(\alpha)$ for actual net fund returns is above the average simulation 99th percentile, and then only slightly. For the $250 million group, the percentiles of three-factor $t(\alpha)$ for actual net fund returns are all below the averages from the simulations. Figure 1 shows the actual and average simulated CDFs for the $5 million AUM group.

Evidence of skill sufficient to cover costs is even weaker with an adjustment for momentum exposure. In the tests that use the four-factor model, the percentiles of the $t(\alpha)$ estimates for actual net fund returns are always below the average values from the simulations. In other words, the averages of the percentile values of four-factor $t(\alpha)$ from the simulations of net returns (where

TABLE III. Percentiles of t(α) estimates for actual and simulated fund returns: January 1984 to September 2006

The table shows values of $t(\alpha)$ at selected percentiles (Pct) of the distribution of $t(\alpha)$ estimates for actual (Act) net and gross fund returns. The table also shows the percent of the 10,000 simulation runs that produce lower values of $t(\alpha)$ at the selected percentiles than those observed for actual fund returns (% < Act). Sim is the average value of $t(\alpha)$ at the selected percentiles from the simulations. The period is January 1984 to September 2006 and results are shown for the three- and four-factor models for the $5 million, $250 million, and $1 billion AUM fund groups. There are 3,156 funds in the $5 million group, 1,422 in the $250 million group, and 660 in the $1 billion group.

| Pct | 5 Million | | | 250 Million | | | 1 Billion | | |
	Sim	Act	%<Act	Sim	Act	%<Act	Sim	Act	%<Act
3-Factor Net Returns									
1	−2.50	−3.87	0.08	−2.45	−3.87	0.10	−2.39	−4.39	0.01
2	−2.17	−3.42	0.06	−2.13	−3.38	0.13	−2.09	−3.55	0.09
3	−1.97	−3.15	0.07	−1.94	−3.15	0.12	−1.91	−3.36	0.07
4	−1.83	−2.99	0.06	−1.80	−3.04	0.10	−1.78	−3.16	0.07
5	−1.71	−2.84	0.08	−1.69	−2.91	0.10	−1.67	−2.99	0.10
10	−1.32	−2.34	0.05	−1.31	−2.37	0.10	−1.30	−2.53	0.08
20	−0.87	−1.74	0.03	−0.86	−1.87	0.04	−0.86	−1.98	0.03
30	−0.54	−1.27	0.06	−0.54	−1.41	0.06	−0.54	−1.59	0.02
40	−0.26	−0.92	0.05	−0.27	−1.03	0.07	−0.27	−1.19	0.02
50	−0.01	−0.62	0.04	−0.01	−0.71	0.06	−0.01	−0.82	0.03
60	0.25	−0.29	0.11	0.25	−0.39	0.19	0.24	−0.51	0.05
70	0.52	0.08	0.51	0.52	−0.08	0.25	0.52	−0.20	0.08
80	0.85	0.50	3.20	0.84	0.37	1.68	0.84	0.25	0.85
90	1.30	1.01	8.17	1.29	0.89	5.19	1.28	0.82	4.81
95	1.68	1.54	30.55	1.66	1.36	14.17	1.64	1.34	17.73
96	1.80	1.71	40.06	1.76	1.49	17.24	1.74	1.52	26.33
97	1.94	1.91	49.35	1.90	1.69	25.92	1.87	1.79	42.86
98	2.13	2.17	58.70	2.08	1.90	30.43	2.04	2.02	50.07
99	2.45	2.47	57.42	2.36	2.29	43.92	2.31	2.40	63.11
4-Factor Net Returns									
1	−2.55	−3.94	0.04	−2.47	−3.94	0.08	−2.40	−4.22	0.01
2	−2.20	−3.43	0.04	−2.14	−3.43	0.09	−2.09	−3.48	0.08
3	−2.00	−3.08	0.13	−1.95	−3.07	0.25	−1.91	−3.11	0.23
4	−1.85	−2.88	0.13	−1.80	−2.88	0.22	−1.77	−2.95	0.21
5	−1.73	−2.74	0.12	−1.69	−2.78	0.18	−1.66	−2.86	0.14
10	−1.33	−2.23	0.14	−1.30	−2.34	0.14	−1.29	−2.48	0.07
20	−0.86	−1.67	0.10	−0.85	−1.80	0.11	−0.84	−1.96	0.05
30	−0.53	−1.25	0.12	−0.52	−1.39	0.10	−0.52	−1.54	0.04
40	−0.25	−0.88	0.21	−0.25	−1.04	0.14	−0.25	−1.23	0.05
50	0.01	−0.60	0.18	0.01	−0.76	0.11	0.01	−0.87	0.07
60	0.26	−0.29	0.25	0.27	−0.42	0.29	0.26	−0.49	0.19
70	0.54	0.02	0.37	0.54	−0.13	0.24	0.54	−0.18	0.24
80	0.87	0.44	1.76	0.86	0.27	0.72	0.86	0.17	0.45
90	1.33	1.04	10.62	1.31	0.86	4.40	1.30	0.86	7.07
95	1.72	1.53	23.82	1.69	1.37	14.35	1.67	1.31	14.13
96	1.84	1.67	28.21	1.80	1.51	18.23	1.78	1.45	17.16
97	1.99	1.84	31.30	1.94	1.65	18.62	1.91	1.57	17.05
98	2.19	2.09	39.12	2.12	1.79	15.57	2.08	1.76	18.86
99	2.52	2.40	36.96	2.42	2.22	29.88	2.36	2.26	42.00

(*Continued*)

TABLE III. (Continued)

Pct	5 Million Sim	Act	%<Act	250 Million Sim	Act	%<Act	1 Billion Sim	Act	%<Act
3-Factor Gross Returns									
1	−2.49	−3.07	4.11	−2.45	−3.16	3.16	−2.39	−3.29	1.88
2	−2.17	−2.68	4.79	−2.13	−2.67	6.01	−2.09	−2.70	5.64
3	−1.97	−2.48	4.20	−1.94	−2.51	4.47	−1.91	−2.51	5.12
4	−1.83	−2.31	4.41	−1.80	−2.35	4.68	−1.78	−2.33	5.77
5	−1.71	−2.19	4.15	−1.69	−2.18	5.99	−1.67	−2.18	6.52
10	−1.32	−1.72	5.75	−1.31	−1.77	5.94	−1.30	−1.86	4.15
20	−0.87	−1.10	13.61	−0.86	−1.24	7.18	−0.86	−1.43	2.52
30	−0.54	−0.71	20.03	−0.54	−0.79	15.10	−0.54	−1.00	4.28
40	−0.26	−0.36	29.74	−0.27	−0.43	23.84	−0.27	−0.59	10.25
50	−0.01	−0.06	38.87	−0.01	−0.15	26.28	−0.01	−0.28	13.48
60	0.25	0.28	56.05	0.25	0.14	31.47	0.24	0.05	21.21
70	0.52	0.63	71.81	0.52	0.48	43.62	0.52	0.35	26.70
80	0.85	1.06	85.21	0.84	0.88	58.14	0.84	0.79	44.31
90	1.30	1.59	90.01	1.29	1.41	69.39	1.28	1.34	60.63
95	1.68	2.04	92.10	1.66	1.81	72.89	1.64	1.78	70.37
96	1.80	2.20	93.73	1.76	1.93	73.44	1.74	1.96	77.00
97	1.94	2.44	95.97	1.90	2.19	84.36	1.87	2.22	85.47
98	2.13	2.72	97.29	2.08	2.47	89.30	2.04	2.37	83.72
99	2.45	3.03	96.66	2.36	2.83	90.95	2.31	2.97	94.63
4-Factor Gross Returns									
1	−2.55	−3.06	5.49	−2.47	−3.02	6.72	−2.40	−3.34	1.67
2	−2.20	−2.71	4.99	−2.14	−2.63	7.84	−2.09	−2.48	14.14
3	−2.00	−2.46	5.46	−1.95	−2.43	7.33	−1.91	−2.40	8.43
4	−1.85	−2.27	6.39	−1.80	−2.33	5.73	−1.77	−2.25	8.66
5	−1.73	−2.11	7.71	−1.69	−2.12	8.62	−1.66	−2.11	9.52
10	−1.33	−1.62	12.27	−1.30	−1.71	8.63	−1.29	−1.85	4.69
20	−0.86	−1.09	16.23	−0.85	−1.19	11.13	−0.84	−1.34	5.29
30	−0.53	−0.65	28.46	−0.52	−0.75	19.76	−0.52	−0.92	8.75
40	−0.25	−0.33	35.43	−0.25	−0.45	22.31	−0.25	−0.57	12.54
50	0.01	−0.02	44.53	0.01	−0.16	26.29	0.01	−0.29	14.40
60	0.26	0.28	53.17	0.27	0.09	25.86	0.26	0.05	22.48
70	0.54	0.62	64.90	0.54	0.48	43.11	0.54	0.36	27.78
80	0.87	0.98	70.19	0.86	0.85	50.07	0.86	0.82	47.07
90	1.33	1.58	84.76	1.31	1.36	58.66	1.30	1.41	65.72
95	1.72	2.05	88.77	1.69	1.87	73.81	1.67	1.83	70.55
96	1.84	2.21	91.03	1.80	2.01	76.27	1.78	1.95	70.91
97	1.99	2.39	92.01	1.94	2.21	81.22	1.91	2.04	66.61
98	2.19	2.58	91.20	2.12	2.43	83.35	2.08	2.30	74.26
99	2.52	3.01	93.44	2.42	2.72	81.41	2.36	2.57	71.98

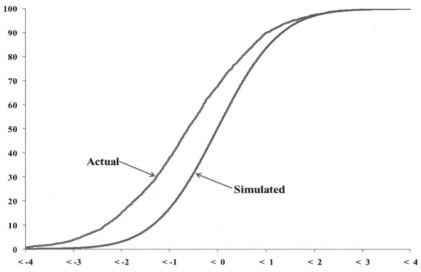

Figure 1. Simulated and actual cumulative density function
of three-factor t(α) for net returns, 1984–2006

by construction skill suffices to cover costs) always beat the corresponding percentiles of $t(\alpha)$ for actual net fund returns.

There is a glimmer of hope for investors in the tests on net returns. Even in the four-factor tests, the 99th and, for the $5 million group, the 98th percentiles of the $t(\alpha)$ estimates for actual fund returns are close to the average values from the simulations. This suggests that some fund managers have enough skill to produce expected benchmark-adjusted net returns that cover costs. This is, however, a far cry from the prediction of Berk and Green (2004) that most if not all fund managers can cover their costs.

B.2. Gross Returns

It is possible that the fruits of skill do not show up more generally in net fund returns because they are absorbed by expenses. The tests on gross returns in Table III show that adding back the costs in expense ratios pushes up $t(\alpha)$ for actual fund returns. For all AUM groups, however, the left tail of three-factor $t(\alpha)$ estimates for actual gross fund returns is still to the left of the average from the simulations. For example, in the simulations the average value of the fifth percentile of $t(\alpha)$ for gross returns for the $5 million group is -1.71, but the actual fifth percentile from actual fund returns is much lower, -2.19. Thus, the left tails of the CDFs of three-factor $t(\alpha)$ suggest that when returns

[277]

are measured before expenses, there are inferior fund managers whose actions result in negative true α relative to passive benchmarks.

Conversely, the right tails of three-factor $t(\alpha)$ suggest that there are superior managers who enhance expected returns relative to passive benchmarks. For the $5 million AUM group, the CDF of $t(\alpha)$ estimates for actual gross fund returns moves to the right of the average from the simulations at about the 60th percentile. For example, the 95th percentile of $t(\alpha)$ for funds in the $5 million group averages 1.68 in the simulations, but the actual 95th percentile is higher, 2.04. For the two larger AUM groups the crossovers occur at higher percentiles, around the 80th percentile for the $250 million group and the 90th percentile for the $1 billion group. Figure 2 graphs the results for the three-factor benchmark and the $5 million AUM group.

The four-factor results for gross returns in Table III are similar to the three-factor results, with a minor nuance. Adding a momentum control tends to shrink slightly the left and right tails of the cross-sections of $t(\alpha)$ estimates for actual fund returns. This suggests that funds with negative three-factor α estimates tend to have slight negative MOM_t exposure and funds with positive three-factor α tend to have slight positive exposure. Controlling for momentum pulls the α estimates toward zero, but only a bit.

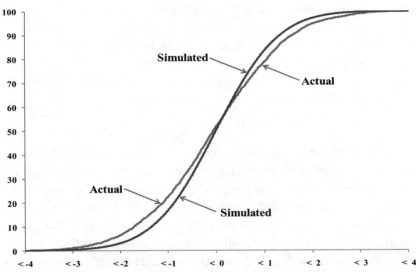

*Figure 2. Simulated and actual cumulative density function
of three-factor $t(\alpha)$ for gross returns, 1984–2006*

Finally, the average simulation distribution of $t(\alpha)$ for the \$5 million fund group is like a t distribution with about 24 degrees of freedom. The average sample life of these funds is 112 months, so we can probably conclude that the simulation distributions of $t(\alpha)$ are more fat-tailed than can be explained by degrees of freedom. This may be due in part to fat-tailed distributions of stock returns (Fama (1965)). A referee suggests that active trading may also fatten the tails of fund returns. And properties of the joint distribution of fund returns may have important effects on the cross-section of $t(\alpha)$ estimates—a comment of some import in our later discussion of Kosowski et al. (2006).

C. Likelihoods

Comparing the percentiles of $t(\alpha)$ estimates for actual fund returns with the simulation averages gives hints about whether manager skill affects expected returns. Table III also provides likelihoods, in particular, the fractions of the 10,000 simulation runs that produce lower values of $t(\alpha)$ at selected percentiles than actual fund returns. These likelihoods allow us to judge more formally whether the tails of the cross-section of $t(\alpha)$ estimates for actual fund returns are extreme relative to what we observe when true α is zero.

Specifically, we infer that some managers lack skill sufficient to cover costs if low fractions of the simulation runs produce left tail percentiles of $t(\alpha)$ below those from actual net fund returns, or equivalently, if large fractions of the simulation runs beat the left tail $t(\alpha)$ estimates from actual net fund returns. Likewise, we infer that some managers produce benchmark-adjusted expected returns that more than cover costs if large fractions of the simulation runs produce right tail percentiles of $t(\alpha)$ below those from actual net fund returns. The logic is similar for gross returns, but the question is whether there are managers with skill sufficient to cover the costs (primarily trading costs) missing from expense ratios.

There are two problems in drawing inferences from the likelihoods in Table III. (i) Results are shown for many percentiles so there is a multiple comparisons issue. (ii) The likelihoods for different percentiles are correlated. One way to address these problems is to focus on a given percentile of each tail of $t(\alpha)$, for example, the 5th and the 95th percentiles, and draw inferences entirely from them. But this approach discards lots of information. We prefer to examine all the likelihoods, with emphasis on the extreme tails, where performance is most likely to be identified. As a result, our inferences from the formal likelihoods are somewhat informal.

C.1. Net Returns

The likelihoods in Table III confirm that skill sufficient to cover costs is rare. Below the 80th percentile, the three-factor $t(\alpha)$ estimates for actual net fund returns beat those from the simulations in less than 1.0% of the net return simulation runs. For example, the 70th percentile of the cross-section of three-factor $t(\alpha)$ estimates from the net returns of $5 million funds (our full sample) is 0.08, and only 0.51% (about half of one percent) of the 10,000 simulation runs for this group produce 70th percentile $t(\alpha)$ estimates below 0.08. It seems safe to conclude that most fund managers do not have enough skill to produce benchmark-adjusted net returns that cover costs. This again is bad news for Berk and Green (2004) since their model predicts that skill sufficient to cover costs is the general rule.

The likelihoods for the most extreme right tail percentiles of the three-factor $t(\alpha)$ estimates in Table III also confirm our earlier conclusion that some managers have sufficient skill to cover costs. For the $5 million group, the 97th, 98th, and 99th percentiles of the cross-section of three-factor $t(\alpha)$ estimates from actual net fund returns are close to the average values from the simulations, and 49.35% to 58.70% of the $t(\alpha)$ estimates from the 10,000 simulation runs are below those from actual net returns. The likelihoods that the highest percentiles of the $t(\alpha)$ estimates from the net returns of funds in the $5 million group beat those from the simulations drop below 40% when we use the four-factor model to measure α, but the likelihoods nevertheless suggest that some fund managers have enough skill to cover costs.

Some perspective is helpful. For the $5 million group, about 30% of funds produce positive net return α estimates. The likelihoods in Table III tell us, however, that most of these funds are just lucky; their managers are not able to produce benchmark-adjusted expected returns that cover costs. For example, the 90th percentile of the $t(\alpha)$ estimates for actual net fund returns is near 1.00. The average standard error of the α estimates is 0.28% (monthly), which suggests that funds around the 90th percentile of $t(\alpha)$ beat our benchmarks by more than 3.3% per year for the entire period they are in the sample. These managers are sure to be anointed as highly skilled active investors. But about 90% of the net return simulation runs produce 90th percentiles of $t(\alpha)$ that beat those from actual fund returns. It thus seems that, like funds below the 90th percentile, most funds around the 90th percentile do not have managers with sufficient skill to cover costs; that is, true net return α is negative.

The odds that managers have enough skill to cover costs are better for funds at or above the 97th percentile of the $t(\alpha)$ estimates. In the $5 million group, funds at the 97th, 98th, and 99th percentiles of three-factor $t(\alpha)$ estimates do about as well as would be expected if all fund managers were able to produce benchmark-adjusted expected returns that cover costs. But this just means that our estimate of true net return three-factor α for these funds is close to zero. If we switch to the four-factor model, the estimate of true α is negative for all percentiles of the $t(\alpha)$ estimates since the percentiles from actual net fund returns beat those from the simulations in less than 40% of the simulation runs.

What mix of active funds might generate the net return results in Table III? Suppose there are two groups of funds. Managers of good funds have just enough skill to produce zero α in net returns; bad funds have negative α. When the two groups are mixed, the expected cross-section of $t(\alpha)$ estimates is entirely to the left of the average of the cross-sections from the net return simulation runs (in which all managers have sufficient skill to cover costs). Even the extreme right tail of the $t(\alpha)$ estimates for actual net fund returns will be weighed down by bad managers who are extremely lucky but have smaller $t(\alpha)$ estimates than if they were extremely lucky good managers. In our tests, most of the cross-section of $t(\alpha)$ estimates for actual net fund returns is way left of what we expect if all managers have zero true α. Thus, most funds are probably in the negative true α group. At least for the $5 million AUM sample, the 97th, 98th, and 99th percentiles of the three-factor $t(\alpha)$ estimates for actual net fund returns are similar to the simulation averages. This suggests that buried in the results are fund managers with more than enough skill to cover costs, and the lucky among them pull up the extreme right tail of the net return $t(\alpha)$ estimates. Unfortunately, these good funds are indistinguishable from the lucky bad funds that land in the top percentiles of the $t(\alpha)$ estimates but have negative true α. As a result, our estimate of the three-factor net return α for a portfolio of the top three percentiles of the $5 million group is near zero; the positive α of the lucky (but hidden) good funds is offset by the negative α of the lucky bad funds. And when we switch to the four-factor model, our estimate of true α turns negative even for the top three percentiles of the $t(\alpha)$ estimates.

Finally, our tests exclude index funds, but we can report that for 1984 to 2006 the net return three-factor α estimate for the VW portfolio of index funds (in which large, low cost funds get heavy weight) is -0.16% per year (-0.01% per month, $t = -0.61$), and four-factor α is 0.01% per year ($t = 0.02$). Since large, low cost index funds are not subject to the vagaries of active management, it seems reasonable to infer that the net return true α for a portfolio of these funds is close to zero. In other words, going forward we expect that a portfolio of low cost index funds will perform about as well as a portfolio of the top three percentiles of past active winners, and better than the rest of the active fund universe.

C.2. Gross Returns

The simulation tests for net returns ask whether active managers have sufficient skill to cover all their costs. In the tests on gross returns, the bar is lower. Specifically, the issue is whether managers have enough skill to at least cover the costs (primarily trading costs) missing from expense ratios.

The three-factor gross return simulations for the $5 million AUM group suggest that most funds in the left tail of three-factor $t(\alpha)$ estimates do not have enough skill to produce benchmark-adjusted expected returns that cover trading costs, but many managers in the right tail have such skill. For the 40th and lower percentiles, the three-factor $t(\alpha)$ estimates for the actual gross returns of funds in the $5 million group beat those from the simulations in less than 30% of the simulation runs, falling to less than 6% for the 10th and lower percentiles. Conversely, above the 60th percentile, the three-factor $t(\alpha)$ estimates for actual gross fund returns beat those from the simulations in at least 56% of the simulation runs, rising to more than 90% for the 96th and higher percentiles. As usual, the results are weaker when we switch from three-factor to four-factor benchmarks, but the general conclusions are the same.

For many readers, the important insight of Berk and Green (2004) is their assumption that there are diseconomies of scale in active management, not their detailed predictions about net fund returns (which are rejected in our tests). The right tails of the $t(\alpha)$ estimates for gross returns suggest diseconomies. The extreme right tail percentiles of $t(\alpha)$ are typically lower for the $250 million and $1 billion groups than for the $5 million group, and more of the simulation runs beat the extreme right tail percentiles of the $t(\alpha)$ estimates for the larger AUM funds. In the world of Berk and Green (2004), however, the weeding out of unskilled managers should also lead to left tails for $t(\alpha)$ estimates that are less extreme for larger funds. This prediction is not confirmed in our results. The left tails of the $t(\alpha)$ estimates for the $250 million and $1 billion groups are at least as extreme as the left tail for the $5 million group. This contradiction in the left tails of the $t(\alpha)$ estimates makes us reluctant to interpret the right tails as evidence of diseconomies of scale.

The tests on gross returns point to the presence of skill (positive and negative). We next estimate the size of the skill effects. A side benefit is evidence on the power of the simulation tests.

IV. ESTIMATING THE DISTRIBUTION OF
TRUE α IN GROSS FUND RETURNS

To examine the likely size of the skill effects in gross fund returns we repeat the simulations but with α injected into fund returns. We then examine (i) how much α is necessary to reproduce the cross-section of $t(\alpha)$ estimates for actual gross fund returns, and (ii) levels of α too extreme to be consistent with the $t(\alpha)$ estimates for actual fund returns.

Given the evidence that, at least for the $5 million group (our full sample), the distribution of $t(\alpha)$ estimates in gross fund returns is roughly symmetric about zero (Table III), it is reasonable to assume that true α is distributed around zero. It is also reasonable to assume that extreme levels of skill (good or bad) are rare. Concretely, we assume that each fund is endowed with a gross return α drawn from a normal distribution with a mean of zero and a standard deviation of σ per year.

The new simulations are much like the old. The first step again is to adjust the gross returns of each fund, setting α to zero for the three-factor and four-factor benchmarks and each of the three AUM groups. But now, before drawing the random sample of months for a simulation run, we draw a true α from a normal distribution with mean zero and standard deviation σ per year—the same α for every combination of benchmark model and AUM group for a given fund, but an independent drawing of α for each fund.

It seems reasonable that more diversified funds have less leeway to generate true α. To capture this idea, we scale the α drawn for a fund by the ratio of the fund's (three-factor or four-factor) residual standard error to the average standard error for all funds. We add the scaled α to the fund's benchmark-adjusted returns. We then draw a random sample (with replacement) of 273 months, and for each fund we estimate three-factor and four-factor regressions on the adjusted gross returns of the fund's three AUM samples. The simulations thus use returns that have the properties of actual fund returns, except we know true α has a normal distribution with mean zero and (for the "average" fund) standard deviation σ per year. We do 10,000 simulation runs, and a fund gets a new drawing of α in each run. To examine power, we vary σ, the standard deviation of true α, from 0.0% to 2.0% per year, in steps of 0.25%.

Table IV shows percentiles of the cross-section of $t(\alpha)$ estimates for actual gross fund returns (from Table III) and the average $t(\alpha)$ estimates at the same percentiles from the 10,000 simulation runs, for each value of σ. These are useful for judging how much dispersion in true α is consistent with the actual cross-section of $t(\alpha)$ estimates. For each σ, the table also shows the fraction of the simulation runs that produce percentiles of $t(\alpha)$ estimates below those from actual fund returns. We use these for inferences about the amount of dispersion in true α we might rule out as too extreme.

A. Likely Levels of Performance

If true α comes from a normal distribution with mean zero and standard deviation σ, Table IV provides two slightly different ways to infer the value of σ. We can look for the value of σ that produces average simulation percentile values of $t(\alpha)$ most like those from actual fund returns. Or we can look for the σ that produces simulation $t(\alpha)$ estimates below those for actual returns in about 50% of the simulation runs. If α has a normal distribution with mean zero and standard deviation σ, we expect the effects of the level of σ to become stronger as we look further into the tails of the cross-section of $t(\alpha)$. Thus, we are most interested in values of σ that match the extreme tails of the $t(\alpha)$ estimates for actual gross fund returns.

The normality assumption for true α is an approximation. We do not expect that a single value of σ (the standard deviation of true α) completely captures the tails of the $t(\alpha)$ estimates for actual fund returns, even if we allow a different σ for each tail. With this caveat, the three-factor and four-factor simulations for the $5 million group suggest that σ around 1.25% to 1.50% per year captures the extreme left tail of the $t(\alpha)$ estimates for actual gross fund returns, and 1.25% works for the right tail. For the $250 million and $1 billion groups, the three-factor simulations again suggest σ around 1.25% to 1.50% per year for the left tail of the $t(\alpha)$ estimates for gross fund returns, but for the right tail σ is lower, 0.75% to 1.00% per year. In the four-factor simulations for the $250 and $1 billion groups $\sigma = 1.25\%$ per year seems to capture the extreme left tail of the $t(\alpha)$ estimates for gross fund returns, but the estimate of σ for the right tail is again lower, 0.75% per year. (To save space, Table IV shows results only for the $5 million and $1 billion AUM groups.)

The estimates do not suggest much performance, especially for larger funds. Thus, $\sigma = 1.25\%$ says that about one-sixth of funds have true gross return α greater than 1.25% per year (about 0.10% per month) and only about 2.4% have true α greater than 2.50% per year (0.21% per month). For perspective, the average of the OLS standard errors of individual fund α estimates—the average imprecision of α estimates—is 0.28% per month (3.4% per year). Moreover, much lower right tail σ estimates for the $250 million and $1 billion funds say that a lot of the right tail performance observed in the full ($5 million) sample is due to tiny funds.

Our gross fund returns are net of trading costs. Returning trading costs to funds (if that is deemed appropriate) would increase the t(α) estimates in both the left and the right tails, which, depending on the (unknown) magnitudes, may move them toward more similar estimates of σ.

B. Unlikely Levels of Performance

What levels of σ can we reject? The answer depends on how confident we wish to be about our inferences. Suppose we are willing to accept a 20% chance of setting a lower bound for σ that is too high and a 20% chance of setting an upper bound that is too low. These bounds imply a narrower range than we would have with standard significance levels, but they are reasonable if our goal is to provide perspective on likely values of σ.

Under the 20% rule, the lower bound for the left tail estimate of σ is the value that produces left tail percentile t(α) estimates below those from actual fund returns in about 20% of the simulation runs. The upper bound for the left tail σ is the value that produces left tail percentiles of t(α) below those from actual fund returns in about 80% of the simulation runs. Conversely, under the 20% rule, the lower bound for the right tail σ estimate produces right tail percentile t(α) estimates below those from actual fund returns in about 80% of the simulation runs. And the upper bound for the right tail σ produces right tail percentiles of t(α) below those from actual fund returns in about 20% of the simulation runs.

In brief, applying the 20% rule leads to intervals for σ that are equal to the point estimates of the preceding section plus and minus 0.5%. For example, 1.25% per year works fairly well as the left tail estimate of σ for all AUM groups and for the three-factor and four-factor models, and the interval for the left tail σ estimates is 0.75% to 1.75%. For the $5 million group, σ = 1.25% also works for the right tail, and the interval is again 0.75% to 1.75%. For the $250 million and $1 billion groups, the right tail estimate of a drops to about 0.75% per year, and the 20% rule leads to an interval for σ from 0.25% to 1.25% per year.

What do these results say about the power of the simulation approach? The upper bound on σ for the $5 million group, 1.75% per year, translates to a monthly σ for the cross-section of true α of about 0.146%. Suppose the standard error of each fund's α estimate is 0.28% per month (the sample average).

TABLE IV. Percentiles of t(α) estimates for actual and simulated gross fund returns with injected α

The table shows values of t(α) at selected percentiles (Pct) of the distribution of t(α) estimates for Actual gross fund returns (repeated from Table III). The table also shows the average values of the t(α) estimates at the same percentiles from the 10,000 simulations, for seven values of σ (the annual standard deviation of injected α). The final seven columns of the table show, for each value of σ, the percent of the 10,000 simulation runs that produce lower t(α) estimates at the selected percentiles than actual fund returns. The period is January 1984 to September 2006 and results are shown for the three- and four-factor models for the $5 million and $1 billion AUM fund groups.

Pct	Actual t(α)	Average t(α) from Simulations							Percent of Simulations below Actual						
		0.50	0.75	1.00	1.25	1.50	1.75	2.00	0.50	0.75	1.00	1.25	1.50	1.75	2.00
3-Factor α, AUM>5 Million															
1	-3.07	-2.63	-2.78	-2.99	-3.24	-3.54	-3.87	-4.23	7.46	15.74	36.37	69.29	92.13	99.00	99.94
2	-2.68	-2.27	-2.38	-2.52	-2.69	-2.89	-3.10	-3.34	8.03	13.67	26.30	49.41	76.25	93.77	99.04
3	-2.48	-2.06	-2.15	-2.27	-2.40	-2.55	-2.72	-2.91	6.55	10.94	19.32	35.16	57.73	80.85	94.54
4	-2.31	-1.91	-1.99	-2.08	-2.20	-2.33	-2.47	-2.62	6.85	10.63	17.71	30.94	49.77	71.63	88.96
5	-2.19	-1.78	-1.85	-1.94	-2.04	-2.16	-2.28	-2.41	6.36	9.68	15.54	26.25	41.95	61.44	80.67
10	-1.72	-1.37	-1.42	-1.48	-1.55	-1.62	-1.70	-1.78	7.86	10.82	15.39	22.37	32.27	44.75	59.63
90	1.59	1.35	1.40	1.46	1.53	1.60	1.68	1.76	86.35	81.64	74.23	64.06	51.23	36.75	22.61
95	2.04	1.75	1.83	1.92	2.02	2.13	2.26	2.39	88.27	82.46	72.10	56.14	36.57	18.02	5.63
96	2.20	1.87	1.96	2.06	2.17	2.30	2.45	2.60	90.76	85.40	74.75	57.87	36.04	16.06	4.08
97	2.44	2.03	2.12	2.23	2.37	2.53	2.70	2.88	93.73	89.76	80.72	63.35	38.59	15.13	3.39
98	2.72	2.23	2.35	2.49	2.66	2.85	3.07	3.31	95.29	91.75	82.56	61.96	32.18	8.75	1.24
99	3.03	2.58	2.74	2.95	3.20	3.49	3.82	4.18	93.48	85.84	63.90	29.57	5.82	0.41	0.02

Pct	Actual t(α)	Average t(α) from Simulations							Percent of Simulations below Actual						
		0.25	0.50	0.75	1.00	1.25	1.50	1.75	0.25	0.50	0.75	1.00	1.25	1.50	1.75
3-Factor α, AUM > 1 Billion															
1	−3.29	−2.42	−2.54	−2.73	−2.99	−3.31	−3.68	−4.09	2.20	3.63	8.89	22.71	48.69	76.60	92.24
2	−2.70	−2.12	−2.21	−2.34	−2.52	−2.73	−2.98	−3.25	6.27	9.11	15.83	28.78	51.16	75.26	90.50
3	−2.51	−1.94	−2.01	−2.12	−2.27	−2.44	−2.63	−2.84	5.82	8.10	13.21	22.97	39.66	61.21	80.93
4	−2.33	−1.80	−1.87	−1.97	−2.09	−2.23	−2.40	−2.57	6.43	8.75	13.73	22.41	36.16	55.28	74.51
5	−2.18	−1.69	−1.75	−1.84	−1.95	−2.08	−2.22	−2.37	7.42	9.81	14.45	22.65	35.12	51.86	70.08
10	−1.86	−1.32	−1.36	−1.42	−1.49	−1.58	−1.67	−1.77	4.46	5.54	7.88	11.48	17.22	25.15	36.41
90	1.34	1.29	1.34	1.40	1.47	1.55	1.64	1.74	58.48	52.67	43.86	34.00	23.16	13.78	6.93
95	1.78	1.66	1.72	1.81	1.92	2.04	2.18	2.33	67.79	60.84	49.40	35.18	20.70	9.71	3.14
96	1.96	1.77	1.83	1.93	2.05	2.19	2.35	2.53	74.69	68.02	56.45	40.71	24.10	11.07	3.42
97	2.22	1.90	1.97	2.08	2.23	2.39	2.58	2.78	84.12	79.12	68.67	52.24	32.34	14.98	4.56
98	2.37	2.07	2.16	2.29	2.46	2.67	2.90	3.16	82.02	75.12	61.59	41.62	21.00	6.82	1.56
99	2.97	2.35	2.46	2.64	2.88	3.18	3.52	3.90	93.92	90.90	81.49	61.18	32.94	11.99	2.84

(Continued)

TABLE IV. (Continued)

4-Factor α, AUM > 5 Million

Pct	Actual t(α)	Average t(α) from Simulations						Percent of Simulations below Actual						
	0.50	0.75	1.00	1.25	1.50	1.75	2.00	0.50	0.75	1.00	1.25	1.50	1.75	2.00
1	−3.06	−2.85	−3.06	−3.33	−3.63	−3.97	−4.34	10.99	22.26	47.07	78.71	95.82	99.64	99.97
2	−2.71	−2.42	−2.57	−2.74	−2.94	−3.16	−3.41	8.36	14.61	28.65	52.04	78.54	94.44	99.25
3	−2.46	−2.18	−2.30	−2.44	−2.60	−2.77	−2.96	8.82	14.08	25.32	42.58	66.01	86.35	96.53
4	−2.27	−2.01	−2.11	−2.23	−2.36	−2.51	−2.66	9.85	15.06	24.90	39.73	60.10	80.07	93.38
5	−2.11	−1.87	−1.96	−2.07	−2.18	−2.31	−2.45	11.46	16.87	26.22	39.83	57.77	76.75	90.48
10	−1.62	−1.43	−1.49	−1.56	−1.64	−1.72	−1.80	16.05	21.02	27.97	37.70	49.46	63.12	76.66
90	1.58	1.43	1.50	1.56	1.64	1.72	1.80	79.81	74.21	66.46	55.96	43.49	30.25	18.17
95	2.05	1.87	1.96	2.07	2.18	2.31	2.44	83.71	76.60	66.13	50.01	31.99	15.33	4.86
96	2.21	2.00	2.11	2.22	2.36	2.50	2.66	86.46	79.25	68.28	50.91	30.64	12.88	3.36
97	2.39	2.17	2.29	2.43	2.59	2.76	2.95	87.10	79.52	66.70	46.44	24.15	7.38	1.23
98	2.58	2.41	2.55	2.72	2.92	3.14	3.38	85.21	75.29	57.57	32.34	10.71	1.74	0.15
99	3.01	2.81	3.02	3.28	3.58	3.91	4.27	88.10	75.85	49.98	19.30	3.25	0.19	0.01

4-Factor α, AUM > 1 Billion

Pct	Actual t(α)	Average t(α) from Simulations							Percent of Simulations below Actual						
	0.25	0.50	0.75	1.00	1.25	1.50	1.75	2.00	0.25	0.50	0.75	1.00	1.25	1.50	1.75
1	−3.34	−2.44	−2.56	−2.76	−3.03	−3.36	−3.74	−4.16	2.00	3.35	8.55	22.91	48.31	75.80	92.22
2	−2.48	−2.12	−2.22	−2.36	−2.54	−2.77	−3.02	−3.30	16.25	22.21	35.17	54.99	75.98	91.84	97.93
3	−2.40	−1.93	−2.01	−2.13	−2.28	−2.46	−2.66	−2.88	9.63	13.33	20.63	34.25	54.13	74.16	89.62
4	−2.25	−1.80	−1.87	−1.97	−2.10	−2.25	−2.42	−2.60	9.86	13.41	19.68	30.72	47.91	66.77	83.79
5	−2.11	−1.68	−1.75	−1.84	−1.96	−2.09	−2.24	−2.40	10.76	13.64	19.81	29.76	44.52	62.13	78.56
10	−1.85	−1.30	−1.35	−1.41	−1.49	−1.58	−1.67	−1.78	5.10	6.48	8.67	12.86	19.05	27.52	38.83
90	1.41	1.32	1.36	1.43	1.50	1.59	1.69	1.79	63.74	58.42	50.10	40.62	29.70	19.17	10.28
95	1.83	1.69	1.76	1.85	1.96	2.09	2.24	2.40	68.10	61.80	50.88	37.12	22.46	10.67	3.71
96	1.95	1.80	1.87	1.97	2.10	2.25	2.41	2.59	68.50	61.33	49.38	34.72	19.04	7.98	2.30
97	2.04	1.94	2.02	2.13	2.28	2.45	2.64	2.86	64.06	55.68	41.85	26.04	11.89	3.83	0.74
98	2.30	2.12	2.21	2.35	2.53	2.74	2.98	3.25	71.76	62.55	47.39	28.62	11.89	3.45	0.70
99	2.57	2.40	2.52	2.71	2.96	3.26	3.61	4.00	68.67	57.31	38.54	18.10	5.17	0.98	0.11

With a monthly σ of 0.146%, the standard deviation of the cross-section of α estimates—caused by measurement error and dispersion in true α—is $(0.146^2 + 0.28^2)^{1/2} = 0.316\%$. This is only a bit bigger than 0.299%, the standard deviation implied by our estimate of σ for the $5 million group, 1.25% per year. The fact that the simulations assign a relatively low probability to $\sigma \geq 1.75\%$ despite the small difference between the implied standard deviations of the α estimates for $\sigma = 1.25\%$ (the point estimate) and $\sigma = 1.75\%$ suggests that the simulations have power. The source of the power is our large sample of funds (3,156 in the $5 million group). With so many funds, the percentiles of $t(\alpha)$ are estimated precisely, which produces power to draw inferences about σ. (We thank a referee for this insight.)

V. KOSOWSKI ET AL. (2006)

The paper closest to ours is Kosowski et al. (2006). They use bootstrap simulations to draw inferences about performance in the cross-section of four-factor $t(\alpha)$ estimates for net fund returns. Their main inference is more positive than ours. They find that the 95th and higher percentiles of four-factor $t(\alpha)$ estimates for net fund returns are above the same simulation percentiles in more than 99% of simulation runs. This seems like strong evidence that among the best funds, many have more than sufficient skill to cover costs. Our simulations on net returns uncover much less evidence of skill. Two features of their tests account for their stronger results—simulation approach and time period.

We jointly sample fund (and explanatory) returns, whereas Kosowski et al. (2006) do independent simulations for each fund. The benefit of their approach is that the number of months a fund is in a simulation run always matches the fund's actual number of months of returns. The cost is that their simulations do not take account of the correlation of α estimates for different funds that arises because a benchmark model does not capture all common variation in fund returns. They summarize but do not show simulations that jointly sample the four-factor residuals of funds. But they never jointly sample fund returns and explanatory returns, which means (for example) they miss any effects of correlated movement in the volatilities of four-factor explanatory returns and residuals. In fact, in the results they show, the explanatory returns do not vary across simulation runs; the historical sequence of explanatory returns is used in every run.

Their rules for including funds in the simulation tests are also different. They include the complete return histories of all funds that survive more than

60 months (so there is survival bias). We include funds after they pass $5 million in AUM if they have at least 8 months of returns thereafter (less survival bias).

Table V shows simulation results for their 1975 to 2002 period using (i) their rules for including funds and (ii) our rules. Note that both sets of simulations use our approach to drawing simulation samples, that is, a simulation run uses the same random sample of months for all funds, which allows for all effects implied by the joint distribution of fund returns, and of fund and explanatory returns.

The rules used to include funds affect the cross-section of $t(\alpha)$ estimates for actual fund returns. Specifically, the right tail $t(\alpha)$ estimates for actual

TABLE V. Percentiles of four-factor $t(\alpha)$ for actual and simulated fund returns: 1975 to 2002

The table shows values of four-factor $t(\alpha)$ at selected percentiles (Pct) of the distribution of $t(\alpha)$ for actual (Act) net and gross fund returns for funds selected using the exclusion rules of Kosowski et al. (2006) and for funds in our $5 million AUM group selected using our exclusion rules. The period is 1975 to 2002 (as in Kosowski et al. (2006)). The table also shows the fraction (%<Act) of the 10,000 simulation runs that produce lower values of $t(\alpha)$ at the selected percentiles than those observed for actual fund returns. Sim is the average value of $t(\alpha)$ at the selected percentiles from the simulations.

Pct	Kosowski et al. Exclusion Rules			Our Exclusion Rules		
	Sim	Act	%<Act	Sim	Act	%<Act
1	−2.48	−3.69	0.18	−2.46	−3.70	0.16
2	−2.16	−3.25	0.19	−2.14	−3.17	0.30
3	−1.96	−2.87	0.53	−1.95	−2.80	0.70
4	−1.82	−2.55	1.34	−1.80	−2.63	0.69
5	−1.70	−2.36	1.90	−1.69	−2.41	1.36
10	−1.31	−1.92	2.17	−1.30	−1.95	1.66
20	−0.85	−1.41	2.15	−0.85	−1.41	2.17
30	−0.52	−1.01	3.18	−0.52	−1.00	3.54
40	−0.25	−0.65	5.75	−0.24	−0.66	5.35
50	0.01	−0.33	9.19	0.01	−0.34	8.50
60	0.27	−0.02	12.20	0.27	−0.03	11.92
70	0.55	0.29	16.51	0.55	0.27	14.86
80	0.87	0.73	32.80	0.87	0.69	28.11
90	1.32	1.44	68.19	1.32	1.34	56.29
95	1.69	1.97	82.42	1.69	1.81	68.32
96	1.80	2.18	88.38	1.80	2.00	75.70
97	1.94	2.38	90.73	1.94	2.25	83.74
98	2.12	2.59	91.38	2.12	2.51	87.57
99	2.40	3.07	95.79	2.42	2.83	88.37

fund returns are less extreme for our sample. This suggests that their rule that a fund must have at least 60 months of returns produces more survival bias than our 8-month rule. Another possibility is that some funds have high returns when they are tiny but do not do as well after they pass $5 million. This may be due in part to an incubation bias in the fund sample of Kosowski et al. (2006), since they include a fund's entire return history if the fund survives for 60 months.

For either sample of funds, joint sampling of fund returns (our approach) affects the simulation results. Kosowski et al. (2006) report that more than 99% of their simulation runs produce 95th percentile four-factor $t(\alpha)$ estimates below the 95th percentile from actual net fund returns. In Table V, the number drops to 82.42% for the fund sample selected using their rules and 68.32% using our rules. Skipping the details, we can report that the stronger performance results from the fund sample chosen using their rules is due to the 60-month survival rule. If the survival rule is reduced to 8 months, their rules for including funds produce simulation results close to ours. The important point, however, is that whatever inclusion rules are used, failure to account for the joint distribution of fund returns, and of fund and explanatory returns, biases the inferences of Kosowski et al. (2006) toward positive performance. (Cuthbertson, Nitzche, and O'Sullivan (2008) apply the simulation approach of Kosowski et al. to U.K. mutual funds, with similar results and, we guess, similar problems.)

Time period is also an important source of differences in results. Our simulations for 1984 to 2006 produce much less evidence of funds with sufficient skill to cover costs. In Table III, the CDFs of four-factor $t(\alpha)$ estimates for the net fund returns of 1984 to 2006 are always to the left of the average CDFs from the net return simulations (in which funds have sufficient skill to cover costs). Even in the extreme right tail of four-factor $t(\alpha)$ for net returns, more than 60% of the simulation runs beat the $t(\alpha)$ estimates for actual fund returns. But when our approach is applied to the 1975 to 2002 period of Kosowski et al. (2006), the 90th and higher percentiles of $t(\alpha)$ for net fund returns are above the average values from the simulations (Table V). And for the 97th and higher percentiles, less than 20% of the simulation runs beat the $t(\alpha)$ estimates for actual fund returns.

What do we make of the stronger results for 1975 to 2002 versus 1984 to 2006? One story is that in olden times there were fewer funds and a larger percentage of managers with sufficient skill to cover costs. Over time the skilled managers lost their edge or went on to more lucrative pursuits (e.g., hedge funds). Or perhaps, the entry of hordes of mediocre managers posing as skilled (Cremers and Petajisto (2009)) buries the tracks of true skill. Stronger results for 1975 to 2002 may also be due to biases in the CRSP data that are more prevalent in earlier years (Elton et al. (2001)). Whatever the explanation, the stronger evidence for performance during 1975 to 2002 is interesting, but irrelevant for today's investors.

VI. CONCLUSIONS

For 1984 to 2006, when the CRSP database is relatively free of biases, mutual fund investors in aggregate realize net returns that underperform CAPM, three-factor, and four-factor benchmarks by about the costs in expense ratios. Thus, if there are fund managers with enough skill to produce benchmark-adjusted expected returns that cover costs, their tracks are hidden in the aggregate results by the performance of managers with insufficient skill.

When we turn to individual funds, the challenge is to distinguish skill from luck. With 3,156 funds in our full ($5 million AUM) sample, some do extraordinarily well and some do extraordinarily poorly just by chance. To distinguish between luck and skill, we compare the distribution of $t(\alpha)$ estimates from actual fund returns with the distribution from bootstrap simulations in which all funds have zero true α. The tests on net returns say that few funds have enough skill to cover costs. The distribution of three-factor $t(\alpha)$ estimates from net fund returns is almost always to the left of the zero α distribution. The extreme right tail of the three-factor $t(\alpha)$ estimates for net fund returns, however, is roughly in line with the simulated distribution. This suggests that some managers do have sufficient skill to cover costs. But the estimate of net return three-factor true α is about zero even for the portfolio of funds in the top percentiles of historical three-factor $t(\alpha)$ estimates, and the estimate of four-factor true α is negative. Moreover, the estimate of true α for funds in the top percentiles is no better than the estimated α (also near zero) for large, efficiently managed passive funds.

The simulation results for gross fund returns say that when returns are measured before the costs in expense ratios, there is stronger evidence of manager skill, negative as well as positive. For our $5 million AUM sample, true three-factor or four-factor gross return α seems to be symmetric about zero with a cross-section standard deviation of about 1.25% per year (about 10 basis points per month). For larger ($250 million and $1 billion AUM) funds, the standard deviation for the left tail is again about 1.25% per year, but the right tail standard deviation of true α falls to about 0.75%.

APPENDIX A: MEASUREMENT ISSUES IN GROSS RETURNS

The question in the tests on gross fund returns is whether managers have skill that causes expected returns to differ from those of comparable passive benchmarks. For this purpose, we would like to have fund returns measured before all costs but net of non-return income like revenues from securities lending. This would put funds on the same pure return basis as the benchmark explanatory returns, so the tests could focus on the effects of skill. Our gross fund returns are before the costs in expense ratios, but they are net of other costs, primarily trading costs, and they include income from securities lending.

We could attempt to add trading costs to our estimates of gross fund returns. Funds do not report trading costs, however, and even when turnover is available, estimates of trading costs are subject to large errors (Carhart (1997)). For example, trading costs are likely to vary across funds because of differences in style tilts, trading skill, and the extent to which a fund is actively managed and demands immediacy in trade execution. Trading costs can also vary through time because of changes in a fund's management and general changes in the costs of trading. All this leads us to conclude that estimates of trading costs for individual funds, especially actively managed funds, are fraught with error and potential bias, and so can be misleading. As a result, we do not take that route in our tests on gross returns.

An alternative approach (suggested by a referee) is to put the passive benchmarks produced by combining the explanatory returns in (1) in the same units as the gross fund returns on the left of (1). This involves taking account of the costs (primarily trading costs) not covered in expense ratios that would be borne by an efficiently managed passive benchmark with the same style tilts as the fund whose gross returns are to be explained.

Vanguard's index funds are good candidates for this exercise since, except for momentum, Vanguard provides index funds (Total Stock Market Index Fund, Growth Index Fund, Value Index Fund, Small-Cap Index Fund, Small-Cap Growth Index Fund, and Small-Cap Value Index Fund) that track well-defined target passive portfolios much like the market portfolio and the components of SMB_t and HML_t in (1). (We thank an Associate Editor for this insight.) Because the Vanguard index funds closely track their targets and stock picking skill is not an issue, we can estimate the average annual costs not included in a fund's expense ratio. Specifically, we add a fund's expense ratio to its reported average annual return for the 10 years through 2008 and then subtract the result from the average annual return of the fund's target for the same period. (The same calculation for an actively managed fund would include the effects of skill, as well as the costs not in expense ratios.) For every Vanguard index fund, this estimate of the costs missed in expense ratios is negative; that is, the fund's target return, which is before all costs, beats the fund's actual net return by less than the fund's expense ratio. If anything, Vanguard's small cap index funds do better on this score than its large cap funds—a clear warning that presumptions about trading costs can be misleading.

The Vanguard results are probably not unusual. We can report that the CAPM, three-factor, and four-factor α estimates for 1984 to 2006 for the net returns on a VW portfolio of index funds (which is dominated by large funds with low expense ratios) are close to zero, 0.08%, −0.16%, and 0.01% per year ($t = 0.18$, −0.61, and 0.02). In other words, in aggregate, wealth invested in index funds seems to earn average returns that cover costs, including trading costs.

Passive mutual funds that focus on momentum do not as yet exist, so we do not have estimates of trading costs for such funds. Existing work (Grundy and Martin (2001), Korajczyk and Sadka (2004)) suggests that the costs are significant. In our tests, however, the cross-sections of four-factor α estimates for funds are similar to the cross-sections of three-factor estimates, and the three-factor and four-factor tests produce much the same inferences. Given the large average MOM_t return, these results suggest that nontrivial long-term exposure to MOM_t is rare, so ignoring MOM_t trading costs is inconsequential. Moreover, the discussion of results in the text centers primarily on the three-factor model. The four-factor results are primarily a robustness check.

The Vanguard evidence and the results for a VW portfolio of index funds suggest that for the market and the components of SMB_t and HML_t, comparable efficiently managed passive mutual funds can enhance returns through trading, securities lending, and perhaps in other ways, so that their total costs are close to their expense ratios. Thus, our three-factor α estimates for the gross returns of funds would hardly change if we adjusted their passive benchmarks for the costs missed in expense ratios.

This does not mean our tests on gross returns capture the pure effects of skill. Though expense ratios seem to capture the total costs of efficiently managed passive funds, this is less likely to be true for actively managed funds. The typical active fund trades more than the typical passive fund, and active funds are likely to demand immediacy in trading that produces positive costs. Because of their high turnover, active funds also have fewer opportunities to generate revenues via securities lending (which are also trivial for the Vanguard funds). In short, it seems more likely that for active funds the costs not included in expense ratios are positive. Thus, our tests on the gross returns of funds produce α estimates that capture the effects of skill, less any costs missed by the expense ratios of the funds.

Equivalently, our tests on gross returns say that a fund's management has skill only if the fund's expected gross returns are sufficient to cover the costs (primarily trading costs) not included in its expense ratio. This is a reasonable definition of skill since a comparable efficiently managed passive fund would apparently avoid these costs. More important, this definition of skill is the only one we can accurately test in the absence of accurate estimates of the trading costs of active funds (impossible with available data).

It is fortuitous that efficiently managed passive benchmarks do not seem to have substantial costs missed in their expense ratios since accurate adjustment for such costs is nontrivial, perhaps impossible. For example, consider an actively managed small value fund. The passive benchmark for the fund produced by the three-factor version of (1) is likely to imply positive weights on the market, *SMB*, and *HML*, which implies positive weights on the market (*M*), small stocks (*S*), and value stocks (*H*) and negative weights on big stocks (*B*) and growth stocks (*L*). Suppose that (contrary to our estimates) efficiently managed passive funds have nontrivial trading costs. We might then increase the three-factor gross return α estimate for an active fund for the trading costs of the long positions in *M, S*, and *H* and the short positions in *B* and *L* that passively replicate the small value style of the active fund. But this is overkill. The three-factor model produces a passive clone for an actively managed fund by inefficiently combining five passive portfolios. A small value fund simply buys a diversified portfolio of small value stocks and only bears the trading costs of these stocks. As a result, even a passive small value fund evaluated with the three-factor model is likely to produce a positive α estimate if we enhance the estimate with positive trading costs for the five components of its three-factor clone.

If we wish to adjust the tests on gross returns for the trading costs of an efficiently managed passive fund with the same style tilts as the active fund to be evaluated, the correct procedure is to add an estimate of the trading costs of a comparable efficiently managed passive fund to the active fund's gross return α estimate. For example, a small value active fund would be reimbursed for the trading costs (more precisely, for all the costs missed in the expense ratio) of an efficiently managed passive fund with the same style tilts. This is nontrivial since a style group includes active funds with widely different style tilts, and we need an efficiently managed passive clone for every active fund. Fortunately, the costs missed in expense ratios are apparently close to zero for efficiently managed passive funds, and ignoring them (as we do in our tests) is inconsequential for inferences.

APPENDIX B: CAPM BOOTSTRAP SIMULATIONS

Table AI replicates the bootstrap simulations in Table III for a CAPM benchmark, that is, regression (1) with the excess market return as the only explanatory variable. The CAPM results are different. The CAPM tests on net returns produce what seems like strong evidence that some fund managers have sufficient skill to cover costs. Thus, for percentiles above the 90th, the CAPM $t(\alpha)$ estimates for actual net fund returns are always above the averages from the net return simulations (in which all managers have sufficient skill to cover costs), and the $t(\alpha)$ estimates for actual fund returns typically beat those from the simulations in more than 80% of simulation runs. Relative to the three-factor and four-factor tests in Table III, the CAPM tests on gross returns in Table AI also produce what seems like stronger evidence that some managers have skill that leads to positive true α, while others have negative true α.

In fact, the CAPM results just illustrate well-known patterns in average returns that cause problems for the CAPM during our sample period. Actual mutual fund returns contain the effects of size, value-growth, and momentum tilts in fund portfolios that are missed by the CAPM. Thus, even passive funds that tilt toward small stocks, value stocks, or positive momentum stocks are likely to produce positive α estimates in CAPM tests, despite the fact that their managers make no effort to pick individual stocks. The CAPM simulations allow for the relation between average return and market exposure, but they wash out all other patterns in average returns when they subtract each fund's CAPM α estimate from its returns. As a result, the CAPM simulations say that actual fund returns have nonzero true α.

Which patterns in average returns left unexplained by the CAPM are most responsible for the differences between the CAPM simulation results and the results for the three-factor and four-factor models? Table III says that adding the momentum factor to the three-factor model has minor effects on estimates of $t(\alpha)$. Since the momentum return MOM_t has the highest average premium during our sample period, we infer that long-term exposure to momentum is probably rare among mutual funds. The average size (SMB_t) premium is trivial during our 1984 to 2006 sample period (0.03% per month, Table I), so size tilts probably are not driving the different results for the CAPM. That leaves the value (HML_t) premium as the focus of the story. Funds in the right tail of the CAPM $t(\alpha)$ estimates are more likely to have positive HML_t exposure that makes them look good in CAPM tests, and funds in the left tail are likely to have negative HML_t exposure.

In short, the CAPM tests are a lesson about how failure to account for common patterns in returns and average returns can affect inferences about the skill of fund managers.

TABLE AI. Percentiles of CAPM $t(\alpha)$ estimates for actual and simulated fund returns

The table shows values of $t(\alpha)$ at selected percentiles (Pct) of the distribution of CAPM $t(\alpha)$ estimates for actual (Act) net and gross fund returns. The table also shows the percent of the 10,000 simulation runs that produce lower values of $t(\alpha)$ at the selected percentiles than those observed for actual fund returns (%<Act). Sim is the average value of $t(\alpha)$ at the selected percentiles from the simulations. The period is January 1984 to September 2006 and results are shown for the $5 million, $250 million, and $1 billion AUM fund groups.

Pct	5 Million			250 Million			1 Billion		
	Sim	Act	%<Act	Sim	Act	%<Act	Sim	Act	%<Act
Net Returns									
1	−2.36	−3.72	0.25	−2.30	−3.70	0.40	−2.27	−4.10	0.08
2	−2.06	−3.28	0.45	−2.02	−3.29	0.58	−2.00	−3.50	0.24
3	−1.88	−3.00	0.64	−1.85	−3.02	0.79	−1.84	−3.29	0.23
4	−1.75	−2.84	0.62	−1.72	−2.92	0.65	−1.71	−3.18	0.19
5	−1.65	−2.69	0.74	−1.62	−2.76	0.77	−1.62	−3.00	0.27
10	−1.29	−2.16	1.08	−1.28	−2.18	1.64	−1.28	−2.47	0.46
20	−0.86	−1.48	1.93	−0.86	−1.58	1.98	−0.87	−1.79	0.70
30	−0.54	−1.05	2.09	−0.55	−1.11	2.30	−0.56	−1.35	0.44
40	−0.26	−0.65	3.84	−0.27	−0.75	2.50	−0.28	−0.88	0.48
50	0.00	−0.29	8.05	0.00	−0.36	5.23	−0.01	−0.46	1.29
60	0.26	0.08	20.79	0.26	0.06	19.86	0.26	−0.10	4.02
70	0.53	0.49	46.40	0.53	0.47	43.16	0.54	0.31	18.52
80	0.84	0.95	71.01	0.84	0.89	61.89	0.84	0.72	36.21
90	1.26	1.66	91.09	1.25	1.49	79.61	1.24	1.42	73.88
95	1.61	2.31	97.29	1.58	2.09	92.39	1.56	1.91	84.74
96	1.71	2.45	97.55	1.67	2.23	93.43	1.66	2.03	85.94
97	1.84	2.68	98.46	1.79	2.43	95.05	1.77	2.22	89.01
98	2.01	2.89	98.69	1.95	2.60	95.07	1.92	2.47	92.06
99	2.29	3.21	98.88	2.21	2.96	96.51	2.16	2.76	92.96

(Continued)

TABLE AI. (Continued)

Pct	5 Million			250 Million			1 Billion		
	Sim	Act	%<Act	Sim	Act	%<Act	Sim	Act	%<Act
Gross Returns									
1	−2.36	−3.04	4.09	−2.30	−3.01	5.35	−2.27	−3.29	2.00
2	−2.06	−2.66	5.29	−2.02	−2.67	6.32	−2.00	−2.93	2.57
3	−1.88	−2.45	5.88	−1.85	−2.45	7.17	−1.84	−2.76	2.37
4	−1.75	−2.26	7.41	−1.72	−2.31	7.54	−1.71	−2.49	3.99
5	−1.65	−2.13	7.82	−1.62	−2.16	8.80	−1.62	−2.34	4.91
10	−1.29	−1.65	11.87	−1.28	−1.66	13.56	−1.28	−1.95	4.93
20	−0.86	−0.95	33.12	−0.86	−1.04	25.14	−0.87	−1.35	7.59
30	−0.54	−0.55	44.63	−0.55	−0.63	35.49	−0.56	−0.88	12.00
40	−0.26	−0.19	62.18	−0.27	−0.26	50.41	−0.28	−0.43	24.27
50	0.00	0.16	77.76	0.00	0.10	67.74	−0.01	−0.05	41.74
60	0.26	0.53	89.27	0.26	0.46	81.45	0.26	0.36	67.57
70	0.53	0.98	96.44	0.53	0.91	91.87	0.54	0.77	82.64
80	0.84	1.44	97.60	0.84	1.37	95.08	0.84	1.18	87.03
90	1.26	2.12	98.96	1.25	1.98	97.29	1.24	1.82	94.23
95	1.61	2.76	99.65	1.58	2.47	98.14	1.56	2.33	96.87
96	1.71	2.89	99.69	1.67	2.72	98.98	1.66	2.46	97.14
97	1.84	3.12	99.77	1.79	2.85	99.01	1.77	2.59	97.16
98	2.01	3.35	99.84	1.95	3.05	99.18	1.92	2.84	98.03
99	2.29	3.72	99.89	2.21	3.37	99.35	2.16	3.34	99.14

REFERENCES

Berk, Jonathan B., and Richard C. Green, 2004, Mutual fund flows in rational markets, *Journal of Political Economy* 112, 1269–1295.

Carhart, Mark M., 1997, On persistence in mutual fund performance, *Journal of Finance* 52, 57–82.

Cremers, Martijn, and Antti Petajisto, 2009, How active is your fund manager? A new measure that predicts performance, *Review of Financial Studies* 22, 3329–3365.

Cuthbertson, K., D. Nitzsche, and N. O'Sullivan, 2008, UK mutual fund performance: Skill or luck? *Journal of Empirical Finance* 15, 613–634.

Dybvig, Philip H., and Stephen A. Ross, 1985, The analytics of performance measurement using a security market line, *Journal of Finance* 40, 401–416.

Elton, Edwin J., Martin J. Gruber, and Christopher R. Blake, 2001, A first look at the accuracy of the CRSP mutual fund database and a comparison of the CRSP and Morningstar mutual fund databases, *Journal of Finance* 56, 2415–2430.

Evans, Richard, 2010, Mutual fund incubator, *Journal of Finance* 65, Forthcoming.

Fama, Eugene F., 1965, The behavior of stock market prices, *Journal of Business* 38, 34–105.

Fama, Eugene F., and Kenneth R. French, 1993, Common risk factors in the returns on stocks and bonds, *Journal of Financial Economics* 33, 3–56.

Ferson, Wayne E., and Rudi W. Schadt, 1996, Measuring fund strategy and performance in changing economic conditions, *Journal of Finance* 51, 425–462.

French, Kenneth R., 2008, The cost of active investing, *Journal of Finance* 63, 1537–1573.

Grinblatt, Mark, and Sheridan Titman, 1992, Performance persistence in mutual funds, *Journal of Finance* 47, 1977–1984.

Gruber, Martin J., 1996, Another puzzle: The growth of actively managed mutual funds, *Journal of Finance* 51, 783–810.

Grundy, Bruce D., and J. Spencer Martin, 2001, Understanding the nature of the risks and the sources of the rewards to momentum investing, *Journal of Financial Studies* 14, 29–78.

Jensen, Michael C., 1968, The performance of mutual funds in the period 1945–1964, *Journal of Finance* 23, 2033–2058.

Korajczyk, Robert A., and Ronnie Sadka, 2004, Are momentum profits robust to trading costs? *Journal of Finance* 59, 1039–1082.

Kosowski, Robert, Allan Timmermann, Russ Wermers, and Hal White, 2006, Can mutual fund "stars" really pick stocks? New evidence from a bootstrap analysis, *Journal of Finance* 61, 2551–2595.

Malkiel, Burton G., 1995, Returns from investing in equity mutual funds: 1971–1991, *Journal of Finance* 50, 549–572.

Sharpe, William F., 1991, The arithmetic of active management, *Financial Analysts Journal* 47, 7–9.

RISK AND RETURN

. . .

RISK AND RETURN

. . .

John H. Cochrane and Tobias J. Moskowitz

While early efficient market work could start with the working hypothesis that expected returns are constant over time, the need for risk adjustment and a "model of market equilibrium" is immediately apparent in the cross-section. There are stocks whose average returns are greater than those of other stocks. But are the high-average-return assets really riskier in the ways described by asset pricing models?

This empirical work is not easy. It took lots of thought and creativity between writing down the theory and evaluating it in the data. The four papers in this section are not only a capsule of how understanding of the facts developed. They more deeply show how Gene, alone, with James MacBeth first, and with Ken French later, shaped how we *do* empirical work in finance.

FAMA AND MACBETH

The CAPM, the subject of Fama and MacBeth's famous paper, states that average returns should be proportional to betas,

$$E(R^{ei}) = \beta_i E(R^{em}) + \alpha_j \qquad (1)$$

where the betas are defined from the time-series regression

$$R_t^{ei} = \alpha_i + \beta_i R_t^{em} + \varepsilon_t^i, \ t = 1, 2, \dots T. \qquad (2)$$

Here, R_t^{ei} is the excess return of any asset or portfolio i, and R_t^{em} is the excess return of the market portfolio.

You run regression (2) first, over time for each i to measure the betas. Then the CAPM relationship (1) says average returns, across i, should be proportional to the betas, with "alphas" as the error term (i.e., the average returns not explained by the model). Though unconventional, we write the alphas as the last term in (1) to emphasize that they are errors to the relationship.

[303]

Now, an empiricist faces many choices. First, one could apply this model to data by just running the time-series regression (2). The mean market premium, the betas, and the alphas are all then estimated, and one can see if the alphas are small.

Fama and MacBeth didn't do that. They estimated the cross-section (1) in a second stage. Why? For many good reasons. First, they wanted, we think, to get past formal estimation and generic testing to see how the model behaves in all sorts of intuitive ways. Sure, all models are models, as Gene frequently reminds us, and all models are false. But even if a glass is statistically 5% empty, we want to really understand the 95%.

The paper tries a nonlinear term in beta in (1), idiosyncratic variances, an intercept, and so forth. These are natural explorations of ways that the model might plausibly be wrong. To explore them, we need to run the cross-sectional regression.

Second, betas are poorly estimated, and betas may vary over time. Fama and MacBeth use portfolios to estimate betas, which reduces estimation error. Portfolios, however, also reduce information, in this case cross-sectional dispersion in betas. (It's like measuring your income by measuring the average income on your block.) Fama and MacBeth used portfolios that maintained dispersion in true betas while also reducing estimation error. They sorted stocks into portfolios based on the stocks' historical betas, but then used the subsequent, post-ranking portfolio beta in the regression equation (2). As is typical with Gene's papers, there is a deep understanding of a complicated problem, solved in a simple yet clever way.

The cross-sectional regression framework easily allows one to use rolling regressions (2) so betas can vary over time.

Forty-five years of econometrics later, we know how to estimate models with time-varying betas, and we know other ways to handle the errors-in-variables problem too. But the transparency and simplicity of the Fama-MacBeth approach still reigns.

The use of portfolios itself is a foundational choice in empirical work. In this paper, you see tables with 1 to 10 marching across the top. That isn't in the theory, which just talks about generic assets. And it isn't in formal econometrics either. (Formal econometrics might call it nonparametric estimation with an inefficient kernel.) Yet this is how we all do empirical finance. It is useful and intuitive.

Most famously, Fama and MacBeth dealt with the problem that the errors are correlated across assets. If Ford has an unusually good stock return this month, it's likely GM has one too. Therefore, the usual formulas for standard errors and tests, which assume observations are uncorrelated across companies as well as over time, are wrong.

This was 1970, before the modern formulas for panel data regressions were invented. Fama and MacBeth found a brilliant way around it, by running a cross-sectional regression at each time period and using the in-sample time-variation of the cross-sectional regression coefficients to compute standard errors. In doing so, they allow for arbitrary cross-correlation of the errors. That this procedure remains in widespread use, despite the existence of econometric formulas that can deal with the problem—sometimes successfully, and sometimes not—is a testament to how brilliant the technique was.

More deeply, Fama and MacBeth's approach to cross-correlation was not to adopt GLS or other statistically "efficient" procedures, which every econometrics textbook of the day and up to just a few years ago would advocate, but instead to run robust, reliable OLS regressions and compute corrected standard errors. That practice has since spread far and wide.

Finally, the Fama and MacBeth procedure has a clever portfolio interpretation. The coefficient in the regression of returns on betas represents the return to a portfolio that has zero weight, unit exposure to beta, and is minimum variance among all such portfolios that satisfy the first two constraints. This description is in essence the market portfolio. Hence, an average of this portfolio's returns is an estimate of the market risk premium. Since returns are close to uncorrelated over time, this interpretation justifies the standard error of that mean return as the standard error of the Fama-MacBeth regression coefficient.

This beautiful insight would allow future researchers to look at other characteristics and other betas in the same way: the coefficients associated with other characteristics (e.g., size or book-to-market ratios) or betas on the right-hand side of the regression are minimum-variance returns of zero cost portfolios with unit exposure to the characteristics and zero exposure to all other variables on the right-hand side.

As with the practice of forming 1–10 test portfolios of assets, this insight allowing researchers to easily translate regressions into portfolios and vice versa would spawn a host of empirical facts and models used in academia and practice.

So, while theorists may think of empirical work as easy and a task for lesser minds, here you see Fama and MacBeth dealing with hard issues of how you do empirical work and interpreting empirical results within the confines of theory. The Fama-MacBeth procedure set a pattern that lasted a generation. We still have 10 portfolios marching across the page, we still compute Fama-MacBeth regressions, and we still use those insights to build efficient portfolios.

Fama and MacBeth's influence was so strong, it extends to the omissions. They refer to linearity of the cross-sectional relation, the statistical significance of the market premium, and the absence of other explanatory variables as "tests" of the model. The actual "test" of the model is whether the alphas are jointly zero. They didn't do that test because it hadn't been invented yet. Curiously, though the Gibbons-Ross-Shanken (GRS) test for joint significance of the alphas was developed for time-series regressions and has come into use, the equally easy (in retrospect) cross-sectional version of the GRS test has never, as far as we know, been used. (Just construct a Fama-MacBeth covariance matrix of the errors $\text{cov}(\hat{\alpha}, \hat{\alpha}') = \text{cov}(\varepsilon, \varepsilon')/T$. Then $\hat{\alpha}'\, \text{cov}(\hat{\alpha}, \hat{\alpha}')^{-1}\, \hat{\alpha}'$ has a χ^2 distribution. Or use GMM, which gives corrections for estimated betas and autocorrelated residuals. Or bootstrap it.) Well, we follow Fama and MacBeth. And the lack of methodological innovation is understandable. When finding new results, one wants to make sure they come from the data, not the method. So method that was innovative in its day, and is transparent, familiar, robust, and good enough now, survives.

THE CROSS-SECTION OF RETURNS

We include three papers on the cross-section of returns, with its primary workhorse the value premium. They represent a remarkable intellectual journey. Gene was both the Newton and Einstein of finance, presiding over the foundation of the field and development of the CAPM, and then presiding over the second revolution, the incorporation and amalgamation of a plethora of anomalies and the emergence of multifactor models, in this case with Ken French.

The CAPM reigned supreme for about a decade after Fama and MacBeth's article was published. Time and again, someone would come up with a clever technique that seemed to make money, and time and again, when examined carefully, either the average returns came from mismeasurement, overfitting, or survivor/selection bias, or the average returns corresponded to a higher beta, so the profits were just as easily made by investing in the market index.

Yet, starting with the size effect in the late 1970s, more and more cross-sectional anomalies cropped up. These are methods for finding securities which have high average returns, but those returns do not correspond to higher betas. Or, less often, they are techniques for finding securities with low betas that do not have low average returns.

"The Cross-Section of Expected Stock Returns" was a bombshell, for it announced Fama and French's certification, after combing through the entrails of the data, that indeed the CAPM fails. On reexamination—where they painstakingly and cleverly try to maximize the information they glean from the data while simultaneously minimizing the noise/error in the data using what became the standard for estimating betas—they find no association between beta and average returns.

Second, Fama and French dug deeply through the trove of expected-return signals and found that size and book-to-market ratio alone captured the information about expected returns from a plethora of signals.

The exercise is in many ways a multiple regression question. Expected returns across assets depend on a vector of forecasting characteristics. Many of those characteristics are significant return forecasters taken one at a time. But in a multiple regression sense, size and book-to-market ratio encompass the information in the other forecasting characteristics.

This paper nicely connects two ways to understand expected returns as a function of characteristics. One can look at the mean returns of portfolios sorted on the characteristic, or one can run cross-sectional forecasting regressions,

$$R_{t+1}^{ei} = a + b'C_t^i + \varepsilon_{t+1}^i$$

where C denotes a vector of characteristics such as size, book-to-market ratio, or beta. Average returns on a portfolio sorted on the basis of C are no more or less than nonparametric estimates of a nonlinear version of this regression—but one that is very simple and intuitive. Portfolio sorts also assuage the worry that regressions of this sort are driven by outliers—a few extreme values of C that happen to have extreme returns.

The way of thinking about asset returns in these papers carries a deeply influential innovation for how we do empirical work. In looking at the theory, you often think of "asset i" as referring to, well, an asset: a stock or bond. In these papers, Fama and French exploit the idea that average returns and betas attach in a stable and strong way to a set of firm *characteristics*, but not to the firm itself. Expected returns and, later, betas, are stable functions of size, book-to-market ratio, and other characteristics. But an individual firm's expected returns and betas vary over time as the firm's characteristics vary, so these statistics are not a stable function of firm name.

That expected returns, betas, and other statistics are stable functions of characteristics, not firm name, is an auxiliary observation about the data. Nothing about this stability is present in the theory. But this auxiliary assumption seems true of the world and makes asset pricing much more interesting and productive. Since characteristics wander over time, there just isn't that much variation in expected returns or betas across firm names. We see that variation as a function of the characteristics, which have a real-world interpretation as portfolio strategies. This procedure also unites "signals," "managed portfolios," and "assets" as just instances of the same thing.

COMMON RISK FACTORS

"Common Risk Factors in the Returns on Stocks and Bonds" took what is, with ex post hindsight, the next and obvious step. To say expected returns are a function of two characteristics, size and book-to-market ratio, is a fine *description* of average returns, but it cannot stand as an *explanation* of average returns, at least not an explanation of any vaguely "rational" sort. For example, if average returns really are a function of the size of the company, we only have to buy a portfolio of small companies, paying high average returns, and finance the purchase by issuing stock of what is now a big company, paying low average returns. Then we retire rich off the difference. "Explanations" must be betas, which are invariant to portfolio formation.

Fama and French then found two "factors" in the covariance matrix of returns, related to size and book-to-market ratio, and found that the expected returns on size and book-to-market sorted portfolios line up beautifully with betas on these two factors, plus a beta of one on the market portfolio. That insight seems obvious, but it really wasn't. There was no guarantee that the covariance structure of the assets would be captured so easily by these two factors. Each size and book-to-market portfolio could have had its own variance devoid of any common structure. But they didn't. The portfolios' returns were tied together by two common sources of variation that were identified by grouping securities based on the two characteristics: size and book-to-market ratio.

With the advantage of hindsight, you can do the same thing by finding the first three principal components of the covariance matrix of the 25 portfolios. You will find those first three principal components explain the vast bulk of co-movement of the 25 portfolios, as reflected in Fama and French's 90–95% R^2 values. The first three principal components are also clearly a "market" portfolio, one that loads on big minus small portfolios, and another that loads on high minus low book-to-market portfolios, as Fama and French's factors do.

Then, you will find that expected returns are almost completely explained by betas on the three principal components. Since the betas or loadings on the "market" factor are all one, though, variation in market betas across portfolios does nothing to explain the cross-sectional variation in average returns.

Viewed this way, the Fama-French model is an arbitrage pricing theory (APT) model, and it certainly is that at least. What Fama and French did *not* do is interesting in that context. Arbitrage pricing models have been around a long time, and they usually met limited success. The typical approach was to factor analyze the covariance matrix of individual stock returns, and then to see if large factors are important drivers of mean returns. But loadings (betas) on factors so derived never did much to explain the cross-section of average returns. Fama and French *first* formed portfolios on the basis of characteristics known to describe average returns, and *then* found the factors that dominate the covariance of returns. Doing so, they made an APT work nicely. At last.

Fama and French also did not try to build some fundamental asset pricing, starting with consumption or state variables for investment opportunities. In retrospect, we see a natural hierarchy for empirical work: First, find how average returns vary with characteristics such as size and book-to-market ratio. Second, see if there is a factor model based on the same characteristics which explains the average returns. Third, see if more "fundamental" factors such as consumption growth or macroeconomic state variables can explain the risk premiums of the empirically derived factors such as Fama and French's HML and SMB.

Seen this way, Fama and French's three-factor model is a remarkable data summary device. The 25 portfolios capture the spread in average returns across thousands of stocks, using book-to-market and size signals. Loadings on the three factors then explain the average returns of the 25 portfolios. As a result, more fundamental approaches need only explain the three factor risk premiums.

As Fama and French emphasize, the three factors should be proxies for something deeper, such as consumption, marginal utility, "state variables of concern to investors," and so forth. Figuring out what those deeper factors are remains a challenge. That challenge has occupied the attention of academic researchers for the better part of three decades now. But by summarizing all the information in stock markets down to three factors, that challenge is enormously easier for theorists.

Interestingly, most authors seem to have missed this point. Most authors test more fundamental models by pricing the 25 portfolios, or they try to see if macro factors drive out, rather than explain, the three Fama and French factors. (And if authors don't do it, referees demand it!) Blindly copying Fama and French's method for this different purpose misses their underlying point. Fama and French did it so you don't have to!

Factor structure itself is a vital point in evaluating book-to-market ratio, size, and other anomalies. It is easy to build stories about why a class of securities should have prices that are too high or too low, and consequently average returns that are subsequently too low or too high. But why in the world should the underpriced securities all move up or down together the next year? Why should they share strong exposures to some risk?

Well, arbitrage. If not, you could earn a fortune holding a diversified portfolio of value stocks. But that means somebody is thinking about the means and variances of diversified portfolios and has driven prices pretty close to the "rational" point where one must hold undiversifiable risk to earn positive returns.

It seems easy in retrospect. It was not. One of us (Cochrane) was there, and I can attest to the fact. I was thinking about cross-sectional versions of dividend-yield forecasts; I was thinking about beta models to explain it. Nothing like what Fama and French did occurred to me. When I first saw the three-factor model, I asked questions that, if anyone remembered, would go down in the history of stupid seminar questions. Isn't it a tautology to "explain" 25 book-to-market portfolios with three book-to-market factors? No. Their genius came in seeing at the time that this was the most natural and simple thing to do. And once again, Fama and French set the stage. Now everyone sorts portfolios and creates factor portfolios to "explain" expected returns.

MULTIFACTOR EXPLANATIONS

"Multifactor Explanations of Asset Pricing Anomalies" is not as famous as the other three papers, but it should be, in our opinion. It is another example of a paper, later in a series, which explains the basic concepts more clearly than earlier papers, without the forest of robustness tests that early papers must have. It is a good paper to recommend that students read first.

Table 1A–B of "Multifactor Explanations" succinctly distills the three-factor model. Panel A shows a strong pattern of average returns across size and book-to-market dimensions, a description in want of an explanation. Panel B shows how the variation across portfolios in betas (b, h, s) on the three factors lines up with the variation in expected returns.

The point of the table is that variation across portfolios in the b, h, s corresponds to the variation across portfolios in average returns shown in Panel A.

Thus, you should read this as a table of *data* for an implicit cross-sectional regression, of 25 average returns (Panel A) on slopes (Panel B). The intercepts (a) of the time-series regression are the errors in this cross-sectional relationship.

The regression in Table 1 has a secondary direct interpretation. The regression and its R^2 tell you how much movements in the factors account for movements in the portfolio returns. The regression and high R^2 tell you that the three-factor model is a good model of return *variance*. They tell you that most of the actual, ex post, returns of the 25 portfolios can be attributed to the actual, ex post, return of the three factors. The size of the alphas, the pattern of betas, and the implied cross-sectional regression tell you the more important fact that this is a good model of *means*.

Read carefully. When Fama and French say this is a good model of "returns and average returns," they repeat "return" for a reason. A good model of "returns" is a good factor model—high R^2 for the first few principal components. It would be a good model no matter how large the intercepts. A good model of "average returns" is one in which mean returns vary a lot across portfolios, but betas vary in the same way as the means, and the intercepts are small. The R^2 is irrelevant to this point. The Fama-French model has both small alphas and large R^2, which makes it both a good model of "returns" and of "average returns."

Table 1 also summarizes a sea change in empirical procedures that occurred in asset pricing, as well as macroeconomics, in the prior 20 years, with Fama alone and with French playing a leading role. In the late 1970s or early 1980s, people wanted to "test" models. Where is the "test" of the Fama-French model? There is one, and only one, such test: whether the 25 alphas are jointly equal to zero. This is the Gibbons-Ross-Shanken test with normal iid returns in time-series regressions, or the GMM overidentifying restrictions test using pricing errors as moment conditions more generally. As reported by Fama and French, that test blows the model out of the water. Fama and French statistically reject the hypothesis that all the alphas are zero at astronomical levels of significance.

How can it be that this, the most successful asset pricing model of a quarter-century at least, is overwhelmingly statistically rejected? What is the rest of Table 1 even doing there if the model is rejected?

Well, formal rejection is no longer that interesting. All models are rejected if you have enough data. The hypothesis that this model is literally true is just not interesting. As Fama and French point out, the residuals are so small that economically small alphas are statistically different from zero. So the model is not 100% true. But it's 95% true!

So the paper proceeds by showing you the 95% that is true: how average returns vary a lot across portfolios; how betas nicely and smoothly vary in the same way; how alphas are by and large an order of magnitude smaller than the average returns; and so forth. That's how we evaluate models now. The focus on "testing" and "not rejecting" led to a lot of models with much larger alphas, but standard errors larger still, so we couldn't statistically reject that the alphas were zero. Or it led us to "rejecting" good models that explained a lot of data, but could be shown not to be 100% perfect.

"Multifactor Explanations" goes on to explain just how *useful* the three-factor model is. Practical usefulness, rather than great theoretical advance, accounts for the astonishing impact of the three-factor model. The point of the CAPM really never was to settle barroom bets about "rationality" or "irrationality." The point of the CAPM was practical—it gave a procedure for quickly and reliably risk-adjusting new findings. If you have a new clever idea for making money, you want to know, is this really something new, or just a way of getting exposure to a known risk? If the higher average return of a new idea corresponds to a higher beta, with no extra alpha, you find the new idea is no better than just investing more in the market index.

The big payoff of the three-factor model is the same sort of practical utility. You find some new procedure for isolating good returns, some new sort or forecasting variable. Is this just a way of buying value stocks, or, more deeply, buying stocks that *behave like* value stocks, and thus don't give any better performance in a portfolio that already includes value stocks? That's a vital question for practice. It lives quite apart from a deep battle over whether value itself represents macroeconomic risk premiums, "distress," or some collective irrationality. Whatever value is, when I look at something new, I want to take out the known value premium. That's what the CAPM was *useful* for, and that's what the three-factor model is useful for.

In addition, the best way to answer the "tautology" charge is to take the three-factor model out for a spin. If you're still worried about explaining value with value, well, let's explain *other* anomalies with value. For both reasons, the heart of the paper is, as the title suggests, showing how the multifactor model addresses other "multifactor anomalies."

To our mind, the sales growth tables are a shining example. Buying stocks of companies with five years of awful sales turns out to give a lot better return than buying stocks of companies whose sales are growing quickly. Apparently, the great sales growth is "priced in" to the stock. Well, this pattern might just be beta—companies with poor sales are going to go down the tubes in the next downturn, no? Well, no, at least as measured by market beta. But HML betas *do* fully explain the sales growth anomaly. The sales losing firms may not *be* value firms, but they *act like* value firms, and they give you no better performance in a portfolio that already includes value.

This paper is also great for showing the practical limits of the model. Momentum is a bust for the three-factor model—momentum average returns go the *opposite way* from value betas. Momentum portfolios can also be "explained" by a momentum factor, but Fama and French shied away from this specification. They didn't want to certify that every anomaly gets a factor. They now provide a momentum factor, UMD, on Ken French's webpage, and they use it for performance evaluation. But they are still reluctant to add it to their view of risk-based factors.

The abysmally low returns of small growth stocks are also a failure of the model. They account in large part for the statistical rejection, and the fact that characteristics are still a better description (but not explanation) of average returns than Fama-French factor betas. To our minds, they are an interesting anomaly awaiting dissection, potentially related to the firm birth-and-death process alluded to in Dennis Carlton's essay, or the fact that much information trading takes place in these mostly new and dynamic companies.

With these momentous papers, Fama and French put the anomaly zoo of the mid-1990s back in the bottle. Their solution was evolutionary, not revolutionary: yes, the CAPM fails. But one look at its assumptions and you expect it to fail. Multiple factors, long anticipated by theory, finally came to life in their empirical hands. By using three factors, just as you would use the CAPM, you can account for the known anomalies except momentum, and you can perform workaday risk adjustment, portfolio evaluation, and anomaly digestion. Compared to calls to throw out all asset pricing and start from scratch with psychology in place of economics, it is a remarkably conservative solution.

Anomalies have broken out again, however. Momentum did not go away. Now there are literally hundreds of claimed additional variables that describe expected returns, in ways that neither size and value characteristics nor size and value betas can account for. The second Fama-French step, finding additional factors, is slowly emerging. Many of the new return-forecasting variables seem to correspond to factors. For example, 10 momentum-sorted portfolio returns are neatly "explained" by a single winner-minus-loser factor. But adding hundreds of new factors is not a satisfactory approach. It's time to do once again what Fama and French did here, to put some order into the emerging chaos. But as happened last time, current off-the-shelf techniques, including Fama and French's, cannot handle the current empirical situation. We have tens or hundreds of right-hand variables, not two or three. It will take the kind of profound, simplifying insight and profound, simplifying innovation in technique that the Fama and French papers showed to put order back in the empirical asset-pricing universe once again.

RISK, RETURN, AND EQUILIBRIUM

EMPIRICAL TESTS

. . .

Eugene F. Fama and James D. MacBeth

This paper tests the relationship between average return and risk for New York Stock Exchange common stocks. The theoretical basis of the tests is the "two-parameter" portfolio model and models of market equilibrium derived from the two-parameter portfolio model. We cannot reject the hypothesis of these models that the pricing of common stocks reflects the attempts of risk-averse investors to hold portfolios that are "efficient" in terms of expected value and dispersion of return. Moreover, the observed "fair game" properties of the coefficients and residuals of the risk-return regressions are consistent with an "efficient capital market"—that is, a market where prices of securities fully reflect available information.

I. THEORETICAL BACKGROUND

In the two-parameter portfolio model of Tobin (1958), Markowitz (1959), and Fama (1965*b*), the capital market is assumed to be perfect in the sense that investors are price takers and there are neither transactions costs nor information costs. Distributions of one-period percentage returns on all assets and portfolios are assumed to be normal or to conform to some other two-parameter member of the symmetric stable class. Investors are assumed to be risk averse and to behave as if they choose among portfolios on the basis of maximum expected utility. A perfect capital market, investor risk aversion, and two-parameter return distributions imply the important "efficient set theorem": The optimal portfolio for any investor must be efficient in the sense that

Reprinted from the *Journal of Political Economy* 81, no. 3 (May–June 1973): 607–36.

Research supported by a grant from the National Science Foundation. The comments of Professors F. Black, L. Fisher, N. Gonedes, M. Jensen, M. Miller, R. Officer, H. Roberts, R. Roll, and M. Scholes are gratefully acknowledged. A special note of thanks is due to Black, Jensen, and Officer.

no other portfolio with the same or higher expected return has lower dispersion of return.[1]

In the portfolio model the investor looks at individual assets only in terms of their contributions to the expected value and dispersion, or risk, of his portfolio return. With normal return distributions the risk of portfolio p is measured by the standard deviation, $\sigma(\tilde{R}_p)$, of its return, $\tilde{R}_p$,[2] and the risk of an asset for an investor who holds p is the contribution of the asset to $\sigma(\tilde{R}_p)$. If x_{ip} is the proportion of portfolio funds invested in asset i, $\sigma_{ij} = \text{cov}(\tilde{R}_i, \tilde{R}_j)$ is the covariance between the returns on assets i and j, and N is the number of assets, then

$$\sigma(\tilde{R}_p) = \sum_{i=1}^{N} x_{ip} \left[\frac{\sum_{j=1}^{N} x_{jp}\sigma_{ij}}{\sigma(\tilde{R}_p)} \right] = \sum_{i=1}^{N} x_{ip} \frac{\text{cov}(\tilde{R}_i, \tilde{R}_p)}{\sigma(\tilde{R}_p)}.$$

Thus, the contribution of asset i to $\sigma(\tilde{R}_p)$—that is, the risk of asset i in the portfolio p—is proportional to

$$\sum_{j=1}^{N} x_{jp}\sigma_{ij}/\sigma(\tilde{R}_p) = \text{cov}(\tilde{R}_i, \tilde{R}_p)/\sigma(\tilde{R}_p).$$

1. Although the choice of dispersion parameter is arbitrary, the standard deviation is common when return distributions are assumed to be normal, whereas an interfractile range is usually suggested when returns are generated from some other symmetric stable distribution.

It is well known that the mean–standard deviation version of the two-parameter portfolio model can be derived from the assumption that investors have quadratic utility functions. But the problems with this approach are also well known. In any case, the empirical evidence of Fama (1965a), Blume (1970), Roll (1970), K. Miller (1971), and Officer (1971) provides support for the "distribution" approach to the model. For a discussion of the issues and a detailed treatment of the two-parameter model, see Fama and Miller (1972, chaps. 6–8).

We also concentrate on the special case of the two-parameter model obtained with the assumption of normally distributed returns. As shown in Fama (1971) or Fama and Miller (1972, chap. 7), the important testable implications of the general symmetric stable model are the same as those of the normal model.

2. Tildes ($\sim$) are used to denote random variables. And the one-period percentage return is most often referred to just as the return.

Note that since the weights x_{jp} vary from portfolio to portfolio, the risk of an asset is different for different portfolios.

For an individual investor the relationship between the risk of an asset and its expected return is implied by the fact that the investor's optimal portfolio is efficient. Thus, if he chooses the portfolio m, the fact that m is efficient means that the weights x_{im}, $i = 1, 2, \ldots, N$, maximize expected portfolio return

$$E(\tilde{R}_m) = \sum_{i=1}^{N} x_{im} E(\tilde{R}_i),$$

subject to the constraints

$$\sigma(\tilde{R}_p) = \sigma(\tilde{R}_m) \text{ and } \sum_{i=1}^{N} x_{im} = 1.$$

Lagrangian methods can then be used to show that the weights x_{jm} must be chosen in such a way that for any asset i in m

$$E(\tilde{R}_i) - E(\tilde{R}_m) = S_m \left[\frac{\sum_{j=1}^{N} x_{jm} \sigma_{ij}}{\sigma(\tilde{R}_m)} - \sigma(\tilde{R}_m) \right], \tag{1}$$

where S_m is the rate of change of $E(\tilde{R}_p)$ with respect to a change in $\sigma(\tilde{R}_p)$ at the point on the efficient set corresponding to portfolio m. If there are nonnegativity constraints on the weights (that is, if short selling is prohibited), then (1) only holds for assets i such that $x_{im} > 0$.

Although equation (1) is just a condition on the weights x_{jm} that is required for portfolio efficiency, it can be interpreted as the relationship between the risk of asset i in portfolio m and the expected return on the asset. The equation says that the difference between the expected return on the asset and the expected return on the portfolio is proportional to the difference between the risk of the asset and the risk of the portfolio. The proportionality factor is S_m, the slope of the efficient set at the point corresponding to the portfolio m. And the risk of the asset is its contribution to total portfolio risk, $\sigma(\tilde{R}_m)$.

II. TESTABLE IMPLICATIONS

Suppose now that we posit a market of risk-averse investors who make portfolio decisions period by period according to the two-parameter model.[3]

---

3. A multiperiod version of the two-parameter model is in Fama (1970a) or Fama and Miller (1972, chap. 8).

We are concerned with determining what this implies for observable properties of security and portfolio returns. We consider two categories of implications. First, there are conditions on expected returns that are implied by the fact that in a two-parameter world investors hold efficient portfolios. Second, there are conditions on the behavior of returns through time that are implied by the assumption of the two-parameter model that the capital market is perfect or frictionless in the sense that there are neither transactions costs nor information costs.

A. Expected Returns

The implications of the two-parameter model for expected returns derive from the efficiency condition or expected return-risk relationship of equation (1). First, it is convenient to rewrite (1) as

$$E(\tilde{R}_i) = \left[E(\tilde{R}_m) - S_m \sigma(\tilde{R}_m) \right] + S_m \sigma(\tilde{R}_m)\beta_i, \tag{2}$$

where

$$\beta_i \equiv \frac{\mathrm{cov}\left(\tilde{R}_i, \tilde{R}_m\right)}{\sigma^2(\tilde{R}_m)} = \frac{\sum\limits_{j=1}^{N} x_{jm}\sigma_{ij}}{\sigma^2(\tilde{R}_m)} = \frac{\mathrm{cov}\left(\tilde{R}_i, \tilde{R}_m\right)/\sigma\left(\tilde{R}_m\right)}{\sigma(\tilde{R}_m)}. \tag{3}$$

The parameter β_i can be interpreted as the risk of asset i in the portfolio m, measured relative to $\sigma(\tilde{R}_m)$, the total risk of m. The intercept in (2),

$$E(\tilde{R}_0) \equiv E(\tilde{R}_m) - S_m \sigma(\tilde{R}_m), \tag{4}$$

is the expected return on a security whose return is uncorrelated with $\tilde{R}_m$—that is, a zero-β security. Since $\beta = 0$ implies that a security contributes nothing to $\sigma(\tilde{R}_m)$, it is appropriate to say that it is riskless in this portfolio. It is well to note from (3), however, that since $x_{im}\sigma_{ii} = x_{im}\sigma^2(\tilde{R}_i)$ is just one of the N terms in β_i, $\beta_i = 0$ does not imply that security i has zero variance of return.

From (4), it follows that

$$S_m = \frac{E(\tilde{R}_m) - E(\tilde{R}_0)}{\sigma(\tilde{R}_m)}, \tag{5}$$

so that (2) can be rewritten

$$E(\tilde{R}_i) = E(\tilde{R}_0) + \left[E(\tilde{R}_m) - E(\tilde{R}_0) \right] \beta_i. \tag{6}$$

In words, the expected return on security i is $E(\tilde{R}_0)$, the expected return on a security that is riskless in the portfolio m, plus a risk premium that is β_i times the difference between $E(\tilde{R}_m)$ and $E(\tilde{R}_0)$.

Equation (6) has three testable implications: (C1) The relationship between the expected return on a security and its risk in any efficient portfolio m is linear. (C2) β_i is a complete measure of the risk of security i in the efficient portfolio m; no other measure of the risk of i appears in (6). (C3) In a market of risk-averse investors, higher risk should be associated with higher expected return; that is, $E(\tilde{R}_m) - E(\tilde{R}_0) > 0$.

The importance of condition C3 is obvious. The importance of C1 and C2 should become clear as the discussion proceeds. At this point suffice it to say that if C1 and C2 do not hold, market returns do not reflect the attempts of investors to hold efficient portfolios: Some assets are systematically underpriced or overpriced relative to what is implied by the expected return-risk or efficiency equation (6).

B. Market Equilibrium and the Efficiency of the Market Portfolio

To test conditions C1–C3 we must identify some efficient portfolio m. This in turn requires specification of the characteristic of market equilibrium when investors make portfolio decisions according to the two-parameter model.

Assume again that the capital market is perfect. In addition, suppose that from the information available without cost all investors derive the same and correct assessment of the distribution of the future value of any asset or portfolio—an assumption usually called "homogeneous expectations." Finally, assume that short selling of all assets is allowed. Then Black (1972) has shown that in a market equilibrium, the so-called market portfolio, defined by the weights

$$x_{im} \equiv \frac{\text{total market value of all units of asset } i}{\text{total market value of all assets}},$$

is always efficient.

Since it contains all assets in positive amounts, the market portfolio is a convenient reference point for testing the expected return-risk conditions C1–C3 of the two-parameter model. And the homogeneous-expectations assumption implies a correspondence between ex ante assessments of return distributions and distributions of ex post returns that is also required for meaningful tests of these three hypotheses.

C. A Stochastic Model for Returns

Equation (6) is in terms of expected returns. But its implications must be tested with data on period-by-period security and portfolio returns. We wish to choose a model of period-by-period returns that allows us to use observed average returns to test the expected-return conditions C1–C3, but one that is nevertheless as general as possible. We suggest the following stochastic generalization of (6):

$$\tilde{R}_{it} = \tilde{\gamma}_{0t} + \tilde{\gamma}_{1t}\beta_i + \tilde{\gamma}_{2t}\beta_i^2 + \tilde{\gamma}_{3t}s_i + \tilde{\eta}_{it}. \tag{7}$$

The subscript t refers to period t, so that $\tilde{R}_{it}$ is the one-period percentage return on security i from $t-1$ to t. Equation (7) allows $\tilde{\gamma}_{0t}$ and $\tilde{\gamma}_{1t}$ to vary stochastically from period to period. The hypothesis of condition C3 is that the expected value of the risk premium $\tilde{\gamma}_{1t}$, which is the slope $[E(\tilde{R}_{mt}) - E(\tilde{R}_{0t})]$ in (6), is positive—that is, $E(\tilde{\gamma}_{1t}) = E(\tilde{R}_{mt}) - E(\tilde{R}_{0t}) > 0$.

The variable β_i^2 is included in (7) to test linearity. The hypothesis of condition C1 is $E(\tilde{\gamma}_{2t}) = 0$, although $\tilde{\gamma}_{2t}$ is also allowed to vary stochastically from period to period. Similar statements apply to the term involving s_i in (7), which is meant to be some measure of the risk of security i that is not deterministically related to β_i. The hypothesis of condition C2 is $E(\tilde{\gamma}_{3t}) = 0$, but $\tilde{\gamma}_{3t}$ can vary stochastically through time.

The disturbance $\tilde{\eta}_{it}$ is assumed to have zero mean and to be independent of all other variables in (7). If all portfolio return distributions are to be normal (or symmetric stable), then the variables $\tilde{\eta}_{it}, \tilde{\gamma}_{0t}, \tilde{\gamma}_{1t}, \tilde{\gamma}_{2t}$ and $\tilde{\gamma}_{3t}$ must have a multivariate normal (or symmetric stable) distribution.

D. Capital Market Efficiency: The Behavior of Returns through Time

C1–C3 are conditions on expected returns and risk that are implied by the two-parameter model. But the model, and especially the underlying assumption of a perfect market, implies a capital market that is efficient in the sense that prices at every point in time fully reflect available information. This use of the word efficient is, of course, not to be confused with portfolio efficiency. The terminology, if a bit unfortunate, is at least standard.

Market efficiency in combination with condition C1 requires that scrutiny of the time series of the stochastic nonlinearity coefficient $\tilde{\gamma}_{2t}$ does not lead to nonzero estimates of expected future values of $\tilde{\gamma}_{2t}$. Formally, $\tilde{\gamma}_{2t}$ must be a fair game. In practical terms, although nonlinearities are observed ex post, because $\tilde{\gamma}_{2t}$ is a fair game, it is always appropriate for the investor to act ex ante under the presumption that the two-parameter model, as summarized by (6), is valid. That is, in his portfolio decisions he always assumes that there is a linear relationship between the risk of a security and its expected return. Likewise, market efficiency in the two-parameter model requires that the non-β risk coefficient $\tilde{\gamma}_{3t}$ and the time series of return disturbances $\tilde{\eta}_{it}$ are fair games. And the fair-game hypothesis also applies to the time series of $\tilde{\gamma}_{1t} - [E(\tilde{R}_{mt}) - E(\tilde{R}_{0t})]$, the difference between the risk premium for period t and its expected value.

In the terminology of Fama (1970b), these are "weak-form" propositions about capital market efficiency for a market where expected returns are generated by the two-parameter model. The propositions are weak since they are only concerned with whether prices fully reflect any information in the time series of past returns. "Strong-form" tests would be concerned with the speed-of-adjustment of prices to all available information.

E. Market Equilibrium with Riskless Borrowing and Lending

We have as yet presented no hypothesis about $\tilde{\gamma}_{0t}$ in (7). In the general two-parameter model, given $E(\tilde{\gamma}_{2t}) = E(\tilde{\gamma}_{3t}) = E(\tilde{\eta}_{it}) = 0$, then, from (6), $E(\tilde{\gamma}_{0t})$ is just $E(\tilde{R}_{0t})$, the expected return on any zero-β security. And market efficiency requires that $\tilde{\gamma}_{0t} - E(\tilde{R}_{0t})$ be a fair game.

But if we add to the model as presented thus far the assumption that there is unrestricted riskless borrowing and lending at the known rate R_{ft}, then one has the market setting of the original two-parameter "capital asset pricing model" of Sharpe (1964) and Lintner (1965). In this world, since $\beta_f = 0$, $E(\tilde{\gamma}_{0t}) = R_{ft}$. And market efficiency requires that $\tilde{\gamma}_{0t} - R_{ft}$ be a fair game.

It is well to emphasize that to refute the proposition that $E(\tilde{\gamma}_{0t}) - \tilde{R}_{ft}$ is only to refute a specific two-parameter model of market equilibrium. Our view is that tests of conditions C1–C3 are more fundamental. We regard C1–C3 as the general expected return implications of the two-parameter model in the sense that they are the implications of the fact that in the two-parameter portfolio model investors hold efficient portfolios, and they are consistent with any two-parameter model of market equilibrium in which the market portfolio is efficient.

F. The Hypotheses

To summarize, given the stochastic generalization of (2) and (6) that is provided by (7), the testable implications of the two-parameter model for expected returns are:

C1 (linearity)—$E(\tilde{\gamma}_{2t}) = 0$.

C2 (no systematic effects of non-β risk)—$E(\tilde{\gamma}_{3t}) = 0$.

C3 (positive expected return-risk tradeoff)—$E(\tilde{\gamma}_{1t}) = E(\tilde{R}_{mt}) - E(\tilde{R}_{0t}) > 0$.

Sharpe-Lintner (S-L) Hypothesis—$E(\tilde{\gamma}_{0t}) = R_{ft}$.

Finally, capital market efficiency in a two-parameter world requires

ME (market efficiency)—the stochastic coefficients $\tilde{\gamma}_{2t}, \tilde{\gamma}_{3t}, \tilde{\gamma}_{1t}$—

$[E(\tilde{R}_{mt}) - E(\tilde{R}_{0t})], \tilde{\gamma}_{0t} - E(\tilde{R}_{0t})$, and the disturbances $\tilde{\eta}_{it}$ are fair games.[4]

III. PREVIOUS WORK[5]

The earliest tests of the two-parameter model were done by Douglas (1969), whose results seem to refute condition C2. In annual and quarterly return data, there seem to be measures of risk, in addition to β, that contribute systematically to observed average returns. These results, if valid, are inconsistent with the hypothesis that investors attempt to hold efficient portfolios. Assuming that the market portfolio is efficient, premiums are paid for risks that do not contribute to the risk of an efficient portfolio.

Miller and Scholes (1972) take issue both with Douglas's statistical techniques and with his use of annual and quarterly data. Using different methods and simulations, they show that Douglas's negative results could be expected even if condition C2 holds. Condition C2 is tested below with extensive monthly data, and this avoids almost all of the problems discussed by Miller and Scholes.

Much of the available empirical work on the two-parameter model is concerned with testing the S-L hypothesis that $E(\tilde{\gamma}_{0t}) = R_{ft}$. The tests of Friend and Blume (1970) and those of Black, Jensen, and Scholes (1972) indicate that, at least in the period since 1940, on average $\tilde{\gamma}_{0t}$ is systematically greater than R_{ft}. The results below support this conclusion.

4. If $\tilde{\gamma}_{2t}$ and $\tilde{\gamma}_{3t}$ are fair games, then $E(\tilde{\gamma}_{2t}) = E(\tilde{\gamma}_{3t}) = 0$. Thus, C1 and C2 are implied by ME. Keeping the expected return conditions separate, however, better emphasizes the economic basis of the various hypotheses.

5. A comprehensive survey of empirical and theoretical work on the two-parameter model is in Jensen (1972).

In the empirical literature to date, the importance of the linearity condition C1 has been largely overlooked. Assuming that the market portfolio m is efficient, if $E(\tilde{\gamma}_{2t})$ in (7) is positive, the prices of high-β securities are on average too low—their expected returns are too high—relative to those of low-β securities, while the reverse holds if $E(\tilde{\gamma}_{2t})$ is negative. In short, if the process of price formation in the capital market reflects the attempts of investors to hold efficient portfolios, then the linear relationship of (6) between expected return and risk must hold.

Finally, the previous empirical work on the two-parameter model has not been concerned with tests of market efficiency.

IV. METHODOLOGY

The data for this study are monthly percentage returns (including dividends and capital gains, with the appropriate adjustments for capital changes such as splits and stock dividends) for all common stocks traded on the New York Stock Exchange during the period January 1926 through June 1968. The data are from the Center for Research in Security Prices of the University of Chicago.

A. General Approach

Testing the two-parameter model immediately presents an unavoidable "errors-in-the-variables" problem: The efficiency condition or expected return-risk equation (6) is in terms of true values of the relative risk measure β_i, but in empirical tests estimates, $\hat{\beta}_i$, must be used. In this paper

$$\hat{\beta}_i \equiv \frac{\widehat{\text{cov}}(\tilde{R}_i, \tilde{R}_m)}{\hat{\sigma}^2(\tilde{R}_m)},$$

where $\widehat{\text{cov}}(\tilde{R}_i, \tilde{R}_m)$ and $\hat{\sigma}^2(\tilde{R}_m)$ are estimates of $\text{cov}(\tilde{R}_i, \tilde{R}_m)$ and $\sigma^2(\tilde{R}_m)$ obtained from monthly returns, and where the proxy chosen for $\tilde{R}_{mt}$ is "Fisher's Arithmetic Index," an equally weighted average of the returns on all stocks listed on the New York Stock Exchange in month t. The properties of this index are analyzed in Fisher (1966).

Blume (1970) shows that for any portfolio p, defined by the weights x_{ip}, $i = 1, 2, \ldots, N$,

$$\hat{\beta}_p \equiv \frac{\widehat{\text{cov}}(\tilde{R}_p, \tilde{R}_m)}{\hat{\sigma}^2(\tilde{R}_m)} = \sum_{i=1}^{N} x_{ip} \frac{\widehat{\text{cov}}(\tilde{R}_i, \tilde{R}_m)}{\hat{\sigma}^2(\tilde{R}_m)} = \sum_{i=1}^{N} x_{ip} \hat{\beta}_i.$$

If the errors in the $\hat{\beta}_i$ are substantially less than perfectly positively correlated, the $\hat{\beta}$'s of portfolios can be much more precise estimates of true β's than the $\hat{\beta}$'s for individual securities.

To reduce the loss of information in the risk-return tests caused by using portfolios rather than individual securities, a wide range of values of portfolio $\hat{\beta}_p$'s is obtained by forming portfolios on the basis of ranked values of $\hat{\beta}_i$ for individual securities. But such a procedure, naïvely executed could result in a serious regression phenomenon. In a cross section of $\hat{\beta}_i$, high observed $\hat{\beta}_i$ tend to be above the corresponding true β_i and low observed $\hat{\beta}_i$ tend to be below the true β_i. Forming portfolios on the basis of ranked $\hat{\beta}_i$ thus causes bunching of positive and negative sampling errors within portfolios. The result is that a large portfolio $\hat{\beta}_p$ would tend to overstate the true β_p, while a low $\hat{\beta}_p$ would tend to be an underestimate.

The regression phenomenon can be avoided to a large extent by forming portfolios from ranked $\hat{\beta}_i$ computed from data for one time period but then using a subsequent period to obtain the $\hat{\beta}_p$ for these portfolios that are used to test the two-parameter model. With fresh data, within a portfolio errors in the individual security $\hat{\beta}_i$ are to a large extent random across securities, so that in a portfolio $\hat{\beta}_p$ the effects of the regression phenomenon are, it is hoped, minimized.[6]

B. Details

The specifics of the approach are as follows. Let N be the total number of securities to be allocated to portfolios and let int($N/20$) be the largest integer equal to or less than $N/20$. Using the first 4 years (1926–29) of monthly return data, 20 portfolios are formed on the basis of ranked $\hat{\beta}_i$ for individual securities. The middle 18 portfolios each has int($N/20$) securities. If N is even, the first and last portfolios each has int($N/20$) + ½[N – 20 int($N/20$)] securities. The last (highest $\hat{\beta}$) portfolio gets an additional security if N is odd.

The following 5 years (1930–34) of data are then used to recompute the $\hat{\beta}_i$, and these are averaged across securities within portfolios to obtain 20 initial

---

6. The errors-in-the-variables problem and the technique of using portfolios to solve it were first pointed out by Blume (1970). The portfolio approach is also used by Friend and Blume (1970) and Black, Jensen, and Scholes (1972). The regression phenomenon that arises in risk-return tests was first recognized by Blume (1970) and then by Black, Jensen, and Scholes (1972), who offer a solution to the problem that is similar in spirit to ours.

portfolio $\hat{\beta}_{pt}$ for the risk-return tests. The subscript t is added to indicate that each month t of the following four years (1935–38) these $\hat{\beta}_{pt}$ are recomputed as simple averages of individual security $\hat{\beta}_i$, thus adjusting the portfolio $\hat{\beta}_{pt}$ month by month to allow for delisting of securities. The component $\hat{\beta}_i$ for securities are themselves updated yearly—that is, they are recomputed from monthly returns for 1930 through 1935, 1936, or 1937.

As a measure of the non-β risk of security i we use $s(\hat{\epsilon}_i)$, the standard deviation of the least-squares residuals $\hat{\epsilon}_{it}$ from the so-called market model

$$\tilde{R}_{it} = a_i + \beta_i \tilde{R}_{mt} + \tilde{\epsilon}_{it}. \tag{8}$$

The standard deviation $s(\hat{\epsilon}_i)$ is a measure of non-β risk in the following sense. One view of risk, antithetic to that of portfolio theory, says that the risk of a security is measured by the total dispersion of its return distribution. Given a market dominated by risk averters, this model would predict that a security's expected return is related to its total return dispersion rather than just to the contribution of the security to the dispersion in the return on an efficient port-folio.[7] If $\beta_i \equiv \text{cov}(\tilde{R}_i, \tilde{R}_m)/\sigma^2 \tilde{R}_m$, then in (8) $\text{cov}(\tilde{\epsilon}_i, \tilde{R}_m) = 0$, and

$$\sigma^2(\tilde{R}_i) = \beta_i^2 \sigma^2(\tilde{R}_m) + \sigma^2(\tilde{\epsilon}_i) + 2\beta_i \text{cov}(\tilde{R}_m, \tilde{\epsilon}_i). \tag{9}$$

Thus, from (9), one can say that $s(\hat{\epsilon}_i)$ is an estimate of that part of the dispersion of the distribution of the return on security i that is not directly related to β_i.

The month-by-month returns on the 20 portfolios, with equal weighting of individual securities each month, are also computed for the 4-year period 1935–38. For each month t of this period, the following cross-sectional regression—the empirical analog of equation (7)—is run:

$$R_{pt} = \hat{\gamma}_{0t} + \hat{\gamma}_{1t}\hat{\beta}_{p,t-1} + \hat{\gamma}_{2t}\hat{\beta}_{p,t-1}^2 + \hat{\gamma}_{3t}\bar{s}_{p,t-1}(\hat{\epsilon}_i) + \hat{\eta}_{pt}, p = 1, 2, \ldots, 20. \tag{10}$$

7. For those accustomed to the portfolio viewpoint, this alternative model may seem so naïve that it should be classified as a straw man. But it is the model of risk and return implied by the "liquidity preference" and "market segmentation" theories of the term structure of interest rates and by the Keynesian "normal backwardation" theory of commodity futures markets. For a discussion of the issues with respect to these markets, see Roll (1970) and K. Miller (1971).

The independent variable $\hat{\beta}_{p,t-1}$ is the average of the $\hat{\beta}_i$ for securities in portfolio p discussed above; $\hat{\beta}_{p,t-1}^2$ is the average of the squared values of these $\hat{\beta}_i$ (and is thus somewhat mislabeled); and $\overline{s}_{p,t-1}(\hat{\varepsilon}_i)$ is likewise the average of $s(\hat{\varepsilon}_i)$ for securities in portfolio p. The $s(\hat{\varepsilon}_i)$ are computed from data for the same period as the component $\hat{\beta}_i$ of $\hat{\beta}_{p,t-1}$, and like these $\hat{\beta}_i$, they are updated annually.

The regression equation (10) is (7) averaged across the securities in a portfolio, with estimates $\hat{\beta}_{p,t-1}$, $\hat{\beta}_{p,t-1}^2$ and $\overline{s}_{p,t-1}(\hat{\varepsilon}_i)$ used as explanatory variables, and with least-squares estimates of the stochastic coefficients $\tilde{\gamma}_{0t}$, $\tilde{\gamma}_{1t}$, $\tilde{\gamma}_{2t}$, and $\tilde{\gamma}_{3t}$. The results from (10)—the time series of month-by-month values of the regression coefficients $\tilde{\gamma}_{0t}$, $\tilde{\gamma}_{1t}$, $\tilde{\gamma}_{2t}$, and $\tilde{\gamma}_{3t}$ for the 4-year period 1935–38—are the inputs for our tests of the two-parameter model for this period. To get results for other periods, the steps described above are repeated. That is, 7 years of data are used to form portfolios; the next 5 years are used to compute initial values of the independent variables in (10); and then the risk-return regressions of (10) are fit month by month for the following 4-year period.

The nine different portfolio formation periods (all except the first 7 years in length), initial 5-year estimation periods, and testing periods (all but the last 4 years in length) are shown in table 1. The choice of 4-year testing periods is a balance of computation costs against the desire to reform portfolios frequently. The choice of 7-year portfolio formation periods and 5–8-year periods for estimating the independent variables $\hat{\beta}_{p,t-1}$ and $\overline{s}_{p,t-1}(\hat{\varepsilon}_i)$ in the risk-return regressions reflects a desire to balance the statistical power obtained with a large sample from a stationary process against potential problems caused by any nonconstancy of the β_i. The choices here are in line with the results of Gonedes (1973). His results also led us to require that to be included in a portfolio a security available in the first month of a testing period must also have data for all 5 years of the preceding estimation period and for at least 4 years

TABLE 1. Porfolio formation, estimation, and testing periods

	Periods				
	1	2	3	4	5
Portfolio formation period	1926–29	1927–33	1931–37	1935–41	1939–45
Initial estimation period	1930–34	1934–38	1938–42	1942–46	1946–50
Testing period	1935–38	1939–42	1943–46	1947–50	1951–54
No. of securities available	710	779	804	908	1,011
No. of securities meeting data requirement	435	576	607	704	751

of the portfolio formation period. The total number of securities available in the first month of each testing period and the number of securities meeting the data requirement are shown in table 1.

C. Some Observations on the Approach

Table 2 shows the values of the 20 portfolios $\hat{\beta}_{p,t-1}$ and their standard errors $s(\hat{\beta}_{p,t-1})$ for four of the nine 5-year estimation periods. Also shown are: $r(R_p, R_m)^2$, the coefficient of determination between R_{pt} and R_{mt}; $s(R_p)$, the sample standard deviation of R_p; and $s(\hat{\epsilon}_p)$, the standard deviation of the portfolio residuals from the market model of (8), not to be confused with $\bar{s}_{p,t-1}(\hat{\epsilon}_i)$, the average for individual securities, which is also shown. The $\hat{\beta}_{p,t-1}$ and $\bar{s}_{p,t-1}(\hat{\epsilon}_i)$ are the independent variables in the risk return regressions of (10) for the first month of the 4-year testing periods following the four estimation periods shown.

Under the assumptions that for a given security the disturbances $\tilde{\epsilon}_{jt}$ in (8) are serially independent, independent of $\tilde{R}_{mt}$, and identically distributed through time, the standard error of $\hat{\beta}_i$ is

$$\sigma(\hat{\beta}_i) = \frac{\sigma(\tilde{\epsilon}_i)}{\sqrt{n}\,\sigma(\tilde{R}_m)},$$

where n is the number of months used to compute $\hat{\beta}_i$. Likewise,

$$\sigma(\tilde{\beta}_{p,t-1}) = \frac{\sigma(\tilde{\epsilon}_p)}{\sqrt{n}\,\sigma(\tilde{R}_m)}.$$

Thus, the fact that in table 2, $s(\hat{\epsilon}_p)$ is generally on the order of one-third to one-seventh $\bar{s}_{p,t-1}(\hat{\epsilon}_i)$ implies that $s(\hat{\beta}_{p,t-1})$ is one-third to one-seventh $s(\hat{\beta}_i)$. Estimates of β for portfolios are indeed more precise than those for individual securities.

TABLE 1. (Continued)

	Periods			
	6	7	8	9
Portfolio formation period	1943–49	1947–53	1951–57	1955–61
Initial estimation period	1950–54	1954–58	1958–62	1962–66
Testing period	1955–58	1959–62	1963–66	1967–68
No. of securities available	1,053	1,065	1,162	1,261
No. of securities meeting data requirement	802	856	858	845

TABLE 2. Sample statistics for four selected estimation periods

Statistic	1	2	3	4	5	6	7	8	9	10
	\multicolumn{10}{c}{Portfolios for Estimation Period 1934–38}									

Portfolios for Estimation Period 1934–38

Statistic	1	2	3	4	5	6	7	8	9	10
$\hat{\beta}_{p,t-1}$	.322	.508	.651	.674	.695	.792	.921	.942	.970	1.005
$s(\hat{\beta}_{p,t-1})$	.027	.027	.025	.023	.028	.026	.032	.029	.034	.027
$r(R_p, R_m)^2$	.709	.861	.921	.936	.912	.941	.932	.946	.933	.958
$s(R_p)$	.040	.058	.072	.074	.077	.087	.101	.103	.106	.109
$s(\hat{\varepsilon}_p)$	.022	.022	.020	.019	.023	.021	.026	.024	.028	.022
$\bar{s}_{p,t-1}(\hat{\varepsilon}_i)$	.085	.075	.083	.078	.090	.095	.109	.106	.111	.097
$s(\hat{\varepsilon}_p)/\bar{s}_{p,t-1}(\hat{\varepsilon}_i)$	.259	.293	.241	.244	.256	.221	.238	.226	.252	.227

Portfolios for Estimation Period 1942–46

Statistic	1	2	3	4	5	6	7	8	9	10
$\hat{\beta}_{p,t-1}$	.467	.537	.593	.628	.707	.721	.770	.792	.805	.894
$s(\hat{\beta}_{p,t-1})$	.045	.041	.044	.037	.027	.032	.035	.035	.028	.040
$r(R_p, R_m)^2$	.645	.745	.753	.829	.919	.898	.889	.898	.934	.896
$s(R_p)$	.035	.037	.041	.041	.044	.046	.049	.050	.050	.057
$s(\hat{\varepsilon}_p)$	.021	0.19	.020	.017	.013	.015	.016	.016	.013	.018
$\bar{s}_{p,t-1}(\hat{\varepsilon}_i)$	.055	.055	.063	.058	.058	.063	.064	.064	.062	.069
$s(\hat{\varepsilon}_p)/\bar{s}_{p,t-1}(\hat{\varepsilon}_i)$	.382	.345	.317	.293	.224	.238	.250	.250	.210	.261

Portfolios for Estimation Period 1950–54

Statistic	1	2	3	4	5	6	7	8	9	10
$\hat{\beta}_{p,t-1}$	.418	.590	.694	.751	.777	.784	.929	.950	.996	1.014
$s(\hat{\beta}_{p,t-1})$	.042	.047	.045	.037	.038	.035	.060	.038	.035	.029
$r(R_p, R_m)^2$	.629	.723	.798	.872	.878	.895	.856	.913	.933	.954
$s(R_p)$	.019	.025	.028	.029	.030	.030	.036	.036	.037	.038
$s(\hat{\varepsilon}_p)$	.012	.013	.013	.010	.010	.010	.014	.011	.010	.008
$\bar{s}_{p,t-1}(\hat{\varepsilon}_i)$	.040	.044	.046	.048	.051	.051	.052	.053	.054	.057
$s(\hat{\varepsilon}_p)/\bar{s}_{p,t-1}(\hat{\varepsilon}_i)$	.300	.295	.283	.208	.196	.196	.269	.208	.185	.140

Portfolios for Estimation Period 1958–62

Statistic	1	2	3	4	5	6	7	8	9	10
$\hat{\beta}_{p,t-1}$	.626	.635	.719	.801	.817	.860	.920	.950	.975	.995
$s(\hat{\beta}_{p,t-1})$	.043	.048	.039	.046	.047	.033	.037	.038	.032	.037
$r(R_p, R_m)^2$	.783	.745	.851	.835	.838	.920	.913	.915	.939	.925
$s(R_p)$	.030	.031	.033	.037	.038	.038	.041	.42	.043	.044
$s(\hat{\varepsilon}_p)$	.014	.016	.013	.015	.015	.011	.012	.012	.011	.012
$\bar{s}_{p,t-1}(\hat{\varepsilon}_i)$	.049	.052	.056	.059	.064	.061	.070	.069	.068	.064
$s(\hat{\varepsilon}_p)/\bar{s}_{p,t-1}(\hat{\varepsilon}_i)$	.286	.308	.232	.254	.234	.180	.171	.174	.162	.188

TABLE 2. (Continued)

	11	12	13	14	15	16	17	18	19	20

Portfolios for Estimation Period 1934–38

	11	12	13	14	15	16	17	18	19	20
$\hat{\beta}_{p,t-1}$	1.046	1.122	1.181	1.192	1.196	1.295	1.335	1.396	1.445	1.458
$s(\hat{\beta}_{p,t-1})$	.028	.031	.035	.028	.029	.032	.032	.053	.039	.053
$r(R_p, R_m)^2$	.959	.956	.951	.969	.966	.966	.967	.922	.958	.927
$s(R_p)$	.113	.122	.128	.128	.129	.140	.144	.154	.156	.160
$s(\hat{\epsilon}_p)$	.023	.026	.029	.023	.024	.026	.026	.043	.032	.043
$\bar{s}_{p,t-1}(\hat{\epsilon}_i)$	.094	.124	.120	.122	.132	.125	.129	.158	.145	.170
$s(\hat{\epsilon}_p)/\bar{s}_{p,t-1}(\hat{\epsilon}_i)$	.245	.210	.242	.188	.182	.208	.202	.272	.221	.253

Portfolios for Estimation Period 1942–46

	11	12	13	14	15	16	17	18	19	20
$\hat{\beta}_{p,t-1}$	.949	.952	1.010	1.038	1.254	1.312	1.316	1.473	1.631	1.661
$s(\hat{\beta}_{p,t-1})$	.031	.036	.040	.030	.034	.039	.041	.084	.083	.077
$r(R_p, R_m)^2$	.942	.923	.917	.954	.958	.951	.945	.839	.867	.887
$s(R_p)$	.059	.060	.063	.064	.077	.081	.081	.097	.105	.106
$s(\hat{\epsilon}_p)$	.014	.016	.018	.014	.016	.018	.019	.039	.038	.036
$\bar{s}_{p,t-1}(\hat{\epsilon}_i)$	.073	.074	.085	.077	.096	.083	.086	.134	.117	.122
$s(\hat{\epsilon}_p)/\bar{s}_{p,t-1}(\hat{\epsilon}_i)$	.192	.216	.212	.182	.167	.217	.221	.291	.325	.295

Portfolios for Estimation Period 1950–54

	11	12	13	14	15	16	17	18	19	20
$\hat{\beta}_{p,t-1}$	1.117	1.123	1.131	1.134	1.186	1.235	1.295	1.324	1.478	1.527
$s(\hat{\beta}_{p,t-1})$	.039	.027	.044	.033	.037	.049	.045	.046	.058	.086
$r(R_p, R_m)^2$	.934	.968	.919	.952	.944	.915	.933	.934	.917	.841
$s(R_p)$	.042	.041	.043	.042	.044	.047	.049	.050	.056	.060
$s(\hat{\epsilon}_p)$	.011	.007	.012	.009	.010	.014	.013	.013	.016	.024
$\bar{s}_{p,t-1}(\hat{\epsilon}_i)$	.066	.057	.066	.060	.064	.064	.065	.068	.076	.088
$s(\hat{\epsilon}_p)/\bar{s}_{p,t-1}(\hat{\epsilon}_i)$	.167	.123	.182	.150	.156	.219	.200	.192	.210	.273

Portfolios for Estimation Period 1958–62

	11	12	13	14	15	16	17	18	19	20
$\hat{\beta}_{p,t-1}$	1.013	1.019	1.037	1.048	1.069	1.081	1.092	1.098	1.269	1.388
$s(\hat{\beta}_{p,t-1})$	.038	.031	.036	.033	.036	.038	.045	.045	.048	.065
$r(R_p, R_m)^2$	.922	.948	.934	.945	.936	.931	.907	.910	.922	.866
$s(R_p)$	.045	.045	.046	.046	.047	.048	.049	.049	.056	.063
$s(\hat{\epsilon}_p)$	.013	.010	.012	.011	.012	.013	.015	.015	.016	.021
$\bar{s}_{p,t-1}(\hat{\epsilon}_i)$	.069	.066	.067	.062	.070	.072	.076	.068	.070	.078
$s(\hat{\epsilon}_p)/\bar{s}_{p,t-1}(\hat{\epsilon}_i)$	.188	.152	.179	.177	.171	.180	.197	.220	.228	.269

Nevertheless, it is interesting to note that if the disturbances $\tilde{\varepsilon}_{jt}$ in (8) were independent from security to security, the relative increase in the precision of the $\hat{\beta}$ obtained by using portfolios rather than individual securities would be about the same for all portfolios. We argue in the Appendix, however, that the results from (10) imply that the $\tilde{\varepsilon}_{it}$ in (8) are interdependent, and the interdependence is strongest among high-β securities and among low-β securities. This is evident in table 2: The ratios $s(\hat{\varepsilon}_p)/\bar{s}_{p,t-1}(\hat{\varepsilon}_i)$ are always highest at the extremes of the $\hat{\beta}_{p,t-1}$ range and lowest for $\hat{\beta}_{p,t-1}$ close to 1.0. But it is important to emphasize that since these ratios are generally less than .33, interdependence among the $\tilde{\varepsilon}_{it}$ of different securities does not destroy the value of using portfolios to reduce the dispersion of the errors in estimated β's.

Finally, all the tests of the two-parameter model are predictive in the sense that the explanatory variables $\hat{\beta}_{p,t-1}$ and $\bar{s}_{p,t-1}(\hat{\varepsilon}_i)$ in (10) are computed from data for a period prior to the month of the returns, the R_{pt}, on which the regression is run. Although we are interested in testing the two-parameter model as a positive theory—that is, examining the extent to which it is helpful in describing actual return data—the model was initially developed by Markowitz (1959) as a normative theory—that is, as a model to help people make better decisions. As a normative theory the model only has content if there is some relationship between future returns and estimates of risk that can be made on the basis of current information.

Now that the predictive nature of the tests has been emphasized, to simplify the notation, the explanatory variables in (10) are henceforth referred to as $\hat{\beta}_p$, $\hat{\beta}_p^2$ and $\bar{s}_p(\hat{\varepsilon}_i)$.

V. RESULTS

The major tests of the implications of the two-parameter model are in table 3. Results are presented for 10 periods: the overall period 1935–6/68; three long subperiods, 1935–45, 1946–55, and 1956–6/68; and six subperiods which, except for the first and last, cover 5 years each. This choice of subperiods reflects the desire to keep separate the pre– and post–World War II periods. Results are presented for four different versions of the risk-return regression equation (10): Panel D is based on (10) itself, but in panels A–C, one or more of the variables in (10) is suppressed. For each period and model, the table shows: $\bar{\hat{\gamma}}_j$, the average of the month-by-month regression coefficient estimates, $\hat{\gamma}_{jt}$; $s(\hat{\gamma}_j)$, the standard deviation of the monthly estimates: and $\bar{r}^2$ and $s(r^2)$, the mean and standard deviation of the month-by-month coefficients of determination,

TABLE 3. Summary results for the regression

$$R_p = \hat{\gamma}_{0t} + \hat{\gamma}_{1t}\hat{\beta}_p + \hat{\gamma}_{2t}\hat{\beta}_p^2 + \hat{\gamma}_{3t}\bar{S}_p(\hat{\epsilon}_i) + \hat{\eta}_{pt}$$

Period	$\bar{\hat{\gamma}}_0$	$\bar{\hat{\gamma}}_1$	$\bar{\hat{\gamma}}_2$	$\bar{\hat{\gamma}}_3$	$\overline{\hat{\gamma}_0 - R_f}$	$s(\hat{\gamma}_0)$	$s(\hat{\gamma}_1)$	$s(\hat{\gamma}_2)$	$s(\hat{\gamma}_3)$	$\rho_0(\hat{\gamma}_0 - R_f)$	$\rho_M(\hat{\gamma}_1)$	$\rho_0(\hat{\gamma}_1)$	$\rho_0(\hat{\gamma}_2)$	$\rho_0(\hat{\gamma}_3)$	$t(\bar{\hat{\gamma}}_0)$	$t(\bar{\hat{\gamma}}_1)$	$t(\bar{\hat{\gamma}}_2)$	$t(\bar{\hat{\gamma}}_3)$	$t(\overline{\hat{\gamma}_0 - R_f})$	$\bar{r}^2$	$s(r^2)$
Panel A:																					
1935–6/68	.0061	.0085	...	...	.0048	.038	.066	...	...	.15	.02	...	...	...	3.24	2.57	...	...	2.55	.29	.30
1935–45	.0039	.0163	...	...	.0037	.052	.098	...	...	.10	−.03	...	...	...	.86	1.92	...	...	.82	.29	.29
1946–55	.0087	.0027	...	...	.0078	.026	.041	...	...	.18	.07	...	...	...	3.71	.70	...	...	3.31	.31	.32
1956–6/68	.0060	.0062	...	...	.0034	.030	.044	...	...	.27	.15	...	...	...	2.45	1.73	...	...	1.39	.28	.29
1935–40	.0024	.0109	...	...	.0023	.064	.116	...	...	.07	−.09	...	...	...	.32	.79	...	...	.31	.23	.30
1941–45	.0056	.0229	...	...	.0054	.034	.069	...	...	.23	.15	...	...	...	1.27	2.55	...	...	1.22	.37	.28
1946–50	.0050	.0029	...	...	.0044	.031	.047	...	...	.20	.04	...	...	...	1.27	.48	...	...	1.10	.39	.33
1951–55	.0123	.0024	...	...	.0111	.019	.035	...	...	.20	.08	...	...	...	5.06	.53	...	...	4.56	.24	.29
1956–60	.0148	−.0059	...	...	.0128	.020	.034	...	...	.37	.18	...	...	...	5.68	−1.37	...	...	4.89	.22	.31
1961–6/68	.0001	.0143	...	...	−.0029	.034	.048	...	...	.22	.09	...	...	...	.03	2.81	...	...	−.08	.32	.27
Panel B:																					
1935–6/68	.0049	.0105	−.0008	...	.0036	.052	.118	.056	...	.03	−.11	−.11	...	...	1.92	1.79	−.29	...	1.42	.32	.31
1935–45	.0074	.0079	.0040	...	.0073	.061	.139	.074	...	−.10	−.31	−.21	...	...	1.39	.65	.61	...	1.36	.32	.30
1946–55	−.0002	.0217	−.0087	...	−.0012	.036	.095	.034	...	.04	.00	.00	...	...	−.79	2.51	−2.83	...	−.38	.36	.32
1956–6/68	.0069	.0040	.0013	...	.0043	.054	.116	.053	...	.17	.07	.03	...	...	1.56	.42	.29	...	.97	.30	.30
1935–40	.0013	.0141	−.0017	...	.0012	.069	.160	.075	...	−.13	−.36	−.35	...	...	.16	.75	−.19	...	.14	.24	.30
1941–45	.0148	.0004	.0108	...	.0146	.050	.111	.073	...	−.04	−.19	−.04	...	...	2.28	.03	1.15	...	2.24	.39	.29
1946–50	−.0008	.0152	−.0051	...	−.0015	.037	.104	.032	...	.14	.04	.00	...	...	−.18	1.14	−1.24	...	−.30	.44	.32
1951–55	.0004	.0281	−.0122	...	−.0008	.030	.085	.035	...	−.17	−.14	−.01	...	...	.10	2.55	−2.72	...	−.20	.28	.29
1956–60	.0128	−.0015	−.0020	...	.0108	.030	.072	.029	...	.35	.11	.26	...	...	3.38	−.16	−.54	...	2.84	.25	.31
1961–6/68	.0029	.0077	.0034	...	−.0000	.066	.138	.064	...	.14	.06	−.01	...	...	.42	.53	.51	...	−.01	.34	.29

(Continued)

TABLE 3. (Continued)

Period	$\bar{\hat{\gamma}}_0$	$\bar{\hat{\gamma}}_1$	$\bar{\hat{\gamma}}_2$	$\bar{\hat{\gamma}}_3$	$\overline{\hat{\gamma}_0 - R_f}$	$s(\hat{\gamma}_0)$	$s(\hat{\gamma}_1)$	$s(\hat{\gamma}_2)$	$s(\hat{\gamma}_3)$	$\rho_0(\hat{\gamma}_0 - R_f)$	$\rho_M(\hat{\gamma}_1)$	$\rho_0(\hat{\gamma}_2)$	$\rho_0(\hat{\gamma}_3)$	$t(\bar{\hat{\gamma}}_0)$	$t(\bar{\hat{\gamma}}_1)$	$t(\bar{\hat{\gamma}}_2)$	$t(\bar{\hat{\gamma}}_3)$	$t(\overline{\hat{\gamma}_0 - R_f})$	$\bar{r}^2$	$s(r^2)$
Panel C:																				
1935–6/68	.0054	.0072	...	.0198	.0041	.052	.065	...	.868	.04	-.12	...	-.04	2.10	2.20	...	.46	1.59	.32	.31
1935–45	.0017	.0104	...	.0841	.0015	.073	.083	...	.921	-.00	-.26	...	-.08	.26	1.41	...	1.05	.24	.32	.31
1946–55	.0110	.0075	...	-.1052	.0100	.032	.056	...	.609	.08	.02	...	-.20	3.78	1.47	...	-1.89	3.46	.34	.32
1956–6/68	.0042	.0041	...	.0633	.0016	.040	.052	...	.984	.12	.08	...	.03	1.28	.96	...	.79	.50	.30	.29
1935–40	.0036	.0119	...	-.0170	.0035	.082	.105	...	.744	-.03	-.26	...	-.18	.37	.97	...	-.19	.36	.25	.30
1941–45	-.0006	.0085	...	.2053	-.0009	.061	.052	...	1.091	.07	-.29	...	-.02	-.08	1.25	...	1.46	-.11	.41	.30
1946–50	.0069	.0081	...	-.0920	.0062	.034	.066	...	.504	.14	.06	...	-.02	1.56	.95	...	-1.41	1.40	.42	.33
1951–55	.0150	.0069	...	-.1185	.0138	.029	.043	...	.702	.06	-.18	...	-.32	4.05	1.24	...	-1.31	3.72	.27	.29
1956–60	.0127	-.0081	...	.0728	.0107	.037	.045	...	1.164	.15	.15	...	.21	2.68	-1.40	...	.48	2.26	.26	.30
1961–6/68	-.0014	.0122	...	.0570	-.0044	.042	.055	...	.850	.10	.00	...	-.19	-.32	2.12	...	.64	-.98	.33	.27
Panel D:																				
1935–6/68	.0020	.0114	-.0026	.0516	.0008	.075	.123	.060	.929	-.09	-.09	-.12	-.10	.55	1.85	-.86	1.11	.20	.34	.31
1935–45	.0011	.0118	-.0009	.0817	.0010	.103	.146	.079	1.003	-.20	-.23	-.24	-.15	.13	.94	-.14	.94	.11	.34	.31
1946–55	.0017	.0209	-.0076	-.0378	.0008	.042	.096	.038	.619	-.10	-.00	-.01	-.20	.44	2.39	-2.16	-.67	.20	.36	.32
1956–6/68	.0031	.0034	-.0000	.0966	.0005	.065	.122	.055	1.061	.12	.03	.01	-.05	.59	.34	-.00	1.11	.10	.32	.29
1935–40	.0009	.0156	-.0029	.0025	.0008	.112	.171	.085	.826	-.16	-.23	-.26	-.12	.07	.78	-.29	.03	.06	.26	.30
1941–45	.0015	.0073	.0014	.1767	.0012	.092	.109	.072	1.181	-.28	-.21	-.22	-.18	.12	.52	.15	1.16	.10	.43	.31
1946–50	.0011	.0141	-.0040	-.0313	.0004	.047	.106	.042	.590	-.10	.03	-.01	-.12	.18	1.03	-.73	-.41	.07	.44	.33
1951–55	.0023	.0277	-.0112	-.0443	.0011	.037	.085	.034	.651	-.11	-.13	-.01	-.28	.48	2.53	-2.54	-.53	.23	.29	.30
1956–60	.0103	-.0047	-.0020	.0979	.0083	.049	.078	.032	1.286	-.16	.19	-.01	.02	1.63	-.47	-.49	.59	1.31	.28	.30
1961–6/68	-.0017	.0088	.0013	.0957	-.0046	.073	.144	.066	.887	.20	.00	.01	-.15	-.21	.58	.19	1.02	-.60	.35	.29

Statistic

r_t^2, which are adjusted for degrees of freedom. The table also shows the first-order serial correlations of the various monthly $\hat{\gamma}_{jt}$ computed either about the sample mean of $\hat{\gamma}_{jt}$ [in which case the serial correlations are labeled $\rho_M(\hat{\gamma}_j)$] or about an assumed mean of zero [in which case they are labeled $\rho_0(\hat{\gamma}_j)$]. Finally, t-statistics for testing the hypothesis that $\bar{\hat{\gamma}}_j = 0$ are presented. These t-statistics are

$$t\left(\bar{\hat{\gamma}}_j\right) = \frac{\bar{\hat{\gamma}}_j}{s\left(\hat{\gamma}_j\right)/\sqrt{n}},$$

where n is the number of months in the period, which is also the number of estimates $\hat{\gamma}_{jt}$ used to compute $\bar{\hat{\gamma}}_j$ and $s(\hat{\gamma}_j)$.

In interpreting these t-statistics one should keep in mind the evidence of Fama (1965a) and Blume (1970) which suggests that distributions of common stock returns are "thick-tailed" relative to the normal distribution and probably conform better to nonnormal symmetric stable distributions than to the normal. From Fama and Babiak (1968), this evidence means that when one interprets large t-statistics under the assumption that the underlying variables are normal, the probability or significance levels obtained are likely to be overestimates. But it is important to note that, with the exception of condition C3 (positive expected return-risk tradeoff), upward-biased probability levels lead to biases toward rejection of the hypotheses of the two-parameter model. Thus, if these hypotheses cannot be rejected when t-statistics are interpreted under the assumption of normality, the hypotheses are on even firmer ground when one takes into account the thick tails of empirical return distributions.

Further justification for using t-statistics to test hypotheses on monthly common stock returns is in the work of Officer (1971). Under the assumption that distributions of monthly returns are symmetric stable, he estimates that in the post–World War II period the characteristic exponent for these distributions is about 1.8 (as compared with a value of 2.0 for a normal distribution). From Fama and Roll (1968), for values of the characteristic exponent so close to 2.0 stable nonnormal distributions differ noticeably from the normal only in their extreme tails—that is, beyond the .05 and .95 fractiles. Thus, as long as one is not concerned with precise estimates of probability levels (always a somewhat meaningless activity), interpreting t-statistics in the usual way does not lead to serious errors.

Inferences based on approximate normality are on even safer ground if one assumes, again in line with the results of Officer (1971), that although they are well approximated by stable non-normal distributions with $\alpha \cong 1.8$, distributions of monthly returns in fact have finite variances and converge—but very slowly—toward the normal as one takes sums or averages of individual returns. Then the distributions of the means of month-by-month regression coefficients from the risk-return model are likely to be close to normal since each mean is based on coefficients for many months.

A. Tests of the Major Hypotheses of the Two-Parameter Model

Consider first condition C2 of the two-parameter model, which says that no measure of risk, in addition to β, systematically affects expected returns. This hypothesis is not rejected by the results in panels C and D of table 3. The values of $t(\bar{\hat{\gamma}}_3)$ are small, and the signs of the $t(\bar{\hat{\gamma}}_3)$ are randomly positive and negative.

Likewise, the results in panels B and D of table 3 do not reject condition C1 of the two-parameter model, which says that the relationship between expected return and β is linear. In panel B, the value of $t(\bar{\hat{\gamma}}_2)$ for the overall period 1935–6/68 is only $-.29$. In the 5-year subperiods, $t(\bar{\hat{\gamma}}_2)$ for 1951–55 is approximately -2.7, but for subperiods that do not cover 1951–55, the values of $t(\bar{\hat{\gamma}}_2)$ are much closer to zero.

So far, then, the two-parameter model seems to be standing up well to the data. All is for naught, however, if the critical condition C3 is rejected. That is, we are not happy with the model unless there is on average a positive tradeoff between risk and return. This seems to be the case. For the overall period 1935–6/68, $t(\bar{\hat{\gamma}}_1)$ is large for all models. Except for the period 1956–60, the values of $t(\bar{\hat{\gamma}}_1)$ are also systematically positive in the subperiods, but not so systematically large.

The small t-statistics for subperiods reflect the substantial month-to-month variability of the parameters of the risk-return regressions. For example, in the one-variable regressions summarized in panel A, for the period 1935–40, $\bar{\hat{\gamma}}_1 = .0109$. In other words, for this period the average incremental return per unit of β was almost 1.1 percent per month, so that on average, bearing risk had substantial rewards. Nevertheless, because of the variability of $\hat{\gamma}_{1t}$—in this period $s(\hat{\gamma}_1)$ is 11.6 percent per month (!)—$t(\bar{\hat{\gamma}}_1)$ is only .79. It takes the statistical power of the large sample for the overall period before values of $\bar{\hat{\gamma}}_1$ that are large in practical terms also yield large t-values.

But at least with the sample of the overall period $t(\bar{\hat{\gamma}}_1)$ achieves values supportive of the conclusion that on average there is a statistically observable positive relationship between return and risk. This is not the case with respect to $t(\bar{\hat{\gamma}}_2)$ and $t(\bar{\hat{\gamma}}_3)$. Even, or indeed especially, for the overall period, these t-statistics are close to zero.

The behavior through time of $\hat{\gamma}_{1t}$, $\hat{\gamma}_{2t}$, and $\hat{\gamma}_{3t}$ is also consistent with hypothesis ME that the capital market is efficient. The serial correlations $\rho_M(\hat{\gamma}_1)$, $\rho_0(\hat{\gamma}_2)$, and $\rho_0(\hat{\gamma}_3)$, are always low in terms of explanatory power and generally low in terms of statistical significance. The proportion of the variance of $\hat{\gamma}_{jt}$ explained by first-order serial correlation is estimated by $\rho(\hat{\gamma}_j)^2$ which in all cases is small. As for statistical significance, under the hypothesis that the true serial correlation is zero, the standard deviation of the sample coefficient can be approximated by $\sigma(\hat{\rho}) = 1/\sqrt{n}$. For the overall period, $\sigma(\hat{\rho})$ is approximately .05, while for the 10- and 5-year subperiods $\sigma(\hat{\rho})$ is approximately .09 and .13, respectively. Thus, the values of $\rho_M(\hat{\gamma}_1)$, $\rho_0(\hat{\gamma}_2)$, and $\rho_0(\hat{\gamma}_3)$ in table 3 are generally statistically close to zero. The exceptions involve primarily periods that include the 1935–40 subperiod, and the results for these periods are not independent.[8]

To conserve space, the serial correlations of the portfolio residuals, $\hat{\eta}_{pt}$, are not shown. In these serial correlations, negative values predominate. But like the serial correlations of the $\hat{\gamma}$'s, those of the $\hat{\eta}$'s are close to zero. Higher-order serial correlations of the $\hat{\gamma}$'s and $\hat{\eta}$'s have been computed, and these also are never systematically large.

In short, one cannot reject the hypothesis that the pricing of securities is in line with the implications of the two-parameter model for expected returns. And given a two-parameter pricing model, the behavior of returns through time is consistent with an efficient capital market.

8. The serial correlations of $\hat{\gamma}_2$ and $\hat{\gamma}_3$ about means that are assumed to be zero provide a test of the fair game property of an efficient market, given that expected returns are generated by the two-parameter model—that is, given $E(\tilde{\gamma}_{2t}) = E(\tilde{\gamma}_{3t}) = 0$. Likewise, $\rho_0(\hat{\gamma}_{0t} - R_{ft})$ provides a test of market efficiency with respect to the behavior of $\hat{\gamma}_{0t}$ through time, given the validity of the Sharpe-Lintner hypothesis (about which we have as yet said nothing). But, at least for $\hat{\gamma}_{2t}$ and $\hat{\gamma}_{3t}$, computing the serial correlations about sample means produces essentially the same results.

To test the market efficiency hypothesis on $\tilde{\gamma}_{1t} - [E(\tilde{R}_{mt}) - E(\tilde{R}_{0t})]$, the sample mean of the $\hat{\gamma}_{1t}$ is used to estimate $E(\tilde{R}_{mt}) - E(\tilde{R}_{0t})$ thus implicitly assuming that the expected risk premium is constant. That this is a reasonable approximation [in the sense that the $\rho_M(\hat{\gamma}_1)$ are small], probably reflects the fact that variation in $E(\tilde{R}_{mt}) - E(\tilde{R}_{0t})$ is trivial relative to the month-by-month variation in $\hat{\gamma}_{1t}$.

Finally, it is well to note that in terms of the implications of the serial correlations for making good portfolio decisions—and thus for judging whether market efficiency is a workable representation of reality—the fact that the serial correlations are low in terms of explanatory power is more important than whether or not they are low in terms of statistical significance.

TABLE 4. The behavior of the market

						Statistic*			
						$\dfrac{\overline{R_m - R_f}}{s(R_m)}$	$\dfrac{\overline{\hat{\gamma}_1}}{s(R_m)}$		
Period	$\overline{R_m}$	$\overline{R_m - R_f}$	$\overline{\hat{\gamma}_1}$	$\overline{\hat{\gamma}_0}$	$\overline{R_f}$			$s(R_m)$	$s(R_m)$
1935–6/68	.0143	.0130	.0085	.0061	.0013	.2136	.1388	.061	.066
1935–45	.0197	.0195	.0163	.0039	.0002	.2207	.1844	.089	.098
1946–55	.0112	.0103	.0027	.0087	.0009	.2378	.0614	.043	.041
1956–6/68	.0121	.0095	.0062	.0060	.0026	.2387	.1560	.040	.044
1935–40	.0132	.0132	.0109	.0024	.0001	.1221	.1009	.108	.116
1941–45	.0274	.0272	.0229	.0056	.0002	.4715	.3963	.058	.069
1946–50	.0077	.0070	.0029	.0050	.0007	.1351	.0564	.052	.047
1951–55	.0148	.0136	.0024	.0123	.0012	.4174	.0735	.033	.035
1956–60	.0090	.0070	−.0059	.0148	.0020	.2080	−.1755	.034	.034
1961–6/68	.0141	.0111	.0143	.0001	.0030	.2567	.3294	.043	.048

* Since $s(R_f)$ is so small relative to $s(R_m)$, $s(R_m - R_f)$, which is not shown, is essentially the same as $s(R_m)$. The standard deviation of $(R_m - R_f)/s(R_m)$, and $\hat{\gamma}_1/s(R_m)$, also not shown, can be obtained directly from $s(R_m - R_f)$, $s(\hat{\gamma}_1)$ and $s(R_m)$. Finally the t-statistics for $\overline{(R_m - R_f)}/s(R_m)$ and $\overline{\hat{\gamma}_1}/s(R_m)$ are identical with those for $\overline{R_m - R_f}$ and $\overline{\hat{\gamma}_1}$.

B. The Behavior of the Market

Some perspective on the behavior of the market during different periods and on the interpretation of the coefficients $\hat{\gamma}_{0t}$ and $\hat{\gamma}_{1t}$ in the risk-return regressions can be obtained from table 4. For the various periods of table 3, table 4 shows the sample means (and with some exceptions), the standard deviations, t-statistics for sample means, and first-order serial correlations for the month-by-month values of the following variables and coefficients: the market return R_{mt}; the riskless rate of interest R_{ft}, taken to be the yield on 1-month Treasury bills; $R_{mt} - R_{ft}$; $(R_{mt} - R_{ft})/s(R_m)$; $\hat{\gamma}_{0t}$ and $\hat{\gamma}_{1t}$, repeated from panel A of table 3; and $\hat{\gamma}_{1t}/s(R_m)$. The t-statistics on sample means are computed in the same way as those in table 3.

If the two-parameter model is valid, then in equation (7), $E(\tilde{\gamma}_{0t}) = E(\tilde{R}_{0t})$, where $E(\tilde{R}_{0t})$ is the expected return on any zero-β security or portfolio. Likewise, the expected risk premium per unit of β is $E(\tilde{R}_{mt}) - E(\tilde{R}_{0t}) = E(\tilde{\gamma}_{1t})$. In fact, for the one-variable regressions of panel A, table 3, that is,

$$R_{pt} = \hat{\gamma}_{0t} + \hat{\gamma}_{1t}\hat{\beta}_p + \hat{\eta}_{pt},\tag{11}$$

we have, period by period,

$$\hat{\gamma}_{1t} = R_{mt} - \hat{\gamma}_{0t}.\tag{12}$$

TABLE 4. (Continued)

Statistic*

$s(\hat{\gamma}_0)$	$s(R_f)$	$t(\bar{R}_m)$	$\overline{t(\bar{R}_m - R_f)}$	$t(\hat{\bar{\gamma}}_1)$	$t(\hat{\bar{\gamma}}_0)$	$\rho_M(R_m)$	$\rho_M(R_m - R_f)$	$\rho_M(\hat{\gamma}_1)$	$\rho_M(\hat{\gamma}_0)$	$\rho_M(R_f)$
.038	.0012	4.71	4.28	2.57	3.24	-.01	-.01	.02	.14	.98
.052	.0001	2.56	2.54	1.92	.86	.07	.07	.03	.10	.88
.026	.0004	2.84	2.60	.70	3.71	.09	.09	.07	.10	.94
.030	.0009	3.72	2.92	1.73	2.45	.14	.14	.15	.25	.92
.064	.0001	1.04	1.04	.79	.32	-.13	-.13	-.09	.07	.72
.034	.0001	3.68	3.65	2.55	1.27	.14	.14	.15	.21	.83
.031	.0003	1.15	1.05	.48	1.27	.09	.09	.04	.18	.97
.019	.0004	3.51	3.22	.53	5.06	-.02	-.01	.08	-.07	.89
.020	.0007	2.07	1.60	-1.37	5.68	.12	.13	.18	.13	.80
.034	.0008	3.08	2.44	2.81	.03	.13	.13	.09	.21	.93

This condition is obtained by averaging (11) over p and making use of the least-squares constraint

$$\sum_p \hat{\eta}_{pt} = 0. \,[9]$$

Moreover, the least-squares estimate $\hat{\gamma}_{0t}$ can always be interpreted as the return for month t on a zero-$\hat{\beta}$ portfolio, where the weights given to each of the 20 portfolios to form this zero-$\hat{\beta}$ portfolio are the least-squares weights that are applied to the R_{pt} in computing $\hat{\gamma}_{0t}$.[10]

In the Sharpe-Lintner two-parameter model of market equilibrium $E(\tilde{\gamma}_{0t}) = E(\tilde{R}_{0t}) = R_{ft}$ and $E(\tilde{\gamma}_{1t}) = E(\tilde{R}_{mt}) - E(\tilde{R}_{0t}) = E(\tilde{R}_{mt}) - R_{ft}$. In the period 1935–40 and in the most recent period 1961–6/68, $\hat{\bar{\gamma}}_{1t}$ is close to $\overline{R_m - R_f}$ and the t-statistics for the two averages are similar. In other periods, and

---

9. There is some degree of approximation in (12). The averages over p of R_{pt} and $\hat{\beta}_p$ are R_{mt} and 1.0, respectively, only if every security in the market is in some portfolio. With our methodology (see table 1) this is never true. But the degree of approximation turns out to be small: The average of the R_{pt} is always close to $\bar{R}_{mt}$ and the average $\hat{\beta}_p$ is always close to 1.0.

10. That $\hat{\gamma}_{0t}$ is the return on a zero-$\hat{\beta}$ portfolio can be shown to follow from the unbiasedness of the least-squares coefficients in the cross-sectional risk-return regressions. If one makes the Gauss-Markov assumptions that the underlying disturbances $\tilde{\eta}_{pt}$ of (11) have zero means, are uncorrelated across p, and have the same variance for all p, then it follows almost directly from the Gauss-Markov Theorem that the least-squares estimate $\hat{\gamma}_{0t}$ is also the return for month t on the minimum variance zero-$\hat{\beta}$ portfolio that can be constructed from the 20 portfolio $\hat{\beta}_p$.

especially in the period 1951–60, $\hat{\bar{\gamma}}_1$ is substantially less than $\overline{R_m - R_f}$. This is a consequence of the fact that for these periods $\hat{\bar{\gamma}}_0$ is noticeably greater than $\bar{R}_f$. In economic terms, the tradeoff of average return for risk between common stocks and short-term bonds has been more consistently large through time than the tradeoff of average return for risk among common stocks. Testing whether the differences between $\overline{R_m - R_f}$ and $\hat{\bar{\gamma}}_1$ are statistically large, however, is equivalent to testing the S-L hypothesis $E(\tilde{\gamma}_{0t}) = R_{ft}$, which we prefer to take up after examining further the stochastic process generating monthly returns.

Finally, although the differences between values of $\overline{R_m - R_f}$ for different periods or between values of $\hat{\bar{\gamma}}_1$ are never statistically large, there is a hint in table 4 that average-risk premiums declined from the pre- to the post–World War II periods. These are average risk premiums per unit of $\hat{\beta}$, however, which are not of prime interest to the investor. In making his portfolio decision, the investor is more concerned with the tradeoff of expected portfolio return for dispersion of return—that is, the slope of the efficient set of portfolios. In the Sharpe-Lintner model this slope is always $[E(\tilde{R}_{mt}) - R_{ft}]/\sigma(\tilde{R}_{mt})$, and in the more general model of Black (1972), it is $[E(\tilde{R}_{mt}) - E(\tilde{R}_{0t})]/\sigma(\tilde{R}_{mt})$ at the point on the efficient set corresponding to the market portfolio m. In table 4, especially for the three long subperiods, dividing $\overline{R_m - R_f}$ and $\hat{\bar{\gamma}}_1$, by $s(R_m)$ seems to yield estimated risk premiums that are more constant through time. This results from the fact that any declines in $\hat{\bar{\gamma}}_1$ or $\overline{R_m - R_f}$ are matched by a quite noticeable downward shift in $s(R_m)$ from the early to the later periods (cf. Blume [1970] or Officer [1971]).

C. Errors and True Variation in the Coefficients $\hat{\gamma}_{jt}$

Each cross-sectional regression coefficient $\hat{\gamma}_{jt}$ in (10) has two components: the true $\tilde{\gamma}_{jt}$ and the estimation error, $\hat{\phi}_{jt} = \hat{\gamma}_{jt} - \tilde{\gamma}_{jt}$. A natural question is: To what extent is the variation in $\hat{\gamma}_{jt}$ through time due to variation in $\tilde{\gamma}_{jt}$ and to what extent is it due to $\hat{\phi}_{jt}$? In addition to providing important information about the precision of the coefficient estimates used to test the two-parameter model, the answer to this question can be used to test hypotheses about the stochastic process generating returns. For example, although we cannot reject the hypothesis that $E(\tilde{\gamma}_{2t}) = 0$, does including the term involving $\hat{\beta}_p^2$ in (10) help in explaining the month-by-month behavior of returns? That is, can we reject the hypothesis that for all t, $\tilde{\gamma}_{2t} = 0$? Likewise, can we reject the hypothesis that month-by-month $\tilde{\gamma}_{3t} = 0$? And is the variation through time in $\hat{\gamma}_{0t}$ due entirely to $\hat{\phi}_{0t}$ and to variation in R_{ft}?

The answers to these questions are in table 5. For the models and time periods of table 3, table 5 shows for each $\hat{\gamma}_j$: $s^2(\hat{\gamma}_j)$, the sample variance of the month-by-month $\hat{\gamma}_{jt}$; $s^2(\tilde{\phi}_j)$, the average of the month-by-month values of $s^2(\tilde{\phi}_{jt})$, where $s(\tilde{\phi}_{jt})$ is the standard error of $\hat{\gamma}_{jt}$ from the cross-sectional risk-return regression of (10) for month t; $s^2(\tilde{\gamma}_j) \equiv s^2(\hat{\gamma}_j) - s^2(\tilde{\phi}_j)$; and the F-statistic $F = s^2(\hat{\gamma}_j)/s^2(\tilde{\phi}_j)$, which is relevant for testing the hypothesis, $s^2(\hat{\gamma}_j)/s^2(\tilde{\phi}_j)$. The numerator of F has $n - 1$ df, where n is the number of months in the sample period; and the denominator has $n(20 - K)$ df, where K is the number of coefficients $\hat{\gamma}_j$ in the model.[11]

One clear-cut result in table 5 is that there is a substantial decline in the reliability of the coefficients $\hat{\gamma}_{0t}$ and $\hat{\gamma}_{1t}$—that is, a substantial increase in $s^2(\tilde{\phi}_0)$ and $s^2(\tilde{\phi}_1)$—when $\hat{\beta}_p^2$ and/or $\bar{s}_p(\hat{\varepsilon}_j)$ are included in the risk-return regressions. The variable $\hat{\beta}_p^2$ is obviously collinear with $\hat{\beta}_p$, and, as can be seen from table 2, $\bar{s}_p(\hat{\varepsilon}_i)$ likewise increases with $\hat{\beta}_p$. From panels B and C of table 5, the collinearity with $\hat{\beta}_p$ is stronger for $\hat{\beta}_p^2$ than for $\bar{s}_p(\hat{\varepsilon}_j)$.

In spite of the loss in precision that arises from multicollinearity, however, the F-statistics for $\hat{\gamma}_2$ (the coefficient of $\hat{\beta}_p^2$) and $\hat{\gamma}_3$ [the coefficient of $\bar{s}_p(\hat{\varepsilon}_j)$] are generally large for the models of panels B and C of table 5, and for the model of panel D which includes both variables. From the F-statistics in panel D, it seems that, except for the period 1935–45, the variation through time of $\tilde{\gamma}_{2t}$ is statistically more noticeable than that of $\tilde{\gamma}_{3t}$, but there are periods (1941–45, 1956–60) when the values of F for both $\tilde{\gamma}_{2t}$ and $\tilde{\gamma}_{3t}$ are large.

11. The standard error of $\hat{\gamma}_{jt}$, $s(\tilde{\phi}_{jt})$ is proportional to the standard error of the risk-return residuals, $\check{\eta}_{pt}$, for month t, which has $20 - K$ df. And n values of $s^2(\tilde{\phi}_{jt})$ are averaged to get $s^2(\tilde{\phi}_j)$, so that the latter has $n(20 - K)$ df. Note that if the underlying return disturbances $\check{\eta}_{pt}$ of (10) are independent across p and have identical normal distributions for all p, then $\hat{\gamma}_{jt}$ is the sample mean of a normal distribution and $s^2(\tilde{\phi}_{jt})$ is proportional to the sample variance of the same normal distribution. If the process is also assumed to be stationary through time, it then follows that $s^2(\hat{\gamma}_{jt})$ and $s^2(\tilde{\phi}_{jt})$ are independent, as required by the F-test. Finally, in the F-statistics of table 5, the values of n are 60 or larger, so that, since K is from 2 to 4, $n(20 - K) \geq 960$. From Mood and Graybill (1963), some upper percentage points of the F-distribution are:

n	$F_{.90}$	$F_{.95}$	$F_{.975}$	$F_{.99}$	$F_{.995}$
60 (120)	1.35	1.47	1.58	1.73	1.83
60 (∞)	1.29	1.39	1.48	1.60	1.69
120 (120)	1.26	1.35	1.43	1.53	1.61
120 (∞)	1.19	1.25	1.31	1.38	1.43

TABLE 5. Components of the variances of the $\hat{\gamma}_{jt}$

Period	$s^2(\hat{\gamma}_0)$	$s^2(\tilde{\gamma}_0)$	$\overline{s^2(\tilde{\phi}_0)}$	F	$s^2(\hat{\gamma}_1)$	$s^2(\tilde{\gamma}_1)$	$\overline{s^2(\tilde{\phi}_1)}$	F
Panel A:								
1935–6/68	.00105	.00142	.00037	3.84	.00401	.00436	.00035	12.46
1935–45	.00182	.00273	.00091	3.00	.00863	.00950	.00087	21.38
1946–55	.00057	.00066	.00009	7.33	.00163	.00171	.00008	21.38
1956–6/68	.00077	.00090	.00013	6.92	.00181	.00193	.00012	16.08
1935–40	.00265	.00404	.00139	2.91	.01212	.01347	.00135	9.98
1941–45	.00086	.00118	.00032	3.69	.00452	.00481	.00029	16.59
1946–50	.00086	.00094	.00008	11.75	.00216	.00224	.00008	28.00
1951–55	.00027	.00036	.00009	4.00	.00113	.00121	.00008	15.12
1956–60	.00032	.00041	.00009	4.56	.00104	.00112	.00008	21.50
1961–6/68	.00100	.00114	.00014	8.14	.00217	.00231	.00014	16.50
Panel B:								
1935–6/68	.00092	.00267	.00175	1.52	.00564	.01403	.00839	1.67
1935–45	.00057	.00377	.00320	1.18	.00372	.01941	.01569	1.24
1946–55	.00053	.00112	.00059	1.90	.00651	.00897	.00245	3.66
1956–6/68	.00155	.00294	.00139	2.12	.00667	.01338	.00671	1.99
1935–40	.00018	.00476	.00458	1.04	.00374	.02555	.02181	1.17
1941–45	.00101	.00254	.00153	1.66	.00389	.01225	.00836	1.46
1946–50	.00084	.00136	.00052	2.62	.00862	.01071	.00209	5.12
1951–55	.00024	.00090	.00066	1.36	.00447	.00729	.00282	2.58
1956–60	.00037	.00087	.00050	1.74	.00289	.00517	.00228	2.27
1961–6/68	.00232	.00431	.00199	2.16	.00928	.01894	.00966	1.96
Panel C:								
1935–6/68	.00192	.00266	.00075	3.55	.00285	.00428	.00142	3.01
1935–45	.00394	.00533	.00139	3.83	.00433	.00717	.00283	2.52
1946–55	.00083	.00101	.00018	5.61	.00261	.00310	.00050	6.20
1956–6/68	.00100	.00164	.00063	2.60	.00178	.00270	.00092	2.93
1935–40	.00473	.00669	.00196	3.41	.00732	.01094	.00362	3.02
1941–45	.00307	.00377	.00070	5.38	.00085	.00274	.00189	1.45
1946–50	.00103	.00117	.00014	8.36	.00386	.00439	.00053	8.28
1951–55	.00061	.00083	.00022	3.77	.00140	.00188	.00047	4.00
1956–60	.00079	.00134	.00055	2.44	.00106	.00204	.00098	2.08
1961–6/68	.00109	.00177	.00068	2.60	.00212	.00300	.00088	3.41
Panel D:								
1935–6/68	.00150	.00566	.00406	1.39	.00608	.01521	.00913	1.66
1935–45	.00233	.01065	.00832	1.28	.00402	.02118	.01716	1.23
1946–55	.00013	.00176	.00163	1.08	.00647	.00916	.00269	3.41
1956–6/68	.00194	.00420	.00226	1.86	.00763	.01485	.00722	2.06
1935–40	.00157	.01263	.01106	1.14	.00457	.02910	.02453	1.19
1941–45	.00340	.00843	.00503	1.68	.00365	.01196	.00832	1.44
1946–50	.00023	.00220	.00197	1.12	.00858	.01119	.00261	4.29
1951–55	.00006	.00136	.00130	1.05	.00442	.00719	.00277	2.60
1956–60	.00092	.00239	.00147	1.62	.00328	.00602	.00274	2.20
1961–6/68	.00260	.00539	.00279	1.93	.01060	.02081	.01021	2.04

TABLE 5. (Continued)

Period	$s^2(\tilde{\gamma}_2)$	$s^2(\hat{\gamma}_2)$	$\overline{s^2(\tilde{\phi}_2)}$	F	$s^2(\tilde{\gamma}_3)$	$s^2(\hat{\gamma}_3)$	$\overline{s^2(\tilde{\phi}_3)}$	F
Panel A:								
1935–6/68	...	...	...	...	...	...	...	...
1935–45	...	...	...	...	...	...	...	...
1946–55	...	...	...	...	...	...	...	...
1956–6/68	...	...	...	...	...	...	...	...
1935–40	...	...	...	...	...	...	...	...
1941–45	...	...	...	...	...	...	...	...
1946–50	...	...	...	...	...	...	...	...
1951–55	...	...	...	...	...	...	...	...
1956–60	...	...	...	...	...	...	...	...
1961–6/68	...	...	...	...	...	...	...	...
Panel B:								
1935–6/68	.00121	.00318	.00197	1.61	...	...	...	...
1935–45	.00171	.00548	.00377	1.45	...	...	...	...
1946–55	.00063	.00112	.00049	2.29	...	...	...	...
1956–6/68	.00122	.00278	.00156	1.78	...	...	...	...
1935–40	.00041	.00566	.00524	1.08	...	...	...	...
1941–45	.00327	.00527	.00201	2.62	...	...	...	...
1946–50	.00066	.00103	.00037	2.78	...	...	...	...
1951–55	.00058	.00120	.00062	1.94	...	...	...	...
1956–60	.00033	.00083	.00050	1.66	...	...	...	...
1961–6/68	.00182	.00410	.00227	1.81	...	...	...	...
Panel C:								
1935–6/68	...	...	...	...	.341	.753	.412	1.83
1935–45	...	...	...	...	.535	.847	.313	2.71
1946–55	...	...	...	...	.165	.370	.206	1.80
1956–6/68	...	...	...	...	.304	.968	.664	1.46
1935–40	...	...	...	...	.270	.553	.282	1.96
1941–45	...	...	...	...	.840	1.189	.349	3.41
1946–50	...	...	...	...	.118	.254	.136	1.87
1951–55	...	...	...	...	.217	.493	.276	1.79
1956–60	...	...	...	...	.622	1.355	.734	1.85
1961–6/68	...	...	...	...	.105	.722	.617	1.17
Panel D:								
1935–6/68	.00061	.00362	.00301	1.21	.276	.864	.588	1.47
1935–45	...	.00624	.00644	.97	.392	1.001	.613	1.63
1946–55	.00061	.00148	.00087	1.70	.028	.383	.355	1.08
1956–6/68	.00134	.00304	.00169	1.80	.374	1.125	.751	1.50
1935–40	...	.00723	.00886	.82	.120	.682	.562	1.21
1941–45	.00162	.00515	.00353	1.46	.720	1.395	.675	2.07
1946–50	.00083	.00180	.00096	1.87	.023	.348	.325	1.07
1951–55	.00039	.00116	.00077	1.51	.038	.424	.386	1.10
1956–60	.00037	.00103	.00066	1.56	.712	1.654	.941	1.76
1961–6/68	.00202	.00440	.00238	1.85	.163	.787	.624	1.26

The F-statistics for $\hat{\gamma}_{1t} = \tilde{\gamma}_{1t} + \tilde{\phi}_{1t}$ also indicate that $\tilde{\gamma}_{1t}$ has substantial varia-tion through time. This is not surprising, however, since $\hat{\gamma}_{1t}$ is always directly related to $\tilde{R}_{mt}$. For example, from equation (12), for the one-variable model of panel A, $\hat{\gamma}_{1t} = \tilde{R}_{mt} - \hat{\gamma}_{0t}$.

Finally, the F-statistics for $\hat{\gamma}_{0t} = \tilde{\gamma}_{0t} + \tilde{\phi}_{0t}$ are also in general large. And the month-by-month variation in $\tilde{\gamma}_{0t}$ cannot be accounted for by variation in R_{ft}. The variance of R_{ft} is so small relative to $s^2(\hat{\gamma}_{0t})$, $s^2(\tilde{\gamma}_{0t})$ and $s^2(\tilde{\phi}_{0t})$ that doing the F-tests in terms of $\hat{\gamma}_{0t} - R_{ft}$ produces results almost identical with those for $\hat{\gamma}_{0t}$.

Rejection of the hypothesis that $\tilde{\gamma}_{0t} - R_{ft} = 0$ does not imply rejection of the S-L hypothesis—to be tested next—that $E(\tilde{\gamma}_{0t}) = R_{ft}$. Likewise, to find that month-by-month $\tilde{\gamma}_{2t} \neq 0$ and $\tilde{\gamma}_{3t} \neq 0$ does not imply rejection of hypotheses C1 and C2 of the two-parameter model. These hypotheses, which we are unable to reject on the basis of the results in table 3, say that $E(\tilde{\gamma}_{2t}) = 0$ and $E(\tilde{\gamma}_{3t}) = 0$.

What we have found in table 5 is that there are variables in addition to $\hat{\beta}_p$ that systematically affect period-by-period returns. Some of these omitted variables are apparently related to $\hat{\beta}_p^2$ and $\bar{s}_p(\tilde{\varepsilon}_i)$. But the latter are almost surely proxies, since there is no economic rationale for their presence in our stochas-tic risk-return model.

D. Tests of the S-L Hypothesis

In the Sharpe-Lintner two-parameter model of market equilibrium one has, in addition to conditions C1–C3, the hypothesis that $E(\tilde{\gamma}_{0t}) = R_{ft}$. The work of Friend and Blume (1970) and Black, Jensen, and Scholes (1972) suggests that the S-L hypothesis is not upheld by the data. At least in the post-World War II period, estimates of $E(\tilde{\gamma}_{0t})$ seem to be significantly greater than R_{ft}.

Each of the four models of table 3 can be used to test the S-L hypothesis.[12]

---

12. The least-squares intercepts $\hat{\gamma}_{0t}$ in the four cross-sectional risk-return regressions can always be interpreted as returns for month t on zero-$\hat{\beta}$ portfolios (n. 10). For the three-variable model of panel D, table 3, the unbiasedness of the least-squares coeffi-cients can be shown to imply that in computing $\hat{\gamma}_{0t}$, negative and positive weights are as-signed to the 20 portfolios in such a way that the resulting portfolio has not only zero-$\hat{\beta}$ but also zero averages of the 20 $\hat{\beta}_p^2$ and of the 20 $\tilde{s}_p(\hat{\varepsilon}_i)$. Analogous statements apply to the two-variable models of panels B and C.

Black, Jensen, and Scholes test the S-L hypothesis with a time series of monthly returns on a "minimum variance zero-$\hat{\beta}$ portfolio" which they derive directly. It turns out, however, that this portfolio is constructed under what amounts to the assumptions of the Gauss-Markov Theorem on the underlying disturbances of the one-variable risk-

The most efficient tests, however, are provided by the one-variable model of panel A, since the values of $s(\tilde{\gamma}_0)$ for this model [which are nearly identical with the values of $s(\hat{\gamma}_0 - R_f)$] are substantially smaller than those for other models. Except for the most recent period 1961–6/68, the values of $\hat{\gamma}_0 - R_f$ in panel A are all positive and generally greater than 0.4 percent per month. The value of $t(\hat{\gamma}_0 - R_f)$ for the overall period 1935–6/68 is 2.55, and the t-statistics for the subperiods 1946–55, 1951–55, and 1956–60 are likewise large. Thus, the results in panel A, table 3, support the negative conclusions of Friend and Blume (1970) and Black, Jensen, and Scholes (1972) with respect to the S-L hypothesis.

The S-L hypothesis seems to do somewhat better in the two-variable quadratic model of panel B, table 3 and especially in the three-variable model of panel D. The values of $t(\hat{\gamma}_0 - R_f)$ are substantially closer to zero for these models than for the model of panel A. This is due to values of $\hat{\gamma}_0 - R_f$ that are closer to zero, but it also reflects the fact that $s(\hat{\gamma}_0)$ is substantially higher for the models of panels B and D than for the model of panel A.

But the effects of $\hat{\beta}_p^2$ and $\bar{s}_p(\hat{\varepsilon}_i)$ on tests of the S-L hypothesis are in fact not at all so clear-cut. Consider the model

$$\tilde{R}_{it} = \tilde{\gamma}_{0t}' + \tilde{\gamma}_{1t}'\beta_i + \tilde{\gamma}_{2t}'(1-\beta_i)^2 + \tilde{\gamma}_{3t}s_i + \tilde{\eta}_{it}. \tag{13}$$

Equations (7) and (13) are equivalent representations of the stochastic process generating returns, with $\tilde{\gamma}_{1t} = \tilde{\gamma}_{1t}' - 2\tilde{\gamma}_{2t}$ and $\tilde{\gamma}_{0t} = \tilde{\gamma}_{0t}' - \tilde{\gamma}_{2t}$. Moreover, if the steps used to obtain the regression equation (10) from the stochastic model (7) are applied to (13), we get the regression equation,

---

return regression (11). With these assumptions the least-squares estimate $\hat{\gamma}_{0t}$, obtained from the cross-sectional risk-return regression of (11) for month t, is precisely the return for month t on the minimum variance zero-$\hat{\beta}$ portfolio that can be constructed from the 20 portfolio $\hat{\beta}_p$. Thus, the tests of the S-L hypothesis in panel A of table 3 are conceptually the same as those of Black, Jensen, and Scholes.

If one makes the assumptions of the Gauss-Markov Theorem on the underlying disturbances of the models of panels B–D of table 3, the regression intercepts for these models can likewise be interpreted as returns on minimum-variance zero-$\hat{\beta}$ portfolios. These portfolios then differ in terms of whether or not they also constrain the averages of the 20 $\hat{\beta}_p^2$ and of the 20 $\bar{s}_p(\hat{\varepsilon}_i)$ to be zero. Given the collinearity of $\hat{\beta}_p$, $\hat{\beta}_p^2$, and $\bar{s}_p(\hat{\varepsilon}_i)$, however, the assumptions of the Gauss-Markov Theorem cannot apply to all four of the models.

$$R_{pt} = \hat{\gamma}'_{0t} + \hat{\gamma}'_{1t}\hat{\beta}_p + \hat{\gamma}_{2t}(1-\hat{\beta}_p)^2 + \hat{\gamma}_{3t}\bar{s}_p(\hat{\varepsilon}_i) + \hat{\eta}_{pt}, \tag{14}$$

where, just as $\hat{\beta}_p^2$ in (10) is the average of $\hat{\beta}_i^2$ for securities i in portfolio p, $(1-\hat{\beta}_p)^2$ is the average of $(1-\hat{\beta}_p)^2$. The values of the estimates $\hat{\gamma}_{2t}$ and $\hat{\gamma}_{3t}$ are identical in (10) and (14); in addition, $\hat{\gamma}_{1t} = \hat{\gamma}'_{1t} - 2\hat{\gamma}_{2t}$ and $\hat{\gamma}_{0t} = \hat{\gamma}'_{0t} + \hat{\gamma}_{2t}$. But although the regression equations (10) and (14) are statistically indistinguishable, tests of the hypothesis $E(\hat{\gamma}_{0t}) = R_{ft}$ from (10) do not yield the same results as tests of the hypothesis $E(\hat{\gamma}'_{0t}) = R_{ft}$ from (14). In panel D of table 3, $\hat{\gamma}_0 - R_f$ is never statistically very different from zero, whereas in tests (not shown) from (14), the results are similar to those of panel A, table 3. That is, $\hat{\gamma}'_0 - R_f$ is systematically positive for all periods but 1961–6/68 and statistically very different from zero for the overall period 1935–6/68 and for the 1946–55, 1951–55, and 1956–60 subperiods.

Thus, tests of the S-L hypothesis from our three-variable models are ambiguous. Perhaps the ambiguity could be resolved and more efficient tests of the hypothesis could be obtained if the omitted variables for which $\bar{s}_p(\hat{\varepsilon}_i)$, $\hat{\beta}_p^2$, or $(1-\hat{\beta}_p)^2$ are almost surely proxies were identified. As indicated above, however, at the moment the most efficient tests of the S-L hypothesis are provided by the one-variable model of panel A, table 3, and the results for that model support the negative conclusions of others.

Given that the S-L hypothesis is not supported by the data, tests of the market efficiency hypothesis that $\tilde{\gamma}_{0t} - E(\tilde{R}_{0t})$ is a fair game are difficult since we no longer have a specific hypothesis about $E(\tilde{R}_{0t})$. And using the mean of the $\hat{\gamma}_{0t}$ as an estimate of $E(\tilde{R}_{0t})$ does not work as well in this case as it does for the market efficiency tests on γ_{1t}. One should note, however, that although the serial correlations $\rho_M(\hat{\gamma}_0)$ in table 4 are often large relative to estimates of their standard errors, they are small in terms of the proportion of the time series variance of $\hat{\gamma}_{0t}$ that they explain, and the latter is the more important criterion for judging whether market efficiency is a workable representation of reality (see n. 8).

VI. CONCLUSIONS

In sum our results support the important testable implications of the two-parameter model. Given that the market portfolio is efficient—or, more specifically, given that our proxy for the market portfolio is at least approximately efficient—we cannot reject the hypothesis that average returns on New York Stock Exchange common stocks reflect the attempts of risk-averse investors to hold efficient portfolios. Specifically, on average there seems to be a positive tradeoff between return and risk, with risk measured from the portfolio viewpoint. In addition, although there are "stochastic nonlinearities" from period to period, we cannot reject the hypothesis that on average their effects are zero and unpredictably different from zero from one period to the next. Thus, we cannot reject the hypothesis that in making a portfolio decision, an investor should assume that the relationship between a security's portfolio risk and its expected return is linear, as implied by the two-parameter model. We also cannot reject the hypothesis of the two-parameter model that no measure of risk, in addition to portfolio risk, systematically affects average returns. Finally, the observed fair game properties of the coefficients and residuals of the risk-return regressions are consistent with an efficient capital market—that is, a market where prices of securities fully reflect available information.

APPENDIX

Some Related Issues
A1. Market Models and Tests of Market Efficiency

The time series of regression coefficients from (10) are, of course, the inputs for the tests of the two-parameter model. But these coefficients can also be useful in tests of capital market efficiency—that is, tests of the speed of price adjustment to different types of new information. Since the work of Fama et al. (1969), such tests have commonly been based on the "one-factor market model":

$$R_{it} = \hat{\alpha}_i + \hat{\beta}_i R_{mt} + \hat{\varepsilon}_{it}. \tag{15}$$

In this regression equation, the term involving R_{mt} is assumed to capture the effects of market-wide factors. The effects on returns of events specific to company i, like a stock split or a change in earnings, are then studied through the residuals $\hat{\varepsilon}_{it}$.

But given that there is period-to-period variation in $\hat{\gamma}_{0t}$, $\hat{\gamma}_{2t}$, and $\hat{\gamma}_{3t}$ in (10) that is above and beyond pure sampling error, then these coefficients can be interpreted as market factors (in addition to R_{mt}) that influence the returns on all securities. To see this, substitute (12) into (11) to obtain the "two-factor market model":

$$R_{pt} = \hat{\gamma}_{0t}(1 - \hat{\beta}_p) + \hat{\beta}_p R_{mt} + \hat{\eta}_{pt}. \tag{16}$$

In like fashion, from equation (10) itself we easily obtain the "four-factor market model":

$$R_{pt} = \hat{\gamma}_{0t}(1-\hat{\beta}_p) + \hat{\beta}_p R_{mt} + \hat{\gamma}_{2t}(\hat{\beta}_p^2 - \hat{\beta}_p \overline{\hat{\beta}^2}) + \hat{\gamma}_{3t}\left[\overline{s}_p(\hat{\varepsilon}_i) - \hat{\beta}_p \overline{\overline{s}}(\hat{\varepsilon}_i)\right] + \hat{\eta}_{pt}, \quad (17)$$

where $\overline{\hat{\beta}^2}$ and $\overline{\overline{s}}(\hat{\varepsilon}_i)$ are the averages over p of the $\hat{\beta}_p^2$ and the $\overline{s}_p(\hat{\varepsilon}_i)$.

Comparing equations (15–17) it is clear that the residuals $\hat{\varepsilon}_{it}$ from the one-factor market model contain variation in the market factors $\hat{\gamma}_{0t}$, $\hat{\gamma}_{2t}$ and $\hat{\gamma}_{3t}$. Thus, if one is interested in the effect on a security's return of an event specific to the given company, this effect can probably be studied more precisely from the residuals of the two- or even the four-factor market models of (16) and (17) than from the one-factor model of (15). This has in fact already been done in a study of changes in accounting techniques by Ball (1972), in a study of insider trading by Jaffe (1972), and in a study of mergers by Mandelker (1972).

Ball, Jaffe, and Mandelker use the two-factor rather than the four-factor market model, and there is probably some basis for this. First, one can see from table 5 that because of the collinearity of $\hat{\beta}_p$, $\hat{\beta}_p^2$, and $\overline{s}_p(\hat{\varepsilon}_i)$, the coefficient estimates $\hat{\gamma}_{0t}$ and $\hat{\gamma}_{1t}$ have much smaller standard errors in the two-factor model. Second, we have computed residual variances for each of our 20 portfolios for various time periods from the time series of $\hat{\varepsilon}_{pt}$ and $\hat{\eta}_{pt}$ from (15), (16), and (17). The decline in residual variance that is obtained in going from (15) to (16) is as predicted: That is, the decline is noticeable over more or less the entire range of $\hat{\beta}_p$ and it is proportional to $(1-\hat{\beta}_p)^2$. On the other hand, in going from the two- to the four-factor model, reductions in residual variance are generally noticeable only in the portfolios with the lowest and highest $\hat{\beta}_p$, and the reductions for these two portfolios are generally small. Moreover, including $\overline{s}_p(\hat{\varepsilon}_i)$ as an explanatory variable in addition to $\hat{\beta}_p$ and $\hat{\beta}_p^2$ never results in a noticeable reduction in residual variances.

A2. Multifactor Models and Errors in the $\hat{\beta}$

If the return-generating process is a multifactor market model, then the usual estimates of β_i from the one-factor model of (15) are not most efficient. For example, if the return-generating process is the population analog of (16), more efficient estimates of β_i could in principle be obtained from a constrained regression applied to

$$\tilde{R}_{it} - \tilde{\gamma}_{0t} = \beta_i(\tilde{R}_{mt} - \tilde{\gamma}_{0t}) + \tilde{\eta}_{it}.$$

But this approach requires the time series of the true $\tilde{\gamma}_{0t}$. All we have are estimates $\hat{\gamma}_{0t}$, themselves obtained from estimates of $\hat{\beta}_p$ from the one-factor model of (15).

It can also be shown that with a multifactor return-generating process the errors in the $\hat{\beta}$ computed from the one-factor market model of (8) and (15) are correlated across securities and portfolios. This results from the fact that if the true process is a multifactor model, the disturbances of the one-factor model are correlated across securities and portfolios. Moreover, the interdependence of the errors in the $\hat{\beta}$ is higher the farther the true β's are from 1.0. This was already noted in the discussion of table 2 where we found that the relative reduction in the standard errors of the $\hat{\beta}$'s obtained by using portfolios rather than individual securities is lower the farther $\hat{\beta}_p$ is from 1.0.

Interdependence of the errors in the $\hat{\beta}_p$ also complicates the formal analysis of the effects of errors-in-the-variables on properties of the estimated coefficients (the $\hat{\gamma}_{jt}$) in the risk-return regressions of (10). This topic is considered in detail in an appendix to an earlier version of this paper that can be made available to the reader on request.

REFERENCES

Ball, R. "Changes in Accounting Techniques and Stock Prices." Ph.D. dissertation, University of Chicago, 1972.

Black, F. "Capital Market Equilibrium with Restricted Borrowing." *J. Bus.* 45 (July 1972): 444–55.

Black, F.; Jensen, M.; Scholes, M. "The Capital Asset Pricing Model: Some Empirical Results." In *Studies in the Theory of Capital Markets,* edited by Michael Jensen. New York: Praeger, 1972.

Blume, M. E. "Portfolio Theory: A Step toward Its Practical Application." *J. Bus.* 43 (April 1970): 152–73.

Douglas, G. W. "Risk in the Equity Markets: An Empirical Appraisal of Market Efficiency." *Yale Econ. Essays* 9 (Spring 1969): 3–45.

Fama, E. F. "The Behavior of Stock Market Prices." *J. Bus.* 38 (January 1965): 34–105. (*a*)

———. "Portfolio Analysis in a Stable Paretian Market." *Management Sci.* 11 (January 1965): 404–19. (*b*)

———. "Multiperiod Consumption-Investment Decisions." *A.E.R.* 60 (March 1970): 163–74. (*a*)

———. "Efficient Capital Markets: A Review of Theory and Empirical Work." *J. Finance* 25 (May 1970): 383–417. (*b*)

———. "Risk, Return and Equilibrium." *J.P.E.* 79 (January/February 1971): 30–55.

Fama, E. F., and Babiak, H. "Dividend Policy: An Empirical Analysis." *J. American Statis. Assoc.* 48 (December 1968): 1132–61.

Fama, E. F.; Fisher, L.; Jensen, M.; Roll, R. "The Adjustment of Stock Prices to New Information." *Internat. Econ. Rev.* 10 (February 1969): 1–21.

Fama, E. F., and Miller, M. *The Theory of Finance.* New York: Holt, Rinehart & Winston, 1972.

Fama, E. F., and Roll, R. "Some Properties of Symmetric Stable Distributions." *J. American Statis. Assoc.* 48 (September 1968): 817–36.

Fisher, L. "Some New Stock Market Indexes." *J. Bus.* 39 (January 1966): 191–225.

Friend, I., and Blume, M. "Measurement of Portfolio Performance under Uncertainty." *A.E.R.* 60 (September 1970): 561–75.

Gonedes, N. J. "Evidence on the Information Content of Accounting Numbers: Accounting-based and Market-based Estimates of Systematic Risk." *J. Financial and Quantitative Analysis* (1973): in press.

Jaffe, J. "Security Regulation, Special Information, and Insider Trading." Ph.D. dissertation, University of Chicago, 1972.

Jensen, M. "The Foundations and Current State of Capital Market Theory." *Bell J. Econ. and Management Sci.* 3 (Autumn 1972): 357–98.

Lintner, J. "The Valuation of Risk Assets and the Selection of Risky Investments in Stock Portfolios and Capital Budgets." *Rev. Econ. and Statis.* 47 (February 1965): 13–37.

Mandelker, G. "Returns to Stockholders from Mergers." Ph.D. proposal, University of Chicago, 1972.

Markowitz, H. *Portfolio Selection: Efficient Diversification of Investments.* New York: Wiley, 1959.

Miller, K. D. "Futures Trading and Investor Returns: An Investigation of Commodity Market Risk Premiums." Ph.D. dissertation, University of Chicago, 1971.

Miller, M., and Scholes, M. "Rates of Return in Relation to Risk: A Re-Examination of Some Recent Findings." In *Studies in the Theory of Capital Markets,* edited by Michael Jensen. New York: Praeger, 1972.

Mood, A. M., and Graybill, F. A. *Introduction to the Theory of Statistics.* New York: McGraw-Hill, 1963.

Officer, R. R. "A Time Series Examination of the Market Factor of the New York Stock Exchange." Ph.D., dissertation, University of Chicago, 1971.

Roll. R. *The Behavior of Interest Rates.* New York: Basic, 1970.

Sharpe, W. F. "Capital Asset Prices: A Theory of Market Equilibrium under Conditions of Risk." *J. Finance* 19 (September 1964): 425–42.

Tobin, J. "Liquidity Preference as Behavior towards Risk." *Rev. Econ. Studies* 25 (February 1958): 65–86.

THE CROSS-SECTION OF
EXPECTED STOCK RETURNS

. . .

Eugene F. Fama and Kenneth R. French

The asset-pricing model of Sharpe (1964), Lintner (1965), and Black (1972) has long shaped the way academics and practitioners think about average returns and risk. The central prediction of the model is that the market portfolio of invested wealth is mean-variance efficient in the sense of Markowitz (1959). The efficiency of the market portfolio implies that (a) expected returns on securities are a positive linear function of their market βs (the slope in the regression of a security's return on the market's return), and (b) market βs suffice to describe the cross-section of expected returns.

There are several empirical contradictions of the Sharpe-Lintner-Black (SLB) model. The most prominent is the size effect of Banz (1981). He finds that market equity, ME (a stock's price times shares outstanding), adds to the explanation of the cross-section of average returns provided by market βs. Average returns on small (low ME) stocks are too high given their β estimates, and average returns on large stocks are too low.

Another contradiction of the SLB model is the positive relation between leverage and average return documented by Bhandari (1988). It is plausible that leverage is associated with risk and expected return, but in the SLB model, leverage risk should be captured by market β. Bhandari finds, however, that leverage helps explain the cross-section of average stock returns in tests that include size (ME) as well as β.

Stattman (1980) and Rosenberg, Reid, and Lanstein (1985) find that average returns on U.S. stocks are positively related to the ratio of a firm's book value of

Reprinted with permission from the *Journal of Finance* 47, no. 2 (June 1992): 427–65. © 1992 by John Wiley and Sons.

We acknowledge the helpful comments of David Booth, Nai-fu Chen, George Constantinides, Wayne Ferson, Edward George, Campbell Harvey, Josef Lakonishok, Rex Sinquefield, René Stulz, Mark Zmijeweski, and an anonymous referee. This research is supported by the National Science Foundation (Fama) and the Center for Research in Security Prices (French).

common equity, BE, to its market value, ME. Chan, Hamao, and Lakonishok (1991) find that book-to-market equity, BE/ME, also has a strong role in explaining the cross-section of average returns on Japanese stocks.

Finally, Basu (1983) shows that earnings-price ratios (E/P) help explain the cross-section of average returns on U.S. stocks in tests that also include size and market β. Ball (1978) argues that E/P is a catch-all proxy for unnamed factors in expected returns; E/P is likely to be higher (prices are lower relative to earnings) for stocks with higher risks and expected returns, whatever the unnamed sources of risk.

Ball's proxy argument for E/P might also apply to size (ME), leverage, and book-to-market equity. All these variables can be regarded as different ways to scale stock prices, to extract the information in prices about risk and expected returns (Keim (1988)). Moreover, since E/P, ME, leverage, and BE/ME are all scaled versions of price, it is reasonable to expect that some of them are redundant for describing average returns. Our goal is to evaluate the joint roles of market β, size, E/P, leverage, and book-to-market equity in the cross-section of average returns on NYSE, AMEX, and NASDAQ stocks.

Black, Jensen, and Scholes (1972) and Fama and MacBeth (1973) find that, as predicted by the SLB model, there is a positive simple relation between average stock returns and β during the pre-1969 period. Like Reinganum (1981) and Lakonishok and Shapiro (1986), we find that the relation between β and average return disappears during the more recent 1963–1990 period, even when β is used alone to explain average returns. The appendix shows that the simple relation between β and average return is also weak in the 50-year 1941–1990 period. In short, our tests do not support the most basic prediction of the SLB model, that average stock returns are positively related to market βs.

Unlike the simple relation between β and average return, the univariate relations between average return and size, leverage, E/P, and book-to-market equity are strong. In multivariate tests, the negative relation between size and average return is robust to the inclusion of other variables. The positive relation between book-to-market equity and average return also persists in competition with other variables. Moreover, although the size effect has attracted more attention, book-to-market equity has a consistently stronger role in average returns. Our bottom-line results are: (a) β does not seem to help explain the cross-section of average stock returns, and (b) the combination of size and book-to-market equity seems to absorb the roles of leverage and E/P in average stock returns, at least during our 1963–1990 sample period.

If assets are priced rationally, our results suggest that stock risks are multi-dimensional. One dimension of risk is proxied by size, ME. Another dimension of risk is proxied by BE/ME, the ratio of the book value of common equity to its market value.

It is possible that the risk captured by BE/ME is the relative distress factor of Chan and Chen (1991). They postulate that the earning prospects of firms are associated with a risk factor in returns. Firms that the market judges to have poor prospects, signaled here by low stock prices and high ratios of book-to-market equity, have higher expected stock returns (they are penalized with higher costs of capital) than firms with strong prospects. It is also possible, however, that BE/ME just captures the unraveling (regression toward the mean) of irrational market whims about the prospects of firms.

Whatever the underlying economic causes, our main result is straightforward. Two easily measured variables, size (ME) and book-to-market equity (BE/ME), provide a simple and powerful characterization of the cross-section of average stock returns for the 1963–1990 period.

In the next section we discuss the data and our approach to estimating β. Section II examines the relations between average return and β and between average return and size. Section III examines the roles of E/P, leverage, and book-to-market equity in average returns. In sections IV and V, we summarize, interpret, and discuss applications of the results.

I. PRELIMINARIES

A. Data

We use all nonfinancial firms in the intersection of (a) the NYSE, AMEX, and NASDAQ return files from the Center for Research in Security Prices (CRSP) and (b) the merged COMPUSTAT annual industrial files of income-statement and balance-sheet data, also maintained by CRSP. We exclude financial firms because the high leverage that is normal for these firms probably does not have the same meaning as for nonfinancial firms, where high leverage more likely indicates distress. The CRSP returns cover NYSE and AMEX stocks until 1973 when NASDAQ returns also come on line. The COMPUSTAT data are for 1962–1989. The 1962 start date reflects the fact that book value of common equity (COMPUSTAT item 60), is not generally available prior to 1962. More important, COMPUSTAT data for earlier years have a serious selection bias; the pre-1962 data are tilted toward big historically successful firms.

To ensure that the accounting variables are known before the returns they are used to explain, we match the accounting data for all fiscal yearends in calendar year $t - 1$ (1962–1989) with the returns for July of year t to June of $t + 1$. The 6-month (minimum) gap between fiscal yearend and the return tests is conservative. Earlier work (e.g., Basu (1983)) often assumes that accounting data are available within three months of fiscal yearends. Firms are indeed required to file their 10-K reports with the SEC within 90 days of their fiscal yearends, but on average 19.8% do not comply. In addition, more than 40% of the December fiscal yearend firms that do comply with the 90-day rule file on March 31, and their reports are not made public until April. (See Alford, Jones, and Zmijewski (1992).)

We use a firm's market equity at the end of December of year $t - 1$ to compute its book-to-market, leverage, and earnings-price ratios for $t - 1$, and we use its market equity for June of year t to measure its size. Thus, to be included in the return tests for July of year t, a firm must have a CRSP stock price for December of year $t - 1$ and June of year t. It must also have monthly returns for at least 24 of the 60 months preceding July of year t (for "pre-ranking" β estimates, discussed below). And the firm must have COMPUSTAT data on total book assets (A), book equity (BE), and earnings (E), for its fiscal year ending in (any month of) calendar year $t - 1$.

Our use of December market equity in the E/P, BE/ME, and leverage ratios is objectionable for firms that do not have December fiscal yearends because the accounting variable in the numerator of a ratio is not aligned with the market value in the denominator. Using ME at fiscal yearends is also problematic; then part of the cross-sectional variation of a ratio for a given year is due to market-wide variation in the ratio during the year. For example, if there is a general fall in stock prices during the year, ratios measured early in the year will tend to be lower than ratios measured later. We can report, however, that the use of fiscal-yearend MEs, rather than December MEs, in the accounting ratios has little impact on our return tests.

Finally, the tests mix firms with different fiscal yearends. Since we match accounting data for all fiscal yearends in calendar year $t - 1$ with returns for July of t to June of $t + 1$, the gap between the accounting data and the matching returns varies across firms. We have done the tests using the smaller sample of firms with December fiscal yearends with similar results.

B. Estimating Market βs

Our asset-pricing tests use the cross-sectional regression approach of Fama and MacBeth (1973). Each month the cross-section of returns on stocks is regressed on variables hypothesized to explain expected returns. The time-series means of the monthly regression slopes then provide standard tests of whether different explanatory variables are on average priced.

Since size, E/P, leverage, and BE/ME are measured precisely for individual stocks, there is no reason to smear the information in these variables by using portfolios in the Fama-MacBeth (FM) regressions. Most previous tests use portfolios because estimates of market βs are more precise for portfolios. Our approach is to estimate βs for portfolios and then assign a portfolio's β to each stock in the portfolio. This allows us to use individual stocks in the FM asset-pricing tests.

B.1. β Estimation: Details

In June of each year, all NYSE stocks on CRSP are sorted by size (ME) to determine the NYSE decile breakpoints for ME. NYSE, AMEX, and NASDAQ stocks that have the required CRSP-COMPUSTAT data are then allocated to 10 size portfolios based on the NYSE breakpoints. (If we used stocks from all three exchanges to determine the ME breakpoints, most portfolios would include only small stocks after 1973, when NASDAQ stocks are added to the sample.)

We form portfolios on size because of the evidence of Chan and Chen (1988) and others that size produces a wide spread of average returns and βs. Chan and Chen use only size portfolios. The problem this creates is that size and the βs of size portfolios are highly correlated (-0.988 in their data), so asset-pricing tests lack power to separate size from β effects in average returns.

To allow for variation in β that is unrelated to size, we subdivide each size decile into 10 portfolios on the basis of pre-ranking βs for individual stocks. The pre-ranking βs are estimated on 24 to 60 monthly returns (as available) in the 5 years before July of year t. We set the β breakpoints for each size decile using only NYSE stocks that satisfy our COMPUSTAT-CRSP data requirements for year $t-1$. Using NYSE stocks ensures that the β breakpoints are not dominated after 1973 by the many small stocks on NASDAQ. Setting β breakpoints with stocks that satisfy our COMPUSTAT-CRSP data requirements guarantees that there are firms in each of the 100 size-β portfolios.

After assigning firms to the size-β portfolios in June, we calculate the equal-weighted monthly returns on the portfolios for the next 12 months, from July to June. In the end, we have post-ranking monthly returns for July 1963 to December 1990 on 100 portfolios formed on size and pre-ranking βs. We then estimate βs using the full sample (330 months) of post-ranking returns on each of the 100 portfolios, with the CRSP value-weighted portfolio of NYSE, AMEX, and (after 1972) NASDAQ stocks used as the proxy for the market. We have also estimated βs using the value-weighted or the equal-weighted portfolio of NYSE stocks as the proxy for the market. These βs produce inferences on the role of β in average returns like those reported below.

We estimate β as the sum of the slopes in the regression of the return on a portfolio on the current and prior month's market return. (An additional lead and lag of the market have little effect on these sum βs.) The sum βs are meant to adjust for nonsynchronous trading (Dimson (1979)). Fowler and Rorke (1983) show that sum βs are biased when the market return is autocorrelated. The 1st- and 2nd-order autocorrelations of the monthly market returns for July 1963 to December 1990 are 0.06 and −0.05, both about 1 standard error from 0. If the Fowler-Rorke corrections are used, they lead to trivial changes in the βs. We stick with the simpler sum βs. Appendix Table AI shows that using sum βs produces large increases in the βs of the smallest ME portfolios and small declines in the βs of the largest ME portfolios.

Chan and Chen (1988) show that full-period β estimates for portfolios can work well in tests of the SLB model, even if the true βs of the portfolios vary through time, if the variation in the βs is proportional,

$$\beta_{jt} - \beta_j = k_t(\beta_j - \beta) \qquad (1)$$

where β_{jt} is the true β for portfolio j at time t, β_j is the mean of β_{jt} across t, and β is the mean of the β_j. The Appendix argues that (1) is a good approximation for the variation through time in the true βs of portfolios (j) formed on size and β. For diehard β fans, sure to be skeptical of our results on the weak role of β in average stock returns, we can also report that the results stand up to robustness checks that use 5-year pre-ranking βs, or 5-year post-ranking βs, instead of the full-period post-ranking βs.

We allocate the full-period post-ranking β of a size-β portfolio to each stock in the portfolio. These are the βs that will be used in the Fama-MacBeth cross-sectional regressions for individual stocks. We judge that the precision of the full-period post-ranking portfolio βs, relative to the imprecise β estimates that would be obtained for individual stocks, more than makes up for the fact that true βs are not the same for all stocks in a portfolio. And note that assigning full-period portfolio βs to stocks does not mean that a stock's β is constant. A stock can move across portfolios with year-to-year changes in the stock's size (ME) and in the estimates of its β for the preceding 5 years.

B.2. β Estimates

Table I shows that forming portfolios on size and pre-ranking βs, rather than on size alone, magnifies the range of full-period post-ranking βs. Sorted on size alone, the post-ranking βs range from 1.44 for the smallest ME portfolio to 0.92 for the largest. This spread of βs across the 10 size deciles is smaller than the spread of post-ranking βs produced by the β sort of *any* size decile. For example, the post-ranking βs for the 10 portfolios in the smallest size decile range from 1.05 to 1.79. Across all 100 size-β portfolios, the post-ranking βs range from 0.53 to 1.79, a spread 2.4 times the spread, 0.52, obtained with size portfolios alone.

Two other facts about the βs are important. First, in each size decile the post-ranking βs closely reproduce the ordering of the pre-ranking βs. We take this to be evidence that the pre-ranking β sort captures the ordering of true post-ranking βs. (The appendix gives more evidence on this important issue.) Second, the β sort is not a refined size sort. In any size decile, the average values of ln(ME) are similar across the β-sorted portfolios. Thus the pre-ranking β sort achieves its goal. It produces strong variation in post-ranking βs that is unrelated to size. This is important in allowing our tests to distinguish between β and size effects in average returns.

II. β AND SIZE

The Sharpe-Lintner-Black (SLB) model plays an important role in the way academics and practitioners think about risk and the relation between risk and expected return. We show next that when common stock portfolios are formed on size alone, there seems to be evidence for the model's central prediction: average return is positively related to β. The βs of size portfolios are, however, almost perfectly correlated with size, so tests on size portfolios are unable to disentangle β and size effects in average returns. Allowing for variation in β that is unrelated to size breaks the logjam, but at the expense of β. Thus, when we subdivide size portfolios on the basis of pre-ranking βs, we find a strong relation between average return and size, but no relation between average return and β.

A. Informal Tests

Table II shows post-ranking average returns for July 1963 to December 1990 for portfolios formed from one-dimensional sorts of stocks on size or β. The portfolios are formed at the end of June each year and their equal-weighted returns are calculated for the next 12 months. We use returns for July to June

TABLE I. Average returns, post-ranking βs and average size for portfolios formed on size and then β: stocks sorted on ME (down) then pre-ranking β (across): July 1963 to December 1990

Portfolios are formed yearly. The breakpoints for the size (ME, price times shares outstanding) deciles are determined in June of year t ($t = 1963–1990$) using all NYSE stocks on CRSP. All NYSE, AMEX, and NASDAQ stocks that meet the CRSP-COMPUSTAT data requirements are allocated to the 10 size portfolios using the NYSE breakpoints. Each size decile is subdivided into 10 β portfolios using pre-ranking βs of individual stocks, estimated with 2 to 5 years of monthly returns (as available) ending in June of year t. We use only NYSE stocks that meet the CRSP-COMPUSTAT data requirements to establish the β breakpoints. The equal-weighted monthly returns on the resulting 100 portfolios are then calculated for July of year t to June of year $t + 1$.

The post-ranking βs use the full (July 1963 to December 1990) sample of post-ranking returns for each portfolio. The pre- and post-ranking βs (here and in all other tables) are the sum of the slopes from a regression of monthly returns on the current and prior month's returns on the value-weighted portfolio of NYSE, AMEX, and (after 1972) NASDAQ stocks. The average return is the time-series average of the monthly equal-weighted portfolio returns, in percent. The average size of a portfolio is the time-series average of monthly averages of ln(ME) for stocks in the portfolio at the end of June of each year, with ME denominated in millions of dollars.

The average number of stocks per month for the size-β portfolios in the smallest size decile varies from 70 to 177. The average number of stocks for the size-β portfolios in size deciles 2 and 3 is between 15 and 41, and the average number for the largest 7 size deciles is between 11 and 22.

The All column shows statistics for equal-weighted size-decile (ME) portfolios. The All row shows statistics for equal-weighted portfolios of the stocks in each β group.

	All	Low-β	β-2	β-3	β-4	β-5	β-6	β-7	β-8	β-9	High-β
					Panel A: Average Monthly Returns (in Percent)						
All	1.25	1.34	1.29	1.36	1.31	1.33	1.28	1.24	1.21	1.25	1.14
Small-ME	1.52	1.71	1.57	1.79	1.61	1.50	1.50	1.37	1.63	1.50	1.42
ME-2	1.29	1.25	1.42	1.36	1.39	1.65	1.61	1.37	1.31	1.34	1.11
ME-3	1.24	1.12	1.31	1.17	1.70	1.29	1.10	1.31	1.36	1.26	0.76
ME-4	1.25	1.27	1.13	1.54	1.06	1.34	1.06	1.41	1.17	1.35	0.98
ME-5	1.29	1.34	1.42	1.39	1.48	1.42	1.18	1.13	1.27	1.18	1.08
ME-6	1.17	1.08	1.53	1.27	1.15	1.20	1.21	1.18	1.04	1.07	1.02
ME-7	1.07	0.95	1.21	1.26	1.09	1.18	1.11	1.24	0.62	1.32	0.76

	All	Low-β	β-2	β-3	β-4	β-5	β-6	β-7	β-8	β-9	High-β
ME-8	1.10	1.09	1.05	1.37	1.20	1.27	0.98	1.18	1.02	1.01	0.94
ME-9	0.95	0.98	0.88	1.02	1.14	1.07	1.23	0.94	0.82	0.88	0.59
Large-ME	0.89	1.01	0.93	1.10	0.94	0.93	0.89	1.03	0.71	0.74	0.56

Panel B: Post-Ranking βs

	All	Low-β	β-2	β-3	β-4	β-5	β-6	β-7	β-8	β-9	High-β
All		0.87	0.99	1.09	1.16	1.26	1.29	1.35	1.45	1.52	1.72
Small-ME	1.44	1.05	1.18	1.28	1.32	1.40	1.40	1.49	1.61	1.64	1.76
ME-2	1.39	0.91	1.15	1.17	1.24	1.36	1.41	1.43	1.50	1.66	1.76
ME-3	1.35	0.97	1.13	1.13	1.21	1.26	1.28	1.39	1.50	1.51	1.75
ME-4	1.34	0.78	1.03	1.17	1.16	1.26	1.28	1.39	1.50	1.51	1.75
ME-5	1.25	0.66	0.85	1.12	1.15	1.16	1.26	1.30	1.43	1.59	1.68
ME-6	1.23	0.61	0.78	1.05	1.16	1.22	1.28	1.36	1.46	1.49	1.70
ME-7	1.17	0.57	0.92	1.01	1.11	1.14	1.26	1.24	1.39	1.34	1.60
ME-8	1.09	0.53	0.74	0.94	1.02	1.13	1.12	1.18	1.26	1.35	1.52
ME-9	1.03	0.58	0.74	0.80	0.95	1.06	1.15	1.14	1.21	1.22	1.42
Large-ME	0.92	0.57	0.71	0.78	0.89	0.95	0.92	1.02	1.01	1.11	1.32

Panel C: Average Size (ln(ME))

	All	Low-β	β-2	β-3	β-4	β-5	β-6	β-7	β-8	β-9	High-β
All	4.11	3.86	4.26	4.33	4.41	4.27	4.32	4.26	4.19	4.03	3.77
Small-ME	2.24	2.12	2.27	2.30	2.30	2.28	2.29	2.30	2.32	2.25	2.15
ME-2	3.63	3.65	3.68	3.70	3.72	3.69	3.70	3.69	3.69	3.70	3.68
ME-3	4.10	4.14	4.18	4.12	4.15	4.16	4.16	4.18	4.14	4.15	4.15
ME-4	4.50	4.53	4.53	4.57	4.54	4.56	4.55	4.52	4.58	4.52	4.56
ME-5	4.89	4.91	4.91	4.93	4.95	4.93	4.92	4.93	4.92	4.92	4.95
ME-6	5.30	5.30	5.33	5.34	5.34	5.33	5.33	5.33	5.33	5.34	5.36
ME-7	5.73	5.73	5.75	5.77	5.76	5.73	5.77	5.77	5.76	5.72	5.76
ME-8	6.24	6.26	6.27	6.26	6.24	6.24	6.27	6.24	6.24	6.24	6.26
ME-9	6.82	6.82	6.84	6.82	6.82	6.81	6.81	6.81	6.81	6.80	6.83
Large-ME	7.93	7.94	8.04	8.10	8.04	8.02	8.02	7.94	7.80	7.75	7.62

TABLE II. Properties of portfolios formed on size or pre-ranking β: July 1963 to December 1990

At the end of June of each year t, 12 portfolios are formed on the basis of ranked values of size (ME) or pre-ranking β. The pre-ranking βs use 2 to 5 years (as available) of monthly returns ending in June of t. Portfolios 2–9 cover deciles of the ranking variables. The bottom and top 2 portfolios (1A, 1B, 10A, and 10B) split the bottom and top deciles in half. The breakpoints for the ME portfolios are based on ranked values of ME for all NYSE stocks on CRSP. NYSE breakpoints for pre-ranking βs are also used to form the β portfolios. NYSE, AMEX, and NAS-DAQ stocks are then allocated to the size or β portfolios using the NYSE breakpoints. We calculate each portfolio's monthly equal-weighted return for July of year t to June of year $t + 1$, and then reform the portfolios in June of $t + 1$.

BE is the book value of common equity plus balance-sheet deferred taxes, A is total book assets, and E is earnings (income before extraor-dinary items, plus income-statement deferred taxes, minus preferred dividends). BE, A, and E are for each firm's latest fiscal year ending in calendar year $t − 1$. The accounting ratios are measured using market equity ME in December of year $t − 1$. Firm size ln(ME) is measured in June of year t, with ME denominated in millions of dollars.

The average return is the time-series average of the monthly equal-weighted portfolio returns, in percent. ln(ME), ln(BE/ME), ln(A/ME), ln(A/BE), E/P, and E/P dummy are the time-series averages of the monthly average values of these variables in each portfolio. Since the E/P dummy is 0 when earnings are positive, and 1 when earnings are negative, E/P dummy gives the average proportion of stocks with negative earnings in each portfolio.

β is the time-series average of the monthly portfolio βs. Stocks are assigned the post-ranking β of the size-β portfolio they are in at the end of June of year t (Table I). These individual-firm βs are averaged to compute the monthly βs for each portfolio for July of year t to June of year $t + 1$.

Firms is the average number of stocks in the portfolio each month.

	1A	1B	2	3	4	5	6	7	8	9	10A	10B
Panel A: Portfolios Formed on Size												
Return	1.64	1.16	1.29	1.24	1.25	1.29	1.17	1.07	1.10	0.95	0.88	0.90
β	1.44	1.44	1.39	1.34	1.33	1.24	1.22	1.16	1.08	1.02	0.95	0.90
ln(ME)	1.98	3.18	3.63	4.10	4.50	4.89	5.30	5.73	6.24	6.82	7.39	8.44
ln(BE/ME)	-0.01	-0.21	-0.23	-0.26	-0.32	-0.36	-0.36	-0.44	-0.40	-0.42	0.51	-0.65
ln(A/ME)	0.73	0.50	0.46	0.43	0.37	0.32	0.32	0.24	0.29	0.27	0.17	-0.03
ln(A/BE)	0.75	0.71	0.69	0.69	0.68	0.67	0.68	0.67	0.69	0.70	0.68	0.62
E/P dummy	0.26	0.14	0.11	0.09	0.06	0.04	0.04	0.03	0.03	0.02	0.02	0.01
E(+)/P	0.09	0.10	0.10	0.10	0.10	0.10	0.10	0.10	0.10	0.10	0.09	0.09
Firms	772	189	236	170	144	140	128	125	119	114	60	64
Panel B: Portfolios Formed on Pre-Ranking β												
Return	1.20	1.20	1.32	1.26	1.31	1.30	1.30	1.23	1.23	1.33	1.34	1.18
β	0.81	0.79	0.92	1.04	1.13	1.19	1.26	1.32	1.41	1.52	1.63	1.73
ln(ME)	4.21	4.86	8.75	4.68	4.59	4.48	4.36	4.25	3.97	3.78	3.52	3.15
ln(BE/ME)	-0.18	-0.13	-0.22	-0.21	-0.23	-0.22	-0.22	-0.25	-0.23	-0.27	-0.31	-0.50
ln(A/ME)	0.60	0.66	0.49	0.45	0.42	0.42	0.45	0.42	0.47	0.46	0.46	0.31
ln(A/BE)	0.78	0.79	0.71	0.66	0.64	0.65	0.67	0.67	0.70	0.73	0.77	0.81
E/P dummy	0.12	0.06	0.09	0.09	0.08	0.09	0.10	0.12	0.12	0.14	0.17	0.23
E(+)/P	0.11	0.12	0.10	0.10	0.10	0.10	0.10	0.09	0.10	0.09	0.09	0.08
Firms	116	80	185	181	179	182	185	205	227	267	165	291

to match the returns in later tests that use the accounting data. When we sort on just size or 5-year pre-ranking βs, we form 12 portfolios. The middle 8 cover deciles of size or β. The 4 extreme portfolios (1A, 1B, 10A, and 10B) split the bottom and top deciles in half.

Table II shows that when portfolios are formed on size alone, we observe the familiar strong negative relation between size and average return (Banz (1981)), and a strong positive relation between average return and β. Average returns fall from 1.64% per month for the smallest ME portfolio to 0.90% for the largest. Post-ranking βs also decline across the 12 size portfolios, from 1.44 for portfolio 1A to 0.90 for portfolio 10B. Thus, a simple size sort seems to support the SLB prediction of a positive relation between β and average return. But the evidence is muddied by the tight relation between size and the βs of size portfolios.

The portfolios formed on the basis of the ranked market βs of stocks in Table II produce a wider range of βs (from 0.81 for portfolio 1A to 1.73 for 10B) than the portfolios formed on size. Unlike the size portfolios, the β-sorted portfolios do not support the SLB model. There is little spread in average returns across the β portfolios, and there is no obvious relation between β and average returns. For example, although the two extreme portfolios, 1A and 10B, have much different βs, they have nearly identical average returns (1.20% and 1.18% per month). These results for 1963–1990 confirm Reinganum's (1981) evidence that for β-sorted portfolios, there is no relation between average return and β during the 1964–1979 period.

The 100 portfolios formed on size and then pre-ranking β in Table I clarify the contradictory evidence on the relation between β and average return produced by portfolios formed on size or β alone. Specifically, the two-pass sort gives a clearer picture of the separate roles of size and β in average returns. Contrary to the central prediction of the SLB model, the second-pass β sort produces little variation in average returns. Although the post-ranking βs in Table I increase strongly in each size decile, average returns are flat or show a slight tendency to decline. In contrast, within the columns of the average return and β matrices of Table I, average returns and βs decrease with increasing size.

The two-pass sort on size and β in Table I says that variation in β that is tied to size is positively related to average return, but variation in β unrelated to size is not compensated in the average returns of 1963–1990. The proper inference seems to be that there is a relation between size and average return, but controlling for size, there is no relation between β and average return. The regressions that follow confirm this conclusion, and they produce another that is stronger. The regressions show that when one allows for variation in β that is unrelated to size, the relation between β and average return is flat, even when β is the only explanatory variable.

B. Fama-MacBeth Regressions

Table III shows time-series averages of the slopes from the month-by-month Fama-MacBeth (FM) regressions of the cross-section of stock returns on size, β, and the other variables (leverage, E/P, and book-to-market equity) used to explain average returns. The average slopes provide standard FM tests for determining which explanatory variables on average have non-zero expected premiums during the July 1963 to December 1990 period.

Like the average returns in Tables I and II, the regressions in Table III say that size, ln(ME), helps explain the cross-section of average stock returns. The average slope from the monthly regressions of returns on size alone is −0.15%, with a t-statistic of −2.58. This reliable negative relation persists no matter which other explanatory variables are in the regressions; the average slopes on ln(ME) are always close to or more than 2 standard errors from 0. The size effect (smaller stocks have higher average returns) is thus robust in the 1963–1990 returns on NYSE, AMEX, and NASDAQ stocks.

In contrast to the consistent explanatory power of size, the FM regressions show that market β does not help explain average stock returns for 1963–1990. In a shot straight at the heart of the SLB model, the average slope from the regressions of returns on β alone in Table III is 0.15% per month and only 0.46 standard errors from 0. In the regressions of returns on size and β, size has explanatory power (an average slope −3.41 standard errors from 0), but the average slope for β is negative and only 1.21 standard errors from 0. Lakonishok and Shapiro (1986) get similar results for NYSE stocks for 1962–1981. We can also report that β shows no power to explain average returns (the average slopes are typically less than 1 standard error from 0) in FM regressions that use various combinations of β with size, book-to-market equity, leverage, and E/P.

C. Can β Be Saved?

What explains the poor results for β? One possibility is that other explanatory variables are correlated with true βs, and this obscures the relation between average returns and measured βs. But this line of attack cannot explain why β has no power when used alone to explain average returns. Moreover, leverage,

TABLE III. Average slopes (*t*-statistics) from month-by-month regressions of stock returns on β, size, book-to-market equity, leverage, and E/P: July 1963 to December 1990

Stocks are assigned the post-ranking β of the size-β portfolio they are in at the end of June of year t (Table I). BE is the book value of common equity plus balance-sheet deferred taxes, A is total book assets, and E is earnings (income before extraordinary items, plus income-statement deferred taxes, minus preferred dividends). BE, A, and E are for each firm's latest fiscal year ending in calendar year $t-1$. The accounting ratios are measured using market equity ME in December of year $t-1$. Firm size ln(ME) is measured in June of year t. In the regressions, these values of the explanatory variables for individual stocks are matched with CRSP returns for the months from July of year t to June of year $t+1$. The gap between the accounting data and the returns ensures that the accounting data are available prior to the returns. If earnings are positive, E(+)/P is the ratio of total earnings to market equity and E/P dummy is 0. If earnings are negative, E(+)/P is 0 and E/P dummy is 1.

The average slope is the time-series average of the monthly regression slopes for July 1963 to December 1990, and the *t*-statistic is the average slope divided by its time-series standard error.

On average, there are 2267 stocks in the monthly regressions. To avoid giving extreme observations heavy weight in the regressions, the smallest and largest 0.5% of the observations on E(+)/P, BE/ME, A/ME, and A/BE are set equal to the next largest or smallest values of the ratios (the 0.005 and 0.995 fractiles). This has no effect on inferences.

β	ln(ME)	ln(BE/ME)	ln(A/ME)	ln(A/BE)	E/P Dummy	E(+)/P
0.15						
(0.46)						
	−0.15					
	(−2.58)					
−0.37	−0.17					
(−1.21)	(−3.41)					
		0.50				
		(5.71)				
			0.50	−0.57		
			(5.69)	(−5.34)		
					0.57	4.72
					(2.28)	(4.57)
	−0.11	0.35				
	(−1.99)	(4.44)				
	−0.11		0.35	−0.50		
	(−2.06)		(4.32)	(−4.56)		
	−0.16				0.06	2.99
	(−3.06)				(0.38)	(3.04)
	−0.13	0.33			−0.14	0.87
	(−2.47)	(4.46)			(−0.90)	(1.23)
	−0.13		0.32	−0.46	−0.08	1.15
	(−2.47)		(4.28)	(−4.45)	(−0.56)	(1.57)

book-to-market equity, and E/P do not seem to be good proxies for β. The averages of the monthly cross-sectional correlations between β and the values of these variables for individual stocks are all within 0.15 of 0.

Another hypothesis is that, as predicted by the SLB model, there is a positive relation between β and average return, but the relation is obscured by noise in the β estimates. However, our full-period post-ranking βs do not seem to be imprecise. Most of the standard errors of the βs (not shown) are 0.05 or less, only 1 is greater than 0.1, and the standard errors are small relative to the range of the βs (0.53 to 1.79).

The β-sorted portfolios in Tables I and II also provide strong evidence against the β-measurement-error story. When portfolios are formed on pre-ranking βs alone (Table II), the post-ranking βs for the portfolios almost perfectly reproduce the ordering of the pre-ranking βs. Only the β for portfolio 1B is out of line, and only by 0.02. Similarly, when portfolios are formed on size and then pre-ranking βs (Table I), the post-ranking βs in each size decile closely reproduce the ordering of the pre-ranking βs.

The correspondence between the ordering of the pre-ranking and post-ranking βs for the β-sorted portfolios in Tables I and II is evidence that the post-ranking βs are informative about the ordering of the true βs. The problem for the SLB model is that there is no similar ordering in the average returns on the β-sorted portfolios. Whether one looks at portfolios sorted on β alone (Table II) or on size and then β (Table I), average returns are flat (Table II) or decline slightly (Table I) as the post-ranking βs increase.

Our evidence on the robustness of the size effect and the absence of a relation between β and average return is so contrary to the SLB model that it behooves us to examine whether the results are special to 1963–1990. The appendix shows that NYSE returns for 1941–1990 behave like the NYSE, AMEX, and NASDAQ returns for 1963–1990; there is a reliable size effect over the full 50-year period, but little relation between β and average return. Interestingly, there is a reliable simple relation between β and average return during the 1941–1965 period. These 25 years are a major part of the samples in the early studies of the SLB model of Black, Jensen, and Scholes (1972) and Fama and MacBeth (1973). Even for the 1941–1965 period, however, the relation between β and average return disappears when we control for size.

III. BOOK-TO-MARKET EQUITY, E/P, AND LEVERAGE

Tables I to III say that there is a strong relation between the average returns on stocks and size, but there is no reliable relation between average returns and β. In this section we show that there is also a strong cross-sectional relation between average returns and book-to-market equity. If anything, this book-to-market effect is more powerful than the size effect. We also find that the combination of size and book-to-market equity absorbs the apparent roles of leverage and E/P in average stock returns.

A. Average Returns

Table IV shows average returns for July 1963 to December 1990 for portfolios formed on ranked values of book-to-market equity (BE/ME) or earnings-price ratio (E/P). The BE/ME and E/P portfolios in Table IV are formed in the same general way (one-dimensional yearly sorts) as the size and β portfolios in Table II. (See the tables for details.)

The relation between average return and E/P has a familiar U-shape (e.g., Jaffe, Keim, and Westerfield (1989) for U.S. data, and Chan, Hamao, and Lakonishok (1991) for Japan). Average returns decline from 1.46% per month for the negative E/P portfolio to 0.93% for the firms in portfolio 1B that have low but positive E/P. Average returns then increase monotonically, reaching 1.72% per month for the highest E/P portfolio.

The more striking evidence in Table IV is the strong positive relation between average return and book-to-market equity. Average returns rise from 0.30% for the lowest BE/ME portfolio to 1.83% for the highest, a difference of 1.53% per month. This spread is twice as large as the difference of 0.74% between the average monthly returns on the smallest and largest size portfolios in Table II. Note also that the strong relation between book-to-market equity and average return is unlikely to be a β effect in disguise; Table IV shows that post-ranking market βs vary little across portfolios formed on ranked values of BE/ME.

On average, only about 50 (out of 2317) firms per year have negative book equity, BE. The negative BE firms are mostly concentrated in the last 14 years of the sample, 1976–1989, and we do not include them in the tests. We can report, however, that average returns for negative BE firms are high, like the average returns of high BE/ME firms. Negative BE (which results from persistently negative earnings) and high BE/ME (which typically means that stock prices have fallen) are both signals of poor earning prospects. The similar average returns of negative and high BE/ME firms are thus consistent with the hypothesis that book-to-market equity captures cross-sectional variation in average returns that is related to relative distress.

B. Fama-MacBeth Regressions
B.1. BE/ME

The FM regressions in Table III confirm the importance of book-to-market equity in explaining the cross-section of average stock returns. The average slope from the monthly regressions of returns on ln(BE/ME) alone is 0.50%, with a t-statistic of 5.71. This book-to-market relation is stronger than the size effect, which produces a t-statistic of -2.58 in the regressions of returns on ln(ME) alone. But book-to-market equity does not replace size in explaining average returns. When both ln(ME) and ln(BE/ME) are included in the regressions, the average size slope is still -1.99 standard errors from 0; the book-to-market slope is an impressive 4.44 standard errors from 0.

B.2. Leverage

The FM regressions that explain returns with leverage variables provide interesting insight into the relation between book-to-market equity and average return. We use two leverage variables, the ratio of book assets to market equity, A/ME, and the ratio of book assets to book equity, A/BE. We interpret A/ME as a measure of market leverage, while A/BE is a measure of book leverage. The regressions use the natural logs of the leverage ratios, ln(A/ME) and ln(A/BE), because preliminary tests indicated that logs are a good functional form for capturing leverage effects in average returns. Using logs also leads to a simple interpretation of the relation between the roles of leverage and book-to-market equity in average returns.

The FM regressions of returns on the leverage variables (Table III) pose a bit of a puzzle. The two leverage variables are related to average returns, but with opposite signs. As in Bhandari (1988), higher market leverage is associated with higher average returns; the average slopes for ln(A/ME) are always positive and more than 4 standard errors from 0. But higher book leverage is associated with lower average returns; the average slopes for ln(A/BE) are always negative and more than 4 standard errors from 0.

The puzzle of the opposite slopes on ln(A/ME) and ln(A/BE) has a simple solution. The average slopes for the two leverage variables are opposite in sign but close in absolute value, e.g., 0.50 and -0.57. Thus it is the difference between market and book leverage that helps explain average returns. But the difference between market and book leverage is book-to-market equity, ln(BE/ME) = ln(A/ME) − ln(A/BE). Table III shows that the average book-to-market slopes in the FM regressions are indeed close in absolute value to the slopes for the two leverage variables.

TABLE IV. Properties of portfolios formed on book-to-market equity (BE/ME) and earnings-price ratio (E/P): July 1963 to December 1990

At the end of each year $t − 1$, 12 portfolios are formed on the basis of ranked values of BE/ME or E/P. Portfolios 2–9 cover deciles of the ranking variables. The bottom and top 2 portfolios (1A, 1B, 10A, and 10B) split the bottom and top deciles in half. For E/P, there are 13 portfolios; portfolio 0 is stocks with negative E/P. Since BE/ME and E/P are not strongly related to exchange listing, their portfolio breakpoints are determined on the basis of the ranked values of the variables for all stocks that satisfy the CRSP-COMPUSTAT data requirements. BE is the book value of common equity plus balance-sheet deferred taxes, A is total book assets, and E is earnings (income before extraordinary items, plus income-statement deferred taxes, minus preferred dividends). BE, A, and E are for each firm's latest fiscal year ending in calendar year $t − 1$. The accounting ratios are measured using market equity ME in December of year $t − 1$. Firm size $\ln(\text{ME})$ is measured in June of year t, with ME denominated in millions of dollars. We calculate each portfolio's monthly equal-weighted return for July of year t to June of year $t + 1$, and then reform the portfolios at the end of year t.

Return is the time-series average of the monthly equal-weighted portfolio returns (in percent). $\ln(\text{ME})$, $\ln(\text{BE/ME})$, $\ln(\text{A/ME})$, $\ln(\text{A/BE})$, $E(+)/P$, and E/P dummy are the time-series averages of the monthly average values of these variables in each portfolio. Since the E/P dummy is 0 when earnings are positive, and 1 when earnings are negative, E/P dummy gives the average proportion of stocks with negative earnings in each portfolio.

β is the time-series average of the monthly portfolio βs. Stocks are assigned the post-ranking β of the size-β portfolio they are in at the end of June of year t (Table I). These individual-firm βs are averaged to compute the monthly βs for each portfolio for July of year t to June of year $t + 1$.

Firms is the average number of stocks in the portfolio each month.

Portfolio	0	1A	1B	2	3	4	5	6	7	8	9	10A	10B
				Panel A: Stocks Sorted on Book-to-Market Equity (BE/ME)									
Return		0.30	0.67	0.87	0.97	1.04	1.17	1.30	1.44	1.50	1.59	1.92	1.83
β		1.36	1.34	1.32	1.30	1.28	1.27	1.27	1.27	1.27	1.29	1.33	1.35
ln(ME)		4.53	4.67	4.69	4.56	4.47	4.38	4.23	4.06	3.85	3.51	3.06	2.65
ln(BE/ME)		-2.22	-1.51	-1.09	-0.75	-0.51	-0.32	-0.14	0.03	0.21	0.42	0.66	1.02
ln(A/ME)		-1.24	-0.79	-0.40	-0.05	0.20	0.40	0.56	0.71	0.91	1.12	1.35	1.75
ln(A/BE)		0.94	0.71	0.68	0.70	0.71	0.71	0.70	0.68	0.70	0.70	0.70	0.73
E/P dummy		0.29	0.15	0.10	0.08	0.08	0.08	0.09	0.09	0.11	0.15	0.22	0.36
E(+)/P		0.03	0.04	0.06	0.08	0.09	0.10	0.11	0.11	0.12	0.12	0.11	0.10
Firms		89	98	209	222	226	230	235	237	239	239	120	117
				Panel B: Stocks Sorted on Earnings-Price Ratio (E/P)									
Return	1.46	1.04	0.93	0.94	1.03	1.18	1.22	1.33	1.42	1.46	1.57	1.74	1.72
β	1.47	1.40	1.35	1.31	1.28	1.26	1.25	1.26	1.24	1.23	1.24	1.28	1.31
ln(ME)	2.48	3.64	4.33	4.61	4.64	4.63	4.58	4.49	4.37	4.28	4.07	3.82	3.52
ln(BE/ME)	-0.10	-0.76	-0.91	-0.79	-0.61	-0.47	-0.33	-0.21	-0.08	0.02	0.15	0.26	0.40
ln(A/ME)	0.90	-0.05	-0.27	-0.16	0.03	0.18	0.31	0.44	0.58	0.70	0.85	1.01	1.25
ln(A/BE)	0.99	0.70	0.63	0.63	0.64	0.65	0.64	0.65	0.66	0.68	0.71	0.75	0.86
E/P dummy	1.00	0.00	0.00	0.00	0.00	0.00	0.00	0.00	0.00	0.00	0.00	0.00	0.00
E(+)/P	0.00	0.01	0.03	0.05	0.06	0.08	0.09	0.11	0.12	0.14	0.16	0.20	0.28
Firms	355	88	90	182	190	193	196	194	197	195	195	95	91

The close links between the leverage and book-to-market results suggest that there are two equivalent ways to interpret the book-to-market effect in average returns. A high ratio of book equity to market equity (a low stock price relative to book value) says that the market judges the prospects of a firm to be poor relative to firms with low BE/ME. Thus BE/ME may capture the relative-distress effect postulated by Chan and Chen (1991). A high book-to-market ratio also says that a firm's market leverage is high relative to its book leverage; the firm has a large amount of market-imposed leverage because the market judges that its prospects are poor and discounts its stock price relative to book value. In short, our tests suggest that the relative-distress effect, captured by BE/ME, can also be interpreted as an involuntary leverage effect, which is captured by the difference between A/ME and A/BE.

B.3. E/P

Ball (1978) posits that the earnings-price ratio is a catch-all for omitted risk factors in expected returns. If current earnings proxy for expected future earnings, high-risk stocks with high expected returns will have low prices relative to their earnings. Thus, E/P should be related to expected returns, whatever the omitted sources of risk. This argument only makes sense, however, for firms with positive earnings. When current earnings are negative, they are not a proxy for the earnings forecasts embedded in the stock price, and E/P is not a proxy for expected returns. Thus, the slope for E/P in the FM regressions is based on positive values; we use a dummy variable for E/P when earnings are negative.

The U-shaped relation between average return and E/P observed in Table IV is also apparent when the E/P variables are used alone in the FM regressions in Table III. The average slope on the E/P dummy variable (0.57% per month, 2.28 standard errors from 0) confirms that firms with negative earnings have higher average returns. The average slope for stocks with positive E/P (4.72% per month, 4.57 standard errors from 0) shows that average returns increase with E/P when it is positive.

Adding size to the regressions kills the explanatory power of the E/P dummy. Thus the high average returns of negative E/P stocks are better captured by their size, which Table IV says is on average small. Adding both size and book-to-market equity to the E/P regressions kills the E/P dummy and lowers the average slope on E/P from 4.72 to 0.87 ($t = 1.23$). In contrast, the average slopes for ln(ME) and ln(BE/ME) in the regressions that include E/P are similar to those in the regressions that explain average returns with only size and book-to-market equity. The results suggest that most of the relation between (positive) E/P and average return is due to the positive correlation between E/P and ln(BE/ME), illustrated in Table IV; firms with high E/P tend to have high book-to-market equity ratios.

IV. A PARSIMONIOUS MODEL FOR AVERAGE RETURNS

The results to here are easily summarized:

(1) When we allow for variation in β that is unrelated to size, there is no reliable relation between β and average return.

(2) The opposite roles of market leverage and book leverage in average returns are captured well by book-to-market equity.

(3) The relation between E/P and average return seems to be absorbed by the combination of size and book-to-market equity.

In a nutshell, market β seems to have no role in explaining the average returns on NYSE, AMEX, and NASDAQ stocks for 1963–1990, while size and book-to-market equity capture the cross-sectional variation in average stock returns that is related to leverage and E/P.

A. Average Returns, Size and Book-to-Market Equity

The average return matrix in Table V gives a simple picture of the two-dimensional variation in average returns that results when the 10 size deciles are each subdivided into 10 portfolios based on ranked values of BE/ME for individual stocks. Within a size decile (across a row of the average return matrix), returns typically increase strongly with BE/ME: on average, the returns on the lowest and highest BE/ME portfolios in a size decile differ by 0.99% (1.63% − 0.64%) per month. Similarly, looking down the columns of the average return matrix shows that there is a negative relation between average return and size: on average, the spread of returns across the size portfolios in a BE/ME group is 0.58% per month. The average return matrix gives life to the conclusion from the regressions that, controlling for size, book-to-market equity captures strong variation in average returns, and controlling for book-to-market equity leaves a size effect in average returns.

B. The Interaction between Size and Book-to-Market Equity

The average of the monthly correlations between the cross-sections of ln(ME) and ln(BE/ME) for individual stocks is −0.26. The negative correlation is also apparent in the average values of ln(ME) and ln(BE/ME) for the portfolios sorted on ME or BE/ME in Tables II and IV. Thus, firms with low market

TABLE V. Average monthly returns on portfolios formed on size and book-to-market equity; stocks sorted by ME (down) and then BE/ME (across): July 1963 to December 1990

In June of each year t, the NYSE, AMEX, and NASDAQ stocks that meet the CRSP-COMPUSTAT data requirements are allocated to 10 size portfolios using the NYSE size (ME) breakpoints. The NYSE, AMEX, and NASDAQ stocks in each size decile are then sorted into 10 BE/ME portfolios using the book-to-market ratios for year $t-1$. BE/ME is the book value of common equity plus balance-sheet deferred taxes for fiscal year $t-1$, over market equity for December of year $t-1$. The equal-weighted monthly portfolio returns are then calculated for July of year t to June of year $t+1$.

Average monthly return is the time-series average of the monthly equal-weighted portfolio returns (in percent).

The All column shows average returns for equal-weighted size decile portfolios. The All row shows average returns for equal-weighted portfolios of the stocks in each BE/ME group.

Book-to-Market Portfolios

	All	Low	2	3	4	5	6	7	8	9	High
All	1.23	0.64	0.98	1.06	1.17	1.24	1.26	1.39	1.40	1.50	1.63
Small-ME	1.47	0.70	1.14	1.20	1.43	1.56	1.51	1.70	1.71	1.82	1.92
ME-2	1.22	0.43	1.05	0.96	1.19	1.33	1.19	1.58	1.28	1.43	1.79
ME-3	1.22	0.56	0.88	1.23	0.95	1.36	1.30	1.30	1.40	1.54	1.60
ME-4	1.19	0.39	0.72	1.06	1.36	1.13	1.21	1.34	1.59	1.51	1.47
ME-5	1.24	0.88	0.65	1.08	1.47	1.13	1.43	1.44	1.26	1.52	1.49
ME-6	1.15	0.70	0.98	1.14	1.23	0.94	1.27	1.19	1.19	1.24	1.50
ME-7	1.07	0.95	1.00	0.99	0.83	0.99	1.13	0.99	1.16	1.10	1.47
ME-8	1.08	0.66	1.13	0.91	0.95	0.99	1.01	1.15	1.05	1.29	1.55
ME-9	0.95	0.44	0.89	0.92	1.00	1.05	0.93	0.82	1.11	1.04	1.22
Large-ME	0.89	0.93	0.88	0.84	0.71	0.79	0.83	0.81	0.96	0.97	1.18

equity are more likely to have poor prospects, resulting in low stock prices and high book-to-market equity. Conversely, large stocks are more likely to be firms with stronger prospects, higher stock prices, lower book-to-market equity, and lower average stock returns.

The correlation between size and book-to-market equity affects the regressions in Table III. Including ln(BE/ME) moves the average slope on ln(ME) from -0.15 ($t = -2.58$) in the univariate regressions to -0.11 ($t = -1.99$) in the bivariate regressions. Similarly, including ln(ME) in the regressions lowers the average slope on ln(BE/ME) from 0.50 to 0.35 (still a healthy 4.44 standard errors from 0). Thus, part of the size effect in the simple regressions is due to the fact that small ME stocks are more likely to have high book-to-market ratios, and part of the simple book-to-market effect is due to the fact that high BE/ME stocks tend to be small (they have low ME).

We should not, however, exaggerate the links between size and book-to-market equity. The correlation (-0.26) between ln(ME) and ln(BE/ME) is not extreme, and the average slopes in the bivariate regressions in Table III show that ln(ME) and ln(BE/ME) are both needed to explain the cross-section of average returns. Finally, the 10×10 average return matrix in Table V provides concrete evidence that, (a) controlling for size, book-to-market equity captures substantial variation in the cross-section of average returns, and (b) within BE/ME groups average returns are related to size.

C. Subperiod Averages of the FM Slopes

The message from the average FM slopes for 1963–1990 (Table III) is that size on average has a negative premium in the cross-section of stock returns, book-to-market equity has a positive premium, and the average premium for market β is essentially 0. Table VI shows the average FM slopes for two roughly equal subperiods (July 1963–December 1976 and January 1977–December 1990) from two regressions: (a) the cross-section of stock returns on size, ln(ME), and book-to-market equity, ln(BE/ME), and (b) returns on β, ln(ME), and ln(BE/ME). For perspective, average returns on the value-weighted and equal-weighted (VW and EW) portfolios of NYSE stocks are also shown.

In FM regressions, the intercept is the return on a standard portfolio (the weights on stocks sum to 1) in which the weighted averages of the explanatory variables are 0 (Fama (1976), chapter 9). In our tests, the intercept is weighted toward small stocks (ME is in millions of dollars so ln(ME) = 0 implies ME = \$1 million) and toward stocks with relatively high book-to-market ratios (Table IV says that ln(BE/ME) is negative for the typical firm, so ln(BE/ME) = 0 is toward the high end of the sample ratios). Thus it is not surprising that the average intercepts are always large relative to their standard errors and relative to the returns on the NYSE VW and EW portfolios.

Like the overall period, the subperiods do not offer much hope that the average premium for β is economically important. The average FM slope for β is only slightly positive for 1963–1976 (0.10% per month, $t = 0.25$), and it is negative for 1977–1990 (-0.44% per month, $t = -1.17$). There is a hint that the size effect is weaker in the 1977–1990 period, but inferences about the average size slopes for the subperiods lack power.

Unlike the size effect, the relation between book-to-market equity and average return is so strong that it shows up reliably in both the 1963–1976 and the 1977–1990 subperiods. The average slopes for ln(BE/ME) are all more than 2.95 standard errors from 0, and the average slopes for the subperiods (0.36 and 0.35) are close to the average slope (0.35) for the overall period. The subperiod results thus support the conclusion that, among the variables considered here, book-to-market equity is consistently the most powerful for explaining the cross-section of average stock returns.

Finally, Roll (1983) and Keim (1983) show that the size effect is stronger in January. We have examined the monthly slopes from the FM regressions in Table VI for evidence of a January seasonal in the relation between book-to-market equity and average return. The average January slopes for ln(BE/ME) are about twice those for February to December. Unlike the size effect, however, the strong relation between book-to-market equity and average return is

TABLE VI. Subperiod average monthly returns on the NYSE equal-weighted and value-weighted portfolios and subperiod means of the intercepts and slopes from the monthly FM cross-sectional regressions of returns on (a) size (ln(ME)) and book-to-market equity (ln(BE/ME)), and (b) β, ln(ME), and ln(BE/ME)

Mean is the time-series mean of a monthly return, Std is its time-series standard deviation, and t(Mn) is Mean divided by its time-series standard error.

	7/63–12/90 (330 Mos.)			7/63–12/76 (162 Mos.)			1/77–12/90 (168 Mos.)		
Variable	Mean	Std	t(Mn)	Mean	Std	t(Mn)	Mean	Std	t(Mn)
NYSE Value-Weighted (VW) and Equal-Weighted (EW) Portfolio Returns									
VW	0.81	4.47	3.27	0.56	4.26	1.67	1.04	4.66	2.89
EW	0.97	5.49	3.19	0.77	5.70	1.72	1.15	5.28	2.82
$R_{it} = a + b_2 ln(ME_{it}) + b_3 ln(BE/ME_{it}) + e_{it}$									
a	1.77	8.51	3.77	1.86	10.10	2.33	1.69	6.67	3.27
b_2	−0.11	1.02	−1.99	−0.16	1.25	−1.62	−0.07	0.73	−1.16
b_3	0.35	1.45	4.43	0.36	1.53	2.96	0.35	1.37	3.30
$R_{it} = a + b_1 \beta_{it} + b_{2t} ln(ME_{it}) + b_3 ln(BE/ME_{it}) + e_{it}$									
a	2.07	5.75	6.55	1.73	6.22	3.54	2.40	5.25	5.92
b_1	−0.17	5.12	−0.62	0.10	5.33	0.25	−0.44	4.91	−1.17
b_2	−0.12	0.89	−2.52	−0.15	1.03	−1.91	−0.09	0.74	−1.64
b_3	0.33	1.24	4.80	0.34	1.36	3.17	0.31	1.10	3.67

not special to January. The average monthly February-to-December slopes for ln(BE/ME) are about 4 standard errors from 0, and they are close to (within 0.05 of) the average slopes for the whole year. Thus, there is a January seasonal in the book-to-market equity effect, but the positive relation between BE/ME and average return is strong throughout the year.

D. β and the Market Factor: Caveats

Some caveats about the negative evidence on the role of β in average returns are in order. The average premiums for β, size, and book-to-market equity depend on the definitions of the variables used in the regressions. For example, suppose we replace book-to-market equity (ln(BE/ME)) with book equity (ln(BE)). As long as size (ln(ME)) is also in the regression, this change will not affect the intercept, the fitted values or the R^2. But the change, in variables increases the average slope (and the t-statistic) on ln(ME). In other words, it increases the risk premium associated with size. Other redefinitions of the β, size, and book-to-market variables will produce different regression slopes and perhaps different inferences about average premiums, including possible resuscitation of a role for β. And, of course, at the moment, we have no theoretical basis for choosing among different versions of the variables.

Moreover, the tests here are restricted to stocks. It is possible that including other assets will change the inferences about the average premiums for β, size, and book-to-market equity. For example, the large average intercepts for the FM regressions in Table VI suggest that the regressions will not do a good job on Treasury bills, which have low average returns and are likely to have small loadings on the underlying market, size, and book-to-market factors in returns. Extending the tests to bills and other bonds may well change our inferences about average risk premiums, including the revival of a role for market β.

We emphasize, however, that different approaches to the tests are not likely to revive the Sharpe-Lintner-Black model. Resuscitation of the SLB model requires that a better proxy for the market portfolio (a) overturns our evidence that the simple relation between β and average stock returns is flat and (b) leaves β as the only variable relevant for explaining average returns. Such results seem unlikely, given Stambaugh's (1982) evidence that tests of the SLB model do not seem to be sensitive to the choice of a market proxy. Thus, if there is a role for β in average returns, it is likely to be found in a multi-factor model that transforms the flat simple relation between average return and β into a positively sloped conditional relation.

V. CONCLUSIONS AND IMPLICATIONS

The Sharpe-Lintner-Black model has long shaped the way academics and prac-titioners think about average return and risk. Black, Jensen, and Scholes (1972) and Fama and MacBeth (1973) find that, as predicted by the model, there is a positive simple relation between average return and market β during the early years (1926–1968) of the CRSP NYSE returns file. Like Reinganum (1981) and Lakonishok and Shapiro (1986), we find that this simple relation between β and average return disappears during the more recent 1963–1990 period. The appendix that follows shows that the relation between β and average return is also weak in the last half century (1941–1990) of returns on NYSE stocks. In short, our tests do not support the central prediction of the SLB model, that average stock returns are positively related to market β.

Banz (1981) documents a strong negative relation between average return and firm size. Bhandari (1988) finds that average return is positively related to leverage, and Basu (1983) finds a positive relation between average return and E/P. Stattman (1980) and Rosenberg, Reid, and Lanstein (1985) document a positive relation between average return and book-to-market equity for U.S. stocks, and Chan, Hamao, and Lakonishok (1992) find that BE/ME is also a powerful variable for explaining average returns on Japanese stocks.

Variables like size, E/P, leverage, and book-to-market equity are all scaled versions of a firm's stock price. They can be regarded as different ways of ex-tracting information from stock prices about the cross-section of expected stock returns (Ball (1978); Keim (1988)). Since all these variables are scaled versions of price, it is reasonable to expect that some of them are redundant for explaining average returns. Our main result is that for the 1963–1990 period, size and book-to-market equity capture the cross-sectional variation in average stock returns associated with size, E/P, book-to-market equity, and leverage.

A. Rational Asset-Pricing Stories

Are our results consistent with asset-pricing theory? Since the FM intercept is constrained to be the same for all stocks, FM regressions always impose a linear factor structure on returns and expected returns that is consistent with the multifactor asset-pricing models of Merton (1973) and Ross (1976). Thus our tests impose a rational asset-pricing framework on the relation between average return and size and book-to-market equity.

Even if our results are consistent with asset-pricing theory, they are not ec-onomically satisfying. What is the economic explanation for the roles of size and book-to-market equity in average returns? We suggest several paths of inquiry.

(a) The intercepts and slopes in the monthly FM regressions of returns on ln(ME) and ln(BE/ME) are returns on portfolios that mimic the underlying common risk factors in returns proxied by size and book-to-market equity (Fama (1976), chapter 9). Examining the relations between the returns on these portfolios and economic variables that measure variation in business conditions might help expose the nature of the economic risks captured by size and book-to-market equity.

(b) Chan, Chen, and Hsieh (1985) argue that the relation between size and average return proxies for a more fundamental relation between expected returns and economic risk factors. Their most powerful factor in explaining the size effect is the difference between the monthly returns on low- and high-grade corporate bonds, which in principle captures a kind of default risk in returns that is priced. It would be interesting to test whether loadings on this or other economic factors, such as those of Chen, Roll, and Ross (1986), can explain the roles of size and book-to-market equity in our tests.

(c) In a similar vein, Chan and Chen (1991) argue that the relation between size and average return is a relative-prospects effect. The earning prospects of distressed firms are more sensitive to economic conditions. This results in a distress factor in returns that is priced in expected returns. Chan and Chen construct two mimicking portfolios for the distress factor, based on dividend changes and leverage. It would be interesting to check whether loadings on their distress factors absorb the size and book-to-market equity effects in average returns that are documented here.

(d) In fact, if stock prices are rational, BE/ME, the ratio of the book value of a stock to the market's assessment of its value, should be a direct indicator of the relative prospects of firms. For example, we expect that high BE/ME firms have low earnings on assets relative to low BE/ME firms. Our work (in progress) suggests that there is indeed a clean separation between high and low BE/ME firms on various measures of economic fundamentals. Low BE/ME firms are persistently strong performers, while the economic performance of high BE/ME firms is persistently weak.

[375]

B. Irrational Asset-Pricing Stories

The discussion above assumes that the asset-pricing effects captured by size and book-to-market equity are rational. For BE/ME, our most powerful expected-return variable, there is an obvious alternative. The cross-section of book-to-market ratios might result from market overreaction to the relative prospects of firms. If overreaction tends to be corrected, BE/ME will predict the cross-section of stock returns.

Simple tests do not confirm that the size and book-to-market effects in average returns are due to market overreaction, at least of the type posited by DeBondt and Thaler (1985). One overreaction measure used by DeBondt and Thaler is a stock's most recent 3-year return. Their overreaction story predicts that 3-year losers have strong post-ranking returns relative to 3-year winners. In FM regressions (not shown) for individual stocks, the 3-year lagged return shows no power even when used alone to explain average returns. The univariate average slope for the lagged return is negative, -6 basis points per month, but less than 0.5 standard errors from 0.

C. Applications

Our main result is that two easily measured variables, size and book-to-market equity, seem to describe the cross-section of average stock returns. Prescriptions for using this evidence depend on (a) whether it will persist, and (b) whether it results from rational or irrational asset-pricing.

It is possible that, by chance, size and book-to-market equity happen to describe the cross-section of average returns in our sample, but they were and are unrelated to expected returns. We put little weight on this possibility, especially for book-to-market equity. First, although BE/ME has long been touted as a measure of the return prospects of stocks, there is no evidence that its explanatory power deteriorates through time. The 1963–1990 relation between BE/ME and average return is strong, and remarkably similar for the 1963–1976 and 1977–1990 subperiods. Second, our preliminary work on economic fundamentals suggests that high-BE/ME firms tend to be persistently poor earners relative to low-BE/ME firms. Similarly, small firms have a long period of poor earnings during the 1980s not shared with big firms. The systematic patterns in fundamentals give us some hope that size and book-to-market equity proxy for risk factors in returns, related to relative earning prospects, that are rationally priced in expected returns.

If our results are more than chance, they have practical implications for portfolio formation and performance evaluation by investors whose primary concern is long-term average returns. If asset-pricing is rational, size and BE/ME must proxy for risk. Our results then imply that the performance of managed portfolios (e.g., pension funds and mutual funds) can be evaluated by comparing their average returns with the average returns of benchmark portfolios with similar size and BE/ME characteristics. Likewise, the expected returns for different portfolio strategies can be estimated from the historical average returns of portfolios with matching size and BE/ME properties.

If asset-pricing is irrational and size and BE/ME do not proxy for risk, our results might still be used to evaluate portfolio performance and measure the expected returns from alternative investment strategies. If stock prices are irrational, however, the likely persistence of the results is more suspect.

APPENDIX

Size versus β: 1941–1990

Our results on the absence of a relation between β and average stock returns for 1963–1990 are so contrary to the tests of the Sharpe-Lintner-Black model by Black, Jensen, and Scholes (1972), Fama and MacBeth (1973), and (more recently) Chan and Chen (1988), that further tests are appropriate. We examine the roles of size and β in the average returns on NYSE stocks for the half-century 1941–1990, the longest available period that avoids the high volatility of returns in the Great Depression. We do not include the accounting variables in the tests because of the strong selection bias (toward successful firms) in the COMPUSTAT data prior to 1962.

We first replicate the results of Chan and Chen (1988). Like them, we find that when portfolios are formed on size alone, there are strong relations between average return and either size or β; average return increases with β and decreases with size. For size portfolios, however, size (ln(ME)) and β are almost perfectly correlated (-0.98), so it is difficult to distinguish between the roles of size and β in average returns.

One way to generate strong variation in β that is unrelated to size is to form portfolios on size and then on β. As in Tables I to III, we find that the resulting independent variation in β just about washes out the positive simple relation between average return and β observed when portfolios are formed on size alone. The results for NYSE stocks for 1941–1990 are thus much like those for NYSE, AMEX, and NASDAQ stocks for 1963–1990.

This appendix also has methodological goals. For example, the FM regressions in Table III use returns on individual stocks as the dependent variable. Since we allocate portfolio βs to individual stocks but use firm-specific values of other variables like size, β may be at a disadvantage in the regressions for individual stocks. This appendix shows, however, that regressions for portfolios, which put β and size on equal footing, produce results comparable to those for individual stocks.

A. Size Portfolios

Table AI shows average monthly returns and market βs for 12 portfolios of NYSE stocks formed on the basis of size (ME) at the end of each year from 1940 to 1989. For these size portfolios, there is a strong positive relation between average return and β. Average returns fall from 1.96% per month for the smallest ME portfolio (1A) to 0.93% for the largest (10B) and β falls from 1.60 to 0.95. (Note also that, as claimed earlier, estimating β as the sum of the slopes in the regression of a portfolio's return on the current and prior month's NYSE value-weighted return produces much larger βs for the smallest ME portfolios and slightly smaller βs for the largest ME portfolios.)

The FM regressions in Table AI confirm the positive simple relation between average return and β for size portfolios. In the regressions of the size-portfolio returns on β alone, the average premium for a unit of β is 1.45% per month. In the regressions of individual stock returns on β (where stocks are assigned the β of their size portfolio), the premium for a unit of β is 1.39%. Both estimates are about 3 standard errors from 0. Moreover, the βs of size portfolios do not leave a residual size effect; the average residuals from the simple regressions of returns on β in Table AI show no relation to size. These positive SLB results for 1941–1990 are like those obtained by Chan and Chen (1988) in tests on size portfolios for 1954–1983.

There is, however, evidence in Table AI that all is not well with the βs of the size portfolios. They do a fine job on the relation between size and average return, but they do a lousy job on their main task, the relation between β and average return. When the residuals from the regressions of returns on β are grouped using the pre-ranking βs of individual stocks, the average residuals are strongly positive for low-β stocks (0.51% per month for group 1A) and negative for high-β stocks (-1.05% for 10B). Thus the market lines estimated with size-portfolio βs exaggerate the tradeoff of average return for β; they underestimate average returns on low-β stocks and overestimate average returns on high-β stocks. This pattern in the β-sorted average residuals for individual stocks suggests that (a) there is variation in β across stocks that is lost in the size portfolios, and (b) this variation in β is not rewarded as well as the variation in β that is related to size.

[378]

B. Two-Pass Size-β Portfolios

Like Table I, Table AII shows that subdividing size deciles using the (pre-ranking) βs of individual stocks results in strong variation in β that is independent of size. The β sort of a size decile always produces portfolios with similar average ln(ME) but much different (post-ranking) βs. Table AII also shows, however, that investors are not compensated for the variation in β that is independent of size. Despite the wide range of βs in each size decile, average returns show no tendency to increase with β. AII

The FM regressions in Table AIII formalize the roles of size and β in NYSE average returns for 1941–1990. The regressions of returns on β alone show that using the βs of the portfolios formed on size and β, rather than size alone, causes the average slope on β to fall from about 1.4% per month (Table AI) to about 0.23% (about 1 standard error from 0). Thus, allowing for variation in β that is unrelated to size flattens the relation between average return and β, to the point where it is indistinguishable from no relation at all.

The flatter market lines in Table AIII succeed, however, in erasing the negative relation between β and average residuals observed in the regressions of returns on β alone in Table AI. Thus, forming portfolios on size and β (Table AIII) produces a better description of the simple relation between average return and β than forming portfolios on size alone (Table AI). This improved description of the relation between average return and β is evidence that the β estimates for the two-pass size-β portfolios capture variation in true βs that is missed when portfolios are formed on size alone.

Unfortunately, the flatter market lines in Table AIII have a cost, the emergence of a residual size effect. Grouped on the basis of ME for individual stocks, the average residuals from the univariate regressions of returns on the βs of the 100 size-β portfolios are strongly positive for small stocks and negative for large stocks (0.60% per month for the smallest ME group, 1A, and -0.27% for the largest, 10B). Thus, when we allow for variation in β that is independent of size, the resulting βs leave a large size effect in average returns. This residual size effect is much like that observed by Banz (1981) with the βs of portfolios formed on size and β.

The correlation between size and β is -0.98 for portfolios formed on size alone. The independent variation in β obtained with the second-pass sort on β lowers the correlation to -0.50. The lower correlation means that bivariate regressions of returns on β and ln(ME) are more likely to distinguish true size effects from true β effects in average returns.

The bivariate regressions (Table AIII) that use the βs of the size-β portfolios

TABLE A1. Average returns, post-ranking βs and Fama-MacBeth regression slopes for size portfolios of NYSE stocks: 1941–1990

At the end of each year $t - 1$, stocks are assigned to 12 portfolios using ranked values of ME. Included are all NYSE stocks that have a CRSP price and shares for December of year $t - 1$ and returns for at least 24 of the 60 months ending in December of year $t - 1$ (for pre-ranking β estimates). The middle 8 portfolios cover size deciles 2 to 9. The 4 extreme portfolios (1A, 1B, 10A, and 10B) split the smallest and largest deciles in half. We compute equal-weighted returns on the portfolios for the 12 months of year t using all surviving stocks. Average Return is the time-series average of the monthly portfolio returns for 1941–1990, in percent. Average firms is the average number of stocks in the portfolios each month. The simple βs are estimated by regressing the 1941–1990 sample of post-ranking monthly returns for a size portfolio on the current month's value-weighted NYSE portfolio return. The sum βs are the sum of the slopes from a regression of the post-ranking monthly returns on the current and prior month's VW NYSE returns.

The independent variables in the Fama-MacBeth regressions are defined for each firm at the end of December of each year $t - 1$. Stocks are assigned the post-ranking (sum) β of the size portfolio they are in at the end of year $t - 1$. ME is price times shares outstanding at the end of year $t - 1$. In the individual-stock regressions, these values of the explanatory variables are matched with CRSP returns for each of the 12 months of year t. The portfolio regressions match the equal-weighted portfolio returns with the equal-weighted averages of β and ln(ME) for the surviving stocks in each month of year t. Slope is the average of the (600) monthly FM regression slopes and SE is the standard error of the average slope. The residuals from the monthly regressions for year t are grouped into 12 portfolios on the basis of size (ME) or pre-ranking β (estimated with 24 to 60 months of data, as available) at the end of year $t - 1$. The average residuals are the time-series averages of the monthly equal-weighted portfolio residuals, in percent. The average residuals for regressions (1) and (2) (not shown) are quite similar to those for regressions (4) and (5) (shown).

Portfolios Formed on Size

	1A	1B	2	3	4	5	6	7	8	9	10A	10B
Ave. return	1.96	1.59	1.44	1.36	1.28	1.24	1.23	1.17	1.15	1.13	0.97	0.93
Ave. firms	57	56	110	107	107	108	111	113	115	118	59	59
Simple β	1.29	1.24	1.21	1.19	1.16	1.13	1.13	1.12	1.09	1.05	1.00	0.98
Standard error	0.07	0.05	0.04	0.03	0.02	0.02	0.02	0.02	0.01	0.01	0.01	0.01
Sum β	1.60	1.44	1.37	1.32	1.26	1.23	1.19	1.17	1.12	1.06	0.99	0.95
Standard error	0.10	0.06	0.05	0.04	0.03	0.03	0.03	0.02	0.02	0.01	0.01	0.01

Portfolio Regressions — Individual Stock Regressions

	(1) β	(2) ln(ME)	(3) β and ln(ME)		(4) β	(5) ln(ME)	(6) β and ln(ME)	
Slope	1.45	-0.137	3.05	0.149	1.39	-0.133	0.71	-0.060
SE	0.47	0.044	1.51	0.115	0.46	0.043	0.81	0.062

Average Residuals for Stocks Grouped on Size

	1A	1B	2	3	4	5	6	7	8	9	10A	10B
Regression (4)	0.17	0.00	-0.04	-0.06	-0.05	-0.04	0.00	-0.03	0.03	0.08	0.01	0.04
Standard error	0.11	0.06	0.04	0.04	0.04	0.04	0.03	0.03	0.03	0.03	0.05	0.06
Regression (5)	0.30	0.02	-0.05	-0.06	-0.08	-0.07	-0.03	-0.04	0.02	0.08	0.01	0.13
Standard error	0.14	0.07	0.04	0.04	0.04	0.04	0.04	0.03	0.03	0.03	0.04	0.07
Regression (6)	0.20	0.02	-0.05	-0.07	-0.08	-0.06	-0.01	-0.02	0.04	0.09	0.00	0.06
Standard error	0.10	0.06	0.04	0.04	0.04	0.04	0.03	0.03	0.03	0.03	0.05	0.05

Average Residuals for Stocks Grouped on Pre-Ranking β

	1A	1B	2	3	4	5	6	7	8	9	10A	10B
Regression (4)	0.51	0.61	0.38	0.32	0.16	0.12	0.03	-0.10	-0.27	-0.31	-0.66	-1.05
Standard error	0.21	0.19	0.13	0.08	0.04	0.03	0.04	0.05	0.09	0.11	0.18	0.23
Regression (5)	-0.10	0.00	0.02	0.09	0.05	0.07	0.05	0.00	-0.03	-0.01	-0.11	-0.33
Standard error	0.11	0.10	0.07	0.05	0.04	0.03	0.03	0.04	0.05	0.07	0.10	0.13
Regression (6)	0.09	0.25	0.13	0.19	0.11	0.14	0.09	0.01	-0.11	-0.12	-0.38	-0.70
Standard error	0.41	0.37	0.24	0.14	0.07	0.04	0.04	0.09	0.16	0.21	0.34	0.43

TABLE AIII. Properties of portfolios formed on size and pre-ranking β: NYSE stocks sorted by ME (down) then pre-ranking β (across): 1941–1990

At the end of year $t-1$, the NYSE stocks on CRSP are assigned to 10 size (ME) portfolios. Each size decile is subdivided into 10 β portfolios using pre-ranking βs of individual stocks, estimated with 24 to 60 monthly returns (as available) ending in December of year $t-1$. The equal-weighted monthly returns on the resulting 100 portfolios are then calculated for year t. The average returns are the time-series averages of the monthly returns, in percent. The post-ranking βs use the full 1941–1990 sample of post-ranking returns for each portfolio. The pre- and post-ranking βs are the sum of the slopes from a regression of monthly returns on the current and prior month's NYSE value-weighted market return. The average size for a portfolio is the time-series average of each month's average value of ln(ME) for stocks in the portfolio. ME is denominated in millions of dollars. There are, on average, about 10 stocks in each size-β portfolio each month. The All column shows parameter values for equal-weighted size-decile (ME) portfolios. The All rows show parameter values for equal-weighted portfolios of the stocks in each β group.

	All	Low-β	β-2	β-3	β-4	β-5	β-6	β-7	β-8	β-9	High-β
					Panel A: Average Monthly Return (in Percent)						
All		1.22	1.30	1.32	1.35	1.36	1.34	1.29	1.34	1.14	1.10
Small-ME	1.78	1.74	1.76	2.08	1.91	1.92	1.72	1.77	1.91	1.56	1.46
ME-2	1.44	1.41	1.35	1.33	1.61	1.72	1.59	1.40	1.62	1.24	1.11
ME-3	1.36	1.21	1.40	1.22	1.47	1.34	1.51	1.33	1.57	1.33	1.21
ME-4	1.28	1.26	1.29	1.19	1.27	1.51	1.30	1.19	1.56	1.18	1.00
ME-5	1.24	1.22	1.30	1.28	1.33	1.21	1.37	1.41	1.31	0.92	1.06
ME-6	1.23	1.21	1.32	1.37	1.09	1.34	1.10	1.40	1.21	1.22	1.08
ME-7	1.17	1.08	1.23	1.37	1.27	1.19	1.34	1.10	1.11	0.87	1.17
ME-8	1.15	1.06	1.18	1.26	1.25	1.26	1.17	1.16	1.05	1.08	1.04
ME-9	1.13	0.99	1.13	1.00	1.24	1.28	1.31	1.15	1.11	1.09	1.05
Large-ME	0.95	0.99	1.01	1.12	1.01	0.89	0.95	0.95	1.00	0.90	0.68

Panel B: Post-Ranking β

	All										
All		0.76	0.95	1.05	1.14	1.22	1.26	1.34	1.38	1.49	1.69
Small-ME	1.52	1.17	1.40	1.31	1.50	1.46	1.50	1.69	1.60	1.75	1.92
ME-2	1.37	0.86	1.09	1.12	1.24	1.39	1.42	1.48	1.60	1.69	1.91
ME-3	1.32	0.88	0.96	1.18	1.19	1.33	1.40	1.43	1.56	1.64	1.74
ME-4	1.26	0.69	0.95	1.06	1.15	1.24	1.29	1.46	1.43	1.64	1.83
ME-5	1.23	0.70	0.95	1.04	1.10	1.22	1.32	1.34	1.41	1.56	1.72
ME-6	1.19	0.68	0.86	1.04	1.13	1.20	1.20	1.35	1.36	1.48	1.70
ME-7	1.17	0.67	0.88	0.95	1.14	1.18	1.26	1.27	1.32	1.44	1.68
ME-8	1.12	0.64	0.83	0.99	1.06	1.14	1.14	1.21	1.26	1.39	1.58
ME-9	1.06	0.68	0.81	0.94	0.96	1.06	1.11	1.18	1.22	1.25	1.46
Large-ME	0.97	0.65	0.73	0.90	0.91	0.97	1.01	1.01	1.07	1.12	1.38

Panel C: Average Size (ln(ME))

	All										
All		4.39	4.39	4.40	4.40	4.39	4.40	4.38	4.37	4.37	4.34
Small-ME	1.93	2.04	1.99	2.00	1.96	1.92	1.92	1.91	1.90	1.87	1.80
ME-2	2.80	2.81	2.79	2.81	2.83	2.80	2.79	2.80	2.80	2.79	2.79
ME-3	3.27	3.28	3.27	3.28	3.27	3.27	3.28	3.29	3.27	3.27	3.26
ME-4	3.67	3.67	3.67	3.67	3.68	3.68	3.67	3.68	3.66	3.67	3.67
ME-5	4.06	4.07	4.06	4.05	4.06	4.07	4.06	4.05	4.05	4.06	4.06
ME-6	4.45	4.45	4.44	4.46	4.45	4.45	4.45	4.46	4.44	4.46	4.45
ME-7	4.87	4.86	4.87	4.86	4.87	4.87	4.88	4.87	4.87	4.85	4.87
ME-8	5.36	5.38	5.38	5.38	5.35	5.36	5.37	5.37	5.36	5.35	5.34
ME-9	5.98	5.96	5.98	5.99	6.00	5.98	5.98	5.97	5.95	5.96	5.96
Large-ME	7.12	7.10	7.12	7.16	7.17	7.20	7.29	7.14	7.09	7.04	6.83

are more bad news for β. The average slopes for ln(ME) are close to the values in the univariate size regressions, and almost 4 standard errors from 0, but the average slopes for β are negative and less than 1 standard error from 0. The message from the bivariate regressions is that there is a strong relation between size and average return. But like the regressions in Table AIII that explain average returns with β alone, the bivariate regressions say that there is no reliable relation between β and average returns when the tests use βs that are not close substitutes for size. These uncomfortable SLB results for NYSE stocks for 1941–1990 are much like those for NYSE, AMEX, and NASDAQ stocks for 1963–1990 in Table III.

C. Subperiod Diagnostics

Our results for 1941–1990 seem to contradict the evidence in Black, Jensen, and Scholes (BJS) (1972) and Fama and MacBeth (FM) (1973) that there is a reliable positive relation between average return and β. The βs in BJS and FM are from portfolios formed on β alone, and the market proxy is the NYSE equal-weighted portfolio. We use the βs of portfolios formed on size and β, and our market is the value-weighted NYSE portfolio. We can report, however, that our inference that there isn't much relation between β and average return is unchanged when (a) the market proxy is the NYSE EW portfolio, (b) portfolios are formed on just (pre-ranking) βs, or (c) the order of forming the size-β portfolios is changed from size then β to β then size.

A more important difference between our results and the earlier studies is the sample periods. The tests in BJS and FM end in the 1960s. Table AIV shows that when we split the 50-year 1941–1990 period in half, the univariate FM regressions of returns on β produce an average slope for 1941–1965 (0.50% per month, $t = 1.82$) more like that of the earlier studies. In contrast, the average slope on β for 1966–1990 is close to 0 (-0.02, $t = 0.06$).

But Table AIV also shows that drawing a distinction between the results for 1941–1965 and 1966–1990 is misleading. The stronger tradeoff of average return for β in the simple regressions for 1941–1965 is due to the first 10 years, 1941–1950. This is the only period in Table AIV that produces an average premium for β (1.26% per month) that is both positive and more than 2 standard errors from 0. Conversely, the weak relation between β and average return for 1966–1990 is largely due to 1981–1990. The strong negative average slope in the univariate regressions of returns on β for 1981–1990 (-1.01, $t = -2.10$) offsets a positive slope for 1971–1980 (0.82, $t = 1.27$).

The subperiod variation in the average slopes from the FM regressions of returns on β alone seems moot, however, given the evidence in Table AIV that adding size always kills any positive tradeoff of average return for β in the subperiods. Adding size to the regressions for 1941–1965 causes the average slope for β to drop from 0.50 ($t = 1.82$) to 0.07 ($t = 0.28$). In contrast, the average slope on size in the bivariate regressions (-0.16, $t = -2.97$) is close to its value (-0.17, $t = -2.88$) in the regressions of returns on ln(ME) alone. Similar comments hold for 1941–1950. In short, any evidence of a positive average premium for β in the subperiods seems to be a size effect in disguise.

D. Can the SLB Model Be Saved?

Before concluding that β has no explanatory power, it is appropriate to consider other explanations for our results. One possibility is that the variation in β produced by the β sorts of size deciles in just sampling error. If so, it is not surprising that the variation in β within a size decile is unrelated to average return, or that size dominates β in bivariate tests. The standard errors of the βs suggest, however, that this explanation cannot save the SLB model. The standard errors for portfolios formed on size and β are only slightly larger (0.02 to 0.11) than those for portfolios formed on size alone (0.01 to 0.10, Table AI). And the range of the post-ranking βs within a size decile is always large relative to the standard errors of the βs.

Another possibility is that the proportionality condition (1) for the variation through time in true βs, that justifies the use of full-period post-ranking βs in the FM tests, does not work well for portfolios formed on size and β. If this is a problem, post-ranking βs for the size-β portfolios should not be highly correlated across subperiods. The correlation between the half-period (1941–1965 and 1966–1990) βs of the size-β portfolios is 0.91, which we take to be good evidence that the full-period β estimates for these portfolios are informative about true βs. We can also report that using 5-year βs (pre- or post-ranking) in the FM regressions does not change our negative conclusions about the role of β in average returns, as long as portfolios are formed on β as well as size, or on β alone.

Any attempt to salvage the simple positive relation between β and average return predicted by the SLB model runs into three damaging facts, clear in Table AII. (a) Forming portfolios on size and pre-ranking βs produces a wide range of post-ranking βs in every size decile. (b) The post-ranking βs closely reproduce (in deciles 2 to 10 they exactly reproduce) the ordering of the

TABLE AIII. Average slopes, their standard errors (SE), and average residuals from monthly FM regressions for individual NYSE stocks and for portfolios formed on size and pre-ranking β: 1941–1990

Stocks are assigned the post-ranking β of the size-β portfolio they are in at the end of year $t-1$ (Table AII). ln(ME) is the natural log of price times shares outstanding at the end of year $t-1$. In the individual-stock regressions, these values of the explanatory variables are matched with CRSP returns for each of the 12 months in year t. The portfolio regressions match the equal-weighted portfolio returns for the size-β portfolios (Table AII) with the equal-weighted averages of β and ln(ME) for the surviving stocks in each month of year t. Slope is the time-series average of the monthly regression slopes from 1941–1990 (600 months); SE is the time-series standard error of the average slope.

The residuals from the monthly regressions in year t are grouped into 12 portfolios on the basis of size or pre-ranking β (estimated with 24 to 60 months of returns, as available) as of the end of year $t-1$. The average residuals are the time-series averages of the monthly equal-weighted averages of the residuals in percent. The average residuals (not shown) from the FM regressions (1) to (3) that use the returns on the 100 size-β portfolios as the dependent variable are always within 0.01 of those from the regressions for individual stock returns. This is not surprising given that the correlation between the time-series of 1941–1990 monthly FM slopes on β or ln(ME) for the comparable portfolio and individual stock regressions is always greater than 0.99.

	Portfolio Regressions				Individual Stock Regressions			
	(1) β	(2) ln(ME)	(3) β and ln(ME)		(4) β	(5) ln(ME)	(6) β and ln(ME)	
Slope	0.22	-0.128	-0.13	-0.143	0.24	-0.133	-0.14	-0.147
SE	0.24	0.043	0.21	0.039	0.23	0.043	0.21	0.039

Average Residuals for Stocks Grouped on Size

	1A	1B	2	3	4	5	6	7	8	9	10A	10B
Regression (4)	0.60	0.26	0.13	0.06	-0.01	-0.03	-0.03	-0.09	-0.10	-0.11	-0.25	-0.27
Standard error	0.21	0.10	0.06	0.04	0.04	0.04	0.04	0.04	0.04	0.05	0.06	0.08
Regression (5)	0.30	0.02	-0.05	-0.06	-0.08	-0.07	-0.03	-0.04	0.02	0.08	0.01	0.13
Standard error	0.14	0.07	0.04	0.04	0.04	0.04	0.04	0.03	0.03	0.03	0.04	0.07
Regression (6)	0.31	0.02	-0.05	-0.06	-0.09	-0.07	-0.03	-0.04	0.02	0.08	0.01	0.13
Standard error	0.14	0.07	0.04	0.04	0.04	0.04	0.04	0.03	0.03	0.03	0.04	0.07

Average Residuals for Stocks Grouped on Pre-Ranking β

	1A	1B	2	3	4	5	6	7	8	9	10A	10B
Regression (4)	-0.08	0.03	-0.01	0.08	0.04	0.08	0.04	0.02	-0.03	0.02	-0.11	-0.32
Standard error	0.07	0.05	0.03	0.03	0.03	0.03	0.04	0.04	0.04	0.04	0.06	0.07
Regression (5)	-0.10	0.00	0.02	0.09	0.05	0.07	0.05	0.00	-0.03	-0.01	-0.11	-0.33
Standard error	0.11	0.10	0.07	0.05	0.04	0.03	0.03	0.04	0.05	0.07	0.10	0.13
Regression (6)	-0.17	-0.07	-0.02	0.07	0.04	0.06	0.05	0.03	0.00	0.04	-0.04	-0.23
Standard error	0.05	0.04	0.03	0.03	0.03	0.03	0.03	0.03	0.04	0.04	0.06	0.07

TABLE AIV. Subperiod average returns on the NYSE value-weighted and equal-weighted portfolios and average values of the intercepts and slopes for the FM cross-sectional regressions of individual stock returns on β and size (ln(ME))

Mean is the average VW or EW return or an average slope from the monthly cross-sectional regressions of individual stock returns on β and/or ln(ME). Std is the standard deviation of the time-series of returns or slopes, and t(Mn) is Mean over its time-series standard error. The average slopes (not shown) from the FM regressions that use the returns on the 100 size-β portfolios of Table AII as the dependent variable are quite close to those for individual stock returns. (The correlation between the 1941–1990 month-by-month slopes on β or ln(ME) for the comparable portfolio and individual stock regressions is always greater than 0.99.)

Panel A

Variable	1941–1990 (600 Mos.)			1941–1965 (300 Mos.)			1966–1990 (300 Mos.)		
	Mean	*Std*	*t(Mn)*	*Mean*	*Std*	*t(Mn)*	*Mean*	*Std*	*t(Mn)*
	NYSE Value-Weighted (VW) and Equal-Weighted (EW) Portfolio Returns								
VW	0.93	4.15	5.49	1.10	3.58	5.30	0.76	4.64	2.85
EW	1.12	5.10	5.37	1.33	4.42	5.18	0.91	5.70	2.77
	$R_{it} = a + b_{1t}\beta_{it} + e_{it}$								
a	0.98	3.93	6.11	0.84	3.18	4.56	1.13	4.57	4.26
b_1	0.24	5.52	1.07	0.50	4.75	1.82	-0.02	6.19	-0.06
	$R_{it} = a + b_{2t}\ln(ME_{it}) + e_{it}$								
a	1.70	8.24	5.04	1.88	6.43	5.06	1.51	9.72	2.69
b_2	-0.13	1.06	-3.07	-0.17	1.01	-2.88	-0.10	1.11	-1.54
	$R_{it} = a + b_{1t}\beta_{it} + b_{2t}\ln(ME_{it}) + e_{it}$								
a	1.97	6.16	7.84	1.80	4.77	6.52	2.14	7.29	5.09
b_1	-0.14	5.05	-0.66	0.07	4.15	0.28	-0.34	5.80	-1.01
b_2	-0.15	0.96	-3.75	-0.16	0.94	-2.97	-0.13	0.99	-2.34

Panel B

NYSE Value-Weighted (VW) and Equal-Weighted (EW) Portfolio Returns

Variable	1941–1950 Mean	1941–1950 t(Mn)	1951–1960 Mean	1951–1960 t(Mn)	1961–1970 Mean	1961–1970 t(Mn)	1971–1980 Mean	1971–1980 t(Mn)	1981–1990 Mean	1981–1990 t(Mn)
VW	1.05	2.88	1.18	3.95	0.66	1.84	0.72	1.67	1.04	2.40
EW	1.59	3.16	1.13	3.76	0.88	1.96	1.04	1.82	0.95	2.01

$$R_{it} = a + b_{1t}\beta_{it} + e_{it}$$

Variable	1941–1950 Mean	1941–1950 t(Mn)	1951–1960 Mean	1951–1960 t(Mn)	1961–1970 Mean	1961–1970 t(Mn)	1971–1980 Mean	1971–1980 t(Mn)	1981–1990 Mean	1981–1990 t(Mn)
a	0.24	0.66	1.41	6.36	0.64	1.94	0.27	0.62	2.35	5.99
b_1	1.26	2.20	-0.19	-0.63	0.32	0.72	0.82	1.27	-1.01	-2.10

$$R_{it} = a + b_{2t}\ln(ME_{it}) + e_{it}$$

Variable	1941–1950 Mean	1941–1950 t(Mn)	1951–1960 Mean	1951–1960 t(Mn)	1961–1970 Mean	1961–1970 t(Mn)	1971–1980 Mean	1971–1980 t(Mn)	1981–1990 Mean	1981–1990 t(Mn)
a	2.63	3.47	1.08	2.73	1.78	2.50	2.18	2.03	0.82	1.20
b_2	-0.37	-2.90	0.03	0.53	-0.17	-2.19	-0.20	-1.57	0.04	0.57

$$R_{it} = a + b_{1t}\beta_{it} + b_{2t}\ln(ME_{it}) + e_{it}$$

Variable	1941–1950 Mean	1941–1950 t(Mn)	1951–1960 Mean	1951–1960 t(Mn)	1961–1970 Mean	1961–1970 t(Mn)	1971–1980 Mean	1971–1980 t(Mn)	1981–1990 Mean	1981–1990 t(Mn)
a	2.14	3.93	1.38	4.03	2.01	4.16	1.50	2.12	2.84	4.25
b_1	0.34	0.75	-0.17	-0.53	-0.11	-0.27	0.41	0.75	-1.14	-2.16
b_2	-0.34	-2.92	0.01	0.20	-0.18	-2.89	-0.16	-1.50	-0.07	-0.84

pre-ranking βs used to form the β-sorted portfolios. It seems safe to conclude that the increasing pattern of the post-ranking βs in every size decile captures the ordering of the true βs. (c) Contrary to the SLB model, the β sorts do not produce a similar ordering of average returns. Within the rows (size deciles) of the average return matrix in Table AII, the high-β portfolios have average returns that are close to or less than the low-β portfolios.

But the most damaging evidence against the SLB model comes from the univariate regressions of returns on β in Table AIII. They say that when the tests allow for variation in β that is unrelated to size, the relation between β and average return for 1941–1990 is weak, perhaps nonexistent, even when β is the only explanatory variable. We are forced to conclude that the SLB model does not describe the last 50 years of average stock returns.

REFERENCES

Alford, Andrew, Jennifer J. Jones, and Mark E. Zmijewski, 1992, Extensions and violations of the statutory SEC Form 10-K filing date, Unpublished manuscript, University of Chicago, Chicago, IL.

Ball, Ray, 1978, Anomalies in relationships between securities' yields and yield-surrogates, *Journal of Financial Economics* 6, 103–126.

Banz, Rolf W., 1981, The relationship between return and market value of common stocks, *Journal of Financial Economics* 9, 3–18.

Basu, Sanjoy, 1983, The relationship betweer. earnings yield, market value, and return for NYSE common stocks: Further evidence, *Journal of Financial Economics* 12, 129–156.

Bhandari, Laxmi Chand, 1988, Debt/Equity ratio and expected common stock returns: Empirical evidence, *Journal of Finance* 43, 507–528.

Black, Fischer, 1972, Capital market equilibrium with restricted borrowing, *Journal of Business* 45, 444–455.

———, Michael C. Jensen, and Myron Scholes, 1972, The capital asset pricing model: some empirical tests, in M. Jensen, ed.: *Studies in the Theory of Capital Markets* (Praeger).

Chan, Louis K., Yasushi Hamao, and Josef Lakonishok, 1991, Fundamentals and stock returns in Japan, *Journal of Finance* 46, 1739–1789.

Chan, K. C. and Nai-fu Chen, 1988, An unconditional asset-pricing test and the role of firm size as an instrumental variable for risk, *Journal of Finance* 43, 309–325.

———, and Nai-fu Chen, 1991, Structural and return characteristics of small and large firms, *Journal of Finance* 46, 1467–1484.

———, Nai-fu Chen, and David A. Hsieh, 1985, An exploratory investigation of the firm size effect, *Journal of Financial Economics* 14, 451–471.

Chen, Nai-fu, Richard Roll, and Stephen A. Ross, 1986, Economic forces and the stock market, *Journal of Business* 56, 383–403.

DeBondt, Werner F. M., and Richard H. Thaler, 1985, Does the stock market overreact, *Journal of Finance* 40, 557–581.

Dimson, Elroy, 1979, Risk measurement when shares are subject to infrequent trading, *Journal of Financial Economics* 7, 197–226.

Fama, Eugene F., 1976, *Foundations of Finance* (Basic Books, New York).

———, and James MacBeth, 1973, Risk, return and equilibrium: Empirical tests, *Journal of Political Economy* 81, 607–636.

Fowler, David J. and C. Harvey Rorke, 1983, Risk measurement when shares are subject to infrequent trading: Comment, *Journal of Financial Economics* 12, 279–283.

Jaffe, Jeffrey, Donald B. Keim, and Randolph Westerfield, 1989, Earnings yields, market values, and stock returns, *Journal of Finance* 44, 135–148.

Keim, Donald B., 1983, Size-related anomalies and stock return seasonality, *Journal of Financial Economics* 12, 13–32.

———, 1988, Stock market regularities: A synthesis of the evidence and explanations, in Elroy Dimson, ed.: *Stock Market Anomalies* (Cambridge University Press, Cambridge).

Lakonishok, Josef, and Alan C. Shapiro, 1986, Systematic risk, total risk and size as determinants of stock market returns, *Journal of Banking and Finance* 10, 115–132.

Lintner, John, 1965, The valuation of risk assets and the selection of risky investments in stock portfolios and capital budgets, *Review of Economics and Statistics* 47, 13–37.

Markowitz, Harry, 1959, *Portfolio Selection: Efficient Diversification of Investments* (Wiley, New York).

Merton, Robert C., 1973, An intertemporal capital asset pricing model, *Econometrica* 41, 867–887.

Reinganum, Marc R., 1981, A new empirical perspective on the CAPM, *Journal of Financial and Quantitative Analysis* 16, 439–462.

Roll, Richard, 1983, Vas ist Das? The turn-of-the-year effect and the return premia of small firms, *Journal of Portfolio Management* 9, 18–28.

Rosenberg, Barr, Kenneth Reid, and Ronald Lanstein, 1985, Persuasive evidence of market inefficiency, *Journal of Portfolio Management* 11, 9–17.

Ross, Stephen A., 1976, The arbitrage theory of capital asset pricing, *Journal of Economic Theory* 13, 341–360.

Sharpe, William F., 1964, Capital asset prices: a theory of market equilibrium under conditions of risk, *Journal of Finance* 19, 425–442.

Stambaugh, Robert F., 1982, On the exclusion of assets from tests of the two-parameter model: A sensitivity analysis, *Journal of Financial Economics* 10, 237–268.

Stattman, Dennis, 1980, Book values and stock returns, *The Chicago MBA: A Journal of Selected Papers* 4, 25–45.

COMMON RISK FACTORS IN THE
RETURNS ON STOCKS AND BONDS

· · ·

Eugene F. Fama and Kenneth R. French

This paper identifies five common risk factors in the returns on stocks and bonds. There are three stock-market factors: an overall market factor and factors related to firm size and book-to-market equity. There are two bond-market factors related to maturity and default risks. Stock returns have shared variation due to the stock-market factors, and they are linked to bond returns through shared variation in the bond-market factors. Except for low-grade corporates, the bond-market factors capture the common variation in bond returns. Most important, the five factors seem to explain average returns on stocks and bonds.

1. INTRODUCTION

The cross-section of average returns on U.S. common stocks shows little relation to either the market βs of the Sharpe (1964)–Lintner (1965) asset-pricing model or the consumption βs of the intertemporal asset-pricing model of Breeden (1979) and others. [See, for example. Reinganum (1981) and Breeden, Gibbons, and Litzenberger (1989).] On the other hand, variables that have no special standing in asset-pricing theory show reliable power to explain the cross-section of average returns. The list of empirically determined average-return variables includes size (*ME*, stock price times number of shares), leverage, earnings/price (*E/P*), and book-to-market equity (the ratio of the book value of a firm's common stock, *BE*, to its market value, *ME*). [See Banz (1981), Bhandari (1988), Basu (1983), and Rosenberg, Reid, and Lanstein (1985).]

Reprinted with permission from the *Journal of Financial Economics* 33, no. 1 (February 1993): 3–56. © 1993 by Elsevier Limited.

The comments of David Booth. John Cochrane, Nai-fu Chen, Wayne Ferson, Josef Lakonishok, Mark Mitchell, G. William Schwert, Jay Shanken, and Rex Sinquefield are gratefully acknowledged. This research is supported by the National Science Foundation (Fama) and the Center for Research in Securities Prices (French).

Fama and French (1992a) study the joint roles of market β, size, *E/P,* leverage, and book-to-market equity in the cross-section of average stock returns. They find that used alone or in combination with other variables, β (the slope in the regression of a stock's return on a market return) has little information about average returns. Used alone, size, *E/P,* leverage, and book-to-market equity have explanatory power. In combinations, size (*ME*) and book-to-market equity (*BE/ME*) seem to absorb the apparent roles of leverage and *E/P* in average returns. The bottom-line result is that two empirically determined variables, size and book-to-market equity, do a good job explaining the cross-section of average returns on NYSE, Amex, and NASDAQ stocks for the 1963–1990 period.

This paper extends the asset-pricing tests in Fama and French (1992a) in three ways.

(a) We expand the set of asset returns to be explained. The only assets considered in Fama and French (1992a) are common stocks. If markets are integrated, a single model should also explain bond returns. The tests here include U.S. government and corporate bonds as well as stocks.

(b) We also expand the set of variables used to explain returns. The size and book-to-market variables in Fama and French (1992a) are directed at stocks. We extend the list to term-structure variables that are likely to play a role in bond returns. The goal is to examine whether variables that are important in bond returns help to explain stock returns, and vice versa. The notion is that if markets are integrated, there is probably some overlap between the return processes for bonds and stocks.

(c) Perhaps most important, the approach to testing asset-pricing models is different. Fama and French (1992a) use the cross-section regressions of Fama and MacBeth (1973); the cross-section of stock returns is regressed on variables hypothesized to explain average returns. It would be difficult to add bonds to the cross-section regressions since explanatory variables like size and book-to-market equity have no obvious meaning for government and corporate bonds.

This paper uses the time-series regression approach of Black, Jensen, and Scholes (1972). Monthly returns on stocks and bonds are regressed on the returns to a market portfolio of stocks and mimicking portfolios for size, book-to-market equity (*BE/ME*), and term-structure risk factors in returns. The time-series regression slopes are factor loadings that, unlike size or *BE/ME*, have a clear interpretation as risk-factor sensitivities for bonds as well as for stocks.

The time-series regressions are also convenient for studying two important asset-pricing issues.

(a) One of our central themes is that if assets are priced rationally, variables that are related to average returns, such as size and book-to-market equity, must proxy for sensitivity to common (shared and thus undiversifiable) risk factors in returns. The time-series regressions give direct evidence on this issue. In particular, the slopes and R^2 values show whether mimicking portfolios for risk factors related to size and *BE/ME* capture shared variation in stock and bond returns not explained by other factors.

(b) The time-series regressions use excess returns (monthly stock or bond returns minus the one-month Treasury bill rate) as dependent variables and either excess returns or returns on zero-investment portfolios as explanatory variables. In such regressions, a well-specified asset-pricing model produces intercepts that are indistinguishable from o [Merton (1973)]. The estimated intercepts provide a simple return metric and a formal test of how well different combinations of the common factors capture the cross-section of average returns. Moreover, judging asset-pricing models on the basis of the intercepts in excess-return regressions imposes a stringent standard. Competing models are asked to explain the one-month bill rate as well as the returns on longer-term bonds and stocks.

Our main results are easy to summarize. For stocks, portfolios constructed to mimic risk factors related to size and *BE/ME* capture strong common variation in returns, no matter what else is in the time-series regressions. This is evidence that size and book-to-market equity indeed proxy for sensitivity to common risk factors in stock returns. Moreover, for the stock portfolios we examine, the intercepts from three-factor regressions that include the excess market return and the mimicking returns for size and *BE/ME* factors are close to o. Thus a market factor and our proxies for the risk factors related to size and book-to-market equity seem to do a good job explaining the cross-section of average stock returns.

The interpretation of the time-series regressions for stocks is interesting. Like the cross-section regressions of Fama and French (1992a), the time-series regressions say that the size and book-to-market factors can explain the differences in average returns across stocks. But these factors alone cannot explain the large difference between the average returns on stocks and one-month bills. This job is left to the market factor. In regressions that also include the size and book-to-market factors, all our stock portfolios produce slopes on the market factor that are close to 1. The risk premium for the market factor then links the average returns on stocks and bills.

For bonds, the mimicking portfolios for the two term-structure factors (a term premium and a default premium) capture most of the variation in the returns on our government and corporate bond portfolios. The term-structure factors also 'explain' the average returns on bonds, but the average premiums for the term-structure factors, like the average excess bond returns, are close to 0. Thus, the hypothesis that all the corporate and government bond portfolios have the same long-term expected returns also cannot be rejected.

The common variation in stock returns is largely captured by three stock-portfolio returns, and the common variation in bond returns is largely explained by two bond-portfolio returns. The stock and bond markets, however, are far from stochastically segmented. Used alone in the time-series regressions, the term-structure factors capture strong variation in stock returns; indeed, the slopes on the term-structure factors in the regressions for stocks are much like those for bonds. But interestingly, when stock-market factors are also included in the regressions, all of our stock portfolios load in about the same way on the two term-structure factors and on the market factor in returns. As a result, a market portfolio of stocks captures the common variation in stock returns associated with the market factor and the two term-structure factors.

The stochastic links between the bond and stock markets do, however, seem to come largely from the term-structure factors. Used alone, the excess market return and the mimicking returns for the size and book-to-market equity factors seem to capture common variation in bond returns. But when the two term-structure factors are included in the bond regressions, the explanatory power of the stock-market factors disappears for all but the low-grade corporate bonds.

In a nutshell, our results suggest that there are at least three stock-market factors and two term-structure factors in returns. Stock returns have shared variation due to the three stock-market factors, and they are linked to bond returns through shared variation in the two term-structure factors. Except for low-grade corporate bonds, only the two term-structure factors seem to produce common variation in the returns on government and corporate bonds.

The story proceeds as follows. We first introduce the inputs to the time-series regressions: the explanatory variables and the returns to be explained (sections 2 and 3). We then use the regressions to attack our two central asset-pricing issues: how do different combinations of variables capture (a) the common variation through time in the returns on bonds and stocks (section 4) and (b) the cross-section of average returns (section 5).

2. THE INPUTS TO THE TIME-SERIES REGRESSIONS

The explanatory variables in the time-series regressions include the returns on a market portfolio of stocks and mimicking portfolios for the size, book-to-market, and term-structure factors in returns. The returns to be explained are for government bond portfolios in two maturity ranges, corporate bond portfolios in five rating groups, and 25 stock portfolios formed on the basis of size and book-to-market equity.

2.1. The Explanatory Returns

The explanatory variables fall into two sets, those likely to be important for capturing variation in bond returns and those likely to be important for stocks. Segmenting the explanatory variables in this way sets up interesting tests of whether factors important in stock returns help to explain bond returns and vice versa.

2.1.1. Bond-Market Factors

One common risk in bond returns arises from unexpected changes in interest rates. Our proxy for this factor, *TERM*, is the difference between the monthly long-term government bond return (from Ibbotson Associates) and the one-month Treasury bill rate measured at the end of the previous month (from the Center for Research in Security Prices, CRSP). The bill rate is meant to proxy for the general level of expected returns on bonds, so that *TERM* proxies for the deviation of long-term bond returns from expected returns due to shifts in interest rates.

For corporate bonds, shifts in economic conditions that change the likelihood of default give rise to another common factor in returns. Our proxy for this default factor, *DEF*, is the difference between the return on a market portfolio of long-term corporate bonds (the Composite portfolio on the corporate bond module of Ibbotson Associates) and the long-term government bond return.

Chen, Roll, and Ross (1986) use *TERM* and a variable like *DEF* to help explain the cross-section of average returns on NYSE stocks. They use the Fama and MacBeth (1973) cross-section regression approach; the cross-section of average stock returns is explained with the cross-section of slopes from time-series regressions of returns on *TERM*, a default factor, and other factors. In their tests, the default factor is the most powerful factor in average stock returns, and *TERM* sometimes has power. We confirm that the tracks of *TERM* and *DEF* show up clearly in the time-series variation of stock returns. We also find that the two variables dominate the common variation in government and corporate bond returns. In contrast to the cross-section regressions of Chen, Roll, and Ross, however, our time-series regressions say that the average premiums for *DEF* and *TERM* risks are too small to explain much variation in the cross-section of average stock returns. [Shanken and Weinstein (1990) make a similar point.]

2.1.2. Stock-Market Factors

Motivation—Although size and book-to-market equity seem like ad hoc variables for explaining average stock returns, we have reason to expect that they proxy for common risk factors in returns. In Fama and French (1992b) we document that size and book-to-market equity are related to economic fundamentals. Not surprisingly, firms that have high *BE/ME* (a low stock price relative to book value) tend to have low earnings on assets, and the low earnings persist for at least five years before and five years after book-to-market equity is measured. Conversely, low *BE/ME* (a high stock price relative to book value) is associated with persistently high earnings.

Size is also related to profitability. Controlling for book-to-market equity, small firms tend to have lower earnings on assets than big firms. The size effect in earnings, however, is largely due to the 1980s. Until 1981, controlling for *BE/ME*, small firms are only slightly less profitable than big firms. But for small firms, the 1980–1982 recession turns into a prolonged earnings depression. For some reason, small firms do not participate in the economic boom of the middle and late 1980s.

The fact that small firms can suffer a long earnings depression that bypasses big firms suggests that size is associated with a common risk factor that might explain the negative relation between size and average return. Similarly, the relation between book-to-market equity and earnings suggests that relative profitability is the source of a common risk factor in returns that might explain the positive relation between *BE/ME* and average return. Measuring the common variation in returns associated with size and *BE/ME* is a major task of this paper.

[397]

The Building Blocks—To study economic fundamentals, Fama and French (1992b) use six portfolios formed from sorts of stocks on *ME* and *BE/ME*. We use the same six portfolios here to form portfolios meant to mimic the underlying risk factors in returns related to size and book-to-market equity. This ensures a correspondence between the study of common risk factors in returns carried out here and our complementary study of economic fundamentals.

In June of each year *t* from 1963 to 1991, all NYSE stocks on CRSP are ranked on size (price times shares). The median NYSE size is then used to split NYSE, Amex, and (after 1972) NASDAQ stocks into two groups, small and big (*S* and *B*). Most Amex and NASDAQ stocks are smaller than the NYSE median, so the small group contains a disproportionate number of stocks (3,616 out of 4,797 in 1991). Despite its large number of stocks, the small group contains far less than half (about 8% in 1991) of the combined value of the two size groups.

We also break NYSE, Amex, and NASDAQ stocks into three book-to-market equity groups based on the breakpoints for the bottom 30% (*Low*), middle 40% (*Medium*), and top 30% (*High*) of the ranked values of *BE/ME* for NYSE stocks. We define book common equity, *BE*, as the COMPUSTAT book value of stockholders' equity, plus balance-sheet deferred taxes and investment tax credit (if available), minus the book value of preferred stock. Depending on availability, we use the redemption, liquidation, or par value (in that order) to estimate the value of preferred stock. Book-to-market equity, *BE/ME*, is then book common equity for the fiscal year ending in calendar year $t-1$, divided by market equity at the end of December of $t-1$. We do not use negative-*BE* firms, which are rare before 1980, when calculating the breakpoints for *BE/ME* or when forming the size–*BE/ME* portfolios. Also, only firms with ordinary common equity (as classified by CRSP) are included in the tests. This means that ADRs, REITs, and units of beneficial interest are excluded.

Our decision to sort firms into three groups on *BE/ME* and only two on *ME* follows the evidence in Fama and French (1992a) that book-to-market equity has a stronger role in average stock returns than size. The splits are arbitrary, however, and we have not searched over alternatives. The hope is that the tests here and in Fama and French (1992b) are not sensitive to these choices. We see no reason to argue that they are.

We construct six portfolios (*S/L, S/M, S/H, B/L, B/M, B/H*) from the intersections of the two *ME* and the three *BE/ME* groups. For example, the *S/L* portfolio contains the stocks in the small-*ME* group that are also in the low-*BE/ME* group, and the *B/H* portfolio contains the big-*ME* stocks that also have high *BE/MEs*. Monthly value-weighted returns on the six portfolios are calculated from July of year t to June of $t + 1$, and the portfolios are reformed in June of $t + 1$. We calculate returns beginning in July of year t to be sure that book equity for year $t - 1$ is known.

To be included in the tests, a firm must have CRSP stock prices for December of year $t - 1$ and June of t and COMPUSTAT book common equity for year $t - 1$. Moreover, to avoid the survival bias inherent in the way COMPUSTAT adds firms to its tapes [Banz and Breen (1986)], we do not include firms until they have appeared on COMPUSTAT for two years. (COMPUSTAT says it rarely includes more than two years of historical data when it adds firms).

Size—Our portfolio *SMB* (small minus big), meant to mimic the risk factor in returns related to size, is the difference, each month, between the simple average of the returns on the three small-stock portfolios (*S/L, S/M,* and *S/H*) and the simple average of the returns on the three big-stock portfolios (*B/L, B/M,* and *B/H*). Thus, *SMB* is the difference between the returns on small- and big-stock portfolios with about the same weighted-average book-to-market equity. This difference should be largely free of the influence of *BE/ME,* focusing instead on the different return behaviors of small and big stocks.

BE/ME—The portfolio *HML* (high minus low), meant to mimic the risk factor in returns related to book-to-market equity, is defined similarly. *HML* is the difference, each month, between the simple average of the returns on the two high-*BE/ME* portfolios (*S/H* and *B/H*) and the average of the returns on the two low-*BE/ME* portfolios (*S/L* and *B/L*). The two components of *HML* are returns on high- and low-*BE/ME* portfolios with about the same weighted-average size. Thus the difference between the two returns should be largely free of the size factor in returns, focusing instead on the different return behaviors of high- and low-*BE/ME* firms. As testimony to the success of this simple procedure, the correlation between the 1963–1991 monthly mimicking returns for the size and book-to-market factors is only -0.08.

True mimicking portfolios for the common risk factors in returns minimize the variance of firm-specific factors. The six size–*BE/ME* portfolios in *SMB* and *HML* are value-weighted. Using value-weighted components is in the spirit of minimizing variance, since return variances are negatively related to size (table 2, below). More important, using value-weighted components results in mimicking portfolios that capture the different return behaviors of small and big stocks, or high- and low-*BE/ME* stocks, in a way that corresponds to realistic investment opportunities.

Market—Finally, our proxy for the market factor in stock returns is the excess market return, *RM–RF. RM* is the return on the value-weighted portfolio of the stocks in the six size–*BE/ME* portfolios, plus the negative-*BE* stocks excluded from the portfolios. *RF* is the one-month bill rate.

2.2. The Returns to Be Explained

Bonds—The set of dependent variables used in the time-series regressions includes the excess returns on two government and five corporate bond portfolios. The government bond portfolios (from CRSP) cover maturities from 1 to 5 years and 6 to 10 years. The five corporate bond portfolios, for Moody's rating groups Aaa, Aa, A, Baa, and LG (low-grade, that is, below Baa) are from the corporate bond module of Ibbotson Associates (provided to us by Dimensional Fund Advisors).

Stocks—For stocks, we use excess returns on 25 portfolios, formed on size and book-to-market equity, as dependent variables in the time-series regressions. We use portfolios formed on size and *BE/ME* because we seek to determine whether the mimicking portfolios *SMB* and *HML* capture common factors in stock returns related to size and book-to-market equity. Portfolios formed on size and *BE/ME* will also produce a wide range of average returns to be explained by competing asset-pricing equations [Fama and French (1992a)]. Later, however, we use portfolios formed on *E/P* (earnings/price) and *D/P* (dividend/price), variables that are also informative about average returns [e.g., Keim (1988)], to check the robustness of our results on the ability of our explanatory factors to capture the cross-section of average returns.

The 25 size–*BE/ME* portfolios are formed much like the six size–*BE/ME* portfolios discussed earlier. In June of each year *t* we sort NYSE stocks by size and (independently) by book-to-market equity. For the size sort, *ME* is measured at the end of June. For the book-to-market sort, *ME* is market equity at the end of December of *t* − 1, and *BE* is book common equity for the fiscal year ending in calendar year *t* − 1. We use NYSE breakpoints for *ME* and *BE/ME* to allocate NYSE, Amex, and (after 1972) NASDAQ stocks to five size quintiles and five book-to-market quintiles. We construct 25 portfolios from the intersections of the size and *BE/ME* quintiles and calculate value-weighted monthly returns on the portfolios from July of *t* to June of *t* + 1. The excess returns on these 25 portfolios for July 1963 to December 1991 are the dependent variables for stocks in the time-series regressions.

Table 1 shows that, because we use NYSE breakpoints to form the 25 size–*BE/ME* portfolios, the portfolios in the smallest size quintile have the most stocks (mostly small Amex and NASDAQ stocks). Although they contain many stocks, each of the five portfolios in the smallest size quintile is on average less

TABLE 1. Descriptive statistics for 25 stock portfolios formed on size and book-to-market equity: 1963–1991, 29 years.[a]

Size	Book-to-market equity (BE/ME) quintiles									
quintile	Low	2	3	4	High	Low	2	3	4	High
	Average of annual averages of firm size					Average of annual B/E ratios for portfolio				
Small	20.6	20.8	20.2	19.4	15.1	0.30	0.62	0.84	1.09	1.80
2	89.7	89.3	89.3	89.9	88.5	0.31	0.60	0.83	1.09	1.71
3	209.3	211.9	210.8	214.8	210.7	0.31	0.60	0.84	1.08	1.66
4	535.1	537.4	545.4	551.6	538.7	0.31	0.61	0.84	1.09	1.67
Big	3583.7	2885.8	2819.5	2700.5	2337.9	0.29	0.59	0.83	1.08	1.56
	Average of annual percent of market value in portfolio					Average of annual number of firms in portfolio				
Small	0.69	0.49	0.46	0.48	0.64	428.0	276.6	263.8	291.5	512.7
2	0.92	0.71	0.65	0.61	0.55	121.6	94.0	86.7	79.8	71.3
3	1.78	1.36	1.26	1.14	0.82	102.7	78.3	73.0	64.5	45.9
4	3.95	3.01	2.71	2.41	1.50	90.1	68.9	60.7	53.1	33.4
Big	30.13	15.87	12.85	10.44	4.61	93.6	63.7	52.7	44.0	23.6
	Average of annual E/P ratios (in percent) for portfolio					Average of annual D/P ratios (in percent) for portfolio				
Small	2.42	7.24	8.26	9.06	2.66	1.00	1.94	2.60	3.13	2.82
2	5.20	8.61	10.16	10.95	9.28	1.59	2.45	3.45	4.25	4.53
3	5.91	8.72	10.43	11.62	10.78	1.56	3.03	4.04	4.68	4.64
4	5.85	8.94	10.45	11.64	11.39	1.80	3.09	4.22	5.01	4.94
Big	6.00	9.07	10.90	12.45	13.92	2.34	3.69	4.68	5.49	5.90

[a]The 25 size–BE/ME stock portfolios are formed as follows. Each year t from 1963 to 1991 NYSE quintile breakpoints for size (ME, stock price times shares outstanding), measured at the end of June, are used to allocate NYSE. Amex, and NASDAQ stocks to five size quintiles. Similarly, NYSE quintile breakpoints for BE/ME are used to allocate NYSE, Amex. and NASDAQ stocks to five book-to-market equity quintiles. The 25 size–BE/ME portfolios are formed as the intersections of the five size and the five BE/ME groups. Book equity, BE, is the COMPUSTAT book value of stockholders' equity, plus balance sheet deferred taxes and investment tax credits (if available), minus the book value of preferred stock. Depending on availability, we use the redemption, liquidation, or par value (in that order) to estimate the book value of preferred stock. Book-to-market equity, BE/ME, for a stock is BE for the fiscal year ending in calendar year $t - 1$, divided by ME at the end of December of $t - 1$.

A portfolio's book-to-market equity, BE/ME, for the portfolio formation year t is the sum of book equity, BE, for the firms in the portfolio for the fiscal year ending in calendar year $t - 1$, divided by the sum of their market equity, ME, in December of $t - 1$. A portfolio's earnings/price ratio (E/P) for year t is the sum of equity income for the firms in the portfolio for the fiscal year ending in calendar year $t - 1$, divided by the sum of their market equity in December of $t - 1$. Equity income is income before extraordinary items, plus income-statement deferred taxes, minus preferred dividends. A portfolio's dividend yield (D/P) for year t is the sum (across firms in the portfolio) of the dividends paid from July of $t - 1$ to June of t, divided by the sum of market equity in June of $t - 1$. We use the procedure described in Fama and French (1988) to estimate dividends.

The descriptive statistics are computed when the portfolio is formed in June of each year, 1963–1991, and are then averaged across the 29 years.

than 0.70% of the combined value of stocks in the 25 portfolios. In contrast, the portfolios in the largest size quintile have the fewest stocks but the largest fractions of value. Together, the five portfolios in the largest *ME* quintile average about 74% of total value. The portfolio of stocks in both the largest size and lowest *BE/ME* quintiles (big successful firms) alone accounts for more than 30% of the combined value of the 25 portfolios. And note that using all stocks, rather than just NYSE stocks, to define the size quintiles would result in an even more skewed distribution of value toward the biggest size quintile.

Table 1 also shows that in every size quintile but the smallest, both the number of stocks and the proportion of total value accounted for by a portfolio decrease from lower- to higher-*BE/ME* portfolios. This pattern has two causes. First, using independent size and book-to-market sorts of NYSE stocks to form portfolios means that the highest-*BE/ME* quintile is tilted toward the smallest stocks. Second, Amex and NASDAQ stocks, mostly small, tend to have lower book-to-market equity ratios than NYSE stocks of similar size. In other words, NYSE stocks that are small in terms of *ME* are more likely to be fallen angels (big firms with low stock prices) than small Amex and NASDAQ stocks.

3. THE PLAYING FIELD

Table 2 summarizes the dependent and explanatory returns in the time-series regressions. The average excess returns on the portfolios that serve as dependent variables give perspective on the range of average returns that competing sets of risk factors must explain. The average returns on the explanatory portfolios are the average premiums per unit of risk (regression slope) for the candidate common risk factors in returns.

3.1. The Dependent Returns

Stocks—The 25 stock portfolios formed on size and book-to-market equity produce a wide range of average excess returns, from 0.32% to 1.05% per month. The portfolios also confirm the Fama–French (1992a) evidence that there is a negative relation between size and average return, and there is a stronger positive relation between average return and book-to-market equity. In all but the lowest-*BE/ME* quintile, average returns tend to decrease from the small- to the big-size portfolios. The relation between average return and book-to-market equity is more consistent. In every size quintile, average returns tend to increase with *BE/ME,* and the differences between the average returns for the highest- and lowest-*BE/ME* portfolios range from 0.19% to 0.62% per month.

Our time-series regressions attempt to explain the cross-section of average returns with the premiums for the common risk factors in returns. The wide range of average returns on the 25 stock portfolios, and the size and book-to-market effects in average returns, present interesting challenges for competing sets of risk factors.

Most of the ten portfolios in the bottom two *BE/ME* quintiles produce average excess returns that are less than two standard errors from 0. This is an example of a well-known problem [Merton (1980)]: because stock returns have high standard deviations (around 6% per month for the size–*BE/ME* portfolios), large average returns often are not reliably different from 0. The high volatility of stock returns does not mean, however, that our asset-pricing tests will lack power. The common factors in returns will absorb most of the variation in stock returns, making the asset-pricing tests on the intercepts in the time-series regressions quite precise.

Bonds—In contrast to the stock portfolios, the average excess returns on the government and corporate bond portfolios in table 2 are puny. All the average excess bond returns are less than 0.15% per month, and only one of seven is more than 1.5 standard errors from 0. There is little evidence in table 2 that (a) average returns on government bonds increase with maturity, (b) long-term corporate bonds have higher average returns than government bonds, or (c) average returns on corporate bonds are higher for lower-rating groups.

The flat cross-section of average bond returns does not mean that bonds are uninteresting dependent variables in the asset-pricing tests. On the contrary, bonds are good candidates for rejecting asset-pricing equations that predict patterns in the cross-section of average returns based on different slopes on the common risk factors in returns.

3.2. The Explanatory Returns

In the time-series regression approach to asset-pricing tests, the average risk premiums for the common factors in returns are just the average values of the explanatory variables. The average value of *RM–RF* (the average premium per unit of market β) is 0.43% per month. This is large from an investment perspective (about 5% per year), but it is a marginal 1.76 standard errors from 0. The average *SMB* return (the average premium for the size-related factor in returns) is only 0.27% per month ($t = 1.73$). We shall find, however, that the slopes on *SMB* for the 25 stock portfolios cover a range in excess of 1.7, so the estimated spread in expected returns due to the size factor is large, about 0.46% per month. The book-to-market factor *HML* produces an average premium of 0.40% per month ($t = 2.91$), that is large in both practical and statistical terms.

TABLE 2. Summary statistics for the monthly dependent and explanatory returns (in percent) in the regressions of tables 3 to 8: July 1963 to December 1991, 342 observations.[a]

| | | | | Autocorr. for lag | | | Correlations | | | | |
Name	Mean	Std.	t(mn)	1	2	12	RM-RF	RMO	SMB	HML	TERM
RM	0.97	4.52	3.97	0.05	-0.05	0.03					
TB	0.54	0.22	45.97	0.94	0.90	0.65					
LTG	0.60	3.03	3.66	0.05	-0.00	0.00					
CB	0.62	2.24	5.10	0.20	-0.04	0.04					
						Explanatory returns					
RM-RF	0.43	4.54	1.76	0.05	-0.04	0.03	0.78				
RMO	0.50	3.55	2.61	-0.10	-0.05	0.02	0.32	1.00			
SMB	0.27	2.89	1.73	0.19	0.07	0.23	-0.38	-0.00	1.00		
HML	0.40	2.54	2.91	0.18	0.06	0.07	0.34	-0.00	-0.08	1.00	
TERM	0.06	3.02	0.38	0.05	-0.00	-0.00	-0.07	0.00	-0.07	-0.05	1.00
DEF	0.02	1.60	0.21	-0.20	-0.04	-0.00	-0.07	-0.00	0.17	0.08	-0.69
				Dependent variables: Excess returns on government and corporate bonds							
1-5G	0.12	1.25	1.71	0.15	-0.08	0.01					
6-10G	0.14	2.03	1.24	0.12	-0.05	0.02					
AAA	0.06	2.34	0.44	0.16	-0.04	0.02					
AA	0.07	2.23	0.58	0.19	-0.04	0.03					
A	0.08	2.25	0.63	0.21	-0.03	0.04					
BAA	0.14	2.35	1.09	0.21	0.00	0.03					
LG	0.13	2.52	0.98	0.23	0.05	0.08					

Dependent variables: Excess returns on 25 stock portfolios formed on ME and BE/ME

Size quintile	Book-to-market equity (BE/ME) quintiles				
	Low	2	3	4	High
	Means				
Small	0.39	0.70	0.79	0.88	1.01
2	0.44	0.71	0.85	0.84	1.02
3	0.43	0.66	0.68	0.81	0.97
4	0.48	0.35	0.57	0.77	1.05
Big	0.40	0.36	0.32	0.56	0.59
	Standard deviations				
Small	7.76	6.84	6.29	5.99	6.27
2	7.28	6.42	5.85	5.33	6.06
3	6.71	5.71	5.27	4.92	5.69
4	5.97	5.44	5.03	4.95	5.75
Big	4.95	4.70	4.38	4.27	4.85
	t-statistics for means				
Small	0.93	1.88	2.33	2.73	2.97
2	1.11	2.05	2.69	2.91	3.11
3	1.18	2.12	2.39	3.04	3.15
4	1.49	1.19	2.08	2.88	3.36
Big	1.50	1.42	1.34	2.43	2.26

[a] RM is the value-weighted monthly percent return on the stocks in the 25 size–BE/ME portfolios, plus the negative-BE stocks excluded from the portfolios. RF is the one-month Treasury bill rate, observed at the beginning of the month. LTG is the long-term government bond return. CB is the return on a proxy for the market portfolio of long-term corporate bonds. $TERM$ is LTG-RF. DEF is CB-LTG. SMB (small minus big) is the difference between the returns on small-stock and big-stock portfolios with about the same weighted average book-to-market equity. HML (high minus low) is the difference between the returns on high and low book-to-market equity portfolios with about the same weighted average size. RMO is the sum of the intercept and residuals from the regression (1) of RM–RF on $TERM$, DEF, SMB, and HML.

The seven bond portfolios used as dependent variables in the excess-return regressions are 1- to 5-year and 6- to 10-year governments (1–5G and 6–10G) and corporate bonds rated Aaa, Aa, A, Baa, and below Baa (LG) by Moody's. The 25 size–BE/ME stock portfolios are formed as follows. Each year t from 1963 to 1991 NYSE quintile breakpoints for size (ME, stock price times shares outstanding), measured at the end of June, are used to allocate NYSE, Amex, and NASDAQ stocks to five size quintiles. Similarly, NYSE quintile breakpoints for BE/ME are used to allocate NYSE, Amex, and NASDAQ stocks to five book-to-market equity quintiles. In BE/ME, BE is book common equity for the fiscal year ending in calendar year t − 1, and ME is for the end of December of t − 1. The 25 size–BE/ME portfolios are formed as the intersections of the five size and the five BE/ME groups. Value-weighted monthly percent returns on the portfolios are calculated from July of year t to June of t + 1.

The average risk premiums for the term-structure factors are trivial relative to those of the stock-market factors. *TERM* (the term premium) and *DEF* (the default premium) are on average 0.06% and 0.02% per month; both are within 0.4 standard errors of 0. Note, though, that *TERM* and *DEF* are about as volatile as the stock-market returns *SMB* and *HML*. Low average premiums will prevent *TERM* and *DEF* from explaining much cross-sectional variation in average returns, but high volatility implies that the two factors can capture substantial common variation in returns. In fact, the low means and high volatilities of *TERM* and *DEF* will be advantageous for explaining bond returns. But the task of explaining the strong cross-sectional variation in average stock returns falls on the stock-market factors, *RM–RF, SMB,* and *HML,* which produce higher average premiums.

We turn now to the asset-pricing tests. In the time-series regression approach, the tests have two parts. In section 4 we establish that the two bond-market returns, *TERM* and *DEF,* and the three stock-market returns, *RM–RF, SMB,* and *HML,* are risk factors in the sense that they capture common (shared and thus undiversifiable) variation in stock and bond returns. In section 5 we use the intercepts from the time-series regressions to test whether the average premiums for the common risk factors in returns explain the cross-section of average returns on bonds and stocks.

4. COMMON VARIATION IN RETURNS

In the time-series regressions, the slopes and R^2 values are direct evidence on whether different risk factors capture common variation in bond and stock returns. We first examine separately the explanatory power of bond-market and stock-market factors. The purpose is to test for overlap between the stochastic processes for stock and bond returns. Do bond-market factors that are important in bond returns capture common variation in stock returns and vice versa? We then examine the joint explanatory power of the bond-and stock-market factors, to develop an overall story for the common variation in returns.

4.1. Bond-Market Factors

Table 3 shows that, used alone as the explanatory variables in the time-series regressions, *TERM* and *DEF* capture common variation in stock and bond returns. The 25 stock portfolios produce slopes on *TERM* that are all more than five standard errors above 0; the smallest *TERM* slope for the seven bond portfolios is 18 standard errors from 0. The slopes on *DEF* are all more than

TABLE 3. Regressions of excess stock and bond returns (in percent) on the bond-market returns, TERM and DEF: July 1963 to December 1991, 342 months.[a]

$$R(t) - RF(t) = a + mTERM(t) + dDEF(t) + e(t)$$

Dependent variable: Excess returns on 25 stock portfolios formed on size and book-to-market equity

Size quintile	Book-to-market equity (BE/ME) quintiles									
	Low	2	3	4	High	Low	2	3	4	High
			m					*t(m)*		
Small	0.93	0.90	0.89	0.86	0.89	5.02	5.50	5.95	6.08	6.01
2	0.99	0.96	0.99	1.01	0.98	5.71	6.32	7.29	8.34	6.92
3	0.99	0.94	0.94	0.95	0.99	6.25	7.10	7.80	8.50	7.60
4	0.92	0.95	0.97	1.05	1.03	6.58	7.57	8.53	9.64	7.83
Big	0.82	0.82	0.80	0.80	0.77	7.14	7.60	8.09	8.26	6.84
			d					*t(d)*		
Small	1.39	1.31	1.33	1.45	1.52	3.96	4.27	4.73	5.45	5.45
2	1.26	1.28	1.35	1.38	1.41	3.84	4.47	5.28	6.05	5.29
3	1.21	1.19	1.25	1.24	1.21	4.05	4.74	5.49	5.89	4.88
4	0.96	1.01	1.13	1.21	1.22	3.65	4.28	5.25	5.89	4.92
Big	0.78	0.73	0.78	0.83	0.89	3.59	3.60	4.18	4.56	4.15
			R^2					*s(e)*		
Small	0.06	0.08	0.09	0.10	0.10	7.50	6.57	6.00	5.68	5.95
2	0.08	0.10	0.13	0.17	0.12	6.97	6.09	5.45	4.87	5.69
3	0.10	0.12	0.15	0.17	0.14	6.38	5.35	4.86	4.48	5.28
4	0.11	0.14	0.17	0.21	0.15	5.63	5.04	4.57	4.39	5.31
Big	0.13	0.15	0.16	0.17	0.12	4.61	4.33	4.00	3.89	4.55

Dependent variable: Excess returns on government and corporate bonds

	1–5G	6–10G	Aaa	Aa	A	Baa	LG
m	0.45	0.72	1.02	0.99	1.00	1.01	0.81
t(m)	31.73	38.80	99.94	130.44	139.80	56.24	18.05
d	0.25	0.27	0.94	0.96	1.02	1.10	1.01
t(d)	9.51	7.85	48.95	67.54	75.74	32.33	11.95
R^2	0.79	0.87	0.97	0.98	0.98	0.90	0.49
s(e)	0.57	0.75	0.41	0.30	0.29	0.72	1.80

[a] TERM is LTG–RF, where LTG is the monthly percent long-term government bond return and RF is the one-month Treasury bill rate, observed at the beginning of the month. DEF is CB–LTG, where CB is the return on a proxy for the market portfolio of corporate bonds.

The seven bond portfolios used as dependent variables in the excess-return regressions are 1- to 5-year and 6- to 10-year governments (1–5G and 6–10G) and corporate bonds rated Aaa, Aa, A, Baa, and below Baa (LG) by Moody's. The 25 size–BE/ME stock portfolios are formed as follows. Each year t from 1963 to 1991 NYSE quintile breakpoints for size (ME, stock price times shares outstanding), measured at the end of June, are used to allocate NYSE, Amex, and NASDAQ stocks to five size quintiles. Similarly, NYSE quintile breakpoints for BE/ME are used to allocate NYSE, Amex, and NASDAQ stocks to five book-to-market equity quintiles. In BE/ME, BE is book common equity for the fiscal year ending in calendar year t − 1, and ME is for the end of December of t − 1. The 25 size–BE/ME portfolios are formed as the intersections of the five size and the five BE/ME groups. Value-weighted monthly percent returns on the portfolios are calculated from July of year t to June of t + 1.

R^2 and the residual standard error, s(e), are adjusted for degrees of freedom.

7.8 standard errors from 0 for bonds, and more than 3.5 standard errors from 0 for stocks.

The slopes on *TERM* and *DEF* allow direct comparisons of the common variation in stock and bond returns tracked by the term-structure variables. Interestingly, the common variation captured by *TERM* and *DEF* is, if anything, stronger for stocks than for bonds. Most of the *DEF* slopes for stocks are bigger than those for bonds. The *TERM* slopes for stocks (all close to 1) are similar to the largest slopes produced by bonds.

As one might expect, however, the fractions of return variance explained by *TERM* and *DEF* are higher for bonds. In the bond regression, R^2 ranges from 0.49 for low-grade corporates to 0.97 and 0.98 for high-grade corporates. In contrast, R^2 ranges from 0.06 to 0.21 for stocks. Thus, *TERM* and *DEF* clearly identify shared variation in stock and bond returns, but for stocks and low-grade bonds, there is plenty of variation left to be explained by stock-market factors.

There is an interesting pattern in the slopes for *TERM*. The slopes increase from 0.45 to 0.72 for 1- to 5-year and 6- to 10-year governments, and then settle at values near 1 for four of the five long-term corporate bond portfolios. (The low-grade portfolio LG, with a slope of 0.81, is the exception.) As one would expect, long-term bonds are more sensitive than short-term bonds to the shifts in interest rates measured by *TERM*. What is striking, however, is that the 25 stock portfolios have *TERM* slopes like those for long-term bonds. This suggests that the risk captured by *TERM* results from shocks to discount rates that affect long-term securities, bonds and stocks, in about the same way.

There are interesting parallels between the *TERM* slopes observed here and our earlier evidence that yield spreads predict bond and stock returns. In Fama and French (1989), we find that a spread of long-term minus short-term bond yields (an ex ante version of *TERM*) predicts stock and bond returns, and captures about the same variation through time in the expected returns on long-term bonds and stocks. We conjectured that the yield spread captures variation in a term premium for discount-rate changes that affect all long-term securities in about the same way. The similar slopes on *TERM* for long-term bonds and stocks observed here seem consistent with that conjecture.

Our earlier work also finds that the return premium predicted by the long-term minus short-term yield spread wanders between positive and negative values, and is on average close to 0. This parallels the evidence here (table 2) that the average premium for the common risk associated with shifts in interest rates (the average value of *TERM*) is close to 0.

The pattern in the *DEF* slopes in table 3 is also interesting. The returns on small stocks are more sensitive to the risk captured by *DEF* than the returns on big stocks. The *DEF* slopes for stocks tend to be larger than those for corporate bonds, which are larger than those for governments. *DEF* thus seems to capture a common 'default' risk in returns that increases from government bonds to corporates, from bonds to stocks, and from big stocks to small stocks. Again, there is an interesting parallel between this pattern in the *DEF* slopes and the similar pattern observed in Fama and French (1989) in time-series regressions of stock and bond returns on an ex ante version of *DEF* (a spread of low-grade minus high-grade bond yields).

Using the Fama–Macbeth (1973) cross-section regression approach and stock portfolios formed on ranked values of size. Chan, Chen, and Hsieh (1985) and Chen, Roll, and Ross (1986) find that the cross-section of slopes on a variable like *DEF* goes a long way toward explaining the negative relation between size and average stock returns. Given the negative relation between size and the slopes on *DEF* in table 3, it is easy to see why the *DEF* slopes work well in cross-section return regressions for size portfolios.

Our time-series regressions suggest, however, that *DEF* cannot explain the size effect in average stock returns. In the time-series regressions, the average premium for a unit of *DEF* slope is the mean of *DEF*, a tiny 0.02% per month. Likewise, the average *TERM* return is only 0.06% per month. As a result, we shall see that the intercepts in the regressions of stock returns on *TERM* and *DEF* leave strong size and book-to-market effects in average returns. We shall also find that when the stock-market factors are added to the regressions, the negative relation between size and the *DEF* slopes in table 3 disappears.

4.2. Stock-Market Factors

The role of stock-market factors in returns is developed in three steps. We examine (a) regressions that use the excess market return, *RM–RF*, to explain excess bond and stock returns, (b) regressions that use *SMB* and *HML*, the mimicking returns for the size and book-to-market factors, as explanatory variables, and (c) regressions that use *RM–RF*, *SMB*, and *HML*. The three-factor regressions work well for stocks, but the one- and two-factor regressions help explain why.

The Market—Table 4 shows, not surprisingly, that the excess return on the market portfolio of stocks, *RM–RF*, captures more common variation in stock returns than the term-structure factors in table 3. For later purposes, however, the important fact is that the market leaves much variation in stock returns

TABLE 4. Regressions of excess stock and bond returns (in percent) on the excess stock-market return, RM–RF: July 1963 to December 1991, 342 months.[a]

$$R(t) - RF(t) = a + b[RM(t) - RF(t)] + e(t)$$

Dependent variable: Excess returns on 25 stock portfolios
formed on size and book-to-market equity

Book-to-market equity (BE/ME) quintiles

Size quintile	Low	2	3	4	High	Low	2	3	4	High
			b					*t(b)*		
Small	1.40	1.26	1.14	1.06	1.08	26.33	28.12	27.01	25.03	23.01
2	1.42	1.25	1.12	1.02	1.13	35.76	35.56	33.12	33.14	29.04
3	1.36	1.15	1.04	0.96	1.08	42.98	42.52	37.50	35.81	31.16
4	1.24	1.14	1.03	0.98	1.10	51.67	55.12	46.96	37.00	32.76
Big	1.03	0.99	0.89	0.84	0.89	51.92	61.51	43.03	35.96	27.75
			R^2					*s(e)*		
Small	0.67	0.70	0.68	0.65	0.61	4.46	3.76	3.55	3.56	3.92
2	0.79	0.79	0.76	0.76	0.71	3.34	2.96	2.85	2.59	3.25
3	0.84	0.84	0.80	0.79	0.74	2.65	2.28	2.33	2.26	2.90
4	0.89	0.90	0.87	0.80	0.76	2.01	1.73	1.84	2.21	2.83
Big	0.89	0.92	0.84	0.79	0.69	1.66	1.35	1.73	1.95	2.69

Dependent variable: Excess returns on government and corporate bonds

	1–5G	6–10G	Aaa	Aa	A	Baa	LG
b	0.08	0.13	0.19	0.20	0.21	0.22	0.30
t(b)	5.24	5.57	7.53	8.14	8.42	8.73	11.90
R^2	0.07	0.08	0.14	0.16	0.17	0.18	0.29
s(e)	1.21	1.95	2.17	2.05	2.05	2.12	2.12

[a]*RM* is the value-weighted monthly percent return on all the stocks in the 25 size–*BE/ME* portfolios, plus the negative-*BE* stocks excluded from the 25 portfolios. *RF* is the one-month Treasury bill rate, observed at the beginning of the month.

The seven bond portfolios used as dependent variables in the excess-return regressions are 1- to 5-year and 6- to 10-year governments (1–5G and 6–10G) and corporate bonds rated Aaa, Aa, A, Baa, and below Baa (LG) by Moody's. The 25 size–*BE/ME* stock portfolios are formed as follows. Each year *t* from 1963 to 1991 NYSE quintile breakpoints for size (*ME*, stock price times shares outstanding), measured at the end of June, are used to allocate NYSE, Amex, and NASDAQ stocks to five size quintiles. Similarly, NYSE quintile breakpoints for *BE/ME* are used to allocate NYSE, Amex, and NASDAQ stocks to five book-to market equity quintiles. In *BE/ME*, *BE* is book common equity for the fiscal year ending in calendar year *t* − 1, and *ME* is for the end of December of *t* − 1. The 25 size–*BE/ME* portfolios are formed as the intersections of the five size and the five *BE/ME* groups. Value-weighted monthly percent returns are calculated from July of year *t* to June of *t* + 1.

R^2 and the residual standard error, *s(e)*, are adjusted for degrees of freedom.

that might be explained by other factors. The only R^2 values near 0.9 are for the big-stock low-book-to-market portfolios. For small-stock and high-*BE/ ME* portfolios. R^2 values less than 0.8 or 0.7 are the rule. These are the stock portfolios for which the size and book-to-market factors, *SMB* and *HML*, will have their best shot at showing marginal explanatory power.

The market portfolio of stocks also captures common variation in bond returns. Although the market βs are much smaller for bonds than for stocks, they are 5 to 12 standard errors from 0. Consistent with intuition, β is higher for corporate bonds than for governments and higher for low-grade than for high-grade bonds. The β for low-grade bonds (LG) is 0.30, and *RM–RF* explains a tidy 29% of the variance of the LG return.

SMB and HML—Table 5 shows that in the absence of competition from the market portfolio, *SMB* and *HML* typically capture substantial time-series variation in stock returns; 20 of the 25 R^2 values are above 0.2 and eight are above 0.5. Especially for the portfolios in the larger-size quintile, however, *SMB* and *HML* leave common variation in stock returns that is picked up by the market portfolio in table 4.

The Market, SMB, and HML—Table 5 says that, used alone, *SMB* and *HML* have little power to explain bond returns. Table 6 shows that when the excess market return is also in the regressions, each of the three stock-market factors captures variation in bond returns. We shall find, however, that adding the term-structure factors to the bond regressions largely kills the explanatory power of the stock-market factors. Thus the apparent role of the stock-market factors in bond returns in table 6 probably results from covariation between the term-structure and stock-market factors.

The interesting regressions in table 6 are for stocks. Not surprisingly, the three stock-market factors capture strong common variation in stock returns. The market βs for stocks are all more than 38 standard errors from 0. With one exception, the *t*-statistics on the *SMB* slopes for stocks are greater than 4; most are greater than 10. *SMB*, the mimicking return for the size factor, clearly captures shared variation in stock returns that is missed by the market and by *HML*. Moreover, the slopes on *SMB* for stocks are related to size. In every book-to-market quintile. the slopes on *SMB* decrease monotonically from smaller- to bigger-size quintiles.

Similarly, the slopes on *HML*, the mimicking return for the book-to-market factor, are systematically related to *BE/ME*. In every size quintile of stocks, the *HML* slopes increase monotonically from strong negative values for the

TABLE 5. Regressions of excess stock and bond returns (in percent) on the mimicking returns for the size (SMB) and book-to-market equity (HML) factors: July 1963 to December 1991, 342 months.[a]

$$R(t) - RF(t) = a + sSMB(t) + hHML(t) + e(t)$$

Dependent variable: Excess returns on 25 stock portfolios formed on size and book-to-market equity

Book-to-market equity (BE/ME) quintiles

Size quintile	Low	2	3	4	High	Low	2	3	4	High
			s					$t(s)$		
Small	1.93	1.73	1.63	1.59	1.67	22.52	21.38	21.88	22.30	22.16
2	1.52	1.46	1.35	1.18	1.40	17.23	17.68	17.08	15.47	16.42
3	1.28	1.12	1.05	0.93	1.16	14.43	13.89	13.42	12.13	13.45
4	0.86	0.82	0.77	0.72	0.95	10.16	9.64	9.29	8.57	10.02
Big	0.28	0.35	0.22	0.29	0.44	3.70	4.39	2.79	3.69	5.02
			h					$t(h)$		
Small	-0.95	-0.57	-0.35	-0.18	0.01	-9.72	-6.19	-4.10	-2.20	0.16
2	-1.23	-0.66	-0.38	-0.16	0.00	-12.25	-7.02	-4.20	-1.82	0.05
3	-1.09	-0.65	-0.31	-0.11	-0.01	-10.84	-7.07	-3.43	-1.23	-0.12
4	-1.11	-0.65	-0.36	-0.11	-0.01	-11.43	-6.69	-3.80	-1.12	-0.09
Big	-1.07	-0.65	-0.42	-0.06	0.08	-12.46	-7.07	-4.64	-0.66	0.81
			R^2					$s(e)$		
Small	0.65	0.60	0.60	0.60	0.59	4.57	4.31	3.98	3.79	4.01
2	0.59	0.53	0.49	0.42	0.44	4.68	4.41	4.20	4.06	4.53
3	0.51	0.43	0.37	0.31	0.35	4.71	4.31	4.19	4.10	4.60
4	0.43	0.30	0.24	0.18	0.23	4.53	4.55	4.40	4.48	5.06
Big	0.34	0.18	0.08	0.04	0.06	4.02	4.27	4.20	4.19	4.69

Dependent variable: Excess returns on government and corporate bonds

	1–5G	6–10G	Aaa	Aa	A	Baa	LG
s	-0.02	-0.06	-0.00	0.00	0.03	0.09	0.19
t(s)	-0.66	-1.50	-0.15	0.22	0.77	1.99	4.19
h	0.00	-0.03	-0.02	-0.01	-0.00	0.02	0.00
t(h)	0.24	-0.71	-0.45	-0.22	-0.05	0.46	0.15
R^2	-0.00	0.00	-0.00	-0.00	-0.00	0.00	0.04
s(e)	1.26	2.03	2.34	2.24	2.25	2.34	2.46

[a]SMB (small minus big), the return on the mimicking portfolio for the common size factor in stock returns, is the difference each month between the simple average of the percent returns on the three small-stock portfolios (S/L, S/M, and S/H) and the simple average of the returns on the three big-stock portfolios (B/L, B/M, and B/H). HML (high minus low), the return on the mimicking portfolio for the common book-to-market equity factor in returns, is the difference each month between the simple average of the returns on the two high-BE/ME portfolios (S/H and B/H) and the average of the returns on the two low-BE/ME portfolios (S/L and B/L).

The seven bond portfolios used as dependent variables in the excess-return regressions are 1- to 5-year and 6- to 10-year governments (1–5G and 6–10G) and corporate bonds rated Aaa, Aa, A, Baa, and below Baa (LG) by Moody's. The 25 size–BE/ME stock portfolios are formed as follows. Each year t from 1963 to 1991 NYSE quintile breakpoints for size (ME, stock price times shares outstanding), measured at the end of June, are used to allocate NYSE, Amex, and NASDAQ stocks to five size quintiles. Similarly, NYSE quintile breakpoints for BE/ME are used to allocate NYSE, Amex, and NASDAQ stocks to five book-to-market equity quintiles. In BE/ME, BE is book common equity for the fiscal year ending in calendar year $t-1$, and ME is for the end of December of $t-1$. The 25 size–BE/ME portfolios are formed as the intersections of the five size and the five BE/ME groups. Value-weighted percent monthly returns on the portfolios are calculated from July of year t to June of $t+1$.

R^2 and the residual standard error, $s(e)$, are adjusted for degrees of freedom.

lowest-*BE/ME* quintile to strong positive values for the highest-*BE/ME* quintile. Except for the second *BE/ME* quintile, where the slopes pass from negative to positive, the *HML* slopes are more than five standard errors from 0. *HML* clearly captures shared variation in stock returns, related to book-to-market equity, that is missed by the market and by *SMB*.

Given the strong slopes on *SMB* and *HML* for stocks, it is not surprising that adding the two returns to the regressions results in large increases in R^2. For stocks, the market alone produces only two (of 25) R^2 values greater than 0.9 (table 4); in the three-factor regressions (table 6), R^2 values greater than 0.9 are routine (21 of 25). For the five portfolios in the smallest-size quintile, R^2 increases from values between 0.61 and 0.70 in table 4 to values between 0.94 and 0.97 in table 6. Even the lowest three-factor R^2 for stocks, 0.83 for the portfolio in the largest-size and highest-*BE/ME* quintiles, is much larger than the 0.69 generated by the market alone.

Adding *SMB* and *HML* to the regressions has an interesting effect on the market βs for stocks. In the one-factor regressions of table 4, the β for the portfolio of stocks in the smallest-size and lowest-*BE/ME* quintiles is 1.40. At the other extreme, the univariate β for the portfolio of stocks in the biggest-size and highest-*BE/ME* quintiles is 0.89. In the three-factor regressions of table 6, the βs for these two portfolios are 1.04 and 1.06. In general, adding *SMB* and *HML* to the regressions collapses the βs for stocks toward 1.0; low βs move up toward 1.0 and high βs move down. This behavior is due, of course, to correlation between the market and *SMB* or *HML*. Although *SMB* and *HML* are almost uncorrelated (-0.08), the correlations between *RM–RF* and the *SMB* and *HML* returns are 0.32 and -0.38.

4.3. Stock-Market and Bond-Market Factors

Used alone, bond-market factors capture common variation in stock returns as well as bond returns (table 3). Used alone, stock-market factors capture shared variation in bond returns as well as stock returns (table 6). These results demonstrate that there is overlap between the stochastic processes for bond and stock returns. We emphasize this point because the joint tests on the stock- and bond-market factors that follow muddy the issue a bit.

First Pass—Table 7 shows that, used together to explain returns, the bond-market factors continue to have a strong role in bond returns and the stock-market factors have a strong role in stock returns. For stocks, adding *TERM* and *DEF* to the regressions has little effect on the slopes on the stock-market factors; the slopes on *RM–RF, SMB,* and *HML* for stocks in table 7a are strong

TABLE 6. Regressions of excess stock and bond returns (in percent) on the excess market return (RM–RF) and the mimicking returns for the size (SMB) and book-to-market equity (HML) factors: July 1963 to December 1991, 342 months.[a]

$$R(t) - RF(t) = a + b[RM(t) - RF(t)] + sSMB(t) + hHML(t) + e(t)$$

Dependent variable: Excess returns on 25 stock portfolios formed on size and book-to-market equity

	Book-to-market equity (BE/ME) quintiles									
Size quintile	Low	2	3	4	High	Low	2	3	4	High
	b									
Small	1.04	1.02	0.95	0.91	0.96	39.37	51.80	60.44	59.73	57.89
2	1.11	1.06	1.00	0.97	1.09	52.49	61.18	55.88	61.54	65.52
3	1.12	1.02	0.98	0.97	1.09	56.88	53.17	50.78	54.38	52.52
4	1.07	1.08	1.04	1.05	1.18	53.94	53.51	51.21	47.09	46.10
Big	0.96	1.02	0.98	0.99	1.06	60.93	56.76	46.57	53.87	38.61
	s					*t(b)*				
Small	1.46	1.26	1.19	1.17	1.23	37.92	44.11	52.03	52.85	50.97
2	1.00	0.98	0.88	0.73	0.89	32.73	38.79	34.03	31.66	36.78
3	0.76	0.65	0.60	0.48	0.66	26.40	23.39	21.23	18.62	21.91
4	0.37	0.33	0.29	0.24	0.41	12.73	11.11	9.81	7.38	11.01
Big	-0.17	-0.12	-0.23	-0.17	-0.05	-7.18	-4.51	-7.58	-6.27	-1.18
	h					*t(s)*				
Small	-0.29	0.08	0.26	0.40	0.62	-6.47	2.35	9.66	15.53	22.24
2	-0.52	0.01	0.26	0.46	0.70	-14.57	0.41	8.56	17.24	24.80
3	-0.38	-0.00	0.32	0.51	0.68	-11.26	-0.05	9.75	16.88	19.39
4	-0.42	0.04	0.30	0.56	0.74	-12.51	1.04	8.83	14.84	17.09
Big	-0.46	0.00	0.21	0.57	0.76	-17.03	0.09	5.80	18.34	16.24
						t(h)				

(Continued)

TABLE 6. (Continued)

Size quintile	Book-to-market equity (BE/ME) quintiles									
	Low	2	3	4	High	Low	2	3	4	High
			R^2					$s(e)$		
Small	0.94	0.96	0.97	0.97	0.96	1.94	1.44	1.16	1.12	1.22
2	0.95	0.96	0.95	0.95	0.96	1.55	1.27	1.31	1.16	1.23
3	0.95	0.94	0.93	0.93	0.93	1.45	1.41	1.43	1.32	1.52
4	0.94	0.93	0.91	0.89	0.89	1.46	1.48	1.49	1.63	1.88
Big	0.94	0.92	0.88	0.90	0.83	1.16	1.32	1.55	1.36	2.02

Dependent variable: Excess returns on government and corporate bonds

	1–5G	6–10G	Aaa	Aa	A	Baa	LG
b	0.10	0.18	0.25	0.25	0.26	0.27	0.34
$t(b)$	6.45	6.75	8.60	9.30	9.46	9.58	12.22
s	−0.06	−0.14	−0.12	−0.11	−0.09	−0.04	0.04
$t(s)$	−2.70	−3.65	−2.89	−2.72	−2.18	−0.91	0.89
h	0.07	0.08	0.14	0.15	0.16	0.20	0.23
$t(h)$	2.66	1.83	2.77	3.26	3.51	4.08	4.75
R^2	0.10	0.12	0.17	0.20	0.20	0.22	0.33
$s(e)$	1.19	1.91	2.13	2.00	2.01	2.08	2.06

[a]RM is the value-weighted percent monthly return on all the stocks in the 25 size–BE/ME portfolios, plus the negative-BE stocks excluded from the 25 portfolios. RF is the one-month Treasury bill rate, observed at the beginning of the month. SMB (small minus big) is the return on the mimicking portfolio for the size factor in stock returns. HML (high minus low) is the return on the mimicking portfolio for the book-to-market factor. (See table 5.)

The seven bond portfolios used as dependent variables are 1- to 5-year and 6- to 10-year governments (1–5G and 6–10G) and corporate bonds rated Aaa, Aa, A, Baa, and below Baa (LG) by Moody's. The 25 size–BE/ME stock portfolios are formed as follows. Each year t from 1963 to 1991 NYSE quintile breakpoints for size, ME, measured at the end of June, are used to allocate NYSE, Amex, and NASDAQ stocks to five size quintiles. Similarly, NYSE quintile breakpoints for BE/ME are used to allocate NYSE, Amex, and NASDAQ stocks to five book-to-market equity quintiles. In BE/ME, BE is book common equity for the fiscal year ending in calendar year $t − 1$, and ME is for the end of December of $t − 1$. The 25 size–BE/ME portfolios are the intersections of the five size and the five BE/ME groups. Value-weighted monthly percent returns on the 25 portfolios are calculated from July of t to June of $t + 1$.

R^2 and the residual standard error, $s(e)$, are adjusted for degrees of freedom.

and much like those in table 6. Similarly, adding *RM–RF, SMB,* and *HML* to the regressions for bonds has little effect on the slopes on *TERM* and *DEF,* which are strong and much like those in table 3.

The five-factor regressions in table 7 do, however, seem to contradict the evidence in tables 3 and 6 that there is strong overlap between the return processes for bonds and stocks. Adding the stock-market factors to the regressions for stocks kills the strong slopes on *TERM* and *DEF* observed in the two-factor regressions of table 3. The evidence in table 6 that bond returns respond to stock-market factors also largely disappears in table 7b. In the five-factor regressions, only the low-grade bond portfolio, LG, continues to produce non-trivial slopes on the stock-market factors.

Table 7 seems to say that the only shared variation in bond and stock returns comes through low-grade bonds. But tables 3 and 6 say there is strong common variation in bond and stock returns when bond- and stock-market factors are used alone to explain returns. Can we reconcile these results? We argue next that the two term-structure factors are indeed common to bond and stock returns. In the five-factor regressions for stocks, however, the tracks of *TERM* and *DEF* are buried in the excess market return, *RM–RF.* In contrast to the two term-structure factors, the three stock-market factors are generally confined to stock returns; except for low-grade bonds, these factors do not spill over into bond returns. In short, we argue that stock returns share three stock-market factors, and the links between stock and bond returns come largely from two shared term-structure factors.

Second Pass: An Orthogonalized Market Factor—If there are multiple common factors in stock returns, they are all in the market return, *RM,* which is just a value-weighted average of the returns on the stocks in the CRSP–COMPUSTAT sample. The regression of *RM–RF* on *SMB, HML, TERM,* and *DEF* for monthly returns of July 1963 to December 1991 illustrates the point:

$$RM - RF = 0.50 + 0.44\,SMB - 0.63\,HML + 0.81\,TERM + 0.79\,DEF + e.$$
$$\quad\ (2.55)\ (6.48)\quad (-8.23)\qquad (9.09)\qquad (4.62) \tag{1}$$

The *t*-statistics are in parentheses below the slopes; the R^2 is 0.38. This regression demonstrates that the market return is a hodgepodge of the common factors in returns. The strong slopes on *TERM* and *DEF* produced by *RM–RF* (the excess return on a proxy for the portfolio of stock-market wealth) are clear evidence that the two term-structure factors capture common variation in stock returns.

The sum of the intercept and the residuals in (1), call it *RMO*, is a zero-investment portfolio return that is uncorrelated with the four explanatory variables in (1). We can use *RMO* as an orthogonalized market factor that captures common variation in returns left by *SMB*, *HML*, *TERM*, and *DEF*. Since the stock-market returns, *SMB* and *HML*, are largely uncorrelated with the bond-market returns, *TERM* and *DEF* (table 2), five-factor regressions that use *RMO*, *SMB*, *HML*, *TERM*, and *DEF* to explain bond and stock returns will provide a clean picture of the separate roles of bond- and stock-market factors in bond and stock returns. The regressions are in table 8.

The story for the common variation in bond returns in table 8b is like that in table 7b. The bond-market factors, *TERM* and *DEF*, have strong roles in bond returns. Some bond portfolios produce slopes on the stock-market factors that are more than two standard errors from 0. But this is mostly because *TERM* and *DEF* produce high R^2 values in the bond regressions, so trivial slopes can be reliably different from 0. As in table 7b, only the low-grade bond portfolio (LG) produces nontrivial slopes on the stock-market factors. Otherwise, the stock-market factors don't add much to the shared variation in bond returns captured by *TERM* and *DEF*.

For the stock portfolios, the slopes on *RMO* in the five-factor regressions of table 8a are identical (by construction) to the large slopes on *RM–RF* in table 7a. The slopes on the size and book-to-market returns in table 8a shift somewhat (up for *SMB*, down for *HML*) relative to the slopes in table 7a. But the spreads in the *SMB* and *HML* slopes across the stock portfolios in table 8a are like those in table 7a, and *SMB* and *HML* again capture strong shared variation in stock returns.

What changes dramatically in the five-factor regressions of table 8, relative to table 7, are the slopes on the term-structure factors for stocks. The slopes on *TERM* are more than 14 standard errors from 0; the *DEF* slopes are more than seven standard errors from 0. The slopes on *TERM* and *DEF* for stocks are like those for bonds. Thus unlike table 7, the five-factor regressions in table 8 say that the term-structure factors capture strong common variation in stock and bond returns.

How do the tracks of the term-structure variables get buried in the five-factor regressions for stocks in table 7a? Table 8a says that stocks load strongly on *RMO*, *TERM*, and *DEF*, but there is little cross-sectional variation in the slopes on these factors. All the stock portfolios produce slopes on *TERM* and

TABLE 7A. Regressions of excess stock returns on 25 stock portfolios formed on size and book-to-market equity (in percent) on the stock-market returns, RM–RF, SMB, and HML, and the bond-market returns, TERM and DEF: July 1963 to December 1991, 342 months.[a]

$$R(t) - RF(t) = a + b[RM(t) - RF(t)] + sSMB(t) + hHML(t) + mTERM(t) + dDEF(t) + e(t)$$

Book-to-market equity (BE/ME) quintiles

Size quintile	Low	2	3	4	High	Low	2	3	4	High
			b					$t(b)$		
Small	1.06	1.04	0.96	0.92	0.98	35.97	47.65	54.48	54.51	53.15
2	1.12	1.06	0.98	0.94	1.10	47.19	54.95	49.01	54.19	59.00
3	1.13	1.01	0.97	0.95	1.08	50.93	46.95	44.57	47.59	46.92
4	1.07	1.07	1.01	1.00	1.17	48.18	47.55	44.83	41.02	41.02
Big	0.96	1.02	0.98	1.00	1.10	53.87	51.01	41.35	48.29	35.96
			s					$t(s)$		
Small	1.45	1.26	1.20	1.15	1.21	37.02	43.42	50.89	51.36	49.55
2	1.01	0.98	0.89	0.74	0.89	32.06	38.10	33.68	32.12	35.79
3	0.76	0.66	0.60	0.49	0.68	25.82	22.97	20.83	18.54	22.32
4	0.38	0.34	0.30	0.26	0.42	12.71	11.36	9.99	8.05	11.07
Big	-0.17	-0.11	-0.23	-0.17	-0.06	-7.03	-4.07	-7.31	-6.07	-1.44
			h					$t(h)$		
Small	-0.27	0.10	0.27	0.40	0.63	-5.95	2.90	9.82	15.47	22.27
2	-0.51	0.02	0.25	0.44	0.71	-14.01	0.69	8.11	16.50	24.61
3	-0.37	-0.00	0.31	0.50	0.69	-10.81	-0.11	9.28	16.18	19.34
4	-0.42	0.04	0.29	0.53	0.75	-12.09	1.10	8.37	14.20	16.88
Big	-0.46	0.01	0.21	0.58	0.78	-16.85	0.38	5.70	18.16	16.59

(Continued)

Book-to-market equity (BE/ME) quintiles

Size quintile	Low	2	3	4	High	Low	2	3	4	High
			m					$t(m)$		
Small	-0.10	-0.11	-0.05	-0.04	-0.06	-1.93	-2.70	-1.49	-1.19	-1.87
2	-0.05	-0.04	0.07	0.14	-0.05	-1.16	-1.12	1.90	4.33	-1.48
3	-0.04	0.02	0.06	0.09	0.01	-0.91	0.53	1.48	2.48	0.25
4	-0.02	0.00	0.08	0.18	-0.01	-0.55	0.19	1.92	3.98	-0.19
Big	0.03	-0.04	-0.00	-0.04	-0.16	0.82	-0.98	-0.06	-0.98	-2.82
			d					$t(d)$		
Small	-0.17	-0.19	-0.10	0.06	0.02	-1.74	-2.70	-1.76	1.06	0.34
2	-0.12	-0.11	0.04	0.15	-0.07	-1.59	-1.83	0.61	2.64	-1.24
3	-0.09	-0.01	0.07	0.10	-0.16	-1.25	-0.17	1.00	1.51	-2.11
4	-0.11	-0.10	0.04	0.13	-0.12	-1.51	-1.44	0.59	1.64	-1.30
Big	0.06	-0.14	-0.02	-0.07	-0.18	0.97	-2.15	-0.25	-1.08	-1.84
			R^2					$s(e)$		
Small	0.94	0.96	0.97	0.97	0.96	1.93	1.43	1.16	1.11	1.20
2	0.95	0.96	0.95	0.95	0.96	1.55	1.27	1.31	1.13	1.23
3	0.95	0.94	0.93	0.93	0.93	1.45	1.41	1.43	1.31	1.50
4	0.94	0.93	0.91	0.90	0.89	1.46	1.47	1.48	1.59	1.88
Big	0.94	0.92	0.87	0.90	0.83	1.17	1.31	1.55	1.36	2.00

[a]See footnote under table 7b.

TABLE 7B. Regressions of excess stock returns on government and corporate bonds (in percent) on the stock-market returns, RM–RF, SMB, and HML, and the bond-market returns, TERM and DEF: July 1963 to December 1991, 342 months.[a]

$$R(t) - RF(t) = a + b[RM(t) - RF(t)] + sSMB(t) + hHML(t) + mTERM(t) + dDEF(t) + e(t)$$

				Bond portfolio			
	1–5G	6–10G	Aaa	Aa	A	Baa	LG
b	−0.02	−0.04	−0.02	0.00	0.00	0.02	0.18
t(b)	−2.84	−3.14	−2.96	0.06	1.05	1.99	7.39
s	0.00	−0.02	−0.02	−0.01	0.00	0.05	0.08
t(s)	0.30	−1.12	−2.28	−2.42	0.40	3.20	2.34
h	0.00	−0.02	−0.02	−0.00	0.00	0.04	0.12
t(h)	0.44	−1.29	−2.46	−0.40	0.90	2.39	3.13
m	0.47	0.75	1.03	0.99	1.00	0.99	0.64
t(m)	30.01	36.84	93.30	117.30	124.19	50.50	14.25
d	0.27	0.32	0.97	0.97	1.02	1.05	0.80
t(d)	9.87	8.77	49.25	65.04	71.51	30.33	9.92
R^2	0.80	0.87	0.97	0.98	0.98	0.91	0.58
s(e)	0.56	0.73	0.40	0.30	0.29	0.70	1.63

[a] RM is the value-weighted monthly percent return on all stocks in the 25 size–BE/ME portfolios, plus the negative-BE stocks excluded from the portfolios. RF is the one-month Treasury bill rate, observed at the beginning of the month. SMB (small minus big) is the difference each month between the simple average of the returns on the three small-stock portfolios (S/L, S/M, and S/H) and the simple average of the returns on the three big-stock portfolios (B/L, B/M, and B/H). HML (high minus low) is the difference each month between the simple average of the returns on the two high-BE/ME portfolios (S/H and B/H) and the average of the returns on the two low-BE/ME portfolios (S/L and B/L). TERM is LTG–RF, where LTG is the long-term government bond return. DEF is CB–LTG, where CB is the return on a proxy for the market portfolio of corporate bonds.

The seven bond portfolios used as dependent variables in the excess-return regressions are 1- to 5-year and 6- to 10-year governments (1–5G and 6–10G) and corporate bonds rated Aaa, Aa, A, Baa, and below Baa (LG) by Moody's. The 25 size–BE/ME stock portfolios are formed as follows. Each year t from 1963 to 1991 NYSE quintile breakpoints for size (ME, stock price times shares outstanding), measured at the end of June, are used to allocate NYSE, Amex, and NASDAQ stocks to five size quintiles. Similarly, NYSE quintile breakpoints for BE/ME are used to allocate NYSE, Amex, and NASDAQ stocks to five book-to-market quintiles. In BE/ME, BE is book common equity for the fiscal year ending in calendar year t − 1, and ME is for the end of December of t − 1. The 25 size–BE/ME portfolios are the intersections of the five size and the five BE/ME groups. Value-weighted monthly percent returns on the portfolios are calculated from July of year t to June of t + 1.

R^2 and the residual standard error, s(e), are adjusted for degrees of freedom.

DEF close to 0.81 and 0.79, the slopes produced by the excess market return in (1). And the stock portfolios all produce slopes close to 1.0 on *RMO* in table 8a, and thus on *RM–RF* in table 7a. Tables 7a and 8a then say that because there is little cross-sectional variation in the slopes on *RM–RF, RMO, TERM,* and *DEF,* the excess market return in table 7a absorbs the common variation in stock returns associated with *RMO, TERM,* and *DEF.* In short, the common variation in stock returns related to the term-structure factors is buried in the excess market return in table 7a.

Is there any reason to prefer the five-factor regressions in table 8 over those in table 7? Only to show that, in addition to the three stock-market factors, there are two bond-market factors in stock returns. Otherwise, the two sets of regressions produce the same R^2 values and thus the same estimates of the total common variation in returns. And the two sets of regressions produce the same intercepts for testing the implications of five-factor models for the cross-section of average stock returns.

5. THE CROSS-SECTION OF AVERAGE RETURNS

The regression slopes and R^2 values in tables 3 to 8 establish that the stock-market returns, *SMB, HML,* and *RM–RF* (or *RMO*), and the bond-market returns, *TERM* and *DEF,* proxy for risk factors. They capture common variation in bond and stock returns. Stock returns have shared variation related to three stock-market factors, and they are linked to bond returns through shared variation in two term-structure factors. We next test how well the average premiums for the five proxy risk factors explain the cross-section of average returns on bonds and stocks.

The average-return tests center on the intercepts in the time-series regressions. The dependent variables in the regressions are excess returns. The explanatory variables are excess returns (*RM–RF* and *TERM*) or returns on zero-investment portfolios (*RMO, SMB, HML,* and *DEF*). Suppose the explanatory returns have minimal variance due to firm-specific factors, so they are good mimicking returns for the underlying state variables or common risk factors of concern to investors. Then the multifactor asset-pricing models of Merton (1973) and Ross (1976) imply a simple test of whether the premiums associated with any set of explanatory returns suffice to describe the cross-section of average returns: the intercepts in the time-series regressions of excess returns on the mimicking portfolio returns should be indistinguishable from 0.[1]

---

1. This implication is only an approximation in the Ross (1976) model. See, for example, Shanken (1982).

TABLE 8A. Regressions of excess stock returns on 25 stock portfolios formed on size and book-to-market equity (in percent) on the stock-market returns, RMO, SMB, and HML, and the bond-market returns, TERM and DEF: July 1963 to December 1991, 342 months.[a]

$$R(t) - RF(t) = a + bRMO(t) + sSMB(t) + hHML(t) + mTERM(t) + dDEF(t) + e(t)$$

Book-to-market equity (BE/ME) quintiles

Size quintile	Low	2	3	4	High	Low	2	3	4	High
			b					$t(b)$		
Small	1.06	1.04	0.96	0.92	0.98	35.97	47.65	54.48	54.51	53.15
2	1.12	1.06	0.98	0.94	1.10	47.19	54.95	49.01	54.19	59.00
3	1.13	1.01	0.97	0.95	1.08	50.93	46.95	44.57	47.59	46.92
4	1.07	1.07	1.01	1.00	1.17	48.18	47.55	44.83	41.02	41.02
Big	0.96	1.02	0.98	1.00	1.10	53.87	51.01	41.35	48.29	35.96
			s					$t(s)$		
Small	1.92	1.72	1.62	1.56	1.64	51.96	62.88	73.21	73.72	71.32
2	1.50	1.45	1.33	1.16	1.38	50.66	59.80	53.02	53.20	58.79
3	1.26	1.11	1.03	0.91	1.16	45.37	40.94	37.83	36.47	40.24
4	0.85	0.81	0.75	0.70	0.94	30.49	28.84	26.42	23.02	26.22
Big	0.26	0.34	0.20	0.28	0.43	11.56	13.69	6.85	10.62	11.17
			h					$t(h)$		
Small	-0.94	-0.56	-0.34	-0.18	0.01	-22.65	-18.19	-13.67	-7.49	0.57
2	-1.22	-0.65	-0.37	-0.15	0.01	-36.52	-23.89	-13.09	-6.22	0.51
3	-1.08	-0.64	-0.30	-0.10	0.00	-34.68	-21.18	-9.82	-3.61	0.16
4	-1.09	-0.64	-0.35	-0.10	0.00	-34.85	-20.12	-10.93	-2.83	0.10
Big	-1.07	-0.63	-0.41	-0.05	0.09	-42.62	-22.46	-12.30	-1.75	2.06

(Continued)

TABLE 8A. (Continued)

Size quintile	Book-to-market equity (BE/ME) quintiles						Book-to-market equity (BE/ME) quintiles				
	Low	2	3	4	High		Low	2	3	4	High
	m						$t(m)$				
Small	0.75	0.73	0.73	0.71	0.73		15.66	20.60	25.32	25.67	24.24
2	0.85	0.82	0.86	0.89	0.84		22.08	25.96	26.40	31.68	27.57
3	0.88	0.84	0.84	0.86	0.88		24.21	23.85	23.73	26.34	23.52
4	0.85	0.87	0.90	0.98	0.94		23.24	23.77	24.35	24.76	20.11
Big	0.80	0.79	0.79	0.77	0.73		27.60	24.17	20.42	22.83	14.66
	d						$t(d)$				
Small	0.67	0.63	0.66	0.78	0.79		7.25	9.20	11.90	14.81	13.73
2	0.76	0.72	0.81	0.89	0.79		10.23	11.94	12.96	16.36	13.57
3	0.80	0.78	0.83	0.84	0.69		11.53	11.64	12.25	13.53	9.63
4	0.74	0.74	0.84	0.91	0.80		10.56	10.48	11.88	12.01	8.98
Big	0.81	0.66	0.75	0.72	0.68		14.56	10.62	10.15	11.04	7.15
	R^2						$s(e)$				
Small	0.94	0.96	0.97	0.97	0.96		1.93	1.43	1.16	1.11	1.20
2	0.95	0.96	0.95	0.95	0.96		1.55	1.27	1.31	1.13	1.23
3	0.95	0.94	0.93	0.93	0.93		1.45	1.41	1.43	1.31	1.50
4	0.94	0.93	0.91	0.90	0.89		1.46	1.47	1.48	1.59	1.88
Big	0.94	0.92	0.87	0.90	0.83		1.17	1.31	1.55	1.36	2.00

aSee footnote under table 8b.

TABLE 8B. Regressions of excess returns on government and corporate bonds (in percent) on the stock-market returns, RMO, SMB, and HML, and the bond-market returns, TERM and DEF: July 1963 to December 1991, 342 months.[a]

$$R(t) - RF(t) = a + bRMO(t) + sSMB(t) + hHML(t) + mTERM(t) + dDEF(t) + e(t)$$

				Bond portfolio			
	1–5G	6–10G	Aaa	Aa	A	Baa	LG
b	−0.02	−0.04	−0.02	0.00	0.00	0.02	0.18
t(b)	−2.84	−3.14	−2.96	0.06	1.05	1.99	7.39
s	−0.00	−0.03	−0.03	−0.01	0.00	0.06	0.16
t(s)	−0.68	−2.30	−3.47	−2.55	0.80	4.09	5.09
h	0.02	−0.00	−0.01	−0.00	0.00	0.03	0.00
t(h)	1.76	−0.00	−1.36	−0.47	0.52	1.72	0.12
m	0.45	0.72	1.02	0.99	1.00	1.01	0.79
t(m)	32.09	39.55	102.65	130.93	139.11	57.34	19.56
d	0.25	0.29	0.95	0.97	1.02	1.07	0.94
t(d)	9.46	8.25	50.04	67.08	74.00	31.77	12.09
R^2	0.80	0.87	0.97	0.98	0.98	0.91	0.58
s(e)	0.56	0.73	0.40	0.30	0.29	0.70	1.63

[a]RMO, the orthogonalized market return, is the sum of intercept and residuals from the regression of RM–RF on SMB, HML, TERM, and DEF. RM is the value-weighted monthly percent return on all stocks in the 25 size–BE/ME portfolios, plus the negative-BE stocks excluded from the portfolios. RF is the one-month Treasury bill rate, observed at the beginning of the month. SMB (small minus big), the return on the mimicking portfolio for the common size factor in stock returns, is the difference each month between the simple average of the returns on the three small-stock portfolios (S/L, S/M, and S/H) and the simple average of the returns on the three big-stock portfolios (B/L, B/M, and B/H). HML (high minus low), the return on the mimicking portfolio for the common book-to-market equity factor in returns, is the difference each month between the simple average of the returns on the two high-BE/ME portfolios (S/H and B/H) and the average of the returns on the two low-BE/ME portfolios (S/L and B/L). TERM is LTG–RF. where LTG is the long-term government bond return. DEF is CB–LTG. where CB is the return on a proxy for the market portfolio of corporate bonds.

The seven bond portfolios used as dependent variables in the excess-return regressions are 1- to 5-year and 6- to 10-year governments (1–5G and 6–10G) and bonds rated Aaa, Aa, A, Baa, and below Baa (LG) by Moody's. The 25 size–BE/ME stock portfolios are formed as follows. Each year t from 1963 to 1991 NYSE quintile breakpoints for size (ME, stock price times shares outstanding), measured at the end of June, are used to allocate NYSE, Amex, and NASDAQ stocks to five size quintiles. NYSE quintile breakpoints for BE/ME are also used to allocate NYSE, Amex, and NASDAQ stocks to five-book-to-market equity quintiles. In BE/ME, BE is book common equity for the fiscal year ending in calendar year t − 1, and ME is for the end of December of t − 1. The 25 size–BE/ME portfolios are the intersections of the five size and the five BE/ME groups. Value-weighted monthly percent returns on the portfolios are calculated from July of year t to June of t + 1.

R^2 and the residual standard error, s(e), are adjusted for degrees of freedom.

Since the stock portfolios produce a wide range of average returns, we examine their intercepts first. We are especially interested in whether the mimicking returns *SMB* and *HML* absorb the size and book-to-market effects in average returns, illustrated in table 2. We then examine the intercepts for bonds. Here the issue is whether different factor models predict patterns in average returns that are rejected by the flat average bond returns in table 2.

5.1. The Cross-Section of Average Stock Returns

RM–RF—When the excess market return is the only explanatory variable in the time-series regressions, the intercepts for stocks (table 9a) show the size effect of Banz (1981). Except in the lowest-*BE/ME* quintile, the intercepts for the smallest-size portfolios exceed those for the biggest by 0.22% to 0.37% per month. The intercepts are also related to book-to-market equity. In every size quintile, the intercepts increase with *BE/ME*; the intercepts for the highest-*BE/ME* quintile exceed those for the lowest by 0.25% to 0.76% per month. These results parallel the evidence in Fama and French (1992a) that, used alone, market βs leave the cross-sectional variation in average stock returns that is related to size and book-to-market equity.

In fact, as in Fama and French (1992a), the simple relation between average return and β for the 25 stock portfolios used here is flat. A regression of average return on β yields a slope of -0.22 with a standard error of 0.31. The Sharpe (1964)–Lintner (1965) model (β suffices to describe the cross-section of average returns and the simple relation between β and average return is positive) fares no better here than in our earlier paper.

SMB and HML—The two-factor time-series regressions of excess stock returns on *SMB* and *HML* produce similar intercepts for the 25 stock portfolios (table 9a). The two-factor regression intercepts are, however, large (around 0.5% per month) and close to or more than two standard errors from 0. Intercepts that are similar in size support the conclusion from the cross-section regressions in Fama and French (1992a) that size and book-to-market factors explain the strong differences in average returns across stocks. But the large intercepts also say that *SMB* and *HML* do not explain the average premium of stock returns over one-month bill returns.

RM–RF, SMB, and HML—Adding the excess market return to the time-series regressions pushes the strong positive intercepts for stocks observed in the two-factor (*SMB* and *HML*) regressions to values close to 0. Only three of the 25 intercepts in the three-factor regressions differ from 0 by more than 0.2% per month; 16 are within 0.1 % of 0. Intercepts close to 0 say that the

TABLE 9A. Intercepts from excess stock return regressions for 25 stock portfolios formed on size and book-to-market equity: July 1963 to December 1991, 342 months.[a]

Size quintile	a					t(a)				
	Low	2	3	4	High	Low	2	3	4	High
(i) $R(t) - RF(t) = a + mTERM(t) + dDEF(t) + e(t)$										
Small	0.31	0.62	0.71	0.80	0.92	0.75	1.73	2.20	2.61	2.87
2	0.35	0.63	0.77	0.75	0.93	0.93	1.91	2.60	2.85	3.03
3	0.34	0.58	0.60	0.73	0.89	1.00	1.99	2.28	3.01	3.11
4	0.41	0.27	0.49	0.69	0.96	1.34	1.01	1.96	2.88	3.35
Big	0.34	0.30	0.25	0.50	0.53	1.35	1.27	1.17	2.36	2.14
(ii) $R(t) - RF(t) = a + b[RM(t) - RF(t)] + e(t)$										
Small	-0.22	0.15	0.30	0.42	0.54	-0.90	0.73	1.54	2.19	2.53
2	-0.18	0.17	0.36	0.39	0.53	-1.00	1.05	2.35	2.79	3.01
1	-0.16	0.15	0.23	0.39	0.50	-1.12	1.25	1.82	3.20	3.19
4	-0.05	-0.14	0.12	0.35	0.57	-0.50	-1.50	1.20	2.91	3.71
Big	-0.04	-0.07	-0.07	0.20	0.21	-0.49	-0.95	-0.70	1.89	1.41
(iii) $R(t) - RF(t) = a + sSMB(t) + hHML(t) + e(t)$										
Small	0.24	0.46	0.49	0.53	0.55	0.97	1.92	2.24	2.52	2.49
2	0.52	0.58	0.64	0.58	0.64	2.00	2.40	2.76	2.61	2.56
3	0.52	0.61	0.52	0.60	0.66	2.00	2.58	2.25	2.66	2.61
4	0.69	0.39	0.50	0.62	0.79	2.78	1.55	2.07	2.51	2.85
Big	0.76	0.52	0.43	0.51	0.44	3.41	2.23	1.84	2.20	1.70

Book-to-market equity (BE/ME) quintiles

(Continued)

TABLE 9A. (Continued)

Size quintile	a					t(a)				
	Low	2	3	4	High	Low	2	3	4	High
(iv) $R(t) - RF(t) = a + b[RM(t) - RF(t)] + sSMB(t) + hHML(t) + e(t)$										
Small	-0.34	-0.12	-0.05	0.01	0.00	-3.16	-1.47	-0.73	0.22	0.14
2	-0.11	-0.01	0.08	0.03	0.02	-1.24	-0.20	1.04	0.51	0.34
3	-0.11	0.04	-0.04	0.05	0.05	-1.42	0.47	-0.47	0.71	0.56
4	0.09	-0.22	-0.08	0.03	0.13	1.07	-2.65	-0.99	0.33	1.24
Big	0.21	-0.05	-0.13	-0.05	-0.16	3.27	-0.67	-1.46	-0.69	-1.41
(v) $R(t) - RF(t) = a + b[RM(t) - RF(t)] + sSMB(t) + hHML(t) + mTERM(t) + dDEF(t) + e(t)$										
Small	-0.35	-0.13	-0.05	0.01	0.00	-3.24	-1.58	-0.79	0.20	0.09
2	-0.11	-0.02	0.08	0.04	0.02	-1.29	-0.24	1.10	0.67	0.29
3	-0.12	0.04	-0.03	0.06	0.05	-1.45	0.48	-0.42	0.79	0.56
4	0.08	-0.22	-0.08	0.04	0.13	1.04	-2.67	-0.94	0.47	1.23
Big	0.21	-0.05	-0.13	-0.06	-0.17	3.29	-0.72	-1.46	-0.73	-1.51

aSee footnote under table 9c.

TABLE 9B. Intercepts from excess bond return regressions for two government and five corporate bond portfolios: July 1963 to December 1991, 342 months.[a]

	1–5G	6–10G	Aaa	Aa	A	Baa	LG
			Bond portfolio				
			(i) $R(t) - RF(t) = a + mTERM(t) + dDEF(t) + e(t)$				
a	0.08	0.09	−0.02	−0.00	−0.00	0.06	0.06
$t(a)$	2.70	2.16	−1.10	−0.55	−0.29	1.42	0.67
			(ii) $R(t) - RF(t) = a + b[RM(t) - RF(t)] + e(t)$				
a	0.08	0.08	−0.03	−0.02	−0.01	0.04	0.00
$t(a)$	1.27	0.76	−0.24	−0.15	−0.11	0.37	0.03
			(iii) $R(t) - RF(t) = a + sSMB(t) + hHML(t) + e(t)$				
a	0.12	0.16	0.07	0.07	0.07	0.11	0.08
$t(a)$	1.70	1.47	0.52	0.58	0.55	0.82	0.58
			(iv) $R(t) - RF(t) = a + b[RM(t) - RF(t)] + sSMB(t) + hHML(t) + e(t)$				
a	0.06	0.07	−0.07	−0.07	−0.08	−0.05	−0.11
$t(a)$	0.89	0.62	−0.62	−0.64	−0.69	−0.41	−1.00
			(v) $R(t) - RF(t) = a + b[RM(t) - RF(t)] + sSMB(t) + hHML(t)$ $+ mTERM(t) + dDEF(t) + e(t)$				
a	0.09	0.11	−0.00	−0.00	−0.00	0.02	−0.07
$t(a)$	2.84	2.77	−0.17	−0.25	−0.57	0.52	−0.77

[a]See footnote under table 9c.

regressions that use *RM–RF*, *SMB*, and *HML* to absorb common time-series variation in returns do a good job explaining the cross-section of average stock returns.

There is an interesting story for the smaller intercepts obtained when the excess market return is added to the two-factor (*SMB* and *HML*) regressions. In the three-factor regressions, the stock portfolios produce slopes on *RM–RF* close to 1. The average market risk premium (0.43% per month) then absorbs the similar strong positive intercepts observed in the regressions of stock returns on *SMB* and *HML*. In short, the size and book-to-market factors can explain the differences in average returns across stocks, but the market factor is needed to explain why stock returns are on average above the one-month bill rate.

TERM and DEF—Table 9a shows that adding the term-structure factors, *TERM* and *DEF*, to the time-series regressions for stocks has almost no effect on the intercepts produced by the three stock-market factors. Likewise,

TABLE 9C. *F-statistics testing the intercepts in the excess-return regressions against 0 and matching probability levels of bootstrap and F-distributions.*[a]

	Regression (from tables 9a and 9b)				
	(i)	(ii)	(iii)	(iv)	(v)
F-statistic	2.09	1.91	1.78	1.56	1.66
Probability level					
Bootstrap	0.998	0.996	0.985	0.951	0.971
F-distribution	0.999	0.996	0.990	0.961	0.975

[a]*RM* is the value-weighted monthly percent return on all stocks in the 25 size-*BE/ME* portfolios, plus the negative-*BE* stocks excluded from the 25 portfolios. *RF* is the one-month Treasury bill rate, observed at the beginning of the month. *SMB* (small minus big), the return on the mimicking portfolio for the common size factor in stock returns, is the difference each month between the simple average of the returns on the three small-stock portfolios (*S/L, S/M,* and *S/H*) and the simple average of the returns on the three big-stock portfolios (*B/L, B/M,* and *B/H*). *HML* (high minus low), the return on the mimicking portfolio for the common book-to-market equity factor in returns, is the difference each month between the simple average of the returns on the two high-*BE/ME* portfolios (*S/H* and *B/H*) and the average of the returns on the two low-*BE/ME* portfolios (*S/L* and *B/L*). *TERM* is *LTG–RF*. where *LTG* is the long-term government bond return. *DEF* is *CB–LTG*, where *CB* is the return on a proxy for the market portfolio of corporate bonds.

The seven bond portfolios used as dependent variables in the excess-return regressions are 1- to 5-year and 6- to 10-year governments (1–5G and 6–10G) and corporate bonds rated Aaa, Aa, A, Baa, and below Baa (LG) by Moody's. The 25 size–*BE/ME* stock portfolios are formed as follows. Each year t from 1963 to 1991 NYSE quintile breakpoints for size (*ME*, stock price times shares outstanding), measured at the end of June, are used to allocate NYSE, Amex, and NASDAQ stocks to five size quintiles. NYSE quintile breakpoints for *BE/ME* are also used to allocate NYSE, Amex, and NASDAQ stocks to five book-to-market equity quintiles. In *BE/ME*, *BE* is book common equity for the fiscal year ending in calendar year $t - 1$, and *ME* is for the end of December of $t - 1$. The 25 size–*BE/ME* portfolios are the intersections of the five size and the five *BE/ME* groups. Value-weighted monthly percent returns on the portfolios are calculated from July of year t to June of $t + 1$.

Regressions (i)–(v) in table 9c correspond to the regressions in tables 9a and 9b. The *F-statisticis*

$$F = (A' \sum\nolimits^{-1} A)(N - K - L + 1)/(L*(N-K)*\omega_{1,1})$$

where $N = 342$ observations, $L = 32$ regressions, K is 1 plus the number of explanatory variables in the regression, A is the (column) vector of the 32 regression intercepts, Σ ($L \times L$) is the unbiased covariance matrix of the residuals from the 32 regressions, and $\omega_{1,1}$ is the diagonal element of $(X'X)^{-1}$ corresponding to the intercept. Gibbons, Ross, and Shanken (1989) show that this statistic has an F-distribution with L and $N - K - L + 1$ degrees of freedom under the assumption that the returns and explanatory variables are normal and the true intercepts are 0.

In the bootstrap simulations, the slopes (with intercepts set to 0), explanatory variables, and residuals from the regressions for July 1963 to December 1991 in tables 3 to 7 are used to generate 342 monthly excess returns for the 25 stock and seven bond portfolios for each regression model. These model returns and the explanatory returns. *RM–RF, SMB, HML, TERM,* and *DEF,* for July 1963 to December 1991, are the population for the simulations. Each simulation takes a random sample, with replacement, of 342 paired observations (the same set of observations for each of the five regression models) on the model returns and the explanatory variables, and estimates the regressions. For each model, the table shows the proportion of 10,000 simulations in which the F-statistic is smaller than the empirical estimate. The table also shows the probability that a value drawn from an F-distribution is smaller than the empirical estimate.

in spite of the strong slopes on *TERM* and *DEF* when they are used alone to explain stock returns (table 3), the two variables produce intercepts close to the average excess returns for the 25 stock portfolios in table 2.

The reason for these results is straightforward. The average *TERM* and *DEF* returns (the average risk premiums for the term-structure factors) are puny, 0.06% and 0.02% per month. The high volatility of *TERM* and *DEF* (table 2) allows them to capture substantial common variation in bond and stock returns in the two-factor regressions of table 3 and the five-factor regressions of table 8. But the low average *TERM* and *DEF* returns imply that the two term-structure factors can't explain much of the cross-sectional variation in average stock returns.

5.2. The Cross-Section of Average Bond Returns

Tables 3, 7b and 8b say that the common variation in bond returns is dominated by the bond-market factors, *TERM* and *DEF*. Only the low-grade bond portfolio (LG) has nontrivial slopes on the stock-market factors when *TERM* and *DEF* are in the bond regressions. Like the average values of *TERM* and *DEF*, the average excess returns on the bond portfolios are close to 0 (table 2), so it is not surprising that the intercepts in the time-series regressions for bonds (table 9b) are close to 0.

Do low average *TERM* and *DEF* premiums imply that the term-structure factors are irrelevant in a well-specified asset-pricing model? Hardly. *TERM* and *DEF* are the dominant variables in the common variation in bond returns. Moreover, Fama and French (1989) and Chen (1991) find that the expected values of variables like *TERM* and *DEF* vary through time and are related to business conditions. The expected value of *TERM*, the term premium for discount-rate risks, is positive around business cycle troughs and negative near peaks. The expected value of the default premium in *DEF* is high when economic conditions are weak and default risks are high, and it is low when business conditions are strong. Thus, the common sensitivity of stocks and bonds to *TERM* and *DEF* implies interesting intertemporal variation in expected stock and bond returns.

5.3. Joint Tests on the Regression Intercepts

We use the *F*-statistic of Gibbons, Ross, and Shanken (1989) to formally test the hypothesis that a set of explanatory variables produces regression intercepts for the 32 bond and stock portfolios that are all equal to 0. The *F*-statistics, and bootstrap probability levels, for the five sets of intercepts produced by the explanatory variables in tables 3 to 8 are in table 9c.

The *F*-tests support the analysis of the intercepts above. The tests reject the hypothesis that the term-structure returns, *TERM* and *DEF*, suffice to explain the average returns on bonds and stocks at the 0.99 level. This confirms the conclusion, obvious from the regression intercepts in table 9a, that the low average *TERM* and *DEF* returns cannot explain the cross-section of average stock returns. The *F*-test rejects the hypothesis that *RM–RF* suffices to explain average returns at the 0.99 level. This confirms that the excess market return cannot explain the size and book-to-market effects in average stock returns. The large positive intercepts for stocks observed when *SMB* and *HML* are the only explanatory variables produce an *F*-statistic that rejects the zero-intercepts hypothesis at the 0.98 level.

In terms of the *F*-test, the three stock-market factors, *RM–RF*, *SMB*, and *HML*, produce the best-behaved intercepts. Nevertheless, the joint test that all intercepts for the seven bond and 25 stock portfolios are 0 rejects at about the 0.95 level. The rejection comes largely from the lowest-*BE/ME* quintile of stocks. Among stocks with the lowest ratios of book-to-market equity (growth stocks), the smallest stocks have returns that are too low (-0.34% per month, $t = -3.16$) relative to the predictions of the three-factor model, and the biggest stocks have returns that are too high (0.21% per month, $t = 3.27$). Put a bit differently, the rejection of a three-factor model in table 9c is due to the absence of a size effect in the lowest-*BE/ME* quintile. The five portfolios in the lowest-*BE/ME* quintile produce slopes on the size factor *SMB* that are strongly negatively related to size (table 6). But unlike the other *BE/ME* quintiles, average returns in the lowest-*BE/ME* quintile show no relation to size (table 2).

Despite its marginal rejection in the *F*-tests, our view is that the three-factor model does a good job on the cross-section of average stock returns. The rejection of the model simply says that because *RM–RF*, *SMB*, and *HML* absorb most of the variation in the returns on the 25 stock portfolios (the typical R^2 values in table 6 are above 0.93), even small abnormal average returns suffice to show that the three-factor model is just a model, that is, it is false. To answer the important question of whether the model can be useful in applications, the interesting result is that only one of the 25 three-factor regression intercepts for stocks (for the portfolio in both the smallest-size and the lowest-*BE/ME* quintiles) is much different from 0 in practical terms.

Indeed, our view is that the three-factor regressions that use *RM–RF, SMB,* and *HML* to explain average returns do surprisingly well, given the simple way the mimicking returns *SMB* and *HML* for the size and book-to-market factors are constructed. The regressions produce intercepts for stocks that are close to 0, even though *SMB* and *HML* surely contain some firm-specific noise as proxies for the risk factors in returns related to size and book-to-market equity.

Adding the term-structure returns, *TERM* and *DEF,* to regressions that also use *RM–RF, SMB,* and *HML* as explanatory variables increases *F*. The larger *F* comes from bonds. The five-factor regression intercepts and R^2 values for stocks are close to those produced by the three stock-market factors. But for bonds, adding *TERM* and *DEF* results in much lower residual standard errors, and the increased precision pushes the five-factor intercepts for the two government bond portfolios beyond two standard errors from 0. The two intercepts are, however, rather small, 0.09% and 0.11% per month.

The three stock-market factors produce a lower *F,* but we think the five-factor regressions provide the best model for returns and average returns on bonds and stocks. *TERM* and *DEF* dominate the variation in bond returns. And the variation in the expected values of *TERM* and *DEF* with business conditions is an interesting part of the variation through time in the expected returns on stocks and bonds that is missed by the *F*-test, which is concerned only with long-term average returns.

6. DIAGNOSTICS

In this section we check the robustness of our inference that five common risk factors explain the cross-section of expected stock and bond returns. We first use the residuals from the five-factor time-series regressions to check that the regressions capture the variation through time in the cross-section of expected returns. We then examine whether our five risk factors capture the January seasonals in stock and bond returns. Next come split-sample regressions that use one set of stocks in the explanatory returns and another, disjoint, set in the dependent returns. These tests address the concern that the evidence of size and book-to-market factors in the regressions above is spurious, arising only because we use size and book-to-market portfolios for both our dependent and explanatory returns. The last and most interesting tests examine whether the stock-market factors that capture the average returns on size–*BE/ME* portfolios work as well on portfolios formed on other variables known to be informative about average returns, in particular, earnings/price and dividend/price ratios.

6.1. *The Predictability of the Regression Residuals*

There is evidence that stock and bond returns can be predicted using (a) dividend yields (*D/P*), (b) spreads of low-grade over high-grade bond yields (default spreads, *DFS*), (c) spreads of long-term over short-term bond yields (term spreads, *TS*), and (d) short-term interest rates. [See Fama (1991) and the references therein.] If our five risk factors capture the cross-section of expected returns, the predictability of stock and bond returns should be embodied in the explanatory returns (the month-by-month risk premiums) in the five-factor regressions. The regression residuals should be unpredictable. To test this hypothesis, we estimate the 32 time-series regressions,

$$
\begin{aligned}
e_p(t+1) &= k_0 + k_1 D(t)/P(t) + k_2 DFS(t) + k_3 TS(t) + k_4 RF(t) \\
&\quad + \eta_p(t+1).
\end{aligned}
\tag{2}
$$

The $e_p(t+1)$ in (2) are the time series of residuals for our 25 stock and seven bond portfolios from the five-factor regressions of table 7. The dividend yield, $D(t)/P(t)$, is dividends on the value-weighted portfolio of NYSE stocks for the year ending in month t divided by the value of the portfolio at the end of t. The default spread, $DFS(t)$, is the difference at the end of month t between the yield on a market portfolio of corporate bonds and the long-term government bond yield (from Ibbotson Associates). The term spread, $TS(t)$, is the difference between the long-term government bond yield at the end of month t and the one-month bill rate, $RF(t)$.

The estimates of (2) produce no evidence that the residuals from the five-factor time-series regressions are predictable. In the 32 regressions, 15 produce negative values of R^2 (adjusted for degrees of freedom). Only four of the 32 R^2 values exceed 0.01; the largest is 0.03. Out of 128 (32×4) slopes in the residual regressions, ten are more than two standard errors from 0; they are split evenly between positive and negative values, and they are scattered randomly across the 32 regressions and the four explanatory variables.

The fact that variables known to predict stock and bond returns do not predict the residuals from our five-factor regressions supports our inference that the five risk factors capture the cross-section of expected stock and bond returns. The residual tests are also interesting information on a key regression specification. Since we estimate regression slopes on returns for the entire 1963–1991 period, we implicitly assume that the sensitivities of the dependent returns to the risk factors are constant. If the true slopes vary through time, the regression residuals may be spuriously predictable. The absence of predictability suggests that the assumption of constant slopes is reasonable, at least for the portfolios used here.

6.2. January Seasonals

Since the work Roll (1983) and Keim (1983), documenting that stock returns, especially returns on small stocks, tend to be higher in January, it is standard in tests of asset-pricing models to look for unexplained January effects. We are leery of judging models on their ability to explain January seasonals. If the seasonals are, in whole or in part, sampling error, the tests can contain a data-snooping bias toward rejection [Lo and MacKinlay (1990)]. Nevertheless, we test for January seasonals in the residuals from our five-factor regressions. Despite our fears, we find that, except for the smallest stocks, residual January seasonals are weak at best. The strong January seasonals in the returns on stocks and bonds are largely absorbed by strong seasonals in our risk factors.

Table 10 shows regressions of returns on a dummy variable that is 1 in January and 0 in other months. The regression intercepts are average returns for non-January months, and the slopes on the dummy measure differences between average January returns and average returns in other months.

The table confirms that there are January seasonals in excess stock returns, and the seasonals are related to size. The slopes on the January dummy are all more than 2.92% per month and more than two standard errors from 0 for the portfolios in the two smallest size quintiles. Controlling for *BE/ME*, the extra January return declines monotonically with increasing size. More interesting, the January seasonal in stock returns is also related to book-to-market equity. In every size quintile, the slopes on the January dummy tend to increase with *BE/ME*. The extra January return for the two highest-*BE/ME* portfolios in a size quintile is always at least 2.38% per month and 2.85 standard errors from 0.

January seasonals are not limited to stock returns. The slopes on the January dummy for corporate bonds increase monotonically from the Aaa to the LG portfolio. The extra January returns are 0.86%, 1.14%, and 1.56% per month for the A, Baa, and LG portfolios, and these extra average returns are at least 1.94 standard errors from 0.

If our five-factor time-series regressions are to explain the January seasonals in stock and bond returns, there must be January seasonals in the risk factors. Table 10 shows that, except for *TERM*, the risk factors have extra January returns in excess of 1 % per month and at least 1.67 standard errors from 0.

TABLE 10. Tests for January seasonals in the dependent returns, explanatory returns, and residuals from the five-factor regressions: July 1963 to December 1991, 342 months.[a]

$$R(t) = a + bJAN(t) + e$$

	a	b	t(a)	t(b)	R²		a	b	t(a)	t(b)	R²
Factor											
	Five-factor explanatory returns							Five-factor regression residuals			
RM–RF	0.31	1.49	1.22	1.67	0.00						
RMO	0.40	1.19	2.03	1.70	0.00						
SMB	0.05	2.74	0.30	4.96	0.06						
HML	0.21	2.29	1.53	4.70	0.06						
TERM	0.10	-0.41	0.56	-0.69	-0.00						
DEF	-0.07	1.10	-0.81	3.56	0.03						
Stock portfolio											
	Excess stock returns										
						Smallest-size quintile					
BE/ME Low	-0.13	6.31	-0.30	4.23	0.05		-0.12	1.51	-1.17	4.09	0.04
BE/ME 2	0.24	5.62	0.63	4.27	0.05		-0.05	0.56	-0.57	2.01	0.00
BE/ME 3	0.31	5.91	0.90	4.93	0.06		-0.06	0.69	-0.88	3.06	0.02
BE/ME 4	0.37	6.29	1.14	5.55	0.08		-0.06	0.76	-1.02	3.57	0.03
BE/ME High	0.40	7.39	1.20	6.31	0.10		-0.09	1.13	-1.41	4.94	0.06
						Size quintile 2					
BE/ME Low	0.20	2.92	0.48	2.04	0.00		0.02	-0.23	0.21	-0.74	-0.00
BE/ME 2	0.37	4.17	1.04	3.34	0.03		0.00	-0.04	0.04	-0.15	-0.00
BE/ME 3	0.53	3.95	1.63	3.48	0.03		0.04	-0.55	0.62	-2.16	0.01
BE/ME 4	0.48	4.32	1.65	4.22	0.05		0.02	-0.22	0.28	-0.97	-0.00
BE/ME High	0.55	5.76	1.66	4.99	0.07		-0.01	0.12	-0.14	0.49	-0.00
						Size quintile 3					
BE/ME Low	0.24	2.35	0.62	1.78	0.00		0.04	-0.49	0.50	-1.74	0.00
BE/ME 2	0.42	2.87	1.31	2.57	0.02		0.03	-0.41	0.42	-1.48	0.00
BE/ME 3	0.43	3.06	1.47	2.99	0.02		0.07	-0.80	0.83	-2.90	0.02
BE/ME 4	0.52	3.51	1.92	3.68	0.04		0.04	-0.46	0.52	-1.80	0.00
BE/ME High	0.60	4.53	1.91	4.12	0.04		0.03	-0.34	0.33	-1.15	0.00

	Size quintile 4									
BE/ME Low	0.39	1.12	1.16	0.95	-0.00	0.04	-0.46	0.46	-1.60	0.00
BE/ME 2	0.21	1.77	0.68	1.65	0.00	0.06	-0.73	0.73	-2.54	0.02
BE/ME 3	0.40	2.08	1.40	2.11	0.01	0.08	-0.93	0.93	-3.27	0.03
BE/ME 4	0.52	3.12	1.88	3.24	0.03	0.03	-0.37	0.34	-1.17	0.00
BE/ME High	0.68	4.45	2.15	4.00	0.04	0.00	-0.03	0.03	-0.09	-0.00
	Biggest-size quintile									
BE/ME Low	0.37	0.34	1.34	0.35	-0.00	-0.03	0.38	-0.48	1.67	0.00
BE/ME 2	0.27	1.11	1.02	1.19	0.00	0.00	-0.00	0.00	-0.02	-0.00
BE/ME 3	0.23	1.11	0.92	1.28	0.00	0.01	-0.17	0.16	-0.57	-0.00
BE/ME 4	0.37	2.38	1.54	2.85	0.02	-0.00	0.08	-0.09	0.31	-0.00
BE/ME High	0.32	3.38	1.17	3.59	0.03	-0.02	0.25	-0.18	0.63	-0.00
Bond portfolio	Excess bond returns					Five-factor regression residuals				
1–5G	0.11	0.05	1.58	0.20	-0.00	0.00	-0.04	0.12	-0.40	-0.00
6–10G	0.16	-0.22	1.35	-0.56	-0.00	0.00	-0.11	0.23	-0.79	-0.00
Aaa	0.03	0.34	0.21	0.74	-0.00	0.01	-0.17	0.62	-2.17	0.01
Aa	0.03	0.51	0.23	1.15	0.00	0.00	-0.11	0.53	-1.85	0.00
A	0.00	0.86	0.05	1.94	0.00	-0.01	0.12	-0.60	2.08	0.01
Baa	0.05	1.14	0.35	2.48	0.01	-0.01	0.14	-0.29	1.01	0.00
LG	0.00	1.56	0.05	3.17	0.03	-0.02	0.19	-0.17	0.58	-0.00

[a] $JAN(t)$ is a dummy variable that is 1 if month t is January and o otherwise. RMO is the sum of the intercept and residuals from the regression of $RM-RF$ on SMB, HML, $TERM$, and DEF. RM is the value-weighted monthly stock-market return. RF is the one-month Treasury bill rate, observed at the beginning of the month. SMB and HML are the returns on the mimicking portfolios for the size and book-to-market equity factors in stock returns. $TERM$ is $LTG-RF$, where LTG is the long-term government bond return. DEF is $CB-LTG$, where CB is the return on a proxy for the market portfolio of corporate bonds.

The seven bond portfolios are 1- to 5-year and 6- to 10-year governments (1–5G and 6–10G) and bonds rated Aaa, Aa, A, Baa, and below Baa (LG) by Moody's. The 25 size–BE/ME portfolios are formed as the intersections of independent sorts of stocks into size and book-to-market equity quintiles in June of each year from 1963–1991. The variables are described in more detail in table 8.

The seasonals in the size and book-to-market factors are especially strong. The average *SMB* and *HML* returns in January are 2.74% and 2.29% per month greater than in other months, and the extra January returns are 4.96 and 4.70 standard errors from 0. Indeed, like the excess returns on the 25 stock portfolios and the five corporate bond portfolios that are the dependent variables in the five-factor regressions, the extra January returns on the risk factors are generally much larger and more reliably different from 0 than the average returns for non-January months.

Finally, table 10 shows that the January seasonals in our risk factors largely absorb the seasonals in stock and bond returns. In the regressions of the five-factor residuals on the January dummy, only the stock portfolios in the smallest-size quintile produce systematically positive slopes; even these slopes are only one-quarter to one-tenth the positive January seasonals in the raw excess returns on the portfolios. If anything, the five-factor residuals for the remaining size quintiles show negative January seasonals, but the slopes on the January dummy for these stock portfolios, and for the bond portfolios, are small and mostly within two standard errors of 0. In short, whether spurious or real, the January seasonals in the returns on stocks and corporate bonds seem to be largely explained by the corresponding seasonals in the risk factors of our five-factor model.

6.3. Split-Sample Tests

In the time-series regressions for stocks, the dependent returns and the two explanatory returns *SMB* and *HML* are portfolios formed on size and book-to-market equity. Many readers worry that the apparent explanatory power of *SMB* and *HML* is spurious, induced by the regression setup. We think this is unlikely, given that the dependent returns are based on much finer size and *BE/ME* sorts (25 portfolios) than the *SMB* and *HML* returns. It also seems unlikely that we have stumbled on two mimicking returns for size and *BE/ME* factors that (a) measure strong common variation in the returns on 25 portfolios when really there is none, and (b) produce exactly the patterns in the regression slopes on *SMB* and *HML* needed to explain the size and book-to-market effects in the average returns on the 25 portfolios. Still, an independent test is of interest.

We split the stocks in each of the 25 size–*BE/ME* portfolios into two equal groups. One group is used to form the 25 dependent value-weighted portfolio returns for the time-series regressions. The other is used to form half-sample versions of the explanatory returns, *RM–RF, SMB,* and *HML.* The roles of the two groups are then reversed, and another set of regressions is run. In this way we have two sets of regressions. In each set, the explanatory and dependent returns are from disjoint groups of stocks.

Without showing all the details, we can report that the results for the two sets of regressions of excess returns for 25 size–*BE/ME* portfolios on disjoint versions of *RM–RF, SMB,* and *HML* are similar to the full-sample results in tables 6 and 9. The slopes on *RM–RF, SMB,* and *HML* in the split-sample regressions are close to those in table 6, and the intercepts, like those for the full-sample three-factor regressions in table 9, are close to 0. In short, the split-sample regressions confirm that there are common risk factors in returns related to size and book-to-market equity. They also confirm that market, size, and book-to-market factors seem to capture the cross-section of average stock returns.

If anything, the split-sample regressions show less power to reject the hypothesis that *RM–RF, SMB,* and *HML* capture the cross-section of average stock returns than the full-sample regressions. Since the 25 dependent portfolio returns in the split-sample regressions use half the available stocks, the portfolios are less diversified than those in table 6. Although the three-factor split-sample regressions produce high values of R^2 (mostly greater than 0.88), they are a bit lower than those in table 6 (mostly greater than 0.9). As a result, the *F*-tests of the zero-intercepts hypothesis are weaker for the split-sample regressions than for the full-sample regressions.

6.4. Portfolios Formed on E/P

The most interesting check on our inferences about the role of size and book-to-market risk factors in returns is to examine whether these variables explain the returns on portfolios formed on other variables known to be informative about average returns. Table 11 shows summary statistics, as well as one-factor (*RM–RF*) and three-factor (*RM–RF, SMB,* and *HML*) regressions for portfolios formed on earnings/price (*E/P*) and dividend/price (*D/P*) ratios.

The average returns on the *E/P* portfolios have the U-shape documented in Jaffe, Keim, and Westerfield (1989) and Fama and French (1992a). The portfolio of firms with negative earnings and the portfolio of firms in the highest-*E/P* quintile have the highest average returns. For the positive-*E/P* portfolios, average return increases from the lowest- to the highest-*E/P* quintile. This pattern is an interesting challenge for our risk factors.

Table 11 confirms the evidence in Basu (1983) that the one-factor Sharpe–Lintner model leaves the relation between average return and E/P largely unexplained. For the positive-E/P portfolios, the intercepts in the one-factor regressions increase monotonically. from -0.20% per month ($t = -2.35$) for the lowest-E/P quintile to 0.46% ($t = 3.69$) for the highest. The failure of the one-factor model has a simple explanation. The market βs for the positive-E/P

TABLE 11. Summary statistics for value-weighted monthly excess returns (in percent) on portfolios formed on dividend price (D/P) and earnings/price (E/P), and regressions of excess portfolio returns on (i) the excess market return (RM–RF) and (ii) the excess market return (RM–RF) and the mimicking returns for the size (SMB) and book-to-market equity (HML) factors: July 1963 to December 1991, 342 months.[a]

$$\text{(i) } R(t) - RF(t) = a + b[RM(t) - RF(t)] + e(t)$$
$$\text{(ii) } R(t) - RF(t) = a + b[RM(t) - RF(t)] + sSMB(t) + hHML(t) + e(t)$$

Portfolio	Portfolios formed on E/P			Portfolios formed on D/P		
	Mean	Std.	t(mn)	Mean	Std.	t(mn)
≤ 0	0.72	7.77	1.72	0.48	7.36	1.20
Low	0.27	5.23	0.96	0.39	5.48	1.30
2	0.47	4.76	1.82	0.44	4.83	1.68
3	0.46	4.68	1.83	0.47	4.65	1.87
4	0.55	4.48	2.27	0.57	4.32	2.42
High	0.86	4.84	3.30	0.56	3.86	2.67

Portfolios formed on E/P

Portfolio	Regression (i)			Regression (ii)				
	a	b	R^2	a	b	s	h	R^2
E/P ≤ 0	0.13	1.37	0.64	−0.30	1.24	1.13	0.46	0.82
	(0.50)	(24.70)		(−1.68)	(27.82)	(17.42)	(6.10)	
Low	−0.20	1.10	0.91	0.04	0.99	−0.01	−0.50	0.96
	(−2.35)	(57.42)		(0.70)	(66.78)	(−0.55)	(−19.73)	
2	0.03	1.01	0.94	0.03	1.01	0.02	−0.00	0.94
	(0.46)	(70.24)		(0.40)	(61.17)	(1.01)	(−0.08)	
3	0.04	0.99	0.92	−0.00	1.00	0.01	0.09	0.92
	(0.50)	(61.62)		(−0.12)	(55.46)	(0.40)	(2.86)	
4	0.15	0.93	0.88	−0.02	0.98	0.05	0.33	0.91
	(1.76)	(49.78)		(−0.28)	(53.57)	(1.95)	(10.44)	
High	0.46	0.94	0.78	0.08	1.03	0.24	0.67	0.91
	(3.69)	(34.73)		(1.01)	(51.56)	(8.34)	(19.62)	

TABLE 11. (Continued)

Portfolios formed on D/P

	Regression (i)			Regression (ii)				
Portfolio	a	b	R^2	a	b	s	h	R^2
D/P = 0	−0.15	1.45	0.80	−0.23	1.20	0.99	−0.21	0.94
	(−0.86)	(37.18)		(−2.30)	(49.45)	(28.09)	(−5.17)	
Low	−0.11	1.15	0.91	0.11	1.03	0.09	−0.48	0.95
	(−1.29)	(59.15)		(1.64)	(65.09)	(3.92)	(−17.92)	
2	−0.01	1.04	0.96	0.06	1.01	−0.01	−0.14	0.96
	(−0.19)	(85.34)		(1.17)	(77.07)	(−0.66)	(−6.49)	
3	0.04	0.99	0.93	−0.03	1.02	0.02	0.14	0.94
	(0.64)	(69.14)		(−0.44)	(64.43)	(0.72)	(5.09)	
4	0.17	0.91	0.91	0.04	0.98	−0.06	0.30	0.94
	(2.45)	(58.42)		(0.59)	(66.51)	(−2.80)	(12.00)	
High	0.24	0.72	0.73	−0.01	0.85	−0.05	0.54	0.84
	(2.22)	(30.16)		(0.16)	(40.08)	(−1.77)	(15.04)	

[a]Portfolios are formed in June of year t, 1963–1991. The dividend yield (D/P) for year t is the dividends paid from July of $t − 1$ to June of t [measured using the procedure described in Fama and French (1988)], divided by market equity in June of $t − 1$. The earnings/price ratio (E/P) for year t is the equity income for the fiscal year ending in calendar year $t − 1$, divided by market equity in December of $t − 1$. Equity income is income before extraordinary items, plus income-statement deferred taxes, minus preferred dividends. The quintile breakpoints for D/P or E/P are determined using only NYSE firms with positive dividends or earnings. Regression t-statistics are in parentheses. See table 7 for definitions of $RM–RF$, SMB, and HML.

portfolios are all close to 1.0, so the one-factor model cannot explain the positive relation between E/P and average return.

In contrast, the three-factor model that uses $RM–RF$, SMB, and HML to explain returns leaves no residual E/P effect in average returns. The three-factor intercepts for the five positive-E/P portfolios are within 0.1 of 0 (t's from −0.12 to 1.01). Interestingly, the three-factor regressions say that the increasing pattern in the average returns on the positive-E/P portfolios is due to their loadings on the book-to-market factor HML. The lowest positive-E/P quintile has an HML slope, −0.50, like those produced by portfolios in the lowest-BE/ME quintile in the three-factor regressions in table 6. The highest-E/P quintile has an HML slope, 0.67, like those for portfolios in the highest-BE/ME quintile in table 6. Table 1 confirms that there is also a positive relation between E/P and BE/ME for our 25 portfolios formed on size and BE/ME.

Fama and French (1992b) find that low BE/ME is characteristic of growth stocks, that is, stocks with persistently high earnings on book equity that result in high stock prices relative to book equity. High *BE/ME,* on the other hand, is associated with distress, that is, persistently low earnings on book equity that result in low stock prices. The loadings on *HML* in the three-factor regressions of table 11 then say that low-*E/P* stocks have the low average returns typical of (low-*BE/ME*) growth stocks, while high-*E/P* stocks have the high average returns associated with distress (high-*BE/ME*).

The negative-*E/P* portfolio produces the only hint of evidence against the three-factor model. In spite of the portfolio's high average excess return (0.72% per month), the three-factor model says that its average return is 0.3% per month too low, given its strong loadings on *SMB* (1.13, like the smallest-size portfolios in table 6) and *HML* (0.46. like the higher-*BE/ME* portfolios in table 6). In other words, according to the three-factor model, the average return on this portfolio should be higher because its return behaves like those of small, relatively depressed, stocks. The three-factor intercept for the negative-*E/P* portfolio is, however, only 1.68 standard errors from 0.

In short, *E/P* portfolios produce a strong spread in average returns, which seems to be absorbed by the three common risk factors in stock returns. The *E/P* portfolios are thus interesting corroboration of our inferences that (a) there are common risk factors in stock returns related to size and book-to-market equity, and (b) *RM–RF, SMB,* and *HML,* the mimicking returns for market, size, and *BE/ME* risk factors, capture the cross-section of average stock returns.

6.5. Portfolios Formed on D/P

Table 11 shows that, as in Keim (1983), average returns on portfolios formed on *D/P* are also U-shaped: they drop from the zero-dividend portfolio to the lowest positive-*D/P* portfolio, and then increase across the positive-*D/P* portfolios. The U-shaped pattern, and the overall spread in average returns, are, however, much weaker for the *D/P* portfolios than for the *E/P* portfolios.

Table 11 also confirms Keim's (1983) finding that the one-factor Sharpe–Lintner model leaves a pattern in average returns that looks like a tax penalty on dividends. The one-factor intercepts increase monotonically from the low-est-to the highest-*D/P* portfolios. This suggests that pre-tax returns on higher-*D/P* stocks must be higher to equalize after-tax risk-adjusted returns.

But the apparent tax effect in average returns does not survive in the three-factor regressions that use *RM–RF, SMB,* and *HML* to explain returns. The three-factor intercepts for the five positive-*D/P* portfolios are close to 0 and show no relation to *D/P.* The three-factor regressions say that the increasing pattern in the average returns on the positive-D/P portfolios is due to the increasing pattern in their loadings on the book-to-market factor HML. The lowest-(positive)-D/P quintile has a strong negative HML slope, -0.48, and the highest-D/P portfolio has a strong positive slope, 0.54. Again, the three-factor model says that low-D/P stocks have the low average returns typical of growth stocks, whereas high-D/P stocks have the high average returns associated with relative distress. Table 1 confirms that there is also a positive relation between D/P and BE/ME for our 25 portfolios formed on size and BE/ME.

The zero-dividend portfolio produces the strongest evidence against the three-factor model. The three-factor model says that the high average excess return on this portfolio (0.48% per month) is 0.23% too low ($t = -2.30$), given its strong loading (0.99) on SMB, the mimicking return for the size factor. In other words, because the return on the zero-dividend portfolio varies like the return on a portfolio of small stocks, the three-factor model says that the high return on this portfolio is not high enough. But the three-factor intercept for the zero-dividend portfolio is small in practical terms. Moreover, the three-factor model produces intercepts for the five positive-D/P portfolios that are all close to 0, both statistically and practically. We conclude that, overall, the D/P portfolios are consistent with our inference that the three stock-market factors, RM–RF, SMB, and HML, capture the cross-section of average stock returns.

7. INTERPRETATION AND APPLICATIONS

This paper studies the common risk factors in stock and bond returns and tests whether these shared risks capture the cross-section of average returns. There are at least five common factors in returns. Three stock-market factors produce common variation in stock returns. Except for low-grade corporate bonds, the stock-market factors have little role in returns on government and corporate bonds. The stock and bond markets are linked, however, through two shared term-structure factors.

7.1. Interpretation

Table 2 shows that the three stock-market factors, RMO, SMB, and HML, are largely uncorrelated with one another and with the two term-structure factors, $TERM$ and DEF. The regressions in table 8 that use RMO, SMB, HML, $TERM$, and DEF to explain stock and bond returns thus provide a good summary of the separate roles of the five factors in the volatility of returns and in the cross-section of average returns.

The 25 stock portfolios produce slopes on the orthogonalized market return, RMO, that are all around 1. Thus RMO, which has a standard deviation of 3.55% per month, accounts for similar common variation in the returns on all the stock portfolios. The average RMO return, 0.50% per month ($t = 2.61$), is also a common part of the average excess returns on stocks. Since the RMO slopes for stocks are all around 1, we can interpret the average RMO return as the premium for being a stock (rather than a one-month bill) and sharing general stock-market risk.

For stocks, the slopes on the two term-structure returns in table 8 are all around 0.8. The standard deviations of $TERM$ and DEF, 3.02% and 1.60% per month (table 2), then say that $TERM$ accounts for similar variation in the returns on all the stock portfolios, on the order of that captured by RMO, while DEF captures less common variation in returns. The average $TERM$ and DEF returns are only 0.06% and 0.02% per month, so they explain almost none of the average excess returns on stocks. But the expected $TERM$ and DEF returns vary through time with business conditions [Fama and French (1989) and Chen (1991)]. Thus $TERM$ and DEF produce interesting time-series variation in expected bond and stock returns.

Except for low-grade corporate bonds, $TERM$ and DEF capture almost all the common variation in bond returns identified in the five-factor regressions of table 8. Thus the low average excess returns on bonds fit nicely with the low average $TERM$ and DEF returns. R^2 values near 1 in tables 3 and 8 say that $TERM$ and DEF explain almost all the variation in high-grade (Aaa, Aa, A) corporate returns. Since the $TERM$ and DEF slopes for corporate bonds (around 1) are similar to the slopes for stocks (around 0.8), we can infer that stocks share almost all the variation in high-grade corporate bond returns. Stocks, however, have substantial additional common volatility due to stock-market factors.

In the five-factor regressions of table 8, the slopes on RMO, $TERM$, and DEF do not vary much across the 25 stock portfolios. As a result, the roles of RMO, $TERM$, and DEF in stock returns are captured well by the excess market return, RM–RF, in table 7. The slopes on RM–RF in table 7 are, however, the same as the slopes on RMO in table 8. Thus, like RMO, $TERM$, and DEF, the excess market return does not explain the strong cross-sectional differences in average stock returns and their volatilities (table 2). That job is left to SMB and HML, the mimicking returns for the risk factors related to size and book-to-market equity.

The slopes on *SMB* in table 8 exceed 1.5 for portfolios in the smallest-size quintile, and they drop to around 0.3 for portfolios in the biggest-size quintile. The standard deviation of *SMB* is large, 2.89% per month. The common size-related factor in returns is thus important in explaining why small-stock returns are much more variable than big-stock returns (table 2). The average *SMB* return is only 0.27% per month ($t = 1.73$). The *SMB* slopes in table 8 range from 1.92 to 0.20, however, so the predicted spread in average returns across the 25 stock portfolios due to the size-related risk factor is large, 0.46% per month.

The slopes on *HML* in table 8 range from about -1 for portfolios in the lowest-book-to-market quintile to values near 0 in the highest-*BE/ME* quintile. *HML* thus tends to increase the volatility of low-*BE/ME* stock returns. Table 2 confirms that, within the size quintiles, the returns on the lowest-*BE/ME* portfolios are more volatile than the highest-*BE/ME* returns, especially for the three smallest-size quintiles, where the five-factor regressions produce R^2 values near 1. The average *HML* return, 0.40% per month ($t = 2.91$, table 2), then says that portfolios in the lowest-*BE/ME* quintile, with *HML* slopes close to -1, have their average returns reduced by about 0.40% per month relative to portfolios in the highest-*BE/ME* quintile, which have *HML* slopes close to 0.

Fama and French (1992b) find that book-to-market equity is related to relative profitability. On average, low-*BE/ME* firms have persistently high earnings and high-*BE/ME* firms have persistently poor earnings. The evidence here then suggests that *HML*, the difference between the returns on high- and low-*BE/ME* stocks, captures variation through time in a risk factor that is related to relative earnings performance. *HML* lowers the average returns on low-*BE/ME* stocks because their negative slopes on *HML* indicate that they hedge against the common factor in returns related to relative profitability.

A caveat is in order, however, about detailed stories for the slopes and average premiums in the time-series regressions. Many transformations of the five explanatory returns yield the same intercepts and R^2 values. Thus they yield the same inferences about the total common variation in returns and the ability of five factors to capture the cross-section of average returns. But different transformations change the slopes and average premiums for the factors. For example, the average value of *RMO*, the orthogonalized market return, is 0.50% per month ($t = 2.61$) versus 0.43% ($t = 1.76$) for *RM–RF*. Using *RMO* rather than *RM–RF* in the five-factor regressions also changes the slopes on *SMB, HML, TERM,* and *DEF* (compare tables 7 and 8). But *RMO* and *RM–RF* produce the same intercepts and R^2 values for testing a five-factor asset-pricing model.

At a minimum, our results show that five factors do a good job explaining (a) common variation in bond and stock returns and (b) the cross-section of average returns. We think there is appeal in the simple way we define mimicking returns for the stock-market and bond-market factors. But the choice of factors, especially the size and book-to-market factors, is motivated by empirical experience. Without a theory that specifies the exact form of the state variables or common factors in returns, the choice of any particular version of the factors is somewhat arbitrary. Thus detailed stories for the slopes and average premiums associated with particular versions of the factors are suggestive, but never definitive.

7.2. Applications

In principle, our results can be used in any application that requires estimates of expected stock returns. The list includes (a) selecting portfolios, (b) evaluating portfolio performance, (c) measuring abnormal returns in event studies, and (d) estimating the cost of capital. The applications depend on the evidence that the five factors provide a good description of the cross-section of average returns, but they do not require that we have identified the true factors.

If the five factors capture the cross-section of average returns, they can be used to guide portfolio selection. The exposures of a candidate portfolio to the five risk factors can be estimated with a regression of the portfolio's past excess returns on the five explanatory returns. The regression slopes and the historical average premiums for the factors can then be used to estimate the (unconditional) expected return on the portfolio. A similar procedure can be used to estimate the expected return on a firm's securities, for the purpose of judging its cost of capital. (We predict, however, that sampling error will be a serious problem in the five-factor parameter estimates for individual securities.)

If our results are taken at face value, evaluating the performance of a managed portfolio is straightforward. The intercept in the time-series regression of the managed portfolio's excess return on our five explanatory returns is the average abnormal return needed to judge whether a manager can beat the market, that is, whether he can use special information to generate average returns greater than those on passive combinations of the mimicking returns for the five risk factors.

Using our results for portfolio formation and performance evaluation is even simpler for portfolios that hold only stocks. Tables 5 to 8 say that a model that uses only the three stock-market factors, *RM–RF, SMB,* and *HML,* does as well as the five-factor model in explaining the common time-series variation in stock returns and the cross-section of average stock returns.

Many continue to use the one-factor Sharpe–Lintner model to evaluate portfolio performance and to estimate the cost of capital, despite the lack of evidence that it is relevant. At a minimum, the results here and in Fama and French (1992a) should help to break this common habit.

Finally, in event studies of the stock-price response to firm-specific information, the residuals from a one-factor regression of the stock's return on a market return are often used to abstract from common variation in returns. Our results suggest that the residuals from three-factor regressions that also use *SMB* and *HML* will do a better job isolating the firm-specific components of returns.

Using a three-factor alternative is especially important if the tests impose a cross-section constraint on average stock returns. For example, Agrawal, Jaffe, and Mandelker (1991) use the residuals from the Sharpe–Lintner model to judge the post-merger stock returns of acquiring firms. Aware that post-merger returns may seem too low because acquiring firms tend to be large, they control for size as well as the excess market return when measuring abnormal returns. Still, they find that the average abnormal returns of acquiring firms are negative and similar in size in each of the five years after mergers.

We conjecture that the persistent negative abnormal returns of acquiring firms are a book-to-market effect. We guess that acquiring firms tend to be successful firms that have high stock prices relative to book value and low loadings on *HML*. In our three-factor model, low loadings on *HML* would reduce the average stock returns of acquiring firms, and produce persistent negative abnormal returns in tests that adjust only for market and size factors.

7.3. Open Questions

Taken together, the results here and in Fama and French (1992b) suggest that there is an economic story behind the size and book-to-market effects in average stock returns. The tests here show that there are common return factors related to size and book-to-market equity that help capture the cross-section of average stock returns in a way that is consistent with multifactor asset-pricing models. Fama and French (1992b) show that size and *BE/ME* are related to systematic patterns in relative profitability and growth that could well be the source of common risk factors in returns.

But our work leaves many open questions. Most glaring, we have not shown how the size and book-to-market factors in returns are driven by the stochastic behavior of earnings. How does profitability, or any other fundamental, produce common variation in returns associated with size and *BE/ME* that is not picked up by the market return? Can specific fundamentals be identified as state variables that lead to common variation in returns that is independent of the market and carries a different premium than general market risk? These and other interesting questions are left to future work.

REFERENCES

Agrawal, Anup, Jeffrey F. Jaffe, and Gershon N. Mandelker. 1991. The post-merger performance of acquired firms: A re-examination of an anomaly. Journal of Finance, forthcoming.

Banz, Rolf W., 1981. The relationship between return and market value of common stocks, Journal of Financial Economics 9, 3–18.

Banz, Rolf W. and William J. Breen, 1986. Sample dependent results using accounting and market data: Some evidence, Journal of Finance 41, 779–793.

Basu, Sanjoy, 1983, The relationship between earnings yield, market value, and return for NYSE common stocks: Further evidence, Journal of Financial Economics 12, 129–156.

Bhandari, Laxmi Chand, 1988. Debt/equity ratio and expected common stock returns: Empirical evidence, Journal of Finance 43, 507–528.

Black, Fischer, Michael C. Jensen, and Myron Scholes, 1972, The capital asset pricing model: Some empirical tests, in: M. Jensen, ed., Studies in the theory of capital markets (Praeger, New York, NY).

Breeden, Douglas T., 1979, An intertemporal asset pricing model with stochastic consumption and investment opportunities, Journal of Financial Economics 7, 265–296.

Breeden, Douglas T., Michael R. Gibbons, and Robert H. Litzenberger, 1989, Empirical tests of the consumption-oriented CAPM, Journal of Finance 44, 231–262.

Chan, K. C., Nai-fu Chen, and David Hsieh, 1985, An exploratory investigation of the firm size effect, Journal of Financial Economics 14, 451–471.

Chen, Nai-fu, 1991, Financial investment opportunities and the macroeconomy, Journal of Finance 46, 529–554.

Chen, Nai-fu, Richard Roll, and Stephen A. Ross, 1986, Economic forces and the stock market, Journal of Business 59, 383–403.

Fama, Eugene F., 1991, Efficient markets: II, Journal of Finance 46, 1575–1617.

Fama, Eugene F. and Kenneth R. French, 1988, Dividend yields and expected stock returns, Journal of Financial Economics 22, 3–25.

Fama, Eugene F. and Kenneth R. French, 1989, Business conditions and expected returns on stocks and bonds, Journal of Financial Economics 25, 23–49.

Fama, Eugene F. and Kenneth R. French, 1992a, The cross-section of expected stock returns, Journal of Finance 47, 427–465.

Fama, Eugene F. and Kenneth R. French, 1992b. The economic fundamentals of size and book-to-market equity, Working paper (Graduate School of Business, University of Chicago, Chicago, IL).

Fama, Eugene F. and James MacBeth, 1973, Risk, return and equilibrium: Empirical tests, Journal of Political Economy 81, 607–636.

Gibbons, Michael R., Stephen A. Ross and Jay Shanken, 1989, A test of the efficiency of a given portfolio, Econometrica 57, 1121–1152.

Jaffe, Jeffrey, Donald B. Keim, and Randolph Westerfield, 1989, Earnings yields, market values and stock returns, Journal of Finance 44, 135–148.

Keim, Donald B., 1983, Size-related anomalies and stock return seasonality, Journal of Financial Economics 12, 13–32.

Keim, Donald B., 1988, Stock market regularities: A synthesis of the evidence and explanations, in: E. Dimson, ed., Stock market anomalies (Cambridge University Press, Cambridge).

Lintner, John, 1965. The valuation of risk assets and the selection of risky investments in stock portfolios and capital budgets. Review of Economics and Statistics 47, 13–37.

Lo, Andrew W. and A. Craig MacKinlay, 1990, Data-snooping biases in tests of financial asset pricing models, Review of Financial Studies 3, 431–467.

Merton, Robert C., 1973, An intertemporal capital asset pricing model, Econometrica 41, 867–887.

Merton, Robert C., 1980, On estimating the expected return on the market: An exploratory investigation, Journal of Financial Economics 8, 323–361.

Reinganum, Marc R., 1981, A new empirical perspective on the CAPM, Journal of Financial and Quantitative Analysis 16, 439–462.

Rosenberg, Barr, Kenneth Reid, and Ronald Lanstein, 1985, Persuasive evidence of market inefficiency, Journal of Portfolio Management 11, 9–17.

Roll, Richard, 1983, Vas ist das? The turn-of-the-year effect and the return premia of small firms, Journal of Portfolio Management 9, 18–28.

Ross, Stephen A., 1976, The arbitrage theory of capital asset pricing, Journal of Economic Theory 13, 341–360.

Shanken, Jay, 1982, The arbitrage pricing theory: Is it testable?, Journal of Finance 37, 1129–1140.

Shanken, Jay and Mark I. Weistein, 1990. Macroeconomic variables and asset pricing: Estimation and tests, Working paper (Simon School of Business Administration, University of Rochester, Rochester, NY).

Sharpe, William F., 1964, Capital asset prices: A theory of market equilibrium under conditions of risk, Journal of Finance 19, 425–442.

MULTIFACTOR EXPLANATIONS OF
ASSET PRICING ANOMALIES

$\cdot\ \cdot\ \cdot$

Eugene F. Fama and Kenneth R. French

Researchers have identified many patterns in average stock returns. For example, DeBondt and Thaler (1985) find a reversal in long-term returns; stocks with low long-term past returns tend to have higher future returns. In contrast, Jegadeesh and Titman (1993) find that short-term returns tend to continue; stocks with higher returns in the previous twelve months tend to have higher future returns. Others show that a firm's average stock return is related to its size (ME, stock price times number of shares), book-to-market-equity (BE/ME, the ratio of the book value of common equity to its market value), earnings/price (E/P), cash flow/price (C/P), and past sales growth. (Banz (1981), Basu (1983), Rosenberg, Reid, and Lanstein (1985), and Lakonishok, Shleifer and Vishny (1994).) Because these patterns in average stock returns are not explained by the capital asset pricing model (CAPM) of Sharpe (1964) and Lintner (1965), they are typically called anomalies.

This paper argues that many of the CAPM average-return anomalies are related, and they are captured by the three-factor model in Fama and French (FF 1993). The model says that the expected return on a portfolio in excess of the risk-free rate $[E(R_i) - R_f]$ is explained by the sensitivity of its return to three factors: (i) the excess return on a broad market portfolio $(R_M - R_f)$; (ii) the difference between the return on a portfolio of small stocks and the return on a portfolio of large stocks (SMB, small minus big); and (iii) the difference between the return on a portfolio of high-book-to-market stocks and the return on a portfolio of low-book-to-market stocks (HML, high minus low). Specifically, the expected excess return on portfolio i is,

Reprinted with permission from the *Journal of Finance* 51, no. 1 (March 1996): 55–84. © 1996 by John Wiley and Sons.

The comments of Clifford Asness, John Cochrane, Josef Lakonishok, G. William Schwert, and René Stulz are gratefully acknowledged.

$$E(R_i) - R_f = b_i[E(R_M) - R_f] + s_i E(SMB) + h_i E(HML), \qquad (1)$$

where $E(R_M)-R_f$, $E(SMB)$, and $E(HML)$ are expected premiums, and the factor sensitivities or loadings, b_i, s_i, and h_i, are the slopes in the time-series regression,

$$R_i - R_f = \alpha_i + b_i(R_M - R_f) + s_i SMB + h_i HML + \varepsilon_i. \qquad (2)$$

Fama and French (1995) show that book-to-market equity and slopes on HML proxy for relative distress. Weak firms with persistently low earnings tend to have high BE/ME and positive slopes on HML; strong firms with persistently high earnings have low BE/ME and negative slopes on HML. Using HML to explain returns is thus in line with the evidence of Chan and Chen (1991) that there is covariation in returns related to relative distress that is not captured by the market return and is compensated in average returns. Similarly, using SMB to explain returns is in line with the evidence of Huberman and Kandel (1987) that there is covariation in the returns on small stocks that is not captured by the market return and is compensated in average returns.

The three-factor model in (1) seems to capture much of the cross-sectional variation in average stock returns. FF (1993) show that the model is a good description of returns on portfolios formed on size and BE/ME. FF (1994) use the model to explain industry returns. Here we show that the three-factor model captures the returns to portfolios formed on E/P, C/P, and sales growth. In a nutshell, low E/P, low C/P, and high sales growth are typical of strong firms that have negative slopes on HML. Since the average HML return is strongly positive (about 6 percent per year), these negative loadings, which are similar to the HML slopes for low-BE/ME stocks, imply lower expected returns in (1). Conversely, like high-BE/ME stocks, stocks with high E/P, high C/P, or low sales growth tend to load positively on HML (they are relatively distressed), and they have higher average returns. The three-factor model also captures the reversal of long-term returns documented by DeBondt and Thaler (1985). Stocks with low long-term past returns (losers) tend to have positive SMB and HML slopes (they are smaller and relatively distressed) and higher future average returns. Conversely, long-term winners tend to be strong stocks that have negative slopes on HML and low future returns.

Equation (1), however, cannot explain the continuation of short-term returns documented by Jegadeesh and Titman (1993). Like long-term losers, stocks that have low short-term past returns tend to load positively on HML; like long-term winners, short-term past winners load negatively on HML. As it does for long-term returns, this pattern in the HML slopes predicts reversal rather than continuation for future returns. The continuation of short-term returns is thus left unexplained by our model.

At a minimum, the available evidence suggests that the three-factor model in (1) and (2), with intercepts in (2) equal to 0.0, is a parsimonious description of returns and average returns. The model captures much of the variation in the cross-section of average stock returns, and it absorbs most of the anomalies that have plagued the CAPM. More aggressively, we argue in FF (1993, 1994, 1995) that the empirical successes of (1) suggest that it is an equilibrium pricing model, a three-factor version of Merton's (1973) intertemporal CAPM (ICAPM) or Ross's (1976) arbitrage pricing theory (APT). In this view, SMB and HML mimic combinations of two underlying risk factors or state variables of special hedging concern to investors.

Our aggressive interpretation of tests of (1) has produced reasonable skepticism, much of it centered on the premium for distress (the average HML return). Kothari, Shanken, and Sloan (1995) argue that a substantial part of the premium is due to survivor bias; the data source for book equity (COMPUSTAT) contains a disproportionate number of high-BE/ME firms that survive distress, so average return for high-BE/ME firms is overstated. Another view is that the distress premium is just data snooping; researchers tend to search for and fixate on variables that are related to average return, but only in the sample used to identify them (Black (1993), MacKinlay (1995)). A third view is that the distress premium is real but irrational, the result of investor over-reaction that leads to underpricing of distressed stocks and overpricing of growth stocks (Lakonishok, Shleifer, and Vishny (1994), Haugen (1995)).

Section VI discusses the competing stories for the successes of the three-factor model. First, however, Sections I to V present the evidence that the model captures most of the average-return anomalies of the CAPM.

I. TESTS ON THE 25 FF SIZE-BE/ME PORTFOLIOS

To set the stage, Table I shows the average excess returns on the 25 Fama-French (1993) size-BE/ME portfolios of value-weighted NYSE, AMEX, and NASD stocks. The table shows that small stocks tend to have higher returns than big stocks and high-book-to-market stocks have higher returns than low-BE/ME stocks.

Table I also reports estimates of the three-factor time-series regression (2). If the three-factor model (1) describes expected returns, the regression intercepts should be close to 0.0. The estimated intercepts say that the model leaves

TABLE I. Summary statistics and three-factor regressions for simple monthly percent excess returns on 25 portfolios formed on size and BE/ME: 7/63–12/93, 366 months

R_f is the one-month Treasury bill rate observed at the beginning of the month (from CRSP). The explanatory returns R_M, SMB, and HML are formed as follows. At the end of June of each year t (1963–1993), NYSE, AMEX, and Nasdaq stocks are allocated to two groups (small or big, S or B) based on whether their June market equity (ME, stock price times shares outstanding) is below or above the median ME for NYSE stocks. NYSE, AMEX, and Nasdaq stocks are allocated in an independent sort to three book-to-market equity (BE/ME) groups (low, medium, or high; L, M, or H) based on the breakpoints for the bottom 30 percent, middle 40 percent, and top 30 percent of the values of BE/ME for NYSE stocks. Six size-BE/ME portfolios (S/L, S/M, S/H, B/L, B/M, B/H) are defined as the intersections of the two ME and the three BE/ME groups. Value-weight monthly returns on the portfolios are calculated from July to the following June. SMB is the difference, each month, between the average of the returns on the three small-stock portfolios (S/L, S/M, and S/H) and the average of the returns on the three big-stock portfolios (B/L, B/M, and B/H). HML is the difference between the average of the returns on the two high-BE/ME portfolios (S/H and B/H) and the average of the returns on the two low-BE/ME portfolios (S/L and B/L). The 25 size-BE/ME portfolios are formed like the six size-BE/ME portfolios used to construct SMB and HML, except that quintile breakpoints for ME and BE/ME for NYSE stocks are used to allocate NYSE, AMEX, and Nasdaq stocks to the portfolios.

BE is the COMPUSTAT book value of stockholders' equity, plus balance sheet deferred taxes and investment tax credit (if available), minus the book value of preferred stock. Depending on availability, we use redemption, liquidation, or par value (in that order) to estimate the book value of preferred stock. The BE/ME ratio used to form portfolios in June of year t is then book common equity for the fiscal year ending in calendar year $t - 1$, divided by market equity at the end of December of $t - 1$. We do not use negative BE firms, which are rare prior to 1980, when calculating the breakpoints for BE/ME or when forming the size-BE/ME portfolios. Also, only firms with ordinary common equity (as classified by CRSP) are included in the tests. This means that ADR's, REIT's, and units of beneficial interest are excluded.

The market return R_M is the value-weight return on all stocks in the size-BE/ME portfolios, plus the negative BE stocks excluded from the portfolios.

	Book-to-Market Equity (BE/ME) Quintiles									
Size	Low	2	3	4	High	Low	2	3	4	High
				Panel A: Summary Statistics						
			Mean				Standard Deviations			
Small	0.31	0.70	0.82	0.95	1.08	7.67	6.74	6.14	5.85	6.14
2	0.48	0.71	0.91	0.93	1.09	7.13	6.25	5.71	5.23	5.94
3	0.44	0.68	0.75	0.86	1.05	6.52	5.53	5.11	4.79	5.48
4	0.51	0.39	0.64	0.80	1.04	5.86	5.28	4.97	4.81	5.67
Big	0.37	0.39	0.36	0.58	0.71	4.84	4.61	4.28	4.18	4.89

(*Continued*)

TABLE 1. (Continued)

Book-to-Market Equity (BE/ME) Quintiles

Size	Low	2	3	4	High	Low	2	3	4	High

Panel B: Regressions: $R_i - R_f = a_i + b_i(R_M - R_f) + s_i SMB + h_i HML + e_i$

Size	Low	2	3	4	High	Low	2	3	4	High
			a					*t(a)*		
Small	−0.45	−0.16	−0.05	0.04	0.02	−4.19	−2.04	−0.82	0.69	0.29
2	−0.07	−0.04	0.09	0.07	0.03	−0.80	−0.59	1.33	1.13	0.51
3	−0.08	0.04	−0.00	0.06	0.07	−1.07	0.47	−0.06	0.88	0.89
4	0.14	−0.19	−0.06	0.02	0.06	1.74	−2.43	−0.73	0.27	0.59
Big	0.20	−0.04	−0.10	−0.08	−0.14	3.14	−0.52	−1.23	−1.07	−1.17
			b					*t(b)*		
Small	1.03	1.01	0.94	0.89	0.94	39.10	50.89	59.93	58.47	57.71
2	1.10	1.04	0.99	0.97	1.08	52.94	61.14	58.17	62.97	65.58
3	1.10	1.02	0.98	0.97	1.07	57.08	55.49	53.11	55.96	52.37
4	1.07	1.07	1.05	1.03	1.18	54.77	54.48	51.79	45.76	46.27
Big	0.96	1.02	0.98	0.99	1.07	60.25	57.77	47.03	53.25	37.18
			s					*t(s)*		
Small	1.47	1.27	1.18	1.17	1.23	39.01	44.48	52.26	53.82	52.65
2	1.01	0.97	0.88	0.73	0.90	34.10	39.94	36.19	32.92	38.17
3	0.75	0.63	0.59	0.47	0.64	27.09	24.13	22.37	18.97	22.01
4	0.36	0.30	0.29	0.22	0.41	12.87	10.64	10.17	6.82	11.26
Big	−0.16	−0.13	−0.25	−0.16	−0.03	−6.97	−5.12	−8.45	−6.21	−0.77
			h					*t(h)*		
Small	−0.27	0.10	0.25	0.37	0.63	−6.28	3.03	9.74	15.16	23.62
2	−0.49	0.00	0.26	0.46	0.69	−14.66	0.34	9.21	18.14	25.59
3	−0.39	0.03	0.32	0.49	0.68	−12.56	0.89	10.73	17.45	20.43
4	−0.44	0.03	0.31	0.54	0.72	−13.98	0.97	9.45	14.70	17.34
Big	−0.47	0.00	0.20	0.56	0.82	−18.23	0.18	6.04	18.71	17.57
			R^2					*s(e)*		
Small	0.93	0.95	0.96	0.96	0.96	1.97	1.49	1.18	1.13	1.22
2	0.95	0.96	0.95	0.95	0.96	1.55	1.27	1.28	1.16	1.23
3	0.95	0.94	0.93	0.93	0.92	1.44	1.37	1.38	1.30	1.52
4	0.94	0.92	0.91	0.88	0.89	1.46	1.47	1.51	1.69	1.91
Big	0.94	0.92	0.87	0.89	0.81	1.19	1.32	1.55	1.39	2.15

a large negative unexplained return for the portfolio of stocks in the smallest size and lowest BE/ME quintiles, and a large positive unexplained return for the portfolio of stocks in the largest size and lowest BE/ME quintiles. Otherwise the intercepts are close to 0.0.

The *F*-test of Gibbons, Ross, and Shanken (GRS 1989) rejects the hypothesis that (1) explains the average returns on the 25 size-BE/ME portfolios at the

0.004 level. This rejection of the three-factor model is testimony to the explanatory power of the regressions. The average of the 25 regression R^2 is 0.93, so small intercepts are distinguishable from zero. The model does capture most of the variation in the average returns on the portfolios, as witnessed by the small average absolute intercept, 0.093 percent (about nine basis points) per month. We show next that the model does an even better job on most of the other sets of portfolios we consider.

A comment on methodology is necessary. In the time-series regression (2), variation through time in the expected premiums $E(R_M) - R_f$, $E(SMB)$, and $E(HML)$ in (1) is embedded in the explanatory returns, $R_M - R_f$, SMB, and HML. Thus the regression intercepts are net of (they are conditional on) variation in the expected premiums. We also judge that forming portfolios periodically on size, BE/ME, E/P, C/P, sales growth, and past returns results in loadings on the three factors that are roughly constant. Variation through time in the slopes is, however, important in other applications. For example, FF (1994) show that because industries wander between growth and distress, it is critical to allow for variation in SMB and HML slopes when applying (1) and (2) to industries.

II. LSV DECILES

Lakonishok, Shleifer, and Vishny (LSV 1994) examine the returns on sets of deciles formed from sorts on BE/ME, E/P, C/P, and five-year sales rank. Table II summarizes the excess returns on our versions of these portfolios. The portfolios are formed each year as in LSV using COMPUSTAT accounting data for the fiscal year ending in the current calendar year (see table footnote). We then calculate returns beginning in July of the following year. (LSV start their returns in April.) To reduce the influence of small stocks in these (equal-weight) portfolios, we use only NYSE stocks. (LSV use NYSE and AMEX.) To be included in the tests for a given year, a stock must have data on all the LSV variables. Thus, firms must have COMPUSTAT data on sales for six years before they are included in the return tests. As in LSV, this reduces biases that might arise because COMPUSTAT includes historical data when it adds firms (Banz and Breen (1986), Kothari, Shanken, and Sloan (1995)).

Our sorts of NYSE stocks in Table II produce strong positive relations between average return and BE/ME, E/P, or C/P, much like those reported by LSV for NYSE and AMEX firms. Like LSV, we find that past sales growth is negatively related to future return. The estimates of the three-factor regression (2) in Table III show, however, that the three-factor model (1) captures these patterns in average returns. The regression intercepts are consistently small.

TABLE II. Summary statistics for simple monthly excess returns (in percent) on the LSV equal-weight deciles: 7/63–12/93, 366 months

At the end of June of each year t (1963–1993), the NYSE stocks on COMPUSTAT are allocated to ten portfolios, based on the decile breakpoints for BE/ME (book-to-market equity), E/P (earnings/price), C/P (cash flow/price), and past five-year sales rank (5-Yr SR). Equal-weight returns on the portfolios are calculated from July to the following June, resulting in a time series of 366 monthly returns for July 1963 to December 1993. To be included in the tests for a given year, a stock must have data on all of the portfolio-formation variables of this table. Thus, the sample of firms is the same for all variables.

For portfolios formed in June of year t, the denominator of BE/ME, E/P, and C/P is market equity (ME, stock price times shares outstanding) for the end of December of year $t-1$, and BE, E, and C are for the fiscal year ending in calendar year $t-1$. Book equity BE is defined in Table I. E is earnings before extraordinary items but after interest, depreciation, taxes, and preferred dividends. Cash flow, C, is E plus depreciation.

The five-year sales rank for June of year t, 5-Yr SR(t), is the weighted average of the annual sales growth ranks for the prior five years, that is,

$$5-Yr\ SR(t) = \sum_{j=1}^{5}(6-j)\times Rank(t-j)$$

The sales growth for year $t-j$ is the percentage change in sales from $t-j-1$ to $t-j$, $\ln[\text{Sales}(t-j)/\text{Sales}(t-j-1)]$. Only firms with data for all five prior years are used to determine the annual sales growth ranks for years $t-5$ to $t-1$.

For each portfolio, the table shows the mean monthly return in excess of the one-month Treasury bill rate (Mean), the standard deviation of the monthly excess returns (Std. Dev.), and the ratio of the mean excess return to its standard error [$t(\text{mean}) = \text{Mean}/(\text{Std. Dev.}/365^{1/2})$]. Ave ME is the average size (ME, in $millions) of the firms in a portfolio, averaged across the 366 sample months.

	Deciles									
	1	2	3	4	5	6	7	8	9	10
BE/ME	Low									High
Mean	0.42	0.50	0.53	0.58	0.65	0.72	0.81	0.84	1.03	1.22
Std. Dev.	5.81	5.56	5.57	5.52	5.23	5.03	4.96	5.06	5.52	6.82
t(Mean)	1.39	1.72	1.82	2.02	2.38	2.74	3.10	3.17	3.55	3.43
Ave. ME	2256	1390	1125	1037	1001	864	838	730	572	362
E/P	Low									High
Mean	0.55	0.45	0.54	0.63	0.67	0.77	0.82	0.90	0.99	1.03
Std. Dev.	6.09	5.62	5.51	5.35	5.14	5.18	4.94	4.88	5.05	5.87
t(Mean)	1.72	1.52	1.89	2.24	2.49	2.84	3.16	3.51	3.74	3.37
Ave. ME	1294	1367	1211	1209	1411	1029	1022	909	862	661
C/P	Low									High
Mean	0.43	0.45	0.60	0.67	0.70	0.76	0.77	0.86	0.97	1.16
Std. Dev.	5.80	5.67	5.57	5.39	5.39	5.19	5.00	4.88	4.96	6.36
t(Mean)	1.41	1.52	2.06	2.37	2.47	2.78	2.93	3.36	3.75	3.47
Ave. ME	1491	1266	1112	1198	990	994	974	951	990	652
5-Yr SR	High									Low
Mean	0.47	0.63	0.70	0.68	0.67	0.74	0.70	0.78	0.89	1.03
Std. Dev.	6.39	5.66	5.46	5.15	5.22	5.10	5.00	5.10	5.25	6.13
t(Mean)	1.42	2.14	2.45	2.52	2.46	2.78	2.68	2.91	3.23	3.21
Ave. ME	937	1233	1075	1182	1265	1186	1075	884	744	434

Despite the strong explanatory power of the regressions (most R^2 values are greater than 0.92), the GRS tests never come close to rejecting the hypothesis that the three-factor model describes average returns. In terms of both the magnitudes of the intercepts and the GRS tests, the three-factor model does a better job on the LSV deciles than it does on the 25 FF size-BE/ME portfolios. (Compare Tables I and III.)

For perspective on why the three-factor model works so well on the LSV portfolios, Table III shows the regression slopes for the C/P deciles. Higher-C/P portfolios produce larger slopes on SMB and especially HML. This pattern in the slopes is also observed for the BE/ME and E/P deciles (not shown). It seems that dividing an accounting variable by stock price produces a characterization of stocks that is related to their loadings on HML. Given the evidence in FF (1995) that loadings on HML proxy for relative distress, we can infer that low BE/ME, E/P, and C/P are typical of strong stocks, while high BE/ME, E/P, and C/P are typical of stocks that are relatively distressed. The patterns in the loadings of the BE/ME, E/P, and C/P deciles on HML, and the high average value of HML (0.46 percent per month, 6.33 percent per year) largely explain how the three-factor regressions transform the strong positive relations between average return and these ratios (Table II) into intercepts that are close to 0.0.

Among the sorts in Table III, the three-factor model has the hardest time with the returns on the sales-rank portfolios. Recall that high sales-rank firms (strong past performers) have low future returns, and low sales-rank firms (weak past performers) have high future returns (Table II). The three-factor model of (1) captures most of this pattern in average returns, largely because low sales-rank stocks behave like distressed stocks (they have stronger loadings on HML). But a hint of the pattern is left in the regression intercepts. Except for the highest sales-rank decile, however, the intercepts are close to 0.0. Moreover, although the intercepts for the sales-rank deciles produce the largest GRS F-statistic (0.87), it is close to the median of its distribution when the true intercepts are all 0.0 (its p-value is 0.563). This evidence that the three-factor model describes the returns on the sales-rank deciles is important since sales rank is the only portfolio-formation variable (here and in LSV) that is not a transformed version of stock price. (See also the industry tests in FF (1994).)

III. LSV DOUBLE-SORT PORTFOLIOS

LSV argue that sorting stocks on two accounting variables more accurately distinguishes between strong and distressed stocks, and produces larger

TABLE III. Three-factor time-series regressions for monthly excess returns (in percent) on the LSV equal-weight deciles: 7/63–12/93, 366 months

$$R_i - R_f = a_i + b_i(R_M - R_f) + s_i \text{SMB} + h_i \text{HML} + e_i$$

The formation of the BE/ME, E/P, C/P, and five-year-sales-rank (5-Yr SR) deciles is described in Table II. The explanatory returns, $R_M - R_f$, SMB, and HML are described in Table I. $t(\,)$ is a regression coefficient divided by its standard error. The regression R^2s are adjusted for degrees of freedom. GRS is the F-statistic of Gibbons, Ross, and Shanken (1989), testing the hypothesis that the regression intercepts for a set of ten portfolios are all 0.0. $p(GRS)$ is the p-value of GRS, that is, the probability of a GRS value as large or larger than the observed value if the zero-intercepts hypothesis is true.

| | | | | | | Deciles | | | | | | |
	1	2	3	4	5	6	7	8	9	10	GRS	p(GRS)
BE/ME	Low									High		
a	0.08	−0.02	−0.09	−0.11	−0.08	−0.03	0.01	−0.04	0.03	−0.00		
t(a)	1.19	−0.26	−1.25	−1.39	−1.16	−0.40	0.15	−0.61	0.43	−0.02	0.57	0.841
R²	0.95	0.95	0.94	0.93	0.94	0.94	0.94	0.94	0.95	0.89		
E/P	Low									High		
a	−0.00	−0.07	−0.07	−0.04	−0.03	0.02	0.06	0.09	0.12	0.00		
t(a)	−0.07	−1.07	−0.94	−0.52	−0.43	0.24	1.01	1.46	1.49	0.05	0.84	0.592
R²	0.91	0.95	0.94	0.94	0.94	0.94	0.94	0.94	0.92	0.92		
C/P	Low									High		
a	0.02	−0.08	−0.07	−0.00	−0.04	0.00	0.00	0.05	0.06	0.01		
b	1.04	1.06	1.08	1.06	1.05	1.04	0.99	1.00	0.98	1.14		
s	0.45	0.50	0.54	0.51	0.55	0.50	0.53	0.48	0.57	0.92		
h	−0.39	−0.18	0.07	0.11	0.23	0.31	0.36	0.50	0.67	0.79		
t(a)	0.22	−1.14	−1.00	−0.04	−0.51	0.00	0.06	0.72	0.92	0.14	0.49	0.898
t(b)	51.45	61.16	62.49	64.15	59.04	61.28	60.02	63.36	58.92	46.49		
t(s)	15.56	20.32	22.11	21.57	21.49	20.72	22.19	21.17	24.13	26.18		
t(h)	−12.03	−6.52	2.56	4.28	7.85	11.40	13.52	19.46	24.88	19.74		
R²	0.93	0.95	0.95	0.95	0.94	0.94	0.94	0.94	0.94	0.92		
5-Yr SR	High									Low		
a	−0.21	−0.06	−0.03	−0.01	−0.04	−0.02	−0.04	0.00	0.04	0.07		
b	1.16	1.10	1.09	1.03	1.03	1.03	1.00	0.99	0.99	1.02		
s	0.72	0.56	0.52	0.49	0.52	0.51	0.50	0.57	0.67	0.95		
h	−0.09	0.09	0.21	0.20	0.24	0.33	0.33	0.36	0.47	0.50		
t(a)	−2.60	−0.97	−0.49	−0.20	−0.61	−0.25	−0.66	0.07	0.47	0.60	0.87	0.563
t(b)	59.01	70.59	67.65	65.34	56.68	68.89	62.49	54.12	50.08	34.54		
t(s)	25.69	25.11	22.59	21.65	20.15	23.64	21.89	21.65	23.65	22.34		
t(h)	−2.88	3.55	8.05	7.98	8.07	13.63	12.80	12.13	14.78	10.32		
R²	0.95	0.96	0.95	0.95	0.93	0.95	0.94	0.93	0.92	0.87		

spreads in average returns. Because accounting ratios with stock price in the denominator tend to be correlated, LSV suggest combining sorts on sales rank with sorts on BE/ME, E/P, or C/P. We follow their procedure and separately sort firms each year into three groups (low 30 percent, medium 40 percent, and high 30 percent) on each variable. We then form sets of nine portfolios as the intersections of the sales-rank sort and the sorts on BE/ME, E/P, or C/P. Confirming their results, Table IV shows that the sales-rank sort increases the spread of average returns provided by the sorts on BE/ME, E/P, or C/P. In fact, the two double-whammy portfolios, combining low BE/ME, E/P, or C/P with high sales growth (portfolio 1–1), and high BE/ME, E/P, or C/P with low sales growth (portfolio 3–3), always have the lowest and highest post-formation average returns.

Table V shows that the three-factor model has little trouble describing the returns on the LSV double-sort portfolios. Strong negative loadings on HML (which has a high average premium) bring the low returns on the 1–1 portfolios comfortably within the predictions of the three-factor model; the most extreme intercept for the 1–1 portfolios is −6 basis points (−0.06 percent) per month and less than one standard error from 0.0. Conversely, because the 3–3 portfolios have strong positive loadings on SMB and HML (they behave like smaller distressed stocks), their high average returns are also predicted by the three-factor model. The intercepts for these portfolios are positive, but again quite close to (less than 8 basis points and 0.7 standard errors from) 0.0.

The GRS tests in Table V support the inference that the intercepts in the three-factor regression (2) are 0.0; the smallest p-value is 0.284. Thus, whether the spreads in average returns on the LSV double-sort portfolios are caused by risk or over-reaction, the three-factor model in equation (1) describes them parsimoniously.

IV. PORTFOLIOS FORMED ON PAST RETURNS

DeBondt and Thaler (1985) find that when portfolios are formed on long-term (three- to five-year) past returns, losers (low past returns) have high future returns and winners (high past returns) have low future returns. In contrast, Jegadeesh and Titman (1993) and Asness (1994) find that when portfolios are formed on short-term (up to a year of) past returns, past losers tend to be future losers and past winners are future winners.

Table VI shows average returns on sets of ten equal-weight portfolios formed monthly on short-term (11 months) and long-term (up to five years of) past returns. The results for July 1963 to December 1993 confirm the strong

TABLE IV. Summary statistics for excess returns (in percent) on the LSV equal-weight double-sort portfolios: 7/63–12/93, 366 months

At the end of June of each year t (1963–1993), the NYSE stocks on COMPUSTAT are allocated to three equal groups (low, medium, and high: 1, 2, and 3) based on their sorted BE/ME, E/P, or C/P ratios for year $t - 1$. The NYSE stocks on COMPUSTAT are also allocated to three equal groups (high, medium, and low: 1, 2, and 3) based on their five-year sales rank. The intersections of the sales-rank sort with the BE/ME, E/P, or E/P sorts are then used to create three sets of nine portfolios (BE/ME & Sales Rank, E/P & Sales Rank, C/P & Sales Rank). Equal-weight returns on the portfolios are calculated from July to the following June. To be included in the tests for a given year, a stock must have data on all of the portfolio-formation variables. The sample of firms is thus the same for all variables. BE/ME (book-to-market equity), E/P (earnings/price), C/P (cash flow/price), and five-year sales rank are defined in Table II. The 1–1 portfolios contain strong firms (high sales growth and low BE/ME, E/P, or C/P), while the 3–3 portfolios contain weak firms (low sales growth and high BE/ME, E/P, or C/P).

For each portfolio, the table shows the mean monthly return in excess of the one-month Treasury bill rate (Mean), the standard deviation of the monthly excess returns (Std. Dev.), and the ratio of the mean excess return to its standard error [t(mean) = Mean/(Std. Dev./$365^{1/2}$)]. Ave. ME is the average size (ME, in $millions) of the firms in a portfolio, averaged across the 366 sample months. Count is the average across months of the number of firms in a portfolio.

	1–1	1–2	1–3	2–1	2–2	2–3	3–1	3–2	3–3
BE/ME and Sales Rank									
Mean	0.47	0.49	0.52	0.64	0.69	0.74	0.93	0.94	1.11
Std. Dev.	5.95	5.19	5.63	5.75	4.97	5.02	6.45	5.59	5.99
t(Mean)	1.52	1.81	1.77	2.11	2.66	2.83	2.76	3.20	3.55
Count	151	109	41	106	180	116	49	118	146
Ave. ME	1530	1867	1061	723	1110	866	482	655	445
E/P and Sales Rank									
Mean	0.41	0.47	0.77	0.63	0.72	0.82	0.80	0.86	1.06
Std. Dev.	6.02	5.44	5.76	5.76	4.94	4.96	6.08	5.33	5.90
t(Mean)	1.31	1.66	2.57	2.10	2.80	3.16	2.51	3.08	3.43
Count	114	98	68	105	163	104	87	145	131
Ave. ME	1394	1524	739	1103	1355	928	651	754	506
C/P and Sales Rank									
Mean	0.44	0.45	0.70	0.62	0.71	0.83	0.85	0.91	1.06
Std. Dev.	6.03	5.26	5.76	5.80	5.01	5.09	6.13	5.34	5.90
t(Mean)	1.40	1.64	2.33	2.03	2.70	3.10	2.64	3.27	3.44
Count	122	107	62	106	166	115	78	134	125
Ave. ME	1365	1527	648	1067	1187	796	615	881	616

TABLE V. Three-factor regressions for monthly excess returns (in percent) on the LSV equal-weight double-sort portfolios: 7/63–12/93, 366 months

$$R_i - R_f = a_i + b_i(R_M - R_f) + s_i SMB + h_i HML + e_i$$

The formation of the double-sort portfolios is described in Table IV. BE/ME (book-to-market equity), E/P (earnings/price), C/P (cash flow/price), and five-year sales rank are described in Table II. The 1–1 portfolios contain strong firms (high sales growth and low BE/ME, E/P, or C/P), while the 3–3 portfolios contain weak firms (low sales growth and high BE/ME, E/P, or C/P). $t()$ is a regression coefficient divided by its standard error. The regression R^2 are adjusted for degrees of freedom. GRS is the F-statistic of Gibbons, Ross, and Shanken (1989), testing the hypothesis that the nine regression intercepts for a set of double-sort portfolios are all 0.0. p(GRS) is the p-value of GRS.

	1–1	1–2	1–3	2–1	2–2	2–3	3–1	3–2	3–3	GRS	p(GRS)
BE/ME and Sales Rank											
a	−0.00	0.00	−0.06	−0.19	−0.00	0.00	−0.19	−0.07	0.07		
b	1.10	1.03	1.00	1.12	1.00	0.99	1.17	1.06	1.01		
s	0.49	0.31	0.55	0.63	0.48	0.50	0.87	0.74	0.97		
h	−0.33	−0.14	−0.04	0.31	0.25	0.32	0.75	0.70	0.68		
$t(a)$	−0.10	0.12	−0.57	−2.59	−0.07	0.12	−1.64	−0.94	0.69	1.22	0.284
$t(b)$	71.67	67.85	35.65	61.81	67.36	51.00	41.29	54.45	38.46		
$t(s)$	22.30	14.32	13.77	24.42	22.44	18.18	21.36	26.62	25.76		
$t(h)$	−13.19	−5.74	−0.94	10.57	10.33	10.17	16.30	22.31	15.91		
R^2	0.96	0.95	0.86	0.94	0.95	0.92	0.89	0.93	0.89		
E/P and Sales Rank											
a	−0.06	−0.06	0.02	−0.09	0.03	0.06	−0.19	−0.06	0.06		
b	1.11	1.04	1.02	1.11	1.01	0.99	1.13	1.04	1.00		
s	0.48	0.45	0.74	0.58	0.43	0.48	0.82	0.65	0.92		
h	−0.34	−0.12	0.18	0.14	0.25	0.39	0.53	0.58	0.61		
$t(a)$	−0.89	−0.87	0.24	−1.23	0.53	0.81	−2.10	−0.82	0.59	1.06	0.394
$t(b)$	62.12	56.09	41.52	58.97	67.48	53.80	51.32	59.05	37.61		
$t(s)$	18.61	17.04	21.07	21.30	20.18	18.13	26.08	25.66	23.98		
$t(h)$	−11.56	−3.86	4.41	4.50	10.46	12.88	14.92	20.49	14.19		
R^2	0.95	0.94	0.90	0.94	0.95	0.92	0.93	0.94	0.89		
C/P and Sales Rank											
a	−0.02	−0.06	−0.02	−0.14	0.00	0.07	−0.17	−0.02	0.04		
b	1.11	1.01	1.02	1.12	1.02	1.00	1.13	1.04	1.00		
s	0.46	0.42	0.72	0.63	0.46	0.53	0.80	0.64	0.92		
h	−0.36	−0.12	0.14	0.17	0.26	0.34	0.62	0.62	0.68		
$t(a)$	−0.27	−1.03	−0.24	−1.93	0.08	0.95	−1.73	−0.34	0.34	1.04	0.405
$t(b)$	64.04	65.82	40.20	63.31	67.96	52.28	45.55	58.48	36.63		
$t(s)$	18.37	19.12	19.86	24.77	21.34	19.47	22.57	25.32	23.47		
$t(h)$	−12.71	−4.90	3.42	5.82	10.61	10.84	15.21	21.64	15.40		
R^2	0.95	0.95	0.89	0.95	0.95	0.92	0.91	0.94	0.88		

TABLE VI. Average monthly excess returns (in percent) on equal-weight NYSE deciles formed monthly based on continuously compounded past returns

At the beginning of each month t, all NYSE firms on CRSP with returns for months $t - x$ to $t - y$ are allocated to deciles based on their continuously compounded returns between $t - x$ and $t - y$. For example, firms are allocated to the 12–2 portfolios for January 1931 based on their continuously compounded returns for January 1930 through November 1930. Decile 1 contains the NYSE stocks with the lowest continuously compounded past returns. The portfolios are reformed monthly, and equal-weight simple returns in excess of the one-month bill rate are calculated for January 1931 (3101) to December 1993 (9312). The table shows the averages of these excess returns for 6307 to 9312 (366 months) and 3101 to 6306 (390 months).

Period	Portfolio Formation Months	Average Excess Returns									
		1	2	3	4	5	6	7	8	9	10
6307–9312	12–2	−0.00	0.46	0.61	0.55	0.72	0.68	0.85	0.90	1.08	1.31
6307–9312	24–2	0.36	0.60	0.59	0.66	0.71	0.81	0.73	0.80	0.93	1.05
6307–9312	36–2	0.46	0.60	0.77	0.69	0.73	0.81	0.69	0.78	0.84	0.97
6307–9312	48–2	0.66	0.70	0.77	0.74	0.71	0.71	0.72	0.71	0.72	0.89
6307–9312	60–2	0.86	0.76	0.73	0.75	0.70	0.71	0.74	0.70	0.66	0.73
6307–9312	60–13	1.16	0.81	0.77	0.76	0.74	0.72	0.72	0.73	0.54	0.42
3101–6306	12–2	1.49	1.52	1.32	1.49	1.39	1.45	1.45	1.55	1.58	1.87
3101–6306	24–2	2.24	1.60	1.57	1.70	1.41	1.31	1.32	1.24	1.26	1.46
3101–6306	36–2	2.31	1.74	1.65	1.46	1.40	1.40	1.32	1.23	1.27	1.36
3101–6306	48–2	2.34	1.81	1.62	1.60	1.37	1.30	1.33	1.22	1.24	1.26
3101–6306	60–2	2.49	1.78	1.74	1.50	1.39	1.33	1.27	1.18	1.28	1.14
3101–6306	60–13	2.62	1.85	1.63	1.61	1.43	1.24	1.34	1.28	1.08	1.01

continuation of short-term returns. The average excess return for the month after portfolio formation ranges from −0.00 percent for the decile of stocks with the worst short-term past returns (measured from 12 to 2 months before portfolio formation) to 1.31 percent for the decile with the best short-term past returns. (Skipping the portfolio formation month in ranking stocks reduces bias from bid-ask bounce.)

Table VI also confirms that average returns tend to reverse when portfolios are formed using returns for the four years from 60 to 13 months prior to portfolio formation. For these portfolios, the average return in the month after portfolio formation ranges from 1.16 percent for the decile of stocks with the worst long-term past returns to 0.42 percent for stocks with the best past returns. In the 1963–1993 results, however, long-term return reversal is observed only when the year prior to portfolio formation is skipped in ranking stocks. When the preceding year is included, short-term continuation offsets long-term reversal, and past losers have lower future returns than past winners for portfolios formed with up to four years of past returns.

Can our three-factor model explain the patterns in the future returns for 1963–1993 on portfolios formed on past returns? Table VII shows that the answer is yes for the reversal of long-term returns observed when portfolios are formed using returns from 60 to 13 months prior to portfolio formation. The regressions of the post-formation returns on these portfolios on $R_M - R_f$, SMB, and HML produce intercepts that are close to 0.0 both in absolute terms and on the GRS test. The three-factor model works because long-term past losers load more on SMB and HML. Since they behave more like small distressed stocks, the model predicts that the long-term past losers will have higher average returns. Thus, the reversal of long-term returns, which has produced so much controversy (DeBondt and Thaler (1985, 1987), Chan (1988), Ball and Kothari (1989), Chopra, Lakonishok, and Ritter (1992)), falls neatly within the predictions of our three-factor model. Moreover, since the model captures the economic essence of long-term winners (strong stocks) and losers (smaller distressed stocks), we speculate that it can explain the stronger reversal of long-term returns observed in the 1931–1963 period (Table VI).

In contrast, Table VII shows that the three-factor model misses the continuation of returns for portfolios formed on short-term past returns. In the three-factor regressions for these portfolios, the intercepts are strongly negative for short-term-losers (low-past-returns) and strongly positive for short-term winners. The problem is that losers load more on SMB and HML (they behave more like small distressed stocks) than winners. Thus, as for the portfolios formed on long-term past returns, the three-factor model predicts reversal for the post-formation returns of short-term losers and winners, and so misses the observed continuation.

As noted earlier, when portfolios are formed on long-term past returns that include the year prior to portfolio formation, short-term continuation offsets long-term reversal, leaving either continuation or little pattern in future returns. Again, however, future returns on long-term losers load more on SMB and HML, so the three-factor model (1) incorrectly predicts return reversal. The regressions in table VII for portfolios formed using returns from two to 48 months prior to portfolio formation are an example.

TABLE VII. Three-factor regressions for monthly excess returns (in percent) on equal-weight NYSE portfolios formed on past returns: 7/63–12/93, 366 months

$$R_i - R_f = a_i + b_i(R_M - R_f) + s_i\text{SMB} + h_i\text{HML} + e_i$$

The formation of the past-return deciles is described in Table VI. Decile 1 contains the NYSE stocks with the lowest continuously compounded returns during the portfolio-formation period (12–2, 48–2, or 60–13 months before the return month). $t()$ is a regression coefficient divided by its standard error. The regression R^2s are adjusted for degrees of freedom. GRS is the F-statistic of Gibbons, Ross, and Shanken (1989), testing the hypothesis that the regression intercepts for a set of ten portfolios are all 0.0. $p(\text{GRS})$ is the p-value of GRS.

	1	2	3	4	5	6	7	8	9	10	GRS	P(GRS)
Portfolio formation months are t-12 to t-2												
a	−1.15	−0.39	−0.21	−0.22	−0.04	−0.05	0.12	0.21	0.33	0.59		
b	1.14	1.06	1.04	1.02	1.02	1.02	1.04	1.03	1.10	1.13		
s	1.35	0.77	0.66	0.59	0.53	0.48	0.47	0.45	0.51	0.68		
h	0.54	0.35	0.35	0.33	0.32	0.30	0.29	0.23	0.23	0.04		
t(a)	−5.34	−3.05	−2.05	−2.81	−0.54	−0.93	1.94	3.08	3.88	4.56	4.45	0.000
t(b)	21.31	33.36	42.03	51.48	61.03	73.62	68.96	62.67	51.75	35.25		
t(s)	17.64	16.96	18.59	20.87	22.06	23.96	21.53	19.03	16.89	14.84		
t(h)	6.21	6.72	8.74	10.18	11.86	13.16	11.88	8.50	6.68	0.70		
R^2	0.75	0.85	0.89	0.92	0.94	0.96	0.95	0.94	0.92	0.86		
Portfolio formation months are t-48 to t-2												
a	−0.73	−0.32	−0.09	−0.08	−0.05	−0.00	0.07	0.10	0.15	0.37		
b	1.16	1.12	1.06	1.05	1.02	1.01	1.00	0.99	1.04	1.11		
s	1.59	0.87	0.64	0.52	0.48	0.42	0.41	0.40	0.42	0.49		
h	0.90	0.60	0.44	0.44	0.36	0.31	0.18	0.11	−0.05	−0.26		
t(a)	−2.91	−2.79	−0.96	−0.99	−0.67	−0.01	1.08	1.46	2.09	3.60	2.02	0.031
t(b)	18.61	39.22	46.55	53.19	57.82	63.78	64.72	58.62	57.02	43.37		
t(s)	17.91	21.36	19.68	18.61	19.17	18.51	18.52	16.61	16.22	13.40		
t(h)	8.91	12.94	11.93	13.78	12.61	11.87	7.34	4.19	−1.55	−6.35		
R^2	0.73	0.88	0.91	0.92	0.93	0.94	0.95	0.93	0.94	0.90		
Portfolio formation months are t-60 to t-13												
a	−0.18	−0.16	−0.13	−0.07	0.00	0.02	0.06	0.10	−0.07	−0.12		
b	1.13	1.09	1.07	1.04	0.99	1.00	1.00	1.01	1.06	1.15		
s	1.50	0.83	0.67	0.59	0.47	0.38	0.35	0.40	0.45	0.50		
h	0.87	0.54	0.50	0.42	0.34	0.29	0.23	0.13	−0.00	−0.26		
t(a)	−0.80	−1.64	−1.69	−0.99	0.02	0.40	0.96	1.43	−0.92	−1.36	1.29	0.235
t(b)	20.24	44.40	55.03	61.09	63.79	65.68	62.58	58.26	60.49	53.04		
t(s)	18.77	23.63	24.09	24.06	21.21	17.44	15.43	16.18	18.06	16.33		
t(h)	9.59	13.67	15.94	15.31	13.46	11.82	8.98	4.46	−0.14	−7.50		
R^2	0.75	0.91	0.93	0.94	0.94	0.94	0.94	0.93	0.94	0.93		

V. EXPLORING THREE-FACTOR MODELS

The tests above suggest that many patterns in average stock returns, so-called anomalies of the CAPM, are captured by the three-factor model of (1). In this section we show that the explanatory returns of the model are not unique. Many other combinations of three portfolios describe returns as well as $R_M - R_f$, SMB, and HML. These results support our conclusion that a three-factor model is a good description of average returns.

We first provide some background. Fama (1994) shows that a generalized portfolio-efficiency concept drives Merton's (1973) ICAPM. Because ICAPM investors are risk averse, they are concerned with the mean and variance of their portfolio return. ICAPM investors are, however, also concerned with hedging more specific state-variable (consumption-investment) risks. As a result, optimal portfolios are multifactor-minimum-variance (MMV): they have the smallest possible return variances, given their expected returns and sensitivities to the state-variables.

In a two-state-variable ICAPM, MMV portfolios are spanned by (they can be generated from) the risk-free security and any three linearly independent MMV portfolios. (With two state variables and a finite number of risky securities, a third MMV portfolio is needed to capture the tradeoff of expected return for return variance that is unrelated to the state variables.) This spanning result has two implications that we test below.

(S1) The expected excess returns on any three MMV portfolios describe the expected excess returns on all securities and portfolios. In other words, the intercepts in regressions of excess returns on the excess returns on any three MMV portfolios are equal to 0.0.

(S2) The realized excess returns on any three MMV portfolios perfectly describe (intercepts equal to 0.0 and R^2 equal to 1.0) the excess returns on other MMV portfolios.

In the usual representation of a three-factor ICAPM, the three explanatory portfolios are the value-weight market and MMV portfolios that mimic the two state variables of special hedging concern to investors. (S1) and (S2) say, however, that any three MMV portfolios can be used to generate MMV portfolios and describe returns.

The tests that follow can also be interpreted in terms of a model in the spirit of Ross' (1976) APT. Suppose (i) investors are risk averse, (ii) there are two common factors in returns, and (iii) the number of risky securities is finite.

Fama's (1994) analysis again implies that optimal portfolios are MMV: they have the smallest possible variances given their expected returns and their loadings on the two common factors. With a finite number of securities, however, the returns on MMV portfolios in general are not perfectly explained by the two common factors in returns. As a result, as in the ICAPM, the risk-free security and three MMV portfolios are needed to span MMV portfolios and describe expected returns. Again, (S1) and (S2) hold.

A. Spanning Tests

In principle, the explanatory variables in the ICAPM (or the APT) are the expected returns on MMV portfolios in excess of the risk-free rate. SMB and HML in (1) are, however, each the difference between two portfolio returns. Equation (1) is still a legitimate three-factor risk-return relation as long as the two components of SMB (S and B) and the two components of HML (H and L) are MMV. $R_B - R_f$ and $R_L - R_f$ are then exact linear combinations of $R_M - R_f$, $R_S - R_f$, and $R_H - R_f$, so subtracting R_B from R_S (to get SMB) and R_L from R_H (HML) has no effect on the intercepts or the explanatory power of the three-factor regressions.

Obviously, we do not presume that our ad hoc size and book-to-market portfolios are truly MMV. We suggest, however, that if $R_M - R_f$, SMB, and HML do a good job describing average returns, then M, S, B, H, and L are close to MMV. (S1) and (S2) say that this hypothesis has two testable implications. (i) All combinations of three of the portfolios M, S, B, H, and L should provide similar descriptions of average returns (S1). (ii) Realized excess returns on any three of the candidate MMV portfolios should almost perfectly describe the excess returns on other candidate MMV portfolios (S2).

Table VIII tests (S2) with regressions that use the four different triplets of $R_M - R_f$, $R_S - R_f$, $R_H - R_f$, and $R_L - R_f$ to explain the excess return on the excluded MMV proxy. (We drop the big-stock portfolio B from the list of MMV proxies because the correlation between R_M and R_B is 0.99.) The results are consistent with (S2). Excess returns on any three of M, S, H, and L almost perfectly describe the excess return on the fourth. The regression intercepts are close to 0.0, and the R^2 values are close to 1.0 (0.98 and 0.99).

Table IX summarizes the intercepts from regressions that use the four different triplets of $R_M - R_f$, $R_S - R_f$, $R_H - R_f$, and $R_L - R_f$ to describe the excess returns on the different sets of portfolios examined in previous sections. As predicted by (S1), different triplets of M, S, L, and H provide equivalent descriptions of returns. Specifically, different three-factor regressions produce

TABLE VIII. Regressions to explain monthly excess returns (in percent) on M, S, L, H, SMB and HML: 7/63–12/93, 366 months

The portfolios (described in Table I) include the market (M), the small-stock portfolio (S), the low-book-to-market portfolio (L), the high-book-to-market portfolio (H), the difference between H and L (HML), and the difference between S and the return on the big-stock portfolio B (SMB). To simplify the notation, the table uses the portfolio labels, rather than explicit notation for their excess returns. The regression R^2 and the residual standard error, $s(e)$, are adjusted for degrees of freedom. The numbers in parentheses are t-statistics (regression coefficients divided by their standard errors).

							R^2	$s(e)$
S	=	0.28	+1.17 M	+e			0.79	2.68
		(1.99)	(36.95)					
L	=	−0.10	+1.20 M	+e			0.92	1.62
		(−1.15)	(62.84)					
H	=	0.46	+0.99 M	+e			0.80	2.16
		(4.08)	(38.73)					
SMB	=	0.19	+0.21 M	+e			0.10	2.74
		(1.32)	(6.54)					
HML	=	0.56	−0.21 M	+e			0.13	2.41
		(4.42)	(−7.53)					
S	=	0.00	−0.83 M	+1.00 L	+0.81 H	+e	0.99	0.65
		(0.17)	(−29.12)	(46.81)	(50.12)			
L	=	−0.03	+0.86 M	+0.86 S	−0.67 H	+e	0.99	0.60
		(−0.90)	(51.83)	(46.81)	(−29.30)			
H	=	0.06	+0.98 M	+1.09 S	−1.05 L	+e	0.98	0.75
		(1.36)	(31.38)	(50.12)	(−29.30)			
M	=	0.00	−0.85 S	+1.03 L	+0.75 H	+e	0.98	0.66
		(0.08)	(−29.12)	(51.83)	(31.38)			

much the same GRS tests, mean absolute and squared intercepts, and average values of R^2. Moreover, the regression intercepts (not shown) are nearly identical for different triplets of explanatory returns. Substantively, Table IX says that different three-factor regressions all miss the continuation of returns for portfolios formed on short-term past returns. On the other hand, every triplet of M, S, L, and H does a similar and excellent job describing the returns on the LSV deciles formed on E/P and sales rank, and the LSV portfolios

TABLE IX. Summary of intercepts from one-factor CAPM excess-return regressions and different versions of the three-factor ICAPM regressions: 7/63–12/93, 366 months

The alternative sets of dependent excess returns (and the tables that describe them) include the 25 size-BE/ME portfolios (Table I), the E/P and five-year sales-rank deciles (Table II), the nine portfolios doubled-sorted on C/P and five-year sales rank (Table IV), the long-term and short-term past return deciles (60–13 and 12–2) (Table VI). The explanatory variables (described in Table I) include the excess returns on the market portfolio (M), the small-stock portfolio (S), the low- and high-book-to-market portfolios (L and H), SMB (the return on S minus the return on the big-stock portfolio B) and HML (H minus L). GRS is the F-statistic of Gibbons, Ross, and Shanken (1989), testing the hypothesis that the regression intercepts for a set of dependent portfolios are all 0.0. p(GRS) is the p-value of GRS. Ave $| a |$ and Ave a^2 are the average absolute and squared values of the intercepts for a set of dependent portfolios, and Ave R^2 is the average of the regression R^2 (adjusted for degrees of freedom).

Dependent Ports.	Explanatory Ports.			GRS	p(GRS)	Ave |a|	Ave a^2	Ave R^2
25 Size-BE/ME	M			2.76	0.000	0.286	0.1140	0.77
25 Size-BE/ME	M	SMB	HML	1.97	0.004	0.093	0.0164	0.93
25 Size-BE/ME	M	S	H	2.06	0.002	0.097	0.0170	0.93
25 Size-BE/ME	M	S	L	2.16	0.001	0.102	0.0183	0.92
25 Size-BE/ME	M	L	H	1.87	0.008	0.094	0.0159	0.92
25 Size-BE/ME	S	L	H	2.06	0.002	0.094	0.0162	0.92
E/P	M			2.85	0.002	0.260	0.1059	0.83
E/P	M	SMB	HML	0.84	0.592	0.051	0.0039	0.93
E/P	M	S	H	0.95	0.488	0.059	0.0051	0.94
E/P	M	S	L	1.02	0.427	0.064	0.0057	0.94
E/P	M	L	H	0.86	0.575	0.052	0.0041	0.93
E/P	S	L	H	0.86	0.571	0.051	0.0040	0.93
Sales Rank	M			2.51	0.006	0.256	0.0821	0.82
Sales Rank	M	SMB	HML	0.87	0.563	0.053	0.0058	0.93
Sales Rank	M	S	H	1.01	0.437	0.055	0.0068	0.94
Sales Rank	M	S	L	0.96	0.474	0.052	0.0059	0.94
Sales Rank	M	L	H	0.92	0.514	0.052	0.0057	0.93
Sales Rank	S	L	H	0.93	0.509	0.052	0.0057	0.93
C/P & Sales Rank	M			2.93	0.002	0.268	0.1007	0.80
C/P & Sales Rank	M	SMB	HML	1.04	0.405	0.062	0.0068	0.93
C/P & Sales Rank	M	S	H	1.13	0.338	0.067	0.0068	0.93
C/P & Sales Rank	M	S	L	1.14	0.333	0.063	0.0064	0.93
C/P & Sales Rank	M	L	H	1.03	0.416	0.061	0.0064	0.92
C/P & Sales Rank	S	L	H	1.05	0.396	0.061	0.0065	0.93

TABLE IX. (Continued)

Dependent Ports.	Explanatory Ports.			GRS	p(GRS)	Ave |a|	Ave a²	Ave R²
60–13	M			2.51	0.006	0.268	0.0899	0.80
60–13	M	SMB	HML	1.29	0.235	0.092	0.0114	0.92
60–13	M	S	H	1.38	0.186	0.094	0.0112	0.92
60–13	M	S	L	1.19	0.299	0.077	0.0074	0.92
60–13	M	L	H	1.29	0.234	0.089	0.0102	0.91
60–13	S	L	H	1.30	0.230	0.090	0.0107	0.91
12–2	M			5.13	0.000	0.337	0.1647	0.79
12–2	M	SMB	HML	4.46	0.000	0.331	0.2097	0.90
12–2	M	S	H	4.45	0.000	0.322	0.2027	0.90
12–2	M	S	L	4.58	0.000	0.329	0.2040	0.90
12–2	M	L	H	4.51	0.000	0.326	0.2047	0.90
12–2	S	L	H	4.46	0.000	0.328	0.2069	0.90

double-sorted on C/P and sales rank. In results not shown in Table IX, excellent three-factor descriptions of returns are also obtained for the LSV BE/ME and C/P deciles, and for portfolios double-sorted on sales rank and BE/ME or E/P. Finally, Table IX shows that all triplets of M, S, L, and H capture the reversal of returns for portfolios formed on long-term past returns.

Table IX says that our original (FF 1993) combination of the market, SMB, and HML fares no better or worse than triplets of M, S, H, and L. But the original set of portfolios has one advantage. Table X shows that $R_M - R_f$, SMB, and HML are much less correlated with one another than $R_M - R_f$, $R_S - R_f$, $R_B - R_f$, $R_H - R_f$, and $R_L - R_f$. This makes three-factor regression slopes easier to interpret, and it is why we use $R_M - R_f$, SMB, and HML in the regressions of Tables I, III, V, and VII.

B. Additional MMV Proxies

M, S, H, and L are not the only portfolios that give equivalent descriptions of returns. We construct explanatory portfolios (MMV proxies) that are simple averages of the returns for the bottom and top three deciles of each of the LSV (BE/ME, E/P, C/P, and sales-rank) sorts and the short- and long-term past-return sorts. For example, the high E/P return (HE/P) is the average of the top three E/P decile returns.

The MMV proxies formed from the LSV BE/ME, E/P, and C/P deciles work much like our L and H (low- and high-BE/ME) portfolios in describing returns. The reason is clear from Table X. Excess returns on the LSV low BE/ME,

TABLE x. Average monthly excess returns (in percent) and correlations of excess returns for MMV proxies: 7/63–12/93, 366 months

The market portfolio (M), the small-stock portfolio (S), the low- and high-book-to-market portfolios (L and H), SMB (the return on S minus the return on the big-stock portfolio B) and HML (H minus L) are described in Table I. LBE/ME, LE/P, LC/P and LSR are the simple averages of the returns on the three lowest LSV BE/ME, E/P, C/P, and five-year-sales-rank deciles, while HBE/ME, HE/P, HC/P, and HSR are the simple averages of the returns on the three highest BE/ME, E/P, C/P, and five-year-sales-rank deciles, described in Table II. L60–13 and H60–13 are the simple averages of the returns on the three lowest and highest long-term-past-return deciles, described in Table VI.

	L	LBE/ME	LE/P	LC/P	HSR	H60–13	H	HBE/ME	HE/P	HC/P	LSR	L60–13	M	SMB	HML
							Average Excess Returns								
Means	0.44	0.48	0.51	0.49	0.60	0.56	0.90	1.03	0.97	1.00	0.90	0.91	0.45	0.28	0.46
Std. Dev.	5.56	5.55	5.63	5.58	5.77	5.47	4.87	5.66	5.18	5.29	5.40	6.41	4.43	2.89	2.59
t(Mn)	1.51	1.67	1.74	1.69	2.00	1.95	3.55	3.47	3.58	3.60	3.18	2.72	1.93	1.88	3.42
							Correlations								
LBE/ME	0.98														
LE/P	0.98	0.99													
LC/P	0.98	0.99	0.99												
HSR	0.97	0.98	0.98	0.98											
H60–13	0.97	0.98	0.97	0.98	0.97										
H	0.88	0.89	0.91	0.90	0.94	0.91									
HBE/ME	0.86	0.87	0.90	0.89	0.93	0.88	0.97								
HE/P	0.88	0.90	0.90	0.91	0.95	0.92	0.97	0.98							
HC/P	0.88	0.89	0.90	0.90	0.95	0.90	0.98	0.97	0.99						
LSR	0.89	0.91	0.93	0.93	0.94	0.91	0.95	0.99	0.95	0.96					
L60–13	0.85	0.86	0.89	0.88	0.91	0.84	0.93	0.97	0.93	0.95	0.97				
M	0.96	0.96	0.95	0.95	0.94	0.95	0.90	0.84	0.88	0.87	0.87	0.81			
SMB	0.53	0.51	0.55	0.54	0.57	0.52	0.56	0.66	0.60	0.61	0.63	0.67	0.32		
HML	-0.48	-0.44	-0.40	-0.41	-0.31	-0.36	-0.02	-0.02	-0.07	-0.04	-0.13	-0.06	-0.37	-0.10	

E/P, and C/P portfolios are correlated 0.99 with each other, and they are correlated 0.98 with our L (low-BE/ME) portfolio. Excess returns on the LSV high BE/ME, E/P, and C/P portfolios are correlated 0.98 and 0.99 with each other, and their correlations with our H portfolio are 0.97 and 0.98. The "high" portfolios are much more correlated with one another than with the "low" portfolios. The MMV proxies produced by the LSV BE/ME, E/P, and C/P sorts also have similar average excess returns, 0.48 to 0.51 for the three "low" portfolios and 0.97 to 1.03 for the three "high" portfolios. These returns are a bit higher than those of our L and H portfolios, 0.44 and 0.90, probably because L and H are constructed from value-weight components.

In short, the "low" and "high" MMV proxies from the LSV BE/ME, E/P, and C/P sorts mimic our L and H portfolios. Thus it is not surprising that they can replace L and H in the three-factor model. Without showing the details, combining the market portfolio M with LBE/ME and HBE/ME, or LE/P and HE/P, or LC/P and HC/P produces three-factor descriptions of returns like those in Table IX.

Ball (1978) argues that scaling stock prices with accounting variables, like earnings, cash flow, or book equity, is a good way to extract the information in stock prices about expected returns. Our tests suggest, more precisely, that MMV proxies formed on E/P, C/P, and BE/ME mimic more or less the same combinations of the underlying common factors in returns.

Unlike the proxies created from the LSV BE/ME, E/P, and C/P sorts, MMV proxies constructed from the LSV sales-rank sort, or from long-term past returns, cannot successfully replace L and H in tests of the three-factor model. There are two possible explanations. (i) Perhaps sorts on sales growth or long-term past return expose variation in expected returns missed by sorts on size, BE/ME, E/P, and C/P. The fact that the three-factor regressions in Table IX have no problem explaining the average returns on the sales-rank and long-term-past-return deciles seems to refute this hypothesis. (ii) The sales-rank and long-term-past-return proxies are not diversified enough. If the proxies are not close to MMV, too much of their return variance is not priced. This diversifiable risk creates an errors-in-variables problem that contaminates tests of three-factor models.

C. The CAPM versus Three-Factor Models

Table IX shows tests of the CAPM in which $R_M - R_f$ is used alone to explain returns. The GRS test always rejects the CAPM at the 0.99 level (p-values less than 0.01). Omitting the details, which are similar to FF (1992) and LSV (1994), the CAPM fails because univariate market βs show little relation to variables like BE/ME, E/P, C/P, and sales rank, that are strongly related to average return. Table IX also shows that, except for portfolios formed on short-term past return, where all models fail, the CAPM is dominated by the three-factor model. The average absolute pricing errors (intercepts) of the CAPM are large (25 to 30 basis points per month), and they are three to five times those of the three-factor model (5 to 10 basis points per month).

Using the ICAPM to interpret the problems of the CAPM is instructive. Fama (1994) shows that the multifactor-minimum-variance (MMV) portfolios that are relevant for ICAPM investors can be characterized as combinations of Markowitz' (1959) mean-variance-efficient (MVE) portfolios and MMV mimicking portfolios for the state variables. Most important, a market equilibrium in the ICAPM implies that the market portfolio M (the aggregate of the MMV portfolios chosen by investors) is MMV. But M almost surely is not MVE. Thus, market βs do not suffice to explain expected returns. More specifically, because ICAPM investors have different tastes for state-variable risks and general sources of return variance, the market βs of some or all MMV state-variable mimicking portfolios cannot explain their expected returns. This means that β alone cannot explain the expected returns on all MMV portfolios.

In contrast, in the CAPM all sources of return variance, including the state-variable or common-factor risks of the ICAPM and the APT, are equivalent to investors. Investors hold mean-variance-efficient portfolios, and the market portfolio is MVE. This means that the expected excess returns on all securities and portfolios, including MMV portfolios, are fully explained by their market βs. Thus, one way to test whether a multifactor return process collapses to CAPM rather than multifactor ICAPM or APT pricing is to test whether the expected excess returns on MMV portfolios are explained by their market βs.

Table VIII shows CAPM time-series regressions in which $R_M - R_f$ is used alone to explain the excess returns on our MMV proxies S, L, and H. The MMV proxies that are seriously mispriced by the CAPM are prime candidates for explaining why three-factor models improve on the CAPM's description of average returns. Table VIII says that the CAPM misprices the low-book-to-market portfolio L by −0.10 percent per month ($t = -1.15$). The pricing error for the small-stock portfolio S is more serious, 0.28 percent per month ($t = 1.99$). The largest CAPM pricing error is for the high-book-to-market portfolio H. The one-factor CAPM regression intercept for H is 0.46 percent per month ($t = 4.08$). The CAPM regressions for SMB and HML confirm that H's high return is the prime embarrassment of the CAPM. Much of the discussion of competing interpretations of our results that follows focuses on stories for H's (or HML's) average return.

VI. INTERPRETING THE RESULTS

Standard tests of the CAPM ask whether loadings on a market proxy can describe the average returns on other portfolios. Algebraically, these are just tests of whether the market proxy is in the set of mean-variance-efficient (MVE) portfolios that can be formed from the returns to be explained (Fama (1976), Roll (1977), Gibbons, Ross, and Shanken (1989)). Similarly, tests of a three-factor ICAPM or APT ask whether loadings on three portfolios can describe the average returns on other portfolios. Such tests in effect ask whether the explanatory portfolios span the three-factor MMV portfolios that can be formed from the returns to be explained (Fama (1994)). Thus, a minimalist (purely algebraic) interpretation of our results is that the portfolios M, S, B, H, and L are in the sets of three-factor-MMV portfolios that can be formed from sorts on size, BE/ME, E/P, C/P, sales rank, and long-term past returns. But our explanatory portfolios cannot span the three-factor-MMV portfolios that can be constructed from sorts on short-term past returns.

The economic interpretation of our results is more contentious. We distinguish three stories. The first says that asset pricing is rational and conforms to a three-factor ICAPM or APT that does not reduce to the CAPM (FF (1993, 1994, 1995)). The second story agrees that a three-factor model describes returns, but argues that it is investor irrationality that prevents the three-factor model from collapsing to the CAPM. Specifically, irrational pricing causes the high premium for relative distress (the average HML return). Proponents of this view include Lakonishok, Shleifer, and Vishny (1994), Haugen (1995), and MacKinlay (1995). The third story says the CAPM holds but is spuriously rejected because (i) there is survivor bias in the returns used to test the model (Kothari, Shanken, and Sloan (1995)), (ii) CAPM anomalies are the result of data snooping (Black (1993), MacKinlay (1995)), or (iii) the tests use poor proxies for the market portfolio.

A. The Case for a Multifactor ICAPM or APT

In FF (1992) we reject the CAPM based on evidence that size and book-to-market-equity (BE/ME) capture cross-sectional variation in average returns that is missed by univariate market βs. We have since tried to infer whether these size and book-to-market effects are generated by a multifactor ICAPM or APT.

One necessary condition for multifactor ICAPM or APT pricing is multiple common (undiversifiable) sources of variance in returns. FF (1993) show that there is indeed covariation in returns related to size and BE/ME (captured by loadings on SMB and HML), above and beyond the covariation explained by the market return. Moreover, FF (1995) show that there are common factors in fundamentals like earnings and sales that look a lot like the SMB and HML factors in returns.

The acid test of the three-factor model is whether it can explain differences in average returns. FF (1993) find that the model describes the average returns on portfolios formed on size and BE/ME. It may not be surprising, however, that portfolios like SMB and HML that are formed on size and BE/ME can explain the returns on other portfolios formed on size and BE/ME (albeit with a finer grid). We address this concern here by testing whether the three-factor model can explain other prominent CAPM average-return anomalies. We find that the patterns in average return produced by forming portfolios on E/P, C/P, sales growth, and long-term past return are absorbed by the three-factor model, largely because they line up with the loadings of the portfolios on HML. The tests of (1) on industries in FF (1994) are also a check on FF (1993).

The three-factor model (1) is also useful in applications. For example, Reinganum (1990) finds that size-adjusted average returns are higher for NYSE stocks than for NASD stocks. Fama, French, Booth, and Sinquefield (1993) use (1) to explain this puzzling result. Controlling for size, NYSE stocks have higher loadings on HML, and thus higher predicted returns. Carhart (1994) finds that the three-factor model (1) provides sharper evaluations of the performance of mutual funds than the CAPM. SMB adds a lot to the description of the returns on small-stock funds, and loadings on HML are important for describing the returns on growth-stock funds. FF (1994) find that the three-factor model (1) signals higher costs of equity for distressed industries than for strong industries, largely because the distressed industries have higher loadings on HML.

One can argue that all of this still falls within a minimalist interpretation of the three-factor model; that is, we have simply found three portfolios that provide a parsimonious description of returns and average returns, and so can absorb most of the anomalies of the CAPM. In other words, without knowing why, we have stumbled on explanatory portfolios that are close to three-factor

MMV. And the main reason many will not go beyond this minimalist story is clear. We have not identified the two state variables of special hedging concern to investors that lead to three-factor asset pricing. Such state variables are necessary in a three-factor ICAPM or APT, if they are not to collapse to the CAPM.

FF (1993) interpret the average HML return as a premium for a state-variable risk related to relative distress. This story is suggested by the evidence in FF (1995) that low book-to-market-equity is typical of firms that have persistently strong earnings, while high-BE/ME is associated with persistently low earnings. Moreover, FF (1994) argue that the variation through time in the loadings of industries on HML correctly reflects periods of industry strength or distress. Industries have strong positive HML loadings in bad times and negative loadings when times are good. Finally, Chan and Chen (1991) present evidence for a risk factor in returns and average returns related to relative-distress.

Why is relative distress a state variable of special hedging concern to investors? One possible explanation is linked to human capital, an important asset for most investors. Consider an investor with specialized human capital tied to a growth firm (or industry or technology). A negative shock to the firm's prospects probably does not reduce the value of the investor's human capital; it may just mean that employment in the firm will expand less rapidly. In contrast, a negative shock to a distressed firm more likely implies a negative shock to the value of specialized human capital since employment in the firm is more likely to contract. Thus, workers with specialized human capital in distressed firms have an incentive to avoid holding their firms' stocks. If variation in distress is correlated across firms, workers in distressed firms have an incentive to avoid the stocks of all distressed firms. The result can be a state-variable risk premium in the expected returns of distressed stocks.

Unfortunately, tracing a common factor in returns to an economic state variable does not in itself imply that the state variable is of special hedging concern to investors, and so carries a special risk premium. For example, in Mayers (1972), covariation with the income return on (nonmarketable) human capital has no special premium. Jagannathan and Wang (1995) argue that human capital (taken to be marketable) is just another asset in the CAPM. Thus, even if we found two state variables that could explain the common variation in returns tracked by portfolios like SMB and HML, we would still face the problem of explaining why the state variables produce special premiums. Merton (1973) clearly recognizes this problem. It lurks on the horizon in all tests of multifactor ICAPM's or APT's.

B. The Distress Premium Is Irrational

Lakonishok, Shleifer, and Vishny (LSV 1994), Haugen (1995), and MacKinlay (1995) argue that the premium for relative distress, the difference between the average returns on high- and low-book-to-market stocks, is too large to be explained by rational pricing. Indeed, LSV and Haugen conclude that the premium is almost always positive and so is close to an arbitrage opportunity. Table XI, which shows the annual $R_M - R_f$, SMB, and HML returns for 1964–1993, provides relevant evidence.

If the premium for relative distress is close to an arbitrage opportunity, the standard deviation of HML should be small. In fact, HML's standard deviation, 13.11 percent per year, is similar to the standard deviations of $R_M - R_f$ and SMB, 16.33 percent and 15.44 percent per year, respectively. The average values of the three annual premiums are also similar: 6.33 percent for HML, 5.94 percent for $R_M - R_f$, and 4.93 percent for SMB. The yearly returns confirm that a high-book-to-market strategy is not a sure thing. HML is negative in ten of the thirty years we study, $R_M - R_f$ is also negative ten times, and SMB is negative nine times. In short, if the relative-distress premium is too high to be explained by rational asset pricing, one must also be suspicious of the market and size premiums.

But the fact that the premium for relative distress is not an arbitrage opportunity does not imply that it is rational. LSV and Haugen argue that the premium is due to investor over-reaction. Specifically, investors do not understand that the low earnings growth of high-BE/ME firms and the high earnings growth of low-BE/ME firms quickly revert to normal levels after portfolios are formed on BE/ME. FF (1995) argue, however, that over-reaction cannot be the whole story, since the high distress premium in returns persists for at least five years after portfolio formation, but the mean reversion of earnings growth is apparent much sooner.

Another LSV argument is that the relative-distress premium is irrational because periods of poor returns on distressed stocks are not typically periods of low GNP growth or low overall market returns. Since the relative-distress premium is not related to these obvious macroeconomic state variables, they conclude that the premium arises simply because investors dislike distressed stocks and so cause them to be underpriced.

The essence of a multifactor model, however, is that covariance with the market return is not sufficient to measure risk. Moreover, our industry work leans us toward the conclusion that the state variable related to relative distress is not a common macro-variable, like GNP. FF (1994) find that industries

TABLE XI. Annual three-factor explanatory returns: $R_M - R_f$, SMB, and HML, 1964–1993, $N = 30$

R_M is the annual market return. R_f is the return obtained by rolling over 12 one-month bills during a year. SMB is the difference between the annual returns on the small-stock portfolio, S, and the big-stock portfolio, B. HML is the difference between the annual returns on the high-book-to-market portfolio, H, and the low-book-to-market portfolio, L. The portfolios M, S, B, H, and L are defined in Table I. t(Mean) is the mean of the annual returns (Mean) divided by its standard error (Std. Dev.)/$29^{1/2}$. Negative is the number of negative annual returns.

Year	$R_M - R_f$	SMB	HML
1964	13.25	1.15	6.32
1965	10.31	22.84	12.54
1966	−13.87	2.47	3.12
1967	22.01	50.84	−6.69
1968	7.92	23.89	16.97
1969	−16.12	−14.14	−8.86
1970	−5.35	−10.98	23.35
1971	11.46	6.46	−12.54
1972	13.92	−12.40	3.39
1973	−22.40	−23.13	19.35
1974	−34.93	0.17	11.18
1975	31.72	16.85	7.34
1976	21.61	13.19	26.01
1977	−7.91	22.32	8.58
1978	2.33	13.97	−0.05
1979	14.52	19.18	−3.21
1980	23.23	6.31	−23.86
1981	−16.91	7.03	24.32
1982	11.78	8.58	12.76
1983	14.66	15.31	20.00
1984	−4.58	−7.90	18.64
1985	24.06	0.17	0.12
1986	9.98	−8.11	8.46
1987	−1.51	−11.99	−1.03
1988	14.31	5.46	14.76
1989	23.74	−12.86	−5.92
1990	−11.28	−15.02	−11.07
1991	28.49	14.34	−14.20
1992	5.73	6.39	22.71
1993	8.07	7.20	17.44
Mean	5.94	4.92	6.33
Std. Dev.	16.33	15.44	13.11
t(Mean)	1.96	1.72	2.60
Negative	10	9	10

fluctuate between strength and distress. The expansions and contractions of the economy are minor compared to the variation in the fortunes of industries. We suspect that product innovation, technology shocks, and changes in tastes dramatically alter the relative prospects of industries without having much effect on aggregate variables like GNP. We also suspect that industries provide a muted version of the changes in the relative prospects of individual firms. (The evidence of Davis and Haltiwanger (1992) that variation in aggregate employment is trivial relative to the gross job creation and destruction that occurs, in good times and bad, at the level of individual firms is consistent with this view.) In other words, although two unidentified state variables lead to common risk factors in returns, they are not the market factor and we should not expect to find their tracks in variables that are important in generating the market factor. Thus, we are not surprised by the LSV evidence that variation in a return spread like HML is not highly correlated with GNP, or with the market return itself.

Finally, LSV argue that the relative distress premium is irrational because diversified portfolios of high- and low-book-to-market firms have similar return variances. Equation (1) provides an explanation. The positive HML slopes of high-BE/ME (distressed) firms raise their return variances and imply higher average returns. The negative HML slopes of low-BE/ME (strong) firms also raise their return variances but imply lower average returns. In any case, in a multifactor ICAPM or APT, different sources of return variance do not carry the same premiums, so variance is not a sufficient statistic for a portfolio's risk.

C. The Distress Premium Is Spurious

The final category of stories for the high relative-distress premium in average returns says that the CAPM holds and the premium is the spurious result of (i) survivor bias, (ii) data snooping, or (iii) a bad proxy for the market portfolio in tests of the CAPM.

Survivor Bias—Kothari, Shanken, and Sloan (KSS 1995) are the prime proponents of a survivor-bias story. They argue that average returns on high-book-to-market portfolios of COMPUSTAT stocks like H are overstated because COMPUSTAT is more likely to include distressed firms that survive and to miss distressed firms that fail. The direct evidence of Chan, Jegadeesh, and Lakonishok (1995) refutes this claim. Moreover, KSS concede that survivor bias is not a major problem for value-weight portfolios, which means that it cannot explain why the high average return of H (or HML) is not captured by the CAPM.

Data Snooping—Lo and MacKinlay (1988), Black (1993), and MacKinlay (1995) argue that CAPM anomalies may be the result of data-snooping. A nontrivial portion of asset pricing research is devoted to dredging for anomalies. As the profession rummages through the same data, we are sure to find patterns in average returns, like the size and book-to-market effects, that are inconsistent with the CAPM, but are sample specific. In this view, it is not surprising that factors like SMB and HML, that are aimed directly at the spurious anomalies, produce multifactor models that "explain" the anomalies in the same data used to unearth them. The data-snooping story predicts that in out-of-sample tests, average SMB and HML (more specifically, average S and H) returns will fall to levels that are consistent with their market βs. Our three-factor model will then reduce to a CAPM in which, like the expected returns on all other securities and portfolios, the expected returns on the MMV mimicking portfolios for the three common factors will be completely explained by their market βs.

Data-snooping bias can never be ruled out, but we suggest four counter arguments. (i) Davis (1994) shows that the distress premium is not special to the post-1962 COMPUSTAT period studied in FF (1992, 1993). Using a sample of large firms, he finds a strong relation between BE/ME and average return from 1941 to 1962. (ii) Tests on international data, which can also be regarded as out-of-sample, produce relations between average return and variables like size, BE/ME, E/P, and C/P much like those observed in U.S. data (e.g., Chan, Hamao, and Lakonishok (1991), Capaul, Rowley, and Sharpe (1993)). (iii) Ball (1978) argues that scaled versions of price like size, BE/ME, E/P, and C/P are proxies for expected return. They are thus excellent for identifying the real failures of asset pricing models like the CAPM. (iv) Our results suggest that data-snooping has not been that effective; there are not so many independent average-return anomalies to explain. Specifically, the message from our results is that, whatever the economic explanation, a three-factor model captures the CAPM anomalies produced by sorts on size, BE/ME, E/P, C/P, sales rank, and long-term past return.

Bad Market Proxies—Finally, there is the ritual argument that the CAPM holds, and its average-return anomalies just expose the shortcomings of empirical proxies for the market portfolio. In this view, multifactor models are just a convenient way to recover CAPM expected returns. Specifically, the spanning result (S1) implies that the loadings on any X linearly independent X-factor-MMV portfolios produce the same expected returns for securities and portfolios as their univariate βs on a mean-variance-efficient portfolio. Thus, if the CAPM holds and the unobserved market portfolio is MVE, any

X linearly independent X-factor-MMV portfolios can be used in a multifactor model to recover CAPM expected returns.

Unfortunately, the bad-market-proxy argument does not justify the way the CAPM is currently applied, for example, to estimate the cost of capital or to evaluate portfolio managers. The bad market proxies that produce spurious anomalies in tests of the CAPM are similar to those used in applications. If the common market proxies are not MVE, applications that use them rely on the same flawed estimates of expected return that undermine tests of the CAPM. In the end, the irony of the bad-market-proxy argument is that if the CAPM is true but the market portfolio is unobservable, multifactor models like ours may provide better estimates of CAPM expected returns.

D. The Continuation of Short-Term Returns

We have saved until last the discussion of the main embarassment of the three-factor model, its failure to capture the continuation of short-term returns documented by Jegadeesh and Titman (1993) and Asness (1994). There are at least three possible stories.

(i)   This particular anomaly is a spurious result of data snooping. The weak continuation of short-term returns in the 1931–1963 period preceding our asset pricing regressions is suggestive (Table 6). Jegadeesh and Titman (1993) show, however, that weak continuation is limited to the 1930's. They find short-term return continuation in the 1941–1964 and post-1964 periods. Still, the fact that the continuation of short-term returns is so far from the contrarian spirit of other CAPM anomalies (like the size, BE/ME, E/P, C/P, and sales-growth effects, or the reversal of long-term returns) suggests that further out-of-sample tests, for example on international data, are desirable.

(ii)   Asset pricing is irrational. Investors underreact to short-term past information, which produces return continuation, but they overreact to long-term past information, which produces return reversal (Lakonishok, Shleifer, and Vishny (1994), Haugen (1995)). Behavioral-finance types should be wary of this explanation. The evidence of Kahneman and Tversky (1982) and others, which forms the foundation of existing behavioral finance models, predicts overreaction and return reversal. (See, for example, DeBondt and Thaler (1985).) The continuation of short-term returns is then as much a challenge to behavioral finance as to our asset-pricing model.

(iii) Asset pricing is rational, but our three-factor model is (alas!) just a model, and the continuation anomaly exposes one of its shortcomings. In this view, future work should look for a richer model, perhaps including an additional risk factor, that encompasses the continuation of short-term returns. We are reluctant to follow this track, however, until robustness checks of the continuation anomaly have run their course.

VII. CONCLUSIONS

Fama and French (1993) find that the three-factor risk-return relation (1) is a good model for the returns on portfolios formed on size and book-to-market-equity. We find that (1) also explains the strong patterns in returns observed when portfolios are formed on earnings/price, cash flow/price, and sales growth, variables recommended by Lakonishok, Shleifer, and Vishny (1994) and others. The three-factor risk-return relation (1) also captures the reversal of long-term returns documented by DeBondt and Thaler (1985). Thus, portfolios formed on E/P, C/P, sales growth, and long-term past returns do not uncover dimensions of risk and expected return beyond those required to explain the returns on portfolios formed on size and BE/ME. Fama and French (1994) extend this conclusion to industries.

The three-factor risk-return relation (1) is, however, just a model. It surely does not explain expected returns on all securities and portfolios. We find that (1) cannot explain the continuation of short-term returns documented by Jegadeesh and Titman (1993) and Asness (1994).

Finally, there is an important hole in our work. Our tests to date do not cleanly identify the two consumption-investment state variables of special hedging concern to investors that would provide a neat interpretation of our results in terms of Merton's (1973) ICAPM or Ross' (1976) APT. The results of Chan and Chen (1991) and Fama and French (1994, 1995) suggest that one of the state variables is related to relative distress. But this issue is far from closed, and multiple competing interpretations of our results remain viable.

REFERENCES

Asness, Clifford S., 1994, The power of past stock returns to explain future stock returns, Manuscript, June.

Ball, Ray, 1978, Anomalies in relationships between securities' yields and yield-surrogates, *Journal of Financial Economics* 6, 103–26.

Ball, Ray, and S. P. Kothari, 1989, Non-stationary expected returns: Implications for tests of market efficiency and serial correlation of returns, *Journal of Financial Economics* 25, 51–74.

Banz, Rolf W., 1981, The relationship between return and market value of common stocks, *Journal of Financial Economics* 9, 3–18.

Banz, Rolf W., and William Breen, 1986, Sample dependent results using accounting and market data: Some evidence, *Journal of Finance* 41, 779–793.

Basu, Sanjoy, 1983, The relationship between earnings yield, market value, and return for NYSE common stocks: Further evidence, *Journal of Financial Economics* 12, 129–156.

Black, Fischer, 1993, Beta and return, *Journal of Portfolio Management* 20, 8–18.

Capaul, Carlo, Ian Rowley, and William F. Sharpe, 1993, International value and growth stock returns, *Financial Analysts Journal,* January-February, 27–36.

Carhart, Mark M., 1994, On persistence in mutual fund performance, Working paper, Graduate School of Business, University of Chicago.

Chan, K. C. 1988, On the contrarian investment strategy, *Journal of Business* 61, 147–163.

Chan, K. C., and Nai-fu Chen, 1991, Structural and return characteristics of small and large firms, *Journal of Finance* 46, 1467–1484.

Chan, Louis K. C., Yasushi Hamao, and Josef Lakonishok, 1991, Fundamentals and stock returns in Japan, *Journal of Finance* 46, 1739–1789.

Chan, Louis K. C., Narasimhan Jegadeesh, and Josef Lakonishok, 1995, Evaluating the performance of value versus glamour stocks: The impact of selection bias, *Journal of Financial Economics* 38, 269–296.

Chopra, N., Josef Lakonishok, and Jay Ritter, 1992, Measuring abnormal performance: Does the stock market overreact? *Journal of Financial Economics* 40, 793–805.

Davis, James, 1994, The cross-section of realized stock returns: The pre-Compustat evidence, *Journal of Finance* 49, 1579–1593.

Davis, Steven J., and John Haltiwanger, 1992, Gross job creation, gross job destruction, and employment reallocation, *Quarterly Journal of Economics* 107, 819–863.

DeBondt, Werner F. M., and Thaler, Richard H., 1985, Does the stock market overreact, *Journal of Finance* 40, 793–805.

DeBondt, Werner F. M., and Thaler, Richard H., 1987, Further evidence on investor overreaction and stock market seasonality, *Journal of Finance* 42, 557–581.

Fama, Eugene F., 1976, *Foundations of Finance* (Basic Books, New York).

Fama, Eugene F., 1994, Multifactor portfolio efficiency and multifactor asset pricing, Manuscript, Graduate School of Business, University of Chicago, revised July 1995.

Fama, Eugene F., and Kenneth R. French, 1992, The cross-section of expected stock returns, *Journal of Finance* 47, 427–465.

Fama, Eugene F., and Kenneth R. French, 1993, Common risk factors in the returns on stocks and bonds, *Journal of Financial Economics* 33, 3–56.

Fama, Eugene F., and Kenneth R. French, 1994, Industry costs of equity, Working paper, Graduate School of Business, University of Chicago, Chicago, IL, revised July 1995.

Fama, Eugene F., and Kenneth R. French, 1995, Size and book-to-market factors in earnings and returns. *Journal of Finance* 50, 131–155.

Fama, Eugene F., Kenneth R. French, David G. Booth, and Rex Sinquefield, 1993, Differences in the risks and returns of NYSE and NASD stocks, *Financial Analysts Journal*, January–February, 37–41.

Gibbons, Michael R., Stephen A. Ross, and Jay Shanken, 1989, A test of the efficiency of a given portfolio, *Econometrica* 57, 1121–1152.

Haugen, Robert, 1995, *The New Finance: The Case against Efficient Markets* (Prentice Hall, Englewood Cliffs, New Jersey.)

Huberman Gur, and Shmuel Kandel, 1987, Mean-variance spanning, *Journal of Finance* 42, 873–888.

Jagannathan, Ravi, and Zhenyu Wang, 1995, The conditional CAPM and the cross-section of expected returns, Manuscript, Carlson Graduate School of Management, University of Minnesota, April.

Jegadeesh, Narasimhan, and Sheridan Titman, 1993, Returns to buying winners and selling losers: Implications for stock market efficiency, *Journal of Finance* 48, 65–91.

Kahneman, Daniel, and Amos Tversky, 1982, Intuitive predictions: Biases and corrective procedures. Reprinted in Kahneman, Slovic, and Tversky, *Judgement under Uncertainty: Heuristics and Biases* (Cambridge University Press, Cambridge, England).

Kothari, S. P., Jay Shanken, and Richard G. Sloan, 1995, Another look at the cross-section of expected stock returns, *Journal of Finance* 50, 185–224.

Lakonishok, Josef, Andrei Shleifer, and Robert W. Vishny, 1994, Contrarian investment, extrapolation, and risk, *Journal of Finance* 49, 1541–1578.

Lintner, John, 1965, The valuation of risk assets and the selection of risky investments in stock portfolios and capital budgets, *Review of Economics and Statistics 47*, 13–37.

Lo, Andrew W., and A. Craig MacKinlay, 1988, Stock market prices do not follow random walks: Evidence from a simple specification test, *Review of Financial Studies* 1, 41–66.

MacKinlay, A. Craig, 1995, Multifactor models do not explain deviations from the CAPM, *Journal of Financial Economics* 38, 3–28.

Markowitz, Harry, 1959, *Portfolio Selection: Efficient Diversification of Investments* (Wiley, New York).

Mayers, David, 1972, Nonmarketable assets and capital market equilibrium under uncertainty, in Michael C. Jensen, Ed., *Studies in the Theory of Capital Markets* (Praeger, New York), 223–248.

Merton, Robert C., 1973, An intertemporal capital asset pricing model, *Econometrica* 41, 867–887.

Reinganum, Marc R., 1990, Market microstructure and asset pricing: An empirical investigation of NYSE and NASDAQ securities, *Journal of Financial Economics* 28, 127–147.

Roll, Richard, 1977, A critique of the asset pricing theory's tests Part I: On past and potential testability of the theory, *Journal of Financial Economics* 4, 129–176.

Rosenberg, Barr, Kenneth Reid, and Ronald Lanstein, 1985, Persuasive evidence of market inefficiency, *Journal of Portfolio Management* 11, 9–17.

Ross, Stephen A., 1976, The arbitrage theory of capital asset pricing, *Journal of Economic Theory* 13, 341–360.

Sharpe, William F., 1964, Capital asset prices: A theory of market equilibrium under conditions of risk, *Journal of Finance* 19, 425–442.

RETURN FORECASTS AND TIME-VARYING RISK PREMIUMS

. . .

RETURN FORECASTS AND
TIME-VARYING RISK PREMIUMS

. . .

John H. Cochrane

The most obvious early efficiency tests examined whether returns on a given security are predictable over time:

$$R^e_{t+1} = a + bx_t + \varepsilon_{t+1}$$

where R^e_{t+1} denotes the excess return on a security, and x_t is any variable that investors might use at time t to forecast returns.

Tests using daily, weekly, or monthly return data found coefficients b that are small, with tiny R^2 values. Thus even some statistically "significant" results were judged economically insignificant. A coin with 51%/49% probabilities is darn close to fair, surely, it would seem, within transactions costs.

In the mid-1970s, Gene started looking at long-run return forecasts and, perhaps more importantly, at forecasts using prices as right-hand variables. Lo and behold, you *can* forecast returns using prices, and these forecasts are particularly striking at longer horizons. The b coefficients are economically large, and the R^2 values rise to impressive values.

Figure 1 illustrates this phenomenon.

The dashed line is the dividend/price ratio of the CRSP value-weighted portfolio. Think of it as prices upside down. The dividend/price ratio goes down in the big price booms, such as the 1960s and 1990s, and goes up in the big busts, such as the 1970s. It also wiggles with business cycles. Among other things, this graph points out the astounding volatility of stock valuations, which Bob Shiller shared the Nobel Prize in part for pointing out.

The solid line is the average return for the seven *following* years. So, times of high prices relative to dividends are reliably followed by seven years of low returns. Times of low prices relative to dividends are reliably followed by seven years of high returns.

The graph is my way of illustrating Fama and French's "Dividend Yields and Expected Stock Returns" regressions,

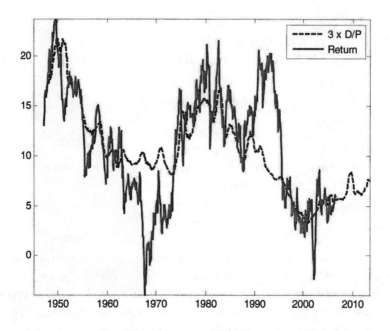

*Figure 1. Dividend yield of value-weighted NYSE stock
portfolio and following seven-year return*

$$R^e_{t,t+7} = a + b\left(\frac{D_t}{P_t}\right) + \varepsilon_{t+7}. \tag{1}$$

These regressions have large R^2 values, visible in the correlation between lines in my graph. By this and other measures, long-run returns can be predicted with economic and statistical significance.

What do we make of this finding? Such a regression means that expected returns vary through time,

$$E\left(R^e_{t,t+7}\middle|\frac{D_t}{P_t}\right) = a + b\left(\frac{D_t}{P_t}\right) \tag{2}$$

It all seems simple in retrospect, but once again the idea that one could just run such simple regressions to measure time-variation in expected returns was not at all obvious at the time. Gene's "life in finance" explains some of the muddy contemporary thinking on the topic. Contemporary thinking revolved around looking for "proxies" for expected return variation. Using ex post returns, as in the left-hand side of this regression, looked fishy from that perspective. Ex post returns contain expected returns plus a large unpredictable component, so they are poor proxies for expected returns. But the forecasting regression doesn't use a proxy concept, and the unpredictable part of returns is uncorrelated with dividend yields, so the regression is valid.

Some of this confusion, I think, comes down to information sets, which are still a source of much confusion. We can think about expected returns given investors' information, given all public information, or given the information in one particular study. (And, to do it properly, one should distinguish conditional expectation from linear projection, which I will gloss over in the interest of simplicity.) Each set is smaller than the previous one, and they are not the same.

When we run a regression like (1) and interpret the "expected returns" as in (2), we measure the expectation given the dividend yield only. We do not measure investors' "true" expectations, or even the expectations we could measure with multiple regressions.

But the measurement in (2) still tells us a lot. By the law of iterated expectations, it gives the expected value of agent's expectations, $E[E(R|A, B)|B] = E(R|B)$. Furthermore, the variation over time of expected returns documented by (1) and (2) is a lower bound for the variation in expected returns conditioned on larger information sets: $var[E(R|A,B)] \geq var[E(R|B)]$. Adding more variables to a regression always increases the R^2.

So, regressions such as (1) do not isolate "the" expected return. But they do inform us about investors' expected returns and provide a lower bound for the variation over time of investors' expected returns.

To this day, many studies "proxy" for investors' information, deriving implications that hold only when investors use exactly the same information that a study uses to forecast returns, and no more. The Fama forecasting regressions, by contrast, "condition down." We start with a theoretical statement that is true based on investors' information, then take conditional expectations on both sides to derive expressions that remain valid based on a subset of that information, such as dividend/price ratios. Investors will always have much more information than we can include in a study, so avoiding proxies is a great advance. In this way, Fama's return-forecasting regressions are the precursor to the first-order condition instrumental variable estimation technique introduced in Hansen (1982) and Hansen and Singleton (1982). They mirror the inversion mentioned in Ray Ball's essay, and the grouping procedure we mentioned in discussing mutual funds. Markets reflect all sorts of information that we will never see, and tests of market efficiency must respect that fact.

After a long controversy, I think it is fair to say that long-horizon regressions are most important for showing the *economic* rather than *statistical* significance of forecasting regressions. The number of nonoverlapping observations declines as the horizon lengthens, so larger standard errors make up for larger coefficients, and there is not really a huge statistical advantage either way.

But that observation does not make the finding any less important. Really, much of the second revolution in finance—predictability, value, and momentum—comes from looking at the same phenomena in different ways that reveal their previously overlooked economic significance, rather than finding new techniques that wring more statistical significance out of the data.

When we unite return regressions with the evolution of the right-hand variable,

$$R^e_{t+1} = a + bx_t + \varepsilon_{t+1}$$

$$x_{t+1} = a_x + \phi x_t + \varepsilon^x_{t+1}.$$

a highly persistent forecasting variable (i.e., ϕ near one) means that regression coefficients b rise with horizon, and R^2 values rise with horizon. So, consider a regression forecast that one might have dismissed in 1970 as having a small b with low R^2, statistically "significant" but on that basis "economically insignificant." Yet, if the forecasting variable is persistent, that regression is exactly equivalent to a long-run forecast with a large b and a large R^2. There is no separate fact at long horizons. The long-horizon regressions are just a consequence of short-horizon regressions and a persistent forecasting variable. But the long-horizon regressions let us see that the fact is economically significant after all.

A better way to demonstrate economic significance, I think with a lot of hindsight, is to compare the variation in expected returns to the level of expected returns, rather than to divide the variation of expected returns by the variance of actual returns in R^2. We will never perfectly forecast returns, so the latter is an unhelpful comparison.

In a regression $r_{t+1} = a + bx_t + \varepsilon_{t+1}$, variation in expected returns is $\sigma(E_t(r_{t+1})) = b\sigma(x_t)$. If stock returns have a 5% unconditional mean, and the conditional mean varies by $\sigma(E_t(r_{t+1})) = 4\%$, that's an economically *huge* variation in expected returns. Expected returns are 5% on average, yet sometimes 0% and sometimes 10%! Such numbers are typical of dividend-yield forecasts such as equation (1). But since stock returns vary by $\sigma(r_{t+1}) = 20\%$, the R^2 of this forecast is only $(4/20)^2 = 0.04$, which seems small.

Unlike R^2, this comparison of the volatility of expected returns with the level of expected returns is not strongly affected by horizon, since the standard deviation of expected returns and the level of expected returns both grow roughly linearly with horizon.

The Fama forecastability papers have something else in common: the right-hand variable contains a price, and there is usually only one right-hand variable. If we were just looking for large variation in expected returns, then any variable could go on the right, and the more the merrier, up to the danger of fishing. Why prices, and why just prices?

In one sense prices are a natural variable. If expected returns are abnormally high on a given date, prices will be low since dividends are discounted at a higher rate. Thus, low prices partially reveal to us the fact that investors have information of high expected returns. If the investors are rational, average returns will be higher following a "low" price. Using prices is a clever way to aggregate and help us see some of the widely dispersed information that investors see.

But the use of prices is deeper. These regressions are not really about documenting variation in expected returns, which we could do by putting anything on the right-hand side. *These regressions tell us why prices move.* They are one more brilliant Fama use of OLS regressions for unusual purposes.

In economics, when you run $y = a + bx + \varepsilon$, it's conventional to think of x as "causing" y. In return-forecasting regressions, causality goes the other way. A rise in risk premium or other event causes expected returns to rise. Higher expected returns means prices fall as they discount the same dividends more strongly. We then see, on average, higher actual returns following the lower price, which is the fact that drives the regression. It is like a regression of Saturday's weather on Friday's forecast. The weather causes the forecast, not the other way around.

Fama's return-forecasting regressions are here not so much to tell us about expected returns but to tell us about *how prices are formed.* They are about what explains variation in the *right*-hand variable, not the *left*-hand variable. We put the "cause" on the "wrong" side because forecast errors are orthogonal to forecasters, and orthogonality, not causality, is the ultimate arbiter of which side each variable should lie on.

The message of the regressions is that variation in expected returns—

variation in discount rates—is an important determinant of the variation in prices.

This interpretation became clearest as return regressions were integrated with volatility tests, the latter made famous by Robert Shiller (1981). In modern expression, volatility tests amount to the observation that regressions of long-run dividend growth on the dividend/price ratio have a coefficient close to zero. They "should," in a constant-expected-return, efficient-market world, have a strong negative coefficient: If prices are lower than current dividends, it should mean that investors think dividends will decline in the future.

An identity links these observations. A high price/dividend ratio must mean higher subsequent dividend growth, lower subsequent returns, or a perpetually rising price/dividend ratio (a "rational bubble," "violation of the transversality condition"). These three items must add up as a matter of arithmetic, by the definition of return. Therefore, the regression coefficient of long-run return, long-run dividend growth, and terminal dividend yield on initial dividend yields must add up to one. The question is, which one is it? The answer is that all variation in price/dividend ratios corresponds to expected returns— and none of it to expected dividend growth (confirming Shiller) or perpetually rising prices ("rational bubbles"). In this sense, the subsequent digestion of Fama and French's regressions has completely united volatility tests and return predictability regressions.

Does return predictability imply that markets are inefficient? No, or at least not necessarily. In 1970, Gene's joint-hypothesis theorem emphasized that you *can* get better returns by shouldering more risk, and the reward for bearing risk can vary over time and across assets. We don't see important forecasts at daily, weekly, or seasonal frequencies, where it would be pretty hard to concoct a theory of time-varying risk premiums. The significant return forecasts seem to line up with business cycles and larger movements in economic activity, just where one might expect variation in economic risk premiums. Of course, that's not proof—one needs to write down and check economic models of time-varying risk premiums. But it certainly is suggestive.

For example, in December 2008, prices fell and, by the regression, expected stock returns rose. In the risk-premium view, typical investors answered, "Yes, I see it's a buying opportunity. But stocks are still risky, and the economy is falling to pieces. I just can't take risks right now. I'm selling." Many university endowments did just that.

There is another possibility: perhaps people were irrationally optimistic in the booms, and irrationally pessimistic in the busts.

And a third, more recent, challenge: perhaps the institutional mechanics of financial intermediation cause variation in the risk premium. When leveraged hedge funds lose money, they sell. If not enough buyers are around, prices fall.

These views agree on the facts so far. So how do we tell them apart? Answer: we need "models of market equilibrium." We are not here to tell stories. We need economic models, psychological models, or institutional models that tie price and expected-return fluctuations to data, in a nontautological way. Gene proved in the 1970 joint hypothesis theorem that there is no test based only on asset prices that can distinguish these explanations. And constructing such models is exactly what a generation of researchers including myself do, which is a measure of the large influence of Fama's forecasting regressions.

The forecastability regressions radically changed our worldview about variation in prices. In the 1970s, we might have thought that variation in market-wide price/dividend or price/earnings ratios came from changing expectations of dividend growth, earnings growth, etc. A high price relative to current dividends means that people expect higher dividends in the future. The return-forecast regressions, together with the "complementary" dividend-growth regressions, mean that variations in the risk premium, rather than variation in expected cash flows, account *entirely* for the volatility of market-wide stock valuations. A high price relative to current dividends entirely means that returns will be lower in the future. (This is a simple, agreed-on fact, not an explanation. The disagreement concerns whether those lower returns represent rationally avoided risk or irrational expectations. I carefully use the word "account," not "cause," here.)

Our worldview changed from "variation in price/dividend ratios corresponds 100% to variation in cash flow expectations with constant expected returns" to "variation in price/dividend ratios corresponds 0% to variation in cash flow expectations and 100% to expected return variation." You can't ask for greater "economic" significance of the point estimates—though you can still argue with statistical significance, and a large literature does.

The fact that the risk premium accounts for *all* variation in valuations changes everything we do in finance and related fields from accounting to macroeconomics. And the fact that variation in risk premiums is so correlated with business cycles tells macroeconomics that recessions have a lot to do with the ability to bear risk, a feature largely missing in current macroeconomic modeling.

A few caveats, because these results are frequently misinterpreted. First, one must be clear about information sets. Dividend growth is unpredictable at annual horizons from dividend/price ratios. That does not mean that dividend growth is unpredictable from other variables. In fact, dividend growth does seem to be predictable about one year ahead, using variables other than dividend/price ratios as predictors. So don't jump from "dividend yields don't predict dividend growth" to "dividend growth is unpredictable!"

Second, one might think that when additional variables show higher dividend growth predictability, they must imply less expected return variability. But adding variables to a regression always increases R^2. When we add other variables, expected returns must vary *even more* than dividend yield regressions indicate. The resolution of this puzzle is that additional dividend growth and additional return forecastability must be perfectly correlated. Any variable that forecasts higher dividend growth, holding dividend yields constant, must *also* forecast higher returns. For example, at the bottom of a recession, current dividends are depressed. Expected dividend growth is high, but expected returns are unusually high as well. The cash flow and discount rates offset each other, leaving no additional effect on prices. Thus, the fact that dividend growth is forecastable means that expected return variation accounts for more than 100% of price/dividend ratio variation!

Third, the fact that variation in *valuations*—price/dividend or price/earnings ratios—are fully accounted for by expected return variation does not mean that variation in *prices* or *returns* have the same sources. Contemporaneous dividend growth shocks account for about half the variance in price changes and returns. Prices and dividends decline together, leaving price/dividend ratios unaffected.

Fourth, these facts hold for time-series variation in the market as a whole. Cross-sectional variation in dividend/price, price/earnings, and book-to-market ratios seems to come about half from variation in expected cash flows and half from variation in expected returns. However, these decompositions are still somewhat overlooked, and a much better job of quantifying them is possible.

We start this section of the volume, however, with the much earlier "Short-Term Interest Rates as Predictors of Inflation." This was the first paper in the series, and it inaugurated the technique of regressing ex post values on prices to see how prices are determined.

This paper investigates the Fisher relationship, which states that the nominal interest rate should equal the real interest rate plus the expected rate of inflation,

$$i_t = r_t + E(\pi_{t+1}|I_t) \tag{3}$$

where I_t denotes the investor's information set. As Gene explains, previous efforts to examine this relationship looked at proxies for expected inflation.

Gene ran it backwards, with the price determined by the market i_t on the right-hand side:

$$\pi_{t+1} = r + bi_t + cx_t + \varepsilon_{t+1} \tag{4}$$

If the real rate is constant—the needed "model of market equilibrium"—then the coefficient b on the interest rate in (4) should be one, and, more importantly, the coefficient on c multiplying any other variable x_t in investors' information sets should be zero. The nominal interest rate should be a sufficient statistic, capturing all available information about future inflation. The nominal interest rate reveals the slice of investors' rich information sets that is useful for forecasting inflation.

Gene's paper found these predictions held quite well in the data sample available at that time. Gene was also sensitive to what we now call "weak instruments." The most interesting sorts of tests are x variables that forecast inflation well in univariate regressions, but should be driven out by the nominal rate i in a multiple regression. Inflation must be forecastable for this test to have any bite. Fortunately, since inflation is persistent, past inflation rates serve quite well in this purpose. Past inflation forecasts future inflation, but interest rates forecast inflation better.

This simple article set off much of the subsequent investigation. For example, Hansen and Singleton (1982) wrote the relation between real and nominal interest rates as

$$1 = E\left[\beta\frac{u'(c_{t+1})}{u'(c_t)}(1+i_t)\frac{\Pi_t}{\Pi_{t+1}}\bigg|I_t\right],$$

using the consumption-based model as the "model of market equilibrium." Writing their instruments as x_t, they tested the relation

$$0 = E\left[\left(\beta\frac{u'(c_{t+1})}{u'(c_t)}(1+i_t)\frac{\Pi_t}{\Pi_{t+1}}-1\right)\times x_t\right].$$

This moment condition is the numerator of a Fama-like regression coefficient. That's how we've done asset pricing ever since.

"Forward Rates as Predictors of Future Spot Rates" really leads off the series of papers by finding stunning expected-return variation, and it investigates the term structure of interest rates.

We included "The Information in Long-Maturity Forward Rates," with Rob Bliss, once again as a paper that came late in the series, less famous and less well cited, but benefiting from nearly a decade of refinement and a much clearer first paper for a modern reader.

The log forward rate $f_t^{(n)}$ is the rate at which you can contract today t to borrow from $t + n - 1$ to $t + n$. The log spot rate is the rate at which you can contract at t to borrow from t to $t + 1$. The simple expectations hypothesis states that the forward rate equals the expected future spot rate, perhaps plus a constant risk premium,

$$f_t^{(n)} = E\left(y_{t+n-1}^{(1)} \mid I_t\right) + c.$$

Following the standard Fama idea of running the regression backwards, Fama and Bliss run

$$y_{t+n-1}^{(1)} - y_t^{(1)} = a_y + b_y\left[f_t^{(n)} - y_t^{(1)}\right] + \varepsilon_{t+n-1}^y$$

and they check for the "efficient market" prediction $b_y = 1$.

Subtracting today's spot rate $y_t^{(1)}$ on both sides is important. If you simply report today's weather as your forecast for tomorrow's weather, over the course of the year you will look like a pretty good weather forecaster. The coefficient in a regression of tomorrow's weather on your forecast will be one, with a very high R^2. To reveal the emptiness of this forecast, we run the regression of the *change* in weather from today to tomorrow on the *difference* between your forecast and today's weather. This is an important step because weather, like forward rates, is highly serially correlated.

The result of this regression is profoundly unsettling. Tables 1 and 2 of "Forward Rates as Predictors of Future Spot Rates" imply that ". . . the martingale model, which simply predicts that the interest rate will remain unchanged, does better in predicting future spot rates than forward rates" (p. 363). Crystallized in "The Information in Long-Maturity Forward Rates," the coefficient is not just a bit less than one. It is *zero*. The forward rate does, essentially, report today's weather as its forecast for tomorrow.

As for dividend yields, there is an identity at work here: the forward-spot spread must correspond to a change in yield or to an ex post excess return:

$$\left[y_{t+n-1}^{(1)} - y_t^{(1)} \right] + \left[p_{t+n-1}^{(1)} - p_t^{(n)} + p_t^{(n-1)} \right] = \left[f_t^{(n)} - y_t^{(1)} \right].$$

The term in the middle is the return from holding an n-period bond from time t to time t + n − 1, financed by holding an n−1 period bond for the same period. Running both sides of this identity on the forward spread, you will find $b_r + b_y = 1$ —exactly, not in expectation, in each sample—where b_r is the coefficient in a regression of excess returns on forward spreads,

$$\left[p_{t+n-1}^{(1)} - p_t^{(n)} + p_t^{(n-1)} \right] = a_r + b_r \left[f_t^{(n)} - y_t^{(1)} \right] + \varepsilon_{t+n-1}^r$$

The forward spread must, mechanically, reflect variation in risk premiums, or variation in expected spot-rate changes. If forward rates do not forecast changes in spot rates, then they correspond to risk premiums.

Comparing "Forward Rates as Predictors of Future Spot Rates" with "The Information in Long-Maturity Forward Rates," we can see Gene's thinking evolve and we see the message become clearer and clearer. The first paper doesn't actually have these regressions. It only interprets tables of variances and autocorrelations in terms that the regressions would later clarify.

In the first paper, you see Gene really trying hard to salvage the view that a lot of forward rate variation comes from variation in expected future spot rates. Noting that forward rates on their own aren't doing a good job, he states that risk premiums merely "obscure" the desired forecast power.

> Any variation over time in the expected premiums . . . tends to obscure the power of the forward rate . . . as a predictor of the spot rate.

He then constructs a model of expected return variation. "After some experimentation" he uses the "average of absolute values of the monthly changes in the spot rate during the year before month t + 1 and during the year following the month t + 1" (p. 366) to measure volatility, and posits expected returns are a linear function of this volatility, an idea that disappeared from later work. The bottom line sounds awfully comforting:

> When forward rates are adjusted for variation through time in expected premiums, they provide predictors of future spot rates as good as those obtained from the information in the time series of spot rates (p. 365).
>
> . . . The market reacts appropriately. . . . This evidence is consistent with the market efficiency proposition (p. 361 [abstract]).

... This evidence is consistent with the market efficiency proposition that in setting bill prices, the market correctly uses at least the information in past spot prices. However, the best support for market efficiency is the direct evidence that in setting bill prices and forward rates the market reacts appropriately to the negative autocorrelation in monthly change in the spot rate and to changes through time in the degrees of this autocorrelation (p. 377 [summary]).

There is some hedging, but you don't come away from this with the idea that all variation in forward spreads comes from expected returns, and none from variation in expected interest rate changes.

"The Information in Long-Maturity Forward Rates," by contrast, cuts to the chase and leads off in Table 1 with return forecasting regressions. At a one year horizon, $b_r = 1$ and $b_y = 0$. End of story. The idea of proxying expected returns by volatility is gone. Similar summary quotes have a dramatically different flavor.

Current 1-year forward rates on 1- to 5-year U.S. Treasury bonds are information about the current term structure of 1-year expected returns on the bonds (p. 680 [abstract]).

We confirm that forward rate forecasts of near-term changes in interest rates are poor (p. 680).

The slopes [b_r] in the term-premium regressions range from 0.91 to 1.42. All are within one standard error of 1.0. We can infer that the slopes (equal to 1-[b_r] ...) in the complementary yield-change regression ... are within one standard error of 0.0. The results suggest that ... variation in current [forward-spot] spreads is mostly variation in the term premiums in current 1-year expected returns, and forward-spot spreads do not predict yield changes 1 year ahead (p. 684).

... 1-year expected returns for U.S. Treasury maturities to 5 years, measured net of the interest rate on a 1-year bond, vary through time. ... This variation in expected term premiums seems to be related to the business cycles (p. 689 [conclusion]).

Some of the difference in language reflects the change of emphasis from levels to differences across time and maturity. But much of the change simply reflects the experience of a whole slew of papers, and over and over again seeing price movements that correspond 100% to variation in expected returns.

"The Information in Long-Maturity Forward Rates," however, shows that at long horizons, the expectations hypothesis actually does work rather well. Five-year forward rates *do* correspond to expected changes in interest rates four years from now, and not to the corresponding risk premium. And Fama and Bliss relate this pattern to the clear cyclical behavior of interest rates. This term structure of risk premiums is now a new and exciting area of research, both in empirical work and in theory.

"Forward and Spot Exchange Rates" is worth reading for several reasons. Coming in between the last two papers, it shows the development of the identity linking the things that "should" be forecastable—yields, dividends, exchange rates—to the thing that "should not" be forecastable—excess returns. It started an immense literature and established one of the handful of founding facts that define international finance. And in doing so, it is a reminder of how pervasive the patterns are across many markets.

A forward exchange rate f_t contract is an obligation to buy foreign currency one period in the future at a set price. The spot exchange rate s_t is the price of the corresponding immediate purchase. Thus, the simple expectations hypothesis predicts that the forward rate is today's expectation of the future spot rate,

$$f_t = E(s_{t+1}|I_t) + c$$

where again I have allowed for a constant risk premium c. Following the usual Fama idea to run the regression backwards, we check if forward rates are set this way by running the change in the spot rate on the spread between today's forward rate and today's spot rate,

$$s_{t+1} - s_t = a_s + b_s(f_t - s_t) + \varepsilon_{t+1}^s,$$

and checking for $b_s = 1$. In words, if the forward rate is higher than the spot rate, and expected returns are constant, we should see, on average, spot rates subsequently rise.

A trader who enters into a forward contract and then sells in the spot market earns an excess log return equal to $f_t - s_{t+1}$. Thus, the identity

$$\left[s_{t+1} - s_t\right] + \left[f_t - s_{t+1}\right] = f_t - s_t$$

says that the forward-spot spread must correspond to a change in spot rate or to an excess return. And running excess returns on the forward spot spread,

$$f_t - s_{t+1} = a_r + b_r(f_t - s_t) + \varepsilon^r_{t+1},$$

we once again have an identity $b_r + b_s = 1$. So a forward-spot spread must forecast the change in spot rate or it must forecast the excess return. The only question is which. (Does this sound repetitive? That's the point! We're seeing the same pattern over and over again.)

Here, Gene found an even more remarkable result. Not only do we not see $b_s = 1$, we see *negative* values of b_s! Correspondingly, b_r is even larger.

If forward rates are higher than spot rates—equivalently, if the foreign interest rate is lower than the domestic rate—it looks like an investment opportunity. Buy forward, or borrow abroad. Exchange rate changes "should" offset this profit opportunity. In fact, they go the "wrong" way and enhance the profit opportunity!

Again, there is a suggestive macroeconomic correlation. Domestic interest rates are low relative to foreign rates in the bottoms of recessions. These are times when all risk premiums are large, so perhaps it makes sense that the risk premium for holding exchange rate risk is large as well. A large number of macroeconomic models have been constructed following this insight to explain this exchange rate premium.

This remains a live field of research. Even the basic facts are not yet completely explored. Fama looked at each country in isolation. We are only starting to see work that ties countries together, considers the difference between time and country fixed effects in these regressions, and examines what factors in exchange rate risk correspond to these expected returns. We are only starting to link currency risk premiums, bond risk premiums, and stock risk premiums. (Lustig, Roussanov, and Verdelhan [2011] stand out in this effort. They form portfolios of countries based on forward-spot exchange rate spreads, they document the average returns of these portfolios, and they show those average returns line up with a slope factor. In doing so, they at last bring different countries together in the analysis. Their watershed paper amounts, however, essentially to implementing Fama and French's "Common Risk Factors in Returns on Stocks and Bonds" [1993] and "Multifactor Explanations of Asset Pricing Anomalies" [1996] techniques to the well-known currency puzzle. That this took 15 years suggests how much low-hanging fruit Fama has left on the trees.)

The patterns shown in these three examples—stocks, bonds, and foreign exchange—are pervasive in financial markets, extending to commodities, corporate bond spreads, real estate, and other assets. In each case, time-series variation in a price/x ratio should, if expected returns are constant over time, forecast changes in x. In each case, it doesn't at all. Instead it forecasts excess returns. Corporate spreads largely forecast returns to bondholders, not larger defaults. Price/rent ratios forecast returns to homeowners, not changes in rent. In each case the result is pretty dramatic, typically a 100%/0% split that turns out to be 0%/100% or more. In each case the risk premium varies slowly over time and is suggestively correlated with business cycles.

Furthermore, there are strong suggestions of common movement across asset classes. The variables that forecast stock returns also forecast bond returns, and the variables that forecast bond returns also forecast stock returns. The business cycle association, multivariate return forecasts, and common component are explored a bit in Fama and French (1989). Yet they have really only scratched the surface.

REFERENCES

Fama, Eugene F., and Kenneth R. French. 1989. "Business Conditions and Expected Returns on Stocks and Bonds." *Journal of Financial Economics* 25, 23–49.

Hansen, Lars Peter. 1982. "Large Sample Properties of Generalized Method of Moments Estimators." *Econometrica* 50 (4), 1029–1054. doi: 10.2307/1912775.

Hansen, Lars Peter, and Kenneth J. Singleton. 1982. "Generalized Instrumental Variables Estimation of Nonlinear Rational Expectations Models." *Econometrica* 50 (5), 1269–1286. doi: 10.2307/1911873.

Lustig, Hanno, Nikolai Roussanov, and Adrien Verdelhan. 2011. "Common Risk Factors in Currency Markets." *Review of Financial Studies* 24 (11), 3731–3777. doi: 10.1093/rfs/hhr068.

Shiller, Robert J. 1981. "Do Stock Prices Move Too Much to Be Justified by Subsequent Changes in Dividends?" *American Economic Review* 71 (3), 421–436.

SHORT-TERM INTEREST RATES AS PREDICTORS OF INFLATION

Eugene F. Fama

Irving Fisher pointed out that with perfect foresight and a well-functioning capital market, the one-period nominal rate of interest is the equilibrium real return plus the fully anticipated rate of inflation. In a world of uncertainty where foresight is imperfect, the nominal rate of interest can be thought of as the equilibrium expected real return plus the market's assessment of the expected rate of inflation.

The relationships between interest rates and inflation have been tested extensively.[1] In line with Fisher's initial work, the almost universal finding is that there are no relationships between interest rates observed at a point in time and rates of inflation subsequently observed. Although the market does not do well in predicting inflation, the general finding is that there are relationships between current interest rates and past rates of inflation. This is interpreted as evidence in favor of the Fisherian view. Thus Fisher concludes:

> We have found evidence, general and specific, . . . that price changes do,
> generally and perceptibly, affect the interest rate in the direction indicated
> by *a priori* theory. But since forethought is imperfect, the effects are
> smaller than the theory requires and lag behind price movements, in some
> periods, very greatly. [p. 451]

Fisher's empirical evidence, and that of most other researchers, is in fact inconsistent with a well-functioning or "efficient" market.[2] An efficient market correctly uses all relevant information in setting prices. If the inflation rate is

Reprinted from the *American Economic Review* 65, no. 3 (June 1975): 269–82.

I am grateful to F. Black, N. Gonedes, M. Jensen, A. Laffer, M. Miller, C. Nelson, H. Roberts, and C. Upton for helpful comments, and to J. MacBeth and D. Garren for computational assistance.

1. For a summary, see Richard Roll.

2. For a discussion of the theory of efficient capital markets and related empirical work, see the author.

to some extent predictable, and if the one-period equilibrium expected real return does not change in such a way as to exactly offset changes in the expected rate of inflation, then in an efficient market there will be a relationship between the one-period nominal interest rate observed at a point in time and the one-period rate of inflation subsequently observed. If the inflation rate is to some extent predictable and no such relationship exists, the market is inefficient: in setting the nominal interest rate, it overlooks relevant information about future inflation.

This paper is concerned with efficiency in the market for one- to six-month U.S. Treasury Bills. Unlike Fisher and most of the rest of the literature, the results presented here indicate that, at least during the 1953–71 period, there are definite relationships between nominal interest rates and rates of inflation subsequently observed. Moreover, during this period the bill market seems to be efficient in the sense that nominal interest rates summarize all the information about future inflation rates that is in time-series of past inflation rates. Finally, another interesting result is that the substantial variation in nominal bill rates during the 1953–71 period seems to be due entirely to variation in expected inflation rates; in other words, expected real returns on bills seem to be constant during the period.

The theory and tests of bill market efficiency are first presented for one-month bills. The results are then extended to bills with longer maturities.

I. INFLATION AND EFFICIENCY IN THE BILL MARKET: THEORY

A. Returns and the Inflation Rate

The nominal return from the end of month $t-1$ to the end of month t on a Treasury Bill with one month to maturity at $t-1$ is

$$R_t = \frac{v_t - v_{t-1}}{v_{t-1}} = \frac{\$1,000 - v_{t-1}}{v_{t-1}} \tag{1}$$

where $v_t = \$1,000$ is the price of the bill at t, and v_{t-1} is its price at $t-1$. Since the bill has one month to maturity at $t-1$, once v_{t-1} is set, R_t is known and can be interpreted as the one-month nominal rate of interest set in the market at $t-1$ and realized at t.

Let p_t be the price level at t, that is, p_t is the price of consumption goods in terms of money, so that the purchasing power of a unit of money, the price of money in terms of goods, is $\pi_t = 1/p_t$. The real return from $t-1$ to t on a one-month bill is then

$$\tilde{r}_t = (v_t \tilde{\pi}_t - v_{t-1} \pi_{t-1}) / v_{t-1} \pi_{t-1} \qquad (2)$$

$$= R_t + \tilde{\Delta}_t + R_t \tilde{\Delta}_t \qquad (3)$$

where tildes (˜) are used to denote random variables, and

$$\tilde{\Delta}_t = (\tilde{\pi}_t - \pi_{t-1}) / \pi_{t-1} \qquad (4)$$

is the rate of change in purchasing power from t − 1 to t. In monthly data, R_t and $\tilde{\Delta}_t$ are close to zero, so that although the equality only holds as an approximation, no harm is done if (3) is reduced to

$$\tilde{r}_t = R_t + \tilde{\Delta}_t \qquad (5)$$

Thus the real return from the end of month t − 1 to the end of month t on a Treasury Bill with one month to maturity at t − 1 is the nominal return plus the rate of change in purchasing power from t − 1 to t.

The fact that $\tilde{r}_t$ is a random variable at t − 1 only because $\tilde{\Delta}_t$ is a random variable explains why bills are attractive for studying how well the market uses information about future inflation in setting security prices. It seems reasonable to assume that investors are concerned with real returns on securities. Since all uncertainty in the real return on a one-month bill is uncertainty about the change in the purchasing power of money during the month, one-month bills are the clear choice for studying how well the market absorbs information about inflation one month ahead. For the same reason, n-month bills are best for studying n-month predictions of inflation.

B. The General Description of an Efficient Market

Market efficiency requires that in setting the price of a one-month bill at t − 1, the market correctly uses all available information to assess the distribution of $\tilde{\Delta}_t$. Formally, in an efficient market,

$$f_m(\Delta_t \mid \phi_{t-1}^m) = f(\Delta_t \mid \phi_{t-1}) \qquad (6)$$

where ϕ_{t-1} is the set of information available at t−1, ϕ_{t-1}^m is the set of information used by the market, $f_m(\Delta_t \mid \phi_{t-1}^m)$ is the market assessed density function for $\tilde{\Delta}_t$, and $f(\Delta_t \mid \phi_{t-1})$ is the true density function implied by ϕ_{t-1}.

When the market sets the equilibrium price of a one-month bill at $t-1$, R_t is also set. Given the relationship among $\tilde{r}_t$, R_t, and $\tilde{\Delta}_t$ of (5), the market's assessed distribution for $\tilde{r}_t$ is implied by R_t and its assessed distribution for $\tilde{\Delta}_t$. If (6) holds, then the market's assessed distribution for $\tilde{r}_t$ is the true distribution

$$f_m(r_t \mid \phi_{t-1}^m, R_t) = f(r_t \mid \phi_{t-1}, R_t) \tag{7}$$

In short, if the market is efficient, then in setting the nominal price of a one-month bill at $t-1$, it correctly uses all available information to assess the distribution of $\tilde{\Delta}_t$. In this sense v_{t-1} fully reflects all available information about $\tilde{\Delta}_t$. Since an equilibrium value of v_{t-1} implies an equilibrium value of R_t, the one-month nominal rate of interest set in the market at $t-1$ likewise fully reflects all available information about $\tilde{\Delta}_t$. Finally, when an efficient market sets R_t, the distribution of the real return $\tilde{r}_t$ that it perceives is the true distribution.

C. A Simple Model of Market Equilibrium

The preceding specification of market efficiency is so general that it is not testable. Since we cannot observe $f_m(\Delta_t \mid \phi_{t-1}^m)$, we cannot determine whether (6) holds, and so we cannot determine whether the the bill market is efficient. What the model lacks is a more detailed specification of the link between $f_m(\Delta_t \mid \phi_{t-1}^m)$ and v_{t-1}; that is, we must specify in more detail how the equilibrium price of a bill at $t-1$ is related to the market-assessed distribution of $\tilde{\Delta}_t$. This is a common feature of tests of market efficiency. A test of efficiency must be based on a model of equilibrium, and any test is simultaneously a test of efficiency and of the assumed model of equilibrium.

The first assumption of the model of bill market equilibrium is that in their decisions with respect to one-month bills, the primary concern of investors is the distribution of the real return on a bill. A market equilibrium depends visibly on a market-clearing value of the nominal price v_{t-1}, but it is assumed that what causes investors to demand the outstanding supply of bills is the implied "equilibrium distribution" of the real return. Testable propositions about market efficiency then require propositions about the characteristics of the market assessed distribution $f_m(r_t \mid \phi_{t-1}^m, R_t)$ that results from an equilibrium price v_{t-1} at $t-1$. As is common in tests of market efficiency, we concentrate on the mean of the distribution, and the proposition about $E_m(\tilde{r}_t \mid \phi_{t-1}^m, R_t)$ is that for all t and ϕ_{t-1}^m,

$$E_m(\tilde{r}_t \mid \phi_{t-1}^m, R_t) = E(\tilde{r}) \qquad (8)$$

Thus the model of bill market equilibrium is the statement that each month the market sets the price of a one-month bill so that it perceives the expected real return on the bill to be $E(\tilde{r})$. In short, the equilibrium expected real return on a one-month bill is assumed to be constant through time.

II. TESTABLE IMPLICATIONS OF MARKET EFFICIENCY WHEN THE EQUILIBRIUM EXPECTED REAL RETURN IS CONSTANT THROUGH TIME

A. The Real Return

In an efficient market (7) holds, and (7) implies

$$E_m(\tilde{r}_t \mid \phi_{t-1}^m, R_t) = E(\tilde{r}_t \mid \phi_{t-1}, R_t) \qquad (9)$$

If market equilibrium is characterized by (8), then with (9) we have

$$E(\tilde{r}_t \mid \phi_{t-1}, R_t) = E(\tilde{r}) \qquad (10)$$

Thus at any time $t-1$ the market sets the price of a one-month bill so that its assessment of the expected real return is the constant $E(\tilde{r})$. Since an efficient market correctly uses all available information, $E(\tilde{r})$ is also the true expected real return on the bill.

The general testable implication of this combination of market efficiency with a model of market equilibrium is that there is no way to use ϕ_{t-1}, the set of information available at $t-1$, or any subset of ϕ_{t-1}, as the basis of a correct assessment of the expected real return on a one-month bill which is other than $E(\tilde{r})$. One subset of ϕ_{t-1} is the time-series of past real returns. If (10) holds,

$$E(\tilde{r}_t \mid r_{t-1}, r_{t-2}, \ldots) = E(\tilde{r}) \qquad (11)$$

That is, there is no way to use the time-series of past real returns as the basis of a correct assessment of the expected real return which is other than $E(\tilde{r})$. If (11) holds, the autocorrelations of $\tilde{r}_t$ for all lags are equal to zero, so that sample autocorrelations provide tests of (11).

Sample autocorrelations of $\tilde{r}_t$ are presented later, but it is well to make one point now. The autocorrelations are joint tests of market efficiency and of the model for the equilibrium expected real return. Thus nonzero autocorrelations of $\tilde{r}_t$ are consistent with a world where the equilibrium expected real return is constant and the market is inefficient, but nonzero autocorrelations are also consistent with a world where the market is efficient and equilibrium expected real returns change through time as a function of the sequence of past real returns. Market efficiency in no way rules out such behavior of the equilibrium expected return.

B. The Nominal Interest Rate as a
Predictor of Inflation

There are tests that distinguish better between the hypothesis that the market is efficient and the hypothesis that the expected real return is constant through time. From (5), the relationship between the market's expectation of the rate of change in purchasing power, the nominal rate of interest, and the market's expectation of the real return is

$$E_m(\tilde{\Delta}_t \mid \phi_{t-1}^m) = E_m(\tilde{r}_t \mid \phi_{t-1}^m, R_t) - R_t \tag{12}$$

If the expected real return is the constant $E(\tilde{r})$, then (12) becomes

$$E_m(\tilde{\Delta}_t \mid \phi_{t-1}^m) = E(\tilde{r}) - R_t \tag{13}$$

If the market is also efficient,

$$E(\tilde{\Delta}_t \mid \phi_{t-1}) = E(\tilde{r}) - R_t \tag{14}$$

Thus a constant expected real return implies that all variation through time in the nominal rate R_t is a direct reflection of variation in the market's assessment of the expected value of $\tilde{\Delta}_t$. If the market is also efficient, then all variation in R_t mirrors variation in the best possible assessment of the expected value of $\tilde{\Delta}_t$. Moreover, once R_t is set at time $t-1$, the details of ϕ_{t-1}, the information that an efficient market uses to assess the expected value of $\tilde{\Delta}_t$, become irrelevant. The information in ϕ_{t-1} is summarized completely in the value of R_t. In this sense, the nominal rate R_t observed at $t-1$ is the best possible predictor of the rate of inflation from $t-1$ to t.

To test these propositions, it is convenient to introduce a new class of models of market equilibrium that includes (8) as a special case. Suppose that at any time $t-1$ the market always sets the price of a one-month bill so that it perceives the expected real return to be

$$E_m(\tilde{r}_t \mid \phi_{t-1}^m, R_t) = \alpha_0 + \gamma R_t \tag{15}$$

If the market is also efficient, we have

$$E(\tilde{r}_t \mid \phi_{t-1}, R_t) = \alpha_0 + \gamma R_t \tag{16}$$

With (5), (15) and (16) imply that

$$E_m(\tilde{\Delta}_t \mid \phi_{t-1}^m) = \alpha_0 + \alpha_1 R_t, \, \alpha_1 = \gamma - 1 \tag{17}$$

$$E_m(\tilde{\Delta}_t \mid \phi_{t-1}) = \alpha_0 + \alpha_1 R_t, \, \alpha_1 = \gamma - 1 \tag{18}$$

In the new model, γ is the proportion of the change in the nominal rate from one month to the next that reflects a change in the equilibrium expected real return, and $-\alpha_1 = 1 - \gamma$ is the proportion of the change in R_t that reflects a change in the expected value of $\tilde{\Delta}_t$. In the special case where the expected real return is constant through time, $\gamma = 0$, $\alpha_1 = -1$, and all variation in R_t mirrors variation in $E(\tilde{\Delta}_t \mid \phi_{t-1})$.

Estimates of α_0 and α_1 in (18) can be obtained by applying least squares to

$$\tilde{\Delta}_t = \alpha_0 + \alpha_1 R_t + \tilde{\varepsilon}_t \tag{19}$$

If the coefficient estimates are inconsistent with the hypothesis that

$$\alpha_0 = E(\tilde{r}) \quad \text{and} \quad \alpha_1 = -1 \tag{20}$$

the model of a constant equilibrium expected real return is rejected. The more general interpretation of (15), that is, with unrestricted values of the coefficients, can then be taken as the model for the equilibrium expected real return, and other results from the estimates of (19) can be used to test market efficiency. Thus, like (14), (18) says that in an efficient market R_t summarizes all the information about the expected value of $\tilde{\Delta}_t$ which is in ϕ_{t-1}. For example, given R_t, the sequence of past values of the disturbance $\tilde{\varepsilon}_t$ in (19) should be of no additional help in assessing the expected value of $\tilde{\Delta}_t$ which implies that the autocorrelations of the disturbance should be zero for all lags.

The approach is easily generalized to obtain other tests of (14). For example, one item of information available at $t-1$ is Δ_{t-1}. If periods of inflation or deflation tend to persist, then Δ_{t-1} is relevant information for assessing the expected value of $\tilde{\Delta}_t$. If the information in Δ_{t-1} is not correctly used by the market in setting R_t, then the coefficient α_2 in

$$\tilde{\Delta}_t = \alpha_0 + \alpha_1 R_t + \alpha_2 \Delta_{t-1} + \tilde{\varepsilon}_t \tag{21}$$

is nonzero. On the other hand, if (14) holds, the market is efficient and the value of R_t set at $t-1$ summarizes all the information available about the expected value of $\tilde{\Delta}_t$, which includes any information in Δ_{t-1} and any information in the past values of $\tilde{\varepsilon}_t$. Thus, in this case, $\alpha_2 = 0$ and the autocorrelations of the disturbance $\tilde{\varepsilon}_t$ in (21) are zero for all lags. Moreover, if (14) holds, the expected real return is constant through time, so that the values of α_0 and α_1 in (21) are as in (20). All of these propositions are tested below with least squares estimates of (21).

C. Reinterpretation of the Proposed Tests

It is well to recognize that all of the tests of market efficiency are different ways to examine whether in assessing the expected value of $\tilde{\Delta}_t$, the market correctly uses any information in the past values $\Delta_{t-1}, \Delta_{t-2} \ldots$. The point is obvious with respect to tests based on the coefficient α_2 in (21). The argument is also direct for the autocorrelations of the disturbances $\tilde{\varepsilon}_t$ in (19) and (21). The disturbance $\tilde{\varepsilon}_t$ in (19) is the deviation of $\tilde{\Delta}_t$ from the market's assessment of its conditional expected value, when $E_m(\tilde{\Delta}_t | \phi_{t-1}^m)$ is given by (17). The autocorrelations of $\tilde{\varepsilon}_t$ tell us whether the past values of these deviations are used correctly by the market when it assesses the expected value of $\tilde{\Delta}_t$. Nonzero autocorrelations imply that the market is inefficient; one can improve on the market's assessment of the expected value of $\tilde{\Delta}_t$ by making correct use of information in past values of Δ_t. Likewise the disturbance $\tilde{\varepsilon}_t$ in (21) is the deviation of $\tilde{\Delta}_t$ from its conditional expected value when the latter is allowed to be a function of Δ_{t-1} as well as of R_t. Finally, if the equilibrium expected real return is constant through time, then the market's assessment of the expected value of $\tilde{\Delta}_t$ is described by (13). From (5) it then follows that

$$\tilde{r}_t - E(\tilde{r}) = \tilde{\Delta}_t + R_t - E(\tilde{r}) \tag{22a}$$

$$= \tilde{\Delta}_t - E_m(\tilde{\Delta}_t | \phi_{t-1}^m) \tag{22b}$$

Thus, the deviation of $\tilde{r}_t$ from its expected value is the deviation of $\tilde{\Delta}_t$ from the market's assessment of its expected value, when the latter is described by (13). Tests of market efficiency based on the autocorrelations of $\tilde{r}_t$, like all the other proposed tests, are concerned with whether the market correctly uses any information in the time-series of past values, $\Delta_{t-1}, \Delta_{t-2}, \ldots$, when it assesses $E_m(\tilde{\Delta}_t | \phi^m_{t-1})$ on which the nominal rate R_t is then based. Any such test must assume some model of market equilibrium, that is, some proposition about the equilibrium expected real return $E_m(\tilde{r}_t | \phi^m_{t-1})$, which in turn implies some proposition about $E_m(\tilde{\Delta}_t | \phi^m_{t-1})$, and this is where the tests differ.

There is, however, no need to apologize for the fact that the tests of market efficiency concentrate on the reaction of the market to information in the time-series of past rates of change in the purchasing power of money. Beginning with the pioneering work of Fisher, researchers in this area have long contended, and the results below substantiate the claim, that past rates of inflation are important information for assessing future rates. Moreover, previous work almost uniformly suggests that the market is inefficient; in assessing expected future rates of inflation, much of the information in past rates is apparently ignored. This conclusion, if true, indicates a serious failing of a free market. The value of a market is in providing accurate signals for resource allocation, which means setting prices that more or less fully reflect available information. If the market ignores the information from so obvious a source as past inflation rates, its effectiveness is seriously questioned. The issue deserves further study.

III. THE DATA

The one-month nominal rate of interest R_t used in the tests is the return from the end of month $t - 1$ to the end of month t on the Treasury Bill that matures closest to the end of month t. The data are from the quote sheets of Salomon Brothers. In computing R_t from (1), the average of the bid and asked prices at the end of month $t - 1$ is used for the nominal price v_{t-1}. The Bureau of Labor Statistics Consumer Price Index (*CPI*) is used to estimate Δ_t, the rate of change in the purchasing power of money from the end of month $t - 1$ to the end of month t. The use of any index to measure the level of prices of consumption goods can be questioned. There is, however, no need to speculate about the effects of shortcomings of the data on the tests. If the results of the tests seem meaningful, the data are probably adequate.

The tests cover the period from January 1953 through July 1971. Tests for periods prior to 1953 would be meaningless. First, during World War II and up to the Treasury-Federal Reserve Accord of 1951, interest rates on Treasury Bills were pegged by the government. In effect, a rich and obstinate investor saw to it that Treasury Bill rates did not adjust to predictable changes in inflation rates. Second, at the beginning of 1953 there was a substantial upgrading of the *CPI*.[3] The number of items in the Index increased substantially, and monthly sampling of major items became the general rule. For tests of market efficiency based on monthly data, monthly sampling of major items in the *CPI* is critical. Sampling items less frequently than monthly, the general rule prior to 1953, means that some of the price changes for month t show up in the Index in months subsequent to t. Since nominal prices of goods tend to move together, spreading price changes for month t into following months creates spurious positive autocorrelation in monthly changes in the Index. This gives the appearance that there is more information about future inflation rates in past inflation rates than is really the case. Since the spurious component of the information in measured inflation rates is not easily isolated, test of market efficiency on pre-1953 data would be difficult to interpret.

The values of the *CPI* from August 1971 to the present (mid-1974) are also suspect. During this period the Nixon Administration made a series of attempts to fix prices. The controls were effective in creating "shortages" of some important goods (who can forget the gas queues of the winter of 1973–74?), so that for this period there are nontrivial differences between the observed values of the *CPI* and the true costs of goods to consumers. For this reason, the tests concentrate on the "clean" precontrols period January 1953 to July 1971.

IV. RESULTS FOR ONE-MONTH BILLS

Table 1 shows sample autocorrelations $\hat{\rho}_\tau$ of Δ_t for lags τ of from one to twelve months. The table also shows sample means and standard deviations of Δ_t, and

$$\sigma(\hat{\rho}_1) = 1/(T-1)^{1/2} \tag{23}$$

where $T-1$ is the number of observations used to compute $\hat{\rho}_1$, and $\sigma(\hat{\rho}_\tau)$ is the approximate standard error of $\hat{\rho}_1$ under the hypothesis that the true autocorrelation is zero. Table 2 shows sample autocorrelations and other statistics for the real return r_t. Although, for simplicity, the development of the theory is

---

3. See ch. 10 of the *BLS* reference.

in terms of the approximation given by (5), the exact expression (3) is used to compute r_t in the empirical work.

Table 3 shows summary statistics for the estimated version of (19). In addition to the least squares regression coefficient estimates a_0 and a_1, the table shows the sample standard errors of the estimates $s(a_0)$ and $s(a_1)$; the coefficient of determination, adjusted for degrees of freedom; $s(e)$, the standard deviation of the residuals; and the first three residual autocorrelations, $\hat{\rho}_1(e)$, $\hat{\rho}_2(e)$, and $\hat{\rho}_3(e)$. Table 4 shows similar summary statistics for the estimated version of (21).

A. The Information in Past Inflation Rates

The market efficiency hypothesis to be tested is that the one-month nominal interest rate R_t set in the market at the end of month $t-1$ is based on correct utilization of all the information about the expected value of $\tilde{\Delta}_t$, which is in the time-series of past values Δ_{t-1}, Δ_{t-2}, ... The hypothesis is only meaningful, however, if past rates of change in purchasing power do indeed have information about the expected future rate of change. The predominance of large estimated autocorrelations of Δ_t in Table 1 indicates that this is the case.

TABLE 1. Autocorrelations of Δ_t: one-month intervals

	1/53–7/71	1/53–2/59	3/59–7/64	8/64–7/71
$\hat{\rho}_1$	.36	.21	−.09	.35
$\hat{\rho}_2$	.37	.28	−.09	.34
$\hat{\rho}_3$	.27	.10	−.25	.26
$\hat{\rho}_4$	.30	.16	−.05	.23
$\hat{\rho}_5$	.29	.01	.03	.33
$\hat{\rho}_6$	.29	−.01	.09	.30
$\hat{\rho}_7$	.25	.05	−.06	.18
$\hat{\rho}_8$	.34	.18	−.20	.37
$\hat{\rho}_9$	.36	.21	.13	.24
$\hat{\rho}_{10}$	.34	.20	.04	.21
$\hat{\rho}_{11}$	.27	.09	−.09	.18
$\hat{\rho}_{12}$	.37	.18	.17	.30
$\sigma(\hat{\rho}_1)$	.07	.12	.13	.11
$\bar{\Delta}$	−.00188	−.00111	−.00108	−.00321
$s(\Delta)$	.00234	.00258	.00169	.00195
$T-1$	222	73	64	83

TABLE 2. Autocorrelations of r_t: one-month bills

	1/53–7/71	1/53–2/59	3/59–7/64	8/64–7/71
$\hat{\rho}_1$	.09	.11	−.04	.10
$\hat{\rho}_2$	.13	.17	.01	.08
$\hat{\rho}_3$	−.02	−.02	−.20	−.01
$\hat{\rho}_4$	−.01	.01	−.06	−.10
$\hat{\rho}_5$	−.02	−.14	.00	.08
$\hat{\rho}_6$	−.02	−.18	.07	.07
$\hat{\rho}_7$	−.07	−.09	−.09	−.15
$\hat{\rho}_8$	.04	.05	−.23	.17
$\hat{\rho}_9$	.11	.11	.09	.04
$\hat{\rho}_{10}$	.10	.12	.07	−.02
$\hat{\rho}_{11}$	.03	.03	−.10	−.07
$\hat{\rho}_{12}$	.19	.16	.19	.15
$\sigma(\hat{\rho}_1)$	.07	.12	.13	.11
$\bar{r}$	.00074	.00038	.00111	.00075
$s(r)$	.00197	.00240	.00172	.00168
$T-1$	222	73	64	83

TABLE 3. Regression tests on one-month bills

$$\Delta_t = a_0 + a_1 R_t + e_t$$

Period	a_0	a_1	$s(a_0)$	$s(a_1)$	Coefficient of Determination	$s(e)$	$\hat{\rho}_1(e)$	$\hat{\rho}_2(e)$	$\hat{\rho}_3(e)$
1/53–7/71	.00070	−.98	.00030	.10	.29	.00196	.09	.13	−.02
1/53–2/59	.00116	−1.49	.00069	.42	.14	.00240	.09	.15	−.05
3/59–7/64	−.00038	−.33	.00095	.42	−.01	.00168	−.09	−.08	−.26
8/64–7/71	.00118	−1.10	.00083	.20	.26	.00167	.09	.06	−.02

In fact, especially for the longer periods 1/53–7/71 and 8/64–7/71, the sample autocorrelations of Δ_t for different lags are similar in size with individual estimates in the neighborhood of .30. This finding is discussed later when the behavior through time of Δ_t is studied in more detail.

B. Market Efficiency

Given that the equilibrium expected real return is constant through time, the market efficiency hypothesis says that the autocorrelations of the real return

$\tilde{r}_t$ are zero for all lags. The sample autocorrelations of r_t in Table 2 are close to zero. Recall from (5) that the real return r_t is approximately the rate of change in purchasing power Δ_t plus the nominal interest rate R_t. The evidence from the sample autocorrelations of Δ_t and r_t in Tables 1 and 2 is that adding R_t to Δ_t brings the substantial autocorrelations of Δ_t down to values close to zero. This is consistent with the hypothesis that R_t, the nominal rate set at $t-1$, summarizes completely the information about the expected value of $\tilde{\Delta}_t$ which is in the time-series of past values, $\Delta_{t-1}, \Delta_{t-2}, \ldots$.

Tables 3 and 4 give further support to the market efficiency hypothesis. When applied to (21), the hypothesis says that α_2, the coefficient of Δ_{t-1}, is zero, and the autocorrelations of the disturbance $\tilde{\varepsilon}_t$ are likewise zero for all lags. The residual autocorrelations in Table 4 are close to zero. The values of a_2, the sample estimates of α_2 in (21), are also small and always less than two standard errors from zero. When applied to (19), the market efficiency hypothesis is again that the autocorrelations of the disturbance $\tilde{\varepsilon}_t$ should be zero. The residual autocorrelations in Table 3 are close to zero. Moreover, comparing the results for the estimated versions of (19) and (21) in Tables 3 and 4 shows that dropping Δ_{t-1} from the model has almost no effect on the coefficients of determination, which is consistent with the implication of market efficiency that the value of R_t set at time $t-1$ summarizes any information in Δ_{t-1} about the expected value of $\tilde{\Delta}_t$.

Closer inspection of the tables seems to provide slight evidence against market efficiency. Except for the 3/59–7/64 period, the first-order sample autocorrelations of r_t, though small, are nevertheless all positive. The estimated regression coefficients a_2 of Δ_{t-1} in Table 4 are likewise small but generally positive, as are the first-order residual autocorrelations in Table 3. It is well to note,

TABLE 4. Regression tests on one-month bills

$$\Delta_t = a_0 + a_1 R_t + a_2 \Delta_{t-1} + e_t$$

Period	a_0	a_1	a_2	$s(a_0)$	$s(a_1)$	$s(a_2)$	Coefficient of Determination	$s(e)$	$\hat{\rho}_1(e)$	$\hat{\rho}_2(e)$	$\hat{\rho}_3(e)$
1/53–7/71	.00059	–.87	.11	.00030	.12	.07	.30	.00195	–.05	.13	–.04
1/53–2/59	.00108	–1.40	.11	.00069	.44	.11	.14	.00238	–.09	.17	–.07
3/59–7/64	–.00054	–.30	–.08	.00097	.42	.13	–.02	.00170	–.01	–.11	–.25
8/64–7/71	.00073	–.89	.14	.00084	.24	.11	.24	.00164	–.04	.05	–.01

however, that even after the upgrading of the *CPI* in 1953, there are some items whose prices are sampled less frequently than monthly; and items that are sampled monthly are not sampled at the same time during the month. Again, since prices of goods tend to move together, these quirks of the sampling process induce spurious positive autocorrelation in measured rates of change in purchasing power. Since an efficient market does not react to "information" that is recognizably spurious, the small apparent discrepancies from efficiency provide more "reasonable" evidence in favor of the efficiency hypothesis than if the data suggested that the hypothesis does perfectly well.

C. The Expected Real Return

The evidence is also consistent with the hypothesis that the expected real return on a one-month bill is constant during the 1953–71 period. First, the sample autocorrelations of the real return r_t are joint tests of the hypotheses that the market is efficient and that the expected real return is constant through time. Since the sample autocorrelations of r_t in Table 2 are close to zero, the evidence is consistent with a world where both hypotheses are valid.

The regression coefficient estimates for (19) and (21) in Tables 3 and 4 are, however, more direct evidence on the hypothesis that the expected value of $\tilde{r}_t$ is constant. The hypothesis implies that in (19) and (21), the intercept α_0 is the constant expected real return $E(\tilde{r})$ and the coefficient α_1 of R_t is -1.0. The coefficient estimates a_1 of α_1 in (19) and (21) are always well within two standard errors of -1.0. And statistical considerations aside, the estimate $a_1 = -.98$ for (19) for the overall period 1/53–7/71 is impressively close to -1.0. Given estimates a_1 of α_1 in (19) and (21) that are close to -1.0, and given the earlier observation that the estimates a_2 of α_2 in (21) are close to zero, equation (5) and the least squares formulas guarantee that the intercept estimates a_0 for (19) and (21) in Tables 3 and 4 are close to the sample means of the real return in Table 2.

Finally, the sample autocorrelations of r_t in Table 2 and the regression coefficient estimates a_0 and a_1 in Tables 3 and 4 are consistent with the world of equation (13) where the equilibrium expected real return is constant and all variation through time in the nominal interest rate R_t mirrors variation in the market's assessment of the expected value of $\tilde{\Delta}_t$. There is, however, another interesting way to check this conclusion. From the discussion of (22) it follows that the standard deviation of the real return r_t is the standard deviation of the disturbance $\tilde{\varepsilon}_t$ in (19) when the coefficients α_0 and α_1 in (19) are constrained to have the values $\alpha_0 = E(r)$ and $\alpha_1 = -1.0$ that are appropriate under the hypothesis that the expected real return is constant through time. If this hypothesis is incorrect, letting the data choose values of α_0 and α_1, as in Table 3, should produce lower estimates of the disturbance variance than when the values of the coefficients are constrained. But the results indicate that, especially for the longer periods, not only are the values of $s(r)$ in Table 2 almost identical to the values of $s(e)$ in Table 3, but the sample autocorrelations of r_t and e_t are almost identical. In short, the hypothesis that the expected real return is constant fits the data so well that the residuals from the estimated version of (19) are more or less identical to the deviations of r_t from its sample mean.

V. THE BEHAVIOR OF $\tilde{\Delta}_t$

The results allow some interesting insights into the behavior through time of $\tilde{\Delta}_t$. The rate of change in purchasing power can always be written as

$$\tilde{\Delta}_t = E(\tilde{\Delta}_t \mid \phi_{t-1}) + \tilde{\varepsilon}_t \qquad (24)$$

Since the evidence is consistent with the hypothesis that the expected real return is constant through time, we can substitute (14) into (24) to get

$$\tilde{\Delta}_t = E(\tilde{r}) - R_t + \tilde{\varepsilon}_t \qquad (25)$$

The conclusion drawn from the residual autocorrelations in Table 3 and the sample autocorrelations of r_t in Table 2 is that the disturbance $\tilde{\varepsilon}_t$ in (25) is uncorrelated through time. The time-series of past values of $\tilde{\varepsilon}_t$ is no real help in predicting the next value. Quite the opposite sort of behavior characterizes the expected value of $\tilde{\Delta}_t$ in (24). Since, as stated in (25), variation in R_t through time mirrors variation in the expected value of $\tilde{\Delta}_t$, the time-series properties of R_t are the time-series properties of $E(\tilde{\Delta}_t \mid \phi_{t-1})$. For the 1/53–7/71 period, the first four sample autocorrelations of R_t are all in excess of .93, and only one of the first twenty-four is less than .9. Sample autocorrelations close to 1.0 are consistent with the representation of R_t as a random walk. Thus in contrast with the evidence for the disturbance $\tilde{\varepsilon}_t$ in (24), the autocorrelations of R_t indicate that there is much persistence through time in the level of R_t and thus in the level of $E(\tilde{\Delta}_t \mid \phi_{t-1})$. The time-series of past values of R_t has substantial information about future values.

This discussion helps explain the behavior of the sample autocorrelations of $\tilde{\Delta}_t$ in Table 1. As stated in (24), $\tilde{\Delta}_t$ has two components. One component of $\tilde{\Delta}_t$, its expected value, behaves like a random walk. The other component of $\tilde{\Delta}_t$, the disturbance $\tilde{\varepsilon}_t$, is essentially random noise. The autocorrelations of its expected value cause the autocorrelations of $\tilde{\Delta}_t$ to likewise have approximately the same magnitude for different lags. The uncorrelated disturbance $\tilde{\varepsilon}_t$, however, causes the autocorrelations of $\tilde{\Delta}_t$, unlike those of R_t, to be far below 1.0.

The sample autocorrelations of R suggest that the expected value of $\tilde{\Delta}_t$ behaves through time much like a random walk. The sample autocorrelations of the month-to-month changes in R_t, shown in Table 5, suggest, however, that we can improve on this description of the behavior of $E(\tilde{\Delta}_t \mid \phi_{t-1})$. For example, the first-order autocorrelations of $R_t - R_{t-1}$ are consistently negative. From the first-order autocorrelations for the longer periods, the change in R_t might reasonably be represented as

$$\tilde{R}_{t+1} - R_t = -.25\,(R_t - R_{t-1}) + \tilde{\eta}_t \qquad (26)$$

Thus the process that generates the nominal rate is no longer just a random walk. The process is slightly regressive so that on average the change in the expected inflation rate from one month to the next reverses itself by about 25 percent.

TABLE 5. Autocorrelations of $R_t - R_{t-1}$

	1/53–7/71	1/53–2/59	3/59–7/64	8/64–7/71
$\hat{\rho}_1$	−.25	−.14	−.41	−.18
$\hat{\rho}_2$	.06	.05	.07	.06
$\hat{\rho}_3$	.01	.07	−.03	.00
$\hat{\rho}_4$	.15	.23	.08	.18
$\hat{\rho}_5$	−.03	−.04	.07	−.13
$\hat{\rho}_6$	−.06	.01	−.12	−.01
$\hat{\rho}_7$	−.13	−.35	−.11	−.05
$\hat{\rho}_8$	.10	.17	.13	.02
$\hat{\rho}_9$	.06	−.03	−.06	.18
$\hat{\rho}_{10}$	−.24	−.26	−.07	−.42
$\hat{\rho}_{11}$	−.05	−.16	−.10	.08
$\hat{\rho}_{12}$	.09	.13	.06	.04
$\sigma(\hat{\rho}_1)$	.07	.12	.13	.11
$\overline{dR}$	.00001	.00000	.00001	.00001
$s(dR)$	.00032	.00028	.00035	.00033
$T-1$	221	72	63	82

VI. RESULTS FOR BILLS WITH LONGER MATURITIES

The presentation of theory and tests of bill market efficiency has concentrated so far on one-month bills and one-month rates of change in the purchasing power of money. As far as the theory is concerned, the interval of time over which the variables are measured is arbitrary. In testing the theory, the fact that the *CPI* is only reported monthly limits us to tests based on intervals that cover an integral number of months. Tests are presented now for one- to six-month intervals. Thus, in these tests the interval from $t - 1$ to t is one, or two, ..., or six months; R_t is the sure one-, or two-, ..., or six-month nominal rate of interest from $t - 1$ to t on a bill with one, or two, ..., or six months to maturity at $t - 1$; and the real return $\tilde{r}_t$ and the rate of change in the purchasing power of money $\tilde{\Delta}_t$ are likewise measured for nonoverlapping one- to six-month intervals.

Since the theory and tests are the same for bills of all maturities, the market efficiency hypothesis is that in setting the nominal rate R_t at time $t - 1$, the market correctly uses any information about the expected value of $\tilde{\Delta}_t$ which is in the time-series of past values $\Delta_{t-1}, \Delta_{t-2}, \ldots$. The model of market equilibrium on which the tests are based is the assumption that the expected real returns on bills with one to six months to maturity are constant through time. The tests of these propositions are in Tables 6 to 9, and the tests are the same as those for one-month bills in Tables 1 to 4. Results for the one- to three-month versions of the variables are shown for the 1/53–7/71 and 3/59–7/71 periods. Since the data for four- to six-month bills are only available beginning in March 1959, results for the four- to six-month versions of the variables are only shown for the 3/59–7/71 period.

Implicit in the tests of market efficiency is the assumption that past rates of change in purchasing power have information about expected future rates of change. The autocorrelations of Δ_t in Table 6 support this assumption. The autocorrelations are large for all six intervals used to measure Δ_t. But consistent with the hypotheses that the market is efficient and that the equilibrium expected real returns on bills with different maturities are constant through time, the autocorrelations of the real returns shown in Table 7 are close to zero. Remember from (5) that the n-month real return on an n-month bill is approximately the n-month rate of change in purchasing power plus the n-month nominal return on the bill. Thus the evidence from the autocorrelations of Δ_t and r_t in Tables 6 and 7 is that when R_t is added to Δ_t, the substantial autocorrelations of Δ_t drop to values close to zero. This is consistent with a world where R_t, the n-month nominal rate set at $t-1$, summarizes all the information about the expected value of the rate of change in purchasing power over the n months from $t-1$ to t which is in the time-series of past rates of changes in purchasing power.

The model gets further support from the regression tests in Table 8. Consistent with the hypothesis that expected real returns are constant through time, the estimates a_1 of α_1 in (19) in Table 8 are all impressively close to -1.0. Consistent with the hypothesis that the market is efficient, the residual autocorrelations in Table 8 are close to zero for bills of all maturities.

The only hint of evidence against the model is in the estimates of (21) for five-and six-month bills in Table 9. As predicted by the model, the values of a_1 and a_2 for one- to four-month bills are close to -1.0 and 0.0, and the residual autocorrelations are close to 0.0. For the five- and six-month bills, however, the values of a_1 are rather far from -1.0 and the values of a_2 are rather far from 0.0. In conducting so many different tests for so many different bills, however, some re-

TABLE 6. Autocorrelations of Δ_t: one- to six-month intervals

| | 1/53–7/71 | | | 3/59–7/71 | | | | | |
| | Interval | | | Interval | | | | | |
	1	2	3	1	2	3	4	5	6
$\hat{\rho}_1$	.36	.50	.53	.40	.55	.58	.67	.84	.86
$\hat{\rho}_2$	.37	.39	.57	.39	.50	.74	.72	.78	.83
$\hat{\rho}_3$	.27	.43	.59	.32	.66	.64	.71	.74	.74
$\hat{\rho}_4$	.30	.45	.54	.36	.57	.70	.71	.73	.81
$\hat{\rho}_5$	.29	.52	.48	.43	.58	.66	.63	.76	.90
$\hat{\rho}_6$	.29	.41	.38	.44	.56	.65	.76	.77	1.03[a]
$\hat{\rho}_7$	.25	.40	.39	.34	.53	.65	.61	.89	.98
$\hat{\rho}_8$	.34	.32	.27	.40	.60	.58	.73	.83	.95
$\hat{\rho}_9$	.36	.36	.32	.44	.55	.73	.70	.94	.45
$\hat{\rho}_{10}$	.34	.30	.08	.40	.49	.42	.65	.79	.32
$\hat{\rho}_{11}$	.27	.28	.35	.34	.54	.84	.54	.14	−.07
$\hat{\rho}_{12}$	.37	.28	.29	.47	.56	.55	.82	.11	.23
$\sigma(\hat{\rho}_i)$	.07	.10	.12	.08	.12	.14	.17	.19	.21
$\overline{\Delta}$	−.00188	−.00368	−.00550	−.00228	−.00445	−.00656	−.00881	−.01105	−.01319
$s(\Delta)$	.00234	.00386	.00521	.00211	.00348	.00485	.00628	.00735	.00857
$T-1$	222	110	73	148	73	49	36	29	24

[a] The sample autocorrelations are estimated as linear regression coefficients. Thus the estimates can be greater than 1.0.

sults are likely to turn out badly even though the model is a valid approximation to the world. This argument gains force from the fact that the autocorrelations of the real returns in Table 7 and the estimates of (19) in Table 8 do not produce evidence for five- and six-month bills that contradicts the model.

VII. INTEREST RATES AS PREDICTORS OF INFLATION: COMPARISONS WITH THE RESULTS OF OTHERS

In a world where equilibrium expected real returns on bills are constant through time, then, aside from the additive constant $E(\tilde{r})$ in (13), the nominal rate R_t set at time $t-1$ is in effect the market's prediction of the rate of change in purchasing power from $t-1$ to t. The coefficients of determination in Table 8 indicate that variation through time in these predictions accounts for 30 percent of the variance of subsequently observed values of Δ_t in the case of one-month bills, and the proportion of the sample variance of Δ_t accounted for by R_t increases to about 65 percent for five- and six-month bills. Thus, nominal interest rates observed at $t-1$ contain nontrivial information about the rate of change in purchasing power from $t-1$ to t. Moreover, the evidence on market efficiency suggests that the market's prediction of $\tilde{\Delta}_t$ is the best that can be made on the basis of information available at time $t-1$; or, more precisely, it is the best that can be done on the basis of information in past rates of change in purchasing power.

As noted earlier, the results reported here differ substantially from those of the rest of the literature on interest rates and inflation. In line with the early work of Fisher, the almost universal finding in other studies is that the market does not perform efficiently in predicting inflation. But the earlier studies, including, of course, Fisher's, are based primarily on pre-1953 data, and the negative results on market efficiency may to a large extent just reflect poor commodity price data. By the same token, the success of the tests reported here is probably to a nonnegligible extent a consequence of the availability of good data beginning in 1953.

Poor commodity price data also probably explain why the empirical literature is replete with evidence in support of the so-called Gibson Paradox—the proposition that there is a positive relationship between the nominal interest rate and the level of commodity prices, rather than the relationship between the interest rate and the rate of change in prices posited by Fisher.[4] With a

---

4. For a discussion of the Gibson Paradox and a review of previous evidence, see Roll. A more recent study is Thomas Sargent.

TABLE 7. Sample autocorrelations of r_t: one- to six-month bills

	1/53–7/71 Bill			3/59–7/71 Bill					
	1	2	3	1	2	3	4	5	6
$\hat{\rho}_1$	.09	.15	.00	.05	.03	−.16	−.17	.02	.07
$\hat{\rho}_2$	.13	−.09	.02	.05	−.15	.16	−.06	−.13	.07
$\hat{\rho}_3$	−.02	−.03	.08	−.08	.18	−.14	.20	−.03	−.05
$\hat{\rho}_4$	−.01	.01	.26	−.07	−.06	.25	.14	.03	.26
$\hat{\rho}_5$	−.02	.18	.16	.06	.00	.11	−.08	.15	.11
$\hat{\rho}_6$	−.02	.10	−.09	.10	.10	.04	.30	−.19	.43
$\hat{\rho}_7$	−.07	.15	.06	−.10	.07	.06	−.22	.33	−.04
$\hat{\rho}_8$	.04	−.01	−.01	.00	.14	.02	.17	−.02	.49
$\hat{\rho}_9$	.11	.06	.08	.09	.08	.18	.16	.25	−.60
$\hat{\rho}_{10}$	.10	.00	−.32	.05	−.07	−.33	−.09	.04	.27
$\hat{\rho}_{11}$	.03	.04	.11	−.04	.08	.36	−.02	−.69	.32
$\hat{\rho}_{12}$	.19	.09	.19	.20	.20	.10	.32	.13	.07
$\sigma(\hat{\rho}_1)$	.07	.10	.12	.08	.12	.14	.17	.19	.21
$\bar{r}$	.00074	.00185	.00306	.00090	.00224	.00373	.00514	.00706	.00882
$s(r)$	.00197	.00292	.00371	.00169	.00236	.00307	.00379	.00375	.00444
$T-1$	222	110	73	148	73	49	36	29	24

TABLE 8. Regression tests on one- to six-month bills

$$\Delta_t = a_0 + a_1 R_t + e_t$$

Period	Bill	a_0	a_1	$s(a_0)$	$s(a_1)$	Coefficient of Determination	$s(e)$	$\hat{\rho}_1(e)$	$\hat{\rho}_2(e)$	$\hat{\rho}_3(e)$
1/53–7/71	1	.00070	−.98	.00030	.10	.29	.00196	.09	.13	−.02
	2	.00161	−.96	.00066	.11	.42	.00296	.15	−.08	−.03
	3	.00228	−.92	.00105	.11	.48	.00380	.00	.03	.10
3/59–7/71	1	.00120	−1.09	.00041	.12	.36	.00169	.04	.05	−.08
	2	.00269	−1.08	.00086	.12	.52	.00245	.02	−.16	.14
	3	.00397	−1.03	.00145	.13	.55	.00330	−.16	.12	−.16
	4	.00543	−1.03	.00216	.14	.58	.00413	−.18	−.10	.14
	5	.00635	−.97	.00236	.12	.68	.00416	.01	−.10	−.02
	6	.00879	−1.01	.00344	.14	.65	.00505	.01	−.01	−.11

TABLE 9. Regression tests on one- to six-month bills

$$\Delta_t = a_0 + a_1 R_t + a_2 \Delta_{t-1} + e_t$$

Period	Bill	a_0	a_1	a_2	$s(a_0)$	$s(a_1)$	$s(a_2)$	Coefficient of Determination	$s(e)$	$\hat{\rho}_1(e)$	$\hat{\rho}_2(e)$	$\hat{\rho}_3(e)$
1/53–7/71	1	.00059	−.87	.11	.00030	.12	.07	.30	.00195	−.05	.13	−.04
	2	.00115	−.78	.17	.00064	.13	.09	.44	.00280	.03	−.06	.02
	3	.00173	−.79	.11	.00107	.15	.12	.48	.00372	−.06	.07	.05
3/59–7/71	1	.00109	−1.01	.07	.00042	.14	.08	.35	.00169	−.03	.05	−.07
	2	.00252	−1.02	.05	.00094	.18	.12	.51	.00248	−.02	−.16	.15
	3	.00390	−1.06	−.04	.00169	.23	.17	.53	.00334	−.10	.11	−.17
	4	.00520	−.97	.07	.00261	.26	.20	.57	.00423	−.23	−.06	.12
	5	.00359	−.57	.40	.00301	.27	.23	.71	.00404	−.13	−.08	−.02
	6	.00263	−.39	.58	.00406	.28	.23	.72	.00461	−.29	.18	−.32

poor price index, the Fisherian relationship between the nominal interest rate and the true inflation rate can be obscured by noise and by spurious autocorrelation in measured inflation rates. But over long periods of time—and the Gibson Paradox is usually posited as a long-run phenomenon—even a poor index picks up general movements in prices. Thus if inflations and deflations tend to persist (an implication of the evidence presented here that $E(\tilde{\Delta}_t \mid \phi_{t-1})$ is close to a random walk), there may well appear to be a relationship between the level of interest rates and the measured level of prices, which merely reflects the more fundamental Fisherian relationship between the interest rate and the rate of change of prices that is obscured by poor data. In this study, which is based on the relatively clean data of the 1953–71 period, the Fisherian relationship shows up clearly.

VIII. CONCLUSIONS

The two major conclusions of the paper are as follows. First, during the 1953–71 period, the bond market seems to be efficient in the sense that in setting one-to six-month nominal rates of interest, the market correctly uses all the information about future inflation rates that is in time-series of past inflation rates. Second, one cannot reject the hypothesis that equilibrium expected real returns on one-to six-month bills are constant during the period. When combined with the conclusion that the market is efficient, this means that one also cannot reject the hypothesis that all variation through time in one- to six-month nominal rates of interest mirrors variation in correctly assessed one- to six-month expected rates of change in purchasing power.

REFERENCES

E. F. Fama, "Efficient Capital Markets: A Review of Theory and Empirical Work," *J. Finance,* May 1970, *25,* 383–417.

I. Fisher, *The Theory of Interest,* New York 1930, reprinted A. M. Kelley, 1965.

R. Roll, "Interest Rates on Monetary Assets and Commodity Price Index Changes," *J. Finance,* May 1972, *27,* 251–77.

T. J. Sargent, "Interest Rates and Prices in the Long Run: A Study of the Gibson Paradox," *J. Money, Credit, Banking,* Feb. 1973, *5,* 385–449.

U.S. Bureau of Labor Statistics, *Handbook of Methods for Surveys and Studies,* Bull. 1458, Washington 1971.

Salomon Brothers, "United States Treasury Securities," New York, issued daily.

FORWARD RATES AS PREDICTORS
OF FUTURE SPOT RATES

. . .

Eugene F. Fama

When adjusted for variation through time in expected premiums, the forward rates of interest that are implicit in Treasury Bill prices contain assessments of expected future spot rates of interest that are about as good as those that can be obtained from the information in past spot rates. Moreover, in setting bill prices and forward rates, the market reacts appropriately to the negative auto-correlation in monthly changes in the spot rate and to changes through time in the degree of this autocorrelation. This evidence is consistent with the market efficiency proposition that in setting bill prices, the market correctly uses the information in past spot rates.

1. INTRODUCTION

Define v_{nt} as the price at the end of month t of a no-coupon bond that has n months to maturity at (the end of month) t and pays \$1 for certain at $t + n$. Define R_{t+1}, the one month continuously compounded spot rate of interest from t to $t + 1$, set in the market at t, as

$$v_{1t} = \exp(-R_{t+1}). \tag{1}$$

The price v_{nt} can then be written

$$v_{nt} = \exp(-R_{t+1} - F_{t+2,t} - \ldots - F_{t+n,t}) \tag{2}$$

where $F_{t+\tau, t}$, the forward rate for month $t + \tau$ set in the market at t, is

$$F_{t+\tau,t} = \ln(v_{\tau-1,t} / v_{\tau t}) \tag{3}$$

Reprinted with permission from the *Journal of Financial Economics* 3, no. 4 (October 1976): 361–77. © 1976 by Elsevier Limited.

This research is supported by a grant from the National Science Foundation. I have had helpful comments from Nicholas Gonedes, Michael Jensen, Reuben Kessel, Richard Roll and Michael Rozeff.

It is usually assumed that $F_{t+\tau, t}$ contains the market's prediction at t of $\tilde{R}_{t+\tau}$, the spot rate for month $t + \tau$ to be set at $t + \tau - 1$.[1] If this is true, then forward rates computed directly from prices observed at t can be used to check how well the market uses information available at t to predict future spot rates. This market efficiency question is the subject of this paper. Specifically, the tests are concerned with whether forward rates contain predictions of future spot rates at least as good as those that can be obtained from the information in past spot rates.[2]

2. A FIRST LOOK

Table 1 shows summary statistics for the difference between $F_{t+\tau, t}$, the forward rate for month $t + \tau$ set in the market at time t, and the subsequently observed spot rate $R_{t+\tau}$. The underlying data are monthly prices of one to six month U.S. Treasury Bills from the quote sheets of Salomon Brothers. The estimate of v_{nt} is the average of the bid and asked prices on the last trading day of month t for the bill that matures closest to the end of month $t + n$. For one to three month bills, the sampling period is January 1953 to June 1974. Data on four to six month bills are only available beginning in March 1959. For each value of τ, the summary statistics shown in table 1 for the time series of monthly values of $F_{t+\tau, t} - R_{t+\tau}$ are means, standard deviations, t-statistics (ratios of means to their standard errors), the first three autocorrelations ($\hat{\rho}_1$, $\hat{\rho}_2$ and $\hat{\rho}_3$), and the sample size T.

The choice of periods in table 1 reflects two considerations. First, results are shown for subperiods as well as for overall periods. Second, the evidence of Fama (1975, 1976b) indicates that the prediction of a future spot rate is largely the assessment of a future expected inflation rate. Beginning in August 1971 the U.S. government engaged in a series of attempts to fix prices. During the period of controls, reported price changes are not good measures of changes in purchasing costs. In the presence of inaccurate data, it may be difficult for the market to assess future expected inflation rates. To bypass problems this might

---

1. The tilde indicates that $\tilde{R}_{t+\tau}$ is a random variable at any time prior to $t + \tau - 1$. Tildes are used in general to denote random variables. When referring to observed or sample values of a random variable, the tilde is dropped.

2. For a discussion of market efficiency and a review of the empirical literature, see Fama (1976a, chs. 5 and 6). Roll (1970) provides the first tests of market efficiency in the Treasury Bill market.

TABLE 1. Summary statistics for forward rate minus subsequently observed spot rate

Period	τ	Mean	Std. dev.	$F_{t+\tau,t} - R_{t+\tau}$ t-Stat.	$\hat{\rho}_1$	$\hat{\rho}_2$	$\hat{\rho}_3$	T
Pre-controls								
1/53–7/71	2	0.00028	0.000343	11.99	0.31	0.19	0.20	223
1/53–7/71	3	0.00044	0.000478	13.73	0.59	0.30	0.25	223
3/59–7/71	2	0.00030	0.000365	10.12	0.34	0.21	0.25	149
3/59–7/71	3	0.00048	0.000500	11.65	0.58	0.35	0.31	149
3/59–7/71	4	0.00041	0.000537	9.29	0.57	0.34	0.21	149
3/59–7/71	5	0.00066	0.000774	10.46	0.59	0.55	0.41	149
3/59–7/71	6	0.00073	0.000857	10.40	0.67	0.53	0.44	149
Controls								
1/53–6/74	2	0.00025	0.000357	11.30	0.29	0.15	0.19	258
1/53–6/74	3	0.00041	0.000508	13.05	0.52	0.25	0.19	257
3/59–6/74	2	0.00026	0.000381	9.38	0.31	0.16	0.23	184
3/59–6/74	3	0.00043	0.000538	10.90	0.50	0.27	0.23	183
3/59–6/74	4	0.00038	0.000583	8.91	0.48	0.30	0.14	182
3/59–6/74	5	0.00060	0.000814	9.88	0.55	0.51	0.39	181
3/59–6/74	6	0.00068	0.000912	10.06	0.65	0.50	0.35	180
Shorter subperiods								
1/53–2/59	2	0.00022	0.000289	6.58	0.18	0.09	0.01	74
1/53–2/59	3	0.00036	0.000425	7.38	0.62	0.14	0.04	74
3/59–7/64	2	0.00033	0.000360	7.36	0.15	0.20	0.59	65
3/59–7/64	3	0.00050	0.000458	8.77	0.67	0.59	0.69	65
3/59–7/64	4	0.00037	0.000460	6.48	0.51	0.52	0.37	65
3/59–7/64	5	0.00074	0.000699	8.50	0.67	0.69	0.71	65
3/59–7/64	6	0.00091	0.000851	8.60	0.80	0.69	0.68	65
8/64–5/69	2	0.00023	0.000271	6.52	0.30	0.24	0.09	58
8/64–5/69	3	0.00035	0.000395	6.83	0.53	0.09	−0.08	58
8/64–5/69	4	0.00035	0.000431	6.22	0.49	0.27	0.07	58
8/64–5/69	5	0.00045	0.000539	6.41	0.46	0.37	0.31	58
8/64–5/69	6	0.00039	0.000676	4.43	0.39	0.22	0.06	58
6/69–6/74	2	0.00022	0.000477	3.67	0.39	0.10	0.07	61
6/69–6/74	3	0.00044	0.000710	4.80	0.40	0.16	0.11	60
6/69–6/74	4	0.00043	0.000800	4.16	0.46	0.24	0.08	59
6/69–6/74	5	0.00059	0.001101	4.06	0.50	0.46	0.24	58
6/69–6/74	6	0.00073	0.001105	4.96	0.62	0.43	0.18	57

cause, results are shown separately for pre-controls periods and for periods that include the price controls.

To judge how well the forward rate $F_{t+\tau, t}$ predicts the future spot rate $\tilde{R}_{t+\tau}$, a standard of comparison is needed. One possibility is a martingale model where the prediction is that $\tilde{R}_{t+\tau}$ will be equal to the current rate R_{t+1}. If the spot rate follows a martingale with respect to its own past values, then at time t the conditional expected value of any future spot rate is

$$E_t (\tilde{R}_{t+\tau}| R_{t+1}, R_t,...) = R_{t+1} \qquad (4)$$

In this world, the prediction that $\tilde{R}_{t+\tau}$ will be equal to R_{t+1} makes the best possible use of the information in the past values of the spot rate.

Summary statistics for the prediction errors of the martingale model are in table 2. With but one exception, the standard deviations of these prediction errors are less than the corresponding standard deviations of forward rates minus subsequently observed spot rates in table 1. This suggests that the martingale model, which simply predicts that the interest rate will remain unchanged

TABLE 2. Summary statistics for the change in the spot rate across τ months

$$R_{t+\tau} - R_{t+1}$$

Period	τ	Mean	Std. dev.	t-Stat.	$\hat{\rho}_1$	$\hat{\rho}_2$	$\hat{\rho}_3$	T
Pre-controls								
1/53–7/71	2	0.00001	0.000321	0.54	−0.24	0.06	0.01	223
1/53–7/71	3	0.00002	0.000396	0.82	0.37	−0.09	0.15	223
3/59–7/71	2	0.00002	0.000340	0.56	−0.28	0.07	−0.01	149
3/59–7/71	3	0.00003	0.000410	0.81	0.34	−0.13	0.11	149
3/59–7/71	4	0.00004	0.000479	0.96	0.49	0.34	−0.01	149
3/59–7/71	5	0.00005	0.000539	1.02	0.64	0.49	0.29	149
3/59–7/71	6	0.00005	0.000614	1.04	0.67	0.54	0.35	149
Controls								
1/53–6/74	2	0.00002	0.000336	0.89	−0.16	0.02	0.00	258
1/53–6/74	3	0.00004	0.000436	1.41	0.42	−0.07	0.09	257
3/59–6/74	2	0.00002	0.000356	0.93	−0.16	0.01	−0.02	184
3/59–6/74	3	0.00005	0.000462	1.46	0.41	−0.10	0.05	183
3/59–6/74	4	0.00008	0.000546	1.93	0.57	0.34	0.02	182
3/59–6/74	5	0.00010	0.000619	2.27	0.71	0.52	0.30	181
3/59–6/74	6	0.00013	0.000703	2.42	0.75	0.58	0.38	180

(*Continued*)

TABLE 2. (Continued)

Period	τ	Mean	Std. dev.	t-Stat.	$\hat{\rho}_1$	$\hat{\rho}_2$	$\hat{\rho}_3$	T
Shorter subperiods								
1/53–2/59	2	0.00000	0.000280	0.12	−0.14	0.05	0.07	74
1/53–2/59	3	0.00001	0.000368	0.24	0.46	0.02	0.25	74
3/59–7/64	2	0.00001	0.000349	0.26	−0.42	0.07	−0.03	65
3/59–7/64	3	0.00002	0.000379	0.49	0.21	−0.26	0.08	65
3/59–7/64	4	0.00003	0.000425	0.65	0.31	0.27	−0.09	65
3/59–7/64	5	0.00004	0.000459	0.76	0.47	0.44	0.29	65
3/59–7/64	6	0.00005	0.000510	0.86	0.57	0.50	0.28	65
8/64–5/69	2	0.00004	0.000283	0.98	−0.30	−0.08	0.01	58
8/64–5/69	3	0.00008	0.000333	1.77	0.25	−0.33	0.03	58
8/64–5/69	4	0.00012	0.000367	2.48	0.43	0.20	−0.20	58
8/64–5/69	5	0.00017	0.000405	3.11	0.58	0.32	0.21	58
8/64–5/69	6	0.00022	0.000468	3.53	0.58	0.42	0.31	58
6/69–6/74	2	0 00003	0.000424	0.49	0.08	−0.00	−0.03	61
6/69–6/74	3	0.00005	0.000627	0.64	0.53	0.02	0.03	60
6/69–6/74	4	0.00009	0.000771	0.85	0.69	0.38	0.08	59
6/69–6/74	5	0.00011	0.000894	0.95	0.81	0.57	0.31	58
6/69–6/74	6	0.00012	0.001022	0.87	0.84	0.65	0.43	57

does better in predicting future spot rates than forward rates. The finding that forward rates are not accurate predictors of future spot rates is consistent with the evidence of Macauley (1938), Hickman (1942) and Culbertson (1957).

The market efficiency issue is, however, not yet closed. The forward rate $F_{t+\tau, t}$ contains the market's prediction of $\tilde{R}_{t+\tau}$, but forward rates also include expected premiums. We shall find that when forward rates are adjusted for variation through time in expected premiums, they provide predictors of future spot rates as good as those obtained from the information in the time series of past spot rates.

3. FORWARD RATES AND EXPECTED PREMIUMS

The return from t to $t+1$ on a bill with τ months to maturity at t is

$$\tilde{H}_{\tau, t+1} = \ln(\tilde{v}_{\tau-1, t+1}/v_{\tau t}). \tag{5}$$

The premium in the bill's return is defined as

$$\tilde{P}_{\tau,t+1} = \tilde{H}_{\tau,t+1} - R_{t+1}. \tag{6}$$

Thus the premium is the difference between the return at $t+1$ on a bill that had τ months to maturity at t and the return at $t+1$ on a bill that had one month to maturity at t.

Fama (1976b) shows that the price at time t of a bill with n months to maturity can be written

$$v_{nt} = \exp(-E_t(\tilde{H}_{n,t+1}) - E_t(\tilde{H}_{n-1,t+2}) - \ldots \\ - E_t(\tilde{H}_{2,t+n-1}) - E_t(\tilde{R}_{t+n})) \tag{7}$$

$$= \exp(-[E_t(\tilde{P}_{t,t+1}) + R_{t+1}] - [E_t(\tilde{P}_{n-1,t+2}) + E_t(\tilde{R}_{t+1})]1 - \ldots \\ - [E_t(\tilde{P}_{2,t+n-1}) + E_t(\tilde{R}_{t+n-1})] - E_t(\tilde{R}_{t+n})). \tag{8}$$

In eq. (7) the price v_{nt} is the present value of the terminal \$1 to be received at $t+n$, where the discount rates are the current expected values of the successive returns on the bill in each of the remaining months of its life. In (8) these expected future returns are broken into the corresponding expected future spot rates and the expected premiums in the returns on the bill during the remaining periods of its life.

When the relevant versions of (8) are substituted for the prices in (3), the expression for the forward rate becomes

$$F_{t+\tau,t} = E_t(\tilde{P}_{\tau,t+1}) + [E_t(\tilde{P}_{\tau-1,t+2}) - E_t(\tilde{P}_{\tau-1,t+1})] + \ldots \\ + [E_t(\tilde{P}_{2,t+\tau-1}) - E_t(\tilde{P}_{2,t+\tau-2})] + E_t(\tilde{R}_{t+\tau}). \tag{9}$$

Thus the forward rate for month $t+\tau$, observed at t, indeed contains $E_t(\tilde{R}_{t+\tau})$, the market's assessment at t of the expected value of the spot rate for month $t+\tau$. However, $F_{t+\tau,t}$ also includes other terms. First there is $E_t(\tilde{P}_{\tau,t+1})$, the expected value at t of the premium in the return from t to $t+1$ on a bill with τ months to maturity at t. Then, for $\tau > 2$, there are the bracketed terms in (9), each of which is the difference between the expected values at t of the premiums to be observed in two successive future months on bills that will have the same number of months to maturity at the beginning of the two successive future months.

Any variation through time in the expected premiums in (9) tends to obscure the power of the forward rate $F_{t+\tau,t}$ as a predictor of the spot rate $\tilde{R}_{t+\tau}$. To focus on the predictive power of the forward rate, we shall first present a model for the expected premium $E_t(\tilde{P}_{\tau,t+1})$ and then use this model to net variation in $E_t(\tilde{P}_{\tau,t+1})$ out of the time series of the forward rate $F_{t+\tau,t}$.

4. ISOLATING VARIATION IN EXPECTED PREMIUMS

4.1. Expected Premiums and Uncertainty about Future Expected Inflation Rates

In Fama (1976b) I argue that variation through time in the expected premium $E_t(\tilde{P}_{\tau,t+1})$ is associated with variation in uncertainty about future expected inflation rates. On the basis of evidence in Fama (1975), I also argue that at least during the 1953–71 period, the expected real return on a one month bill is nearly constant through time so that the uncertainty of future expected inflation rates is the uncertainty of future expected spot rates. After some experimentation, which is discussed briefly later, the measure of the uncertainty of expected spot rates chosen, call it σ_{t+1}, is the average of the absolute values of the monthly changes in the spot rate during the year before month $t+1$ and during the year following month $t+1$. If the relationship between the expected premium $E_t(\tilde{P}_{\tau,t+1})$ and σ_{t+1} is linear, it can then be estimated with a time series regression of the premium $P_{\tau,t+1}$ on σ_{t+1}.

Table 4 shows results from such regressions. For purposes of comparison and perspective, table 3 shows summary statistics for the Treasury Bill premiums themselves. In both tables 3 and 4, the premium $P_{\tau,t+1}$ is, as in (6), the difference between $H_{\tau,t+1}$ (the continuously compounded return for month $t+1$ on a bill with τ months to maturity at t) and R_{t+1} (the spot rate for month $t+1$ set in the market at t). For any given τ, a time series of the premium $P_{\tau,t+1}$ is generated by in effect purchasing a different τ month bill at the end of each month t and selling it at the end of month $t+1$. This generates the time series of returns $H_{\tau,t+1}$, from which one then subtracts R_{t+1} to get the time series of the premium $P_{\tau,t+1}$.

The results in table 3 indicate that longer-term bills generally have larger expected returns than shorter-term bills. The average premiums are always large relative to their standard errors, and they generally increase with maturity τ. Moreover, comparison of tables 3 and 1 shows that for given τ the average value of the premium $P_{\tau,t+1}$ for any given sampling period is quite close to the

TABLE 3. Summary statistics for the premiums in the returns on two to six month bills

Period	Bill (τ)	Mean	Std. dev.	$P_{\tau, t+1}$ t-Stat.	$\hat{\rho}_1$	$\hat{\rho}_2$	$\hat{\rho}_3$	T
Pre-controls								
1/53–7/71	2	0.00027	0.00031	13.15	0.38	0.20	0.17	223
1/53–7/71	3	0.00044	0.00056	11.67	0.31	0.14	0.20	223
3/59–7/71	2	0.00030	0.00034	10.96	0.40	0.22	0.19	149
3/59–7/71	3	0.00047	0.00058	10.05	0.33	0.18	0.29	149
3/59–7/71	4	0.00041	0.00079	6.30	0.26	0.06	0.11	149
3/59–7/71	5	0.00066	0.00104	7.76	0.33	0.16	0.28	149
3/59–7/71	6	0.00072	0.00129	6.77	0.25	0.10	0.21	149
Controls								
1/53–6/74	2	0.00025	0.00032	12.54	0.35	0.17	0.17	258
1/53–6/74	3	0.00042	0.00061	11.14	0.23	0.08	0.12	258
3/59–6/74	2	0.00026	0.00035	10.34	0.36	0.18	0.20	184
3/59–6/74	3	0.00045	0.00064	9.45	0.23	0.09	0.16	184
3/59–6/74	4	0.00041	0.00090	6.23	0.20	−0.05	0.01	184
3/59–6/74	5	0.00062	0.00117	7.16	0.23	0.05	0.16	184
3/59–6/74	6	0.00069	0.00150	6.27	0.18	−0.02	0.10	184
Shorter subperiods								
1/53–2/59	2	0.00022	0.00025	7.56	0.26	0.11	0.03	74
1/53–2/59	3	0.00036	0.00052	5.99	0.25	0.02	−0.03	74
3/59–7/64	2	0.00032	0.00030	8.59	0.26	0.25	0.56	65
3/59–7/64	3	0.00049	0.00055	7.27	0.27	0.17	0.66	65
3/59–7/64	4	0.00037	0.00068	4.42	0.07	−0.01	0.48	65
3/59–7/64	5	0.00074	0.00090	6.64	0.21	0.17	0.63	65
3/59–7/64	6	0.00091	0.00112	6.56	0.18	0.17	0.67	65
8/64–5/69	2	0.00024	0 00026	6.90	0.33	0.22	0.13	58
8/64–5/69	3	0.00037	0.00044	6.31	0.29	0.10	−0.01	58
8/64–5/69	4	0.00037	0.00063	4.43	0.26	0.06	−0.06	58
8/64–5/69	5	0.00049	0.00079	4.67	0.19	0.11	0.10	58
8/64–5/69	6	0.00043	0.00106	3.10	0.17	0.03	−0.06	58
6/69–6/74	2	0.00023	0.00045	4.02	0.41	0.12	0.05	61
6/69–6/74	3	0.00047	0.00085	4.28	0.18	0.04	−0.01	61
6/69–6/74	4	0.00050	0.00125	3.10	0.22	−0.10	−0.11	61
6/69–6/74	5	0.00061	0.00163	2.92	0.23	−0.02	0.03	61
6/69–6/74	6	0.00070	0.00207	2.65	0.15	−0.12	−0.05	61

corresponding average value of the forward rate minus subsequently observed spot rate $F_{t+\tau, t} + R_{t+\tau}$. This suggests that at least on average the bracketed terms in the forward rate expression (9) are close to zero.

In the regressions of the premiums $P_{\tau, t+1}$ on σ_{t+1} in table 4, the coefficients $a_{1\tau}$ of σ_{t+1} are positive; they increase with maturity τ; and, as indicated by their t-statistics, they are always more than two standard errors from zero. This is evidence that expected premiums are positively associated with σ_{t+1}. Moreover, since the intercepts $a_{0\tau}$ are neither systematically positive nor negative and since they are small relative to their standard errors, uncertainty about future expected inflation rates, as measured by σ_{t+1}, seems to account entirely for the levels of the significant average premiums observed in table 3.

Finally, the independent variable σ_{t+1} in the regressions of table 4 is calculated by averaging the absolute values of the monthly changes in the spot

TABLE 4. Summary statistics for premium regressions

$$P_{\tau, t+1} = a_{0\tau} + a_{1\tau}\sigma_{t+1} + e_{t+1}$$

				Coeff. of						
Period	Bill (τ)	$a_{0\tau}$	$a_{1\tau}$	$t(a_{0\tau})$	$t(a_{1\tau})$	det.	s(e)	$\hat{\rho}_1(e)$	$\hat{\rho}_2(e)$	$\hat{\rho}_3(e)$	T^*
Pre-controls											
1/53–7/71	2	−0.00007	1.51	−1.22	6.37	0.17	0.00028	0.26	0.04	0.02	198
1/53–7/71	3	−0.00015	2.58	−1.54	6.29	0.16	0.00049	0.15	−0.07	0.07	198
3/59–7/71	2	0.00002	1.12	0.29	3.93	0.11	0.00029	0.36	0.04	−0.05	124
3/59–7/71	3	−0.00002	1.99	−0.20	4.68	0.15	0.00044	0.18	−0.10	0.02	124
3/59–7/71	4	0.00004	1.50	0.24	2.34	0.04	0.00066	0.19	−0.12	−0.15	124
3/59–7/71	5	0.00003	2.39	0.14	3.01	0.06	0.00082	0.25	−0.05	0.01	124
3/59–7/71	6	−0.00011	3.15	−0.44	3.15	0.07	0.00103	0.15	−0.11	−0.09	124
Controls											
1/53–6/74	2	−0.00004	1.26	−0.59	5.29	0.10	0.00030	0.27	0.09	0.09	233
1/53–6/74	3	−0.00011	2.28	−1.04	5.31	0.11	0.00055	0.18	0.04	0.10	233
3/59–6/74	2	0.00005	0.87	0.69	3.08	0.05	0.00032	0.33	0.09	0.06	159
3/59–6/74	3	0.00001	1.72	0.10	3.59	0.07	0.00054	0.21	0.08	0.07	159
3/59–6/74	4	0.00005	1.44	0.26	2.09	0.02	0.00078	0.19	−0.02	−0.01	159
3/59–6/74	5	0.00003	2.31	0.14	2.50	0.03	0.00104	0.19	0.07	0.15	159
3/59–6/74	6	−0.00007	3.00	−0.25	2.58	0.04	0.00131	0.09	−0.04	0.06	159

*Since the first and last years of any period are used up in computing the first and last values of σ_{t+1}, the numbers of observations used in the regressions do not correspond to the numbers of months in the stampling periods. Given this loss of observations, results for the shorter sub-periods of tables 1 to 3 seem meaningless and so they are not shown.

rate during the year following as well as during the year preceding the month $t + 1$ when the dependent variable, the premium $P_{\tau,t+1}$, is observed. Other regressions in which σ_{t+1} was calculated only from past or only from future changes in the spot rate were also tried. In terms of coefficients of determination, the regressions in which σ_{t+1} was based on future changes in the spot rate gave slightly better results than those in which σ_{t+1} was based on past changes, while past and future changes together yielded slightly stronger relationships than either past or future changes alone. However, the similarities among the results from these experiments were more important than the differences.

In any case, since there are no purely algebraic relationships between the premium $P_{\tau,t+1}$ and the absolute values of changes in the spot rate in months following $t + 1$, it is legitimate to use the future changes to calculate σ_{t+1}, the empirical proxy for the market's assessment of the uncertainty of future expected inflation rates, which, according to the model of Fama (1976b), determines the expected premium $E_t(\tilde{P}_{\tau,t+1})$. The fact that a version of σ_{t+1} based on future as well as past absolute changes in monthly spot rates explains more of the variation in the premium $P_{\tau,t+1}$ than a version of σ_{t+1} based only on past absolute changes in spot rates simply means that the future changes in the spot rate summarize, directly or indirectly, information that the market uses to determine the equilibrium value of the expected premium $E_t(\tilde{P}_{\tau,t+1})$, which it then incorporates into the price of the τ month bill at time t.

4.2. Extracting the Expected Premium $E_t(\tilde{P}_{\tau,t+1})$ from the Forward Rate $F_{t+\tau,t}$

The model for the expected premium $E_t(\tilde{P}_{\tau,t+1})$ estimated in table 4 provides the basis of a method for netting variation in $E_t(\tilde{P}_{\tau,t+1})$ out of the forward rate $F_{t+\tau,t}$ in order to better concentrate on the power of the forward rate as a predictor of the future spot rate $\tilde{R}_{t+\tau}$. Table 5 summarizes time series regressions of the forward rate minus the subsequently observed spot rate $F_{t+\tau,t} - R_{t+\tau}$ on σ_{t+1}. The coefficients $a_{0\tau}$ and $a_{1\tau}$ in table 5 are close to the coefficients $a_{0\tau}$ and $a_{1\tau}$ from the corresponding regressions of the premium $P_{\tau,t+1}$ on σ_{t+1} in table 4. Since, from (9),

$$
\begin{aligned}
F_{t+\tau,t} - \tilde{R}_{t+\tau} = E_t(\tilde{P}_{\tau,t+1}) + [E_t(\tilde{P}_{\tau-1,t+2}) - E_t(\tilde{P}_{\tau-1,t+1})] + \ldots \\
+ [E_t(\tilde{P}_{2,t+\tau-1}) - E_t(\tilde{P}_{2,t+\tau-2})] + E_t(\tilde{R}_{t+\tau}) - \tilde{R}_{t+\tau},
\end{aligned}
\tag{10}
$$

we can conclude that the regressions in table 5 measure the variation through time in the forward rate $F_{t+\tau,t}$ that can be attributed to variation in the expected

TABLE 5. $F_{t+\tau,t} - R_{t+\tau}$ as a function of uncertainty about future expected inflation rates

$$F_{t+\tau,t} - R_{t+\tau} = a_{0\tau} + a_{1\tau}\sigma_{t+1} + e_{t+\tau}$$

Period	τ	$a_{0\tau}$	$a_{1\tau}$	$t(a_{0\tau})$	$t(a_{1\tau})$	Coeff. of det.	$s(e)$	$\hat{\rho}_1(e)$	$\hat{\rho}_2(e)$	$\hat{\rho}_3(e)$
Pre-controls										
1/53–7/71	2	−0.00010	1.62	−1.50	6.18	0.16	0.000314	0.16	0.04	0.07
1/53–7/71	3	−0.00017	2.66	−2.13	8.02	0.24	0.000397	0.43	0.06	0.06
3/59–7/71	2	0.00000	1.19	0.03	3.97	0.11	0.000311	0.31	0.03	−0.05
3/59–7/71	3	−0.00004	2.04	−0.42	5.71	0.20	0.000372	0.36	0.02	0.03
3/59–7/71	4	0.00002	1.57	0.16	3.70	0.09	0.000439	0.35	0.08	−0.03
3/59–7/71	5	0.00002	2.38	0.13	4.53	0.14	0.000546	0.32	0.30	0.24
3/59–7/71	6	−0.00010	3.11	−0.71	5.19	0.17	0.000621	0.39	0.22	0.16
Controls										
1/53–6/74	2	−0.00004	1.27	−0.66	4.82	0.09	0.000338	0.24	0.11	0.12
1/53–6/74	3	−0.00011	2.26	−1.26	6.28	0.14	0.000459	0.52	0.16	0.11
3/59–6/74	2	0.00005	0.83	0.65	2.74	0.04	0.000343	0.35	0.12	0.04
3/59–6/74	3	0.00001	1.65	0.13	4.01	0.09	0.000464	0.51	0.17	0.09
3/59–6/74	4	0.00003	1.45	0.24	3.11	0.05	0.000523	0.47	0.26	0.10
3/59–6/74	5	0.00002	2.26	0.12	3.44	0.07	0.000735	0.47	0.41	0.26
3/59–6/74	6	−0.00007	2.90	−0.40	4.19	0.10	0.000771	0.51	0.34	0.14

premium $E_t(\tilde{P}_{\tau,t+1})$ in about the same way that the regressions in table 4 measure the variation in the premium $\tilde{P}_{\tau,t+1}$ that can be attributed to the expected premium $E_t(\tilde{P}_{\tau,t+1})$. Thus, ignoring for the moment the bracketed terms in (10), we can interpret the residuals from the regressions in table 5 as estimates of the market's prediction error $E_t(\tilde{R}_{t+\tau}) - \tilde{R}_{t+\tau}$ in (10).

4.3. Autoregressive Predictors of Spot Rates

Having gone to some length to isolate the power of forward rates as predictors of future spot rates, we should also take account of the evidence in table 2 that predictions of future spot rates based on the martingale model of (4) do not take full account of the information in past spot rates. The results for $\tau = 2$ in table 2 suggest that in most periods there is negative correlation between monthly changes in spot rates. If we want predictions of future spot rates based on the information in past spot rates, we should take account of this finding.

Table 6 summarizes regressions of $R_{t+\tau} - R_{t+1}$ on $R_{t+1} - R_t$. For any given period, the slope coefficients $a_{1\tau}$ are quite similar for different values of τ. For $\tau = 2$, the autocorrelation of the residuals are close to zero. These two findings are consistent with the evidence from the autocorrelations of $R_{t+2} - R_{t+1}$ in table 2, which suggests that monthly changes in the spot rate can be represented as a first-order autoregressive process but with a coefficient close enough to zero that the relationships between $R_{t+1} - R_t$ and future changes in spot rates become negligible after the change $R_{t+2} - R_{t+1}$. Thus the residuals from the regressions in table 6 can be interpreted as the prediction errors for an autoregressive model that forecasts $\tilde{R}_{t+\tau}$ as the current rate R_{t+1} adjusted for the autocorrelation in the month-to-month changes in the spot rate.

The positive autocorrelation of the residuals in the regressions for $\tau \geq 3$ in table 6 seems inconsistent with this claim. The changes $R_{t+\tau} - R_{t+1}$ are, however, computed for every month t. This means that the successive two month changes in the one month spot rate, $R_{t+3} - R_{t+1}$ and $R_{t+2} - R_t$, both contain the one month change $R_{t+2} - R_{t+1}$. Likewise, successive monthly values of $R_{t+4} - R_{t+1}$ share two monthly changes in the spot rate, etc. In this sense, the autocorrelations of $R_{t+\tau} - R_{t+1}$ for $\tau \geq 3$ in table 2 are spurious indications of predictability, as are the autocorrelations of the residuals for $\tau \geq 3$ in table 6.

TABLE 6. Regression results for changes in spot rates

$$R_{t+\tau} - R_{t+1} = a_{0\tau} + a_{1\tau}(R_{t+1} - R_t) + e_{t+\tau}$$

Period	τ	$a_{0\tau}$	$a_{1\tau}$	$t(a_{0\tau})$	$t(a_{1\tau})$	Coeff. of det.	$s(e)$	$\hat{\rho}_1(e)$	$\hat{\rho}_2(e)$	$\hat{\rho}_3(e)$
Pre-controls										
1/53–7/71	2	0.00001	−0.24	0.71	−3.70	0.05	0.000313	0.00	0.01	0.07
1/53–7/71	3	0.00002	−0.20	0.89	−2.40	0.02	0.000392	0.48	0.03	0.14
3/59–7/71	2	0.00002	−0.28	0.72	−3.49	0.07	0.000328	−0.00	−0.01	0.05
3/59–7/71	3	0.00003	−0.23	0.92	−2.40	0.03	0.000403	0.47	0.01	0.09
3/59–7/71	4	0.00004	−0.25	1.06	−2.18	0.02	0.000474	0.62	0.42	0.10
3/59–7/71	5	0.00005	−0.15	1.07	−1.13	0.00	0.000539	0.69	0.53	0.32
3/59–7/71	6	0.00006	−0.20	1.10	−1.35	0.01	0.000612	0.74	0.57	0.40
Controls										
1/53–6/74	2	0.00002	−0.16	1.06	−2.54	0.02	0.000333	−0.00	−0.01	0.03
1/53–6/74	3	0.00004	−0.15	1.52	−1.79	0.01	0.000435	0.49	0.01	0.09
3/59–6/74	2	0.00003	−0.16	1.09	−2.22	0.02	0.000352	−0.00	−0.02	0.00
3/59–6/74	3	0.00005	−0.16	1.60	−1.69	0.01	0.000459	0.49	−0.01	0.05
3/59–6/74	4	0.00008	−0.17	2.04	−1.45	0.01	0.000544	0.64	0.39	0.08
3/59–6/74	5	0.00011	−0.05	2.29	−0.41	−0.00	0.000620	0.72	0.53	0.31
3/59–6/74	6	0.00013	−0.05	2.43	−0.34	−0.01	0.000704	0.76	0.59	0.39

(Continued)

TABLE 6. (Continued)

Period	τ	$a_{0\tau}$	$a_{1\tau}$	$t(a_{0\tau})$	$t(a_{1\tau})$	Coeff. of det.	$s(e)$	$\hat{\rho}_1(e)$	$\hat{\rho}_2(e)$	$\hat{\rho}_3(e)$
Shorter subperiods										
1/53–2/59	2	0.00001	−0.14	0.19	−1.18	0.01	0.000281	0.01	0.04	0.11
1/53–2/59	3	0.00001	−0.09	0.23	−0.56	−0.01	0.000372	0.51	0.08	0.25
3/59–7/64	2	0.00002	−0.41	0.42	−3.58	0.16	0.000321	−0.05	−0.12	0.03
3/59–7/64	3	0.00003	−0.35	0.61	−2.67	0.09	0.000362	0.40	−0.07	0.01
3/59–7/64	4	0.00004	−0.37	0.76	−2.54	0.08	0.000408	0.52	0.39	0.08
3/59–7/64	5	0.00005	−0.30	0.84	−1.85	0.04	0.000451	0.62	0.52	0.33
3/59–7/64	6	0.00006	−0.23	0.91	−1.28	0.01	0.000507	0.66	0.52	0.33
8/64–5/69	2	0.00005	−0.30	1.34	−2.36	0.07	0.000272	−0.06	−0.19	0.02
8/64–5/69	3	0.00009	−0.35	2.14	−2.31	0.07	0.000321	0.42	−0.12	−0.07
8/64–5/69	4	0.00013	−0.32	2.78	−1.88	0.04	0.000359	0.57	0.29	−0.05
8/64–5/69	5	0.00017	−0.20	3.23	−1.03	0.00	0.000405	0.64	0.37	0.26
8/64–5/69	6	0.00023	−0.30	3.72	−1.39	0.02	0.000464	0.68	0.48	0.37
6/69–6/74	2	0.00002	0.07	0.45	0.55	−0.01	0.000427	0.01	−0.00	−0.03
6/69–6/74	3	0.00005	0.05	0.61	0.25	−0.02	0.000632	0.51	−0.01	0.02
6/69–6/74	4	0.00008	0.05	0.82	0.20	−0.02	0.000777	0.67	0.36	0.06
6/69–6/74	5	0.00011	0.20	0.92	0.70	−0.01	0.000898	0.76	0.53	0.27
6/69–6/74	6	0.00011	0.20	0.83	0.61	−0.01	0.001028	0.81	0.62	0.38

These autocorrelations would largely disappear if non-overlapping values of $R_{t+\tau} - R_{t+1}$ were used.

For $\tau \geq 3$ in table 1, there is similar positive autocorrelation in successive values of the forward rate minus the subsequently observed spot rate, $F_{t+\tau, t} - R_{t+\tau}$, which also shows up in the residuals from the regressions in table 5, but which is of no real predictive value. For example, $F_{t+2, t-1} - R_{t+2}$, the difference between the forward rate for month $t+2$ set at $t-1$ and the spot rate R_{t+2} subsequently observed, reflects information (in particular the change $R_{t+2} - R_{t+1}$ in the spot rate from t to $t+1$) which helps to 'predict' $F_{t+3, t} - R_{t+3}$, but which was not available when the market set the forward rate $F_{t+3,t}$ at the end of month t.

In contrast, since the return $\tilde{H}_{\tau,t+1}$ and the spot rate R_{t+1} that together determine the premium $\tilde{P}_{\tau,t+1}$ in (6) are both realized at $t+1$, there is no similar phenomenon in the premiums. The autocorrelations of the premiums in table 3 and the autocorrelations of the residuals from the premium regressions in table 4 are true indications of predictability, and we have more to say about them shortly.

4.4. Comparisons of Predictions

Comparing tables 5 and 6, one finds that sometimes the autoregressive model produces slightly lower residual standard errors, while sometimes those for the forward rate regressions are lower. If we say that the autoregressive model predicts future spot rates from the information in past spot rates, we can conclude that the forward rate $F_{t+\tau,t}$, adjusted for variation in the expected premium $E_t(\tilde{P}_{\tau,t+1})$, seems to include a prediction of the future spot rate $\tilde{R}_{t+\tau}$ about as good as, but no better than, the prediction that can be obtained from the information in past spot rates.

Since the forward rates do as well as the predictions based on the information in past spot rate, the data are consistent with the hypothesis that the market is efficient. One would be more comfortable with the hypothesis if forward rates contained predictions of future spot rates better than those that can be obtained from the information in past spot rates. But perhaps better predictions are not possible.

Moreover, there are at least two reasons why the tests in tables 5 and 6 might be biased against finding that forward rates contain good predictions of future spot rates. First, there is evidence that we do not have a good model for the expected premium $E_t(\tilde{P}_{\tau,t+1})$ in (9) and (10). The autocorrelations of the residuals from the premium regressions in table 4 are smaller than the autocorrelations of the premiums in table 3, but the first-order residual autocorrelations in table 4 are still noticeably different from zero. There is variation in the expected premium $E_t(\tilde{P}_{\tau,t+1})$ that is not captured by the regressions. From (9) or (10) one can see that any deficiency in the method of abstracting from variation in $E_t(\tilde{P}_{\tau,t+1})$ biases the tests in tables 5 and 6 against concluding that the forward rate $F_{t+\tau,t}$ contains a good prediction of the future spot rate $\tilde{R}_{t+\tau}$. Second, comparison of the means in tables 1 and 3 suggests that the averages of the bracketed terms in (9) or (10) are close to zero during the sampling period, but this does not rule out variation through time in these expected changes in expected premiums. Any such variation also tends to obscure the power of the forward rate $F_{t+\tau,t}$ as a predictor of the future spot rate $\tilde{R}_{t+\tau}$. Thus, perhaps the fact that forward rates hold their own with the autoregressive model based on the information in past spot rates is rather good evidence for market efficiency.

[537]

5. THE RESPONSE OF THE FORWARD RATE TO
THE AUTOREGRESSIVENESS OF SPOT RATES

There is, however, a different and somewhat more direct test of the hypothesis that forward rates correctly reflect the information in past spot rates. The test is different in the sense that it works with $F_{t+\tau} - R_{t+1}$, the difference between the forward rate for month $t + \tau$ set at t and the current spot rate, rather than with $F_{t+\tau,t} - \tilde{R}_{t+\tau}$, the difference between the forward rate and the spot rate for month $t + \tau$ subsequently observed. The test is more direct in the sense that, rather than comparing the variance of the prediction errors of the forward rate with the variance of the prediction errors of a model based on the information in past spot rates, one examines directly the response of the forward rate to the information in past spot rates. Finally, the new test has the important advantage that it does not require a model for the expected premiums in forward rates.

From eq. (9) we know that the forward rate $F_{t+\tau,t}$ contains $E_t(\tilde{R}_{t+\tau})$, the market's assessment at t of the expected value of the spot rate for month $t + \tau$. If the market is efficient, the assessment $E_t(\tilde{R}_{t+\tau})$ that it includes in the forward rate $F_{t+\tau,t}$ should correctly take account of the change in the spot rate from t (the time when the forward rate $F_{t+\tau,t}$ is set) to $t + \tau-1$ (the time when the spot rate $\tilde{R}_{t+\tau}$ is observed) that can be expected on the basis of the autocorrelations of monthly changes in the spot rate. In other words, the prediction of the future spot rate $\tilde{R}_{t+\tau}$ that the market puts into the forward rate $F_{t+\tau,t}$ at time t should directly reflect any information about $\tilde{R}_{t+\tau}$ that is contained in past spot rates.

Consider a regression of the forward rate minus the current spot rate $F_{t+\tau,t} - R_{t+1}$ on the most recent change in the spot rate $R_{t+1} - R_t$. From (9), we have

$$F_{t+\tau,t} - R_{t+1} = E_t(\tilde{P}_{\tau,t+1}) + [E_t(\tilde{P}_{\tau-1,t+2}) - E_t(\tilde{P}_{\tau-1,t+1})] + \dots \\ + [E_t(\tilde{P}_{2,t+\tau-1}) - E_t(\tilde{P}_{2,t+\tau-2})] + E_t(\tilde{R}_{t+\tau}) - R_{t+1}.$$

(11)

Suppose variation through time in the expected premiums in (11) is unrelated to the autocorrelations of the changes in the spot rate. Then the regression of $F_{t+\tau,t} - R_{t+1}$ on $R_{t+1} - R_t$ focuses on the relationship between $E_t(\tilde{R}_{t+\tau}) - R_{t+1}$ (the market's prediction of the change in the spot rate from t to $t + \tau - 1$) and $R_{t+1} - R_t$ (the most recent change in the spot rate).[3] The 'true' information that

3. The point is most transparent when one assumes that all of the expected premiums in (11) are equal to zero, so that the difference between the forward rate and the current

$R_{t+1} - R_t$ contains about the change in the spot rate from t to $t + \tau - 1$, can be estimated with a regression of $R_{t+\tau} - R_{t+1}$ on $R_{t+1} - R_t$. If the market is efficient, that is, if it appropriately adjusts its prediction $E_t(\tilde{R}_{t+\tau}) - R_{t+1}$ of the change in the spot rate to reflect the information in the most recent change $R_{t+1} - R_t$, then the regression of $F_{t+\tau,t} - R_{t+1}$ on $R_{t+1} - R_t$ should show the same slope coefficient as the regression of $R_{t+\tau} - R_{t+1}$ on $R_{t+1} - R_t$.

To emphasize exactly what one is aiming at in this test, note that in regressions of $F_{t+\tau,t} - R_{t+1}$ and $R_{t+\tau} - R_{t+1}$ on $R_{t+1} - R_t$, only comparison of the slope coefficients is relevant. For example, the intercept in the regression of $F_{t+\tau,t} - R_{t+1}$ on $R_{t+1} - R_t$ reflects the average value of the expected premium $E_t(\tilde{P}_{\tau,t+1})$, which has no role at all in the regression of $R_{t+\tau} - R_{t+1}$ on $R_{t+1} - R_t$. Likewise, the residuals from the regression of $F_{t+\tau,t} - R_{t+1}$ on $R_{t+1} - R_t$ reflect the variation through time in the expected premiums in (11), which has nothing to do with the issue of interest—whether the expected change in the spot rate $E_t(\tilde{R}_{t+\tau}) - R_{t+1}$ that the market includes in $F_{t+\tau,t} - R_{t+1}$ correctly reflects the information about the future spot rate $\tilde{R}_{t+\tau}$ which is contained in the most recent change in the spot rate $R_{t+1} - R_t$.

The regressions of $F_{t+\tau,t} - R_{t+1}$ on $R_{t+1} - R_t$ are summarized in table 7. In the regressions of $R_{t+\tau} - R_{t+1}$ on $R_{t+1} - R_t$ in table 6, there are two shorter subperiods, January 1953 to February 1959 and June 1969 to June 1974, when the slope coefficients $a_{1\tau}$ are statistically indistinguishable from zero. In contrast, for the March 1959 to July 1964 and August 1964 to May 1969 periods, the coefficients $a_{1\tau}$ in table 6 are substantially negative, and, at least for the smaller values of τ, the coefficients are large relative to their standard errors. This behavior across subperiods of the slope coefficients in table 6 is reproduced well in the coefficients $a_{1\tau}$ from the forward rate regressions in table 7.

Hamburger and Platt (1975) also find that forward rates contain predictions of future spot rates that are consistent with the time series process generating spot rates. Their data are for three and six month bills, and during their sampling period (1961–71) the three month bill rate is close to a martingale. In this world, correct utilization of the information in past three month spot rates simply requires assessing any expected future three month rate spot as equal to the current rate. Hamburger and Platt conclude that the market incorporates this assessment in the three month forward rate. One can wonder, however, whether this reflects the market's understanding of the process generating spot

---

spot rate, $F_{t+\tau,t} - R_{t+1}$, is just $E_t(\tilde{R}_{t+\tau}) - R_{t+1}$, the market's prediction of the change in the spot rate.

TABLE 7. The reaction of forward rates to the autoregressiveness on spot rates

$$F_{t+\tau, t} - R_{t+1} = a_{0\tau} + a_{1\tau}(R_{t+1} - R_t) + e_{t+1}$$

Period	τ	$a_{0\tau}$	$a_{1\tau}$	$t(a_{0\tau})$	$t(a_{1\tau})$	Coeff. of det.	$s(e)$	$\hat{\rho}_1(e)$	$\hat{\rho}_2(e)$	$\hat{\rho}_3(e)$
Pre-controls										
1/53–7/71	2	0.00029	−0.25	12.54	−3.45	0.05	0.000346	0.20	0.11	0.20
1/53–7/71	3	0.00047	−0.33	17.95	−4.04	0.06	0.000386	0.52	0.28	0.25
3/59–7/71	2	0.00032	−0.33	10.38	−3.60	0.07	0.000379	0.20	0.06	0.16
3/59–7/71	3	0.00051	−0.40	15.43	−4.11	0.10	0.000403	0.49	0.28	0.25
3/59–7/71	4	0.00045	−0.23	14.72	−2.55	0.04	0.000372	0.33	0.02	−0.01
3/59–7/71	5	0.00071	−0.32	14.88	−2.27	0.03	0.000584	0.40	0.38	0.37
3/59–7/71	6	0.00078	−0.15	13.90	−0.93	−0.00	0.000688	0.53	0.41	0.39
Controls										
1/53–6/74	2	0.00027	−0.20	13.09	−3.15	0.03	0.000336	0.18	0.12	0.19
1/53–6/74	3	0.00046	−0.25	18.88	−3.49	0.04	0.000388	0.44	0.25	0.21
3/59–6/74	2	0.00029	−0.24	10.96	−3.24	0.05	0.000363	0.18	0.10	0.15
3/59–6/74	3	0.00049	−0.30	16.41	−3.47	0.06	0.000404	0.40	0.25	0.20
3/59–6/74	4	0.00047	−0.25	16.24	−2.99	0.04	0.000389	0.25	0.09	0.02
3/59–6/74	5	0.00071	−0.24	16.39	−1.97	0.02	0.000580	0.31	0.32	0.33
3/59–6/74	6	0.00081	−0.04	15.88	−0.29	−0.01	0.000685	0.45	0.38	0.33
Shorter subperiods										
1/53–2/59	2	0.00023	−0.02	7.90	−0.16	−0.01	0.000246	0.16	0.15	0.30
1/53–2/59	3	0.00038	−0.12	9.70	−0.85	−0.00	0.000333	0.55	0.20	0.18
3/59–7/64	2	0.00034	−0.31	7.66	−2.39	0.07	0.000362	0.19	0.19	0.39
3/59–7/64	3	0.00053	−0.57	10.37	−3.84	0.18	0.000410	0.65	0.48	0.49
3/59–7/64	4	0.00041	−0.36	9.67	−2.96	0.11	0.000340	0.45	0.28	0.12
3/59–7/64	5	0.00078	−0.15	10.87	−0.73	−0.01	0.000580	0.62	0.63	0.60
3/59–7/64	6	0.00097	−0.40	10.54	−1.52	0.02	0.000740	0.65	0.52	0.49
8/64–5/69	2	0.00029	−0.48	6.97	−3.28	0.15	0.000311	0.12	−0.02	0.26
8/64–5/69	3	0.00045	−0.44	9.67	−2.64	0.09	0.000350	0.56	0.26	0.11
8/64–5/69	4	0.00048	−0.19	10.91	−1.21	0.01	0.000331	0.41	0.21	0.17
8/64–5/69	5	0.00063	−0.24	8.86	−0.97	−0.00	0.000535	0.39	0.35	0.51
8/64–5/69	6	0.00061	0.06	6.95	0.19	−0.02	0.000660	0.39	0.20	0.25
6/69–6/74	2	0.00025	−0.09	4.91	−0.77	−0.01	0.000402	0.21	0.13	−0.14
6/69–6/74	3	0.00049	−0.02	8.95	−0.18	−0.02	0.000425	0.12	0.15	−0.02
6/69–6/74	4	0.00052	−0.19	8.37	−1.26	0.01	0.000480	0.02	−0.07	−0.19
6/69–6/74	5	0.00070	−0.31	8.51	−1.51	0.02	0.000630	−0.07	0.04	−0.12
6/69–6/74	6	0.00084	0.24	10.75	1.24	0.01	0.000588	0.11	0.26	−0.02

rates, or whether the market is fortuitous but naive and would in any case set the prediction of the future spot rate equal to the current spot rate.

In contrast, during most of the period examined here, there is noticeable negative autocorrelation in changes in the spot rate, and the degree of auto-correlation changes through time. The finding that in setting forward rates the market reacts appropriately to the autocorrelation in spot rate changes is then more positive evidence that the market understands the process generating the spot rate.

6. THE COMPONENTS OF A FORWARD RATE

Table 8 summarizes regressions of the forward rate minus the current spot rate, $F_{t+\tau,t} - R_{t+1}$, on both the change in the spot rate, $R_{t+1} - R_t$, and σ_{t+1}, the measure of uncertainty about future expected inflation rates. The regressions give an interesting summary perspective of the view of forward rates that emerges in this paper. In particular the coefficients $a_{1\tau}$ for $R_{t+1} - R_t$ in table 8 are similar to the corresponding $a_{1\tau}$ for the autoregressive models in table 6, while the coefficients $a_{2\tau}$ in table 8 are similar to the corresponding coefficients $a_{1\tau}$ in the premium regressions of table 4.

Thus, the forward rate $F_{t+\tau,t}$ responds to two different and apparently in-dependent influences. In terms of (9) or (11), the expected premium $E_t(\tilde{P}_{\tau,t+1})$ in the forward rate responds to changes in uncertainty about future expected inflation rates, as measured by σ_{t+1}, while the expected future spot rate com-ponent of the forward rate responds to the information in the autoregressive-ness of past spot rates.

7. SUMMARY

This paper is concerned with efficiency in the market for U.S. Treasury Bills. The evidence is that, once they are adjusted for variation in expected premi-ums, the forward rates that are implicit in bill prices contain assessments of expected future spot rates that are about as good as those that can be obtained from extrapolations based on the time series properties of past spot rates. This evidence is consistent with the market efficiency proposition that in setting bill prices, the market correctly uses at least the information in past spot rates. However, the best support for market efficiency is the direct evidence that in setting bill prices and forward rates the market reacts appropriately to the negative autocorrelation in monthly changes in the spot rate and to changes through time in the degrees of this autocorrelation.

TABLE 8. Forward rates, expected premiums and the autoregressiveness of spot rates

$$F_{t+\tau,t} - R_{t+1} = a_{0\tau} + a_{1\tau}(R_{t+1} - R_t) + a_{2\tau}\sigma_{t+1} + e_{t+1}$$

Period	τ	$a_{0\tau}$	$a_{1\tau}$	$a_{2\tau}$	$t(a_{0\tau})$	$t(a_{1\tau})$	$t(a_{2\tau})$	Coeff. of det.	$s(e)$	$\hat{\rho}_1(e)$	$\hat{\rho}_2(e)$	$\hat{\rho}_3(e)$
Pre-controls												
1/53–7/71	2	-0.000036	-0.28	1.48	-0.53	-3.71	5.26	0.17	0.000336	0.10	0.01	0.14
1/53–7/71	3	-0.000052	-0.33	2.37	-0.74	-4.30	8.08	0.30	0.000348	0.36	0.06	0.05
3/59–7/71	2	0.000072	-0.42	1.01	0.90	-4.30	2.99	0.18	0.000347	0.14	-0.10	0.09
3/59–7/71	3	0.000085	-0.39	1.73	1.11	-4.22	5.39	0.29	0.000329	0.26	0.02	-0.02
3/59–7/71	4	0.000181	-0.19	1.12	2.13	-1.83	3.16	0.09	0.000365	0.27	-0.13	-0.11
3/59–7/71	5	0.000246	-0.41	1.76	2.09	-2.86	3.57	0.15	0.000507	0.21	0.18	0.26
3/59–7/71	6	0.000164	-0.17	2.37	1.28	-1.10	4.43	0.14	0.000551	0.31	0.12	0.18
Controls												
1/53–6/74	2	-0.000002	-0.24	1.23	-0.03	-3.62	4.78	0.13	0.000328	0.10	0.04	0.12
1/53–6/74	3	-0.000011	-0.28	2.06	-0.16	-3.90	7.49	0.24	0.000350	0.38	0.07	0.05
3/59–6/74	2	0.000095	-0.34	0.79	1.27	-4.14	2.67	0.13	0.000332	0.12	-0.05	0.06
3/59–6/74	3	0.000112	-0.30	1.48	1.49	-3.70	5.01	0.20	0.000332	0.28	0.03	-0.03
3/59–6/74	4	0.000186	-0.19	1.12	2.25	-2.14	3.45	0.09	0.000364	0.25	-0.05	0.01
3/59–6/74	5	0.000247	-0.32	1.74	2.11	-2.53	3.79	0.11	0.000518	0.12	0.15	0.18
3/59–6/74	6	0.000181	-0.05	2.36	1.45	-0.38	4.80	0.12	0.000553	0.26	0.17	0.16

REFERENCES

Culbertson, J.W., 1957, The term structure of interest rates, Quarterly Journal of Economics, Nov., 485–517.

Fama, E.F., 1976a, Foundations of finance (Basic Books, New York).

Fama, E.F., 1976b, Inflation uncertainty and the expected returns on treasury bills, Journal of Political Economy 84, June, 427–448.

Fama, E.F., 1975, Short-term interest rates as predictors of inflation, American Economic Review 65, June, 269–282.

Hamburger, M.J. and E.N. Platt, 1975, The expectations hypothesis and the efficiency of the Treasury Bill market, Review of Economics and Statistics 57, May, 190–199.

Hickman, W.B., 1942, The term structure of interest rates: An exploratory analysis, mimeo. (National Bureau of Economic Research, New York).

Hicks, J.R., 1946, Value and capital, 2nd ed. (The Clarendon Press, Oxford).

Kessel, R.A., 1965, The cyclical behavior of the term structure of interest rates (National Bureau of Economic Research, New York).

Macauley, F.R., 1938, The movements of interest rates, bond yields and stock prices in the United States since 1859 (National Bureau of Economic Research, New York).

Roll, R., 1970, The behavior of interest rates (Basic Books, New York).

FORWARD AND SPOT EXCHANGE RATES

· · ·

Eugene F. Fama

There is a general consensus that forward exchange rates have little if any power as forecasts of future spot exchange rates. There is less agreement on whether forward rates contain time varying premiums. Conditional on the hypothesis that the forward market is efficient or rational, this paper finds that both components of forward rates vary through time. Moreover, most of the variation in forward rates is variation in premiums, and the premium and expected future spot rate components of forward rates are negatively correlated.

1. INTRODUCTION

There is much empirical work on forward foreign exchange rates as predictors of future spot exchange rates. [See, for example, Hansen and Hodrick (1980), Bilson (1981), and the review article by Levich (1979).] There is also a growing literature on whether forward rates contain variation in premiums. [See, for example, Frankel (1982), Hsieh (1982), Korajczyk (1983), Hansen and Hodrick (1983), Hodrick and Srivastava (1984), and Domowitz and Hakkio (1983).] There is a general concensus that forward rates have little if any power to forecast changes in spot rates. There is less consensus on the existence of time varying premiums in forward rates. Frankel (1982) and Domowitz and Hakkio (1983) fail to identify such premiums, while Hsieh (1982), Hansen and Hodrick (1983), Hodrick and Srivastava (1984), and Korajczyk (1983) find evidence consistent with time varying premiums.

This paper tests a model for joint measurement of variation in the premium and expected future spot rate components of forward rates. Conditional on

Reprinted with permission from the *Journal of Monetary Economics* 14, no. 3 (November 1984): 319–38. © 1984 by Elsevier Limited.

The comments of John Abowd, John Bilson. David Hsieh, John Huizinga, Michael Mussa. Charles Plosser, Richard Roll, and Alan Stockman are gratefully acknowledged. This research is supported by the National Science Foundation.

the hypothesis that the forward market is efficient or rational, we find reliable evidence that both components of forward rates vary through time. More startling are the conclusions that (a) most of the variation in forward rates is variation in premiums, and (b) the premium and expected future spot rate components of forward rates are negatively correlated.

2. THEORETICAL FRAMEWORK

The forward exchange rate f_t observed at time t for an exchange at $t+1$ is the market determined certainty equivalent of the future spot exchange rate s_{t+1}. One way to split this certainty equivalent into an expected future spot rate and a premium is

$$F_t = E(S_{t+1}) + P_t, \tag{1}$$

where $F_t = \ln f_t$, $S_{t+1} = \ln s_{t+1}$, and the expected future spot rate, $E(S_{t+1})$, is the rational or efficient forecast, conditional on all information available at t. Logs are used (a) to make the analysis independent of whether exchange rates are expressed as units of currency i per unit of currency j or units of j per unit of i, and (b) because some models for the premium [for example, Fama and Farber (1979) and Stulz (1981)] can be stated in logs.

Eq. (1) is no more than a particular definition of the premium component of the forward rate. To give the equation economic content, a model that describes the determination of P_t is required. Examples of such models are discussed later. For the statistical analysis of the premium and expected future spot rate components of the forward rate, however, it suffices that the forward rate is the market determined certainty equivalent of the future spot rate.

2.1. Statistics
From (1) the difference between the forward rate and the current spot rate is

$$F_t - S_t = P_t + E(S_{t+1} - S_t). \tag{2}$$

Consider the regressions of $F_t - S_{t+1}$ and $S_{t+1} - S_t$ (both observed at $t+1$) on $F_t - S_t$ (observed at t),

$$F_t - S_{t+1} = \alpha_1 + \beta_1 (F_t - S_t) + \varepsilon_{1, t+1}, \tag{3}$$

$$S_{t+1} - S_t = \alpha_2 + \beta_2 (F_t - S_t) + \varepsilon_{2, t+1}. \tag{4}$$

[545]

Estimates of (4) tell us whether the current forward-spot differential, $F_t - S_t$, has power to predict the future change in the spot rate, $S_{t+1} - S_t$. Evidence that β_2 is reliably non-zero means that the forward rate observed at t has information about the spot rate to be observed at $t + 1$. Likewise, since $F_t - S_{t+1}$ is the premium P_t plus $E(S_{t+1}) - S_{t+1}$, the random error of the rational forecast $E(S_{t+1})$, evidence that β_1 in (3) is reliably non-zero means that the premium component of $F_t - S_t$ has variation that shows up reliably in $F_t - S_{t+1}$.

With the assumption that the expected future spot rate in the forward rate is efficient or rational, the regression coefficients in (3) and (4) are

$$\beta_1 = \frac{\mathrm{cov}(F_t - S_{t+1}, F_t - S_t)}{\sigma^2(F_t - S_t)},$$

$$= \frac{\sigma^2(P_t) + \mathrm{cov}(P_t, E(S_{t+1} - S_t))}{\sigma^2(P_t) + \sigma^2(E(S_{t+1} - S_t)) + 2\mathrm{cov}(P_t, E(S_{t+1} - S_t))},$$

$$\tag{5}$$

$$\beta_2 = \frac{\mathrm{cov}(S_{t+1} - S_t, F_t - S_t)}{\sigma^2(F_t - S_t)}$$

$$= \frac{\sigma^2(E(S_{t+1} - S_t)) + \mathrm{cov}(P_t, E(S_{t+1} - S_t))}{\sigma^2(P_t) + \sigma^2(E(S_{t+1} - S_t)) + 2\mathrm{cov}(P_t, E(S_{t+1} - S_t))}.$$

$$\tag{6}$$

In the special case where P_t and $E(S_{t+1} - S_t)$ are uncorrelated, the regression coefficients β_1 and β_2 split the variance of $F_t - S_t$ into two parts: the proportion due to the variance of the premium and the proportion due to the variance of the expected change in the spot rate. When the two components of $F_t - S_t$ are correlated, the contribution of covariation between P_t and $E(S_{t+1} - S_t)$ to $\sigma^2(F_t - S_t)$ is divided equally between β_1 and β_2. The regression coefficients still include the proportions of $\sigma^2(F_t - S_t)$ due to $\sigma^2(P_t)$ and $\sigma^2(E(S_{t+1} - S_t))$, but the simple interpretation of β_1 and β_2 obtained when P_t and $E(S_{t+1} - S_t)$ are uncorrelated is lost. The troublesome $\mathrm{cov}(P_t, E(S_{t+1} - S_t))$ in (5) and (6) is a central issue in the empirical tests.

Since $F_t - S_{t+1}$ and $S_{t+1} - S_t$ sum to $F_t - S_t$, the sum of the intercepts in (3) and (4) must be zero, the sum of the slopes must be 1.0, and the disturbances, period-by-period, must sum to 0.0. In other words, regressions (3) and (4) contain identical information about the variation of the P_t and $E(S_{t+1} - S_t)$ components of $F_t - S_t$, and in principle there is no need to show both. I contend, however, that joint analysis of the regressions is what makes clear the information that either contains.

Thus, regression (4) of the change in the spot rate, $S_{t+1} - S_t$, on the forward rate minus the current spot rate, $F_t - S_t$, is common in the literature. [See, for example, Bilson (1981) and Levich (1979, table 2).] It is also widely recognized that deviations of β_2 in (4) from 1.0 can somehow be due to a time varying premium in the forward rate. To my knowledge, however, the explicit interpretation of the regression coefficients provided by (5) and (6) is not well known. In particular, it is not widely recognized that, given an efficient or rational exchange market, the deviation of β_2 from 1.0 is a direct measure of the variation of the premium in the forward rate. The complementarity of the regression coefficients in (3) and (4) which is described in (5) and (6) helps us to interpret some of the anomalous results observed for estimates of (4).

2.2. Economics

Since a major conclusion of the empirical work is that variation in forward rates is mostly variation in premiums, some discussion of the economics of premiums is warranted. Using more precise notation, let f_t^{ij} and s_t^{ij} be the forward and spot exchange rates (units of currency i per unit of currency j) observed at t, and let R_{it} and R_{jt} be the nominal interest rates observed at t on discount bonds denominated in currencies i and j. The bonds have either zero or identical default risks, and they have the same maturity as f_t^{ij}.

With open international bond markets, the no arbitrage condition of interest rate parity (IRP) implies

$$f_t^{ij}/s_t^{ij} = (1+R_{it})/(1+R_{jt}).$$

Thus, the difference between the forward and spot exchange rates observed at t is directly related to the difference between the interest rates on nominal bonds denominated in the two currencies. Any premium in the forward rate must be explainable in terms of the interest rate differential.

For example (and keep in mind that it is just an example), suppose (a) that exchanges rates are characterized by complete purchasing power parity (PPP), and (b) that the Fisher equation holds for nominal interest rates. Let V_{it} and V_{jt} be the price levels in the two countries, let $\Delta_{i,t+1} = \ln(V_{i,t+1}/V_{it})$ and $\Delta_{j,t+1} = \ln(V_{j,t+1}/V_{jt})$ be their inflation rates, and let $r_{i,t+1}$ and $r_{j,t+1}$ be the *ex post* continuously compounded real returns on their nominal bonds. Taking logs in (7) and applying the Fisher equation to the resulting continuously compounded nominal interest rates, we have

$$
\begin{aligned}
F_t^{ij} - S_t^{ij} &= [E(r_{i,t+1}) + E(\Delta_{i,t+1})] - [E(r_{j,t+1}) + E(\Delta_{j,t+1})] \\
&= [E(r_{i,t+1}) + E(r_{j,t+1})] + [E(\ln V_{i,t+1}) - E(\ln V_{j,t+1})] \\
&\quad - [\ln V_{it} - \ln V_{jt}].
\end{aligned}
\tag{8}
$$

With complete PPP, $s_t^{ij} = V_{it}/V_{jt}$, that is, the spot exchange rate is the ratio of the price levels in the two countries, and (11) reduces to

$$
F_t^{ij} = [E(r_{i,t+1}) - E(r_{j,t+1})] + E(S_{t+1}^{ij}).
\tag{9}
$$

In words, with the Fisher equation, interest rate parity and purchasing power parity, the premium P_t in the forward rate expression (1) is just the difference between the expected real returns on the nominal bonds of the two countries. Thus, the variables that determine the difference between the expected real returns on the nominal bonds (for example, differential purchasing power risks of their nominal payoffs) also explain the premium in the forward rate. This interpretation applies to any model of international capital market equilibrium characterized by IRP, PPP, and the Fisher equation for nominal interest rates. Examples are the international version of the Sharpe (1964) and Lintner (1965) model discussed by Fama and Farber (1979) or the version of the Lucas (1978) model discussed by Hodrick and Srivastava (1984).

The lock between the premium in the forward exchange rate and the interest rates on the nominal bonds of two countries is the direct consequence of the interest rate parity condition (7) of an open international bond market. For example, using IRP and an international version of the Breeden (1979) model, Stulz (1981) derives an expression for the forward rate similar to (1) or (9), but for a world in which (a) complete PPP does not hold, and (b) differential tastes for consumption goods combine with uncertainty about relative prices to strip the Fisher equation of its meaning.

3. DATA AND SUMMARY STATISTICS

Spot exchange rates and thirty-day forward rates for nine major currencies are taken from the Harris Bank Data Base supported by the Center for Studies in International Finance of the University of Chicago. The rates are Friday closes sampled at four-week intervals. There are 122 observations covering the period August 31, 1973, to December 10, 1982. All rates are U.S. dollars per unit of foreign currency.

Table 1 shows means, standard deviations, and autocorrelations of $S_{t+1} - S_t$ (the four-week change in the spot rate), $F_t - S_{t+1}$ (the thirty-day forward rate minus the spot rate observed four weeks later), and $F_t - S_t$ (the forward rate minus the current spot rate). Since the forward and spot rates are in logs and the differences are multiplied by 100, the three variables are on a percent per month basis.

The standard deviations of $F_t - S_{t+1}$ in table 1 are larger than the standard deviations of $S_{t+1} - S_t$. Thus, in terms of standard deviation of forecast errors, the current spot rate is a better predictor of the future spot rate than the current forward rate. However, variation in the premium component of the forward rate can obscure the power of the prediction of the future spot rate in the forward rate. This is the problem that the complementary regressions (3) and (4) are meant to alleviate.

Consistent with the previous literature, the autocorrelations of changes in spot rates, $S_{t+1} - S_t$, are close to zero. Thus, if the expected component of the changes, $E(S_{t+1} - S_t)$, varies in an autocorrelated way, this is not evident in the behavior of the observed changes. The $F_t - S_{t+1}$ for different countries also show little autocorrelation. $F_t - S_{t+1}$ is the premium, P_t, plus the forecast error, $E(S_{t+1}) - S_{t+1}$, which should be white noise. Thus, any autocorrelation of the premium is not evident in the time series behavior of $F_t - S_{t+1}$.

The autocorrelations of $F_t - S_t$ tell a different story. The first-order autocorrelations are 0.65 or greater, and the decay of the autocorrelations at successive lags suggests a first-order autoregressive process. This is confirmed by the partial autocorrelations (not shown) which are large at lag 1 but close to zero at higher-order lags. Since $F_t - S_t$ is the premium, P_t, plus the expected change in the spot rate, $E(S_{t+1} - S_t)$, the autocorrelations of $F_t - S_t$ indicate that P_t and/or $E(S_{t+1} - S_t)$ vary in an autocorrelated way.

The difference between the behavior of the autocorrelations of $F_t - S_t$ and those of $S_{t+1} - S_t$ and $F_t - S_{t+1}$ is easily explained. The standard deviations of $F_t - S_t$ are between 0.17 and 0.66 percent per month, whereas those of either $S_{t+1} - S_t$ or $F_t - S_{t+1}$ are typically greater than 3.0 percent per month. Thus, the autocorrelation of P_t and/or $E(S_{t+1} - S_t)$, which shows up in the time series behavior of $F_t - S_t$, is buried in the high variability of the unexpected components of $F_t - S_{t+1}$ and $S_{t+1} - S_t$.

TABLE 1. Autocorrelations, means, and standard deviations: 8/31/73–12/10/82, $N = 122$[a]

Country	Autocorrelations												Mean	Std. Dev.
	ρ_1	ρ_2	ρ_3	ρ_4	ρ_5	ρ_6	ρ_7	ρ_8	ρ_9	ρ_{10}	ρ_{11}	ρ_{12}		
							$S_{t+1} - S_t$							
Belgium	0.05	0.08	0.07	-0.03	0.02	-0.03	-0.01	0.06	0.14	-0.07	0.20	0.01	-0.25	3.11
Canada	0.13	-0.24	0.08	0.05	0.03	0.00	-0.16	0.06	0.07	-0.15	0.16	0.03	-0.17	1.12
France	-0.04	0.06	0.14	-0.02	0.14	0.04	0.01	-0.02	0.10	-0.12	0.11	-0.01	-0.43	3.01
Italy	0.01	0.15	-0.03	-0.11	0.09	-0.01	0.09	0.04	0.14	-0.17	0.12	-0.01	-0.73	2.80
Japan	0.16	-0.11	0.03	0.13	0.15	-0.09	-0.04	0.07	0.05	-0.09	-0.10	0.11	0.07	3.05
Netherlands	0.02	0.05	0.05	-0.14	-0.01	-0.01	-0.01	0.04	0.04	-0.06	0.17	-0.02	-0.04	3.01
Switzerland	0.01	0.08	0.03	-0.11	0.09	0.01	-0.05	-0.08	0.01	-0.04	0.07	-0.01	0.26	3.76
United Kingdom	0.15	0.04	0.10	-0.07	0.09	0.04	0.16	0.01	0.02	0.07	0.08	0.14	-0.36	2.58
West Germany	0.01	0.08	0.01	-0.13	0.00	-0.04	0.02	0.06	0.07	-0.05	0.17	-0.00	-0.03	3.08
							$F_t - S_{t+1}$							
Belgium	0.11	0.10	0.08	-0.02	0.02	-0.05	-0.03	0.04	0.11	-0.08	0.19	0.00	0.09	3.22
Canada	0.17	-0.21	0.07	0.04	0.01	-0.01	-0.16	0.04	0.06	-0.14	0.15	0.02	0.08	1.16
France	0.01	0.09	0.16	-0.01	0.14	0.04	0.00	-0.02	0.06	-0.10	0.12	-0.01	0.17	3.10
Italy	0.08	0.17	-0.02	-0.11	0.07	-0.03	0.08	0.03	0.11	-0.17	0.07	-0.03	-0.07	2.95
Japan	0.21	-0.05	0.07	0.13	0.14	-0.09	-0.05	0.05	0.05	-0.07	-0.08	0.12	0.10	3.15
Netherlands	0.07	0.08	0.07	-0.11	0.01	-0.00	-0.00	0.04	0.04	-0.05	0.19	0.01	0.21	3.08
Switzerland	0.05	0.10	0.06	-0.09	0.09	0.01	-0.04	-0.08	0.01	-0.02	0.08	0.01	0.23	3.82
United Kingdom	0.19	0.08	0.12	-0.06	0.09	0.03	0.15	0.01	0.01	0.05	0.07	0.13	0.13	2.65
West Germany	0.03	0.09	0.03	-0.12	0.00	-0.04	0.02	0.05	0.07	-0.04	0.18	0.02	0.33	3.12

	$F_t - S_t$													
Belgium	0.67	0.44	0.33	0.33	0.18	0.04	-0.01	0.01	0.00	-0.01	0.00	-0.01	-0.16	0.41
Canada	0.82	0.63	0.49	0.38	0.36	0.32	0.33	0.36	0.36	0.35	0.26	0.23	-0.09	0.17
France	0.65	0.45	0.36	0.28	0.24	0.18	0.17	0.18	0.23	0.28	0.26	0.23	-0.25	0.44
Italy	0.68	0.47	0.37	0.28	0.23	0.19	0.18	0.19	0.19	0.14	0.03	0.04	-0.80	0.66
Japan	0.85	0.69	0.61	0.47	0.34	0.30	0.22	0.16	0.21	0.24	0.22	0.20	0.17	0.64
Netherlands	0.72	0.55	0.40	0.28	0.24	0.20	0.20	0.23	0.22	0.21	0.15	0.09	0.17	0.32
Switzerland	0.86	0.73	0.61	0.52	0.47	0.46	0.48	0.49	0.50	0.49	0.44	0.40	0.48	0.37
United Kingdom	0.87	0.75	0.64	0.51	0.43	0.36	0.31	0.28	0.25	0.20	0.16	0.15	-0.23	0.35
West Germany	0.78	0.56	0.39	0.26	0.20	0.20	0.26	0.34	0.42	0.46	0.40	0.33	0.30	0.24

[a] All exchange rates are U.S. dollars per unit of foreign currency. $S_{t+1} - S_t$ is the four-week change in the spot exchange rate; $F_t - S_{t+1}$ is the thirty-day forward rate minus the spot rate observed four weeks later; $F_t - S_t$ is the forward rate minus the current spot rate. The means and standard deviations of the variables are on a percent per month basis. Under the hypothesis that the true autocorrelations are 0.0, the standard error of the sample autocorrelations is about 0.09.

4. REGRESSION TESTS

4.1. OLS Estimates

Table 2 shows the estimated regressions of $F_t - S_{t+1}$ and $S_{t+1} - S_t$ on $F_t - S_t$. Only one set of coefficient standard errors, residual standard errors and residual autocorrelations is shown for each country. This reflects the complementarity of the $F_t - S_{t+1}$ and $S_{t+1} - S_t$ regressions for each country. The intercept estimates in the two regressions sum to zero, the slope coefficients sum to one, and the sum of the two residuals is zero on a period-by-period basis.

Since the regressor $F_t - S_t$ has low variation relative to $F_t - S_{t+1}$ and $S_{t+1} - S_t$, the coefficients of determination (R_1^2 and R_2^2) for the regressions are small, and they are smaller for the $S_{t+1} - S_t$ regressions than for the $F_t - S_{t+1}$ regressions. The regression residuals, like the dependent variables, show little autocorrelation.

The anomalous numbers in table 2 are the estimates of the regression slope coefficients, $\hat{\beta}_1$ and $\hat{\beta}_2$. According to (5) and (6), the slope coefficient in the regression of $F_t - S_{t+1}$ on $F_t - S_t$ contains the proportion of the variance of $F_t - S_t$ due to variation in its premium component, P_t, while the slope coefficient in the regression of $S_{t+1} - S_t$ on $F_t - S_t$ contains the proportion of the variance of $F_t - S_t$ due to variation in the expected change in the spot rate, $E(S_{t+1} - S_t)$. The coefficients clearly cannot be interpreted in terms of these proportions alone, since the coefficients in the $S_{t+1} - S_t$ regressions are always negative so that those in the $F_t - S_{t+1}$ regressions are greater than 1.0.

Inspection of (5) and (6) indicates an explanation for the strange estimates of β_1 and β_2. Since $\sigma^2(E(S_{t+1} - S_t))$ in (6) must be non-negative, a negative estimate of β_2 implies that $cov(P_t, E(S_{t+1} - S_t))$ is negative and larger in magnitude than $\sigma^2(E(S_{t+1} - S_t))$. The complementary estimate of $\beta_1 > 1$ then implies that $cov(P_t, E(S_{t+1} - S_t))$ is smaller in absolute magnitude than $\sigma^2(P_t)$, and thus that $\sigma^2(P_t)$ is larger than $\sigma^2(E(S_{t+1} - S_t))$.

The non-zero covariance between P_t and $E(S_{t+1} - S_t)$ prevents us from using the regression coefficients to estimate the levels of $\sigma^2(P_t)$ and $\sigma^2(E(S_{t+1} - S_t))$. With (5) and (6), however, we can estimate the difference between the two variances as a proportion of $\sigma^2(F_t - S_t)$,

$$\beta_1 - \beta_2 = \frac{\sigma^2(P_t) - \sigma^2(E(S_{t+1} - S_t))}{\sigma^2(F_t - S_t)} \tag{10}$$

The differences between the estimates of β_1 and β_2 in table 2 range from 1.58 (Japan) to 4.16 (Belgium). Except for Japan, all the differences between the

TABLE 2. OLS regressions: 8/31/73–12/10/82, N = 122[a]

$$F_t - S_{t+1} = \hat{\alpha}_1 + \hat{\beta}_1(F_t - S_t) + \hat{\epsilon}_{1,t+1}, \quad S_{t+1} - S_t = \hat{\alpha}_2 + \hat{\beta}_2(F_t - S_t) + \hat{\epsilon}_{2,t+1}$$

Country	$\hat{\alpha}_1$	$\hat{\beta}_1$	$\hat{\alpha}_2$	$\hat{\beta}_2$	$s(\hat{\alpha})$	$s(\hat{\beta})$	R_1^2	R_2^2	$s(\hat{\epsilon})$	Residual autocorrelations					
										ρ_1	ρ_2	ρ_3	ρ_4	ρ_5	ρ_6
Belgium	0.50	2.58	-0.50	-1.58	0.30	0.68	0.11	0.04	3.05	0.01	0.06	0.06	-0.03	0.02	0.02
Canada	0.25	1.87	-0.25	-0.87	0.11	0.61	0.07	0.01	1.12	0.12	-0.23	0.10	0.07	0.06	0.03
France	0.64	1.87	-0.64	-0.87	0.31	0.63	0.07	0.01	3.00	-0.07	0.04	0.13	-0.03	0.15	0.04
Italy	1.14	1.51	-1.14	-0.51	0.40	0.38	0.11	0.01	2.79	-0.00	0.16	-0.01	-0.09	0.10	0.01
Japan	-0.12	1.29	0.12	-0.29	0.29	0.43	0.07	0.00	3.06	0.15	-0.12	0.03	0.13	0.16	-0.08
Netherlands	-0.21	2.43	0.21	-1.43	0.31	0.86	0.06	0.01	2.99	-0.03	0.03	0.02	-0.17	-0.01	-0.02
Switzerland	-0.81	2.14	0.81	-1.14	0.56	0.92	0.04	0.00	3.75	-0.02	0.06	0.01	-0.12	0.10	0.02
United Kingdom	0.57	1.90	-0.57	-0.90	0.28	0.66	0.06	0.01	2.57	0.13	0.03	0.11	-0.06	0.10	0.05
West Germany	-0.36	2.32	0.36	-1.32	0.44	1.15	0.03	0.00	3.08	-0.01	0.07	0.00	-0.13	0.01	-0.03

[a] R_1^2 and R_2^2 are the coefficients of determination (regression R^2) for the $F_t - S_{t+1}$ and $S_{t+1} - S_t$ regressions. The complete complementarity of the $F_t - S_{t+1}$ and $S_{t+1} - S_t$ regressions for each country means that the standard errors $s(\hat{\alpha})$ and $s(\hat{\beta})$ of the estimated regression coefficients, the residual standard error $s(\hat{\epsilon})$, and the residual autocorrelations, ρ_i, are the same for the two regressions. Under the hypothesis that the true autocorrelations are zero, the standard error of the estimated residual autocorrelations is about 0.09.

estimated coefficients are greater than 2.0. Thus, the point estimates are that the difference between the variance of the premium, P_t, and the variance of the expected change in the spot rate, $E(S_{t+1} - S_t)$, in $F_t - S_t$ is typically more than twice the variance of $F_t - S_t$. Moreover, since $\hat{\beta}_1$ and $\hat{\beta}_2$ sum to 1.0, the estimates of the regression coefficients are perfectly negatively correlated, and the standard error of their difference is twice their common standard error. Only the estimates of $\beta_1 - \beta_2$ for Japan, Switzerland, and West Germany are less than two standard errors from zero, and all are more than 1.5 standard errors from zero. Thus, we can conclude that $\sigma^2(P_t)$ is reliably greater than $\sigma^2(E(S_{t+1} - S_t))$.

In short, negative covariation between P_t and $E(S_{t+1} - S_t)$ attenuates the variability of $F_t - S_t$ and obscures the interpretation of the regression slope coefficients in (3) and (4). Nevertheless the regression slope coefficients provide the interesting information that both the premium, P_t, and the expected change in the spot rate, $E(S_{t+1} - S_t)$, in $F_t - S_t$ vary through time, and $\sigma^2(P_t)$ is large relative to $\sigma^2(E(S_{t+1} - S_t))$.

A good story for negative covariation between P_t and $E(S_{t+1} - S_t)$ is difficult to tell. For example, in the PPP model for the exchange rate underlying (9), the dollar is expected to appreciate relative to a foreign currency, that is, $E(S_{t+1} - S_t)$ is negative, when the expected inflation rate in the U.S. is lower than in the foreign country. (Remember that the exchange rates are all expressed as dollars per unit of foreign currency.) A negative $\text{cov}(P_t, E(S_{t+1} - S_t))$ then implies a higher purchasing power risk premium in the expected real returns on dollar denominated bonds relative to foreign currency bonds when the anticipated U.S. inflation rate is low relative to the anticipated foreign inflation rate.

We return to economic interpretations of the negative covariance between the P_t and $E(S_{t+1} - S_t)$ components of $F_t - S_t$ after exploring some purely statistical possibilities.

4.2. SUR Estimates

The apparent negative covariation between P_t and $E(S_{t+1} - S_t)$ may be sampling error. All the slope coefficients in the $F_t - S_{t+1}$ regressions are more than two standard errors above 0.0, but only one (Belgium) is more than two standard errors above 1.0. Equivalently, only one of the negative slope coefficients in the $S_{t+1} - S_t$ regressions (Belgium) is more than two standard errors below zero. Perhaps the appropriate conclusion is that all variation through time in $F_t - S_t$ is variation in premiums, and there is no variation in expected changes in spot rates.

Individually testing the $\hat{\beta}_1$ coefficients in table 2 against 1.0 (or the $\hat{\beta}_2$ coefficients against 0.0) does not provide the appropriate joint test that all $\beta_1 = 1.0$ (or all $\beta_2 = 0$). An appropriate joint test takes into account the high correlation of $F_t - S_{t+1}$ (or $S_{t+1} - S_t$) across currencies, documented in table 3. Such cross-correlation is to be expected given that (a) all exchange rates are measured relative to the U.S. dollar, and (b) most of the European countries are involved in attempts to control the movements of their exchange rates relative to one another during the sample period. Table 3 also indicates that, with the possible exception of Canada, the correlations of the regressor variable $F_t - S_t$ across countries are generally lower than the correlations of $S_{t+1} - S_t$ or $F_t - S_{t+1}$ across the countries. Thus, there is reason to suspect that joint estimation of the $F_t - S_{t+1}$ (or the $S_{t+1} - S_t$) regressions for different countries will improve the precision of the coefficient estimates.

The coefficient estimates obtained when Zellner's (1962) 'seemingly unrelated regression' (SUR) technique is used to estimate either the $F_t - S_{t+1}$ regressions for different countries or the $S_{t+1} - S_t$ regressions are summarized in part A of table 4. As anticipated, joint estimation substantially improves the precision of the estimated slope coefficients. The $s(\hat{\beta})$ in table 4 are often less than half those for the OLS estimates in table 2. Moreover, the slope coefficients in the SUR versions of the $S_{t+1} - S_t$ regressions are generally closer to zero than in the OLS regressions which means that the coefficients in the complementary $F_t - S_{t+1}$ regressions are generally closer to 1.0. (Canada and Switzerland are exceptions.)

Table 4 also shows F tests on various joint hypotheses on the coefficients. The hypothesis that all the slope coefficients β_2 in the $S_{t+1} - S_t$ regressions (or all the slope coefficients β_1 in the $F_t - S_{t+1}$ regressions) are equal is consistent with the data. However, the hypothesis that all $\beta_2 = 0.0$ (or all $\beta_1 = 1.0$) yields a test statistic far out in the tail of the F distribution (beyond the 0.997 fractile) which suggests rejection of the hypothesis. Thus, we are left with the uncomfortable conclusion that the negative estimates of β_2 in the regressions of $S_{t+1} - S_t$ on $F_t - S_t$ are the result of negative covariation between the P_t and $E(S_{t+1} - S_t)$ components of $F_t - S_t$.

Finally, since the hypothesis that the slope coefficients in the $S_{t+1} - S_t$ (or $F_t - S_{t+1}$) regressions are equal across countries is consistent with the data, we can use the SUR technique to estimate the regressions subject to the equality constraint. The results for the $S_{t+1} - S_t$ regressions are shown in part B of table 4. For all but three countries (France, Italy and Japan) the constrained

TABLE 3. Correlations of $S_{t+1} - S_t$, $F_t - S_{t+1}$ and $F_t - S_t$ across countries[a]

$S_{t+1} - S_t$

	Belgium	Canada	France	Italy	Japan	Netherlands	Switzerland	United Kingdom	West Germany
Belgium	1.00								
Canada	0.19	1.00							
France	0.84	0.18	1.00						
Italy	0.69	0.10	0.77	1.00					
Japan	0.52	0.04	0.56	0.48	1.00				
Netherlands	0.94	0.19	0.85	0.72	0.50	1.00			
Switzerland	0.81	0.13	0.76	0.64	0.53	0.81	1.00		
United Kingdom	0.57	0.18	0.54	0.54	0.46	0.56	0.51	1.00	
West Germany	0.94	0.17	0.84	0.71	0.54	0.96	0.85	0.53	1.00

$F_t - S_{t+1}$

	Belgium	Canada	France	Italy	Japan	Netherlands	Switzerland	United Kingdom	West Germany
Belgium	1.00								
Canada	0.20	1.00							
France	0.85	0.16	1.00						
Italy	0.69	0.07	0.74	1.00					
Japan	0.51	0.07	0.55	0.46	1.00				
Netherlands	0.94	0.20	0.85	0.71	0.51	1.00			
Switzerland	0.80	0.14	0.76	0.61	0.55	0.80	1.00		
United Kingdom	0.55	0.16	0.51	0.51	0.47	0.56	0.50	1.00	
West Germany	0.93	0.18	0.84	0.69	0.56	0.96	0.85	0.53	1.00

$F_t - S_t$

	Belgium	Canada	France	Italy	Japan	Netherlands	Switzerland	United Kingdom	West Germany
Belgium	1.00								
Canada	0.55	1.00							
France	0.57	0.43	1.00						
Italy	0.59	0.43	0.51	1.00					
Japan	0.31	0.12	0.36	0.32	1.00				
Netherlands	0.54	0.40	0.31	0.49	0.49	1.00			
Switzerland	0.38	0.25	0.51	0.43	0.77	0.59	1.00		
United Kingdom	0.45	0.36	0.31	0.47	0.65	0.74	0.63	1.00	
West Germany	0.49	0.50	0.52	0.49	0.73	0.69	0.88	0.72	1.00

[a]$S_{t+1} - S_t$ is the four-week change in the spot exchange rate: $F_t - S_{t+1}$ is the thirty-day forward rate minus the spot rate observed four weeks later; $F_t - S_t$ is the forward rate minus the current spot rate.

TABLE 4. SUR regressions: 8/31/73–12/10/82, $N = 122^a$

$$F_t - S_{t+1} = \hat{\alpha}_1 + \hat{\beta}_1(F_t - S_t) + \hat{\varepsilon}_{1,t+1}, \qquad S_{t+1} - S_t = \hat{\alpha}_2 + \hat{\beta}_2(F_t - S_t) + \hat{\varepsilon}_{2,t+1}$$

Part A: Unconstrained

	$\hat{\alpha}_2(=-\hat{\alpha}_1)$	$\hat{\beta}_2(=1-\hat{\beta}_1)$	$s(\hat{\alpha})$	$s(\hat{\beta})$
Belgium	-0.36	-0.72	0.28	0.24
Canada	-0.26	-1.04	0.11	0.59
France	-0.48	-0.21	0.28	0.30
Italy	-1.08	-0.44	0.32	0.24
Japan	0.12	-0.28	0.28	0.35
Netherlands	0.10	-0.78	0.27	0.25
Switzerland	0.81	-1.15	0.42	0.50
United Kingdom	-0.52	-0.69	0.26	0.51
West Germany	0.23	-0.89	0.29	0.32

F tests			
	1. All β_2 (or β_1) equal	$F = 0.73$	P level = 0.66
	2. All α_2 (or α_1) equal	$F = 5.14$	P level = 0.0001
	3. All $\beta_2 = 0.0$ (or $\beta_1 = 1.0$)	$F = 2.81$	P level = 0.003

Part B: Constrained

$$S_{t+1} - S_t = \hat{\alpha}_B + \hat{\alpha}_C + \hat{\alpha}_F + \hat{\alpha}_I + \hat{\alpha}_J + \hat{\alpha}_N + \hat{\alpha}_S + \hat{\alpha}_{UK} + \hat{\alpha}_{WG} + \hat{\beta}_2 \ (F_t - S_t)$$

	$\hat{\alpha}_B$	$\hat{\alpha}_C$	$\hat{\alpha}_F$	$\hat{\alpha}_I$	$\hat{\alpha}_J$	$\hat{\alpha}_N$	$\hat{\alpha}_S$	$\hat{\alpha}_{UK}$	$\hat{\alpha}_{WG}$	$\hat{\beta}_2$
	-0.34	-0.22	-0.57	-1.20	0.17	0.07	0.54	-0.49	0.14	-0.58
	(0.28)	(0.10)	(0.27)	(0.27)	(0.28)	(0.27)	(0.35)	(0.23)	(0.28)	(0.13)

F test	All α equal	$F = 5.68$	P level = 0.0001

[a]Like the OLS regressions in table 2, the SUR regressions are completely complementary; that is, the intercepts in the $F_t - S_{t+1}$ and $S_{t+1} - S_t$ regressions sum to 0.0, the slopes sum to 1.0, and the residuals sum to 0.0 period-by-period. The subscripts on the $\hat{\alpha}$ in the constrained $S_{t+1} - S_t$ regressions indicate countries.

estimate of β_2, -0.58, is closer to 0.0 than the unconstrained estimate in part A of the table. However, constraining the estimate of β_2 to be equal across countries so lowers the standard error of the estimate that $\hat{\beta}_2$ is now more than four standard errors from 0.0.

4.3. Subperiod Results

Some argue that the nature of the flexible exchange rate system during our sample period is not well understood by market participants until the late 1970's. [See, for example, Hansen and Hodrick (1983).] Thus, the properties of forward exchange rates as predictors of future spot rates may be different during later years. To check on this possibility, the tests in tables 1 to 4 are replicated for the two 61-month subperiods covered by the data. The results are summarized in tables 5 to 7. The subperiod results also help to alleviate any statistical problems caused by changes in variance during the sample period.

There are some differences between the two subperiods. For example, the summary statistics of table 5 document an increase in the variability of $S_{t+1} - S_t$ and $F_t - S_{t+1}$ for the later period. There is no corresponding increase in the variability of $F_t - S_t$. The implied conclusion is that the higher variability of $S_{t+1} - S_t$ and $F_t - S_{t+1}$ in later years reflects increased uncertainty about the *ex post* change in the spot rate with no corresponding increase in the variability of the *ex ante* $E(S_{t+1} - S_t)$ and P_t components of $F_t - S_t$.

The mean values of the variables do not suggest improved market forecasts of future spot rates during the later subperiod. The mean of $F_t - S_t$ more often has the same sign as the mean of $S_{t+1} - S_t$ during the earlier subperiod (seven of nine versus five of nine for the later period). Moreover, although the dollar appreciates relative to all nine currencies during the later period (the means of $S_{t+1} - S_t$ are all negative), all the means of $F_t - S_t$ move upward. Thus, either the forward rate on average becomes a less rational predictor of the future spot rate during the later period, or, as suggested by the regression results, there is opposite movement in the premium component of $F_t - S_t$ which more than offsets movement in the expected change in the spot rate.

On the other hand, the key aspects of the regression results in tables 6 and 7 are similar for the two subperiods. The slope coefficients in the regressions of $S_{t+1} - S_t$ on $F_t - S_t$ are generally negative, which means that the coefficients in the complementary regressions of $F_t - S_{t+1}$ on $F_t - S_t$ are generally greater than 1.0. In the SUR tests, the hypothesis that all the slope coefficients in the $S_{t+1} - S_t$ regressions are 0.0 (or that the coefficients in the $F_t - S_{t+1}$ regressions are 1.0) is easily rejected in either subperiod.

Under the maintained hypothesis that the market assessments of $E(S_{t+1} - S_t)$ in $F_t - S_t$ are efficient or rational, the subperiod results confirm the earlier conclusions that (a) there is variation in both the P_t and $E(S_{t+1} - S_t)$ components of $F_t - S_t$, (b) the variance of the premium component of $F_t - S_t$ is large relative to the variance of the expected change in the spot rate, and (c) negative covariation between P_t and $E(S_{t+1} - S_t)$ dominates the variance of $E(S_{t+1} - S_t)$ to produce negative slope coefficients in the regressions of $S_{t+1} - S_t$ on $F_t - S_t$.

TABLE 5. Autocorrelations, means and standard deviations for 61-month subperiods[a]

	First subperiod: 8/31/73–4/7/78 Autocorrelations						Second subperiod: 5/5/78–12/10/82 Autocorrelations					
Country	ρ_1	ρ_2	ρ_3	ρ_4	Mean	Std. dev.	ρ_1	ρ_2	ρ_3	ρ_4	Mean	Std. dev.
			$S_{t+1} - S_t$						$S_{t+1} - S_t$			
Belgium	0.11	0.16	0.05	-0.13	0.20	2.57	-0.00	0.01	0.06	-0.01	-0.69	3.48
Canada	0.19	-0.05	0.28	0.23	-0.21	1.00	0.11	-0.33	-0.04	-0.07	-0.13	1.23
France	0.09	0.05	0.13	-0.04	-0.16	2.49	-0.11	0.04	0.11	-0.06	-0.69	3.42
Italy	0.19	0.25	-0.18	-0.23	-0.63	2.56	-0.12	0.08	0.08	-0.04	-0.83	3.00
Japan	0.21	0.04	-0.10	-0.06	0.30	2.15	0.15	-0.18	-0.01	0.10	-0.17	3.70
Netherlands	0.07	0.03	0.04	-0.18	0.30	2.66	-0.02	0.07	0.04	-0.13	-0.37	3.27
Switzerland	0.08	0.26	0.13	-0.13	0.69	2.84	-0.03	-0.03	-0.03	-0.13	-0.18	4.43
United Kingdom	0.14	0.18	0.03	-0.16	-0.48	2.31	0.15	-0.06	0.16	0.02	-0.24	2.80
West Germany	0.15	0.13	-0.00	-0.19	0.25	2.64	0.09	0.05	0.01	-0.11	-0.32	3.42
			$F_t - S_{t+1}$						$F_t - S_{t+1}$			
Belgium	0.17	0.21	0.07	-0.14	-0.49	2.68	0.02	0.00	0.05	0.01	0.66	3.56
Canada	0.21	-0.03	0.30	0.24	0.10	1.02	0.16	-0.30	-0.06	-0.09	0.07	1.27
France	0.12	0.08	0.14	-0.03	-0.30	2.59	-0.08	0.05	0.11	-0.07	0.64	3.45
Italy	0.26	0.26	-0.17	-0.21	-0.44	2.74	-0.08	0.07	0.08	-0.06	0.30	3.08
Japan	0.22	0.02	-0.17	-0.21	-0.50	2.19	0.19	-0.13	0.03	0.12	0.71	3.77
Netherlands	0.10	0.04	0.04	-0.18	-0.29	2.72	0.02	0.09	0.06	-0.10	0.70	3.30
Switzerland	0.10	0.26	0.12	-0.14	-0.48	2.83	-0.01	-0.02	-0.02	-0.13	0.93	4.47
United Kingdom	0.13	0.16	-0.01	-0.21	0.06	2.33	0.22	0.02	0.20	0.07	0.20	2.91
West Germany	0.16	0.13	-0.00	-0.20	-0.11	2.67	-0.08	0.05	0.02	-0.11	0.77	3.43

(Continued)

TABLE 5. (Continued)

Country	First subperiod: 8/31/73–4/7/78						Second subperiod: 5/5/78–12/10/82					
	Autocorrelations				Mean	Std. dev.	Autocorrelations				Mean	Std. dev.
	ρ_1	ρ_2	ρ_3	ρ_4			ρ_1	ρ_2	ρ_3	ρ_4		
			$F_t - S_t$						$F_t - S_t$			
Belgium	0.70	0.52	0.28	0.17	−0.28	0.39	0.56	0.20	0.18	0.31	−0.03	0.38
Canada	0.91	0.82	0.74	0.71	−0.12	0.17	0.70	0.39	0.14	−0.07	−0.06	0.16
France	0.46	0.02	−0.06	−0.08	−0.46	0.36	0.63	0.50	0.35	0.18	−0.05	0.40
Italy	0.61	0.36	0.36	0.25	−1.06	0.70	0.60	0.36	0.03	−0.09	−0.53	0.49
Japan	0.73	0.47	0.37	0.15	−0.20	0.66	0.82	0.65	0.41	0.24	0.54	0.33
Netherlands	0.60	0.43	0.29	0.12	0.01	0.30	0.65	0.33	0.04	−0.11	0.33	0.24
Switzerland	0.67	0.42	0.20	−0.00	0.21	0.26	0.69	0.32	−0.03	−0.27	0.76	0.23
United Kingdom	0.83	0.69	0.54	0.35	−0.41	0.29	0.78	0.59	0.42	0.26	−0.04	0.31
West Germany	0.61	0.32	0.12	−0.16	0.14	0.16	0.62	0.18	−0.18	−0.37	0.45	0.21

[a] All exchange rates are U.S. dollars per unit of foreign currency. $S_{t+1} - S_t$ is the four-week change in the spot exchange rate: $F_t - S_{t+1}$ is the forward rate minus the spot rate observed four weeks later; $F_t - S_t$ is the forward rate minus the current spot rate. The means and standard deviations of the variables are on a percent per month basis. Under the hypothesis that the true autocorrelations are zero, the standard error of the sample autocorrelation ρ_τ is approximately 0.13.

TABLE 6. OLS regressions for 61-month subperiods[a]

$$F_t - S_{t+1} = \hat{\alpha}_1 + \hat{\beta}_1(F_t - S_t) + \hat{\varepsilon}_{1,t+1}, \qquad S_{t+1} - S_t = \hat{\alpha}_2 + \hat{\beta}_2(F_t - S_t) + \hat{\varepsilon}_{2,t+1}$$

Country	$\hat{\alpha}_2(=-\hat{\alpha}_1)$	$\hat{\beta}_2(=1-\hat{\beta}_1)$	$s(\hat{\alpha})$	$s(\hat{\beta})$	R_1^2	R_2^2	$s(\hat{\varepsilon})$	ρ_1
				First subperiod: 8/31/73–4/7/78				
Belgium	-0.20	-1.42	0.40	0.83	0.13	0.05	2.56	0.05
Canada	-0.25	-0.32	0.16	0.77	0.05	0.00	1.01	0.19
France	-0.79	-1.38	0.51	0.87	0.11	0.04	2.48	0.06
Italy	-1.17	-0.51	0.60	0.47	0.15	0.02	2.58	0.17
Japan	0.37	0.31	0.29	0.42	0.04	0.01	2.18	0.20
Netherlands	0.31	-1.22	0.34	1.14	0.06	0.02	2.68	0.04
Switzerland	0.52	0.81	0.47	1.40	0.00	0.01	2.88	0.10
United Kingdom	-0.47	0.02	0.52	1.04	0.02	0.00	2.35	0.14
West Germany	0.62	-2.60	0.45	2.12	0.05	0.03	2.65	0.14
				Second subperiod: 55/78–12/10/82				
Belgium	-0.74	-1.32	0.45	1.18	0.06	0.02	3.50	-0.02
Canada	-0.23	-1.64	0.17	0.98	0.11	0.05	1.22	0.06
France	-0.70	-0.22	0.45	1.11	0.02	0.00	3.47	-0.12
Italy	-1.15	-0.60	0.58	0.80	0.06	0.01	3.04	-0.12
Japan	0.82	-1.84	0.92	1.46	0.06	0.03	3.72	0.11
Netherlands	0.02	-1.18	0.73	1.77	0.03	0.01	3.32	-0.06
Switzerland	1.66	-2.44	1.98	2.50	0.03	0.02	4.47	-0.06
United Kingdom	-0.36	-2.83	0.35	1.12	0.17	0.10	2.71	-0.03
West Germany	-0.30	-0.04	1.05	2.10	0.00	0.00	3.48	-0.09

[a]R_1^2 and R_2^2 are the coefficients of determination (regression R^2) for the $F_t - S_{t+1}$ and $S_{t+1} - S_t$ regressions. The complete complementarity of the $F_t - S_{t+1}$ and $S_{t+1} - S_t$ regressions for each country means that the standard errors $s(\hat{\alpha})$ and $s(\hat{\beta})$ of the estimated regression coefficients, the residual standard error $s(\hat{\varepsilon})$, and the residual autocorrelation ρ_1 are the same for the two regressions.

TABLE 7. SUR regressions for 61-month subperiods[a]

$$F_t - S_{t+1} = \hat{\alpha}_1 + \hat{\beta}_1(F_t - S_t) + \hat{\varepsilon}_{1, t+1}, \qquad S_{t+1} - S_t = \hat{\alpha}_2 + \hat{\beta}_2(F_t - S_t) + \hat{\varepsilon}_{2, t+1}$$

Country	$\hat{\alpha}_2(= -\hat{\alpha}_1)$	$\hat{\beta}_2(= 1 - \hat{\beta}_1)$	$s(\hat{\alpha})$	$s(\hat{\beta})$
	First subperiod: 8/31/73–4/7/78			
Belgium	0.00	−0.72	0.33	0.22
Canada	−0.22	−0.01	0.15	0.71
France	−0.37	−0.45	0.41	0.56
Italy	−1.04	−0.39	0.52	0.37
Japan	0.35	0.24	0.29	0.33
Netherlands	0.31	−0.53	0.34	0.31
Switzerland	0.78	−0.41	0.40	0.73
United Kingdom	−0.54	−0.16	0.45	0.79
West Germany	0.57	−2.23	0.35	0.59

F tests
1. All β_2 (or β_1) equal $F = 2.56$ P level = 0.0095
2. All $\beta_2 = 0$ (or $\beta_1 = 1$) $F = 3.22$ P level = 0.0009
3. All α_2 (or α_1) equal $F = 3.92$ P level = 0.0002

Country	$\hat{\alpha}_2(= -\hat{\alpha}_1)$	$\hat{\beta}_2(= 1 - \hat{\beta}_1)$	$s(\hat{\alpha})$	$s(\hat{\beta})$
	Second subperiod: 5/5/78–12/10/82			
Belgium	−0.71	−0.41	0.45	0.41
Canada	−0.24	−1.78	0.16	0.82
France	−0.68	0.24	0.45	0.32
Italy	−1.11	−0.52	0.41	0.22
Japan	1.08	−2.32	0.78	1.15
Netherlands	−0.03	−1.03	0.44	0.37
Switzerland	1.87	−2.71	1.09	1.23
United Kingdom	−0.37	−3.06	0.35	0.78
West Germany	−0.11	−0.46	0.48	0.40

F tests
1. All β_2 (or β_1) equal $F = 3.17$ P level = 0.0016
2. All $\beta_2 = 0$ (or $\beta_1 = 1$) $F = 4.20$ P level = 0.0001
3. All α_2 (or α_1) equal $F = 3.92$ P level = 0.0002

[a]Like the OLS regressions, the SUR regressions are completely complementary; that is, the intercepts in the $F_t - S_{t+1}$ and $S_{t+1} - S_t$ regressions sum to 0.0, the slopes sum to 1.0 and the residuals sum to 0.0 period-by-period.

5. INTERPRETATIONS

Various explanations of the results are suggested by the existing literature and by readers of earlier versions of this paper. Some of these explanations are discussed now. No explanation is necessarily complete, and they are not mutually exclusive. Moreover, generous readers of earlier drafts are not responsible for my paraphrasing of their comments.

5.1. An Inefficient Foreign Exchange Market

The interpretation of the results above is based on the hypothesis that the assessment of $E(S_{t+1} - S_t)$ in $F_t - S_t$ is efficient or rational. An alternative hypothesis is that the negative slope coefficients in the regressions of $S_{t+1} - S_t$ on $F_t - S_t$ reflect assessments of $E(S_{t+1} - S_t)$ that are consistently perverse relative to the true expected value of the change in the spot rate. The large positive coefficients in the $F_t - S_{t+1}$ regressions are then a simple consequence of the complementarity of the $F_t - S_{t+1}$ and $S_{t+1} - S_t$ regressions rather than manifestation of movement in rationally determined premiums. Under this interpretation, the similarity of the regression results for the two subperiods indicates that market irrationality in forecasting exchange rates is not cured by continued experience with flexible exchange rates.

5.2. Government Intervention in the Spot Exchange Market

A kind of 'market inefficiency', suggested by Richard Roll, can result from government intervention in the spot foreign exchange market. For example, suppose forward rates are determined by the interest rate parity condition (7) and interest rates in different countries rationally reflect their expected inflation rates. Left to the open market forces suggested by purchasing power parity, spot exchange rates would tend to move in the direction implied by the forward-spot differential $F_t - S_t$. Government logic and obstinacy, however, may be inversely related to natural market forces. Governments may support their currencies more vigorously (through open market operations, trade restrictions, and restrictions on capital flows) the stronger are the market forces, like differential expected inflation rates, which indicate that the currency should depreciate. They may try to move back toward a free market equilibrium by changing the direction of the underlying factors pressuring the exchange rate, like differential inflation rates, rather than by letting adjustments take place through the exchange rate.

5.3. The Doomsday Theory

Michael Mussa suggests that there are episodes, often brief, during which the distribution of anticipated changes in exchange rates is highly skewed. For example, market participants may assess a small probability that a country will change its monetary policy so that its inflation rate will rise dramatically relative to other countries. The result may be a highly skewed distribution of anticipated inflation rates, which in turn increases interest rate differentials and forward-spot exchange rate differentials between this country and other countries. Since the phenomenon centers on skewness that exists for brief periods, the *ex post* drawings from the distributions of anticipated inflation rates and changes in exchange rates are likely to be below the *ex ante* means. This creates negative sample correlations between changes in exchange rates and forward-spot differentials which would not be observed if the skewed distributions were sampled over longer periods.

5.4. Stochastic Deviations from Purchasing Power Parity

Stockman (1980) and Lucas (1982) develop international models in which shocks to real activity work in part through money demand functions to drive changes in inflation and exchange rates. Fama (1982) also argues that through the workings of a standard money demand function and inertia in money supply, variation in anticipated real activity in the U.S. leads to variation in expected inflation of the opposite sign. Fama and Gibbons (1982) argue that expected real returns on U.S. nominal bonds are also driven by and move in the same direction as anticipated real activity. With a somewhat different story in which monetary shocks cause changes in real variables, Tobin (1965) and Mundell (1963) likewise conclude that the expected real and expected inflation components of nominal interest rates are negatively correlated.

Suppose (a) interest rate parity holds; (b) expected changes in exchange rates reflect expected inflation differentials; and (c) the expected real components of nominal interest rates can vary somewhat independently across countries in response to purely domestic factors. These conditions, along with either the Tobin–Mundell or Fama–Gibbons stories for negative correlation between the expected real and expected inflation components of nominal interest rates, imply negative correlation between the premium, P_t, and the expected change in the spot rate, $E(S_{t+1} - S_t)$, in the forward-spot differential, $F_t - S_t$.

To complete this story, however, we need a subplot to explain how the expected real returns on the nominal bonds of a country can vary in response to domestic factors that do not necessarily imply variation in the risks of the bonds. Segmented international capital markets can produce this result, but then the interest rate parity part of the story is likely to be lost. Alternatively, John Bilson suggests that such independent variation in the expected real returns on the nominal bonds of different countries can arise in open international capital markets when stochastic deviations from purchasing power parity (PPP) lead to strong preferences for borrowing and lending contracts denominated in one's domestic unit of account. Stulz (1981) provides a formal version of this kind of model in which deviations from PPP are due to the existence of nontraded goods. The Stulz model, in turn, can be viewed as a generalization of the Stockman (1980) and Lucas (1978, 1982) models.

6. CONCLUSIONS

Large positive autocorrelations of the difference between the forward rate and the current spot rate indicate variation through time in either the premium component of $F_t - S_t$ or in the assessment of the expected change in the spot rate. Moreover, slope coefficients in the regressions of $F_t - S_{t+1}$ and $S_{t+1} - S_t$ on $F_t - S_t$ that are reliably different from zero imply variation in both components of $F_t - S_t$. However, negative covariation between P_t and $E(S_{t+1} - S_t)$ leads to negative slope coefficients in the regressions of $S_{t+1} - S_t$ on $F_t - S_t$ and preempts accurate measurement of the variances of P_t and $E(S_{t+1} - S_t)$. Given market efficiency or rationality, the only conclusion we can draw from the negative slope coefficients in the $S_{t+1} - S_t$ regressions and slope coefficients greater than 1.0 in the complementary regressions of $F_t - S_{t+1}$ on $F_t - S_t$ is that the variance of the P_t component of $F_t - S_t$ is much larger than the variance of $E(S_{t+1} - S_t)$.

Any forward rate can be interpreted as the sum of a premium and an expected future spot rate. Thus, our regression approach to examining the components of forward rates has broad applicability to financial and commodity market data. In Fama (1984), I apply the approach to forward and spot interest rates on U.S. Treasury bills, with somewhat more success. For example, unlike the forward exchange rate, which seems primarily to reflect variation in its premium component, the difference between the forward one month interest rate for one month ahead and the current one month spot interest rate, $F_t - R_t$, splits roughly equally between variation in its premium component and variation in the expected change in the one month spot interest rate. Moreover, in the interest rate data, $F_t - R_t$ sometimes has a larger variance than the *ex post* change in the one month spot interest rate, $R_{t+1} - R_t$. Perhaps as a consequence, the *ex ante* $F_t - R_t$ explains from 15 to 70 percent of the variance of the *ex post* change in the spot interest rate, $R_{t+1} - R_t$. All of this is in striking contrast to the weak and somewhat perplexing picture that emerges from the exchange rate data, where variation in the *ex ante* forward-spot differential, $F_t - S_t$, is always small relative to the variation of the *ex post* change in the spot rate, $S_{t+1} - S_t$.

REFERENCES

Bilson, John F.O., 1981, The speculative efficiency hypothesis, Journal of Business 54, July, 435–451.

Breeden, Douglas T., 1979, An intertemporal asset pricing model with stochastic consumption and investment opportunities, Journal of Financial Economics 7, Sept., 265–296.

Domowitz, Ian and Craig S. Hakkio, 1983, Conditional variance and the risk premium on the foreign exchange market, Manuscript, Sept.

Fama, Eugene F., 1982, Inflation, output and money, Journal of Business 55, April, 201–231.

Fama, Eugene F., 1984, The information in the term structure, Journal of Financial Economics 13, forthcoming.

Fama, Eugene F. and André Farber, 1979, Money, bonds, and foreign exchange. American Economic Review 69, Sept., 269–282.

Fama, Eugene F. and Michael R. Gibbons, 1982, Inflation, real returns, and capital investment, Journal of Monetary Economics 9, May, 297–327.

Frankel, Jeffrey A., 1982, It. search of the exchange risk premium: A six currency test assuming mean variance optimization, Journal of International Money and Finance 1, Dec., 255–274.

Hansen, Lars P. and Robert J. Hodrick, 1980, Forward exchange rates as optimal predictors of future spot rates: An econometric analysis, Journal of Political Economy 88, Oct. 829–853.

Hansen, Lars P. and Robert J. Hodrick, 1983, Risk averse speculation in the forward foreign exchange market: An econometric analysis of linear models, in: J.A. Frenkel, ed., Exchange rates and international economics (University of Chicago Press for the National Bureau of Economic Research, Chicago, IL).

Hodrick, Robert J. and Sanjay Srivastava, 1984, An investigation of risk and return in forward foreign exchange, Journal of International Money and Finance 3, 5–29.

Hsich, David A., 1982, Tests of rational expectations and no risk premium in forward exchange markets, National Bureau of Economic Research working paper no, 843, Jan.

Korajczyk, Robert A., 1983, The pricing of forward and futures contracts for foreign exchange, Ph.D. thesis, May (Graduate School of Business, University of Chicago, Chicago, IL).

Levich, Richard M., 1979, On the efficiency of markets for foreign exchange, in: R. Dornbusch and J.A. Frenkel, eds., International economic policy: Theory and evidence, Ch. 7 (Johns Hopkins University Press. Baltimore, MD).

Lintner, John. 1965. The valuation of risk assets and the selection of risky investments in stock portfolios and capital budgets, Review of Economics and Statistics 47, Feb., 13–27.

Lucas, Robert E., Jr., 1978, Asset pricing in an exchange economy, Econometrica 46, Nov., 1429–1445.

Lucas, Robert E., Jr., 1982, Interest rates and currency prices in a two country world. Journal of Monetary Economics 10, Nov., 335–359.

Mundell, Robert, 1963. Inflation and real interest, Journal of Political Economy 71, June, 280–283.

Sharpe, William F., 1964, Capital asset prices: A they of market equilibrium under conditions of risk. Journal of Finance 19, Sept., 425–442.

Stockman, Alan C., 1980. A theory of exchange rate determination, Journal of Political Economy 88, Aug., 673–698.

Stulz, René M., 1981. A model of international asset pricing, Journal of Financial Economics 9, Dec., 383–406.

Tobin, James, 1965. Money and economic growth, Econometrica 33, Oct., 671–684.

Zellner, Arnold, 1962. An efficient method for estimating seemingly unrelated regressions and tests for aggregation bias, Journal of the American Statistical Association 57, June, 348–368.

DIVIDEND YIELDS AND
EXPECTED STOCK RETURNS

. . .

Eugene F. Fama and Kenneth R. French

The power of dividend yields to forecast stock returns, measured by regression R^2, increases with the return horizon. We offer a two-part explanation. (1) High autocorrelation causes the variance of expected returns to grow faster than the return horizon. (2) The growth of the variance of unexpected returns with the return horizon is attenuated by a discount-rate effect—shocks to expected returns generate opposite shocks to current prices. We estimate that, on average, the future price increases implied by higher expected returns are just offset by the decline in the current price. Thus, time-varying expected returns generate 'temporary' components of prices.

1. INTRODUCTION

There is much evidence that stock returns are predictable. The common conclusion, usually from tests on monthly data, is that the predictable component of returns, or equivalently, the variation through time of expected returns, is a small fraction (usually less than 3%) of return variances. See, for example, Fama and Schwert (1977), Fama (1981), Keim and Stambaugh (1986), and French, Schwert, and Stambaugh (1987). Recently, however, Fama and French (1987a) find that portfolio returns for holding periods beyond a year have strong negative autocorrelation. They show that under some assumptions about the nature of the price process, the autocorrelations imply that time-varying expected

Reprinted with permission from the *Journal of Financial Economics* 22, no. 1 (October 1988): 3–25. © 1988 by Elsevier Limited.

This research is supported by the National Science Foundation (Fama), the Center for Research in Security Prices (French), and Batterymarch Financial Management (French). We have had helpful comments from David Booth, Nai-fu Chen, John Cochrane, Bradford Corneli, Michael Hemler, Merton Miller, Kevin Murphy, Rex Sinquefield, Robert Stambaugh, and especially the editor, G. William Schwert, and the referee, James Poterba.

returns explain 25–40% of three- to five-year return variances. Using variance-ratio tests, Poterba and Summers (1987) also estimate that long-horizon stock returns have large predictable components.

Univariate tests on long-horizon returns are imprecise. Although their point estimates suggest strong predictability, Poterba and Summers (1987) cannot reject the hypothesis that stock prices are random walks, even with variance ratios estimated on returns from 1871 to 1985. Fama and French (1987a) find reliable negative autocorrelation in tests on long-horizon returns for the 1926–1985 period, but subperiod results suggest that the autocorrelation is largely due to the 1926–1940 period. Because sample sizes for long-horizon returns are small, however, it is impossible to make reliable inferences about changes in their time-series properties.

We use dividend/price ratios (D/P), henceforth called dividend yields, to forecast returns on the value- and equal-weighted portfolios of New York Stock Exchange (NYSE) stocks for return horizons (holding periods) from one month to four years. Our tests confirm existing evidence that the predictable (expected) component of returns is a small fraction of short-horizon return variances. Regressions of returns on yields typically explain less than 5% of monthly or quarterly return variances. More interesting, our results add statistical power to the evidence that the predictable component of returns is a larger fraction of the variation of long-horizon returns. Regressions of returns on D/P often explain more than 25% of the variances of two- to four-year returns. In contrast to the univariate tests of Fama and French (1987a) and Poterba and Summers (1987), regressions of returns on yields provide reliable evidence of forecast power for subperiods as well as for the 1927–1986 sample period.

The hypothesis that D/P forecasts returns has a long tradition among practitioners and academics [for example, Dow (1920) and Ball (1978)]. The intuition of the 'efficient markets' version of the hypothesis is that stock prices are low relative to dividends when discount rates and expected returns are high, and vice versa, so that D/P varies with expected returns. There is also evidence, primarily for annual returns, that supports the hypothesis. See, for example, Rozeff (1984), Shiller (1984), Flood, Hodrick, and Kaplan (1986), and Campbell and Shiller (1987). Thus, neither the hypothesis nor the evidence that D/P forecasts returns is new. What we offer are (a) evidence that forecast power increases with the return horizon, (b) an economic story to explain this result, and (c) evidence consistent with the explanation.

Part of the story for why the predictable component of returns becomes more important for longer return horizons is easy to document. If expected returns have strong positive autocorrelation, rational forecasts of one-year returns one to four years ahead are highly correlated. As a consequence, the variance of expected returns grows faster with the return horizon than the variance of unexpected returns—the variation of expected returns becomes a larger fraction of the variation of returns. Our results, like those of others, indicate that expected returns are highly autocorrelated.

The second part of the story for forecast power that increases with the return horizon is more interesting. It starts from the observation that residual variances for regressions of returns on yields (the unexpected returns estimated from the regressions) increase less than in proportion to the return horizon. Our explanation centers on what we call the discount-rate effect, that is, the offsetting adjustment of current prices triggered by shocks to discount rates and expected returns. We find that estimated shocks to expected returns are indeed associated with opposite shocks to prices. The cumulative price effect of these shocks is roughly zero; on average, the expected future price increases implied by higher expected returns are offset by the immediate decline in the current price.

These results are consistent with models [for example, Summers (1986)] in which time-varying expected returns generate mean-reverting components of prices. The interesting economic question, motivated but unresolved by our results, is whether the predictability of returns implied by such temporary price components is driven by rational economic behavior (the investment opportunities of firms and the tastes of investors for current versus risky future consumption)—or by animal spirits.

2. DIVIDEND YIELDS

Consider a discrete-time perfect-certainty model in which $D(t)$, the dividend per share for the time period from $t-1$ to t, grows at the constant rate g, and the market interest rate that relates the stream of future dividends to the stock price $P(t-1)$ at time $t-1$ is the constant r. In this model, the price $P(t-1)$ is

$$P(t-1) = \frac{D(t)}{1+r}\left(1 + \frac{1+g}{1+r} + \frac{(1+g)^2}{(1+r)^2} + \dots\right) = \frac{D(t)}{r-g} \qquad (1)$$

The dividend yield is the interest rate less the dividend growth rate,

$$\frac{D(t)}{P(t-1)} = r - g. \qquad (2)$$

In the certainty model, the interest rate r is the discount rate for dividends and the period-by-period return on the stock. The transition from certainty to a model that (a) accommodates uncertain future dividends and discount rates and (b) shows the correspondence between discount rates and time-varying expected returns is difficult. See Campbell and Shiller (1987) and Poterba and Summers (1987). The direct relation between the dividend yield and the interest rate in the certainty model (2) suffices, however, to illustrate that yields are likely to capture variation in expected returns.

3. VARIABLES FOR THE BASIC REGRESSIONS

3.1. Returns and Dividend Yields

Fama and French (1987a) find that the predictability of long-horizon returns implied by negative autocorrelation is stronger for portfolios of small firms. They also find that the return behavior of large- and small-firm portfolios is typified by the value- and equal-weighted portfolios of NYSE stocks constructed by the Center for Research in Security Prices (CRSP). Our tests use continuously compounded returns $r(t, t + T)$ on the two market portfolios for return horizons T of one month, one quarter, and one to four years. The monthly, quarterly, and annual returns are nonoverlapping. The two- to four-year returns are overlapping annual (end-of-year) observations. The sample period for the returns is 1927–1986.

The tests center on regressions of the future return, $r(t, t + T)$, on two measures of the time t dividend yield, $Y(t)$,

$$r(t, t + T) = \alpha(T) + \beta(T)Y(t) + \varepsilon(t, t + T) \tag{3}$$

The yields are constructed from returns, with and without dividends, provided by CRSP. Consider a one-dollar investment in either the value- or equal-weighted market portfolio at the end of December 1925. If dividends are not reinvested, the value of the portfolio at the end of the month m is

$$P(m) = \exp[r_0(1) + r_0(2) + r_0(3) + \ldots + r_0(m)] \tag{4}$$

where $r_0(m)$ is the continuously compounded without-dividend return for month m. If the continuously compounded with-dividend return is $r(m)$, the dividend on the portfolio in month m is

$$D(m) = P(m-1)\exp[r(m)] - P(m) \tag{5}$$

EUGENE F. FAMA AND KENNETH R. FRENCH

Two dividend yields, $D(t)/P(t-1)$ and $D(t)/P(t)$, are computed by summing the monthly dividends, from (5), for the year preceding time t and dividing by the value of the portfolio at the beginning or end of the year, from (4). We use annual yields to avoid seasonal differences in dividend payments. The annual yields are used in the estimates of (3) for all return horizons.

3.2. Estimation Problems and the Definition of the Yield

The certainty model (2) shows that the dividend yield is a noisy proxy for expected returns because it also reflects expected dividend growth. Variation in the dividend yield, $Y(t)$, due to changes in the expected growth of dividends can cloud the information in the yield about time-varying expected returns. More generally, any variation in $Y(t)$ that is unrelated to variation in the time t expected return, $E_t r(t, t+T)$, is noise that tends to cause the regression of $r(t, t+T)$ on $Y(t)$ to miss some of the variation in expected returns—it shows up in the regression residuals.

On the other hand, when expected returns vary through time, the discount-rate effect tends to cause estimates of (3) to overstate the variation of expected returns. Suppose an expected return shock at t increases discount rates. If the discount-rate increases are not offset by increases in expected dividends, the expected return shock causes an unexpected decline in $P(t)$. If dividend yields forecast returns, the expected return shock also causes an unexpected increase in $Y(t)$. Thus, because of the discount-rate effect, expected return shocks produce a negative correlation between unexpected returns and contemporaneous yield shocks that tends to produce upward biased slopes in regressions of returns on yields. [See Stambaugh (1986)]. This bias arises only when yields track time-varying expected returns. It does not bias the tests toward false conclusions that yields have forecast power.

Upward bias of the estimated slope in (3) due to the discount-rate effect and downward bias due to variation in $Y(t)$ unrelated to $E_t r(t, t+T)$ can arise for any definition of the yield. Other problems in estimating (3) are specific to the definition of $Y(t)$ as $D(t)/P(t)$ or $D(t)/P(t-1)$. For example, because we would like a yield with up-to-date but known information about expected returns for periods forward from t, $D(t)/P(t)$ is a natural choice. Because stock prices are forward-looking, however, $D(t)$ is old relative to the dividend forecasts in $P(t)$. Good news about future dividends produces a high price $P(t)$ relative to the current dividend $D(t)$ and a low dividend yield $D(t)/P(t)$. Good news about dividends also produces a high return $r(t-T, t)$. The result is a negative correlation between the disturbance $\varepsilon(t-T, t)$ and the time t shock to $D(t)/P(t)$

that again tends to produce upward-biased slopes in regressions of $r(t, t+T)$ on $D(t)/P(t)$.

Table 1 shows that the cross-correlations between one-year stock returns and dividend changes more than a year ahead are close to 0.0. These results suggest that stock prices do not forecast dividend charges more than a year ahead. Thus, variation in the dividend yield due to a denominator price that looks beyond the dividend in the numerator is substantially reduced when $Y(t)$ is defined as $D(t)/P(t-1)$, where $P(t-1)$ is the price at the beginning of the year covered by $D(t)$. If stock prices do not forecast dividend changes more than a year ahead, the dividend forecasts in $P(t-1)$ will not produce variation in $D(t)/P(t-1)$, and they will not produce upward-biased slopes in regressions of $r(t, t+T)$ on $D(t)/P(t-1)$.

Confident conclusions that $D(t)/P(t)$ or $D(t)/P(t-1)$ produces regressions that overstate or understate the variation of expected returns can not be made on *a priori* grounds. $D(t)/P(t-1)$ is more conservative. Any upward bias in the slopes it produces occurs only when expected returns vary through time (the discount-rate effect). Thus, regressions that use $D(t)/P(t-1)$ are more likely to avoid a false positive conclusion that yields track expected returns. They are,

TABLE 1. Cross-correlations between one-year continuously-compounded returns and current and future one-year changes in the log of annual dividends for the CRSP value-weighted and equal-weighted NYSE portfolios

$$\mathrm{Cor}[r(t-1, t), \ln D(t+i) - \ln D(t+i-1)]$$

Period	Lead i					$s(0)^a$
	0	1	2	3	4	
	Value-weighted nominal returns					
1927–1986	0.10	0.68	0.22	0.03	−0.16	0.13
1927–1956	0.13	0.78	0.26	0.08	−0.18	0.18
1957–1986	−0.09	0.37	0.05	−0.29	−0.10	0.18
1941–1986	−0.12	0.26	0.00	−0.16	−0.05	0.15
	Equal-weighted nominal returns					
1927–1986	0.17	0.72	0.21	0.04	−0.20	0.13
1927–1956	0.19	0.80	0.23	0.08	−0.22	0.18
1957–1986	0.09	0.46	0.13	−0.11	−0.10	0.18
1941–1986	0.03	0.46	0.11	−0.01	−0.12	0.15

$^a s(0)$ is the asymptotic standard error of the contemporaneous cross-correlation, that is, $n^{-0.5}$, when n is the sample size. Real returns produce correlations similar to those shown for nominal returns.

however, also more likely to be too conservative. The deviation of $D(t)$ from its expected value at $t-1$ is noise that tends to cause regressions of $r(t, t+T)$ on $D(t)/P(t-1)$ to understate the variation of expected returns. Moreover, because $P(t-1)$ can only reflect information about expected returns available at $t-1$, $D(t)/P(t-1)$ is about a year out of date with respect to expected returns measured forward from t. If current shocks have a decaying effect on expected returns, using an 'old' yield to track expected returns is likely to understate the variation of expected returns. We present results for the more timely measure, $D(t)/P(t)$, as well as for $D(t)/P(t-1)$.

4. SUMMARY STATISTICS

Table 2 shows summary statistics for one-year nominal and real returns on the value- and equal-weighted portfolios. Standard deviations of returns are about 50% higher during the 1927–1956 period than during the 1957–1986 period. As in Blume (1968), the high variability of returns for 1927–1956 is largely due to the 1927–1940 period. The standard deviations of returns are similar for 1957–1986 and 1941–1986. We shall find that the regression results are also similar for these periods.

Like stock returns, dividend changes are more variable toward the beginning of the sample. The standard deviations of year-to-year changes in the logs of annual dividends on the value- and equal-weighted portfolios for 1957–1986 are about 25% of those for 1927–1956. Dividend variability declines relative to that of returns. During the 1927–1956 period, dividend changes are almost as variable as returns. After 1940 returns are more than 2.4 times as variable as dividend changes.

Dividend variability also declines relative to the variability of earnings. For the 1927–1956 period, the standard deviation of annual changes in the log of annual earnings on the Standard and Poor's (S&P) Composite Index (0.259) is about 43% greater than that of changes in annual Index dividends (0.181). For 1957–1986, the standard deviation of changes in earnings (0.113) is more than three times that of dividend changes (0.037).

The estimated speed of adjustment of dividends to target dividends in Lintner's (1956) dividend model also declines over the sample period. Lintner postulates that a firm's target dividend $D^{*}(t)$ for year t is a constant fraction of earnings $E(t)$,

$$D^{*}(t) = kE(t) \qquad (6)$$

TABLE 2. Summary statistics for one-year nominal and real returns, dividend yields, and changes in the logs of annual dividends for the CRSP value-weighted and equal-weighted NYSE portfolios[a]

			Autocorrelations							Autocorrelations				
Period	Mean	S.D.	1	2	3	4	5	Mean	S.D.	1	2	3	4	5
	Value-weighted nominal returns							*Equal-weighted nominal returns*						
1927–1986	0.092	0.206	0.10	−0.20	−0.07	−0.15	−0.02	0.125	0.280	0.13	−0.18	−0.14	−0.23	−0.11
1927–1956	0.088	0.244	0.21	−0.10	−0.18	−0.44	−0.03	0.124	0.336	0.19	−0.11	−0.23	−0.51	−0.12
1957–1986	0.096	0.163	−0.16	−0.39	0.19	0.30	0.06	0.125	0.216	−0.04	−0.36	0.13	0.26	−0.07
1941–1986	0.112	0.155	−0.08	−0.33	0.03	0.27	0.10	0.143	0.210	0.04	−0.28	−0.07	0.17	−0.01
	Value-weighted real returns							*Equal-weighted real returns*						
1927–1986	0.062	0.208	0.04	−0.24	−0.08	−0.09	0.05	0.094	0.282	0.08	−0.22	−0.15	−0.19	−0.04
1927–1956	0.074	0.239	0.11	−0.17	−0.22	−0.40	0.06	0.109	0.334	0.13	−0.15	−0.26	−0.47	−0.04
1957–1986	0.050	0.174	−0.10	−0.38	0.18	0.29	0.06	0.079	0.224	−0.03	−0.39	0.11	0.26	−0.05
1941–1986	0.068	0.173	−0.01	−0.29	−0.01	0.24	0.16	0.099	0.223	0.04	−0.31	−0.12	0.15	0.05
	Value-weighted $\ln D(t+1) - \ln D(t)$							*Equal-weighted* $\ln D(t+1) - \ln D(t)$						
1927–1986	0.041	0.133	0.30	−0.10	−0.17	−0.20	−0.00	0.079	0.220	0.31	−0.15	−0.16	−0.28	−0.20
1927–1956	0.028	0.184	0.28	−0.13	−0.21	−0.23	−0.00	0.083	0.304	0.30	−0.18	−0.17	−0.30	−0.21
1957–1986	0.055	0.041	0.54	0.30	0.22	0.08	−0.19	0.075	0.077	0.55	0.37	0.12	−0.09	−0.22
1941–1986	0.058	0.058	0.25	0.10	0.11	−0.21	−0.34	0.089	0.087	0.33	0.21	0.14	0.12	0.02
	Value-weighted $D(t)/P(t-1)$							*Equal-weighted* $D(t)/P(t-1)$						
1926–1985	0.047	0.012	0.81	0.59	0.48	0.44	0.39	0.044	0.013	0.78	0.51	0.36	0.30	0.28
1926–1955	0.053	0.009	0.64	0.18	−0.14	−0.25	−0.10	0.048	0.015	0.79	0.50	0.26	0.18	0.28
1956–1985	0.040	0.010	0.79	0.65	0.64	0.58	0.41	0.040	0.010	0.65	0.34	0.32	0.30	0.10
1940–1985	0.046	0.013	0.84	0.67	0.57	0.50	0.41	0.046	0.014	0.78	0.51	0.39	0.40	0.38

[a]The one-year value- and equal-weighted portfolio returns are continuously compounded. Real returns are calculated by summing the differences between monthly continuously compounded nominal returns and the one-month inflation rate, calculated from the U.S. Consumer Price Index (CPI). $D(t)/P(t-1)$ is the ratio of dividends for year t to the value of the portfolio at the end of year $t-1$. The time periods for $D(t)/P(t-1)$ are those for $D(t)$. The periods for $D(t)$ match the periods to be used in the regressions of one-year returns on the yields. For example, the returns for 1927–1986 are regressed on the yields for 1926–1985.

The change in the actual dividends from $t-1$ to t is assumed to follow a partial adjustment model,

$$D(t)-D(t-1) = a + s \, [D^*(t)-D(t-1)] + u(t) \qquad (7)$$

When this model is fitted to the annual S&P earnings and dividends, the estimated speed of adjustment s drops from 49% per year for 1927–1956 to 12% per year for 1941–1986, and 11% for 1957–1986.

In short, the data suggest systematic changes in the dividend policies of firms (toward dividends that are smoother relative to earnings) during the sample period. For our purposes, changes in dividend policy are important because they can produce variation in yields that obscures information about expected returns or causes the relation between the yield and expected returns to change through time.

Finally, table 2 shows summary statistics for end-of-year observations on the yield $D(t)/P(t-1)$, the explanatory variable in regressions of $r(t,\, t+T)$ on $D(t)/P(t-1)$ for one- to four-year returns. The first-order autocorrelations of $D(t)/P(t-1)$ are large, but the autocorrelations decay across longer lags. If yields track expected returns, high first-order autocorrelation implies persistence in expected returns. The decay of the autocorrelations across longer lags then suggests the appealing conclusion that, though highly autocorrelated, expected returns have a mean-reverting tendency.

5. REGRESSIONS FOR NOMINAL
AND REAL RETURNS

The change in return variability around 1940 suggests that a weighted least squares (WLS) approach that deflates the observations by estimates of return variability will produce more efficient estimates of regressions of returns on dividend yields. Some of our more interesting analysis, however, involves explaining why the expected return variation tracked by yields is a larger fraction of the variation of returns for longer return horizons. WLS estimates would complicate the analysis by changing the meaning of what is being explained. Thus the text uses ordinary least squares (OLS) estimates. WLS regressions produce slopes that are similar to OLS slopes, however, and so produce similar estimates of the variation in expected returns. In fact, for periods that overlap the shift in return variances around 1940 (for example, 1927–1986 and 1927–1956), WLS estimates actually give a stronger view of the statistical reliability of return forecasts from yields. The WLS estimates are available on request.

Tables 3 and 4 summarize the OLS regressions of the value- and equal-weighted portfolio returns, $r(t, t + T)$, on their *ex ante* yields, $D(t)/P(t-1)$ and $D(t)/P(t)$. Because the regressions are the central evidence on the variation of expected returns, the results are shown in some detail. Each table splits the 1927–1986 sample into 30-year periods (1927–1956 and 1957–1986). Results for the 1941–1986 period of roughly constant return variances are also shown. Estimates of regression slopes and their t-statistics for 1946–1986 and 1936–1986 (not shown) are close to those for 1941–1986. Finally, to illustrate that the results are similar for different definitions of returns, regressions for nominal and real returns are shown.

5.1. Nominal Returns

All the regression slopes in tables 3 and 4 are positive. For value-weighted nominal returns, regressions that use the less timely $D(t)/P(t-1)$ as the explanatory variable produce only one slope less than 1.8 standard errors from 0.0. Slopes for value-weighted nominal returns more than 2.0 standard errors from 0.0 are the rule, and slopes more than 2.5 standard errors from 0.0 are common. For 1941–1986, the longest period of roughly constant return variances, all the slopes for value-weighted nominal returns are more than 2.4 standard errors from 0.0.

Except for the 1927–1956 period, the regressions of equal-weighted nominal returns on $D(t)/P(t-1)$ are also strong evidence that expected returns vary through time. For the 1927–1986 sample period and the 1941–1986 and 1957–1986 subperiods, the regression slopes for equal-weighted nominal returns are typically more than 2.0 standard errors from 0.0. Moreover, the weak results for equal-weighted returns for 1927–1956 are a consequence of the high variability of returns in the early years of the sample. The slopes for 1927–1956 are similar to those for the 1941–1986 period of lower return variances, and the 1941–1986 slopes are all more than 2.6 standard errors from 0.0.

Regressions that use the more timely $D(t)/P(t)$ to explain nominal returns also produce strong evidence of forecast power for the 1927–1986 period and especially for 1941–1986 and 1957–1986. For the two post-1940 periods, the slopes for $D(t)/P(t)$ are more than 2.5 standard errors from 0.0 for both market portfolios and for all return horizons. Slopes more than 4.0 standard errors from 0.0 are common.

TABLE 3. Regressions of nominal and real CRSP value-weighted NYSE portfolio returns on dividend yields[a]

$$r(t, t+T) = a + bY(t) + e(t, t+T)$$

Return horizon		Nominal returns								Real returns							
		$Y(t) = D(t)/P(t-1)$				$Y(t) = D(t)/P(t)$				$Y(t) = D(t)/P(t-1)$				$Y(t) = D(t)/P(t)$			
T	N	b	t(b)	R^2	s(e)	b	t(b)	R^2	s(e)	b	t(b)	R^2	s(e)	b	t(b)	R^2	s(e)
							1927–1986										
M	720	0.53	2.99	0.01	0.06	0.21	1.40	0.00	0.06	0.49	2.76	0.01	0.06	0.28	1.83	0.00	0.06
Q	240	1.12	1.87	0.01	0.11	1.07	2.10	0.01	0.11	1.04	1.71	0.01	0.11	1.26	2.48	0.02	0.11
1	60	5.37	2.40	0.07	0.20	2.47	1.27	0.01	0.20	5.32	2.35	0.07	0.20	3.35	1.72	0.03	0.20
2	59	9.10	2.18	0.10	0.29	7.38	2.04	0.09	0.29	9.08	2.31	0.11	0.28	8.77	2.59	0.15	0.28
3	58	11.56	2.14	0.13	0.33	9.94	2.21	0.13	0.33	11.73	2.51	0.15	0.31	11.53	2.93	0.21	0.30
4	57	12.68	1.93	0.13	0.37	12.86	2.43	0.19	0.36	13.44	2.46	0.17	0.33	14.43	3.25	0.29	0.31
							1927–1956										
M	360	0.93	2.77	0.02	0.07	0.17	0.69	-0.00	0.07	0.78	2.33	0.01	0.07	0.27	1.08	0.00	0.07
Q	120	1.79	1.55	0.01	0.14	1.16	1.41	0.01	0.14	1.38	1.20	0.00	0.14	1.42	1.75	0.02	0.13
1	30	11.04	2.49	0.15	0.22	1.50	0.46	-0.03	0.25	9.61	2.16	0.11	0.23	2.62	0.83	-0.01	0.24
2	29	22.49	2.88	0.28	0.33	8.92	1.49	0.07	0.37	19.43	2.65	0.23	0.32	10.16	1.89	0.13	0.34
3	28	29.24	2.86	0.33	0.39	15.27	2.21	0.18	0.43	24.73	2.74	0.29	0.36	15.94	2.73	0.26	0.36
4	27	28.16	2.25	0.24	0.46	20.86	3.14	0.30	0.44	23.00	2.21	0.22	0.40	20.39	3.70	0.40	0.35

1957–1986

	N																
M	360	0.53	2.31	0.01	0.04	0.68	2.66	0.02	0.04	0.42	1.79	0.01	0.04	0.51	1.95	0.01	0.04
Q	120	1.40	1.82	0.02	0.08	2.33	2.78	0.05	0.08	1.11	1.40	0.01	0.08	1.87	2.14	0.03	0.08
1	30	5.60	1.86	0.08	0.16	9.32	3.02	0.22	0.14	4.58	1.39	0.03	0.17	7.74	2.21	0.12	0.16
2	29	7.51	1.89	0.09	0.20	16.40	4.04	0.45	0.16	5.68	1.10	0.02	0.23	14.06	2.53	0.25	0.20
3	28	10.41	3.01	0.21	0.19	17.12	4.12	0.51	0.15	8.16	1.38	0.08	0.23	14.03	2.05	0.24	0.21
4	27	15.05	3.37	0.38	0.18	19.69	3.87	0.57	0.15	12.48	1.57	0.17	0.24	16.21	1.83	0.26	0.23

1941–1986

	N																
M	552	0.39	2.95	0.01	0.04	0.36	2.59	0.01	0.04	0.37	2.73	0.01	0.04	0.32	2.20	0.01	0.04
Q	184	1.07	2.47	0.03	0.08	1.20	2.64	0.03	0.08	1.04	2.28	0.02	0.08	1.07	2.23	0.02	0.08
1	46	4.46	2.62	0.12	0.15	5.09	2.88	0.14	0.14	4.40	2.29	0.09	0.17	4.82	2.38	0.09	0.16
2	45	7.15	3.04	0.17	0.19	10.34	4.18	0.35	0.17	7.21	2.36	0.13	0.23	10.26	3.15	0.25	0.21
3	44	9.42	4.77	0.29	0.19	12.94	5.68	0.51	0.15	9.66	2.91	0.21	0.24	13.10	3.53	0.36	0.21
4	43	12.75	5.49	0.49	0.17	15.35	5.62	0.64	0.14	13.34	3.18	0.36	0.23	15.71	3.31	0.45	0.22

[a] N is the number of observations. $P(t)$ is the time t price. $D(t)$ is the dividend for the year preceding t, $r(t, t + T)$ is the continuously compounded return from t to $t + T$. The regressions for $T =$ one month (M), one quarter (Q), and one year use nonoverlapping returns. The regressions for two- to four-year returns use overlapping annual observations. The standard errors in the t-statistic $t(b)$ for the two- to four-year slopes are adjusted for the sample autocorrelation of overlapping residuals with the method of Hansen and Hodrick (1980). Regression slopes and t-statistics for 1946–1986 and 1936–1986 (not shown) are close to those for 1941–1986.

TABLE 4. Regressions of nominal and real CRSP equal-weighted NYSE portfolio returns on dividend yields[a]

$$r(t, t+T) = a + bY(t) + e(t, t+T)$$

Return horizon T	N	Nominal returns								Real returns							
		$Y(t)=D(t)/P(t-1)$				$Y(t)=D(t)/P(t)$				$Y(t)=D(t)/P(t-1)$				$Y(t)=D(t)/P(t)$			
		b	t(b)	R^2	s(e)	b	t(b)	R^2	s(e)	b	t(b)	R^2	s(e)	b	t(b)	R^2	s(e)
										1927–1986							
M	720	0.52	2.40	0.01	0.07	0.21	0.97	-0.00	0.07	0.45	2.10	0.00	0.07	0.24	1.15	0.00	0.08
Q	240	1.07	1.41	0.00	0.15	1.28	1.74	0.01	0.15	0.91	1.19	0.00	0.16	1.40	1.90	0.01	0.15
1	60	5.87	2.21	0.06	0.27	2.69	1.06	0.00	0.28	5.48	2.04	0.05	0.27	3.38	1.33	0.01	0.28
2	59	10.75	2.14	0.10	0.40	9.91	2.15	0.10	0.40	10.06	2.05	0.09	0.40	11.23	2.54	0.14	0.39
3	58	13.60	2.09	0.12	0.47	14.68	2.63	0.17	0.46	12.38	2.02	0.10	0.46	16.08	3.14	0.22	0.43
4	57	14.28	1.96	0.11	0.53	17.96	2.95	0.21	0.49	12.64	1.86	0.09	0.50	18.91	3.47	0.27	0.45
										1927–1956							
M	360	0.49	1.50	0.00	0.09	0.06	0.20	-0.00	0.09	0.38	1.18	0.00	0.09	0.10	0.34	-0.00	0.09
Q	120	0.85	0.73	-0.00	0.19	0.91	0.83	-0.00	0.19	0.56	0.48	-0.01	0.19	1.03	0.95	-0.00	0.19
1	30	5.14	1.25	0.02	0.33	0.38	0.10	-0.04	0.34	4.21	1.02	0.00	0.33	1.13	0.31	-0.03	0.34
2	29	11.97	1.45	0.09	0.50	7.86	1.11	0.03	0.52	10.18	1.28	0.06	0.49	8.97	1.35	0.06	0.49
3	28	16.05	1.44	0.11	0.61	14.92	1.73	0.13	0.61	12.92	1.23	0.07	0.59	15.65	2.00	0.17	0.56
4	27	13.92	1.11	0.05	0.71	19.35	2.03	0.19	0.65	9.58	0.84	0.01	0.66	18.93	2.23	0.22	0.59

M	360	0.87	2.76	0.02	0.05	0.99	2.80	0.02	0.05	0.76	2.37	0.01	0.05	0.82	2.30	0.01	0.05
Q	120	2.24	2.08	0.03	0.10	3.68	3.18	0.07	0.10	1.97	1.78	0.02	0.11	3.28	2.75	0.05	0.10
1	30	10.01	2.68	0.18	0.20	12.58	3.28	0.25	0.19	9.31	2.35	0.13	0.21	11.56	2.79	0.19	0.20
2	29	13.02	2.39	0.16	0.28	23.85	4.59	0.51	0.21	11.82	1.93	0.11	0.30	22.86	3.83	0.42	0.24
3	28	16.22	2.66	0.22	0.29	23.87	3.84	0.45	0.24	14.77	2.14	0.17	0.31	22.84	3.30	0.39	0.26
4	27	21.99	3.01	0.35	0.30	25.98	3.39	0.42	0.28	20.26	2.47	0.28	0.32	24.85	3.00	0.32	0.30

M	552	0.51	3.21	0.02	0.05	0.45	2.57	0.01	0.05	0.51	3.18	0.02	0.05	0.44	2.49	0.01	0.05
Q	184	1.42	2.64	0.03	0.10	1.64	2.78	0.04	0.10	1.47	2.64	0.03	0.10	1.63	2.67	0.03	0.10
1	46	6.75	3.35	0.19	0.19	7.05	3.15	0.17	0.19	6.99	3.24	0.17	0.20	7.27	3.03	0.15	0.21
2	45	10.38	3.15	0.22	0.27	14.64	4.02	0.37	0.24	10.89	3.07	0.21	0.29	15.51	4.00	0.36	0.26
3	44	11.90	2.94	0.23	0.30	17.71	4.02	0.43	0.26	12.37	2.96	0.22	0.32	18.99	4.25	0.45	0.27
4	43	13.68	2.76	0.26	0.32	19.00	3.60	0.43	0.28	14.19	2.90	0.27	0.33	20.50	3.97	0.47	0.28

[a]N is the number of observations. $P(t)$ is the time t price. $D(t)$ is the dividend for the year preceding t, $r(t, t+T)$ is the continuously compounded return from t to $t+T$. The regressions for $T=$ one month (M), one quarter (Q), and one year use nonoverlapping returns. The regressions for two- to four-year returns use overlapping annual observations. The standard errors in the t-statistic $t(b)$ for the two- to four-year slopes are adjusted for the sample autocorrelation of overlapping residuals with the method of Hansen and Hodrick (1980). Regression slopes and t-statistics for 1946–1986 and 1936–1986 (not shown) are close to those for 1941–1986.

5.2. *Real Returns*

The slopes for real returns in tables 3 and 4 are typically close to those for nominal returns. Because the real and nominal regressions have the same explanatory variable, similar slopes indicate that variation in expected nominal returns translates into similar variation in expected real returns. If the market is efficient, the results indicate that dividend yields signal variation in equilibrium expected real returns.

Fama and French (1987b) show regressions of excess stock returns on dividend yields. Excess returns for horizons beyond a month are calculated by cumulating the differences between monthly nominal stock returns and the one-month U.S. Treasury bill rate. The results for excess returns are similar to those for real returns in tables 3 and 4. Thus the variation in expected real stock returns tracked by dividend yields is also present in the expected premiums of stock returns over one-month bill returns.

5.3. *The Behavior of the Regression Slopes*

The slopes in the regressions of real or nominal returns $r(t, t+T)$ on $Y(t)$ increase with the return horizon T. When the explanatory variable is $D(t)/P(t-1)$, the increase in the slopes is roughly proportional to T for horizons to one year, but less than proportional to T for two- to four-year returns. For the more timely $D(t)/P(t)$ and for periods after 1940, the slopes increase roughly in proportion to T for return horizons to four years, but more slowly thereafter.

This behavior of the slopes has an appealing explanation. The slope in the regression of the T-period return $r(t, t+T)$ on $Y(t)$ is the sum of the slopes in the T regressions of the one-period returns, $r(t, t+1), \ldots, r(t+T-1, t+T)$, on $Y(t)$. Slopes in regressions of $r(t, t+T)$ on $Y(t)$ that increase in proportion to T for horizons of one or two years thus imply that variation in $Y(t)$ signals similar variation in one-period expected returns out to one or two years. Slopes that increase less than in proportion to T for longer return horizons suggest that $Y(t)$ signals less variation in more distant one-period expected returns. This behavior of the slopes suggests that expected returns are highly autocorrelated but slowly mean-reverting. The decay of the autocorrelations of $D(t)/P(t-1)$ in table 2 also suggests slow mean reversion.

5.4. *Other Tests*

The intuition of the hypothesis that dividend yields forecast returns is that stock prices are low relative to dividends when discount rates and expected returns are high, and vice versa, so that yields capture variation in expected returns. There is a similar intuition for earnings/price ratios (E/P).

We have estimated regressions (available on request) of value- and equal-weighted NYSE returns, $r(t, t + T)$, on $E(t)/P(t - 1)$ and $E(t)/P(t)$. $E(t)$ is earnings per share on the Standard and Poor's (S&P) Composite Index for calendar year t, as reported by S&P. $P(t)$ is the value of the index at the end of the year. In many ways the E/P results are similar to the D/P results. For example, the regression slopes and R^2 produced by E/P increase with the return horizon. The t's for the slopes suggest that E/P has reliable forecast power. E/P tends, however, to have less explanatory power than D/P.

Earnings are more variable than dividends. (See section 4). If this higher variability is unrelated to the variation in expected returns, E/P is a noisier measure of expected returns than D/P. This 'numerator noise' argument may also explain why the forecast power of dividend yields is higher in the periods after 1940, when the variability of dividends declines substantially relative to the variability of returns.

It would seem that a solution to problems caused by noise in the numerator of E/P or D/P is to use $1/P$ as the forecast variable. Miller and Scholes (1982) show that the cross-section of $1/P$ for common stocks helps explain the cross-section of expected returns. Suppose, however, that reinvestment of earnings causes stock prices to have an upward-drifting nonstationary component. Then $1/P$ is nonstationary (it tends to drift downward), and it is not a good variable for tracking expected returns in time-series tests. In fact, for the value- and equal-weighted NYSE portfolios, regressions (not shown) of $r(t, t + T)$ on $1/P(t)$, where $P(t)$ is the value of the portfolio at t produce slopes and R^2 close to 0.0.

6. OUT-OF-SAMPLE FORECASTS

The slopes in tables 3 and 4 are apparently strong evidence that yields signal variation in expected returns. Given the uncertainty about the bias of the slopes, however, further testing is in order. One approach is to use the regressions to forecast out-of-sample returns. We forecast returns for the 20-year period 1967–1986. Each forecast is from a regression of $r(t, t + T)$ on $Y(t)$ estimated with returns that begin and end in the preceding 30-year period. For example, to forecast the first one-year return (1967), we use coefficients estimated with the 30 one-year returns for 1937–1966. To forecast the first four-year return (1967–1970), we use coefficients estimated with the 27 overlapping annual observations on the four-year returns that begin and end in the

1937–1966 period. For monthly and quarterly returns, the 30-year estimation period rolls forward in monthly or quarterly steps. For one- to four-year returns, the estimation period rolls forward in annual increments.

We start the estimation periods in 1937 because of the evidence that returns and yields behave differently during the first ten years of the sample. Because the overlap of annual observations on multiyear returns reduces effective sample sizes, we judge that estimation periods shorter than 30 years would not produce meaningful forecasts of two- to four-year returns. The 1937 starting date and the choice of 30-year estimation periods then limit the forecast period to 1967–1986. For this 20-year forecast period, there are only five nonoverlapping forecasts of four-year returns.

6.1. Perspective

With respect to possible bias of the regression slopes, the out-of-sample tests are conservative. They correct for bias that causes the in-sample slopes to overstate the variation of expected returns, but they leave the estimation problems that cause the regressions to understate the variation of expected returns.

Thus, section 3 argues that negative correlation between shocks to returns and yields (because of the discount-rate effect or because yields and returns respond to dividend forecasts) produces positive bias in the slope estimates for dividend yields, with possibly more bias in the slopes for $D(t)/P(t)$ than in the slopes for $D(t)/P(t-1)$. The bias means that in-sample R^2 tend to overstate explanatory power. The bias decreases out-of-sample forecast power, however, so out-of-sample tests are appropriately punitive.

On the other hand, yields contain noise (variation unrelated to expected returns) that tends to cause estimates of (3) to understate the variation of expected returns. Since the noise reduces both in-sample and out-of-sample forecast power, out-of-sample tests do not correct for this source of error. Likewise, if regressions of $r(t, t+T)$ on the less timely $D(t)/P(t-1)$ understate the variation of expected returns, the understatement remains in out-of-sample forecasts.

6.2. Results

Table 5 summarizes the mean squared errors (MSE) of the out-of-sample forecasts. To compare the forecasts with the in-sample fit of the regressions, the MSE are reported as R^2. Specifically, the MSE R^2 in table 5 is $1 - (MSE/s^2[r(t, t+T)])$, where $s^2[r(t, t+T)]$ is the out-of-sample variance of the forecasted return. The out-of-sample forecasts cover 1967–1986. The in-sample

TABLE 5. Mean squared error R^2 for out-of-sample forecasts for NYSE portfolio returns for 1967–1986 and R^2 for in-sample forecasts for 1957–1986[a]

Return horizon	$D(t)/P(t-1)$		$D(t)/P(t)$		$D(t)/P(t-1)$		$D(t)/P(t)$	
T	Out	In	Out	In	Out	In	Out	In
	Value-weighted nominal returns				Value-weighted real returns			
M	0.01	0.01	0.02	0.02	0.01	0.01	0.01	0.01
Q	0.03	0.02	0.06	0.05	0.01	0.01	0.03	0.03
1	0.13	0.08	0.33	0.22	0.07	0.03	0.13	0.12
2	0.20	0.09	0.43	0.45	0.05	0.02	0.22	0.25
3	0.24	0.21	0.48	0.51	-0.18	0.08	0.00	0.24
4	0.35	0.38	0.50	0.57	-0.38	0.17	-0.26	0.26
	Equal-weighted nominal returns				Equal-weighted real returns			
M	0.01	0.02	0.01	0.02	0.01	0.01	0.01	0.01
Q	0.02	0.03	0.04	0.07	0.02	0.02	0.04	0.05
1	0.17	0.18	0.16	0.25	0.17	0.13	0.15	0.19
2	0.18	0.16	0.34	0.51	0.18	0.11	0.35	0.42
3	0.16	0.22	0.35	0.45	0.10	0.17	0.36	0.38
4	0.23	0.35	0.36	0.42	0.09	0.28	0.36	0.37

[a]The out-of-sample (Out) mean squared error R^2 is $1 - (\mathrm{MSE}/s^2[r(t, t+T)])$. Each out-of-sample forecast is made with coefficients estimated using the previous 30 years of returns and yields. Monthly (M), quarterly (Q), and one-year forecasts are for nonoverlapping periods. The two- to four-year forecasts are overlapping annual observations. The in-sample regressions are in tables 3 and 4.

R^2 for 1957–1986, the most comparable period in tables 3 and 4, are also shown in table 5.

For horizons out to two years, the MSE R^2 for the 1967–1986 out-of-sample return forecasts from $D(t)/P(t-1)$ and $D(t)/P(t)$ are close to the in-sample R^2 for 1957–1986. The signs of the differences between the in-sample R^2 and the out-of-sample MSE R^2 are random. The MSE R^2 for forecasts of three- and four-year value-weighted nominal returns from $D(t)/P(t-1)$ are also similar to the in-sample R^2. Otherwise, the MSE R^2 produced by $D(t)/P(t-1)$ deteriorate relative to the in-sample R^2 in three- and four-year forecasts. (The obvious worst cases are the negative MSE R^2 for forecasts of value-weighted three- and four-year real returns.) The results for longer return horizons are less reliable, however, because they involve fewer independent returns during the 20-year forecast period. The uniform similarity of in- and out-of-sample forecast power for horizons to two years suggests that regressions of $r(t, t + T)$ on either $D(t)/P(t-1)$ or $D(t)/P(t)$ do not produce strongly biased slopes and thus biased estimates of explanatory power.

The out-of-sample forecasts do not confirm that $D(t)/P(t)$ slopes are more biased than $D(t)/P(t-1)$ slopes. The out-of-sample forecast power of $D(t)/P(t)$ actually matches in-sample explanatory power better than $D(t)/P(t-1)$. Only the out-of-sample MSE R^2 for forecasts of three- and four-year value-weighted real returns from $D(t)/P(t)$ are much less than the in-sample R^2. Thus there is no evidence in the out-of-sample tests that slope estimates for the more timely $D(t)/P(t)$ exaggerate the variation in expected returns.

On the other hand, like the in-sample R^2, the MSE R^2 for out-of-sample forecasts from $D(t)/P(t)$ are higher, often much higher, than those for forecasts from $D(t)/P(t-1)$. For example, the MSE R^2 for forecasts of two-to four-year returns from $D(t)/P(t)$ commonly exceed 0.35, while those for forecasts from $D(t)/P(t-1)$ are typically less than 0.20. The out-of-sample forecasts thus confirm that using the less timely $D(t)/P(t-1)$ to avoid false positive conclusions about forecast power produces regressions that understate the variation of expected returns.

7. WHY DOES FORECAST POWER INCREASE WITH THE RETURN HORIZON?

The out-of-sample MSE R^2 tend to confirm the more extensive evidence from the in-sample R^2 in tables 3 and 4 that the explanatory power of the regressions increases with the return horizon. The in-sample R^2 in tables 3 and 4 and the out-of-sample MSE R^2 in table 5 are 0.07 or less for monthly and quarterly returns, but they are often greater than 0.25 for two- to four-year returns. That the same yields capture more return variance for longer forecast horizons is an interesting and challenging result.

Algebraically, the regression R^2 increase with the return horizon because the variance of the fitted values grows more quickly than the horizon, whereas the variance of the residuals generally grows less quickly than the horizon. Our goal is to explain why.

7.1. The Regression Fitted Values and Residuals

In the regressions of returns on dividend yields, the explanatory variable is the same for all return horizons. Thus, as return horizon increases, the variance of the fitted values grows in proportion to the square of the regression slopes. The slopes in tables 3 and 4 increase roughly in proportion to the return horizon out to one or two years, and then more slowly. As noted earlier, this behavior suggests that short-horizon expected returns are autocorrelated but slowly mean-reverting. The persistence of short-horizon expected returns implied by slow mean reversion causes the variances of multiperiod expected returns to grow more than in proportion to the return horizon.

On the other hand, tables 3 and 4 show that for periods after 1940, the residual variances in regressions of $r(t, t + T)$ on $Y(t)$ grow less than in proportion to the return horizon, at least for one- to four-year returns. For example, the residual standard errors for four-year returns never come close to twice the one-year standard errors. The residual in the regression of the multiyear return $r(t, t + T)$ on $Y(t)$ is the sum of the residuals from regressions of the one-year returns, $r(t, t + 1), \ldots, r(t + T - 1, t + T)$, on $Y(t)$. If multiyear residual variances grow less than in proportion to the return horizon, the correlations of the residuals from the one-year regressions must on average be negative. The negative correlation is documented in table 6. It has an economic explanation that, along with the persistence of expected returns, completes the story for the predictability of long-horizon returns.

7.2. Stock Prices and Expected Return Shocks

Suppose there is a shock at $t + 1$ that increases expected returns. Since the shock occurs after the yield $Y(t)$ is set, fitted values from regressions of $r(t + 1, t + 2), \ldots, r(t + T - 1, t + T)$ on $Y(t)$ will tend to underestimate returns after $t + 1$, and the residuals will tend to be positive. On the other hand, if expected return shocks generate opposite unexpected changes in prices (the discount-rate effect), the positive shock to expected returns at $t + 1$ will tend to produce

TABLE 6. Correlations of residuals from regressions of one-year real CRSP value- and equal-weighted NYSE returns on the dividend yield D(t)/P(t–1)[a]

$$r(t+i-1, t+i) = a + bD(t)/P(t-1) + e(t+i-1, t+i)$$

$$\text{Cor}[e(t+i-1, t+i), e(t+j-1, t+j)], \quad i=2,3,4 \quad j=1,2,3$$

Lead	Value-weighted returns; Lead j			Equal-weighted returns; Lead j		
i	1	2	3	1	2	3
			1927–1986			
2	–0.05			–0.00		
3	–0.30	–0.05		–0.29	–0.00	
4	–0.14	–0.31	0.1	–0.20	–0.26	0.09
			1941–1986			
2	–0.15			–0.18		
3	–0.39	–0.09		–0.43	–0.00	
4	–0.08	–0.39	–0.05	–0.17	–0.35	0.02

[a]The residuals are from regressions that use $D(t)/P(t-1)$ to forecast one-year returns one, two, three, and four years ahead.

$\text{Cor}[e(t+i-1, t+i), e(t+j-1, t+j)]$ is the correlation between the residual for the regression forecast of the one-year return i years ahead and the residual for the regression forecast of the one-year return j years ahead.

The correlations for nominal returns and for the other subperiods in tables 3 and 4 are similar to those shown. Using $D(t)/P(t)$ as the forecast variable produces similar results.

---

a negative residual in the regression of the one-year return $r(t, t+1)$ on $Y(t)$. Thus, because of the discount-rate effect, the residual from the regression of $r(t, t+1)$ on $Y(t)$ is negatively correlated with the residuals from regressions of $r(t+1, t+2), \ldots, r(t+T-1, t+T)$ on $Y(t)$. A similar argument implies that the residuals from the regression of $r(t+k-1, t+k)$ on $Y(t)$ tend to be negatively correlated with the residuals from regressions of one-year returns after $t+k$ on $Y(t)$.

The next section presents further tests for the discount-rate effect, based on estimates of the relation between contemporaneous return and dividend yield shocks.

8. YIELDS AND TEMPORARY COMPONENTS OF STOCK PRICES

8.1. Yield Shocks, Price Shocks, and Future Expected Returns

Table 1 suggests that one-year returns are uncorrelated with dividend changes more than one year ahead. This suggests that $D(t+1)$ is an unbiased (but noisy) measure of the information in $P(t)$ about future dividends, so that $D(t+1)/P(t)$ is relatively free of variation due to dividend forecasts. Thus, the unexpected component of $D(t+1)/P(t)$ can be interpreted as a (noisy) measure of the shock to expected returns at t.

Preliminary tests (not shown) indicated that the highly autocorrelated yields on the value- and equal-weighted portfolios are approximated well by first-order autoregressions (AR1s), with AR1 parameters close to the first-order autocorrelations in table 2. We use residuals from AR1s estimated on end-of-year yields to measure yield shocks,

$$D(t+1)/P(t) = \alpha + \phi D(t)/P(t{-}1) + v(t-1, t). \qquad (8)$$

We use the yield shock $v(t-1, t)$ as a proxy for the expected return shock from $t-1$ to t.

The discount-rate effect implies a negative relation between expected return shocks and contemporaneous returns; an unexpected increase in expected returns drives the current price down. We measure this relation with the slope δ in the regression of $r(t-1, t)$ on $v(t-1, t)$,

$$r(t-1, t) + \gamma + \delta v(t-1, t) + u(t-1, t). \qquad (9)$$

We interpret δ as the response of $P(t)$ per unit of the time t yield shock. The slope $\beta(T)$ in the regression of $r(t, t+T)$ on $D(t)/P(t-1)$ then measures the T-period expected future price change due to the changes in expected returns implied by a yield shock. Comparing estimates of δ and $\beta(T)$ allows us to judge the relative magnitudes of the current and expected future price responses to yield shocks. The logic of this approach is that we want estimates of $\beta(T)$ for a long return horizon (we use $T = 4$ years), since the autocorrelation of expected returns implies that a yield shock has a slowly decaying effect on one-period expected future price changes.

Estimates of δ in (9) must be interpreted cautiously. The lack of correlation between returns and dividend changes more than a year ahead suggests that $D(t+1)/P(t)$ is relatively free of variation due to dividend forecasts. But this does not mean that all variation in $D(t+1)/P(t)$ is due to expected returns. Moreover, whatever its source, variation in $P(t)$ that results in variation in $D(t+1)/P(t)$ tends to produce a negative correlation between $r(t-1, t)$ and the yield shock $v(t-1, t)$. Thus negative estimates of δ are not per se evidence of a discount-rate effect. To infer that negative estimates of δ reflect offsetting changes in current prices related to changes in expected future returns, we need the complementary evidence from estimates of $\beta(T)$ that yields track expected returns so that yield shocks imply expected future price changes of the same sign.

8.2. The Estimates

Table 7 shows estimates of δ for real returns on the NYSE value- and equal-weighted portfolios. The estimates are always negative, less than -17.0, and more than 2.9 standard errors from 0.0. Table 7 also shows estimates of $\beta(T)$ for $T = 4$ years. Despite large standard errors, the estimates are usually more than 2.0 standard errors above 0.0. We conclude from the estimates of δ and $\beta(4)$ that dividend yield shocks are associated with (a) contemporaneous price changes of the opposite sign and (b) expected future price changes of the same sign.

TABLE 7. Tests for a discount-rate effect in stock returns

Comparisons of the relation between contemporaneous real returns and dividend yield shocks (δ) and the relation between future returns and current dividend yields (b).[a]

$$D(t+1)/P(t) = \alpha + \phi D(t)/P(t-1) + v(t-1, t)$$

$$r(t-1, t) = \gamma + \delta v(t-1, t) + u(t-1, t)$$

$$r(t, t+4) = a + bY(t) + e(t, t+4)$$

					$Y(t) = D(t)/P(t-1)$		$Y(t) = D(t)/P(t)$	
Period		δ	$s(\delta)$	$b(4)$	$s[b(4)]$		$b(4)$	$s[b(4)]$
				Value-weighted real returns				
1927–1986		−22.27	2.71	13.44	5.47		14.43	4.44
1927–1956		−20.42	4.69	23.00	10.40		20.39	5.51
1957–1986		−25.72	2.44	12.48	7.94		16.21	8.88
1941–1986		−20.10	2.15	13.34	4.19		15.71	4.75
				Equal-weighted real returns				
1927–1986		−20.42	3.48	12.64	6.81		18.91	5.45
1927–1956		−17.80	5.95	9.58	11.45		18.93	8.47
1957–1986		−24.73	3.17	20.26	8.22		24.85	8.29
1941–1986		−20.37	2.23	14.19	4.90		20.50	5.16

[a] δ, the contemporaneous response of the return $r(t-1, t)$ to the yield shock $v(t-1, t)$ is estimated with regressions of annual observations on one-year returns on the residuals from a first-order autoregression for the yield. The estimates of $b(4)$, interpreted as the response of future one-year returns to a current yield shock, are from tables 3 and 4, $s(\delta)$ and $s[b(4)]$ are standard errors. The results for nominal returns are similar.

The positive estimates of $\beta(4)$ from regressions of $r(t, t + T)$ on $D(t)/P(t-1)$ are large but typically smaller in magnitude than the negative estimates of δ. The out-of-sample forecasts in table 5 suggest, however, that the $D(t)/P(t-1)$ slopes understate the variation of expected returns because the information in $D(t)/P(t-1)$ is about a year out of date for expected returns measured forward from t. The estimates of $\beta(4)$ for regressions of $r(t, t+4)$ on the more timely $D(t)/P(t)$ are closer in magnitude to (usually within 1.0 standard error of) the estimates of δ.

We interpret the estimates of δ and $\beta(4)$ as suggesting that, on average, the expected future price increases implied by higher expected returns are just offset by the immediate price decline due to the discount-rate effect. Thus, as postulated in Summers (1986) and Fama and French (1987a), positively auto-correlated expected returns generate mean-reverting components of prices. We consider next competing scenarios for such temporary price components.

8.3. Temporary Price Components

Temporary components of prices and the forecast power of yields are consis-tent with an efficient market. Suppose investor tastes for current versus risky future consumption and the stochastic evolution of firms' investment oppor-tunities result in equilibrium expected returns that are highly autocorrelated but mean-reverting. Suppose shocks to expected returns and shocks to ratio-nal forecasts of dividends are independent. Then a shock to expected returns has no effect on expected dividends or expected returns in the distant future. Thus, the shock has no long-term effect on expected prices. The cumulative effect of a shock on expected returns must be exactly offset by an opposite adjustment in the current price. It follows that mean-reverting equilibrium expected returns can give rise to mean-reverting (temporary) components of stock prices. See Poterba and Summers (1987) for a formal analysis.

On the other hand, temporary components of prices and the forecast power of yields are also consistent with common models of an inefficient market, such as Keynes (1936), Shiller (1984), DeBondt and Thaler (1985), and Sum-mers (1986), in which stock prices take long temporary swings away from fun-damental values. In this view, high D/P ratios signal that future returns will be high because stock prices are temporarily irrationally low. Conversely, low D/P ratios signal irrationally high prices and low future returns.

As always, market efficiency per se is not testable. It must be tested jointly with restrictions on the behavior of equilibrium expected returns. [See Fama

(1970).] One reasonable restriction is that equilibrium in an efficient market never implies predictable price declines (negative expected nominal returns) for the value- and equal-weighted NYSE portfolios. The behavior of the fitted values for the regressions in tables 3 and 4 supports this hypothesis.

The fitted values from the regressions of nominal returns on dividend yields are rarely negative. For example, when the explanatory variable is the more timely $D(t)/P(t)$, the regressions for equal-weighted returns for all horizons produce a total of six negative fitted values during the 1927–1986 period and no negative fitted values during the 1941–1986 period. The regressions of value-weighted nominal returns on $D(t)/P(t)$ produce no negative fitted values in either period. In both the $D(t)/P(t)$ and the $D(t)/P(t-1)$ regressions, no negative fitted value is close to 2.0 standard errors from 0.0. As a rule at least two-thirds of the return forecasts are more than 2.0 standard errors above 0.0.

A stronger hypothesis is that equilibrium in an efficient market never implies negative expected real returns for the value- and equal-weighted NYSE portfolios. The regression fitted values are more often negative for real returns than for nominal returns, but again no negative forecast of real returns is more than 2.0 standard errors from 0.0, whereas typically more than half of the forecasts are more than 2.0 standard errors above 0.0.

In short, low dividend yields forecast that nominal returns will be relatively low, but they do not forecast that prices will decline. Likewise, the strong forecast power of yields does not imply that expected real returns are ever reliably negative.

8.4. Dividend Yields and the Autocorrelation of Returns

Autocorrelated expected returns and the opposite response of prices to expected return shocks (the discount-rate effect) can combine to produce mean-reverting components of stock prices. Fama and French (1987a) show that mean-reverting price components tend to induce negative autocorrelation in long-horizon returns. Thus, the negative autocorrelation of long-horizon returns in the earlier work is consistent with the positive autocorrelation of expected returns documented here.

But a mean-reverting, positively autocorrelated expected return does not necessarily imply negative autocorrelated returns or a mean-reverting component of prices. If shocks to expected returns and expected dividends are positively correlated, the opposite response of prices to expected return shocks can disappear. In this case, the positive autocorrelation of expected returns will imply positively autocorrelated returns, and time-varying expected returns will not generate mean-reverting price components. Moreover, changes through time in the autocorrelation of expected returns, or in the relation between shocks to expected returns and expected dividends, can change the time-series properties of returns and obscure tests of forecast power based on autocorrelation.

In contrast, as long as yields move with expected returns, regressions of returns on yields can document time-varying expected returns irrespective of changes in the autocorrelation of returns. This may explain why yields have strong forecast power in post-1940 periods, when the autocorrelations of returns in Fama and French (1987a) give weak indications of time-varying expected returns.

Does the variation of expected returns tracked by yields subsume the predictability of long-horizon returns implied by the negative autocorrelation in Fama and French (1987a)? We have estimated multiple regressions of $r(t, t + T)$ on $D(t)/P(t)$ and the lagged return $r(t-T, t)$. The lagged return rarely has marginal explanatory power. Negative slopes for the lagged return are typically less than 1.0 standard error from 0.0. In contrast, as in the univariate regressions, the slopes for the dividend yield in the multiple regressions increase with the return horizon and are typically more than 2.0 standard errors from 0.0 for the 1927–1986 period and for all periods after 1935. Thus including the lagged return in the regressions has no effect or the conclusion that dividend yields have systematic forecast power across different time periods and return horizons.

9. CONCLUSIONS

Like previous work, our regressions of returns on dividend yields indicate that time variation in expected returns accounts for small fractions of the variances of short-horizon returns. Dividend yields typically explain less than 5% of the variances of monthly or quarterly returns. An interesting and challenging feature of our evidence is that time variation in expected returns accounts for more of the variation of long-horizon returns. Dividend yields often explain more than 25% of the variances of two- to four-year returns. We offer a simple explanation.

The persistence (high positive autocorrelation) of expected returns causes the variance of expected returns, measured by the fitted values in the regressions of returns on dividend yields, to grow more than in proportion to the return horizon. On the other hand, the growth of the variance of the regression residuals is attenuated by a discount-rate effect: shocks to expected returns are associated with opposite shocks to current prices.

The cumulative price effect of an expected return shock and the associated price shock is roughly zero. On average, the expected future price increases implied by higher expected returns are just offset by the immediate decline in the current price. Thus the time variation of expected returns gives rise to mean-reverting or temporary components of prices.

REFERENCES

Ball, Ray, 1978, Anomalies in relationships between securities' yields and yield-surrogates, Journal of Financial Economics 6, 103–126.

Blume, Marshall E., 1968, The assessment of portfolio performance: An application of portfolio theory, Ph.D. dissertation (University of Chicago, Chicago, IL).

Campbell, John Y. and Robert Shiller, 1987, The dividend–price ratio and expectations of future dividends and discount factors, Unpublished manuscript (Princeton University, Prineon, NJ).

DeBondt, Werner F.M. and Richard Thaler, 1985, Does the stock market overreact?, Journal of Finance 40, 793–805.

Dow, Charles H., 1920, Scientific stock speculation, The Magazine of Wall Street (New York).

Fama, Eugene F., 1970, Efficient capital markets: A review of theory and empirical work, Journal of Finance 25, 383–417.

Fama, Eugene F., 1981, Stock returns, real activity, inflation, and money, American Economic Review 71, 545–565.

Fama, Eugene F. and Kenneth R. French, 1987a, Permanent and temporary components of stock prices, Journal of Political Economy 96, 246–273.

Fama, Eugene F. and Kenneth R. French, 1987b, Forecasting returns on corporate bonds and common stocks, Working paper (Center for Research in Security Prices, Graduate School of Business, University of Chicago, Chicago, IL).

Fama, Eugene F. and G. William Schwert, 1977, Asset returns and inflation, Journal of Financial Economics 5, 115–146.

Flood, Robert P., Robert J. Hodrick, and Paul Kaplar, 6, An evaluation of recent evidence on stock market bubbles, Unpublished manuscript (National Bureau of Economic Research, Cambridge, MA).

French, Kenneth R., G. William Schwert, and Robert Stambaugh, 1987, Expected stock returns and volatility, Journal of Financial Economics 19, 3–29.

Hansen, Lars P. and Robert J. Hodrick, 1980, Forward exchange rates as optimal predictors of future spot rates: An econometric analysis, Journal of Political Economy 88, 829–853.

Keim, Donald B. and Robert F. Stambaugh, 1986, Predicting returns in the stock and bond markets, Journal of Financial Economics 17, 357–390.

Keynes, John M., 1936, The general theory of employment, interest, and money (Harcourt, Brace and Company, New York, NY).

Lintner, John, 1956, Distribution of incomes of corporations among dividends, retained earnings and taxes, American Economic Review 46, 97–113.

Miller, Merton H. and Myron S. Scholes, 1982, Dividends and taxes: Some empirical evidence, Journal of Political Economy 90, 1118–1141.

Poterba, James M and Lawrence Summers, 1987, Mean reversion in stock returns: Evidence and implications, Unpublished manuscript (National Bureau of Economic Research, Cambridge, MA).

Rozeff, Michael, 1984, Dividend yields are equity risk premiums, Journal of Portfolio Management, 68–75.

Shiller, Robert J., 1984, Stock prices and social dynamics, Brookings Papers on Economic Activity 2, 457–498.

Stambaugh, Robert F., 1986, Bias in regressions with lagged stochastic regressors, Unpublished manuscript (University of Chicago, Chicago, IL).

Summers, Lawrence H., 1986, Does the stock market rationally reflect fundamental values?, Journal of Finance 41, 591–601.

THE INFORMATION IN LONG-MATURITY
FORWARD RATES

· · ·

Eugene F. Fama and Robert R. Bliss

Current 1-year forward rates on 1- to 5-year U.S. Treasury bonds are information about the current term structure of 1-year expected returns on the bonds, and forward rates track variation through time in 1-year expected returns. More interesting, 1-year forward rates forecast changes in the 1-year interest rate 2- to 4-years ahead, and forecast power increases with the forecast horizon. We attribute this forecast power to a mean-reverting tendency in the 1-year interest rate.

Much of the empirical work on the term structure of interest rates is concerned with two questions. (a) Do current forward rates forecast future interest rates? (b) Do current forward rates have information about the structure of current expected returns on bonds with different maturities? Much of the empirical work on these questions uses U.S. Treasury bills and so is restricted to maturities less than a year. This paper studies the information in forward rates about future interest rates and current expected returns for annual U.S. Treasury maturities to 5 years.

Our results on expected bond returns are novel. Past tests typically fail to produce reliable inferences about the structure of expected returns for maturities beyond a year. (See, for example, Reuben Kessel, 1965; J. Huston McCulloch, 1975; and Fama, 1984b.) Using the regression approach in Fama (1984a, 1986), we are able to infer that 1-year expected returns for maturities to 5 years, measured net of the interest rate on a 1-year bond, vary through time. These expected premiums swing from positive to negative, however. On average,

Reprinted from the *American Economic Review* 77, no.4 (September 1987): 680–92.

The helpful comments of John Cochrane, Bradford Cornell, Wayne Ferson, Kenneth French, Merton Miller, Richard Roll, and two referees are gratefully acknowledged. This research is supported by the National Science Foundation (Fama) and the Center for Research in Security Prices (Bliss).

the term structure of 1-year expected returns on 1- to 5-year Treasury bonds is flat.

Differences in expected returns are usually interpreted as rewards for risk. In this view, our evidence that the ordering of expected returns across maturities changes through time implies changes in the ordering of risks. This behavior of expected returns is inconsistent with simple term structure models, like the liquidity preference hypothesis of John Hicks (1946) in which expected returns always increase with maturity. The evidence poses an interesting challenge to models like those of Robert Merton (1973), John Long (1974), Douglas Breeden (1979), and John Cox et al. (1985), that allow time-varying expected returns.

Our results on the forecast power of forward rates are also novel. Previous tests find little evidence that forward rates can forecast future interest rates. For example, Michael Hamburger and E. N. Platt (1975) and Robert Shiller et al. (1983) conclude that forward rates have no forecast power. Fama (1984a) finds some power to forecast 1-month interest rates 1 month ahead. We confirm that forward rate forecasts of near-term changes in interest rates are poor. When the forecast horizon is extended, however, forecast power increases. The 1-year forward rate calculated from the prices of 4- and 5-year bonds explains 48 percent of the variance of the change in the 1-year interest rate 4 years ahead. We argue that this forecast power is largely due to a slow mean-reverting tendency in interest rates which is more apparent over longer horizons.

The hypothesis that interest rates are mean reverting is prominent in old and new models of the term structure, for example, F. A. Lutz (1940) and Cox et al. Unlike other recent work (for example, Charles Nelson and Charles Plosser, 1982, and Fama and Michael Gibbons, 1984), our results offer supporting evidence.

I. REGRESSION TESTS: THEORY

Treasury bonds with maturities longer than a year are not issued on a regular basis, and only irregularly spaced maturities are available. To estimate a term structure for regularly spaced maturities, some method of interpolation must be used. We use such a method (see the Appendix) to construct end-of-month prices for 1- to 5-year discount bonds. From the prices, we calculate forward rates, returns, and interest rates for annual maturities to 5 years.

The tests of the information in forward rates about current expected returns and future interest rates are simple regressions of future returns and changes in interest rates on current forward rates. As in most term structure work, however, even simple tests require a tedious notation.

A. Definitions of Variables

The return on an x-year discount bond bought at time t and sold at $t + x - y$, when it has y years to maturity, is defined as

$$h(x,y : t + x - y) = \ln p(y : t + x - y) - \ln p (x : t), \tag{1}$$

where ln indicates a natural log, and $p(x : t)$ is the price of the bond at t. Symbols before a colon are the maturities that define a variable. The symbol after the colon is the time the variable is observed. Since most of the empirical variables are annual, time is measured in annual increments. For example, $h(5, 4 : t + 1)$ is the 1-year return from t to $t + 1$ on a 5-year bond.

The yield $r(x : t)$ on a discount bond with \$1 face value and x years to maturity at t is defined as

$$r(x : t) = - \ln p (x : t). \tag{2}$$

The yield $r(1 : t)$ on a 1-year bond is called the 1-year spot rate. It has a prominent role in the tests.

The time t 1-year forward rate for the year from $t + x - 1$ to $t + x$ is

$$\begin{aligned} f(x, x - 1 : t) &= \ln p(x - 1 : t) - \ln p(x : t) \\ &= r(x : t) - r(x - 1 : t). \end{aligned} \tag{3}$$

For example, $f(5, 4 : t)$ is the forward rate for the year from $t + 4$ to $t + 5$.

The time t price of an x-year discount bond that pays \$1 at maturity is the present value of the \$1 payoff discounted at the time t expected values (E_t) of the future 1-year returns on the bond,

$$\begin{aligned} p(x : t) = \exp[- E_t h(x, x - 1 : t + 1) - E_t h(x - 1, x - 2 : t + 2) \\ - \ldots - E_t r (1 : t + x - 1)]. \end{aligned} \tag{4}$$

Equation (4) is a tautology, implied by the definition of returns. It acquires testable content when we add the hypothesis that the expected returns in (4) are rational forecasts used by the market to set $p(x : t)$. Equation (4) then says that the price contains rational forecasts of equilibrium expected returns. This hypothesis about the price is the basis of the tests.

B. Forward Rates and Future Spot Rates

For example, the forward rate $f(x, x-1 : t)$ can be viewed as the rate set at t on a contract to purchase a 1-year bond at $t + x - 1$. Motivated by this view, the literature has long been concerned with the hypothesis that the forward rate rationally forecasts the 1-year spot rate, $r(1 : t + x - 1)$, to be observed at $t + x - 1$. To focus on the forecast of the spot rate in $f(x, x - 1 : t)$, we sum the first $x - 1$ expected returns in (4) and write the price as

$$p(x : t) = \exp[-E_t h(x, 1 : t + x - 1) - E_t r(1 : t + x - 1)]. \tag{5}$$

Substituting (5) into (3) and subtracting the 1-year spot rate $r(1 : t)$ gives

$$f(x, x-1 : t) - r(1 : t) = [E_t r(1 : t + x-1) - r(1 : t)] \\ + [E_t h(x, 1 : t + x - 1) - r(x - 1 : t)]. \tag{6}$$

We call $f(x, x - 1 : t) - r(1 : t)$ the forward-spot spread. Our tests of the information in the forward rate $f(x, x - 1 : t)$ about the future spot rate $r(1 : t + x - 1)$ then center on the slope in the forecasting regression,

$$r(1 : t + x - 1) - r(1 : t) = a_1 + b_1 [f(x, x - 1 : t) - r(1 : t)] + u_1(t + x - 1). \tag{7}$$

Evidence that b_1 is greater than 0.0 implies that the forward-spot spread observed at time t has power to forecast the change in the 1-year spot rate $x - 1$ years ahead.

Equation (6) holds for realized returns as well as expected values,

$$f(x, x - 1 : t) - r(1 : t) = [r(1 : t + x - 1) - r(1 : t)] \\ + [h(x, 1 : t + x - 1) - r(x - 1 : t)]. \tag{8}$$

It follows that the regression (7) is complementary to the regression

$$h(x, 1 : t + x - 1) - r(x - 1 : t) = -a_1 + (1 - b_1)[f(x, x - 1 : t) - r(1 : t)] \\ - u_1(t + x - 1). \tag{9}$$

As indicated, the intercepts in (7) and (9) sum to 0.0, the residuals sum to 0.0 every period, and, most interesting, the slopes sum to 1.0. Thus, the slope in (7) estimates the split of variation in the forward-spot spread between the two terms of (6): (*i*) the forecasted change in the 1-year spot rate from t to $t + x - 1$; and (*ii*) the premium of the $(x-1)$-year expected return on an x-year bond over the time t yield on an $(x-1)$-year bond.

Since b_1 is a constant, the estimated split of variation in the forward-spot spread does not change through time. This means that (7) can tell us that the forward-spot spread has power to forecast the change in the spot rate; but the regression fitted values only track all variation in the forecasts when the expected change in the spot rate and the expected premium in (6) always vary in fixed proportion. This is a limitation of (7) and of similar regressions outlined below.

Expression (6) for the forward-spot spread combines expected returns in (4) to focus on information in the time t price, $p(x : t)$, about the return, $h(x, 1 : t + x - 1)$, and the spot rate, $r(1 : t + x - 1)$, to be observed at the beginning of the last year in the life of the x-year bond. We turn now to a different grouping of the expected returns in (4) which focuses on the information in $p(x : t)$ about the 1-year return, $h(x, x - 1 : t + 1)$, and the yield, $r(x - 1 : t + 1)$, to be observed in 1 year.

C. Forward Rates and 1-Year Expected Returns

If we sum the last $x - 1$ expected returns in (4), the price of an x-year bond is

$$p(x : t) = \exp[- E_t h(x, x - 1 : t + 1) - E_t r(x - 1 : t + 1)]. \tag{10}$$

Substituting (10) into (3) and subtracting the spot rate $r(1 : t)$ gives

$$f(x, x - 1 : t) - r(1 : t) = [E_t h(x, x - 1 : t + 1) - r(1 : t)] \\ + [E_t r(x - 1 : t + 1) - r(x - 1 : t)]. \tag{11}$$

Thus, when (10) is used for the price of an x-year bond, the forward-spot spread contains $E_t(x, x - 1 : t + 1) - r(1 : t)$, the time t expected premium of the 1-year return on an x-year bond over the 1-year spot rate. But the forward-spot spread also contains the expected change from t to $t + 1$ in the yield on $(x-1)$-year bonds. If yields are random walks, the expected yield change in (10) is 0.0, and $f(x, x - 1 : t) - r(1 : t)$ is $E_t h(x, x - 1 : t + 1) - r(1 : t)$. The common finding that forward rates have little power to forecast interest rates suggests a world where yields are close to random walks.

We call $h(x, x - 1 : t + 1) - r(1 : t)$ the term premium in the 1-year return on

TABLE 1. Term premium regressions: estimates of (12): 1964–85

$$h(x, x-1 : t+1)-r(1 : t) = a_2 + b_2[f(x, x-1 : t)-r(1 : t)] + u_2(t+1)$$

Dependent	a_2	$s(a)$	b_2	$s(b)$	R^2	Residual Autos (Yearly Lag)				
						1	2	3	4	5
$h(2, 1 : t+1) - r(1 : t)$	−.21	.41	.91	.28	.14	−.01	−.12	−.07	−.17	−.01
$h(3, 2 : t+1) - r(1 : t)$	−.51	.68	1.13	.37	.11	−.18	−.12	.03	−.17	−.05
$h(4, 3 : t+1) - r(1 : t)$	−.91	.92	1.42	.45	.11	−.23	−.10	.02	−.14	−.08
$h(5, 4 : t+1) - r(1 : t)$	−1.06	1.31	.93	.53	.05	−.17	−.11	.03	−.17	−.10

Note: $r(1 : t)$ is the 1-year spot rate observed at t; $h(x, x-1 : t+1)$ is the 1-year return (t to $t+1$) on an x-year bond, and $h(x, x-1 : t+1) - r(1 : t)$ is the term premium in the 1-year return. $f(x, x-1 : t)$ is a 1-year forward rate observed at t, and $f(x, x-1 : t) - r(1 : t)$ is the forward-spot spread. The regression estimates the expected value of the term premium to be observed at $t+1$, conditional on the forward-spot spread observed at t. The standard errors, $s(a)$ and $s(b)$, of the regression coefficients are adjusted for possible heteroscedasticity and for the autocorrelation induced by the overlap of monthly observations on annual returns. (See Halbert White, 1980, and Lars Peter Hansen, 1982.) The regression R^2 is adjusted for degrees of freedom. The sample size is 252, corresponding to the period January 1964 to December 1984 for the forward-spot spreads and January 1965 to December 1985 for the term premiums. If the true autocorrelations are 0.0, the standard error of the estimated residual autocorrelations is about 0.065. The data are derived from the U.S. Government Bond File of the Center for Research in Security Prices (CRSP) of the University of Chicago. See the Appendix.

an x-year bond. Our tests of the information in time t forward rates about time t 1-year expected returns then center on the slope in the regression,

$$h(x, x-1 : t+1)-r(1 : t) = a_2 + b_2[f(x, x-1 : t)-r(1 : t)] + u_2(t+1). \quad (12)$$

Evidence that b_2 is positive implies that the expected value of the term premium varies through time. Moreover, like (6), (11) holds for the realized returns, $h(x, x-1 : t+1)$ and $r(x-1 : t+1)$, as well as for their expected values. It follows that $1 - b_2$ in (12) is the slope in the complementary regression,

$$r(x-1 : t+1) - r(x-1 : t) = -a_2 + (1-b_2)[f(x, x-1 : t)-r(1 : t)]$$
$$-u_2(t+1). \quad (13)$$

Evidence that b_2 differs from 1.0 means that the forward-spot spread forecasts the change in the $(x-1)$-year yield 1 year ahead.

In short, the slope in (12) splits variation in the forward-spot spread between the 1-year expected term premium and expected yield change in (11), just as the slope in (7) splits variation in the forward-spot spread between the two multiyear forecasts in (6).

II. EXPECTED TERM PREMIUMS

A. Time-Varying Expected Term Premiums

Estimates of the term-premium regression (12) are in Table 1. Three slopes are more than 3.0 standard errors from 0.0, and the fourth is 1.75 standard errors from 0.0. We infer that expected term premiums in 1-year returns for maturities to 5 years vary through time, and so are typically nonzero. The results are in contrast to previous work of Kessel, McCulloch, Fama (1984b), and others that finds no convincing evidence of incremental expected returns for maturities beyond a year. The tests extend to longer maturities the conclusion of Richard Startz (1982), Shiller et al., and Fama (1984a, 1986), that expected bill returns contain time-varying maturity premiums. The evidence also confirms Shiller's (1979) claim that if bond prices are rational, the high variability of yields on longer-term bonds implies time-varying expected returns.

The slopes b_2 in the term-premium regressions range from 0.91 to 1.42. All are within one standard error of 1.0. We can infer that the slopes (equal to $1 - b_2$ and with the same standard errors as b_2) in the complementary yield-change regression (13) are within one standard error of 0.0. The results suggest that when forward-spot spreads are viewed as in (11), variation in current spreads is mostly variation in the term premiums in current 1-year expected returns, and forward-spot spreads do not predict yield changes 1 year ahead. The evidence extends to longer maturities Fama's (1984a, 1986) conclusion for bills that forward rates are close to current expected returns.

B. The Behavior of Expected Term Premiums

Kessel, McCulloch, Fama (1984b), and others show that inferences from average returns about average expected returns on longer-maturity bonds are imprecise because of the high variability of returns. An alternative approach is to use the term-premium regressions as a license to infer average expected returns from average forward rates. The average forward rates in Table 2 show no strong tendency to increase or decrease across longer maturities. The average value of the 4- to 5-year forward rate, $f(5, 4 : t)$, only exceeds the average value of the 1-year spot rate, $r(1 : t)$, by 0.25 percent per year.

However, the structure of forward rates varies through time, and the picture provided by average forward rates is misleading. Figure 1 plots the 5-year forward-spot spread. General patterns of variation are similar for other ma-

TABLE 2. Autocorrelations, means, and standard deviations: 1964–85

Variable	$\bar{x}$	$s(x)$	Autocorrelations (Monthly Lag)										
			1	2	3	4	5	6	12	24	36	48	60
			Spot and Forward Rates: $r(1:t)$ and $f(x, x-1:t)$										
$r(1:t)$	7.49	2.90	.97	.93	.89	.86	.84	.81	.71	.48	.31	.15	.09
$f(2,1:t)$	7.59	2.81	.97	.94	.92	.89	.87	.86	.75	.59	.43	.24	.12
$f(3,2:t)$	7.74	2.69	.96	.94	.92	.90	.89	.87	.75	.59	.41	.23	.11
$f(4,3:t)$	7.80	2.79	.96	.94	.92	.91	.89	.87	.75	.59	.44	.24	.11
$f(5,4:t)$	7.74	2.65	.93	.90	.89	.88	.87	.85	.75	.60	.41	.26	.12
			Term Premiums: $h(x, x-1:t+1) - r(1:t)$										
$h(2,1:t+1) - r(1:t)$	−.11	2.18	.90	.80	.72	.65	.59	.53	.08	−.10	−.16	−.24	−.05
$h(3,2:t+1) - r(1:t)$	−.23	3.75	.89	.79	.70	.63	.56	.49	−.01	−.09	−.11	−.22	−.09
$h(4,3:t+1) - r(1:t)$	−.46	5.13	.89	.80	.71	.64	.57	.48	−.04	−.08	−.09	−.21	−.10
$h(5,4:t+1) - r(1:t)$	−.83	6.36	.89	.80	.73	.66	.58	.49	−.04	−.07	−.08	−.22	−.13
			Forward-spot spreads: $f(x, x-1:t) - r(1:t)$										
$f(2,1:t) - r(1:t)$	.10	.91	.82	.78	.71	.64	.59	.53	.34	−.12	−.42	−.22	.03
$f(3,2:t) - r(1:t)$	.26	1.13	.78	.66	.57	.51	.48	.45	.29	−.14	−.39	−.23	.01
$f(4,3:t) - r(1:t)$	.31	1.22	.74	.66	.62	.53	.51	.48	.33	−.10	−.39	−.25	−.03
$f(5,4:t) - r(1:t)$	.25	1.54	.77	.62	.53	.52	.53	.47	.32	−.14	−.34	−.23	−.09
			Residual from Spot Rate Autoregression (14)										
$e(t)$	.00	.69	.15	−.08	−.12	−.11	.08	−.08	−.07	.06	−.07	−.02	−.04

Note: $r(1:t)$ is the 1-year spot rate observed at t; $h(x, x-1:t+1)$ is the 1-year return (t to $t+1$) on an x-year bond; $f(x, x-1:t)$ is a 1-year forward rate observed at t; $e(t)$ is the residual from the first-order autoregression (14) fit to the monthly time series of $r(1:t)$. The sample size is 252, corresponding to the period January 1964 to December 1984 for the forward-spot spreads and the period January 1965 to December 1985 for the term premiums in 1-year returns. If the true autocorrelations are 0.0, the standard error of the estimated autocorrelations is about 0.065. The data are derived from the CRSP U.S. Government Bond File. See the Appendix.

turities. If forward-spot spreads are expected term premiums in 1-year returns, Figure 1 shows the general path of the variation through time of expected term premiums. The forward-spot spread is characterized by alternating runs of positive and negative values. At least after 1970, there seems to be a relation between the sign of the forward-spot spread and the business cycle. Positive forward-spot spreads in Figure 1 tend to be associated with periods of strong business activity, for example, 1970–72, 1975–78, 1983–85. Negative spreads tend to occur during the recessions of 1973–74 and 1979–82.

In short, the average forward rates in Table 2 suggest that the term structure of expected 1-year returns on 1- to 5-year Treasury bonds is on average flat. But Figure 1 shows that a flat term structure of forward rates is not typical. The path of the forward-spot spread in Figure 1 suggests that expected term premiums are typically nonzero and vary between positive and negative values. Such

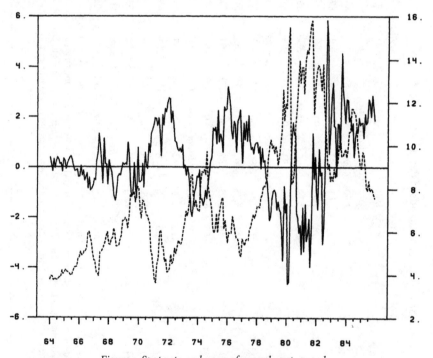

Figure 1. Spot rate and 5-year forward-spot spread

Note: 5-year forward-spot spread, $f(5, 4 : t) - r(1 : t)$ (solid line), and 1-year spot rate, $r(1 : t)$ (dashed line). The left vertical axis is the scale (percent per year) for the spread, and the right is the scale for the spot rate. The horizontal axis is the date t.

changes in the ordering of expected returns, and their apparent relation to the business cycle, pose an interesting challenge to term structure models that can accommodate time-varying expected returns.

C. The Effects of Measurement Error

A caveat about the term-premium regressions is in order. The spot rate $r(1 : t)$ is obtained from a 1-year bill, but the implied prices of discount bonds used to estimate forward rates and returns for longer maturities involve interpolation that can produce measurement error. Errors in the long-maturity price $p(x : t)$ in $f(x, x-1 : t)$ tend to bias the slope in the term-premium regression (12) toward 1.0, since $p(x : t)$ is the purchase price for the return $h(x, x-1 : t+1)$. Errors in the short-maturity price $p(x-1 : t)$ in $f(x, x-1 : t)$ tend to bias the slope in (12) toward 0.0 since $-\ln p(x-1 : t)$ is the yield $r(x-1 : t)$ in the complementary yield change regression (13). The net effect of measurement error on the slopes in the term-premium regressions is thus difficult to predict.

It is easier to predict the effect of measurement error on the spot-rate forecasting regression (7). The future spot rate $r(1 : t+x-1)$ is calculated from the price of a 1-year bill at $t+x-1$. Measurement errors in the time t prices in $f(x, x-1 : t)$ tend to bias the slope in (7) toward 0.0 and so attenuate our ability to identify forecast power in the forward rate. The forecast power we find in the tests that follow is thus in spite of any bias due to measurement error in forward rates.

III. FORECASTS OF 1-YEAR SPOT RATES

A. Estimates of the Spot-Rate Forecasting Regression

Since slopes close to 1.0 in the estimates of the term-premium regression (12) suggest that forward rates do not forecast yields 1 year ahead, intuition suggests that they will not forecast longer-term changes in rates. Intuition is not confirmed by the slope estimates for regression (7) in Table 3. The slopes are more than 2.6 standard errors from 0.0 for all forecasts beyond a year. The forward-spot spread, $f(x, x-1 : t) - r(1 : t)$, forecasts the change in the 1-year spot rate, $r(1 : t+x-1) - r(1 : t)$, 2 to 4 years ahead. Moreover, forecast power improves with the forecast horizon: $f(3, 2 : t) - r(1 : t)$ explains 8 percent of the variance of the change in the spot rate 2 years ahead; $f(4, 3 : t) - r(1 : t)$ explains 24 percent of the variance of the 3-year change; $f(5, 4 : t) - r(1 : t)$ explains 48 percent of the variance of the 4-year change.

Figure 2 plots 4-year changes in the 1-year spot rate and the fitted values

TABLE 3. Regression forecasts of the change in the spot rate

Dependent	a	$s(a)$	b_1	$s(b_1)$	b_2	$s(b_2)$	R^2	Residual Autos (Yearly Lag)				
								1	2	3	4	5
$r(1:t+x-1) - r(1:t) = a + b1\,[f(x, x-1:t) - r(1:t)] + u(t+x-1)$												
$r(1:t+1) - r(1:t)$	.21	.41	.09	.28			.00	-.11	-.12	-.07	-.17	-.01
$r(1:t+2) - r(1:t)$	.40	.73	.69	.26			.08	.39	-.21	-.36	-.33	-.08
$r(1:t+3) - r(1:t)$	.57	.75	1.30	.10			.24	.52	.04	-.40	-.46	-.25
$r(1:t+4) - r(1:t)$	1.12	.61	1.61	.34			.48	.38	.09	-.09	-.23	-.27
$r(1:t+x-1) - r(1:t) = a + b2\,[[\hat{r}(1:t+x-1) - r(1:t)] + u(t+x-1)$												
$r(1:t+1) - r(1:t)$	.03	.44			.87	.40	.16	-.01	-.05	-.02	-.12	.03
$r(1:t+2) - r(1:t)$	.16	.70			.88	.20	.26	.43	-.08	-.15	-.10	.04
$r(1:t+3) - r(1:t)$	.22	.84			.90	.13	.33	.57	.16	-.15	-.14	-.04
$r(1:t+4) - r(1:t)$	.37	.80			.91	.21	.36	.58	.29	.03	-.18	-.10
$r(1:t+x-1) - r(1:t) = a + b1\,[f(x, x-1:t) - r(1:t)] + b2[\hat{r}(1:t+x-1) - r(1:t)] + u(t+x-1)$												
$r(1:t+1) - r(1:t)$	.04	.43	-.14	.24	.90	.39	.16	-.03	-.04	-.00	-.09	.05
$r(1:t+2) - r(1:t)$	.15	.74	.19	.30	.82	.17	.26	.44	-.07	-.17	-.15	.01
$r(1:t+3) - r(1:t)$	.22	.84	.76	.43	.69	.22	.40	.56	.19	-.15	-.27	-.17
$r(1:t+4) - r(1:t)$	.79	.79	1.21	.45	.38	.20	.51	.47	.19	.03	-.14	-.23

Note: $r(1:t)$ is the 1-year spot rate observed at t; $f(x, x-1:t)$ is a 1-year forward rate observed at t; $\hat{r}(1:t+x-1)$ is the time t forecast of $r(1:t+x-1)$ from the first-order autoregression (14) fit to the time-series of $r(1:t)$. The standard errors of the regression coefficients are adjusted for possible heteroscedasticity and for the autocorrelation induced by the overlap of monthly observations on annual or multiyear changes in the spot rate. See White and Hansen. The sample size in the regressions for the 1-year change in the spot rate, $r(1:t+1) - r(1:t)$ is 252, corresponding to the period January 1964 to December 1984 for the forward-spot spread and the period January 1965 to December 1985 for the 1-year changes in the 1-year spot rate. An additional year (12 months) of data is lost each time the forecast horizon $t + x - 1$ is extended an additional year. Thus, the regressions for the 4-year change, $r(1:t+4) - r(1:t)$, have 216 observations. Under the hypothesis that the true autocorrelations are 0.0, the standard error of the estimated residual autocorrelations is about 0.065. The data are derived from the CRSP U.S. Government Bond File. See the Appendix.

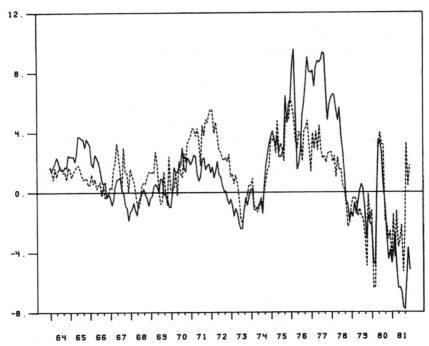

Figure 2. 4-year change in spot rate and forecast from regression (7)
Note: 4-year change in the spot rate, $r(1 : t+4) - r(1 : t)$ (solid line), and the forecasted change (dashed line) from the regression (7) of $r(1 : t+4) - r(1 : t)$ on the forward-spot spread $f(5, 4 : t) - r(1 : t)$. The vertical axis is percent per year and the horizontal axis is t, the date of the forecast.

from the regression of $r(1 : t + 4) - r(1 : t)$ on $f(5, 4 : t) - r(1 : t)$. The figure suggests that the high R^2 (0.48) of the regression reflects consistent long-term forecast power during the sample period. We argue that long-term forecast power is largely due to slow mean reversion of the spot rate.

B. Forecast Power and Mean Reversion

The autocorrelations of $r(1 : t)$ in Table 2 are close to 1.0 at short lags, but they decay across longer lags. The pattern suggests that month-to-month levels of the 1-year spot rate are highly autocorrelated, but the spot rate has a slow mean-reverting tendency.

The Appendix shows that if the 1-year spot rate is mean-reverting (stationary), then for long forecast horizons the expected change in the spot rate due to mean reversion explains half the variance of the actual change. If the spot rate is slowly mean reverting, the expected change explains more of the variance of the change for longer forecast horizons. Recall that the proportions of the variance of the change in the 1-year spot rate explained by forward-spot spreads in the estimates of (7) increase with the forecast horizon and reach 0.48 for 4-year changes. Thus, the forecast power of forward-spot spreads conforms to what is predicted by slow mean reversion.

It is also easy to show that if the spot rate is highly autocorrelated but slowly mean reverting, the correlation of the nonoverlapping changes, $r(1 : t + T) - r(1 : t)$ and $r(1 : t) - r(1 : t-T)$, is close to 0.0 for small values of T but approaches -0.5 for large values of T. The correlations between nonoverlapping 1-, 2-, 3-, and 4-year changes in the 1-year spot rate are -0.13, -0.29, -0.51, and -0.52.

C. Forecast Power and Mean Reversion: Direct Evidence

Although slow mean reversion of the spot rate is sufficient to explain the long-term forecast power of forward rates, the pattern of decay of the autocorrelations of the spot rate suggests that a first-order autoregression (AR1) is a reasonable model for the 1964–85 period. Fitting an AR1 to monthly observations on the 1-year spot rate yields

$$r(1 : t) = .257 + .968r(1 : t - 1) + e(t),$$
$$(.121) \quad (.015) \tag{14}$$

where the numbers in parentheses are standard errors. The autocorrelations of the residuals (Table 2) are generally close to 0.0. The first-order residual autocorrelation, 0.15, suggests that the model can be improved by adding a (1-month) moving-average term. Since we are interested in forecasts of spot-rate changes over long horizons, and since our goal is to document a mean-reverting tendency in a simple way, we stick with the AR1.

We use (14), fit to monthly levels of the 1-year spot rate, to forecast changes 1 to 4 years ahead. Regressions of actual on forecasted changes test for forecast power due to slow mean reversion. If the spot rate has a slow mean-reverting tendency which is well-approximated by the estimated AR1, the regressions of changes on the changes forecast by the AR1 will have forecast power that increases with the forecast horizon. Note, however, that the estimated AR1 slope, 0.968, is barely 2.0 standard errors from 1.0. If the spot rate is actually a random walk, the regressions of changes on the changes forecast by the estimated AR1 will have no power.

Regression intercepts (Table 3) that are all within 1.0 standard error of 0.0 and slopes within 1.0 standard error of 1.0 suggest that the AR1 forecasts of spot-rate changes are unbiased. As predicted by slow mean reversion, the forecasts explain more of the variance of spot-rate changes for longer forecast horizons. Explained variance rises from 16 percent for 1-year changes to 36 percent for 4-year changes. However, variance explained never reaches 50 percent, the limit predicted by mean reversion. An AR1 may not be the best model for the spot rate. But the AR1 serves its purpose. Its power to forecast spot-rate changes is consistent with a tendency toward mean reversion of the spot rate.

D. Forward Rate vs. AR1 Forecasts

Is the forecast power of forward rates solely due to mean reversion of the spot rate? Multiple regressions (Table 3) of spot-rate changes on forward-spot spreads and the AR1 forecasts are a test. In the regressions for 1- and 2-year changes, the slopes for the forward-spot spread are close to 0.0, while the slopes for the AR1 forecasts are close to 1.0 and more than 2.0 standard errors from 0.0. In the multiple regressions for 3- and 4-year changes, both the forward-spot spreads and the AR1 forecasts have marginal explanatory power (slopes almost or more than 2.0 standard errors from 0.0).

The fact that the AR1 dominates forward-spot spreads in the 1- and 2-year regressions does not necessarily mean that the market misses some of the mean reversion of the spot rate. We know from (6) that $f(x, x-1 : t) - r(1 : t)$ contains both the spot-rate forecast, $E_t r(1 : t+x-1) - r(1 : t)$, and the premium, $E_t h(x, 1 : t+x-1) - r(x-1 : t)$. If the expected change in the spot rate is a varying proportion of the forward-spot spread, the fixed-coefficient regression of $r(1 : t+x-1) - r(1 : t)$ on $f(x, x-1 : t) - r(1 : t)$ will not track all the information in the forward rate about the future spot rate.

There is evidence that variation in forward rates is not due entirely to forecasts of a mean-reverting spot rate. Although forward-spot spreads move opposite the spot rate, the correlations of the spot rate with 2- to 5-year forward-spot spreads (-0.25, -0.37, -0.30, and -0.42) are far from -1.0. If forward rates were driven only by mean reversion of the spot rate, our longest maturity forward rate, $f(5, 4 : t)$, would be much less variable than the spot rate. Table 2 shows that the standard deviation of $f(5, 4 : t)$ is within 10 percent of that of $r(1 : t)$.

On the other hand, the fact that forward-spot spreads have marginal explanatory power relative to the AR1 in 3- and 4-year regression forecasts may reflect deficiencies of the AR1. One possibility is that reversion to a constant mean is not a complete story for the spot rate. Such mean reversion predicts that forward-spot spreads are positive (the spot rate is expected to increase) when the spot rate is low and negative when the spot rate is high. The plots of the spot rate and the 5-year forward-spot spread in Figure 1 confirm this prediction for most of the sample period. However, some of the lowest values of the spot rate occur in 1964–68. Mean reversion predicts positive expected changes in spot rates for this period, but forward-spot spreads are not systematically positive. Likewise, when the spot rate drops in 1982, it remains above its sample mean. Simple mean reversion predicts that forward-spot spreads should not become positive, but they do.

Scott Ulman and John Wood (1983) suggest that the mean of the spot rate rises with the end of the gold standard in 1971 because a fiduciary currency means higher average inflation rates. A rise in the mean of the spot rate is consistent with the behavior of the spot rate and the forward-spot spread in Figure 1. John Campbell and Shiller (1984) suggest a time-series model for the spot rate that includes mean reversion, but toward a mean that can change through time.

The important point for our purposes is that the Table 3 regressions are sufficient to conclude that much of the forecast power of forward rates is due to a mean-reverting tendency of the spot rate. But we cannot infer on the basis of our simple tests that the forecast power of forward rates is better or worse than expected on the basis of the mean reversion of the spot rate.

Finally, the autocorrelations of forward rates (Table 2) are close to those of the spot rate. The same slow decay is observed in autocorrelations of 1- to 5-year yields (not shown). A slow mean-reverting tendency is apparently a general property of interest rates—an appealing conclusion with strong roots in term structure theory. However, because the autocorrelations of interest rates are close to 1.0 for short lags, recent empirical studies (for example, Nelson-Plosser and Fama-Gibbons) tend to conclude that interest rates are approximately random walks. Our evidence that long-term changes in rates are predictable suggests that the slow decay of the autocorrelations should instead be emphasized.

IV. CONCLUSIONS

A. Forward Rates and the Term Structure of Expected Returns

The estimates of the term-premium regression (12) allow us to infer that 1-year expected returns for U.S. Treasury maturities to 5 years, measured net of the interest rate on a 1-year bond, vary through time. Moreover, at least during the 1964–85 period, this variation of expected term premiums seems to be related to the business cycle. Expected term premiums are mostly positive during good times but mostly negative during recessions.

Differences in expected returns are usually interpreted as rewards for risk. Our evidence, like that for shorter maturities in Fama (1986), suggests that the ordering of risks and rewards changes with the business cycle. This behavior of expected returns is inconsistent with simple term structure models, like the liquidity preference hypothesis of Hicks and Kessel in which expected returns always increase with maturity. Perhaps it can be explained by models, like those of Merton, Long, Breeden, and Cox et al., that allow time-varying expected returns. The challenge is apparent.

B. Forward Rates and Future Spot Rates

Like earlier work, we find little evidence that forward rates can forecast near-term changes in interest rates. When the forecast horizon is extended, however, forecast power improves, and 1-year forward rates forecast changes in the 1-year spot rate 2 to 4 years ahead. We conclude that this forecast power reflects a slow mean-reverting tendency of interest rates.

Like any interest rate, the 1-year spot rate on Treasury bonds can be split into an expected real return and an expected inflation rate. The mean reversion of the spot rate likely implies that both of its components are mean reverting, a hypothesis with strong economic appeal. However, theory does not suggest that the processes that generate expected inflation and expected real returns should be the same, or that the processes should not change through time. We interpret the mean reversion of interest rates documented here as a tendency with details to be documented by future work.

APPENDIX

A. Data

The U.S. Government Bond File of the Center for Research in Security Prices (CRSP) has end-of-month data for all U.S. Treasury securities. We use the data to estimate end-of-month term structures for taxable, noncallable bonds for annual maturities to 5 years. The approach is outlined below. Our data are available to subscribers to the CRSP bond file.

Each month a term structure of 1-day continuously compounded forward rates is first calculated from available maturities. Bills are used for maturities to a year. To extend beyond a year, the pricing assumption is that the daily forward rate for the interval between successive maturities is the relevant discount rate for each day in the interval. Suppose daily forward rates for month t are calculated for maturities to T and the next bond matures at $T + k$. Coupons on the bond to be received prior to T are priced with the daily forward rates from t to each payment date. Coupons and the principal to be received after T are priced with the daily forward rates from t to T and with the (solved for) daily forward rate for T to $T + k$ that equates the price of the bond at t to the value of all payments. These calculations generate a step-function term structure in which 1-day forward rates are the same between successive maturities.

Prior to the recent large deficits, the number of noncallable, fully taxable bonds available each month is small. From 1964 onward there is at least one bond in each 1-year maturity interval to 5 years, but often there are few bonds beyond 5 years. We sum the daily forward rates to generate end-of-month term structures of yields for annual maturities to 5 years. The yields are used to calculate implied prices of 1- to 5-year discount bonds, from which we calculate the term-structure variables used in the tests.

B. Forecast Power and Mean Reversion

We use a first-order autoregression (AR1) to illustrate that predictable changes in the spot rate due to slow mean reversion are more apparent over longer horizons. Suppose $z(t)$ is an AR1 with parameter ϕ and mean μ,

$$z(t) = \delta + \phi z(t - 1) + \varepsilon(t),$$
$$\mu = \delta/(1 - \phi) \tag{A1}$$

The time t expected value of $z(t + T)$ is (see Nelson, 1973, p. 148)

$$E_t z(t + T) = \mu + \phi^T [z(t) - \mu], \tag{A2}$$

and the expected change in $z(t)$ from t to $t + T$ is

$$E_t z(t + T) - z(t) = [z(t) - \mu](\phi^T - 1). \tag{A3}$$

If ϕ is close to 1.0, the expected change in $z(t)$ is small for small values of T. The expected change in $z(t)$ increases with the forecast horizon and approaches $\mu - z(t)$: $z(t)$ is expected to revert to its mean μ.

The variance of the expected change in $z(t)$ is

$$\sigma^2[E_t z(t + T) - z(t)] = \sigma^2(z)(\phi^T - 1)^2, \tag{A4}$$

which grows with T and approaches $\sigma^2(z)$. How much of the variance of the T-period change is explained by the expected change? Since $\text{cov}[z(t + T), z(t)]$ approaches 0.0 for large values of T, the variance of $z(t + T) - z(t)$ approaches $2\sigma^2(z)$. Since $\sigma^2[E_t z(t + T) - z(t)]$ approaches $\sigma^2(z)$, for long forecast horizons the expected change in $z(t)$ due to the mean reversion of $z(t)$ explains half the variance of $z(t + T) - z(t)$. This result is a general property of stationary processes; it is not special to an AR1.

For an AR1 with ϕ close to 1.0, the ratio of the variance of the expected change to the variance of the change approaches 0.5 from below. For example, if $\phi = 0.95$, $\sigma^2[E_t z(t + 1) - z(t)]$ is $0.025\sigma^2[z(t + 1) - z(t)]$. Thus, the expected change explains more of the variance of the change for longer horizons. This is a rather general implication of slow mean reversion.

REFERENCES

Breeden, Douglas T., "An Intertemporal Asset Pricing Model with Stochastic Consumption and Investment Opportunities," *Journal of Financial Economics,* September 1979, *7,* 265–96.

Campbell, John Y. and Shiller, Robert J., "A Simple Account of the Behavior of Long-Term Interest Rates," *American Economic Review* Proceedings, May 1984, *74,* 44–48.

Cox, John C., Ingersoll Jonathan E., Jr. and Ross, Stephen A., "A Theory of the Term Structure of Interest Rates," *Econometrica,* March 1985, *53,* 385–407.

Fama, Eugene F., (1984a) "The Information in the Term Structure," *Journal of Financial Economics,* December 1984, *13,* 509–28.

———, (1984b) "Term Premiums in Bond Returns," *Journal of Financial Economics,* December 1984, *13,* 529–46.

———, "Term Premiums and Default Premiums in Money Markets," *Journal of Financial Economics,* September 1986, *17,* 175–96.

——— and Gibbons, Michael R., "A Comparison of Inflation Forecasts," *Journal of Monetary Economics,* May 1984, *13,* 327–48.

Hamburger, Michael J. and Platt, E. N., "The Expectations Hypothesis and the Efficiency of the Treasury Bill Market," *Review of Economics and Statistics,* May 1975, *57,* 190–99.

Hansen, Lars Peter, "Large Sample Properties of Generalized Method of Moments Estimators," *Econometrica,* June 1982, *50,* 1029–54.

Hicks, John R., *Value and Capital,* 2nd ed., London: Oxford University Press, 1946.

Kessel, Reuben A., "The Cyclical Behavior of the Term Structure of Interest Rates," NBER, Occasional Paper No. 91, 1965.

Long, John, "Stock Prices, Inflation, and the Term Structure of Interest Rates," *Journal of Financial Economics,* July 1974, *1,* 131–70.

Lutz, F. A., "The Structure of Interest Rates," *Quarterly* Journal *of Economics,* November 1940, *55,* 36–63.

McCulloch, J. Huston, "An Estimate of the Liquidity Premium," Journal *of Political Economy,* February 1975, *83,* 95–119.

Merton, Robert C., "An Intertemporal Capital Asset Pricing Model," *Econometrica,* September 1973, *41,* 867–87.

Nelson, Charles R., *Applied Time Series Analysis,* San Francisco: Holden-Day, 1973.

―――― and Plosser, Charles I., "Trends and Random Walks in Macroeconomic Time Series," *Journal of Monetary Economics,* September 1982, *10,* 139–62.

Shiller, Robert J., "The Volatility of Long-term Interest Rates and Expectations Models of the Term Structure," *Journal of Political Economy,* December 1979, *87,* 1190–219.

――――, Campbell John Y. and Schoenholtz, Kermit L., "Forward Rates and Future Policy: Interpreting the Term Structure of Interest Rates," *Brookings Papers on Economic Activity,* 1:1983, 173–217.

Startz, Richard, "Do Forecast Errors or Term Premia Really Make the Difference between Long and Short Rates?," *Journal of Financial Economics,* November 1982, *10,* 323–29.

White, Halbert, "A Heteroscedasticity-Consistent Covariance Matrix Estimator and a Direct Test for Heteroscedasticity," *Econometrica,* May 1980, *48,* 817–38.

Ulman, Scott and Wood, John H., "Monetary Regimes and the Term Structure of Interest Rates," manuscript, University of Minnesota, January 1983.

CORPORATE FINANCE AND BANKING

· · ·

CORPORATE FINANCE

· · ·

Amit Seru and Amir Sufi

Modigliani and Miller (1958) argued that, under certain conditions, the value of a firm is determined only by the value of its real projects, and that value is independent of the securities the firm issues to finance its real projects. Since real projects might be related to organizational form, in the Modigliani and Miller world, financing is irrelevant to organization of the firm as well.

Many researchers attribute the origins of the field of corporate finance to this seminal study. It seems that one must find frictions, violations of the Modigliani-Miller assumptions, to resurrect the view that the financial structure of a firm matters for its value and its organizational form—really, for corporate finance to have anything interesting to say. The evolution of corporate finance over the past 50 years has been shaped by this search for such frictions.

But the Modigliani-Miller logic is strong. In our view, the Modigliani-Miller theorem is better seen not as the origin of the field, the motivator for frictions to revive its importance, but as a menacing shadow over the field, constantly suggesting to researchers working within corporate finance that their search for frictions is in vain, or at least that frictions are subject to constant attack by alternative forces.

Gene Fama's research has played an important role in the back and forth that has defined corporate finance since its inception. Broadly, the core question of Gene's research in this area has been: Do the frictions used to assert value implications of financial structure really matter? Or does the evidence support the general idea in Modigliani and Miller (1958)—that financing is a second-order consideration for firm value and its organization? Gene's work has concentrated on agency problems, dividend policy, and equity issuances.

AGENCY PROBLEMS

While the original attack on the Modigliani-Miller theorem emphasized the importance of taxes and the costs of financial distress (e.g., Scott 1976), the field later converged on the importance of *agency problems* and *incentive conflicts*. For example, Jensen and Meckling (1976) argued that debt could help improve incentives of managers by giving them a larger share of the returns to their effort, but debt could also lead to conflicts of interests between shareholders and creditors. (When a firm is near bankruptcy, shareholders will want to bet the farm on the chance the firm recovers, while bondholders will bear larger losses if the bet fails.) The implication: too little debt means the manager will shirk; too much debt means creditor-shareholder conflict will emerge. In either case, a firm's leverage will impact its overall value.

In "Agency Problems and the Theory of the Firm," published in the *Journal of Political Economy* in 1980, Gene contends that the incentive conflicts literature, which largely studied games between investors and management of a given firm, was ignoring the important role of external competition in reducing agency problems. As he put it:

> The firm is disciplined by competition from other firms, which forces the evolution of devices for efficiently monitoring the performance of the entire team and of its individual members. In addition, individual participants in the firm, and in particular its managers, face both the discipline and opportunities provided by the markets for their services, both within and outside of the firm.

In particular, Gene argues that the managerial labor market plays an important role. For large corporations, hiring and firing and reputation are the primary forms of discipline. Managers that shirk are revealed to the market. This threat of ex post "settling up" in the labor market effectively reduces the agency problem that a manager might shirk in his or her current job. As Gene puts it:

> The important general point is that in any scenario where the weight of the wage revision process is at least equivalent to full ex post settling up, managerial incentive problems—the problems usually attributed to the separation of security ownership and control of the firm—are resolved.

The implication of Gene's study is that the capital structure of the firm may not need to be used to discipline managers.

This study was provocative and became a central part of the debate on managerial agency problems. For example, Bengt Holmström (1999) wrote one of his most cited studies on dynamic managerial agency problems. His motivation was in part the gauntlet thrown by Gene:

[Fama] argues that market forces alone will frequently remove moral hazard problems, because managers will be concerned about their reputations in the labor market. . . . The purpose of this paper is to investigate in some more detail Fama's rather provocative but interesting idea that career concerns induce efficient managerial behavior.

Holmström builds a model in his study in which a competitive labor market may not induce efficient behavior by managers, even when there is no discounting and the manager is risk-neutral.

Ultimately, whether the labor market provides the necessary discipline for managers is an empirical question. A large body of evidence speaks to this debate. Many studies find that competition and the threat of being fired reduces managerial agency problems, while others find that capital structure continues to play an important disciplinary role. We do not have a definitive conclusion, but Gene's study represents a very important contribution to the debate. Before scholars get carried away with the importance of incentive problems in corporate finance—typically studying interactions between a fixed set of players—they must take into account whether competition and market forces resolve these problems. Yet another shadow over the field!

Gene wrote another influential study in this area together with Michael Jensen: "Separation of Ownership and Control," published in the *Journal of Law and Economics*. They published it in 1983, when agency theory started to heavily influence corporate finance. It is an ambitious study which tries to offer principles for thinking through the classic agency problem within an organization: "we are concerned with the survival of organizations in which important decision agents do not bear a substantial share of the wealth effects of their decisions."

Broadly, we see this study too as being motivated from the perfect world envisioned by Modigliani-Miller in which the role of a firm or its organization has no effect on firm value. Fama and Jensen move beyond treating the firm as a black box with a set of real projects, financed by debt and equity. Instead, they explore agency-theory-based explanation for why and how the projects and people running them could be organized within the same firm.

Fama and Jensen discuss the interaction of three roles in an organization: bearing risk, initiating and implementing actions ("decision management"), and ratifying and monitoring actions ("decision control"). They argue for two main principles in optimal organizational form: if residual risk bearing is separated from those implementing actions (as in a large corporation with specialized managers and external shareholders), then corporate governance requires that ratification and monitoring be done by agents other than those implementing actions (such as a board of directors looking over managers). In contrast, if those implementing decisions are the same agents as those monitoring the decisions, then residual risk bearing must be concentrated among the same agents as in a partnership.

They use this framework to explain a number of different organizational forms. Open corporations, for example, have a separation of risk bearing from implementation decisions. As a result, an important monitoring role must be played by the stock market, the takeover market, or expert boards. Small professional partnerships restrict residual claims to a limited group of experts who both implement decisions and monitor others. Financial mutuals separate implementation from risk bearing. As a result, they must rely on a board of directors and the ability of investors to easily redeem their claims at face value to discipline the agents implementing actions. Their wide-ranging analysis even takes on the organizational structure of the Catholic Church.

The framework offered by Fama and Jensen was foundational to the literature exploring organizational form in the presence of agency problems. It also helps us understand a variety of organizational forms we witness in practice.

DIVIDEND POLICY

Gene also made large contributions to our understanding of corporate dividend policy. In one of his earliest studies with Harvey Babiak, he empirically examined dividend policy for a large set of firms ("Dividend Policy: An Empirical Analysis," published in the *Journal of the American Statistical Association* in 1968). Starting with the partial adjustment model of Lintner (1956), Fama and Babiak conducted a statistical analysis of the dividend policy of 400 firms from 1946 to 1964. Their main conclusion was that the Lintner two-variable model is a reasonable benchmark: a constant, lagged dividends, and concurrent earnings explain current dividends at a firm quite well. They find some evidence that lagged earnings helped improve the explanatory power of the model, which suggests that firms pay attention to a sequence of earnings shocks rather than just the most recent one.

In our view, the most remarkable aspect of the study is how advanced the statistical analysis was for its time. The authors use *panel* data (data that runs both over time and across firms) to estimate the model, going beyond the aggregate regressions that were common during the 1950s and 1960s. The use of panel data from Compustat is the norm in empirical corporate finance research today; this study was among the earliest to do so. Further, Fama and Babiak took a number of steps to avoid bias in coefficient estimates. For example, "to avoid spurious results that could follow from the extensive data-dredging involved in finding 'good-fitting' dividend models, only half of the available firms are used in the original search, the remaining firms serving as a check on the findings." They also used simulations to help guard against bias caused by the autoregressive nature of dividend policy.

This early study demonstrated characteristics of Gene's empirical research that would carry on through the years: first-rate data, rigorous and innovative estimation techniques, and careful consideration of biases that naturally arise in statistical tests.

In a 2001 study published in the *Journal of Financial Economics*, Gene together with frequent collaborator Ken French studied the phenomenon of disappearing dividends. Gene and Ken have always had an elite ability to uncover the key patterns in an ocean of data; the study exemplifies this skill.

They start with a striking feature of the data: the fraction of public firms paying dividends plummeted from two-thirds in 1978 to only one-fifth in 1999. They then show that the main reason for this striking change is an evolution of the composition of firms that are publicly traded. More specifically, from 1978 to 1999, small firms with low profitability and strong growth opportunities made up a higher proportion of publicly traded firms, and these characteristics are typical of firms that do not pay dividends.

But Gene and Ken point out that this is not the entire explanation of disappearing dividends. In the second half of the study, they show that even firms that typically pay dividends were less likely to do so toward the end of the sample. As they put it, "the decline in aggregate profitability hides the fact that an increasing fraction of firms with positive earnings—firms that in the past would typically pay dividends—now choose not to pay." They quantify this argument by using the early period to obtain estimates of the effects of certain characteristics (such as profitability or growth opportunities) on the likelihood of paying a dividend. They then project the expected probability of paying dividends in the later part of the sample based on the estimates from the early part. When they compare the expected to the actual likelihood of paying dividends, they find large positive gaps. In the 1980s and 1990s, even firms with the same characteristics as firms in the 1960s and 1970s were much less likely to pay dividends.

Gene and Ken do not offer a strong view on *why* these patterns have occurred. But their exceptional empirical skills help elucidate the key features of the data that can help guide research exploring why dividends are disappearing.

EQUITY ISSUANCE

The pecking-order theory of Myers and Majluf (Myers 1984; Myers and Majluf 1984) is one of the main proposed theories of why capital structure is relevant for firm value. According to this view, capital structure has important value implications because of the information asymmetry that managers know more than outsiders know. Firms should be hesitant to issue securities with payoffs that are highly sensitive to private information because outsiders will distrust those securities. This view implies that firms should first rely on cash, then bank debt, then bonds, and equity last. As Myers (1984) puts it, "If external finance is required, firms issue the safest security first. That is, they start with debt, then possibly hybrid securities such as convertible bonds, then perhaps equity as a last resort."

In their 2005 article in the *Journal of Financial Economics*, Gene and Ken take on the pecking-order theory by examining empirically one of its central predictions: the issuance of equity by publicly traded firms should be rare. Previous research supported this argument by showing that seasoned equity offerings are uncommon. But as Gene and Ken point out, "In addition to SEOs, firms issue equity in mergers and through private placements, convertible debt, warrants, direct purchase plans, rights issues, and employee options, grants, and benefit plans."

The article is short and concise, and it quickly gets to the heart of the matter: firms issue equity all the time. As Gene and Ken write, "during 1973 to 1982, on average 67% of our sample firms issue some equity each year, and the proportion rises to 74% for 1983 to 1992 and 86% for 1993 to 2002." If the unaltered pecking order theory were the correct model of capital structure for the universe of firms, there would not be nearly as many firms issuing equity.

As Gene and Ken acknowledge, this result does not say that information asymmetry plays no role in corporate finance. There is likely a subset of firms for which the pecking order is the best model of capital structure decisions. Further, equity issuances to corporate insiders likely fit within the pecking order framework. But Gene and Ken refute the argument that the pecking order is the best description of capital structure policy for the universe of publicly traded firms, and they refute the bandied stylized fact that firms rarely issue equity. Information asymmetry no doubt plays some role in corporate capital structure, but Gene and Ken place some appropriate limits on how extensive its presence is. Their work has had one more important effect—it has stopped researchers from running horse races between predictions of the pecking order theory with its main competing theory, the trade-off model. As Gene and Ken suggested, and we agree, "Perhaps it is best to regard the two models as stable mates with each having elements of truth that help explain some aspects of financing decisions."

REFERENCES

Holmström, Bengt. 1999. "Managerial Incentive Problems: A Dynamic Perspective." *Review of Economic Studies* 66 (1), 169–182. doi: 10.1111/1467-937X.00083.

Lintner, John. 1956. "Distribution of Incomes of Corporations among Dividends, Retained Earnings, and Taxes." *American Economic Review* 46 (2), 97–113. Available at http://www.jstor.org/stable/1910664.

Modigliani, Franco, and Merton H. Miller. 1958. "The Cost of Capital, Corporation Finance and the Theory of Investment." *American Economic Review* 48 (3), 261–97. Available at http://www.jstor.org/stable/1809766.

Myers, Stewart C. 1984. "The Capital Structure Puzzle." *Journal of Finance* 39, 574–592. doi: 10.1111/j.1540-6261.1984.tb03646.x.

Myers, Stewart C., and Nicholas S. Majluf. 1984. "Corporate Financing and Investment Decisions when Firms Have Information That Investors Do Not Have." *Journal of Financial Economics* 13 (2), 187–221.

AGENCY PROBLEMS AND THE THEORY OF THE FIRM

. . .

Eugene F. Fama

This paper attempts to explain how the separation of security ownership and control, typical of large corporations, can be an efficient form of economic organization. We first set aside the presumption that a corporation has owners in any meaningful sense. The entrepreneur is also laid to rest, at least for the purposes of the large modern corporation. The two functions usually attributed to the entrepreneur—management and risk bearing—are treated as naturally separate factors within the set of contracts called a firm. The firm is disciplined by competition from other firms, which forces the evolution of devices for efficiently monitoring the performance of the entire team and of its individual members. Individual participants in the firm, and in particular its managers, face both the discipline and opportunities provided by the markets for their services, both within and outside the firm.

Economists have long been concerned with the incentive problems that arise when decision making in a firm is the province of managers who are not the firm's security holders.[1] One outcome has been the development of "behavioral"

Reprinted from the *Journal of Political Economy* 88, no.2 (April 1980): 288–307.
© 1980 by The University of Chicago.

This research is supported by the National Science Foundation. Roger Kormendi has contributed much, and the comments of A. Alchian, S. Bhattacharya, G. Becker, F. Black, M. Blume, M. Bradley, D. Breeden, N. Gonedes, B. Horwitz, G. Jarrell, E. H. Kim, J. Long, H. Manne, W. Meckling, M. H. Miller, M. Scholes, C. Smith, G. J. Stigler, R. Watts, T. Whisler, and J. Zimmerman are gratefully acknowledged. Presentations at the finance, labor economics, and industrial organization workshops of the University of Chicago and the workshop of the Managerial Economics Research Center of the University of Rochester have been helpful. The paper is largely an outgrowth of discussions with Michael C. Jensen.

1. Jensen and Meckling (1976) quote from Adam Smith (1776). The modern literature on the problem dates back at least to Berle and Means (1932).

and "managerial" theories of the firm which reject the classical model of an entrepreneur, or owner-manager, who single-mindedly operates the firm to maximize profits, in favor of theories that focus more on the motivations of a manager who controls but does not own and who has little resemblance to the classical "economic man." Examples of this approach are Baumol (1959), Simon (1959), Cyert and March (1963), and Williamson (1964).

More recently the literature has moved toward theories that reject the classical model of the firm but assume classical forms of economic behavior on the part of agents within the firm. The firm is viewed as a set of contracts among factors of production, with each factor motivated by its self-interest. Because of its emphasis on the importance of rights in the organization established by contracts, this literature is characterized under the rubric "property rights." Alchian and Demsetz (1972) and Jensen and Meckling (1976) are the best examples. The antecedents of their work are in Coase (1937, 1960).

The striking insight of Alchian and Demsetz (1972) and Jensen and Meckling (1976) is in viewing the firm as a set of contracts among factors of production. In effect, the firm is viewed as a team whose members act from self-interest but realize that their destinies depend to some extent on the survival of the team in its competition with other teams. This insight, however, is not carried far enough. In the classical theory, the agent who personifies the firm is the entrepreneur who is taken to be both manager and residual risk bearer. Although his title sometimes changes—for example, Alchian and Demsetz call him "the employer"—the entrepreneur continues to play a central role in the firm of the property-rights literature. As a consequence, this literature fails to explain the large modern corporation in which control of the firm is in the hands of managers who are more or less separate from the firm's security holders.

The main thesis of this paper is that separation of security ownership and control can be explained as an efficient form of economic organization within the "set of contracts" perspective. We first set aside the typical presumption that a corporation has owners in any meaningful sense. The attractive concept of the entrepreneur is also laid to rest, at least for the purposes of the large modern corporation. Instead, the two functions usually attributed to the entrepreneur, management and risk bearing, are treated as naturally separate factors within the set of contracts called a firm. The firm is disciplined by competition from other firms, which forces the evolution of devices for efficiently monitoring the performance of the entire team and of its individual members. In addition, individual participants in the firm, and in particular its managers, face both the discipline and opportunities provided by the markets for their services, both within and outside of the firm.

THE IRRELEVANCE OF THE CONCEPT
OF OWNERSHIP OF THE FIRM

To set a framework for the analysis, let us first describe roles for management and risk bearing in the set of contracts called a firm. Management is a type of labor but with a special role—coordinating the activities of inputs and carrying out the contracts agreed among inputs, all of which can be characterized as "decision making." To explain the role of the risk bearers, assume for the moment that the firm rents all other factors of production and that rental contracts are negotiated at the beginning of each production period with payoffs at the end of the period. The risk bearers then contract to accept the uncertain and possibly negative difference between total revenues and costs at the end of each production period.

When other factors of production are paid at the end of each period, it is not necessary for the risk bearers to invest anything in the firm at the beginning of the period. Most commonly, however, the risk bearers guarantee performance of their contracts by putting up wealth ex ante, with this front money used to purchase capital and perhaps also the technology that the firm uses in its production activities. In this way the risk bearing function is combined with ownership of capital and technology. We also commonly observe that the joint functions of risk bearing and ownership of capital are repackaged and sold in different proportions to different groups of investors. For example, when front money is raised by issuing both bonds and common stock, the bonds involve a combination of risk bearing and ownership of capital with a low amount of risk bearing relative to the combination of risk bearing and ownership of capital inherent in the common stock. Unless the bonds are risk free, the risk bearing function is in part borne by the bondholders, and ownership of capital is shared by bondholders and stockholders.

However, ownership of capital should not be confused with ownership of the firm. Each factor in a firm is owned by somebody. The firm is just the set of contracts covering the way inputs are joined to create outputs and the way receipts from outputs are shared among inputs. In this "nexus of contracts" perspective, ownership of the firm is an irrelevant concept. Dispelling the tenacious notion that a firm is owned by its security holders is important because it is a first step toward understanding that control over a firm's decisions is not necessarily the province of security holders. The second step is setting aside the equally tenacious role in the firm usually attributed to the entrepreneur.

MANAGEMENT AND RISK BEARING:
A CLOSER LOOK

The entrepreneur (manager–risk bearer) is central in both the Jensen-Meckling and Alchian-Demsetz analyses of the firm. For example, Alchian-Demsetz state: "The essence of the classical firm is identified here as a contractual structure with: 1) joint input production; 2) several input owners; 3) one party who is common to all the contracts of the joint inputs; 4) who has the right to renegotiate any input's contract independently of contracts with other input owners; 5) who holds the residual claim; and 6) who has the right to sell his central contractual residual status. The central agent is called the firm's owner and the employer" (1972, p. 794).

To understand the modern corporation, it is better to separate the manager, the agents of points 3 and 4 of the Alchian-Demsetz definition of the firm, from the risk bearer described in points 5 and 6. The rationale for separating these functions is not just that the end result is more descriptive of the corporation, a point recognized in both the Alchian-Demsetz and Jensen-Meckling papers. The major loss in retaining the concept of the entrepreneur is that one is prevented from developing a perspective on management and risk bearing as separate factors of production, each faced with a market for its services that provides alternative opportunities and, in the case of management, motivation toward performance.

Thus, any given set of contracts, a particular firm, is in competition with other firms, which are likewise teams of cooperating factors of production. If there is a part of the team that has a special interest in its viability, it is not obviously the risk bearers. It is true that if the team does not prove viable factors like labor and management are protected by markets in which rights to their future services can be sold or rented to other teams. The risk bearers, as residual claimants, also seem to suffer the most direct consequences from the failings of the team. However, the risk bearers in the modern corporation also have markets for their services—capital markets—which allow them to shift among teams with relatively low transaction costs and to hedge against the failings of any given team by diversifying their holdings across teams.

Indeed, portfolio theory tells us that the optimal portfolio for any investor is likely to be diversified across the securities of many firms.[2] Since he holds the securities of many firms precisely to avoid having his wealth depend too much on any one firm, an individual security holder generally has no special interest in personally overseeing the detailed activities of any firm. In short, efficient allocation of risk bearing seems to imply a large degree of separation of security ownership from control of a firm.

On the other hand, the managers of a firm rent a substantial lump of wealth—their human capital—to the firm, and the rental rates for their human capital signaled by the managerial labor market are likely to depend on the success or failure of the firm. The function of management is to oversee the contracts among factors and to ensure the viability of the firm. For the purposes of the managerial labor market, the previous associations of a manager with success and failure are information about his talents. The manager of a firm, like the coach of any team, may not suffer any immediate gain or loss in current wages from the current performance of his team, but the success or failure of the team impacts his future wages, and this gives the manager a stake in the success of the team.

The firm's security holders provide important but indirect assistance to the managerial labor market in its task of valuing the firm's management. A security holder wants to purchase securities with confidence that the prices paid reflect the risks he is taking and that the securities will be priced in the future to allow him to reap the rewards (or punishments) of his risk bearing. Thus, although an individual security holder may not have a strong interest in directly overseeing the management of a particular firm, he has a strong interest in the existence of a capital market which efficiently prices the firm's securities. The signals provided by an efficient capital market about the values of a firm's securities are likely to be important for the managerial labor market's revaluations of the firm's management.

We come now to the central question. To what extent can the signals provided by the managerial labor market and the capital market, perhaps along with other market-induced mechanisms, discipline managers? We first discuss, still in general terms, the types of discipline imposed by managerial labor markets, both within and outside of the firm. We then analyze specific conditions under which this discipline is sufficient to resolve potential incentive

2. Detailed discussions of portfolio models can be found in Fama and Miller (1972, chaps. 6 and 7), Jensen (1972), and Fama (1976, chaps. 7 and 8).

problems that might be associated with the separation of security ownership and control.

The outside managerial labor market exerts many direct pressures on the firm to sort and compensate managers according to performance. One form of pressure comes from the fact that an ongoing firm is always in the market for new managers. Potential new managers are concerned with the mechanics by which their performance will be judged, and they seek information about the responsiveness of the system in rewarding performance. Moreover, given a competitive managerial labor market, when the firm's reward system is not responsive to performance the firm loses managers, and the best are the first to leave.

There is also much internal monitoring of managers by managers themselves. Part of the talent of a manager is his ability to elicit and measure the productivity of lower managers, so there is a natural process of monitoring from higher to lower levels of management. Less well appreciated, however, is the monitoring that takes place from bottom to top. Lower managers perceive that they can gain by stepping over shirking or less competent managers above them. Moreover, in the team or nexus of contracts view of the firm, each manager is concerned with the performance of managers above and below him since his marginal product is likely to be a positive function of theirs. Finally, although higher managers are affected more than lower managers, all managers realize that the managerial labor market uses the performance of the firm to determine each manager's outside opportunity wage. In short, each manager has a stake in the performance of the managers above and below him and, as a consequence, undertakes some amount of monitoring in both directions.

All managers below the very top level have an interest in seeing that the top managers choose policies for the firm which provide the most positive signals to the managerial labor market. But by what mechanism can top management be disciplined? Since the body designated for this function is the board of directors, we can ask how it might be constructed to do its job. A board dominated by security holders does not seem optimal or endowed with good survival properties. Diffuse ownership of securities is beneficial in terms of an optimal allocation of risk bearing, but its consequence is that the firm's security holders are generally too diversified across the securities of many firms to take much direct interest in a particular firm.

If there is competition among the top managers themselves (all want to be the boss of bosses), then perhaps they are the best ones to control the board of directors. They are most directly in the line of fire from lower managers when the markets for securities and managerial labor give poor signals about the performance of the firm. Because of their power over the firm's decisions, their market-determined opportunity wages are also likely to be most affected by market signals about the performance of the firm. If they are also in competition for the top places in the firm, they may be the most informed and responsive critics of the firm's performance.

Having gained control of the board, top management may decide that collusion and expropriation of security holder wealth are better than competition among themselves. The probability of such collusive arrangements might be lowered, and the viability of the board as a market-induced mechanism for low-cost internal transfer of control might be enhanced, by the inclusion of outside directors. The latter might best be regarded as professional referees whose task is to stimulate and oversee the competition among the firm's top managers. In a state of advanced evolution of the external markets that buttress the corporate firm, the outside directors are in their turn disciplined by the market for their services which prices them according to their performance as referees. Since such a system of separation of security ownership from control is consistent with the pressures applied by the managerial labor market, and since it likewise operates in the interests of the firm's security holders, it probably has good survival properties.[3]

This analysis does not imply that boards of directors are likely to be composed entirely of managers and outside directors. The board is viewed as a market-induced institution, the ultimate internal monitor of the set of contracts called a firm, whose most important role is to scrutinize the highest decision makers within the firm. In the team or nexus of contracts view of the firm, one cannot rule out the evolution of boards of directors that contain many different factors of production (or their hired representatives), whose

3. Watts and Zimmerman (1978) provide a similar description of the market-induced evolution of "independent" outside auditors whose function is to certify and, as a consequence, stimulate the viability of the set of contracts called the firm. Like the outside directors, the outside auditors are policed by the market for their services which prices them in large part on the basis of how well they resist perverting the interests of one set of factors (e.g., security holders) to the benefit of other factors (e.g., management). Like the professional outside director, the welfare of the outside auditor depends largely on "reputation."

common trait is that their marginal products are affected by those of the top decision makers. On the other hand, one also cannot conclude that all such factors will naturally show up on boards since there may be other market-induced institutions, for example, unions, that more efficiently monitor managers on behalf of specific factors. All one can say is that in a competitive environment lower-cost sets of monitoring mechanisms are likely to survive. The role of the board in this framework is to provide a relatively low-cost mechanism for replacing or reordering top managers; lower cost, for example, than the mechanism provided by an outside takeover, although, of course, the existence of an outside market for control is another force which helps to sensitize the internal managerial labor market.

The perspective suggested here owes much to, but is nevertheless different from, existing treatments of the firm in the property rights literature. Thus, Alchian (1969) and Alchian and Demsetz (1972) comment insightfully on the disciplining of management that takes place through the inside and outside markets for managers. However, they attribute the task of disciplining management primarily to the risk bearers, the firm's security holders, who are assisted to some extent by managerial labor markets and by the possibility of outside takeover. Jensen and Meckling (1976) likewise make control of management the province of the firm's risk bearers, but they do not allow for any assistance from the managerial labor market. Of all the authors in the property-rights literature, Manne (1965, 1967) is most concerned with the market for corporate control. He recognizes that with diffuse security ownership management and risk bearing are naturally separate functions. But for him, disciplining management is an "entrepreneurial job" which in the first instance falls on a firm's organizers and later on specialists in the process of outside takeover.

When management and risk bearing are viewed as naturally separate factors of production, looking at the market for risk bearing from the viewpoint of portfolio theory tells us that risk bearers are likely to spread their wealth across many firms and so not be interested in directly controlling the management of any individual firm. Thus, models of the firm, like those of Alchian-Demsetz and Jensen-Meckling, in which the control of management falls primarily on the risk bearers, are not likely to allay the fears of those concerned with the apparent incentive problems created by the separation of security ownership and control. Likewise, Manne's approach, in which the control of management relies primarily on the expensive mechanism of an outside takeover, offers little comfort. The viability of the large corporation with diffuse security ownership is better explained in terms of a model where the primary disciplining of managers comes through managerial labor markets, both within and outside of the firm, with assistance from the panoply of internal and external monitoring devices that evolve to stimulate the ongoing efficiency of the corporate form, and with the market for outside takeovers providing discipline of last resort.

THE VIABILITY OF SEPARATION OF SECURITY OWNERSHIP AND CONTROL: DETAILS

The preceding is a general discussion of how pressure from managerial labor markets helps to discipline managers. We now examine somewhat more specifically conditions under which the discipline imposed by managerial labor markets can resolve potential incentive problems associated with the separation of security ownership and control of the firm.

To focus on the problem we are trying to solve, let us first examine the situation where the manager is also the firm's sole security holder, so that there is clearly no incentive problem. When he is sole security holder, a manager consumes on the job, through shirking, perquisites, or incompetence, to the point where these yield marginal expected utility equal to that provided by an additional dollar of wealth usable for consumption or investment outside of the firm. The manager is induced to make this specific decision because he pays directly for consumption on the job; that is, as manager he cannot avoid a full ex post settling up with himself as security holder.

In contrast, when the manager is no longer sole security holder, and in the absence of some form of full ex post settling up for deviations from contract, a manager has an incentive to consume more on the job than is agreed in his contract. The manager perceives that, on an ex post basis, he can beat the game by shirking or consuming more perquisites than previously agreed. This does not necessarily mean that the manager profits at the expense of other factors. Rational managerial labor markets understand any shortcomings of available mechanisms for enforcing ex post settling up. Assessments of ex post deviations from contract will be incorporated into contracts on an ex ante basis; for example, through an adjustment of the manager's wage.

Nevertheless, a game which is fair on an ex ante basis does not induce the same behavior as a game in which there is also ex post settling up. Herein lie the potential losses from separation of security ownership and control of a firm. There are situations where, with less than complete ex post settling up, the manager is induced to consume more on the job than he would like, given that on average he pays for his consumption ex ante.

Three general conditions suffice to make the wage revaluation imposed by the managerial labor market a form of full ex post settling up which resolves the managerial incentive problem described above. The first condition is that a manager's talents and his tastes for consumption on the job are not known with certainty, are likely to change through time, and must be imputed by managerial labor markets at least in part from information about the manager's current and past performance. Since it seems to capture the essence of the task of managerial labor markets in a world of uncertainty, this assumption is no real restriction.

The second assumption is that managerial labor markets appropriately use current and past information to revise future wages and understand any enforcement power inherent in the wage revision process. In short, contrary to much of the literature on separation of security ownership and control, we impute efficiency or rationality in information processing to managerial labor markets. In defense of this assumption, we note that the problem faced by managerial labor markets in revaluing the managers of a firm is much entwined with the problem faced by the capital market in revaluing the firm itself. Although we do not understand all the details of the process, available empirical evidence (e.g., Fama 1976, chaps. 5 and 6) suggests that the capital market generally makes rational assessments of the value of the firm in the face of imprecise and uncertain information. This does not necessarily mean that information processing in managerial labor markets is equally efficient or rational, but it is a warning against strong presumptions to the contrary.

The final and key condition for full control of managerial behavior through wage changes is that the weight of the wage revision process is sufficient to resolve any potential problems with managerial incentives. In this general form, the condition amounts to assuming the desired result. More substance is provided by specific examples.

Example 1: Marketable Human Capital

Suppose a manager's human capital, his stream of future wages, is a marketable asset. Suppose the manager perceives that, because of the consequent revaluations of future wages, the current value of his human capital changes by at least the amount of an unbiased assessment of the wealth changes experienced by other factors, primarily the security holders, because of his current deviations from contract. Then, as long as the manager is not a risk preferrer, these revaluations of his human capital are a form of full ex post settling up. The manager need not be charged ex ante for presumed ex post deviations from contract since the weight of the wage revision process is sufficient to neutralize his incentives to deviate.

It is important to consider why the manager might perceive that the value of his human capital changes by at least the amount of an unbiased assessment of the wealth changes experienced by other factors due to his deviations from contract. Note first that the market's assessment of such wealth changes is also its assessment of the difference between the manager's ex post marginal product and the marginal product he contracted to deliver ex ante. However, any assessment of the manager's marginal product is likely to include extraneous noise which has little to do with his talents and efforts. Without specific details on what the market takes to be the statistical process governing the evolution of the manager's talents and his tastes for consumption on the job, one cannot say exactly how far it will go in adjusting his future wages to reflect its most recent measurement of his marginal product. Assuming the market uses information rationally, the adjustment is closer to complete the larger the signal in the most recent measurement relative to the noise, but as long as there is some noise in the process, the adjustment is less than complete.[4]

Although his next wage may not adjust by the full amount of an unbiased assessment of the current cost of his deviations from contract, a manager with a multiperiod horizon may perceive that the implied current wealth change, the present value of likely changes in the stream of future wages, is at least as great as the cost of his deviations from contract. In this case, the contemporaneous change in his wealth implied by an eventual adjustment of future wages is a form of full ex post settling up which results in full enforcement of his contract. Moreover, the wage revision process resolves any potential problems about a manager's incentives even though the implied ex post settling up need not involve the firm currently employing the manager; that is, lower or higher future wages due to current deviations from contract may come from other firms.

Of course, changes in a manager's wealth as a consequence of anticipated future wage revisions are not always equivalent to full ex post settling up. When a manager does not expect to be in the labor market for many future periods, the weight of future wage revisions due to current assessments of performance may amount to substantially less than full ex post settling up. However, it is just as important to recognize that the weight of anticipations about future wages may amount to more than full ex post settling up. There may

---

4. Specific illustrations of this point are provided later.

be situations where the personal wealth change perceived by the manager as a consequence of deviations from contract is greater than the wealth change experienced by other factors. Since many readers have had trouble with this point, it is well to bring it closer to home.

Economists (especially young economists) easily imagine situations where the effects of higher or lower quality of a current article or book on the market value of human capital, through enhancement or lowering of "reputation," are in excess of the effects of quality differences on the market value of the specific work to any publisher. Managers can sometimes have similar perceptions with respect to the implications of current performance for the market value of their human capital.

Example 2: Stochastic Processes for Marginal Products

The next example of ex post settling up through the wage revision process is somewhat more formal than that described above. We make specific assumptions about the stochastic evolution of a manager's measured marginal product and about how the managerial labor market uses information from the process to adjust the manager's future wages—in a manner which amounts to precise, full ex post settling up for the results of past performance.

Suppose the manager's measured marginal product for any period t is composed of two terms: (i) an expected value, given his talents, effort exerted during t, consumption of perquisites, etc.; and (ii) random noise. The random noise may in part result from measurement error, that is, the sheer difficulty of accurately measuring marginal products when there is team production, but it may also arise in part from the fact that effort exerted and talent do not yield perfectly certain consequences. Moreover, because of the uncertain evolution of the manager's talents and tastes, the expected value of his marginal product is itself a stochastic process. Specifically, we assume that the expected value, $\bar{z}_t$, follows a random walk with steps that are independent of the random noise, ε_t, in the manager's measured marginal product, z_t. Thus, the measured marginal product,

$$z_t = \bar{z}_t + \varepsilon_t, \tag{1}$$

is a random walk plus white noise. For simplicity, we also assume that this process describes the manager's marginal product both in his current employment and in the best alternative employment.

The characteristics (parameters) of the evolution of the manager's marginal product depend to some extent on endogenous variables like effort and per-quisites consumed, which are not completely observable. Our purpose is to set up the managerial labor market so that the wage revision process resolves any potential incentive problems that may arise from the endogeneity of z_t in a sit-uation where there is separation of security ownership and control of the firm.

Suppose next that risk bearers are all risk neutral and that 1-period market interest rates are always equal to zero. Suppose also that managerial wage con-tracts are written so that the manager's wage in any period t is the expected value of his marginal product, $\bar{z}_t$, conditional on past measured values of his marginal product, with the risk bearers accepting the noise ε_t, in the ex post measurement of the marginal product. We shall see below that this is an op-timal arrangement for our risk-neutral risk bearers. However, it is not neces-sarily optimal for the manager if he is risk averse. A risk-averse manager may want to sell part of the risk inherent in the uncertain evolution of his expected marginal product to the risk bearers, for example, through a long-term wage contract.

We avoid this issue by assuming that, perhaps because of the more extreme moral hazard problems in long-term contracts (remember that $\bar{z}_t$ is in part un-der the control of the manager) and the contracting costs to which these moral hazard problems give rise, simple contracts in which the manager's wage is reset at the beginning of each period are dominant, at least for some nontrivial subset of firms and managers.[5] If we could also assume away any remaining moral hazard (managerial incentive) problems, then with risk-averse manag-ers, risk-neutral risk bearers, and the presumed fixed recontracting period, the contract which specifies ex ante that the manager will be paid the current ex-pected value of his marginal product dominates any contract where the man-ager also shares the ex post deviation of his measured marginal product from its ex ante expected value (see, e.g., Spence and Zeckhauser 1971).

However, contracts which specify ex ante that the manager will be paid the

5. Institutions like corporations, that are subject to rapid technological change with a large degree of uncertainty about future managerial needs, may find that long-term managerial contracts can only be negotiated at high cost. On the other hand, institu-tions like governments, schools, and universities may be able to forecast more reliably their future needs for managers (and other professionals) and so may be able to offer long-term contracts at relatively low cost. These institutions can then be expected to at-tract the relatively risk-averse members of the professional labor force, while the riskier employment offered by corporations attracts those who are willing to accept shorter-term contracts.

current expected value of his marginal product seem to leave the typical moral hazard problem that arises when there is less than complete ex post enforcement of contracts. The noise ε_t in the manager's marginal product is borne by the risk bearers. Once the manager's expected marginal product $\bar{z}_t$ (= his current wage) has been assessed, he seems to have an incentive to consume more perquisites and provide less effort than are implied in $\bar{z}_t$.

A mechanism for ex post enforcement is, however, built into the model. With the expected value of the manager's marginal product wandering randomly through time, future assessments of expected marginal products (and thus of wages) will be determined in part by ε_t, the deviation of the current measured marginal product from its ex ante expected value. In the present scenario, where $\bar{z}_t$ is assumed to follow a random walk, Muth (1960) has shown that the expected value of the marginal product evolves according to

$$\bar{z}_t = \bar{z}_{t-1} + (1-\phi)\varepsilon_{t-1}, \tag{2}$$

where the parameter ϕ ($0 < \phi < 1$) is closer to zero the smaller the variance of the noise term in the marginal product equation (1) relative to the variance of the steps in the random walk followed by the expected marginal product.

In fact, the process by which future expected marginal products are adjusted on the basis of past deviations of marginal products from their expected values leads to a precise form of full ex post settling up. This is best seen by writing the marginal product z_t in its inverted form, that is, in terms of past marginal products and the current noise. The inverted form for our model, a random walk embedded in random noise, is

$$z_t = (1-\phi)z_{t-1} + \phi(1-\phi)z_{t-2} + \phi^2(1-\phi)z_{t-3} + \ldots + \varepsilon_t, \tag{3}$$

so that

$$\bar{z}_t = (1-\phi)z_{t-1} + \phi(1-\phi)z_{t-2} + \phi^2(1-\phi)z_{t-3} + \ldots \tag{4}$$

(see, e.g., Nelson 1973, chap. 4, or Muth 1960).

For our purposes, the interesting fact is that, although he is paid his ex ante expected marginal product, the manager does not get to avoid his ex post marginal product. For example, we can infer from (4) that z_{t-1} has weight $1 - \phi$ in $\bar{z}_t$; then it has weight $\phi(1-\phi)$ in $\bar{z}_{t+1}$, $\phi^2(1-\phi)$ in $\bar{z}_{t+2}$, and so on. In the end, the sum of the contributions of z_{t-1} to future expected marginal products, and thus to future wages, is exactly z_{t-1}. With zero interest rates, this means that the risk bearers simply allow the manager to smooth his marginal product across future periods at the going opportunity cost of all such temporal wealth transfers. As a consequence, the manager has no incentive to try to bury shirking or consumption of perquisites in his ex post measured marginal product.

Since the managerial labor market is presumed to understand the weight of the wage revision process, which in this case amounts to precise full ex post settling up, any potential managerial incentive problems in the separation of risk bearing, or security ownership, from control are resolved. The manager can contract for and take an optimal amount of consumption on the job. The wage set ex ante need not include any allowance for ex post incentives to deviate from the contract since the wage revision process neutralizes any such incentives. Note, moreover, that the value of ϕ in the wage revision process described by (4) determines how the observed marginal product of any given period is subdivided and spread across future periods, but whatever the value of ϕ, the given marginal product is fully accounted for in the stream of future wages. Thus, it is now clear what was meant by the earlier claim that although the parameter ϕ in the process generating the manager's marginal product is to some extent under his control, this is not a matter of particular concern to the managerial labor market.

A somewhat evident qualification is in order. The smoothing process described by (4) contains an infinite number of terms, whereas any manager has a finite working life. For practical purposes, full ex post settling up is achieved as long as the manager's current marginal product is "very nearly" fully absorbed by the stream of wages over his future working life. This requires a value of ϕ in (4) which is sufficiently far from 1.0, given the number of periods remaining in the manager's working life. Recall that ϕ is closer to 1.0 the larger the variance of the noise in the manager's measured marginal product relative to the variance of the steps of the random walk taken by the expected value of his marginal product. Intuitively, when the variance of the noise term is large relative to that of the changes in the expected value, the current measured marginal product has a weak signal about any change in the expected value of the marginal product, and the current marginal product is only allocated slowly to expected future marginal products.

SOME EXTENSIONS

Having qualified the analysis, let us now indicate some ways in which it is robust to changes in details of the model.

1. More Complicated Models for the Manager's Marginal Product

The critical ingredient in enforcing precise full ex post settling up through wage revisions on the basis of reassessments of expected marginal products is that when the marginal product and its expected value are expressed in inverted form, as in (3) and (4), the sum of the weights on past marginal products is exactly 1.0. This will be the case (see, e.g., Nelson 1973, chap. 4) whenever the manager's marginal product conforms to a nonstationary stochastic process, but the changes from period to period in the marginal product conform to some stationary ARMA (mixed autoregressive moving average) process. The example summarized in equations (1)–(4) is the interesting but special case where the expected marginal product follows a random walk so that the differences of the marginal product are a stationary, first-order moving average process. The general case allows the expected value of the marginal product to follow any more complicated nonstationary process which has the property that the differences of the marginal product are stationary, so that the marginal product and its expected value can be expressed in inverted form as

$$z_t = \pi_1 z_{t-1} + \pi_2 z_{t-2} + \ldots + \varepsilon_t \tag{5}$$

$$\overline{z}_t = \pi_1 z_{t-1} + \pi_2 z_{t-2} + \ldots \tag{6}$$

with

$$\sum_{i=1}^{\infty} \pi_i = 1. \tag{7}$$

These can be viewed as the general conditions for enforcing precise full ex post settling through the wage revision process when the manager's wage is equal to the current expected value of his marginal product.[6]

2. Risk-Averse Risk Bearers

In the framework summarized in equations (5)–(7), if the manager switches firms, the risk bearers of his former firm are left with the remains of his measured marginal products not previously absorbed into the expected value of

---

6. When $\overline{z}_t$ follows a stationary process, the long-run average value toward which the process always tends will eventually be known with near perfect certainty. Thus, the case of a stationary expected marginal product is of little interest, at least for the purposes of ex post settling up enforced by the wage revision process.

his marginal product. Nevertheless, in the way we have set up the world, the risk bearers realize that the manager's next firm continues to set his wage according to the same stochastic process as the last firm. Since this results in full ex post settling up on the part of the manager, the motive for switching firms cannot be to avoid perverse adjustments of future wages on the basis of past performance. On average, the switching of managers among firms does not result in gains or losses to risk bearers, which means that the switches are a matter of indifference to our presumed risk-neutral risk bearers.

It is, however, interesting to examine how the analysis might change when the risk bearers are risk averse and switching of managers among firms is not a matter of indifference. Suppose, for the moment, that the risk bearers offer managers contracts where, as before, the manager's wage tracks the expected value of his marginal product, but each period there is also a fixed discount in the wage to compensate the risk bearers for the risks of unfinished ex post settling up with the firm as a consequence of a possible future shift by the manager to another firm. Such an arrangement may satisfy the risk bearers, but it will not be acceptable to the manager. As long as his marginal product evolves according to equations (5)–(7), both in his current firm and in the best alternative, the manager is subject to full ex post settling up. Thus, any risk adjustment of his wage to reflect the fact that the settling up may not be with his current firm is an uncompensated loss which he will endeavor to avoid.

The manager can avoid any risk discount in his wage, and maintain complete freedom to switch among firms, by himself bearing all the risk of his marginal product; that is, he contracts to accept, at the end of each period, his ex post measured marginal product rather than its ex ante expected value so that there is, period by period, full ex post settling up with his current firm. There is such a presumption against the optimality of immediate, full ex post settling up in the literature on optimal contracting that it behooves us to examine how and why it works, and is optimal, in the circumstances under examination.

CONTRACTUAL SETTLING UP

The literature on optimal contracting, for example, Harris and Raviv (1978, 1979), Holmström (1979), and Shavell (1979), suggests uniformly that when there is noise in the manager's marginal product, that is, when the deviation of measured marginal product from its expected value cannot be traced unambiguously and costlessly to the manager's actions (talents, effort exerted, and consumption on the job), then a risk-averse manager will always choose to share part of the uncertainty in the evaluation of his performance with the firm's risk bearers. He will agree to some amount of ex post settling up, but always less than 100 percent of the deviation of his measured marginal product from its ex ante expected value. In short, the contracting models suggest that we must learn to live with the incentive problems that arise when there is less than complete ex post enforcement of contracts.

The contracting literature is almost uniformly concerned with 1-period models. In a 1-period world, there can be no enforcement of contracts through a wage revision process imposed by the managerial labor market. The existence of this form of ex post settling up in a multiperiod world affects the manager's willingness to engage in explicit contractual ex post settling up.

For example, in the model summarized in equations (5)–(7), the manager's wage in any period is the expected value of his marginal product assessed at the beginning of the period, and the manager does not immediately share any of the deviation of his ex post marginal product from its ex ante expected value. However, because it contains information about future expected values of his marginal product, eventually the manager's current measured marginal product is allocated in full to future expected marginal products. Equivalently, in the wage revision process described by equations (5)–(7), the managerial labor market in effect acts as a financial intermediary. It withdraws portions of past accumulated measured marginal products to pay the manager a dividend on his human capital equal to the expected value of his marginal product, and implicitly provides the lending arrangements which allow the manager to spread his current measured marginal product over future periods in precisely the way the current marginal product will contribute to expected future marginal products.

Looked at from this perspective, however, the manager might simply contract to take the ex post measured value of his marginal product as his wage and then himself use the capital market to smooth his measured marginal product over future periods. Since the same asset (his human capital) is involved, the manager should be able to carry out these smoothing transactions via the capital market on the same terms as can be had in the managerial labor market. The advantage to the manager in smoothing through the capital market, however, is that he can then contract to accept full ex post settling up period by period (he is paid his measured marginal product), which means he can avoid any risk discount in his wage that might be imposed when he is paid the expected value of his marginal product with the possibility of unantici-pated switches to other firms.[7]

It is important to recognize that using the capital market in the manner described above allows the manager to "average out" the random noise in his measured marginal product. Thus, when he is instead paid the expected value of his marginal product each period, and when the process generating his marginal product is described by equations (5)–(7), the manager's current measured marginal product is eventually allocated in full to future expected marginal products. This happily, but only coincidentally, resolves incentive problems by imposing full ex post settling up. The allocation of the current marginal product to future expected marginal products in fact occurs because the current marginal product has information about future expected marginal products. The weights π_i in equations (5)–(7) are precisely those that optimally extract this information and so optimally smooth or average out the purely random noise in the manager's measured marginal product. The manager can achieve the same result by contracting to be paid the measured value of his marginal product and then using the capital market to smooth his marginal product. This power of the capital market to reduce the terror in full con-tractual ex post settling up is lost in the 1-period models that dominate the contracting literature.

CONCLUSIONS

The model summarized by equations (5)–(7) is one specific scenario in which the wage revision process imposed by the managerial labor market amounts to full ex post settling up by the manager for his past performance. The impor-tant general point is that in any scenario where the weight of the wage revision process is at least equivalent to full ex post settling up, managerial incentive

7. With positive interest rates, contracting to be paid his measured marginal product and then using the capital market to smooth the marginal product over future periods dominates the contract in which the manager is paid the expected value of his marginal product. Equivalence can be restored by adjusting the expected marginal product $\bar{z}_t$ in eq. (6) for accumulated interest on the past marginal products, $z_{t-1}, z_{t-2}, \ldots$, or by prepaying the present value of interest on the deferrals of the current marginal product over future periods. Suffice it to say, however, that either accumulation or prepayment of interest complicates the problems posed by possible shifts of the manager to other firms and so may lean the system toward contracts in which the manager is paid his measured marginal product and then uses the capital market to achieve optimal smoothing.

problems—the problems usually attributed to the separation of security ownership and control of the firm—are resolved.

No claim is made that the wage revision process always results in a full ex post settling up on the part of the manager. There are certainly situations where the weight of anticipated future wage changes is insufficient to counterbalance the gains to be had from ex post shirking, or perhaps outright theft, in excess of what was agreed ex ante in a manager's contract. On the other hand, precise full ex post settling up is not an upper bound on the force of the wage revision process. There are certainly situations where, as a consequence of anticipated future wage changes, a manager perceives that the value of his human capital changes by more than the wealth changes imposed on other factors, and especially the firm's security holders, by his current deviations from the terms of his contract.

The extent to which the wage revision process imposes ex post settling up in any particular situation is, of course, an empirical issue. But it is probably safe to say that the general phenomenon is at least one of the ingredients in the survival of the modern large corporation, characterized by diffuse security ownership and the separation of security ownership and control, as a viable form of economic organization.

REFERENCES

Alchian, Armen A. "Corporate Management and Property Rights." In *Economic Policy and the Regulation of Corporate* Securities, edited by Henry G. Manne. Washington: American Enterprise Inst. Public Policy Res., 1969.

Alchian, Armen A., and Demsetz, Harold. "Production, Information Costs, and Economic Organization." *A.E.R.* 62 (December 1972): 777–95.

Baumol, William J. *Business Behavior, Value and Growth.* New York: Macmillan, 1959.

Berle, Adolph A., Jr., and Means, Gardiner C. *The Modern Corporation and Private Property.* New York: Macmillan, 1932.

Coase, Ronald H. "The Nature of the Firm." *Economica,* n.s. 4 (November 1937): 386–405.

——— "The Problem of Social Cost." *J. Law and Econ.* 3 (October 1960): 1–44.

Cyert, Richard M., and March, James G. *A Behavioral Theory of the Firm.* Englewood Cliffs, N.J.: Prentice-Hall, 1963.

Fama, Eugene F. *Foundations of Finance.* New York: Basic, 1976.

Fama, Eugene F., and Miller, Merton H. *The Theory of Finance.* New York: Holt, Rinehart & Winston, 1972.

Harris, Milton, and Raviv, Artur. "Some Results on Incentive Contracts with Applications to Education and Employment, Health Insurance, and Law Enforcement." *A.E.R.* 68 (March 1978): 20–30.

———. "Optimal Incentive Contracts with Imperfect Information." Working Paper no. 70-75-76, Carnegie-Mellon Univ., Graduate School of Indus. Admin., April 1976 (rev. January 1979), forthcoming in *J. Econ. Theory.*

Holmström, Bengt. "Moral Hazard and Observability." *Bell J. Econ.* 10 (Spring 1979): 74–91.

Jensen, Michael C. "Capital Markets: Theory and Evidence." *Bell J. Econ. and Management Sci.* 3 (Autumn 1972): 357–98.

Jensen, Michael C., and Meckling, William H. "Theory of the Firm: Managerial Behavior, Agency Costs and Ownership Structure." *J. Financial Econ.* 3 (October 1976): 305–60.

Manne, Henry G. "Mergers and the Market for Corporate Control." *J.P.E.* 73, no. 2 (April 1965): 110–20.

——— "Our Two Corporate Systems: Law and Economics." *Virginia Law Rev.* 53 (March 1967): 259–85.

Muth, John F. "Optimal Properties of Exponentially Weighted Forecasts." *J. American Statis. Assoc.* 55 (June 1960): 299–306.

Nelson, Charles R. *Applied Time Series Analysis for Managerial Forecasting.* San Francisco: Holden-Day, 1973.

Shavell, Steven. "Risk Sharing and Incentives in the Principal and Agent Relationship." *Bell J. Econ.* 10 (Spring 1979): 55–73.

Simon, Herbert A. "Theories of Decision Making in Economics and Behavioral Science." *A.E.R.* 49 (June 1959): 253–83.

Smith, Adam. *The Wealth of Nations.* 1776. Cannan ed. New York: Modern Library, 1937.

Spence, Michael, and Zeckhauser, Richard. "Insurance, Information and Individual Action." *A.E.R.* 61 (May 1971): 380–87.

Watts, Ross L., and Zimmerman, Jerold. "Auditors and the Determination of Accounting Standards, an Analysis of the Lack of Independence." Working Paper GPB 7806, Univ. Rochester, Graduate School of Management, 1978.

Williamson, Oliver E. *The Economics of Discretionary Behavior: Managerial Objectives in a Theory of the Firm.* Englewood Cliffs, N.J.: Prentice-Hall, 1964.

SEPARATION OF OWNERSHIP AND CONTROL

· · ·

Eugene F. Fama and Michael C. Jensen

I. INTRODUCTION

Absent fiat, the form of organization that survives in an activity is the one that delivers the product demanded by customers at the lowest price while covering costs.[1] Our goal is to explain the survival of organizations characterized by separation of "ownership" and "control"—a problem that has bothered students of corporations from Adam Smith to Berle and Means and Jensen and Meckling.[2] In more precise language, we are concerned with the survival of organizations in which important decision agents do not bear a substantial share of the wealth effects of their decisions.

We argue that the separation of decision and risk-bearing functions observed in large corporations is common to other organizations such as large professional partnerships, financial mutuals, and nonprofits. We contend that separation of decision and risk-bearing functions survives in these organiza-

Reprinted from the *Journal of Law and Economics* 26, no. 2 (June 1983): 301–25.
© 1983 by The University of Chicago.

This paper is a revision of parts of our earlier paper, The Survival of Organizations (September 1980). In the course of this work we have profited from the comments of R. Antle, R. Benne, F. Black, F. Easterbrook, A. Farber, W. Gavett, P. Hirsch, R. Hogarth, C. Holderness, R. Holthausen, C. Home, J. Jeuck, R. Leftwich, S. McCormick, D. Mayers, P. Pashigian, M. Scholes, C. Smith, G. Stigler, R. Watts, T. Whisler, R. Yeaple, J. Zimmerman, and especially A. Alchian, W. Meckling, and C. Plosser. Financial support for Fama's participation is from the National Science Foundation. Jensen is supported by the Managerial Economics Research Center of the University of Rochester.

1. Armen A. Alchian, Uncertainty, Evolution and Economic Theory, 58 J. Pol. Econ. 211 (1950), is an early proponent of the use of natural selection in economic analysis. For a survey of general issues in the analysis of organizations, see Michael C. Jensen, Organization Theory and Methodology, 50 Accounting Rev. (1983).

2. Adam Smith, The Wealth of Nations (Cannan ed. 1904) (1st ed. London 1776); Adolf A. Berle & Gardiner C. Means, The Modern Corporation and Private Property (1932); Michael C. Jensen & William H. Meckling, Theory of the Firm: Managerial Behavior, Agency Costs and Ownership Structure, 3 J. Financial Econ. 305 (1976).

tions in part because of the benefits of specialization of management and risk bearing but also because of an effective common approach to controlling the agency problems caused by separation of decision and risk-bearing functions. In particular, our hypothesis is that the contract structures of all of these organizations separate the ratification and monitoring of decisions from initiation and implementation of the decisions.

II. RESIDUAL CLAIMS AND DECISION PROCESSES

An organization is the nexus of contracts, written and unwritten, among owners of factors of production and customers.[3] These contracts or internal "rules of the game" specify the rights of each agent in the organization, performance criteria on which agents are evaluated, and the payoff functions they face. The contract structure combines with available production technologies and external legal constraints to determine the cost function for delivering an output with a particular form of organization.[4] The form of organization that delivers the output demanded by customers at the lowest price, while covering costs, survives.

The central contracts in any organization specify (1) the nature of residual claims and (2) the allocation of the steps of the decision process among agents. These contracts distinguish organizations from one another and explain why specific organizational forms survive. We first discuss the general characteristics of residual claims and decision processes. We then present the major hypotheses about the relations between efficient allocations of residual claims and decision functions. The analysis focuses on two broad types of organizations—those in which risk-bearing and decision functions are separated and those in which they are combined in the same agents. We analyze only private organizations that depend on voluntary contracting and exchange.

A. Residual Claims

The contract structures of most organizational forms limit the risks undertaken by most agents by specifying either fixed promised payoffs or incentive payoffs tied to specific measures of performance. The residual risk—the risk of the difference between stochastic inflows of resources and promised payments to agents—is borne by those who contract for the rights to net cash flows. We

3. See Jensen & Meckling, *supra* note 2.
4. Michael C. Jensen & William H. Meckling, Rights and Production Functions: An Application to Labor-managed Firms and Codetermination, 52 J. Bus. 469 (1979).

call these agents the residual claimants or residual risk bearers. Moreover, the contracts of most agents contain the implicit or explicit provision that, in exchange for the specified payoff, the agent agrees that the resources he provides can be used to satisfy the interests of residual claimants.

Having most uncertainty borne by one group of agents, residual claimants, has survival value because it reduces the costs incurred to monitor contracts with other groups of agents and to adjust contracts for the changing risks borne by other agents. Contracts that direct decisions toward the interests of residual claimants also add to the survival value of organizations. Producing outputs at lower cost is in the interests of residual claimants because it increases net cash flows, but lower costs also contribute to survival by allowing products to be delivered at lower prices.

The residual claims of different organizational forms contain different restrictions. For example, the least restricted residual claims in common use are the common stocks of large corporations. Stockholders are not required to have any other role in the organization; their residual claims are alienable without restriction; and, because of these provisions, the residual claims allow unrestricted risk sharing among stockholders. We call these organizations *open* corporations to distinguish them from *closed* corporations that are generally smaller and have residual claims that are largely restricted to internal decision agents.[5]

B. *The Decision Process*

By focusing on entrepreneurial firms in which all decision rights are concentrated in the entrepreneur, economists tend to ignore analysis of the steps of the decision process. However, the way organizations allocate the steps of the decision process across agents is important in explaining the survival of organizations.

In broad terms, the decision process has four steps:

1. *initiation*—generation of proposals for resource utilization and structuring of contracts;
2. *ratification*—choice of the decision initiatives to be implemented;

---

5. The terms "public corporation" and "close corporation," which are common in the legal literature, are not used here. "Closed corporation" seems more descriptive than "close corporation." The term "public corporation" best describes government-owned corporations such as Amtrak and the TVA. In contrast, what we call "open corporations" are private organizations.

3. *implementation*—execution of ratified decisions; and
4. *monitoring*—measurement of the performance of decision agents and implementation of rewards.

Because the initiation and implementation of decisions typically are allocated to the same agents, it is convenient to combine these two functions under the term *decision management*. Likewise, the term *decision control* includes the ratification and monitoring of decisions. Decision management and decision control are the components of the organization's decision process or decision system.

III. FUNDAMENTAL RELATIONS BETWEEN RISK-BEARING AND DECISION PROCESSES

We first state and then elaborate the central complementary hypotheses about the relations between the risk-bearing and decision processes of organizations.

1. Separation of residual risk bearing from decision management leads to decision systems that separate decision management from decision control.
2. Combination of decision management and decision control in a few agents leads to residual claims that are largely restricted to these agents.

A. The Problem

Agency problems arise because contracts are not costlessly written and enforced. Agency costs include the costs of structuring, monitoring, and bonding a set of contracts among agents with conflicting interests. Agency costs also include the value of output lost because the costs of full enforcement of contracts exceed the benefits.[6]

Control of agency problems in the decision process is important when the decision managers who initiate and implement important decisions are not the major residual claimants and therefore do not bear a major share of the wealth effects of their decisions. Without effective control procedures, such decision managers are more likely to take actions that deviate from the interests of residual claimants. An effective system for decision control implies, almost by definition, that the control (ratification and monitoring) of decisions is to some extent separate from the management (initiation and implementation) of decisions. Individual decision agents can be involved in the manage-

6. This definition of agency costs comes from Jensen & Meckling, *supra* note 2.

ment of some decisions and the control of others, but separation means that an individual agent does not exercise exclusive management and control rights over the same decisions.

The interesting problem is to determine when separation of decision management, decision control, and residual risk bearing is more efficient than combining these three functions in the same agents. We first analyze the factors that make combination of decision management, decision control, and residual risk bearing efficient. We then analyze the factors that make separation of these three functions efficient.

B. Combination of Decision Management, Decision Control, and Residual Risk Bearing

Suppose the balance of cost conditions, including both technology and the control of agency problems, implies that in a particular activity the optimal organization is noncomplex. For our purposes, *noncomplex* means that specific information relevant to decisions is concentrated in one or a few agents. (Specific information is detailed information that is costly to transfer among agents.)[7] Most small organizations tend to be noncomplex, and most large organizations tend to be complex, but the correspondence is not perfect. For example, research oriented universities, though often small in terms of assets or faculty size, are nevertheless complex in the sense that specific knowledge, which is costly to transfer, is diffused among both faculty and administrators. On the other hand, mutual funds are often large in terms of assets but noncomplex in the sense that information relevant to decisions is concentrated in one or a few agents. We take it as given that optimal organizations in some activities are noncomplex. Our more limited goal is to explain the implications of noncomplexity for control of agency problems in the decision process.

If we ignore agency problems between decision managers and residual claimants, the theory of optimal risk bearing tells us that residual claims that allow unrestricted risk sharing have advantages in small as well as in large

7. Specific information is closely related to the notions of "information impactedness" and "bounded rationality" discussed in Oliver E. Williamson, Markets and Hierarchies: Analysis and Antitrust Implications (1975) and The Modern Corporation: Origins, Evolution, Attributes, 19 J. Econ. Literature 1537 (1981). Friedrich A. von Hayek, The Use of Knowledge in Society, 35 Am. Econ. Rev. 519 (1945) uses specific information to discuss the role of markets in complex economies. See also Thomas Sowell, Knowledge and Decisions 13–14 (1980). Our analysis of the relations between specific information and efficient decision processes owes much to ongoing work with William Meckling.

organizations.[8] However, in a small noncomplex organization, specific knowledge important for decision management and control is concentrated in one or a few agents. As a consequence, it is efficient to allocate decision control as well as decision management to these agents. Without separation of decision management from decision control, residual claimants have little protection against opportunistic actions of decision agents, and this lowers the value of unrestricted residual claims.

A feasible solution to the agency problem that arises when the same agents manage and control important decisions is to restrict residual claims to the important decision agents. In effect, restriction of residual claims to decision agents substitutes for costly control devices to limit the discretion of decision agents. The common stocks of closed corporations are this type of restricted residual claim, as are the residual claims in proprietorships and partnerships. The residual claims of these organizations (especially closed corporations) are also held by other agents whose special relations with decision agents allow agency problems to be controlled without separation of the management and control of decisions. For example, family members have many dimensions of exchange with one another over a long horizon and therefore have advantages in monitoring and disciplining related decision agents. Business associates whose goodwill and advice are important to the organization are also potential candidates for holding minority residual claims of organizations that do not separate the management and control of decisions.[9]

Restricting residual claims to decision makers controls agency problems between residual claimants and decision agents, but it sacrifices the benefits of unrestricted risk sharing and specialization of decision functions. The decision process suffers efficiency losses because decision agents must be chosen on the basis of wealth and willingness to bear risk as well as for decision skills. The residual claimants forgo optimal risk reduction through portfolio diversification so that residual claims and decision making can be combined in a small number of agents. Forgone diversification lowers the value of the residual claims and raises the cost of risk-bearing services.

---

8. See, for example, Kenneth J. Arrow, The Role of Securities in the Optimal Allocation of Risk Bearing, 31 Rev. Econ. Stud. 91 (1964); or Eugene F. Fama, Foundations of Finance chs. 6 & 7 (1976).

9. In contrast, the analysis predicts that when venture equity capital is put into a small entrepreneurial organization by outsiders, mechanisms for separating the management and control of important decisions are instituted.

Moreover, when residual claims are restricted to decision agents, it is generally rational for the residual claimant–decision makers to assign lower values to uncertain cash flows than residual claimants would in organizations where residual claims are unrestricted and risk bearing can be freely diversified across organizations. As a consequence, restricting residual claims to agents in the decision process leads to decisions (for example, less investment in risky projects that lower the costs of outputs) that tend to penalize the organization in the competition for survival.[10]

However, because contracts are not costlessly written and enforced, all decision systems and systems for allocating residual claims involve costs. Organizational survival involves a balance of the costs of alternative decision systems and systems for allocating residual risk against the benefits. Small noncomplex organizations do not have demands for a wide range of specialized decision agents; on the contrary, concentration of specific information relevant to decisions implies that there are efficiency gains when the rights to manage and control decisions are combined in one or a few agents. Moreover, the risk-sharing benefits forgone when residual claims are restricted to one or a few decision agents are less serious in a small noncomplex organization than in a large organization, because the total risk of net cash flows to be shared is generally smaller in small organizations. In addition, small organizations do not often have large demands for wealth from residual claimants to bond the payoffs promised to other agents and to purchase risky assets. As a consequence, small noncomplex organizations can efficiently control the agency problems caused by the combination of decision management and control in one or a few agents by restricting residual claims to these agents. Such a combining of decision and risk-bearing functions is efficient in small noncomplex organizations because the benefits of unrestricted risk sharing and specialization of decision functions are less than the costs that would be incurred to control the resulting agency problems.

The proprietorships, partnerships, and closed corporations observed in small scale production and service activities are the best examples of classical entrepreneurial firms in which the major decision makers are also the major residual risk bearers. These organizations are evidence in favor of the hypoth-

---

10. These propositions are developed in Eugene F. Fama & Michael C. Jensen, Organizational Forms and Investment Decisions (Working Paper No. MERC 83–03, Univ. Rochester, Managerial Economics Research Center 1983).

esis that combination of decision management and decision control in one or a few agents leads to residual claims that are largely restricted to these agents.

We analyze next the forces that make separation of decision management, decision control, and residual risk bearing efficient—in effect, the forces that cause the classical entrepreneurial firm to be dominated by organizational forms in which there are no decision makers in the classical entrepreneurial sense.

C. Separation of Decision Management,
Decision Control, and Residual Risk Bearing

Our concern in this section is with the organizational forms characterized by separation of decision management from residual risk bearing—what the literature on open corporations calls, somewhat imprecisely, separation of ownership and control. Our hypothesis is that all such organizations, including large open corporations, large professional partnerships, financial mutuals, and nonprofits, control the agency problems that result from separation of decision management from residual risk bearing by separating the management (initiation and implementation) and control (ratification and monitoring) of decisions. Documentation of this hypothesis takes up much of the rest of the paper.

1. *Specific Knowledge and Diffusion of Decision Functions.* Most organizations characterized by separation of decision management from residual risk bearing are *complex* in the sense that specific knowledge relevant to different decisions—knowledge which is costly to transfer across agents—is diffused among agents at all levels of the organization. Again, we take it as given that the optimal organizations in some activities are complex. Our theory attempts to explain the implications of complexity for the nature of efficient decision processes and for control of agency problems in the decision process.

Since specific knowledge in complex organizations is diffused among agents, diffusion of decision management can reduce costs by delegating the initiation and implementation of decisions to the agents with valuable relevant knowledge. The agency problems of diffuse decision management can then be reduced by separating the management (initiation and implementation) and control (ratification and monitoring) of decisions.

In the unusual cases where residual claims are not held by important decision managers but are nevertheless concentrated in one or a few residual claimants, control of decision managers can in principle be direct and simple, with the residual claimants ratifying and monitoring important decisions and setting rewards.[11] Such organizations conform to our hypothesis, because top-level decision control is separated from top-level decision managers and exercised directly by residual claimants.

However, in complex organizations valuable specific knowledge relevant to decision control is diffused among many internal agents. This generally means that efficient decision control, like efficient decision management, involves delegation and diffusion of decision control as well as separation of decision management and control at different levels of the organization. We expect to observe such delegation, diffusion, and separation of decision management and control below the top level of complex organizations, even in those unusual complex organizations where residual claims are held primarily by top-level decision agents.

2. *Diffuse Residual Claims and Delegation of Decision Control.* In the more common complex organizations, residual claims are diffused among many agents. Having many residual claimants has advantages in large complex organizations because the total risk of net cash flows to be shared is generally large and there are large demands for wealth from residual claimants to bond the payoffs promised to a wide range of agents and to purchase risky assets. When there are many residual claimants, it is costly for all of them to be involved in decision control and it is efficient for them to delegate decision control. For example, some delegation of decision control is observed even in the large professional partnerships in public accounting and law, where the residual claimants are expert internal decision agents. When there are many partners it is inefficient for each to participate in ratification and monitoring of all decisions.

Nearly complete separation and specialization of decision control and residual risk bearing is common in large open corporations and financial mutuals where most of the diffuse residual claimants are not qualified for roles in the decision process and thus delegate their decision control rights to other agents. When residual claimants have no role in decision control, we expect to observe separation of the management and control of important decisions at all levels of the organization.

Separation and diffusion of decision management and decision control—in effect, the absence of a classical entrepreneurial decision maker—limit the power of individual decision agents to expropriate the interests of residual claimants. The checks and balances of such decision systems have costs, but

11. Armen A. Alchian & Harold Demsetz, Production, Information Costs, and Economic Organization, 62 Am. Econ. Rev. 777 (1972).

they also have important benefits. Diffusion and separation of decision management and control have benefits because they allow valuable knowledge to be used at the points in the decision process where it is most relevant and they help control the agency problems of diffuse residual claims. In complex organizations, the benefits of diffuse residual claims and the benefits of separation of decision functions from residual risk bearing are generally greater than the agency costs they generate, including the costs of mechanisms to separate the management and control of decisions.

3. *Decision Control in Nonprofits and Financial Mutuals.* Most organizations characterized by separation of decision management from residual risk bearing are complex. However, separation of the management and control of decisions contributes to the survival of any organization where the important decision managers do not bear a substantial share of the wealth effects of their decisions—that is, any organization where there are serious agency problems in the decision process. We argue below that separation of decision management and residual risk bearing is a characteristic of nonprofit organizations and financial mutuals, large and small, complex and noncomplex. Thus, we expect to observe separation of the management and control of important decisions even in small noncomplex nonprofits and financial mutuals where, ignoring agency problems in the decision process, concentrated and combined decision management and control would be more efficient.

4. *Common General Features of Decision Control Systems.* Our hypothesis about the decision systems of organizations characterized by separation of decision management and residual risk bearing gets support from the fact that the major mechanisms for diffusing and separating the management and control of decisions are much the same across different organizations.

Decision hierarchies. A common feature of the diffuse decision management and control systems of complex organizations (for example, large nonprofit universities as well as large open corporations) is a formal decision hierarchy with higher level agents ratifying and monitoring the decision initiatives of lower level agents and evaluating their performance.[12] Such hierarchical parti-

---

12. See Max Weber, The Theory of Social and Economic Organization (1947); Peter M. Blau, Bureaucracy in Modern Society (1956); Herbert A. Simon, The Architecture of Complexity, 106 Proc. Am. Philosophical Soc'y 467 (1962); and the titles by Williamson, *supra* note 7. The historical development of hierarchies in open corporations is analyzed in Alfred D. Chandler, The Visible Hand (1977); and Alfred D. Chandler & Herman Daems, Managerial Hierarchies (1980).

tioning of the decision process makes it more difficult for decision agents at all levels of the organization to take actions that benefit themselves at the expense of residual claimants. Decision hierarchies are buttressed by organizational rules of the game, for example, accounting and budgeting systems, that monitor and constrain the decision behavior of agents and specify the performance criteria that determine rewards.[13]

Mutual monitoring systems. The formal hierarchies of complex organizations are also buttressed by information from less formal mutual monitoring among agents. When agents interact to produce outputs, they acquire low-cost information about colleagues, information not directly available to higher level agents. Mutual monitoring systems tap this information for use in the control process. Mutual monitoring systems derive their energy from the interests of agents to use the internal agent markets of organizations to enhance the value of human capital.[14] Agents choose among organizations on the basis of rewards offered and potential for development of human capital. Agents value the competitive interaction that takes place within an organization's internal agent market because it enhances current marginal products and contributes to human capital development. Moreover, if agents perceive that evaluation of their performance is unbiased (that is, if they cannot systematically fool their evaluators) then they value the fine tuning of the reward system that results from mutual monitoring information, because it lowers the uncertainty of payoffs from effort and skill. Since the incentive structures and diffuse decision control systems that result from the interplay of formal hierarchies and less formal mutual monitoring systems are also in the interests of residual claimants, their survival value is evident.

Boards of directors. The common apex of the decision control systems of organizations, large and small, in which decision agents do not bear a major share of the wealth effects of their decisions is some form of board of directors. Such boards always have the power to hire, fire, and compensate the top-level decision managers and to ratify and monitor important decisions. Exercise of

13. The separation of decision management from decision control that we emphasize is reflected in the auditing profession's concern with allocating operating and accounting responsibility to different agents. For instance, it is recommended that an agent with responsibility for billing should not have a role in receiving or recording customer payments. See, for example, Charles Horngren, Cost Accounting: A Managerial Emphasis ch. 27 (1982); or Howard P. Stettler, Auditing Principles chs. 4 & 8 (1977).

14. Eugene F. Fama, Agency Problems and the Theory of the Firm, 88 J. Pol. Econ. 288 (1980).

these top-level decision control rights by a group (the board) helps to ensure separation of decision management and control (that is, the absence of an entrepreneurial decision maker) even at the top of the organization.[15]

IV. THE SPECTRUM OF ORGANIZATIONS

A. Introduction

Organizations in which important decision agents do not bear a major share of the wealth effects of their decisions include open corporations, large professional partnerships, financial mutuals, and nonprofits. We are concerned now with analyzing the data each of these organizations provides to test the hypothesis that separation of decision management functions from residual risk bearing leads to decision systems that separate the management and control of decisions.

To motivate the discussion of specific organizational forms, we also outline a set of more specialized propositions to explain the survival value of the special features of their residual claims. These more specialized hypotheses about the survival of specific organizational forms in specific activities are developed in our paper "Agency Problems and Residual Claims."[16]

B. Open Corporations

1. *Unrestricted Common Stock Residual Claims.* Most large nonfinancial organizations are open corporations. The common stock residual claims of such organizations are unrestricted in the sense that stockholders are not required to have any other role in the organization, and their residual claims are freely alienable. As a result of the unrestricted nature of the residual claims of open corporations, there is almost complete specialization of decision management and residual risk bearing. Even managers who own substantial blocs of stock, and thus are residual risk bearers, may elect to sell these shares.

Unrestricted common stock is attractive in complicated risky activities where substantial wealth provided by residual claimants is needed to bond the large aggregate payoffs promised to many other agents. Unrestricted common

---

15. Decision functions can be delegated in two general ways: (1) joint delegation to several agents (as in a committee), or (2) partitioning and delegation of the parts to different agents. Boards of directors are examples of the former approach; decision hierarchies are examples of the latter.

16. Eugene F. Fama & Michael C. Jensen, Agency Problems and Residual Claims, in this issue.

stock, with its capacity for generating large amounts of wealth from residual claimants on a permanent basis, is also attractive in activities more efficiently carried out with large amounts of risky assets owned within the organization rather than rented. Moreover, since decision skills are not a necessary consequence of wealth or willingness to bear risk, the specialization of decision management and residual risk bearing allowed by unrestricted common stock enhances the adaptability of a complex organization to changes in the economic environment. The unrestricted risk sharing and diversification allowed by common stock also contributes to survival by lowering the cost of risk-bearing services.

2. *Control of the Agency Problems of Common Stock.* Separation and specialization of decision management and residual risk bearing leads to agency problems between decision agents and residual claimants. This is the problem of separation of ownership and control that has long troubled students of corporations. For example, potential exploitation of residual claimants by opportunistic decision agents is reflected in the arguments leading to the establishment of the Securities and Exchange Commission and in the concerns of the modern corporate governance movement. Less well appreciated, however, is the fact that the unrestricted nature of common stock residual claims also allows special market and organizational mechanisms for controlling the agency problems of specialized risk bearing.

The stock market. The unrestricted alienability of the residual claims of open corporations gives rise to an external monitoring device unique to these organizations—a stock market that specializes in pricing common stocks and transferring them at low cost. Stock prices are visible signals that summarize the implications of internal decisions for current and future net cash flows. This external monitoring exerts pressure to orient a corporation's decision process toward the interests of residual claimants.

The market for takeovers. External monitoring from a takeover market is also unique to the open corporation and is attributable to the unrestricted nature of its residual claims.[17] Because the residual claims are freely alienable and separable from roles in the decision process, attacking managers can circumvent existing managers and the current board to gain control of the decision process, either by a direct offer to purchase stock (a tender offer) or by an appeal for stockholder votes for directors (a proxy fight).

---

17. Monitoring from the takeover market is emphasized in Henry Manne, Mergers and the Market for Corporate Control, 73 J. Pol. Econ. 110 (1965).

Expert boards. Internal control in the open corporation is delegated by residual claimants to a board of directors. Residual claimants generally retain approval rights (by vote) on such matters as board membership, auditor choice, mergers, and new stock issues. Other management and control functions are delegated by the residual claimants to the board. The board then delegates most decision management functions and many decision control functions to internal agents, but it retains ultimate control over internal agents—including the rights to ratify and monitor major policy initiatives and to hire, fire, and set the compensation of top level decision managers. Similar delegation of decision management and control functions, at the first step to a board and then from the board to internal decision agents, is common to other organizations, such as financial mutuals, nonprofits, and large professional partnerships, in which important decision agents do not bear a major share of the wealth effects of their decisions.

However, the existence of the stock market and the market for takeovers, both special to open corporations, explains some of the special features of corporate boards, in particular: (1) why inside manager board members are generally more influential than outside members, and (2) why outside board members are often decision agents in other complex organizations.[18]

Since the takeover market provides an external court of last resort for protection of residual claimants, a corporate board can be in the hands of agents who are decision experts. Given that the board is to be composed of experts, it is natural that its most influential members are internal managers since they have valuable specific information about the organization's activities. It is also natural that when the internal decision control system works well, the outside members of the board are nominated by internal managers. Internal managers can use their knowledge of the organization to nominate outside board members with relevant complementary knowledge: for example, outsiders with expertise in capital markets, corporate law, or relevant technology who provide an important support function to the top managers in dealing with specialized decision problems.

However, the board is not an effective device for decision control unless it limits the decision discretion of individual top managers. The board is the top-level court of appeals of the internal agent market,[19] and as such it must

18. See Edward S. Herman, Corporate Control, Corporate Power ch. 2 (1981), for data on the characteristics of corporate boards.

19. See Fama, *supra* note 14.

be able to use information from the internal mutual monitoring system. To accomplish this and to achieve effective separation of top-level decision management and control, we expect the board of a large open corporation to include several of the organization's top managers. The board uses information from each of the top managers about his decision initiatives and the decision initiatives and performance of other managers. The board also seeks information from lower level managers about the decision initiatives and performance of top managers.[20] This information is used to set the rewards of the top managers, to rank them, and to choose among their decision initiatives. To protect information flows to the board, we expect that top managers, especially those who are members of the board, can effectively be fired only with consent of the board and thus are protected from reprisals from other top managers.

The decision processes of some open corporations seem to be dominated by an individual manager, generally the chief executive officer. In some cases, this signals the absence of separation of decision management and decision control, and, in our theory, the organization suffers in the competition for survival. We expect, however, that the apparent dominance of some top managers is more often due to their ability to work with the decision control systems of their organizations than to their ability to suppress diffuse and separate decision control. In any case, the financial press regularly reports instances where apparently dominant executives are removed by their boards.

Corporate boards generally include outside members, that is, members who are not internal managers, and they often hold a majority of seats.[21] The outside board members act as arbiters in disagreements among internal managers and carry out tasks that involve serious agency problems between internal managers and residual claimants, for example, setting executive compensation or searching for replacements for top managers.

Effective separation of top-level decision management and control means that outside directors have incentives to carry out their tasks and do not col-

---

20. For example, Horngren, *supra* note 13, at 911, describes the role of the audit committee of the board (generally composed of outside board members) as a collector and conduit of information from the internal mutual monitoring system: "The objective of the audit committee is to oversee the accounting controls, financial statements, and financial affairs of the corporation. The committee represents the full board and provides personal contact and communication among the board, the external auditors, the internal auditors, the financial executives, and the operating executives."

21. See Herman, *supra* note 18, at ch. 2.

lude with managers to expropriate residual claimants. Our hypothesis is that outside directors have incentives to develop reputations as experts in decision control. Most outside directors of open corporations are either managers of other corporations or important decision agents in other complex organizations.[22] The value of their human capital depends primarily on their performance as internal decision managers in other organizations. They use their directorships to signal to internal and external markets for decision agents that (1) they are decision experts, (2) they understand the importance of diffuse and separate decision control, and (3) they can work with such decision control systems. The signals are credible when the direct payments to outside directors are small, but there is substantial devaluation of human capital when internal decision control breaks down and the costly last resort process of an outside takeover is activated.

C. Professional Partnerships

1. *Mutual Monitoring, Specific Knowledge, and Restricted Residual Claims.* The residual claims of professional partnerships in activities such as law, public accounting, medicine, and business consulting are restricted to the major professional agents who produce the organization's services. This restriction increases the incentives of agents to monitor each other's actions and to consult with each other to improve the quality of services provided to customers. Such mutual monitoring and consulting are attractive to the professional agents in service activities where responsibility for variation in the quality of services is easily assigned and the value of professional human capital is sensitive to performance. The monitoring and consulting are likely to be effective when professional agents with similar specialized skills agree to share liability for the actions of colleagues.

In both large and small partnerships, individuals or small teams work on cases, audits, and so forth. Because of the importance of specific knowledge about particular clients and circumstances, it is efficient for the teams to make most decisions locally. At this level, however, decision management and decision control are not separate. To control the resulting agency problems, the residual claims in professional partnerships, large and small, are restricted to the professional agents who have the major decision-making roles. This is consistent with our hypothesis that combination of decision management and

22. *Id.*

control functions leads to restriction of residual claims to the agents who both manage and control important decisions.

2. *Large Professional Partnerships.* The partners in large professional partnerships are diffuse residual claimants whose welfare depends on the acts of agents they do not directly control. Thus, these organizations provide a test of our hypothesis that separation of residual risk bearing and decision management induces decision systems that separate the management and control of important decisions. The major decision control devices of large professional partnerships are similar to those of other organizations with diffuse residual claims. For example, residual claimants in large partnerships delegate to boards the ratification and monitoring of important decisions above the level of individual cases and audits. Moreover, the sharing of liability and residual cash flows among important decision agents (the partners) ensures that large partnerships have strong versions of the mutual monitoring systems that we contend are common to the decision control systems of complex organizations.

The boards of large partnerships have special features that relate to the restriction of the residual claims to important internal agents. The residual claimants are experts in the organization's activities, and they observe directly the effects of actions taken by the board of managing partners. Thus, unlike the stockholders of open corporations, the residual claimants in large partnerships have little demand for outside experts to protect their interests, and their boards are composed entirely of partners.

The board is involved in decisions with respect to the management of the partnership, for example, where new offices should be opened, who should be admitted to the partnership, and who should be dismissed. The board is also involved in renegotiating the shares of the partners. Here, as in other decisions, the boards of large partnerships combine the valuable specific knowledge available at the top level with information from partner–residual claimants. The role of the board is to develop acceptable consensus decisions from this information. Thus, the boards of large professional partnerships are generally called committees of managing partners rather than boards of directors. The idea is that such committees exist to manage agency problems among partners and to study and determine major policy issues in a manner that is less costly than when performed jointly by all partners.

Since the residual claims in a large professional partnership are not alienable, unfriendly outside takeovers are not possible. Inside takeovers by dissident partners are possible, however, because the managing boards of these organizations are elected by the partner–residual claimants.

D. Financial Mutuals

A common form of organization in financial activities is the mutual. An unusual characteristic of mutuals is that the residual claimants are customers, for example, the policyholders of mutual insurance companies, the depositors of mutual savings banks, and the shareholders of mutual funds. Like the diffuse stockholders of large nonfinancial corporations, most of the diffuse depositors, policyholders, and mutual fund shareholders of financial mutuals do not participate in the internal decision process. Thus, financial mutuals provide another test of our hypothesis that substantial separation of decision management and residual risk bearing leads to decision systems that separate the management and control of decisions.

1. *The Control Function of Redeemable Claims.* For the purpose of decision control, the unique characteristic of the residual claims of mutuals is that they are redeemable on demand. The policyholder, depositor, or shareholder can, on demand, turn in his claim at a price determined by a prespecified rule. For example, the shareholder of an open-end mutual fund can redeem his claim for the market value of his share of the fund's assets, while the whole life or endowment insurance policyholder, like the shareholder of a mutual savings bank, can redeem his claim for its specified value plus accumulated dividends.

The decision of the claim holder to withdraw resources is a form of partial takeover or liquidation which deprives management of control over assets. This control right can be exercised independently by each claim holder. It does not require a proxy fight, a tender offer, or any other concerted takeover bid. In contrast, customer decisions in open non-financial corporations and the repricing of the corporation's securities in the capital market provide signals about the performance of its decision agents. Without further action, however, either internal or from the market for takeovers, the judgments of customers and of the capital market leave the assets of the open nonfinancial corporation under the control of the managers.

2. *The Board of Directors.* Like other organizations characterized by substantial separation between decision management and residual risk bearing, the top-level decision control device in financial mutuals is a board of directors. Because of the strong form of diffuse decision control inherent in the redeemable residual claims of financial mutuals, however, their boards are less important in the control process than the boards of open nonfinancial corporations.

The reduced role of the board is especially evident in mutual savings banks and mutual funds, which are not complex even though often large in terms of assets. Moreover, the residual claimants of mutuals show little interest in their boards and often do not have the right to vote for board members.[23] Outside board members are generally chosen by internal managers. Unlike open corporations, the boards of financial mutuals do not often impose changes in managers. The role of the board, especially in the less complex mutuals, is largely limited to monitoring agency problems against which redemption of residual claims offers little protection, for example, fraud or outright theft of assets by internal agents.

E. Nonprofit Organizations

When an organization's activities are financed in part through donations, part of net cash flows is from resources provided by donors. Contracts that define the share of residual claimants in net cash flows are unlikely to assure donors that their resources are protected from expropriation by residual claimants. In a nonprofit organization, however, there are no agents with alienable rights in residual net cash flows and thus there are no residual claims. We argue in "Agency Problems and Residual Claims" that the absence of such residual claims in nonprofits avoids the donor-residual claimant agency problem and explains the dominance of nonprofits in donor-financed activities.[24]

The absence of residual claims in nonprofits avoids agency problems between donors and residual claimants, but the incentives of other internal agents to expropriate donations remain. These agency problems between donors and decision agents in nonprofits are similar to those in other organizations where important decision managers do not bear a major share of the wealth effects of their decisions. Our hypothesis predicts that, like other organizations characterized by separation of decision management from residual risk bearing, nonprofits have decision systems that separate the management (initiation and

23. See Edward S. Herman, Conflict of Interest in the Savings and Loan Industry, in A Study of the Savings and Loan Industry 789 (Irwin Friend ed. 1969), for documentation of such lack of interest. For example, he describes situations where in more than a decade only four depositors in total attended the annual meetings of two savings and loan associations and other situations where management did not even bother to collect proxies.

24. Fama & Jensen, Agency Problems and Residual Claims, in this issue. See Henry B. Hansmann, The Role of Nonprofit Enterprise, 89 Yale L. J. 835 (1980), for a general discussion of nonprofits.

implementation) and control (ratification and monitoring) of decisions. Such decision systems survive in donor nonprofits because of the assurances they provide that donations are used effectively and are not easily expropriated.

1. *Nonprofit Boards.* In small nonprofits delegation of decision management to one or a few agents is generally efficient. For example, in nonprofit cultural performing groups, an artistic director usually chooses performers, does the primary monitoring of their outputs, and initiates and implements major decisions. Nevertheless, the important decision agents in these organizations are chosen, monitored, and evaluated by boards of directors. Boards with similar decision control rights are common to other small nonprofits characterized by concentrated decision management, such as charities, private museums, small private hospitals, and local Protestant and Jewish congregations. Boards are also observed at the top of the decision control systems of complex nonprofits, such as private universities, in which both decision management and decision control are diffuse.

Although their functions are similar to those of other organizations, nonprofit boards have special features that are due to the absence of alienable residual claims. For example, because of the discipline from the outside takeover market, boards of open corporations can include internal decision agents, and outside board members can be chosen for expertise rather than because they are important residual claimants. In contrast, because a nonprofit lacks alienable residual claims, the decision agents are immune from ouster (via takeover) by outside agents. Without the takeover threat or the discipline imposed by residual claimants with the right to remove members of the board, nonprofit boards composed of internal agents and outside experts chosen by internal agents would provide little assurance against collusion and expropriation of donations. Thus, nonprofit boards generally include few if any internal agents as voting members, and nonprofit boards are often self-perpetuating, that is, new members are approved by existing members. Moreover, nonprofit board members are generally substantial donors who serve without pay. Willingness to provide continuing personal donations of wealth or time is generally an implicit condition for membership on nonprofit boards. Acceptance of this condition certifies to other donors that board members are motivated to take their decision control task seriously.

2. *The Roman Catholic Church.* To our knowledge the only nonprofit organization that is financed with donations but lacks a board of important continuing donors with effective decision control rights is the Roman Catholic church. Parish councils exist in local Catholic churches, but unlike their Protestant and

Jewish counterparts, they are only advisory. The clerical hierarchy controls the allocation of resources, and the papal system does not seem to limit the discretion of the Pope, the organization's most important decision agent.

Other aspects of the contracts of the Catholic clergy in part substitute for the control of expropriation of donations that would be provided by more effective donor-customer constraints on decisions. For example, the vows of chastity and obedience incorporated into the contracts of the Catholic clergy help to bond against expropriation of donations by avoiding conflicts between the material interests of a family and the interests of donor-customers. In addition, the training of a Catholic priest is organization-specific. For example, it involves a heavy concentration on (Catholic) theology, whereas the training of Protestant ministers places more emphasis on social service skills. Once certified, the Catholic priest is placed by the hierarchy. He cannot offer his services on a competitive basis. In exchange for developing such organization-specific human capital, the Catholic priest, unlike his Protestant and Jewish counterparts, gets a lifetime contract that promises a real standard of living. The organization-specific nature of the human capital of the Catholic clergy and the terms of the contract under which it is employed act as a bond to donor-customers that the interests of the Catholic clergy are closely bound to the survival of the organization and thus to the interests of donor-customers.

Although Protestantism arose over doctrinal issues, the control structures of Protestant sects—in particular, the evolution of lay councils with power to ratify and monitor resource allocation decisions—can be viewed as a response to breakdowns of the contract structure of Catholicism, that is, expropriation of Catholic donor-customers by the clergy. The evolution of Protestantism is therefore an example of competition among alternative contract structures to resolve an activity's major agency problem—in this case monitoring important agents to limit expropriation of donations.

There is currently pressure to allow Catholic priests to marry, that is, to drop the vow of chastity from their contracts. We predict that if this occurs, organizational survival will require other monitoring and bonding mechanisms, for example, control over allocation of resources by lay councils similar to those observed in Protestant and Jewish congregations.

3. *The Private University and Decision Systems in Complex Nonprofits.* In complex nonprofits we observe mechanisms for diffuse decision control similar to those of other complex organizations. For example, large private universities, like large open corporations, have complicated decision hierarchies and active internal agent markets with mutual monitoring systems that generate

information about the performance of agents. Again, however, the decision control structures of complex nonprofits have special features attributable to the absence of alienable residual claims.

For example, a university's trustees are primarily donors rather than experts in the details of education or research. In ratifying and monitoring decision initiatives presented by internal decision agents (presidents, chancellors, provosts, etc.), and in evaluating the agents themselves, boards rely on information from the internal diffuse decision system—for example, reports from faculty senates and appointments committees—and on external peer reviews.

Moreover, the structure of internal diffuse decision control systems is a more formal part of a university's contract structure (its charter or bylaws) than in large for-profit organizations such as open corporations. For example, unlike corporate managers, university deans, department heads, provosts, and presidents are generally appointed for fixed terms. The end of a contract period activates a process of evaluation, with search committees chosen according to formal rules and with rules for passing their recommendations on to the board. A more formal structure of diffuse decision management and control is helpful to trustees who do not have specialized knowledge about a university's activities. It also helps to assure donors that the absence of discipline from an outside takeover market is compensated by a strong system for internal decision control.

V. SUMMARY

The theory developed in this paper views an organization as a nexus of contracts (written and unwritten). The theory focuses on the contracts that (1) allocate the steps in an organization's decision process, (2) define residual claims, and (3) set up devices for controlling agency problems in the decision process. We focus on the factors that give survival value to organizational forms that separate what the literature imprecisely calls ownership and control.

A. The Central Hypotheses

An organization's decision process consists of decision management (initiation and implementation) and decision control (ratification and monitoring). Our analysis produces two complementary hypotheses about the relations between decision systems and residual claims:

1. Separation of residual risk bearing from decision management leads to decision systems that separate decision management from decision control.

2. Combination of decision management and decision control in a few agents leads to residual claims that are largely restricted to these agents.

B. Combination of Decision Management and Control

When it is efficient to combine decision management and control functions in one or a few agents, it is efficient to control agency problems between residual claimants and decision makers by restricting residual claims to the decision makers. This proposition gets clear support from the proprietorships, small partnerships, and closed corporations observed in small-scale production and service activities. These organizations are all characterized by concentrated decision systems and residual claims that are restricted to decision agents.

C. Separation of Residual Risk Bearing from Decision Management

1. *The Role of Specific Knowledge.* In contrast, most of the organizations characterized by separation of residual risk bearing from decision management are complex in the sense that specific information valuable for decisions is diffused among many agents throughout the organization. Thus in a complex organization separation of residual risk bearing from decision management arises in part because efficient decision systems are diffuse. Benefits from better decisions can be achieved by delegating decision functions to agents at all levels of the organization who have relevant specific knowledge, rather than allocating all decision management and control to the residual claimants. Control of the agency problems of such diffuse decision systems is then achieved by separating the ratification and monitoring of decisions (decision control) from initiation and implementation (decision management). The efficiency of such decision systems is buttressed by incentive structures that reward agents both for initiating and implementing decisions and for ratifying and monitoring the decision management of other agents.

2. *The Role of Diffuse Residual Claims.* In most complex organizations, residual claims are diffused among many agents. When there are many residual claimants, it is costly for all of them to be involved in decision control. As a consequence there is separation of residual risk bearing from decision control, and this creates agency problems between residual claimants and decision agents. Separation of decision management and decision control at all levels of the organization helps to control these agency problems by limiting the power of individual agents to expropriate the interests of residual claimants. Thus diffusion and separation of decision management and control have survival value in complex organizations both because they allow valuable specific knowledge

to be used at the points in the decision process where it is most relevant and because they help control the agency problems of diffuse residual claims.

3. *Common Features of Decision Control Systems.* What we call separation of residual risk bearing from decision management is the separation of ownership and control that has long bothered students of open corporations. We argue that separation of decision and risk bearing functions is also common to other organizations like large professional partnerships, financial mutuals, and nonprofits. Moreover, our central hypothesis about control of the agency problems caused by separation of residual risk bearing from decision management gets support from the fact that the major mechanisms for separating decision management and decision control are much the same across organizations.

The common central building blocks of the diffuse decision control systems of complex organizations of all types are formal decision hierarchies in which the decision initiatives of lower level agents are passed on to higher level agents, first for ratification and then for monitoring. Such decision hierarchies are found in large open corporations, large professional partnerships, large financial mutuals, and large nonprofits. Formal decision hierarchies are buttressed by less formal mutual monitoring systems that are a by-product of interaction that takes place to produce outputs and develop human capital.

The common apex of the decision control systems of organizations, large and small, in which decision agents do not bear a major share of the wealth effects of their decisions is a board of directors (trustees, managing partners, etc.) that ratifies and monitors important decisions and chooses, dismisses, and rewards important decision agents. Such multiple-member boards make collusion between top-level decision management and control agents more difficult, and they are the mechanism that allows separation of the management and control of the organization's most important decisions.

BIBLIOGRAPHY

Alchian, Armen A. "Uncertainty, Evolution and Economic Theory." *Journal of Political Economy* 58, no. 3 (June 1950): 211–21.

Alchian, Armen A., and Demsetz, Harold. "Production, Information Costs, and Economic Organization." *American Economic Review* 62, no. 5 (December 1972): 777–95.

Arrow, Kenneth J. "The Role of Securities in the Optimal Allocation of Risk Bearing." *Review of Economic Studies* 31, no. 86 (April 1964): 91–96.

Berle, Adolf A., and Means, Gardiner C. *The Modern Corporation and Private Property.* New York: Macmillan Publishing Co., 1932.

Blau, Peter M. *Bureaucracy in Modern Society*. New York: Random House, 1956.

Chandler, Alfred D., Jr. *The Visible Hand*. Cambridge, Mass.: Harvard University Press, 1977.

Chandler, Alfred D., Jr., and Daems, Herman. *Managerial Hierarchies*. Cambridge, Mass.: Harvard University Press, 1980.

Fama, Eugene F. *Foundations of Finance*. New York: Basic Books, 1976.

Fama, Eugene F. "Agency Problems and the Theory of the Firm." *Journal of Political Economy* 88, no. 2 (April 1980): 288–307.

Fama, Eugene F., and Jensen, Michael C. "Agency Problems and Residual Claims." *Journal of Law and Economics* 26 (June 1983): 327–49.

Fama, Eugene F., and Jensen, Michael C. "Organizational Forms and Investment Decisions." Managerial Economics Research Center Working Paper no. MERC 83–03. Rochester, N.Y.: University of Rochester, Graduate School of Management, 1983.

Hansmann, Henry B. "The Role of Nonprofit Enterprise." *Yale Law Journal* 89, no. 5 (April 1980): 835–901.

Hayek, Freidrich A. "The Use of Knowledge in Society." *American Economic Review* 35, no. 4 (September 1945): 519–30.

Herman, Edward S. "Conflict of Interest in the Savings and Loan Industry." In *A Study of the Savings and Loan Industry*, edited by Irwin Friend. Washington, D.C.: Federal Home Loan Board, 1969.

Herman, Edward S., *Corporate Control, Corporate Power*. Twentieth Century Fund Study. New York: Cambridge University Press, 1981.

Horngren, Charles. *Cost Accounting: A Managerial Emphasis*. Englewood Cliffs, N.J.: Prentice-Hall, Inc., 1982.

Jensen, Michael C. "Organization Theory and Methodology." *Accounting Review* 50, no. 2 (April 1983): 319–39.

Jensen, Michael C., and Meckling, William H. "Theory of the Firm: Managerial Behavior, Agency Costs and Ownership Structure." *Journal of Financial Economics* 3, no. 4 (October 1976): 305–60.

Jensen, Michael C., and Meckling, William H. "Rights and Production Functions: An Application to Labor-Managed Firms and Codetermination." *Journal of Business* 52, no. 4 (October 1979): 469–506.

Manne, Henry. "Mergers and the Market for Corporate Control." *Journal of Political Economy* 73, no. 2 (April 1965): 110–20.

Simon, Herbert A. "The Architecture of Complexity." *Proceedings of the American Philosophical Society* 106 (December 1962): 467–82.

Smith, Adam. *The Wealth of Nations*. 1776. Edited by Edwin Cannan, 1904. Reprint. New York: Modern Library, 1937.

Sowell, Thomas. *Knowledge and Decisions*. New York: Basic Books, 1980.

Stettler, Howard P. *Auditing Principles*. Englewood Cliffs, N.J.: Prentice-Hall, Inc., 1977.

Weber, Max. *The Theory of Social and Economic Organization*, edited by T. Parsons. Glencoe, Ill.: Free Press, 1947.

Williamson, Oliver E. Markets and Hierarchies: Analysis and Antitrust Implications. New York: Free Press, 1975.

Williamson, Oliver E. "The Modern Corporation: Origins, Evolution, Attributes." *Journal of Economic Literature* 19, no. 4 (December 1981): 1537–68.

DIVIDEND POLICY

AN EMPIRICAL ANALYSIS

· · ·

Eugene F. Fama and Harvey Babiak

Starting with the "partial adjustment model" suggested by Lintner [10, 11], this paper examines the dividend policies of individual firms. The Lintner model, in which the change in dividends from year $t-1$ to year t is regressed on a constant, the level of dividends for $t-1$, and the level of profits for t, explains dividend changes for individual firms fairly well relative to other models tested. But a model in which the constant term is suppressed and the level of earnings for $t-1$ is added, provides the best predictions of dividends on a year of data not used in fitting the regressions.

Though the dividend policy of individual firms is certainly a subject of economic interest, perhaps much of the novelty of the paper is methodological: specifically, the way in which a validation sample, simulations, and prediction tests are used to investigate results obtained from a pilot sample. To avoid spurious results that could follow from the extensive data-dredging involved in finding "good-fitting" dividend models, only half of the available firms are used in the original search, the remaining firms serving as a check on the findings. In addition, since the models tested are autoregressive, their statistical properties cannot always be evaluated analytically. This problem is surmounted to some extent by using simulations to study the results and conclusions obtained from the data for individual firms. The novelty in this use of simulations is that they are directed towards checking specific empirical results rather than establishing the properties of some general model. Finally, the conclusions drawn from the regression analysis and from the simulations are again checked by

Reprinted from the *Journal of the American Statistical Association* 63, no. 324 (December 1968): 1132–61. © 1968 by the American Statistical Association.

We have benefitted from the comments of P. Brown, Z. Griliches, H. Thornber, A. Zellner, and especially H. Roberts and R. Roll. The study was financed with funds granted to the Graduate School of Business, University of Chicago, by the Ford Foundation and by a grant from the National Science Foundation.

using the various models to predict dividend changes for a new year of data. The coherence in the results obtained with these various tests justifies strong conclusions with respect to the "best" dividend models and their properties.

1. INTRODUCTION

This paper studies the determinants of dividend payments by individual firms. The starting point is the work of Lintner [10, 11], recently extended by Brittain [2, 3]. Lintner's model is an application of the partial adjustment model (cf. [16]). For any year t the target dividends (D_{it}^*) for firm i are related to profits (E_{it}) according to

$$D_{it}^* = r_i E_{it},$$ (1)

where r_i is the firm's target ratio of dividends to profits. In any given year the firm will only partially adjust to the target dividend level, so that the change in dividend payments from year $t-1$ to year t is assumed to be

$$\Delta D_{it} = D_{it} - D_{i,t-1} = a_i + c_i(D_{it}^* - D_{i,t-1}) + u_{it},$$ (2)

where c_i is the "speed-of-adjustment coefficient" and u_{it} is an error term. Substitution of (1) into (2) yields[1]

$$\Delta D_{it} = a_i + c_i r_i E_{it} - c_i D_{i,t-1} + u_{it},$$ (3)

or

$$\Delta D_{it} = \alpha_i + \beta_{1i} D_{i,t-1} + \beta_{2i} E_{it} + u_{it},$$ (4)

where $\alpha_i = a_i$, $\beta_{1i} = -c_i$, and $\beta_{2i} = c_i r_i$.

Although Lintner and Brittain develop (4) to explain dividend decisions of individual firms, most of their empirical work involves aggregate data. In this study the model will be applied to data for individual firms. The problem will be approached as follows:

---

1. Lintner was led to the partial adjustment model (2) as a result of interviews with the managements of 28 firms. But the partial adjustment model is not the only behavioral justification of (4). For a discussion see [2, pp. 27–31].

(a)   Most of the behavioral models consistent with (4) imply that the current dividend is a function of current and past earnings. Section 2 provides a rough test of this postulated distributed lag effect.

(b)   Sections 3 and 4 are concerned more directly with testing (4) as a description of dividend changes. Issues that arise in estimating the coefficients of (4) will be considered, and alternative models will be examined.

(c)   In Section 5 Monte Carlo experiments will be used to study statistical properties of the various dividend models that cannot be examined analytically.

(d)   Finally, in Section 6 a new year of data will be used to compare the predictions of the "best" regression models with those of various "naive" forecasting procedures.

2. DIVIDENDS AND DISTRIBUTED LAGS: A PRELIMINARY TEST

Most dividend models implicitly assume that the current dividend payments of the firm are a distributed lag function of current and past profits. Before examining models that assume specific lag structures, it is appropriate to test whether the data lend any support to the notion of a lagged response. Table 1 provides distributions by sign of ΔD_{it}, conditional on the signs of the per share profits changes ΔE_{it} (Panel A), ΔE_{it} and $\Delta E_{i, t-1}$ (Panel B), and ΔE_{it}, $\Delta E_{i, t-1}$ and $\Delta E_{i, t-2}$ (Panel C). The table is taken from pooled annual data on 392 major industrial firms for the 19 years 1946–64.[2]

Table 1 seems to provide evidence for a distributed lag relationship between profits and dividend changes. In Panel A when $\Delta E_{it} > 0$, in 65.8 per cent of the cases $\Delta D_{it} > 0$. In Panel B when both ΔE_{it} and $\Delta E_{i,t-1}$ are positive, the proportion of positive dividend changes is 74.8, while when ΔE_{it} is positive but $\Delta E_{i,t-1}$ is negative, there are only 54.1 per cent dividend increases. Finally, in Panel C, in 80.7 per cent of the cases where there were three consecutive increases in annual profits, the current dividend per share was also increased;

2. The basic data file consists of annual financial statement information on 900 major industrial firms for the period 1946–64, as reported on the Compustat tapes of the Standard Statistics Corporation. Our sample includes only the 392 firms for which 19 years of complete data on all variables needed in the various tests are available. The profits variable in Table 1 is net income per share (income after depreciation and taxes divided by an adjusted measure of number of shares outstanding). The reported number of shares outstanding is adjusted to eliminate the effect of stock dividends and splits.

TABLE 1. Distribution by sign of ΔD_t, conditional on ΔE_t, ΔE_{t-1}, and ΔE_{t-2}

			ΔD_t −		ΔD_t 0		ΔD_t +				
ΔE_t	ΔE_{t-1}	ΔE_{t-2}	#	% of Row Total	#	% of Row Total	#	% of Row Total	Total	% of Column Total	Expected %
Panel A											
+			752	20.3	517	13.9	2,437	65.3	3,706	59.3	
−			1,002	39.5	455	17.9	1,083	42.6	2,540	40.7	
		Totals	1,754	28.1	972	15.5	3,520	56.4	6,246	100.0	
Panel B											
+	+		288	13.8	238	11.4	1,562	74.8	2,088	33.4	35.2
+	−		464	28.7	279	17.2	875	54.1	1,618	25.9	24.1
−	+		515	33.4	261	16.9	766	49.7	1,542	24.7	24.1
−	−		487	48.8	194	19.4	317	31.8	998	16.0	16.6
		Totals	1,754	28.1	972	15.5	3,520	56.4	6,246	100.0	100.0
Panel C											
+	+	+	131	10.9	101	8.4	967	80.7	1,199	19.2	20.9
+	+	−	157	17.7	137	15.4	595	66.9	889	14.2	14.3
+	−	+	234	25.0	159	17.0	542	58.0	935	15.0	14.3
−	+	+	262	31.5	123	14.8	447	53.7	832	13.3	14.3
+	−	−	230	33.7	120	17.6	333	48.7	683	10.9	9.8
−	+	−	253	35.6	138	19.4	319	44.9	710	11.4	9.8
−	−	+	323	48.4	111	16.6	233	34.9	667	10.7	9.8
−	−	−	164	49.5	83	25.1	84	25.4	331	5.3	6.7
		Totals	1,754	28.1	972	15.5	3,520	56.4	6,246*	100.0	100.0

* Note that the total number of observations should be 16×392 = 6,272. The missing 26 observations are the cases where $\Delta E = 0$. Since there were so few of them, we simply excluded these cases from the tabulation.

on the other hand, two successive profits increases preceded by a decrease resulted in an increased current dividend in 66.9 per cent of the cases. Similar statements apply to dividend and profit decreases. Further support for some sort of distributed lag dividend model is the evidence in Table 1 that the effects of a given change in profits on the dividend stream decline over time. For example, if two out of three of the profits changes $(\Delta E_{it}, \Delta E_{i,\,t-1}, \Delta E_{i,\,t-2})$ are negative, the proportion of negative ΔD_{it} for the sequence $(- - +)$ is higher than for the sequence $(- + -)$ which in turn is higher than for the sequence $(+ - -)$.

Finally, a parenthetical comment. Table 1 provides some evidence that earnings changes, or at least their signs, are nearly independent. The last column of Panels B and C shows the expected percentages of different profits sequences under the assumption that successive changes in profits are independent, with the estimated probabilities of positive and negative changes given by the observed relative frequencies $P(+) = .593$ and $P(-) = .407$. The observed percentages of each sequence of earnings changes are shown in the second last column of the table. The differences between the actual and expected percentages are small.

In the adaptive expectations model, an alternative behavioral model often used to derive (4), it is assumed that dividends are linearly related to long-run expected profits

$$D_{it} = r_i E_{it}^* + u_{it},$$

and the change at t in long-run expected profits is related to profits observed at t by

$$E_{it}^* - E_{i,t-1}^* = \lambda_i (E_{it} - E_{i,t-1}^*).$$

But if successive earnings changes are independent, the optimal value of λ_i is 1, and

$$D_{it} - D_{i,t-1} = \alpha_i + r_i E_{it} - D_{i,t-1} + u_{it}.$$

Thus the coefficient of the lagged dividend term is -1. In fact, the estimated average value of this coefficient (Table 2 Panel A) is $-.37$, which suggests that adaptive expectations is an inappropriate specification.

3. INITIAL TESTS OF THE LINTNER MODEL

In this section we begin to examine (4) as a description of the dividend behavior of firms. We shall be concerned with (a) the fact that (4) contains a lagged dependent variable as an explanatory variable, (b) determination of the appropriate measure of profits; and finally (c) whether the intercept in (4) is 0 or close to it.

a. Design of Tests

The available data were used to test many different models. In such data-dredging there is the danger that a particular model works well (in terms of multiple R^2) only because it happens by chance to conform to the random elements in the sample at hand. Two steps were taken in this study to guard against this result. First, the data for half of the available firms were used in "screening" for the best models; data for the remaining firms were used to "validate" the initial results. Second, when the "best" models had been chosen, their predictive value was examined (see Section 6) by applying them to a new year of data.

The procedure used in allocating firms to one-half of the sample or the other was as follows. First we attempted to determine in advance all the variables that would be required in the models to be examined. Then those companies with nineteen years of data on all variables were selected, ordered alphabetically within each industry, and allocated alternately into one-half of the sample or the other. Originally 412 firms were identified as having full information. Predictably, after testing a few models, additional models were suggested; as a result, the two subsamples eventually dwindled to 201 and 191 firms.

The first four panels of Table 2 summarize the cross-sectional distributions of parameter estimates obtained when least squares was used to estimate the coefficients of different versions of

$$\Delta D_{it} = \alpha_i + \beta_{1i} D_{i,t-1} + \beta_{2i} E_{it} + \beta_{3i} A_{it} + u_{it}, \quad t = 1947-1964, \tag{5}$$

for each of the 392 firms in the total sample. D_{it} is dividends per share paid by firm i during year t, E_{it} is profits per share, A_{it} is depreciation per share, and u_{it} is a random disturbance term. In Panels A, C, and D the profits variable E_{it} is net income, whereas in Panel B it is cash flow (net income plus depreciation). In Panels A, B, and D the depreciation variable A_{it} is suppressed, and in Panel D the constant term α_i is also suppressed.

TABLE 2. Cross-sectional distributions of regression coefficients for the models of (5)*

	(1) P	(2) R^2	(3) $\hat{\alpha}$	(4) $t(\hat{\alpha})$	(5) $\hat{\beta}_1$	(6) $t(\hat{\beta}_1)$	(7) $\hat{\beta}_2$	(8) $t(\hat{\beta}_2)$	(9) $\hat{\beta}_3$	(10) $t(\hat{\beta}_3)$	(11) $\hat{\rho}_1$	(12) $\hat{\rho}_2$	(13) $\hat{\rho}_3$
Panel A $\bar{P}$	.432	.062	.26	-.366	-3.10	.168	3.39				-.093	-.094	-.057
$E_t=$ Net $\hat{\sigma}(P)$	.236	.390	2.04	.386	2.41	.112	2.05				.227	.239	.255
Income .10	.094	-.158	-1.39	-.664	-5.31	.048	1.00				-.382	-.405	-.403
.25	.270	-.054	-.68	-.490	-3.91	.091	1.89				-.243	-.255	-.231
.50	.439	.010	.13	-.303	-2.74	.155	3.17				-.094	-.083	-.047
.75	.615	.094	.99	-.201	-1.92	.225	4.49				.061	.053	.125
.90	.725	.307	1.79	-.127	-1.18	.294	5.70				.195	.228	.245
Panel B $\bar{P}$	.409	.038	.22	-.428	-3.19	.136	3.14				-.027	-.077	-.057
$E_t=$ Net $\hat{\sigma}(P)$	.226	.480	2.28	.421	2.47	.111	1.99				.235	.231	.238
Income + .10	.094	-.279	-1.95	-.710	-5.28	.033	.98				-.341	-.372	-.350
Depreciation .25	.245	-.106	--97	-.540	-3.88	.075	1.90				-.184	-.232	-.220
.50	.406	.003	.03	-.382	-2.94	.122	2.95				-.025	-.081	-.061
.75	.561	.117	1.22	-.254	-1.94	.187	4.13				.137	.070	.104
.90	.700	.355	2.22	-.174	-1.33	.256	5.36				.271	.224	.245
Panel C $\bar{P}$	.466	.109	.45	-.452	-2.99	.160	3.04	.061	.46	-.111	-.128	-.092
$E_t=$ Net $\hat{\sigma}(P)$	.226	.494	2.06	.376	2.29	.120	2.11	.294	1.52	.213	.235	.247
Income .10	.150	-.214	-1.44	-.789	-5.25	.032	.68	-.177	-1.29	-.379	-.437	-.405
.25	.309	-.060	-.69	-.597	-3.72	.084	1.65	-.043	-.45	-.263	-.287	-.267
.50	.471	.028	.34	-.402	-2.67	.147	2.68	.040	.40	-.115	-.120	-.104
.75	.632	.180	1.30	-.266	-1.72	.220	4.14	.144	1.36	.003	.024	.086
.90	.749	.501	2.20	-.158	-1.06	.294	5.47	.315	2.26	.183	.180	.221
Panel D $\bar{P}$	.377			-.317	-3.38	.165	4.03				-.067	-.059	-.022
$E_t=$ Net $\hat{\sigma}(P)$	.241			.351	1.91	.099	2.07				.234	.240	.251
Income .10	.027			-.537	-5.69	.056	1.80				-.356	-.386	-.352
.25	.206			-.415	-4.32	.096	2.82				-.230	-.220	-.202
.50	.383			-.280	-3.13	.146	3.72				-.058	-.049	-.011
.75	.542			-.182	-2.23	.211	4.89				.101	.092	.158
.90	.672			-.110	-1.24	.278	6.36				.218	.228	.293
Panel E $\bar{P}$	.392			-.342	-3.47	.165	4.16				-.075	-.090	-.041
"Screening" $\hat{\sigma}(P)$	.244			.463	1.90	.099	2.13				.222	.249	.263
Subsample .10	.029			-.554	-5.67	.054	1.99				-.350	-.415	-.397
$E_t=$ Net .25	.214			-.442	-4.36	.097	2.86				-.238	-.257	-.227
Income .50	.414			-.285	-3.14	.148	3.87				-.071	-.092	-.052
.75	.580			-.183	-2.38	.215	5.09				.077	.082	.153
.90	.681			-.113	-1.43	.288	6.36				.212	.225	.295
Panel F $\bar{P}$	.360			-.290	-3.29	.164	3.91				-.059	-.025	-.002
"Validation" $\hat{\sigma}(P)$	.236			.162	1.90	.098	1.99				.246	.226	.236
Subsample .10	.025			-.506	-5.69	.059	1.73				-.383	-.345	-.339
$E_t=$ Net .25	.205			-.397	-4.18	.096	2.63				-.226	-.166	-.182
Income .50	.361			-.275	-3.04	.146	3.62				-.042	-.024	.023
.75	.536			-.182	-2.13	.209	4.74				.116	.129	.169
.90	.672			-.095	-1.04	.273	6.36				.241	.250	.272

* The regression equation is $\Delta D_t = \hat{\alpha} + \hat{\beta}_1 D_{t-1} + \hat{\beta}_2 E_t + \hat{\beta}_3 A_t + \hat{u}_t$. To simplify the notation, the firm subscript i that appears in (5) is omitted.

The cross-sectional distributions of the estimated regression coefficients of (5) are in columns (3), (5), (7) and (9) of Table 2, while the distributions of their "*t*" values (ratios of coefficients to estimated standard errors) are in columns (4), (6), (8) and (10). Column (1) shows the distribution of the coefficient of determination (R^2), while columns (11)–(13) present the autocorrelation coefficients ($\hat{\rho}_1, \hat{\rho}_2, \hat{\rho}_3$) of the estimated regression residuals for one, two, and three year lags. For each parameter or its corresponding "*t*" value, Table 2 presents seven summary statistics: the mean and standard deviation ($\bar{P}$ and $\hat{\sigma}(P)$), and five fractiles (the .10, .25, .50, .75, and .90). (Note that a single line of the table does not correspond to the regression for a given company. For example, the .5 fractile line does not summarize the results for the "median company" but rather shows the medians of each of the parameter distributions.)

The tests of (5) will be discussed in terms of the entire sample of 392 firms. But, as noted above, the research procedure was first to study the results obtained for the 201 firms in the "screening" subsample and then to check these on the 191 firms in the "validation" subsample. For the models of Panels A–D of Table 2, the results for the two subsamples were almost identical. A sample comparison is provided by Panels E and F, which summarize the model of Panel D for the two separate subsamples.

b. Some Statistical Issues

Equation (5) contains a lagged value of the dependent variable as an explanatory variable.[3] In finite samples this leads to bias of unknown magnitude in the ordinary least squares regression coefficients. If there is also serial dependence in the error term u_t, the regression coefficients will not even be consistent. For the moment we shall not be concerned with the bias in the estimated coefficients. In Section 5, after obtaining evidence about the "best" form of dividend model, simulations will be used to study the properties of the sampling distributions of the coefficients.

But the existence of bias or inconsistency or both is not in itself sufficient reason for rejecting ordinary least squares. From a sampling theory viewpoint, biased coefficients do not necessarily lead to biased predictions of the dependent variable, and estimating techniques (such as instrumental variables) designed to produce consistency often lead to regression coefficients with larger small sample dispersion than the inconsistent least squares estimates (cf. [12]).

3. If the lagged dividend term on the left of (5) is transferred to the right, the coefficients of E_t and A_t will be the same as in (5), and the coefficient of D_{t-1} will be $1 + \beta$.

From a Bayesian or decision theory viewpoint, in choosing point estimators, the only consideration is expected loss; bias and inconsistency are never of direct concern.

c. The Earnings Variable

We turn now to a comparison of the results for the different models summarized in Table 2. First, for all models both lagged dividends and some measure of current profits are important variables in explaining dividend changes. For example, in Panel A, which is the Lintner model (4), more than 75 per cent of the estimated coefficients of D_{t-1} (expected to be negative) have "t" values less than -1.92, and 75 per cent of the estimated coefficients of E_t (expected to be positive) have "t" values greater than 1.89.[4]

Brittain [2, 3] argues that in the war and postwar periods the changes in the tax laws with respect to depreciation (five-year equipment writeoffs, allowances for accelerated depreciation, etc.) invalidate reported depreciation figures as either, estimates or proxies for the economic costs associated with capital usage. He contends that after 1941, instead of net income, firms were more likely either to use cash flow (net income plus depreciation) as the measure of their ability to pay dividends, or to use net income and depreciation separately, presumably paying out a smaller proportion of the latter since part of the measured depreciation figure is true amortization of capital.[5]

Unlike his aggregate data for all manufacturing corporations and for individual industries, Brittain's data for individual firms lend little support to his profits hypothesis. The results in Table 2 confirm this negative conclusion. All five fractiles of the distribution of adjusted R^2 in the net income model of Panel A are at least as large as the corresponding fractiles for the cash flow model of Panel B.[6] But the differences between the values of R^2 are small. Similarly, all

4. Given the lagged variable issue, and the possibility of serial correlation in the disturbances, the "t" values provide only rough indications of the "importance" of the variables.

5. Brittain's primary goal in [2] is to relate changes over time in target payout ratios to public policy factors. In addition to his results with respect to depreciation tax laws, he finds that in the entire 1920–60 period changes in target payout ratios can in part be accounted for by changes in personal income tax rates, and especially changes in the tax treatment of dividends and capital gains. Since most of the changes in the personal income tax laws were enacted prior to 1946, we can avoid this issue here.

6. Let $\bar{R}^2$ be the ratio of the "explained" sum of squares from the regression to the total sum of squares. Then R^2, adjusted for degrees of freedom, is

five fractiles of the distribution of adjusted R^2 in Panel C, in which net income and depreciation are included as separate variables, are greater than the corresponding fractiles for the net income model of Panel A, but again the differences are small. Panel C shows quite clearly why the cash flow model of Panel B performs relatively poorly. The cash flow model constrains the coefficients of net income and depreciation to be equal. The distributions of $\hat{\beta}_2$ and $\hat{\beta}_3$, the estimated coefficients of net income and depreciation, in Panel C indicate that there is no correspondence between the values of the two coefficients. Whereas the net income variable enters strongly into the model, the "t" values for the coefficients of the depreciation variable are generally of trivial magnitude.

In the remainder of the paper we follow Lintner and use net income as the measure of profits. As a check, when various models are used in Section 6 to predict a new year of dividend data, depreciation will be included as an explanatory variable in some of the models.

d. The Constant Term in the Lintner Model

Lintner [11, p. 107] argues that a constant term (expected to be positive) should be included in (5) "to reflect the greater reluctance to reduce than to raise dividends which was commonly observed as well as the influence of the specific desire for a gradual growth in dividend payments found in about a third of the companies visited." In Panel A of Table 2 the mean and median values of $t(\hat{\alpha})$ for the different firms are indeed positive, though close to o. Under the assumption that the $t(\hat{\alpha})$ are independent drawings from a t distribution with mean o and $18-3=15$ degrees of freedom, 80 per cent of the observed values would be expected to fall between $t(\hat{\alpha})=\pm$ 1.34 and 50 per cent between $t(\hat{\alpha})=\pm$ .69. The actual distribution in column (4) of Panel A deviates only slightly (in the positive direction) from this.[7] But when the constant is suppressed in Panel D, the distribution of adjusted R^2 shifts downward. For example, the median value of R^2 falls from .439 to .383. Since this evidence is somewhat conflicting, we defer further consideration of the role of the con-

---

$$R^2 = 1 - (1 - \bar{R}^2)\frac{T-\delta}{T-K-\delta},$$

where T is the sample size (always 18 in our case), K is the number of explanatory variables, and δ is 1 if the model includes a constant and o otherwise. (Cf. [6, p. 217].)

7. The values of α depend on the levels of the dividend and profits variables for each firm. The standardization implicit in the "t" ratio makes the estimates roughly comparable from firm to firm.

stant until Sections 5 and 6, where simulations and predictive tests will be used to judge the importance of the constant term in dividend models.

4. TESTS OF THE LAG STRUCTURE

Griliches [7] suggests that in cases where (4) may seem appropriate on the basis of behavioral considerations, the underlying lag structure which (4) implies can be tested against a wide range of alternatives simply by comparing the results obtained when (4) is applied to the data with those obtained from estimating equations involving additional lagged values of one or both of the earnings and dividend variables. Panels A–D of Table 3 summarize the cross-sectional distributions of estimates obtained when the model

$$\Delta D_{it} = \alpha_i + \beta_{1i} D_{i,t-1} + \beta_{2i} D_{i,t-2} + \beta_{3i} E_{it} + \beta_{4i} E_{i,t-1} + u_{it} \tag{6}$$

was applied to each of the 392 firms in the sample.

A plausible dividend model can be derived by combining the partial adjustment and adaptive expectations models. Dividend changes follow the partial adjustment model

$$\Delta D_t = \alpha + c(D_t^* - D_{t-1}) + u_t,$$

but now target dividends are proportional to long-run expected earnings,

$$D_t^* = rE_t^*,$$

and long-run expected earnings are given by,

$$E_t^* - E_{t-1}^* = b(E_t - E_{t-1}^*).$$

Waud [19] shows that if $b \neq 1$ the estimating equation for this model will contain a constant, E_t, D_{t-1} and D_{t-2}, i.e., the model of Panel A Table 3. Comparison of Panel A Table 3 with Panel A Table 2 indicates that adding the lagged dividend D_{t-2} does not improve upon the explanation of annual dividend changes provided by the Lintner model. The mean and median values of adjusted R^2 for the two models are almost identical. The fact that this model performs no better than the simple partial adjustment model of (1)–(4) suggests that the optimal value of the smoothing constant b is in general close to 1. This is consistent with the tentative hypothesis, advanced in Section 2, that year-to-year changes

TABLE 3. Cross-sectional distributions of regression coefficients for the models of (6)*

Panel	(1) P	(2) R^2	(3) $\hat\alpha$	(4) $t(\hat\alpha)$	(5) $\hat\beta_1$	(6) $t(\hat\beta_1)$	(7) $\hat\beta_2$	(8) $t(\hat\beta_2)$	(9) $\hat\beta_3$	(10) $t(\hat\beta_3)$	(11) $\hat\beta_4$	(12) $t(\hat\beta_4)$	(13) $\hat\rho_1$	(14) $\hat\rho_2$	(15) $\hat\rho_3$
Panel A	$\bar P$	.432	.061	.14	−.381	−1.79	.003	.06	.166	3.11			−.100	−.139	−.045
	$\hat\sigma(P)$	.241	.431	1.44	.447	1.69	.340	1.20	.122	2.08			.192	.222	.242
	.10	.122	−.170	−1.34	−.741	−3.77	−.278	−1.40	.040	.84			−.362	−.425	−.358
	.25	.259	−.062	−.62	−.559	−2.66	−.144	−.76	.085	1.72			−.233	−.283	−.215
	.50	.440	.009	.09	−.351	−1.61	.022	.13	.156	2.94			−.096	−.133	−.035
	.75	.607	.104	.86	−.156	−.67	.172	.87	.232	4.10			.032	.000	.122
	.90	.735	.327	1.76	−.028	−.14	.320	1.62	.304	5.51			.146	.131	.255
Panel B	$\bar P$	.469	.056	.16	−.402	−2.70			.150	2.74	.043	.65	−.077	−.078	−.075
	$\hat\sigma(P)$	.238	.383	1.77	.344	1.85			.128	2.06	.121	1.55	.216	.238	.243
	.10	.138	−.170	−1.56	−.759	−4.33			.025	.50	−.078	−1.06	−.348	−.397	−.392
	.25	.317	−.066	−.79	−.530	−3.40			.072	1.29	−.020	−.28	−.217	−.238	−.237
	.50	.487	.006	.08	−.333	−2.58			.138	2.42	.035	.53	−.086	−.067	−.085
	.75	.643	.093	.94	−.208	−1.79			.206	3.89	.096	1.44	.079	.080	.093
	.90	.772	.294	1.70	−.137	−1.15			.287	5.21	.172	2.44	.204	.212	.248
Panel C	$\bar P$	.467	.036	−.01	−.473	−1.77	.055	.29	.142	2.46	.061	.78	−.047	−.151	−.071
	$\hat\sigma(P)$	.250	.422	1.42	.423	1.30	.320	1.14	.139	2.09	.130	1.49	.153	.225	.234
	.10	.124	−.254	−1.80	−.849	−3.35	−.236	−1.11	.011	.14	−.066	−1.04	−.224	−.443	−.370
	.25	.294	−.089	−.90	−.671	−2.53	−.100	−.45	.060	1.09	−.009	−.11	−.131	−.309	−.221
	.50	.493	−.004	−.04	−.437	−1.69	.069	.30	.129	2.18	.045	.67	−.041	−.144	−.063
	.75	.645	.092	.77	−.260	−.92	.231	1.09	.204	3.54	.121	1.44	.036	−.011	.087
	.90	.781	.345	1.70	−.074	−.31	.362	1.63	.293	4.86	.205	2.53	.136	.152	.228
Panel D	$\bar P$	.416			−.339	−2.76			.149	3.07	.028	.46	−.047	−.039	−.033
	$\hat\sigma(P)$	.244			.300	1.43			.116	2.31	.129	1.64	.222	.240	.243
	.10	.081			−.610	−4.53			.033	.77	−.105	−1.39	−.350	−.371	−.345
	.25	.254			−.443	−3.57			.072	1.48	−.031	−.48	−.204	−.192	−.221
	.50	.433			−.299	−2.70			.139	2.71	.025	.41	−.042	−.041	−.026
	.75	.592			−.179	−1.91			.209	4.15	.083	1.30	.099	.114	.141
	.90	.739			−.102	−1.08			.284	5.80	.147	2.32	.243	.260	.289
Panel E "Screening Subsample"	$\bar P$	.433			−.374	−2.96			.145	3.04	.040	.63	−.045	−.060	−.052
	$\hat\sigma(P)$	.252			.371	1.56			.115	2.28	.138	1.63	.216	.245	.244
	.10	.071			−.658	−4.86			.035	.80	−.080	−1.16	−.353	−.399	−.352
	.25	.261			−.484	−3.87			.071	1.48	−.016	−.28	−.190	−.210	−.237
	.50	.467			−.321	−2.78			.136	2.63	.030	.47	−.035	−.057	−.055
	.75	.622			−.191	−1.91			.204	4.30	.098	1.43	.098	.106	.100
	.90	.739			−.119	−1.35			.274	5.56	.161	2.71	.241	.249	.273
Panel F "Validation Subsample"	$\bar P$	.398			−.302	−2.56			.154	8.09	.016	.27	−.050	−.017	−.012
	$\hat\sigma(P)$	.235			.192	1.37			.118	2.33	.117	1.62	.229	.231	.241
	.10	.105			−.567	−4.10			.029	.72	−.112	−1.73	−.343	−.335	−.336
	.25	.254			−.411	−3.24			.074	1.49	−.047	−.72	−.226	−.156	−.172
	.50	.396			−.289	−2.54			.142	2.76	.016	.32	−.044	−.002	.004
	.75	.549			−.163	−1.90			.219	4.09	.069	1.22	.108	.127	.171
	.90	.741			−.089	−.80			.312	6.42	.136	2.00	.253	.278	.298

* The regression equation is $\Delta D_t = \hat\alpha + \hat\beta_1 D_{t-1} + \hat\beta_2 D_{t-2} + \hat\beta_3 E_t + \hat\beta_4 E_{t-1} + \hat u_t$.

in net income are nearly independent. This negative conclusion with respect to the role of D_{t-2} is also supported by comparison of Panels B and C of Table 3. Again adding D_{t-2} to the equation leads to no noticeable improvement in R^2.

For the lagged profits variable E_{t-2} the results are slightly more positive. Comparing Panel A Table 2 with Panel B Table 3, we see that addition of the lagged profits term raises the mean R^2 by .037, about a nine per cent improvement. The low "t" values for $\hat{\beta}_4$, which seem to indicate that lagged profits do not have "significant" explanatory power, may be due to multicollinearity between E_t and E_{t-1}. This is supported by the fact that the "t" values for the coefficient of E_t also drop substantially when E_{t-1} is added to the model.[8]

One model that is consistent with the partial adjustment hypothesis and that can be used to explain the presence of a lagged profits term in the dividend model assumes that the process generating the annual profits of firm i can be represented as

$$E_{it} = (1 + \lambda_i) E_{i,t-1} + v_{it}, \tag{7}$$

where v_{it} is a serially independent error term. Target dividends are still

$$D_{it}^* = r_i E_{it}, \tag{8}$$

but now it is assumed that there is full adjustment of dividends to the expected earnings change $\lambda_i E_{i,t-1}$ and partial adjustment to the remainder:

$$\Delta D_{it} = a_i + c_i [r_i (E_{it} - \lambda_i E_{i,t-1}) - D_{i,t-1}] + r_i \lambda_i E_{i,t-1} + u_{it}, \tag{9}$$

or

$$\Delta D_{it} = a_i - c_i D_{i,t-1} + c_i r_i E_{it} + r_i \lambda_i (1 - c_i) E_{i,t-1} + u_{it}. \tag{10}$$

This interpretation of the lagged earnings model will be examined more fully in the next two sections.

The tests of the lag structure have been discussed in terms of the sample of 392 firms. In fact the research procedure was first to study the results obtained for the 201 firms in the "screening" subsample and then to check these

---

8. Note that successive levels of profits may be highly correlated, even though (as suggested in Section 2) changes in profits are nearly independent.

on the 191 firms in the "validation" subsample. For the models of Panels A–D of Table 3, the results for the two subsamples were again almost identical. A sample comparison is provided by Panels E and F of Table 3, which summarize the model of Panel D for the two separate subsamples.

In the course of this study many other dividend models were tried, but without much success. For example, past, current, and future capital expenditure variables (levels and changes) were introduced separately and in combination into (5) and (6). In no case did the capital expenditure variables produce an improvement of as much as .02 in the average value of adjusted R^2. We have also tried models in which the current dividend change is considered a function of current and past *changes* in earnings and dividends; by the R^2 criterion, none of these performed as well as the Lintner model (4).

5. SIMULATIONS

In this section Monte Carlo experiments will be used to study some statistical issues mentioned earlier. The simulations will be concerned with (a) the effects on the sampling distributions of the estimated regression coefficients of the fact that models (5) and (6) contain lagged values of the dependent variable as explanatory variables; (b) the effects of fitting dividend models with constant terms when the constant is inappropriate; (c) the effects of misspecification of distributed lag structures; (d) measuring the serial dependence in the disturbances of these lagged variable models; and (e) determining efficient procedures for estimating various parameters of economic interest in the models.

Throughout these simulations we shall be concerned with the sampling distributions of estimated regression parameters, given the underlying population values of these parameters. Thus our analysis is in the context of the "sampling theory" approach to statistics. By contrast, in the Bayesian and "likelihood theory" approaches, interest would center around the distributions of the population values of the parameters, given the observed sample values. It is interesting to note that lagged variable models provide one case where the "sampling theory" and Bayesian (or likelihood theory) approaches lead to different views of estimation problems, even when the Bayesian uses diffuse prior distributions. (Cf. [1], [18], [22].)

a. Design of the Tests

We stress that the goal of the simulations is limited: to obtain insights into the empirical results for the firm data presented in the previous sections. Thus the simulation process will be designed to capture as many features as possible of the firm data. For example, the sample size and coefficient values will correspond closely to the firm data, and distributions of disturbance terms will be chosen to produce cross-sectional distributions of R^2 close to those observed in the firm data.

The data for the initial simulations are generated by the model

$$\Delta D_t = -.45D_{t-1} + .15E_t + u_t,$$ (11)

$$E_t = (1+\lambda)E_{t-1} + e_t.$$ (12)

Expression (11) can be interpreted as the Lintner "partial adjustment" model of (3) and (4) with intercept $\alpha = 0$, "speed of adjustment coefficient" $c = -\beta_1 = .45$, and target payout ratio $r = -\beta_2/\beta_1 = .33$. In (12) two values of λ will be used in the tests: $\lambda = 0$, and $\lambda = .1$.

To generate simulated "data" samples for (11) and (12) it is necessary to choose starting values, E_0 and D_0, and to specify the process generating the disturbance terms u_t and e_t. Initially successive values of u_t and e_t will be independent, identically distributed random variables with mean 0. In half of the simulations u_t and e_t are normal with SIQ(u), the semi-interquartile range of the distribution of u, equal to 1.0 and SIQ(e) = .21. In the other half u and e are generated from symmetric stable distributions with characteristic exponent $\theta = 1.7$, again with SIQ(u) = 1.0 and SIQ(e) = .21. The stable and normal samples are related in the sense that a single random sample of "cumulative probabilities" (random numbers uniformly distributed over the interval 0–1) was generated, and then inverse functions for the normal and stable $\theta = 1.7$ distributions were used to get the two samples of u. The same procedure was used for e. Generating the disturbance terms in this way should enable us to isolate the effects of distributional assumptions.[9]

---

9. The normal distribution is itself symmetric stable or stable Paretian with characteristic exponent $\theta = 2.0$, The normal is the only stable distribution for which second and higher order moments exist. For $\theta < 2$, moments or order less than θ exist, while those of order equal to and greater than θ do not. Heuristically, nonnormal symmetric stable distributions have higher densities around their medians and in their extreme tails than the normal—properties which seem to describe empirical distributions for many economic variables. (Cf. [4], [14], and [17]. Since variances of nonnormal stable distributions do not exist, least squares estimating procedures would seem inappropriate.

Under each distributional assumption 201 samples of 20 observations on u_t and e_t have been generated. For each sample $E_0 = 1.0$ and $D_0 = .33$ and then (11) and (12) are used to generate D_1 through D_{20} and E_1 through E_{20}, first for $\lambda = 0$ and then for $\lambda = .1$. Thus there are four sets of data (201 samples per set and 20 observations per sample), each set corresponding to a pair of assumptions concerning the distributions of the disturbance terms and the trend in earnings. Least squares is then used to estimate the coefficients of

$$\Delta D_t = \alpha + \beta_1 D_{t-1} + \beta_2 E_t + u_t, \quad t = 1, 2, \dots, 20, \tag{13}$$

for each sample of 20 observations. The cross-sectional distributions of the estimates are presented in Table 4 and 5. To check that the results do not depend critically on the choice of starting values, the models in Table 4 were replicated using randomly selected values of E_0 and D_0. The results were almost identical.

b. Lagged Variable Bias

Given that the model is otherwise correctly specified, how does the presence of a lagged value of the dependent variable as an explanatory variable affect the distributions of the estimated regression coefficients of (13)? The question can be answered by reference to Panel A Table 4. The sampling distribution of $\hat{\beta}_1$, with a mean value of $-.493$ and a median of $-.471$, is centered to the left of the true value $\beta_1 = -.45$. On the other hand, the sampling distribution of $\hat{\beta}_2$ is centered to the right of the true value $\beta_2 = .15$, with a mean of .160 and a median of .155.

Panel B Table 4 presents results for the same model as Panel A but for the case where all random variables are generated by stable $\theta = 1.7$ rather than normal distributions. This change has little effect on the sampling distributions of the regression coefficients. The mean values of the coefficients are close to those for the normal model in Panel A, and the fractiles of the cross-sectional distributions are similar. On the other hand, the cross-sectional distributions of the "t" values for the coefficients are much more disperse in the stable $\theta = 1.7$ case. For example, for the normal model of Panel A Table 4 the interquartile

---

Though they are certainly inefficient, some justification for their use has been provided by Wise [21]. Further justification will be provided by the results of our simulations.

It would have been desirable to study the distributions of the residuals u_{it} for the dividend models fit to the firm data. But with samples of 18, the results would not be meaningful.

TABLE 4. Cross-sectional distributions of regression coefficients for simulations of (13) with no earnings trend*

		(1)	(2)	(3)	(4)	(5)	(6)	(7)	(8)
	Parameter	R^2	$\hat{\alpha}$	$t(\hat{\alpha})$	$\hat{\beta}_1$	$t(\hat{\beta}_1)$	$\hat{\beta}_2$	$t(\hat{\beta}_2)$
Panel A	$\bar{P}$	.436			−.493	−3.91	.160	4.29
$\theta = 2.0$	$\hat{\sigma}(P)$	.160			.145	1.25	.041	1.38
	.10	.199			−.704	−5.44	.113	2.63
	.25	.328			−.598	−4.67	.129	3.27
	.50	.448			−.471	−3.83	.155	4.22
	.75	.547			−.392	−3.04	.188	5.21
	.90	.624			−.317	−2.41	.218	5.86
Panel B	$\bar{P}$	.466			−.501	−4.40	.160	4.89
$\theta = 1.7$	$\hat{\sigma}(P)$	.208			.147	2.38	.050	2.99
	.10	.177			−.669	−6.57	.113	2.15
	.25	.313			−.584	−5.18	.134	3.20
	.50	.482			−.479	−4.06	.155	4.46
	.75	.618			−.408	−2.95	.188	5.84
	.90	.740			−.345	−2.33	.228	7.55
Panel C	$\bar{P}$	.476	.034	.16	−.533	−3.92	.161	3.79
$\theta = 2.0$	$\hat{\sigma}(P)$	.147	.187	1.21	.157	1.19	.055	1.49
	.10	.288	−.155	−1.25	−.727	−5.33	.104	2.23
	.25	.381	−.076	−.67	−.625	−4.53	.128	2.83
	.50	.486	.014	.12	−.512	−3.82	.159	3.82
	.75	.585	.123	1.00	−.423	−3.16	.195	4.64
	.90	.647	.258	1.70	−.359	−2.50	.225	5.50
Panel D	$\bar{P}$	.507	.048	.14	−.539	−4.35	.157	4.27
$\theta = 1.7$	$\hat{\sigma}(P)$	.192	.314	1.21	.157	2.09	.082	2.81
	.10	.265	−.183	−1.23	−.737	−6.52	.103	1.73
	.25	.356	−.096	−.71	−.637	−5.02	.129	2.67
	.50	.521	.008	.06	−.516	−4.05	.156	3.91
	.75	.648	.149	.87	−.434	−3.14	.195	5.33
	.90	.755	.293	1.81	−.352	−2.46	.230	6.92

* The regression equation is $\Delta D_t = \hat{\alpha} + \hat{\beta}_1 D_{t-1} + \hat{\beta}_2 E_t + \hat{u}_t$. The data are generated by the model of (11) and (12) with $\lambda = 0$ in (12). Thus the population values of the coefficients are $\alpha = 0$, $\beta_1 = -.45$ and $\beta_2 = .15$.

range of the distribution of $t(\hat{\beta}_1)$ is 1.63, whereas for the stable model of Panel B it is 2.23. Thus when the disturbances are generated by a stable distribution with $\theta = 1.7$, the distributions of the ordinary least squares regression coefficients are well-behaved (in the sense of being close to those obtained when the disturbances are normal), but inferences based on the normal regression model will be misleading. The problem arises from the fact that the estimates of the standard errors of the regression coefficients computed under the normality assumption are downward biased estimates of dispersion when the disturbances are stable with characteristic exponent $\theta < 2$.[10]

The simulations summarized in Table 4 are for $\lambda = 0$ in (12), i.e., no earnings trend. But during 1946–64 a majority of firms had positive earnings trends. The results for $\lambda = .1$, summarized in Panels A and B of Table 5, indicate that any such trend effects are minor; the cross-sectional distributions of coefficient estimates and their "t" values in Table 5 are close to those for the corresponding models in Panels A and B of Table 4.

c. The Constant Term

The simulations summarized in Tables 4 and 5 also provide evidence on the effects of estimating the dividend model with a constant term when the population value of the constant is 0. Some of the pertinent results are presented in Table 6, along with corresponding results for the Compustat firm data from Panels A and D of Table 2. In several respects the simulations reproduce fairly well the results for the firm data. As in the firm data, including the constant in the estimating equation in the simulations leads to an increase in the values of adjusted R^2. In the firm data the average value of $\hat{\beta}_1$, the coefficient of D_{t-1}, goes from $-.317$ to $-.366$ when the constant is added to the model. In the simula-

---

10. Consider the model
$$y_t = \beta x_t + u_t \quad t = 1, 2, \dots, n,$$
where the x_t are fixed numbers and the u_t are independent drawings from a symmetric stable distribution with $\theta \leq 2$. If σ is the semi-interquartile range of the distribution of u, the least squares estimate of β will have a symmetric stable distribution with the same characteristic exponent θ as u and with semi-interquartile range

$$\sigma(\hat{\beta}) = \sigma \frac{\sum\limits_{t=1}^{n} |x_t|^\theta}{\left(\sum\limits_{t=1}^{n} x_t^2\right)^\theta} \qquad \text{(Wise [21])}. \quad (14)$$

If in general $\sum x_t^2 > |x_t|$, then $\sigma(\hat{\beta})$ is a decreasing function of θ for $\theta > 1$. Thus if we apply standard normal regression theory (i.e., assume $\theta = 2$) when in fact $\theta < 2$, estimates of the dispersion in the distribution of β will be downward biased. (Moreover, the bias will *increase* with the sample size n.) In the simulations the values of x_t are not fixed; outliers from the distribution of x_t will tend to occur more frequently in the stable $\theta = 1.7$ model than in the normal model, accentuating the effects discussed above.

TABLE 5. Cross-sectional distributions of regression coefficients for simulations of (13) with earnings trend*

	(1)	(2)	(3)	(4)	(5)	(6)	(7)	(8)
	Parameter	R^2	$\hat{\alpha}$	$t(\hat{\alpha})$	$\hat{\beta}_1$	$t(\hat{\beta}_1)$	$\hat{\beta}_2$	$t(\hat{\beta}_2)$
Panel A	$\bar{P}$	.464			−.513	−3.85	.165	4.58
$\theta = 2.0$	$\hat{\sigma}(P)$	.165			.146	1.24	.040	1.40
	.10	.246			−.698	−5.55	.122	2.87
	.25	.360			−.604	−4.67	.138	3.65
	.50	.461			−.496	−3.70	.160	4.29
	.75	.580			−.427	−3.03	.187	5.44
	.90	.673			−.352	−2.57	.213	6.56
Panel B	$\bar{P}$	.468			−.513	−4.15	.168	5.00
$\theta = 1.7$	$\hat{\sigma}(P)$	.206			.139	2.15	.046	3.37
	.10	.217			−.708	−6.48	.121	2.75
	.25	.287			−.601	−5.02	.139	3.28
	.50	.444			−.502	−3.64	.160	4.26
	.75	.610			−.415	−2.83	.187	5.83
	.90	.751			−.363	−2.43	.218	7.62
Panel C	$\bar{P}$	.502	−.004	−.05	−.561	−3.87	.176	4.20
$\theta = 2.0$	$\hat{\sigma}(P)$	.160	.158	1.23	.164	1.26	.051	1.41
	.10	.287	−.200	−1.58	−.774	−5.51	.112	2.59
	.25	.399	−.112	−.98	−.675	−4.70	.145	3.21
	.50	.508	−.006	−.04	−.534	−3.69	.172	3.96
	.75	.620	.098	.81	−.454	−3.00	.207	5.06
	.90	.701	.162	1.36	−.365	−2.53	.238	6.12
Panel D	$\bar{P}$	.508	.002	−.06	−.560	−4.13	.182	4.59
$\theta = 1.7$	$\hat{\sigma}(P)$	.194	.345	1.20	.159	1.89	.073	3.22
	.10	.266	−.260	−1.58	−.779	−6.44	.122	2.33
	.25	.354	−.130	−.99	−.666	−4.82	.143	3.03
	.50	.502	−.011	−.05	−.540	−3.77	.169	3.94
	.75	.654	.110	.74	−.444	−2.89	.205	5.34
	.90	.763	.250	1.47	−.376	−2.50	.236	7.06

* The model is $\Delta D_t = \hat{\alpha} + \hat{\beta}_1 D_{t-1} + \hat{\beta}_2 E_t + \hat{u}_t$. The data are generated by (11) and (12) with $\lambda = .1$ in (12). Thus the population values of the coefficients are $\alpha = 0$, $\beta_1 = -.45$ and $\beta_2 = .15$.

TABLE 6. Comparisons of cross-sectional distributions of regression parameters for firm data and simulations, and for models which include and exclude the constant term*

(1) Parameter Model	(2) Firm Data R^2 With Constant	(3) Firm Data R^2 Without Constant	(4) Simulations R^2 With Constant	(5) Simulations R^2 Without Constant	(6) Firm Data $t(\hat{\alpha})$ With Constant	(7) Simulations $t(\hat{\alpha})$ With Constant	(8) Firm Data $\hat{\beta}_1$ With Constant	(9) Firm Data $\hat{\beta}_1$ Without Constant	(10) Simulations $\hat{\beta}_1$ With Constant	(11) Simulations $\hat{\beta}_1$ Without Constant	(12) Firm Data $\hat{\beta}_2$ With Constant	(13) Firm Data $\hat{\beta}_2$ Without Constant	(14) Simulations $\hat{\beta}_2$ With Constant	(15) Simulations $\hat{\beta}_2$ Without Constant
$\hat{P}$	.432	.377	.502	.464	.26	-.05	-.366	-.317	-.561	-.513	.168	.165	.176	.165
$\hat{\sigma}(P)$	.236	.241	.160	.165	2.04	1.23	.386	.351	.164	.146	.112	.099	.051	.040
.10	.094	.027	.287	.246	-1.39	-1.58	-.664	-.537	-.774	-.698	.048	.056	.112	.122
.25	.270	.206	.399	.360	-.68	-.98	-.490	-.415	-.675	-.604	.091	.096	.145	.138
.50	.439	.383	.508	.461	.13	-.04	-.303	-.280	-.534	-.496	.155	.146	.172	.160
.75	.615	.542	.620	.580	.99	.81	-.201	-.182	-.454	-.427	.225	.211	.207	.187
.90	.725	.672	.701	.673	1.79	1.36	-.127	-.110	-.365	-.352	.294	.278	.238	.213

* The regression model is $\Delta D_t = \hat{\alpha} + \hat{\beta}_1 D_{t-1} + \hat{\beta}_2 E_t + \hat{u}_t$. In the simulations the population values of the coefficients are $\alpha = 0$, $\beta_1 = -.45$, $\beta_2 = .15$; the values of E_t are generated by $E_t = 1.1 E_{t-1} + v_t$. The results for the firm data are from panels A and D of Table 2 while the simulation results are from the normal models of Panels A and C of Table 5.

tions, including the constant seems to increase the downward bias of $\hat{\beta}_1$; the average value goes from $-.513$ to $-.561$. Finally, there is also some similarity between the distributions of $t(\hat{\alpha})$ for the firm and the simulated data.

The success of the simulations in reproducing results observed in the firm data suggests that for most firms the constant in the dividend model is close to zero. But, as in all simulations, there is the danger that the success of the simulations in capturing features of the empirical data may result from factors other than the constant term that were overlooked in the analysis. Fortunately, independent evidence on the role of the constant term will be obtained in the prediction tests of Section 6.

d. Testing the Lag Structure

We saw in Section 4 that in the data for individual firms, including a lagged earnings variable in the dividend model increases adjusted R^2, though the increases are small. Simulations can be used to examine the effects of the lagged earnings variable both when the true dividend generating process involves this variable and when it does not. In the latter case we simply examine the effects of including a lagged earnings variable in the estimating equation when in fact the data are generated by (11), which does not involve the lagged earnings variable. The relevant results appear in Table 7. The underlying data samples are the same as those in Tables 4 and 5. For a dividend generating process involving the lagged earnings variable we return to (10), setting $\lambda = .1$, $a = 0$, $c = .45$, and $r = .33$. Thus the process is

$$\Delta D_t = \beta_1 D_{t-1} + \beta_2 E_t + \beta_3 E_{t-1} + u_t \tag{15}$$

$$= -.45 D_{t-1} + .15 E_t + .018 E_{t-1} + u_t \tag{16}$$

where $\beta_1 = -c = -.45$, $\beta_2 = cr = .15$, $\beta_3 = r\lambda(1-c) = .018$. The same samples of disturbances used in the previous simulations were used to obtain observations on (16). The regressions for this model are summarized in Table 8. In both Tables 7 and 8 the model fit to the data is (15).

When the data for individual firms are used to estimate the coefficients of (15), the average value of R^2 is $.416$ (Panel D Table 3) versus $.377$ when the lagged earnings variable E_{t-1} is excluded (Panel D Table 2). In the simulations a systematic increase in R^2 is only observed in Table 8, where the dividend generating process involves the lagged earnings variable directly. In Table 7, where the dividend generating process does not involve E_{t-1}, no such systematic increase in R^2 is observed when this variable is included in the estimating equation. In Panels B and D of Table 7 the average values of R^2 (.467 and .474) are slightly higher than the values in Panel B Table 4 (.466) and Panel B Table 5 (.468) for the corresponding models in which E_{t-1} is excluded. But in Panels A and C of Table 7 the average values of R^2 (.433 and .450) are slightly lower than the values (.436 and .464) for the corresponding models of Panel A Table 4 and Panel A Table 5. On the other hand, when the dividend generating process in the simulations involves E_{t-1} directly, including this variable in the estimating equation increases the values of adjusted R^2, though only very slightly. From Panel A Table 8 to Panel C the average R^2 increases from .458 to .466, while from Panel B to Panel D the increase is from .486 to .493. Thus the simulations support the evidence in the firm data that the lagged earnings variable has explanatory value.

e. Testing for Serial Dependence in the Estimated Regression Residuals

Griliches [7] has shown that common measures of dependence like the auto-correlation coefficient often do not provide a powerful test of independence for the residuals from lagged variable regression models. In such models the estimated autocorrelation coefficient is substantially biased towards 0. In Monte Carlo experiments on the model

$$y_t = \alpha + \beta_1 y_{t-1} + \beta_2 x_t + u_t, \quad x_t \text{ exogenous,}$$
$$u_t = .5 u_{t-1} + \varepsilon_t, \qquad \varepsilon_t \text{ normal and serially uncorrelated,}$$

Malinvaud [12] documents the bias of the autocorrelation coefficient estimated from the $\hat{u}_t$. Though the population value of the coefficient is .5, the sample values are widely dispersed about a mean of .3. Nevertheless, Malinvaud's results indicate that, though the power of the test of independence provided by the autocorrelation coefficient is weakened when the regression model contains lagged endogenous variables, the test still provides fairly reliable information concerning the direction (positive or negative) of any serial dependence in the residuals and will produce values systematically different from 0 when the serial dependence is strong.

In this section we shall try to obtain evidence on the degree of serial dependence in the residuals of our dividend models by comparing the cross-sectional distribution of residual autocorrelation coefficients obtained for the Lintner model (4) from the Compustat firm data with the distributions obtained from a simulated model of the same form but with various levels of

TABLE 7. Cross-sectional distribution of regression coefficients for simulations of (15) where true value of $\beta_3 = 0$*

	(1) Parameter	(2) R^2	(3) $\hat{\beta}_1$	(4) $t(\hat{\beta}_1)$	(5) $\hat{\beta}_2$	(6) $t(\hat{\beta}_2)$	(7) $\hat{\beta}_3$	(8) $t(\hat{\beta}_3)$
Panel A	$\bar{P}$	.433	−.543	−2.95	.144	2.85	.033	.49
$\theta = 2.0$	$\hat{\sigma}(P)$	.186	.203	1.16	.057	1.35	.079	1.13
No Earnings	.10	.190	−.827	−4.35	.074	1.29	−.065	−.92
Trend	.25	.318	−.674	−3.52	.106	1.96	−.012	−.19
	.50	.464	−.516	−2.75	.143	2.80	.034	.45
	.75	.557	−.383	−2.23	.181	3.64	.080	1.12
	.90	.649	−.310	−1.69	.219	4.68	.124	1.78
Panel B	$\bar{P}$	.467	−.551	−3.17	.145	3.37	.032	.46
$\theta = 1.7$	$\hat{\sigma}(P)$	.230	.201	1.51	.072	2.58	.091	1.18
No Earnings	.10	.159	−.841	−4.86	.059	.80	−.066	−.99
Trend	.25	.300	−.672	−3.75	.111	1.89	−.019	−.26
	.50	.500	−.536	−2.84	.143	2.92	.033	.41
	.75	.629	−.415	−2.27	.177	4.61	.083	1.04
	.90	.751	−.312	−1.79	.218	6.02	.143	1.71
Panel C	$\bar{P}$	.450	−.532	−2.88	.149	3.01	.026	.37
$\theta = 2.0$	$\hat{\sigma}(P)$	.184	.199	1.00	.058	1.37	.079	1.09
With	.10	.213	−.815	−4.11	.080	1.38	−.078	−.97
Earnings	.25	.337	−.656	−3.45	.111	2.09	−.033	−.42
Trend	.50	.473	−519	−2.77	.148	2.96	.033	.44
	.75	.582	−.376	−2.16	.183	3.82	.080	1.06
	.90	.661	−.296	−1.66	.220	4.83	.114	1.67
Panel D	$\bar{P}$	.474	−.535	−3.09	.150	3.55	.024	.31
$\theta = 1.7$	$\hat{\sigma}(P)$	.224	.201	1.36	.073	2.60	.093	1.15
With	.10	.167	−.796	−4.61	.072	1.06	−.079	−1.13
Earnings	.25	.347	−.637	−3.67	.121	1.95	−.031	−.41
Trend	.50	.493	−.521	−2.82	.151	3.13	.024	.34
	.75	.636	−.385	−2.30	.181	4.78	.067	.96
	.90	.753	−.305	−1.74	.227	6.08	.143	1.63

* The regression model is $\Delta D_t = \hat{\beta}_1 D_{t-1} + \hat{\beta}_2 E_t + \hat{\beta}_3 E_{t-1} + \hat{u}_t$. In the data generating process the values of the coefficients are $\beta_1 = -.45$, $\beta_2 = .15$, $\beta_3 = 0$.

serial dependence in the disturbances. The process generating the simulation data is again (11) but with the additional specification

$$u_t = \rho u_{t-1} + v_t. \tag{17}$$

Three values of ρ are used: 0, −.2, and .2. The 201 normal samples of 20 observations each obtained earlier for u_t in (11) are used here for v_t. The equa-

TABLE 8. Cross-sectional distribution of regression coefficients for simulations of (15) where true value of $\beta_3 = .018$*

	(1) Parameter	(2) R^2	(3) $\hat{\beta}_1$	(4) $t(\hat{\beta}_1)$	(5) $\hat{\beta}_2$	(6) $t(\hat{\beta}_2)$	(7) $\hat{\beta}_3$	(8) $t(\hat{\beta}_3)$
Panel A	$\bar{P}$	.458	-.456	-3.74	.169	4.63		
$\theta = 2.0$	$\hat{\sigma}(P)$	.180	.134	1.20	.039	1.35		
	.10	.217	-.642	-5.32	.125	2.83		
	.25	.350	-.540	-4.56	.139	3.62		
	.50	.479	-.442	-3.62	.164	4.62		
	.75	.601	-.366	-2.85	.193	5.54		
	.90	.664	-.282	-2.24	.223	6.32		
Panel B	$\bar{P}$	.486	-.465	-4.23	.170	5.22		
$\theta = 1.7$	$\hat{\sigma}(P)$	.219	.133	2.14	.043	2.87		
	.10	.200	-.658	-6.40	.126	2.58		
	.25	.334	-.540	-4.99	.142	3.38		
	.50	.504	-.449	-3.82	.164	4.77		
	.75	.625	-.378	-2.88	.193	6.17		
	.90	.754	-.310	-2.28	.228	7.87		
Panel C	$\bar{P}$	.466	-.519	-3.04	.149	3.03	.043	.59
$\theta = 2.0$	$\hat{\sigma}(P)$	.188	.190	1.06	.057	1.37	.081	1.11
	.10	.218	-.783	-4.38	.083	1.43	-.055	-.81
	.25	.342	-.642	-3.61	.113	2.07	-.016	-.22
	.50	.505	-.499	-2.92	.149	2.93	.045	.62
	.75	.606	-.371	-2.34	.183	3.85	.098	1.34
	.90	.677	-.288	-1.79	.215	4.95	.132	1.86
Panel D	$\bar{P}$	.493	-.522	-3.32	.150	3.55	.041	.58
$\theta = 1.7$	$\hat{\sigma}(P)$	.226	.184	1.58	.073	2.60	.092	1.18
	.10	.190	-.763	-4.87	.075	1.02	-.063	-.84
	.25	.356	-.623	-3.97	.122	1.98	-.014	-.19
	.50	.517	-.504	-2.93	.152	3.12	.043	.52
	.75	.657	-.383	-2.43	.183	4.79	.091	1.16
	.90	.772	-.306	-1.82	.225	6.13	.155	1.92

* The regression model is $\Delta D_t = \hat{\beta}_1 D_{t-1} + \hat{\beta}_2 E_t + \hat{\beta}_3 E_{t-1} + \hat{u}_t$. In the data generating process the values of the coefficients are $\beta_1 = -.45$, $\beta_2 = .15$, and $\beta_3 = .018$.

tion fit to the data is (4) but with the constant suppressed. The cross-sectional distributions of $\hat{\rho}$, the first order autocorrelation of the estimated regression residuals, are presented in Table 9. The results for the Compustat firm data in column (1) are from Panel D Table 2.

It seems safe to conclude that positive autocorrelation of order $\rho = .2$ or greater is not a general phenomenon for the Compustat firms. In the simula-

TABLE 9. Cross-sectional distributions of first order autocorrelation coefficients for Compustat firms and for simulations*

	Compustat Firms	Simulations† $\rho = 0$	$\rho = -.2$	$\rho = .2$
	(1)	(2)	(3)	(4)
$\bar{\rho}$	−.067	−.057	−.174	.061
$\sigma(\hat{\rho})$	.234	.189	.179	.197
.10	−.356	−.297	−.388	−.197
.25	−.230	−.188	−.313	−.080
.50	−.058	−.066	−.183	.064
.75	.101	.076	−.060	.208
.90	.218	.181	.063	.289

* The regression model is

$$\Delta D_t = \hat{\beta}_1 D_{t-1} + \hat{\beta}_2 E_t + \hat{u}_t .$$

Data for the simulations are generated by

$$\Delta D_t = -.45 D_{t-1} + .15 E_t + u_t \quad u_t = \rho u_{t-1} + v_t$$
$$E_t = E_{t-1} + e_t ; \quad e_t \text{ and } v_t \text{ serially independent and normal.}$$

† In the *absence* of the lagged variable problem, the estimated autocorrelation of the residuals would have bias of order approximately $-1/N$ (Cf. [8] or [20]), which in samples of size 20 is about −.05. If the mean values of $\hat{\rho}$ for $\rho = -.2$, (−.174), and for $\rho = .2$, (.061), are corrected for bias, they will be close in absolute value. If the mean of $\hat{\rho}$ for $\rho = 0$ were likewise corrected, it would be close to 0.

---

tions, the mean and fractiles of the distribution of $\hat{\rho}$ obtained when $\rho = .2$ are much larger than for the firm data in column (1). In fact the cross-sectional distribution of $\hat{\rho}$ for the firms seems to be somewhere between those for $\rho = 0$ and $\rho = -.2$ in the simulations, and indeed somewhat closer to that for $\rho = 0$ in the simulations than for $\rho = -.2$.

Comparisons of cross-sectional distributions of $\hat{\rho}$ have been carried out for stable $\theta = 1.7$ models as well as for normal models. They have also been carried out for lagged variable dividend equations of the form of (6). The results support completely the conclusions drawn here.

On balance the comparisons of $\hat{\rho}$ for the simulations and the firm data seem to support the following conclusions concerning the magnitude of the autocorrelations in the disturbances for the dividend models fit to the firm data. When autocorrelations for firms are nonzero, they will generally be negative and somewhere between 0 and −.2. More important, strong positive *or* negative serial dependence in the disturbances of the dividend models fit to the firm data is certainly not a general phenomenon.

f. Speed of Adjustment Coefficients, Target Payout
Ratios, and the Rate of Growth of Earnings

Simulations can provide valuable evidence on properties of the estimates of three parameters of economic interest in the various dividend models: the speed-of-adjustment coefficient c, the target payout ratio r, and the rate of growth of earnings λ. Table 10 summarizes the cross-sectional distributions of $\hat{c}$, $\hat{r}$, and $\hat{\lambda}$ for different simulation models and provides the mean square error (M.S.E.) for each of the distributions. The table allows us to examine the distributions of these parameters both in cases where the regression equation fit to the data is of the same form as the model generating the data and in cases where the regression model is misspecified in some way. Except for column (15), Table 10 concentrates entirely on normal models. The results for the corresponding stable $\theta = 1.7$ models are again almost identical. Table 11 presents distributions of the three parameters obtained from the Compustat firm data.

The simulation data used to obtain the distributions of the speed-of-adjustment coefficient $\hat{c}$ and the target payout ratio $\hat{r}$ in columns (1) and (8) of Table 10 were generated by the two variable model (11) and (12) with serially independent disturbances and no earnings trend. The regression equation fit to the data is also the two variable Lintner model with the constant suppressed, so that the data-generating process and the regression equation have the same form. The M.S.E. for the distribution of $\hat{c}$ is .0228 with .0210 due to the variance of the estimates and .0018 due to bias. The M.S.E. for the distribution of $\hat{r}$ is .0069 but all of it is due to variance since the bias is essentially o. The absence of bias in the estimates of r is interesting. Malinvaud [13] shows that the estimates of β_1 and β_2 in (15) are negatively correlated. But it is nevertheless surprising that this apparently causes the ratio of the coefficients to provide an unbiased estimate of the target payout ratio, in spite of the fact that both of the coefficients are themselves biased.

In the model of columns (2) and (9) of Table 10 the data generating process (and in fact the data themselves) are the same as in column (1), but the regression equation is the two variable Lintner model with the constant. Including the constant when this is inappropriate causes the dispersion in the distributions of $\hat{c}$ and $\hat{r}$ to increase. The bias of $\hat{c}$ is also increased and bias is now apparently also present in the estimates of r. The net effect is an increase in the M.S.E. of both coefficients. Similar results, at least with respect to the dispersion of $\hat{c}$ and $\hat{r}$, are also observed in the firm data of Table 11; suppressing the constant leads to substantial reductions in dispersion.

Next we consider the effects of autocorrelation in the disturbances on the

TABLE 10. Cross-sectional distributions of speed-of-adjustment coefficients (ĉ), target payout ratios (r̂), and the rate of growth of earnings (λ̂)*

Model of	Speed of Adjustment Coefficient (ĉ)							Target Payout Ratios (r̂)						Rate of Growth (λ̂)	
	(1) Panel A Table 4	(2) Panel C Table 4	(3) Panel A Table 5	(4) Panel A Table 7	(5) Panel A Table 8	(6) Panel C Table 8	(7)	(8) Panel A Table 4	(9) Panel C Table 4	(10) Panel A Table 7	(11) Panel A Table 8	(12) Panel C Table 8	(13)	(14) Panel C Table 8	(15) Panel D Table 8
$\bar{P}$	.493	.533	.513	.543	.456	.519	.543	.337	.316	.308	.384	.329	.324	.044	-5.593
$\hat{\sigma}(P)$	.145	.157	.146	.203	.134	.190	.152	.083	.112	.214	.089	.183	.062	18.119	58.650
.10	.317	.359	.352	.310	.282	.288	.360	.255	.197	.136	.324	.159	.257	-.193	-.294
.25	.392	.423	.427	.383	.366	.371	.433	.299	.267	.196	.350	.208	.298	-.080	-.093
.50	.471	.512	.496	.516	.442	.499	.526	.334	.322	.261	.369	.284	.326	.269	.165
.75	.598	.625	.604	.674	.540	.642	.626	.364	.373	.377	.397	.423	.350	1.106	.824
.90	.704	.727	.698	.827	.642	.783	.765	.419	.427	.521	.444	.567	.386	2.480	2.840
$\hat{\sigma}^2(P)$	.0210	.0246	.0213	.0412	.0180	.0361	.0231	.0069	.0125	.0458	.0079	.0335	.0038	328.2981	3439.8225
$(\bar{P}-P)^2$	.0018	.0069	.0040	.0086	.0000	.0048	.0086	.0000	.0002	.0005	.0029	.0000	.0000	.0031	32.4102
M.S.E.	.0228	.0315	.0253	.0498	.0180	.0409	.0317	.0069	.0127	.0463	.0108	.0335	.0038	328.3012	3472.2327

* For all columns except (5), (6), (11), (12), (14) and (15) the dividend generating process is

(11) $\Delta D_t = -.45 D_{t-1} + .15 E_t + u_t$;　(12) $E_t = (1+\lambda) E_{t-1} + e_t$;　(17) $u_t = \rho u_{t-1} + v_t$.

For columns (5), (6), (11), (12), (14) and (15) the process is (12) and (17) plus

(18) $\Delta D_t = -.45 D_{t-1} + .15 E_t + .0183 E_{t-1} + u_t$.

In the models of columns (3), (5), (6), (11), (12), (14) and (15), $\lambda = .1$ in (12), while for all others $\lambda = 0$. The first order coefficient $\rho = 0$ in (17) for all columns except (7) and (13) and for these $\rho = -.2$.

The regression equation fit to the data is $\Delta D_t = \hat{\alpha} + \hat{\beta}_1 D_{t-1} + \hat{\beta}_2 E_t + \hat{u}_t$ for columns (1), (2), (3), (5), (7), (8), (9), (11), (13) with $\hat{\alpha}$ constrained to be 0 for all columns except (2) and (9). For the models of columns (4), (6), (10), (12), (14) and (15) the regression equation is

$$\Delta D_t = \hat{\beta}_1 D_{t-1} + \hat{\beta}_2 E_t + \hat{\beta}_3 E_{t-1} + \hat{u}_t.$$

distributions of $\hat{c}$ and $\hat{r}$. In the model of columns (7) and (13) of Table 10 the dividend generating process is the same as that used in obtaining columns (1) and (8) except that the disturbances follow a first order process with $\rho = -.2$. The regression equation fit to the data is the two variable model with the constant suppressed, the same as in columns (1) and (8). Autocorrelation in the disturbances has about the same effect on the speed of adjustment coefficient $\hat{c}$ as including the constant in the estimating equations when this is inappropriate; the distributions of $\hat{c}$ in columns (2) and (7) are very similar in terms of bias and dispersion, both of which are slightly higher than for the correctly specified regression equation of column (1). For the target payout ratio $\hat{r}$, however, things are much different. Autocorrelation in the disturbances in the form of a first order process with $\rho = -.2$ apparently *improves* the estimates of r. In column (13) Table 10 the mean value $\hat{\bar{r}} = .324$ is close to the true value $r = .333$, and the dispersion in the distribution of $\hat{r}$ is lower than for any other model. The M.S.E. of $\hat{r}$ is .0038 versus .0069 in column (8) for the same model without serial correlation.

Table 10 also shows the effects of misspecification of the lag structure on the distributions of the estimates of $\hat{c}$ and $\hat{r}$. Consider first the case where the dividend data are generated by the two-variable model (11) with no trend in earnings or autocorrelated disturbances, but a three-variable regression equation, including the "unnecessary" lagged earnings variable E_{t-1}, is fit to the data. The resulting distributions of $\hat{c}$ and $\hat{r}$ are in columns (4) and (10) of Table 10. The M.S.E.'s of both $\hat{c}$ and $\hat{r}$ are substantially higher than those of any other model. Thus, including the lagged earnings variable in the regression model when this is inappropriate leads to problems in estimating the coefficients c and r.

Suppose now the dividend generating process includes the lagged earnings variable E_{t-1} directly and this variable is also included in the estimating equation. The distributions of $\hat{c}$ and $\hat{r}$ obtained in this case are in columns (6) and (12) of Table 10. Though the estimating equation includes exactly the same variables as the equation generating the data, the M.S.E.'s of the distributions of $\hat{c}$ and $\hat{r}$ are high relative to those of other models, and this is primarily a result of the high degree of dispersion in these distributions. The high dispersion relative to two-variable models can be traced directly to increased multicollinearity between the variables in the estimating equation when E_{t-1} is included. For example, for the model without the lagged earnings variable summarized in Panel A Table 4, the average values of $t(\hat{\beta}_1)$ and $t(\hat{\beta}_2)$ are -3.91 and 4.29 respectively. For the corresponding model with the lagged earnings variable, summarized in Panel A Table 7, the average values of $t(\hat{\beta}_1)$ and $t(\hat{\beta}_2)$ are -2.95 and 2.85 respectively.

In fact, at least in these simulations, better estimates (in terms of M.S.E.) of c and r are obtained by omitting E_{t-1} from the estimating equation, even though the dividend generating process involves this variable. In column (5) Table 10 the distribution of $\hat{c}$ has smaller bias, variance, and M.S.E. than the distribution for the "correct" three-variable estimating equation in column (6). The corresponding distribution of $\hat{r}$ for the two-variable estimating equation in column (11) shows estimates with higher bias than those obtained with the three-variable equation in column (12), but the low variance obtained with the two-variable model more than offsets the increased bias: the M.S.E. of the distribution of $\hat{r}$ for the two-variable model is less than one-third that of the three-variable model. These results suggest that perhaps in the firm data the two-variable dividend model, involving D_{t-1} and E_t, should sometimes be used to estimate the parameters c and r even though one may suspect that the generating process also involves the lagged earnings variable E_{t-1}. This anomalous conclusion, however, results from the high degree of multicollinearity between successive values of E that was incorporated into the simulations. In a study concerned with precise estimation of c and r for the firm data, one would want to check the degree of multicollinearity. Certainly an optimal procedure would be contingent on the observed levels of dependence.

Finally, columns (14) and (15) of Table 10 present the cross-sectional distributions of the rate of growth of earnings $\hat{\lambda}$ obtained when the dividend data are generated according to the three variable model (16) and the three variable equation (15) is fit to the data. The estimated values of $\hat{\lambda}$ are given by $\hat{\lambda} = -\hat{\beta}_1 \hat{\beta}_3 / \hat{\beta}_2 (1 + \hat{\beta}_1)$, and the true value is $\lambda = .1$. In the model of column (14) the disturbances in (16) are normal, while in the model of column (15) they are stable $\theta = 1.7$. We conclude immediately that the regression model does not provide meaningful estimates of $\hat{\lambda}$. Apparently the complicated function of random variables (the $\hat{\beta}$'s) used to estimate λ produces a sampling distribution which provides very little information about the rate of growth parameter. This conclusion is also supported by the distribution of $\hat{\lambda}$ obtained for the Compustat firm data in column (8) Table 11.

6. PREDICTIONS OF 1965 DIVIDENDS

In this section we examine the results obtained when various dividend models are used to predict the changes in dividends per share paid by indi-

TABLE 11. Cross-sectional distributions of the speed-of-adjustment coefficient ($\hat{c}$), the target payout ratio ($\hat{r}$) and the rate of growth of earnings ($\hat{\lambda}$) for the 392 Compustat firms*

Model	$\Delta D_t = \hat{\alpha} + \hat{\beta}_1 D_{t-1}$ $+ \hat{\beta}_2 E_t + \hat{u}_t$		$\Delta D_t = \hat{\beta}_1 D_{t-1}$ $+ \hat{\beta}_2 E_t + \hat{u}_t$		$\Delta D_t = \hat{\beta}_1 D_{t-1} + \hat{\beta}_2 E_t$ $+ \hat{\beta}_3 E_{t-1} + \hat{u}_t$		
(1)	(2)	(3)	(4)	(5)	(6)	(7)	(8)
P	$\hat{c}$	$\hat{r}$	$\hat{c}$	$\hat{r}$	$\hat{c}$	$\hat{r}$	$\hat{\lambda}$
$\bar{P}$	.366	.816	.317	.604	.339	.404	.147
$\hat{\sigma}$ (P)	.386	5.044	.351	.445	.300	2.941	10.522
.10	.127	.157	.110	.369	.102	.081	−.163
.25	.201	.337	.182	.476	.179	.248	−.056
.50	.303	.509	.280	.574	.299	.440	.059
.75	.490	.683	.415	.660	.443	.719	.402
.90	.664	.974	.537	.774	.610	1.159	1.558

* $\hat{c} = -\hat{\beta}_1, \hat{r} = -\hat{\beta}_2/\hat{\beta}_1$, and $\hat{\lambda} = -(\hat{\beta}_1\hat{\beta}_3)/[\hat{\beta}_2(1+\hat{\beta}_1)]$. The fact that $\hat{r}$ and $\hat{\lambda}$ involve products and ratios of the regression coefficients (which are themselves random variables) seems to destroy the value of the mean and standard deviation as measures of location and dispersion for the distributions of $\hat{r}$ and $\hat{\lambda}$.

---

vidual firms during 1965. Let $\hat{D}_{i,65}$ be the predicted and $D_{i,65}$ the actual dividend for firm i for 1965. The raw prediction error is then

$$\hat{u}_{i,65} = (\hat{D}_{i,65} - D_{i,64}) - (D_{i,65} - D_{i,64})$$

$$= \hat{D}_{i,65} - D_{i,65}.$$

The dispersion of the distribution of $\hat{u}$ for any given dividend model will vary from firm to firm. To construct meaningful cross-sectional distributions of prediction errors, it is necessary to "standardize" the units used in measuring the errors. We therefore define the standardized prediction error

$$\varepsilon_i = \frac{\hat{u}_{i,65}}{M_i}$$

In half the tests $M_i = \hat{\sigma}(\Delta D_i)$, the standard deviation of the dividend changes of firm i over the period 1946–64, while in the other half $M_i = IQ(\Delta D_i)$, the interquartile range of the annual dividend changes.

The five "naive" models (N1–N5) and nine regression models (R1–R9) used to make dividend predictions for 1965 are presented in Table 12. The coefficient estimates for R_1–R_3 are from the regressions used in constructing Panels A, C, and D of Table 2. The coefficients for R_5 and R_6 are from the regressions used in constructing Panels B and D of Table 3. For each firm R_7 is that model of the models R_1–R_6 which had the highest multiple R^2 in the regression analyses. Thus, the actual model used for R_7 differs from firm to firm. Similarly, for each firm R_8 is the "best" of R_1, R_2, and R_5, the regression models which include a constant, while R_9 is the "best" of R_3, R_4, and R_6, the models in which the constant is suppressed. For each of the models Table 13 provides the number of firms (N) for which a forecast of 1965 dividends was made, the average absolute value of the standardized prediction errors ($\sum_{i=1}^{N} |\varepsilon_i| / N$), the mean square prediction error ($\sum_{i=1}^{N} \varepsilon_i^2 / N$), the average ($\bar{\varepsilon}$), squared average ($\bar{\varepsilon}^2$), standard deviation $\hat{\sigma}(\varepsilon)$, variance $\hat{\sigma}^2(\varepsilon)$, interquartile range $IQ(\varepsilon)$, and inter-decile range $ID(\varepsilon)$ of the errors, along with five fractiles of the cross-sectional distribution of ε.

How do these prediction tests compare to the earlier results concerning the "best" dividend models? Table 13 includes results for four criteria (average absolute error, mean square error, and the interquartile and interdecile ranges) for judging the predictive power of the various dividend models. For each criterion two versions of the standardized prediction error are used, making a total of eight summary comparisons of the models. If for the moment we exclude the summary models R_7–R_9, in five of these comparisons the regression model R_6 produces the minimum value of the test criterion, and R_6 ranks no lower than fourth in the remaining three comparisons. In the regressions on the firm data the best model, in terms of average R^2, was R_5, the model with the constant and lagged earnings variable. In the predictions R_6, the same lagged earnings model *but with the constant suppressed,* is best.

This negative result with respect to the importance of the constant term is supported by the forecasting tests for the other regression models. R_3 (the Lintner model with the constant suppressed) outperforms R_1 (the same model with the constant) in six out of eight of the summary comparisons of distributions of prediction errors. The constant-suppressed model R_4 outperforms R_2 in every comparison. These results confirm the earlier conclusions drawn from the simulations (which were concerned with models R_1, R_3, R_5 and R_6). In the simulations, including the constant term in the regression models led to a slight increase in R^2, though the data generating process did not involve the constant.

The evidence uniformly suggests that, for a majority of firms, models with the constant suppressed provide better predictions of dividend changes than

TABLE 12. Descriptions of dividend prediction models

NAIVE MODELS

Model	Description	Predicted 1965 Dividend Change $(\hat{D}_{i,65} - D_{i,64})$ Equals	Exceptions
N1	No change	0	—
N2	Same dollar change	$D_{i,64} - D_{i,63}$	If $\hat{D}_{i,65} < 0$, let $\hat{D}_{i,65} = 0$
N3	Average dollar change	$\dfrac{D_{i,64} - D_{i,46}}{18}$	If $\hat{D}_{i,65} < 0$, let $\hat{D}_{i,65} = 0$
N4	Average rate of growth	$D_{i,64}(e^r - 1); r = \dfrac{\log D_{i,64} - \log D_{i,46}}{18}$	If $D_{i,46} = 0$, the first positive dividend is used in the numerator and the denominator is correspondingly reduced
N5	Same percentage change	$D_{i,64}\left(\dfrac{D_{i,64}}{D_{i,63}} - 1\right)$	If $D_{i,63} = 0$ and $D_{i,64} > 0$, no prediction is made. If $D_{i,63} = 0$ and $D_{i,64} = 0$, let $\hat{D}_{i,65} = 0$

REGRESSION MODELS

Model	Predicted 1965 Dividend Change $(\hat{D}_{i,65} - D_{i,64})$ Equals
R1	$\hat{\alpha}_i + \hat{\beta}_{1i} D_{i,64} + \hat{\beta}_{2i} E_{i,65}$
R2	$\hat{\alpha}_i + \hat{\beta}_{1i} D_{i,64} + \hat{\beta}_{2i} E_{i,65} + \hat{\beta}_{3i} A_{i,65}$
R3	$\hat{\beta}_{1i} D_{i,64} + \hat{\beta}_{2i} E_{i,65}$
R4	$\hat{\beta}_{1i} D_{i,64} + \hat{\beta}_{2i} E_{i,65} + \hat{\beta}_{3i} A_{i,65}$
R5	$\hat{\alpha}_i + \hat{\beta}_{1i} D_{i,64} + \hat{\beta}_{2i} E_{i,65} + \hat{\beta}_{3i} E_{i,64}$
R6	$\hat{\beta}_{1i} D_{i,64} + \hat{\beta}_{2i} E_{i,65} + \hat{\beta}_{3i} E_{i,64}$
R7	Best of R1–R6 for each individual firm.
R8	Best of R1, R2 or R5 (i.e., with constants)
R9	Best of R3, R4 or R6 (i.e., without constants)

models in which the value of the constant is left completely free. But from a Bayesian viewpoint, our treatment of the constant throughout the paper has considered only the extreme cases of diffuse and dogmatic prior beliefs. If we had chosen the Bayesian route, we would have been forced to admit that our *a priori* feelings concerning the constant would have been summarized by a distribution closely but not completely concentrated about zero. Imposing such a prior distribution on the data would guarantee that the posterior distribution of the constant was also closely concentrated about zero. Since it would rule

TABLE 13. Cross-sectional distributions of 1965 prediction errors for naive models (N) and various "good fitting" regression models (R)

(1) Model	(2) N	(3) $\bar{\varepsilon}$	(4) $\frac{\Sigma|\varepsilon_i|}{N}$	(5) $\frac{\Sigma\varepsilon_i^2}{N}$	(6) $\hat{\sigma}^2(\varepsilon)$	(7) $\bar{\varepsilon}^2$	(8) $\hat{\sigma}(\varepsilon)$	(9) $IQ(\varepsilon)$	(10) $ID(\varepsilon)$	(11) .10	(12) .25	(13) Fractiles .50	(14) .75	(15) .90
Panel A														
Prediction error														
for firm i is di-														
vided by $\hat{\sigma}(\Delta D_i)$														
N1	369	-1.05	1.24	3.29	2.19	1.10	1.48	1.64	3.07	-3.04	-1.66	-.77	-.01	.03
N2	369	-.29	.94	2.20*	2.12	.08	1.45	1.17*	2.92	-1.87	-.89	-.07	.28	1.05
N3	369	-.68	1.07	2.44	1.98*	.46	1.41*	1.40	3.04	-2.52	-1.24	-.47	.15	.52
N4	369	-.26	1.06	2.29	2.22	.07	1.49	1.49	3.21	-2.00	-1.01	-.18	.47	1.21
N5	366	-.08	1.06	3.01	3.00	.01	1.73	1.31	3.32	-1.75	-.85	-.02	.46	1.57
R1	369	-.10	.93	3.64	3.63	.01	1.90	1.21	2.62	-1.38	-.60	.03	.61	1.24
R2	369	-.10	1.02	3.56	3.55	.01	1.88	1.35	2.83	-1.50	-.67	.07	.68	1.33
R3	369	-.06	.90	3.32	3.32	.00	1.82	1.25	2.54	-1.34	-.57	.08	.67	1.20
R4	369	-.01*	.96	3.04	3.04	.00	1.74	1.27	2.70	-1.47	-.54	.19	.73	1.23
R5	369	-.04*	.92	2.80	2.80	.00	1.67	1.21	2.59	-1.34	-.55	.05	.66	1.25
R6	369	-.02	.88*	2.36	2.36	.00	1.54	1.24	2.50*	-1.31	-.56	.10	.68	1.19
R7	369	-.05	.99	3.48	3.48	.00	1.87	1.23	2.72	-1.38	-.57	.10	.66	1.34
R8	369	-.06	.99	3.48	3.48	.00	1.87	1.27	2.72	-1.38	-.59	.10	.68	1.34
R9	369	.01*	.93	2.94	2.94	.00	1.72	1.25	2.64	-1.36	-.52	.11	.73	1.28
Panel B														
Prediction error														
for firm i is di-														
vided by $IQ(\Delta D_i)$														
N1	361	-1.06	1.28	4.77	3.65	1.12	1.91	1.54	2.79	-2.76	-1.57	-.72	-.02	.03
N2	361	-.31	1.00	3.72	3.62	.10	1.90	1.16	2.64	-1.80	-.87	-.07	.29	.84
N3	361	-.72	1.13	3.87	3.36	.51	1.83	1.37	2.81	-2.32	-1.20	-.46	.17	.49
N4	361	-.36	1.10	3.45	3.32	.13	1.82	1.47	3.18	-2.04	-.97	-.19	.51	1.14
N5	359	.05	1.28	12.88	12.88	.00	3.59	1.25	2.96	-1.61	-.81	-.03	.45	1.35
R1	361	.07	1.00	3.14	3.13	.01	1.77	1.09*	2.81	-1.36	-.51	.06	.58	1.45
R2	361	.04*	1.06	3.23	3.23	.00	1.80	1.32	2.67	-1.31	-.63	.10	.69	1.36
R3	361	.14	.96	2.82	2.80	.02	1.67	1.14	2.55	-1.18	-.52	.10	.61	1.37
R4	361	.19	1.03	3.17	3.13	.04	1.77	1.15	2.51	-1.21	-.47	.18	.69	1.30
R5	361	.10	.99	2.75	2.74	.01	1.66	1.14	2.65	-1.17	-.51	.06	.63	1.48
R6	361	.14	.93*	2.32*	2.30*	.02	1.52*	1.15	2.49	-1.08	-.49	.11	.66	1.41
R7	361	.08	1.03	2.85	2.84	.01	1.69	1.27	2.70	-1.24	-.58	.13	.69	1.46
R8	361	.07	1.03	2.83	2.82	.01	1.68	1.30	2.70	-1.24	-.58	.13	.72	1.46
R9	361	.17	.95	2.36	2.33	.03	1.53	1.14	2.47*	-1.11	-.44	.12	.69	1.35

*Minimum value for column and panel.

Note: In the annual date for 1946–64 the total number of firms was 392. During 1965, 23 of these firms "disappeared" from the Compustat tapes. No predictions were made for these firms. In addition, for 8 of the remaining firms $IQ(\Delta D_i) = 0$; that is, each of these firms changed dividends per share less than 9 times during the period 1946–64.

out wild values of the estimated constant, this approach could lead to even better predictions of dividend changes than simply suppressing the constant.

The prediction tests also confirm the earlier conclusions with respect to the relevant measure of earnings to be used in dividend model. Following the suggestions of Brittain [2, 3], $R2$ and $R4$ contain both net income and depreciation as explanatory variables; following Lintner [11], $R1$ and $R3$ contain only net income. For six of eight of the summary measures of prediction error, model $R1$ is better than $R2$, and $R3$ outperforms $R4$ in seven of eight comparisons. Thus, for most firms the depreciation variable adds little to the prediction of dividends.

Can predictions of dividend changes be improved by using the model that has the highest R^2 for each firm? The results for models $R7$–$R9$ in Table 13 indicate that the answer is negative. $R9$ produces the minimum prediction error in column (10) Panel B, but in the remaining seven tests models $R7$–$R9$ are dominated by one of the other models (usually $R6$).

In most of the tests the naive model $N2$ (same dollar change) performs well relative to the various regression models. When testing many naive models, however, one is likely to find by chance alone at least one that performs well. The reason for the good performance of $N2$ is easy to find. For the Compustat firms the average change in net income from 1964–65 was very close to the change from 1963–64. $N2$ would not perform so well in years when this was not the case.

Finally, the four summary measures (average absolute error, mean square error, and the interquartile and interdecile ranges) of the distributions of prediction errors are certainly not of equal value. The primary concern here is determining which of the various dividend models works best for a large majority of firms; it is unreasonable to expect that any given model will be appropriate for all firms. If a model works well for most firms but is completely inappropriate for a few firms, this is the best we can expect. We certainly do not want to give heaviest weight to the prediction errors of the few firms for which the model examined is completely inappropriate. But since these firms are likely to have the largest prediction errors, the mean square error criterion gives them heaviest weight. For our purposes the interquartile and interdecile ranges provide a more representative picture of the cross-sectional distributions of prediction errors produced by each model, but these also have their shortcomings. Any interfractile range criterion puts heavy weight on just two points of the distribution. The average absolute error criterion provides a much more even weighting of individual prediction errors than either mean square error or interfractile ranges.

The rankings of the models (excluding the summary models $R7$–$R9$) by size of average absolute error are as follows.

Rank	1	2	3	4	5	6	7	8	9	10	11
$M_i = \hat{\sigma}(\Delta D_i)$	R6	R3	R5	R1	N2	R4	R2	N4	N5	N3	N1
$M_i = IQ(\Delta D_i)$	R6	R3	R5	R1	N2	R4	R2	N4	N3	N5	N1

It is clear that for this criterion the rankings of the various models do not depend much on whether the prediction errors are measured in units of standard deviation of dividend changes or in units of the interquartile ranges.

7. CONCLUSIONS

The regressions on the firm data, the simulations, and the prediction tests provide consistent evidence on dividend models for individual firms. The two variable Lintner model (4), including a constant term, D_{t-1}, and E_t, performs well relative to other models; in general, however, deleting the constant and adding the lagged profits variable E_{t-1} leads to a slight improvement in the predictive power of the model. In applying dividend models to the data of most firms, net income seems to provide a better measure of profits than either cash flow or net income and depreciation included as separate variables in the model. Finally, in the models tested here, serial dependence in the disturbances does not seem to be a serious problem.

REFERENCES

[1] Barnard, G. A., Jenkins, G. M., and Winsten, C. B., "Likelihood Inference and Time Series," *Journal of the Royal Statistical Society,* Series A (General), Vol. 125 (1962), 321–72.

[2] Brittain, John A., *Corporate Dividend Policy* (Washington: The Brookings Institution, 1966).

[3] Brittain, John A., "The Tax Structure and Corporate Dividend Policy," *American Economic Review* (May, 1964), 272–87.

[4] Fama, Eugene F., "The Behavior of Stock Market Prices," *Journal of Business* (January, 1965), 34–105.

[5] Fama, Eugene F., and Roll, Richard, "Some Properties of Symmetric Stable Distributions," *Journal of the American Statistical Association* (September, 1968).

[6] Goldberger, Arthur S., *Econometric Theory* (New York: John Wiley and Sons, 1964).

[7] Griliches, Zvi, "Distributed Lags: A Survey", *Econometrica* (January, 1967), 16–49.

[8] Kendall, M. G., "Note on Bias in the Estimation of Autocorrelation," *Biometrika* (1954), 403–04.

[9] Koyck, L. M., *Distributed Lags and Investment Analysis* (Amsterdam: North Holland Publishing Co., 1954).

[10] Lintner, John, "The Determinants of Corporate Saving," in *Savings in the Modern Economy*, edited by W. W. Heller (Minneapolis: University of Minnesota Press, 1963), 230–55.

[11] Lintner, John, "Distribution of Incomes of Corporations among Dividends, Retained Earnings and Taxes," *American Economic Review* (May, 1956), 97–113.

[12] Malinvaud, Edmond, "Estimation et Prévision dans les Modèles Économiques Autoregressifs," *Revue de l'Institut International de Statistique* Vol. 29, No. 2 (1961), 1–32.

[13] Malinvaud, Edmond, *Statistical Methods of Econometrics* (Amsterdam: North Holland Publishing Co., 1966), Chs. 13–15.

[14] Mandelbrot, Benoit, "The Variation of Certain Speculative Prices," *Journal of Business* (October, 1963), 394–419.

[15] Miller, Merton H., and Modigliani, Franco, "Dividend Policy, Growth and the Valuation of Shares," *Journal of Business* (October, 1961), 411–33.

[16] Nerlove, Marc, *Distributed Lags and Demand Analysis* (Washington: U.S.D.A. Agriculture Handbook No. 141, 1958).

[17] Roll, Richard, "The Efficient Market Model Applied to U. S. Treasury Bill Rates," unpublished Ph.D. thesis, Graduate School of Business, University of Chicago, March, 1968.

[18] Thornber, Hodson, "Finite Sample Monte Carlo Studies: An Autoregressive Illustration," *Journal of the American Statistical Association* (September, 1967), 801–18.

[19] Waud, Roger N., "Small Sample Bias Due to Misspecification in the 'Partial Adjustment' and 'Adaptive Expectations' Models," *Journal of the American Statistical Association* (December, 1966), 1130–52.

[20] White, John S., "Asymptotic Expansions for the Mean and Variance of the Serial Correlation Coefficient," *Biometrika* (1961), 85–94.

[21] Wise, John, "Linear Estimators for Linear Regression Systems Having Infinite Residual Variances," unpublished paper presented to the Berkeley-Stanford Mathematical Economics Seminar (October, 1963).

[22] Zellner, Arnold, and Tiao, George C., "Bayesian Analysis of the Regression Model with Autocorrelated Errors," *Journal of the American Statistical Association* (September, 1964), 763–78.

DISAPPEARING DIVIDENDS

CHANGING FIRM CHARACTERISTICS OR

LOWER PROPENSITY TO PAY?

. . .

Eugene F. Fama and Kenneth R. French

1. INTRODUCTION

Dividends have long been an enigma. Since they are taxed at a higher rate than capital gains, the common presumption is that dividends are less valuable than capital gains. In this view, firms that pay dividends are at a competitive disadvantage since they have a higher cost of equity than firms that do not pay. The fact that many firms pay dividends is then difficult to explain.

Using CRSP and Compustat, we study the incidence of dividend payers during the 1926–99 period, with special interest in the period after 1972, when the data cover NYSE, AMEX, and NASDAQ firms. The percent of firms paying dividends declines sharply after 1978. In 1973, 52.8% of publicly traded non-financial non-utility firms pay dividends. The proportion of payers rises to a peak of 66.5% in 1978. It then falls rather relentlessly. In 1999, only 20.8% of firms pay dividends.

The decline after 1978 in the percent of firms paying dividends raises three questions. (i) What are the characteristics of dividend payers? (ii) Is the decline in the percent of payers due to a decline in the prevalence of these characteristics among publicly traded firms, or (iii) have firms with the characteristics typical of dividend payers become less likely to pay? We address these questions.

We use logit regressions and summary statistics to examine the characteristics of dividend payers. Both approaches suggest that three characteristics

Reprinted with permission from the *Journal of Financial Economics* 60, no. 1 (April 2001): 3–43. © 2001 by Elsevier Limited.

We acknowledge the comments of John Graham, Douglas Hannah, Anil Kashyap, Tobias Moskowitz, G. William Schwert (the editor), Andrei Shleifer, Janice Willett, Paul Zarowin, and seminar participants at Harvard University, the University of Chicago, the National Bureau of Economic Research, the University of Rochester, and Virginia Polytechnical Institute. The referees, Harry DeAngelo and René Stulz, were particularly helpful.

affect the decision to pay dividends: profitability, investment opportunities, and size. Larger firms and more profitable firms are more likely to pay dividends. Dividends are less likely for firms with more investments.

The summary statistics provide details on the nature of dividend payers, former payers, and firms that have never paid. Former payers tend to be distressed. They have low earnings and few investments. Firms that have never paid dividends are more profitable than former payers and they have strong growth opportunities. Dividend payers are, in turn, more profitable than firms that have never paid. But firms that have never paid invest at a higher rate, do more R&D, and have a higher ratio of the market value of assets to their book value (V_t/A_t, a proxy for Tobin's Q) than dividend payers. The investments of dividend payers are on the order of pre-interest earnings, but the investments of firms that have never paid exceed earnings. Finally, payers are about 10 times as large as non-payers.

The decline after 1978 in the percent of firms paying dividends is due in part to an increasing tilt of publicly traded firms toward the characteristics of firms that have never paid—low earnings, strong investments, and small size. This tilt in the population of firms is driven by an explosion of newly listed firms, and by the changing nature of the new firms. The number of publicly traded non-financial non-utility firms grows from 3,638 in 1978 to 5,670 in 1997, before declining to 5,113 in 1999. Newly listed firms always tend to be small, with extraordinary investment opportunities (high asset growth rates and high V_t/A_t). What changes after 1978 is their profitability. Before 1978, new lists are more profitable than seasoned firms. In 1973–77, the earnings of new lists average a hefty 17.79% of book equity, versus 13.68% for all firms. The profitability of new lists falls throughout the next 20 years. The earnings of new lists in 1993–98 average 2.07% of book equity, versus 11.26% for all firms.

The decline in the profitability of new lists is accompanied by a decline in the percent of new lists that pay dividends. During 1973–77, one-third of newly listed firms pay dividends. In 1999, only 3.7% of new lists pay dividends. The surge in numbers and the changing nature of new lists produce a swelling group of small firms with low profitability but large investments that have never paid dividends. This group of firms is a big factor in the decline in the percent of firms paying dividends.

It is perhaps obvious that investors have become more willing to hold the shares of small, relatively unprofitable growth companies. But the resulting tilt of the publicly traded population toward such firms is only half of the story for the declining incidence of dividend payers. Our more striking finding is that firms have become less likely to pay dividends, whatever their characteristics. We characterize the decline in the likelihood that a firm pays dividends, given its characteristics, as a lower propensity to pay. What we mean is that the perceived benefits of dividends (whatever they are) have declined through time.

We use two approaches to quantify how characteristics and propensity to pay combine to produce the decline in the percent of dividend payers. One approach works with logit regressions. The other uses relative frequencies of payers in portfolios formed on profitability, investment opportunities, and size. Both approaches say that lower propensity to pay is at least as important as changing characteristics in explaining the decline in the percent of dividend payers.

Lower propensity to pay is quite general. For example, the percent of dividend payers among firms with positive earnings declines after 1978. But the percent of payers among firms with negative earnings also declines. Small firms become much less likely to pay dividends after 1978, but there is also a lower incidence of dividend payers among large firms. Firms with many investment opportunities become much less likely to pay dividends after 1978, but dividends also become less likely among firms with fewer investments.

The effects of changing characteristics and propensity to pay vary across dividend groups. The characteristics of dividend payers (large, profitable firms) do not change much after 1978, and controlling for characteristics, payers become only a bit more likely to stop paying. Changing characteristics and lower propensity to pay show up more clearly in the dividend decisions of former payers and firms that have never paid. For example, after 1978, lower profitability and abundant growth opportunities produce much lower expected rates of dividend initiation by firms that have never paid. But controlling for characteristics, firms that have never paid also initiate dividends at much lower rates after 1978, and former payers become much less likely to resume dividends.

Share repurchases jump in the 1980s, and it is interesting to examine the role of repurchases in the declining incidence of dividend payers. We show that because repurchases are largely the province of dividend payers, they leave the decline in the percent of payers largely unexplained. Instead, the primary effect of repurchases is to increase the already high earnings payouts of cash dividend payers.

Our story proceeds as follows. Section 2 presents the facts about dividends to be explained. Section 3 documents the characteristics of dividend payers and the progressive tilt of the population of publicly traded firms toward the characteristics of firms that have never paid. Section 4 presents qualitative evidence on the reduced propensity to pay dividends. Section 5 quantifies the effects of characteristics and propensity to pay. Section 6 examines share repurchases. Section 7 concludes.

2. TIME TRENDS IN CASH DIVIDENDS

Our goal is to explain the decline after 1978 in the incidence of dividend payers among NYSE, AMEX, and NASDAQ firms. We begin by examining the behavior of dividends for the longer 1926–99 period covered by CRSP. Fig. 1 shows the total number of non-financial non-utility firms on CRSP each year, and the number of firms that (i) pay cash dividends, (ii) do not pay, (iii) formerly paid, and (iv) have never paid. Fig. 2 shows percents of the total number of firms in the four dividend groups. We exclude utilities from the tests to avoid the criticism that their dividend decisions are a byproduct of regulation. We also exclude financial firms. The data to come on the characteristics of dividend

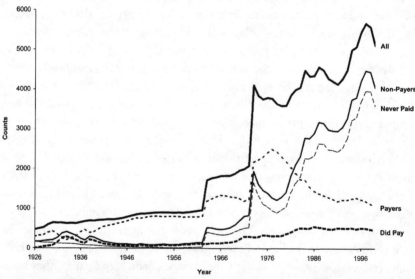

Figure 1. The number of CRSP firms in different dividend groups.
The CRSP sample includes NYSE, AMEX, and NASDAQ securities with share codes of 10 or 11. A firm must have market equity data (price and shares outstanding) for December of year t to be in the sample for that year. We exclude utilities (SIC codes 4900–4949) and financial firms (SIC codes 6000–6999). Payers pay dividends in year t; non-payers do not. The two subgroups of non-payers are firms that have never paid and former payers (firms that do not pay in year t but did pay in a previous year).

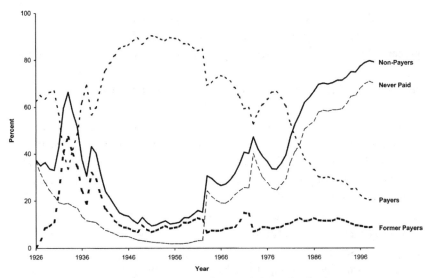

Figure 2. The percent of CRSP firms in different dividend groups.
The CRSP sample includes NYSE, AMEX, and NASDAQ securities with share codes
of 10 or 11. A firm must have market equity data (price and shares outstanding) for
December of year *t* to be in the sample for that year. We exclude utilities (SIC codes
4900–4949) and financial firms (SIC codes 6000–6999). Payers pay dividends in year *t*;
non-payers do not. The two subgroups of non-payers are firms that have never paid and
former payers (firms that do not pay in year *t* but did pay in a previous year).

payers are from Compustat, and Compustat's historical coverage of financial
firms is spotty. Until mid-1962, CRSP covers only NYSE firms. The jumps in
the total number of firms in 1963 and 1973 in Fig. 1 are due to the addition of
AMEX and then NASDAQ firms.

The proportion of NYSE non-financial non-utility firms paying dividends
falls by half during the early years of the Great Depression, from 66.9% in 1930
to 33.6% in 1933 (Fig. 2). Thereafter, the percent paying rises. In every year from
1943 to 1962, more than 82% of NYSE firms pay dividends. More than 90%
pay dividends in 1951 and 1952. With the addition of AMEX firms in 1963, the
proportion of payers drops to 69.3%. The addition of NASDAQ firms in 1973
lowers the proportion of payers to 52.8%, from 59.8% in 1972. It then rises to
66.5% in 1978, the peak for the post-1972 period of NYSE-AMEX-NASDAQ
coverage. The proportion paying declines sharply after 1978, to 30.3% for 1987.
It continues to decline thereafter, though less rapidly. In 1999, only 20.8% of
firms pay dividends.

Both the numerator (the number of dividend payers) and the denominator (the number of sample firms) contribute to the decline after 1978 in the percent of firms paying dividends. Swelling numbers of new listings cause the CRSP sample to expand by about 40%, from 3,638 firms in 1978 to 5,113 in 1999 (Fig. 1). New lists average 5.2% of listed firms (114 per year) during 1963–77, versus 9.6% (436 per year) for 1978–99 (Table 1).

More interesting, the population of dividend payers shrinks by more than 50% after 1978. There are 2,419 dividend payers in 1978 but only 1,182 in 1991 and 1,063 in 1999 (Fig. 1). The decline in the number of payers means that payers added to the sample fail to replace those lost. Dividend payers are lost when firms stop paying dividends or disappear from CRSP due to merger or delisting. Payers are added to the sample when former payers resume dividends, firms that have never paid initiate dividends, or new firms pay dividends in the year of listing.

Table 2 provides details on the change in the number of payers. The rate at which dividend payers are lost from the sample (due to dividend terminations, mergers, and delistings) rises from 6.8% per year for 1963–77 to 9.8% for 1978–99. Much of the increase is due to mergers. There is no clear trend in the rate at which dividend payers terminate dividends. During 1978–99, on average 5.0% of payers stop paying each year. This is higher than the termination rate for 1963–77, 3.5% per year, but it is lower than the rate for 1927–62, 5.4% per year. A relatively steady termination rate is consistent with the evidence in DeAngelo and DeAngelo (1990) and DeAngelo et al. (1992) that only distressed firms (with strongly negative earnings) terminate dividends. In contrast, during 1978–99, dividend payers merge into other firms at the rate of 3.9% per year. This is higher than the merger rates for 1927–62 (0.6% per year) and 1963–77 (2.7% per year). Dividend payers delist at the rate of 0.9% per year during 1978–99, versus 0.3% for 1927–62 and 0.8% for 1963–77.

Dividend payers disappear at a higher rate during 1978–98, but the more important factor in the decline in the number of payers is the failure of new payers to replace those that are lost. Former payers (always a relatively small group) resume dividends at an average rate of 11.8% per year during 1963–77; this rate falls to 6.2% per year for 1978–99 and 2.5% for 1999. New lists surge after 1978, but the proportion paying dividends in the year of listing declines from 50.8% for 1963–77 to 9.0% for 1978–99 and only 3.7% in 1999 (Table 1). New lists feed a swelling group of firms that never get around to paying dividends. The initiation rate for firms that have never paid dividends drops from 7.1% per year for 1963–77 to 1.8% for 1978–99 and a tiny 0.7% for 1999.

TABLE 1. Counts and percents of CRSP and Compustat firms in different dividend groups

Payers pay dividends in year t; non-payers do not. The two subgroups of non-payers are firms that have never paid and former payers (firms that do not pay in year t but did pay in a previous year). A new list is a firm that first appears on CRSP or Compustat in year t. (See the appendix for more complete definitions of payers, non-payers, and new lists.) New Lists that Pay is the percent of newly listed firms that pay in year t. The numbers are averages of annual values for the indicated time periods.

Counts of CRSP firms	1926–62	1963–99	1963–77	1978–99	1963–67	1968–72	1973–77	1978–82	1983–87	1988–92	1993–98	1999
All firms	762	3,679	2,528	4,464	1,779	1,948	3,856	3,735	4,357	4,276	5,208	5,113
New lists	25	305	114	436	99	140	103	286	515	352	584	322
Counts of Compustat firms		1963–98	1963–77	1978–98	1963–67	1968–72	1973–77	1978–82	1983–87	1988–92	1993–98	
All firms		2,919	1,823	3,702	1,024	1,600	2,847	2,883	3,301	3,566	4,831	
New lists		205	69	302	61	100	45	112	283	261	511	
Percents of CRSP firms	1926–62	1963–99	1963–77	1978–99	1963–67	1968–72	1973–77	1978–82	1983–87	1988–92	1993–98	1999
Payers	74.7	47.6	65.5	35.5	71.6	64.6	60.3	58.2	36.1	29.4	23.5	20.8
Non-payers	25.3	52.4	34.5	64.5	28.4	35.4	39.7	41.8	63.9	70.6	76.5	79.2
Never paid	10.0	42.2	25.4	53.7	20.9	23.7	31.6	31.8	51.7	58.7	66.6	70.1
Former payers	15.3	10.1	9.1	10.8	7.4	11.7	8.2	10.0	12.1	11.9	9.8	9.1
New lists	3.5	7.8	5.2	9.6	5.6	7.2	2.7	7.5	11.7	8.2	11.2	6.3
New lists that pay	83.0	25.9	50.8	9.0	72.1	47.3	33.1	15.7	8.8	7.9	5.2	3.7
Percents of Compustat firms		1963–98	1963–77	1978–98	1963–67	1968–72	1973–77	1978–82	1983–87	1988–92	1993–98	
Payers		51.2	68.5	38.8	74.5	66.6	64.3	62.7	40.0	31.9	23.6	
Non-payers		48.8	31.5	61.2	25.5	33.4	35.7	37.3	60.0	68.1	76.4	
Never paid		39.7	23.1	51.7	19.4	23.0	26.8	28.6	49.7	58.1	67.1	
Former payers		9.1	8.5	9.6	6.1	10.5	8.9	8.7	10.2	10.0	9.3	

TABLE 2. What happens in year t to CRSP firms that do and do not pay dividends in year $t-1$ Firms that Continue to Pay pay dividends in years $t-1$ and t. Firms that Stop Paying pay dividends in $t-1$ and not in t. Firms that Merge are delisted in year t with a CRSP delist code between 200 and 299. Delist includes all other firms delisted in year t. The numbers are averages of annual values for the indicated time periods.

	1927–62	1963–99	1963–77	1978–99	1963–67	1968–72	1973–77	1978–82	1983–87	1988–92	1993–98	1999
What happens in year t to firms that pay dividend in year t − 1 (percent)												
Continue to pay	93.7	91.3	93.1	90.1	94.1	91.3	94.0	90.8	88.1	89.4	91.9	89.6
Stop paying	5.4	4.4	3.5	5.0	2.6	4.5	3.3	4.1	5.7	6.0	4.5	4.2
Merge	0.6	3.4	2.7	3.9	2.6	3.5	1.9	3.9	4.4	3.8	3.2	5.5
Delist	0.3	0.8	0.6	0.9	0.8	0.5	0.5	1.1	1.7	0.8	0.4	0.5
What happens in year t to firms that do not pay dividend in year t − 1 (percent)												
Start paying	15.0	5.2	8.8	2.7	9.9	4.1	12.3	5.0	2.5	2.4	1.5	0.9
Do not pay	81.2	86.0	84.9	86.8	84.3	90.3	80.0	86.4	86.3	85.5	89.3	82.3
Merge	0.8	3.2	2.3	3.8	2.1	2.5	2.3	3.7	2.8	3.5	4.2	7.3
Delist	2.9	5.1	3.5	6.3	3.6	2.5	4.3	4.1	7.7	8.1	4.9	9.3
Percent of non-payers in year t − 1 that start paying in year t												
All non-payers in $t-1$	15.0	5.2	8.8	2.7	9.9	4.1	12.3	5.0	2.5	2.4	1.5	0.9
Never paid in $t-1$	8.5	4.0	7.1	1.8	6.9	3.2	11.3	3.6	1.4	1.7	1.0	0.7
Former payers in $t-1$	16.9	8.5	11.8	6.2	14.1	6.2	15.1	9.4	6.5	5.8	4.3	2.5

Although mergers contribute to the decline in the number of dividend payers, they are not important in the decline in the percent of payers. During the critical 1978–99 period, non-payers merge into other firms at about the same rate (3.8% per year) as payers (3.9% per year), so mergers have little effect on the percent of firms paying dividends. Non-payers delist at a higher rate (6.3% per year for 1978–99) than payers (0.9% per year). Thus, delistings reduce the number of firms paying dividends, but they actually increase the percent of firms paying.

Fig. 2 gives a simple view of the factors that contribute to the decline in the percent of firms paying dividends. Terminations by dividend payers and resumptions by former payers have little net effect. Terminations and resumptions determine the population of former payers, which grows from 319 firms in 1978 to 466 in 1999 (Fig. 1). Because the number of listed firms also grows, the proportion of all firms accounted for by former payers only rises from 8.8% in 1978 to 9.1% in 1999 (Fig. 2). As a result, the decline in the proportion of firms paying dividends (from 66.5% in 1978 to 20.8% in 1999) almost matches the growth in the proportion that have never paid (from 24.7% in 1978 to 70.1% in 1999). This group (new lists that never become dividend payers) is a big factor in both the decline in the numerator of the percent of dividend payers (the number of payers) and the increase in the denominator (the number of sample firms).

The rest of the paper addresses two questions raised by the declining incidence of dividend payers: (i) Has the population of firms drifted toward a lower frequency of firms with the characteristics typical of payers, or (ii) have firms with the characteristics typical of payers become less likely to pay dividends? We start by establishing the characteristics of dividend payers, and the declining incidence of these characteristics among publicly traded firms.

3. CHARACTERISTICS OF DIVIDEND PAYERS

Our evidence on the characteristics of dividend payers and non-payers is from Compustat. The time period, 1963–98, is shorter than the 1926–99 CRSP period examined above, but the Compustat data cover the post-1972 NYSE-AMEX-NASDAQ period and the post-1978 period of most interest to us.

On average, the CRSP sample has about 750 more firms than the Compustat sample in their shared 1963–98 period (Table 1). The difference between the samples is due to CRSP's more complete coverage and the data requirements we impose on the Compustat sample (see the appendix). But the Compustat sample does show the sharp decline in the percent of dividend payers observed in the CRSP sample. Dividend payers average 64.3% of Compustat firms in 1973–77 and 23.6% in 1993–98 (Table 1). The averages for CRSP are 60.3% in 1973–77 and 23.5% in 1993–98.

Our initial discussion of the characteristics of dividend payers focuses on the evidence from summary statistics that payers and non-payers differ in terms of profitability, investment opportunities, and size. The evidence from the summary statistics is then confirmed with logit regressions.

3.1. Profitability

Table 3 details the characteristics of firms in various dividend groups. Dividend payers have higher measured profitability than non-payers. For the full 1963–98 period, E_t/A_t (the ratio of aggregate earnings before interest to aggregate assets) averages 7.82% per year for payers versus 5.37% for non-payers. Among non-payers, E_t/A_t averages 4.54% per year for former dividend payers. This is lower than the profitability of firms that have never paid dividends, 6.11% per year, which in turn is below the profitability of dividend payers, 7.82% per year.

Earnings before interest, E_t, are the payoff on a firm's assets, but earnings available for common, Y_t, may be more relevant for the decision to pay dividends. Table 3 shows that the gap between the profitability of payers and non-payers is wider when profitability is measured as Y_t/BE_t (aggregate common stock earnings over aggregate book equity). For 1963–98, Y_t/BE_t averages 12.75% for dividend payers, versus 6.15% for non-payers. Among non-payers, Y_t/BE_t averages 7.94% for firms that have never paid dividends and only 3.18% for former payers.

Low profitability becomes more common in the second half of the 1963–98 period. The plots of the decile breakpoints for E_t/A_t in Fig. 3 provide perspective. Initially the breakpoints drift upward, peaking around 1979 or 1980. After the peak years, profitability declines. The decline is marginal in the higher profitability deciles, but it is large in the lower profitability deciles. The lowest breakpoint (the tenth percentile) switches from consistently positive to consistently negative in 1982. At least 20% of firms have negative earnings before interest after 1984. In the last three years, 1996–98, negative earnings before interest afflict more than 30% of the firms.

Many of the firms that are unprofitable later in the sample period are new listings. Until 1978, more than 90% of new lists are profitable (Fig. 4). Thereafter, the fraction with positive earnings falls. In 1998, only 51.5% of new lists have positive common stock earnings. Table 3 shows that before 1982, new lists—even new lists that do not pay dividends—tend to be more profitable

TABLE 3. Average firm size, and ratios of aggregate earnings, investment, firm value, and liabilities to aggregate assets and book equity, for different dividend groups and for new lists

A_t, BE_t, ME_t, $L_t = A_t - BE_t$, and $V_t = L_t + ME_t$ are assets, book common equity, market value of common equity, book liabilities, and total market value, at the end of fiscal year t. E_t, Y_t, D_t, and RD_t are earnings before interest but after taxes, after-tax earnings to common stock, dividends, and R&D expenditures for fiscal year t. Investment, dA_t, is $A_t - A_{t-1}$. The ratios shown are ratios of the year t aggregate values of the variables for the firms in a group, averaged over the years in a period. Results are shown for all firms and for firms grouped according to dividend status. Results are also shown for all new lists and for newly listed dividend payers and non-payers.

	1963–98	1963–67	1968–72	1973–77	1978–82	1983–87	1988–92	1993–98
E_t/A_t (percent)								
All firms	7.59	8.45	7.38	7.69	9.02	8.04	6.45	6.35
Payers	7.82	8.58	7.54	7.81	9.13	8.37	6.64	6.88
Non-payers	5.37	5.34	5.37	5.94	7.01	4.90	4.94	4.30
Never paid	6.11	5.94	6.07	7.02	9.58	5.54	5.10	3.95
Former payers	4.54	4.57	4.51	4.62	4.32	3.89	4.64	5.13
All new lists	7.56	9.05	7.94	10.10	10.49	5.71	6.70	3.69
Payers	9.04	9.27	8.17	11.13	11.18	10.69	6.75	6.59
Non-payers	6.97	8.06	7.74	9.03	10.60	4.97	6.19	3.00
Y_t/BE_t (percent)								
All firms	12.04	12.55	11.58	13.68	14.36	11.37	9.62	11.26
Payers	12.75	12.69	11.87	14.04	14.60	12.07	10.46	13.41
Non-payers	6.15	7.95	7.37	7.67	8.96	3.96	3.44	4.12
Never paid	7.94	9.61	9.20	9.82	13.73	5.70	4.64	3.70
Former payers	3.18	5.91	4.77	4.55	0.67	-0.40	0.46	5.78
All new lists	10.71	14.73	12.63	17.79	16.08	7.09	6.29	2.07
Payers	13.52	14.51	12.54	18.73	17.50	14.78	6.78	10.41
Non-payers	9.88	15.65	13.20	16.21	15.76	5.25	4.75	0.27
dA_t/A_t (percent)								
All firms	9.25	9.35	9.70	9.93	10.44	7.11	9.28	9.00
Payers	8.78	9.32	9.52	10.16	10.44	6.57	9.20	6.65
Non-payers	11.62	10.10	13.53	6.47	10.32	12.43	9.62	17.67
Never paid	16.50	13.98	17.98	10.12	17.35	18.20	13.80	22.82
Former payers	4.67	5.46	7.80	1.64	2.85	3.33	3.42	7.61
All new lists	23.29	15.57	21.22	17.87	30.15	28.79	16.04	31.71
Payers	13.42	12.75	16.55	13.38	17.54	14.93	6.50	12.50
Non-payers	30.28	24.62	29.27	25.94	38.43	33.15	22.93	36.38
V_t/A_t								
All firms	1.40	1.71	1.52	1.12	1.06	1.24	1.35	1.72
Payers	1.39	1.72	1.53	1.14	1.05	1.22	1.34	1.69
Non-payers	1.42	1.42	1.47	0.99	1.25	1.42	1.42	1.86
Never paid	1.64	1.62	1.70	1.09	1.52	1.65	1.65	2.13
Former payers	1.10	1.17	1.16	0.86	0.94	1.07	1.12	1.34
All new lists	1.76	1.86	1.86	1.32	1.81	1.61	1.68	2.09
Payers	1.51	1.80	1.76	1.27	1.32	1.46	1.39	1.55
Non-payers	1.90	1.93	2.05	1.33	2.16	1.71	1.85	2.20

(*Continued*)

TABLE 3. (Continued)

	1963–98	1963–67	1968–72	1973–77	1978–82	1983–87	1988–92	1993–98
RD_t/A_t								
All firms	1.67	0.65	1.08	1.35	1.66	2.36	2.17	2.27
Payers	1.61	0.64	1.11	1.35	1.62	2.30	2.05	2.09
Non-payers	2.07	0.76	0.74	1.33	2.38	2.89	3.19	3.03
Never paid	2.76	0.72	0.83	1.67	3.15	3.93	4.67	4.07
Former payers	1.03	0.80	0.62	0.90	1.52	1.24	1.04	1.08
All new lists	1.44	0.51	0.53	1.19	1.96	1.57	1.79	2.36
Payers	1.05	0.45	0.53	0.94	1.10	0.94	0.81	2.31
Non-payers	1.70	0.68	0.53	1.46	2.62	1.86	2.42	2.23
A_t								
All firms	577.06	270.85	336.75	367.40	544.63	584.55	877.91	977.27
Payers	1,389.18	348.33	471.41	533.72	838.59	1,345.67	2,452.04	3,343.61
Non-payers	110.43	43.75	71.71	65.89	70.88	92.44	143.87	255.46
Never paid	81.68	31.14	57.71	49.09	47.53	68.40	99.20	195.88
Former payers	262.42	84.34	101.04	116.79	148.30	211.73	399.68	689.62
All new lists	70.24	45.61	56.67	25.89	23.96	65.96	96.32	159.43
Payers	323.21	50.34	78.09	58.73	64.34	208.77	608.28	1,048.80
Non-payers	52.98	36.22	37.78	15.57	15.69	55.76	63.66	130.62
L_t/A_t								
All firms	0.55	0.41	0.51	0.57	0.54	0.52	0.64	0.62
Payers	0.54	0.40	0.50	0.57	0.53	0.52	0.64	0.64
Non-payers	0.60	0.57	0.62	0.63	0.63	0.57	0.62	0.56
Never paid	0.55	0.57	0.60	0.60	0.54	0.51	0.54	0.51
Former payers	0.67	0.57	0.63	0.66	0.72	0.68	0.73	0.66
All new lists	0.53	0.47	0.51	0.55	0.55	0.56	0.53	0.54
Payers	0.52	0.43	0.47	0.51	0.57	0.45	0.60	0.58
Non-payers	0.55	0.61	0.57	0.58	0.51	0.58	0.51	0.53

than all publicly traded firms. After 1982 the profitability of new lists falls. The deterioration occurs as the number of new lists explodes, and it is dramatic for the increasingly large group of new lists that do not pay dividends. By 1993–98 (when there are 511 Compustat new lists per year and only 5.2% pay dividends), the common stock earnings of newly listed non-payers average only 0.27% of book equity, versus 11.26% for all firms. The low profitability of new lists later in the sample period is in line with similar evidence on the low post-issue profitability of IPO firms (Jain and Kini, 1994; Mikkelson et al., 1997).

After 1977, more than 85% of new lists trade on NASDAQ. One might suspect that the declining incidence of dividend payers is a NASDAQ phenomenon, driven by looser listing standards. In fact, all three exchanges contribute to the growth of unprofitable new lists. Among firms that begin trading between 1978 and 1998, 10.7% of NYSE new lists, 29.0% of AMEX new lists, and 23.6% of NASDAQ new lists have negative common stock earnings. Fig. 5 shows that all three exchanges experience large declines in the percent of payers after 1978. The fraction of NYSE firms paying dividends drops from 88.6% in 1979 to 52.0% in 1999, a level not seen since the Great Depression. AMEX and NASDAQ payers drop from peaks of 63.4 and 54.1% in 1978 and 1977 to 16.9 and 8.6% in 1999. Thus, although it coincides with the explosion of unprofitable NASDAQ new lists, the decline in the percent of firms paying dividends is not limited to NASDAQ.

3.2. Investment Opportunities

Like profitability, investment opportunities differ across dividend groups. Firms that have never paid dividends have the best growth opportunities. Table 3 shows that they have much higher asset growth rates for 1963–98 (16.50% per year) than dividend payers (8.78%) or former payers (4.67%). V_t/A_t (the ratio of the aggregate market value to the aggregate book value of assets) is also higher for firms that have never paid (1.64) than for payers (1.39) or former payers (1.10). The R&D expenditures of firms that have never paid are on

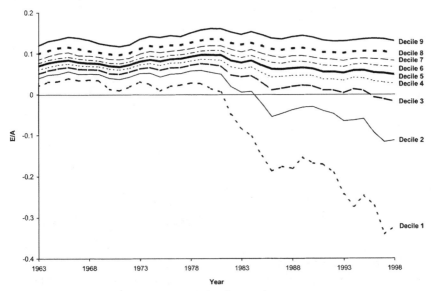

Figure 3. Decile breakpoints for E_t/A_t.

The sample of Compustat firms for calendar year t, 1963–98, includes non-financial non-utility firms with fiscal year-ends in t that satisfy the data requirements described in the appendix. E_t is earnings before interest but after taxes in year t. A_t is the book value of assets in year t.

average 2.76% of their assets, versus 1.61% for dividend payers and 1.03% for former payers. Thus, though firms that have never paid seem to be less profitable than dividend payers, they have better growth opportunities. In contrast, former payers are victims of a double whammy—low profitability and poor investment opportunities.

Newly listed firms are again of interest. Dividend-paying new lists invest at a higher rate during 1963–98 (13.42% per year, Table 3) than all dividend payers (8.78%). There is an even larger spread between the asset growth rates of non-paying new lists and all non-paying firms. The 1963–98 average growth rate for non-paying new lists—an extraordinary 30.28% per year—is almost twice the high 16.50% average growth rate for all firms that have never paid dividends. Similarly, V_t/A_t is higher for newly listed non-payers than for all firms that have never paid dividends. Thus, although newly listed non-payers suffer from low profitability later in the period, they have abundant investments.

Figure 4. Percent of newly listed firms with positive earnings on common stock, $Y_t > 0$.
A firm in the Compustat sample is defined as a new list in calendar year *t* if it is added to the CRSP database between January and December of year *t*. NYSE firms added to the CRSP database in December 1925, AMEX firms added in July 1962, and NASDAQ firms added between December 1972 and February 1973 are not defined as new lists. Earnings on common stock, Y_t, is earnings after interest, taxes, and preferred dividends.

Figure 5. Percent of CRSP firms paying dividends.
The CRSP sample includes NYSE, AMEX, and NASDAQ securities with share codes
of 10 or 11. A firm must have market equity data (price and shares outstanding) for
December of year t to be in the sample for that year. We exclude utilities (SIC codes
4900–4949) and financial firms (SIC codes 6000–6999).

Some readers express a preference for capital expenditures (roughly the
change in long-term assets), rather than the change in total assets, to measure
investment. Our view is that short-term assets are investments. Just as they
invest in machines, firms invest in cash, accounts receivable, and inventory to
facilitate their business activities. And when cash is retained for future long-
term investments, the resources for these investments are committed when the
cash is acquired.

Finally, a caveat is in order. The investment evidence suggests that, measured by E_t/A_t, the profitability advantage of dividend payers over firms that
have never paid is probably exaggerated, for three reasons. (i) If investments
take time to reach full profitability, E_t/A_t understates profitability for growing firms. And firms that have never paid grow faster than dividend payers.
(ii) When R&D is a multiperiod asset, mandatory expensing of R&D causes us
to understate earnings and assets. If R&D is growing, E_t/A_t understates profitability. RD_t/A_t is higher for firms that have never paid dividends than for
dividend payers. And the RD_t/A_t spread grows through time, from 0.32% in

1973–77 to 1.98% in 1993–98 (Table 3). (iii) Since firms that have never paid dividends grow faster, their assets are on average younger than those of dividend payers. Inflation is then likely to cause us to overstate the profitability advantage of dividend payers relative to firms that have never paid.

3.3. Size

Dividend payers are much larger than non-payers. During 1963–67, the assets of payers average about eight times those of non-payers (Table 3). In the non-payer group, former payers are about three times the size of firms that have never paid. In later years, as the Compustat sample grows and the number of payers declines, payers become even larger relative to non-payers. During 1993–98, the assets of payers average more than 13 times those of non-payers.

Table 4 gives a different perspective on the relative size of dividend payers and non-payers. The table shows that payers account for 93.5–95.8% of the aggregate book and market values of assets and common stock during 1973–77, when 64.3% of firms in the Compustat sample pay dividends. Even during 1993–98, when fewer than one-quarter of Compustat firms pay dividends, payers account for more than three-quarters of aggregate book and market values.

TABLE 4. Percent of aggregate values accounted for by firms paying dividends

A_t, BE_t, ME_t, $L_t = A_t - BE_t$, and $V_t = L_t + ME_t$ are assets, book common equity, market value of common equity, book liabilities, and total market value, at the end of fiscal year t. $dA_t = A_t - A_{t-1}$ is the change in assets in fiscal year t. E_t, Y_t, SP_t, and SI_t are earnings before interest but after taxes, after-tax earnings to common stock, stock purchases, and stock issues for fiscal year t. dT_t is the change in treasury stock. The table shows average values for the indicated periods of the year t percents of the aggregate values of the variables (sums over all Compustat firms in the sample) accounted for by firms that pay dividends.

	1963–98	1971–98	1983–98	1963–67	1968–72	1973–77	1978–82	1983–87	1988–92	1993–98
Y_t	96.4	96.0	95.2	98.1	96.7	96.8	97.8	97.3	97.2	91.7
E_t	93.5	92.6	90.6	97.4	94.9	94.9	96.3	94.3	91.7	86.7
dA_t	85.5	83.2	74.2	95.7	91.8	95.9	95.1	80.0	85.5	60.0
A_t	90.7	89.4	86.2	95.9	92.8	93.5	95.1	90.5	88.9	80.3
V_t	90.3	88.8	84.9	96.6	93.3	94.3	94.3	89.1	88.2	78.7
BE_t	90.8	89.2	85.1	97.0	94.3	94.3	96.0	91.5	88.3	77.1
ME_t	90.3	88.5	83.8	97.3	94.4	95.8	94.2	88.8	87.4	76.7
L_t	90.3	89.3	86.7	94.2	91.3	92.9	94.3	89.6	89.2	82.2
SP_t		88.0	88.9			84.4	91.4	90.9	89.1	87.1
SI_t		68.4	53.6			90.4	88.0	67.3	61.3	35.8
dT_t			92.2					100.3	84.7	91.7

Dividend payers are more profitable and non-payers derive more of their market value from expected growth, so the share of dividend payers in aggregate earnings is even higher than their share of assets and market values. During each of the four five-year periods from 1973 to 1992, payers account for about 97% of common stock earnings (Table 4). For 1993–98, the 23.6% of firms that pay dividends account for all but 8.3% of aggregate earnings.

The fact that, even at the end of the sample period, dividend payers account for a large fraction of aggregate earnings, is, however, a bit misleading. Firms with negative earnings (mostly non-payers) become more common later in the sample period. As a result, we shall see that dividend payers can continue to account for a large fraction of aggregate earnings even though an increasing fraction of profitable firms, that in earlier times would be dividend payers, are now non-payers.

Finally, firms that do not pay dividends are big issuers of equity. During 1971–98 (when data on stock purchases and issues are available on Compustat), the aggregate net stock issues of non-payers average 2.80% of the aggregate market value of their common stock, versus a trivial −0.05% for dividend payers. Dividend payers' share of gross stock issues drops from 90.4% for 1973–77 to 35.8% for 1993–98 (Table 4). Thus, though much less important on other dimensions, firms that do not pay dividends currently account for almost two-thirds of the aggregate value of stock issues. This is not surprising, given that the non-payer group tilts increasingly toward growth firms with investment outlays much in excess of their earnings.

3.4. Synopsis

The evidence suggests that three fundamentals—profitability, investment opportunities, and size—are factors in the decision to pay dividends. Dividend payers tend to be large, profitable firms with earnings on the order of investment outlays (Table 3). Firms that have never paid are smaller and they seem to be less profitable than dividend payers, but they have more investment opportunities (higher asset growth rates, higher V_t/A_t, and higher RD_t/A_t), and their investment outlays are much larger than their earnings. The salient characteristics of former dividend payers are low earnings and few investments.

The steady decline after 1978 in the percent of firms paying dividends is in part due to an increasing tilt of the population of publicly traded firms toward the characteristics typical of firms that have never paid. The source of the tilt is new lists. There is a surge in newly listed firms after 1977, and they differ from earlier new lists. During the early years of the 1963–98 period, new lists tend to be small, profitable firms with abundant investments. After 1977, new lists continue to be small and to grow rapidly. But their profitability deteriorates, and new lists that pay dividends become increasingly rare. The new breed of new lists feeds a swelling group of small firms with low earnings and strong growth opportunities—the timeworn characteristics of firms that have never paid dividends.

3.5. Confirmation from Logit Regressions

Table 5 summarizes annual logit regressions that document more formally the marginal effects of size, profitability, and investment opportunities on the likelihood that a firm pays dividends. The size of an NYSE, AMEX, or NASDAQ firm for a given year is its NYSE percentile, NYP_t, that is, the percent of NYSE firms that have the same or smaller market capitalization. This size measure is meant to neutralize any effects of the growth in typical firm size through time. Profitability is measured as the ratio of a firm's earnings before interest to its total assets, E_t/A_t. The proxies for investment opportunities are a firm's rate of growth of assets, dA_t/A_t, and its market-to-book ratio, V_t/A_t. Rather than one overall regression, we estimate the logit regressions year-by-year. In the spirit of Fama and MacBeth (1973), we use the time-series standard deviations of the annual coefficients, which allow for correlation of the regression residuals across firms, to make inferences about average coefficients.

The full-period (1963–98) average slopes from the regressions confirm our inferences about the roles of size, profitability, and investment opportunities in the decision to pay dividends. Larger firms are more likely to pay dividends; the average slope on NYP_t is 37.84 standard errors from zero. More profitable firms are more likely to pay dividends; the average slope on E_t/A_t is 12.20 standard errors from zero. And firms with more investments are less likely to pay dividends; the average slopes on V_t/A_t and dA_t/A_t are -16.93 and -6.50 standard errors from zero. Strong negative average slopes for V_t/A_t (more than eight standard errors from zero) and strong positive slopes for NYP_t and E_t/A_t (more than nine standard errors from zero) are also observed in every five-year subperiod. The average slope for dA_t/A_t is negative in every subperiod, but the small five-year sample size makes the weaker negative marginal effect of investment outlays less consistently reliable in the subperiods.

Our results on the characteristics of dividend payers and non-payers complement the evidence in Fama and French (1999) that among dividend payers, larger and more profitable firms have higher payout ratios, and firms with more investments have lower payouts. And all these results are consistent with

TABLE 5. Logit regressions to explain which firms pay dividends

We estimate logit regressions for each year t of the 1963–98 period. The dependent variable is 1.0 in year t if a firm pays dividends, 0.0 otherwise. The explanatory variables are profitability (E_t/A_t), the growth rate of assets (dA_t/A_t), the market-to-book ratio (V_t/A_t), and the percent of NYSE firms with the same or lower market capitalization (NYP_t). The year t regressions are estimated for all Compustat firms with the required data items. The table shows means (across years) of the regression intercepts (Int) and slopes, and t-statistics for the means, defined as the mean divided by its standard error (the times-series standard deviation of the regression coefficient divided by the square root of the number of years in the period).

	Average coefficient					t-statistic				
	Int	NYP_t	V_t/A_t	dA_t/A_t	E_t/A_t	Int	NYP_t	V_t/A_t	dA_t/A_t	E_t/A_t
1963–98	-0.48	5.03	-0.83	-0.97	10.47	-4.17	37.84	-16.93	-6.50	12.20
1963–77	-0.11	4.56	-0.85	-0.88	15.09	-1.18	22.14	-8.82	-2.99	11.67
1978–98	-0.75	5.36	-0.81	-1.04	7.17	-4.53	39.65	-16.21	-6.84	27.66
1963–67	-0.20	4.35	-0.66	-0.70	16.71	-2.24	24.67	-10.39	-1.56	12.07
1968–72	-0.27	3.84	-0.62	-1.90	18.63	-1.31	21.27	-11.02	-5.68	9.31
1973–77	0.14	5.48	-1.27	-0.03	9.93	1.03	31.17	-8.14	-0.08	9.13
1978–82	0.40	5.69	-1.15	-0.55	8.08	5.60	44.62	-20.88	-2.43	17.41
1983–87	-0.62	5.58	-0.77	-1.23	7.51	-3.00	40.19	-9.59	-5.43	16.55
1988–92	-1.32	5.83	-0.72	-0.48	6.00	-82.55	52.15	-20.94	-2.51	11.93
1993–98	-1.33	4.51	-0.65	-1.75	7.09	-17.59	34.25	-14.31	-9.95	21.78
1963–98	-1.20	4.26		-1.55	7.21	-10.07	35.69		-8.92	14.61
1963–77	-0.63	3.83		-1.31	9.71	-11.53	26.28		-4.18	12.46
1978–98	-1.61	4.58		-1.73	5.43	-11.07	32.03		-8.82	25.47
1963–67	-0.62	3.81		-1.00	11.22	-6.14	23.38		-2.31	9.59
1968–72	-0.63	3.29		-2.33	11.39	-4.66	34.03		-5.60	14.14
1973–77	-0.63	4.37		-0.59	6.51	-12.51	21.78		-1.17	9.09
1978–82	-0.58	4.74		-1.54	5.59	-5.09	30.47		-3.63	21.07
1983–87	-1.52	4.93		-2.00	6.27	-11.19	24.97		-6.18	15.02
1988–92	-2.12	5.06		-0.85	4.38	-166.29	26.73		-2.41	9.92
1993–98	-2.11	3.75		-2.38	5.45	-49.00	25.53		-13.24	28.15

a pecking-order model in which firms are reluctant to issue risky securities because of asymmetric information problems (Myers and Majluf, 1984; Myers, 1984) or simply because of high transactions costs. Bigger asymmetric information problems and higher costs when issuing securities can also explain why smaller firms are less likely to pay dividends. That more profitable firms pay more dividends while firms with more investments pay less is also consistent with the propositions of Easterbrook (1984) and Jensen (1986) about the role of dividends in controlling the agency costs of free cash flow.

4. THE PROPENSITY TO PAY DIVIDENDS: QUALITATIVE EVIDENCE

The surge in new listings in the 1980s and 1990s, and the changing nature of new lists, cause the population of publicly traded firms to tilt increasingly toward the characteristics—small size, low profitability, and strong growth opportunities—of firms that have never paid dividends. But this is not the whole story for the decline in the percent of dividend payers. Our more interesting result is that, given their characteristics, firms have become less likely to pay dividends. This section presents some preliminary qualitative evidence. Section 5 then quantifies how the changing characteristics of firms combine with lower propensity to pay to explain the decline in the incidence of dividend payers.

If the decline in the percent of dividend payers is due entirely to the changing characteristics of firms, firms with particular characteristics should be as likely to pay dividends now as in the past. Fig. 6 suggests that this is not the case. The figure shows time series plots of the percent of dividend payers among (i) firms with positive common stock earnings, $Y_t > 0$, (ii) firms with negative Y_t, (iii) firms with earnings before interest that exceed investment outlays, $E_t > dA_t$, and (iv) firms with $E_t < dA_t$. In all four groups, firms become less likely to pay dividends later in the sample period.

In 1978, 72.4% of firms with positive common stock earnings pay dividends. In 1998, 30.0% of profitable firms pay dividends, less than half the fraction for 1978. The proportion of payers among firms with $E_t > dA_t$ falls from 68.4% in 1978 to 32.4% in 1998. These results suggest that dividends become less likely among firms with the characteristics (positive earnings and earnings in excess of investment) of dividend payers. But unprofitable firms and firms with investment outlays that exceed earnings also become less likely to pay. For firms with $E_t < dA_t$, the proportion paying dividends falls from 68.6% in 1978 to 15.6% in 1998. Dividends are never common among unprofitable firms. But

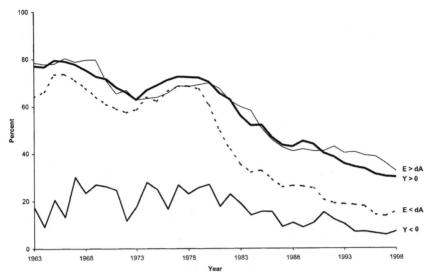

Figure 6. Percent of payers among firms with (i) positive and negative earnings on common stock, $Y_t > 0$ and $Y_t < 0$; and (ii) earnings before interest but after taxes greater than and less than investment, $E_t > dA_t$ and $E_t < dA_t$.

The sample of Compustat firms for calendar year *t*, 1963–98, includes non-financial non-utility firms with fiscal year-ends in *t* that satisfy the data requirements described in the appendix. Y_t, earnings on common stock, is earnings after interest, taxes, and preferred dividends in year *t*; E_t is earnings before interest but after taxes in year *t*; and dA_t, investment, is the change in the book value of assets from *t*–1 to *t*.

these firms also become less likely to pay dividends in the 1980s and 1990s. Before 1983, about 20% of firms with negative common stock earnings pay dividends. In 1998, only 7.2% of unprofitable firms pay dividends. In short, the evidence suggests that firms become less likely to pay dividends, whatever their characteristics.

It is worth dwelling a bit on these results. The surge in unprofitable non-paying new lists causes the aggregate profitability of firms that do not pay dividends to fall in the 1980s and 1990s (Table 3). But Fig. 6 says that this decline in aggregate profitability hides the fact that an increasing fraction of firms with positive earnings—firms that in the past would typically pay dividends—now choose not to pay. Similarly, for non-payers the spread of aggregate investment over aggregate earnings widens later in the sample period, again largely as a result of new lists. But Fig. 6 says that an increasing fraction of firms with earnings that exceed investment—firms that in the past would typically pay dividends—are now non-payers. In short, the surge in unprofitable new lists with investment outlays far in excess of earnings causes the aggregate characteristics of non-payers, documented in Table 3, to mask widespread evidence of a lower propensity to pay dividends.

5. CHANGING CHARACTERISTICS AND PROPENSITY TO PAY: QUANTITATIVE EFFECTS

This section quantifies the effects of changing characteristics and propensity to pay on the percent of dividend payers. The approach is simple. We first estimate the probabilities that firms with given characteristics (size, profitability, and investment opportunities) pay dividends during 1963–77, the 15-year period of Compustat coverage preceding the 1978 peak in the percent of dividend payers. We then apply the probabilities from the 1963–77 base period to the samples of firm characteristics observed in subsequent years to estimate the expected percent of dividend payers for each year after 1977. Since the probabilities associated with characteristics are fixed at their base period values, variation in the expected percent of payers after 1977 is due to the changing characteristics of sample firms. We then use the difference between the expected percent of payers for a year (calculated using the base period probabilities) and the actual percent to measure the change in the propensity to pay dividends. A decline in the propensity to pay implies a positive difference between expected and actual percents of payers.

We use two approaches to estimate the probability function for the base period, logit regressions and relative frequencies of dividend payers in portfolios formed on profitability, investment opportunities, and size. We show results that use 1963–77 as the base period, but using 1973–77 (the first five-year period of NYSE-AMEX-NASDAQ coverage) as the base period produces similar results.

5.1. Regression Estimates

Table 6 shows the expected percents of dividend payers obtained by applying the average coefficients from year-by-year logit regressions for 1963–77 to the samples of firm characteristics of subsequent years. Two sets of results are shown. In one, the regressions use size (NYSE percentile, NYP_t), profitability (E_t/A_t), and two measures of investment opportunities (V_t/A_t and dA_t/A_t) to explain the probability that a firm pays dividends. In the other, V_t/A_t is dropped, leaving dA_t/A_t as the sole measure of investment opportunities. (The base period regressions are summarized in Table 5.)

Why two sets of results? Our approach to measuring the effects of changing characteristics on the incidence of dividend payers presumes that the proxies for profitability, investment opportunities, and size have constant meaning through time. This presumption is especially suspect for V_t/A_t. V_t/A_t drifts up in the 1980s and 1990s (Table 3). With rational pricing, the drift in V_t/A_t is due to some mix of (i) increasing profitability of assets in place, (ii) more profitable or more abundant expected investments, or (iii) lower discount rates for expected cash flows. Profitability (E_t/A_t) and investment outlays (dA_t/A_t) show no clear tendency to increase during the 1980s and 1990s (Table 3). It is reasonable to conclude that declining discount rates have a role in the drift in V_t/A_t. For our purposes, upward drift in V_t/A_t that is not due to improved investment opportunities causes us to overestimate the decline in the percent of payers due to changing characteristics and to understate the decline due to propensity to pay.

Consider first the regressions that use NYP_t, E_t/A_t, and both V_t/A_t, and dA_t/A_t to explain the probability that a firm pays dividends. Since we use the same 1963–77 average regression function to estimate the expected percent of payers in each of the following years, changes in the expected percent after 1977 are due to the changing characteristics of sample firms. When the average regression function for 1963–77 is applied to the sample of firm characteristics for 1978, the expected proportion of payers is 70.0%. The proportion of dividend payers for 1963–77 is 68.5%. Thus, roughly speaking, the characteristics of firms in 1978 are similar to those of the base period. The expected proportion of payers falls after 1978, reaching 44.6% in 1998. The 25.4 percentage point decline in the expected proportion of payers, from 70.0% in 1978 to 44.6% in 1998, is an estimate of the effect of changing characteristics on the percent of firms paying dividends.

The actual percent of dividend payers for a given year of the 1978–98 period is also the expected percent that would be produced by a logit regression estimated on that year's sample of firms. Thus, by comparing the actual percent of payers for a year and the expected percent produced with the regression function for the 1963–77 base period, we can infer the effect of changes in the regression function, or equivalently, changes in the propensity to pay dividends. In 1978, the actual percent of payers is only 1.5 percentage points below the expected. The spread between the expected and actual percent widens thereafter. By 1998, when the regression function for 1963–77 predicts that 44.6% of firms pay dividends, only 21.3% actually pay. The difference, 23.3 percentage points, between the expected and actual percents for 1998 estimates the end-of-sample shortfall in the percent of dividend payers due to reduced propensity to pay.

TABLE 6. Estimates from logit regressions of the effect of changing characteristics and declining propensity to pay on the percent of firms paying dividends

We use all firms for each year of the 1963–77 base period to estimate logit regressions that explain whether a firm pays dividends. The explanatory variables are profitability (E_t/A_t), the growth rate of assets (dA_t/A_t), the market-to-book ratio (V_t/A_t), and the percent of NYSE firms with the same or lower market capitalization (NYP_t). Firms is the number of firms in the sample for a year, or the average for a period. Payers is the number (or average number) of dividend payers. Actual Percent is the percent of payers (the ratio of payers to firms, times 100). The Expected Percent of payers for a year t is estimated by applying the average logit regression coefficients for 1963–77 to the values of the explanatory variables for each firm for year t, summing over firms, dividing by the number of firms, and then multiplying by 100. The evolution of Expected Percent measures the effects of changing characteristics on the percent of dividend payers. Expected–Actual measures the effect of propensity to pay. There are two sets of results. One uses V_t/A_t and dA_t/A_t to control for investment opportunities; the second uses only dA_t/A_t.

| | | | | V_t/A_t and dA_t/A_t | | dA_t/A_t | |
	Firms	Payers	Actual Percent	Expected Percent	Expected –Actual	Expected Percent	Expected –Actual
1963–77	1,823	1,218	68.5				
1978	2,901	1,988	68.5	70.0	1.5	66.9	−1.6
1979	2,819	1,918	68.0	69.7	1.7	67.3	−0.7
1980	2,806	1,825	65.0	67.9	2.9	67.9	2.9
1981	2,917	1,698	58.2	65.3	7.1	65.9	7.7
1982	2,974	1,596	53.7	61.5	7.8	62.5	8.8
1983	3,127	1,470	47.0	54.1	7.1	60.1	13.1
1984	3,239	1,393	43.0	56.9	13.9	58.9	15.9
1985	3,196	1,319	41.3	53.4	12.1	57.6	16.3
1986	3,357	1,220	36.3	48.7	12.4	54.1	17.8
1987	3,587	1,162	32.4	49.0	16.6	53.8	21.4
1988	3,526	1,151	32.6	52.0	19.4	55.4	22.8
1989	3,429	1,144	33.4	52.5	19.1	57.0	23.6
1990	3,451	1,131	32.8	55.2	22.4	57.9	25.1
1991	3,582	1,115	31.1	50.7	19.6	57.2	26.1
1992	3,845	1,137	29.6	48.7	19.1	55.7	26.1
1993	4,265	1,143	26.8	45.5	18.7	53.4	26.6
1994	4,558	1,168	25.6	47.3	21.7	53.3	27.7
1995	4,768	1,177	24.7	45.9	21.2	53.9	29.2
1996	5,211	1,157	22.2	43.3	21.1	52.1	29.9
1997	5,278	1,113	21.1	42.6	21.5	51.2	30.1
1998	4,906	1,045	21.3	44.6	23.3	52.1	30.8

As predicted, when we drop V_t/A_t from the 1963–77 base period regressions, changing characteristics make a smaller contribution to the decline in the percent of dividend payers. The expected proportion of payers now declines from 66.9% in 1978 to 52.1% in 1998. This 14.8 percentage point decline (due to changing NYP_t, E_t/A_t, and dA_t/A_t characteristics) compares to the estimated 25.4 percentage point decline obtained when V_t/A_t is used along with dA_t/A_t to measure investment opportunities. Conversely, when we drop V_t/A_t from the base period regressions, lower propensity to pay gets more weight in explaining the declining percent of dividend payers. In 1978 and 1979, the actual percent of payers is slightly higher than the expected percent. Thereafter, the expected percent exceeds the actual, and by increasing amounts. The final (1998) shortfall in the proportion of dividend payers due to lower propensity to pay, 30.8%, is 7.5 percentage points higher than the 23.3% estimate obtained when V_t/A_t is also included in the base period regressions.

One can quarrel about whether excluding V_t/A_t as a control variable provides cleaner estimates of the decline in the percent of dividend payers due to changing characteristics. But there is no need. The important point is that, with or without V_t/A_t, the regression approach uncovers the tracks of a potentially elusive phenomenon—the lower propensity of firms to pay dividends, given their characteristics.

5.2. Regressions for Different Dividend Groups

There is a missing variable in the regressions underlying Table 6—lagged dividend status. Table 7 summarizes annual logit regressions estimated separately for firms classified as payers, former payers, and firms that have never paid as of the previous year. The full-period (1963–98) average coefficients show that the decision to pay dividends in year t depends on dividend status in $t-1$. Dividend payers produce a large positive average intercept (1.26, $t = 8.94$), but the intercepts for former payers and firms that have never paid are strongly negative (-3.38, $t = -21.84$; and -2.16, $t = -8.37$). The regression slopes confirm that there is inertia in dividend decisions. Skipping the details, for given positive values of the explanatory variables [size (NYP_t), profitability (E_t/A_t), and investment opportunities (V_t/A_t and dA_t/A_t)], the probability that a dividend payer continues to pay is higher than the probability that a non-payer with the same characteristics starts paying.

The regressions for the three dividend groups allow us to examine how the effects of changing characteristics and propensity to pay differ across the groups. Table 8 uses the average 1963–77 logit coefficients for each dividend group to estimate expected percents of payers for each group in subsequent years. The proportion of year $t-1$ dividend payers expected to continue paying in year t only falls from 97.9% in 1978 to 97.0% in 1998. Thus, roughly speaking, the characteristics of dividend payers do not change much through time. In all but one year of the 1978–98 period, the actual percent of continuing payers falls short of the expected. But the annual differences (the effect of lower propensity to pay) average only 1.2% for 1978–98. This small decline in the propensity to pay nevertheless has a nontrivial cumulative effect on the payer population. The annual spreads between expected and actual percents of payers for 1978–98 cumulate to about 320 payers lost due to lower propensity to pay.

Changing characteristics and lower propensity to pay have bigger effects on the dividend decisions of former payers. When the average coefficients of the 1963–77 regressions for former payers are applied to the former payer samples of later years, the expected proportion of those resuming dividends falls (due to changes in characteristics) from 17.4% in 1978 to 9.9% in 1998. Given their characteristics, the propensity of former payers to resume dividends is also lower after 1978; the difference between expected and actual percents resuming is positive after 1979, and the average difference for 1978–98 is 3.1 percentage points. In 1998, 9.9% of former payers are expected to resume, but only 4.0% (less than half the expected number) actually do.

Changing characteristics and lower propensity to pay also have strong separate effects on the dividend decisions of firms that have never paid. Changes in characteristics cause the expected proportion of initiators among firms that have never paid to fall from 11.3% in 1978 to 5.2% in 1998, a decline of more than half. The consistently positive differences between the expected and actual percents of initiators after 1978 then say that controlling for characteristics, firms that have never paid dividends become less likely to start. For 1978–98, the difference averages 3.8 percentage points (6.8% expected versus 3.0% actual). In 1998, 5.2% of the never paid are expected to start paying dividends, but only 0.8% (less than one-sixth the expected number) actually do—rather strong evidence of a declining propensity to initiate dividends.

The regressions estimated separately for payers, former payers, and firms that have never paid are useful for documenting that, to different degrees, changing characteristics and lower propensity to pay affect the dividend decisions of all three groups. But the regressions are inappropriate for estimating how the decline in the overall percent of dividend payers splits between characteristics and propensity to pay. Suppose we estimate the overall expected percent of payers for a year as the sum of the expected number of payers in

TABLE 7. Logit regressions to explain which firms pay dividends

The logit regressions are estimated separately for each year t of the 1963–98 period for (i) firms that paid dividends in year $t-1$ (Dividend Payers), (ii) firms that have Never Paid as of year $t-1$, and (iii) firms that did not pay in $t-1$ but did pay in an earlier year (Former Payers). The dependent variable is 1.0 in year t if a firm pays dividends, 0.0 otherwise. The explanatory variables are NYSE percentile (NYP_t), the market-to-book ratio (V_t/A_t), the rate of growth of assets (dA_t/A_t), and profitability (E_t/A_t). The table shows means (across years) of the regression intercepts (Int) and slopes, and t-statistics for the means, defined as the mean divided by its standard error (the times-series standard deviation of the regression coefficient divided by the square root of the number of years in the period).

	Average coefficient					t-statistic				
	Int	NYP_t	V_t/A_t	dA_t/A_t	E_t/A_t	Int	NYP_t	V_t/A_t	dA_t/A_t	E_t/A_t
Dividend Payers										
1963–98	1.26	5.54	0.32	1.57	13.51	8.94	5.64	2.11	3.69	8.26
1963–77	1.04	6.85	0.54	2.03	21.19	4.22	2.96	1.72	2.06	7.75
1978–98	1.41	4.60	0.17	1.24	8.02	8.75	13.27	1.25	5.89	9.74
1963–67	0.63	10.71	1.10	1.07	26.47	0.95	1.53	1.44	0.37	4.25
1968–72	1.13	4.61	−0.16	1.42	24.32	5.06	4.48	−0.86	2.68	7.75
1973–77	1.36	5.23	0.68	3.59	12.80	5.05	6.70	1.50	4.60	7.49
1978–82	1.83	6.19	−0.36	1.34	12.72	8.01	11.76	−2.14	2.70	9.68
1983–87	1.28	4.14	0.40	1.68	7.66	2.86	7.09	1.00	3.21	5.57
1988–92	1.17	5.03	0.17	1.19	6.82	6.09	7.44	1.47	2.62	4.54
1993–98	1.38	3.32	0.41	0.82	5.40	3.84	8.39	1.83	3.27	10.26
Former Payers										
1963–98	−3.38	2.19	−0.60	0.14	10.41	−21.84	10.91	−7.47	0.85	10.41
1963–77	−2.81	1.59	−0.83	0.79	14.95	−10.32	5.89	−5.42	2.59	9.32
1978–98	−3.78	2.62	−0.43	−0.33	7.16	−30.96	10.49	−6.66	−3.75	10.69
1963–67	−2.00	1.77	−1.19	1.25	15.77	−5.29	6.93	−3.46	1.76	7.57
1968–72	−3.89	0.94	−0.37	0.17	15.96	−11.87	1.43	−2.04	0.38	3.70
1973–77	−2.53	2.07	−0.94	0.95	13.11	−10.76	6.41	−9.38	2.83	7.86
1978–82	−2.98	1.29	−0.51	−0.21	7.18	−14.13	7.27	−3.55	−0.91	5.47
1983–87	−4.20	2.62	−0.21	−0.20	7.87	−43.61	5.06	−3.29	−1.37	6.67
1988–92	−3.97	3.61	−0.35	−0.36	6.72	−37.82	13.91	−7.13	−3.20	6.84
1993–98	−3.94	2.92	−0.63	−0.50	6.92	−28.84	7.41	−4.20	−2.61	3.73
Never Paid										
1963–98	−2.16	0.72	−1.28	0.63	14.84	−8.37	2.11	−3.64	2.04	5.82
1963–77	−1.60	0.18	−1.98	0.82	22.23	−3.27	0.26	−2.66	1.23	4.04
1978–98	−2.57	1.10	−0.78	0.48	9.56	−10.32	3.69	−3.09	2.07	9.51
1963–67	−0.66	−0.14	−3.58	1.03	30.34	−0.54	−0.08	−1.74	0.52	1.95
1968–72	−2.81	−0.26	−0.86	0.76	22.34	−4.77	−0.26	−1.29	0.99	4.05
1973–77	−1.33	0.95	−1.51	0.69	14.00	−5.64	1.50	−3.80	1.71	4.17
1978–82	−1.56	2.07	−1.94	1.22	14.03	−2.04	7.47	−2.49	2.00	4.90
1983–87	−2.63	1.51	−0.59	0.20	8.32	−5.33	1.76	−1.68	0.63	11.89
1988–92	−3.09	1.00	−0.16	−0.01	8.32	−14.21	6.38	−1.02	−0.04	4.80
1993–98	−2.92	0.04	−0.49	0.51	7.88	−14.28	0.08	−1.76	1.10	5.64

each dividend group divided by the total number of firms (Table 8). With separate regressions, the probability that a payer continues to pay is higher than the probability that an otherwise similar non-payer initiates dividends. The expected number of payers for a year thus depends on the distribution of firms across dividend groups in the preceding year. Toward the end of the sample period, many firms are non-payers because of the lower propensity to pay. As a result, the decline from 1978 to 1998 in the overall expected percent of payers combines the effects of changing characteristics and lower propensity to pay, and the 1998 difference between the overall actual and expected percents of payers understates the cumulative effect of propensity to pay.

We are interested in long-term dividend patterns. Under reasonable assumptions, the regression approach that ignores lagged dividend status (Table 6) does a better job capturing the long-term effects of changing characteristics and propensity to pay. If propensity to pay, given a firm's characteristics, is constant prior to 1978, the average allocations of firms across dividend groups during the 1963–77 base period should largely be driven by characteristics rather than by lagged dividend status. In this situation, the base period average regression function that ignores lagged dividend status captures the pre-1978 long-term propensity to pay, given characteristics. And applying the base period regression function to the samples of firm characteristics of subsequent years produces estimates of the long-term effects of changing characteristics and propensity to pay.

5.3. Estimates of Base Period Probabilities from Portfolios

The logit regressions use a functional form for the base period relation between characteristics and the likelihood that a firm pays dividends that may be misspecified. Our second approach addresses this problem by allowing the base period probabilities to vary with characteristics in an unrestricted way.

Each year from 1963 to 1977, we form 27 portfolios as the intersections of independent sorts of firms on profitability (E_t/A_t), investment opportunities (V_t/A_t or dA_t/A_t), and size. We sort firms into three equal groups on E_t/A_t, V_t/A_t, and dA_t/A_t, but we do not form equal groups on size. Instead, we use the 20th and 50th percentiles of market capitalization for NYSE firms to allocate NYSE, AMEX, and NASDAQ firms to portfolios. We use NYSE percentiles to prevent the growing population of small NASDAQ firms from changing the meaning of small, medium, and large over the sample period. The 20th and 50th NYSE percentiles lead to similar average numbers of firms in the medium and large groups (and many more in the small group). To have a manageable

TABLE 8. Estimates from logit regressions of the effect of changing characteristics and propensity to pay on the percent of firms paying dividends

The logit regressions are estimated separately for each year t of the 1963–77 period for (i) firms that paid dividends in year $t-1$ (Payers), (ii) firms that have Never Paid as of year $t-1$, and (iii) firms that did not pay in $t-1$ but did pay in an earlier year (Former Payers). The explanatory variables are NYSE percentile (NYP_t), profitability (E/A_t), the growth rate of assets (dA/A_t), and the market-to-book ratio (V/A_t). Act is the actual percent of payers (the ratio of payers to firms, times 100). Exp is the expected percent of payers for a year, estimated by applying the average logit regression coefficients for 1963–77 to the values of the explanatory variables for each firm for year t, summing over firms, dividing by the number of firms, and then multiplying by 100. The evolution of Exp measures the effect of changing characteristics on the percent of dividend payers. Exp − Act (expected minus actual) measures the effects of propensity to pay. Exp for Payers + Never Paid + Former is the sum of the weighted Exp's of dividend payers, firms that have never paid, and former payers, where the weights are the year t proportions of all firms in the three dividend groups.

	Payers			Never Paid			Former Payers			Payers + Never Paid + Former		
	Act	Exp	Exp–Act	Act	Exp	Exp–Act	Act	Exp	Exp–Act	Act	Exp	Exp–Act
1963–77	97.3			9.1			13.0			68.5		
1978–98	95.7	96.9	1.2	3.0	6.8	3.8	8.3	11.4	3.1	38.8	41.5	2.7
1978	97.2	97.9	0.7	11.3	11.3	0.0	18.1	17.4	-0.7	68.5	68.9	0.4
1979	97.7	98.0	0.3	5.1	11.3	6.2	18.4	18.2	-0.2	68.0	69.8	1.8
1980	96.4	97.6	1.2	4.2	9.7	5.5	13.8	15.3	1.5	65.0	67.4	2.4
1981	95.4	97.9	2.5	3.8	9.8	6.0	8.9	16.6	7.7	58.2	62.3	4.1
1982	95.7	96.6	0.9	3.2	8.7	5.5	6.9	14.5	7.6	53.7	56.9	3.2
1983	94.1	96.4	2.3	2.4	5.9	3.5	6.7	10.5	3.8	47.0	49.9	2.9
1984	96.3	97.1	0.8	3.1	7.9	4.8	10.5	13.9	3.4	43.0	46.0	3.0
1985	96.8	96.8	0.0	2.2	6.5	4.3	8.2	10.4	2.2	41.3	43.6	2.3
1986	94.8	95.5	0.7	2.2	5.6	3.4	6.1	8.4	2.3	36.3	38.7	2.4
1987	95.2	96.5	1.3	2.5	5.8	3.3	6.9	10.0	3.1	32.4	35.0	2.6
1988	95.5	97.1	1.6	3.8	6.7	2.9	8.4	9.7	1.3	32.6	35.0	2.4
1989	95.6	97.5	1.9	3.2	6.6	3.4	10.6	12.2	1.6	33.4	36.1	2.7
1990	95.3	97.2	1.9	2.6	7.1	4.5	6.2	10.5	4.3	32.8	36.4	3.6
1991	94.8	95.6	0.8	2.0	5.5	2.5	4.7	8.5	3.8	31.1	33.8	2.7
1992	94.8	95.8	1.0	2.5	5.1	2.6	7.8	9.0	1.2	29.6	31.6	2.0
1993	95.0	96.2	1.2	2.3	4.6	2.3	5.6	7.4	1.8	26.8	28.8	2.0
1994	95.3	97.2	1.9	2.1	5.5	3.4	6.6	8.8	2.2	25.6	28.5	2.9
1995	97.3	97.1	-0.2	1.6	5.1	3.5	5.9	9.9	4.0	24.7	27.4	2.7
1996	96.4	97.4	1.0	1.2	4.8	3.6	6.4	10.0	3.6	22.2	25.3	3.1
1997	95.0	96.6	1.6	1.2	4.7	3.5	3.0	8.6	5.6	21.1	24.3	3.2
1998	96.2	97.0	0.8	0.8	5.2	4.4	4.0	9.9	5.9	21.3	25.1	3.8

number of portfolios, each with many firms, we use V_t/A_t or dA_t/A_t (but not both) to control for investment opportunities.

We estimate the base period probabilities that firms in each of the 27 portfolios pay dividends as the sum of the number of payers in a portfolio during the 15 years of 1963–77 divided by the sum of the number of firms in the portfolio. These base period probabilities are free of assumptions about the form of the relation between characteristics and the probability that a firm pays dividends (except, of course, that all firms in a portfolio are assigned the same probability). The number of observations in the base period probability estimates is always at least 45, and it is 165 or greater for all but one portfolio.

The base period probabilities vary across portfolios in a familiar way (Table 9). Larger firms are more likely to pay dividends; controlling for profitability (E_t/A_t) and investment opportunities (V_t/A_t or dA_t/A_t), the 1963–77 probability that a firm pays dividends increases across size portfolios. More profitable firms are more likely to pay dividends; controlling for size and V_t/A_t or dA_t/A_t, high E_t/A_t portfolios have higher percents of payers in 1963–77 than low E_t/A_t portfolios. Finally, firms with more investments are less likely to pay dividends; the high V_t/A_t (or dA_t/A_t) portfolio in a size-E_t/A_t group typically has a lower base period percent of dividend payers than the low V_t/A_t (or dA_t/A_t) portfolio.

We form portfolios each year after 1977 using breakpoints designed to have the same economic meaning as those of the 1963–77 base period. For profitability and investment opportunities, we assume that values of E_t/A_t, V_t/A_t, and dA_t/A_t have constant meaning. (Again, this assumption is shaky for V_t/A_t.) Thus, in forming portfolios after 1977, the E_t/A_t, V_t/A_t, and dA_t/A_t breakpoints are averages (across years) of the breakpoints for 1963–77. Holding breakpoints constant means that outside the base period, the split of firms across E_t/A_t, V_t/A_t, and dA_t/A_t groups varies with changes in the distribution of these characteristics across firms. Finally, we assume that the 20th and 50th percentile breakpoints for NYSE market capitalization, allowed to vary through time, are measures of size with relatively constant economic meaning. The proportions of firms in the three size groups vary through time with the size and number of AMEX and NASDAQ firms relative to NYSE firms.

The expected percent of dividend payers for a given year t after 1977 is

$$Ep_t = \frac{\sum_{i=1}^{27} n_{it} p_i}{N_t} \times 100,$$

where n_{it} is the number of firms in portfolio i in year t, N_t is the total number of firms, and p_i is the expected proportion of dividend payers in portfolio i, estimated as the actual proportion for 1963–77. Since the expected proportion of payers in a portfolio is fixed at the 1963–77 base value, the aggregate expected percent of payers varies through time because changes in the characteristics of firms alter the allocation of firms across the 27 portfolios. The evolution of the expected percent of payers after 1977 can thus be attributed to changing characteristics. The difference between the expected percent of payers for a year and the actual percent then measures the effect of changes in the propensity to pay dividends.

When V_t/A_t is used to measure investment opportunities, the expected proportion of payers for 1978 produced by the portfolio approach is 70.0% (Table 10). The expected proportion falls over the next 20 years, to 53.3% in 1998. Thus, when V_t/A_t measures investment opportunities, the portfolio approach says that changes in the characteristics of firms cause the proportion of payers to drop by 16.7 percentage points from 1978 to 1998. The actual proportion of firms paying dividends in 1978, 68.5%, is close to the expected 70.0%. Thereafter, the spread between expected and actual widens. In the final year, 1998, 53.3% of firms are expected to pay dividends but only 21.3% actually pay. The difference, 32.0 percentage points, is the end-of-sample estimate of the decline in the percent of payers due to reduced propensity to pay dividends.

Using dA_t/A_t rather than V_t/A_t to measure investment opportunities lowers our estimate of the effect of changing characteristics on the decline in the percent of dividend payers. The expected proportion of payers now falls by only 6.8 percentage points, from 65.1% in 1978 to 58.3% in 1998. Conversely, using dA_t/A_t rather than V_t/A_t to form portfolios increases the share of the decline in the percent of payers attributed to lower propensity to pay. In 1978, the actual proportion of payers is 3.5 percentage points above the expected. After 1979, however, the expected percent exceeds the actual, and by increasing amounts. In 1998, 58.3% of firms are expected to pay dividends, but only 21.3% in fact pay. Thus, the end-of-sample shortfall in the proportion of dividend payers due to lower propensity to pay is 37.0 percentage points.

In short, like the logit tests, the portfolio approach says that changing characteristics and lower propensity to pay both have roles in the decline in the percent of firms paying dividends. And lower propensity to pay is at least as important as changing characteristics.

TABLE 9. Percents of dividend payers in 27 portfolios formed on size, profitability, and either market-to-book ratio or investment outlays

Each year we form two sets of 27 portfolios of NYSE, AMEX, and NASDAQ firms, using sorts on profitability (E_t/A_t), market-to-book ratio (V_t/A_t), investment (dA_t/A_t), and size (market capitalization, ME_t). In each of the 15 base years, 1963–77, firms are sorted into three equal groups on E_t/A_t, V_t/A_t, and dA_t/A_t. In the years after 1977, we use the average breakpoints for 1963–77 to assign firms to the three E_t/A_t, V_t/A_t, and dA_t/A_t groups. The breakpoints for the three size groups for year t are the 20th and 50th NYSE percentiles of ME_t for that year. Big firms have ME_t above the median ME_t of NYSE firms; medium-sized firms are between the 20th and 50th percentiles; small firms are below the 20th NYSE percentile. The 27 portfolios are the intersections of the size, E_t/A_t, and V_t/A_t, or dA_t/A_t, groups. The table shows annual values and averages of annual values of the percents of the firms in the portfolios that pay dividends.

	Investment variable is V_t/A_t									Investment variable is dA_t/A_t								
	Low E_t/A_t			Medium E_t/A_t			High E_t/A_t			Low E_t/A_t			Medium E_t/A_t			High E_t/A_t		
	Low	V_t/A_t	High	Low	V_t/A_t	High	Low	V_t/A_t	High	Low	dA_t/A_t	High	Low	dA_t/A_t	High	Low	dA_t/A_t	High
Small firms																		
1963–77	48.5	31.0	13.6	72.3	58.7	32.5	66.9	65.2	51.1	36.4	47.2	36.6	60.4	69.4	52.9	58.3	71.2	51.8
1978	45.8	21.7	7.5	70.2	49.3	8.6	72.3	57.3	42.9	30.6	52.0	41.1	56.2	73.3	58.6	56.3	73.2	57.2
1978–82	44.7	24.1	3.5	66.7	44.4	15.3	66.8	56.0	36.6	32.3	46.5	24.2	57.4	65.3	47.8	57.8	67.1	46.4
1983–87	25.9	17.3	3.6	47.0	39.0	18.6	37.0	39.2	24.2	16.8	22.0	9.3	40.9	50.7	24.1	38.4	45.6	21.7
1988–92	17.8	12.7	2.4	24.7	26.9	12.6	23.7	24.8	17.6	12.9	16.3	5.7	27.7	25.0	15.1	25.0	31.6	13.0
1993–98	15.7	10.6	1.5	29.1	25.8	11.5	16.1	18.2	17.0	8.8	12.9	4.4	29.9	26.4	12.9	22.3	28.2	11.0
1998	10.7	7.4	1.6	19.0	24.7	11.5	11.8	15.6	20.5	6.0	10.7	5.1	24.8	27.2	12.6	23.0	23.2	13.1
Medium-sized firms																		
1963–77	80.4	67.9	43.4	92.8	85.7	63.1	91.5	85.0	75.2	68.5	77.9	61.5	86.4	89.0	72.4	86.5	89.1	69.5
1978	84.3	66.7	12.5	97.6	71.4	66.7	95.2	86.2	79.2	59.3	81.2	82.4	91.7	89.7	84.3	80.0	95.2	83.3
1978–82	88.8	68.2	19.7	94.9	79.3	52.9	95.1	87.5	67.6	73.7	86.7	60.9	90.8	91.4	75.1	84.1	91.8	72.0
1983–87	66.3	61.5	17.6	90.3	77.9	44.4	81.3	77.8	56.3	57.4	60.0	28.7	86.9	76.5	52.4	78.6	81.5	50.4
1988–92	58.3	52.4	13.2	65.4	63.1	36.8	67.3	55.0	42.4	49.1	46.4	23.3	67.0	66.8	34.8	65.1	57.4	31.2
1993–98	52.1	43.1	11.5	63.9	55.3	30.3	22.8	44.5	32.5	38.3	38.7	12.6	62.8	55.0	24.7	57.8	51.5	21.1
1998	39.1	32.1	8.8	39.1	53.0	28.8	25.0	47.1	29.5	28.3	32.3	11.1	52.7	58.8	24.0	61.7	44.4	19.5
Big firms																		
1963–77	89.1	87.4	82.5	96.8	95.1	90.1	96.6	96.6	92.4	84.2	90.4	87.1	96.6	96.9	85.5	97.5	97.2	87.9
1978	95.6	77.8	50.0	98.9	88.9	100.0	99.0	97.8	90.9	90.0	92.3	85.7	95.0	95.5	97.8	100.0	99.4	92.4
1978–82	93.8	89.8	36.7	97.1	96.4	84.9	99.2	97.5	85.2	92.9	92.3	79.4	94.9	95.4	93.7	97.8	98.7	84.7
1983–87	86.6	85.2	56.3	95.1	92.1	77.7	99.5	95.9	84.7	85.9	83.1	70.7	94.4	93.3	78.7	95.2	95.4	79.1
1988–92	85.3	88.9	53.4	90.4	87.6	77.6	76.0	82.2	81.8	85.6	86.0	58.2	90.7	87.4	69.8	89.5	93.3	66.7
1993–98	66.3	68.4	45.5	66.0	81.4	61.7	54.6	70.5	60.7	73.7	66.3	36.7	85.5	76.8	48.0	84.7	80.3	37.5
1998	67.7	56.8	37.8	62.5	76.6	47.5	50.0	53.3	56.4	75.6	55.7	28.4	78.6	62.7	40.6	78.2	73.0	33.6

TABLE 10. Effects of changing characteristics and propensity to pay on the percent of firms paying dividends, estimated from 27 portfolios formed on size, profitability (E_t/A_t), and either market-to-book ratio (V_t/A_t) or investment outlays (dA_t/A_t)

Firms is the number of firms in the sample for a year, or the average for a period. Actual Percent is the percent of payers (the ratio of payers to firms, times 100). The Expected Percent of payers for a year is the number of firms in each of the 27 size-E_t/A_t – V_t/A_t portfolios (or the 27 size-E_t/A_t – dA_t/A_t portfolios) for the year times the proportion of dividend payers in the portfolio during the 1963–77 base period, summed over the 27 portfolios, divided by the total of firms in the 27 portfolios for the year, and then multiplied by 100. The expected percents change through time due to changes in the characteristics (size, E_t/A_p, and V_t/A_t or dA_t/A_t) of sample firms. Expected–Actual, the difference between the expected and actual percents of payers, measures the effect of changing propensity to pay.

| | | | V_t/A_t | | dA_t/A_t | |
	Firms	Actual Percent	Expected Percent	Expected –Actual	Expected Percent	Expected –Actual
1963–77	1,823	66.8				
1978	2,901	68.5	70.0	1.5	65.1	–3.5
1979	2,819	68.0	69.5	1.5	65.0	–3.0
1980	2,806	65.0	68.3	3.2	65.7	0.6
1981	2,917	58.2	65.9	7.7	64.4	6.1
1982	2,974	53.7	63.0	9.4	62.0	8.4
1983	3,127	47.0	57.6	10.6	61.2	14.2
1984	3,239	43.0	59.1	16.1	60.3	17.3
1985	3,196	41.3	56.4	15.1	59.3	18.0
1986	3,357	36.3	53.6	17.2	57.6	21.3
1987	3,587	32.4	53.6	21.2	57.3	24.9
1988	3,526	32.6	55.4	22.7	58.1	25.5
1989	3,429	33.4	55.2	21.8	58.7	25.3
1990	3,451	32.8	58.6	25.8	59.4	26.6
1991	3,582	31.1	56.5	25.3	59.4	28.3
1992	3,845	29.6	53.9	24.3	59.1	29.5
1993	4,265	26.8	50.3	23.5	57.4	30.6
1994	4,558	25.6	51.9	26.3	57.8	32.2
1995	4,768	24.7	52.2	27.5	58.4	33.7
1996	5,211	22.2	50.6	28.4	57.9	35.7
1997	5,278	21.1	49.3	28.2	57.3	36.2
1998	4,906	21.3	53.3	32.0	58.3	37.0

5.4. Propensity to Pay: Entrails from the Portfolio Approach

What kinds of firms do not pay dividends in 1998 that would have paid in earlier years? The answer from Table 9 is—all kinds. Lower propensity to pay cuts across all size, profitability, and investment groups. Table 9 shows percents of dividend payers in the portfolios formed on size, E_t/A_t, and V_t/A_t or dA_t/A_t. A portfolio's expected percent of payers after 1977 is the actual percent for the 1963–77 base period. Thus, the time path of the percent of payers for a portfolio traces the effects of propensity to pay dividends for firms with given size, E_t/A_t, and V_t/A_t or dA_t/A_t characteristics.

The results for the 27 portfolios formed on size, E_t/A_t, and dA_t/A_t are easiest to judge since each of these portfolios has at least 47 firms in 1998. The percents of dividend payers in the 27 portfolios are often higher in 1978 than in 1963–77. After 1978, the propensity to pay declines. For every portfolio, the percent of payers is lower in 1998 than in 1978. The results for the 27 portfolios formed on size, E_t/A_t, and V_t/A_t are similar; the percent of dividend payers declines (due to lower propensity to pay) in all but one portfolio. The only exception, small firms with medium E_t/A_t and high V_t/A_t, occurs because the percent of payers in 1978 is abnormally low. The 1998 proportion, 11.5%, is well below the average for 1963–77, 32.5%.

At the 1978 peak, most big stocks pay dividends whatever their characteristics. When dA_t/A_t is used to control for growth opportunities, the 1978 proportion of payers exceeds 85.0% in all nine big-stock portfolios, and it is above 92.0% in seven of the nine (Table 9). But even among big stocks, the propensity to pay declines sharply after 1978. When dA_t/A_t is used to measure growth opportunities, the 1998 proportion of payers never reaches 80.0% in any big-stock portfolio, it is below 65.0% for five of the nine, and the 1998 proportion of payers is 40.6% or less in three big-stock portfolios.

The decline in the propensity to pay dividends is even larger among small stocks. When dA_t/A_t is used to measure growth opportunities, the 1978 proportion of payers is less than 40.0% in only one of nine small-stock portfolios and it is 52.0% or higher in seven (Table 9). In contrast, the 1998 proportion of dividend payers exceeds 20.0% only in the four small-stock portfolios with medium or high profitability and low or medium investment outlays. In the five small-stock portfolios with low profitability or high investment outlays, dividend payers are an endangered species; the 1998 proportion of payers is 13.1% or less.

Finally, controlling for size and investment opportunities, the percent of dividend payers declines after 1978 in each of the three profitability groups, but there is no particular pattern across E_t/A_t groups. In contrast, controlling for size and profitability, the propensity to pay declines more from 1978 to 1998 for firms with high investment outlays. In other words, investment outlays become more of a deterrent to dividends (a result that seems in line with the logit regressions in Table 5). The big-stock portfolios provide striking examples. In 1978, 85.7%, 97.8%, and 92.4% of the firms in the three big-stock portfolios with high dA_t/A_t pay dividends. In 1998, only 28.4%, 40.6%, and 33.6% pay. Clearly, rapidly growing large firms no longer feel compelled to pay dividends.

6. SHARE REPURCHASES

Declining propensity to pay suggests that firms have become aware of the tax disadvantage of dividends. Consistent with this view, Table 11 confirms earlier evidence (Bagwell and Shoven, 1989; Dunsby, 1995) that share repurchases surge in the mid-1980s. For 1973–77 and 1978–82, aggregate share repurchases average 3.37% and 5.12% of aggregate earnings. For 1983–98, repurchases are 31.42% of earnings. Bagwell and Shoven (1989) argue that the increase in repurchases indicates that firms have learned to substitute repurchases for dividends in order to generate lower-taxed capital gains for stockholders. But subsequent tests of this hypothesis produce mixed results (DeAngelo et al., 2000; Jagannathan et al., 2000; Grullon and Michaely, 2000).

For our purposes, repurchases turn out to be rather unimportant. In particular, we show that because repurchases are primarily the province of dividend payers, they leave most of the decline in the percent of payers unexplained. Instead, the primary effect of repurchases is to increase the already high cash payouts of dividend payers.

We first address a problem. Previous papers treat all share repurchases as non-cash dividends, that is, a repackaging of shareholder wealth that substitutes capital value for cash dividends. There are two cases where repurchases do not have this effect: (i) repurchased stock is often reissued to employee stock ownership plans (ESOPs) and as executive stock options, and (ii) repurchased stock is often reissued to the acquired firm in a merger. [Allen and Michaely (1995) show that the surge in repurchases after 1983 lines up with a surge in mergers.] An acquiring firm repurchases stock when it wishes to finance a merger with retained earnings or debt but the acquired firm (for tax reasons) prefers stock. Repurchases to complete mergers simply help finance this form of investment. Like other investments, mergers allow firms to transform earnings into capital value rather than dividends. But repurchases of stock to

TABLE 11. Aggregate dividends, share repurchases, share issues, and changes in treasury stock as percents of aggregate earnings and market equity

We calculate annual ratios as the aggregate value of the numerator divided by the aggregate value of the denominator, and then average the ratios over the years in a period. D_t and Y_t are dividends and after-tax earnings to common stock for fiscal years that end in calendar year t. ME_t is the market value of common equity at the end of fiscal year t. SP_t, SI_t, and dT_t are gross share repurchases, share issues, and the change in treasury stock for fiscal year t. Net share repurchases, NP_t, are $SP_t - SI_t$. Results are for all firms and, where indicated, for firms grouped according to dividend status. Data on share repurchases and share issues are not available until 1971. The change in treasury stock is not available until 1983.

Aggregate dividends as a percent of aggregate earnings, D_t/Y_t

	1963–98	1963–67	1968–72	1973–77	1978–82	1983–87	1988–92	1993–98
All firms	43.27	50.71	47.29	33.95	34.86	40.73	56.86	39.31
Payers	44.78	51.69	48.91	35.05	35.63	41.84	58.02	42.71

Aggregate dividends as a percent of aggregate market equity, D_t/ME_t

	1963–98	1963–67	1968–72	1973–77	1978–82	1983–87	1988–92	1993–98
All firms	2.95	2.91	2.66	3.68	4.39	3.09	2.62	1.56
Payers	3.22	2.99	2.82	3.84	4.66	3.47	3.00	2.02

Aggregate share repurchases, share issues, and changes in treasury stock as percents of aggregate earnings for all firms

	1971–98	1983–98	1973–77	1978–82	1983–87	1988–92	1993–98
SP_t/Y_t	19.71	31.42	3.37	5.12	27.98	30.02	35.46
SI_t/Y_t	24.64	33.71	8.90	14.93	26.00	35.91	38.29
NP_t/Y_t	-4.93	-2.28	-5.54	-9.80	1.98	-5.89	-2.83
dT_t/Y_t		14.95			14.92	11.76	17.63

Aggregate change in treasury stock as a percent of aggregate market equity, dT_t/ME_t

	1983–98	1983–87	1988–92	1993–98
All firms	0.80	1.10	0.67	0.66
Payers	0.89	1.19	0.72	0.79
Non-payers	0.28	0.36	0.27	0.23
Never paid	0.24	0.25	0.30	0.18
Former payers	0.52	0.91	0.17	0.49

finance a merger are not a source of additional capital value, beyond what is produced by the merger.

A better measure of repurchases that qualify as non-cash dividends is the annual change in treasury stock. Treasury stock captures the cumulative effects of stock repurchases and reissues, and it is not affected by new issues of stock (seasoned equity offerings). Treasury stock data are not available on Compustat before 1982, so the first change is for 1983. But the treasury stock data do cover the period of strong repurchase activity. Some firms use the retirement method, rather than treasury stock, to account for repurchases. Our aggregate changes in treasury stock include the net repurchases of these firms, measured (for each firm) as the difference between purchases and sales of stock, when the difference is positive, and zero otherwise. (See the appendix for details.)

During 1983–98, the annual change in treasury stock, dT_t, is less than half of gross share repurchases, SP_t; specifically, dT_t and SP_t average 14.95% and 31.42% of earnings (Table 11). Cash dividends are 45.24% of earnings, so if gross repurchases are treated as an additional payout of earnings, the total payout for 1983–98 averages 76.66% of earnings. Substituting the more appropriate annual change in treasury stock drops the payout to (a still high) 60.19% of earnings.

Aggregate changes in treasury stock are substantial relative to aggregate earnings, but they fall far short of explaining the decline in the percent of dividend payers due to lower propensity to pay. The problem is that the fraction of non-payers with positive dT_t is low. During 1983–98, on average only 14.5% of non-payers have positive dT_t (Table 12). And the percent of firms with positive dT_t overstates the extent to which firms substitute repurchases for dividends. Consider a firm that repurchases shares in one fiscal year and reissues them as part of an ESOP, executive compensation plan, or merger in the next. Because the repurchase and reissue are spread across two fiscal years, they cause a positive change in dT_t in the first year and a negative change in the second. Although the repurchase just accommodates a reissue, a simple count of firms with positive dT_t misclassifies the repurchase as a substitute for a cash dividend. On average, 6.9% of non-payers have negative dT_t during 1983–98. The results for 1993–98 are similar; 14.5% of non-payers have positive dT_t and 6.6% have negative dT_t.

On average, 76.4% of Compustat firms do not pay dividends during 1993–98. Thus, even if we use our upper bound of 14.5% to estimate the fraction of non-payers that use share repurchases as a substitute for dividends, this group is only 11.1% (0.764*0.145) of all firms. This is about one-third of the

TABLE 12. Percent of firms with positive and negative changes in treasury stock

The change in treasury stock, dT_t, is measured from the end of fiscal year $t-1$ to the end of fiscal year t. The reported percent of firms with a positive change in treasury stock, $dT_t > 0$, or a negative change in treasury stock, $dT_t < 0$, is the average of the annual percents. Positive changes in treasury stock include firms that use the retirement method to account for repurchases if their repurchases for fiscal year t exceed their stock issues. Negative changes in treasury stock do not include firms that use the retirement method and have negative net repurchases. The results are shown for all firms and for firms grouped according to dividend status.

	1983–98	1983–87	1988–92	1993–98
All				
Net $dT > 0$	20.1	19.0	22.0	19.5
Net $dT < 0$	10.1	10.1	11.5	9.0
Payers				
Net $dT > 0$	33.4	28.9	34.5	36.2
Net $dT < 0$	17.2	16.1	19.0	16.5
Non-payers				
Net $dT > 0$	14.5	12.8	16.1	14.5
Net $dT < 0$	6.9	6.0	8.0	6.6
Never paid				
Net $dT > 0$	13.5	12.0	15.3	13.3
Net $dT < 0$	5.6	4.8	6.5	5.5
Former payers				
Net $dT > 0$	20.5	16.9	21.1	23.0
Net $dT < 0$	14.5	12.1	17.0	14.5

smaller estimate (32.0) of the shortfall in the percent of payers that the portfolio approach of the preceding section attributes to lower propensity to pay dividends. Thus, lower propensity to pay must be related to other aspects of the investment and financing decisions of non-payers.

Net repurchases are larger and more prevalent among dividend payers. On average, 33.4% of dividend payers have positive dT_t during 1983–98, versus 14.5% for non-payers (Table 12). The aggregate dT_t of dividend payers averages 0.89% of their aggregate market equity, versus 0.28% for non-payers (Table 11). Aggregate cash dividends average 2.78% of the aggregate market equity of dividend payers during 1983–98. Thus, dividend payers use share repurchases rather than dividends for about 25% of their cash payments to shareholders.

The cash dividend payout ratio of dividend payers shows no tendency to decline. The aggregate dividends of payers are 47.22% of their aggregate earnings in 1983–98, versus 44.78% for 1963–98. And on average, 92.2% of the annual aggregate change in treasury stock during 1983–98 is by firms that also pay dividends (Table 4). We infer that the large share repurchases of 1983–98 are mostly due to an increase in the desired payout ratios of dividend payers, which they are reluctant to satisfy with cash dividends. Table 3 then shows that the higher payout ratios of dividend payers during 1983–98 are associated with lower rates of investment (dA_t/A_t) and higher book leverage (L_t/A_t).

Finally, even during the 1993–98 period, when dividend payers are only 23.6% of Compustat firms (Table 1), they nevertheless account for 91.7% of common stock earnings (Table 4). It is thus not surprising that the aggregate payout ratio D_t/Y_t (the ratio of aggregate dividends to aggregate common stock earnings) for all firms is basically the same as the ratio for dividend payers—and likewise shows no tendency to decline through time. Confirming Dunsby (1995), Table 11 shows that the aggregate payout ratio for all firms actually increases from 33.95% in 1973–77, when 64.3% of firms pay dividends, to 39.31% in 1993–98, when only 23.6% of firms pay dividends.

We emphasize, however, that the aggregate payout ratio says nothing about the propensity of firms to pay dividends. As noted earlier, the surge in unprofitable non-paying new lists in the 1980s and 1990s keeps the aggregate profits of non-payers low even though the non-payer group includes an increasing fraction of firms with positive earnings—firms that in the past would have paid dividends. As a result, the aggregate payout ratio for all firms masks the kind of widespread evidence of lower propensity to pay dividends, among individual firms of all types, that is obvious in Tables 6, 8, and (especially) 9.

7. CONCLUSIONS

From a post-1972 peak of 66.5% in 1978, the proportion of dividend payers among NYSE, AMEX, and NASDAQ non-financial non-utility firms falls to 20.8% in 1999. The decline in the incidence of dividend payers is in part due to an increasing tilt of publicly traded firms toward the characteristics of firms that have never paid dividends—small size, low earnings, and large investments relative to earnings. This change in the nature of publicly traded firms is driven by a surge in new listings after 1978 and by the changing nature of new lists. Before 1978, newly listed firms have strong investment opportunities (high asset growth rates and high market value of assets relative to book value) and they are more profitable than seasoned firms. After 1978, new lists continue to have high V_t/A_t and high asset growth rates, but their profitability falls. The surge in new lists and their changing characteristics produce a swelling group of small firms with low profitability but strong investment opportunities that never pay dividends.

The change in the characteristics of firms is important in the declining incidence of dividend payers. But it is only half the story. Our more interesting result is that given their characteristics, firms have become less likely to pay dividends. We use logit regressions and a portfolio approach to document that characteristics and propensity to pay make large separate contributions to the decline in the percent of payers. When V_t/A_t is used to measure investment opportunities, characteristics and propensity to pay are roughly equal partners in the decline in the percent of dividend payers. When only actual investment outlays, dA_t/A_t, are used to measure investment opportunities, propensity to pay has the larger role.

Lower propensity to pay is quite general. The percent of dividend payers among firms with positive earnings declines after 1978. But the percent of payers among firms with negative earnings also declines. Small firms become much less likely to pay dividends after 1978, but there is also a lower incidence of dividend payers among large firms. Firms with many investments become much less likely to pay dividends after 1978, but dividends also become less likely among firms with fewer investments.

The effects of changing characteristics and propensity to pay vary across dividend groups. The characteristics of dividend payers (large, profitable firms) do not change much after 1978, and controlling for characteristics, payers become only slightly more likely to stop paying. Changing characteristics and lower propensity to pay show up more clearly in the dividend decisions of former payers and firms that have never paid. Lower profitability and strong growth opportunities produce much lower expected rates of dividend initiation by firms that have never paid. But controlling for characteristics, firms that have never paid also initiate dividends at much lower rates after 1978, and former payers become much less likely to resume dividends.

The evidence that, controlling for characteristics, firms become less likely to pay dividends says that the perceived benefits of dividends have declined through time. Some (but surely not all) of the possibilities are: (i) lower transactions costs for selling stocks for consumption purposes, in part due to an increased tendency to hold stocks via open end mutual funds; (ii) larger holdings of stock options by managers who prefer capital gains to dividends; and (iii) better corporate governance technologies (e.g., more prevalent use of stock options) that lower the benefits of dividends in controlling agency problems between stockholders and managers.

APPENDIX. DATA AND VARIABLE DEFINITIONS

The Compustat sample for calendar year t, 1963–98, includes those firms with fiscal year-ends in t that have the following data (Compustat data items in parentheses): total assets (6), stock price (199) and shares outstanding (25) at the end of the fiscal year, income before extraordinary items (18), interest expense (15), dividends per share by ex date (26), preferred dividends (19), and (a) preferred stock liquidating value (10), (b) preferred stock redemption value (56), or (c) preferred stock carrying value (130). Firms must also have (a) stockholder's equity (216), (b) liabilities (181), or (c) common equity (60) and preferred stock par value (130). Total assets must be available in years t and $t-1$. The other items must be available in t. We also use, but do not require, balance sheet deferred taxes and investment tax credit (35), income statement deferred taxes (50), purchases of common and preferred stock (115), sales of common and preferred stock (108), and common treasury stock (226). We exclude firms with book equity (BE$_t$) below $250,000 or assets ($A_t$) below $500,000. To ensure that firms are publicly traded, the Compustat sample includes only firms with CRSP share codes of 10 or 11, and we use only the fiscal years a firm is in the CRSP database at its fiscal year-end.

The CRSP sample, used in Tables 1 and 2 and Figs. 1, 2, and 5, includes NYSE, AMEX, and NASDAQ securities with CRSP share codes of 10 or 11. A firm must have market equity data (price and shares outstanding) for December of year t to be in the CRSP sample for that year. We exclude utilities (SIC codes 4900–4949) and financial firms (SIC codes 6000–6999) from both samples.

A.1. Derived Variables

Preferred Stock = Preferred Stock Liquidating Value (10) [or Preferred Stock Redemption Value (56), or Preferred Stock Par Value (130)];

Book Equity (BE$_t$) = Stockholder's Equity (216) [or Common Equity (60) + Preferred Stock Par Value (130) or Assets (6) − Liabilities (181)] − Preferred Stock + Balance Sheet Deferred Taxes and Investment Tax Credit (35) if available − Post Retirement Asset (330) if available;

Market Equity (ME$_t$) = Stock Price (199) times Shares Outstanding (25);

Market Value of Firm (V_t) = Assets (6) − Book Equity + Market Equity;

Earnings Before Interest (E_t) = Earnings Before Extraordinary Items (18) + Interest Expense (15) + Income Statement Deferred Taxes (50) if available;

Earnings Available for Common (Y_t) = Earnings Before Extraordinary Items (18) − Preferred Dividends (19) + Income Statement Deferred Taxes (50) if available.

A.2. Dividend Payers and Non-Payers

A firm in the Compustat sample is defined as a dividend payer in calendar year t if it has positive dividends per share by the ex date (26) in the (last) fiscal year that ends in t. A firm in the CRSP sample is defined as a dividend payer in calendar year t if its with-dividend return exceeds its without-dividend return in any month of year t. A CRSP firm must have at least seven months of good returns in year t to be classified as a non-payer. A firm is included in only the All Firms category for a year if it has fewer than seven good returns and there is no month when its with-dividend and without-dividend returns differ.

A.3. Newly Listed Firms

A firm in the CRSP sample is defined as a new list in calendar year t if it is added to the CRSP database between June of year $t − 1$ and May of t. A firm in the Compustat sample is defined as a new list in calendar year t if it is added to the CRSP database between January and December of year t. Compustat firms must be in the CRSP database to be new lists. Moreover, NYSE firms added to the CRSP database in December 1925, AMEX firms added in July 1962, and NASDAQ firms added between December 1972 and February 1973 are not defined as new lists in either the CRSP or Compustat samples.

A.4. Change in Treasury Stock

The change in treasury stock for year t is defined as the change in the value of common treasury stock (Compustat data item 226) from year $t − 1$ to year t. When a firm uses the retirement method to account for repurchases, however, we replace the change in treasury stock by the maximum of zero and the difference between purchases (115) and sales (108) of common and preferred stock in year t.

Compustat indicates that a firm uses the retirement method in year t by setting annual footnote 45 equal to TR. But a check of the database reveals many TR firms with fiscal years in which (i) footnote 45 does not indicate the retirement method, (ii) treasury stock is zero, and (iii) purchases of common and preferred stock exceed sales. We infer that the firm uses the retirement method in these "non-TR" years. Thus, we assume that a firm uses the retirement method in any year in which footnote 45 is "TR", and in all contiguous years in which common treasury stock is zero. For example, if footnote 45 is "TR" in year t and the treasury stock is zero from $t-5$ to $t+3$, we measure net repurchases for years $t-5$ to $t+4$ as the maximum of zero and the difference between purchases and sales. (We cannot use the change in treasury stock in year $t+4$ because we need a start-up year to measure the annual difference.)

REFERENCES

Allen, F., Michaely, R., 1995. Dividend policy. In: Jarrow, R., Maksimovic, V., Ziemba, W. (Eds.), Handbooks in Operations Research and Management Science: Finance. North-Holland, Amsterdam, pp. 793–838.

Bagwell, L., Shoven, J., 1989. Cash distributions to shareholders. Journal of Economic Perspectives 3, 129–149.

DeAngelo, H., DeAngelo, L., 1990. Dividend policy and financial distress: an empirical examination of troubled NYSE firms. Journal of Finance 45, 1415–1431.

DeAngelo, H., DeAngelo, L., Skinner, D., 1992. Dividends and losses. Journal of Finance 47, 1837–1863.

DeAngelo, H., DeAngelo, L., Skinner, D., 2000. Special dividends and the evolution of dividend signaling. Journal of Financial Economics 57, 309–354.

Dunsby, A., 1995. Share repurchases, dividends, and corporate distribution policy. Ph.D. Thesis, The Wharton School, University of Pennsylvania, Philadelphia.

Easterbrook, F., 1984. Two agency-cost explanations of dividends. American Economic Review 74, 650–659.

Fama, E., French, K., 1999. Testing tradeoff and pecking order predictions about dividends and debt. Unpublished working paper, Sloan School of Management, MIT, Cambridge, MA.

Fama, E., MacBeth, J., 1973. Risk, return, and equilibrium: empirical tests. Journal of Political Economy 81, 607–636.

Grullon, G., Michaely, R., 2000. Dividends, share repurchases, and the substitution hypothesis. Unpublished manuscript, Cornell University, Ithaca, NY.

Jagannathan, M., Stephens, C., Weisbach, M., 2000. Financial flexibility and the choice between dividends and stock repurchases. Journal of Financial Economics 57, 355–384.

Jain, B., Kini, O., 1994. The post-issue operating performance of IPO firms. Journal of Finance 49, 1699–1726.

Jensen, M., 1986. Agency costs of free-cash-flow, corporate finance, and takeovers. American Economic Review 76, 323–329.

Mikkelson, W., Partch, M., Shah, K., 1997. Ownership and operating performance of companies that go public. Journal of Financial Economics 44, 281–307.

Myers, S., 1984. The capital structure puzzle. Journal of Finance 39, 575–592.

Myers, S., Majluf, N., 1984. Corporate financing and investment decisions when firms have information the investors do not have. Journal of Financial Economics 13, 187–221.

FINANCING DECISIONS

WHO ISSUES STOCK?

. . .

Eugene F. Fama and Kenneth R. French

1. INTRODUCTION

The modern corporate finance literature focuses on two competing models to explain the financing decisions of firms. In the tradeoff model, firms identify optimal leverage by weighing the costs and benefits of an additional dollar of debt. The benefits of debt include, for example, the tax deductibility of interest and the reduction of free-cash-flow agency problems. The costs of debt include potential bankruptcy costs and agency conflicts between stockholders and bondholders. At the leverage optimum, the benefit of the last dollar of debt just offsets the cost.

Myers (1984) advocates an alternative theory, the pecking order model. The pecking order arises if the costs of issuing risky securities—transactions costs and especially the costs created by management's superior information about the value of the firm's risky securities—overwhelm the costs and benefits proposed by the tradeoff model. The costs of issuing risky securities spawn the pecking order: firms finance new investments first with retained earnings, then with safe debt, then risky debt, and finally, but only under duress, with outside equity.

The pecking order sequence for financing decisions leads to a prediction about capital structures. Specifically, variation in a firm's leverage is driven not by the tradeoff model's costs and benefits of debt or equity, but more simply, by the firm's financing deficit (dividends plus investment outlays minus

Reprinted with permission from the *Journal of Financial Economics* 76 (June 2005): 549–82. © 2004 by Elsevier Limited.

We acknowledge the helpful comments of Elroy Dimson, Michael Katz, Stewart Myers, Richard Roll, Richard Sansing René Stulz, workshop participants at Dartmouth, the University of Chicago, Yale, and the NBER, and especially Clyde Stickney and two anonymous referees. We thank Michael McWilliams and especially Savina Rizova for excellent research assistance.

earnings). Quoting Myers (1984), "The crucial difference between this and the static tradeoff story is that, in the modified pecking order story, observed debt ratios will reflect the cumulative requirement for external financing—a requirement cumulated over an extended period".

In short, Myers (1984) presents the pecking order model as a theory both about how firms finance themselves and about the capital structures that result from pecking order financing. Subsequent tests of the model follow these two routes. For example, Shyam-Sunder and Myers (1999), Fama and French (2002), and Frank and Goyal (2003) test the model's predictions about the securities firms issue to cover financing deficits, while Titman and Wessels (1988), Rajan and Zingales (1995), Shyam-Sunder and Myers (1999), Fama and French (2002), and Huang and Song (2003) test the model's predictions about capital structures.

This earlier work mainly uses cross-section regressions to test the pecking order model. Cross-section regressions measure average responses of financing decisions and capital structures to variables such as growth and profitability (the ingredients of the financing deficit). But average responses may conceal important details relevant for judging the model. We take a more direct approach. We test pecking order predictions about financing decisions by examining how often and under what circumstances firms issue and repurchase equity. We uncover what seem to be pervasive contradictions of the model.

The first important result is striking evidence against the pecking order prediction that firms rarely issue stock. As motivation for the pecking order, Myers (1984) emphasizes that aggregate net new issues of equity are small relative to net new debt. It is also well-known that seasoned equity offerings (SEOs) are rare. But the aggregate level of equity financing and the scarcity of SEOs are misleading. In addition to SEOs, firms issue equity in mergers and through private placements, convertible debt, warrants, direct purchase plans, rights issues, and employee options, grants, and benefit plans. During 1973 to 1982, on average 67% of our sample firms issue some equity each year, and the proportion rises to 74% for 1983 to 1992 and 86% for 1993 to 2002. During much of the sample period, however, repurchases by some firms offset the equity issues of others, and aggregate annual net new equity is small. This result, along with the low frequency of SEOs, leads to the misleading impression that new issues of stock are rare.

In fact, most firms issue, repurchase, or do both every year. And our examination of the firms that issue or retire equity shows that equity decisions often violate the pecking order. Thus, equity issuers are not typically under duress;

net issues are common among firms with moderate leverage and financing surpluses (earnings exceed the sum of dividends and investment). Also in violation of the pecking order, repurchases are not limited to firms with low demand for outside financing; many firms with financing deficits repurchase stock. We estimate that during 1973 to 2002, the year-by-year equity decisions of more than half of our sample firms contradict the pecking order.

Moreover, annual net issues of equity are material. For example, on average 61.5% of small firms (total assets below the NYSE median) make net issues of stock each year from 1983 to 1992, and the average rises to 73.7% for 1993 to 2002. These annual net stock issues average 6.0% of assets during 1983 to 1992 and 12.6% for 1993 to 2002, both larger than the annual net new debt of these firms, which averages 5.2% and 6.4% of assets for the two periods. On average 66.5% of big firms make net stock issues each year of the 1993 to 2002 period, and their net equity issues are about the same magnitude, 7.5% of assets, as their net issues of debt, 7.9%.

The fact that equity issues and repurchases are commonplace and commonly not in line with the pecking order seems like a telling blow to the argument of Myers (1984) and Myers and Majluf (1984) that asymmetric information problems drive the capital structures of firms. Myers (1984) and Myers and Majluf (1984) do not allow for equity issues that do not have an asymmetric information problem. One story for our results is that there are important ways to issue equity that avoid this problem. If so, the pecking order, as the stand-alone model of capital structure proposed by Myers (1984), is dead: financing with equity is not a last resort, and asymmetric information problems are not the sole (or perhaps even an important) determinant of capital structures. This does not mean the asymmetric information problem disappears. But its implications become quite limited: firms do not follow the pecking order in financing decisions; they simply avoid issuing equity in ways that involve asymmetric information problems.

Our measure of equity issues is all encompassing, including any transaction that increases the number of (split-adjusted) shares outstanding. This leads some readers to argue that our results say nothing about the pecking order because we include stock issues that do not have asymmetric information problems. But again, the pecking order is proposed by Myers (1984) and Myers and Majluf (1984) as a complete model of capital structures, so our broad measure of equity issues is relevant for analyzing its predictions about how capital structures are determined. For example, issues of stock to employees via options and grants play a big role in our results on the frequency of equity issues.

Stock issues to employees may not have an asymmetric information problem. A firm nevertheless alters its capital structure when it compensates employees with stock instead of cash—and chooses not to offset the stock issues with repurchases. In short, if the pecking order model can only handle ways of issuing equity that involve large asymmetric information problems, it is not a model of capital structure.

The breakdown of the pecking order does not require that equity can be issued with minor asymmetric information problems. Anything that produces the result that equity is not a last resort will do. For example, agency problems may sometimes lead managers to ignore the costs of issuing equity (Jung et al., 1996). It is also likely that some equity issues have benefits that outweigh their costs, i.e., tradeoff effects. For example, getting stock in a merger can have tax benefits for shareholders of the acquired firm that lead them to accept a lower price for their shares. Similarly, stock issued to employees may have motivation benefits that outweigh any asymmetric information costs. The important point is that any forces that cause firms to deviate systematically from pecking order financing (retained earnings, then debt, and equity only as a last resort) imply that the pecking order model, on its own, cannot explain capital structures.

Our story proceeds as follows. Section 2 outlines the pecking order model. Section 3 documents how the profitability and growth characteristics of firms, which are important for understanding financing decisions, change through time. Our main empirical results are in Sections 4–6. The theme of these sections is that violations of the pecking order become more evident when financing decisions are examined at more disaggregated levels. Section 4 examines financing decisions at the level of the market, where we find little evidence against the pecking order model, except later in the sample period. Section 5, the paper's centerpiece, disaggregates firms into 12 groups formed on size, profitability, and growth, and examines in detail how equity issuers in the 12 groups differ from repurchasers. Here we find widespread evidence of pecking order violations. Section 6 provides evidence on the mechanisms firms use to issue equity. The concluding section discusses the implications of our findings.

2. THE PECKING ORDER MODEL

Myers (1984) uses Myers and Majluf (1984) to motivate the pecking order. In Myers and Majluf (1984), managers use private information to issue risky securities when they are overpriced. Investors are aware of this asymmetric information problem, and the prices of risky securities fall when new issues are announced. Managers anticipate the price declines, and may forego profitable investments if they must be financed with risky securities. To avoid this distortion of investment decisions, managers follow what Myers (1984) calls the pecking order. They finance projects first with retained earnings, which have no asymmetric information problem, then with low-risk debt, for which the problem is negligible, then with risky debt. Equity is issued only under duress, or when investment so far exceeds earnings that financing with debt would produce excessive leverage. Myers (1984) also posits that in the short term, dividends are (for unspecified reasons) sticky, leaving variation in net cash flows to be absorbed mainly by debt.

Myers (1984) largely ignores share repurchases. Shyam-Sunder and Myers (1999) address the issue, and argue that the asymmetric information problem of new common stock applies to repurchases. If a firm announces a repurchase, investors assume managers have positive information not reflected in the stock price, causing the price to rise. This can deter the repurchase if the price rises above what managers consider the equilibrium level. More important, debt capacity is a valuable option for future financing. Thus, when firms use financing surpluses to retire securities, they first retire debt. They retire equity only when leverage is low or when poor investment opportunities (relative to earnings) lower the value of debt capacity. In short, repurchases should be limited to firms with little or no leverage, few investment opportunities, or both.

Two additional points about the pecking order are pertinent for interpreting our empirical results. First, Myers (1984) emphasizes asymmetric information problems, but he recognizes that transactions costs alone can produce pecking order financing if they are higher for debt than for retained earnings and higher yet for equity. In other words, asymmetric information may be unnecessary.

Second, in Myers (1984) and Myers and Majluf (1984), the pecking order arises through an implicit assumption that there is no way to issue equity that avoids asymmetric information problems. If firms find ways to issue equity without such problems, asymmetric information may not constrain equity issues. As a result, pecking order financing can disappear; that is, financing with equity is not a last resort, the incentive to avoid repurchases to maintain debt capacity is gone, and asymmetric information problems do not drive capital structures. This does not mean asymmetric information is irrelevant. But its implications become quite limited. Firms do avoid issuing risky securities in ways that involve asymmetric information problems, but financing decisions do not follow the pecking order.

The capital structure literature focuses on SEOs as the source of outside equity. There are at least seven other ways firms issue equity: (1) mergers via an exchange of stock, (2) employee stock options, grants, and other employee benefit plans, (3) subscription rights issued to stockholders, (4) warrants attached to other securities, (5) convertible bonds, (6) dividend reinvestment and other direct purchase plans, and (7) private placements. Do some of the mechanisms for issuing equity involve low transactions costs and minor asymmetric information problems?

Consider transactions costs. SEOs, warrants, and convertible bonds have large underwriting costs. The large price concessions in private placements of equity (Wruck, 1989; Hertzel et al., 2002) are also a high transaction cost. In contrast, rights offerings are not costly (Smith, 1977). Issuing stock to employees via grants, options, and other benefit plans also probably involves low transactions costs. The same is true for direct purchase plans. Negotiating mergers is costly, but the marginal cost of carrying out an exchange of stock may not be high. In short, four of the alternatives for issuing stock seem to involve low transactions costs.

Asymmetric information is a stickier issue. Myers (1984) posits that stock price declines in response to announcements of equity issues reflect asymmetric information problems. If so, the problems are severe for SEOs (Masulis and Korwar, 1986), and present but weaker for convertible bonds (Mikkelson and Partch, 1986). Wruck (1989) and Hertzel et al. (2002) find that the stock price response to private placements is positive. Though their samples are small, Smith (1977) and Eckbo and Masulis (1992) find no evidence of a reliable negative price response to announcements of rights issues. The price responses to initiations of dividend reinvestment plans (Peterson et al., 1987; Allen et al., 1995) and ESOP plans (Chaplinsky and Niehaus, 1994) also seem to be small. Moeller et al. (2004) find that the negative price responses to stock-financed mergers are limited to acquisitions of publicly traded firms by big publicly traded firms. Otherwise, mergers financed with stock do not seem to have negative price effects.

Stock issues in direct purchase plans are initiated by the purchasers (mostly existing stockholders), not by managers, so asymmetric information problems may be absent. Asymmetric information problems may be minor in stock-financed mergers because mergers are negotiated between informed parties. Likewise, asymmetric information may not be important in grants of stock and options to employees because employees are informed or the issues are a matter of routine. And stock issues in mergers and to employees are important in our later evidence on the frequency and magnitude of issues.

But asymmetric information problems can never be ruled out. Firms can always use repurchases to offset stock issues to employees, in mergers, and in direct purchase plans. The decision not to repurchase may be interpreted as evidence that managers think the stock is overvalued—an asymmetric information problem. As always, the information conveyed by any action depends on the market's expectations. Unfortunately, event studies cannot settle the matter unambiguously since price responses to announcements may not be due solely to asymmetric information problems.

We are not arguing that asymmetric information problems are unavoidable. Indeed, it is likely that the asymmetric information problems that arise with some ways of issuing stock (most notably SEOs) do not lead to pecking order financing (equity is not a last resort and asymmetric information problems do not drive capital structures) because firms can issue equity in other ways that largely avoid asymmetric information problems. The discussion above suggests that the prime candidates for breaking the grip of the pecking order are stock issues to employees, with perhaps a minor assist from rights offerings and direct purchase plans, and a big assist from stock-financed mergers.

Breaking the grip of the pecking order does not require that equity can be issued with minor asymmetric information problems and low transactions costs. Any forces that produce the result that equity is not a last resort will do. One possibility is that agency problems sometimes lead managers to ignore equity issuing costs (Jung et al., 1996). A potentially important alternative is that equity issues can have benefits that outweigh their costs, i.e., tradeoff effects. For example, an exchange of stock in a merger can create a tax benefit that offsets asymmetric information costs. By paying with stock, the acquiring firm allows target shareholders to postpone capital gains taxes, which should lead the shareholders to accept a lower price for their shares. Similarly, the motivation benefits of stock issued to employees may outweigh asymmetric information costs if there are any. The important point is that any forces that cause firms to deviate systematically from pecking order financing (retained earnings, then debt, and equity only as a last resort) imply that the pecking order model cannot alone explain capital structures.

Finally, in developing the pecking order model, Myers (1984) takes dividend decisions as given and outside the purview of the model. This is a patch on the model, a tacit admission that tradeoff forces or other factors are important in dividend decisions since the asymmetric information story in itself would predict that dividends (like repurchases) are rare. There is a second important patch. The concluding sections of Myers (1984) and Myers and Majluf (1984) argue that firms want to avoid debt that may result in distress that prevents them from exercising future investment options. As a result, firms with large current and expected investments relative to earnings may issue equity even though leverage is moderate. This patch on the pecking order model allows firms with large current and expected financing deficits to opt out of simple pecking order behavior, causing such firms to look more like those predicted by the tradeoff model (they incur current asymmetric information costs because of expected future benefits).

In evaluating the empirical results that follow, we largely let the pecking order retain these two patches, to give the model its best shot at explaining the evidence.

3. THE CHARACTERISTICS OF SAMPLE FIRMS

The profitability and growth characteristics of firms are central in evaluating their financing decisions. Thus, we begin the empirical work with a brief description of the changing characteristics of listed firms. The data are from CRSP and Compustat, the period is 1973 to 2002 (when Compustat's coverage of listed firms is fairly complete), and the sample includes NYSE, AMEX, and Nasdaq firms. We exclude financial firms and utilities. Financial intermediaries do not seem relevant for testing models of financing decisions, and during much of the sample period, regulation is important in the capital structure decisions of utilities.

The number of listed non-financial, non-utility firms with the necessary data for later tests rises from an average of 2,951 for 1973 to 1982, to 4,417 for 1993 to 2002 (Table 1). The increase is primarily among small firms, defined as NYSE, AMEX, and Nasdaq firms with total assets below the NYSE median. The number of big firms only rises from an average of 617 for 1973 to 1982, to 712 for 1993 to 2002.

To illustrate the changing characteristics of firms, Table 1 separately allocates small and big firms to portfolios formed as the intersections of three profitability and two growth groups. The breakpoints for the profitability and growth groups are averages of NYSE annual medians for 1973 to 2002. The three profitability groups for each year include firms with (i) negative earnings before interest (E), (ii) low profitability (earnings relative to total assets, E/A, below the average median for NYSE firms with positive E), and (iii) high profitability (E/A above the average NYSE median). The two growth groups include firms with (i) low asset growth for year t ($dA/A = (A_t - A_{t-1})/A_t$ below the average median for NYSE firms) and (ii) high asset growth (dA/A above

TABLE 1. Average number of firms in size-profitability-growth groups

Each year's sample of all firms includes all non-financial (SIC codes between 6000 and 6999), non-utility (4900–4949) firms with the necessary CRSP and Compustat data for that year (see the appendix). Firms are assigned to the Small and Big portfolios and to the 12 size-profitability-growth portfolios in year t based on their characteristics at the end of their fiscal year in calendar year t. The assets of small and big firms in year t are below or above those of the median NYSE firm in t. The breakpoints for growth and positive profitability are the averages of the annual NYSE medians for 1973 to 2002. A firm is assigned to the low- or high-growth group for year t if its growth in assets, $dA/A = (A_t - A_{t-1})/A_t$, is below or above the average median for 1973 to 2002. A profitable firm is assigned to the low- or high-profitability group for t if its earnings relative to assets, E/A, is below or above the 1973 to 2002 average median of NYSE firms with positive profitability.

	All firms	Small	Big
1973–1982	2951	2334	617
1983–1992	3672	3126	545
1993–2002	4417	3704	712

		Small						Big				
E/A:		Negative E		Low E/A		High E/A		Negative E		Low E/A		High E/A	
	dA/A:	Low	High	Low	High	Low	High	Low	High	Low	High	Low	High
1973–1982		186	47	459	412	340	887	11	2	130	154	71	246
1983–1992		757	224	579	518	329	717	38	8	144	109	93	152
1993–2002		1018	398	606	676	298	707	54	33	191	185	104	142

the NYSE average median). The appendix contains precise definitions of E/A, dA/A, and our other variables.

There are fairly general increases in the number of big firms in different profitability and growth groups. The group of big firms with high profitability and high growth is the only one that shrinks, from an average of 246 for 1973 to 1982, to 142 for 1993 to 2002. Thus, the population of profitable, rapidly growing big firms contracts through time, but all other big groups expand.

The number of small firms (mostly on Nasdaq) explodes during the sample period, but the increases are not uniform across groups. The notable surges are for small unprofitable firms and small firms with positive but low profitability. The number of small highly profitable firms actually declines, from an average of 1,227 for 1973 to 1982, to 1,005 for 1993 to 2002.

In short, the number of listed firms increases from 1973 to 2002, largely due to an influx of unprofitable and low-profitability firms. The number of highly profitable firms actually declines. These patterns are common to both small and big firms, but for groups with increasing numbers of firms, the increases among small firms dwarf those for big firms.

Lemmon and Zender (2002) argue that equity issues by fast-growing firms with low profitability are rational opt-outs allowed by the pecking order (via the patch discussed above). They argue that the increased frequency of such firms, obvious in Table 1, explains the apparent evidence against the pecking order of Frank and Goyal (2003). When we later examine equity issuers and repurchasers in the 12 size-profitability-growth groups in detail, however, we find that violations of the pecking order are pervasive. The violations are not limited to fast-growing low-profitability firms.

4. THE MARKET

Table 2 summarizes the aggregate financing decisions of all sample firms, the market. The variables in Table 2 (and in later tables) are ratios, and the denominator is total assets. Specifically, the variables are book leverage (total liabilities over total assets, L/A), the market-to-book ratio for total assets (V/A, a proxy for Tobin's Q), profitability (E/A), asset growth (dA/A), net debt issues (dL/A), the change in balance sheet retained earnings (dRE/A), and two measures of net equity issues (dSB/A and dSM/A). The ratios are calculated as the aggregate value of the numerator divided by aggregate assets, which in effect treats the entire sample as a single firm. Equivalently, the ratios are size-weighted averages of the ratios for firms, where a firm's ratio is weighted by its assets relative to aggregate assets. Finally, the ratios are multiplied by 100, and thus are expressed as percents of assets.

Our results center on pecking order predictions about which firms issue equity. We show two measures of annual equity issues. The first, dSB, is the change in the book value of stockholders' equity in excess of the change in Compustat's adjusted balance sheet retained earnings,

$$dSB = dSE - dRE \qquad (1)$$

The change in stockholders' equity, dSE, combines (i) issues and repurchases of equity, (ii) the change in retained earnings, and (iii) "dirty surplus" transactions such as foreign currency translation adjustments. Since dirty surplus transactions do not flow through the income statement, they do not affect

TABLE 2. Average characteristics of all firms

Each year's sample includes all non-financial, non-utility firms with the necessary CRSP and Compustat data for that year (see the appendix). We report the average ratio of the annual aggregate value of the numerator for a portfolio divided by the aggregate value of assets, in percent. Thus, leverage, $L/A(t)$, is the sum of total liabilities in year t (Compustat item 181) divided by the sum of assets in year t (6); $L/A(t-1)$ is L/A for the previous fiscal year, $t-1$; dL/A is the aggregate change in liabilities from $t-1$ to t divided by the sum of assets at t; dA/A is the aggregate growth in assets from $t-1$ to t divided by the sum of year t assets; profitability, E/A, is the aggregate of the sum of income before extraordinary items (18), interest expense (15), and extraordinary income (48) if available, divided by aggregate assets; dRE/A is the sum of the change in Compustat's adjusted retained earnings (36) from $t-1$ to t divided by aggregate assets at t; the financing deficit, Def/A, is the difference between the growth in assets and the change in retained earnings, $dA/A-dRE/A$; the book measure of net equity issued, dSB/A, is the financing deficit minus the change in liabilities, $Def/A-dL/A$; and the market-based measure of net stock issued, dSM, is the split-adjusted change in Compustat shares outstanding (25) during the fiscal year times the average of the beginning and ending split-adjusted Compustat stock prices (199). The market-to-book ratio for total assets, V/A, is the aggregate of the sum of book value of debt and the market value of equity divided by aggregate assets.

	Firms	dSM/A	dSB/A	dL/A	dRE/A	dA/A	V/A	L/A		E/A	Def/A
								t	$t-1$		
1973–1982	2951	0.8	0.7	6.5	3.0	10.3	110.5	57.5	56.9	7.7	7.2
1983–1992	3672	0.5	0.3	6.6	1.1	8.0	132.4	64.4	62.8	6.5	6.9
1993–2002	4417	4.0	2.4	6.2	0.5	9.1	186.2	68.0	68.0	5.0	8.6

a firm's reported value of retained earnings. These transactions are typically incorporated, however, in Compustat's adjusted value of retained earnings (data item 36), so we use this measure to compute dSB.

Both pooling of interests mergers and employee stock options cause dSB to understate stock issues. In a pooling of interests merger, stockholders' equity increases by the book value of the acquired firm's stock, not by the (typically greater) market value of the shares issued to the acquired firm's shareholders. When stock options are exercised, stockholders' equity rises by the strike price plus the taxes saved because of the exercise, not by the (typically greater) market value of the shares issued.[1] Stock dividends also contaminate dSB. When a firm pays a stock dividend, it transfers the market value of the shares issued from its retained earnings account to its contributed capital account. As a result, dSB misclassifies stock dividends as new equity issued.

Our second measure of equity issued during a fiscal year, dSM, is the (split-adjusted) change in the number of shares outstanding over the fiscal year times the average of the (split-adjusted) stock prices at the beginning and end of the fiscal year. (See the appendix for details.) Since the market-based dSM does not suffer from the accounting problems of dSB, it is a more accurate measure of equity financing, and thus is the central variable in the tests below. But we also show dSB because it balances financing sources and investment,

$$dL/A + dSB/A + dRE/A = dA/A \qquad (2)$$

and it produces the financing deficit in Table 2,

$$Def/A = dA/A - dRE/A = dL/A + dSB/A. \qquad (3)$$

Both dSB/A and dSM/A are superior to another measure of outside equity financing, net cash from stock issued—the difference between inflows from new issues and outflows for repurchases, from the statement of cash flows.

---

1. The tax effect arises because of differences between the way options are expensed for tax and financial reporting purposes. During our sample period, few firms recognize the cost of executive options in their financial statements. When an option is exercised, however, the difference between the market value of the stock and the strike price is an expense for tax purposes. This expense reduces the firm's tax liability and drives a permanent wedge between the tax expense reported in the financial statements and the actual taxes paid. The tax savings are credited to stockholders' equity without flowing through the income statement.

This measure, used by Frank and Goyal (2003) and Lemmon and Zender (2002), understates equity issued because the statement of cash flows does not show stock issued in mergers or outright grants of stock to employees because such issues produce no cash flows. The change in Treasury stock used by Fama and French (2001) has similar problems.

The aggregate profitability and growth of sample firms change through time. Profitability, E/A, falls from an average of 7.7% for 1973 to 1982, to 5.0% for 1993 to 2002 (Table 2). Earnings in excess of dividends (dRE/A) also fall, averaging 3.0% of assets for 1973 to 1982 and 0.5% for 1993 to 2002. Asset growth declines, but less, from 10.3% per year to 9.1%. Since asset growth declines less than the change in retained earnings, outside financing increases. The increase is not met with new debt, which falls a bit; dL/A averages 6.5% per year for 1973 to 1982, and 6.2% for 1993 to 2002. New issues of equity fill the void. During 1973 to 1982 and 1983 to 1992, annual aggregate net new equity averages 0.8% and 0.5% of assets, and most outside financing is debt. Myers (1984) uses the relatively low level of aggregate equity financing to motivate the pecking order. Confirming Frank and Goyal (2003), however, during 1993 to 2002 equity financing is important, even at the aggregate level; annual net new equity, dSM/A, averages a substantial 4.0% of assets, which is about two-thirds as large as net new debt (6.2% per year).

Aggregate results are, however, largely irrelevant for judging the predictions of the pecking order. The pecking order is a model of financing decisions by individual firms. Because aggregate results hide much variation in the financing of individual firms, aggregate results can be misleading. When we next examine financing decisions at a more disaggregated level, we find lots of behavior inconsistent with the pecking order—throughout the 1973 to 2002 period.

5. WHO ISSUES STOCK?

In the pecking order model, transactions costs and asymmetric information problems lead firms to finance first with internal funds and then with debt. Equity is issued only under duress or when investment so far exceeds earnings that financing with debt would produce excessive leverage. Since pecking order predictions about when firms issue equity are the lynchpin of the model, this section examines the evidence in detail.

5.1. Incidence and Materiality of Equity Issues

The pecking order model predicts that few firms issue or repurchase shares. In fact, most firms issue, repurchase, or do both every year. Table 3 shows average annual percents of sample firms with net repurchases (dSM < 0), net issues (dSM > 0), or neither (dSM = 0)—mutually exclusive categories. The table also shows percents of firms with gross issues and gross repurchases. These groups are not mutually exclusive; a firm can be in one, both, or neither of the groups. In addition to results for all sample firms, Table 3 shows separate results for small and big firms.

Raising immediate suspicions about the extent to which financing decisions follow the pecking order (equity as a last resort), the average fraction of sample firms with no net equity issues (dSM = 0) falls from a rather low 24% per year for 1973 to 1982, to 8% per year for 1993 to 2002. Big firms almost always make annual net issues or net repurchases. The fraction of big firms with no net issues is 11% per year for 1973 to 1982 and 2% for 1993 to 2002. Despite the literature's emphasis on repurchases, the fraction of all sample firms with net repurchases hovers around a modest 20% per year. During the last 20 years of the sample (1983 to 2002), a more impressive 30% per year of big firms make net repurchases.

Most firms make annual net issues of equity. The average annual fraction of sample firms with net issues (dSM > 0) rises from more than half (54% per year) for 1973 to 1982, to 62% for 1983 to 1992, and an impressive 72% for 1993 to 2002. The increase in net issuers among all sample firms is driven by small firms. The fraction of big firms with net issues of equity is *always* high, averaging 72%, 66%, and 67% per year for the three ten-year periods of Table 3.

The pecking order model is silent on why firms pay dividends, but issuing stock to pay dividends seems like a problem. Specifically, if asymmetric information means stock must be issued at below equilibrium value, issuing stock to pay dividends decreases the wealth of current shareholders. In contrast, reducing dividends does not cause permanent wealth losses for long-term shareholders even if asymmetric information problems cause the stock price to fall temporarily below its equilibrium value.

Dividend payers are more likely to repurchase than non-payers, especially during 1983 to 2002. For example, though not shown in Table 3, during 1993 to 2002, on average 37% of each year's dividend payers make net repurchases, versus 15% for non-payers. And firms that do not pay dividends are more likely to issue equity than dividend payers. Nevertheless, in apparent contradiction of the pecking order, during 1973 to 2002 on average about 58% of each year's dividend payers make net issues of equity.

The fractions of firms with net equity issues or net repurchases each year are high, but they understate the frequency of issues and repurchases. Many

TABLE 3. Average percents of firms that issue and repurchase equity and average issues and repurchases as percents of total assets

Each year's sample (All) includes all non-financial, non-utility firms with the necessary CRSP and Compustat data for that year (see the appendix). Firms are assigned to the Small or Big category in year t if their assets are below or above those of the median NYSE firm in t. The market-based measure of net stock issued, dSM, is the split-adjusted change in Compustat shares outstanding during the fiscal year times the average of the beginning and ending split-adjusted Compustat stock prices. Thus, net stock issuers have a positive split-adjusted growth in shares, dSM > 0, and net stock repurchasers have a negative growth in shares, dSM < 0. Gross stock repurchases, GR, is Compustat annual item 115. Gross stock issues, GI, is net issues, dSM, plus gross repurchases.

	% in dSM group			% with GI > 0			% with GR > 0			% with GI/A > 1%		
	All	Small	Big	All	Small	Big	All	Small	Big	All	Small	Big
Part A: percent of firms in dSM categories that issue and repurchase												
All dSM groups												
1973–1982	100	100	100	67	63	83	30	29	32	24	23	25
1983–1992	100	100	100	74	71	89	33	29	52	40	40	37
1993–2002	100	100	100	86	84	91	42	39	59	57	58	51
dSM < 0												
1973–1982	21	22	18	56	55	60	83	83	86	11	10	12
1983–1992	20	18	29	56	50	75	88	86	93	18	15	28
1993–2002	20	18	31	64	59	78	92	90	96	26	23	34
dSM = 0												
1973–1982	24	28	11	6	6	8	6	6	8	1	1	1
1983–1992	18	20	4	4	3	10	4	3	10	1	1	2
1993–2002	8	9	2	6	5	24	6	5	24	2	1	8
dSM > 0												
1973–1982	54	50	72	100	100	100	19	18	23	38	41	32
1983–1992	62	61	66	100	100	100	23	21	37	58	61	43
1993–2002	72	74	67	100	100	100	33	31	43	71	73	61

	dSM/A			GI/A			GR/A		
	All	Small	Big	All	Small	Big	All	Small	Big
Part B: issues and repurchases as percents of assets									
All dSM groups									
1973–1982	0.8	1.2	0.8	1.1	1.7	1.0	0.3	0.5	0.2
1983–1992	0.5	3.3	0.2	1.7	4.2	1.5	1.2	1.0	1.3
1993–2002	4.0	7.9	3.5	5.6	9.4	5.2	1.7	1.4	1.7
dSM < 0									
1973–1982	−0.9	−1.7	−0.8	0.2	0.1	0.2	1.1	1.8	1.0
1983–1992	−2.3	−3.4	−2.2	0.6	0.1	0.6	2.9	3.5	2.9
1993–2002	−2.6	−4.7	−2.5	0.9	0.4	0.9	3.5	5.1	3.4
dSM = 0									
1973–1982	0.0	0.0	0.0	0.0	0.1	0.0	0.0	0.1	0.0
1983–1992	0.0	0.0	0.0	0.1	0.0	0.1	0.1	0.0	0.1
1993–2002	0.0	0.0	0.0	0.6	0.1	0.8	0.6	0.1	0.8
dSM > 0									
1973–1982	1.4	2.7	1.3	1.5	2.8	1.4	0.1	0.1	0.1
1983–1992	2.3	6.1	1.9	2.6	6.3	2.2	0.3	0.3	0.3
1993–2002	8.2	12.6	7.5	8.8	13.0	8.2	0.6	0.4	0.7

firms that are net issuers in a given year repurchase in the same year, and most firms that make net repurchases also issue. On average, 19% of the firms that make net issues of equity during 1973 to 1982 repurchase in the same year, and the average rises to 33% for 1993 to 2002 (Table 3). As a result, the fraction of all sample firms making gross repurchases (30% per year, rising to 42%) is much higher than the fraction making net repurchases. More impressive, of each year's sample of firms with net repurchases (dSM $<$ 0), 56% issue equity in the same year during 1973 to 1982 and the fraction rises to 64% during 1993 to 2002 (Table 3). As a result, most sample firms (67% per year for 1973 to 1982 and 86% for 1993 to 2002) issue some equity each year.[2] Big firms are especially active. The fractions with gross issues of equity, gross repurchases, and both issues and repurchases are higher for big firms than for small firms (Table 3).

Some equity issues are tiny, so it is interesting to examine the frequency of issues above a non-trivial threshold, say 1% of assets. The fraction of all sample firms with gross issues that exceed 1% of assets rises from 24% per year for 1973 to 1982, to 40% for 1983 to 1992, and 57% for 1993 to 2002 (Table 3). More impressive, among the high fractions of firms that make net issues of equity, in a typical year 38% of the 1973 to 1982 sample make equity issues that exceed 1% of assets, and the fraction rises to 58% for 1983 to 1992 and 71% for 1993 to 2002.

A caveat is in order. We see later that for individual firms, the equity issuing process is lumpy, with smaller issues during most years but large issues during some years, the result of relatively infrequent SEOs and mergers. The distribution of equity issues is thus skewed right, and tabulating annual percents of firms that make issues above some threshold (1% of assets) gives a misleadingly low impression of the cumulative effects of issues. A better picture of cumulative effects is obtained (next) by comparing average annual equity issues with average debt issues.

Consider the firms that are net issuers of equity in a given year, dSM $>$ 0. Their annual net equity issues average 1.4% of assets during 1973 to 1982, 2.3% for 1983 to 1992, and an impressive 8.2% for 1993 to 2002 (Part B of Table 3). Their gross issues are larger, averaging 1.5%, 2.6%, and 8.8% of assets. The an-

2. Note that Compustat reports zero gross repurchases for some firms making net repurchases (dSM $<$ 0). Compustat's gross repurchases are from the Statement of Cashflows. A cashless repurchase can occur in a variety of ways. For example, a shareholder (typically an employee) can deliver shares as payment on a loan from the company, the firm can exchange other property for outstanding shares, or an employee can forfeit non-vested shares when leaving the firm. Some cases, however, are probably Compustat errors (reporting zero cash repurchases when they are in fact positive).

nual net new debt of these firms averages about 7.0% of assets (Table 4). Thus, for firms that make net issues of equity, the issues are substantial relative to new issues of debt, especially during the last 20 years of the sample period. For the seven of ten sample firms that make annual net equity issues during 1993 to 2002, aggregate net new equity exceeds net new debt.

The aggregate issues of all net issuers quoted above are dominated by big firms, so it is interesting to examine small firms. The net equity issues of small firms that are net issuers tend to be even more substantial, averaging 2.7% of assets for 1973 to 1982, 6.1% for 1983 to 1992, and 12.6% for 1993 to 2002 (Table 3). In contrast, the net new debt for these firms averages about 6.0% of assets, and net new debt is less than net new equity during both 1983 to 1992 and 1993 to 2002 (Table 4).

In short, during the last 20 years of the sample, on average about two-thirds of each year's firms make net equity issues. For big firms that are net issuers, net new issues of equity are on average about one-third the size of net new debt during 1983 to 1992, and they are about as large as new debt during 1993 to 2002 (Table 4). For small firms that make net equity issues, the issues are on average larger than net new debt for the entire 1983 to 2002 period. And it is worth adding that the evidence for small firms cannot be dismissed as unimportant for judging the pecking order model since the asymmetric information problems that generate its predictions about financing decisions are probably more serious for smaller firms.

Though net issuers outnumber repurchasers about three to one, firms that retire equity tend to be larger. As a result, for the sample as a whole, aggregate net new equity averages just 0.8% of assets for the first ten years of the sample (1973 to 1982) and 0.5% for 1983 to 1992 (Table 3). These aggregates are clearly misleading, however. They are not due to the paucity of equity issues predicted by the pecking order. On the contrary, they are the result of equity issues by a large fraction of firms that are offset by repurchases by others. During 1993 to 2002, even aggregate net new equity is no longer small, averaging 4.0% of the assets of sample firms and 8.2% of the assets of net issuers (as compared to about 6.2% for net new debt).

5.2. The Characteristics of Firms that Make Net Issues or Repurchases

Since the pecking order model leads us to expect that equity issues and repurchases are rare, the fact that almost all firms do one or the other—or both— every year suggests that many firms violate the model's predictions about equity decisions. The key variables in the predictions are profitability and growth, the main ingredients of the financing deficit. Thus, to examine the extent to which equity decisions conform to the model, we break the sample into groups of firms with similar profitability and growth. Specifically, as in Table 1, we allocate firms to 12 groups each year based on size (big and small), profitability (negative, low, and high E/A), and growth (low and high dA/A). Table 4 summarizes the characteristics of the net equity issuers and net repurchasers in the overall sample, for small and big firms separately, and for each of the 12 size-profitability-growth groups.

The market-to-book ratios, V/A, in Table 4 are normalized. Fama and French (2001) find that the upward drift in market V/A after 1980, apparent in Table 2, is not matched by drift in aggregate profitability or growth. Based on this evidence, they conclude that the drift in V/A reflects a decline in expected returns (discount rates) rather than better investment opportunities that might affect financing decisions. Thus, to better isolate the information in V/A about the investment opportunities of our 12 groups, we normalize by dividing the values of V/A for year t by market V/A for t.

The pecking order model predicts that equity issuers are highly levered and repurchasers have little debt. But Part A of Table 4 shows that when we aggregate across all sample firms, net issuers and net repurchasers have similar leverage at the beginning of the year (before the year's financing decisions). Equity issuers do differ from repurchasers in other respects. Issuers as a whole are less profitable and grow faster, especially during 1993 to 2002. And lower profitability and faster growth lead equity issuers to issue more debt (dL/A is higher). As a result, net issuers and repurchasers have similar leverage after as well as before the financing decisions of year t (which might be viewed as a hint of tradeoff behavior).

The fact that in aggregate net equity issuers are less profitable and grow faster than firms that repurchase seems to support Lemmon and Zender (2002). They argue that though equity issuers may have moderate leverage, they face larger current and expected financing deficits, which put them among the rational opt-outs allowed by the (patched version of the) pecking order. Advocates of the pecking order model should, however, be uncomfortable with the argument that this version allows large fractions of our sample firms (54% for 1973 to 1982, rising to 72% for 1993 to 2002) to opt out of the pecking order and make annual net equity issues. But there is no need to quarrel. Closer examination of our 12 size-profitability-growth groups shows that large fractions of firms of all types make equity decisions that seem inconsistent with the pecking order.

TABLE 4. Average characteristics of firms that make net repurchases (dSM < 0) or net issues (dSM > 0)

Each year's sample (All firms) includes all non-financial, non-utility firms with the necessary CRSP and Compustat data for that year (see the appendix). Firms are assigned to the 12 size-profitability-growth groups in year t based on their characteristics at the end of their fiscal year in calendar year t. The assets of small and big firms in year t are below or above those of the median NYSE firm in t. The breakpoints for growth (dA/A) and positive profitability (E/A) are the averages of the annual NYSE medians for 1973 to 2002. We report the average ratio of the annual aggregate value of the numerator for a group divided by the aggregate value of assets, in percent. Thus leverage, $L/A(t)$, is the sum of total liabilities in year t divided by the sum of assets in year t; $L/A(t-1)$ is L/A for the previous fiscal year, $t-1$; dL/A is the aggregate change in liabilities from $t-1$ to t divided by the sum of year t assets; dA/A is the aggregate growth in assets from $t-1$ to t divided by the sum of year t assets; profitability, E/A, is the aggregate sum of income before extraordinary items, interest expense, and extraordinary income if available, divided by aggregate assets; dRE/A is the sum of the change in Compustat's adjusted retained earnings from $t-1$ to t divided by aggregate assets at t; the financing deficit, Def/A, is the difference between the growth in assets and the change in retained earnings, $dA/A - dRE/A$; and the market-based measure of net stock issued, dSM, is the split-adjusted change in Compustat shares outstanding during the fiscal year times the average of the beginning and ending split-adjusted Compustat stock prices. The % of Group is the average of the annual percents of All firms and of firms in the 12 size-profitability-growth groups with dSM < 0 (Net repurchases) and dSM > 0 (Net issues). The market-to-book ratio for total assets, V/A, is the aggregate of the sum of book value of debt and the market value of equity divided by aggregate assets. We standardize V/A by dividing each year's V/A for a group by V/A for all firms.

| | % of | | | | | | | L/A | | | |
	Firms	Group	dSM/A	dSB/A	dL/A	dRE/A	dA/A	V/A	t	t-1	E/A	Def/A
Part A: average characteristics of all sample firms												
All firms: dSM < 0												
1973–1982	622	21.3	-0.9	-0.4	5.6	3.1	8.3	95.2	55.1	54.0	8.3	5.2
1983–1992	737	20.0	-2.3	-1.6	8.1	1.8	8.3	103.0	63.1	60.1	7.6	6.5
1993–2002	873	19.7	-2.6	-1.8	4.0	2.0	4.2	103.1	69.0	67.8	7.3	2.2

All firms: dSM > 0												
1973–1982	1608	54.3	1.4	1.1	6.9	3.2	11.2	103.2	57.3	56.7	7.8	8.0
1983–1992	2284	62.3	2.3	1.5	5.7	0.7	7.9	100.3	64.9	64.2	6.1	7.2
1993–2002	3202	72.5	8.2	5.1	7.7	-0.3	12.5	99.4	67.3	68.0	3.7	12.8
Small firms: dSM < 0												
1973–1982	514	22.3	-1.7	-0.6	4.4	3.1	6.9	91.3	50.5	49.5	8.5	3.8
1983–1992	578	18.4	-3.4	-1.7	3.9	1.2	3.4	107.5	52.1	49.9	6.7	2.2
1993–2002	647	17.5	-4.7	-2.8	2.9	1.5	1.7	90.8	51.0	49.0	6.0	0.2
Small firms: dSM > 0												
1973–1982	1165	49.6	2.7	2.0	6.8	4.2	13.0	114.5	52.3	52.4	8.9	8.8
1983–1992	1920	61.5	6.0	4.5	5.2	0.9	10.7	123.4	54.4	55.0	5.4	9.8
1993–2002	2730	73.7	12.6	8.7	6.4	-2.9	12.2	112.5	52.3	52.4	0.3	15.1
Big firms: dSM < 0												
1973–1982	108	17.6	-0.8	-0.3	5.8	3.1	8.6	96.0	55.7	54.6	8.3	5.5
1983–1992	158	29.3	-2.2	-1.6	8.3	1.9	8.6	102.7	63.8	60.8	7.7	6.7
1993–2002	226	31.4	-2.5	-1.8	4.1	2.0	4.4	104.1	70.3	69.2	7.4	2.3
Big firms: dSM > 0												
1973–1982	443	71.8	1.3	1.0	6.9	3.1	11.0	102.2	57.7	57.1	7.7	7.9
1983–1992	364	66.6	1.9	1.1	5.8	0.6	7.5	97.4	66.3	65.4	6.2	6.9
1993–2002	471	66.5	7.5	4.5	7.9	0.1	12.5	97.6	69.4	70.2	4.2	12.4

Part B: average characteristics of high-growth firms

Small, unprofitable, high-growth firms: dSM < 0

1973–1982	4	13.5	-1.1	-0.5	28.5	-10.2	17.9	143.8	72.9	53.8	-5.8	28.1
1983–1992	11	5.1	-5.6	1.9	31.0	-9.8	23.1	93.6	63.7	44.1	-5.9	32.9
1993–2002	12	3.2	-10.6	2.3	29.3	-9.0	22.6	87.2	63.2	43.9	-5.4	31.6

(*Continued*)

TABLE 4: (Continued)

	% of		dSM/A	dSB/A	dL/A	dRE/A	dA/A	V/A	L/A		E/A	Def/A
	Firms	Group							t	$t-1$		
Small, unprofitable, high-growth firms: dSM > 0												
1973–1982	31	57.4	12.5	8.1	25.0	-10.7	22.3	149.4	68.9	56.6	-6.9	33.0
1983–1992	189	84.1	25.0	19.7	22.6	-13.6	28.7	153.3	57.7	49.3	-10.6	42.3
1993–2002	371	93.1	38.2	32.1	23.0	-18.3	36.8	134.8	50.7	43.9	-15.6	55.1
Big, unprofitable, high-growth firms: dSM < 0												
1973–1982	0	7.3	-0.2	0.4	10.8	-2.5	8.7	93.8	63.6	57.8	-1.1	11.2
1983–1992	0	6.3	-0.6	-0.5	30.9	-8.1	22.3	88.2	79.6	61.4	-2.0	30.4
1993–2002	2	5.6	-2.2	0.8	25.5	-9.9	16.4	89.4	71.3	55.0	-5.9	26.3
Big, unprofitable, high-growth firms: dSM > 0												
1973–1982	1	70.8	0.3	0.9	19.3	-7.5	12.6	82.4	71.2	59.7	-4.0	20.2
1983–1992	7	89.8	6.5	9.0	24.2	-10.5	22.7	93.1	78.2	70.5	-6.0	33.2
1993–2002	31	93.7	28.0	26.2	25.8	-8.0	44.0	92.2	64.2	67.7	-5.5	52.0
Small, low-profitability, high-growth firms: dSM < 0												
1973–1982	88	21.1	-0.8	-0.1	13.9	1.9	15.8	79.7	59.1	53.6	6.0	13.8
1983–1992	79	15.3	-2.0	-0.5	16.5	1.8	17.8	89.1	61.2	54.4	5.6	16.0
1993–2002	87	13.1	-2.7	-1.5	16.4	2.3	17.2	73.0	58.5	50.8	5.6	15.0
Small, low-profitability, high-growth firms: dSM > 0												
1973–1982	209	51.4	2.5	2.3	14.9	2.3	19.4	94.8	59.7	55.7	6.2	17.2
1983–1992	355	68.7	7.1	5.9	16.9	2.5	25.3	104.8	56.4	52.9	5.6	22.8
1993–2002	538	79.9	13.3	9.1	16.0	2.9	28.0	101.4	52.5	50.7	5.1	25.1

Period	N											
Big, low-profitability, high-growth firms: dSM <0												
1973–1982	25	15.4	−0.7	−0.4	14.1	1.6	15.2	85.4	71.4	67.9	5.0	13.6
1983–1992	24	21.4	−1.3	−0.8	18.6	1.1	18.8	84.2	75.9	70.3	4.7	17.8
1993–2002	35	18.7	−1.0	−0.5	13.7	1.5	14.8	76.0	82.0	80.0	4.5	13.2
Big, low-profitability, high-growth firms: dSM >0												
1973–1982	111	73.6	1.2	1.2	11.1	1.7	14.0	87.6	66.3	64.2	5.7	12.3
1983–1992	81	75.1	2.1	1.9	16.8	1.2	20.0	85.6	71.4	67.9	5.4	18.8
1993–2002	147	79.9	8.4	5.2	16.9	1.6	23.7	82.8	73.4	73.7	4.5	22.1
Small, high-profitability, high-growth firms: dSM <0												
1973–1982	166	19.1	−1.5	−0.3	8.9	6.6	15.2	107.1	46.4	44.2	12.1	8.6
1983–1992	121	16.7	−4.0	−1.3	9.9	7.1	15.6	146.5	46.3	43.2	12.7	8.5
1993–2002	114	16.8	−4.8	−2.8	9.0	9.5	15.7	128.6	46.0	43.9	13.8	6.2
Small, high-profitability, high-growth firms: dSM >0												
1973–1982	558	61.8	3.6	2.6	10.0	7.3	19.9	137.5	47.5	46.9	11.9	12.6
1983–1992	509	71.6	7.1	4.7	8.8	8.3	21.8	165.6	45.0	46.3	12.2	13.5
1993–2002	555	78.2	12.1	6.1	7.6	10.4	24.1	163.8	41.1	44.1	12.7	13.7
Big, high-profitability, high-growth firms: dSM <0												
1973–1982	38	15.6	−0.8	−0.3	7.4	5.3	12.3	110.9	48.6	47.0	11.3	7.1
1983–1992	45	29.7	−2.5	−1.7	10.0	5.3	13.6	143.8	54.3	51.3	11.9	8.3
1993–2002	45	31.6	−3.3	−1.7	8.8	6.2	13.3	167.2	58.4	57.2	13.4	7.2
Big, high-profitability, high-growth firms: dSM >0												
1973–1982	194	78.6	2.0	1.3	7.7	5.6	14.6	129.7	48.9	48.2	10.8	9.0
1983–1992	101	66.6	3.6	1.8	9.4	5.9	17.2	139.1	54.1	54.0	11.1	11.3
1993–2002	94	66.5	11.9	4.0	9.2	8.1	21.3	180.5	52.5	54.9	12.2	13.2

(Continued)

TABLE 4. (Continued)

	Firms	% of Group	dSM/A	dSB/A	dL/A	dRE/A	dA/A	V/A	L/A t	L/A t–1	E/A	Def/A
Part C: average characteristics of low-growth firms												
Small, unprofitable, low-growth firms: dSM<0												
1973–1982	28	16.3	-1.3	-0.6	-6.2	-13.9	-20.7	80.8	60.8	55.5	-9.1	-6.8
1983–1992	104	13.7	-2.9	-1.8	-2.2	-15.6	-19.6	84.6	59.9	52.0	-11.2	-4.0
1993–2002	126	12.0	-3.7	-2.1	-5.3	-18.1	-25.4	68.7	55.0	48.2	-15.2	-7.3
Small, unprofitable, low-growth firms: dSM>0												
1973–1982	73	36.3	2.5	2.2	-11.1	-15.2	-24.1	98.4	71.1	65.4	-9.4	-8.9
1983–1992	431	57.1	4.8	3.6	-5.7	-20.3	-22.5	102.1	66.3	58.7	-15.5	-2.1
1993–2002	776	76.1	10.5	7.6	-3.5	-29.0	-25.0	92.9	59.9	51.0	-25.0	4.0
Big, unprofitable, low-growth firms: dSM<0												
1973–1982	1	9.3	-0.4	-0.3	-6.8	-10.3	-17.3	82.0	76.0	69.9	-6.6	-7.0
1983–1992	6	16.1	-3.7	-2.7	0.9	-16.1	-18.0	93.1	71.5	59.5	-10.3	-1.8
1993–2002	10	21.0	-3.4	-2.4	0.5	-13.9	-15.8	78.0	70.1	60.1	-8.0	-1.9
Big, unprofitable, low-growth firms: dSM>0												
1973–1982	7	61.2	0.3	0.7	2.0	-9.1	-6.4	74.1	68.7	62.6	-4.8	2.7
1983–1992	29	77.8	0.9	1.0	-0.5	-11.9	-11.3	81.3	73.8	66.8	-7.1	0.6
1993–2002	42	76.7	3.3	2.7	-1.2	-18.4	-16.9	90.5	74.4	64.8	-12.5	1.5
Small, low-profitability, low-growth firms: dSM<0												
1973–1982	127	27.4	-1.2	-0.7	-2.1	0.6	-2.1	73.8	52.4	53.3	5.3	-2.8
1983–1992	163	28.2	-2.5	-1.8	-2.0	0.2	-3.5	81.7	51.6	51.8	5.1	-3.8
1993–2002	178	29.4	-3.1	-2.2	-1.4	1.2	-2.4	67.8	50.4	50.6	5.0	-3.6

Small, low-profitability, low-growth firms: dSM > 0												
1973–1982	152	34.1	0.8	0.6	-2.9	0.8	-1.5	81.5	55.9	58.0	5.6	-2.3
1983–1992	265	45.8	1.7	1.4	-3.8	-0.2	-2.6	87.0	56.3	58.6	4.9	-2.4
1993–2002	341	56.3	2.1	1.3	-4.4	0.5	-2.6	68.6	58.2	61.0	4.7	-3.1
Big, low-profitability, low-growth firms: dSM < 0												
1973–1982	26	19.7	-0.7	-0.3	-0.6	1.2	0.3	77.9	57.6	58.2	5.7	-0.9
1983–1992	40	29.8	-1.6	-1.4	1.6	0.3	0.6	85.1	63.3	62.1	6.1	0.3
1993–2002	68	36.1	-1.8	-1.7	-1.2	0.4	-2.5	78.5	70.4	69.7	5.1	-2.9
Big, low-profitability, low-growth firms: dSM > 0												
1973–1982	79	61.3	0.4	0.4	1.2	1.1	2.6	81.0	61.4	61.8	5.2	1.6
1983–1992	96	65.0	1.0	-0.7	-3.7	-1.5	-5.9	85.8	66.9	67.1	5.4	-4.4
1993–2002	117	60.7	1.1	0.5	-1.4	0.2	-0.6	73.6	72.8	73.7	4.6	-0.8
Small, high-profitability, low-growth firms: dSM < 0												
1973–1982	98	29.7	-3.7	-1.3	-3.5	4.1	-0.8	98.2	44.4	47.5	11.4	-4.9
1983–1992	97	29.5	-5.3	-3.3	-4.1	3.8	-3.6	124.1	47.4	49.7	12.1	-7.5
1993–2002	127	42.2	-8.7	-5.2	-3.7	5.8	-3.1	111.5	49.4	51.5	12.7	-8.9
Small, high-profitability, low-growth firms: dSM > 0												
1973–1982	141	40.6	1.3	0.7	-6.0	5.1	-0.1	99.7	49.5	55.5	11.1	-5.3
1983–1992	169	51.4	3.1	2.2	-10.2	4.2	-3.8	113.7	59.4	66.9	12.1	-8.1
1993–2002	146	49.6	4.1	1.9	-12.5	7.0	-3.6	100.9	61.6	71.6	13.6	-10.6
Big, high-profitability, low-growth firms: dSM < 0												
1973–1982	16	25.0	-1.6	-0.8	-0.7	3.8	2.3	100.8	49.4	51.2	10.3	-1.5
1983–1992	42	44.7	-4.5	-2.8	0.1	2.3	-0.3	119.5	58.6	58.3	10.9	-2.7
1993–2002	63	60.5	-4.6	-3.5	-2.2	3.8	-2.0	133.9	64.0	64.8	11.7	-5.8
Big, high-profitability, low-growth firms: dSM > 0												
1973–1982	49	66.1	1.3	0.4	-1.3	3.9	3.0	97.2	51.1	54.0	9.9	-1.0
1983–1992	48	51.8	1.6	0.7	-3.6	2.9	0.0	110.7	64.1	67.6	10.5	-3.0
1993–2002	39	37.7	2.4	0.3	-9.7	2.6	-6.8	116.3	66.9	71.4	10.6	-9.4

Consider fast-growing firms, which consistently have large financing deficits. The fact that most unprofitable fast-growing firms make net equity issues each year (Part B of Table 4) can be viewed as consistent with at least the patched version of the pecking order. If they did not issue equity, the leverage of these firms would quickly be far above average. One might draw the same inference about the more than 73% of big rapidly-growing firms with positive but low profitability that make net equity issues each year, since these firms have relatively high leverage.

Annual net equity issues by more than half (more than two-thirds during 1983 to 2002) of small, low-profitability, fast-growing firms are, however, a problem for the pecking order. The issuing firms in this group start the year with low leverage, and leverage would be moderate even if no equity were issued. Likewise, on average more than 61% of each year's highly profitable fast-growing firms issue equity (Part B of Table 4). This is a clear problem for the pecking order since the leverage of issuers would be low even if they issued no equity.

Equity issues by some groups of fast-growing firms may be consistent with the pecking order, but repurchases are a contradiction. Fast-growing firms in all size-profitability groups have large financing deficits and they issue lots of debt. Thus, they have a clear demand for debt capacity, and issuing debt to retire equity is a problem for the pecking order. Few unprofitable fast-growing firms retire equity, but net repurchases are more common among profitable high-growth firms. On average about 14% of small fast-growing firms with low profitability and about 17% with high profitability make annual net repurchases during 1983 to 2002. The numbers for big fast-growing firms are higher. About 20% of those with low profitability and about 30% of the highly profitable make annual net repurchases during 1983 to 2002.

Part C of Table 4 shows the characteristics of low-growth firms that issue or retire equity each year. Without showing the details, we can report that, examined at a more aggregate level (that is, if one does not separately examine net issuers and repurchasers), low-growth firms do not seem to present serious problems for the pecking order model. For example, in aggregate, low-growth firms with positive profitability do not issue or retire much equity, and they typically have financing surpluses which they use to retire debt, all of which is consistent with the pecking order.

Once again, however, aggregates are misleading. Part C of Table 4 shows that most low-growth firms issue or retire equity each year. Among low-growth firms with positive profitability, 20% to 61% make net repurchases each year and 34–66% make net issues. Repurchases by profitable low-growth firms may be consistent with the pecking order since these firms tend to have financing surpluses, moderate leverage, and so apparently little need for more debt capacity. But net equity issues by large fractions of these firms are a pecking order problem; profitable low-growth firms with financing surpluses and moderate leverage should not issue equity to retire additional debt. Finally, the equity issues of large fractions of unprofitable low-growth firms are consistent with the pecking order since these firms are under duress (they are quite unprofitable and are rapidly disgorging assets). But then the fact that 9–21% of such firms make net repurchases seems like a pecking order problem.

Table 5 summarizes the evidence from Table 4 about how well the pecking order explains equity issues and repurchases. Net issues and repurchases by firms in the 12 size-profitability-growth groups are counted as consistent (Y) or inconsistent (N) with the model based on its predictions about equity (discussed above) for firms in each group. Firms that are neither net issuers nor repurchasers are taken to be consistent with the pecking order. The last two columns of the table show the average percents of total sample firms that can be counted for or against the model.

Despite the decline through time in the incidence of firms that neither issue nor repurchase equity and the increase in the incidence of firms that make net issues, the average percent of firms whose equity decisions are consistent with the pecking order rises from 41% for 1973 to 1982, to 49% for 1993 to 2002. The improved performance of the pecking order is largely due to the increasing numbers of small unprofitable firms whose net equity issues are taken to be consistent with the model. But the important point is that even during 1993 to 2002, more than half of the net issues and repurchases of sample firms run counter to the model. In short, the pecking order does a poor job describing the equity decisions of individual firms.

Without showing the details, we can also report that bigger firms are more likely to violate the pecking order. The firms whose equity decisions obey the pecking order account for 25%, 32%, and 43% of the market capitalization of sample firms during the three ten-year periods of 1973 to 2002, leaving 75%, 68%, and 57% as model failures. These results are surprising, given the evidence in Frank and Goyal (2003) and Lemmon and Zender (2002) that the pecking order works better for bigger firms. The earlier papers examine financing decisions at a higher level of aggregation than Tables 4 and 5. One of our messages

TABLE 5. Average percents of total firms that are consistent with the predictions of the pecking order model

After splitting each size-profitability-growth group into firms making net repurchases (dSM<0), issues (dSM>0), or neither (dSM=0), we categorize their financing decisions as consistent (Y) or inconsistent (N) with the pecking order model based on the evidence in Table 4. The Percent of all firms shows the fraction of the sample firms in each size-profitability-growth group. The blocks for dSM<0, dSM=0, and dSM>0 show the fraction of the sample firms whose behavior is consistent or inconsistent with the pecking order model. The Total percent for these blocks aggregates the other columns in the block and shows the fraction of all sample firms that are net repurchasers, issuers, or neither, and are consistent or inconsistent with the pecking order. The Total percent for all firms aggregates the Total percent results for dSM<0, dSM=0, and dSM>0, and thus shows the fraction of all sample firms whose behavior is consistent or inconsistent with the pecking order model.

		Small						Big						Total percent	
Market — E/A:		Negative E		Low E/A		High E/A		Negative E		Low E/A		High E/A			
dA/A:		Low	High	Low	High	Low	High	Low	High	Low	High	Low	High	Y	N
Percent of all firms															
1973–1982	100.0	6.1	1.6	15.5	14.2	11.4	30.2	0.4	0.1	4.4	5.4	2.4	8.4	40.9	59.0
1983–1992	100.0	20.6	6.1	15.8	14.1	9.0	19.6	1.0	0.2	3.9	3.0	2.5	4.1	46.9	52.8
1993–2002	100.0	23.3	8.9	13.9	15.1	6.7	15.8	1.3	0.8	4.4	4.2	2.4	3.2	48.8	51.2
dSM<0															
Pecking order behavior?		N	N	Y	N	Y	N	N	N	Y	N	Y	N	Y	N
1973–1982	21.3	1.0	0.2	4.3	3.1	3.3	5.7	0.0	0.0	0.9	0.9	0.5	1.3	9.0	12.2
1983–1992	20.0	2.8	0.3	4.4	2.2	2.6	3.3	0.2	0.0	1.1	0.7	1.1	1.2	9.2	10.7
1993–2002	19.7	2.9	0.3	4.1	2.0	2.9	2.6	0.3	0.0	1.6	0.8	1.4	1.0	10.0	9.9
dSM=0															
Pecking order behavior?		Y	Y	Y	Y	Y	Y	Y	Y	Y	Y	Y	Y	Y	N
1973–1982	24.4	2.8	0.4	6.1	4.0	3.4	5.6	0.1	0.0	0.9	0.6	0.2	0.5	24.4	0.0
1983–1992	17.7	6.0	0.6	4.1	2.3	1.7	2.4	0.1	0.0	0.2	0.1	0.1	0.2	17.7	0.0
1993–2002	7.7	2.6	0.3	2.0	1.1	0.5	0.8	0.0	0.0	0.1	0.1	0.0	0.1	7.7	0.0
dSM>0															
Pecking order behavior?		Y	Y	N	N	N	N	Y	Y	N	Y	N	N	Y	N
1973–1982	54.3	2.4	1.0	5.1	7.2	4.7	18.9	0.2	0.0	2.7	3.9	1.6	6.6	7.5	46.8
1983–1992	62.3	11.7	5.1	7.2	9.7	4.6	13.9	0.8	0.2	2.6	2.2	1.3	2.8	20.0	42.1
1993–2002	72.5	17.8	8.3	7.8	12.1	3.3	12.4	1.0	0.7	2.7	3.3	0.9	2.1	31.1	41.3

is that results for broad aggregates can give a misleading impression of the success of the pecking order, which, after all, is a model of the financing decisions of individual firms.

If, keeping in mind the caveat discussed earlier, we count only net issues and net repurchases that exceed 1% of assets, the fractions of each year's firms that make annual issues or repurchases that are inconsistent with the pecking order are smaller but substantial—20.8% for 1973 to 1982, 27.2% for 1983 to 1992, and 31.0% for 1993 to 2002. Big firms are again more likely to violate the model than small firms. The firms whose equity issues or repurchases violate the pecking order model by more than 1% of assets account for 28.1%, 33.1%, and 37.5% of total market equity during our three ten-year periods.

The summary of pecking order violations in Table 5 is conservative. For example, we classify net repurchases by low-growth firms with positive profitability as consistent with the pecking order since these firms tend to have financing surpluses and little apparent need for debt capacity. But the debt of these firms averages around 50% of assets. If there is any chance that investment opportunities will be more abundant in the future, in a strict pecking order world these firms would retire more debt, not equity. About 10% of sample firms are in this category. Moreover, Table 5 ignores dividend status. We argue earlier that net equity issues by dividend payers are inconsistent with the pecking order, and there are many dividend payers among the net issuers classified as consistent with the pecking order in Table 5. Finally, many firms issue and repurchase equity in the same year. Though their net issues or repurchases may be consistent with the pecking order, the fact that they both issue and repurchase can imply pecking order problems. For example, since the fast-growing firms that make annual net equity issues in Table 4 have a clear demand for debt capacity, the fact that on average about 25% of them also repurchase is a contradiction of the pecking order, which goes uncounted in Table 5.

6. HOW DO FIRMS ISSUE EQUITY?

The results above raise an obvious question: given that most firms issue some equity every year, what mechanisms do they use? We offer two types of evidence, (i) incomplete results for all sample firms for 1983 to 2002, and (ii) complete results for a sample of big firms (the S&P 100) for three years.

6.1. Partial Results for All Sample Firms
The results for all sample firms are from Thompson Financial's SDC database, which provides data on mergers, SEOs, and private placements. We suspect

that Thompson's coverage is less complete early in our sample, so we drop 1973 to 1982 from the tabulated results. We complement Thompson with Compustat data on cash inflows and outflows from equity sales and repurchases (data items 115 and 108). Recall that cash inflows from the sale of equity are not a good measure of total equity issued because they miss stock issues that do not generate cash, such as mergers financed with stock, outright grants of stock to employees, and conversions of other securities into stock. This variable does, however, include the net cash from SEOs, private placements, direct purchases, sale of stock to employees, and exercises of rights and warrants. The results for all sample firms, for small and big firms, and for the net issuers and net repurchasers in the three groups are in Table 6.

For all groups in Table 6, Compustat's cash inflow from the sale of equity is larger than the sum of Thompson's proceeds from SEOs and private placements. The detailed results for the S&P 100 presented later suggest that the difference is due primarily to employee option exercises (not on Thompson), but SEOs and private placements missed by Thompson may also be a factor. Private placements are larger for small firms than big firms, but they are always relatively unimportant.

Not surprisingly, firms that make net issues of equity (dSM>0) have larger cash inflows from the sale of equity. And the difference between inflows from equity issues and the sum of SEOs and private placements is larger for net issuers. This suggests that net issuers have bigger cash inflows from option exercises by employees. Cash inflows from the sale of equity by small firms that are net issuers are a much larger percent of assets than for big firms, primarily due to larger SEOs. Still, cash from the sale of equity by big firms that are net issuers is non-trivial, averaging 1.14% and 1.30% of the assets of these firms during 1983 to 1992 and 1993 to 2002 (versus a more impressive 3.51% and 5.20% for small firms). For net issuers of equity, stock issued in mergers is much higher for 1993 to 2002 than for 1983 to 1992. The large increase in net issues by big firms that are net issuers (from 1.87% to 7.53% of assets) is mostly due to the jump in stock-financed mergers. For small net issuers, SEOs are also important, averaging 2.11% of assets per year for 1983 to 1992 and 3.48% for 1993 to 2002.

Given the importance of SEOs, especially for small firms, and given the importance of stock-financed mergers during the last ten years of the sample, the evidence on the incidence of mergers and SEOs in Table 6 is interesting. Almost all big firms and most small firms do one or more acquisitions during each of the table's two ten-year periods. On average, more than half of the big firms have an acquisition in any given year. Not all mergers involve equity financing, however, and even among net equity issuers, the fractions of firms that issue stock to finance mergers in any given year are low. For example, equity issued in mergers is substantial during 1993 to 2002, but only 12% of the small firms and 19% of the big firms that are net equity issuers in any given year do stock-financed mergers that year.

Similarly, about 30% of small firms and 40% of big firms do an SEO sometime during each of the ten-year periods of Table 6, but only about 8% and 11% of the small and big net issuers of a given year do an SEO that year. Since proceeds from SEOs are a larger fraction of assets for small firms than for big firms, we can infer that though big firms do SEOs more often, the SEOs of small firms tend to be relatively larger.

In sum, SEOs always account for large fractions of the equity issues of small firms that make net issues, and stock-financed mergers account for large fractions of the equity issues of the small and big net issuers of 1993 to 2002. But small fractions of each year's net issuers do stock-financed mergers or SEOs. Thus, the distribution of net equity issues for any year is skewed right, the result of large issues by the firms that do SEOs or stock-financed mergers. We also know, however, that equity issues exceed 1% of assets for large fractions (58% for 1983 to 1992 and 71% for 1993 to 2002) of each year's net issuers. What is the source of the relatively large equity issues left unexplained by SEOs and mergers? Our guess, informed by the more detailed evidence for the S&P 100 that follows, is employee options, grants, and benefit plans.

6.2. Complete Results for the S&P 100

Table 7 provides a detailed breakdown of equity issues and repurchases for 1999, 2000, and 2001 for firms in the S&P 100 in 2001. (The sample includes only 99 firms in 1999 because Goldman Sachs did not go public until November of that year.) These firms are special—they are big and successful—and the time period is short, but the advantage of the sample is that the breakdown of equity issues by source is near complete (hand-collected from annual reports).

Like the full sample, more of the firms in the S&P 100 make net issues than net repurchases. More important, like firms in the full sample, S&P 100 firms are quite active in the equity market. Every firm issues shares every year and most also repurchase. (Gross repurchases are positive in 224 of 299 firm-years.) Not surprisingly, S&P 100 firms that are net issuers of equity have larger equity issues of all sorts than net repurchasers, whereas the latter, of course, do more repurchasing. But the interesting fact is that there is lots of issuing and

TABLE 6. Sources of equity financing for all firms, small firms, and big firms, and for firms making net repurchases (dSM < o) and net issues (dSM > o)

Each year's sample (All firms) includes all non-financial, non-utility firms with the necessary CRSP and Compustat data for that year (see the appendix). The assets of small and big firms in year t are below or above those of the median NYSE firm in t. The table shows average annual equity financing as a percent of assets, by source. The sources are mergers, SEOs, and private placements (all from Thompson SDC), and cash flow from sales and repurchases of equity (Compustat items 115 and 108). The table also shows percents of firms with mergers, equity financed mergers, and SEOs during any year of a subperiod, and average annual percents per year (This yr.) for each subperiod.

	Percent of firms	dSM/A	Sources of equity financing as percent of assets				Cash flow from equity		Percent of firms with					
									Mergers		Equity mergers		SEOs	
			Mergers	SEOs	Private placements	Sale	Repurchase	Net	Any yr.	This yr.	Any yr.	This yr.	Any yr.	This yr.
Part A: all firms														
1983–1992	100.0	0.52	0.35	0.34	0.01	1.05	1.22	-0.17	63.0	20.7	15.6	2.6	31.9	5.7
1993–2002	100.0	3.99	3.33	0.56	0.02	1.30	1.66	-0.36	81.4	34.7	42.3	9.9	33.6	6.3
dSM<0														
1983–1992	20.0	-2.32	0.10	0.07	0.00	0.49	2.89	-2.40	72.1	28.8	12.8	1.1	26.6	1.6
1993–2002	19.7	-2.60	0.29	0.09	0.00	0.54	3.49	-2.95	85.9	37.7	32.4	2.5	24.9	1.2
dSM>0														
1983–1992	62.3	2.33	0.56	0.50	0.02	1.41	0.30	1.11	66.1	22.0	18.9	3.7	37.9	8.3
1993–2002	72.5	8.16	5.35	0.86	0.03	1.79	0.63	1.16	82.0	36.2	47.2	12.9	37.7	8.2
Part B: small firms														
1983–1992	100.0	3.29	0.61	1.54	0.07	2.51	0.96	1.55	57.7	15.9	12.9	2.3	29.5	5.3
1993–2002	100.0	7.93	3.13	2.61	0.14	3.93	1.44	2.49	78.6	29.8	40.2	9.1	32.2	5.9

dSM < 0														
1983–1992	18.4	−3.40	0.18	0.40	0.01	0.56	3.51	−2.95	66.0	20.8	8.9	0.8	24.4	1.4
1993–2002	17.5	−4.71	0.17	0.45	0.01	0.86	5.12	−4.26	81.8	29.6	27.9	2.0	23.9	1.1
dSM > 0														
1983–1992	61.5	6.04	0.84	2.11	0.09	3.51	0.25	3.25	60.9	17.5	16.2	3.3	35.5	7.9
1993–2002	73.7	12.58	4.38	3.48	0.18	5.20	0.42	4.78	79.7	32.0	45.3	11.9	36.1	7.7
Part C: big firms														
1983–1992	100.0	0.22	0.32	0.21	0.01	0.89	1.25	−0.37	93.1	48.7	31.0	4.8	45.3	7.9
1993–2002	100.0	3.52	3.35	0.31	0.00	0.99	1.69	−0.70	95.8	60.0	53.2	13.7	40.7	7.9
dSM < 0														
1983–1992	29.3	−2.25	0.10	0.05	0.00	0.48	2.86	−2.38	94.5	58.1	27.5	2.0	34.7	2.3
1993–2002	31.4	−2.45	0.30	0.07	0.00	0.52	3.38	−2.86	97.6	61.1	45.1	4.1	27.6	1.7
dSM > 0														
1983–1992	66.6	1.87	0.54	0.31	0.01	1.14	0.31	0.83	93.2	46.5	33.7	6.3	50.5	10.3
1993–2002	66.5	7.53	5.49	0.48	0.00	1.30	0.66	0.64	95.3	60.9	58.4	19.0	47.1	11.0

TABLE 7. Components of the change in equity, dSM/A, for all S&P 100 firms, for net issuers (dSM > 0), and for net repurchasers (dSM < 0), 1999–2001

The sample is firms in the S&P 100 in 2001. The ratios for each year are the aggregate value of the numerator divided by the aggregate value of the denominator, multiplied by 100. The ratios for 1999–2001 are the averages of the annual ratios. The market-based measure of net stock issued, dSM, is the split-adjusted change in shares outstanding during the fiscal year times the average of the beginning and ending split-adjusted stock prices; dL is the change in total liabilities during the fiscal year; and dRE is the change in adjusted retained earnings. These variables and the assets used in the denominator of all ratios are from Compustat. The other data are collected from the individual companies' annual reports for 1999 to 2001. SEOs is the value of shares sold through seasoned equity offerings and private placements; Executive compensation is the value of shares issued to employees as part of executive compensation plans, employee stock option plans, or through the exercise of employee stock options; Mergers is the value of shares issued to complete equity financed mergers; Convert debt is the value of shares issued through the retirement of debt or the conversion of debt or preferred stock; Exercise warrants is the value of shares issued through the exercise of warrants and other options not included in Executive compensation and Convert debt; and Share repurchases is the value of shares acquired for cash or in exchange for other assets. The sample includes only 99 firms in 1999 because Goldman Sachs did not go public until November of that year.

	Firms	dSM/A	SEOs	Executive compensation	Mergers	Convert debt	Exercise warrants	Share repurchases	dL/A	dRE/A
All S&P 100 firms										
1999–2001	100	3.57	0.09	1.05	3.68	0.14	0.05	-1.44	10.07	1.37
1999	99	4.37	0.10	1.15	4.55	0.20	0.09	-1.71	9.35	2.34
2000	100	4.29	0.06	1.23	4.31	0.14	0.03	-1.48	13.42	1.51
2001	100	2.05	0.09	0.78	2.19	0.07	0.04	-1.12	7.42	0.25
dSM > 0										
1999–2001	54	7.45	0.14	1.31	6.42	0.22	0.06	-0.70	13.67	1.41
1999	54	10.06	0.20	1.59	8.70	0.38	0.13	-0.94	12.98	3.04
2000	51	8.14	0.07	1.53	7.03	0.17	0.02	-0.68	18.02	1.50
2001	58	4.15	0.15	0.81	3.54	0.11	0.02	-0.47	10.01	-0.33
dSM < 0										
1999–2001	45	-1.53	0.02	0.73	0.10	0.03	0.05	-2.46	5.05	1.43
1999	45	-1.61	0.00	0.68	0.17	0.01	0.04	-2.51	5.54	1.60
2000	49	-1.74	0.06	0.77	0.05	0.08	0.04	-2.74	6.23	1.53
2001	42	-1.23	0.01	0.73	0.08	0.01	0.07	-2.14	3.39	1.15

repurchasing in both groups. For these firms, the equity valve is always open, and the flow is almost always in both directions—hardly the picture one expects to observe in a pecking order world (where issues and repurchases are rare).

The equity financing that S&P 100 net issuers get from SEOs, conversion of bonds and other securities into stock, and exercise of warrants and rights is small, but combined equity financing from these sources averages 0.42% per year of assets for the three-year sample period. This pales in comparison to equity issues to employees (1.31% per year), which in turn pale relative to equity issued in mergers (6.42% of assets per year). Thus, as in the results for all big firms that are net issuers of equity, mergers are important, at least in these later years. What we learn in addition from the S&P 100 is that stock issues to employees are important and other sources are less important.

S&P 100 firms that make net repurchases also issue substantial stock to employees, though only about half as much (0.73% of assets per year) as net equity issuers (1.31%). For net repurchasers, other kinds of equity issues are small, and equity issues are much more than offset by repurchases. In contrast, less than 10% of the equity issues of net issuers are offset with repurchases. And firms that make net repurchases do so despite the fact that they issue substantial net new debt. Issuing debt to repurchase stock is, of course, unacceptable behavior from the perspective of the pecking order.

How would the results in Table 7 change if we instead examined a sample of small firms? Table 6 says that new equity from SEOs is a larger percent of assets for small net issuers than for big net issuers. Table 6 also says that net equity issues left unexplained by mergers and cash inflows from the sale of equity are larger for small firms. Although some of the small firms' unexplained equity issues are probably omissions from the Thompson database, our bet is that stock issues to employees (not covered by Thompson) are more important for small firms.

7. DISCUSSION AND CONCLUSIONS

The presumption of the pecking order model of Myers (1984) and Myers and Majluf (1984) is that the costs of issuing equity—transactions costs and especially the costs arising from asymmetric information problems—are high. This is what gives rise to the pecking order itself. Specifically, because the costs of issuing equity are high, investments are financed first with retained earnings, then debt, and with equity only as a last resort. Because debt capacity is valuable for avoiding the costs of issuing equity, the pecking order model predicts that repurchases of equity are also rare, and they are restricted to firms with few investment opportunities relative to earnings, and thus little need for debt capacity.

Contradicting these predictions, we find that equity issues are common-place. During 1973 to 1982, 54% of our sample firms make net equity issues each year, rising to 62% for 1983 to 1992 and 72% for 1993 to 2002. The fractions of firms making gross equity issues are much higher, 67%, 74%, and 86%. Given that equity issues are so pervasive, it is not surprising that they are commonly done by firms that are not under duress. Repurchases are less common than equity issues, but they are far from rare. About 20% of sample firms retire equity each year, and the fractions of firms making gross repurchases are much higher. Moreover, many of the firms making net repurchases have financing deficits that, in a pecking order world, should make debt capacity valuable. In short, our results reject the pecking order's central predictions about how often and under what circumstances firms issue and repurchase equity.

Equity issues are on average material. During 1983 to 1992 and 1993 to 2002, the net equity issues of net issuers among small firms are on average larger than their net new issues of debt. The net equity issues of big firms that are net issuers are about one-third the size of their net debt issues during 1983 to 1992, and they are on the order of net debt issues during 1993 to 2002. The equity issuing process is lumpy, however, resulting in a distribution of issues that is right skewed. Year in and year out, stock issues to employees are probably the most consistent source of important amounts of new equity, for big as well as small firms. SEOs are infrequent, but when they hit they are large, and they are important in the average annual net stock issues (and thus in the cumulative issues) of smaller firms. Mergers financed with stock are also infrequent but large, and at least during 1993 to 2002, they are important in average annual net issues of stock, especially for bigger firms.

One story for our results is that the pecking order breaks down (equity is not a last resort) at least in part because there are ways to issue equity with low transactions costs and modest asymmetric information problems. Three of the alternatives to SEOs for issuing equity (issues to employees, rights issues, and direct purchase plans) seem to have both low transactions costs and minor asymmetric information problems, and a fourth (mergers financed with stock) may fall into this category. At least during the last ten years of the sample period, mergers are important in explaining the magnitude of equity issues, and issues to employees are probably important in explaining both the magnitude and frequency of issues throughout the sample period.

If there are ways to issue equity that avoid the costs assumed by the pecking order, there is potentially a gaping hole in the model: transactions costs and asymmetric information problems may not seriously constrain equity issues. In this case, equity issues are not a last resort, the incentive to avoid repurchases to maintain debt capacity disappears, and the asymmetric information problems that are the focus of the pecking order are not the sole or perhaps even an important determinant of capital structures.

Breaking the grip of the pecking order does not require, however, that equity can be issued with low transactions costs and minor asymmetric information problems. Any forces leading to the result that equity is not a last resort will do. A plausible alternative (or complementary) story is that equity issues often have benefits that outweigh their costs, i.e., tradeoff considerations. For example, exchanges of stock in mergers often have tax benefits that can offset transactions costs and any asymmetric information problems. Stock issued to employees may have motivation benefits that outweigh issuing costs. In short, any forces that cause firms to systematically deviate from pecking order financing (retained earnings, then debt, and equity only as a last resort) imply that the pecking order, as the complete model of capital structure proposed by Myers (1984) and Myers and Majluf (1984), is dead.

Although we disagree with Shyam-Sunder and Myers (1999) about the success of the pecking order model, we agree with their conclusion that its main competitor, the tradeoff model, has serious problems. Like asymmetric information, tradeoff considerations (for example, the bankruptcy costs of debt) surely play a role in financing decisions. But there are important aspects of the tradeoff model that get little empirical support. For example, the negative relation between leverage and profitability documented in much previous work (e.g., Kester, 1986; Titman and Wessels, 1988; Rajan and Zingales, 1995; Fama and French, 2002) is a serious contradiction of the model's central predictions about the tax and agency benefits of debt. The tax benefits of debt in enhancing market values have also proven elusive in direct tests (Fama and French, 1998). Other work (Auerbach, 1985; Jalilvand and Harris, 1984; Fama and French, 2002) suggests that if firms have the leverage targets posited by the tradeoff model, reversion to the targets is quite slow, leading Shyam-Sunder and Myers (1999) to question the existence of targets. Finally, the survey evidence of Graham and Harvey (2001) suggests that if firms have leverage targets, the targets are quite soft.

In short, both the tradeoff model and the pecking order model have serious problems. Thus, it is probably time to stop running empirical horse races between them as stand-alone stories for capital structures. Perhaps it is best to regard the two models as stable mates, with each having elements of truth that help explain some aspects of financing decisions.

APPENDIX A. DATA

The data are from CRSP and Compustat. To be included in the sample for calendar year t, a firm must have total assets (Compustat item 6) for the last fiscal year in t and for the previous fiscal year ($t-1$), liabilities (181) for t and $t-1$, Compustat's adjusted value of balance sheet retained earnings (36) for t and $t-1$, interest expense (15) for t, income before extraordinary items (18) for t, and a stock price (199) and shares outstanding (25) for the fiscal year-ends in t and $t-1$. Moreover, the change in the Compustat split adjustment factor (27) from $t-1$ to t must match the change implied by the CRSP share factors (FACSHR) for stock splits and stock dividends (distribution codes 5510–5559) distributed between the fiscal year-ends for $t-1$ to t. We exclude utilities (SIC codes 4900–4949) and financial firms (6000–6999).

Our measure of earnings, E, is income before extraordinary items (Compustat item 18), plus interest expense (15), plus extraordinary income (48) if available. The financing deficit, Def, is the growth in assets (6) minus the change in Compustat's adjusted value of balance sheet retained earnings (36),

$$\text{Def} = (A_t - A_{t-1}) - (\text{RE}_t - \text{RE}_{t-1}). \tag{A.1}$$

The book measure of net equity issued, dSB, is the financing deficit, Def, minus the change in liabilities, dL. Equivalently, it is the change in stockholders' equity minus the change in retained earnings,

$$\text{dSB} = \text{Def} - dL = \text{dSE} - \text{dRE} \tag{A.2}$$

We compute the market measure of net equity issued, dSM, for fiscal year t as the product of (i) the split-adjusted growth in shares and (ii) the average of the split-adjusted stock price at the beginning and end of the fiscal year, both from Compustat,

$$\text{dSM}_t = (\text{Shares}_t\,\text{Adjust}_t - \text{Shares}_{t-1}\,\text{Adjust}_{t-1}) \tag{A.3}$$
$$\times (\text{Price}_{t-1}/\text{Adjust}_{t-1} + \text{Price}_t/\text{Adjust}_t)/2,$$

where Price_t, Shares_t, and Adjust_t are the Compustat price, shares outstanding, and split adjustment factor at the end of fiscal year t.

REFERENCES

Allen, G.C., Brooks, L.D., Moore, W.T., 1995. Informativeness of the equity financing decision: dividend reinvestment versus the public offer. Journal of Financial and Strategic Decisions 8, 97–104.

Auerbach, A.J., 1985. Real determinants of corporate leverage. In: Friedman, B.J. (Ed.), Corporate Capital Structures in the United States. University of Chicago Press, Chicago.

Chaplinsky, S., Niehaus, G., 1994. The role of ESOPs in takeover contests. Journal of Finance 49, 1451–1470.

Eckbo, B.E., Masulis, R.W., 1992. Adverse selection and the rights offer paradox. Journal of Financial Economics 32, 293–332.

Fama, E.F., French, K.R., 1998. Taxes, financing decisions, and firm value. Journal of Finance 53, 819–843.

Fama, E.F., French, K.R., 2001. Disappearing dividends: changing firm characteristics or lower propensity to pay? Journal of Financial Economics 60, 3–43.

Fama, E.F., French, K.R., 2002. Testing tradeoff and pecking order predictions about dividends and debt. Review of Financial Studies 15, 1–33.

Frank, M.Z., Goyal, V.K., 2003. Testing the pecking order theory of capital structure. Journal of Financial Economics 67, 217–248.

Graham, J.R., Harvey, C.R., 2001. The theory and practice of corporate finance: evidence from the field. Journal of Financial Economics 60, 187–243.

Hertzel, M., Lemmon, M., Linck, J.S., Rees, L., 2002. Long-run performance following private placements of equity. Journal of Finance 57, 2595–2617.

Huang, S.G.H., Song, F.M., 2003. The determinants of capital structure: evidence from China. Unpublished working paper, University of Hong Kong.

Jalilvand, A., Harris, R.S., 1984. Corporate behavior in adjusting to capital structure and dividend targets: an econometric study. Journal of Finance 39, 127–145.

Jung, K., Kim, Y., Stulz, R.M., 1996. Timing, investment opportunities, managerial discretion, and the security issue decision. Journal of Financial Economics 42, 159–185.

Kester, W.C., 1986. Capital and ownership structure: a comparison of United States and Japanese manufacturing corporations. Financial Management 15, 5–16.

Lemmon, M.L., Zender, J.F., 2002. Debt capacity and tests of capital structure theories. Unpublished working paper, University of Utah and University of Colorado at Boulder.

Masulis, R.W., Korwar, A.W., 1986. Seasoned equity offerings: an empirical investigation. Journal of Financial Economics 15, 91–118.

Mikkelson, W.H., Partch, M.M., 1986. Valuation effects of security offerings and the issuance process. Journal of Financial Economics 15, 31–60.

Moeller, S.B., Schlingemann, F.P., Stulz, R.M., 2004. Firms size and the gains from acquisitions. Journal of Financial Economics 73, 201–228.

Myers, S.C., 1984. The capital structure puzzle. Journal of Finance 39, 575–592.

Myers, S.C., Majluf, N.S., 1984. Corporate financing and investment decisions when firms have information the investors do not have. Journal of Financial Economics 13, 187–221.

Peterson, P.P., Peterson, D.R., Moore, N.H., 1987. The adoption of new-issue dividend reinvestment plans and shareholder wealth. The Financial Review 22, 221–232.

Rajan, R.G., Zingales, L., 1995. What do we know about capital structure? Some evidence from international data. Journal of Finance 50, 1421–1460.

Shyam-Sunder, L., Myers, S.C., 1999. Testing static tradeoff against pecking order models of capital structure. Journal of Financial Economics 51, 219–244.

Smith, C.W., 1977. Alternative methods for raising capital: rights versus underwritten offerings. Journal of Financial Economics 5, 273–307.

Titman, S., Wessels, R., 1988. The determinants of capital structure choice. Journal of Finance 43, 1–19.

Wruck, K.H., 1989. Equity ownership concentration and firm value: evidence from private equity financing. Journal of Financial Economics 23, 3–18.

BANKING IN THE THEORY OF FINANCE
. . .

Eugene F. Fama

Banks are financial intermediaries that issue deposits and use the proceeds to purchase securities. This paper argues that when banking is competitive, these portfolio management activities in principle fall under the Modigliani–Miller theorem on the irrelevance of pure financing decisions. It follows that there is no need to control the deposit creation or security purchasing activities of banks to obtain a stable general equilibrium with respect to prices and real activity. In practice, however, banks are forcibly involved in the process by which a pure nominal commodity or unit of account is made to play the role of numeraire in a monetary system. The paper examines the nature of such a nominal commodity and how, through reserve requirements, banks get involved in making it a real economic good.

1. INTRODUCTION

This paper studies commercial banking from the viewpoint of the theory of finance. We take the main function of banks in the transactions industry to be the maintenance of a system of accounts in which transfers of wealth are carried out with bookkeeping entries. Banks also provide the service of exchanging deposits and other forms of wealth for currency, but in modern banking this is less important than the accounting system of exchange. Moreover, although both can be used to carry out transactions, one of our main points is that currency and an accounting system are entirely different methods for

Reprinted with permission from the *Journal of Monetary Economics* 6, no. 1 (January 1980): 39–57. © 1980 by Elsevier Limited.

Theodore O. Yntema, Professor of Finance, Graduate School of Business, the University of Chicago. This research is supported by a grant from the National Science Foundation. The comments of F. Black, A. Drazen, N. Gonedes, M. Jenson, R. Lucan, D. Patinkin, and M. Scholes, and the insightful prodding of M.H. Miller are gratefully acknowledged.

exchanging wealth. Currency is a physical medium which can be characterized as money. An accounting system works through bookkeeping entries, debits and credits, which do not require any physical medium or the concept of money.

In principle, providing an accounting system of exchange does not require that banks hold the wealth being exchanged. In practice, the costs of operating the system—replenishment costs for depositors and costs to banks and transactors of determining when transactions are feasible—are probably smaller when this is the case. Thus, banks assume a second major function, portfolio management. They issue deposits and use the proceeds to purchase securities. A basic point of this paper is that when banking is competitive, the portfolio management activities of banks are the type of pure financing decisions covered by the Modigliani–Miller (1958) theorem. From this result we can infer that there is no need to control either the deposit creation or the security purchasing activities of banks for the purpose of obtaining a stable general equilibrium with respect to prices and real activity.

In examining the nature of banking, it is helpful to start with the assumption that banks are unregulated. This case provides the clearest view of the characteristics of an accounting system of exchange and of the fact that the concept of money plays no essential role in such a system. The unregulated case also provides the clearest application of the Modigliani–Miller theorem to the deposit creation and asset management decisions of banks. Having analyzed unregulated banking, we then study the effects of two main forms of bank regulation, reserve requirements and the limitation of direct interest payments on deposits.

Finally, much of the analysis centers on the argument that in principle the banking industry has no special role in the determination of prices. In practice, however, banks are forcibly involved in the process by which a pure nominal commodity or unit of account is made to play the role of numeraire in a real world monetary system. Our last task is to examine the nature of such a pure nominal commodity and how banks get involved in making it a real economic good.

2. AN UNREGULATED BANKING SYSTEM

To get an understanding of the microeconomic structure of an unregulated banking industry, let us, for the moment, take the economy's pricing process as given. For concreteness, let us assume there is a numeraire, some real good, in terms of which prices are stated, leaving the issues connected with the pricing process for later. Finally, to focus on the issues of immediate interest let us also assume, temporarily, that currency does not exist.

With unregulated banking, we might expect to observe a competitive banking system like that described by Johnson (1968) or Black (1970). In brief, banks pay competitive returns on deposits, that is, they pay the returns that would be earned by depositors on securities or portfolios that have risk equivalent to that of the deposits, less a competitively determined management fee; and banks charge for the transactions services they provide, again according to the competitively determined prices of these services. It is fruitful, however, to examine more closely both the transactions mechanism and the likely nature of unregulated deposits.

2.1. Bank Deposits as Portfolio Assets

In the unregulated environment described by Black and Johnson, there is nothing special about bank deposits as portfolio assets since deposits pay the same returns as other managed portfolios with the same risk. Although Black and Johnson presume that bank deposits would be low risk portfolio assets, Tobin's (1963) conjecture seems more valid; that is, in an unregulated environment there is unlikely to be a clear distinction between banks and other portfolio managers. Although banks may be more interested in supplying transactions services, competition will induce them to provide different types of portfolios against which their depositors can hold claims. Although other financial institutions, like mutual funds, may be more interested in managing portfolios, competition will induce them to provide the transactions services normally associated with banks. In the end, one will observe financial institutions, all of which can be called banks, that provide accounts with different degrees of risk and allow individuals to carry out exchanges of wealth through their accounts.

In cases where individuals choose to hold deposits against risky portfolios, the value of an account fluctuates because of withdrawals and deposits and because of fluctuations in the market values of the portfolio assets on which the account has claim. For example, some banks may offer deposits which are nothing more than claims against an open end mutual fund. Such funds now issue and redeem shares on demand at the current market value of the portfolio. In a more open environment, they would allow the same thing to be done by check or any other mechanism coincident with the tastes of 'depositors' and whose costs the depositors are willing to bear.

One might also expect to observe banks that provide personalized portfolios of assets for the deposits of individual investors. The 'general accounts' maintained by New York Stock Exchange brokers for their customers could easily be transformed into such personalized bank accounts. As currently operated, an investor can borrow on demand, usually with a phone call to the broker, against a general account. When the broker's check is received, it can be endorsed over to an arbitrary third party. It is a short step from this to allowing investors to write checks against their accounts, with the checks covered, according to the choice of the investor, either with an automatic loan against the account or by the sale of specified assets from the account. There are similar simple mechanisms whereby the recipient of the check can instruct his broker–banker to use the addition to his account either to purchase new portfolio assets or draw down existing loans.

There will also be riskless deposits, that is, deposits not subject to capital gains or losses, where the value of the deposit varies only because of transactions executed and the accumulation of interest. Such riskless deposits might be direct claims against a portfolio of short-term riskless securities, in effect, a riskless mutual fund. Or a bank may issue both riskfree and risky deposits against a given portfolio of assets, with any capital gains or losses in the portfolio absorbed by those holding the risky deposits. The latter scenario would look more familiar if we assumed instead that the risk in the portfolio is borne by stockholders. However, our risky deposits are common stock with the additional benefits provided by access to the bank's transactions services.

2.2. An Accounting System of Exchange

Consider a transaction in which wealth is to be transferred from one economic unit to another. In a complicated world where there are many types of portfolio assets and a spectrum of consumption goods and services, the form of wealth one economic unit chooses to give up in a transaction does not generally correspond to the form of wealth that the other eventually chooses to hold. Thus, one transaction generally gives rise to a set of transactions involving transfers of portfolio assets or consumption goods among many economic units. In a currency type system, each transaction in this resettling of wealth involves the intervention of a physical medium of exchange which serves as a temporary abode of purchasing power, but which is soon given up for consumption goods or new holdings of portfolio assets. In contrast, in a pure accounting system of exchange, the notion of a physical medium or temporary abode of purchasing power disappears. Its role in the transactions sequence is replaced by bookkeeping entries, that is, debits and credits to the deposits of the economic units involved.

Thus, when one economic unit wishes to transfer a given amount of wealth to another, he signals his broker–banker with a check or some more modern way of accessing the bank's bookkeeping system. The broker–banker debits the sending account and the same or another broker–banker credits the receiving account for the amount of the transaction. The debit to the sending account generates a sale of securities from the portfolio against which the sending depositor has claim while the credit to the receiving account generates a purchase of securities for the portfolio against which the receiving depositor has claim. All prices, including prices of securities, are stated in terms of a numeraire, which we have assumed is one of the economy's real goods, but the numeraire never appears physically in the process of exchange described above. The essence of an accounting system of exchange is that it operates through debits and credits, which do not require any physical medium.

Of course, the existing checking system is not as free as the unregulated one we have described. There are regulations concerning what types of securities can be held in the bank portfolios against which deposits represent claims; there are regulations limiting the returns that can be paid on deposits; and for banks in the Federal Reserve system, there are regulations concerning how the bookkeeping entries generated by transactions move through the accounts that individual banks must keep with Federal Reserve banks. Nevertheless, the checking mechanism still operates through debits and credits that generate sales and purchases of securities from the portfolios against which the deposits involved have claims. Both in our unrestricted environment and in the real world's regulated environment, the accounting system of exchange provided by banks operates without the intervention of a physical medium of exchange or temporary abode of purchasing power.

2.3. Deposits, Prices, and Real Activity

Although an accounting system of exchange involves no physical medium, like any system of exchange its efficiency is improved when all prices are stated in units of a common numeraire. For the purposes of a pure accounting system, the numeraire need not be portable or storable. It could well be tons of fresh cut beef or barrels of crude oil. However, in the type of unregulated banking system we have described, there is no meaningful way in which deposits can be the numeraire since deposits can be tailored to have the characteristics of any form of marketable wealth. Unregulated banks provide an accounting system in which organized markets and bookkeeping entries are used to allow economic units to exchange one form of wealth for another. But the deposits of the system are not a homogeneous good in which prices of all goods and securities might be stated.

The point is more than semantic. For example, after an insightful analysis of the social optimality of an unregulated banking system, Johnson (1968, p. 976) concludes that such a system would produce an upward spiralling price level:

> 'The analysis thus far has been concerned with the efficiency of the banking system, considered as an industry like any other industry. The banking system cannot, however, in strict logic, be so treated, because of the special characteristics that distinguish its product—money, the means of payment—from the products of other private enterprises—real goods and services ... Less abstractly, a competitive banking system would be under constant incentive to expand the nominal money supply and thereby initiate price inflation.
>
> Stability in the trend of prices (a special case of which is price stability) and in the trend of expectations about the future course of prices—which are generally agreed to be important to the social welfare—requires social control over the total quantity of money supplied by the banking system.'

Johnson is bothered by the fact that the deposits of an unregulated banking system involve no opportunity cost. There is no reason for investors to limit their holdings of deposits, and the supply of deposits is limited only by the economy's total invested wealth. However, the appropriate conclusion is not that prices measured in units of deposits will tend upward without limit, but rather that it makes no sense to try to force deposits to be numeraire in a system where 'deposits' is a rubric for all the different forms of portfolio wealth that have access to the accounting system of exchange provided by banks. Moreover, in a system where deposits can take on the characteristics of any form of invested wealth, deposits are a means of payment only in the sense that all forms of wealth are a means of payment, and the banking system is best understood without the mischief introduced by the concept of money.

The point in quoting from Johnson (1968) is not to single him out for special criticism. Other treatments of unregulated banking agree that determination of the price level is a special problem in such systems. Like Johnson, Pesek and Saving (1967) conclude that with unregulated banking, the price level will tend to spiral upward, while Gurley and Shaw (1960) and Patinkin (1961) argue that the price level is indeterminate. In all of these analyses, the problem of price level determinacy arises from treating unregulated deposits as 'money' and then trying to force this money to be the numeraire.

Since the economy in which we have embedded our competitive unregulated banking system is basically non-monetary, with some real good serving as numeraire, price level determinacy reduces to a standard problem concerning the existence of a stable general equilibrium in a non-monetary system. We examine now the role of banks in a general equilibrium, that is, in the determination of prices, real activity and the way that activity is financed.

In the world we are examining, banks have two functions. They provide transactions services, allowing depositors to carry out exchanges of wealth through their accounts, and they provide portfolio management services. The transactions services of banks allow economic units to exchange wealth more efficiently than if such services were not available, and in this way they are a real factor in a general equilibrium. However, there is no reason to suppose that these services are subject to special supply and demand conditions which would make them troublesome to price. Rather, the concern with banks in macroeconomics centers on their role as portfolio managers, whereby they purchase securities from individuals and firms (and a loan is, after all, just a purchase of securities) which they then offer as portfolio holdings (deposits) to other individuals and firms. Thus, banks are in the center of the process by which the economy chooses its real activities and the way those activities are financed.

In spite of their apparently strategic position, from the viewpoint of the theory of finance the portfolio management decisions of banks are the type of pure financing decisions that can be subject to the Modigliani–Miller (1958) theorem. The theorem has a strong form and a weak form, and we consider below how each can be applied to the portfolio management activities of banks. But the common message in both forms of the theorem is that as portfolio managers, banks are financial intermediaries with no special control over the details of a general equilibrium.[1]

Suppose that in purchasing securities from investors or firms and in issuing portfolios that represent claims against these securities, banks have no special privileges or comparative advantages vis à vis investors, firms or other financial intermediaries. Given such equal access to the capital market on the part

---

1. A discussion of the Modigliani–Miller theorem, covering both the 'equal access' and 'perfect substitutes' approaches used in what follows, is in Fama (1978).

of all economic units, the standard proof of the Modigliani–Miller theorem implies that the portfolios offered to depositors by banks can be refinanced by the depositors or their intermediaries so as to allow the depositors to achieve portfolio holdings that conform best to their tastes. In short, in an equal access market, a strong form of the Modigliani–Miller theorem holds. The basic constraints on portfolio opportunities are defined by the real production-investment decisions of firms. The way firms finance these decisions, or the way they are refinanced by intermediaries, including banks, neither expands nor contracts the set of portfolio opportunities available to investors. In this world, banks hold portfolios on behalf of their depositors because this probably allows them to provide transactions services (the accounting system of exchange) more efficiently, but the portfolio management activities of banks affect nothing, including prices and real activity.

Under the equal access assumption, the portfolio management decisions of the entire banking sector are of no consequence. However, the equal access assumption is stronger than is necessary for the weaker conclusions that each and every bank is subject to the Modigliani–Miller theorem (its portfolio decisions are of no consequence to investors) and that the banking sector is at most a passive force in the determination of prices and real activity. Thus, suppose access to the capital market for individuals is more limited than for banks, but among banks access to the market is competitive in the sense that an individual bank cannot offer to purchase securities and provide deposits which cannot also be purchased and offered by other banks. In other words, there are always actual or potential perfect substitutes for the portfolio management activities of any bank. As pointed out by Tobin (1963), if a bank is to survive, it must attract depositors, which means providing portfolios against which depositors are willing to hold claims. Moreover, competitive banks simply turn over the returns on their portfolios to their depositors, less a competitively determined management fee. Banks are concerned with the fees they earn rather than with the types of portfolios they provide, so in a competitive equilibrium they provide, in aggregate, portfolios to the point where each different type produces management fees at the same rate.

Suppose now that, for whatever reason, one bank perturbs the equilibrium by arbitrarily providing more deposits of a given type and less of another. If other banks do not respond, deposits of different types no longer produce management fees at the same rate. Thus, other banks respond by exactly offsetting the changes in the portfolio management decisions of the perturbing bank and in this way restore the original general equilibrium. It follows that the portfolio management decisions of individual banks are of no consequence to investors, that is, no bank can by itself alter the portfolio opportunities available to investors, and individual banks are subject to the Modigliani–Miller theorem.

The essence of the story is that even when they have comparative advantages in the capital market vis à vis individual investors, competitive unregulated banks end up simply bringing together demanders and suppliers of portfolio assets and then acting as repositories for the securities that are thereby created. If all or most portfolio wealth is managed by banks, this means that banks succeed, under the impetus of competition, in eliciting securities from individuals and firms and in transforming these securities into portfolio holdings that conform to the opportunities and tastes of the ultimate suppliers and demanders of securities. Since banks just respond to the tastes and opportunities of demanders and suppliers of portfolio assets, banks are simple intermediaries, and the role of a competitive banking sector in a general equilibrium is passive. The controlling forces in the economic activity that takes place, the way that activity is financed, and the prices of securities and goods are the tastes and endowments of individual economic units and the state of the economy's technology.

Finally, a rigorous development of the Modigliani–Miller theorem [see, for example, Fama (1978)] would require, among other assumptions, that there are no transactions costs in purchasing and selling securities. In the strong form of the theorem, which is based on equal access to the capital market on the part of both individuals and firms, the optimizing portfolio rearrangements undertaken by individuals must be costless. In the weak form of the theorem, which in our analysis is based on the assumption that there are perfect substitutes among banks for the portfolio management activities of any individual bank, the offsetting portfolio rearrangements that take place among banks to return the system to a general equilibrium in response to a perturbation must be costless.

However, the rigorous application of perfect competition to any industry always involves a similar assumption about frictionless reallocations of resources. The standard scientific hope is that the major conclusions drawn from simplified scenarios are robust in the face of real world complications. For our purposes, the complications introduced by transactions costs in trading securities are not likely to overturn the general conclusions that a competitive banking sector is largely a passive participant in the determination of a general equilibrium, with no special control over prices or real activity, which in turn means that there is nothing in the economics of this sector that makes it a special candidate for government control.

3. A REGULATED BANKING SYSTEM

Understanding unregulated banking makes analysis of the major forms of bank regulation straightforward. We consider first a reserve requirement and then a limitation on direct payments of returns to deposits. For the moment, we maintain the assumption that the numeraire is one of the economy's real goods and that there is no currency. The role of banks in defining a pure nominal commodity or unit of account which serves as numeraire is taken up subsequently.

3.1. Reserve Requirements

Suppose banks, that is, intermediaries that offer deposits that provide access to an accounting system of exchange, are required to keep a minimum fraction of their assets 'on reserve' at the government's central bank, with the return on these reserves passing to the central bank. Such a reserve requirement is a direct tax on deposit returns since it lowers the return on deposits by the fraction of deposits that must be held as reserves. Deposits now involve opportunity costs, that is, lower returns than non-deposit assets with the same risk. Investors and firms are induced to economize their holdings of deposits and so to incur replenishment and other costs that would be unnecessary in the absence of a reserve requirement. Moreover, the reserve requirement causes some intermediaries to choose not to provide access to the accounting system of exchange, so the reserve requirement has the effect of differentiating banks from other intermediaries.

However, there are important conclusions on which a reserve requirement has no effect. It is still true that the payments mechanism provided by banks is a pure accounting system of exchange wherein transfers of wealth take place via debits and credits that give rise to sales and purchases of securities in the portfolios against which the sending and receiving accounts have claim. The reserve requirement simply means that there must also be a resettling of the reserve accounts that the banks involved must keep with the central bank.

Moreover, aside from the fact that they are taxed, there is still nothing special about deposits as portfolio assets. In the absence of further restrictions, deposits can represent claims against any form of invested wealth. If banks are competitive, deposits pay returns just like comparable non-deposit portfolios, less, of course, the tax imposed by the reserve requirement. Thus, deposits are still not a homogeneous good and they are not an appropriate candidate for numeraire.

Most important, if banking is competitive, banks remain passive intermediaries, with no control over any of the details of a general equilibrium. With respect to these issues, the 'perfect substitutes' analysis of unregulated banking can be applied intact. In brief, because they are concerned with management fees and not with the types of portfolios they manage, in their portfolio management decisions, banks simply cater to the tastes and opportunities of suppliers of securities and demanders of deposits. Thus, the real activity that takes place, the way it is financed, and the prices of securities and goods are not controlled either by individual banks or by the banking sector.

3.2. Limitation of Interest Payments on Deposits

Suppose that in addition to a reserve requirement, there is a complete restriction on the payment of explicit returns on deposits. The restriction is complete in the sense that capital gains and losses on deposits as well as interest payments are not allowed and the value of a deposit is fixed, at least in units of whatever the system uses as numeraire. Since deposits must now be riskfree, a bank either limits its asset portfolio to riskfree securities or it has stockholders that absorb any variation in the market value of its portfolio. In short, except for the units in which they are denominated, deposits now look much like those of real world commercial banks.

If banks remain competitive, the restriction of interest payments on deposits does not yield them monopoly profits. One thing that is likely to happen, and which we in fact observe, is that banks charge less than cost for the transactions services they provide. In general, banks will now compete in finding ways to pass back returns on portfolio assets in the form of services to depositors. This special task of transforming ordinary interest bearing securities into securities (deposits) that pay returns in kind further differentiates banks from other financial intermediaries. However, if banks are competitive, the services they provide to depositors use up returns equivalent to those on non-deposit riskfree portfolio assets.[2]

2. If the limitation of interest payments on deposits does not generate either profits for competitive banks or taxes for the government, one can wonder why sufficient political pressure has not been generated to cause this restriction to be eliminated. One possibility is that the limitation has tax advantages. For individuals, interest received from banks would be taxable but payments for transactions services, like other expenses involved in generating consumption, would not be tax deductible. Thus, when banks transform interest payments into 'free' transactions services, they are in effect allowing individuals to realize tax-free returns on their deposits. Note that this form of tax avoid-

Because they pay returns in kind, deposits are not perfect substitutes for non-deposit portfolio assets with the same risk. Thus, the size of the banking sector is limited on the demand side by the incentives of investors to restrict their holdings of deposits. On the supply side, there is nothing special about the actions of any individual bank in transforming returns earned on portfolio assets into returns paid to depositors as services, so that this activity is likely to be characterized by constant returns to scale, at least at the industry level. Thus, the 'perfect substitutes' approach to the Modigliani–Miller theorem again holds. Perturbations to the overall equilibrium of the banking sector by any individual bank are offset by other banks, making the activities of any individual bank of no consequence. The banking sector as a whole just passively responds to the demands of investors for its particular type of financial intermediation.

In short, the limitation of direct payment of returns on deposits differentiates the portfolio management activities of banks from those of other financial intermediaries. Banks get into the business of transforming ordinary securities into special securities, deposits, that pay returns in the form of services. Nevertheless, as in the earlier cases, competitive banks end up as passive intermediaries fully subject to the Modigliani-Miller theorem, which means that there is no need to control their activities for the purpose of obtaining a stable general equilibrium with respect to prices and real activity.

4. BANKING WHEN THE NUMERAIRE IS A PURE NOMINAL OR UNIT OF ACCOUNT

In large part, the analysis of banking presented above can be viewed as a development of Tobin's (1963) insight that banking is just another industry whose equilibrium is subject to standard economic analysis. Elaborating this point has been simplified by the fact that we have so far treated banking in a non-monetary economy, which also allows us to give content to Tobin's conjecture that the special characteristics of banks as financial intermediaries derive more from regulations, for example, restrictions on returns paid on deposits, than from any role played by banks with respect to money.

On the other hand, we have so carefully kept anything resembling money out of banking that our analysis so far has nothing to say about how banks get involved in the process by which a pure nominal commodity or unit of ac-

---

ance tends to offset the implicit taxes that the government collects from the banking sector through the imposition of a reserve requirement.

count is made to play the role of numeraire in a real world monetary system. We turn now to this issue. First we consider the case where the unit of account is introduced through a fiat currency. We then consider how a reserve requirement can be used to force on deposits the problem of transforming a unit of account into a well-defined economic good.

4.1. Currency

Suppose that for some transactions a hand-to-hand medium of exchange is more efficient than an accounting system. Let us jump right to a system where the physical medium is a non-interest-bearing fiat currency produced monopolistically by the government. Assume also that the government chooses to supply currency to the private sector via banks; it supplies currency to banks in exchange for securities or deposits. Banks, in turn, inventory currency on behalf of their depositors; they provide the currency convertibility service, allowing depositors to 'turn in' deposits for currency and vice versa.

Having described how currency gets into an economic system and how banks get involved in its distribution, the problem now is to give economic content to the pure nominal unit of account (say, a dollar) in which currency is measured, that is, to make this unit of account a good that can serve as numeraire. Applying the analysis of Patinkin (1961), the problem is to ensure that the nominal commodity, currency in the present case, is subject to sufficiently well-defined demand and supply functions to give the unit in which it is measured determinate prices in terms of other goods.[3]

Since currency produces real services in allowing some exchanges to be carried out with lower transactions costs, currency has a demand function. For example, one might hypothesize that there is an aggregate demand for real currency which depends on (i) the opportunity cost of currency, the interest rate on a short-term bond whose promised pay-off in the nominal unit (say dollars) in which currency is measured is certain, (ii) some measure of real transactions activity of the type in which currency has a comparative advantage, and (iii) the minimum real costs of executing these transactions through methods other than currency.

---

3. Since our goal is just to examine how banks get involved in introducing a pure nominal unit of account into the economy, we mean to bypass the type of price level determinacy issue, discussed by Brock (1974) and others, which arises when currency is treated as an asset with an infinite life. Let us just assume that the currency in our model will be expropriated and destroyed at some distant future date.

As the wording suggests, in most models the demand for currency is expressed in real terms, units of goods and services, rather than in the nominal unit of account in which currency is denominated. To get a well-defined equilibrium in the currency market, that is, a price for the unit of account in terms of goods and services, the supply function for currency must be stated in terms of the unit of account. One possibility is that the government fixes the supply of nominal currency in terms of units of account, and then lets the public's demand function for the services of real currency determine the price level or the real value of a unit of account.

When the currency market is used to transform the unit of account into a real economic good, there is no need for government control of banking. Thus, suppose the unit in which currency is measured is the economy's numeraire, and currency exists side-by-side with an accounting system of exchange. Suppose the government monopolizes the production of currency but the banking sector is uncontrolled and competitive in the sense of section 2: Banks pass the returns they earn on portfolio assets over to depositors, they charge depositors for portfolio management and transactions services according to competitively determined fees, they allow deposits to be claims against portfolios with any degree of risk desired by depositors, and they allow depositors to participate in two kinds of transactions services, the currency convertibility privilege and access to an accounting system of exchange.

Since the nominal unit (say, a dollar) in which currency is measured is assumed to be the numeraire, the value of deposits like the value of all securities and goods, is expressed in this same nominal unit. However, in the present scenario, transforming the unit of account into a real economic good takes place in the currency market, via well-specified demand and supply functions for currency. For deposits, the analysis of section 2 holds intact. The portfolio management decisions of banks, that is, their decisions to issue deposits and purchase securities, are subject to the Modigliani–Miller theorem, which means that there is no reason to control these financing decisions of competitive banks for the purpose of obtaining equilibrium with respect to prices and real activity.

4.2. A Reserve Requirement

Although currency alone could be used to define a nominal unit of account as a separate good in an economic system, this function can also be imposed on deposits. One possible device is a reserve requirement. When an abstract nominal unit (a dollar) is numeraire, a regulation which says that a minimum fraction of the portfolio against which deposits represent claims must be non-interest bearing reserves issued by a central bank in effect requires that a minimum fraction of the value of the portfolio must be held in pure nominal units of account 'issued' by the central bank.

As in the case of currency, if the unit of account is to be defined through reserves, reserves must have demand and supply functions. The demand for currency arises from the direct transactions services that it provides as a physical medium of exchange. In contrast, the demand for required reserves arises because of the reserve requirement: By making non-interest bearing reserves a required part of an accounting system of exchange which yields valuable transactions services, the government creates a demand for non-interest bearing central bank reserves which would not exist in the absence of the reserve requirement.

The point bears emphasis. Even in a competitive unregulated system, there may be securities that can be exchanged among banks at lower transactions costs than other portfolio assets. Such securities might be convenient for re-settling accounts within and among banks. As a consequence, depositors may generally choose to have some amount of such low transactions cost assets in the portfolios against which their deposits have claim in order to reduce the charges they must bear when transactions through deposits require purchases or sales of assets. Thus, such low transactions cost assets may come to play the role of 'reserves'. However, these 'reserves' of an unregulated competitive system would be interest bearing since they would be ordinary securities for which competitive trading involved low transactions costs.[4]

Currency and the accounting system of exchange maintained by banks are substitutes but not perfect substitutes as methods of executing transactions. Thus, currency and reserves have separate demand functions. It follows that by controlling the nominal supply of currency alone, the government could continue to use currency alone to render the real value of the unit of account (the price level) determinate. The government could follow a passive policy with respect to reserves, allowing banks to exchange securities (but not currency) for

4. There would be no particular problem in the arrangement of competitive interest payments on reserves, even though they may be continuously shifting among banks. For example, the federal funds market now provides an efficient mechanism whereby banks can earn competitive interest, on a day-to-day basis on any reserves they may happen to have in excess of the legal minimum. In earlier times, banks paid interest on the deposits kept with them by other banks to resettle accounts in response to transactions among their depositors.

reserves on demand. In this situation, the earlier analysis of the reserve require-ment would apply: The reserve requirement is simply a tax on deposit returns which does not imply a need to control the level of either reserves or deposits.

Alternatively, since currency and reserves have separate demand functions, the government could choose to define the unit of account through reserves alone, controlling the nominal quantity of reserves, but following a passive policy with respect to currency, that is, allowing banks to exchange currency for ordinary securities (but not reserves) on demand. Finally, the government could choose to follow a passive policy with respect to the mix of currency and reserves, allowing banks to exchange currency for reserves on demand. In this case, there is no separate supply function for either currency or reserves, but determinacy of the real value of the unit of account can be obtained by controlling the sum of currency and reserves. This last possibility seems to correspond best to the stated policy of the central bank in the U.S.

4.3. Patinkin and the Price Level

The preceding draws heavily on the analysis of Patinkin (1961), who in turn builds on the work of Gurley and Shaw (1960, ch. 7). However, Patinkin and Gurley and Shaw always tie control of the supply of units of account to con-trol of bank reserves or deposits, in which case determinacy of the price level implies controlled banking. It is clear from the analysis above that currency alone could be used to define the unit of account and so obtain a determinate price level. The government could leave reserves uncontrolled or the reserve requirement could be dropped; that is, the assets (if any) that banks choose to hold as reserves to resettle accounts in response to transactions executed through their accounting system of exchange could be left unregulated, and all other aspects of banking could also be left unregulated.

Patinkin, at least, does not seem to be misled on this matter. At the end of his review of the Gurley and Shaw (1960) book, he states (1961, p. 116):

'The general conclusion that we can draw from all this is that, in the absence of distribution effects, the necessary conditions for rendering a monetary system determinate are that there be an exogenous fixing of (1) some nominal quantity and (2) some rate of return. It follows that if we were to extend the argument to an economy with both inside and outside money (something G–S do not do) it would suffice to fix the quantity of outside money and its rate of return (say, at zero). In such an economy the price level would be determinate even if the central bank were to fix

[804]

nothing, . . . subject to the restriction that the quantity of outside money is fixed.'

If the term 'outside money' is interpreted as currency, and 'inside money' is taken to mean unregulated deposits, then the contention of Patinkin's statement is exactly our conclusion that controlling the supply of currency alone is sufficient to render the price level (the real value of the unit of account) determinate.[5]

The fact that Patinkin may not be misled does not mean that the implications of his analysis about the feasibility of uncontrolled banking are clear. We saw in the earlier quote from Johnson (1968) that he felt that a determinate price level requires government control over the total quantity of money, including the fully interest-bearing deposits of competitive banks, and Johnson explicitly considered a system where non-interest bearing, government-produced currency exists side-by-side with the deposits issued by competitive banks. Moreover, in a later comment on the Pesek and Saving (1967) book, Johnson (1969) re-iterates his position and indicates that he sees it to be consistent with Patinkin's:

'This analysis shows that reduction of the alternative opportunity cost of holding money to zero and reduction of the purchasing power of money to zero are two extremely different things involving different policies. The confusion between them has probably been fostered by an ambiguity in the concept of 'competition' among banks as providers of the money supply. If deposits cost nothing to create and yet the assets held against them yield a positive return, banks subject to no restraint on the nominal quantity of money they can create in the aggregate will be

---

5. We might note that when he applies his results to reserves, Patinkin's analysis is incomplete. He concludes that the real value of the unit of account becomes determinate when the government fixes the supply of reserves and the interest rate paid on them, leaving the fraction of deposits held as reserves to the discretion of the banks. In other words, he concludes that there is no need for a reserve requirement. However, since his analysis implies that the interest rate fixed for reserves must be below what a free market would pay, the optimal strategy for banks is to hold no central bank reserves. When reserves pay less than a competitive return banks must be forced to hold them. This is the function of a reserve requirement. Alternatively, a demand for reserves can be created by making central bank reserves the only eligible security for settling accounts among banks in response to transactions among customers. However, such a regulation would probably be more difficult to enforce than a reserve requirement.

under competitive pressure to expand the nominal money supply until its purchasing power is reduced to zero. At best the money supply so determined will be in neutral equilibrium.

On the other hand, if banks are competitive but subject either to a quantitative restraint on the aggregate money supply they can create or to a policy of stabilization of the aggregate price level mediated through control of the aggregate money supply, competition among them will force them to pay interest to their depositors and so optimize the supply of real balances without reducing the real value of money to zero . . .

In conclusion, it may be noted that Figure 4.4 can be used to establish in a simple way the proposition, which emerged from Patinkin's critique of Gurley and Shaw's work that the monetary authority needs to control both a nominal magnitude and an interest rate to control the price level.'

The confusion in Johnson's interpretation of Patinkin probably arises in part from the fact that Patinkin, like everyone but Black (1970), treats unregulated competitively produced deposits as money. Even though he distinguishes between this 'inside money' and 'outside money', like currency, which is produced exogenously, and even though he is clear on the point that controlling only the quantity of outside money (and the interest paid on it) can render the price level determinate, the temptation is there for others to treat all things called money alike, and, like Johnson, to conclude that price level determinacy requires that competitive banks are 'subject either to a quantitative restraint on the aggregate money supply they can create or to a policy of stabilization of the aggregate price level mediated through control of the aggregate money supply.'

Perhaps a more important source of confusion is that Patinkin consistently uses phrases like 'the necessary conditions for *rendering a monetary system determinate* are that there be an exogenous fixing of (1) some nominal quantity and (2) some rate of return' [Patinkin (1961, p. 116), italics mine]. The precise problem is not rendering a monetary system determinate, but rather giving content to a pure nominal unit of account (a dollar) as a separate, well-defined economic good. It turns out, of course, that the unit of account is generally defined through parts of what is usually referred to as the monetary system, and, more specifically, through currency and the non-interest bearing reserves that member banks are required to hold with central banks. Nevertheless, when the price level determinacy problem is focused directly on the unit of account, one is less likely to fall into the error of concluding that price level determinacy requires control over all parts of the monetary system. One might even be tempted to conclude that the price level determinacy problem could be solved and the efficiency of the transactions and portfolio management industries could be improved if the government got out of the banking business, that is, if the activities of banks in managing portfolios (issuing deposits and purchasing securities) and in providing an accounting system of exchange were deregulated, and if the problem of defining a unit of account were focused solely on the currency end of the transactions industry.

5. A CONCLUDING PARABLE

Finally, let us consider a scenario in which it is clear that, at least in principle, the problem of defining a nominal unit of account is not coincident with the problem of rendering a monetary system determinate. Suppose we have a completely unregulated banking system in the sense of section 2, and an advanced society in which it is economic to carry out all transactions through the accounting system of exchange provided by banks. The system finds no need for currency or other physical mediums of exchange, and its numeraire has long been a real good, say steel ingots. The society is so advanced that terms like money, medium of exchange, means of payment, and temporary abode of purchasing power have long ago fallen from its vocabulary, and all written accounts of the ancient 'monetary age' were long ago recycled as part of an ecology movement.

Suppose now that, for whatever reason, the government of this society decides that it would be more aesthetic to replace steel ingots as numeraire with a pure nominal commodity which will be called a 'unit' but which has no physical representation. Although monetary theory has long since passed away, value theory has strengthened with time, and the government's economists realize that the 'unit' cannot be established as numeraire by simple decree. It must be a well-defined economic good, that is, the 'unit' needs demand and supply functions which can determine its equilibrium value in terms of other goods.

Controlling the supply of 'units' is no problem, but creating a demand for them is another matter since they have no intrinsic usefulness. The solution hit upon by the authorities is to use a reserve requirement to forcibly join the holding of 'units' with something that does provide valuable services. In the monetary age the appropriate industry to burden with the reserve requirement would have been clear, but in the new more enlightened age it is evident that there are many potential candidates. In the end, the government imposes the reserve requirement on spaceship owners. Every spaceship owner has to keep a reserve of X 'units' with the central 'unit' authority. Since most citizens of the society desire the transportation services of private spaceships, the reserve requirement creates a real demand for 'units'. The government then renders the price of the 'unit' determinate by fixing the interest rate paid on 'units', perhaps at zero, and controlling the supply of 'unit' reserves.

The reserve requirement, of course, has a depressing effect on the spaceship industry. Because X 'units' must be purchased along with every spaceship, people economize more on their holdings of spaceships, existing spaceships are used more intensively, and alternative forms of transportation services are substituted to some extent for spaceships. On the other hand, sales of 'units' by the government can substitute for other forms of taxation. Indeed, most of the citizens of this enlightened society feel this new form of taxation is the major reason for the government's interest in replacing the ingot as numeraire with the 'unit'.

REFERENCES

Black, Fischer, 1970, Banking and interest rates in a world without money, Journal of Bank Research, Autumn, 9–20.

Brock, William A., 1974, Money and growth: The case of long-run perfect foresight, International Economic Review 15, Oct., 750–777.

Fama, Eugene F., 1978, The effects of a firm's investment and financing decisions on the welfare of its securityholders, American Economic Review 68, June, 272–284.

Gurley, John G. and Edward S. Shaw, 1960, Money in a theory of finance (The Brookings Institution, Washington, DC); chapter 7 of the book is most relevant for the purposes of this paper.

Johnson, Harry G., 1968, Problems of efficiency in monetary management. Journal of Political Economy 76, Sept./Oct., 971–990.

Johnson, H.G., 1969, A comment on Pesek and Saving's theory of money and wealth, Journal of Money, Credit and Banking 1, Aug., 535–537.

Modigliani, Franco and Merton H. Miller, 1958, The cost of capital, corporation finance, and the theory of investment, American Economic Review 48, June, 261–297.

Patinkin, Don, 1961, Financial intermediaries and the logical structure of monetary theory, American Economic Review 51, March, 95–116.

Pesek, Boris and Thomas R. Saving, 1967, Money, wealth and economic theory (Macmillan, New York).

Tobin, James, 1963, Commercial banks as creators of 'money', in: Dean Carson, ed., Banking and monetary studies (Irwin, Homewood, IL) 408–419.

OUR COLLEAGUE

. . .

John H. Cochrane and Tobias J. Moskowitz

This volume is dedicated to Gene's written intellectual contributions. We conclude by sharing some thoughts on what it is like to be Gene's colleague at the University of Chicago. We complement Ken French's thoughts on Gene as a coauthor, and Bill Schwert and René Stultz's observations about Gene as a professional colleague and coeditor.

Between the two of us, we have enjoyed being Gene's colleague at the University of Chicago for almost 50 years. Our interaction and friendship with Gene, as well as his scholarship, personal examples, and values, have profoundly shaped our lives and careers. We would not have a fraction of our own modest accomplishments in finance without Gene. We also write as representatives of many colleagues who have been affected similarly and profoundly over Gene's long and illustrious career. These are some reasons this quiet man inspires so much loyalty.

Gene doesn't say much, or ever tell you what to do. He just sets an example, so profoundly influential that people, and the culture of an institution, follow.

As Ken French writes, Gene is a model of how to be a good colleague. Commenting on papers is a key part of that interaction. If you ask for comments, consistent with his philosophy in life, Gene will typically return your paper in a day. It will often be riddled with red scribbles that might contain a word ("What?!") or a short phrase ("Doesn't look right") with a number circled. Once in a great while you might earn a simple "not bad," which is high praise. (Toby is proud of once—once—receiving a "pretty good.") But mostly, you can count that Gene will get to the central idea and find weak points you haven't thought of.

The point: Research is always imperfect and can always be improved. Research is about mulling it over, boiling it down to the essential point, finding the one clearest way to see the data or express an idea. Research is about thinking through a thousand objections and misunderstandings, and checking the thousand ways that it could be wrong. If Gene objects that something seems wrong, take that as it is intended, as the most helpful and constructive advice anyone could give you. If you want bland praise and feel-good support for half-baked ideas, you won't get it from Gene. Gene's comments are about seeking the truth and improving the research.

Gene will often comment even if you don't give him the paper directly. If you sign up for an internal seminar and circulate your paper, or even just the tables, Gene will often read them and comment. He views that as part of his job and just elementary proper behavior.

Reading and commenting is a two-way street. We reacted immediately and in kind, sending Gene similarly critical comments on his papers. Only in retrospect does it occur to us that maybe mid-20s assistant professors with the ink barely dry on their diplomas are not supposed to tear apart tables, equations, and even prose of the senior star of their department. But this brash egalitarianism was as natural to Gene as it was to us.

He applies those same criteria to his own work, always pushing to do better. He is grateful if you point out a weakness. He's even grateful when we make harebrained comments, figuring if one of us could get something so wrong it is up to him to explain it better. He models how to receive comments as well as how to give them.

The finance seminar is the second great social ritual that defines Gene's collegiality. Gene presents every one of his papers in the internal workshops and encourages feedback, with only occasional impatience at silly questions. He demonstrates an ideal seminar style: no 45 minutes of preview, motivation, and chit-chat before getting to the point. The typical Fama seminar starts with "Here is Table 1." By presenting his own work at an early stage and adapting and refining it later, we all get the message: "If *Fama* feels he needs to vet his research first, how could I possibly think otherwise about my own work?"

Gene attends every finance workshop, no matter the topic. "You might learn something, even if it's bad." He sits in the front row and doesn't play with his iPhone. He doesn't charge in during the introduction, but waits patiently for the presenter to get to the point. Then he quickly finds the important weaknesses. He sets the rule: it's not personal. A paper can be silly, but that doesn't mean the person is silly. The point of finding weaknesses is to help improve the work. Gene is impatient with people who try to score points, are rude, grandstand, or otherwise treat a discussion as a personal one-upmanship game rather than a collective effort to produce good work, or at least to understand the limitations of the evidence before us.

Gene's office door is always open. If you have an interesting research question, it doesn't matter whether you're a PhD student, junior faculty member, or Nobel Prize winner—you have Gene's attention. Toby remembers in his second year at Chicago having what he thought was a simple question about the Fama-MacBeth procedure. After some consternation about bothering Gene with what was likely a very simple issue, he decided to approach Gene because, well, who would know better? (Also, he was in the office next door. Geographical proximity and regular hours matter.) The question turned out to be not so simple, and 3½ hours later he emerged from Gene's office with a whole new perspective on the methodology. And, as Gene would tell him later, Gene learned something, too. That was the first time Toby realized that even Eugene Fama was still learning; that being a colleague isn't just a one-way street of senior faculty educating and helping junior faculty; that we are all in this together to learn something. John spent most of his first 10 years at Chicago bouncing between Gene's office and Lars Hansen's, putting together two apparently different views of the same thing, and learning most of what he (John) knows about the theory and facts of finance along the way. And discovering, too, that every now and then something about his questions illuminated things for Gene and Lars.

But if you come to Gene's office to gossip, you're standing in the wrong door. Gene guards his time preciously. His shadow price for research discussions is extremely low, but that for academic gossip and chit-chat is nearly infinite. (With a few exceptions. Toby notes that Gene is an avid sports fan and loves talking about sports analytics and numbers. But this is so close to his research interests that it doesn't count. And John did waste a few office hours looking with Gene at weather forecasts for windsurfing outings. Chicago, it turns out, is not a reliably windy city.)

Gene is always at the daily faculty lunch gathering. If you're a nervous assistant professor, just show up and you'll soon get to know him. The conversation isn't always research, and often turns to sports, politics, or wine. But with Gene there, everyone else shows up too.

Gene works with PhD students, which many people consider a chore. As René Stulz and Bill Schwert document, Gene has advised more than 100 students, many of whom have gone on to fame and fortune. His involvement in mentoring doctoral students continues today. Hint: you should, too.

Participation in recruitment and promotion decisions is one of the most important duties of a scholar and a colleague. Here, Gene profoundly affected the Booth School and the University of Chicago, by action and by example.

To Gene, the quality of the ideas and the work supporting them is all that has ever mattered. Gene comes to appointments and promotion meetings completely prepared, and he talks about the papers—not the gossip, not others' opinions, not numbers, not citations, not conclusions, not silly comments made at seminars (thank goodness, in both our cases) or early presentations that didn't go so well, but the papers, in their final published form. We doubt there are many business schools where all-school senior-faculty appointment meetings will spend a half hour on the specification of a regression, with the table before us. Following Gene's example, this is how discussions are conducted at the Booth School.

Gene also has faced many difficult decisions, where it was time for accomplished scholars, who had become close personal friends, to leave Chicago. Painful as it was, when that was the right decision, Gene did not hesitate.

What matters to Gene is the quality of the argument, not the ideology, "Chicago-school" conformity, or the academic or public politics of the conclusions. There has never been a hint of argument from authority—I, Gene Fama, like this work or not.

One example speaks for a lifetime: With Gene's support, the Booth School hired, and worked hard to get and to keep, Richard Thaler, one of Gene's most outspoken intellectual critics. Well, behavioral finance is important, so Chicago should have the best of behavioral finance. Thaler's empirical work was innovative and solid. Facts are facts. If Gene disagrees with Thaler's interpretation, and if young people are following Thaler, well, Gene's sense of ethics would never allow him to object to an appointment on that basis. And Gene golfs with Dick, perhaps just to remind the rest of us how one should behave personally toward intellectual antagonists.

Gene has supported many other prominent advocates of behavioral finance, market inefficiencies, and many other surprising conclusions—when the work was first-rate. As a result of this culture instilled and exemplified by Gene, the Booth School has become the best research business school by far.

Not everyone has prospered at Chicago. Many younger faculty don't offer Gene the same feedback he offers them, or otherwise seem not to appreciate incisive comments. They find that Gene's services tail off. Some expect "mentoring," that Gene and other senior faculty members will be gently supportive, praise weak work, guide careers, pull strings with editors or promotion committees, or tell them what to work on. Such people can find Chicago disappointing.

Gene has never suggested what research we should do, what conclusions we should look for, or even what general areas we should focus on. He knows he didn't get famous by following suggestions of his senior colleagues. And don't try flattery or obsequiousness, or to ingratiate yourself with Gene by shoddy work that seems to support his. We've seen people try! Gene reacts with a stare of bored annoyance that we dub the "why don't you get out of my office" look. Gene would rather read and discuss brilliant work that disproves or refutes his own than mediocre work that supports his view of the world. Truth above all else, and let the data speak.

Gene is a leader—by example, not by giving directions. Gene comes into the office seven days a week, by 8 a.m. every morning, including Saturday and Sunday. As a junior faculty member you realize, "Wow, if *Fama* comes in every day, what excuse do I have to goof off?" Gene works hard on teaching and with PhD students. You look and realize, "If Fama finds the time, why can't I?" But he never took us or anyone else aside and said, "Here is how you behave, young whippersnapper." The most he offers are occasional pithy one-liners. To John, wondering how to deal with a malicious public attack: "Don't get in a pissing match with a skunk." To Toby, seeking advice on a referee's suggestion: "If you have to hold your nose, don't do it."

The underlying thread is that Gene is a deeply ethical person. He does what he does because it's the right thing to do, even when it's difficult. Whether it is committee work, promotions cases, hiring decisions, curriculum, relations with colleagues, or teaching, he applies the same principles that guide him: respect data, value your time, seek the truth, and always improve. Respect people, but also treat all ideas critically, ignoring rank and honors. Gene is famous for saying no to endless invitations and managing his time efficiently. But here, too, he is just treating people with respect. Saying no quickly, not promising things you can't deliver, and doing promptly what tasks you do take on, is ultimately far more respectful than the hemming and hawing and late shoddy work that the overcommitted (like, too often, ourselves) ultimately deliver.

When Gene received the call from Stockholm that he had won the Nobel Prize, Toby asked what he was going to do that morning. Gene replied simply, "I have to prepare for class. I teach in an hour." The dozens of reporters trying to reach him got the same answer. Even the University of Chicago, scrambling to hold a press conference in his honor, was delayed by several hours waiting for Gene to finish class. His intellectual life, and his duties to students, come before honors and accolades, even the Nobel Prize.

We have watched and tried hard to follow Gene's example in so many things, and to pass on the same values he exemplified. We have done so imperfectly, but we're still learning and trying—and we are grateful.

That is what it is like to be Gene Fama's colleague. This volume is one small way to try to say thank you, Gene.

CONTRIBUTORS

. . .

Clifford S. Asness
Managing and Founding Principal
AQR Capital Management
Greenwich, CT 06830

Ray Ball
Sidney Davidson Distinguished
Service Professor of Accounting
Booth School of Business
University of Chicago
Chicago, IL 60637

Dennis Carlton
David McDaniel Keller Professor
of Economics
Booth School of Business
University of Chicago
Chicago, IL 60637

John H. Cochrane
Senior Fellow
Hoover Institution
Stanford University
Stanford, CA 94305

Kenneth R. French
Roth Family Distinguished Professor
of Finance
Tuck School of Business
Dartmouth Etna
Hanover, NH 03755

Campbell R. Harvey
J. Paul Sticht Professor of International
Business
Fuqua School of Business
Duke University
Durham, NC 27708

John Liew
Founding Principal
AQR Capital Management
Greenwich, CT 06830

Yan Liu
Assistant Professor of Finance
Mays School of Business
Texas A&M University
College Station, Texas 77843

Tobias J. Moskowitz
Fama Family Professor of Finance
Booth School of Business
University of Chicago
Chicago, IL 60637

G. William Schwert
Distinguished University Professor
and Professor of Finance and
Statistics
Simon Business School
University of Rochester
Rochester, NY 14627

Amit Seru
Dennis and Karen Chookaszian
Professor of Finance and the David G.
Booth Faculty Fellow
Booth School of Business
University of Chicago
Chicago, IL 60637

René M. Stulz
Everett D. Reese Chair of Banking and
Monetary Economics
Ohio State University
Columbus, OH 43210

Amir Sufi
Bruce Lindsay Professor of Economics
and Public Policy
Booth School of Business
University of Chicago
Chicago, IL 60637